THE SYMPHONIC REPERTOIRE
VOLUME V

THE SYMPHONIC REPERTOIRE

VOLUME 5

The Symphony in the Americas

EDITED BY
BRIAN HART

WITH

A. Peter Brown
Founding Editor

INDIANA UNIVERSITY PRESS

This book is a publication of

Indiana University Press
Office of Scholarly Publishing
Herman B Wells Library 350
1320 East 10th Street
Bloomington, Indiana 47405 USA

iupress.org

© 2023 by Indiana University Press

All rights reserved

No part of this book may be reproduced or utilized in any form or by any means, electronic or mechanical, including photocopying and recording, or by any information storage and retrieval system, without permission in writing from the publisher. The paper used in this publication meets the minimum requirements of the American National Standard for Information Sciences—Permanence of Paper for Printed Library Materials, ANSI Z39.48–1992.

Manufactured in the United States of America

First Printing 2023

Cataloging information is available from the Library of Congress.

ISBN 978-0-253-06753-1 (hardcover)
ISBN 978-0-253-06754-8 (ebook)

CONTENTS

PREFACE   vii

ACKNOWLEDGMENTS   ix

LIST OF ABBREVIATIONS   xi

1. Introduction to the Symphonic Repertoire of the United States and Latin America · **BRIAN HART**   1

2. The First Generation of Symphonists in the United States · **DOUGLAS W. SHADLE**   60

3. The Second New England School and Their Contemporaries · **E. DOUGLAS BOMBERGER**   123

4. The Symphonic Works of Charles Ives · **J. PETER BURKHOLDER**   175

5. From 1920 to 1950 in the United States: The Symphony in a World Upended · **SUSAN KEY, WITH DREW MASSEY**   309

6. Forgotten Modernisms: The Symphony in the United States from 1950 to 1970 · **KATHERINE BABER**   484

7. The Symphony in South America · **CAROL A. HESS**   665

8. The Symphony in Mexico, Central America, and the Spanish-Speaking Caribbean · **CAROL A. HESS**   735

9. The Symphony in the United States since 1970 · **MATTHEW MUGMON**   793

LIST OF CONTRIBUTORS   951

INDEX   953

PREFACE

Brian Hart

When A. Peter Brown conceived *The Symphonic Repertoire*, he intended the final installment of the series—the symphony in Europe from ca. 1930 to today, as well as a comprehensive overview of the genre in the Western Hemisphere—to comprise the work of multiple specialists. As he stated in the Preface to the Series (reprinted in volumes 2 through 4), it would consider "the 'afterlife' of the genre as seen in European composers who have continued in or reformulated the tradition; in American composers who in Leonard Bernstein's words have pursued the 'great American symphony'; and in Latin-American composers who have attempted to incorporate their own regional idioms into the symphony tradition. It will be a symposium with contributions on the symphonic repertoire for various regions and national groups."

He left no specific plans for the volume beyond that statement.

At the gracious invitation of Peter's widow, Carol Vanderbilt Brown, as well as the music editor of Indiana University Press, I agreed to serve as organizer and editor of the present volume. From the outset, we decided to devote it exclusively to the symphony in the United States and Latin America, saving the post-1930 European symphony for a future volume 6.

As we hope to demonstrate in this volume, a sizable body of worthy and stimulating symphonies has been produced in the Western Hemisphere and, to this day, many younger composers continue to embrace the genre with enthusiasm, especially in the United States. Recordings and scores of numerous works are now available; but, while one finds studies of individual composers and periods, no comprehensive scholarly examination of the symphony in the Americas exists, and certainly not one of the scope found in *The Symphonic Repertoire*. The moment then is propitious for adding this volume to the series.

In previous installments, which cover the European symphonic repertoire of a specific chronological period, individual chapters have considered either the output of a single composer or the works within a particular nation or region. Since volume 5, by contrast, devotes itself exclusively to the full symphonic history of one geographic entity, the United States and Latin America, its chapters follow a different format. With the exception of the works of Charles Ives—the singularity, complexity, and significance of which justified giving them their own chapter—I have partitioned the symphonic history of the United States into six chronological and conceptually organized chapters, recognizing both that the divisions are necessarily arbitrary and that some chapters, especially the fifth and ninth, consider a much larger number of symphonists (and consequently at shorter individual length) than others. The two chapters on the Latin American symphony examine the repertoires of South America and of Mexico, Central America, and the Spanish-speaking Caribbean nations, respectively. As in previous volumes, a composer's complete symphonic output is considered "at one sitting," as it were, even when the works span more than one chronological unit; in such cases I have assigned the symphonist to the time period that I believe covers his or her most significant

Preface

achievements with the genre, whether as composers or as advocates; thus, for example, Roger Sessions, William Schuman, and Leonard Bernstein appear in the 1950–70 period, even though their earliest and arguably most famous symphonies properly belong to the timespan of the previous chapter, which covers 1920–50.

Each author, in consultation with me, made the final selection of the composers to receive extended attention. For each, at least one representative or historically important symphony is covered at length—including composition history, analysis, and early reception—with any remaining works treated in a more summary manner. In view of the wide scope of this volume, however, most discussions of symphonies save those by Ives cannot probe as deeply as those in previous installments. Also as before, the authors include orchestral compositions that, regardless of title, they deem to possess symphonic "weight"—e.g., George Whitefield Chadwick's *Symphonic Sketches*, Ives's Orchestral Sets 1 and 2, Alberto Ginastera's *Pampeana No. 3*, John Adams's *Harmonielehre*, and the works of Mason Bates. Although this volume attempts to present a comprehensive history of the development of the symphony in the United States and Latin America, as well as a thorough accounting of many of its finest and most important contributions, it cannot pretend to be exhaustive, and accordingly symphonists such as Henry Hadley, Daniel Gregory Mason, "Duke" Ellington, Vittorio Giannini, Nicolas Flagello, Wallingford Riegger, Glenn Branca, David Maslanka, Kamran Ince, and Kevin Puts receive at best passing notice (chapters 5 and 6 conclude with "brief mentions" of many of these composers active between 1920 and 1970, and chapter 9 refers to many symphonists besides the 22 covered). Nevertheless, we trust that the consideration of these composers who are included and the contextual questions surrounding their work will lay the foundation on which others will build with profit.

The text retains many of the analytical abbreviations, labels, and symbols used in earlier volumes, though the authors adopt individual methodologies for dealing with post-tonal symphonies; in the Ives chapter, for example, the analytical tools highlight the depth and complexity of the counterpoint. As before, the bibliography follows the format designed by William S. Newman in *History of the Sonata Idea* and is mostly restricted to works cited, although each chapter closes with an overview of the pertinent literature. In a departure from earlier practice, the bibliographies appear at the end of every chapter rather than in one master file, and so repetitions will occur.

In addition to writing this preface and the first chapter, I created the composer tables for chapters 5, 6, 7 (Villa-Lobos), and 8 (Chávez), as well as the "Brief Mentions" in chapter 6, and the responsibility for any faulty information therein is mine. At the author's request, I also undertook the majority of the final revisions for chapter 6.

ACKNOWLEDGMENTS

First thanks are due to Carol Vanderbilt Brown and the successive music editors of Indiana University Press—Jane Behnken, Raina Polivka, Janice Frisch, and Allison Chaplin—for their faith in me to carry on Peter's legacy in this volume. They have provided consistent encouragement and support to me and all our authors as we have navigated the sometimes-tortuous path of bringing this book to realization, patiently enduring delays, complications, and other obstacles, not least of them a pandemic.

As we began this project, I consulted numerous colleagues for feedback on the chapter divisions and on recommendations for potential authors. I would especially like to thank Peter Burkholder, Carol Oja, Howard Pollack, and Doug Bomberger for their help in assembling what I consider an exceptionally strong team of specialists. I am grateful to all the authors for their hard work and endurance, as well as their forbearance with me—the one person on this project whose research specialty lies outside the Western Hemisphere—and my at times decidedly interventionist editing! It has been a joy to work with and learn from each of them. My thanks also for the very helpful advice from the various chapter readers.

Northern Illinois University provided a sabbatical in which I was able to read and edit the first drafts of most of the contributions and familiarize myself with the symphonic contributions of all the composers featured in these pages aside from the brief mentions (with invaluable assistance from Interlibrary Loan, YouTube, and the Naxos website!). It was a great delight to discover so many enjoyable and often uplifting and moving symphonies from the Americas. My thanks go also to Mary Sue Morrow for giving me extremely useful guidance from her experiences in coediting volume 1 of *The Symphonic Repertoire*, as well as to Carlo Caballero for his insightful reading and critique of chapter 1. Many other friends and colleagues have given continuous support and encouragement throughout this process, among whom I would cite Keith Clifton, Andreas Giger, and John Novak. I will forever be grateful for the never-ending love and care of my dear mother, Gayle Hart, who to my great sorrow passed away in March 2023 while the volume was in final production.

My final thanks go to Peter Brown—for all he taught me during my years of graduate study, for the support he gave during my early years of teaching, and for his confidence in inviting me to contribute to his series in volume 3B. It was his vision that made this volume possible, and it, like volume 1, is dedicated to his memory.

ABBREVIATIONS

A	Part form refrain
A Clar.	Clarinet in A
Aclar.	Alto clarinet
Aflt.	Alto flute
Asax.	Alto saxophone
B	Part form episodes
B♭Ssax.	Soprano saxophone in B-flat
B♭Tsax.	Tenor saxophone in B-flat
Barhr.	Baritone horn
Barsax.	Baritone saxophone
Bclar.	Bass clarinet
BD	Bass drum
Bflt.	Bass flute
Bssn.	Bassoon
Btpt.	Bass trumpet
Btrom.	Bass trombone
Btuba	Bass tuba
ca.	circa
Cb.	Contrabass
Cbclar.	Contrabass clarinet
Cbssn.	Contrabassoon
Cbtrom.	Contrabass trombone
Cel.	Celesta
Clar.	Clarinet
Cor.	Cornet
CT	Countertheme
Cym.	Cymbals
Dev.	Development section
E♭ Aclar.	Alto clarinet in E-flat
E♭ Asax.	Alto saxophone in E-flat
E♭ Barsax.	Baritone saxophone in E-flat
E♭ Clar.	Clarinet in E-flat
E♭ Picc.	Piccolo in E-flat
EH	English horn
Euph.	Euphonium
Expo.	Exposition
Flt.	Flute

Abbreviations

GP	Grand pause
Glsp.	Glockenspiel
Gui.	Guitar
Hr.	Horn
Intro.	Introduction
K	Closing material
m. (mm.)	Measure(s)
Mand.	Mandolin
mod.	Modulatory (modulation)
Mrb.	Marimba
mvt.	Movement
N	New material
O	Introductory material
Ob.	Oboe
Org.	Organ
P	Primary material in the tonic key
Perc.	Percussion
Picc.	Piccolo
Pno.	Piano
Recap.	Recapitulation
Reh.	Rehearsal number
retrans.	Retransition
S	Secondary material presented initially in a related key
Sax.	Saxophone
SD	Snare drum
Sopsax.	Soprano saxophone
Strgs.	Strings
T	Transition material usually of a modulatory nature
Tamb.	Tambourine
Timp.	Timpani
Tpt.	Trumpet
trans.	Transition of a smaller-dimension level than a *T*
Tri.	Triangle
Trom.	Trombone
Tsax.	Tenor saxophone
Vbp.	Vibraphone
Vla.	Viola
Vlc.	Violoncello
Vln.	Violin
Xylo.	Xylophone

Tuba, harp, and unlisted percussion instruments are spelled out in full.

Orchestral Instrumentation

Full	1 or 2 Flt., 2 Ob., 2 Clar., 2 Bssn., 2 Hr., 2 Tpt., Timp., and Strgs.
Grand	2 Flt., 2 Ob., 2 Clar., 2 Bssn., 4 Hr., 2 Tpt., 3 Trom., Timp., and Strgs.

Analytical Symbols

Previous volumes in this series have employed analytical symbols for movements in sonata and related forms that derive from the system developed in Jan LaRue, *Guidelines for Style Analysis*, 2nd ed. (Warren, MI: Harmonie Park, 1992); although these symbols are less useful for post-tonal idioms and structures, they will appear where applicable or helpful.

In the LaRue system, *P, T, S, K,* and *N* stand for primary, transitional, secondary, closing, and new functions, respectively. Letters preceded by Arabic numerals define constituent parts of a function (e.g., *1P, 2P*). Lowercase letters *a, b, c, d*, etc., following uppercase letters indicate phrases or smaller-dimension portions of a function; while *x, y, z* following *a, b, c, d*, etc. identify a still-smaller component. Thus, the initial motive of the beginning of a primary section of an exposition would be *Pax*; the second idea of the second phrase of the second motive of the secondary area would be *2Sby*. Parentheses are for derivations: *S(P)* means that the secondary area derives from the primary material. Superscript numerals signal variants: e.g., Pa^1 indicates a variant of *Pa*. The superscript *k* (e.g., P^k) denotes a closing function at the end of the main function. I/1P and similar designations indicate that the *1P* material from the first movement appears in a subsequent movement. For forms other than sonata form, the standard uppercase and lowercase letters are used (e.g., ternary form: *A-B-A*).

THE SYMPHONIC REPERTOIRE
VOLUME V

CHAPTER ONE

Introduction to the Symphonic Repertoire of the United States and Latin America

Brian Hart

From relatively modest though by no means negligible beginnings, the symphony has become a central genre for composers of concert music in the United States; in terms of numbers, in fact, few nations contributed more to the symphonic repertoire in the twentieth century, and symphonies and orchestral works of similar breadth continue to proliferate in the twenty-first.[1] Why has the symphony appealed so strongly to American temperaments? At first, enthusiasts embraced it as the voice of Beethoven, whose music to them embodied the American democratic ideal at work. As John Sullivan Dwight wrote in 1845, "'we are all *one*, though many,' [Beethoven's] notes seem to say."[2] Throughout the nineteenth century, composers continued to respond to the almost mythic aura of the genre: as a young man enthusiastically hearing John Knowles Paine's First Symphony in 1876, George Whitefield Chadwick confessed, "To me there was something Godlike in the very name of Symphony."[3] Through the symphony, American audiences could partake of the best of European tradition while composers had the opportunity to contribute meaningfully to it. Speaking in 1873, Paine challenged his compatriots to make the development of a reputable American symphonic repertoire "the mission of our own land."[4]

Throughout much of the twentieth century, the symphony flourished in the United States. Many composers valued its stature as "a full orchestral piece for the concert hall that makes a serious statement" (Aaron Copland's words), especially as its formal and stylistic conventions loosened.[5] William Schuman asserted that "symphonies will always be written as long as composers wish to use large instrumental forces to say what they have to say."[6] In the present century, composers of all generations continue to regard the symphony as the default for "making serious statements." William Bolcom (born 1938) stated in 2008 that "I suppose I still write them in this late day because some things can only be expressed in a symphony, at least by me. I cannot imagine having written my Eighth in a lesser form than that of a symphony."[7] Five years later, Kevin Puts (born 1972) wrote an essay explaining why he continues to compose symphonies, despite the practical obstacles:

> The symphony is not a trifle. It is not cute or hip or light. It says something important—about life and death and cosmic stuff—and it does so without embarrassment. What it needs to say cannot be said in a few minutes; it is not short attention span music. It is music for the patient listener. . . .

> I feel [Symphony No. 1] was my earliest attempt at speaking with utmost sincerity, at digging as deeply as I could emotionally. . . . I need a private place where I can express the spiritual, the epic, the heartbreaking without shame or embarrassment. My Symphony No. 1 led me to this place. . . .
>
> Since writing my first symphony, I have written three others. . . . They are rarely played. In fact, I can count the number of performances of each of these, with the possible exception of my Symphony No. 2, on one hand. . . .
>
> Strangely, this doesn't bother me the way it probably should. I feel very fortunate for the opportunities I had to write the pieces and the symphonic genre has led me to some wonderful places. . . .
>
> For me, the genre continues to feel right and true to who I am. I owe a lot to it.[8]

Finally, Mohammed Fairouz, born in 1985 and, as of this writing, already the composer of five highly varied symphonies, stated in 2015 that "I don't think that the poetry of the form has even begun to be exploited to its full potential."[9] Popular imagination continues to privilege the genre as well, even extending to concert nomenclature: as Annegret Fauser and others have observed, Americans go not to orchestral concerts but "to the symphony."[10]

Despite its largeness and high quality, much of the symphonic repertoire of the United States has generally been regarded as little more than a postscript to the history of the genre. Nineteenth-century symphonies of the Second New England School and even more those of the antebellum period have mostly been ignored and not infrequently derided. The boldness and vision of Charles Ives's symphonies are appreciated, but their construction and expressive goals are often misunderstood. A few midcentury compositions, particularly the Third Symphonies of Aaron Copland and Roy Harris, receive dutiful mention, with others cited for special status (William Grant Still's *Afro-American Symphony* as the first recognized concert work by a Black composer, Howard Hanson's "Romantic" Symphony as an emblem of archconservatism). Symphonies written in the decades after World War II have been widely dismissed as desperate or defiant refusals to embrace postwar modernism. Finally, some commentators have characterized more recent symphonies as little more than exercises in nostalgia except when they address issues of current interest.[11] For its part, the Latin American symphony has been treated as still more of an afterthought: only Carlos Chávez's *Sinfonía India* is heard with anything approaching regularity, and even listeners invested in music of the region know comparatively few other works of symphonic scope emanating from Central or South America.

The present volume of *The Symphonic Repertoire* seeks to address these issues of neglect and misapprehension by presenting a thorough account of the flourishing of symphonic music in the United States and Latin America. It will examine the contributions of numerous composers (primarily native-born figures but also selected émigrés) working from the 1820s to the early 2020s and the diverse symphonic languages they created; the chapters will also explore the singular historical and contextual issues that have set the development of the symphony in the Western Hemisphere apart from that of its European counterparts. Since most of this volume concentrates on the music of one nation, chapters have been apportioned primarily according to chronological and topical divisions, with composers assigned to the division in which they exercised their most important influence on the symphony, whether as contributors or as advocates. Chapters 2 and 3 cover the nineteenth century roughly up to World War I, and chapter 4 focuses on Ives. Chapter 5 considers the American symphony from circa 1920 to 1950, which thrived against the backdrop of modernist experimentation in the 1920s, the emergence of radio and other mass media, and composers' responses to the great social traumas of the Depression and World War II. Chapter 6 examines symphonic production between circa 1950 and 1970 in the light of postwar reactions, the emergence of the musical avant-garde, and the growth of institutional patronage. Two chapters consider the symphonic repertoire of Latin America: chapter 7 examines works from South America and chapter 8 explores Mexico and the Spanish-speaking regions of Central America and the Caribbean. Returning to the United States, the final chapter looks at the continuing vitality of the symphony since circa 1970 and the ever more divergent paths composers have followed.[12]

Readers who take this journey will reap many revelatory insights about the development of the symphony in the Western Hemisphere: the richness of the antebellum repertoire and the extent to which it was erased from American musical consciousness, beginning in the composers' own lifetimes; the equally varied and individual responses of Second New England School symphonists to the culture of their day; the impeccable craftsmanship of Charles Ives's earliest symphonic works as well as the Romantic expressiveness of the most radical ones; the fervent embrace of the symphony as a response to the Depression and World War II and the continued vibrancy (rather than the expected decline) of the genre in the postwar decades; the diverse Latin American approaches to the symphony from identity-conscious works to those redolent of the European mainstream; and, as noted earlier, the passion with which composers continue to embrace the symphony into the twenty-first century, as they explore an unprecedented array of languages and styles.

Diversity, in fact, will be a constant refrain throughout the history of the symphony in the Americas, as is so often the case with music of the Western Hemisphere. Antebellum symphonies included European mainstream works, programmatic pieces, and exotic compositions, while the Second New England School encompassed Paine's cosmopolitanism, Chadwick's infusion of American popular styles, and Amy Beach's celebration of Celtic roots. Each of Ives's symphonies represents a sharply different conception of the genre. Between 1920 and 1950, composers veered between folk or popular nationalism, "abstract" nationalism (i.e., identifiably American music created without recourse to vernacular idioms), and cosmopolitanism. After World War II, symphonists added to their palettes atonal, twelve-tone, and non-Western languages. Since 1970, choices have expanded even more to include minimalism, contemporary popular music, and a variety of postmodern expressions. As the foregoing suggests, the symphony in the United States resists attempts to be defined by a single evolutionary trajectory or distinctly American style of symphony—indeed, one of the clearest lessons of this volume is that such constructs are illusory. One narrative about the genre, however, has had a dominant and lingering effect for good or ill—mostly the latter—on the development and image of the symphony in the United States, at least until recent years, and this is the search for the Great American Symphony.

The "Great American Symphony" Albatross

In the mid-nineteenth century, many stateside observers concurred with a famous European taunt that "America is only a land of steam engines"—technologically pioneering but culturally primitive.[13] In 1854, Dwight asked, "Who can point us to one American composition, great or small, with much assurance that it is destined to become classical and to be treasured in the world's repertory?"[14] Almost forty years later, another critic voiced a similar complaint after hearing Chadwick's Second Symphony at the 1893 World's Columbian Exposition in Chicago: "From a musical point of view America has as yet had no message to deliver to the world."[15] This artistic inferiority complex played no little role in driving the quixotic quest for the "Great American Symphony," a phrase popularized by Leonard Bernstein but already in use in the late nineteenth century.[16] The anxiety to create a work commonly understood to "reconcil[e] European tradition and recognizably American music" preoccupied the thoughts of many symphonists in the United States between circa 1880–1970; it arguably influenced a number of their compositional choices and unquestionably colored the critical reception of their works.[17]

The key word is indeed *critical*. As Julie Schnepel and Douglas W. Shadle have compellingly demonstrated, reviewers and other writers on music served both as the prime advocates for the Great American Symphony and its self-appointed selection committee.[18] Granting themselves the authority to determine its essential elements, they demanded, sometimes quite peremptorily, that composers observe them.[19] Yet, to the latter's chagrin, the standards proved to be as inconstant as they were inflexible, with fundamental components subject to change every generation. Symphonists active before the Civil War faced the aptly named "Beethoven problem," while those following had Wagner to contend with as well. As in Europe, the Music of the Future debate pit defenders of absolute music against proponents of programmatic compositions.[20] Then, in the 1890s, Henry Krehbiel and similar-minded critics urged American composers to follow Antonín Dvořák in enriching the traditional Germanic forms with folk idioms. Every time values shifted, reviewers who supported them censured composers who in their view failed to follow suit, so that symphonists found themselves held to what Douglas Bomberger calls "nearly unattainable" standards of perfection.[21] When, as often happened, the public embraced a work the reviewers dismissed, they airily ascribed it to listeners' lack of sophistication.[22]

In the decades after World War I, according to Schnepel, critics settled on three general conditions a symphony had to meet in order to aspire to the title of Great American Symphony. Above all, it had to demonstrate transcendence, exhibiting both the power to make a strong impact on the emotions of present-day listeners—to transport them "out of ourselves and beyond ourselves," as critic Paul Rosenfeld put it—and also the potential to continue doing so in the future.[23] Second, whether through thematic interconnections, an intangible "inner unity," or some other means (most critics did not specify a method), the symphony formed an organic whole, its structure, thematic profile, and growth process conveying appropriate "breadth and dignity." Finally, the symphony radiated an "American" character, defined variously as pioneering in spirit, self-reliant, and forward-looking. Such qualities, however, were never to be achieved at the expense of universality: "although they welcomed the musical expression of the American spirit, critics expected these works to be first and foremost great symphonies."[24] Composers thus labored under dual and contradictory burdens: to personify the "American Beethoven" who created transcendent works according to European standards while also embodying the "musical Walt Whitman" who manifested the national identity through stylistic innovation.[25]

In every period, the critics' idealistic, inconsistent, and intractable standards resulted in each new work falling short of the glory of the Great American Symphony, even when they could not articulate precisely where the fault lay. As Louis Elson's 1894 review of Chadwick's prize-winning Third Symphony concludes, "All in all, one finds much to praise in the work, but at the end must confess that the great American symphony is not yet written."[26] Shadle poignantly sums up the dilemma faced by nineteenth-century symphonists: "No matter how good the work was, it was not good enough for some reason or other."[27] The generation after World War I saw qualified improvement. Critics generally regarded the First Symphony of

Samuel Barber, the Second of Randall Thompson, and the Third Symphonies of Harris, Copland, and Schuman—the most visible symphonies of the 1930s and 1940s—as fine and honorable works; but as the embodiment of the Great American Symphony, they judged each work to be an unsuccessful attempt or, more benevolently, one not quite arrived. The works of Harris and Copland came closest to the mark—the former on account of its originality, the latter for its tangibly high quality.[28] (Schnepel speculates that, had they known it better, the critics might well have hailed Ives's Fourth Symphony as their dream work that merged Beethovenian universality and Whitmanesque singularity; in 1942, Bernard Herrmann declared it "the great American symphony that our critics and conductors have cried out for."[29]) By the 1950s, Leonard Bernstein and others asked despairingly whether composing a viable—never mind "great"—American symphony was even possible anymore, given the postwar dominance of nontonal systems. With Neoromanticism and the resurgence of tonality came a firm rejection of the Great American Symphony paradigm, and its abandonment has contributed significantly to the rich and highly varied flourishing of the symphony genre after 1970.

What impact did the quest for the Great American Symphony have on the development of the genre in the United States? While its specter obviously did not deter composers from writing symphonies, a disproportionately large number of works fell short of achieving the recognition they might have gained had they not been constantly measured against a chimeric ideal and found wanting. Undoubtedly, the fraught critical reception accorded most American symphonies reinforced the predisposition of conductors and orchestras to favor canonic European repertory; furthermore, the present-day neglect of many of these works, both in the concert hall and in scholarship, likely stems at least in part from their unmerited reputation as so many failures.[30]

"An *American* Symphony or an American *Symphony*?"[31]

As we observed, advocates for the Great American Symphony set composers a near-insurmountable task in requiring them to be both universalist (especially) and American (as currently defined). Even before the quest began, though, composers themselves tended to favor one identity over the other. In 1853, William Henry Fry forcefully argued that only by transforming European procedures into a peculiarly American idiom could symphonists in the United States find their voice: "Until . . . American composers shall discard their foreign liveries and found an American school—and until the American public shall learn to support American artists, Art will not become indigenous to this country, but will only exist as a feeble exotic, and we shall continue to be provincial in Art. The American composer should not allow the name of Beethoven, or Handel, or Mozart to prove an eternal bugbear."[32]

Composers of the next generation largely rejected Fry's admonition. Paine, the most celebrated symphonist in the land in the late nineteenth century, stated that "We have not now national, but international music, and it makes no difference whether I compose here or in St. Petersburg, so long as I express myself in my own way."[33] Edward MacDowell repeatedly resisted enticements to musical nationalism (including participating in all-American concerts), believing that it, rather than cosmopolitanism, would lead to the provincialism Fry feared.[34]

Both positions found adherents in the mid-twentieth century. Roger Sessions and Paul Creston echoed Paine. As Sessions stated, "You create music and if it's genuine and spontaneous music written by an American, why then it's American music. . . . For me nationalism is the wrong approach."[35] Harris, the preeminent "Americanist" symphonist, dissented in terms Fry would have appreciated: "Musical literature never has been and never will be valuable to society as a whole until it is created as an authentic and characteristic culture of and from the people it expresses. History reveals that the great music has been produced only by staunch individuals who sank their roots deeply into the social soil which they accepted as their own."[36]

Apologists for the Americanist symphony faced a vexing question: How could a single symphony represent the vast expanse of the nation? Many nationalistic works focused on one region: Ives for example specified that the *Holidays Symphony* and Orchestral Set No. 1 concerned life and rituals in New England, however similar they might have been elsewhere in the country. Most symphonies before 1930, in fact, mirrored to various degrees the culture of the East Coast, particularly the New York–Boston corridor. Enthusiasts of Harris's symphonies seized on their supposedly midwestern character (open spaces, frontier spirit), which to them embodied a more comprehensive and authentic Americana.[37] In contrast to the supposedly rural spirit of Harris and Copland, Schuman and Bernstein cultivated a language designed again to point eastward, this time to contemporary urban life in New York City rather than small-town New England.[38]

Just as one symphony was hard-pressed to represent all of the United States geographically, still less could any one vernacular idiom—whether folk, popular, or patriotic in origin—reflect the full extent of the nation's highly heterogeneous racial and ethnic makeup. It was on these grounds that Amy Beach contested Dvořák's recommendation to base an American nationalist music on Black sources. As a national wellspring, she argued, a spiritual was as foreign intrinsically to Americans of Anglo-Celtic heritage such as herself as to Bohemians, and American composers could not draw on a broadly shared musical heritage in the way that many European nationalists could.[39] As Schnepel observes, a fundamental flaw of the Great American Symphony paradigm was that it presupposed a standard national style that cannot exist.[40] Ethnic diversity has, in fact, inspired a number of American symphonies in which composers explored their personal heritage (Beach's "Gaelic" Symphony, Hanson's "Nordic" Symphony, William Levi Dawson's *Negro Folk Symphony*, Aaron Jay Kernis's "Symphony of Meditations") or that of another culture (the Sixteenth Symphonies of Henry Cowell and Alan Hovhaness, inspired by Iceland and Korea, respectively). In recent decades, works like Lou Harrison's Fourth Symphony and Philip Glass's Fifth freely and eclectically combine unhomogenized idioms of multiple cultures.

Patronage

Symphonists in the United States have frequently faced an obstacle even more formidable than malcontent critics holding them to unrealistic ideals: the reluctance, when not outright refusal, of orchestras to perform their works on any regular basis. As early as the 1850s, Fry and George Frederick Bristow charged the New York Philharmonic (founded in 1842) with systematically ignoring homegrown music, especially works of substantial breadth; defenders of its programming, whether German by birth or by sympathy, responded with barbs about the poverty of native talent. The American symphony took shape against the backdrop of this increasingly ethnically tinged feud.[41] Until 1917, ensembles consisted largely of Central European players and conductors—rehearsals, in fact, were routinely held in German—who, with a few exceptions, emphasized a Germanic canon.[42]

Following World War I, however, some European conductors working in the United States began to champion American music, none more enthusiastically than Serge Koussevitzky (1874–1951). During his tenure at the Boston Symphony Orchestra from 1924 to 1949, the Russian-born conductor aggressively commissioned, performed (repeatedly), and promoted numerous American symphonies. As Joseph Horowitz states, "Koussevitzky, convinced that 'the next Beethoven vill from Colorado come,' retooled an orchestra into a laboratory for American music."[43] He particularly favored works radiating a heroic spirit that his student Bernstein would come to label the "Koussevitzky manner," but he did not restrict his patronage to compositions in that style. Walter Piston paid tribute to the conductor's genuine passion for supporting native-born composers:

> Of course the great event for American music at that time was the coming of Serge Koussevitzky. When I returned from France [1926] I felt pretty gloomy about the situation of the composer in America. I knew conductors were not interested in what we composers were doing, so I was writing only chamber music. Edward Burlingame Hill spoke to Koussevitzky about me and Koussevitzky asked to see me. He asked, "Why you no write for orchestra?" I said, "Because nobody would play it." And he said, "Write, and I will play." So I wrote and he played. I would get through with one piece and he would say, "Now what are you writing? Now the next score. Where is the next?" And it was the same story with other American composers.[44]

Aaron Copland also had effusive praise for the conductor: "I've never seen anything like Koussevitzky's enthusiasm for new music before or since. . . . It is not by chance that during the twenty-five years of Koussevitzky's leadership, from 1924 to 1949, American symphonic music came of age. . . . It would not please Koussevitzky to know that he set no precedent by his custom of keeping contemporary works in the repertoire."[45]

Outside of Boston, according to Copland, most American compositions—including, of course, symphonies—debuted in "an atmosphere of distrust and indifference"; Koussevitzky, by contrast, regarded each new work as "a fresh adventure."[46] Tables 1.1a and b list symphonies by composers from the United States and Latin America—both natives and émigrés—performed by the Boston Symphony Orchestra during Koussevitzky's tenure; 1.1a indicates premieres while 1.1b lists symphonies first heard elsewhere but played by the orchestra in this period.

Three Hungarian conductors also supported American symphonies in midcentury: Antal Dorati (Dallas Symphony Orchestra, Minneapolis Symphony Orchestra), Eugene Ormandy (Philadelphia Orchestra), and George Szell (Cleveland Orchestra). Native champions included Howard Hanson with the Eastman-Rochester Orchestra, Leonard Bernstein with the New York Philharmonic, and Robert Whitney with the Louisville Orchestra; the latter organization received a generous Rockefeller Grant in the 1950s to commission and record symphonies.

Further patronage arose through commissioning organizations. From its inception, the Koussevitzky Music Foundation (created in 1942 by the conductor as a memorial to his recently deceased wife Natalie) and its successor, the Serge Koussevitzky Foundation in the Library of Congress (established in 1950), has commissioned symphonies and other notable works from composers throughout the Americas and Europe; many bear dedications to the memory of Natalie or, after 1951, to both Koussevitzkys. Table 1.2 lists symphonies from the United States and Latin America sponsored by the Koussevitzky foundations; as it shows, the 1950s–1954 in particular—proved especially fruitful for the genre.

Since the 1950s, additional support has come through commissions from various orchestras as well as arts centers and foundations; besides the aforementioned Rockefeller Foundation, the latter have included the Lincoln Center for the Performing Arts, the John F. Kennedy Center for the Performing Arts, the Ford Foundation, the John D. and Catherine T. MacArthur Foundation, and the Andrew W. Mellon Foundation's Meet the Composer. Most of

Table 1.1a American and Latin American Symphonies Premiered by the Boston Symphony Orchestra during the Tenure of Serge Koussevitzky (1924–49)

Composer and work	**Date of performance** (conductors other than Koussevitzky are noted after the date)
Roger Sessions: Symphony No. 1 in E Minor	April 22, 1927
Edward Burlingame Hill: Symphony No. 1 in B-flat Major	March 30, 1928
*Vladimir Dukelsky: Symphony No. 2 in D-flat Major	April 25, 1930
Howard Hanson: Symphony No. 2, "Romantic"	November 28, 1930
Edward Burlingame Hill: Symphony No. 2 in C Minor	February 27, 1931
Louis Gruenberg: Symphony No. 1	February 10, 1933
Roy Harris: *Symphony 1933* [Symphony No. 1]	January 26, 1934
*Nicolai Berezowsky: Symphony No. 2	February 16, 1934
Roy Harris: Symphony No. 2	February 28, 1936 (Richard Burgin)
*Werner Josten: Symphony in F	November 13, 1936 (composer)
Edward Burlingame Hill: Symphony No. 3 in G Major	December 3, 1937
Walter Piston: Symphony No. 1	April 8, 1938 (composer)
Roy Harris: Symphony No. 3	February 24, 1939
David Stanley Smith: Symphony No. 4	April 14, 1939 (composer)
Howard Hanson: Symphony No. 3	November 3, 1939
*Nicolai Lopatnikoff: Symphony No. 2	December 22, 1939
William Schuman: Symphony No. 3	October 17, 1941
*Arthur Lourié: Symphony No. 2, "Kormtchaia"	November 7, 1941
*Bohuslav Martinů: Symphony No. 1	November 13, 1942
Roy Harris: Symphony No. 5	February 26, 1943
*Nicolai Berezowsky: Symphony No. 4	October 22, 1943 (composer)
William Schuman: Symphony for Strings (Symphony No. 5)	November 12, 1943
Gardner Read: Symphony No. 2	November 26, 1943 (composer)
Howard Hanson: Symphony No. 4, "Requiem"	December 3, 1943 (composer)
Samuel Barber: Symphony No. 2	March 3, 1944
Roy Harris: Symphony No. 6	April 14, 1944
David Diamond: Symphony No. 2	October 13, 1944
*Bohuslav Martinů: Symphony No. 3	October 12, 1945
Aaron Copland: Symphony No. 3	October 18, 1946
Henry Cowell: *Short Symphony* [Symphony No. 4]	October 24, 1947 (composer)
Walter Piston: Symphony No. 3	January 8, 1948
David Diamond: Symphony No. 4	January 22, 1948 (Leonard Bernstein)
Harold Shapero, Symphony for Classical Orchestra	January 30, 1948 (Leonard Bernstein)
Leo Sowerby: Symphony No. 4 in B	January 7, 1949
Leonard Bernstein: Symphony No. 2, *The Age of Anxiety*	April 8, 1949

Sources: Smith/KOUSSEVITZKY, Appendix A; Leichtentritt/KOUSSEVITZKY; Boston Symphony Orchestra/ARCHIVES
*Denotes an émigré composer.

Table 1.1b American and Latin American Symphonies Not Premiered by Koussevitzky but Performed during His Tenure

Composer and work	Years of performance (conductors other than Koussevitzky are noted after the date)
Aaron Copland: Symphony for Organ and Orchestra	1925
Henry Hadley: Symphony No. 4 in D Minor	1925 (composer)
Daniel Gregory Mason: Symphony No. 1 in C Minor	1928
*Ernest Bloch: *America: An Epic Rhapsody*	1928–29, 1939
*Vladimir Dukelsky: Symphony No. 1 in F Major	1929
Howard Hanson: Symphony No. 1 in E Minor, "Nordic"	1929 (composer)
George Whitefield Chadwick: Sinfonietta in D Major	1930
*Nicolai Berezowsky: Symphony No. 1	1931 (composer)
Randall Thompson: Symphony No. 2 in E Minor	1934, 1939–40
Aaron Copland: Symphony No. 1 (revision of Symphony for Organ and Orchestra)	1935
Carlos Chávez: *Sinfonía de Antígona* [Symphony No. 1]	1936 (composer)
Carlos Chávez: *Sinfonía India* [Symphony No. 2]	1936 (composer)
*Nicolai Berezowsky: Symphony No. 3	1937, 1940–41, 1946 (composer)
Henry Hadley: Andante from Symphony No. 3 in B Minor	1938 (performed as memorial to Hadley)
William Schuman: Symphony No. 2	1939
Arthur Shepherd: Symphony No. 2 in D Minor	1940 (composer)
Roy Harris: *Folk-Song Symphony* [Symphony No. 4]	1941
*Nicolai Lopatnikoff: Sinfonietta	1942 (Richard Burgin)
Walter Piston: Sinfonietta	1942 (Richard Burgin)
Walter Piston: Symphony No. 2	1944 (G. Wallace Woodworth)
Leonard Bernstein: Symphony No. 1, *Jeremiah*	1944 (composer)
Paul Creston: Symphony No. 2	1945 (Richard Burgin)

Sources: Smith/KOUSSEVITZKY, Appendix A; Leichtentritt/KOUSSEVITZKY; Boston Symphony Orchestra/ARCHIVES
*Denotes an émigré composer.

Schuman's later symphonies originated as commissions from major orchestras, including the Sixth (Dallas), Seventh (Boston), Eighth (New York), and Tenth (National Symphony Orchestra). By the same token, Peter Mennin's commissions included the Fifth Symphony (Dallas), Sixth (Louisville), Seventh (Cleveland), and Ninth (National Symphony Orchestra). Universities have also sponsored works such as Sessions's Seventh Symphony (University of Michigan), Vincent Persichetti's Sixth (Washington University Wind Ensemble) and Eighth (Baldwin-Wallace College), and John Corigliano's Symphony No. 3 "Circus Maximus" (University of Texas Wind Ensemble). Some symphonists have enjoyed the support of specific conductors or orchestras, such as Glass (Dennis Russell Davies) and John Harbison (Boston Symphony Orchestra). Patronage increasingly takes place through combined efforts—for example, Christopher Rouse wrote his Third Symphony as the result of a joint commission by the orchestras

Table 1.2 American and Latin American Symphonies Created through Grants by the Koussevitzky Music Foundation and the Serge Koussevitzky Foundation in the Library of Congress

Year commissioned	Composer and work	Library of Congress receipt of score
1942	*Bohuslav Martinů, Symphony No. 1	1942
1942	*Nicolai Berezowsky, Symphony No. 4	1943
1943	William Schuman, Symphony for Strings (Symphony No. 5)	1943
1944	*Darius Milhaud, Symphony No. 2	1944
1944	Aaron Copland, Symphony No. 3	1946
1945	David Diamond, Symphony No. 4	1945
1945	Harold Shapero, Symphony for Classical Orchestra	1947
1946	Walter Piston, Symphony No. 3	1947
1947	Roy Harris, Symphony No. 7	1952
1951	Leo Smit, Symphony No. 1	1955
1951	*Alexander Tcherepnin, Symphony No. 4	1965
1952	Carlos Chávez, Sinfonía No. 5 for Strings	1953
1952	*Ernest Bloch, *Sinfonia breve*	1953
1953	*Aaron Avshalomov, Symphony No. 3	1954
1953	Walter Sinclair Harvey, Chamber Symphony	1954
1954	Walter Piston, Symphony No. 6	1955
1954	Heitor Villa-Lobos, Symphony No. 11	1955
1954	Hall Overton, Symphony for Strings	1955
1954	Roger Sessions, Symphony No. 3	1957
1954	William Schuman, Symphony No. 7	1960
1954	Leonard Bernstein, Symphony No. 3, *Kaddish*	1963
1956	Lukas Foss, *Symphony of Chorales* [Symphony No. 2]	1958
1958	William Russo, Symphony No. 2, "Titans"	1958
1958	Ross Lee Finney, Symphony No. 2	1959
1959	Henry Cowell, Symphony No. 14	1960
1963	Lester Trimble, Symphony No. 2	1968
1973	Lou Harrison, Symphony No. 2, "Elegiac"	1976
1983	William Thomas McKinley, Symphony No. 3 for Chamber Ensemble, "Romantic"	1984
1983	Samuel Adler, Symphony No. 6	1985
1985	Martin Boykan, Symphony	1989
1988	George Walker, Sinfonia No. 2	1990
1990	Gerald Levinson, Symphony No. 2	1997
1996	Charles Wuorinen, Symphony Six	1997
1998	Wynton Marsalis, *All Rise* [Symphony No. 1]	2003
2002	Gregory D'Alessio, Symphony	2004
2003	Tison Street, *Symphony V: Colonial Scenes*	2004
2006	Donald Harris, Symphony No. 2	2012

Sources: Koussevitzky/FOUNDATION, Gottlieb, and Mauskapf/FOUNDATIONS
*Denotes an émigré composer.

of St. Louis, Baltimore, Stockholm, and Singapore—and through individual donations, one of which subsidized Ellen Taaffe Zwilich's Second Symphony.

Despite the varied resources for patronage, the symphonists' dilemma continues. While commissioned pieces generally receive a premiere from the supporting orchestra or orchestras (sometimes followed by a commercial recording), the problem remains securing the next performance. Works such as Ives's Second, Hanson's Second, Chávez's *Sinfonía India*, Copland's Third, and Corigliano's First appear with a certain degree of frequency, but most American and Latin American symphonies continue to suffer from severe underexposure in the concert hall. Declining financial resources for the orchestras and traditionally tepid governmental support for the arts in the United States (save during the Depression and World War II) clearly compound the problem—one which the ongoing fallout from the COVID-19 pandemic obviously will do nothing to ameliorate. Nevertheless, as Kevin Puts indicated, such trials have not always deterred symphonists: Glass may have said in 1987 that composers had little pragmatic or financial incentive to write symphonies, yet he has finished fourteen to date, one of which premiered in 2022.[47]

Though too often absent from live performance, the American symphony has found a home in the recording studio. A considerable number of works are commercially available, and others not yet preserved on disc can be heard on archival radio broadcasts posted on YouTube.[48] Three labels have devoted extensive coverage to American symphonies. Through the auspices of its Rockefeller Grant, the Louisville Symphony Orchestra founded its own label, First Edition, which issued recordings from 1955 to 1992 (a second label, First Edition Music, reissued some of these discs in new compilations between 2001 and 2006). The first thirteen symphonies it released were commissioned through the Rockefeller grant, but the orchestra continued to record old and new works after the grant expired; the catalogue eventually grew to fifty-five symphonies by native-born, immigrant, and Latin American composers, mostly conducted by Robert Whitney or Jorge Mester.[49]

The year before the founding of First Edition, Otto Luening, Douglas Moore, and Oliver Daniel established Composers Recording, Inc. (CRI), which from 1954 to 2003 released more than six hundred recordings of contemporary American music, including almost sixty symphonies. More impressive still is the Naxos label, which, as of this writing, has produced recordings of more than 175 symphonies by composers in the United States and Latin America, performed by numerous ensembles and conductors.

During their respective tenures with the Eastman-Rochester Orchestra and New York Philharmonic, Hanson and Bernstein each recorded sixteen symphonies—some well-known, some less so—written between 1900 and 1970 (including composer-led readings of the first five of Hanson's and all of Bernstein's). Starting in the 1980s, Gerard Schwarz and the Seattle Symphony produced a series of compact discs for the Delos label dedicated to symphonists active primarily in the mid-twentieth century—Ernest Bloch, Hanson, Piston, Creston, Schuman, Hovhaness, David Diamond, and Mennin. Most have been reissued on Naxos, and Schwarz has since added other performances on that label; in all, he has recorded thirty-four symphonies to date, including the complete works of Hanson and Schuman. At the same time, Estonian conductor Neeme Järvi and the Detroit Symphony Orchestra combined well-known works like Barber's First and Harris's Third with lesser-known symphonies by nineteenth-century figures (Bristow, Chadwick, Beach) and Black composers (Still and Dawson, as well as concert works by Duke Ellington)—again a total of sixteen symphonies. Finally, New World Records, a label devoted exclusively to American music of various folk, popular, and classical

Table 1.3 Commercial Recordings of American and Latin American Symphonies: A Selected List by Chronology (First Editions) or Composer (the rest)

FIRST EDITION RECORDS (LOUISVILLE ORCHESTRA)

Conducted by Robert Whitney (1955–67)

Henry Cowell, Symphony No. 11, "The Seven Rituals of Music" (1955)[a]
Peter Mennin, Symphony No. 6 (1955)[a]
Vincent Persichetti, Symphony No. 5 for Strings (1955)[a]
Robert Sanders, Little Symphony No. 2 in B-flat (1955)[a]
Alberto Ginastera, *Pampeana No. 3* (1955)[a]
Paul Nordoff, *Winter Symphony* (1957)[a]
John Vincent, Symphony in D: A Festive Piece in One Movement (1957)[a]
Meyer Kupferman, Fourth Symphony (1958)[a]
Gail Kubik, Symphony No. 2 in F (1958)[a]
*Colin McPhee, Symphony No. 2, "Pastoral" (1959)[a]
Halsey Stevens, *Sinfonia breve* (1959)[a]
*Benjamin Lees, Symphony No. 2 (1959)[a]
*Paul Hindemith, Sinfonietta in E (1960)[a]
Elliott Carter, Symphony No. 1 (1961)
Peter Mennin, Symphony No. 5 (1961)
Robert Kurka, Symphony No. 2 (1961)
Henry Cowell, Symphony No. 15, "Thesis" (1961)
*Juan Orrego-Salas, Symphony No. 2, "To the Memory of a Wanderer" (1962)

Ross Lee Finney, Symphony No. 2 (1962)
Ross Lee Finney, Symphony No. 3 (1962?)
Hall Overton, Symphony No. 2 in One Movement (1963)
George Rochberg, Symphony No. 1 (three-movement version) (1963)
Ray Luke, Symphony No. 2 (1963)
Robert Sanders, Little Symphony No. 1 in G (1963)
Quincy Porter, Symphony No. 2 (1964)
*Alexander Tcherepnin, Symphony No. 2 (1964)
Wallingford Riegger, Symphony No. 4 (1964)
Ross Lee Finney, Symphony No. 1, "Communiqué 1943" (1965)
Daniel Pinkham, Symphony No. 2 (1965)
Walter Piston, Symphony No. 5 (1965)
Roy Harris, Symphony No. 5 (1965)
*Ernst Toch, Symphony No. 5 "Jeptha" (1966)
Alan Hovhaness, Symphony No. 15, "The Silver Pilgrimage" (1966)
Irwin Bazelon, Short Symphony, "Testament to a Big City" (1966)

Conducted by Jorge Mester (1967–79)

Henry Cowell, Sinfonietta (1968)
William Schuman, Symphony No. 4 (1969)
Vincent Persichetti, Symphony No. 8 (1970)
Gustavo Becerra-Schmidt, Symphony No. 1 (1970)
John J. Becker, *Symphonia brevis* (Symphony No. 3) (1970)
Walter Piston, Symphony No. 7 (1974)

Walter Piston, Symphony No. 8 (1974)
*Benjamin Lees, Symphony No. 3 (1975)
Blas Galindo, Symphony No. 2 (1976)
Roy Harris, *Symphony 1933* [Symphony No. 1] (1978)
*Roque Cordero, Symphony No. 2 (1979)
Walter Piston, Symphony No. 1 (1979)

Other Conductors (in Parentheses)

George Antheil, Symphony No. 5 (Richard Duffalo, 1980)
Roger Sessions, Symphony No. 7 (Peter Leonard, 1981)
Thomas Ludwig, Symphony No. 1 (Akira Endo, 1983)
Boris Pillin, Symphony No. 3 (Lawrence Leighton Smith, 1986)

Ellen Taaffe Zwilich, Symphony No. 2, "Cello" (Lawrence Leighton Smith, 1990)
Karl Korte, Symphony No. 3 (Lawrence Leighton Smith, 1990)
William Bolcom, Symphony No. 1 (Lawrence Leighton Smith, 1992)
William Bolcom, Symphony No. 3 (Lawrence Leighton Smith, 1992)

Introduction to the Symphonic Repertoire of the United States and Latin America

NAXOS RECORDINGS (NAXOS AMERICAN CLASSICS)

Conducted by Marin Alsop (various ensembles)[b]

Samuel Barber, Symphony No. 1 (in One Movement) (Royal Scottish NO, 2000)
Samuel Barber, Symphony No. 2 (Royal Scottish NO, 2000)
Leonard Bernstein, Symphony No. 1, *Jeremiah* (Baltimore SO, 2017)
Leonard Bernstein, Symphony No. 2, *The Age of Anxiety* (Baltimore SO, 2017)
Leonard Bernstein, Symphony No. 3, *Kaddish* (Vocalists, Baltimore SO, 2015)
Aaron Copland, Symphony No. 1 (Bournemouth SO, 2008)
Aaron Copland, *Short Symphony* (Symphony No. 2) (Bournemouth SO, 2008)
Philip Glass, Symphony No. 2 (Bournemouth SO, 2004)
Philip Glass, Symphony No. 3 (Bournemouth SO, 2004)
Philip Glass, Symphony No. 4, "Heroes" (Bournemouth SO, 2007)
Roy Harris, Symphony No. 3 (Colorado Symphony, 2006)
Roy Harris, *Folk-Song Symphony* (Symphony No. 4) (Colorado Symphony, 2006)
Roy Harris, Symphony No. 5 (Bournemouth SO, 2010)
Roy Harris, Symphony No. 6, "Gettysburg" (Bournemouth SO, 2010)
Michael Hersch, Symphony No. 1 (Bournemouth SO, 2006)
Michael Hersch, Symphony No. 2 (Bournemouth SO, 2006)
Aaron Jay Kernis, Second Symphony (Peabody SO, 2019)
Kevin Puts, Symphony No. 2 "Island of Innocence" (Peabody SO, 2016)

Conducted by JoAnn Falletta (various ensembles)[b]

Edward Kennedy "Duke" Ellington, *Black, Brown, and Beige*, arr. Maurice Peress (Buffalo Philharmonic, 2013)
Jack Gallagher, Symphony No. 1 in One Movement, "Threnody" (London SO, 2010)
Jack Gallagher, Symphony No. 2, "Ascendant" (London SO, 2015)
Adolphus Hailstork, Symphony No. 1 (Virginia Symphony, 2012)
John Knowles Paine, Symphony No. 1 (Ulster Orchestra, 2013)
John Knowles Paine, Symphony No. 2 (Ulster Orchestra, 2015)

Conducted by Gerard Schwarz (with the Seattle Symphony Unless Otherwise Noted)

*Ernest Bloch, *America: An Epic Rhapsody* (2012)[c]
Paul Creston, Symphony No. 5 (2004)[c]
Richard Danielpour, Symphony No. 3, "Journey without Distance" (2012)[c]
David Diamond, Symphony No. 1 (2003)[c]
David Diamond, Symphony No. 2 (2004)[c]
David Diamond, Symphony No. 3 (2004)[c]
David Diamond, Symphony No. 4 (2004)[c]
David Diamond, Symphony No. 8 (2004)[c]
Howard Hanson, Symphony No. 1 (2011)[c]
Howard Hanson, Symphony No. 2 (2011)[c]
Howard Hanson, Symphony No. 3 (2011)[c]
Howard Hanson, Symphony No. 4, "Requiem" (2011)[c]
Howard Hanson, Symphony No. 5, "Sinfonia sacra" (2011)[c]
Howard Hanson, Symphony No. 6 (2012)[c]
Howard Hanson, Symphony No. 7, "A Sea Symphony" (2012)[c]
Alan Hovhaness, Symphony No. 1, "Exile" (2012)[c]
Alan Hovhaness, Symphony No. 22, "City of Light" (Seattle Symphony conducted by the composer, 2004)[c]
Alan Hovhaness, Symphony No. 48, "Vision of Andromeda" (Eastern Music Festival Orchestra, 2015)
Alan Hovhaness, Symphony No. 50, "Mount St. Helens" (2012)[c]
Alan Hovhaness, Symphony No. 60, "To the Appalachian Mountains" (Berlin Radio SO, 2006)
Samuel Jones, Symphony No. 3, "Palo Duro Canyon" (2009)
*Henri Lazarof, Symphony No. 2 (2003)
Peter Mennin, Symphony No. 3 (2012)[c]

Table 1.3 *continued*

Peter Mennin, Symphony No. 7, "Variation-Symphony" (2012)c	William Schuman, Symphony No. 5 (2006)c
Walter Piston, Symphony No. 2 (2003)c	William Schuman, Symphony No. 6 (2009)
Walter Piston, Symphony No. 4 (2003)c	William Schuman, Symphony No. 7 (2005)
Walter Piston, Symphony No. 6 (2003)c	William Schuman, Symphony No. 8 (2010)
William Schuman, Symphony No. 3 (2006)	William Schuman, Symphony No. 9, "Le fosse ardeatine" (2005)
William Schuman, Symphony No. 4 (2005)	William Schuman, Symphony No. 10 (2005)

Recorded by the Nashville Symphony Orchestra,
Conducted by Kenneth Schermerhorn or Giancarlo Guerrero

John Adams, *Harmonielehre* (Guerrero, 2021)	Charles Ives, Symphony No. 2 (Schermerhorn, 2000)
Amy Beach, Symphony in E Minor, "Gaelic" (Schermerhorn, 2003)	Aaron Jay Kernis, Symphony No. 4, "Chromelodeon" (Guerrero, 2020)
Elliott Carter, Symphony No. 1 (Schermerhorn, 2004)	Jonathan Leshnoff, Symphony No. 4, "Heichalos" (Guerrero, 2019)
Michael Daugherty, *Metropolis* Symphony (Guerrero, 2009)	Christopher Rouse, Symphony No. 5 (Guerrero, 2020)
Howard Hanson, Symphony No. 1, "Nordic" (Schermerhorn, 2000)	Roberto Sierra, Sinfonía No. 4 (Guerrero, 2013)

Recorded by the National Orchestral Institute Philharmonic,
Conducted by David Alan Miller or James Ross

Samuel Barber, Symphony No. 1 (in One Movement) (Ross, 2017)	Walter Piston, Symphony No. 5 (Miller, 2020)
John Corigliano, Symphony No. 1 (Miller, 2016)	Randall Thompson, Symphony No. 2 (Ross, 2017)
John Harbison, Symphony No. 4 (Miller, 2018)	

Recorded by the Ukraine National Symphony Orchestra,
Conducted by Theodore Kuchar or John McLaughlin Williams

George Antheil, Symphony No. 4 (Kuchar, 2000)	Nicolas Flagello, *Missa sinfonica* (Williams, 2008)
George Antheil, Symphony No. 6 (Kuchar, 2000)	Henry Hadley, Symphony No. 4, "North, East, South, and West" (Williams, 2001)
John Alden Carpenter, Symphony No. 1 (Williams, 2001)	Roy Harris, Symphony No. 7 (Kuchar, 2002)
John Alden Carpenter, Symphony No. 2 (Williams, 2001)	Roy Harris, Symphony No. 9 (Kuchar, 2002)
George Whitefield Chadwick, Symphony No. 2 (Kuchar, 2005)	*Benjamin Lees, Symphony No. 4, "Memorial Candles" (Kuchar, 1999)
George Whitefield Chadwick, *Symphonic Sketches* (Kuchar, 2005)	George Frederick McKay, Sinfonietta No. 4 (Williams, 2004)
Paul Creston, Symphony No. 1 (Kuchar, 2000)	Arnold Rosner, Symphony No. 5, "Missa sine Cantoribus super Salve Regina" (Williams, 2008)
Paul Creston, Symphony No. 2 (Kuchar, 2000)	
Paul Creston, Symphony No. 3, "Three Mysteries" (Kuchar, 2000)	

Miscellaneous Performances by Ensembles outside the United States[b]

Steven Albert, *RiverRun* (Symphony No. 1) (Russian PO/Paul Polivnick, 2007)	*Leonardo Balada, *Sinfonia en negro: Homage to Martin Luther King* (Symphony No. 1) (Málaga PO/Edmon Colomer, 2013)
Steven Albert, Symphony No. 2 (Russian PO/Paul Polivnick, 2007)	

*Leonardo Balada, Symphony No. 4, "Lausanne" (Barcelona Symphony/Salvador Mas Conde, 2004)

*Leonardo Balada, Symphony No. 5, "American" (Seville Royal SO/Eduardo Alonso-Crespo, 2006)

*Leonardo Balada, Symphony No. 6, "Symphony of Sorrows" (Galicia SO/Jesús López-Cobos, 2014)

*George Barati, Symphony No. 1, "Alpine Symphony" (Budapest PO/Lászlo Kováks, 2001)

Leonard Bernstein, Symphony No. 1, *Jeremiah* (New Zealand SO/James Judd, 2003)

Peter Boyer, Symphony No. 1 (London PO/composer, 2014)

Gloria Coates, Symphony No. 1, "Music on Open Strings" (Siegerland Orchestra/Jorge Rotter, 2006)

Gloria Coates, Symphony No. 7 (Bavarian Radio SO/Olaf Henzold, 2006)

Gloria Coates, Symphony No. 14, "Symphony in Microtones" (Munich Chamber Orchestra/Christoph Poppen, 2006)

Gloria Coates, Symphony No. 15, "Homage to Mozart" (ORF Vienna Radio Symphony/Michael Boder, 2007)

James Cohn, Symphony No. 2 (Slovak Radio SO/Kirk Trevor, 2008)

James Cohn, Symphony No. 7 (Slovak Radio SO/Vakhtang Jordania, 2008)

Carson Cooman, Symphony No. 2, "Litanies of Love and Rain" (Slovak Radio SO/Kirk Trevor, 2007)

Carson Cooman, Symphony No. 3, "Ave Maria Stella" (Slovak Radio SO/Kirk Trevor, 2007)

Aaron Copland, Symphony No. 3 (New Zealand SO/James Judd, 2002)

Richard Danielpour, Symphony for Strings (Russian String Orchestra/Mischa Rachlevsky, 2019)

William Henry Fry, *Santa Claus: Christmas Symphony* (Royal Scottish NO/Tony Rowe, 2000)

William Henry Fry, *Niagara* (Royal Scottish NO/Tony Rowe, 2000)

William Henry Fry, *The Breaking Heart* (Royal Scottish NO/Tony Rowe, 2000)

Vittorio Giannini, Symphony No. 4 (Bournemouth SO/Daniel Spalding, 2009)

Alan Hovhaness, Symphony No. 63, "Loon Lake" (Royal Scottish NO/Stewart Robertson, 2008)

Kamran Ince, Symphony No. 2, "Fall of Constantinople" (Bilkent Symphony/composer, 2011)

Kamran Ince, Symphony No. 3, "Siege of Vienna" (Prague Symphony/composer, 2005)

Kamran Ince, Symphony No. 4, "Sardis" (Prague Symphony/composer, 2005)

Kamran Ince, Symphony No. 5, "Galatasaray" (Bilkent Symphony/composer, 2011)

Charles Ives, Symphony No. 1 (Irish National SO/James Sinclair, 2003)

Charles Ives, Symphony No. 3, "The Camp Meeting" (Northern Sinfonia/James Sinclair, 2003)

Ian Krouse, Symphonies of Strings No. 1, Op. 33b, "La follia" (Seocho Philharmonic/Jong Hoon Bae, 2021)

Ian Krouse, Symphonies of Strings No. 2, Op. 30b, "Dror Yikro, 'Song of Freedom'" (Seocho Philharmonic/Jong Hoon Bae, 2021)

Ian Krouse, Symphony No. 5, "A Journey towards Peace" (Seocho Philharmonic/Jong Hoon Bae, 2021)

Dan Locklair, *Symphony of Seasons* (Slovak Radio SO/Kirk Trevor, 2007)

Edward MacDowell, Suite No. 1 for Large Orchestra (Ulster Orchestra/Takuo Yuasa, 2000)

Edward MacDowell, Suite No. 2 for Large Orchestra, "Indian" (Ulster Orchestra/Takuo Yuasa, 2000)

Florence Price, Symphony No. 3 in C Minor (ORF Vienna Radio Symphony/John Jeter, 2021)

George Rochberg, Symphony No. 1 (complete five-movement version) (Saarbrücken German Radio PO/Christopher Lyndon-Gee, 2007)

George Rochberg, Symphony No. 2 (Saarbrücken German Radio PO/Christopher Lyndon-Gee, 2005)

George Rochberg, Symphony No. 5 (Saarbrücken German Radio PO/Christopher Lyndon-Gee, 2003)

Cláudio Santoro, Symphony No. 5 (Goiás Philharmonic/Neil Thomson, 2022)

Cláudio Santoro, Symphony No. 7, "Brasília" (Goiás Philharmonic/Neil Thomson, 2022)

Table 1.3 *continued*

Cláudio Santoro, Symphony No. 11 (Goiás Philharmonic/Neil Thomson, 2022)
Cláudio Santoro, Symphony No. 12 (Goiás Philharmonic/Neil Thomson, 2022)
*José Serebrier, Symphony No. 1 (Bournemouth SO/composer, 2010)
*José Serebrier, Symphony No. 2, "Partita" (London PO/composer, 2007)
*José Serebrier, Symphony No. 3, "Symphonie mystique" (Toulouse National Chamber Orchestra/composer, 2003)
George Templeton Strong, Symphony No. 2, "Sintram" (Moscow SO/Adriano, 1999)
Virgil Thomson, *Symphony on a Hymn Tune* (New Zealand SO/James Sedares, 1999)
Virgil Thomson, Symphony No. 2 (New Zealand SO/James Sedares, 1999)
Virgil Thomson, Symphony No. 3 (New Zealand SO/James Sedares, 1999)
Heitor Villa-Lobos, Complete Symphonies (São Paulo SO/Isaac Karabtchevsky, 2020) box set in 6 volumes, 1–2; 3–4; 6–7; 8–9-11; 10; 12 (Symphony #5 is lost)
Meredith Willson, Symphony No. 1, "A Symphony of San Francisco" (Moscow SO/William Stromberg, 1999)
Meredith Willson, Symphony No. 2, "The Missions of California" (Moscow SO/William Stromberg, 1999)

Miscellaneous Performances by American Ensembles[b]

Leonard Bernstein, Symphony No. 2, *The Age of Anxiety* (Florida PO/James Judd, 2002)
Gloria Coates, Symphony No. 10 (CalArts Orchestra/Susan Allen, 2018)
David Diamond, Symphony No. 6 (Indiana University PO/Arthur Fagen, 2018)
Louis Moreau Gottschalk, Symphony No. 1, *La nuit des tropiques* (Hot Springs Music Festival SO/Richard Rosenberg, 2007)
Louis Moreau Gottschalk, Symphony No. 2, *À Montevideo* (Hot Springs Music Festival SO/Richard Rosenberg, 2007)
Adolphus Hailstork, Symphony No. 2 (Grand Rapids Symphony/David Lockington, 2007)
Adolphus Hailstork, Symphony No. 3 (Grand Rapids Symphony/David Lockington, 2007)
Jonathan Leshnoff, Symphony No. 1, "Forgotten Chants and Refrains" (IRIS Orchestra/Michael Stern, 2010)
Cindy McTee, Symphony No. 1 (Detroit SO/Leonard Slatkin, 2013)
Florence Price, Symphony No. 1 (Fort Smith Orchestra/John Jeter, 2019)
Florence Price, Symphony No. 4 (Fort Smith Orchestra/John Jeter, 2019)
Roberto Sierra, Sinfonía No. 3, "La Salsa" (Puerto Rico SO/Maximiano Valdés, 2016)
William Grant Still, *Afro-American Symphony* (Symphony No. 1) (Fort Smith Orchestra/John Jeter, 2005)
William Grant Still, Symphony No. 2, "Song of a New Race" (Fort Smith Orchestra/John Jeter, 2011)
William Grant Still, Symphony No. 3, "The Sunday Symphony" (Fort Smith Orchestra/John Jeter, 2011)
William Grant Still, Symphony No. 4, "Autochthonous" (Fort Smith Orchestra/John Jeter, 2009)
William Grant Still, Symphony No. 5, "Western Hemisphere" (Fort Smith Orchestra/John Jeter, 2009)

Symphonies for Wind Ensemble (Wind Band Classics series)[b]

William Bolcom, First Symphony for Band (Middle Tennessee State Univ. WE/Reed Thomas, 2011)
John Corigliano, Symphony No. 3, "Circus Maximus" (Univ. of Texas WE/Jerry Junkin, 2009)
Mohammed Fairouz, Symphony No. 4, "In the Shadow of No Towers" (Univ. of Kansas WE/Paul Popiel, 2013)
Nicolas Flagello, Symphony No. 2, "Symphony of the Winds" (Univ. of Houston WE/David Bertman, 2013)
Vittorio Giannini, Symphony No. 3 (Univ. of Houston WE/Tom Bennett, 2006)
Morton Gould, Symphony No. 4, "West Point" (Univ. of Kansas WE/Scott Weiss, 2011)

Ira Hearshen, Symphony on Themes by John Philip Sousa (United States Air Force Band/Lowell Graham, 2013)

Alan Hovhaness, Symphony No. 4 (Royal Scottish Academy of Music and Drama WO/Keith Brion, 2005)

Alan Hovhaness, Symphony No. 7, "Nanga Parvat" (Trinity College of Music WO/Keith Brion, 2010)

Alan Hovhaness, Symphony No. 14, "Ararat" (Trinity College of Music WO/Keith Brion, 2010)

Alan Hovhaness, Symphony No. 20, "Three Journeys to a Holy Mountain" (Royal Scottish Academy of Music and Drama WO/Keith Brion, 2005)

Alan Hovhaness, Symphony No. 23, "Ani" (Trinity College of Music WO/Keith Brion, 2010)

Alan Hovhaness, Symphony No. 53, "Star Dawn" (Royal Scottish Academy of Music and Drama WO/Keith Brion, 2005)

David Maslanka, Symphony No. 3 (University of Miami Frost WE/Gary D. Green, 2007)

Arnold Rosner, Symphony No. 8, "Trinity" (Univ. of Houston WE/David Bertman, 2013)

Frank Ticheli, Symphony No. 2 (Middle Tennessee State University WE/Reed Thomas, 2011)

Kevin Walczyk, Symphony No. 5, "Freedom from Fear—Images from the Shoreline" (Univ. of Kansas WE/Paul Popiel, 2020)

NEW WORLD RECORDS/COMPOSERS RECORDINGS, INC. (CRI)

Daniel Asia, Symphony No. 2 "Celebration" (Phoenix Symphony/James Sedares, 1993)

Daniel Asia, Symphony No. 3 (Phoenix Symphony/James Sedares, 1993)

*Leonardo Balada, *Steel Symphony* (Symphony No. 3; Pittsburgh SO/Lorin Maazel, 1987)

Samuel Barber, Symphony No. 1 (in One Movement) (Japan Philharmonic SO/William Strickland, 2010)[d]

Irwin Bazelon, Symphony No. 5 (Indianapolis Symphony/Izler Solomon, 2007)[d]

Jack Beeson, Symphony No. 1 (Polish National Radio Orchestra/William Strickland, 2010)[d]

Gordon Binkerd, Symphony No. 2 (Oslo Philharmonic Orchestra/George Barati, 2010)[d]

Easley Blackwood, Symphony for Fourteen Chamber Instruments (Contemporary Chamber Ensemble/Arthur Weisberg, 2010)[d]

*Ernest Bloch, Symphony for Trombone and Orchestra (Howard Prince, trom.; Portland Youth Philharmonic/Jacob Avshalomov, 2007)[d]

John Boda, Sinfonia (Knoxville SO/David Van Vactor, 2010)[d]

William Bolcom, Symphony No. 4 (Saint Louis SO/Leonard Slatkin, 1988)

George Frederick Bristow, Symphony No. 2, "Jullien" (Royal Northern Sinfonia/Rebecca Miller, 2016)

Robert Carl, Symphony No. 4, "The Ladder" (Hartt SO/Christopher Zimmerman, 2016)

Elliott Carter, Symphony No. 1 (American Composers Orchestra/Paul Dunkel, 2007)

George Whitefield Chadwick, Symphony No. 2 (Albany SO/Julius Hegyi, 1986)

Gloria Coates, Symphony No. 8, "Indian Sounds" (soloists with Musica-viva-ensemble Dresden/Jürgen Wirrmann, 2002)

Paul Cooper, Symphony No. 4, "Landscape" (concertino soloists, Houston SO/Samuel Jones, 2007)

Henry Cowell, Symphony No. 7 (Vienna SO/William Strickland, 2010)[d]

Henry Cowell, Symphony No. 16, "Icelandic" (Iceland SO/William Strickland, 1997)[d]

David Del Tredici, *An Alice Symphony* (Phyllis Bryn-Julson, soprano; Tanglewood Music Center Orchestra/Oliver Knussen, 2007)[d]

David Diamond, Symphony No. 4 (New York Philharmonic/Leonard Bernstein, 1977)

David Diamond, Symphony No. 5 (Juilliard Orchestra/Christopher Keene, 1990)

*Marcel Dick, Symphony for Strings (London Sinfonietta/David Atherton, 2010)[d]

*Johan Franco, Symphony No. 5, "The Cosmos" (North Holland Philharmonic/Henri Arends, 2010)[d]

Miriam Gideon, *Symphonia brevis* (Radio Orchestra of Zurich/Jacques Monod, 2010)[d]

Roger Goeb, Symphony No. 3 (Leopold Stokowski and His Orchestra, 2010)[d]

Table 1.3 *continued*

Louis Moreau Gottschalk, Symphony No. 1, *La nuit des tropiques* (two-piano transcription, Anthony and Joseph Paratore, 1978)

Ray Green, *Sunday Sing Symphony* (Symphonie-Orkester des Hessischen Rundfunks/David Van Vactor, 2010)[d]

Gene Gutschë, Fifth Symphony for Strings (Cincinnati SO/Max Rudolf, 2010)[d]

John Harbison, Symphony No. 1 (Boston SO/Seiji Ozawa, 1985)

Lou Harrison, Symphony on G (Royal Philharmonic Orchestra/Gerhard Samuel, 1996)[d]

Stephen Hartke, Symphony No. 2 (Riverside Symphony/George Rothman, 1993)

Stephen Hartke, Symphony No. 3 (Hilliard Ensemble, New York Philharmonic/Lorin Maazel, 2006)

Herbert Haufrecht, Symphony for Brass and Timpani (Brass Ensemble Society of New York/Simon Karasick, 2010)[d]

Anthony Philip Heinrich, *The Ornithological Combat of Kings* (Syracuse SO/Christopher Keene, 1978)

Robert Helps, Symphony No. 1 (Columbia SO/Zoltan Rozsnyai, 2017)[d]

Andrew Imbrie, Symphony No. 3 (London SO/Harold Farberman, 2007)[d]

Charles Ives, *Holidays Symphony* (various ensembles/William Strickland, 2010)[d]

*Werner Josten, Symphony in F (Polish National Radio Orchestra/William Strickland, 2007)[d]

Ulysses Kay, Sinfonia in E (Oslo PO/George Barati, 2010)[d]

Homer Keller, Symphony No. 3 (Japan Philharmonic SO/William Strickland, 2010)[d]

Robert Kelly, Symphony No. 2 (Japan Philharmonic SO/Akeo Watanabe, 2010)[d]

Ellis Kohs, Symphony No. 1 (Vienna Orchestra/F. Charles Adler, 2010)[d]

Anthony Korf, Symphony No. 2, "Blue Note" (Riverside Symphony/George Rothman, 1990)

Dai-Keong Lee, Symphony No. 1 (Nürnberg Symphony Orchestra/George Barati, 2010)[d]

Robert Hall Lewis, Symphony No. 2 (London SO/composer, 2007)

Robert Hall Lewis, Symphony No. 4 (Philharmonia Orchestra of London/composer, 1993)

Peter Mennin, Symphony No. 3 (New York Philharmonic/Dimitri Mitropoulos, 1997)[d]

Peter Mennin, Symphony No. 7, "Variation-Symphony" (Chicago SO/Jean Martinon, 1977)

Peter Mennin, Symphony No. 8 (Columbus SO/Christian Badea, 1989)

Peter Mennin, Symphony No. 9 (Columbus SO/Christian Badea, 1989)

Douglas Moore, Symphony in A (Japan Philharmonic SO/William Strickland, 2010)[d]

John Knowles Paine, Symphony No. 1 (New York Philharmonic/Zubin Mehta, 1989)

John Knowles Paine, Symphony No. 2 (New York Philharmonic/Zubin Mehta, 1987)

Stephen Paulus, Symphony for Strings (Atlanta SO/Yoel Levi, 1990)

Vincent Persichetti, Symphony No. 5 for Strings (Philadelphia Orchestra/Riccardo Muti, 1990)

Walter Piston, Symphony No. 6 (Boston SO/Charles Munch, 1977)

John Pozdro, Third Symphony (Oklahoma City SO/Guy Fraser Harrison, 2010)[d]

Leland Procter, Symphony No. 1 (Polish National Radio Orchestra/Włodzimiertz Ormicki, 2010)[d]

Gardner Read, Symphony No. 4 (Cleveland Orchestra/Lorin Maazel, 1997)[d]

Wallingford Riegger, Symphony No. 3 (Eastman-Rochester SO/Howard Hanson, 2007)[d]

George Rochberg, Symphony No. 2 (New York Philharmonic/Werner Torkanowsky, 1997)[d]

Ned Rorem, String Symphony (Atlanta SO/Robert Shaw, 1988)

Robert Sanders, Symphony in A (Knoxville SO/David Van Vactor, 2010)[d]

*Anthony Louis Scarmolin, Symphony No. 1 (Slovak Radio SO/Joel Eric Suben, 1995)

*Anthony Louis Scarmolin, Symphony No. 2 (Slovak Radio SO/Joel Eric Suben, 1995)

*Anthony Louis Scarmolin, *Sinfonia breve* (Symphony No. 3) (Polish Radio National SO/Joel Eric Suben, 1995)

William Schuman, Symphony No. 7 (Pittsburgh SO/Lorin Maazel, 1987)

Roger Sessions, Symphony No. 1 (Japan PO/Akeo Wantanabe, 2007)[d]

Roger Sessions, Symphony No. 2 (New York Philharmonic/Dimitri Mitropoulos, 2007)[d]

Roger Sessions, Symphony No. 3 (Royal PO/Igor Buketoff, 2011)[d]
Roger Sessions, Symphony No. 4 (Columbus SO/Christian Badea, 1987)
Roger Sessions, Symphony No. 5 (Columbus SO/Christian Badea, 1987)
Roger Sessions, Symphony No. 8 (American SO/Leon Botstein, 2005)
Harold Shapero, Symphony for Classical Orchestra (Los Angeles Philharmonic/André Previn, 1988)
Elie Siegmeister, Symphony No. 3 (Oslo PO/composer, 2010)[d]
Halsey Stevens, Symphony No. 1 (Japan Philharmonic SO/Akeo Watanabe, 2010)[d]
Howard Swanson, Short Symphony (Vienna State Opera Orchestra/Franz Litschauer, 2010)[d]
Virgil Thomson, Symphony No. 3 (New Hampshire SO/James Bolle, 2017)[d]
Francis Thorne, Symphony No. 5 (American Composers Orchestra/Dennis Russell Davies, 2007)[d]
*George Tremblay, Symphony in One Movement (Hamburg SO/Frederic Balazs, 2010)[d]
Lester Trimble, Symphony in Two Movements (Japan Philharmonic SO/Akeo Watanabe, 2010)[d]
Lester Trimble, Symphony No. 3, "The Tricentennial" (Albany SO/Julius Hegyi, 2007)[d]
Gilbert Trythall, Symphony No. 1 (Knoxville SO/David Van Vactor, 2010)[d]
David Van Vactor, Symphony No. 1 (Frankfurt Radio SO/composer, 1995)[d]
David Van Vactor, Symphony No. 2 (Hessian Radio SO/composer, 2010)[d]
David Van Vactor, Symphony No. 3 (Hessian Radio SO/composer, 1995)[d]
Andrew Waggoner, Symphony No. 2 (Bohuslav Martinů Philharmonic/Petr Pololanik, 2007)[d]
Robert Ward, Symphony No. 2 (Japan PO/William Strickland, 2010)[d]
Robert Ward, Symphony No. 3 (Iceland SO/Igor Buketoff, 2010)[d]
Ben Weber, Symphony on Poems of William Blake (Leopold Stokowski and His Orchestra; Warren Galjour, bar., 2010)[d]
Frank Wigglesworth, Symphony No. 1 (Vienna Orchestra/F. Charles Adler, 1996)[d]
Olly Wilson, Sinfonia (Boston SO/Seiji Ozawa, 1985)
*Stefan Wolpe, Symphony (Orchestra of the 20th Century/Arthur Weisberg, 2007)[d]
Charles Wuorinen, Symphony No. 3 (Japan Philharmonic SO/Akeo Watanabe, 2010)
Charles Wuorinen, *Two-Part Symphony* (American Composers Orchestra/Dennis Russell Davies, 2013)
Rolv Yttrehus, Symphony No. 1 (Polish National Radio Orchestra/Joel Suben, 2007)[d]
Ellen Taaffe Zwilich, Chamber Symphony (Boston Musica Viva/Richard Pittman, 2007)[d]
Ellen Taaffe Zwilich, Symphony No. 1 (Indianapolis SO/John Nelson, 1986)

LEONARD BERNSTEIN AND THE NEW YORK PHILHARMONIC
(ON SONY UNLESS OTHERWISE NOTED)

Leonard Bernstein, Symphony No. 1, *Jeremiah* (1961)[e]
Leonard Bernstein, Symphony No. 2, *The Age of Anxiety* (1950, 1965)[c]
Leonard Bernstein, Symphony No. 3, *Kaddish* (1964)[f]
Marc Blitzstein, *Airborne Symphony* (1966)[g]
Carlos Chávez, *Sinfonía India* (1961)
Aaron Copland, Symphony No. 1 (1967)
Aaron Copland, Symphony No. 3 (1966)[h]
David Diamond, Symphony No. 4 (1958)
Roy Harris, Symphony No. 3 (1960)[h]
Charles Ives, *Holidays Symphony* (1963–68; pieces recorded separately)
Charles Ives, Symphony No. 2 (1987; on Deutsche Grammophon)
William Schuman, Symphony No. 3 (1960)[h]
William Schuman, Symphony No. 5 (1966)
William Schuman, Symphony No. 6 (1958)
William Schuman, Symphony No. 8 (1962)
Randall Thompson, Symphony No. 2 (1968)

Table 1.3 *continued*

HOWARD HANSON AND THE EASTMAN-ROCHESTER ORCHESTRA (MERCURY AND MERCURY LIVING PRESENCE)

Samuel Barber, Symphony No. 1 (in One Movement) (1954)
George Whitefield Chadwick, *Symphonic Sketches* (1956)
Aaron Copland, Symphony No. 3 (1965)
Henry Cowell, Symphony No. 4 (1956)
Howard Hanson, Symphony No. 1 (1960)
Howard Hanson, Symphony No. 2 (1961)
Howard Hanson, Symphony No. 3 (1966)
Howard Hanson, Symphony No. 4 (1953)
Howard Hanson, Symphony No. 5, "Sinfonia sacra" (1954)
Roy Harris, Symphony No. 3 (1953)
Charles Ives, Symphony No. 3 "The Camp Meeting" (1959)
Edward MacDowell, Suite No. 1 for Large Orchestra (1966)
Edward MacDowell, Suite No. 2 for Large Orchestra, "Indian" (1956)
Peter Mennin, Symphony No. 5 (1964)
Walter Piston, Symphony No. 3 (1956)
Virgil Thomson, *Symphony on a Hymn Tune* (1965)

NEEMI JÄRVI AND THE DETROIT SYMPHONY ORCHESTRA (CHANDOS)

Samuel Barber, Symphony No. 1 (in One Movement) (1991)
Samuel Barber, Symphony No. 2 (1993)
Amy Beach, Symphony in E Minor, "Gaelic" (1991)
George Frederick Bristow, Symphony No. 3 (1993)
George Whitefield Chadwick, *Symphonic Sketches* (1995)
George Whitefield Chadwick, Symphony No. 2 (1995)
George Whitefield Chadwick, Symphony No. 3 (1994)
Aaron Copland, Symphony No. 3 (1996)
Paul Creston, Symphony No. 2 (1995)
William Levi Dawson, *Negro Folk Symphony* (1993)
Roy Harris, Symphony No. 3 (1996)
Charles Ives, Symphony No. 1 (1992)
Charles Ives, Symphony No. 2 (1995)
William Grant Still, *Afro-American Symphony* (Symphony No. 1) (1993)
William Grant Still, Symphony No. 2, "Song of a New Race" (1993)
Randall Thompson, Symphony No. 2 (1996)

GERARD SCHWARZ AND THE SEATTLE SYMPHONY (DELOS)

See above under Naxos.

*Émigré composer.
a. Commissioned by the Louisville Orchestra with the support of the Rockefeller Foundation.
b. Ensemble abbreviations: NO = National Orchestra, PO = Philharmonic Orchestra, SO = Symphony Orchestra, WE = Wind Ensemble, WO = Wind Orchestra.
c. Originally a Delos release.
d. Originally released on CRI records; after the label ceased, New World Records obtained the rights to their recordings and has made them available on demand.
e. Also in 1945 with St. Louis Symphony Orchestra on RCA Victor and in 1977 with Israel Philharmonic Orchestra on Deutsche Grammophon.
f. Also in 1977 with Israel Philharmonic Orchestra on Deutsche Grammophon.
g. Also in 1946 on RCA Victor.
h. Also in 1985 on Deutsche Grammophon.

traditions, has produced discs of twenty-four symphonies ranging from Bristow to Zwilich and Daniel Asia; all were first recordings, although those of Paine and Chadwick have since received additional recordings. After CRI ceased production in 2003, New World Records obtained the rights to their recordings and has made them available on demand. To give an idea of the diversity of symphonies that are available on disc, Table 1.3 lists recordings from First Edition, Naxos, and New World Records/CRI, as well as the recordings made by Bernstein, Hanson, Järvi, and Schwarz.[50]

Models

What European works had the strongest impact on American symphonists? In the nineteenth century, composers of course drew on the German Romantic legacy of Beethoven (e.g., Paine Symphony No. 1, 1876), Mendelssohn (Bristow Symphony No. 3, 1859), and Brahms (Chadwick Symphony No. 3, 1894); Berlioz arguably provided a subsidiary stimulus to Fry (*Santa Claus: Christmas Symphony*, 1853) and Louis Moreau Gottschalk (Symphony No. 1, *La nuit des tropiques* (A Night in the Tropics, 1859). Two works from the European nationalist tradition deeply affected the course of the twentieth-century American symphony. Dvořák's "New World" Symphony (1893) electrified those who saw a folk-based music as the way forward for the nation: as critic W. J. Henderson wrote, "We Americans should thank and honor the Bohemian master who has shown us how to build our national school of music."[51] Its supposed folk borrowings, pentatonic language, and orchestration (especially the English horn in the Largo) left discernible marks on contemporary works such as Beach's "Gaelic" Symphony (1896) and Ives's First Symphony (1897–1902). Dvořák's composition also strongly inspired the first generation of Black symphonists, especially Florence Price (Symphony No. 1 in E Minor, 1933) and Dawson (*Negro Folk Symphony*, 1934).[52]

Thirty years later, Jean Sibelius's music made an even greater impact, and that influence continues into the present century. Immensely popular in America in the 1920s and 1930s, when he was widely seen as a viable modernist alternative to Arnold Schoenberg and Igor Stravinsky, the Finnish master greatly appealed to both audiences and composers.[53] Hanson, Hovhaness, Rouse, Steven Stucky, and John Adams, among others, have openly admitted their admiration for and debts to Sibelius (Hovhaness named his daughter Jean Christina in honor of the Finnish composer, who served as her godfather).[54] Several American symphonies allude to specific Sibelius works: the third movement of George Antheil's Third Symphony (1936–39) quotes the opening theme of the Finale of the Fifth Symphony, and George Rochberg's Fifth Symphony (1984) prominently features a motive from the tone poem *Lemminkäinen in Tuonela* (from the *Lemminkäinen Suite: Four Legends of the Kalevala*).[55]

By far, Sibelius's greatest influence on American music was through his Seventh Symphony (1924) and its single-movement form. While symphonies in one movement date as far back as the antebellum works of Fry and Anthony Philip Heinrich, Sibelius's work directly stimulated numerous explorations of that structure; some, like Harris's Third Symphony (1938), enclose discrete sections within a continuous division, while others, such as Schuman's Sixth (1948), consist of a single uninterrupted span. American symphonists who have explicitly cited the Seventh as an inspiration include Barber (First Symphony, 1936), Schuman (Second Symphony, 1937), Bolcom (Second Symphony, 1965), and Lowell Liebermann (Third Symphony, 2010); the works of Schuman and Bolcom even adopt its tonal center of C. At least six of Hovhaness's sixty-seven symphonies follow one-movement structures, as do Rochberg's Fifth and Rouse's First (1986).[56] Table 1.4 lists more than ninety American symphonies that have adopted a monopartite structure.

According to John Harbison, Sibelius's abstract and structuralist concept of the symphony ("severity of form and the profound logic that create[s] an inner connection between all the motives") has proved, perhaps surprisingly, more congenial to the American symphonic temperament than Gustav Mahler's global and philosophical approach ("The symphony must be like the world. It must be all-embracing").[57] By and large, dimensions of American symphonies have tended more toward Sibelius's concision than Mahler's expansiveness, particularly in the period between 1920 and 1970, when the average length of most symphonies lay between 20 and 35 minutes. Still, the Austrian master has not lacked notable adherents, especially starting in the 1960s.[58] With the advent of neoromanticism and its emphasis on post-Wagnerian language, structures, and forces, a significant number of composers have written large-scale symphonies for vocal soloists, chorus, and orchestra that deal overtly with momentous topics such as world conflict (Fairouz Symphony No. 3, "Poems and Prayers," 2010), existential questions (Bernstein Symphony No. 3, *Kaddish*, 1963), personal loss (Kernis, "Symphony of Meditations," 2007–9), ethnic or religious heritage (Asia Symphony No. 5, "Of Songs and Psalms," 2008), and so forth. Examples of other composers who have written symphonies of Mahlerian scope are David Del Tredici (several large-scale works inspired by *Alice in Wonderland*), Tobias Picker, and Liebermann. Furthermore, the intentional eclecticism of many "postmodern" symphonies naturally echoes Mahler's world-embracing approach. As with Sibelius, numerous symphonies—including works by Bernstein (all three symphonies), Rochberg (Symphonies 4, 5, and 6), Corigliano (1 and 2), Bolcom (3 and 5), and Adams (*Harmonielehre*)—make audible references to Mahlerian processes and sometimes allude to specific works.[59]

During World War II, another European C-major symphony had a strong, if more limited, impact. Premiering the year America entered the conflict, Dmitri Shostakovich's Seventh Symphony, "Leningrad," became the emblematic war symphony on account of the circumstances of its creation, its classical approach (despite the Mahlerian length), and its stature as a "solemn and majestic" symphony with the rallying power to "kill Hitler," as one reviewer colorfully expressed it.[60] Although Harris publicly deplored its overshadowing impact on native composers, his own Fifth Symphony (1942) shows the effects of the "Leningrad" by sharing its tonic, focus on counterpoint with a simplified harmonic language, and epic tone.[61] According to Marc Blitzstein, Shostakovich's composition put music "on the map as a positive weapon in winning the war," and he sought to make a similar contribution with his *Airborne Symphony*.[62] Antheil's war-inspired Symphony No. 4, "1942," betrays obvious debts to Shostakovich's sound world and thematic profiles.[63] Similarly, Copland's Third (1946) shares its tonal orientation, conventional framework, and monumental finale. Virgil Thomson called Copland's symphony militaristic in the Russian composer's manner (this was not a compliment), and another reviewer sardonically termed the work "Shostakovich in the Appalachians."[64]

Among homegrown influences, Ives looms as the obvious model, but because of the belated dates at which his symphonies became known, he exercised minimal influence on the development of the genre until about the last quarter of the twentieth century. Since then, however, we can find various Ivesian procedures and concepts at work in American symphonies. In the first and last movements of Corigliano's Symphony No. 1 (1990), for example, Isaac Albéniz's Tango in D is superimposed over the orchestra on an offstage piano, specifically to conjure memory. The middle movement of Adams's *Naïve and Sentimental Music* (1999) sets an electric guitar solo over slowly shifting string sonorities, recalling *The Unanswered Question* and similar compositions (for Adams, by origin a fellow New Englander, Ives's mixture of "the sublime with the vulgar and sentimental, [juxtaposed] with a freedom and insouciance that could only be done by an American, has always been a model for me").[65] The third movement of Fairouz's Fourth Symphony ("In the Shadow of No Towers," 2012) applies Ives's habit of layering unrelated streams of music for programmatic purposes—in this case, representing the split of the United States into "red" and "blue" zones that shout at each other rather than converse. Fairouz divides the ensemble into two groups that, in his words, are "pitted relentlessly against the other with the two sides not listening to one another."[66]

Distinctive Qualities in Symphonies from the United States

As this book will repeatedly demonstrate, composers in the United States have experimented widely with the linguistic, rhythmic, and formal conventions of the symphony. While the authors make no claims for a uniquely American symphonic identity—quite the opposite, in fact—we can nevertheless isolate certain features that appear with some consistency in symphonies from the United States (and often Latin America as well): these include eclectic mixtures of styles, extroverted brass and percussion scoring, energetic syncopated rhythms, and a flexible approach to symphonic structure.

However controversial today, the "melting pot" metaphor fairly describes much American music (both classical and popular), which frequently merges idioms from heterogeneous cultural, racial, and ethnic sources on more or less equal footings. Ives's Second and Fourth Symphonies combine nineteenth-century American popular styles with hymnody, the European classical tradition, and experimental techniques. Cowell's symphonies blend Yankee tunesmith practices such as fuguing tunes with modernist rhythmic and sonic innovations (tone clusters, sliding tones, polymeters). Lou Harrison merges Western idioms such as the medieval estampie dance with the modes and sounds of the gamelan and other Asian musics, as well as with original percussive timbres such as the tack piano.

Thomson's enthusiastic review of Antheil's Fourth Symphony ("1942") could serve as an encomium of American eclecticism: the "Symphony is about the most complete musical picture of an American success that has ever been made. There is everything in it—military band music, waltzes, sentimental ditties, a Red Army song, a fugue, eccentric dancing. . . . It is bright, hard, noisy, busy, bumptious, efficient, and incredibly real. It is 'Columbia the Gem of the Ocean' orchestrated in red, white, and blue. . . . And its tunes can all be remembered."[67]

The neoromantic or postmodern languages of Rochberg, Corigliano, Bolcom, and Adams are self-consciously diverse, freely joining styles and quotations from unrelated artistic periods within the same piece. Kyle Gann describes this approach as a reaction against the Romantic insistence on stylistic unity: "a pluralistic society demand[s] pluralistic music not held hostage to a Germanic idea of organic form." He quotes Corigliano as follows: "If I have my own style, I'm not aware of it. . . . I don't think of style as the basic unifying factor in music. . . . I feel very strongly that a composer has a right to do anything he feels is appropriate, and that stylistic consistency is not what makes a piece impressive."[68]

Corigliano demonstrates his point in the Symphony No. 1 (1990), written to memorialize friends and colleagues lost to the AIDS epidemic. The first movement ("Apologue: Of Rage and Remembrance") juxtaposes assorted twentieth-century procedures to convey the two moods of the title. "Rage" he portrays by superimposing the practices of two prominent postwar Polish masters. The strings play tone clusters in the style of Krzysztof Penderecki: the instruments sound all the pitches within a specified range and move as monolithic entities. Above these string clusters, selected winds, brass, and the piano employ Witold Lutosławski's aleatoric counterpoint, playing notated passages *ad libitum* without synchronization. The previously cited Ivesian quotation of Albéniz's Tango symbolizes "remembrance"; under it, a broad and plaintive melody in high violins recalls such Shostakovichian melodies as the English horn cantilena from the first-movement recapitulation of his Eighth Symphony. Meanwhile, the fearsome distortion of the familiar in the second movement and the climactic funeral march of the third—the culmination of the entire symphony—unmistakably summon Mahler. For Corigliano and other postmodern figures, style and personal expression are located in the linguistic and procedural choices made for each work and the individual manner in which the composer juxtaposes these options or links them together.

Pioneering scoring appears in the American symphony as early as 1853, when Fry incorporated toy instruments and the newly invented saxophone in his *Santa Claus Symphony*; he used the saxophone in other works as well. Ives employed a Jew's harp in *Washington's Birthday*; zither, accordions, and theremin in the Orchestral Set No. 2; and a quarter-tone piano and theremin (or "ether organ," as he calls it) in Symphony No. 4. Many American symphonies from Ives forward have favored large and highly varied arrays of pitched and unpitched percussion; even when the battery is small, the composer often features it prominently. Harbison's Symphony No. 3 (1990) exemplifies the imaginative use of percussion. It requires four players on the following instruments:

Player 1: four suspended cymbals, triangle, four tom-toms, high bell, chimes, crotales, xylophone

Player 2: tambourine, timbales, lujon, temple blocks, marimba

Player 3: tenor drum, snare drum, brake drums, vibraphone

Player 4: cowbell, bass drum, wood block, log drum, tam-tam, glockenspiel[69]

In addition, to an arguably greater extent than their counterparts in Europe, many twentieth- and twenty-first-century American symphonists include the piano as a regular member of the ensemble, whether or not other percussion is present.

American symphonies also tend to highlight what might be described as extroverted and "splashy" writing for the brass. As early as 1886, a critic complimented Chadwick's "affection for the brasses, without which he could scarcely be called American."[70] Such scoring figures prominently in Harris's Third Symphony: in an often-cited profile from 1941, Copland praised his orchestration as "crude and unabashed at times, with occasional blobs and yawps of sound that Whitman would have approved of"—a description that would equally fit Schuman's Third Symphony, Bernstein's Symphony No. 2, *The Age of Anxiety*, Rochberg's Fifth Symphony (which features an extended cadenza for a quartet of horns), and Adams's *Harmonielehre*, not to mention Copland's own Third Symphony.[71] Dynamic brass and outsized percussion batteries, including indigenous instruments from the nation's folk and popular traditions, also figure in many Latin American works, such as Chávez's *Sinfonía India*, Silvestre Revueltas's *La noche de los Mayas*, and Heitor Villa-Lobos's Tenth Symphony. Finally, a number of mid-century composers, such as Harris and Schuman, routinely engage families of instruments in antiphonal dialogues.

The widespread success of Harris's Third Symphony—of which Koussevitzky remarked, "I think that nobody has expressed with such genius the American life, the vitality, the greatness, the strength of this country"—earned it a reputation as the embodiment of an intrinsically

Table 1.4 American Symphonies of Less than Three or More than Four Movements, by Structure and Date

ONE MOVEMENT

*Anthony Philip Heinrich, *The Columbiad: Grand American National Chivalrous Symphony* (1837)
*Anthony Philip Heinrich, *The Indian Carnival* (ca. 1845)
*Anthony Philip Heinrich, *To the Spirit of Beethoven* (1845)
*Anthony Philip Heinrich, *The Tomb of Genius, to the Memory of Mendelssohn-Bartholdy* (ca. 1847)
William Henry Fry, *The Breaking Heart* (1852–53)
William Henry Fry, *A Day in the Country* (1852–53)
William Henry Fry, *Santa Claus: Christmas Symphony* (1853)
William Henry Fry, *Niagara* (1854)
Charles Ives, *Universe Symphony* (1915–28)
John J. Becker, Symphony No. 2, "*Fantasie tragica*, A Short Symphony in One Movement" (1920, rev. 1937)
*Colin McPhee, Symphony No. 1 (1930; lost)
Aaron Copland, *Short Symphony* (Symphony No. 2, 1932–33)
Samuel Barber, Symphony No. 1 (in One Movement) (1936)
Anthony Louis Scarmolin, Symphony in E Minor (Symphony No. 1, 1936)
William Schuman, Symphony No. 2 (1937)
Roy Harris, Symphony No. 3 (1938)
Halsey Stevens, Symphony No. 1 (1945)
Hubert Klyne Headley, Symphony No. 1 for Radio (1946)
Alan Hovhaness, Symphony No. 8, "Arjuna" (1947)
Constant Vauclain, Symphony in One Movement (1947)
William Schuman, Symphony No. 6 (1948)
*George Tremblay, Symphony in One Movement (1949)
Vittorio Giannini, Symphony No. 1 (1950)
Roy Harris, Symphony for Band, "West Point" (1952)
Roy Harris, Symphony No. 7 (1952)
Anthony Louis Scarmolin, *Sinfonia breve* (Symphony No. 3, 1952)
Alan Hovhaness, Symphony No. 13 (1953)
Vincent Persichetti, Symphony No. 5 for Strings (1953)
Howard Hanson, Symphony No. 5, "Sinfonia sacra" (1954)
John Vincent, Symphony in D: A Festive Piece in One Movement (1954, rev. 1956)
George Rochberg, Symphony No. 2 (1955–56; one movement in four sections)
José Serebrier, Symphony No. 1 (1956)
Halsey Stevens, *Sinfonia breve* (1957)
Vincent Persichetti, Symphony No. 7, "Liturgical" (1958; one movement in five sections)
Alan Hovhaness, Symphony No. 6, "Celestial Gate" (1959)
Elie Siegmeister, Symphony No. 3 (in One Movement) (1959)
Julia Perry, Symphony in One Movement for Violas and String Basses (1961)
Irwin Bazelon, Symphony No. One in One Movement (1961)
Hall Overton, Symphony No. 2 in One Movement (1962)
Roy Harris, Symphony No. 8, "San Francisco Symphony" (1962; one movement with five interconnected parts)
Dorothy Rudd Moore, Symphony No. 1 (1962–63)
Alan Hovhaness, Symphony No. 18, "Circe" (1963)
William Bolcom, Symphony No. 2, "Oracles" (1962–64)
Vittorio Giannini, Symphony No. 5 (1964)
Peter Mennin, Symphony No. 7, "Variation-Symphony" (1964; one movement in five sections)
Alan Hovhaness, Symphony No. 19, "Vishnu" (1966)
Howard Hanson, Symphony No. 6 (1967; in six sections)
Roy Harris, Symphony No. 11 (1967)
William Schuman, Symphony No. 9, "Le fosse ardeatine" (1968; one movement in three sections)
George Rochberg, Symphony No. 3 (1966–69)
Vincent Persichetti, *Sinfonia: Janiculum* (Symphony No. 9, 1970)
David Maslanka, Symphony No. 1 (1971)
Robert Hall Lewis, Symphony No. 2 (1971)

Table 1.4 *continued*

*Leonardo Balada, *Steel Symphony* (Symphony No. 3, 1972)
Alan Hovhaness, Symphony No. 25, "Odysseus" (1973)
Elliott Carter, *A Symphony of Three Orchestras* (1976)
Alan Hovhaness, Symphony No. 34 (1977)
William Thomas McKinley: Symphony No. 1 in One Movement (1977)
William Thomas McKinley: Symphony No. 2, "Of Time and Future Monuments" (1978)
Ellen Taaffe Zwilich, Chamber Symphony (1979)
Paul Creston, Symphony No. 6 for Organ and Orchestra (1981)
Warren Benson, Symphony No. 2, "Lost Songs" (1983; for wind enesmble)
George Rochberg, Symphony No. 5 (1984, rev. 1985–86)
Christopher Rouse, Symphony No. 1 (1986)
Richard Danielpour, Symphony No. 3, "Journey without Distance" (1990; one movement in two parts)
Jack Gallagher, Symphony No. 1 in One Movement, "Threnody" (1991)
*Leonardo Balada, Symphony No. 4, "Lausanne" (1992)
Irwin Bazelon, Symphony No. 9, "Sunday Silence" (1992)
Charles Wuorinen, *Microsymphony* (1992)
Samuel Jones, Symphony No. 3, "Palo Duro Canyon" (1992)
David Maslanka, Symphony No. 4 (1994; for wind ensemble)
Rolv Yttrehus, Symphony No. 1 (1997, rev. 1998; one movement in ten short sections)
Michael Hersch, Symphony No. 1 (1998)
Benjamin Lees, Symphony No. 5, "Kalmar Nyckel" (1998)
Lowell Liebermann, Symphony No. 2 (1999)
Kevin Puts, Symphony No. 1 (1999)
Kevin Puts, Symphony No. 2, "Island of Innocence" (2002)
Stephen Hartke, Symphony No. 3 (2003; one movement in four sections)
Carson Cooman, Symphony No. 2, "Litanies of Love and Rain" (2004)
*Leonardo Balada, Symphony No. 6, "Symphony of Sorrows" (2005)
*Lera Auerbach, *Requiem for a Poet* (Symphony No. 2, 2007; one movement in 10 sections)
John Adams, *Doctor Atomic Symphony* (2007; revised version)
Robert Carl, Symphony No. 4, "The Ladder" (2008)
Lowell Liebermann, Symphony No. 3 (2010)
George Walker, Sinfonia No. 4, "Strands" (2011)
William Bolcom, Symphony No. 9 (2011–12)
Steven Stucky, Symphony (2012)
*Wang Jie, Symphony No. 2, "To and from Dakini" (2013)
Stephen Hartke, Symphony No. 4 (2009–14; one movement in three sections)
Carson Cooman, *Liminal* (Symphony No. 4, 2014)
Christopher Rouse, Symphony No. 5 (2015)
Lowell Liebermann, Symphony No. 4 (2015)
George Walker, Symphony No. 5, " Visions" (2015–16)
Wang Jie, *The Winter that United Us* (Symphony No. 3, 2020–22)
Wang Jie, *Flying on the Scaly Backs of Our Mountains* (Symphony No. 4, 2020–22)
Carson Cooman: Symphony No. 5 (2022)

TWO MOVEMENTS OR DIVISIONS

*Leopold Meignen, *Symphonie militaire* (1845)
Louis Moreau Gottschalk, Symphony No. 1, *La nuit des tropiques* (1858–59)
Louis Moreau Gottschalk, Symphony No. 2, *À Montevideo* (1868)
John J. Becker, Symphony No. 3, *Sinfonia brevis* (1929–31)
*Werner Josten, Symphony in F (1936)
William Schuman, Symphony No. 3 (1941; four movements in two divisions)
John J. Becker, Symphony No. 5, "Homage to Mozart" (1942)
Paul Creston, Symphony No. 2 (1944)
Leonard Bernstein, Symphony No. 2, *The Age of Anxiety* (1949; six movements in two divisions)
Alan Hovhaness, Symphony No. 9, "St. Vartan" (1950; 24 short sections divided in two divisions)
Lester Trimble, Symphony in Two Movements (1951)

Miriam Gideon, *Symphonia brevis* (1953)
Gordon Binkerd, Symphony No. 2 (1957)
Gardner Read, Symphony No. 4 (1951–58)
Charles Wuorinen, Symphony No. 3 (1959)
Henry Cowell, Symphony No. 15, "Thesis" (1960)
David Diamond, Symphony No. 8 (1960)
David Diamond, Symphony No. 5 (1951–64)
Richard Yardumian, Symphony No. 2, "Psalms" (1947–64)
Julia Perry, Symphony No. 5, "Integration" (1966–67; lost)
Roger Sessions, Symphony No. 8 (1968)
Roy Harris, Symphony No. 12, "Père Marquette Symphony" (1968, rev. 1969; five movements in two divisions)
Alan Hovhaness, Symphony No. 24, "Manjun" (1973)
Julia Perry, Symphony No. 12 (also titled *Simple Symphony* and *Children's Symphony*, 1973)
*Tomáš Svoboda, Symphony No. 4, "Apocalyptic" (1975)
Frank Ezra Levy, Symphony No. 3 (1977)
Charles Wuorinen, *Two-Part Symphony* (1978)
Irwin Bazelon, Symphony No. 7 in Two Parts, "Ballet for Orchestra" (1980)
Tobias Picker, Symphony No. 1 (1982)
Alan Hovhaness, Symphony No. 53, "Star Dawn" (1983)
George Walker, Sinfonia No. 1 (1984, rev. 1996)
David Diamond, Symphony No. 9 (1977–85)
William Bolcom, Symphony No. 4 (1986)
George Rochberg, Symphony No. 6 (1986–87)
Alan Hovhaness, Symphony No. 63, "Loon Lake" (1988, rev. 1991)
*Henri Lazarof, Symphony No. 2 (1990)
Charles Wuorinen, Symphony Seven (1997)
Carson Cooman, Symphony No. 3, "Ave Maris Stella" (2005)
Richard Danielpour, *Rocking the Cradle:* Symphony in Two Movements for Orchestra (2007)
Christopher Rouse, Symphony No. 3 (2011)
Christopher Rouse, Symphony No. 4 (2013)
Jonathan Leshnoff, Symphony No. 4, "Heichalos" (2018)

FIVE MOVEMENTS

*Anthony Philip Heinrich, *Schiller: Grande sinfonia dramatica* (1834, rev. 1847, 1856)
Charles Ives, Symphony No. 2 (1899–1909)
John Alden Carpenter, Symphony in C (1940)
Ray Green, *Sunday Sing Symphony* (1946)
George Rochberg, Symphony No. 1 (1948–49; written as five-movement symphony; revised in 1957 as three-movement symphony; other two movements restored in the 1970s)
Henry Cowell, Symphony No. 9 (1953)
George Rochberg, Symphony No. 2 (1955–56)
Homer Keller, Symphony No. 3 (1956)
Nicolas Flagello, *Missa sinfonica* (1957)
Henry Cowell, Symphony No. 13, "Madras" (1956–58)
Ned Rorem, Symphony No. 3 (1958)
Henry Cowell, Symphony No. 16, "Icelandic" (1962)
Henry Cowell, Symphony No. 17 (1963)
Henry Cowell, Symphony No. 18 (1963–64)
Henry Cowell, Symphony No. 19 (1964–65)
Julia Perry, *Symphony U.S.A.* (Symphony No. 7, 1967; lost?)
Arthur Rosner, Symphony No. 5, "Missa sine Cantoribus super Salve Regina" (1973)
Lou Harrison, Symphony No. 2, "Elegiac" (1975, rev. 1988)
Roy Harris, *Bicentennial Symphony 1976* (Symphony No. 13, 1975–76)
Alan Hovhaness, Symphony No. 28 (1976)
Alan Hovhaness, Symphony No. 38 (1978)
Ned Rorem, String Symphony (1985)
Richard Danielpour, Symphony No. 2, "Visions" (1986)
Daniel Asia, Symphony No. 1 (1987)
Tobias Picker, Symphony No. 3 for String Orchestra (1988)
Aaron Jay Kernis, *Symphony in Waves* (Symphony No. 1, 1989)
Daniel Asia, Symphony No. 2, "Celebration Symphony" (1988–90)
John Harbison, Symphony No. 3 (1990)
David Maslanka, Symphony No. 3 (1991; for wind ensemble)
Michael Daugherty, *Metropolis Symphony* (1988–93; movements can be performed separately)
Kamran Ince, Symphony No. 2, "Fall of Constantinople" (1994)
Kamran Ince, Symphony No. 4, "Sardis" (2000)
John Corigliano, Symphony No. 2 (2000)

Table 1.4 *continued*

John Harbison, Symphony No. 4 (2003, rev. 2006)

David Maslanka, Symphony No. 6, "Living Earth" (2004; for wind ensemble)

Jonathan Leshnoff, Symphony No. 1, "Forgotten Chants and Refrains" (2004)

Mason Bates, *The B-Sides* (2009)

David Maslanka, Symphony No. 9 (2011; for wind ensemble)

Adam Schoenberg, *American Symphony* (2011)

Philip Glass, Symphony No. 10 (2011–12)

SIX MOVEMENTS

Henry Cowell, Symphony No. 10 (1953)

Leonard Bernstein, Symphony No. 3, *Kaddish* (1963; seven named movements in three divisions, but the sixth and seventh are performed as one)

Alan Hovhaness, Symphony No. 27 (1976)

Alan Hovhaness, Symphony No. 43 (1979)

Philip Glass, Symphony No. 4, "Heroes" (1996)

Wynton Marsalis, Symphony No. 4, "The Jungle" (2014)

Mason Bates, *The Anthology of Fantastic Zoology* (2014)

SEVEN MOVEMENTS

*Anthony Philip Heinrich, *The Empress Queen of the Magyars* (1848, rev. 1855)

Roy Harris, *Folk-Song Symphony* (Symphony No. 4, 1940, rev. 1942)

Henry Cowell, Symphony No. 11, "Seven Rituals of Music" (1953)

Julia Perry, *A Suite Symphony* (1965–70)

Alan Hovhaness, Symphony No. 31 (1976–77)

Tobias Picker, Symphony No. 2 (1986)

*Lera Auerbach, Symphony No. 1, "Chimera" (2006)

Michael Hersch, Symphony No. 3 (2009)

Wynton Marsalis, Symphony No. 2, "Blues Symphony" (2009, rev. 2015)

Wynton Marsalis, Symphony No. 3, "Swing Symphony" (2010, rev. 2013)

Mason Bates, *Children of Adam* (2017–18)

Philip Glass, Symphony No. 12, "Lodger" (2018)

EIGHT OR MORE MOVEMENTS

Kamran Ince, Symphony No. 3, "Siege of Vienna" (1995; 8 movements)

William Thomas McKinley: Symphony No. 7 "The Cosmos" (2004; 8 movements)

John Corigliano, Symphony No. 3, "Circus Maximus" (2004; for wind ensemble in 8 movements)

*Anthony Philip Heinrich, *The Columbiad: Migration of American Passenger Pigeons* (9 movements [possibly 10—see chapter 2]; 1858)

*Lera Auerbach, *The Infant Minstrel and His Peculiar Menagerie*: "Symphony No. 3" for Violin, Choir and Orchestra (2016; 9 movements)

*Lera Auerbach, *ARCTICA*: Symphony No. 4 for Piano, Chorus, and Orchestra (2019; 10 movements)

Wynton Marsalis, *All Rise* (Symphony No. 1, 1999; 12 movements)

Philip Glass, Symphony No. 5 (1999; 12 movements)

*Anthony Philip Heinrich, *Symphony to the Spirit of Beethoven* (1845; 13 movements)

Alan Hovhaness, Symphony No. 57, "Cold Mountain" (1983; 15 movements)

Daniel Asia, Symphony No. 5, "Of Songs and Psalms" (2008; 15 movements)

*indicates émigré composer

and recognizably American symphonic sound world realized without overt appeal to folk or popular idioms.[72] In addition to his scoring practices, Harris achieved the style of his Third Symphony through an idiosyncratic approach to thematic evolution, harmonic progression, and rhythm. He described his melodies as autogenetic, or self-generating—flowing and open-ended themes spun from an initial gesture. They combine a free mix of modes within a chordal system based on the overtone series that favors perfect intervals and open chords progressing by common-tone pivots. In his aforementioned essay, Copland stated that "American, too, is [Harris's] melodic gift, perhaps his most striking characteristic. His music comes nearest to a distinctively native melos of anything yet done, at least in the ambitious forms. Celtic folk songs and Protestant hymns are its basis, but they have been completely reworked, lengthened, malleated."[73]

While slower themes tend to move in even rhythms, Harris's faster melodies often feature shifting accents within steady meters, producing what Copland called an "American" rhythm with a "jerky, nervous quality that is peculiarly our own."[74] Harris himself insisted that Americans' "sense of rhythm is less symmetrical than the European rhythmic sense. . . . [Our] asymmetrical balancing of rhythmic phrases is in our blood; it is not in the European blood."[75] Indeed, the majority of American symphonists have adopted complex, propulsive, and variedly uneven rhythmic profiles, including polyrhythmic and polymetric writing (Ives and Cowell); syncopated quintuple or septuple meters (Hanson and Thompson); multimeter (Copland's *Short Symphony*) or shifting accents within simple divisions (Persichetti); "swing" and "dance" rhythms (Still and Creston); spirited "urban" motions (Schuman and Bernstein); high-octane energy (Mennin); and "American English rhythms" (Libby Larsen).[76] While syncopations and vigorous rhythms obviously are not exclusive to composers working in the United States, their treatment has been such that Elliott Carter could write, "Owing to the influence of Copland, Harris, and Sessions, many [American composers] seem to have an innate rhythmic sense that is different from that of European composers."[77]

From the beginning, American symphonists have explored an extensive variety of formal structures. As noted earlier, one-movement symphonies form a prominent feature of the American approach to the genre. (Although Harris characteristically avoided acknowledging Sibelius's influence, three symphonies besides the Third—the Seventh, Eighth, and Eleventh—unfold in a single movement, following an archlike pattern.[78]) While many follow the traditional divisions of three or four movements, others use only two movements or else five or more—sometimes considerably more, as in the fifteen-movement symphonies of Hovhaness (No. 57, "Cold Mountain") and Asia (Symphony No. 5, "Of Songs and Psalms"). To give an idea of the striking formal variety of symphonies from the United States, table 1.4 lists symphonies that consist of less than three movements or more than four.

Chapter Summaries

The survey begins with Douglas W. Shadle's examination of the symphony in mid-nineteenth-century America (ca. 1830–80). Each of the four composers featured took an individual approach to the genre. Anthony Philip Heinrich, an early representative of the American maverick tradition, created symphonies notable for extravagant titles and ambitious subject matter (e.g., *Manitou Mysteries, The Empress Queen of the Magyars, The Ornithological Combat of Kings*); many of them blend European idioms, including those of his native Bohemia, with American folk and popular styles. Partners in defending American music, George Frederick Bristow and William Henry Fry pursued opposite paths as symphonists: Bristow's first three followed the "conservative" Germanic tradition whereas Fry created "progressive" program symphonies and symphonic poems at the same time as Liszt. Finally, Louis Moreau Gottschalk's first symphony features Afro-Caribbean local color, and his second celebrates Pan-American ideals; his mixture of indigenous and European idioms presages twentieth-century developments in Latin American music. At this early stage, then, the American symphony already made room for cosmopolitan, nationalist, exotic, and (to an extent) experimental languages that later generations would continue to explore; innovation in the American symphony, traditionally understood to be the invention of composers of Charles Ives's generation, in fact dates from the beginnings of the genre.

The works of this period remain little known and suffer from an unjust reputation as mere historical curiosities and precursors. For this, institutional refusal to embrace the repertory from the start bears much of the blame; as Shadle states elsewhere, "None of this music survived as part of the standard performance repertoire after the turn of the century because its most powerful potential cultivators—critics and conductors—had maintained inhospitable attitudes toward it before it had a chance to thrive."[79]

E. Douglas Bomberger explores the symphonies written by members of the Second New England School and their contemporaries (ca. 1875–1915). Continuing the variety of approaches seen in the antebellum period, John Knowles Paine, George Whitefield Chadwick, and Amy Beach each reckon with the European tradition in their own ways. In contrast to Paine's universalist orientation, Chadwick's symphonies and symphonic suites occasionally incorporated lighthearted references to pentatonic motives and subject matter from contemporary popular entertainment, making the works a "reflection of the vibrant American culture in which they were created."[80] Meanwhile, Beach responded to Dvořák's call for a folk-based nationalism by quoting Irish tunes in her "Gaelic" Symphony. As noted previously, the continental conflict over absolute versus programmatic music found an echo in America, as Edward MacDowell and George Templeton Strong aligned themselves forcefully with the New German School against the "dryasdust" Second New England School (as Strong sarcastically called it), with Strong composing program symphonies and MacDowell an orchestral suite of symphonic breadth.

Bomberger also examines the opportunities that newly formed orchestras such as the Boston Symphony Orchestra and the Chicago Symphony Orchestra provided for symphonists as well as the obstacles erected by Eurocentric conductors, most notably Theodore Thomas.[81] Although the symphonies of Paine, Chadwick, and Beach won widespread public approbation—even John Sullivan Dwight welcomed Paine's Second Symphony with an unabashed display of enthusiasm—uncompromising critics, having already commenced their hunt for the Great American Symphony, rebuked the composers for whatever stylistic choices they made. They accused the cosmopolitan Paine of servile imitation while charging the (somewhat) nationalist Chadwick with flippancy because he included vernacular idioms—the latter an early portent of the reception awaiting later symphonists found to privilege "American" qualities over "greatness." (Perhaps mindful of this, Beach did not disclose that the "Gaelic" Symphony quoted actual Irish melodies until after the premiere; at any rate, despite its title and obvious folk atmosphere, most critics ignored this aspect of the work—probably, as Adrienne Fried Block wryly notes, because they were too occupied with discussing her gender.[82])

In his chapter, J. Peter Burkholder addresses a number of misperceptions about Charles Ives's accomplishment as a symphonist. Because his four numbered symphonies premiered largely in reverse chronological order, his most advanced music came to public attention first, and enthusiastic listeners hailed him as an iconoclast, the long-hoped-for sonic counterpart to Whitman.[83] In doing so, however, they missed Ives's fundamentally nineteenth-century creative goal of communicating personal emotions and experiences through traditional European genres and procedures (intricate polyphony, developing variation, and rigorous if subtle cyclic connections, all employed with an exceptionally sound technique for which he is often not given credit). Burkholder hopes to "recapture a sense of Ives as a Romantic composer . . . who gradually developed his own highly personal modernist idiom in order to convey what at heart is a Romantic experience through music."[84]

Ives's symphonies embody American diversity, as each represents a markedly different conception of the genre. The First (ca. 1897–1902) synthesizes themes and languages of various nineteenth-century European symphonies—among them Beethoven's Ninth, Schubert's "Unfinished," Tchaikovsky's "Pathétique," and Dvořák's "New World"—to create an original composition that firmly stakes his claim to a place in the symphonic tradition. The Second (ca. 1899–1909) fuses allusions to Bach, Beethoven, Wagner, and Tchaikovsky with quotations from sundry American popular repertories: parlor songs, minstrel music, fiddle tunes, college songs, patriotic melodies, traditional New England hymnody, and contemporary gospel songs. (Burkholder describes the work as "a celebration of American music and of its place as part of a broader transatlantic musical world.")[85] In the Third Symphony (ca. 1901–11), Ives focuses on hymnody, which serves as the thematic matter for his distinctive structural innovation of cumulative form.

While palpably the most advanced linguistically, the Fourth Symphony (ca. 1912–25) is in a sense also the most Romantic, for its vast array of innovative procedures (polytonality, quarter tones, simultaneous streams of music, etc.)—combined with the largest mass of quotations he ever employed—serves to enact a philosophical program comparable to that of Mahler, Strauss, and other post-Wagnerian composers. The first movement asks the meaning of existence, the following two movements symbolize "false paths," and the Finale proclaims that the true path lies in "religious experience." Such a program makes the Fourth the epitome of the kind of ethical symphony that possessed "community-building power," in the phrase of the influential German critic Paul Bekker.[86] For their part, the programmatic *Holidays Symphony* and the orchestral sets employ quotation as symbols of past experiences, whether festive celebrations in his childhood (e.g., the Fourth of July) or recent national traumas (the sinking of the *Lusitania*). In the unfinished *Universe Symphony*, Ives unleashes his largest arsenal of experimental techniques to suggest the ineffable regions of time, space, and the beyond—the ultimate use of music to, as Ralph Vaughan Williams put it, "stretch out to the ultimate realities through the medium of beauty."[87]

Susan Key's chapter considers the period Aaron Copland described as the "coming of age" of the American symphony (1920 to 1950).[88] The flourishing took place at a time of major aesthetic and social upheavals that left their marks on the works. The modernist experimentation of the 1920s is reflected both in works of considerable complexity (Copland's *Short Symphony*) and subversive simplicity (Thomson's *Symphony on a Hymn Tune*). In the 1930s, amid the sufferings of the Depression—compounded by anxieties over increasing global tensions—composers felt an intense obligation to connect with audiences; in this endeavor, they received unprecedented support from the government through the short-lived Federal Music Project. Because of its perceived power to move and uplift, speak truth, give comfort, and build community, many composers in the United States, as in Europe, defaulted to the symphony during the war; as Marc Blitzstein wrote to David Diamond, "of course symphonies must be written now."[89] Accordingly, a number of symphonies express the wartime mood (Piston Second, Antheil Fourth, Harris Fifth), suggest specific imagery (Blitzstein *Airborne*, Barber Second) or reflect the emotions arising from the end of hostilities (Copland Third). It is not surprising that the 1930s and 1940s also marked the apex of the search for the Great American Symphony. As noted earlier, the critics embraced the Third Symphonies of Harris and Copland and, to a lesser extent, the Third of William Schuman, as strong candidates, though, in the end, each contender was denied the prize for one reason or another.

Sharing the composers' burdens, a number of orchestras (not just Boston's) became more willing in this period to perform American works. Equally decisive was the advent of the radio, with its new possibilities for audience development: concerts were routinely broadcast and ensembles like the NBC Symphony Orchestra were directly sponsored by radio networks. It was the development of the radio and advances in recording technology, as much as the social cataclysms, that prompted erstwhile modernists to repurpose their languages into more audience-friendly mediums without sacrificing their own voices—as Copland memorably put it, "to see if I couldn't say what I had to say in the simplest possible terms."[90]

Key considers fifteen composers divided into three groups according to their training. (With the larger number of composers and works covered in this chapter's period, analyses of individual symphonies of necessity will generally be shorter than in surrounding chapters; the same comment pertains to chapter 9.) Although European institutions remained the desired destination for many aspiring composers, the focus shifted from Germany to Nadia Boulanger's classes at the American Conservatory at Fontainebleau as well as the American Academy of Rome. Broadly stated, the first generations of composers belonging to the *Boulangerie*, as it became known,[91] such as Copland, Piston, Thomson, Harris, and Blitzstein, pursued a relatively progressive style, and those who further espoused a national identity tended to favor a "prairie" sound over that of a hard-driven "urban" Americana. The best-known Rome-based composers, Barber and Hanson, cultivated a conservative and cosmopolitan "Romantic" style, though others such as Thompson and Leo Sowerby made room for vernacular idioms .

The 1920–50 period also witnessed the rise of composers whose education, like that of Beach and Ives before them, was confined to the United States. The symphonists among them pursued various styles. George Antheil filled a traditional symphonic frame with eclectic content laid out in a quirky growth process derived in part from his work in film. Henry Cowell availed himself of an even more diverse palette in which American vernacularisms, non-Western idioms, and ultramodernist rhythmic and sonic experiments could stand side by side, often within unconventional structures.

Four prominent home-trained composers were Black, and in quick succession between 1930 and 1934, they produced symphonies that were played by major orchestras and welcomed by listeners and critics of both races. Each work reflected their heritage in a distinct way. William Grant Still's *Afro-American Symphony* (1930) included original themes in the style of blues, spirituals, and ring shouts, while in her Symphony No. 1 (1933), Florence Price alluded to African-based rhythms and modes and set the third movement as a juba; both thus followed the tradition of nationalist symphonists like Dvořák who favored newly written melodies in folk style and ethnic dances for the Scherzo. By contrast, William Levi Dawson's *Negro Folk Symphony* (1934) incorporated authentic spirituals, though he placed them within an otherwise abstract work (he added titles for the movements only at the behest of the conductor).

These three symphonies premiered during the Harlem Renaissance, and theorists of the New Negro movement, such as Alain Locke and James Weldon Johnson, embraced them as realizations of its aspiration to achieve "the symphonic elevation of black 'folk' musical traditions."[92] Popular idioms of Harlem appealed much less to them.[93] Nevertheless, James P. Johnson and "Duke" Ellington pursued the development of a "concert jazz" that brought the sounds of Harlem's theaters and dance clubs to the concert hall; as Key's study of Johnson's *Harlem Symphony* (1932) vividly demonstrates, popular song form, musical theater instrumentation, and stride proved just as adaptable to symphonic treatment in Johnson's hands as spirituals and folk dances.

The turmoil in Europe brought many noted émigré composers to American shores in the 1930s and 1940s, and a number of them likewise turned to the symphony—some for the first time—to express emotions arising from their personal upheavals. Key's chapter will include brief considerations of the works of Ernest Bloch, Paul Hindemith, Bohuslav Martinů, Darius Milhaud, and Igor Stravinsky, and their contributions to the American symphonic repertoire. The chapter concludes with fifty-one brief mentions of other symphonists (native and émigré) active at the time.

As relief over the end of World War II gave way socially to Cold War tensions and artistically to the assertive rise of the avant-garde, the hope for the Great American Symphony turned decidedly pessimistic. As we have seen, Bernstein questioned whether the genre itself would survive, while Copland observed in 1967 that younger composers "show no signs of wishing to build on the work of the older American-born composers, the generation of the '20s and '30s. Today's gods live elsewhere."[94] Yet the symphony retained considerable cultural prestige and received widespread patronage, not least from Bernstein himself; and, contrary to the common portrayal of the period as one of "relentless forward motion" by antitraditional forces, a large body of very fine symphonies emerged in the United States in the 1950s and 1960s, as Katherine Baber's chapter shows.[95]

As in previous periods, composers pursued opposing paths: Roger Sessions, Paul Creston, and Peter Mennin chose cosmopolitanism, while Bernstein, William Schuman, Vincent Persichetti, and David Diamond consciously sought to be "American," at least at points in their careers. A few symphonists continued in the heroic "Koussevitzky manner," though others rejected that paradigm. The "urban" style cultivated by Bernstein and Schuman—arguably the central symphonists of the period—offered an alternative to the "music of the open spaces" associated with Harris and Copland.

Although by and large they embraced the traditional aesthetic associations of the genre, symphonists of this period were not reactionaries: to various degrees, they adapted current trends to their individual voices. Schuman, Bernstein, Persichetti, and Mennin incorporated row structures, or at least fully chromatic themes, into essentially tonal works, while Sessions and Diamond (in his midperiod symphonies) fully adopted twelve-tone writing in nondoctrinaire ways. Julia Perry combined serialist procedures with Black vernacular musics, though she drew on the language of 1960s popular styles such as rhythm and blues or rock instead of spirituals or jazz. Alan Hovhaness looked both to the distant past and to Asia, combining modal and fugal counterpoint with Armenian and East Asian idioms in sixty-seven uniquely dissimilar works (Baber will examine three). Critical responses remained discouraging: reviewers reproached Creston for being stylistically retrograde and dismissed modernists like Sessions and middle-period Diamond as hermetic and inaccessible. Bernstein and Hovhaness, for their part, were rewarded for their nascent (though starkly different) postmodern approaches with accusations of shallowness, derivativeness, and cheap populism. Perry's symphonies were simply ignored altogether, and they remain so today.

As Baber argues, all of these midcentury symphonists (Bernstein excepted) continue to languish because they do not conform to the received image of postwar composers as either committed atonal serialists or neo-tonal nationalists. Rather, they pursued alternate but equally progressive paths that she terms "forgotten modernisms": personal adaptations of serial techniques within tonal contexts; mergers of serialism and contemporary vernacular music; and intentional eclecticism. Only when American musical institutions acknowledge and affirm these alternate routes will the achievements of midcentury symphonists receive their due appreciation. Like chapter 5, this one closes with brief mentions of twenty-seven additional symphonists active during the 1950–70 period.

Symphonies also flourished in Latin America, if for a relatively limited time. Carol A. Hess examines the symphonic repertoire of South America in chapter 7 and of Mexico, Central America, and the Spanish-speaking Caribbean in chapter 8. As she surveys the orchestral music traditions of each land from its colonial period to the present day, Hess finds the following trajectory holding true: "a strong indigenous heritage, concerted Catholic church music after the conquest, the growth of instrumental music through philharmonic societies and orchestras during the nineteenth century, a flowering of symphonic music in the twentieth, and new directions in orchestral music in the present century."[96] Although composing symphonies in Latin America was not unheard of before World War I—three practitioners were León Ribeiro (Uruguay), Ignacio Cervantes (Cuba), and Julián Carrillo (Mexico)—the great majority of symphonies emanating from Spanish- and Portuguese-speaking regions appeared between circa 1920 and circa 1960. After 1945, Latin American composers increasingly questioned the value of following either nationalism (whether based on folk or popular idioms) or cosmopolitanism; and with the rise of serialism, electroacoustic music, and other avant-garde strategies, they came to write fewer symphonies—and many who continued to do so, such as Juan Orrego-Salas and Roque Cordero, emigrated to the United States. As a result, the genre lies largely dormant in that region today.[97]

Except for Astor Piazzolla, all the internationally celebrated midcentury Latin American composers wrote symphonies or works of related scope. Carlos Chávez and Heitor Villa-Lobos created the most significant bodies, though Villa-Lobos's nonsymphonic orchestral music is much better known. Save for the *Sinfonía India* (1936), certainly an identity-conscious work, Chávez favored universalist, mostly neoclassic, strategies tinged with elements associated with primitivism, such as nondevelopmental repetition of motivic fragments and ostinati.[98] Villa-Lobos's twelve symphonies run the gamut from cosmopolitanism in his war-inspired Third through Fifth Symphonies ("War," "Victory," "Peace," 1919–20; the last-named is lost) to nationalism, as in the oratorio-like Symphony No. 10, *Sumé pater patrium: Sinfonia ameríndia com coros* (1952). Other prominent symphonists were Alberto Williams (Argentina), Mozart Camargo Guarnieri and Cláudio Santoro (Brazil), Guillermo Uribe Holguín (Colombia), Domingo Santa Cruz and Juan Orrego-Salas (Chile), and Roque Cordero (Panama), all of whose symphonies and other orchestral works Hess surveys. Alberto Ginastera's *Pampeana* No. 3 (1954) and Silvestre Revueltas's *La noche de los Mayas* (arranged in 1960 by José Yves Limantour from a 1939 film score) figure among the most important quasi-symphonies. Hess also examines orchestral music by Juan José Castro and Juan Carlos Paz (Argentina), Juan Bautista Plaza and Antonio Estévez Aponte (Venezuela), Luis Abraham Delgadillo

Introduction to the Symphonic Repertoire of the United States and Latin America

(Nicaragua), Andrés Carrizo (Panama), and Alejandro García Caturla and Julián Orbón (Cuba), among others.

Hess's chapters cover many more nonsymphonic pieces—symphonic poems, concert overtures, orchestral dances—than is typical for this series. In part, her coverage reflects the relative scarcity of accessible sources for a number of the symphonists, but it also serves a larger project. As Hess has pointedly asserted, Latin American music suffers general neglect both in scholarship and in the classroom, though a number of prominent conductors from that region are increasingly exposing its music to wider attention. She therefore seizes this promising moment to reveal the full panoply of orchestral music from the Latin American and Caribbean regions, in all its richness and exciting diversity.

The final chapter examines the symphony in the United States from circa 1970 forward. Whatever the portents of the 1950–70 period, the genre has flourished since that time in a manner that compares favorably with the symphonic production of the interwar years. Matthew Mugmon attributes this happy circumstance to several factors: first, the resurgence of tonality; second, the opportunity to incorporate post-1945 techniques (aleatory, clusters, extended techniques, electronica, etc.), even more non-Western idioms, and the sounds and styles of contemporary popular music; and finally, and perhaps most important, the demise of the obsession with the Great American Symphony, which has liberated composers to follow their own paths without feeling obliged—whether by critics or by their own consciences—to create an iconic national emblem. In striking contrast to Bernstein's ambivalence and the initial resistance of older symphonists like Philip Glass and John Corigliano, many younger composers have enthusiastically embraced the challenge of contributing to the "grand symphonic tradition" with its structural and expressive connotations.

As in the preceding chapters, the number of composers and symphonies considered is necessarily selective, but Mugmon's broad survey covers twenty-two composers of various backgrounds. Some symphonists, such as John Adams and Libby Larsen, seek to reflect American heritage or culture, while others, like Elliott Carter and George Walker, placed less emphasis on a national symphonic identity. Some composers continue to explore the Sibelian "absolute" symphony from diverse angles: Carter and Wang Jie experiment with various methods of organizing sound in a large structure; Walker and John Harbison seek to "make a serious statement" through the working out of formal challenges; Lou Harrison finds meaning in juxtaposing incongruous materials; and Philip Glass unites classical and popular idioms in his "Low," "Heroes," and "Lodger" Symphonies. At the same time, George Rochberg, Ellen Taaffe Zwilich, John Corigliano, Christopher Rouse, and Aaron Jay Kernis, among others, have employed the symphony to convey strong personal feelings of commemoration, nostalgia, or loss (as we have seen with Corigliano's Symphony No. 1); voice sociopolitical commentary or protest (Corigliano's Symphony No. 3, Kernis's Second Symphony, Bolcom's Symphony No. 8, and Fairouz's Symphony No. 4); or celebrate their ethnic, racial, or religious heritage (the Second Symphonies of Adolphus Hailstork, Daniel Asia, and Wynton Marsalis). In addition, many composers, such as Adams and Mason Bates, continue to create works that clearly convey the breadth of the symphony but without its title. Despite its checkered history in the nation, the symphony remains a vibrant element of American music, perhaps more than ever. As Mugmon writes at the conclusion of his study: "One need only take into account the blossoming of the symphony in the different approaches, or 'wellsprings,' of the three youngest composers above—Wang Jie's poetic organicism, Mason Bates's far-reaching expansion of the orchestral palette, and Mohammed Fairouz's cosmopolitan and message-oriented musical perspective—to predict that the genre's future seems bright."

Aspirations and Disclaimers

As we have seen, whether out of Eurocentric prejudice, institutional conservatism, composers' alleged failure to deliver the Great American Symphony, or something else, most symphonies written in the United States have commanded minimal attention in the concert hall and in scholarship. Nineteenth-century symphonies, which encompass innovative and idiosyncratic languages (Heinrich, Fry), fluent cosmopolitanism (Bristow, Paine, Beach), and skillfully integrated vernacular inflections (Gottschalk, Chadwick), deserve to be valued on their own terms and not condescendingly dismissed as works of America's musical "kindergarten," as Bernstein phrased it.[99] Ives's works should be seen as the product of an accomplished master of the Romantic symphony, not simply a modernist visionary with questionable technique. The chapters on the twentieth-century symphony seek to inspire examinations of lesser-known compositions by familiar figures—Hanson beyond the "Romantic"; Still beyond the *Afro-American*; Harris, Schuman, and Copland beyond their Thirds; and Chávez beyond the *Sinfonia India*—as well as explorations of the work of Piston, Thompson, Barber, Price, Antheil, Cowell, Diamond, Mennin, Villa-Lobos, and many other composers throughout the Americas. Similarly, the final chapter should stimulate new appreciation for underrated symphonists such as Rochberg; composers like Corigliano and Zwilich, whose first symphonies have overshadowed later contributions; Wang Jie, Fairouz, and other young symphonists; and nontraditional symphonic works created by Walker, Adams, Marsalis, and Bates.

This introduction closes with two disclaimers. First, this volume is entitled *The Symphony in the Americas* with keen awareness that it includes no chapter on the symphony in Canada. Many of the most notable Canadian composers, such as Healy Willan, Claude Champagne, Harry Somers, and R. Murray Schafer wrote only one or two symphonies, often (though not always) early in their careers, while others—Ernest MacMillan, John Beckwith, Henry Brant, and Claude Vivier, for example—avoided the genre entirely.

Composer Michael Matthews cited the following reasons for many of his colleagues' ambivalence toward symphonic expression:

> For many composers of my time the symphony as a form has fallen out of favour. For some this is a practical matter, since the difficulties of having large symphonic works performed are remarkably daunting . . . [because of] the reluctance of Canadian orchestras to encourage the creation of large symphonic compositions. . . . [B]ut it is not the only reason that there are relatively few contemporary symphonies, particularly in Canada. The other reason is a sense shared by many composers that the "symphony" as a form or structural entity is anachronistic, a museum-piece remnant from the 18th and 19th centuries . . . [while] for others it represents something more insidious, such as the exploitation of the working class or a throwback to a Eurocentric view of the arts.[100]

Nonetheless, as the accompanying table will show, a sizable number of Canadian composers (native-born and émigré) have written symphonies, and a few have contributed prolifically to the genre. Works ranking among the most respected Canadian symphonies include the following: Champagne's *Symphonie gaspésienne* (1945), Somers's Symphony No. 1 (1951), Barbara Pentland's *Symphony for Ten Parts* (Symphony No. 3, 1957), and the Second and Third Symphonies of Jacques Hétu (1961, 1971). The vast majority of Canadian symphonies remain

Table 1.5 Symphonies by Canadian Composers: A Selected List, by Birthdate

Entries marked CMC indicate that a score and/or non-commercial recording are available through the Canadian Music Centre (https://www.musiccentre.ca/). Scores are available for loan, rental, or purchase, and many are digitized on the site, albeit with the CMC logo superimposed. Some symphonies are published commercially through Canadian companies (Berandol, Counterpoint Music Library Services, Leeds Music Canada, Doberman-Yppan), while selected symphonies are recorded on the CMC house label, Centrediscs, and a few other labels.

Composer and works	Score and Recording
*Healey Willan (1880–1968) from England; moved to Canada in 1913	
Symphony No. 1 in D Minor (1936)	CMC[a]
Symphony No. 2 in C Minor (1941, rev. 1948)	CMC; also recorded on CBC Records SMCD 5123[a]
Claude Champagne (1891–1965)	
Symphonie gaspésienne (1945)	CMC; score also published by Berandol[a]
*Sophie-Carmen Eckhardt-Gramatté (1899–1974) from Russia; moved to Canada in 1954	
Symphony No. 1 in C Major (1939)	CMC[a]
Symphony-Concerto for Piano and Orchestra (1967)	CMC[a]
Symphony No. 2, "Manitoba" (1970)	CMC[a]
*Arnold Walter (1902–73) from the Czech Republic; moved to Canada in 1937	
Symphony in G Minor (1942)	CMC (score only)
*Janis Kalnins (1904–2000) from Latvia; moved to Canada in 1948	
Symphony No. 1 (1947)	CMC (score only)
Symphony of the Beatitudes (Symphony No. 2, 1972)	CMC (score only)
Symphony No. 3 (1972)	CMC (score only)
Symphony No. 4 (1977)	CMC (score only)
*León Zuckert (1904–92) from Ukraine; moved to Canada in 1929	
Symphony No. 1 (1949)	CMC
Symphony No. 2 (1962)	CMC (score only)
Murray Adaskin (1906–2002)	
Ballet Symphony (1951, rev. 1972)	CMC
Algonquin Symphony (1957)	CMC; also published by Counterpoint Music Library Services
Jean Coulthard (1908–2000)	
Symphony No. 1 (1951)	CMC; also published by Berandol[a]
This Land: Symphony No. 2 for chorus and orchestra (1967)	CMC (score only)
Lyric Symphony: Symphony No. 3 for bassoon and orchestra (1975)	CMC (score only)
Autumn Symphony: Symphony No. 4 for stringed orchestra (1984)	CMC

Table 1.5 *continued*

Composer and works	Score and Recording
Barbara Pentland (1912–2000)	
Symphony No. 1 (1948)	CMC (score only)
Symphony No. 2 (1950)	CMC[a]
Symphony for Ten Parts (Symphony No. 3, 1957)	CMC; also published by Berandol and recorded on Centrediscs CD 814[a]
Symphony No. 4 (1959)	CMC[a]
Violet Archer (1913–2000)	
Symphony No. 1 (1946)	CMC; also published by Berandol[a]
Sinfonietta (1968)	CMC; also published by Berandol[a]
Alexander Brott (1915–2005)	
Symphony in Two Movements (1936)	CMC (score only)
Jean Papineau-Couture (1916–2000)	
Symphony No. 1 in C Major (1948, rev. 1956)	CMC
James Gayfer (1916–97)	
Symphony No. 1 in B-flat (1947)	CMC
Symphony No. 2 in E-flat (1953)	CMC
Samuel Dolin (1917–2002)	
Symphony No. 1, "Elk Falls" (1956)	CMC (score only)
Symphony No. 2 (1957)	CMC; also published by Berandol
Symphony No. 3 (1976)	CMC
***Oskar Morawetz (1917–2007) from the Czech Republic; moved to Canada in 1940**	
Symphony No. 1 (1953)	CMC
Symphony No. 2 (1959)	CMC[a]
Sinfonietta for Winds and Percussion (1965)	CMC
Sinfonietta for Strings (1988)	CMC
***Richard Johnston (1917–97) from the United States; moved to Canada in 1947**	
Symphony No. 1 (1950, rev. 1972)	CMC; also published by Berandol
Lorne Betts (1918–85)	
Symphony No. 1 (1954)	CMC (score only)
Symphony No. 2 (1961)	CMC (score only)
***István Anhalt (1919–2012) from Hungary; moved to Canada in 1949**	
Symphony (1958)	CMC; also published by Berandol
Symphony of Modules (1967)	CMC (score only)
***Tālivaldis Ķeniņš (1919–2008) from Latvia; moved to Canada in 1951**	
Symphony No. 1 for Chamber Orchestra (1959)	CMC; also recorded on Ondine ODE 1350-2[a]
Second Symphony: Sinfonia concertante for Flute, Oboe, Clarinet, and Orchestra (1967)	CMC[a]

Composer and works	Score and Recording
Symphony No. 3 (1970)	CMC[a]
Symphony No. 4 (1972)	CMC; also published by Berandol and recorded on Centrediscs CD 9403, Ondine ODE 1354–2[a]
Symphony No. 5 (1975)	CMC; also recorded on Ondine ODE 1388–2[a]
Simfonietta (1976)	CMC
Sinfonia notturna (1978)	CMC
Sinfonia ad fugam (Symphony No. 6, 1978)	CMC; also recorded on Ondine ODE 1354-2[a]
Symphony No. 7 for Mezzo-soprano and Orchestra (1980)	CMC
Symphony No. 8, Sinfonia concertata for Organ and Orchestra (1986)	CMC; also recorded on Ondine ODE 1388-2[a]
Andrew Twa (1919–2009)	
Symphony (1953)	CMC
Robert Turner (1920–2012)	
Symphony for Strings (1960)	CMC; also published by Berandol
Symphony No. 2 in One Movement, "Gift from the Sea" (1983)	CMC (score only)[a]
Third Symphony (1990)	CMC; also recorded on Centrediscs CD 9704[a]
***Kaljo Raid (1921–2005) from Estonia; moved to Canada by 1954**	
Symphony No. 1 in C Minor (1944)	CMC (recording only); also recorded on Chandos 8525[a]
Symphony No. 2, "Stockholm Symphony" (1946)	CMC; also recorded on Music Manufacturing Services KRCD 01
Symphony No. 3, "Traditional" (1995)	CMC (score only)
Symphony No. 4, "Postmodern" (1997)	No score or recording
***George Fiala (1922–2017) from Ukraine; moved to Canada in 1949**	
Symphony No. 4, "Ukrainian" (1973)	CMC (score only)
Symphony No. 5, "Sinfonia breve" (1981)	No score or recording
Harry Freedman (1922–2005) born in Poland; moved to Canada at age 3	
Symphony No. 1 (1960)	CMC
A Little Symphony (1967)	CMC; also published by Leeds Music Canada
Symphony No. 3 (1983)	CMC (recording only)[a]
Leslie Mann (1923–77)	
Symphony No. 1 (1973)	CMC
Symphony No. 2 (1974)	CMC
Nicholas Slater (1925–94)	
Symphony No. 1 (n.d.)	CMC (complete score; recording of first two movements); also published by Berandol

Table 1.5 *continued*

Composer and works	Score and Recording
Harry Somers (1925–99)	
Symphony No. 1 (1951)	CMC; also published by Berandol and recorded on Centrediscs CD 11306[a]
Symphony for Winds, Brass, and Percussion (1961)	CMC
***Gerhard Wuensch (1925–2007) from Austria; moved to Canada in 1964**	
Symphony for Band, Op. 14 (1960)	CMC (score only)
Symphony, Op. 35 (1967)	CMC (score only)
Clermont Pépin (1926–2006)	
Symphony No. 1 in B Minor (1948)[d]	No score or recording
Symphony No. 2 (1957)	CMC[a]
Symphony No. 3, "Quasars" (1967)	CMC; also published by Leeds Music Canada[a]
Symphony No. 4, "La Messe sur la monde" (1975, rev. 1990)	CMC (score only)
Symphony No. 5, "Implosion" (1983)	CMC (recording only)[a]
Donald Cochrane (born 1928)	
Symphony No. 1 (1982)	CMC (recording only)
Symphony No. 2 (1983)	No score or recording
Symphony No. 3 (1988)	CMC
Symphony No. 4 (1990)	No score or recording
Symphony No. 5 (1991)	CMC (recording only)[a]
Symphony No. 6 (1992)	No score or recording
Symphony No. 7 (1996)	No score or recording
Symphony No. 8 (2002)	No score or recording
Symphony No. 9 (2004)	No score or recording
Symphony No. 10 (2005)	No score or recording
Alfred Kunz (1929–2019)	
Chamber Symphony (1976)	CMC (score only)
Sinfonietta No. 1 (1957)	CMC (score only)
Sinfonietta No. 2: A Symphony for Young People (1961)	CMC (score only)
Milton Barnes (1931–2001)	
Symphony No. 1 (1964)	CMC (score only)
Symphony No. 2 for Strings (1976)	CMC
Symphony No. 3, "Symphonic Portrait" (1987)	CMC (score only)
Frederick R. C. Clarke (1931–2009)	
Symphony (1999)	CMC (score only)
Paul McIntyre (1931–2020)	
Symphonia sacra (1958)	CMC (score only)

Introduction to the Symphonic Repertoire of the United States and Latin America

Composer and works	Score and Recording
Jean de Brébeuf Symphony (1962)	CMC (score only)
A Windsor Symphony (2006)	CMC (score only)
Charles Wilson (1931–2019)	
Symphony in A (1954)	CMC (score only)
Sinfonia (1972)	CMC (score only)
Symphony No. 1 (1998)	CMC (score only)
***Lothar Klein (1932–2004) from Germany; moved to Canada in 1968**	
Symphony No. 1 (1955)	CMC
Symphony No. 2 (1965)	CMC
Symphonic Etudes: Symphony No. 3 for Wind Ensemble (1972)	CMC; also published by Theodore Presser and recorded on Centrediscs CD 548
Michael Miller (born 1932)	
Spirit of Dancing Symphony (2002)	CMC
Walter Buczynski (born 1933)	
Symphony No. 1 (1986)	CMC (score only)
R. Murray Schafer (1933–2021)	
Symphony No. 1 in C Minor (2011)	CMC (recording only)
Srul Irving Glick (1934–2002)	
Symphony No. 1 for Chamber Orchestra (1966)	CMC
Symphony No. 2 (1967)	CMC
The Hour Has Come: A Choral Symphony (1984, rev. 1987)	CMC; also published by Counterpoint Music Library Services
Paul Douglas (1936–2010)	
Helvetia: A First Symphony for Orchestra (1993)	CMC; also published by Skylark Music
La Cévenole: A Second Symphony for Orchestra—A Rocky Mountain Symphony (1998)	CMC (score only)
***Malcolm Forsyth (1936–2011) from South Africa; moved to Canada in 1968**	
Symphony No. 1 (1972)	CMC; also published by Counterpoint Music Library Services
Symphony No. 2 . . . *a host of nomads* . . . (1976)	CMC; also published by Counterpoint Music Library Services
African Ode (Symphony No. 3, 1981)	CMC (score only); also published by Counterpoint Music Library Services
Michael Conway Baker (born 1937)	
Symphony (1977)	CMC
Sinfonia for Strings (1985)	CMC (score only)
Symphony No. 2, "Century Symphony" (1993)	CMC (score only)

Table 1.5 *continued*

Composer and works	Score and Recording
*Thomas Schudel (born 1937) from the United States; moved to Canada in 1964	
Symphony No. 1 (1971)	CMC
Symphony No. 2 (1983)	CMC
Jacques Hétu (1938–2010)	
Symphonie pour cordes (Symphony No. 1, 1959)	CMC; also published by Berandol (under the name Clark and Cruickshank)[a]
Symphony No. 2 (1961)	CMC; also published by Berandol (under the name Clark and Cruickshank)[a]
Symphony No. 3 (1971, rev. 1978)	CMC; also published by Berandol and recorded on Centrediscs CD 710
Symphony No. 4 (1995)	CMC; also published by Doberman-Yppan[a]
Symphony No. 5 (2010)	CMC; also published by Doberman-Yppan[a]
Lloyd Burritt (born 1940)	
Symphony in One Movement (1962)	CMC (score only)
David Hemsley (1940–2000)	
Symphony in A Major (1985)	CMC
Alan Heard (born 1942)	
Sinfonietta (1993)	CMC (score only)
Symphony No. 2 (1984)	CMC (score only)
Allan Rae (1942–2022)	
Symphony No. 1, "In the Shadow of Atlantis" (1972)	CMC (score only)
Symphony No. 2, "Winds of Change" (1978)	CMC (score only)
Symphony #three [*sic*]: *Alam-Al-Mithal* (1980)	CMC (score only)
*David Zhang (born 1942) from China; moved to Canada after 1990	
Symphony No. 1, "Dragon Legends" (2019)	No score or recording
Symphony No. 2, "Fight the Covid 19" (2022)	CMC
*E. John Robertson (born 1943) from New Zealand; moved to Canada in 1967	
Symphony No. 1 (1986)	CMC; also recorded on Navona NV6167[a]
Symphony No. 2 (2014)	No score or recording
Symphony No. 3 (2017)	No score or recording
Symphony No. 4 (2017)	No score or recording
Symphony No. 5 (2018)	No score or recording
*Maya Badian (born 1945) from Romania; moved to Canada in 1987	
Holocaust—In Memoriam, Symphony (1987, rev. 1998, 2011)	CMC; also published by Éditions Lucian Bedian and recorded on Centrediscs CD 515[a]

Introduction to the Symphonic Repertoire of the United States and Latin America

Composer and works	Score and Recording
Ronald Hannah (born 1945)	
Symphony No. 1, "Jasmine" (2004)	CMC (score only)
Clifford Ford (born 1947)	
Ganymede Symphony (1992, rev. 2003)	Self-published; recording available on composer's website
Steven Gellman (born 1947)	
Symphony in Two Movements (1971)	CMC; also published by Counterpoint Music Library Services
Symphony II (1973)	CMC (score only)
Universe Symphony (1986)	CMC[a]
*Michael S. Horwood (born 1947) from United States; moved to Canada in 1971	
Symphony No. 1 (1984)	CMC; also recorded on Albany Troy 943
Symphony No. 2, "Visions of a Wounded Earth" (1995)	CMC (score only)
Symphony No. 3, "Andromeda" (1996)	CMC (score only)
*Peter Koprowski (born 1947) from Poland; moved to Canada in 1971	
Sinfonia da camera (1989)	CMC (recording only)
Sinfonia concertante (1992)	No score or recording
Sinfonia mystica (1993)	CMC (recording only)
Symphony of Nordic Tales (1995)	CMC (score only)
*Nikolai Korndorf (1947–2001) from Russia; moved to Canada in 1991	
Symphony No. 1 (1975)	No score or recording
Symphony No. 2 (1980)	CMC[a]
Symphony No. 3 (1988)	CMC (score only)[a]
Underground Music: Symphony No. 4 (1996)	CMC[a]
Stephen Brown (born 1948) from England; moved to Canada in 1952	
Symphony in A Minor, "The Northern Journey" (1986–89, rev. 1992, 2018–19)	CMC (score only)
Symphony No. 2, "Fear and Loathing" (2019)	CMC (score only)[a]
Symphony No. 3, "Combustion" (n.d.)	CMC (score only)[a]
Symphony No. 4, "Under the Curse of Darkness" (n.d.)	CMC (score only)[a]
Stewart Grant (born 1948)	
Symphony, "Et in terra" (1993)	CMC
Symphonie estrienne for strings (1997)	CMC
*Marjan Mozetich (born 1948) from Slovenia; moved to Canada in 1982	
Symphony No. 1, "A Romantic Rhapsody" (1983)	CMC

Table 1.5 *continued*

Composer and works	Score and Recording
Harold Wevers (born 1949)	
Symphony in D (1984)	CMC
Symphony No. 2 (1995)	CMC (recording only)
Symphony No. 3 (2000)	CMC (recording only)
Symphony No. 4 (2007)	CMC
***Edward Arteaga (born 1950) from the United States; moved to Canada in 1972**	
Symphony No. 1 (1980)	CMC (complete score, but recording of first movement only)
Symphony No. 2 for Chorus and Orchestra, Dedicated to the Victims of Violence (2002)	CMC (score only)
Symphony No. 3 (2005)	CMC (score only)
Symphony No. 4 (2009)	CMC (score only)
Symphony No. 5 (2018)	CMC (score only)
Symphony No. 6 (2021)	CMC (score only)
Michael Matthews (born 1950)	
Symphony No. 1 (1997)	CMC; also recorded on TNC Records
Symphony No. 2 (2001)	CMC
Symphony No. 3 (2005)	CMC (score only)
David Tanner (born 1950)	
Pocket Symphony (2011)	CMC
Alan Belkin (born 1951)	
Symphony No. 1 (1981)	CMC (score only)
Symphony No. 2 (1990)	CMC (score only)
Symphony No. 3 (1990?)	CMC (recording only)[a]
Symphony No. 4 (1990, rev. 2012)	CMC (score only)[a]
Symphony No. 5 (1991)	CMC[a]
Symphony No. 6 (1997, rev. 2014)	CMC (score only)[a]
Symphony No. 7 (1997, rev. 2013)	CMC (score only)[a]
Symphony No. 8 (2018)[d]	No score or recording[a]
Ted Dawson (born 1951)	
Symphony No. 1 (1993)	CMC
Peter Ware (born 1951)	
Symphony No. 1, "Ancient Evenings" (2002?)	CMC (partial recording only); self-published
Frederick Schipizky (born 1952)	
Symphony No. 1 (1985)	CMC (score only)
Symphony No. 2 for Chamber Orchestra (1988)	CMC
Symphony No. 3, "Symphonic Messaging" (by 2014)	CMC (recording only)[a]

Composer and works	Score and Recording
David MacIntyre (born 1952)	
Symphony No. 1 (1979)	CMC (score only)
Glenn Buhr (born 1954)	
Symphony No. 1, "de Joie" (1997)	CMC (recording only)[a]
Symphony No. 2, "Adagio pathétique" (2001)	No score or recording
Symphony No. 3 (2008)	CMC (recording only)
Gary Kulesha (born 1954)	
Symphony (No. 1, 1997)	CMC; also published by Counterpoint Music Library Services
Second Symphony (2005)	No score or recording
Third Symphony (2006)	CMC; also published by Counterpoint Music Library Services
Neil Currie (born 1955)	
Symphony (1999)	No score or recording in CMS; score available through Australian Music Centre
Timothy Brady (born 1956)	
Symphony No. 0: Chamber Symphony (1983)	CMC (score only)
Playing Guitar: Symphony No. 1 (solo electric guitar, 15 musicians, live electronics, 1997)	CMC; also recorded on Ambiances magnétiques 125
The Choreography of Time: Symphony No. 2 (saxophone quartet and orchestra, 2004–10)	CMC (recording only, as Four Saxophones)
Guess Who Symphony (amplified singer and orchestra, 2010)	CMC (recording only)
Atacama: Symphony No. 3 (choir and chamber orchestra, 2007–12)	CMC; also recorded on ATMA Classique 22676[a]
The How and the Why of Memory: Symphony No. 4 (orchestra, 2004–10)	CMC; also recorded on Centrediscs CD 1691
The Same River Twice: Symphony 5.0 (electric guitar quartet, 2013)	CMC
Symphonie 5.1 (multimedia with dance and interactive videos. 2014–16)	No score or recording
The Luxury of Time: Symphony No. 6 (orchestra, 2012–15)	No score or recording
Eight Songs About: Symphony No. 7 (soprano and baritone soloists and chamber orchestra, 2016–17)	CMC (recording only); also recorded on Starkland ST-230[a]
Where Motion Sounds: Symphony No. 8 (12 solo voices, violin, electric guitar, percussion, 2016–18)	No score or recording
For as Many Strings as Possible, Playing: Symphony No. 9 (150 electric guitars divided into 6 groups, 2018)	No score or recording[a]

Table 1.5 *continued*

Composer and works	Score and Recording
SILENCES: Symphony No. 10 (chamber orchestra, 4 electric guitars, 4 choirs, 4 conductors, 2019)	No score or recording
This One is Broken in Pieces: Symphony No. 11 (8 electric guitars, 2 sopranos, 2 mezzo-sopranos, 2019–20)	No score or recording
BECAUSE EVERYTHING WILL CHANGE: Symphony No. 12 (104 electric guitars, 6 percussionists and orchestra divided into two sections; 6 conductors required, 2018)	No score or recording
Symphony in 18 Parts for solo electric guitar (2021)	No score or recording
T. Patrick Carrabré (born 1958)	
Symphony No. 1, "The War of Angels" (1996)	CMC (score only); also recorded on Centrediscs CD 18513
Of Heroes and Legends . . .: Symphony #2 (2000)	No score or recording
Symphony No. 3 (2003)	CMC (score only); also recorded on Centrediscs CD 18513
Andrew Paul MacDonald (born 1958)	
Symphony No. 1, "The Red Guru" (2003–05)	No score or recording
Symphony No. 2, "The Great Wave" (2007)	CMC
Rodney Sharman (born 1958)	
Symphony (2000)	CMC
Second Symphony (2012)	No score or recording
***Nic Gotham (1959–2013) from England**	
Nightscapes: A Chamber Symphony (2012)	CMC (score only)
John Burge (born 1961)	
Symphony No. 1, "The Clarion" (1997)	CMC
E. Scott Wilkinson (1962–2011)	
Symphony No. 1 for Cowbells and Band in C Major (1971)	CMC (score only)
Symphony of the North (1988)	CMC (score only)
Matthew de Lacey Davidson (born 1964)	
Symphony No. 1 in 20 Keys, "Letter to the World" (2014)	CMC (score only)
John Estacio (born 1966)	
A Farmer's Symphony (1994)	CMC[a]
***Airat Ichmouratov (born 1973) from Russia; moved to Canada in 1973**	
Symphony No. 1 in A Major, "On the Ruins of an Ancient Fort" (2017)	CMC (score only); recorded on Chandos 20172

Composer and works	Score and Recording
Derek Charke (born 1974)	
Symphony No. 1, "Transient Energies" (2010)	CMC
Symphony No. 2 for Chorus and Orchestra, "Earth Airs" (2015)	CMC (score only)
Robert Rival (born 1975)	
Symphony No. 1, "Maligne Range" (2009)	CMC (score only)
Symphony No. 2, "Water" (2013)	CMC (score only)
Heather Schmidt (born 1975)	
Sinfonietta (1996)	No score or recording
Symphony No. 1, "Manufactured Landscapes" (2005)	CMC (recording only)[a]
Vincent Ho (born 1975)	
Arctic Symphony (2010)	CMC; also published by Promethean Editions and recorded on Centrediscs CD 24317[a]
Christopher Nickel (born 1978)	
Symphony No. 1 for Strings (2014)	CMC (score only)
Symphony No. 2 (2016)	CMC (score only); also recorded on Avie 2456
Symphony for Flute Choir (2017)	CMC (score only); also recorded on Centrediscs CD 27019
Samy Moussa (born 1984)	
Symphony No. 1 "Concordia" (2016–17)	Published by Éditions Durand (score available for hire); recording available on composer's website
Symphony No. 2 (2022)	No score or recording
Daniel Mehdizadeh (born 1987)	
Symphony No. 1 (2012)	No score or recording
Symphony No. 2 (2020)	CMC
Martial Sauvé (no dates provided)	
Symphony No. 1, "Crescendo" (2004)	CMC[a]
Symphony No. 2, "Tout le ciel" (2011)	CMC (score only)
Michel Edward (no dates provided)	
Symphony No. 2, "Sinfonia canadensis" (2012)	CMC (score only)[a]
Symphony No. 3 "Une symphonie de guerre" (2016)	CMC (score only)
Symphony No. 4 for Strings	CMC (score only)

*denotes émigré composers. (Canadian-born composers who have worked primarily in the United States are not included in this table.)
a. Uploaded, either as a recording or live performance, on YouTube as of March 2023.

unpublished, however, and appear to have received few performances outside their premieres. The Canadian Music Centre possesses scores for many of these compositions (usually the holograph), which are available for loan, rental, or purchase; many of the scores are also digitized on the site, but the scans are heavily imprinted by the Centre's logo, rendering analytical study impractical. About thirty symphonies are published commercially, usually through Canadian companies, but few are readily available in libraries. The Centre also houses archival copies of live performances for a number of these works, which can be heard through the website (https://www.musiccentre.ca) and occasionally on YouTube. Some symphonies have been recorded on the CMC house label Centrediscs, while a few are represented on other labels; most are available on Spotify. In light of the relatively limited availability of resources overall, for reasons of time and space, it was decided with regret to omit Canada from the volume. Table 1.5 offers an extensive list of Canadian symphonies, with the resources available for each work.

Second, as all but two of the following chapters concern symphonists working specifically in the United States, they will employ the adjective "American"—as I have done throughout much of this introduction—while acknowledging that such a restrictive use of the word represents a sensitive issue in Latin American communities. As Gilbert Chase eloquently stated in the preface to his 1955 book *America's Music from the Pilgrims to the Present*, the term is "more properly applicable to the Western Hemisphere as a whole . . . [and a] symbolic name that binds us all to common ideals of peace, friendship, and cooperation."[101] Unfortunately, as Hess points out, English lacks a viable adjectival equivalent to the Spanish *estadounidense* or Portuguese *estadunidense* ("of the United States")—the term "Usonian" favored by Frank Lloyd Wright and others has not found wide favor—to say nothing of designators to distinguish the nation before and after 1848.[102] Chase lamented to Alberto Ginastera, "We are not North Americans because so are Mexicans and Canadians. If we don't call ourselves 'Americans,' in the national sense, we're left without any name at all. Sad fate for a great country!"[103] Following Chase, we have adopted the more limited meaning for the sake of concision and elegant writing—as he put it, for "euphony and convenience, supported by a literary tradition that has ample precedent."[104]

Bibliographic Overview

The first significant overview of the symphony in the United States is Korn/SYMPHONY, a chapter from the two-volume compendium *The Symphony*, edited by Robert Simpson. A sympathetic study by a German-American symphonist, it concentrates on the period from 1920 to 1960. The author does not consider any earlier American symphonies worth hearing, including those by Ives (he makes tepid allowances for the Third Symphony). Korn regards Piston as the greatest symphonist of the nation, and Harris's Third, Barber's First, Bernstein's "Jeremiah," and Sessions's Second as the best individual works by others. He finds Mennin the most promising composer of the younger generation, though he devotes more space to émigré Ernst Toch than to most native-born composers. The compendium includes no chapter on Latin America.

Butterworth/SYMPHONY is the only monograph-length survey to precede the present volume. The author attempts to account for virtually every symphony composed in the United States up to 1999, and his book includes a mammoth *catalogue raisonné* of works by native composers as well as émigrés (pp. 197–302; European symphonists who resided only temporarily in America, such as Hindemith, Martinů, and Milhaud, are not included, nor is Stravinsky). The value of this source, however, is severely undermined by superficial discussions, insufficient citations, mechanical lapses, and distressingly elementary factual errors.[105]

Its principal virtue lies in providing at least a few words about many composers and works not covered anywhere else.

Shadle/ORCHESTRATING characterizes the nineteenth-century American symphonic repertoire as a victim of immediate, willful, and decisive neglect. Although the Great American Symphony trope did not form as such until later in the century, it was effectively already in operation during the antebellum period; as his strongly-researched narrative demonstrates, critics and conductors (though not the public) usually concluded *a priori* that each new symphony would not measure up and responded accordingly. Shadle's account, on the other hand, leaves us with a strong desire to hear these works.

Two sources concentrate on the Great American Symphony, and citations from their work appear prominently throughout this volume. Schnepel/GREAT, an excellent dissertation from Indiana University—advised by Peter Brown with Peter Burkholder as a committee member—focuses on the critics who drove the search between circa 1890–1950 and the unfortunate consequences for the composers. Tawa/GREAT considers the music itself. He studies the work of eighteen symphonists active during the Depression and World War II, usually emphasizing one emblematic work (he makes an exception for Barber, devoting separate chapters to each symphony).[106] Although the analyses rarely penetrate below the surface and include no examples, Tawa provides an important contextual background and framework for the flourishing of the symphony between 1920 and 1970.

Several general histories of music in the United States include passages on the symphony in the 1930s and 1940s. Chase/AMERICA 1987 singles out Copland, Sessions, and Harris as the three who accomplished "the most personal creative extension of the Grand Tradition."[107] Hamm/MUSIC reprints valuable quotations regarding Copland and Harris.[108] Starr/TONAL explains how Hanson, Harris, Piston, and others have been misrepresented by textbook labels that oversimplify the breadth of their achievements.[109] Bernard/TONAL examines the variety of symphonic styles from 1960 to the 1990s through four groups: the "old guard" who never abandoned tonality; "converts" from serialism to tonality; minimalists; and "new and newer Romantics."

Taruskin/OXFORD offers a penetrating discussion of Ives's marriage of a "maximalist" modernism to a fundamentally Romantic aesthetic. He considers Harris's "rugged individualist" style—melodic breadth, dissonant but basically diatonic harmonies, asymmetrical rhythms, and sonorous, often percussion-heavy orchestration—as the paradigm of what he calls the "WPA School."[110] He also includes a section on symphonies of the late twentieth century. As Carol Hess points out, however, the series ignores Latin America completely.[111] Save for brief and generally dismissive asides, no American symphonies appear at any length in Horton/SYMPHONY (and no Latin American symphonies at all).

The primary textbooks on the symphony devote a chapter to the United States. Cuyler/SYMPHONY discusses the symphonies of Ives (especially the Third), as well as Hanson (No. 1), Piston (No. 1), Harris (No. 3), Barber (No. 2), and Copland (a brief survey). In addition to passing comments about other works, the more extended treatment in Stedman/SYMPHONY includes short analyses of symphonies by Ives (No. 4), Harris (No. 7), Schuman (No. 3), Copland (No. 3), Wallingford Riegger (No. 3), Sessions (No. 7), and Zwilich (No. 1), with numerous examples. Steinberg/SYMPHONY offers detailed and informative program-note descriptions of individual symphonies by Copland (No. 2), Hanson (No. 4), Harbison (No. 2), Ives (No. 4), Piston (Nos. 2 and 6), Schuman (Nos. 3 and 6) and Sessions (No. 2). Again, none of these sources consider Latin American symphonies.

Hess/REPRESENTING discusses changing perceptions of Latin American music in the United States throughout the twentieth century; "snapshots" of episodes in the careers of Chávez, Villa-Lobos, and Ginastera illustrate how shifting cultural and political climates affected the reception and interpretation of Latin American music, including symphonies, on both continents. Two widely read textbooks on Latin American music, Béhague/LATIN and Moore and Clark/LATIN, give minimal attention to symphonies except for Chávez's *Sinfonía India*; Hess/EXPERIENCING, a more recent textbook, discusses that symphony along with three non-symphonic orchestral works by Revueltas, Villa-Lobos, and Ricardo Lorenz.

Notes

1. Neil Butterworth estimates that in the twentieth century, only the Soviet Union and, to a lesser extent, Great Britain compare (Butterworth/SYMPHONY, p. 1).
2. Quoted in Shadle/ORCHESTRATING, p. 26. Emphasis in original. It was commonly thought at the time that the diverse timbres and polyphonic layers working together in a symphony served as an apt metaphor for people of various ethnic backgrounds joining to form a united and democratic America (Shadle/NEW WORLD, p. 60).
3. From Chadwick's unpublished memoirs of 1876, quoted in White/CHADWICK, p. 90.
4. Quoted in Shadle/ORCHESTRATING, p. 180.
5. Copland/SINCE 1943, p. 69. Similarly, Dan Stehman speculates that Roy Harris gravitated to the symphony because of "its importance in the tradition, its potential for large-scale utterance, and the increasing freedom with which composers of the nineteenth and early twentieth centuries had treated its formal components" (Stehman/HARRIS, p. 48).
6. Quoted in Schnepel/GREAT, pp. 473–74.
7. Bolcom/PROPHETIC, p. 19. The Eighth Symphony (2005–7) sets poetry of William Blake for soloists, chorus, and orchestra. See chapter 9 in this book for a study of Bolcom's symphonies.
8. Puts/PULITZER.
9. Fairouz/INTERVIEW. See chapter 9 for Fairouz's symphonies.
10. Fauser/SOUNDS, p. 256.
11. For example, Bernard Holland criticized Ellen Taaffe Zwilich's Symphony No. 3 (1992) for supposedly failing to engage "pressing matters" with an "appropriate topical agenda"; Holland/COMPOSERS, quoted in chapter 9. On the other hand, John Corigliano's Symphony No. 1 (1988) received wide praise as a masterful musical response to the AIDS crisis.
12. The final section of the present chapter addresses the absence of Canada from this volume.
13. With this notorious remark, piano professor Pierre Zimmerman summarily rejected Louis Moreau Gottschalk's application to the Paris Conservatoire in 1842 (Starr/BAMBOULA, p. 50).
14. Quoted in Alexander/STRETCH, p. 180.
15. Quoted in Faucett/CHADWICK SYMPHONIC, p. 59.
16. Bernstein/GREAT.
17. Schnepel/GREAT, p. 1. The phrase originated in an 1868 essay by John William DeForest, promoting what he called the "Great American Novel." Some of DeForest's literary criteria are reflected in the requirements adopted for the Great American Symphony. But while Mark Twain was widely regarded as having achieved the Great American Novel with *The Adventures of Huckleberry Finn* (1885), the search for the Great American Symphony remained frustratingly elusive. Ironically, perhaps, music critics consistently invoked Walt Whitman—rather than a master of prose such as Twain, Nathaniel Hawthorne, or Herman Melville—as the proper literary model for composers; they celebrated Whitman as the creator of a uniquely American literature that combined tradition (poetry), innovation (free verse), and patriotism (overt celebration of the nation).

18. See Shadle/ORCHESTRATING for the impact of critics in the nineteenth century and Schnepel/GREAT for their influence in the first half of the twentieth.

19. Schnepel/GREAT, p. 543. For example, Lawrence Morton censured William Schuman's Third Symphony for reputedly lacking "the [thematic] tensions and oppositions and conflict *that we are entitled to expect*" (p. 479; my emphasis).

20. Shadle/NEW WORLD, pp. 48–50, cites four reviews from New York in the 1880s. The first two alternately praise and criticize Dvořák for not admitting Wagnerian influences into his Sixth Symphony, while the second two in turn censure and compliment him for doing precisely that in the Seventh Symphony.

21. See chapter 3, p. 145.

22. "Critics could always decry an uncultivated public, and they frequently did" (Shadle/ORCHESTRATING, p. 220). For example, a review for the *Boston Post* stated that Chadwick's Second Symphony possessed "neither the breadth nor the dignity that are demanded of such a piece of music" because, among other things, the first movement included what the critic heard as a waltz melody: "Such things help perhaps to make a work popular with the indiscriminate, but they are to be unreservedly condemned from a just point of view"; quoted in Faucett/CHADWICK SYMPHONIC, p. 53. Complicating matters further, critics in New York and Boston frequently crossed swords aesthetically, so that a work favored in one place might for the same reasons receive a frosty reception in the other. Such was Chadwick's experience with his Third Symphony (1894), which won a composition prize in New York but garnered withering reviews in his hometown of Boston. See chapter 3, pp. 146–47.

23. Schnepel/GREAT, p. 109.

24. Ibid., pp. 392, 448. Otherwise, as Philip Hale observed, local color served merely for "covering mediocrity with a cloak of patriotism"; ibid., p. 273.

25. Ibid., pp. 3, 241. Schnepel defines their predicament as "the dilemma of writing a distinctively American work under the rubric of a European tradition, of balancing the standards of that tradition with the expectations for originality and individuality, and of fusing recognizably American musics (and the atmosphere or spirit of American life) with not only European musics of the past but with modern musical idioms" (p. 540).

26. Ibid., p. 251.

27. Shadle/ORCHESTRATING, p. 269. He cites William Cadwalader Hudson's contradictory assessments of George Frederick Bristow's Symphony No. 4 ("Arcadian," 1872): praising the programmatic work for its explicitly American subject matter in advance publicity, he reversed himself after hearing a rehearsal and condemned Bristow's attempt to impose an "American" identity on an inherently cosmopolitan genre (pp. 176–77).

28. Schnepel/GREAT, chapter 10, especially pp. 524–25. In addition to the aforementioned symphonies, she examines the reception of Amy Beach's "Gaelic" Symphony.

29. Ibid., p. 539. Although the first two movements were performed in 1927, the complete symphony did not premiere until 1965.

30. See, for example, Fanning/SINCE MAHLER, which summarily dismisses most American symphonies as "ephemeral" and "feeble-minded" in comparison to Russian, Nordic, and British works (pp. 119, 121).

31. Chase/AMERICA 1987, pp. 572–73. The quote, meant to distinguish between symphonies of cosmopolitan and nationalist orientations, is by William Brooks (emphasis in original).

32. Quoted in Tick/USA, pp. 162–63. Shadle calls the process "translation" and discusses it in chapter 3 of Shadle/ORCHESTRATING, especially p. 57.

33. *Boston Herald*, April 26, 1896; quoted in Schmidt/PAINE, p. 197.

34. Bomberger/MACDOWELL, pp. 117–18, 181–85. See also Shadle/NEW WORLD, p. 87.

35. Stated in 1983 (COPLAND/1900-42, p. 149). For his part, Creston declared that "I make no special effort to be American: I conscientiously work to be my true self, which is Italian by parentage, American by birth and cosmopolitan by choice" (Butterworth/SYMPHONY, p. 135).

36. Cowell/AMERICAN, p. 165.

37. Schnepel/GREAT, pp. 509–10. See also Levy/FRONTIER.

38. See chapter 6 for more on the "urban" style of Schuman and Bernstein.

39. See chapter 3 for more on her response to Dvořák. Later, Beach herself would write compositions based on non-Celtic sources, such as her Variations on Balkan Themes (1904) and String Quartet (1929), one of several works employing Native American melodies (Inuit in this case). For more on the Quartet, see Block/BEACH, pp. 126–27, 238; also Block/MUSIC.

40. Schnepel/GREAT, p. 542.

41. See chapter 2 of this volume as well as chapter 5 of Shadle/ORCHESTRATING for further details. This situation was not unique to the United States. Composers in mid-nineteenth-century France received similar treatment from conductors who restricted their programs to "great" (i.e., Germanic) works. As Jules Pasdeloup reportedly told Camille Saint-Saëns in the 1860s, "Write symphonies like Beethoven and I'll play them!" Even after the foundation of the prestigious Colonne and Lamoureux orchestras in the 1870s amid a national drive to promote native concert music, Ernest Chausson lamented that young French composers had no chance finding a place on programs dominated by Beethoven, Wagner, and Berlioz. For more, see Hart/FRENCH, pp. 559, 562–63.

42. Shadle/ORCHESTRATING, p. 272. Bomberger/1917 discusses the rapid collapse of Austro-German domination of American musical culture after the nation's entry into World War I.

43. Horowitz/EXILE, p. 191. Koussevitzky's prophecy is also quoted in Copland/1900–1942, p. 109.

44. Piston and Westergaard/PISTON, p. 9.

45. Copland/1900–1942, pp. 106, 109. Copland benefited strongly from Koussevitzky's patronage and support ("There is no doubt about it—[Copland's Third] is the greatest American symphony. It goes from the heart to the heart"; Copland/SINCE 1943, p. 68). Others included Barber, Hanson, Harris, Hill, and Schuman. Despite his hospitality, though, even Koussevitzky was selective: for reasons not specified, he declined Florence Price's repeated requests to perform her music, although he examined her Third Symphony (Brown/HEART, pp. 186–88, reprints three of her letters to him). He did, however, conduct William Grant Still's *In Memoriam: The Colored Soldiers Who Died for Democracy* (1943), as well as music by Germaine Tailleferre and Mabel Daniels. See chapter 5 for Price's symphonies.

46. Horowitz/EXILE, p. 191.

47. See chapter 9 for a survey of Glass's symphonies.

48. As of this writing, the list of unrecorded works includes symphonies by Heinrich, Bristow, Harris, Cowell, Creston, Hovhaness, Diamond, Rochberg, and Bolcom (a few await a premiere as well). Symphonies available only by radio broadcast on YouTube include Schuman's Second Symphony, Creston's Sixth, Diamond's Tenth, and Rochberg's Third.

49. Carlos Chávez's Fourth Symphony (*Sinfonía romántica*) and George Perle's Second Symphony were also commissioned by the Louisville Orchestra but not recorded on its label. For more on the grant and the commissions, see Belfy/LOUISVILLE, especially Appendix D.

50. Of Latin American symphonies, those of Carlos Chávez are available on the Vox label (the London Symphony Orchestra conducted by Eduardo Mata) and Heitor Villa-Lobos on Naxos (the São Paulo Symphony led by Isaac Karabtchevsky). Assorted works by Brazilian symphonists M. Camargo Guarnieri and Cláudio Santoro are available on the BIS label, again with the São Paulo Symphony, conducted by John Neschling.

51. Quoted in Shadle/ORCHESTRATING, p. 243.

52. See chapters 3, 4, and 5 for discussions of these works and the impact of the "New World." As Douglas Bomberger will demonstrate, Beach conceived of her symphony in some ways as a correction

of what she saw as compositional and philosophical defects in Dvořák's work. A much unhappier legacy of the symphony was the acrimonious and often plainly racist statements it elicited from those critics who either denied or denounced the presence of folk (read: Black) idioms in the symphony. See Shadle/NEW WORLD, especially pp. 129–34.

53. For an account of Sibelius's influence in America in the 1920s and 1930s, as well as reasons for its subsequent decline starting in the 1940s, see Goss/SIBELIUS and Pollack/SIBELIUS (pp. 179–84).

54. "He would find a melody or a motif, more often it was more a motif than an actual melody, and the process of composing was creating this larger form out of this atom; like a gene growing perfectly from its little DNA information. [In his music,] there's a real economy of ideas, which is, for me, one of the reasons why Sibelius has been, along with Beethoven, such [an] extremely important figure for me" (Kallio/ADAMS).

55. The symphonies of Antheil and Rochberg are discussed in chapters 5 and 9, respectively.

56. These compositions are discussed in chapters 5, 6, and 9, respectively.

57. See chapter 9. These famous phrases come from a conversation Sibelius allegedly had with Mahler in 1907; the Finnish composer recounted it to his first biographer, Karl Ekman. See Mäkelä/SIBELIUS, pp. 267–68.

58. For a study of Mahler's influence on midcentury composers, specifically Copland, see Mugmon/COPLAND.

59. See chapter 9 for more on the compositions mentioned in this paragraph, save Del Tredici's (Bernstein is covered in chapter 6). As examples of specific quotes or allusions, Rochberg's Fifth Symphony repeatedly invokes the Finale of Mahler's Ninth Symphony and the climax of the central movement of Adams's *Harmonielehre* makes unambiguous reference to the famous "scream" from the Adagio of Symphony No. 10.

60. Fauser/SOUNDS, p. 257.

61. Ibid., p. 260.

62. Ibid., p. 261.

63. Tawa/GREAT, pp. 91, 93. See chapter 5 for discussions of Blitzstein's and Antheil's symphonies.

64. Fauser/SOUNDS, pp. 266–67.

65. From Adams's program notes to his whimsically titled orchestral fantasy *My Father Knew Charles Ives* (2003), available on the John Adams Earbox website (Adams/EARBOX).

66. All three of these Ives-influenced symphonies are analyzed in chapter 9.

67. Tawa/GREAT, p. 98.

68. Gann/AMERICAN, p. 221.

69. See chapter 9.

70. Faucett/CHADWICK SYMPHONIC, p. 57.

71. Copland/NEW, pp. 119–20; reprinted in Copland/OUR NEW, p. 165.

72. For Koussevitzky's remark, see Perlis/VOICES, p. 331. In creating this sound, Harris was not rejecting vernacularisms; his Fourth Symphony (1940), in fact, consists of choral settings of folk songs of various provenances, including cowboy songs, Civil War songs, and spirituals.

73. Copland/NEW, pp. 119–20; Copland/OUR NEW, p. 166.

74. Copland/NEW, pp. 119–20; Copland/OUR NEW, p. 165.

75. Quoted in Butterworth/SYMPHONY, p. 85.

76. All of these practices will be discussed in their respective chapters.

77. Quoted in Schnepel/GREAT, p. 335.

78. Harris's "idiosyncratic handling of the one-movement type is perhaps his most significant contribution to the history of the [symphony]" (Stehman/HARRIS, p. 68). See chapter 2 of Stehman/HARRIS for a discussion of Harris's general style.

79. Shadle/ORCHESTRATING, p. 263.

80. See chapter 3.

81. Shadle/ORCHESTRATING, pp. 272–73, assesses Thomas's impact on American symphonists.
82. Block/BEACH, p. 101.
83. Although the Fourth Symphony was not heard in its complete form until 1965, the New York Philharmonic had played the first two movements—by far the most radical—in 1927. The Third Symphony premiered in 1946, the Second in 1951, and the First in 1953. The *Holidays Symphony* was first heard complete in 1954, although the first three movements premiered on separate occasions in 1931–32. The Orchestral Set No. 1 received its first performance in 1931, the Second in 1967.
84. See chapter 4.
85. Ibid.
86. Quoted in Fanning/SINCE MAHLER, p. 96.
87. "A Musical Autobiography," reprinted in Vaughan Williams/NATIONAL, p. 189.
88. Copland, 1900–1942, p. 109.
89. Quoted in Fauser/SOUNDS, p. 262.
90. From a 1939 autobiographical essay, "Composer from Brooklyn," quoted in Crist/COPLAND, p. 14. As an illustration of how he preserved his essential style while rendering it more accessible, compare the so-called "clean" textures of *Appalachian Spring* (1944) with the spare, often single-line textures of the highly modernist Piano Variations (1930).
91. Copland/1900–1942, p. 70.
92. Howland/CONCERT JAZZ, p. 55.
93. "Locke . . . distinguishes between the symphonic employment of themes derived from 'folk jazz' and folk music, on the one hand, and concert works based on the idiomatic language of contemporary nonfolk commercial jazz, on the other. . . . It was the former, so-called romantic musical tradition that received the greatest attention from the spokesmen of the Harlem Renaissance" (ibid., p. 56).
94. Quoted in Hamm/MUSIC, p. 446.
95. Chapter 6.
96. Chapter 8.
97. Hess/REPRESENTING, p. 187; the book provides a full accounting of the postwar aesthetic shift. Musical infrastructure has also factored into Latin American symphonic composition: several countries have lacked sufficient concert halls, funding for salaries, and ticket-paying audiences to support such an ambitious genre. Two latter-day practitioners of the symphony include Florentin Giménez of Paraguay, whose final symphony dates from 2016, and Roberto Sierra of Puerto Rico, who has resided for much of his career on the U.S. mainland (his sixth symphony premiered in 2021).
98. Hess/REPRESENTING refers to this language as *ur-classicism*, in which, see pp. 25–26.
99. "Actually, our real serious American music didn't even begin until about seventy-five years ago. At that time the few American composers we did have, were imitating European composers, like Brahms and Liszt and Wagner and all those. We might call that the kindergarten period of American music; our composers then were like happy, innocent little kids in kindergarten. For instance, we had a very fine composer named George W. Chadwick, who wrote expert music, and also deeply felt music, but you could almost not tell it apart from the music of Brahms, Wagner, or other Europeans" (Bernstein, *Young People's Concert: What Is American Music?*, reprinted in Shadle/ORCHESTRATING, pp. 264–65).
100. Matthews/PROGRAM.
101. Chase/AMERICA 1955, p. xxii. This statement was not retained in the second edition (1966) nor in Richard Crawford's foreword to Chase/AMERICA 1987.
102. Hess/REPRESENTING, pp. 14–15.
103. Quoted in ibid., p. 14.
104. Chase/AMERICA 1955, p. xxii.
105. Three examples of the latter: Charles Ives was born in "Danbury, Massachusetts" [*recte* Connecticut] (p. 38; he corrects this elsewhere); George Ives died "in November 1884, when Charles was

ten years old" [*recte* 1894, when Charles was 20] (p. 36); Easley Blackwood "studied . . . with Bernard Heiden at Indianapolis University" [*recte* Indiana University, Bloomington] (p. 173).

106. The composers include Barber, Hanson, Harris, Schuman, John Alden Carpenter, Thomson, Cowell, Antheil, Diamond, Bernstein, Piston, Blitzstein, Douglas Moore, Mennin, Thompson, Copland, Creston, and Sessions.

107. Chase/AMERICA 1987, p. 568.
108. Hamm/MUSIC, especially pp. 443–46.
109. Starr/TONAL, pp. 490–94.
110. Taruskin/OXFORD, pp. 638, 648.
111. Hess/REPRESENTING, p. 243n42.

Bibliography

Adams/EARBOX	Adams, John. Program note, *My Father Knew Charles Ives*. Earbox. https://www.earbox.com/my-father-knew-charles-ives/.
Alexander/STRETCH	Alexander, J. Heywood, ed. *To Stretch Our Ears: Readings in American Music*. New York: W. W. Norton, 2001.
Béhague/LATIN	Béhague, Gerard. *Music in Latin America: An Introduction*. Prentice-Hall History of Music Series. Englewood Cliffs, NJ: Prentice-Hall, 1979.
Belfy/LOUISVILLE	Belfy, Jeanne Marie. "The Commissioning Project of the Louisville Orchestra, 1948–58: A Study of the History and Music." PhD diss., University of Louisville, 1986.
Bernard/TONAL	Bernard, Jonathan W. "Tonal Traditions in Art Music since 1960." In *The Cambridge History of American Music*, edited by David Nicholls, pp. 535–66. Cambridge: Cambridge University Press, 1998.
Bernstein/GREAT	Bernstein, Leonard. "Whatever Happened to That Great American Symphony?" In *The Joy of Music*, pp. 40–51. New York: Simon and Schuster, 1980.
Block/BEACH	Block, Adrienne Fried. *Amy Beach, Passionate Victorian: The Life and Work of an American Composer*. New York: Oxford, 1998.
Block/MUSIC	Block, Adrienne Fried. "Amy Beach's Music on Native American Themes." *American Music*, 8 (Summer 1990): pp. 141–66.
Bolcom/PROPHETIC	Bolcom, William. "A Prophetic Symphony." *Symphony: The Magazine of the League of American Orchestras*, 59, no. 1 (January–February 2008): pp. 15–19.
Bomberger/MACDOWELL	Bomberger, E. Douglas. *MacDowell*. Master Musicians Series. New York: Oxford University Press, 2013.
Bomberger/1917	Bomberger, E. Douglas. *Making Music American: 1917 and the Transformation of Culture*. New York: Oxford University Press, 2018.

Boston Symphony Orchestra/ARCHIVES	Boston Symphony Orchestra: Database "HENRY," BSO Performance History Search. http://archives.bso.org/.
Brown/HEART	Brown, Rae Linda. *The Heart of a Woman: The Life and Music of Florence B. Price*. Edited by Guthrie P. Ramsey Jr. Urbana: University of Illinois Press, 2020.
Butterworth/SYMPHONY	Butterworth, Neil. *The American Symphony*. Brookfield, VT: Ashgate, 1998.
Chase/AMERICA 1955	Chase, Gilbert. *America's Music: From the Pilgrims to the Present*. New York: McGraw-Hill, 1955.
Chase/AMERICA 1987	Chase, Gilbert. *America's Music: From the Pilgrims to the Present*. 3rd ed. With a foreword by Richard Crawford and a discographical essay by William Brooks. Urbana: University of Illinois Press, 1987.
Copland/NEW	Copland, Aaron. *The New Music, 1900–1960*. Rev. ed. New York: W. W. Norton, 1968.
Copland/1900–1942	Copland, Aaron, with Vivian Perlis. *Copland, 1900 through 1942*. New York: St. Martin's, 1984.
Copland/OUR NEW	Copland, Aaron. *Our New Music: Leading Composers in Europe and America*. New York: McGraw-Hill, 1941.
Copland/SINCE 1943	Copland, Aaron, with Vivian Perlis. *Copland since 1943*. New York: St. Martin's, 1989.
Cowell/AMERICAN	Cowell, Henry. *American Composers on American Music: A Symposium*. Stanford, CA: Stanford University Press, 1933; repr., New York: Ungar, 1962.
Crist/COPLAND	Crist, Elizabeth B. *Music for the Common Man: Aaron Copland during the Depression and War*. New York: Oxford University Press, 2005.
Cuyler/SYMPHONY	Cuyler, Louise. *The Symphony*. 2nd ed. Warren, MI: Harmonie Park, 1995.
Fairouz/INTERVIEW	Fairouz, Mohammed. Telephone interview with Matthew Mugmon (the author of chapter 9). February 27, 2015.
Fanning/SINCE MAHLER	Fanning, David. "The Symphony since Mahler: National and International Trends." In *The Cambridge Companion to the Symphony*, edited by Julian Horton, pp. 96–129. New York: Cambridge University Press, 2013.
Faucett/CHADWICK SYMPHONIC	Faucett, Bill F. *George Whitefield Chadwick: His Symphonic Works*. Composers of North America Series No. 19. Lanham, MD: Scarecrow, 1996.
Fauser/SOUNDS	Fauser, Annegret. *Sounds of War: Music in the United States during World War II*. New York: Oxford University Press, 2013.
Floyd/HARLEM	Floyd, Samuel A. Jr. "Music in the Harlem Renaissance: An Overview." In *Black Music in the Harlem*

	Renaissance: A Collection of Essays, edited by Samuel A. Floyd Jr., pp. 1–27. New York: Greenwood, 1990.
Gann/AMERICAN	Gann, Kyle. *American Music in the Twentieth Century.* New York: Schirmer, 1997.
Goss/SIBELIUS	Goss, Glenda Dawn. *Jean Sibelius and Olin Downes: Music, Friendship, Criticism.* Boston: Northeastern University Press, 1995.
Gottlieb and Mauskapf/FOUNDATIONS	Gottlieb, Jane, and Michael Mauskapf. "Koussevitzky Foundations." *Grove Music Online.*
Hamm/MUSIC	Hamm, Charles. *Music in the New World.* New York: W. W. Norton, 1983.
Hart/FRENCH	Hart, Brian. "The French Symphony after Berlioz: From the Second Empire to the First World War." In *The Symphonic Repertoire.* Vol. 3, part B, *The European Symphony, from ca. 1800 to ca. 1930: Great Britain, Russia, and France*, edited by A. Peter Brown with Brian Hart, 527–755. Bloomington: Indiana University Press, 2007.
Hess/EXPERIENCING	Hess, Carol A. *Experiencing Latin American Music.* Oakland: University of California Press, 2018.
Hess/REPRESENTING	Hess, Carol A. *Representing the Good Neighbor: Music, Difference, and the Pan American Dream.* New York: Oxford University Press, 2013.
Holland/COMPOSERS	Holland, Bernard. "From Two American Composers." *New York Times.* March 4, 1993, p. C20.
Horowitz/EXILE	Horowitz, Joseph. *Artists in Exile: How Refugees from Twentieth-Century War and Revolution Transformed the American Performing Arts.* New York: Harper Perennial, 2008.
Horton/SYMPHONY	Horton, Julian, ed. *The Cambridge Companion to the Symphony.* New York: Cambridge University Press, 2013.
Howland/CONCERT JAZZ	Howland, John. *"Ellington Uptown": Duke Ellington, James P. Johnson, and the Birth of Concert Jazz.* Ann Arbor: University of Michigan Press, 2009.
Kallio/ADAMS	Kallio, Jari. "From a New Opera to Old Synthesizers—Interview with John Adams." *Adventures in Music*, February 5, 2021. https://jarijuhanikallio.wordpress.com/2021/02/05/from-a-new-opera-to-old-synthesizers-interview-with-john-adams/.
Korn/SYMPHONY	Korn, Peter Jona. "The Symphony in America." In *Elgar to the Present Day*, edited by Robert Simpson, pp. 243–67. Volume 2 of *The Symphony*. Middlesex, UK: Penguin, 1967.
Koussevitzky/FOUNDATION	Koussevitzky Music Foundation. "Works Commissioned by the Serge Koussevitzky Music Foundation."

	Last updated June 2022. http://www.koussevitzky.org/grantscomplete.html.
Leichtentritt/KOUSSEVITZKY	Leichtentritt, Hugo. *Serge Koussevitzky: The Boston Symphony Orchestra and the New American Music.* Cambridge, MA: Harvard University Press, 1947.
Levy/FRONTIER	Levy, Beth E. *Frontier Figures: American Music and the Mythology of the American West.* Berkeley: University of California Press, 2012.
Mäkelä/SIBELIUS	Mäkelä, Tomi. *Jean Sibelius.* Translated by Steven Lindberg. Woodbridge, UK: Boydell, 2011.
Matthews/PROGRAM	Matthews, Michael. Program note to Symphony No. 3. https://michaelmatthews.net/composition/symphony-no-3.
Moore and Clark/LATIN	Moore Robin, and Walter Aaron Clark, eds. *Musics of Latin America.* New York: W. W. Norton, 2012.
Mugmon/COPLAND	Mugmon, Matthew. *Aaron Copland and the American Legacy of Gustav Mahler.* Rochester, NY: University of Rochester Press, 2019.
Perlis/VOICES	Perlis, Vivian, and Libby Van Cleve. *Composers' Voices from Ives to Ellington: An Oral History of American Music.* New Haven, CT: Yale University Press, 2005.
Piston and Westergaard/PISTON	Piston, Walter, and Peter Westergaard. "Conversation with Walter Piston." *Perspectives of New Music* 7 (Autumn–Winter 1968): pp. 3–17.
Pollack/SIBELIUS	Pollack, Howard. "Samuel Barber, Jean Sibelius, and the Making of an American Romantic." *Musical Quarterly* 84 (2000): pp. 175–205.
Puts/PULITZER	Puts, Kevin. "A Pulitzer Winner Asks: Why Write Symphonies?" *Deceptive Cadence from NPR Radio*, August 5, 2013. http://www.npr.org/sections/deceptivecadence/2013/08/05/208280751/a-pulitzer-winner-asks-why-write-symphonies.
Schmidt/PAINE	Schmidt, John C. *The Life and Works of John Knowles Paine.* Studies in Musicology No. 34. Ann Arbor, MI: UMI Research Press, 1980.
Schnepel/GREAT	Schnepel, Julie. "The Critical Pursuit of the Great American Symphony, 1893–1950." PhD diss., Indiana University, 1995.
Shadle/NEW WORLD	Shadle, Douglas W. *Antonín Dvořák's* New World Symphony. Oxford Keynotes Series. New York: Oxford University Press, 2021.
Shadle/ORCHESTRATING	Shadle, Douglas W. *Orchestrating the Nation: The Nineteenth-Century American Symphonic Enterprise.* New York: Oxford University Press, 2016.
Smith/KOUSSEVITZKY	Smith, Moses. *Koussevitzky.* New York: Allen, Towne and Heath, 1947.

Starr/BAMBOULA	Starr, S. Frederick. *Bamboula! The Life and Times of Louis Moreau Gottschalk*. New York: Oxford University Press, 1995.
Starr/TONAL	Starr, Larry. "Tonal Traditions in Art Music from 1920 to 1960." In *The Cambridge History of American Music*, edited by David Nicholls, pp. 471–95. Cambridge: Cambridge University Press, 1998.
Stedman/SYMPHONY	Stedman, Preston. *The Symphony*. 2nd ed. Upper Saddle River, NJ: Prentice-Hall, 1979.
Stehman/HARRIS	Stehman, Dan. *Roy Harris: An American Musical Pioneer*. Boston: Twayne, 1984.
Steinberg/SYMPHONY	Steinberg, Michael. *The Symphony: A Listener's Guide*. New York: Oxford University Press, 1995.
Taruskin/OXFORD	Taruskin, Richard. *The Oxford History of Western Music*. Vol. 5, *The Early Twentieth Century*. New York: Oxford University Press, 2005.
Tawa/GREAT	Tawa, Nicholas E. *The Great American Symphony: Music, the Depression, and War*. Bloomington: Indiana University Press, 2009.
Tick/USA	Tick, Judith, ed., with Paul Beaudoin. *Music in the USA: A Documentary Companion*. New York: Oxford University Press, 2008.
Vaughan Williams/NATIONAL	Vaughan Williams, Ralph. *National Music and Other Essays*. 2nd ed. Oxford: Oxford University Press, 1987.
White/CHADWICK	White, Kathryn Joann. "George Whitefield Chadwick and the American Vernacular in His Chamber Works." Ph.D. diss., Indiana University, 2012.

CHAPTER TWO

The First Generation of Symphonists in the United States

Douglas W. Shadle

The US public did not hold the genre of the symphony in especially high regard during the half-century between the American Revolution and the death of Ludwig van Beethoven in 1827. As in much of the Old World, any symphonic movements on concert programs would have appeared alongside opera excerpts, choral numbers, chamber works, and even popular tunes from the sheet music market. Symphonies were entertainment. In this situation, the first standing orchestras in the British colonies were formed by musicians themselves for their own personal musical enjoyment and, to a lesser extent, for financial gain. Orchestra personnel ranged from wealthy amateurs to highly skilled freelance professionals, and they had to balance their own interests carefully with those of audiences to stay financially viable. Wealthy civic philanthropists and their brainchild, the endowed corporate professional orchestra, emerged only much later in the century, when beliefs about the power of music to uplift communities gained a stronger foothold among the elite class.[1]

Critics and historians throughout Europe developed myths about the genius of so-called masters such as Haydn, Mozart, and Beethoven that dramatically changed the intellectual landscape surrounding the symphonic repertoire in the first several decades of the nineteenth century. As participants in these intellectual changes, curious American audiences (still relatively small in comparison to other entertainments) slowly increased their demand for symphonies in the years leading up to the Civil War. Responding to this new demand, leading musicians—American residents and touring European visitors alike—offered them selections of the available symphonic repertoire, old and new. Patterns of immigration to the United States and the circulation of information led to a period of synchronization between the cultures of symphonic music throughout the Atlantic world that would extend well into the twentieth century, as later chapters in this volume illustrate.

Within this institutional context, aspiring symphonic composers of the early nineteenth century did not necessarily conceive of their position in the United States as fundamentally different from that of their counterparts overseas. Regarding compositional style, they often considered themselves contributors to broader transatlantic trends rather than representatives of a unique cultural or national milieu. Only when a critical mass of American composers converged in the same location, New York City, in the early 1850s did writers and musicians begin to ask fundamental questions about the specific and potentially different roles that US composers might play in the development of the symphonic repertoire.

Even so, a truly shared sense of transatlantic belonging did not begin to unravel until the last two decades of the nineteenth century, when, as the next chapter explains, musicians increasingly speculated about ways to construct a distinctly American "school" of composition. At the same time, the steady circulation of musicians (and their students) between the United States and Europe created stronger ties than ever. The changing values during this period allowed deceased antebellum composers to fall out of the public imagination. And throughout the twentieth century, the composers highlighted in this chapter continued to languish in relative obscurity despite the efforts of prominent advocates.

The First US Orchestras

The oldest surviving symphony orchestra in the United States, the Philharmonic Society of New-York (now called the New York Philharmonic), was founded in 1842—the same year as its counterpart in Vienna. In the century prior to its establishment, however, a handful of highly regarded concert societies along the Eastern Seaboard occasionally programmed symphonies and symphonic movements. The purposes and trajectories of these early orchestras reflected cultural differences among their founders and members. In each case, they foundered under unfavorable economic conditions or changed institutional missions to meet the changing musical needs of their respective communities.

Charleston, South Carolina, had become the bustling hub of the southern colonies by the middle of the eighteenth century. Like other British colonial centers, the city's musical culture mirrored that of London in key ways. A group of "gentlemen amateurs" from the city formed the St. Cecilia Society in 1766 "to indulge a common taste and to pass an agreeable hour"— a purpose reminiscent of similar associations in Britain. Over the next decade, the society's membership grew to include a twenty-piece orchestra with roughly equal numbers of amateurs and professionals. Like their counterparts in London, the society's musicians established a regular annual concert series and assisted at charity events, balls, and other occasions befitting their well-to-do status. Music for these concerts included a mixed array of genres, and when symphonies were performed, programming followed London trends. Recent works by J. C. Bach, Carl Friedrich Abel, Anton Filtz, and Friedrich Schwindl figured prominently until the 1780s, and those by Joseph Haydn, Wolfgang Amadeus Mozart, Ignaz Pleyel, Adalbert Gyrowetz, and Franz Krommer later supplanted them. The St. Cecilia Society absorbed a significant number of French-speaking professional musicians in the wake of the 1791 slave rebellion on the island of Saint-Domingue and flourished for the next two decades. But it fizzled by 1820 as many of the professionals were able to find more lucrative employment in the city's theater orchestras.[2]

Bethlehem, Pennsylvania, a town founded in 1741, also became an important center of musical activity in the colonial era. Throughout the seventeenth and early eighteenth centuries, German-speaking musicians in Europe established local ensembles called *collegia musica*. Like many British groups, their purpose was primarily musical enjoyment but they also had an educational dimension. German-speaking Moravian settlers in the American colonies continued this practice by forming *collegia* within their own fellowship communities, including Bethlehem.

From the outset, the Bethlehem *collegium* fulfilled the practical purpose of improving the quality of music in worship gatherings. As the group began to include secular instrumental music in its repertoire, its function became subsumed into the community's general ethos of religious devotion. Dated manuscripts of works performed at *collegium* events in the 1760s and 1770s include symphonies by composers from the same stylistic orbit as those featured by

Charleston's St. Cecilia Society, including Anton Filtz and Carl Friedrich Abel. As in Charleston, the *collegium* also remained remarkably current as key leaders, particularly Johann Friedrich Peter (1746–1813), acquired or made copies of recent symphonies by Wolfgang Amadeus Mozart, Joseph Haydn, Andreas Romberg, and Anton Eberl. By 1820, the year of Charleston's St. Cecilia Society's dissolution, professional musicians within the *collegium* reorganized the group into a "Philharmonic Society," an ensemble founded for the mutual benefit of the players that required membership dues. This change reflected the increasing professionalization of American concert music culture.[3]

The First American Symphonists

Although local composers appear to have contributed occasional works to their respective repertories, neither the St. Cecilia Society of Charleston nor the Bethlehem *collegium* cultivated symphonies from within their own ranks. In larger cosmopolitan centers such as Philadelphia and New York, prolific immigrant composers, including Benjamin Carr (1768–1831), Alexander Reinagle (1756–1809), and James Hewitt (1770–1827), earned notoriety for their overtures, keyboard works, songs, and pieces in other small genres. But none wrote symphonies in the contemporary Viennese style that had gained popularity around the beginning of the nineteenth century. Other leading composers, such as John Christopher Moller (1755–1803), a British immigrant of German heritage, and Filippo Trajetta (1777–1854), an Italian immigrant, wrote works with the title "sinfonia" in a style that would have seemed archaic next to pieces by Joseph Haydn or Anton Eberl.

The first organization to support local composers, at least in theory, was the Musical Fund Society of Philadelphia. Much like the St. Cecilia Society, the Musical Fund Society's first leaders were gentlemen amateurs and friendly professionals who had gathered informally "for musical enjoyment and cultivation." Once they decided to organize formally, in 1820, the founders sought to establish a fund that would provide financial relief to injured or aging musicians; the acts of incorporation also included a clause noting the group's desire to "cultivate skill and diffusion of taste in music."[4] Although the size of the original informal group is difficult to determine, the Musical Fund Society's first official roster included nearly fifty professional musicians and more than three times as many amateurs—a number far exceeding Charleston's St. Cecilia Society.

Prominent Philadelphia composers such as Benjamin Carr, Benjamin Cross, Charles Hupfeld, and Raynor Taylor joined the society as professional members, but the organization's founding documents did not make any specific provisions for premiering or sustaining their compositions. These individuals occasionally provided orchestral accompaniments for vocal numbers and smaller original compositions during the group's early years, but no symphonies. The reason for this omission is unclear, because the society's first concert included symphonies (or perhaps just movements) by Beethoven (Op. 21) and Andreas Romberg (Op. 6), both of whom were still alive at the time. And the ensemble would continue to perform symphonies on the handful of programs offered each year.

Within five years of its founding, the Musical Fund Society began to distribute "premiums" for "meritorious" original compositions, but these works evidently did not include symphonies either. The first member of the society to compose a symphony was Charles Hommann (1803–ca. 1870), a young professional and brother-in-law of Charles Hupfeld, the orchestra's concertmaster, or "leader" (See table 2.1). Hommann, however, dedicated the work not to the Musical Fund Society, but to the Philharmonic Society of Bethlehem, the former Moravian *collegium*

Table 2.1 The Symphony of Charles Hommann (1803–ca. 1870)

Date	Title	Movements	Instrumentation	Comments
ca. 1820s	Symphony in E♭ Major	I. Adagio—Allegro con brio II. Andante sostenuto III. Menuetto (Allegro)—Trio IV. Finale: Allegro assai	Flt., 2 Ob., 2 Clar., Bssn., 2 Hr., Strgs.	Dedicated to the Philharmonic Society of Bethlehem, Pennsylvania, an ensemble of Moravian settlers. Performed by them at an unknown date. Score published in an edition by Joanne Swenson-Eldridge (Middleton, WI: A-R Editions, 2007).

musicum that had professionalized in 1820. The Musical Fund Society never performed the work despite its other efforts to encourage local composers.[5]

Why the Musical Fund Society did not acknowledge Hommann's symphony with a prize or, at the very least, perform it on one of its programs, is unknown. The work itself is in a stylistic idiom reminiscent of the symphonic programming popular at the time: later Haydn and Mozart, early Beethoven, and other contemporaries like Andreas Romberg. The scoring is relatively light, with two oboes and clarinets (but only a single flute and bassoon, probably because of a lack of personnel), two trumpets, no trombones or timpani, and a full complement of strings. The work's form follows the standard four-movement plan: a sonata-allegro opening movement preceded by a slow introduction, a songlike adagio, a minuet and trio, and a rapid finale. Hommann's tonal planning was conservative, in that three of the four movements are in the work's home key of E-flat major. Little distinguishes Hommann's symphony from the society's current repertoire, suggesting that style and quality were not the sole reasons behind its neglect.[6]

Beginning in 1840, the Musical Fund Society shifted its focus from "lighter compositions" in favor of "classic and more elaborate productions of the masters of the art," including newer symphonies.[7] This turn aligned with changes elsewhere in the country. In Boston, for example, an organization called the Academy of Music had begun featuring orchestral music more prominently on its programs in a calculated effort to stimulate interest in the repertoire. And in New York, musicians organized a Philharmonic Society in 1842 to serve essentially the same purpose. Perhaps, then, Hommann had written his symphony at the wrong time: it would have fit well in the 1830s, but, by the 1840s, the Haydnesque style of his music was losing its cachet to the more challenging symphonic writing of Beethoven's mature middle-period works.[8]

The first composer to receive a hearing of his own symphony at a Musical Fund Society concert was Leopold Meignen (1793–1873), a long-serving administrator for the group who was elected as chief conductor in 1844. Meignen was an Alsatian immigrant who had once served as a regimental band member in Napoleon Bonaparte's imperial army. He immigrated to Philadelphia in 1828 and joined the Musical Fund Society five years later. Shortly thereafter, he also established the amateur Philharmonic Society (which, incidentally, would later award Hommann a prize) and became a partner to the prominent publisher Augustus Fiot, a relationship that continued until 1842.[9]

During his inaugural season as conductor, Meignen premiered his symphony on a program that also featured Beethoven's First. Unlike the Beethoven symphony, the most Haydnesque

Douglas W. Shadle

Table 2.2 The Symphony of Leopold Meignen (1793–1873)

Title (date)	Movements	Instrumentation	Comments
Symphonie militaire (1845)	I. "The Sentinel" (Andante—Allegro agitato) II. "The Dream" (Allegro)	Grand + Picc., Cor.	Program symphony depicting a soldier on duty who falls asleep and dreams of a battle. First performance: April 1845, by the Musical Fund Society of Philadelphia, conducted by the composer. Score published in *American Orchestral Music, 1800 through 1879*, ed. Sam Dennison (Boston: G. K. Hall, 1992).

of his nine, Meignen's *Symphonie militaire* (1845) is a "characteristic" work that resembles other symphonic pieces from the era, particularly in the French-speaking musical world, which had long pushed the genre's boundaries (table 2.2).[10] A notice given in a Philadelphia newspaper provided the following plot: "A soldier is on guard at midnight: soft music describes the time and scene, the measured tread, the sentinel's challenge, &c. The midnight service of a neighboring church is heard: it reminds the soldier of the scenes of his home; he becomes weary and falls asleep; he dreams of a battle, which is gloriously represented by the confusion of a *double figure* [*recte* fugue], as it is called by musicians; the battle ceases; the retreat bugle sounds; and the dreaming sentinel awakes to the sound of a drum."[11]

Example 2.1 Meignen, *Symphonie militaire:* (A) Mvt. I, Instrumental Recitative; (B) Mvt. II, "Double Fugue"

Example 2.1 *continued*

The symphony is in two movements, "The Sentinel" and "The Dream." Both are episodic and contain frequent changes of tempo and character. A creative orchestrator, Meignen also employed unusual instrumental effects, such as a lengthy recitative-like solo for clarinet, string players sitting away from their respective sections, and a solo bugler sounding the retreat to the accompaniment of a drummer (example 2.1). Meignen's position as the conductor of the Musical Fund Society ensured that he could obtain a platform for his symphony, whereas Hommann, in an entrepreneurial fashion, had to seek support from a neighboring ensemble. (There is no evidence indicating that the Bethlehem Philharmonic performed Meignen's symphony.)

Between the two Philadelphians, Hommann's experience appears to have been more typical. Even composers with close ties to an ensemble ran into difficulty finding an outlet for their works and needed to self-fund benefit concerts with an extemporaneously assembled ensemble, much as Beethoven had to do in 1808 for the premieres of his Fifth and Sixth Symphonies (not an uncommon practice). Simon Knaebel, for example, a charter member and violinist of the New York Philharmonic, had to hire Philharmonic players separately from their regular concert season when he wished to stage a performance of his gigantic symphony marking the seventy-fifth anniversary of the Battle of Bunker Hill (1851). Like Meignen's work of 1845, this piece drew from the characteristic symphonic tradition—in this case, by depicting specific events in the battle itself. The score no longer survives, but one newspaper reported that it elicited "the most unqualified applause" and "received the 'broad seal' of perfect success."[12] The New York Philharmonic never programmed this or any other of Knaebel's compositions.

The Early New York Philharmonic

When he joined the New York Philharmonic as a charter member, Knaebel probably did not guess that it would not support his compositional ambitions. The orchestra's mission, given in the original constitution published in 1842, was "the advancement of Instrumental Music." And beyond this goal, bylaws published a year later included an important article recommending support of local composers: "If any Grand Orchestral Compositions, such as Overtures or Symphonies, shall be presented to the Society, they being composed in this country, the Society shall perform one every season, provided a Committee of five, appointed by the government, shall have approved and recommended the composition."[13] Unlike previous organizations, the Philharmonic's founders believed that supporting local symphonists fell squarely under its purview.

Although the clause encouraging local compositions was unique to the Philharmonic, the ensemble's general organization was typical. As a self-governing body, the orchestra was designed to benefit the musicians themselves. The group sold tickets on a subscription basis or for individual events. Revenues exceeding the mandated annual salary (and of course all other expenses) were then distributed equally to the players as a dividend at the end of the season; the modest annual salary was dropped later in the century, leaving only the dividend for compensation. To induce solidarity, the orchestra levied fines for lateness or absenteeism and, like the Musical Fund Society, established a separate account to aid ailing musicians—or "their widows and children" in the event of a death.

Since the Philharmonic sought to maximize revenue, its programming practices mirrored those of other ensembles around the United States and Europe, such as the Musical Fund Society of Philadelphia or the Royal Philharmonic Society of London. To appeal to a variety of tastes, symphonies and overtures joined eclectic mixtures with concertos, chamber works, opera arias or ensembles, and other vocal numbers. But the group's emphasis on large orchestral works was clear: with one exception, every concert during the Philharmonic's first decade began with a complete symphony.

During its first decade, the Philharmonic performed twenty-two different symphonies, including eight by Beethoven (only the First was missing), three each by Mozart and Louis Spohr, two by Mendelssohn, and one each by Haydn, Schubert, Niels Gade, Franz Lachner, and Johann Wenzel Kalliwoda. Some of these works, particularly Gade's First and Spohr's Seventh, were remarkably recent, as was a small proportion of the orchestra's nonsymphonic repertoire, including overtures by Kalliwoda, Peter Josef von Lindpaintner, and Henry Litolff. Though risky in terms of ticket sales and expensive in terms of procuring and copying scores, the breadth of the Philharmonic's early repertoire reflects the musicians' self-interest as players. They enjoyed the challenge of learning new music and improving their execution of older works.[14]

Despite the liberality of the Philharmonic's programming practices, only two works written by local composers appeared on subscription concerts during the group's first decade: overtures by English conductor George Loder (1846) and New York–born George Frederick Bristow (1847), a multi-instrumentalist and conductor as well as a composer. Two music journals that began operations in 1849—*Saroni's Musical Times* and the *Message Bird*—noticed this fact shortly into the orchestra's 1849–50 season. Writers for both magazines complained about the lack of support for American composers and insinuated that certain members of the orchestra felt snubbed by their associates.[15]

Reflecting on the situation a few months later, critic Hermann Saroni (1824–1900) noted that the mentality of the Philharmonic's governing board had changed in the years since its founding. He accused them of favoring "masters" at the expense of local composers even if the works of these masters included overtures such as "La Gazza Ladra, Joco the Brazilian ape, and any amount of factory ware from the prolific pen of Kalliwoda."[16] He wondered why the orchestra included these potboilers when there were much better options available from composers like Bristow. Capitulating to the pressure, the Philharmonic eventually scheduled Bristow's new symphony, his first, at a public rehearsal at the end of the season.

Reminiscing in 1879 about his family's participation in the orchestra's founding, bandmaster Harvey B. Dodworth (1822–91) recalled in an interview with the *American Art Journal* that, in addition to "the encouragement of art," the orchestra was intended to establish "an American school of musical composition," particularly since "it was required that at least one American work should be performed during each season." He went on to say that "at the start the Philharmonic was the most cosmopolitan thing you ever saw. There were in it Italians, French, English, Germans, and Americans. Not one-fourth of them were Germans." Bristow, it seems, was the first local composer to ingratiate himself to this cosmopolitan bunch when he submitted his overture for consideration in 1847. "Now" Dodworth added, "it is exclusively a German organization."[17] Although Dodworth's "now" was 1879, the shift in the Philharmonic's ethnic makeup had occurred much earlier—at the very moment when critics took notice that it wasn't programming American compositions.

Ethnic Conflict and the Early American Symphony

The revolutions sweeping the European continent in 1848 had a dramatic effect on immigration to the United States, particularly among people from German-speaking lands. Although

Germans from all social classes fled the turmoil for the United States during and after the revolutionary period, an educated class of immigrants, often called Forty-Eighters, brought a wealth of musical experience (both practical and intellectual) to the New World. Throughout the 1840s, German immigrants had been establishing neighborhood choral societies, German-language theaters, beer gardens, and other musical venues that would have required the services of skilled amateurs or trained professionals; New York City became a hub of such activity and, over the course of the nineteenth century, could claim to be the third-largest German-speaking community in the world. The Philharmonic was a natural landing place for some of the most talented German musicians, and the arrival of music lovers with the means to pay for tickets helped spur demand for concerts.

From 1842 to 1850, Germans played another important role in the development of orchestral music culture in the United States: as touring musicians. Private entrepreneurial ensembles from German-speaking regions led lengthy tours (typically along the Eastern Seaboard) that exposed many Americans to high-quality orchestral music for the first time. The most important of these ensembles was the Germania Musical Society, a group of idealist revolutionaries who traveled to the United States from Berlin in 1848 and performed nearly one thousand concerts before disbanding in 1854. Its repertoire, like that of the Philharmonic, was a mixture of serious and light works. Critics throughout its touring radius, which extended as far west as St. Louis, agreed that its performances, particularly of purely instrumental works, set a new standard in the United States.[18]

The coalescence of fresh demand for symphonic music and the desire for higher standards of performance led the Philharmonic for the first time, in 1849, to elect a single conductor to lead the orchestra for much of the season. In this case, the orchestra chose Theodore Eisfeld (1816–82), a Forty-Eighter and former *Kapellmeister* who had arrived in New York the previous year. With a recent German immigrant at the helm, rather than one of the various members who had previously conducted the ensemble, the Philharmonic faced political challenges that led to immediate criticism in the press.

Harvey Dodworth's retrospective comment that the Philharmonic became an "exclusively German organization" had roots in the election of Eisfeld as chief conductor in 1849, after which critics questioned the organization's motives. By the end of the 1850–51 season, certain critics had begun to theorize that ethnic conflict was a broad source of problems. Although art is by nature universal, one critic claimed, national interests in the practice of art should be protected against intruders who "seek our shores [and] come not in that spirit of liberality in which [we] would gladly welcome them, but with 'minds made up' as to the inferiority of our arts, education, and social institutions." These men, he added, had come to the United States not seeking universality in art but rather to flaunt their status as members of national European communities. "Why, if they are truly men of genius, do they band themselves together, and establish lines of nationality in our midst?"[19]

The situation would have a dramatic effect on American composers. Three of the four composers whose works are profiled below—Anthony Philip Heinrich, George Frederick Bristow, and William Henry Fry—engaged in a lengthy feud with the Philharmonic over this precise issue during Eisfeld's early tenure as conductor. Heinrich's case was the most benign, since he had played cat-and-mouse games with his music for decades. In 1845, for example, he contacted the Philharmonic about performing parts of an oratorio but withdrew the request in a matter of days. Three years later, however, he approached the orchestra with greater sincerity about a performance of an evocative new symphony. The orchestra tacitly declined despite Heinrich's offer to provide half the required expenses in advance. Heinrich responded bitterly that the group "clings to the works of celebrated masters" rather than allowing "young aspirants plentiful aid and hearing." By this early date, it had become clear to Heinrich (as it had to the Philharmonic's critics) that the orchestra was more interested in performing European music, particularly symphonies by celebrated masters, than in cultivating local compositions.[20]

Tempers subsided until the autumn of 1853, when the famed London conductor Louis Antoine Jullien (1812–60) arrived in New York City with an orchestra of virtuosos. After several performances in town, he led a lengthy multicity tour that extended into June of the following year. As an engaging celebrity performer, Jullien was bound to attract broad public interest, but, perhaps in a calculated effort to draw even greater receipts, he also chose to program symphonic music by two of the country's leading composers: George Frederick Bristow and William Henry Fry. Moreover, he enticed both composers—either with financial commissions or the promise of exposure (the evidence is spotty on this point)—to compose new music for his orchestra. And both obliged. Within a matter of months, Jullien had provided them with significant opportunities that the Philharmonic had failed to offer.

Tempers began to rekindle after Jullien's orchestra performed a movement from Bristow's First Symphony that October. Reviewing the concert, William Henry Fry urged the Philharmonic to program the work in full, "as their object should be to encourage art on the spot." When someone has composed a work of high quality, Fry argued, "he has a right to be heard, and the public should insist on hearing him, instead of like low provincials taking works exclusively at second-hand."[21] Because of the conservative style of Bristow's music, Fry could think of no reason why the Philharmonic would not want to support music by one of its own, save for an ignorant public and national prejudice among its members. He spat more bile at the Philharmonic once Jullien had performed several new works by locals to great public acclaim. Arguing that it had never performed any music by American composers (a slight overstatement), he called the organization "an incubus on art." It was a high crime, he thought, for local music to depend "upon the accidental presence" a renowned figure like Jullien.[22]

Two prominent critics, John Sullivan Dwight of Boston (1813–93) and Richard Storrs Willis of New York (1819–1900), did not agree. And this was not the first time: only a few months earlier, they had upbraided Fry for wanting to establish a distinctly American school of composition.[23] In this new debate, however, Dwight argued that true genius was destined to be discovered; only audiences and time could confer greatness on a composer. But he did not explain how the public was supposed to make these determinations without repeated exposure to the music. As a composer himself, Fry understood that repeated performances—not time alone—allowed audiences to reach conclusions about the inherent worth of a piece. Willis, for his part, refused to believe that national chauvinism would drive the Philharmonic to reject local works. From his vantage, Fry appeared to be seeking a free pass for his music simply because he was American. Willis urged him to consider that his music may not be up to the Philharmonic's standards (despite Fry's contention that it was good enough for Jullien).

Taking offense at Willis's blind faith in the Philharmonic, Bristow himself, who served on its board of directors, offered a rebuttal. He clarified that his overture was the only piece by an American-born composer that had ever appeared on the Philharmonic's concert programs (George Loder being English-born). He then argued that national chauvinism was the underlying problem. "If all their artistic affections are unalterably German," he mused, "let them pack back to Germany and enjoy the police and bayonets and aristocratic kicks and cuffs of that land, where an artist is a serf to a nobleman, as the history of all their great composers shows."[24] From Bristow's perspective, the orchestra's neglect of American composers amounted to a conspiracy against them.

Weighing Bristow's accusations, Willis requested proof of a conspiracy and the board of directors issued a joint statement claiming that the orchestra had in fact performed *eleven* works by resident Americans. (Only two of the eleven were performed at official concerts and only three had been written by US-born musicians.) These performances, they asserted, fulfilled the orchestra's obligations under the bylaws. But Ureli Corelli Hill (1802–75), the board's vice president, claimed that the author of the statement had forged his, Hill's, signature and explained that he disagreed with the rest of the board's conclusion. Bristow then responded by reiterating that the orchestra had "fallen under the control of German cliques, who still retain control, and whose acts have uniformly showed their disposition to crush and extinguish everything American."[25] After several more weeks of bitter exchanges, Bristow angrily resigned his position in the orchestra, and the matter was eventually dropped.

The place of *new* symphonic music was a flash point in this conflict, and battle lines were drawn between critics who preferred older European music and US-born composers who wanted their new works to have a fair public hearing. Although they understood that orchestras needed to perform pieces several times for listeners to comprehend them fully, conservative critics rarely lobbied for revivals of new works. Composers, on the other hand, knew that a concert series could hold only so many pieces: the Philharmonic typically staged only four concerts a year. The choice to program Beethoven or another master on every program would virtually guarantee the exclusion of American composers, but the fact that some programs included music by lesser Europeans was especially galling.

Moreover, not everyone seemed to understand equally that ethnic tension between individuals underlay this conflict. Dwight and Willis were the most naïve, operating under the assumption that musical genius would be valued universally, regardless of ethnicity. They did not appear to consider that the supposed universality of the German symphony, epitomized by Beethoven's music, was itself a German national construction. Meanwhile, Bristow and Fry criticized the German musical community for remaining insular and cliquish. Their opinion of Germans in the Old World was not high either, for both emphasized the repressiveness of the political regimes in German-speaking lands in the wake of the failed revolutions of 1848–49. But the supporters of German universality fought back with equally chauvinist invective. A correspondent for the *Niederrheinsiche Musik-Zeitung*, a journal housed in Cologne under the editorship of Ludwig Bischoff (1794–1867), wrote about the situation in New York and suggested that Jullien was merely attempting to capitalize on the prevailing patriotic sentiment rather than giving a just appraisal of Bristow's and Fry's works.[26] Another critic's remarks about American composers in relation to their German counterparts were even more malicious, comparing aspiring American symphonists to minstrel troupes and Chinese cigar sellers.[27]

With these battle lines drawn, local composers like Fry and Bristow stood at a distinct disadvantage against the Philharmonic's heavy German majority. Once Jullien returned to London in 1854, however, he championed their works overseas and earned Bristow a sound reputation in Great Britain that persisted until his death in 1898. In the United States, however, composers would continue to struggle to find even an ounce of recognition.[28]

Anthony Philip Heinrich (1781–1861)

In the heat of his feud with the Philharmonic, George Frederick Bristow claimed that no Germans had been involved in its formation. But he may not have known exactly how to categorize Anthony Philip Heinrich, a German-speaking Bohemian by birth who made the United States his adopted home during the 1810s. As Bristow almost certainly knew, Heinrich had presided over the meeting that formally established the Philharmonic Society in 1842. That Heinrich occupied this honorary position, a fact noted in most biographical literature, nevertheless obscures his protracted and ultimately fruitless struggle to earn a sound public reputation as a composer. At no point during Heinrich's lifetime (or at any point after) did the Philharmonic perform his music.

Heinrich began his musical career relatively late in life. He inherited a lucrative business from an uncle but lost his fortune in the wake of the Napoleonic Wars and immigrated to the United States. After a brief tenure as a theater music director in Pittsburgh, Heinrich moved to Kentucky in 1818. There he led occasional ensemble performances and focused most of his energy on developing his compositional technique. Between 1820 and 1823, he published three volumes of music that included vocal numbers and chamber works: *The Dawning of Music in Kentucky* (1820, rev. 1820–23), *The Western Minstrel* (1820, rev. 1820–23), and *The Sylviad* (1823, rev. 1825–26). A favorable review written by Bostonian critic John Rowe Parker (1777–1844) in *The Euterpiad*, one of the country's first periodicals devoted to music, dubbed Heinrich "the Beethoven of America."[29]

Perhaps recognizing that the Kentucky wilderness did not provide a favorable environment for an aspiring professional musician, Heinrich moved to Boston in 1823 and left the United States three years later for an extended stay in Europe. The trip lasted for nearly a decade and included only intermittent returns to New England. During this European sojourn, Heinrich's home base was London, where he performed as a violinist in the Drury Lane Theatre orchestra and purportedly met Felix Mendelssohn briefly during one of Mendelssohn's many visits to Great Britain. The decade also proved to be particularly fruitful for Heinrich as a composer. He began or completed no fewer than thirteen orchestral works and nearly twice as many pieces in smaller genres. The professional high point of this period included the performance of one of his symphonies, *The Ornithological Combat of Kings*, at a concert in Graz, Austria, which received a favorable review in 1836.[30]

After a harrowing journey back to the Atlantic coast of Europe, Heinrich returned to the United States in 1837 and decided to make New York City, rather than Boston, his permanent home. Over the next twenty years, he staged four large benefit concerts (three in New York, one in Boston) that showcased his larger works, particularly excerpts from a grand oratorio that told the story of the American nation from the arrival of the Pilgrims through the Revolutionary War. Despite his lack of success at securing performances of his large orchestral works, Heinrich composed nine more symphonies between 1837 and 1857 and heavily revised two others during the same period. Current events and cultural trends inspired most of these new pieces.

Having saved enough money for the journey, Heinrich returned to Europe in 1857 and achieved his greatest success to that date at a concert series in Prague. And, for the first time in more than two decades, audiences heard his symphonies. The keynote work at the concert series was Heinrich's new symphony, *The Columbiad*, which was a reworking of a short symphony of the same name, and his older *Ornithological Combat of Kings*. As in the Graz concert of 1836, commentators found much to like in the work, especially its peculiar narrative construction and the quotations from American national melodies (discussed in more detail in the next section).

At a Grand Valedictory Concert, given in 1853 as Heinrich was preparing for his final trip to Europe, the septuagenarian left his audience with these bittersweet thoughts: "An ancient troubadour, whose harp must shortly be hung up forever on the willows, acknowledges your kindly greeting. He is about to leave the land of his adoption, and the home of his heart, for the country which gave him birth: and it is no wonder that his breast throbs with emotion, and that his eyes are dim with tears. America has been indeed the home of my affections; but it has likewise been *the grave of many hopes*."[31]

Heinrich had indeed never found true acceptance among the country's musical communities, and his outsider status was only accentuated upon his return to the United States in 1860. Heinrich's health rapidly declined, and friends begged the public for aid. The *Abendzeitung* of New York, for example, noted that he "is too illustrious a person to be suffered to make his debut before the world in the character of a beggar. . . . I trust that the German-American part of our population will see to it that this venerable old man is not only relieved but done justice to."[32] He died a little more than a month later.

Commenting on Heinrich's Grand Valedictory Concert, critic Richard Storrs Willis described Heinrich's overture, *The Wildwood Troubadour*, with language that captures the composer's general style well: "Without any of the sombre harmonies or sudden transitions, which are peculiar to the Beethoven and von Weber school, it gives the impartial, unprejudiced listener a faithful picture of the forest home of the self-reliant Western man, by means of simple harmonies united to melodies highly florid. New and fantastic passages of imitation are distributed among the different instruments of the orchestra in a style entirely the composer's own. The harmony reminds one of Mozart and Haydn; but the orchestral treatment is to the last degree original."[33]

Heinrich developed this idiosyncratic style in his earliest published works, which include a musical palindrome (*Avance et Retraite*), harmonically adventurous pieces with sudden changes of character (*A Chromatic Ramble*), wild variations on familiar tunes (*God Save the Emperor* and *The Yankee Doodleiad*), and pieces that describe detailed narrative plots (*Krásná Pocestná*). He employed all these techniques in his symphonies, which he often scored for "all the known instruments"—a choice that ultimately led most of them to remain unperformed.[34]

Heinrich's career quickly faded from memory after his death, but his legacy began to be restored when Oscar Sonneck (1873–1928), head of the Library of Congress Music Division, acquired his prodigious musical corpus along with an extraordinarily large scrapbook.[35] The dazzling array of American subjects that inspired Heinrich's symphonies (among many other works) has led subsequent scholars to emphasize his participation in the construction of an American musical identity during the antebellum era.[36] But this emphasis has obscured the fact that Heinrich also drew from non-American subjects with equal enthusiasm and tailored them to specific environmental circumstances, often by merely reworking music he had already composed. His contemporaries perceived this tendency and often poked fun at him for it.[37] Even so, Heinrich was one of the most prolific American composers of the antebellum era. His symphonies can be divided into four broad categories according to their titles: American national symphonies, national symphonies with other countries for themes, symphonies on specifically Native American subjects, and symphonies written in honor of a historical figure (see table 2.3).

Table 2.3 The Symphonies of Anthony Philip Heinrich (1781–1861)

Title (dates)	Movements	Instrumentation	Comments
Schiller: Grande sinfonia dramatica (1834, rev. 1847 and 1856)	I. Adagio misterioso II. Allegro patetico concertante III. Minuetto e trio, a chromatic ramble IV. Romanza V. "For the Curious: Finale Doppio"; or, "Avance et Retraite" (Andante largo. Allegro moderato)	Grand + Picc., Cbssn., 2 Tpt, Tuba (doubling Serpent), Perc. (SD, BD, Tamb., Cym., Tri., Gong), Org.	Unperformed. Score published by Andrew Stiller (Philadelphia: Kallisti, 2003).
Gran sinfonia eroica (1835)	I. "The Voice of War" (Allegro comodo) II. "The Counsel" (Adagio) III. "The Resolve" (Finale. Vivace)	Grand + Picc., Cbssn., 2 Tpt, Serpent, Btuba, Ophicleide, Perc. (Tri., Cym., Tamb., BD, SD)	Passages of opening movement transferred into the first two movements of *The Ornithological Combat of Kings*. Unperformed. Unpublished.
The Ornithological Combat of Kings; or, The Condor of the Andes and the Eagle of the Cordilleras (1836, rev. 1847 and 1856)	I. "The Conflict of the Condor in the Air" (Allegro) II. "The Repose of the Condor" (Andante sostenuto, quasi adagio) III. "The Combat of the Condor on Land" (Allegro) IV. "Victory of the Condor" (Finale: Vivace brillante)	Grand + Picc., Cbssn., 2 Tpt, Serpent, Ophicleide, Perc. (Tri., Cym., BD, SD)	Material for the first two movements drawn in part from the *Gran sinfonia eroica*. Premiered in part by the Musik-Verein in Graz, Austria, June 1836. Recorded by the Syracuse Symphony Orchestra, conducted by Christopher Keene, New World Records 80208-2. Unpublished.
The Columbiad, Grand American National Chivalrous Symphony (1837)	One movement: Allegro—Andante maestoso—Allegro—Adagio, quasi largo—Allegro moderato	Grand + Picc., Cbssn., 2 Tpt, Serpent, Ophicleide, Perc. (Tri., Cym., BD, SD)	Partial performance in Graz, Austria, 1836. Unpublished.

Table 2.3 *continued*

Title (dates)	Movements	Instrumentation	Comments
Victoria's and Albion's Young Hope, the Prince of Wales: A Royal Symphony; or, National Memories; or, Gran Sinfonia Britanica (1844)	"Introduzione. National Memories" (Andante, ben sostenuto) I. Andante sostenuto—Allegro assai II. Andantino romantico III. Scherzo. Allegretto IV. Finale. Allegro assai	Grand + Picc., Cbssn., 2 Tpt., Serpent, Ophicleide, Perc. (Tri., Cym., BD, SD)	Score sent to Queen Victoria under the title *The American Eagle's Musical Flight to the World's Fair* in honor of the Great Exhibition of London in 1851. Scheduled for a performance at the Grand Valedictory Concert of 1853 in New York City but dropped at the last minute. The first movement was performed in Prague in 1857. Unpublished.
The Indian Carnival; or, "The Indian Festival of Dreams," sinfonia eratico-fantachia (ca. 1844–45)	One movement: Andante ben sostenuto—Adagio, quasi ad libitum—Allegro ma non tanto, con brio—Tempo con moto—Coda, quasi presto.	Grand + Picc., Cbssn., 2 Tpt., Serpent, Ophicleide, Perc. (Tri., Cym., BD, SD)	First of three symphonies on Native American subjects. Inspired by John McIntosh's *The Origin of the North American Indians* (1843). The symphony describes an Iroquois festival. Unperformed. Unpublished.
Manitou Mysteries; or, the Voice of the Great Spirit. Gran sinfonia misteriosa-indiana (ca. 1845)	I. Adagio assai II. Allegro giusto III. [untitled] IV. Finale: Allegro assai, quasi presto	Grand + Picc., 2 Tpt., Serpent, Ophicleide, Perc. (Tri., Cym., BD, SD)	Inspired by John McIntosh's account of Algonquin religion. Unperformed in Heinrich's lifetime. A modern performance by the Staatsphilharmonie Rheinland-Pfalz (Howard Griffith, cond.) is available on YouTube. Unpublished.
The Mastodon (ca. 1845)	I. "Black Thunder, or the Patriarch of the Fox Tribe" (Allegro ma non tanto, più posto andantino) II. "The Elkhorn Pyramid, or the Indian's Offering to the Spirit of the Prairies" (Adagio) III. "Shenandoah, or Oneida Chief" (Introduzione concertante—Marcia con spirito)	Grand + 2 Tpt., Ophicleide, Bombardon, Perc. (Tri., Cym., BD, SD)	Outer movements inspired by the speeches given by the Native American leaders Mackkatananamakee (Black Thunder) and Oskanondonha (Shenandoah) to leaders of the US government, which McIntosh reprinted in his volume. Inner movement inspired by a religious ritual described by Prince Maximilian von Wied-Neuwied in *Travels in the Interior of North America* (1843). Unperformed. Score published in an edition by Andrew Stiller (Philadelphia: Kallisti Music, 2000).

Symphony to the Spirit of Beethoven (1845)

I. "Hail to the Citizens of Bonn" (Andantino, con moto)
II. "The Musical Procession and the People" (Andantino)
III. "The Approach of the Clergy"
IV. "The Commotion of the Multitude Discovering the Royal Cortege" (Allegro moderato)
V. "The Melodious Outpourings of the Celestial Genius Hovering over the Monument" (Allegretto, ma non tanto, quasi andantino)
VI. "The Greeting of the Genius to the Assembled Host of Admiring Visitors" (Andantino)
VII. "Arrival of the King of Russia, the Queen of England, the Royal Consorts, and Dignitaries of the Courts at the Monument" (Larghetto grandioso)
VIII. "Hail to Beethoven!" (Andantino grandioso. Moderato assai)
IX. "The Uncovering of the Monument" (Poco più lento)
X. "The Enthusiastic Admiration and Praise of the Convention" (Allegro)
XI. "The Triumph of Beethoven's Glory" (Andantino eroico—Allegro animato—Più moderato, quasi andantino—Allegro assai quasi presto)
XII. "The Last Homage to the Shades of Beethoven" (Coda religiosa. Grave)
XIII. "Farewell and Salutation" (Andante con moto)

Grand + Picc., Cbssn., Ophicleide, Perc. (Tri., Cym., BD, SD, Gong), Pno.

Written in honor of the unveiling of a bronze Beethoven memorial in Bonn in 1845. Scheduled for a performance by a pickup orchestra in New York in 1846 but canceled at the last minute. Otherwise unperformed. Score published in *American Classical Music, c. 1799–1845: Works by Moravian-American Composers*, ed. Kenneth Cooper (New York: Garland, 1988).

Table 2.3 *continued*

Title (dates)	Movements	Instrumentation	Comments
The Tomb of Genius, to the Memory of Mendelssohn-Bartholdy, Sinfonia Sacra por Grande Orchestra (ca. 1847)	One movement: Adagio—Andante largo—Allegro, ma non tanto—Andante—Allegro—Adagio (cadenza dolorosa)	Grand + 2 Tpt., Ophicleide, BTuba, Org., Pno.	Inspired by the death of Felix Mendelssohn in November 1847. Unperformed Unpublished.
Bohemia, sinfonia romántica; or, Bohemia, A Heroic Symphony in Three Movements for Full Orchestra (by 1848)	I. "Prayers and Sensations on the Ocean" (*Gebeth und Empfindungen aus den Ocean [sic]*) (Introduzione: Andantino—Adagio, quasi grave sempre ben sostenuto) II. Scherzo. "Hope for a Reunion" (*Hoffnung auf Wiedersehen*) (Vivace scherzando) III. Sympathy (*Sympathie*) (Finale: Allegro, più tosto moderato)	Grand + Picc., Eb Clar, 2 Tpt., Cor., Ophicleide, Bombardon, Org.	Dedicated to Emperor Ferdinand I of Austria. The manuscript has two title pages: the first title is in Heinrich's hand, and the second title is in a copyist's hand. Unperformed Unpublished.

Title	Movements	Instrumentation	Notes
The Empress Queen of the Magyars (1848, rev. 1855)	I. "The Convocation of the Hungarians" (Adagio, quasi lento, sempre sostenuto) II. "The Empress Queen, bearing her Infant, enters the Hall of the Diet, followed by her Cortege" (Andante) III. "Maria Theresia's Appeal" (Adagio sostenuto) IV. "The [illegible] Response of the Magnates" (Allegro) V. "The Warriors March to the Battlefield" (Andante. Allegro moderato) VI. "The Enthusiasm and Heroism of the Hungarian Hussars" (Scherzo) VII. "The Austrian Eagle Crowns the Armies of the Empress Queen and the Child King (afterward Joseph II) with Victory and a General Exultation" (Coda)	Grand + Picc., Cbssn., 2 Tpt., Serpent, Ophicleide, Perc. (Tri, Cym, BD, SD)	Program symphony depicting Maria Theresa's appeal to the Hungarian Diet for aid in the early days of the War of the Austrian Succession. Performed at the Conservatory in Prague in 1857, according to a note in Heinrich's scrapbook. Unpublished.
The Columbiad; or, Migration of American Passenger Pigeons (completed in 1858)	See table 2.4.	Grand + Picc., 2 Tpt., Tuba (doubling Serpent), Ophicleide, Perc. (BD, SD, Tri, Cym, Gong)	Freely expands and reworks material from the 1837 *Columbiad* as well as *The Ornithological Combat of Kings*. Partial performance in Prague, 1857. First US performance by the Yale Symphony Orchestra on October 11, 2014; the recording is available on YouTube. Unpublished.

AMERICAN NATIONAL SYMPHONIES

Heinrich wrote three symphonies with a purely American patriotic or national ethos: *The Ornithological Combat of Kings* (ca. 1835, rev. 1847 and 1856) and two works that share the title *The Columbiad* (1835 and 1857). The three share a musical relationship that reflected Heinrich's lifelong propensity to revise works by reusing or reframing old material. It is useful, therefore, to consider these works a single musical entity rather than distinct pieces.

In 1835, well into Heinrich's European residency, he submitted a symphony to a contest sponsored by the Concert Spirituel of Vienna. No evidence of what musical materials he sent is available, but he completed a three-movement work with the title *Gran sinfonia eroica* around that time. Although the symphony has no national theme, each movement does bear an evocative title: "The Voice of War," "The Counsel," and "The Resolve." The opening movement begins with a stormy introduction to a lengthy allegro. A stately P pervades the first half of the allegro and appears in many guises, either through motivic fragmentation or harmonic modulation. Heinrich typically preferred to organize movements into blocked sections of melodic elaboration rather than conventional forms, such as sonata-allegro. A second, more lyrical S appears halfway through the movement, but, after a restatement in a different key, the stately P returns. The movement closes with radically altered versions of P—first in a sinewy adagio and finally as a quick maestoso march. The other two movements are a slow fantasia on a song published in *The Dawning of Music in Kentucky* ("Sensibility") and a rapid vivace that reworks material from the opening movement.

Heinrich adapted the opening movement of *Gran sinfonia eroica* into the first two movements of a new piece, *The Ornithological Combat of Kings, or the Condor of the Andes and the Eagle of the Cordilleras*, which he began in 1836 and eventually finished in 1847. The completed symphony comprises four movements, each of which bears a descriptive title:

I. Allegro—"The Conflict of the Condor in the Air"

II. Andante sostenuto quasi adagio—"The Repose of the Condor"

III. Allegro—"The Combat of the Condor on Land"

IV. Finale. Vivace brilliante—"The Victory of the Condor"

It is unclear why Heinrich focused on birds of South America (the Andean condor and the golden eagle) and not on a bird native to the United States, but all indications suggest that his goal was to evoke the scenery of the "entire New World."[38]

While constructing this piece, Heinrich transplanted the stormy introduction of the earlier symphony into the opening of the first movement, which maintains an unsettled character. P also appears in this movement and serves as a leitmotif for the condor in this new descriptive context. Heinrich pasted the lyrical theme from *Gran sinfonia eroica* into the second movement of *The Ornithological Combat*, a lush andante that is occasionally interrupted by a stately condor motif derived from P. This motif recurs in the third movement, which is martial in character and has the closest topical alignment with the scene it depicts. The rustic finale celebrates the condor's victory in battle against the golden eagle. After a tutti climax, it closes with a delicate solo flute cadenza that restores the condor's repose.

The Musik-Verein of Graz performed parts of this symphony (probably the opening movement) at a concert in June 1836. August Mandel, the organization's secretary, remarked in a printed review that the symphony was the most interesting piece on the program. He was taken by the work's drama: Heinrich "has sought nature in her workshop," he claimed, "where she produces her mighty works, where great bridges of rock are thrown across streams; where rivers, broad as seas, flow out of undiscovered sources over hundreds of miles to the ocean itself." Mandel believed that Heinrich had captured nature effectively with the sounds of the orchestra alone and had avoided the cheap trick of "seeking reinforcement by bells and cannon."[39] With this generous review in hand, Heinrich had achieved the international success he was seeking.

On his journey back to the French Atlantic coast in 1837, Heinrich completed the first of his two symphonies called *The Columbiad*. The subtitle marked it as a clear homage to the United States: *Grand American National Chivalrous Symphony*. The symphony comprises only one movement but is divided into several episodes, including statements of the patriotic tune "Hail Columbia" and variations on "Yankee Doodle" that exploit a wide timbral palette. Elaborate sections labeled "canone" also appear throughout the work, but they are not strict fugal passages. The symphony ends with a rousing *fortissimo* coda.

When Heinrich returned to Europe in 1857, he drew from his pool of earlier symphonies and combined *The Ornithological Combat* with the original *Columbiad* into a second symphony also called *The Columbiad*. But this time it bore a new subtitle: *Migration of American Wild Passenger Pigeons*. Heinrich's interest in American avian life was stimulated principally by the writings and drawings of the American ornithologist John James Audubon (1785–1851), a close friend whose widow, Lucy (1787–1874), supported the composer during the months leading up to his death.[40]

Heinrich secured a performance of the avian *Columbiad* in Prague in 1857. The program for the performance listed nine separate movements (see table 2.4).[41] The manuscript score includes an opening section that is not listed in the program—"the assembling of the American wild passenger pigeons in the far West for their grand flight or migration." It is marked "Adagio," not andante as indicated in the program, and it is unclear whether this music was included at the concert. In any case, the section is a dreamy and fluid septet for strings, with violins *divisi a 3*, violas, cellos *divisi a 2*, and basses, all marked "con sordini." The Allegro

Table 2.4 The Movements of *The Columbiad; or, Migration of American Passenger Pigeons*

I. *Andante ed Allegro*. "The flitting of birds and thunder-like flappings of a passing phalanx of American wild pigeons"

II. "The aerial armies alight on the primeval forest trees, which bend and crash beneath their weight."

III. *Andante ed Andantino*. "A twilight scene. The cooing of the doves [*sic*], previous to their nightly repose."

IV. *Allegro mosso*. "With Aurora comes the conflict for the beechnuts."

V. *Adagio ed Allegretto cantabile*. "The vast conclave in grand council resolve to migrate elsewhere."

VI. *Molto animato*. "Sudden rise and flight of the myriad winged emigrants."

VII. *Più mosso*. "The crash of hunters startles the multitudinous array.—The wounded and dying birds sink tumultuously earthward."

VIII. *Allegro agitato*. "In brooding agitation, the Columbines continue their flight, darkening the welkin as they utter their aerial Requiem, but passing onward, ever onward, to the goal of their nomadic wandering: the green savannas."

IX. *Finale*. "The Columbiad." *Marcia grande ed a passo doppio*. American folk tunes: "Hail Columbia!" and "Yankee Doodle."

reworks the first movement of *The Ornithological Combat of Kings*, complete with the stormy opening gesture and *P*. The movement proceeds directly into Movement II, a brief section in which the strings tumble down a D major scale and grow in volume until the trees presumably crash to the ground with a fortissimo bang sounded by the full orchestra.

In subsequent movements, Heinrich borrowed directly and then more freely from *The Ornithological Combat of Kings*, thus giving the entire symphony the appearance of being an expanded version of the earlier piece. To create a sense of dramatic unity, Heinrich also reworked earlier themes and motifs into these later movements. To close the symphony, however, Heinrich essentially pasted the entirety of the original *Columbiad* as an appendix. It is unclear how this music is dramatically related to the earlier sections or whether Heinrich intended it to be. In effect, though, the addition of this movement granted the work a patriotic aura that was lacking in *The Ornithological Combat*.

Prague critics greeted the work warmly. Since Heinrich had borrowed material that had also been performed in Graz twenty years earlier, it is possible to compare the Prague remarks with those of August Mandel. One Prague writer claimed to hear "the primitive beginnings" of the new concept of "Programmusik" in Heinrich's music—a term that had been coined only recently by Franz Liszt. Though couching the response in these up-to-date terms, the critic agreed with Mandel that Heinrich had been "absolutely untouched by any fundamental art culture" and was "forced to rely sole upon [his] exceedingly sensitive and innately expressive spirit."[42] Another critic found Heinrich's statements of American national "folk tunes"—"Hail Columbia" and "Yankee Doodle"—most noteworthy. And although at least one commentator described Heinrich as "our compatriot" ("von unserm Landsmann"), no one remarked on passages in the music that bear traces of Central or Eastern European dance music, such as a polkalike section in the first movement.[43] Even so, Heinrich could once again leave Europe having achieved a degree of success and acclaim that had not been afforded him in the United States.

OTHER "NATIONAL" SYMPHONIES

Heinrich directed a significant amount of energy toward American patriotic symphonies, but he also composed three symphonies that exhibit patriotism for *other* countries. In each case, he evidently intended to secure patronage from leading political figures but ultimately failed to do so. As with Heinrich's other symphonic works, evidence of performances is spotty at best.

Heinrich began writing the first of these symphonies in 1844, calling it *Victoria's and Albion's Young Hope, the Prince of Wales; A Royal Symphony*. In honor of London's Great Exhibition of 1851, he sent it to Queen Victoria herself under the title *The American Eagle's Musical Flight to the World's Fair*. The queen's entourage received the work and deposited it into the Royal Music Library. Heinrich kept a second copy of the symphony on hand and later retitled it *National Memories: Grand British Symphony*. It was slated for performance at the Grand Valedictory Concert of 1853 (in New York) but was dropped at the last minute. The first movement, however, found its way onto the program of an 1857 concert in Prague.

The original symphony, *Victoria*, opens with a series of well over a dozen variations on "God Save the King," each of which is separated by freely composed connecting episodes. For the 1853 performance, Heinrich appended a fantasia-like introduction, which he called a "Heroic Overture." The second movement is a bucolic andantino that evokes the British countryside; a clarinet cadenza represents the call of a shepherd's pipe (example 2.2). The scherzo is short and

Example 2.2 Heinrich, *Victoria*, II, Clarinet Cadenza

unremarkable, while the thickly scored finale returns to the pomp of the opening movement. One commentator who had seen the score prior to the scheduled New York performance remarked that the work "might cause a zealous Briton to shout aloud, and throw himself at the composer's feet in patriotic ecstasy."[44]

Heinrich's second non-American patriotic symphony was called *Bohemia*, dedicated to Emperor Ferdinand I of Austria (1793–1875). Since Ferdinand's reign ended in 1848 and the score mentions that it was completed in "New York," Henrich likely wrote it in the 1840s, when he composed most of his other symphonic works. The manuscript has two title pages—one in Heinrich's hand calling the work *Bohemia, sinfonia romantica* and one in a copyist's hand calling it *Bohemia, A Heroic Symphony in Three Movements for Full Orchestra*. This second title page also gives the following movement names:

I. "Prayer and Sensations on the Ocean" (*Gebeth und Empfindungen auf dem Ocean* [sic])
II. Scherzo. "Hope for a Reunion" (*Hoffnung auf Wiedersehen*)
III. Sympathy (*Sympathie*)

Unlike his other symphonies, the first movement is entirely slow and somber. It begins with an andante introduction but proceeds at an adagio tempo until it is interrupted briefly by an andante fanfare given by a solo cornet. Lightly scored throughout, the movement features meandering solos by the flute, cornet, and violas. The quick scherzo builds in intensity until it reaches a sustained fortissimo, but a light coda in the original tempo rounds out the form. The finale is exceptionally long and ranges in character from rustic to martial in Heinrich's typical stream-of-consciousness style. A cornet solo partway through the movement is evocative of an ethnic dance or folk tune with an unusual melodic contour and syncopated downbeats (example 2.3). The movement closes with a substantial multipart coda.

Heinrich composed *The Empress Queen of the Magyars*, the third symphony of this group, in 1848 and revised it in 1855. According to a note in his scrapbook, it was performed at the conservatory in Prague two years later, around the time of the passenger pigeon *Columbiad*

Example 2.3 Heinrich, *Bohemia*, Cornet Solo

Example 2.4 Heinrich, *Empress Queen*, violin cadenza

premiere but not at the same concert.[45] The symphony depicts Maria Theresa's appeal to the Hungarian Diet for aid during the early stages of the War of the Austrian Succession. Heinrich might have written it to show solidarity with the political figures who were leading the charge for Hungarian independence in 1848, such as Lajos Kossuth (1802–94).

Mirroring the approach Heinrich adopted in his second *Columbiad*, each section of the symphony depicts a specific narrative event, such as the "Convocation of the Hungarian Diet" and "The Austrian eagle crowns the armies of the Empress queen and the Hungarian child king (afterwards Joseph II) with victory, and a general exaltation ensues." Perhaps the most arresting moment of the work is a lengthy and difficult violin cadenza that represents Maria Theresa making her impassioned plea to the diet while holding her infant child (example 2.4).[46] After the scenes in the hall of the diet (which compose the entirety of the first movement), the symphony changes character dramatically as the subsequent movements depict the march to battle, the "enthusiasm and heroism of the Hungarian Hussars" (scherzo), and "the Blessing of the God of War." All contain appropriately rousing and martial music.[47]

SYMPHONIES ON NATIVE AMERICAN SUBJECTS

Heinrich maintained an interest in Native American culture throughout his career and wrote several works on related subjects, including a concerto grosso called *The Treaty of William Penn with the Indians* (1834) and fantasias called *Pushmataha* (1831) and *Pocahontas* (1837). Interest in Native American culture among white Americans skyrocketed after the release of two ethnological studies published in 1843, just a few years after Heinrich returned from Europe in 1837: *Travels in the Interior of North America* by the German naturalist Prince Maximilian von Wied-Neuwied (1782–1867) and *The Origin of the North American Indians* by the American ethnographer John McIntosh. Inspired by passages in these books, Heinrich wrote three symphonies on Native American subjects shortly after their publication.

McIntosh's writing directly inspired the first of these symphonies, *The Indian Carnival; or, "The Indian Festival of Dreams"* (subtitled *sinfonia eratico-fantachia*). In McIntosh's account, town residents would don costumes and play pranks on one another during an annual Iroquois festival while their victims could avoid the shenanigans by correctly guessing a prankster's dreams. Though it comprises several distinct sections, Heinrich's symphony is essentially a one-movement work. It begins with a slow introduction that concludes with cadenza-like arpeggiated solos in the flute, clarinet, and oboe. The central section, marked Allegro con brio, moves forward relentlessly until it is interrupted by a sustained chord played by the full orchestra. The speed picks up again, only to be stopped twice more, as if the revelers are encountering new victims. Once the festivities return to full swing, they culminate in an even faster coda that builds to a dramatic conclusion. The relaxed character of the symphony's opening returns briefly as the pranksters finally come to rest.

McIntosh also inspired the second of Heinrich's Native American symphonies, *Manitou Mysteries*, with a passage describing Algonquin religion and spirituality. The direct connection to Native American culture is not as clear, however, for the symphony has a conventional four-movement shape and lacks descriptive movement titles. The first movement begins with a bucolic introduction in F major that evokes the sunrise, complete with flitting birdlike passages in the flute and oboe. The introduction closes on an ominous F minor chord before returning to the major in a lilting, equally rustic allegro. As in Heinrich's other works, melodic variation achieved through changes of instrumentation, rhythm, and mode propel the movement forward, while rigorous Beethovenian motivic development is nearly absent. The allegro concludes with a brilliant brassy fanfare. The second movement is an elegant waltzlike dance that occasionally includes exotic percussion such as the triangle and cymbals. A broad adagio

Example 2.5 Heinrich, *The Mastodon*, Elkhorn Pyramid

movement recalls the pastoral character of the opening, while the brisk finale recalls the revelry of *The Indian Carnival*.

The title of Heinrich's third symphony, *The Mastodon*, likewise bears little resemblance to the assigned subject matter of each movement. The outer movements were inspired by two Native American leaders, Mackkatananamakee (or "Black Thunder") and Oskanondonha (sometimes called "Shenandoah"), whose speeches before US government officials became famous after they were circulated widely in print throughout the era; McIntosh reprinted them in his volume, which is perhaps how Heinrich encountered them for the first time. Neither of these movements deviate from the cinematic, stream-of-consciousness style Heinrich had developed in his previous works. The inner movement ("The Elkhorn Pyramid"), however, refers to a religious ritual described by Prince Maximilian and includes an unusual fugato passage that seems to be Heinrich's attempt to depict the interlocked horns of the pyramid made from the antlers of elk (example 2.5).[48]

MEMORIAL SYMPHONIES

Departing from national connotations of any kind, Heinrich composed three symphonies with titles honoring historical figures: *Schiller* (1834, rev. 1847 and 1856), *To the Spirit of Beethoven* (1845), and *The Tomb of Genius; To the Memory of Mendelssohn-Bartholdy* (ca. 1847). Each of these figures was a beloved cultural icon among German speakers throughout the West, but they also held positions of great esteem among English speakers in the United States and Great Britain. Heinrich wrote these pieces at moments when public interest in these individuals was particularly high. There is no evidence that Heinrich managed to stage performances of any of these works, however, and what Heinrich intended to accomplish with them is unclear, particularly since they lack the patriotic elements of his other symphonies.

Heinrich finished the first version of *Schiller* in 1834, not long after an updated version of Scottish writer Thomas Carlyle's biography of Friedrich Schiller prompted a flurry of reviews to appear in American and British magazines. The symphony's connection to the poet otherwise remains a mystery. Heinrich initially conceived the work as an overture but added movements over the course of several years to round out its shape as a full-length symphony in five movements. The first and fourth, both of which are slow and relaxed in character, function as introductions to the unremarkable second and the more colorful fifth, which is a heavily orchestrated and revised version of the musical palindrome Heinrich had included in *The Dawning of Music in Kentucky*. The third movement is a minuet and trio marked by pervasive chromatic melodies and adventurous harmonies—another combination he had explored in his first published volumes from the 1820s.

Whereas *Schiller*'s relationship to the poet is unclear, Heinrich wrote *To the Spirit of Beethoven* in honor of the 1845 unveiling of a bronze Beethoven memorial in Bonn. Because he occasionally sent works abroad, it is possible that Heinrich intended for the symphony to be performed at the Beethoven Festival that preceded the unveiling. But there is no evidence suggesting as much. Instead, the symphony was slated to appear at a New York concert in 1846 but had to be canceled at the last minute because the orchestra, a group assembled for the occasion, could not prepare it in time.

To the Spirit of Beethoven differs dramatically in character from most of his other symphonies. Matching the structures of *The Columbiad* and *The Empress Queen of the Magyars*, it is divided into several relatively brief sections that presumably depict (or evoke) specific scenes at the unveiling ceremony. It begins with a "Hail to the Citizens of Bonn," for example, which is followed by the arrival of musicians, a procession of clergy, the "commotion of the multitude discovering the royal cortege," and so on. A single gong strike separates each movement from the next. Unlike Heinrich's other works, the musical topics (or *topoi*) that he employed usually have an obvious connection to the scene. The "commotion" section, for example, is highly chromatic and rhythmically busy, whereas the arrival of heads of state is appropriately regal.

Heinrich wrote his third memorial symphony, *The Tomb of Genius*, in the wake of Felix Mendelssohn's untimely death in 1847. Though continuous, the symphony is divided into several sections, most of which are slow and somber. The inclusion of an organ obbligato heightens the seriousness of the mood. Among the most striking passages in the work is a lengthy fugal section written for the organ and the piano (another obbligato instrument) to which Heinrich added colorful doublings throughout the rest of the orchestra. And prior to the closing allegro, Heinrich added a section marked "cadenza dolorosa," in which sustained dissonances in the organ serve as an emotional climax for the entire work. Although the manuscript is sumptuously bound, there is no indication that Heinrich ever sought a performance.

Interest in Heinrich's maverick persona led to niche revivals of his music more than a century after his death. Musicians Neely Bruce and Christopher Keene, for example, recorded a handful of Heinrich's works, including *The Ornithological Combat of Kings*, on LP records in the 1970s, which were later reissued on compact disc. Composer Andrew Stiller began self-publishing a complete edition of Heinrich's music in the 1990s, leading to the relatively wide availability of full scores for several important orchestral pieces. Pavel Farský, a musician in Prague, established the International Anthony Philip Heinrich Society in 2011 to reincorporate Heinrich's legacy into contemporary Czech cultural life. And, finally, Heinrich's 1857 *Columbiad* received its US premiere in 2014 at a Yale symposium dedicated to the passenger pigeon; a similar event was held shortly thereafter in Madison, Wisconsin. But Heinrich was all but forgotten by his contemporaries soon after his death. The difficulty and strangeness of his music, coupled with widespread critical antipathy toward programmaticism, proved to be insurmountable obstacles to achieving success among the antebellum American music-loving public.

George Frederick Bristow (1825–98)

Unlike Anthony Philip Heinrich, the New York–born George Frederick Bristow enjoyed the praise of his contemporaries, who feted him as one of the country's most distinguished musicians and composers. From the earliest days of his compositional career, his sound reputation also extended overseas. But that is not to say it all came easily for him. Despite being esteemed among both the English-speaking and German-speaking communities of New York, Bristow depended on the kindness and support of specific individuals throughout his career to earn and maintain his status.

Bristow was born into a musical family. His father, William Bristow (1803–67), was a clarinetist and entrepreneur who flourished in the complex musical marketplace of the New York metropolis. With a home base in Brooklyn, William staged occasional benefit concerts and, like many of the best professional players, eventually joined a theater orchestra to secure steady performance work. George, a violinist, followed in his father's footsteps and played alongside him at New York's Olympic Theatre beginning in the late 1830s. At the Olympic, they both worked with the English conductor George Loder (1816–68), who would later become one of the chief conductors of the New York Philharmonic. Around this same time, Bristow took lessons in rudimentary theory from Henry Christian Timm (1811–92), a German-born pianist who would also become a leading figure in the Philharmonic.

George joined the Philharmonic during its second season (1843–44) and, save for a brief hiatus in 1854 and 1855, would stay on the roster of violinists until March 1882, when he gave his final performance in the regular subscription series.[49] Early in his Philharmonic career, Bristow occasionally stepped out of his role as a section violinist and served as a soloist with the orchestra on both violin and piano. He also performed frequently at benefit concerts staged by other musicians and even sat in the orchestra that accompanied Jenny Lind during her New York appearances in 1850 and 1851. An indefatigable performer, he later joined the violin section of the Brooklyn Philharmonic, an organization founded in 1857 that shared many players with its New York cousin and, for a time, also shared principal conductors and repertory.[50]

Like so many other successful musicians of the nineteenth century, Bristow capitalized on his musical talents in areas outside of instrumental performance. In 1851, for example, he took over the directorship of the New York Harmonic Society, a leading choral organization, and retained that position until 1862, after which time he began directing similar groups, such as the Mendelssohn Union and Harlem Mendelssohn Union. Bristow's distinction in several branches of practical musicianship undoubtedly helped him earn positions in the city's public schools (which he held for over forty years—he died in a classroom) and as lead organist at some of the city's most renowned churches.

With Bristow's prolific activities as an instrumentalist, conductor, and teacher, it should come as no surprise that he also excelled in a variety of compositional idioms. Part of his extensive catalog includes functional pieces such as organ voluntaries, anthems, and other choral service music. Catering to the amateur marketplace, he also wrote domestic music such as songs, solo piano pieces, and chamber works. But Bristow also found ample time to write in larger genres. He became most famous for his 1855 opera *Rip Van Winkle*, excerpts of which were published and sold as sheet music, and the oratorio *Daniel* (1866–67). In addition, he composed several concert overtures and five symphonies, all of which received performances during his lifetime—some on more than one occasion, or even repeatedly (a rarity for a US-born composer). Bristow's integration into all facets of the city's musical marketplace allowed him to succeed on multiple compositional fronts simultaneously.

Although he had wide knowledge of old and new repertoires, Bristow's compositional style was generally conservative. During his long career, he carefully experimented with European trends as they moved into the United States. His earliest overtures, written in 1845 and 1856, drew freely from the dramatic instrumental style common in curtain-raisers preceding an opera. By 1861, however, Bristow had begun to conceive of the overture as a truly standalone genre. The program note for his *Columbus* overture, for example, explains that "the design of this overture is to present in dramatic form, a series of tone pictures, illustrating some of the incidents connected with the discovery of this continent by Columbus, without however pretending to follow all the events, or to introduce them in strict order of occurrence." Bristow continued to write overtures with American subject matter: *The Great Republic* (1876) and *Jibbenainosay* (1889), the latter of which was inspired by the violent frontier novel *Nick of the Woods* (1837) by Robert Montgomery Bird. Bristow wrote his five symphonies across a forty-year period, and the works followed the stylistic trajectory described as they became increasingly narrative and national (table 2.5). Certain critics hailed Bristow as the first great American composer, but he quickly lost that cachet as musical values changed rapidly during the final two decades of the nineteenth century and into the next.

Table 2.5 The Symphonies of George Frederick Bristow (1825–98)

Opus	Key	Dates	Title	Movements	Instrumentation	Comments
10	E♭	1848–49	Sinfonia No. 1 in E-flat Major	I. Allegro vivace II. Adagio III. Menuetto IV. Allegro	Full + Trom.	First performance: May 25, 1850, at a public rehearsal of the New York Philharmonic. Unpublished.
24	D minor	1853	Symphony No. 2, "Jullien"	I. Allegro appassionato II. Allegretto III. Adagio IV. Allegro agitato	Full + 2 Hr, 3–4, Trom.	Written for Louis Antoine Jullien's orchestra and named after the conductor. Jullien performed excerpts from the symphony on numerous occasions, beginning in December 1853. He took it to Britain the next year, where it was received warmly. Full performance by the New York Philharmonic on March 1, 1856, conducted by Carl Bergmann. Recorded by the Royal Northern Sinfonia, conducted by Rebecca Miller on New World Records 80768–2. Score published in an edition by Katherine K. Preston (Middleton, WI: A-R Editions, 2011).
26	F♯ minor	1858–59	Symphony No. 3	I. Allegro moderato II. Scherzo: "The Butterfly's Frolic" III. Nocturno IV. Finale—allegro con fuoco	Grand + Hp (only 2 Trom.)	First performance: March 26, 1859, by the New York Philharmonic, conducted by Carl Bergmann. In the program, Bristow accompanied each movement with an evocative poem (reprinted in table 2.6). Recorded by the Detroit Symphony Orchestra, conducted by Neeme Järvi on Chandos Records 9169. Unpublished.

Table 2.5 *continued*

Opus	Key	Dates	Title	Movements	Instrumentation	Comments
50	E minor	1872	Symphony No. 4, "Arcadian"	I. Allegro appassionato—"Emigrants' Journey across the Plains" II. Andante religioso—"Halt on the Prairie" III. Allegro ma non troppo—"Indian War Dance and Attack by Indians" IV. Allegro con spirito—"Arrival at the New Home, Rustic Festivities, and Dancing"	Grand + Picc., Tuba, Perc. (Cym., Tri.)	Program symphony about the settling of the Midwest (Bristow's program is reprinted in table 2.7). First performance: February 8, 1873, by the Brooklyn Philharmonic, conducted by Carl Bergmann. A performance by the Royal Philharmonic Orchestra of London, conducted by Karl Krueger, is available on YouTube. Unpublished.
62	C Major	1893	Symphony No. 5, "Niagara"	I. Allegro II. Adagio III. A Breakdown (Allegro) IV. See table 2.8	Grand + Picc., Cbssn., Tuba, SATB chorus	Orchestral symphony with a cantata-like choral finale. Texts compiled by Bristow. Premiered in Carnegie Hall on April 11, 1898, by the Manuscript Society of New York, conducted by the composer. Fourth movement published in an edition by Timothy J. Cloeter (DMA diss., University of Arizona, 2016).

SINFONIA [SYMPHONY NO. 1] IN E-FLAT MAJOR, OP. 10

Following on the heels of the successful Philharmonic premiere of his first concert overture (1847), Bristow immediately set to work on a piece of much larger scope, his First Symphony, which he completed in 1848. As noted earlier, he became entangled in the ensuing maelstrom of ethnic conflict and subsequently ran into difficulty staging a premiere. Amid outcry from the press, the Philharmonic eventually bowed to demands for a hearing and programmed the symphony at an extra public rehearsal on May 25, 1850.

The symphony itself is cast in a conventional four-movement mold. The opening movement begins with a slow introduction (no tempo is given) reminiscent of Mozart's Symphony No. 39 in E-flat. Loud tutti passages and soft, lyrical responses alternate in rapid succession before arriving on a chromatic prolongation of the dominant. The Allegro proper is in sonata form. *P* is introduced in the first violins and then restated by the full orchestra after intervening eighth-note passagework in the upper strings. *S* is insipid by comparison. Bristow chose *P* over *S* for exploration in the development section but, probably because of his inexperience, marked a new key signature for each successive tonal area. The recapitulation sneaks in almost imperceptibly with a pianissimo dynamic but builds to a rousing conclusion.

The symphony's later movements are equally standard. The Adagio presents a series of variations on a dreamy melody in A-flat major. Bristow's interest in writing for a variety of textural combinations is evident throughout, particularly in the rhythmic vitality of the string parts. The third movement is a conventional minuet that features an ongoing melodic dialogue between the strings and woodwinds; the two-part trio is otherwise unremarkable. Bristow adopted the sonata-allegro form in the finale. Like the first movement, it includes a slow introduction, but, in this case, the woodwinds take more of a leading melodic role in the Allegro. The movement concludes with the full orchestra spinning into a loud codetta.

The symphony made a strong impression on critics, who dedicated a significant amount of space to it in various periodicals. Writing for the *Message Bird*, Frederick Nicholls Crouch (1808–96) found much to like and wrote a two-part review. Summarily wagging his finger at the Philharmonic for not bringing out the work sooner, he explained that audiences might not suspect that an American composer could have attained "sufficient knowledge and skill to construct a *Grand Symphony*, . . . Mr. Bristow, however, has grown up, as it were, in an orchestra." This "education," Crouch added, allowed him to "hear and study many of the best modes of instrumental composition."[51]

In the second installment of his essay, describing the music itself, Crouch noted that he enjoyed the Adagio best: "There is a dreamy romance and placid beauty in this strain, which attracts and soothes the listener, almost in spite of his will." The "vigorous effort" of the finale, along with Bristow's selection of a "strong motive, treated in alternate strict and free styles," also greatly pleased Crouch, but he was least satisfied with the slow introduction of the first movement—the element that followed the Mozartean model most closely. In all, Crouch concluded, Bristow should remain steadfast against the "unmanly censure of jealous contemporaries." As long as Bristow did not try too much too soon, he would be successful.[52]

Hermann Saroni, who had agitated for the production in the first place, was much less satisfied. He compared the work "to a musical chessboard, with a field for each composer from the time of Haydn to Mendelssohn Bartholdy." On top of that, "almost every sixteen bars, the composer seems to come to a dead halt" and "begins a new [theme], which has not the remotest connection with the former." And, finally, "Another mistake is, that the four movements

... are all in *major*, thus shedding a monotony over the whole composition, which is anything but pleasant." Saroni did like the opening of the finale, but little else. He urged Bristow "to be content with compositions of less extent" and suggested that Bristow should give up on symphonies altogether. Reacting strongly to this snide dismissal, Bristow canceled his subscription to Saroni's magazine.[53]

SYMPHONY NO. 2 IN D MINOR, OP. 24, "JULLIEN"

Going against Saroni's advice, Bristow did not give up on his symphonic ambitions. During the following concert season, the famed soprano Jenny Lind enlisted Bristow to perform in her New York orchestra, and she reciprocated by programming selections from his symphony. Reviewing one of these concerts, Saroni reminded readers that these selections were superb, and he reiterated his grievances against the Philharmonic.[54] As we saw earlier, though, little would change in the Philharmonic over the next two years, and Bristow would once again rely on the generosity of recent arrivals from Europe for public exposure: William Henry Fry, who was returning to the United States after several years abroad, and Louis Antoine Jullien, who was visiting for the first time.

As I explain in more detail later, Fry had been living and working in Paris since 1846. When he returned in 1852, he staged a series of lectures designed to illustrate the history and theory of music. During one of these lectures, he enlisted the help of a full orchestra to perform selections from Bristow's symphony and, in doing so, kept it alive within the public imagination. Jullien arrived in the United States a few months later and picked up the symphony's minuet movement for his own concert series. His decision added fuel to the fire in the brewing feud with the Philharmonic after Fry reviewed the work in the *Tribune*. In the meantime, Jullien had taken works by Bristow and Fry on his lengthy autumn tour.[55]

In turn, Bristow wrote a new symphony specifically for Jullien's orchestra. The circumstances surrounding this supposed commission are unknown, but Bristow named the symphony after his benefactor. Jullien first programmed a movement in December 1853 and later added a second before going on tour. When his tour concluded in the following July, Jullien took the piece back to Britain, where it was received warmly. In the meantime, Bristow had severed relations with the Philharmonic, but, after a cooling-off period, resumed his duties during the 1855–56 concert season. Carl Bergmann (1821–76), whose programming choices tended to be more progressive than Theodore Eisfeld's, directed the symphony's Philharmonic premiere on March 1, 1856.

Bristow continued to adopt the conventional four-movement structure in this new symphony but reversed the order of the inner movements. The work begins with a fiery triadic gesture in D minor that introduces a brooding P in the violoncellos and bassoons. The opening energy does not flag until a tastefully decorated cantabile melody in F major, stated initially in the strings and then by the full choir of doubled woodwinds, emerges as S. The moodiness of the opening returns in K, which presents fragments of P in the new key. The middle section of the movement develops P but is halted momentarily by a triumphant restatement of S scored for full orchestra; the passage is marked "con grand forte e meno mosso." As in Bristow's earlier symphony, the recapitulation begins softly but builds to a grand conclusion.

Later movements display Bristow's efforts to place an individual stylistic stamp on the work. The second movement is not a standard minuet or scherzo but instead resembles a polka or schottische in its rhythmic profile. Jullien had become famous for performing these dance styles at his concerts, and it is possible that Bristow made this choice as a nod to his patron.

Example 2.6 Bristow, Symphony No. 2, Trombone solo

The main melody of the third movement, a luscious adagio in B-flat major, begins with the unusual sonority of a solo trombone (which appears at various other moments throughout the symphony; example 2.6). Over the course of the movement, Bristow reorchestrated this theme with a wide palette of instrumental combinations. The quick finale, in 6/4 time, has a scherzo-like character but fits into the standard sonata-allegro form. A wind chorale with furious string accompaniment closes the work.

The first movement garnered favorable reviews after Jullien's premiere performance. Richard Storrs Willis described the opening theme as "well-conceived and skilfully developed" and praised Bristow's transitions. He also noted that it was a marked improvement over the previous symphony.[56] After the Philharmonic premiered the entire work in 1856, Willis remained pleased with it. Of the four movements, he liked the inner two the best but remarked that the symphony suffered generally from "excess modulation and lack of harmonic unity" and "needs scissoring." Still, he congratulated Bristow on the accomplishment and pointed out that every movement drew hearty applause from the audience.[57]

William Henry Fry, Bristow's avid supporter in the Philharmonic controversy, was overjoyed. After noting that the symphony followed the conventional four-movement scheme and was a "success," he focused his attention on the unusual second movement: "The second movement is the only approach to innovation. In place of having a minuetto—which was in Haydn's and Mozart's time the dance, and as such suggested to every auditor what a polka does now—Mr. Bristow has, according to a hint we expressed long ago, for the laws of progressive aesthetics in music, adopted the spirit and accent of the polka instead of the now vitally unsuggestive minuet."[58]

The polka's populist ethos appealed to Fry because he believed that orchestral music should be accessible to a wide audience. Commenting on the third movement, Fry also situated the work within broader international trends: "There is nothing in the 'music of the future,' or any other theory which can justly be against a clear, square, vocal melody." He ultimately believed the symphony was a credit to Bristow and had marked the beginning of a new era for the Philharmonic to champion American music.

Theodore Hagen (1823–71), a German critic who had once written for Robert Schumann's *Neue Zeitschrift für Musik* before emigrating to the United States in 1854, held an entirely different opinion. He claimed that Bristow's "very ordinary music, very ordinarily worked out" belonged "in our theaters between the acts, or in the so-called promenade concerts, where they may give pleasure on account of the appropriate frame in which they appear." Next to a masterpiece, such a work was doomed to failure. Bristow's melodies, instrumentation, and polyphony were subpar, and, as far as Hagen was concerned, "all goes on with as little artistical effort as possible, reminding us of the so-called symphonies of Küffner, and similar composers, whose compositions were formerly played by some bands of amateurs, or in some garden-concerts." Bristow's choice to write a polkalike dance for the scherzo movement was poor, he claimed, since composers like Haydn, Mozart, and Beethoven had never debased their symphonies by incorporating a popular dance. And while Hagen appreciated the fact that the Philharmonic was supporting American composers, he urged the ensemble to be more judicious in its selections, particularly with only a handful of concerts available per season.[59]

Writers for other magazines, all Americans rather than Germans, followed in Hagen's footsteps. The New York correspondent for *Dwight's Journal of Music* claimed that the symphony's "chief fault is a pretty serious one: a decided want of originality." Elaborating at length on the claim, this writer described the listening experience in great detail: "It is full of reminiscences of other composers, Weber, Mendelssohn, Spohr, Haydn, Mozart, and I know not what others, seem to be playing ball with snatches of their melodies, and tossing them to and fro in merry confusion. 'What is that? Where have I heard this? I surely know this melody,' etc.; and the same experience has been related to me by many friends."[60]

Perhaps one of these friends was the critic for *Frank Leslie's Illustrated Newspaper*, who added that the symphony "exhibits talent of a moderate order, but we do not find in it any individuality, or any evidence of an original train of thought. Nothing that could lead us to speak of Mr. Bristow's manner, or style, or school."[61] But neither writer presented suggestions for how Bristow might find an individual voice while writing within a shared stylistic idiom, and it did not seem to occur to them that, up to a point, the works by the composers they mentioned sound similar to one another. These accusations of plagiarism cloaked their lack of willingness to fuse Bristow into a transatlantic compositional "school" that included Germans as well. A British critic in Manchester, who had heard the slow movement at one of Jullien's performances in 1855, had no problem doing so: "Mr. Bristow's model has evidently been Mendelssohn. His melodial phrases are graceful and expressive, and his instrumentation clear and musician-like."[62] For an unprejudiced critic not in the thick of bitter ethnic conflict, the resemblance to Mendelssohn was an asset, not a liability.

SYMPHONY NO. 3 IN F-SHARP MINOR, OP. 26

The personal attention that Bristow's music received from leading conductors like Jullien and Bergmann catapulted his reputation during the latter half of the 1850s. In March 1859, for example, musicians from the Philharmonic and distinguished soloists, such as pianist William Mason (1829–1908), hosted a "Grand Testimonial Concert" in his honor. The advertisement claimed that, "As a classical musician and composer[,] Mr. George F. Bristow has long ranked among the highest in the profession. His claims to this position are recognized in Europe, where his symphonies have been repeatedly performed—an honor which has never been paid to any other AMERICAN COMPOSER."[63] Honoring Bristow yet again, Bergmann programmed the premiere of his next symphony—his third—later that month at the Philharmonic's final concert of the season.

Although the new symphony retains the conventional four-movement structure, Bristow also chose to print stanzas of evocative poetry in the Philharmonic program (see table 2.6). Each poem corresponds to the musical character of each movement. Louis Spohr had employed this strategy in his popular Fourth Symphony (*Die Weihe der Töne*, 1832), which the Philharmonic had programmed six times since 1842, though it is clear that the poems appended to Bristow's symphony are more epigrammatic in character than Spohr's, rather than foundational for understanding the piece.[64] I/P resembles that of the second symphony. It is

Table 2.6 The Poems of Bristow's Symphony No. 3

Movement	Text

I. Allegro moderato	My soul is dark—oh! quickly string
	    The harp I yet can brook to hear;
	And let thy gentle fingers fling
	    Its melting murmurs o'er mine ear.
	If in this heart a hope be dear,
	    That sound shall charm it forth again:
	If in these eyes there lurk a tear,
	    'Twill flow, and cease to burn my brain
	But bid the strain be wild and deep
	    Nor let thy notes of joy be first;
	I tell thee, minstrel, I must weep,
	    Or else this heavy heart will burst;
	For it hath been by sorrow nursed,
	    And ached in sleepless silence long;
	And now 'tis doomed to know the worst
	    And break at once—or yield to song.
	        —Lord Byron

II. Scherzo—"The Butterfly"	Gay being, born to flutter through the day;
	    Sport in the sunshine of the present hour;
	On the sweet rose thy painted wings display,
	    And cull the fragrance of the opening flow'r.
	        —J. B. Sale

III. Nocturno—Calm	Pure was the temperate air, and even calm Perpetual reign'd, save what the zephyrs bland Breathed o'er the blue expanse. —From James Thomson's *Seasons*

IV. Allegro con fuoco—Anger	Next anger rushed, his eyes on fire,
	    In lightnings own'd his secret stings,
	In one rude clash he struck the lyre
	    And swept with hurried hand the strings.
	        —From William Collins's *The Passions*

dark, brooding, and presented by the lower strings but appears as if *in medias res* with no introduction. The contrasting *S* is a bright melody with running scalar motifs traded by the first violins and first clarinet (example 2.7). In keeping with the poetic verse given for the movement ("My soul is dark—Oh! quickly string / The harp I yet can brook to hear"), a harp accompanies the melody. In the Philharmonic's performance, however, a piano was substituted instead, according to local custom in New York and elsewhere. The transitional and closing passages of the exposition have distinct melodic identities and become the basis for further development later in the movement. Changing course from his previous symphonies, Bristow

Douglas W. Shadle

Example 2.7 Bristow, Symphony No. 3, I/S

shrouded the end of the movement in mystery as the opening theme becomes rhythmically augmented and fades to nothingness to the accompaniment of a light harp arpeggio.

The second movement, "The Butterfly's Frolic," is a fairylike scherzo in B minor that greatly resembles the scherzo of Mendelssohn's popular incidental music to *A Midsummer Night's Dream*; the main theme of the trio is a rustic melody in the parallel major.[65] While effective, the third and fourth movements—a pulsating nocturne in 9/8 and a stormy sonata-allegro finale—likewise fit into the stylistic milieu of Schumann and Mendelssohn, particularly with thick and brassy orchestration.

Critics generally found the symphony to be Bristow's most praiseworthy to date. Willis called the evening's program "very good" because of "the fact that it included a creditable composition, in classic proportions, by a native composer . . . not simply because the composition was good, nor because it was of American origin, but because it was American and good." The New York correspondent for *Dwight's Journal of Music* claimed that Bristow's work "has the happy quality of being popular enough to please the multitude, and yet possessing sufficient depth and intrinsic worth to preserve it from being trivial." And Theodore Hagen, the German-born critic who had thrashed Bristow's previous effort, added that the symphony was "well received, and deservedly so, for it points, on the part of the author, to hard studies, which we feel confident will be crowned with ultimate and legitimate success."[66] Bristow had finally convinced even the most skeptical critics that he was a legitimate contributor to the vaunted European symphonic tradition.

Carl Bergmann continued to support Bristow by programming the symphony across the East River during the Brooklyn Philharmonic's 1870–71 concert season. According to news reports, Bristow revised the work, but the extent of the revisions is not at present known. A writer for the *Brooklyn Daily Eagle* remarked that the work "deserves to hold a place in the repertoire," especially when considered alongside pieces by lesser figures such as Lindpaintner. Commenting on the audience's reaction at the performance, the *Brooklyn Daily Union* noted that the work aroused "repeated applause" and caused "Mr. Bergmann to agitate the elbow and palm of the composer, who remained as composed as possible."[67]

SYMPHONY NO. 4 IN E MINOR, OP. 50, "ARCADIAN"

The success attending the revival of the Third Symphony prompted Bristow to return to the genre in 1872. To honor his status within the New York musical community after a decade of continued triumph, the Brooklyn Philharmonic offered him $100 to compose a new symphony, which would become his fourth. This was likely the first time that a standing ensemble in the United States had commissioned a US-born composer to write a symphony for it; Carl Bergmann, Bristow's most avid supporter, was still the Philharmonic's director.[68] And although $100 was not an inconsiderable amount at the time, extra rehearsals for the orchestra apparently cost Bristow $200. (And it should be noted that conductor Theodore Thomas [1835–1905] paid Richard Wagner the princely sum of $5,000 for a potboiler to be used at the 1876 centennial festivities in Philadelphia.)

Subtitled "Arcadian," Bristow's Fourth Symphony was his most programmatic to date. Originally conceived as a multimovement introduction to a cantata called *The Pioneer*, the symphony depicts a group of settlers journeying across the western American frontier in search of a new home (See table 2.7). In addition to providing a synopsis to the symphonic version of the score, the printed program noted that the synopsis "is not pretended to give more than an outline of the composer's meaning; enough, simply, to enable the attentive listener

Table 2.7 Bristow's Program for Symphony No. 4

"In this work, Mr. Bristow has chosen for his subject a peculiarly American theme, the passage of emigrants across the plains, and their arrival, after various incidents, at the new Arcadia.

"The first movement (*Allegro Appassionato*) is intended to describe the journey of the emigrants through the unbroken waste, with its weariness and monotony, interspersed with recollections of home and the enjoyments of civilization which they have left.

"In the second movement (*Andante Religioso*) is depicted the halt on the Prairie. Evening is at hand, and the weary travelers prepare to encamp for the night. Then ensues the evening song, Tallis' familiar and beautiful Hymn serving as the theme. The evening prayer is said, the strain sinks to *piannissimo* [sic], and the fatigued and unsuspecting travelers fall asleep.

"The scene changes to an Indian encampment, where the savages are engaged in a war dance, preliminary to an attack. The third movement (*Allegro ma non troppo*) depicts the commotion among the Indians, who, at the conclusion of the dance, fall upon the encampment of emigrants, and after a violent conflict are repulsed.

"The fourth movement (*Allegro con spirito*) is meant to describe their arrival at their Arcadian home, and great rejoicing and merry-making take possession of all. The second subject may be construed as a rude dance. As it progresses it increases to a *presto*. Though the *tempo* is very quick, it is nevertheless intended to be grand, as expressing great gratitude as well as joy at the happy termination of their long and arduous toil. In the brief space allotted to a description of this character, it is not pretended to give more than an outline of the composer's meaning; enough, simply, to enable the attentive listener to understand and appreciate the composition."

---

to understand and appreciate the composition." With this disclaimer, Bristow was hoping to avoid a negative barrage from the many American critics who despised the very concept of program music. With a narrative structure drawn from an American theme, Bristow moved in an even more programmatic direction than in the third symphony a decade earlier, thus aligning his approach to the *Columbus* overture, as well as with certain composers affiliated with the New German School, particularly Joachim Raff (1822–82).[69]

In keeping with the practice of the day, Bristow's first movement is much larger than those of his previous symphonies, though it retains the general outline of sonata-allegro form. Evoking the desolation of a westward journey, it opens with an unaccompanied solo viola melody (*P*) in the instrument's upper register. After a broad development and full recapitulation, the movement ends with the return of *P*, this time in the viola's husky lower register. Capturing the settlers' relaxation after an arduous day's journey, the second movement opens with the calm mood that closed the first. After a brief moment that sets the scene, the trombones enter with a direct quotation of "Tallis's Evening Hymn," a well-known tune that Bristow's audiences almost certainly would have recognized immediately. The tune returns in the French horns near the end of the movement after a series of richly scored passages that match the character of Bristow's previous adagios.

The third movement, which depicts a Native American war dance and an attack on the settlers, was easily Bristow's most adventurous to that date. The opening scherzo is filled with exoticisms: sinewy chromatic lines in the woodwinds, unusual percussion instruments such as the cymbal and triangle, and of course a ubiquitous pulsing drumbeat in the lower strings (example 2.8). The trio presents the settlers' resistance to the attack with a boisterous melody in the trumpets accompanied by a soaring countermelody in the lower strings. The conventions of form dictated the return of the warlike music in the scherzo, but the exuberant opening of

The First Generation of Symphonists in the United States

Example 2.8 Bristow, Symphony No. 4, III

the finale reveals that the settlers defeated their attackers and have begun to rejoice at the discovery of their new home. It closes with an appropriately celebratory gesture.

Public anticipation for Bristow's symphony ran high after the announcement that he was receiving a commission for it, leading a critic for the *Daily Eagle* to point out that, "if Mr. Bristow can catch something of the old time atmosphere [of pioneer life] and give it a fitting art setting, he will accomplish a worthy success." Over the course of the Philharmonic's rehearsals, however, the critic's interest turned sour as questions about music's general ability to depict scenes clouded discussions of the piece. While praising its "scholarship and practical knowledge," the writer noted that these qualities were "not helped by a struggle after elaborate descriptive expression, of which, from the very nature of things, music is incapable."[70]

After the concert performance, the *Eagle* unleashed a tirade against Bristow for opting to tell a story with the symphony. The negativity eventually softened: "Putting aside the preposterous descriptive element, the 'Arcadian' will be pronounced a fluid and finished work. The controlling themes are easily apprehended, and the progress of each movement is readily followed." Despite these favorable remarks, the *Eagle's* ultimate judgment was that the symphony was "not strikingly original, but it is the work of an accomplished musician, well educated in orchestral effects." A critic for the *Daily Union* did not agree and proclaimed the work "a splendid success." Indeed, the symphony "was so enthusiastically received that Mr. Bristow, who occupied his seat in the orchestra, was compelled to acknowledge the plaudits of the audience at the conclusion of the first, third, and fourth movements."[71]

The mixed reception in Brooklyn exemplified a widening rift between audiences who adored Bristow's music and the critics who were lukewarm toward it. Preferring to please his audiences, Bergmann programmed the work the following season on the New York Philharmonic's regular concert series. New York critics, most of whom appear not to have heard the Brooklyn premiere, were much more positive than their counterparts across the river. Myron Cooney of the *New York Herald* believed "the entire work reflects the highest credit on the renowned composer and on the society for presenting before the metropolitan public a vivid musical picture of Western life." News of the performance even reached London, as a correspondent for the *London Musical Standard* described the symphony as "exceedingly clever, showing traces of severe and well-directed study in the best schools." Commenting on the ethnic conflict that still colored the city's musical climate, this writer explained to Londoners that Bristow's "countrymen may well point to him as a proof that they possess a man quite able to hold his own against many greatly inferior composers, who, mainly owing to their Teutonic origin, are lauded to the skies—especially in New York."[72]

SYMPHONY NO. 5, OP. 62, "NIAGARA"

Bristow redoubled his compositional efforts after relinquishing his duties as a Philharmonic violinist in 1882. Among other activities, he joined the Manuscript Society of New York, a loosely organized affiliation of American composers whose mission was to provide a forum for the exchange of ideas and, ultimately, for performances of new works. During the 1880s, Bristow's reputation had started to wane after younger Bostonian composers, such as John Knowles Paine and George Whitefield Chadwick, both of whom had studied at European conservatories, had risen to national prominence. Even so, he found a new key supporter in the charismatic conductor Anton Seidl (1850–98), who programmed his shorter works at several summer concerts on Brighton Beach. Like Bergmann, Seidl was one of the most esteemed musicians in New York during his tenure as music director of both the Metropolitan Opera and the New York Philharmonic.

As a New York area resident, Bristow also would have been fully aware of Antonín Dvořák's 1892 arrival in the city to direct Jeannette Thurber's National Conservatory of Music. A few months into his term as director, Dvořák shocked American musicians by suggesting publicly that US composers should use "negro melodies" as the basis for developing a national style, or school, of composition. His comments generated discussion throughout the United States and Europe for several months. Although there is no evidence that Bristow published his opinions on the matter, Brooklyn writers rushed to his defense and pointed out that he had already developed a national style in his Fourth and Fifth Symphonies.[73]

Prior to Dvořák's arrival, Bristow had indeed been working on one of his most ambitious compositions to date: a four-movement choral symphony called "Niagara." He completed the work in 1893—the same year as the Dvořák discussion in the press—but it was not premiered until 1898, the year of Bristow's death. Seidl, who was slated to direct the piece in a Manuscript Society concert, died unexpectedly just days before the performance. Bristow himself, now seventy-three years of age, had to take over direction of both the chorus and the orchestra at the final rehearsals and concert after preparing only the chorus earlier.

The structural plan of the "Niagara" symphony is conventional except for the choral finale, whose scope is closer to the finale of Mendelssohn's Second Symphony ("Lobgesang") than to that of Beethoven's Ninth, another obvious inspiration. The first movement of Bristow's symphony is in a broad sonata-allegro form and begins with an unaccompanied trombone call. As the call dies away, tremolo strings quietly enter the texture and support a foreboding C minor melody in the cellos and basses. As the theme concludes, the entire orchestra begins to appear with swells, scalar passages, and chromatic motion evoking the waterfall's roughness. These gestures recur throughout the movement and eventually build into a glorious C major coda that closes with tremendous force. The second movement, a lilting adagio in 12/8, gathers emotional intensity with complex rhythms and chromaticism but fades gently to nothingness after a brief climax.

Following a path he had taken in the "Arcadian" symphony, Bristow approached the third movement with a spirit of innovation. As some of the commentary surrounding Dvořák's music and ideas suggested, Bristow attempted to construct an American-sounding style in this movement and called it a "breakdown"—a reference to vernacular dance. Cast as a rondolike scherzo, the movement alternates between statements of a fiery main theme reminiscent of the devilish style in the finales of Liszt's *Faust* symphony (1857) and Hector Berlioz's *Symphonie fantastique* (1830) and lyrical contrasting themes that draw from the melodic and harmonic vocabulary of hymnody and fiddle tunes. In one passage, Bristow directly quoted "Near the Lake Where Drooped the Willow" (1837), a parlor ballad that Charles E. Horn (1786–1849) had adapted from a well-known nostalgic song called "Long, Long Time Ago."[74]

The finale, however, is the most distinctive movement of all. It comprises six numbered sections that include solo arias, duets, and choruses with intervening passages for the full orchestra; a schoolteacher and amateur poet named Charles Walker Lord supplied the text (see table 2.8). Bristow employed overt quotations of familiar music throughout the finale, including the hymn tune "Old Hundredth" and the "Hallelujah Chorus" from Handel's *Messiah*. Rounding out the entire symphony, it closes with a glorious reconfiguration of the materials from the first movement that evoked the awesome force of Niagara Falls.

Table 2.8 Numbers for the Choral Finale of Bristow's Symphony No. 5, "Niagara"

I. Maestoso, "Let ev'ry pow'r of heart and tongue"
II. Allegro, "Niagara! o'erwhelmed with awe and wonder"
III. Andante, "With reverence I bow, thy word believing"
IV. Allegro, "Superior, Huron, Michigan, and Erie"
V. Allegro furioso, "Ye rapids, sparkling, foaming, dashing, wildly"
VI. Allegro furioso, "Thou cataract, thou king, thou king of Nature's wonders"

Although it took place in Carnegie Hall, a venue built in 1891, the grand symphony's premiere in 1898 received scant notice in the press, though critic William Thoms, one of Bristow's longtime advocates in the press, had printed a preperformance description. Tensions with Spain over the sinking of the *USS Maine* dominated national headlines at the time. A writer for the *New York World* remarked briefly, however, that the symphony was a piece of "substantial merit deserving of further consideration." A correspondent to the *Musical Courier* did not respond as kindly: *Niagara* "reminded me of the phrase: 'Sweetness long drawn out,' only with the sweetness omitted. In this the composer makes clever use of various ideas, but repeats and repeats to weariness."[75] The critic neglected to remark on the symphony's blatant patriotism. Thoms reprinted his analytical description to honor Bristow's death, but the symphony was never performed again.[76]

Despite his compositional productivity over nearly half a century, Bristow has been remembered primarily for his courageous stand against the New York Philharmonic early in his career. For that reason, several music historians have perpetuated the myth that the younger John Knowles Paine's First Symphony (1876), which is discussed in the next chapter, was the first American work in the classical tradition to garner widespread recognition.[77] Even so, interest in Bristow's music developed rapidly in the second half of the twentieth century and is reaching new highs in the opening decades of the twenty-first.

The German American conductor Karl Krueger (1894–1979) recorded Bristow's Second, Third, and Fourth Symphonies with the Royal Philharmonic Orchestra for the Society for the Preservation of the American Musical Heritage; to date these LP records have not been rereleased in contemporary formats. Scholar Delmer Rogers assisted with the preservation of Bristow's music manuscripts, now held at the New York Public Library for the Performing Arts, in the 1960s; the library acquired further valuable materials related to Bristow's life and career in 2010. Under the direction of Rebecca Miller, the Royal Northern Sinfonia recorded Bristow's Second Symphony, "Jullien," for New World Records using the contemporary critical edition prepared by Katherine K. Preston. And, in recent years, Bristow and his music have been the subject of several doctoral dissertations (including a critical edition of the fourth movement of the "Niagara" symphony, prepared by Tim Cloeter), as well as a comprehensive biography by Preston.[78] The New York Philharmonic, meanwhile, has not performed any of Bristow's music since it gave the local premiere of his Fourth Symphony in 1874, enabling a professional training ensemble called Orchestra Now, directed by Leon Botstein, to resurrect it at Carnegie Hall in 2021 using an edition prepared by composer Kyle Gann.

William Henry Fry (1813–64)

Unlike the other antebellum symphonists profiled here, William Henry Fry did not pursue an exclusively musical career. The son of a newspaper printer and editor in Philadelphia, he became a journalist in his twenties and would continue to write for newspapers until his death in 1864. Fry's first assignments included writing concert reviews for his father's paper, and music criticism became a lifelong vocation. During this early period, Fry also took composition lessons with Leopold Meignen, the French émigré who helped establish Philadelphia's amateur Philharmonic Society and who would later become chief conductor of the Musical Fund Society. Under Meignen's tutelage, Fry began composing overtures, at least one of which won a Philharmonic Society contest.

But opera, not orchestral music, proved to be Fry's compositional lodestar. After failing to produce his first opera, *Aurelia the Vestal*, Fry and his brother Joseph staged a lavish production of Vincenzo Bellini's *Norma* that included Joseph's translation of the libretto. It was so successful during its initial run in 1841 that they staged it again in New York City a year later. Building on this success, they produced their next original opera, *Leonora*, in 1845. It was the first full-length opera written in the grand Italian style (with accompanied recitatives) by a US-born creative team. Most critics greeted it warmly, and, in the preface to a published piano-vocal reduction, Fry argued incisively for the cultivation of an American school of composition founded on English-language operas.[79]

Fry also developed a special interest in the symphony when Meignen's *Symphonie militaire* premiered just a few weeks before *Leonora*. He was so moved by the performance that he reflected at length on the work's importance for musical life in the United States. "We may, and must, import true models from Europe," he wrote, "but taking as our standard the recognized excellence or perfection of the masters in Art of that country, we must then originate, re-create, and accord our derived taste and skill to the genius of our own hemisphere. . . . Every work like that of the symphony in question, being produced here by an American citizen, is a national work."[80] Fry urged his readers to support Meignen and artists like him to keep the United States from becoming a "beggarly, cent-per-cent, money-grubbing concern."

Hoping to find support for his compositional career in Europe, Fry left for Paris the following summer and would stay there until 1852. Shortly after his arrival, he began sending correspondence to the *Philadelphia Public Ledger* and reported on a variety of political and cultural affairs, including the 1848 revolutions. Later during his European residency, Fry also began to correspond with the *New York Tribune*, a leading daily, and the *Message Bird*, one of the New York City music magazines that had helped to stoke the flames of the early conflict between Bristow and the New York Philharmonic roughly a year earlier. The opportunity to write these voluminous letters allowed Fry to develop and articulate a philosophy of music akin to the writers of Young America, who wished to create a national literary style. According to Fry, art music would continue to flourish only within an American-style democracy, since the cost of an autocratic regime was simply too great to bear. And any new musical style must reflect the country's democratic ethos.[81]

Fry put his theories into practice upon his return to the United States in 1852, when he staged an extensive series of lectures on the history and theory of music at New York's Metropolitan Hall that featured live performances from vocal soloists, instrumental groups, and even an orchestra conducted by George Frederick Bristow.[82] At the final lecture, Fry presented a vision of a musical future with some of his own works—including a symphony—and an excerpt from Bristow's First. Fry eagerly expressed his desire for public support of American composers so that the country might be recognized as an international leader in music. Responses to the lecture series were mixed, and Fry engaged in a heated discussion with critics Richard Storrs Willis and John Sullivan Dwight about the value of bringing out new music, particularly by Americans. While they were not opposed to the effort, both Willis and Dwight agreed that new music should never supplant works by the so-called masters.[83]

The matter was dropped until Louis Antoine Jullien arrived in New York and began programming the works of both Fry and Bristow. As we saw earlier, Fry's review of Bristow's music opened a new chapter in the brewing press firestorm about the Philharmonic's lack of support for American composers. But the controversy that ensued during the 1853–54 concert season also revolved around Fry's latest work, *Santa Claus: Christmas Symphony*. The exchange between Fry and Willis, which concerned Fry's dogged advocacy of programmatic instrumental music, lasted for several weeks before Bristow's entry into the discussion turned the attention back to the Philharmonic. The controversy, explained in more detail later, anticipated the better-known aesthetic debates between Eduard Hanslick, who favored abstract instrumental music, and Franz Liszt, who had pioneered the genre of the symphonic poem and had even coined the term "program music."

After Jullien's departure, Fry's compositional productivity wavered while his activity as a writer and political speaker intensified. Between 1854 and his death a decade later, his only important works were two overtures and a second grand opera, *Notre Dame of Paris*, which premiered in Philadelphia in 1864 under the baton of Theodore Thomas, who had played violin in the New York Philharmonic and Jullien's orchestra during its New York residency.[84] In the meantime, Fry had also become a promoter of the new Republican Party and actively stumped for Abraham Lincoln during the 1860 election cycle. President Lincoln later rewarded him

Table 2.9 The Symphonies of William Henry Fry (1813–64)

Title and date	Movements	Instrumentation	Comments
The Breaking Heart (1852–53)	Adagio sostenuto	Grand + Tuba	Manuscript bears the title *Adagio sostenuto*.
			Written and performed as an illustration for a lecture series Fry gave on the history of music in New York in the winter of 1852–53.
			Performed by Jullien's orchestra in New York in 1854. A program for that performance suggests that the work captures the scene of a young woman dying of heartbreak in a cathedral.
			Unpublished.
			Recorded by the Royal Scottish National Orchestra, conducted by Tony Rowe, on Naxos 8.559057.
A Day in the Country (1852–53)	I. Adagio II. Allegro non tanto III. Meno mosso—andante sostenuto	Grand (1 Bssn. only) + Perc.	Written and performed as part of the same lecture series as *The Breaking Heart*. Performed also by Jullien's orchestra in 1854.
			Programmatic work depicting a village festival from morning to sunset.
			Unpublished.
Santa Claus: Christmas Symphony (1853)	See table 2.10	Grand + Picc., Sopsax., 2 Tpt., 2 Cor., Perc. (Tri., Cym., BD, SD, Tubular Bell, Sleigh Bells, Whip)	Written for Jullien's orchestra. First performance: Christmas Eve, 1853, by Jullien's orchestra, conducted by Louis Antoine Jullien.
			Fry's very detailed program for the symphony is reprinted in Upton/FRY, pp. 335–38.
			Score is published in *American Orchestral Music, 1800 through 1879*, ed. Sam Dennison (Boston: G. K. Hall, 1992).
			Recorded by the Royal Scottish National Orchestra, conducted by Tony Rowe, on Naxos 8.559057.
Childe Harold (1854)			First performance in 1854 by Jullien's Orchestra, in New York City. The score is lost. According to a review, the work gave a leading role to the saxophone.

Niagara (1854)	Largo assai, grave	Grand + Picc., Cbssn., Tuba, Ophicleide, Bombardons, 4 Timp., 2–5, Drums (1 Flt. only)	Vivid musical depiction of Niagara Falls. Not performed in the composer's lifetime. Unpublished. Recorded by the Royal Scottish National Orchestra, conducted by Tony Rowe, on Naxos 8.559057.
Sacred Symphony No. 3—Hagar in the Wilderness (1854)	Largo	2 Flt., 2 Ob., Clar., Sax., Bssn., Timp., Strgs.	Unperformed.
The Dying Soldier (undated)	Largo	Picc., 1 Flt., 2 Ob., 1 Clar., Sopsax., 2 Bssn., 4 Hr., 3 Tpt., 2 Trom., Btrom., Euph., Tuba, Timp., Perc. (BD, SD, Cym.), Strgs.	Based on an unpublished art song by Fry, a dying soldier's last wish is that his slaves should be freed. Unperformed.

with a diplomatic assignment in Italy. But Fry, having contracted tuberculosis during the election season, had to decline the appointment because of his failing health. He died on the island of Santa Cruz (now St. Croix in the Virgin Islands) a few months after the premiere of *Notre Dame of Paris*.[85]

Fry was stylistically progressive in his instrumental music and believed that the standard four-movement template of the symphony was outmoded. Hoping to replace the four-movement convention, he wrote symphonies with evocative titles that suggest pictorial or narrative themes (table 2.9). Like Berlioz's *Symphonie fantastique* and other progressive symphonies of the age, most of his works of this sort were also accompanied by an explanatory synopsis distributed to listeners or proclaimed from the stage at performances. In the preface to *Leonora*, Fry had asserted that "the chief interest of all instrumental music . . . lies in the dramatic expression derived originally from the universal lyrical delineations of the stage." He held fast to this belief in his own work and wrote seven symphonies that translated the drama of opera into a purely instrumental idiom.

THE BREAKING HEART AND A DAY IN THE COUNTRY

Fry wrote his first two symphonies, *The Breaking Heart* and *A Day in the Country*, to use as illustrations in his lecture series given at Metropolitan Hall during the winter of 1852–53. He revised them for Jullien's orchestra the following autumn. In both works, Fry experimented with instrumental music's capacity to depict or represent nonmusical objects, ideas, and stories—the theory he developed in the preface to *Leonora*.

The Breaking Heart does not appear to tell a story but instead captures the emotional content of a scene, as in a painted still-life portrait. A program for an 1854 performance gave the following cryptic synopsis:

> Scene—A Cathedral—"Unrequited Affection." Adagio Passionate Choral—"Angel Whispers." Agitato—"Sad Musings,"—"Spirit Wanderings,"—"Lament—Despair;" the Heroine falls at the foot of the altar, as the organ peals forth with the last pulsations of "The Breaking Heart."

Although there is no extant manuscript with the title *The Breaking Heart*, a score found in Fry's manuscripts, labeled *Adagio sostenuto*, loosely matches the trajectory found in the printed synopsis.

The symphony opens with a pulsing eight-bar introduction that establishes the tonic of A-flat major; the pulsations, in 12/8, represent a beating heart. The introduction leads directly to an arialike melody, given in the first violins, that symbolizes a young woman alone in a cathedral (example 2.9). The pulsating gesture returns and elongates the melody but is rudely interrupted by bleating fortissimo unisons played by the entire orchestra—presumably the "unrequited affection" of the synopsis. This unsettled section moves quickly to a horn and trombone chorale that is repeated by the full orchestra after a brief intervening section. The pulsing eventually returns but is accompanied by rapid scales in the woodwinds and lower strings, perhaps representing the "angel whispers."

The character of the symphony changes dramatically as the initial arialike melody becomes deformed into the minor mode. Before the melody finishes, it leads into a passage marked "agitato"—the only point in the score that clearly aligns with Fry's synopsis. The melody eventually returns to its original shape, this time in E major. Scored for bassoon and low strings, it takes on the quality of "sad musings" in the new context. A modulation back to A-flat major

The First Generation of Symphonists in the United States

Example 2.9 Fry, *Breaking Heart*, Aria-like Melody

ushers in a restatement of the melody given by the oboe, which is accompanied by a flitting solo flute suggestive of "spirit wanderings." The only true secondary melody appears in the following section, and, as before, Fry's scoring for bassoon, viola, and cello grants it a plaintive and particularly Italianate quality. A pulsating diminished chord played by the entire orchestra interrupts this melody, and the beating heart finally stops as a rhythmically augmented version of the heroine's motif signals that she has fallen at the altar. The organ, here represented by trombones, horns, and bassoons, concludes the work with soft and somber chords.

Unlike *The Breaking Heart*, Fry's *A Day in the Country* contains a detailed narrative plot. A description in the extant manuscript explains that the work depicts a village festival from morning to sunset. The element of passing time added narrative depth to Fry's approach in *The Breaking Heart*, which remains static. As in the earlier work, though, several distinct sections, or "movements," flow from one to the next without pause.

The first section, marked Adagio, depicts the sunrise, complete with bird calls given by a bassoon, trumpet, and clarinet. A beautiful Italianate "hymn to nature," scored for four horns, is one of the most striking moments in Fry's *oeuvre* (example 2.10). After the full orchestra restates the hymn, the opening section blends seamlessly into a rustic 6/8 dance in E-flat. The

Example 2.10 Fry, *Day in the Country*, Hymn to Nature

music stops and starts as "the lads and lassies in their best array are about to join the dance." The dance grinds to a halt, however, with the entrance of a somber tune in the low woodwinds and strings that depicts "the jealous pangs of a disappointed swain." Undeterred by his grumblings, the villagers soon resume their dancing. As the sun sets, a group of soldiers arrives, and the symphony closes with an even more boisterous tune sounded by a trombone and the cellos.

Critics enjoyed the work when a full orchestra performed it during a part of Fry's lecture devoted to the rudiments of music. But the tenor of their discussions would change significantly after Jullien revived it. Fry's program note indicated that "symphonies have usually four distinct, and musically disconnected, movements, so that each of them can be given as a separate piece, which is often done. This symphony, however, is so composed, that the different movements are all connected, making an unbroken musical discourse."[86] Focusing on this structural aspect of the piece, critics disagreed with one another about the viability of Fry's approach. Only Charles Burkhardt, a writer for *The Albion*, gave his full support: "we look upon [the piece] in an aesthetic point of view as a cheering sign, indicative of *progress* in the right direction, of an attempt to throw off the shackles of the time-honored conservatism and scientific legitimacy, which have sat brooding, like ill-omened birds, over every attempt to develop, by the extended resources of art, the new ideas of the age." Fry had clearly found an aesthetic ally.[87]

SANTA CLAUS: CHRISTMAS SYMPHONY

The conversation about aesthetic "progress" would continue after Jullien premiered Fry's magnum opus, *Santa Claus*, on Christmas Eve, 1853. Cast in a series of uninterrupted vignettes, the form of *Santa Claus* closely follows the detailed synopsis presented to audiences at performances (see table 2.10). The synopsis also indicates that Fry wrote the work with Jullien's individual performers in mind. Concerning the Largo movement (IV), for example, Fry wrote, "Of all the instruments it was lately conceded that the most melancholy is the Violoncello, but the genius of M. [Giovanni] Bottesini having elevated Double Violoncello or Double Bass to the rank of a solo instrument, sombre pathos yet unachieved in the history of instrumental art can be depicted by this great master of expression. The woe and wail of the Perishing Traveler are therefore entrusted to this Double-Bass player."[88]

Critics even wondered whether the piece could survive Jullien's departure, since its style was tailored so closely to the performers themselves. Questions of performance aside, *Santa Claus* is a tour de force in narrative symphonic writing, as every detail of the score appears to match elements in the synopsis.

The symphony opens with brassy fanfares that represent the heavenly host of angels announcing the "glad tidings of the Saviour's coming birth." That section is followed immediately by a cantabile line for a solo cornet that would transfer well into an operatic context; its Italianate melodic trappings are supported by the marking "colla parte" throughout the score. After a repetition of the cornet tune sounded by the full orchestra, a difficult clarinet cadenza brings the scene from heaven to earth, where villagers dance at a Christmas Eve celebration. Scotch snaps grant the melody a particularly rustic quality that matches the analogous scene in *A Day in the Country*. Windy snow flurries, represented by rapid and high chromatic passages in the violins, briefly interrupt the festivities, but the dancing (preceded by the cadenza) resumes before the villagers head home.

The character of the symphony changes as the scene moves indoors. In an unusual gesture, reminiscent of the finale of Beethoven's Ninth (as well as an analogous passage in Meignen's *Symphonie militaire*), the new section begins with an instrumental recitative in the upper strings that follows the traditional English translation of the *Pater noster* prayer (i.e., "Our father, who art in heaven, . . ."—the Lord's Prayer). A lilting lullaby "sung" by a solo saxophone—one of the first uses of the instrument in the context of the full orchestra—immediately follows the prayer. At the conclusion of the lullaby, the winter storm returns in full force, and the double bass solo described earlier enters, depicting a homeless vagrant dying in the cold before a clock tower strikes midnight. At the stroke of midnight, Santa Claus appears in

Table 2.10 The Structure of Fry's *Santa Claus: Christmas Symphony*

    I. Andante maestoso—Heaven; choirs of angels
  IIa. Allegro non troppo—Christmas dance
  IIb. Moderato assai e grazioso—Joy of homecoming after absence
  IIc. Allegro–allegro non troppo—Snowstorm; reprise of the dance
  III. Andante sostenuto—Domestic evening rituals
  IV. Largo grave—Snowstorm; death of vagrant
   V. Allegro non tanto—Arrival of Santa Claus
  VI. Finale: Allegro—Adeste fideles: "Choral" Finale

the form of a jolly solo bassoon melody accompanied by sleigh bells, pizzicato strings, and a wooden slapstick to create the sound of a whip.

The finale is also reminiscent of Beethoven's Ninth Symphony. It begins with the quiet introduction of the Christmas hymn "Adeste fideles" played *tremolando* in the upper strings; this gesture parallels Beethoven's soft introduction of the "An die Freude" in the cellos. Rather than work the theme into a series of variations, however, Fry interrupts it sharply by shifting the scene to children waking up on Christmas morning and finding their toys, here represented by toy instruments such as rattles, whistles, and trumpets. After a brief transition, the full orchestra returns with a resounding rendition of "Adeste fideles" that thrilled Fry's original audiences.

Critics were much more lukewarm. Charles Burkhardt, Fry's erstwhile ally, called it a "capital musical Christmas piece" but felt that its style did not befit the title of symphony. Richard Storrs Willis agreed. It was a "good Christmas piece," he thought, "but hardly a composition to be gravely criticized like an earnest work of Art." Both Burkhardt and Willis liked *Santa Claus*, but they were not willing to accept Fry's claim that it should be called a symphony.[89] Fry had different ideas about the piece's worth and seriousness. Fresh off his tirade against the New York Philharmonic, he responded bitterly to Burkhardt's and Willis's blithe dismissals by writing a letter to Willis that, when published, occupied nearly four full pages of his magazine.

During the next several weeks, Willis and Fry went back and forth over the true definition of a symphony. Should it have four movements? Could it depict scenes and stories? Did it need unity across movements? And did any of this matter for the future of American music? Fry, the progressive, was a lone voice in the desert against conservatives such as Willis and John Sullivan Dwight, who eventually entered the fray. Willis condescendingly explained, "To call [*Santa Claus*] a symphony, where terms have, among artists, so definite a signification, is like calling a cat a dog, or a house a barn. You can do so, but nobody will understand you."[90] Fry retorted that he had "discovered in musical composition the falsity of some old modes and the processes of correcting them." And, despite being such a leader of "original American Art," he claimed that "my discovery is denied and I am held up to ridicule by the only journals devoted in this country to musical art."[91] When the aesthetic discussion came to a standstill in the subsequent weeks, Bristow threw his hat into the ring with renewed accusations of anti-Americanism in the ranks of the Philharmonic.[92]

CHILDE HAROLD AND *NIAGARA*

Fry, meanwhile, wrote at least three (and possibly four) more of his narrative "symphonies" in the months following the *Santa Claus* premiere: *Childe Harold*, *Niagara*, and *Hagar in the Wilderness*. Though Jullien performed it in 1854, the score for *Childe Harold* does not survive. If Jullien took the manuscript with him to London, it is possible that it burned in the Covent Garden fire of 1856. In any case, extant reviews of the piece indicate that it was conceptually similar to Fry's previous works. As the title suggests, Lord Byron's epic poem *Childe Harold* inspired the symphony, and the reviews reveal that the third stanza of the third canto was the precise source. Byron's verse certainly aligns with the seriousness of purpose that colored Fry's earlier works. (It is unclear whether Fry knew Berlioz's *Harold en Italie* [1834], which is also based on Byron's verse.)

According to an especially detailed review of the symphony by Theodore Hagen, a saxophone served "as the impersonation of the *Childe* or *Knight* Harold of the middle ages—the instruments of Blondel, perchance—and renders songs of chivalric lorn love better than any other wind instrument." And, after "stormy passages" for the bass section, "the piece ends with some farther outworkings, where the highest notes of the violins dialogue with the deepest notes of the bassoons, the whole vanishing in upper harmonics"—the "baseless fabric of a vision." Fry had used each of these techniques in earlier works but refashioned them in new combinations that led Hagen to claim that the symphony "will take high rank as a first-class composition, and in time be classed among the classics of the art."[93]

Niagara exhibits several of the same qualities. Fry finished it early in 1854, probably with the hope that Jullien's orchestra would perform it at the so-called Musical Congress, a large festival held at New York's Crystal Palace in June. The opening concert at the Congress included a performance of *The Breaking Heart*, but Fry did not manage to secure a reading of *Niagara* at any point during the festival. Even though it was never performed, the score survives, and it is perhaps the most vivid pictorial symphony in Fry's *oeuvre*.

The symphony is divided into three parts, the third of which is a wholesale repetition of the first. It opens with four timpani rolling softly on a diminished seventh sonority. They are soon joined by tremolo strings, low brass, and bassoons that move the harmony to a G dominant seventh as they gather intensity. By the time they reach a *forte* dynamic, the chords resolve brilliantly as the entire orchestra resounds with a C major triad. Representing the billowing foam of the waterfall, the orchestra then moves through a series of major triads that ends once again on a sustained G major. This time, however, the resolution of the dominant marks the beginning of a majestic tune given by the entire complement of woodwind and brass instruments. Drawing once again from his operatic background, Fry harmonized the tune with subtle traces of the Italian bel canto repertoire—mild chromaticism and juicy appoggiaturas (example 2.11).

Example 2.11 Fry, *Niagara*, Majestic Tune

Once the tune concludes, the strings take over with rapid arpeggiated figurations outlining a diminished seventh that dissolve into equally rapid chromatic undulations that represent the movement of the water. The woodwinds and low brass soon join the strings in this gesture, and the first section of the symphony closes with the entire orchestra sustaining a dissonant chord that fades to silence. The brief B section introduces a quiet hymnlike melody in the flutes, trumpets, and first violins that is harmonized by the full orchestra. The B section is repeated before a brief transition reintroduces the billowing foam and the A section returns. Had New Yorkers heard the piece given by Jullien's large ensemble, they would have had no trouble imagining the grandeur of Niagara Falls. But it is striking that both Fry and Bristow, albeit nearly forty years apart, chose this magnificent natural phenomenon as the basis for pieces that exhibited some of their most idiosyncratic musical ideas.[94]

THE DYING SOLDIER AND HAGAR IN THE WILDERNESS

Fry's other symphonies, *The Dying Soldier* (n.d.) and *Hagar in the Wilderness* (1854), are essentially orchestral songs without words. In the former case, an unpublished art song called "The

Dying Soldier," available in Fry's manuscripts, serves as the melodic foundation for the symphony. The tune itself appears in whole or in fragments among a wide array of instruments, including the soprano saxophone, flute, woodwind choir, euphonium, first violins, and trumpet. Each statement of the song is sandwiched between dramatic episodes that feature a wide timbral palette. *Hagar in the Wilderness* is structured in a similar way, though there is no known source for the melody that recurs throughout the symphony. Why Fry chose these subjects for symphonic treatment is unclear, but the fourth stanza of "The Dying Soldier" offers a clue:

> Oh, if thou pray'st, pray not for me,
> But for each breathing slave;
> 'Tis better far, not living free,
> To perish with the brave!

Fry was an ardent antislavery advocate who published a treatise in 1860 that argued for its eventual dissolution. "The Dying Soldier" captures this sentiment, as does the story of Hagar, the Old Testament slave whom God protected after she and her son Ishmael were banished by her owner, Sarah, the wife of Abraham. Despite their political potency, there is no extant evidence that audiences heard either of these symphonies in performance.

∽

Like George Fredrick Bristow, Fry is remembered today primarily for his ardent defense of American composers during his 1853 lecture series and the controversy ensuing the premiere of *Santa Claus* later that year. Political historians have virtually ignored his contributions to New York politics and the cause of antislavery during the period leading up the Civil War. Even so, justice for Fry was served in 1959, when conductor and Columbia professor Howard Shanet (1918–2006) gave the New York Philharmonic premiere of *Santa Claus* at one of the orchestra's Young People's Concerts. Looking back on the event, critic Harold Schonberg remarked that the symphony is "mad and it's bad—so bad that it is actually wonderful, and it should be part of New York's Christmas festivities year after year after year."[95] Although no orchestra has followed Schonberg's suggestion, the Royal Scottish National Orchestra and conductor Tony Rowe recorded high-quality performances of *Santa Claus* and two other Fry symphonies (*Niagara* and *The Breaking Heart*) for Naxos Records in 1999 (catalog number 8.559057). Under the direction of Robin Fountain, the Vanderbilt University Orchestra presented the contemporary premiere of *Day in the Country* in 2021 with an edition prepared by Julia Moss and Douglas Shadle.

Louis Moreau Gottschalk (1829–69)

The career of Louis Moreau Gottschalk, one of the most famous pianists of the nineteenth century, began to intersect with those of Anthony Philip Heinrich, George Frederick Bristow, and William Henry Fry when he returned from Europe in 1853, the year of Louis Antoine Jullien's orchestral concert tour. There is no evidence that Gottschalk was involved in the Philharmonic controversy, but he later gave his support to an organization devoted to American composers that Charles Jerome Hopkins (1836–98), a young pianist from Vermont who had recently arrived in New York, established in response. Over the next fifteen years, Gottschalk toured throughout the Western Hemisphere, including the United States, the Caribbean islands, and South America, where he was an especially beloved figure.

Table 2.11 The Symphonies of Louis Moreau Gottschalk (1829–69)

Title and date	Movements	Instrumentation	Comments
Symphonie romantique: La nuit des tropiques (1858–59)	I. "La nuit des tropiques" (Andante) II. "Une fête sous les tropiques: Fiesta criolla" (Allegro moderato)	Picc., 2 Flt., 2 Ob., E♭Clar., 4 Clar., 2 Bssn., Barsax., 4 Hr., Barhr., 3 Tpt., 2 Trom., Tuba, Timp., Afro-Cuban Perc. ensemble, Strgs.	Premiered at a musical festival in Havana, Cuba, February 1860, with the ensemble conducted by the composer. Score published in an edition by Gaylen Hatton, who reconstructed and orchestrated the last 36 measures, which are missing in the full score (New York: Boosey and Hawkes, 1965). An arrangement for two pianos by John Kirkpatrick is also available. Critical edition by Laura Moore Pruett forthcoming from A-R Editions.
À Montevideo: 2me Symphonie-romantique pour grand orchestre (1868)	I. Andante II. Presto III. Maestoso	Full + Picc., 2 Trom., Oph.	The third movement incorporates the Uruguayan national anthem but also prominently features "Yankee Doodle" and "Hail, Columbia!" First performance at a festival in Montevideo, Uruguay, November 1869, with the ensemble conducted by the composer. Critical edition by Laura Moore Pruett forthcoming from A-R Editions.

Unlike most musicians of the day, Gottschalk participated directly in political arenas, especially in South America. His memoirs exhibit his deep interest in the well-being of the newly formed republics, and he raised money for local organizations that supported progressive causes such as public education and care for orphans. He also believed strongly in music's ability to serve as an agent of ennoblement for individuals and communities. In an essay written for the *Atlantic Monthly*, which was later reprinted in his memoirs, he explained that there are listeners "who recognize in the artist the privileged instrument of a moral and civilizing influence; who appreciate art because they derive from it pure and ennobling inspirations; [and] who respect it because it is the highest expression of human thought, aiming at the absolute ideal." In both of Gottschalk's surviving symphonies, he attempted to lead his listeners to this ideal (table 2.11).[96]

SYMPHONIE ROMANTIQUE: LA NUIT DES TROPIQUES

Gottschalk embarked on a six-year tour of the Caribbean in 1856 that included stops in Cuba, Puerto Rico, Martinique, and Guadeloupe. The period was especially fertile for him in that he found boundless compositional inspiration in the vernacular musical styles he encountered on the Caribbean islands. Along his tour, Gottschalk would occasionally mount large festivals that featured his music and included dozens, if not hundreds, of local performers. It was for one of these festivals, mounted in Havana, Cuba, that Gottschalk wrote his first extant symphony, *Symphonie romantique: La nuit des tropiques* (1858–59), or *The Night in the Tropics*, as it is commonly known in English translation.[97]

Gottschalk began composing *The Night in the Tropics* while living in the village of Matouba on the island of Guadeloupe in the French Antilles. It consists of two movements, an Andante in 6/8 and a raucous finale marked "Allegro moderato." The first movement, from which the symphony derives its name, paints a stunning portrait of Gottschalk's tropical paradise. It opens with lazy pulsations in the French horns and low strings that support a breezy melody in the first violins, which is later taken up by the violas. As in several passages by William Henry Fry, this moment is reminiscent of Berlioz's music; both Fry and Gottschalk had lived in Paris for extended periods and likely encountered Berlioz's music there, but we have no evidence suggesting any direct influence.

A cantabile tune played by a cornet eventually intrudes on the peaceful atmosphere but is soon interrupted by agitation in the upper winds signaling the arrival of storm winds. Shortly thereafter, the low strings enter the texture with a brooding melody in C minor that suggests the rumble of thunder. As the storm reaches its climax, this melody returns gloriously in E-flat major as the full complement of brass instruments joins the low strings. Once the storm has passed, the cornet melody returns to the accompaniment of tremolos in the upper register of the violins. It sounds as if dawn has broken and the rain-soaked tropical forest shimmers in sunlight (example 2.12).

The second movement, called *Une fête sous les tropiques* (A Festival in the Tropics), contrasts sharply with the pictorialism of the first. For the Havana festival where the symphony premiered, Gottschalk secured the services of an Afro-Cuban drumming ensemble from Santiago to add the distinct local color of the *tumba francesca* tradition to the large gathering of instrumentalists. In addition to this specifically Cuban timbre, two rhythmic cells associated with Cuban dance—the *cinquillo* and the *habanera*—pervade the score.[98] The movement reaches several climactic moments that include combinations of these rhythms underneath soaring angular melodies in the upper strings and woodwinds. A tune reminiscent of Stephen Foster's

Example 2.12 Gottschalk, *Night in the Tropics*, I, Melodies

Example 2.13 Gottschalk, *Night in the Tropics*, II

"Camptown Races," complete with parlor-style accompaniment in the low strings, provides contrast partway through the movement. This tune blends seamlessly into a fugato section that draws from the rhythmic vitality of the opening. As the counterpoint draws to a close, the festiveness of the opening returns and the orchestra builds to a final climax (example 2.13).

Like Anthony Philip Heinrich, Gottschalk occasionally recycled musical material in new performance venues and adapted it to local taste. One of few extant reviews of *The Night in the Tropics* followed a performance in Santiago, Chile, in which Gottschalk had removed the second movement altogether, since he did not have access to a Cuban drumming ensemble and audiences might not have identified with the dance rhythms. The review, which was published in the United States, claimed that the music was "fresher and more clear than those of the eccentric 'musician of the future' [Richard Wagner] but equal to the works of the great 'Novator' as far as the instrumentation and novel effects were concerned." According to the reviewer, these effects were "most poetical and impressive" and left the audience spellbound.[99]

À MONTEVIDEO

Upon his return to the United States in 1862, Gottschalk found himself touring in a war-torn republic. An ardent supporter of the Union, the New Orleans–born pianist traveled throughout the northern states and earned great public acclaim. In the spring of 1865, he ventured west to California, where he was beset by a scandal that involved insinuations of impropriety with a young lady in San Francisco. The rumormongering eventually compelled Gottschalk to flee the country for South America, where he remained for the rest of his life.[100] When Gottschalk's travels through South America took him to Montevideo, Uruguay, in the autumn of 1868, he planned a series of extravagant concerts. As was his custom, he composed several new works for the festival, including an entirely new symphony, which is commonly called *À Montevideo* (1868) but, showing kinship with its predecessor, also bears the more official sounding subtitle of *2me symphonie romantique*.[101]

Unlike *The Night in the Tropics*, *À Montevideo* consists of three movements performed without pause (although the first and second are separated by a fermata). In the slow first movement (Andante), a languid and meandering melody alternating between the strings and woodwinds projects the tropical atmosphere of the earlier symphony. The second movement (Presto), by contrast, is rapid and light. The primary melody is mildly reminiscent of the conclusion of the overture to Jacques Offenbach's *Orphée aux enfers* (*Orpheus in the Underworld*), and the character of operetta persists throughout the movement. The rapid accompaniment figures in the movement bleed almost imperceptibly into the finale marked Maestoso, which begins with a statement of the Uruguayan national anthem. After a lengthy fantasia on the tune that closes with a rousing rendition given by the whole orchestra, Gottschalk introduced a direct quotation of "Hail Columbia," a national tune associated with the United States, which is followed by "Yankee Doodle" in the flutes. The symphony closes with the return of the opening line in the Uruguayan anthem and an appropriately pompous concluding phrase. Gottschalk never explained why he chose to include the American national tunes alongside the Uruguayan anthem, but their juxtaposition reflected his pan-American political ideals.

Gottschalk's two symphonies exhibit stylistic proclivities that he had developed in his earlier piano music. Local coloring figures prominently in works like *Le banjo* (1854–55) and *Souvenir de Porto Rico* (1857–58), while Gottschalk's patriotism was on full display in *Union* (1852–62), a virtuosic showpiece that combines quotations of "The Star-Spangled Banner," "Hail Columbia," and "Yankee Doodle." But it was in his symphonies that he was able to manifest the breadth of his coloristic imagination.

Through the efforts of pianist Jeanne Behrend (1911–88), Gottschalk's music, particularly the piano works, experienced a significant revival in the 1950s and 1960s. With momentum in his favor, Howard Shanet reconstructed *Night in the Tropics* and gave its New York premiere with the Columbia University Orchestra in 1955; he later revived the piece with the New York Philharmonic at a 1959 Young People's Concert that also featured William Henry Fry's *Santa Claus*. André Kostelanetz (1901–80), the Russian-born British conductor best known for his efforts to bring orchestral music to a broad public, performed Shanet's reconstruction with relative frequency during the Philharmonic's Leonard Bernstein and Pierre Boulez eras. Sensing the work's versatility, Kostelanetz programmed it alongside other American pieces or "exotic" work from areas outside Western Europe. None other than Leopold Stokowski (1882–1977) led the New York premiere of *À Montevideo* for the centenary of the composer's death in 1969. This performance fell on the heels of the work's ostensible US premiere given by the New Orleans Philharmonic-Symphony earlier that year. Recordings of both symphonies are now available on two collections—one released by VoxBox in 1990 with performances by the Vienna State Opera Orchestra and the Berlin Symphony Orchestra, and a second produced for Naxos by the Hot Springs (Arkansas) Festival Orchestra under the direction of Gottschalk advocate Richard Rosenberg.[102] Musicologist Laura Moore Pruett has prepared critical editions of both symphonies for the Music of the United States of America series published by A-R Editions, and the Reading (Pennsylvania) Symphony Orchestra gave the world premiere of Pruett's in-progress edition of *À Montevideo* in 2019.

Conclusion

With the relatively wide availability of recordings and performing editions of several works described in this chapter, as well as ongoing efforts to create scholarly critical editions of still others, the twenty-first century may yet become the first "golden age" of antebellum American symphonies. But, in a sense, this dawning will still come too late. Erasing the damage done to the legacies of these composers over the past century and a half will undoubtedly prove to be a difficult task should anyone attempt it.

As the next chapter explains, the center of gravity of American symphonic composition moved toward Boston in the decades after the Civil War. Composers there, many of whom were trained in Europe, entered new stylistic rivalries with younger generations of Europeans. Symphonists John Knowles Paine, George Whitefield Chadwick, and Amy Beach developed institutional relationships with the city's leading orchestra, the Boston Symphony, with much greater ease than their older New York counterparts, and achieved greater success in the public eye both during and after their lifetimes. With their own careers, reputations, and legacies at stake, they also did little to promote earlier American music; in certain cases, it seems clear that they barely knew of its existence.

Likewise, throughout the twentieth century, prominent musicians consistently downplayed the importance of the nineteenth-century composers to boost their own reputations as innovators and true musical patriots. Both Leonard Bernstein and Aaron Copland critiqued nineteenth-century symphonists like Paine and Chadwick on the grounds that they sounded too German. It seems likely that they knew few if any of the most colorful pieces described in this chapter. If they did, they cleverly chose to ignore it, to the detriment of the legacy of the earliest American symphonic repertoire.

Bibliographic Overview

The published literature on the antebellum American symphonic repertoire generally lacks the cohesion found in work on later generations of musicians. Most of this research has tended to focus on a single composer, city, or institution. But this level of focus has led to extraordinarily valuable depth in coverage. Broyles/MUSIC (on Boston), Butler/VOTARIES (on Charleston, South Carolina), Knouse/COLLEGIA (on Bethlehem, Pennsylvania), and Lawrence/STRONG (on New York City) are standard overviews of the important early musical centers along the Eastern Seaboard. Likewise, Newman/GOOD, Spitzer/AMERICAN, Swenson-Eldrige/MUSICAL, and Broyles/MUSIC offer detailed case studies of various American orchestras, both resident and touring. Though not cited directly in this essay, Howard Shanet's 1975 history of the New York Philharmonic (Shanet/PHILHARMONIC) is the most comprehensive source available on this institution.

Studies on individual composers cover an eclectic array of topics, from pure biographical coverage to analytical or hermeneutic interpretations of specific pieces. Anthony Philip Heinrich's zany life and music have inspired the most coverage, including Chmaj/HEINRICH, Gibbons/AUDUBON, Maust/SYMPHONIES, Heinrich/MASTODON, Broyles/MAVERICKS, and Upton/HEINRICH. Rogers/BRISTOW (though dated), Preston/JULLIEN, and Preston/BRISTOW offer the most comprehensive data about George Frederick Bristow. Upton/FRY and Lawrence/FRY are currently the best sources that focus specifically on William Henry Fry, and Starr/GOTTSCHALK is the standard biography of Louis Moreau Gottschalk. Finally, Swenson-Eldridge/HOMMANN is an outstanding biography of the cryptic composer Charles Hommann and offers further analytical insight into his orchestral works.

Building on the topical items described earlier in this overview, Von Glahn/SOUNDS, Shadle/SANTA, Preston/BRISTOW, and Shadle/ORCHESTRATING present more comprehensive portraits of musical life in the antebellum period. Von Glahn/SOUNDS connects pieces by Heinrich, Fry, and Bristow—all inspired by Niagara Falls—to the broader themes of democracy, manifest destiny, and an emerging sense of nationhood built on the vast natural landscape. Shadle/SANTA addresses William Henry Fry and George Frederick Bristow's controversy with the New York Philharmonic through the lens of transatlantic periodicals and networks of information exchange. Since Fry was composing in an idiom similar to innovative symphonic composers in France and the German-speaking lands, Laudon/DRAMATIC and Will/CHARACTERISTIC are strong supplemental sources for the European context of Fry's ideas; though uncited earlier, Mark Evan Bonds's monumental history of the idea of absolute music (2014) is another excellent supplement. Shadle/ORCHESTRATING is the first large-scale history of the antebellum symphonic repertoire. This resource demonstrates how the lives and music of Heinrich, Bristow, Fry, and Gottschalk became intertwined in the decades leading up to the Civil War and then how their legacies rapidly dissolved after the end of the nineteenth century. Finally, Preston/BRISTOW is the first deep exploration of the social, artistic, and economic circumstances surrounding journeyman musicians like George Frederick Bristow, who composed, taught, and performed throughout his career.

Primary sources for studying the antebellum American symphonic repertoire—both periodicals and archival documents—are abundantly available but not always easy to access. *Dwight's Journal of Music, Musical World and Times*, and *Saroni's Musical Times* are all accessible through Répertoire international de la presse musicale (RIPM), and the *Brooklyn Daily Eagle* is available for no charge on the World Wide Web; other important periodicals are stored in electronic or microfilm databases like the American Periodicals Series. Core archival materials like scores, diaries, and letters are available in research libraries in New York City (Bristow, Gottschalk), Philadelphia (Hommann, Fry), and Washington, DC (Heinrich).

Notes

1. Spitzer/AMERICAN, pp. 25–52.
2. Butler/VOTARIES.
3. Claypool/ARCHIVAL; Knouse/COLLEGIA. Knouse explains that a similar ensemble flourished during roughly the same period in the sister settlement of Salem, North Carolina.
4. Swenson-Eldridge/MUSICAL, pp. 23–26.
5. The surviving manuscripts are undated, but Swenson-Eldridge has reasoned that the work was probably composed in the mid-1820s; see Swenson-Eldridge/HOMMANN, p. lxi.
6. The full score is available in Swenson-Eldridge/HOMMANN.
7. Musical Fund Society Annual Report (1840), quoted in Swenson-Eldridge/HOMMANN, xlii.
8. On Boston, see Broyles/MUSIC, pp. 182–214.
9. On Meignen, Hommann, and the Musical Fund Society, see Swenson-Eldridge/MUSICAL and Swenson-Eldridge/HOMMANN.
10. On this repertoire, see Will/CHARACTERISTIC and Laudon/DRAMATIC.
11. "The Musical Fund Society," *Philadelphia Public Ledger*, April 17, 1845.
12. "Knaebel's National Concert," *Brooklyn Daily Eagle*, April 15 1851.
13. Constitution and By-Laws of the Philharmonic Society of New-York, Adopted April, 1843 (New York: Printed by S. W. Benedict, 1843).
14. Spitzer/AMERICAN, pp. 435–50.
15. "New York Philharmonic Society," *Message Bird*, November 15, 1850, p. 130; "The Philharmonic Society," *Saroni's Musical Times*, November 17, 1850, p. 88.
16. "Musical Season Over," *Saroni's Musical Times*, May 25, 1850, p. 411.
17. Dodworth, his father, and two of his brothers were founding members of the orchestra. "Founding of the Philharmonic," *American Art Journal*, July 5, 1879, p. 150; for a caveat on the reliability of this account, see Shanet/PHILHARMONIC, pp. 423–24.

18. Preston/JULLIEN, pp. xxxi–xxxv; Newman/GOOD.
19. "Art National and Art Universal," *Journal of the Fine Arts*, May 1, 1851, pp. 50–51.
20. Maust/SYMPHONIES, pp. 40–44.
21. "Music. Jullien," *New-York Daily Tribune*, October 14, 1853.
22. "A Letter from Mr. Fry," *Musical World and Times*, January 21, 1854, p. 29.
23. See Lawrence/FRY.
24. "The Philharmonic Society," *Musical World and Times*, March 4, 1854, p. 100.
25. "The Philharmonic Society," *Musical World and Times*, March 18, 1854, pp. 121–22; "The Philharmonic Again," *Musical World and Times*, March 25, 1854, p. 133; "Second Letter from Mr. Bristow," *Musical World and Times*, April 1, 1854, p. 148.
26. "Musicalische Zustände in den Vereinigten Staaten von Nordamerica. II," *Niederrheinische Musik-Zeitung für Kunstfreunde und Künstler*, April 15, 1854, p. 116.
27. "New York Philharmonic Society," *Dwight's Journal of Music*, March 11, 1854, pp. 181–82.
28. See also Lawrence/STRONG, pp. 2:479–94; Preston/JULLIEN, pp. lxx–lxxx; and Shadle/ORCHESTRATING, pp. 81–89.
29. [John Rowe Parker], "Criticism. The Dawning of Music in Kentucky," *Euterpiad*, April 13, 1822, p. 46.
30. See Shadle/ORCHESTRATING, pp. 36–44.
31. "Music," *Literary World*, April 30, 1853, p. 359.
32. Abendzeitung quoted in "A. P. Heinrich," *Dwight's Journal of Music*, March 23, 1861, p. 415.
33. "Weekly Report of Music. New York," *Musical World and Times*, April 30, 1853, p. 273.
34. Heinrich/DAWNING.
35. Library/REPORT, pp. 61–64.
36. Upton/HEINRICH; Chmaj/HEINRICH; Broyles/MAVERICKS, pp. 39–70.
37. See, for example, "Musical Chit-Chat," *Dwight's Journal of Music*, May 19, 1860, p. 63.
38. Gibbons/AUDUBON, p. 473.
39. Quoted in Upton/HEINRICH, p. 143.
40. Gibbons/AUDUBON, pp. 481–82.
41. Translations adapted from Upton/HEINRICH, p. 231.
42. Quoted in ibid., pp. 232–33.
43. "Feuilleton. Aus Prag im März," *Wiener Zeitung*, March 27, 1857, p. 277.
44. "Grand Farewell Concert of Anthony Philip Heinrich," *Musical World and Times*, December 18, 1852, p. 251.
45. Upton/HEINRICH, p. 230.
46. Shadle/ORCHESTRATING, pp. 118–19.
47. More than in the other works discussed here, the manuscript is in poor physical shape and the total number of movements is difficult to discern.
48. See the preface to Heinrich/MASTODON.
49. Rogers/BRISTOW, p. 71. Rogers states that Bristow's career with the Philharmonic ended in 1879, but extant programs show that he was still on the roster in 1882.
50. On Bristow's early career, see Preston/BRISTOW, pp. 3–19.
51. [Frederick Nicholls Crouch], "New York Philharmonic Society. Mr. Bristow's Symphony," *Message Bird*, June 15, 1850, p. 362.
52. [Frederick Nicholls Crouch], "Symphony in E-flat Major. Composed by Geo. F. Bristow," *Message Bird*, July 1, 1850, p. 377.
53. "Domestic Compositions," *Saroni's Musical Times*, June 1, 1850, p. 422; "Bristow versus Musical Times," *Saroni's Musical Times*, June 8, 1850, pp. 436.
54. "Jenny Lind's Concerts," *Saroni's Musical Times,* May 24, 1851, p. 91.
55. Preston/JULLIEN, p. lxviii.

56. "Musical News from Everywhere," *Musical World and Times*, January 7, 1854, pp. 5–6.
57. "The Philharmonic Society," *Musical World and Times*, March 8, 1856, p. 110.
58. "Musical. The Philharmonic Society," *New-York Daily Tribune*, March 3, 1856.
59. "Third Philharmonic Concert," *Musical Review and Gazette*, March 8, 1856, pp. 68–69.
60. "Musical Correspondence," *Dwight's Journal of Music*, March 8, 1856, p. 180.
61. "Music," *Frank Leslie's Illustrated Newspaper*, March 15, 1856, p. 215.
62. "M. Jullien's Concert at the Philharmonic Hall," *Manchester Times* (UK), February 14, 1855.
63. Advertisement, *New York Tribune*, March 5, 1859, p. 2.
64. Preston/BRISTOW, pp. 59–63.
65. The ordering of movements presented here matches the original performance; a 1993 recording of the piece (Neeme Järvi and Detroit Symphony Orchestra, Chandos) reversed the order of the inner two movements.
66. "The Philharmonic Society," *Musical World*, April 2, 1859, p. 210; "New York," *Dwight's Journal of Music*, April 2, 1859, p. 6; "Music in New York. Fourth Philharmonic Concert," *Musical Review and Gazette*, April 2, 1859, p. 99.
67. "Philharmonic," *Brooklyn Daily Eagle*, March 30, 1871; "The Philharmonic Concert," April 10, 1871.
68. "Concerning Music," *Brooklyn Daily Eagle*, October 4, 1872.
69. See Shadle/ORCHESTRATING, pp. 167–71.
70. "Philharmonic," *Brooklyn Daily Eagle*, January 14, 1873; "Philharmonic. The Society's New Symphony," *Brooklyn Daily Eagle*, January 16, 1873.
71. "Philharmonic. Seventy-Sixth Concert," *Brooklyn Daily Eagle*, February 10, 1873; "Amusements. Third Philharmonic Concert," *Brooklyn Daily Eagle*, February 10, 1873.
72. "Amusements. Philharmonic Rehearsal—Bristow's New Symphony," *New York Herald*, February 7, 1874; Musical Standard quoted in "Mr. Howard Glover on 'Lohengrin' 'The Musical Season in America' (meaning New York)," *Dwight's Journal of Music*, June 27 1874, p. 251.
73. Shadle/ORCHESTRATING, pp. 257–58.
74. Preston/BRISTOW, p. 145.
75. "Manuscript Society Concert," *New York World*, April 12, 1898; "Gotham Gossip," *Musical Courier*, April 20, 1898, p. 28.
76. See also Preston/BRISTOW, pp. 143–49.
77. On the historiographical reception of Paine, see Shadle/ORCHESTRATING, pp. 221–22.
78. Preston/BRISTOW.
79. Fry/LEONORA.
80. "Mr. Meignen's Concert," *Philadelphia Public Ledger*, April 21, 1845.
81. Shadle/ORCHESTRATING, pp. 63–66.
82. Preston/BRISTOW, pp. 26–28.
83. Lawrence/FRY.
84. Fry's Overture to MacBeth is available on a 2000 recording of Tony Rowe conducting the Royal Scottish National Orchestra (Naxos 8.559057).
85. For more on Fry's biography, see Upton/FRY.
86. Quoted in "Jullien's Benefit Concert," *Musical World and Times*, October 1, 1853, p. 34.
87. "Amusements," *New York Times*, October 1, 1853; Gemotice [James Otis], "Musical Notes," *Spirit of the Times*, September 24, 1853, p. 373; "Music," *Albion*, September 24, 1853, p. 464.
88. Reprinted in Upton/FRY, pp. 335–38.
89. "Music. Jullien's Concerts: Mr. Fry's New Symphony," *Albion*, December 31, 1853, p. 632; "Musical News from Everywhere. New York," *Musical World and Times*, January 7, 1854, p. 6.
90. "Reply to Mr. Fry, of the Tribune," *Musical World and Times*, January 28, 1854, p. 38.
91. "Rejoinder from Mr. Fry," *Musical World and Times*, February 18, 1854, p. 75.

92. For more on the controversy's specifics, see Shadle/SANTA and Preston/JULLIEN.
93. "Fry's New Symphony," *New York Musical Review*, June 8, 1854, p. 201.
94. See Von Glahn/SOUNDS, pp. 17–63.
95. Schonberg, "Sounds of Christmas: Messiah and More," *New York Times*, December 13, 1985.
96. Gottschalk/NOTES, 177; see also Shadle/ORCHESTRATING, pp. 144–46.
97. On the Caribbean tour, see Starr/GOTTSCHALK, pp. 257–309.
98. Baur/GROOVES.
99. "Correspondence," *American Art Journal*, September 27, 1866, p. 364.
100. Starr/GOTTSCHALK, pp. 368–83.
101. Ibid., pp. 414–15.
102. VoxBox CDX 5009 and Naxos 8.559036 (1999).

Bibliography

Baur/GROOVES	Baur, Steven. "Gottschalk's Grooves." *Dalhousie University Fountain School of Performing Arts Blog.* https://fsparesearchcreativity.wordpress.com/2021/07/05/gottschalks-grooves/.
Broyles/MAVERICKS	Broyles, Michael. *Mavericks and Other Traditions in American Music.* New Haven, CT: Yale University Press, 2004.
Broyles/MUSIC	Broyles, Michael. *"Music of the Highest Class": Elitism and Populism in Antebellum Boston.* New Haven, CT: Yale University Press, 1992.
Butler/VOTARIES	Butler, Nicholas Michael. *Votaries of Apollo: The St. Cecilia Society and the Patronage of Concert Music in Charleston, South Carolina, 1766–1820.* Columbia: University of South Carolina Press, 2007.
Chmaj/HEINRICH	Chmaj, Betty E. "Father Heinrich as Kindred Spirit; or, How the Log-House Composer of Kentucky Became the Beethoven of America." *American Studies* 24 (1983): 35–57.
Claypool/ARCHIVAL	Claypool, Richard D. "Archival Collections of the Moravian Music Foundation and Some Notes on the Philharmonic Society of Bethlehem." *Fontes Artes Musicae* 23 (1976): 177–90.
Fry/LEONORA	Fry, William Henry. *Leonora.* New York: E. Ferrett, 1846.
Gibbons/AUDUBON	Gibbons, William. "The Musical Audubon: Ornithology and Nationalism in the Symphonies of Anthony Philip Heinrich." *Journal of the Society for American Music* 3 (2009): 465–91.
Gottschalk/NOTES	Gottschalk, Louis Moreau. "Notes of a Pianist." *Atlantic Monthly* (February 1865): 177–82.
Heinrich/DAWNING	Heinrich, Anthony Philip. *The Dawning of Music in Kentucky and the Western Minstrel.* New York: Da Capo, 1970.

Heinrich/MASTODON	Heinrich, Anthony Philip. *The Mastodon*. Edited by Andrew Stiller. Philadelphia, PA: Kallisti Music, 2000.
Knouse/COLLEGIA	Knouse, Nola Reed. "The *collegia musica*: Music of the Community." In *The Music of the Moravian Church in America*, edited by Nola Reed Knouse, 189–211. Rochester, NY: University of Rochester Press, 2008.
Laudon/DRAMATIC	Laudon, Robert Tallant. *The Dramatic Symphony: Issues and Explorations from Berlioz to Liszt*. Hillsdale, NY: Pendragon, 2012.
Lawrence/FRY	Lawrence, Vera Brodsky. "William Henry Fry's Messianic Yearnings: The Eleven Lectures, 1852–53." *American Music* 7 (1989): 382–411.
Lawrence/STRONG	Lawrence, Vera Brodsky. *Strong on Music: The New York Music Scene in the Days of George Templeton Strong*. 3 vols. Chicago: University of Chicago Press, 1995.
Library/REPORT	Library of Congress, *Report of the Librarian of Congress*. Washington, DC: Government Printing Office, 1917.
Maust/SYMPHONIES	Maust, Wilbur R. "The Symphonies of Anthony Philip Heinrich Based on American Themes." PhD diss., Indiana University, 1973.
Newman/GOOD	Newman, Nancy. *Good Music for a Free People: The Germania Musical Society in Nineteenth-Century America*. Rochester, NY: University of Rochester Press, 2010.
Preston/BRISTOW	Preston, Katherine K. *George Frederick Bristow*. Urbana: University of Illinois Press, 2020.
Preston/JULLIEN	Preston, Katherine K. *George Frederick Bristow: Symphony No. 2 in D Minor, Op. 24 ("Jullien")*. Middleton, WI: A-R Editions, 2011.
Rogers/BRISTOW	Rogers, Delmer D. "Nineteenth-Century Music as Reflected in the Career of George Frederick Bristow." PhD diss., University of Michigan, 1967.
Shadle/ORCHESTRATING	Shadle, Douglas W. *Orchestrating the Nation: The Nineteenth-Century American Symphonic Enterprise*. New York: Oxford University Press, 2016.
Shadle/SANTA	Shadle, Douglas W. "How Santa Claus Became a Slave Driver: The Role of Print Culture in a Nineteenth-Century Musical Controversy." *Journal of the Society for American Music* 8 (2014): 501–37.
Shanet/PHILHARMONIC	Shanet, Howard. *Philharmonic: A History of New York's Orchestra*. New York: Doubleday, 1975.
Spitzer/AMERICAN	Spitzer, John, ed. *American Orchestras in the Nineteenth Century*. Chicago: University of Chicago Press, 2012.

Starr/GOTTSCHALK	Starr, S. Frederick. *Louis Moreau Gottschalk*. Urbana: University of Illinois Press, 2000.
Swenson-Eldrige/HOMMANN	Swenson-Eldridge, Joanne, ed. *Charles Hommann: Surviving Orchestral Works*. Edited by Joanne Swenson-Eldrige. Middleton, WI: A-R Editions, 2007.
Swenson-Eldrige/MUSICAL	Swenson-Eldridge, Joanne. "The Musical Fund Society of Philadelphia and the Emergence of String Chamber Music Genres Composed in the United States (1820–1860)." PhD diss., University of Colorado at Boulder, 1995.
Upton/FRY	Upton, William Treat. *William Henry Fry: American Journalist and Composer-Critic*. New York: Thomas Crowell, 1954.
Upton/HEINRICH	Upton, William Treat. *Anthony Philip Heinrich: A Nineteenth-Century Composer in America*. New York: Columbia University Press, 1939.
Von Glahn/SOUNDS	Von Glahn, Denise. *The Sounds of Place: Music and the American Cultural Landscape*. Boston: Northeastern University Press, 2003.
Will/CHARACTERISTIC	Will, Richard. *The Characteristic Symphony in the Age of Haydn and Beethoven*. Cambridge: Cambridge University Press, 2002.

CHAPTER THREE

The Second New England School and Their Contemporaries

E. Douglas Bomberger

In the decades after the Civil War, conditions for the production of a mature symphonic repertoire in the United States were greatly enhanced by the establishment of a stable group of orchestras to perform that repertoire. This goal was finally achieved in the last quarter of the nineteenth century, when America's explosive economic growth allowed many cities to invest in cultural institutions. During that era, museums and libraries were established in major American cities with the goal of preserving and disseminating the masterworks of art and literature. The parallel in music was the idealization of classical orchestral music, deemed by John Sullivan Dwight and other critics to be the pinnacle of musical achievement. Cities vied to outdo each other in founding permanent civic orchestras, but in contrast with Europe, the federal government did not concern itself with supporting orchestras.

The institution of a permanent nontouring orchestra devoted to the masterworks of orchestral music and not attached to an opera company may not have been invented in the United States, but it quickly developed into a uniquely American phenomenon. The symphony orchestra encapsulated Gilded Age views of elite culture, elevating classical instrumental music to a sacred status and thereby imbuing the concert hall with the aura of a place of worship. For America's wealthiest citizens, this new institution allowed them to practice conspicuous consumption under the guise of cultural and moral edification. For American music lovers of all income levels, the expansion of orchestral concerts created an unprecedented opportunity to hear professional performances of symphonic masterworks.

The most influential leader in the popularization of orchestral concerts was conductor Theodore Thomas (1835–1905). His concerts in New York during the 1860s and 1870s were crucial in developing a taste for symphonic music in that city. He established patterns of programming and standards of performance that were emulated throughout the country, aided by his indefatigable touring in the 1870s and 1880s. The Chicago Symphony Orchestra was created for him in 1891, and he devoted the rest of his life to the concerts of that organization. Thomas introduced American audiences to the major orchestral works of Richard Wagner (1813–83), Franz Liszt (1811–86), Johannes Brahms (1833–97), Pyotr Ilyich Tchaikovsky (1840–93), Johann Strauss (1825–99), and numerous other European composers. He was less enthusiastic about new works by Americans, but, over the course of his long career, he premiered more of their works than any other conductor.[1]

The prime example of a civic orchestra, and the model for many other orchestras in the country, was the Boston Symphony Orchestra. Since the mid-nineteenth century, Boston had never lacked for orchestral concerts, led mostly by itinerant pickup orchestras. Such performances were uneven, however, as the ensembles lacked consistent leadership, reliable players, and an overall sense of artistic vision. Bostonians prided themselves on their traditions of art and literature, while recognizing that music lagged behind. If New York had more concerts, Bostonians aspired to have better concerts.

The establishment of a permanent orchestra was the brainchild of Henry Lee Higginson (1834–1919), a Civil War veteran who developed a taste for orchestral music during his years of study in Europe. He made his fortune working in his father's brokerage and banking company, but his goal was to use his wealth to raise the quality of orchestral music in Boston while maintaining affordable ticket prices. In a visionary statement written in spring 1881, he outlined his plan for the ensemble. He would hire sixty players and a conductor, paying them each an annual salary. In exchange for this security, he expected them to make a commitment to the orchestra for the entire year, and he forbade them from playing dances or light music on concert days. The conductor was given authority to hire and fire musicians, and he was urged to create concerts of the best classical repertoire during the winter season. This arrangement was fundamentally different from that of the New York Philharmonic, which at the time was a cooperative orchestra whose members elected the conductor annually. Higginson recognized that the Boston Symphony Orchestra could not sustain itself financially on ticket income alone, and he planned from the start to contribute at least $50,000 (over $1 million in today's dollars) of his own money annually to establish the orchestra on a solid footing. The notion of making money was never an expectation.[2]

The initial group of players was recruited locally in order to build goodwill with Boston's musicians, but Higginson felt that the conductor should be drawn from outside the community. Therefore, he hired Georg Henschel (1850–1934), a young German composer and singer who had recently married American soprano Lillian Bailey. Henschel later recalled his discussions about the repertoire to be played: "I submitted to Mr. Higginson my idea of what I thought the programmes of such concerts should be, viz.: in the first part: Overture, a Solo, either vocal or instrumental, and the Symphony; the second part to be short and of considerably lighter, popular character. He approved of that, as also of my plan of giving—in so long a series of concerts—every one of the nine Beethoven Symphonies, of course in numerical order."[3]

Henschel conducted the first three seasons of the Boston Symphony Orchestra, from 1881 to 1884. He was followed by the Austrian Wilhelm Gericke from 1884 to 1889, the Hungarian Arthur Nikisch from 1889 to 1893, the Austrian Emil Paur from 1893 to 1898, Gericke again from 1898 to 1906, and the German-born Karl Muck (1906–8 and 1912–18) and Max Fiedler (1908–12). The fact that no American conductor served as music director until James Levine (2004–11) reflects the Eurocentric orientation of the orchestra, an example followed by the vast majority of American orchestras.[4] It is not surprising that the language used in rehearsals from the founding until World War I was German.

The orchestra was very successful in raising the standards of instrumental performance in Boston and inspiring a host of similar orchestras in American cities, including Chicago (1891), Cincinnati (1895), Pittsburgh (1896), and Philadelphia (1900). Henschel's format of building programs around major European symphonies, as well as the obvious educational agenda implied by programming all nine Beethoven symphonies in order, remained consistent throughout the orchestra's history. Supporting the high performance standards and repertoire choices were erudite program notes written by a succession of scholars, notably William F. Apthorp from 1892 to 1901 and Philip Hale from 1901 to 1933. Hale's engaging notes established the peculiar literary genre of program notes as an essential component of American concert life.

Conspicuously absent in Higginson's ambitious project was any provision for the promotion of works by local composers. Indeed, like John Sullivan Dwight before him, Higginson and many of his wealthy compatriots believed that European music was, by definition, superior to anything produced by American composers. The European conductors of the orchestra were not averse to hearing American works, and Gericke and Nikisch were especially generous to local composers, but their principal loyalty was to their colleagues back home. A poem by critic Louis C. Elson in March 1884 reflects the repertoire choices of the first Boston Symphony Orchestra conductor:

> Oh, Henschel, cease thy higher flight,
> And give the public something light!
> Let no more Wagner themes thy bill enhance,
> And give the native workers just one chance.
> Don't give the Dvořák symphony again;
> If you would give us joy, oh, give us Paine![5]

Compounding this perceived prejudice was the fact that the most prominent American composers had studied in European conservatories, where they honed their craft by hearing and emulating (chiefly) German music. As we shall see repeatedly in this chapter, American composers of the late nineteenth century found themselves in a double bind: if they wrote music in cosmopolitan style, they could be accused of blindly following German models with no originality of their own; if their music was based on American folk materials, they could be dismissed as provincial or accused of choosing the wrong source material because of America's lack of cultural homogeneity. Under these circumstances, it is remarkable that a group of thoroughly professional American composers emerged in the decades after the Civil War; it is not surprising, however, that such a group should have coalesced in the rich cultural milieu of Boston.

Historians vacillated for decades on a name for this group of composers, but the current consensus seems to favor the term "Second New England School" (the "First" having been the Yankee composers of the late eighteenth century) as a neutral designation for the most prominent composers of the era.[6] John Knowles Paine (1839–1906), George Whitefield Chadwick (1854–1931), Amy Beach (1867–1944), Horatio Parker (1863–1919), and Arthur Foote (1853–1937) are the core members of the group, but only the first three wrote works in symphonic form. The most successful composer of the era, Edward MacDowell (1860–1908), resolutely avoided fraternizing with this group—he was invited to meet with Chadwick and Foote in February 1890 to discuss a composer's club for the mutual exchange of ideas, but he grew so disgusted with their petty backbiting that he stood up and excused himself with the words "I don't think I care to swap."[7] His philosophical differences will be discussed later.

The emergence of the Second New England School coincided with the era that Carl Dahlhaus dubbed "The Second Age of the Symphony." After a hiatus of nearly 20 years after Robert Schumann's Third Symphony (1850) and revised Fourth (1851)—during which time the symphony languished as a musical form and the symphonic poem was established—the genre was revived by Brahms, Anton Bruckner (1824–96), Tchaikovsky, Joachim Raff (1822–82), and other contemporary composers.[8] The symphonies of the late nineteenth century reflect new aesthetic concerns and incorporate techniques from the symphonic poem. Most notable are new formal structures, greater use of programmatic content, an array of allusions and quotations, and the adoption of cyclic structures.[9] American symphonies from this era mirror the characteristics of European symphonies, in some cases preceding their appearance on the other side of the Atlantic.

The era also saw a rich variety of alternatives to the symphony. Many Americans experimented with the new genre of the symphonic poem. Strongly influenced by his contact with Franz Liszt, MacDowell produced four symphonic poems: *Hamlet and Ophelia*, Op. 22 (1885), *Lancelot and Elaine*, Op. 25 (1888), *Lamia*, Op. 29 (composed in 1887–88 but not published or performed until 1908), and a pair of "fragments after The Song of Roland" entitled *Die Sarazenen* and *Die schöne Aldâ*, Op. 30 (1891). His most successful orchestral works were his two piano concertos, Opp. 15 (1884) and 23 (1889), and his two orchestral suites, Opp. 42 (1888–91) and 48 (1891–95). Only the title page of a symphony survives, which may have been an earlier version of the Op. 30 pieces. Foote likewise wrote several orchestral suites that were performed by the Boston Symphony Orchestra, but he did not complete a symphony.[10]

It is an irony of American musical history that the most enduring symphony written in America during this era was by a European visitor. The Bohemian composer Antonín Dvořák (1841–1904) was hired as director of the National Conservatory of Music in New York, where he taught composition from 1892 to 1895. During his residence in America he was outspoken in his views on American music, recommending that composers of the United States follow the Bohemian model by basing their art music on folk models. Within eight months of his arrival in New York, he came to the conclusion that Americans would be best served by using African American folk music as raw material for their compositions. This prescription met with vehement opposition in Boston, where the most prominent composers cultivated a cosmopolitan aesthetic. The *Boston Herald* solicited responses to Dvořák's statements from local composers, whose reactions varied from cautious skepticism to outright dismissal. In his usual blunt manner, Chadwick wrote, "I am not sufficiently familiar with the real negro melodies to be able to offer any opinion on the subject. Such negro melodies as I have heard, however, I should be sorry to see become the basis of an American school of musical composition."[11] New York critics, led by Henry E. Krehbiel (1854–1923), embraced Dvořák's views and helped to publicize his ideas before he had composed any new works on American soil.[12] Dvořák further promoted his ideals by sponsoring composition contests through the National Conservatory in 1892 and 1893. The contests offered prizes for the best compositions in various genres, including symphonies. The winner of the $500 first prize in 1892 was Henry Schoenefeld's "Rural" Symphony, and the 1893 winner was Chadwick's Third Symphony.

It was the December 1893 premiere of Dvořák's Symphony No. 9 in E Minor, "From the New World," however, that changed the landscape of American music. The powerful work immediately captivated American audiences, and it remains popular to this day. More important was the debate it spawned about its thematic content. Though it has not been proven unequivocally that the composer drew on African American source materials for his themes, it is likely that his thinking about American folk materials and his intention to write an opera on Longfellow's *The Song of Hiawatha* influenced the compositional process on some level. Dvořák's achievement became a subject of wide discussion among American critics, and his views inspired a generation of American compositions incorporating folk materials, such as MacDowell's "Indian" Suite, Op. 48 (1891–95) and the extensive catalogs of Henry Gilbert (1868–1928) and Arthur Farwell (1872–1952). Dvořák's work single-handedly forced American composers to confront the issues of Americanism and exoticism as they pertained to concert music in the European tradition.[13] As we will see, Amy Beach's reaction to Dvořák's symphony had a direct impact on the writing of her own symphony. She took his example to heart but modified it to suit her own aesthetic goals.

Beach's approach typifies the efforts of her American contemporaries, who were strongly aware of European developments but chose to embrace or depart from them in unique and unpredictable ways. They knew that their work would be compared simultaneously to the European symphonic tradition, to the most recent developments in European composition, and to a hypothetical American art music based on native folk materials. As Julie Schnepel has observed, the efforts of American composers to create "the Great American Symphony" were complicated by critics who kept changing the definitions of "great" and "American."[14] The symphonic works of Paine, Chadwick, and Beach are interesting precisely because of the way each composer negotiated the conflicting demands of contemporary critics and audience members to create a repertoire unlike any other in symphonic history.

John Knowles Paine

John Knowles Paine (1839–1906) was the elder statesman of the Second New England School, a man whose career established the pattern for subsequent composers for decades to follow. He was born and raised in Portland, Maine, where he received his early training with a German immigrant teacher, Hermann Kotzschmar (1829–1909). He studied in Berlin from 1858 to 1861, where his principal teacher was the organist Carl August Haupt (1810–91). He also studied orchestration with Friedrich Wilhelm Wieprecht (1802–72). Upon his return to the United States, he was hired as organist and choirmaster at Harvard University. He began offering courses in music and eventually was appointed the first professor of music at Harvard in 1875, despite the well-known opposition of faculty members such as historian Francis Parkman. Rupert Hughes summarized Paine's reputation for conservatism in 1900:

> There is one thing better than modernity—it is immortality. So while I am a most ardent devotee of modern movements, because they are at worst experiments, and motion is necessary to life, I fail to see why it is necessary in picking up something new always to drop something old, as if one were an awkward, butter-fingered parcel-carrier. If a composer writes empty stuff in the latest styles, he is one degree better than the purveyor of trite stuff in the old styles; but he is nobody before the high thinker who finds himself suited by the general methods of the classic writers [i.e., referring to Paine].[15]

In Boston, more than anywhere else in America, European models were highly valued, and connections with the past—whether the plays of Sophocles, the paintings of Peter Paul Rubens, or the symphonies of Ludwig von Beethoven—were actively cultivated. In a telling summary of his view of cosmopolitan style in the late nineteenth century, Paine wrote, "We have not now national, but international music, and it makes no difference whether I compose here or in St. Petersburg, so long as I express myself in my own way."[16] Paine understood what his audience wanted, and his two symphonies set the standard for his era (table 3.1).

SYMPHONY NO. 1 IN C MINOR, OP. 23

The agenda of Paine's first symphony, premiered on January 26, 1876, was the emulation of Beethoven's Fifth and Ninth Symphonies. Like Brahms, whose own Symphony No. 1 was first heard ten months later (November 4, 1876), Paine had delayed his first symphonic essay until

Table 3.1 The Symphonies of John Knowles Paine (1839–1906)

Title and date	Key	Movements	Instrumentation	Comments
Symphony No. 1, Op. 23 (1872–75)	C minor	1. Allegro con brio ¢ (530 mm.) 2. Allegro vivace 3/4 (678 mm.) C major 3. Adagio 3/4 (172 mm.) A-flat major 4. Allegro vivace ¢ (543 mm.) C major	Grand	Premiered January 26, 1876, Theodore Thomas Orchestra in Boston. Published by Breitkopf & Härtel, 1908.
Symphony No. 2, "Spring," Op. 34 (1879)	A major	1. Introduction. Adagio sostenuto ("Departure of Winter")—Allegro ma non troppo ("Awakening of Nature") 4/4 (56 mm.) A minor —> 2/4 (496 mm.) A major 2. Scherzo. Allegro. ("Maynight Fantasy") 3/4 (600 mm.) D minor 3. Adagio. ("A Romance of Springtime") 4/4 (172 mm.) F major 4. Allegro giojoso. ("The Glory of Nature") ¢ (472 mm.) A major	Grand	Premiered March 10, 1880, Boston Philharmonic Society, conducted by Bernhard Listemann. Published by Arthur P. Schmidt under the title *Im Frühling*, 1880.

Example 3.1 John Knowles Paine, Symphony No. 1, first movement, mm. 1–11

Example 3.1 *continued*

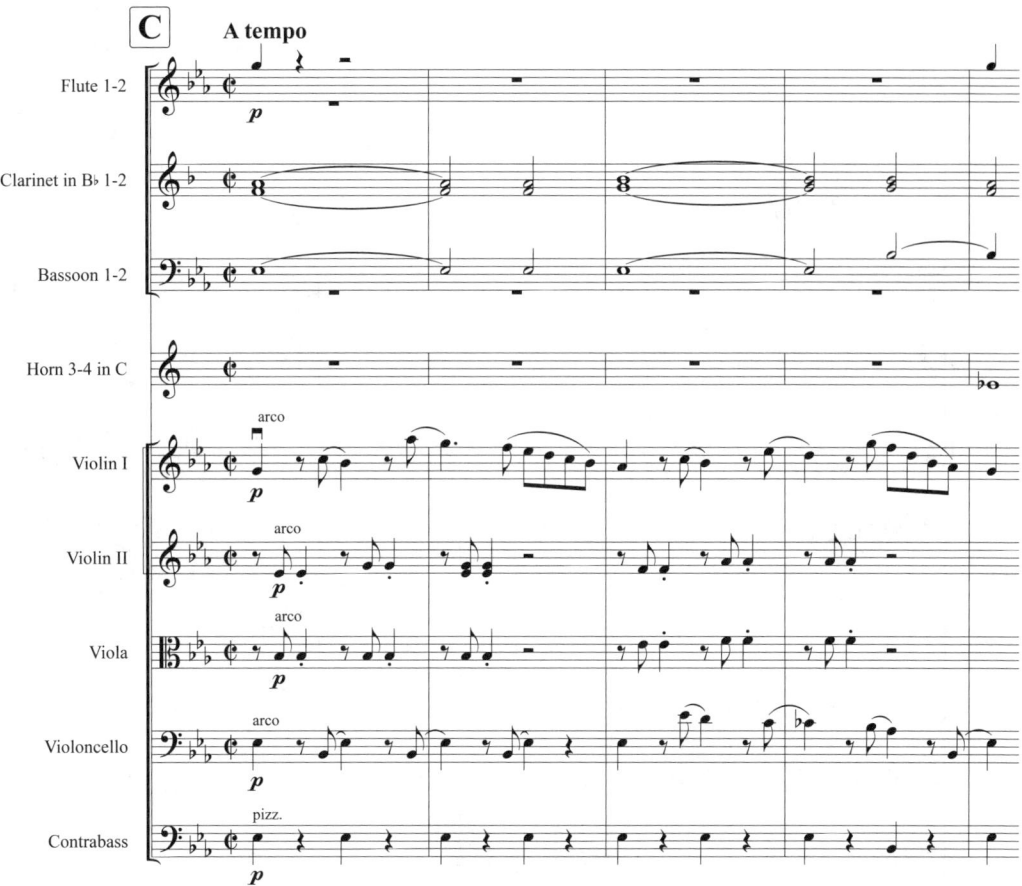

Example 3.2 Paine, Symphony No. 1, first movement, mm. 74–77

after he was well established in his career. Also like Brahms, he included in his first symphony several unmistakable allusions to Beethoven (not least the key) that caused listeners to associate the work with the most eminent of predecessors. We do not have documentary evidence to support the sort of anxiety over Beethoven's influence that Brahms so freely admitted, but Paine's score contains ample evidence that Beethoven's symphonies were not far from his mind as he wrote.

The first movement begins with *P*, a vigorous rocket theme that propels the listener forward and promises possibilities for development (mm. 1–11; example 3.1). A reviewer for the *Atlantic* characterized *P* with a simile that has often been repeated in descriptions of the work: "Whatever anxiety or lack of entire faith one may have felt beforehand must have been removed by the very first phrase, which with its rushing bass and powerful stroke of chords (as if with some resistless hammer of Thor) proclaims at once the technical skill and boldness of design that belong only to masters of symphonic writing."[17] After this arresting opening, a transitional section introduces a lyrical theme in the lower strings that is subsequently repeated and extended by the woodwinds. The section goes on for so long that it has been labeled by some analysts as

Example 3.3 Paine, Symphony No. 1, first movement, mm. 104–23

S, but its restless character and lack of tonal stability mark it clearly as transitional. The true *S* in the relative major appears at Reh. C, with a jaunty dotted rhythm that again makes it ripe for development (mm. 74–77; example 3.2). The tune is the one that preoccupies the composer most extensively, as he embarks on a lengthy exploration of its rhythmic and sequential possibilities. In the middle of the section he takes a detour to the key of B major, introducing a new key signature for twelve measures. (The detour does not sound as jarring as it looks, since C-flat major [the enharmonic of B major] is the flat VI of E-flat major.) This is an erudite bit of *Augenmusik*, an allusion to the similar brief swerve to B major in the first movement of Beethoven's Ninth Symphony that would be evident only to those steeped in the master's works. While in this B-major section, Paine introduces an even clearer Beethoven allusion in the French horns: the famous rhythmic motive that opens Beethoven's Fifth Symphony. This motive becomes ever more insistent after the key returns to E-flat major, until only the most musically unsophisticated listener could fail to recognize the allusion (mm. 104–23; example

Example 3.3 *continued*

3.3). The development section is occupied with the motivic implications of the dotted *S*, as the rhythmic motive is eventually reduced to falling two-note fragments that prompt comparisons with the first movement of Beethoven's Ninth. In the recapitulation, *P* and *S* are shortened, but Paine loses any advantage by tacking on a seventy-five-measure coda whose length dissipates the energy the rest of the movement has accumulated. Though not excessively long at just over eleven minutes, the overall effect of the movement is one of too many digressions, like a lecture undermined by the professor's tangential allusions.

The second movement Scherzo begins with a charming and brief A section followed by a much longer and developmental B section. The rhythmic motives and falling arpeggiated figures again call to mind the first movement of Beethoven's Ninth Symphony. The third movement opens with one of Paine's most beautiful lyrical melodies. Romantic but not sentimental, chromatic but not excessively unstable, the melody sets up a long movement in modified rondo form that demonstrates Paine's mastery of orchestral color.

Example 3.3 *continued*

The final movement, like the concluding movements of Beethoven's Fifth and Brahms's First, is in C major. It is in sonata form but is significantly shorter than the first movement with fewer subsidiary themes. As a consequence, it moves more decisively toward the conclusion. *P* resembles *I//P* with its rising scalar passage that starts on an offbeat and ends on a strong beat. The movement contains more polyphony than any of the previous movements, and the contrapuntal interest is enhanced by a variety of orchestral colors. The result is a satisfying conclusion to the forty-five-minute symphony, moving inexorably toward the triumphant final measures combining the sacred sound of a 4–3 suspension with ornamented resolution and Beethovenian *ff* punctuations of the tonic.

Paine's orchestration is dominated by the strings and woodwinds, often in dialogue with each other. Although the score calls for four French horns, two trumpets, and three trombones, the composer never allows them to dominate the texture, and thus he misses the dramatic potential exploited to such great effect in the last movement of Beethoven's Fifth. Paine's score has great variety and some imaginative moments but, unlike many American symphonists who followed him, at no point does he allow the orchestra to reach a truly dramatic, brassy climax.

The critical response to the premiere was generally positive, as Paine was well connected with the Boston establishment and the work was given a stellar performance by the Theodore Thomas orchestra. Critics noted the strong resemblance to Beethoven, and the reviewer for the *Boston Globe* took him to task for it: "We are compelled to record as our conviction, that, apart from movements two and three, we did not find that originality of treatment which we ought to look for from Mr. Paine; and some places were so decidedly suggestive of Beethoven as to seem a reproduction of his very *forms*, rather than a simple enlargement upon the *spirit* of his works, which a student of his symphonies might reasonably be supposed to acquire."[18]

Christopher Reynolds has shown that modeling a work closely after a distinguished predecessor was an accepted means of planning large-scale formal structures in the nineteenth century.[19] The proportions of Paine's first movement are much closer to those of Beethoven's Ninth than to those of his Fifth. The motivic allusions, however, are drawn primarily from the Fifth: the familiar opening gesture from that work is quoted so often as to be unmistakable. In Reynolds's typology, this quotation is an assimilative allusion, in which the composer pays homage to the spirit of the original work by quoting it in a context that is similar in mood and meaning to the source.[20] Brahms, by contrast, takes a more polemical approach to the Beethoven quotation in the Finale of his First Symphony by confronting both the vocal transcendence of the "Ode to Joy" theme in Beethoven's Ninth and Wagner's claim that his music dramas were the legitimate heir to Beethoven's innovations.[21]

SYMPHONY NO. 2 IN A MAJOR, "SPRING," OP. 34

Between the successful premieres of his First Symphony in 1876 and his Second in 1880, Paine wrote two shorter orchestral works that foreshadowed a new direction for him. The *Overture to "As You Like It"* (1876) is a short, tuneful work that is not explicitly programmatic in thematic content, despite the connection with Shakespeare's play. The symphonic poem *Shakespeare's Tempest* (1877), on the other hand, delineates characters and events with a precision not previously found in Paine's works. When he returned to the symphonic genre, his Second Symphony, Op. 34 (1880), was conceived with programmatic titles for its four movements:

1. Introduction. Adagio sostenuto. (Departure of Winter.)
   Allegro ma non troppo. (Awakening of Nature.)
2. Scherzo. Allegro. (Maynight Fantasy.)
3. Adagio. (A Romance of Springtime.)
4. Allegro giojoso. (The Glory of Nature.)[22]

Table 3.2 Comparison of Spring Symphonies by Schumann, Raff, and Paine

Mvt.	Schumann (1841)	Raff (1878)	Paine (1880)
I	"Spring's Awakening"	"Nature's Awakening"	"Departure of Winter" / "Awakening of Nature"
II	"Evening"	"Walpurgis Night Revel"	"Maynight Fantasy"
III	"Merry Playmates"	"First Blossoms of Spring"	"A Romance of Springtime"
IV	"Full Spring"	"The Joys of Wandering"	"The Glory of Nature"

It is curious that Paine chose not to print the extramusical titles in the concert program of the premiere performance on March 10, 1880, perhaps in deference to the Bostonian distaste for such modernisms. The full score was published simultaneously in Boston and Hamburg in 1880 with the name "Im Frühling" (In Spring) but without the individual movement titles. The programmatic content was generally known among musicians, however, and within a few years it became standard practice to include the movement titles in concert programs.

Paine's Second Symphony is one of a group of symphonies on the topic of spring. Schumann's First Symphony and Raff's Eighth Symphony are also subtitled "Spring," and the titles of their four movements are similar to Paine's (table 3.2). These three works take similar approaches to the problem of portraying spring in a symphony, except that Schumann places the slow movement before the scherzo. Paine's depiction of spring is generalized rather than explicit, making it difficult to identify specific programmatic events beyond the broadest outlines suggested by the titles. In addition to this newfound interest in program music, Paine expanded his harmonic palette by choosing more distant keys for the middle movements and by modulating to less conventional secondary tonal areas in the first and last movements. The work also experiments with cyclic form by reprising themes from the first three movements in the Finale. The length is substantial at nearly an hour without cuts. All told, the work makes a decisive break from the Beethovenian model and explores techniques more characteristic of midcentury Romanticism, albeit with an orchestra that is identical in size to that employed in Paine's First Symphony.

The first movement begins Adagio sostenuto in the key of A minor. Violas and cellos intone a melancholy theme over the throbbing accompaniment of contrabasses. Tension mounts in this opening section, climaxing with stentorian horn calls and rushing violin scales. The mood relaxes into hushed expectation, allowing the first violins to effect a transition to A major and the Allegro ma non troppo that will prevail for the remainder of the movement, which is in sonata-allegro form. The secondary key of the movement is F major, a third relationship more characteristic of later Romantics than of Beethoven. P is less memorable than the opening motive, and its lack of rhythmic variety prevents it from grabbing the listener's attention in its multiple entrances. Paine adds interest by using the winter theme as a countersubject at points throughout the movement. As is often the case in Paine's orchestral textures, the overuse of dotted rhythms lends a sameness to the melodic materials that is only occasionally relieved by contrasting themes. The fifteen-minute movement is a tour de force of orchestral and contrapuntal techniques but lacks memorable melodies and dramatic force.

The Scherzo is in D minor, the minor subdominant. It opens with scales in the first violins, echoing the transition to the Allegro of the first movement. Despite the minor key, this movement is the airiest of the four, with a variety of melodies and clever and abrupt harmonic twists that can be heard as evocative of the sounds of spring. The woodwinds are used primarily as a choir, with few opportunities for solo melodies except for a few well-placed phrases for flute. The third movement Adagio is in the key of F major, foreshadowed by *1/S*; it is long but tuneful, featuring a contrasting middle section in F minor that makes effective use of blended timbres.

The Finale, in sonata-allegro form like the first movement, begins with a distinctive melody in the strings. The movement is in A major, with *S* in C major, the mediant of the parallel minor. The development section features a startling modulation from C major to a false recapitulation of *P* in A-flat major, an effective moment reflecting Paine's technical skill and Haydnesque sense of humor. The Meno mosso e maestoso theme is a broad, dignified melody that effectively contrasts with *P* and brings the symphony to a satisfying conclusion.

Paine's principal biographer, John C. Schmidt, has pointed out that the Second Symphony reflects his tendency to blur the outlines of small-scale units like motives and phrases in order to integrate them into the whole: "Many Paine themes reveal his studied avoidance of small-term melodic symmetry, preferring instead units of irregular length that de-emphasize formal joinings and contribute instead to a sense of larger-scale growth."[23] His preference for asymmetrical phrases reflects both his affinity for the music of Johann Sebastian Bach and contemporary trends in orchestral writing. It is this feature of the Second Symphony that distinguishes it most from the First, so that while the Second is clearly more advanced and in tune with current trends, the First has tauter themes and consequently more rhythmic energy.

The reaction to the Boston premiere on March 10, 1880, was unprecedented in American music history. Richard Aldrich famously described the reception thus: "Ladies waved handkerchiefs, men shouted in approbation, and the highly respected John S. Dwight, arbiter in Boston of criticism, if not of manners, stood on his seat, frantically opening and shutting his umbrella as an expression of uncontrollable enthusiasm."[24] Dwight was equally laudatory in his review: "We cannot but regard this 'Spring' Symphony as a remarkable, a noble work, by far the happiest and ripest product, thus far, of Prof. Paine's great learning and inventive faculty, and marking the highest position yet reached in these early stages of American creative art in music. It is worthy to hold a place among the works of masters, and will reward many hearings wherever the symphonic art can find appreciative audience."[25] The *Boston Transcript* stated, "As it marks a new departure in [Paine's] own career, it also marks an epoch in the development of art in America, and sets the standard of excellence on the very highest plane."[26] Within a year, the complete score and parts were published simultaneously in Boston and Hamburg. It was the first publication of the full score of a symphony by an American, a sign of both the significance of the work and the publisher Arthur P. Schmidt's gratitude to his adopted home.

The work was played often in Boston in the years following, but in the words of Rupert Hughes, "not half enough."[27] When the American conductor Franz Xavier Arens (1856–1932) played the work during his 1892 tour of Berlin, Dresden, Weimar, Leipzig, and Vienna, he omitted the Adagio in all but one of his concerts in order to reduce the length. Critics were most impressed by the Scherzo but were generally positive in their assessments of the other movements as well. They noted especially the influence of Felix Mendelssohn (1809–47), in both the spirit and structure of the work. Paine received much praise for his technique, particularly his handling of form and motivic development. On a program with younger contemporaries, Paine's maturity was evident, and critics repeatedly singled out the excerpts from his symphony as the strongest works on the concerts.[28] It is curious that the absence of a slow movement led several reviewers to wonder whether persons in North America experience spring differently from people in Leipzig or Wiesbaden; two critics who heard Paine's work in Dresden—apparently without realizing that the slow movement was omitted—claimed that he depicted the topic differently than a German would have:

> How differently the American portrays spring as opposed to the German! The printed titles of the individual movements are indeed approximately the same: Winter's Departure, Awakening of Nature, May Night (presented here as a scherzo), the Glory of Nature. Upon hearing such music, we Germans miss the picture of blooming, buzzing, and budding; we would wax poetic, sing, dream, and revel. Not so the American—he seems hardly to know and hastily skips over the deeper nature of spring. [*Dresdner Anzeiger*][29]

> The German thinks of the poetry of a May night, like that portrayed by the scherzo of the *Spring Symphony* of John Knowles Paine, more dreamily and wispily, but not so coarsely American. The above-mentioned symphony, the most outstanding work of the evening, is nevertheless so skillfully worked out and so effectively constructed, so rich in thrilling details, that the European art world should not look away from such appearances of overseas origin. [*Dresdner Nachrichten*][30]

CONCLUSION

Paine's importance should not be underestimated. In earning a professorship in music at Harvard where none had existed previously, in achieving success as a composer of symphonies before the founding of the Boston Symphony Orchestra, and in serving as a teacher of many composers of the following generation, he was an important role model for American musicians. His choice to participate in the mainstream of European stylistic development was perhaps his most important contribution. Writing cosmopolitan music in the age of nationalism established a pattern that would be crucial for American composers in the following decades, staking a claim to an aesthetic high ground that has not always been understood or appreciated by historians and audiences after the beginning of the twentieth century.

George Whitefield Chadwick

Among the audience members at the premiere performance of Paine's Symphony No. 1 on January 26, 1876, was a young man from Lawrence, Massachusetts, by the name of George Whitefield Chadwick (1854–1931). The aspiring composer and future director of the New England Conservatory recalled the concert as a seminal event in his development. He immediately sought lessons from Paine but abandoned them because of the difficulty of commuting to the professor's home in Cambridge. His interest in orchestral music persisted, though, and he became the most successful and prolific orchestral composer of the Second New England School (table 3.3).

After sporadic early training in organ and composition, Chadwick traveled to Germany in his mid-twenties, where he studied composition in Leipzig with Salomon Jadassohn and Carl Reinecke and briefly in Munich with Josef Rheinberger. While in Leipzig, he composed three works that received public performances in the conservatory's public examination concerts [*Prüfungen*]: his first two string quartets and an overture on *Rip Van Winkle*. The last work (1879) earned glowing reviews in the Leipzig journals and was performed in Boston after his return from Europe. Despite its American title, the work was cosmopolitan in style—so much so that the composer revised it to insert more "Americanisms" into the score when it was published in 1930, a time when cosmopolitan music of the Second New England School was derided by younger musicians.[31] After experiencing so much acclaim in Leipzig, Chadwick

Table 3.3 The Symphonic Works of George Whitefield Chadwick (1854–1931)

Title		Date	Movements	Instrumentation	Comments
Symphony No. 1, Op. 5	C major	1877–81	1. Allegro molto e sostenuto—Presto 3/4 (715 mm.) 2. Scherzo: Allegro molto vivace 3/4 (394 mm.) C minor 3. Adagio molto espressivo 4/4 (124 mm.) A-flat major 4. Finale: Introduction—Allegro molto—Presto 4/4 (745 mm.)	Grand	Dedicated to Susan Collins Chadwick, the composer's stepmother. Premiered February 23, 1882, in Boston by the Harvard Musical Association, conducted by Chadwick. Unpublished (holograph in New England Conservatory library; facsimile available through PETRUCCI).
Symphony No. 2, Op. 21	B-flat major	1883–85	1. Andante non troppo 4/4 (473 mm.) 2. Allegretto scherzando 2/4 (251 mm.) F major 3. Largo e maestoso 3/4—Assai con fuoco 2/4—Tempo I (216 mm.) D minor—D major 4. Allegro molto animato 4/4 (332 mm.)	Grand	Dedicated to A. T. Scott. Movement 2 premiered March 8, 1884, with the Boston Symphony Orchestra, conducted by Georg Henschel. Movement 1 premiered April 29, 1885, with the Apollo Club, conducted by Chadwick. Entire work premiered December 10, 1886, with the Boston Symphony Orchestra, conducted by Chadwick. Published by Arthur P. Schmidt, 1888.
Symphony No. 3	F major	1893–94	1. Allegro sostenuto 3/4 (428 mm.) 2. Andante cantabile 3/4 (193 mm.) B-flat major 3. Vivace non troppo 6/8, 2/4 (339 mm.) D minor 4. Finale: Allegro molto energico 6/4, 4/4 (369 mm.)	Grand	Dedicated to Theodore Thomas. Winner, National Conservatory competition, 1894. Premiered October 19, 1894, with the Boston Symphony Orchestra, conducted by Chadwick. Published by Arthur P. Schmidt, 1896.

Table 3.3 continued

Title	Key	Date	Movements	Instrumentation	Comments
Symphonic Sketches	A major	1895 1895 1904 1896	1. "Jubilee" (Allegro molto vivace) 6/4, 4/4 (333 mm.) 2. "Noël" (Andante con tenerezza) 3/4 (143 mm.) D-flat major 3. "Hobgoblin" (Allegro vivace) 3/4 (500 mm.) F major 4. "A Vagrom Ballad" (Moderato) Alla burla A minor 2/4—Molto vivace—Prestissimo A major 6/8 (301 mm.)	Grand plus Picc., EH, Bclar, 4 extra Perc., and Harp	Dedicated to Frederick S. Converse. Each movement prefaced with a poem by Chadwick. The four movements premiered separately in 1903–04. Complete work premiered February 7, 1908, in Boston, with the Boston Symphony Orchestra, conducted by Karl Muck. Published by G. Schirmer, 1907.
Sinfonietta	D major	1904	1. Risolutamente 3/4 (318 mm.) 2. "Canzonetta" (Allegretto) 2/4 (162 mm.) A minor 3. Scherzino vivacissimo e leggiero 9/8 (129 mm.) F major 4. Finale: Assai animato 2/4 (260 mm.)	Grand plus Picc., 1 extra Perc., and Harp	Premiered November 21, 1904, in Boston, with the Boston Symphony Orchestra, conducted by Chadwick. Published by G. Schirmer, 1906.
Suite Symphonique	E-flat major	1905–09	1. Allegro molto animato ¢ (416 mm.) 2. "Romanza" (Andantino espressivo) 4/4 (117 mm.) B-flat major 3. "Intermezzo e humoreske" (Poco allegretto) 2/4 (302 mm.) G minor 4. Finale: Allegro molto e energico 6/4 (276 mm.)	Grand plus Picc., 1 Tpt., extra Perc., and Harp	Dedicated to Frederick A. Stock and the Theodore Thomas Orchestra of Chicago. Winner of National Federation of Music Clubs competition, 1911. Premiered March 29, 1911, in Philadelphia, by the Philadelphia Symphony Orchestra, conducted by Chadwick. Published by Arthur P. Schmidt, 1911.

found Rheinberger's counterpoint classes dull and withdrew at midyear, but he later acknowledged the value of the classes and recommended Rheinberger as a teacher to his own students who wanted to study abroad.

Returning to Boston in early 1880, Chadwick established himself as an organist at a series of churches. He eventually took a teaching position at the New England Conservatory, serving as director of that institution from 1897 to 1930. His long residence in the city allowed him to build connections with local conductors, first with Carl Zerrahn and B. J. Lang and later with the conductors of the Boston Symphony Orchestra after its founding in 1881. He also impressed America's most powerful conductor, Theodore Thomas, who frequently performed his works in New York, Boston, Chicago, and on tours throughout the country. Thomas had the reputation of being unsympathetic to American works, but he countered that he played many American works when they met his high artistic standards. Chadwick's ready access to these conductors gave him an incentive to compile a substantial body of orchestral works, and it also afforded him the opportunity to refine his technique and to learn from his mistakes.

Chadwick's works were also shaped by his own personal experiences as a conductor. There were few opportunities for training in that discipline at the Leipzig Conservatory, but after his return to Boston he conducted many of his own and others' works with the Boston Handel and Haydn Society and other local organizations. He eventually served as director of the Springfield Festival from 1890 to 1899 and the Worcester Festival from 1898 to 1901. As Victor Yellin points out, however, the establishment of the Boston Symphony Orchestra and Higginson's insistence on European conductors effectively put a glass ceiling on Chadwick's conducting aspirations for the rest of his career, and his memoirs chronicle his bitterness over his lost opportunities.[32] Nonetheless, he conducted the premieres of all the works described in this chapter except the *Symphonic Sketches*.[33]

SYMPHONY NO. 1 IN C MAJOR, OP. 5

The completion of Chadwick's first symphony was evidently not a high priority for him, because it kept getting pushed aside for other projects. He started it in the winter of 1877 in Leipzig, and by October 1879 he reported to a friend that the first movement was nearly done. He did not add the other three movements until after relocating to Boston the following year. He conducted the premiere at a concert of the Harvard Musical Association Orchestra on February 23, 1882. The score calls for a medium-sized orchestra similar in size to those used by Paine.

The first movement, in C major and triple meter, emphasizes third relations in modulations and includes a brief section of fugato. The second movement is a fast Scherzo in the parallel key of C minor, again emphasizing mediant modulations. The third movement, marked Adagio molto espressivo, is in A-flat major. Chadwick uses the solo woodwinds extensively to achieve a preponderance of chamber-music effects. The Allegro moderato Finale is back in the tonic key, and, like the first movement, it introduces a section of fugato. The sonata-allegro structures of both the first and last movements are thrown out of balance with excessively long multisection codas.

The premiere was treated as a major event, and most critics were supportive. Naturally, there were comparisons to Paine, as in this comment by Louis C. Elson: "When we think that Chadwick is a very young man, and that Professor Paine, the leading American composer, in my eyes, had not achieved as much at his age, we find that there is great hope and promise in the already prominent composer."[34] With characteristic flippancy, the composer later recalled in his memoirs that "The work was very much praised by the critics, especially the parts which deserved it the least."[35] The score was not published, and its only other performance was a partial one in 1886.

SYMPHONY NO. 2 IN B-FLAT MAJOR, OP. 21

Chadwick's Second Symphony fared much better than his First, despite being again written over a period of years and premiering piecemeal. The eventual second movement, a scherzo in F major, was first heard on March 8, 1884. The first movement began life as an Overture in B-flat at its initial performance on April 29, 1885. He composed the remaining two movements over the next year and a half, and the Boston Symphony Orchestra played the newly assembled four-movement symphony for the first time on December 10, 1886. Chadwick achieved a major success with his Second Symphony, one of the strongest American orchestral works of the nineteenth century. Arthur P. Schmidt published the full score in 1888, making it easily available for repeat performances throughout the country.

Victor Yellin has noted that the first, third, and fourth movements are closely related through the use of several recurring motives that give these movements "an audible and satisfying organic unity."[36] The Scherzo, on the other hand, shows few connections with its companions, functioning well as an independent composition in its own right. The movement was an immediate success on its first performance, and its infectious exuberance helps to make the Second Symphony an attractive composition. William F. Apthorp responded to the 1884 premiere of the Scherzo with high praise: "Mr. Chadwick's new Scherzo is a gem. The themes on which it is built up are both original and taking—the first theme, with its quasi-Irish humorousness (it positively winks at you), is peculiarly happy. The working up of the movement sounds clear and coherent, even at first hearing; the piquant charm of the whole is irresistible. The orchestration is that of a master, and is full of delicious bits of color, without ever becoming outrageous."[37]

Example 3.4 Chadwick, Symphony No. 2, first movement, mm. 1–4

The first movement opens with a lone French horn intoning *O*, a theme that will recur in the third and fourth movements (mm. 1–4; example 3.4). It uses a characteristic pattern that is reminiscent of a pentatonic scale but is more accurately called gapped because it omits only one rather than two of the seven notes of the major scale. Chadwick uses some variation of this pattern in many of his works, one of the factors contributing to the folk-music quality of his style. In this case, he enhances the natural tendency of pentatonic patterns to obscure tonality by using an F diatonic pentatonic scale and ending the melody on D. This harmonic uncertainty persists throughout the Andante introduction, in which a series of modulations leads to a cadence on D major, the opening key of the following Allegro con brio. The tonic of the symphony, B-flat major, is not established until the thirteenth measure of the Allegro con brio (two and a half minutes into the movement), with a vigorous *P* based on the horn call *O* (mm. 50–53; example 3.5). *S*, a lyrical melody in the dominant F major, is played first by the

Example 3.5 Chadwick, Symphony No. 2, first movement, mm. 50–53

horn and then taken up by the woodwinds. The development section is unusually brief at just over one-fifth of the movement's total length. A short coda (starting at Assai animato eight measures before Reh. W) stays firmly in the tonic but accelerates to a thrilling conclusion in Presto tempo.

The ebullient second-movement Scherzo contains several examples of themes that exemplify Chadwick's "quasi-Irish humorousness." The first theme, which Apthorp explicitly identified with this label, is firmly in F major but omits the fourth degree of the scale. This gives it the feel of a pentatonic melody even though, as in the first movement, the presence of the seventh degree makes it more accurately considered as a gapped scale. The syncopated ending of the first phrase enhances its jauntiness (mm. 4–12; example 3.6). The coda begins with a new theme in the oboe and horn accompanied by fragments of the principal theme (Reh. M; example 3.7). This melody also uses a pentatonic-sounding gapped scale, along with syncopated phrase endings. Yellin has described this "short-long" syncopation pattern (also known as the Scotch snap) as prosodic syncopation, "because it refers specifically to a rhythmic stress pattern that characterizes Anglo-Celtic speech."[38] In his view it is a musical reflection of the peculiar speech rhythms of American English.

The third movement, Largo e maestoso in D minor, begins with an audible connection to I/O. The lyrical *A* makes prominent use of the Scotch snap, which, in such a slow tempo, is reminiscent of a funeral march. The overall form of the movement is ABCDA, with the dignified march of the first section contrasted by an extended fourth section in Allegro tempo featuring stirring brass fanfares. The movement features an impressive array of timbres, with the brass playing a more prominent role than is typical in slow movements. In addition, the length of the Allegro is striking, giving the movement a strong sense of turbulent motion.

The vigorous Allegro molto animato Finale is back in the key of B-flat major and follows a standard sonata form, albeit again with an abbreviated development section. Chadwick introduces audible reminiscences of the themes of Movements I and III, a cyclical practice not unusual in late-century symphonies. The helter-skelter quality of this extremely fast movement proved disagreeable to some critics; for instance, the reviewer for the *Boston Post* commented that "the constant changes of tonality and tempo give this movement a certain patchwork character which is much to be regretted."[39] What the reviewer missed in unity, though, is more than compensated for by the movement's kaleidoscopic brilliance. Chadwick's command of orchestral color is on full display, with the horns again featured prominently.

The Second Symphony was well received by the public, but the critical response highlights the challenge faced by Chadwick early in his career. In the review quoted above, William F. Apthorp, influential critic of the *Boston Transcript*, praised the "quasi-Irish humorousness" of the Scherzo when it was performed as an independent work. This review was one of many in the same vein that Apthorp wrote of Chadwick's works over the years. But the critic often treated Chadwick's penchant for writing tuneful melodies as a double-edged sword, admonishing the composer for a lack of seriousness. In his review of the symphony as a whole, he called the work brilliant but frivolous, stating that "it seems as if the composer had not yet sufficiently drilled his powers to cope with so severe a task as a symphony."[40] In response a year later, to the most serious of Chadwick's orchestral works, the dramatic overture *Melpomene*, Apthorp would state approvingly, "he has plainly trusted less to that fatal facility of his, and has put more thought and real energy into his work."[41] Chadwick's memoirs reveal how such references to "fatal facility" and "quasi-Irish humorousness" stung his ego. Chadwick

Example 3.6 Chadwick, Symphony No. 2, second movement, mm. 4–12

Example 3.7 Chadwick, Symphony No. 2, second movement, rehearsal letter M

was dogged by the expectations of Boston's conservative critics for a perfect balance between tunefulness, seriousness of purpose, and structural integrity. The genre of the symphony and its aura of transcendence especially seems to have prompted the critics to set nearly unattainable standards of perfection for Chadwick and other American composers. The reviewer for the *Boston Post* echoed Apthorp's tone: "Mr. Chadwick, who is capable of better things, has sacrificed artistic truth to a desire to please and to produce brilliant effects; and he will come to grief if he persists in writing symphonies, at any rate, in this vein."[42]

SYMPHONY NO. 3 IN F MAJOR

The Third Symphony was written under the shadow of Dvořák in more ways than one. Chadwick began the composition in 1892 or 1893, and it was incomplete at the time of the premiere of the "New World" Symphony. Chadwick finished the work in time to submit it for the National Conservatory's second American composition contest in 1894. Although sponsored by the conservatory and judged by Dvořák, the competition was national in scope. Chadwick learned in mid-April in a letter from Dvořák himself that he had won the prize for best symphony. He dedicated it to Theodore Thomas and tried to convince him to perform the premiere, but that honor went instead to the Boston Symphony Orchestra on October 19, 1894. In characteristic fashion, the Boston critics were not inclined to listen sympathetically to a work that had been endorsed in a New York competition, and Chadwick suffered some of the worst reviews of his career. Further, the symphony was compared to Dvořák's and critiqued on the basis of its "Americanism."

The first movement in F major (Allegro sostenuto) is in sonata-allegro form. It opens with stentorian chords in woodwinds and brass that emulate the sound of a full organ. Perhaps because of the chordal opening in the key of F major as well as the modal ambivalence of the second chord, many of the initial reviews compared the work to the opening of Brahms's Third Symphony. Indeed, that work had been played five times in Boston between 1884 and 1892, making it possible that Chadwick knew it well. After the powerful opening gesture, the texture becomes thick and complex. In the words of Yellin, "Directly following is a melodic line that vitiates this powerful thrust in fussy elaboration; like a once-powerful stream in a sandy desert, all the force is absorbed in this welter of busy notes going everywhere at the same time."[43] Like the first movements of his previous two symphonies, this one is in triple meter. Chadwick favors mediant relationships for his principal thematic areas, and S is a syncopated tune in A minor presented first by the horns.

The 3/8 Andante cantabile is one of Chadwick's most effective slow movements. The opening theme is played primarily by the strings, with discreet echoes from the woodwind choir. The form is a large ABA with a coda. The contrasting B section is characterized by energetic dotted rhythms emulating a march. When the cantabile melody of the A section returns, Chadwick develops the singing lines to a more intense lyrical statement that grows naturally out of the opening ideas. The coda fades away to a calm pianissimo.

The third movement Vivace non troppo vacillates between 6/8 and 2/4. Early in the movement, Chadwick highlights this discrepancy by having the strings play in compound duple meter while the winds play in simple duple. Approximately two-thirds of the way through the movement, the meter changes to 2/2 while the quarter note stays the same, effectively doubling the tempo. This energetic section introduces new themes, which are immediately treated contrapuntally, taxing the listener's ability to retain so much thematic material. When the original tempo returns, the texture becomes increasingly sparse as the dynamic level dies away to nothing, followed by a headlong presto rush to the final cadence.

The Allegro molto energico Finale opens with the sort of syncopated, brassy theme that made Chadwick an audience favorite but earned him jabs from the critics. Philip Hale wrote, "I like the broad and flowing second theme, the dramatic effects of the syncopation. Yet other passages in this finale seemed dull and unnecessarily noisy."[44] The theme mentioned by Hale is introduced by the strings in the dominant key. In its eight-measure period structure, this is the squarest and most traditional theme in this movement, which may be why it attracted Hale at first hearing. Again, the composer indulges in stretches of dense contrapuntal elaboration, along with frequent changes of meter between the opening 6/4 and 4/4. The last two minutes constitute a continual crescendo and accelerando to the thrilling climax.

The Third Symphony has many brilliant moments but lacks a sense of continuity. This may be attributed in large part to Chadwick's metrical decisions. Each movement is in either triple or compound meter and features numerous metrical changes. As a result, one is never quite comfortable with the rhythmic basis, despite many energetic themes and clever syncopations. Hale perhaps alluded to this problem when he wrote, "The symphony is strong in the matter of rhythm, occasionally too strong, as when rhythm is tortured till it shrieks."[45] Hale also took the composer to task for his influences: "Mr. Chadwick has been sitting at the feet of Mr. Johannes Brahms. He has also listened—no doubt unconsciously—to the pleasing performance of Mr. Anton Dvořák on the celebrated instrument known as the Negro-Indian American pipe, which I believe is the invention of Messrs. Krehbiel & Company."[46] Here the composer was caught in the crossfire of a running battle between the New York and Boston critics, whose differing opinions on both Brahms and Dvořák were well known. Henry E. Krehbiel served as apologist for Dvořák, especially in his lengthy article in advance of the premiere of the "New World" Symphony, while the Boston critics were skeptical of the work. Likewise, Krehbiel embraced the music of Brahms earlier than his Boston colleague Hale, who reputedly stated that the fire exits in Boston's Symphony Hall should read, "Exit in case of Brahms."[47]

The symphony is varied and shows impressive skill at orchestration and counterpoint. Chadwick was the most gifted American symphonic composer at the time, and the symphony prize was earned honestly. But the work's failure to impress was summarized by Louis C. Elson: "It is a symphony in which the composer has exerted all his ingenuity, and studied from the manuscript it must contain many points of profound interest to the musician, but it is quite another matter to the auditor, who lets many a bit of augmentation, of diminution, and of contrary motion slip by unperceived." In the conclusion of his review, Elson, like the majority of Boston critics, damned the work with faint praise: "All in all, one finds much to praise in the work, but at the end must confess that the great American symphony is not yet written."[48] In an ironic postscript, a 1905 performance of the Third Symphony in Leipzig (conducted by the composer) led one reviewer to assert in the strongest terms that, in his opinion, Chadwick had in fact achieved just that, and more: "I declare that I consider this symphony the best of all that have been written since Brahms.... From this symphony I hold George W. Chadwick to be the most important living Anglo-American composer—Edward Elgar not excepted."[49] One wonders what the local critics thought when the *Boston Globe* reprinted this German assessment of the work they had judged unable to stand alongside the European canon.

SYMPHONIC SKETCHES

An eminently practical man, Chadwick abandoned his attempt—if it had ever been his goal—to write the "great American symphony." Instead, he turned to other genres that were more conducive to his unique musical style. He continued to produce significant orchestral works in the decades after the appearance of the Third Symphony, some of which are clearly symphonies in all but name. Without the imposing title of "symphony" to distract them—or the preconceptions the name carried—critics and audiences proved much more receptive to these works. Chief among his subsequent orchestral works, and one that has continued to enjoy success, is the set of four *Symphonic Sketches* (1895–1904).

In this work, Chadwick retains the four-movement structure and characteristic key scheme of the symphony but adds descriptive titles and programmatic content. The title is purposely vague, referring perhaps to artists' sketches or to the literary form that was popular with nineteenth-century American authors (e.g., Washington Irving's *Sketch Book*).[50] The programmatic content of the works is not interconnected but rather presents four separate vignettes from American life. Chadwick selected events and scenes that he considered to be characteristically American. This context allowed him full rein to indulge his penchant for syncopated pentatonic melodies and bold, brassy orchestration.

The opening number, "Jubilee," is prefaced by this poetic epigraph written by the composer:

> No cool gray tones for me!
> Give me the warmest red and green,
> A cornet and a tambourine,
> To paint MY jubilee!
> For, when pale flutes and oboes play,
> To sadness I become a prey;
> Give me the violets and the May,
> But no gray skies for me!

The text is generally believed to refer to the National Peace Jubilee organized by bandmaster Patrick Gilmore in Boston in 1869. The event brought together eleven thousand singers and one thousand instrumentalists from across the country in a massive musical concert celebrating the end of the Civil War and reconciliation between North and South. In Gilmore's history of the event, he notes, "The Jubilee was also a crowning triumph of an experiment in art and acoustics, and in musical magnitude was far greater than had ever before been realized, or even attempted; and it fully and successfully demonstrated the feasibility of combining and controlling thousands, ay tens of thousands of musicians—vocal and instrumental—in one harmonious body."[51] The 1869 Peace Jubilee was especially meaningful for the teenaged Chadwick because several of his relatives sang in the massed choir, and he had the opportunity to attend as an audience member.

The movement begins with a jubilant burst of sound from the full orchestra. The effect of all the players attacking the downbeat fortissimo is startling and sets the tone for this crowd-pleasing movement. The bold *P* in A major is homophonic and emphasizes the strong beats of the 6/4 meter. Both the marchlike rhythms of the opening theme and the prominence of winds, triangle, tambourine, and other percussion are redolent of Gilmore's band. There is a hint of syncopation and hemiola in *P*, but the transitional passage that follows makes full use of the characteristic syncopations of minstrel music (mm. 28–34; example 3.8). The contrasting *S* in C major (another instance of Chadwick's preference for mediant relationships) is labeled "cantabile" and introduces a singing melody that is traded back and forth between the strings and solo winds.

This lyrical tune features the kind of gapped scale that reminded reviewers of Irish music. Its overt sentimentality reflects the second stanza of his epigraphic poem, providing a noticeable contrast with the brash opening. The brief development section demonstrates the potential of *P*, as Chadwick treats it with Mendelssohnian lightness before whipping it back into a propulsive frenzy. In the recapitulation, *S* is presented in F major, the submediant of the home key.

The ending of the movement is particularly effective. Chadwick begins with the light-textured version of *P*, building it up to a *ff* fermata D-flat major six-four chord. The oboe

Example 3.8 Chadwick "Jubilee" from *Symphonic Sketches*, mm. 28–34

then sings a soulful rendition of *S* in lento espressivo tempo at Reh. L, gradually augmented by the addition of the rest of the woodwind choir and the strings; it builds to a sentimental climax before dying away to **pp** whole notes in the strings. This tranquil moment is rudely interrupted by the final **ff** statement of *P* in presto tempo leading a mad rush to the double bar. This juxtaposition of unabashed sentimentality and boisterous high spirits will return in the final movement and was the subject of much comment from reviewers.

The second movement, "Noël" (Andante con tenerezza), has a double meaning, invoking both the Christmas story and the composer's love for his son Noel. The dichotomy is reflected in the epigraph:

> Through the soft, calm moonlight comes a sound;
> A mother lulls her babe, and all around
> The gentle snow lies glistening;
> On such a night the virgin mother mild
> In dreamless slumber wrapped the Holy Child,
> While angel-hosts were listening.

The opening solo in the English horn recalls the timbre of the famous Largo of Dvořák's "New World" Symphony. The movement traces a long arch from **_pp_** to a stirring **_ff_**, evoking an angelic choir and back to a whispering conclusion for solo violin and harp accompanied by the rest of the strings **_pp_**. Yellin describes the movement evocatively: "'Noël' is more like a Currier and Ives print than a short story or vaudeville skit. Timeless as a rustic snow-covered landscape under a clear night sky with a full moon, the movement depicts rays of warm light coming from a farmhouse window that frames a mother and child."[52]

The third movement, "Hobgoblin: Scherzo Capriccioso," was written in 1904, nearly a decade after the others. It borrows its epigraph from Shakespeare's *A Midsummer Night's Dream*: "That shrewd and knavish sprite called Robin Good-fellow." This movement is the shortest of the four, and one could be forgiven for expecting a Mendelssohnian scherzo after hearing the elfin passages in "Jubilee" and noting the reference to the play that Mendelssohn immortalized with his incidental music. The quality of this scherzo is heavier, though, with a solid, at times stomping, rhythm that Faucett calls a brisk Celtic jig and Yellin describes as having "an unmistakable Gallic flavor in both harmony and orchestration."[53] The prominence of the brass section and the constant rhythmic back-and-forth (including an overabundance of hemiola) contributes to the inability of this movement to take flight.

The final movement, "A Vagrom Ballad," was Chadwick's personal favorite, of which he wrote, "I was highly elated by the effect of the Vagrom Ballad. I knew I had said something in that piece!"[54] The movement depicts a group of hoboes in the woods that Chadwick had seen from the window of a train as he traveled from Boston to Springfield. His epigraph, written in common meter and reminiscent of English ballad form, alludes to this inspiration:

> A tale of tramps and railway ties,
> Of old clay pipes and rum,
> Of broken heads and blackened eyes
> And the "thirty days" to come!

The movement is even more mercurial than "Jubilee," flitting through a series of moods, folk-inflected tunes, and timbre changes that imply a much more detailed programmatic story than the epigraph supplies. The tempo marking "Alla burla" sets the high-spirited tone of the movement and may suggest hobo routines in the popular burlesque and vaudeville entertainments of the day.

After using formal structures typical of the symphony in his first three movements, Chadwick chooses an unconventional form for "A Vagrom Ballad." It consists of five sections that are only loosely connected thematically. Already in the first two pages, the kaleidoscopic mood contrasts are established, first with an extended cadenza for bass clarinet (a parody of a well-known recitative passage from Act V of Meyerbeer's *Les Huguenots*), and then with a lumbering theme for bass clarinet and contrabassoon. The colorful orchestration features brass fanfares, the bright sound of the xylophone (mimicking the subject of Bach's Fantasia and Fugue in G Minor), ragtime rhythms, and dramatic contrasts between high and low timbres. Chadwick uses an ending similar to that of the first movement, only arguably even more effective. The penultimate section is an extended Lento misterioso that builds to a heartfelt climax (à la vaudeville sentimentalism) in strings and harp before devolving into sighing two-note phrases in the strings. This is followed by another cadenza for bass clarinet ending on a single note with a fermata. The molto vivace coda follows immediately, with a good-natured helter-skelter accelerando to the prestissimo ending.

The Boston critics lavished praise on the work after its February 7, 1908, premiere and in the decades that followed. Philip Hale heard in the work "an originality, a swing, an audacity, a recklessness, an irreverence . . . a joyous extravagance, a rollicking humor, a boastfulness tempered slightly by appreciation of the ridiculous; an utter absence of self-consciousness, and inability to take oneself or one's achievements too seriously," all traits that he associated with the best in American literature (including Walt Whitman).[55] Henry T. Parker heard in the mercurial mood shifts of the first and last movements qualities that distinguished the American temperament from its European counterpart:

> Americans "fool," Americans "jolly," and European observers are fain to lament these ingrained habits in us. Is Mr. Chadwick's final "sketch"—"The Vagrom Ballad" of "clay pipes and rum and broken heads and blackened eyes and thirty days to come"—anything else than musical "fooling" and musical "jollying," American in spirit and expression, and often at its loudest and most careless? Comes the slow, mysterious, sober song near the end. The inevitable "contrasting passage," the merely academic may call it. As it seems to us, it is far more a just musical incarnation of the tendency in the American temperament to turn suddenly serious, and deeply and unaffectedly so, in the midst of its "fooling," to run away into sober fancies and moods, and then as quickly turn "jolly" again.[56]

The progression from the First Symphony to the *Symphonic Sketches* is noteworthy. Chadwick began his career writing in cosmopolitan style and developed his orchestral technique through the course of his three symphonies. It was only in the *Symphonic Sketches*, though, that he achieved a true critical success, attributable to the unabashed nationalism of the work. Though critics had identified American thematic elements in his symphonies, the freedom from generic expectations coupled with explicit American programmatic designations allowed them to appreciate his eclectic, kaleidoscopic work on its own terms.

SINFONIETTA

The diminutive Sinfonietta was sketched in the summer of 1903 and premiered at an all-Chadwick concert on November 21, 1904, in honor of the composer's fiftieth birthday. Its gestation period was thus shorter than that of any of his previous symphonic works. Olin Downes noted that "the four movements have coherency of thought and style which is genuinely symphonic to a far greater degree than the 'Symphonic Sketches.'"[57] The work is unpretentious both in its brevity and in its simplicity. A reviewer of a repeat performance of the work in 1910 wrote, "There was no pitfall for the unwary, no concealed meanings, no pathological or other -ological subtleties, but just a bit of lovely musical landscape, filled with the sunshine of a happy disposition and vocal with the songs of spontaneous fancy."[58] The work has occasional echoes of French impressionism, especially in the employment of modal scales and orchestration reminiscent of exoticism.

The first movement, labeled simply "Risolutamente," opens with a gapped syncopated scale characteristic of the composer's fast movements. The D major key is remarkably stable, and the modulations are not nearly as complex or surprising as those in the Third Symphony and *Symphonic Sketches*, despite the "Chinoise" effects that appear briefly.[59] The second movement in duple meter establishes a marchlike Allegretto that does not fluctuate except for a single fermata on the final chord of the first section. *A*, in A minor, is simple and stable both rhythmically and harmonically. The string and wind families alternate in the opening pages before blending their timbres in the closing measure of the section. *B* features a closely related theme

Example 3.9 Chadwick *Sinfonietta*, third movement "Scherzino," mm. 1–3

in A major, with timpani, tambourine, triangle, and cymbals added to enliven the orchestration. *A* returns in A minor to create a rounded structure. A distinctive feature of the movement is the extensive use of solo viola at the end of both A sections. The end is particularly arresting, as a solo viola plays arpeggios leading to an A above the treble staff, which the instrument holds for seven and one-half measures while two French horns play "in lontananza" (at a distance).

In the third movement, "Scherzino," Chadwick eschews the metrical changes so prevalent in his previous works in favor of a consistent triple meter. Although the time signature shifts from 9/8 to 3/4, the underlying pulse is consistent throughout, with a slight relaxation of the tempo in the Trio. A five-note opening motive (mm. 1–3; example 3.9) is used as a unifying device throughout the A section, and the Trio introduces a contrasting lyrical theme that prominently features fourths. The sparkling movement is brief and unpretentious but all the more satisfying because of its thematic unity. The Finale exemplifies Chadwick's kaleidoscopic style. It opens with an introduction that moves from B minor through E major and A major before arriving at the principal theme in D major. The theme features the prosodic syncopation noted in the Second Symphony as typical of the composer's "American" style. The movement is sectional, with contrasting tempos and themes leading to a grand pause and another wistful melody followed by the now-familiar headlong rush (più mosso and presto) to a noisy conclusion with timpani. The reviewer for the *Boston Transcript* singled out the last two movements as characteristic of Chadwick's best work:

Mr. Chadwick seems preeminently a composer of scherzos and brilliant finales. In this line he has something personal to say, and a distinctly personal way of saying it, very far removed from the commonplace which he is like to approach in his slow music, and also far away from an imitation of German orthodox composers, of which so much of our American effort consists. In Mr. Chadwick's compositions where a keen sense of rhythm, humor, brilliancy and warmth of emotion have play, as in the scherzino and finale of the sinfonietta, the sketches called Jubilee and the Vagrom Ballad, and the vivace and finale of the [Third] symphony, we at last have music by an American composer that is more than skillful, intelligent, earnest work after the pattern of French and German musicians who happen to be in the fashion.[60]

As a whole, the Sinfonietta contrasts with Chadwick's other symphonies and quasi-symphonies. It is light where they are boisterous, short where they are long, and unified where they are eclectic. As is so often the case with Chadwick, his Yankee cussedness led him to defy the conventions of his day, and this charming work was little appreciated in the era of musical modernism. When it was reprised in 1910, reviewers found it to be old-fashioned, and audience members did not take to its effervescent qualities when paired with a long and serious Anton Bruckner symphony. Of all the orchestral works of Chadwick, this one most deserves to be reassessed in the twenty-first century.

SUITE SYMPHONIQUE

The first decade of the twentieth century brought a taste for all things French to Boston. As Americans became increasingly disenchanted with Germany, they embraced French fashions, impressionistic art, and the music of Claude Debussy (1862–1918) and Maurice Ravel (1875–1937). The composer and violinist Charles Martin Loeffler (1861–1935) was crucial in establishing this trend. He was born in Germany but renounced his fatherland after his father was imprisoned by German authorities and died before being released. Loeffler claimed to be Alsatian for the entirety of his long career in Boston. He played violin in the Boston Symphony Orchestra from 1882 to 1903 before resigning to devote his full attention to composition. His French-inflected works were as important as those of Debussy and Ravel in influencing Boston's tastes.

Chadwick was not immune to this French influence. He began work on the *Suite Symphonique* during a visit to Lausanne, in the French-speaking region of Switzerland, but, like many of his orchestral works, it was completed in fits and starts over a period of years. He submitted the first movement under the title *La Vie joyeuse* to the National Federation of Music Clubs competition in 1910, but it did not win. The following year, the newly completed *Suite Symphonique* was named "Best Orchestral Work by an American Composer" in the same competition, affording Chadwick a modicum of vindication along with a generous $700 prize (approximately $15,000 in today's currency). As with the Third Symphony, the suite's prize-winning status dampened the enthusiasm of the critics at the premiere, but it fared better in later performances.

The *Suite Symphonique*, like the *Symphonic Sketches* and Sinfonietta, is a symphony in all but name. Its four movements follow the traditional four-movement structure with characteristic tempos and keys:

I. Allegro molto animato (E-flat major)
II. Romanza: Andantino espressivo (B-flat major)
III. Intermezzo e humoreske: Poco allegretto (G minor)
IV. Finale: Allegro molto e energico (E-flat major)

The score contains numerous echoes of impressionist techniques and sonorities, but commentators have generally found it to be one of the most American of Chadwick's works, in large part because of the quotations and allusions in the third movement.

The first movement opens with the sort of sweeping flourish in the strings that would later become a staple of film scoring. The eleven-minute movement features numerous tempo changes as it juxtaposes two contradictory ideas: soaring melodies in the upper strings and jaunty melodies built of his characteristic prosodic syncopations. When he combines them, as he does at various points throughout the movement, the energy of the syncopated patterns sustains the spacious sweep of the soaring melodies. Chadwick again demonstrates his skill at bringing a movement to a thrilling conclusion with an effective crescendo in the final pages.

Not known for his slow movements, Chadwick nonetheless offers a memorable second-movement Romanza. The frankly sentimental melody in the alto saxophone is in his Irish vein, but without the flippant quality of his scherzos. The simple tunefulness of the principal theme contrasts with a middle section that exploits the shimmering orchestration of Debussy. A whole-tone oboe melody over the accompaniment of harp arpeggios and violin harmonics near the end of the middle section inevitably calls to mind the French composer's *Prelude to the Afternoon of a Faun*. A brief cadenza for saxophone sets up a partial recapitulation of the principal melody in the closing section.

The third movement, Intermezzo e humoreske, displays the humor and kaleidoscopic textures of his best scherzos. It features numerous tempo and meter changes, including two brief excursions into 5/4. Chadwick makes liberal use of the xylophone and triangle in a sparkling score that demonstrates his mastery of Debussyan impressionistic textures and includes a delicious whole-tone parody of "Yankee Doodle" (mm. 196–99; example 3.10).

The Finale begins with rising scales in the strings reminiscent of the first movement. The 6/4 meter is Chadwick's favorite, perhaps, as Yellin has suggested, because of the potential for duple and triple patterns and inherent cross-rhythms. The energy of the opening is not sustained in the lengthy sonata form. Again, Chadwick pauses periodically to invoke impressionist sonorities, which mitigates against the forward motion, despite a rousing accelerando and crescendo to the end.

The suite was premiered to generally positive reviews in Philadelphia on March 29, 1911.[61] When it was repeated by the Boston Symphony Orchestra two weeks later, however, the critics in Chadwick's hometown were ruthless. The notoriously hard-to-please Henry T. Parker, whose reviews were signed "H.T.P.," paradoxically noted, "Mr. Chadwick did not write it for the competition, arranged by the Federation of Musical Clubs in which it lately won a prize. Having the music finished and in hand, he merely submitted it. Yet more than once it does not escape the easy obviousness of prize music, and still more does it suggest an effort to do again what Mr. Chadwick did so interestingly, individually and stirringly in his first Symphony [sic] Suite."[62] The other Boston critics concurred with the opinion that it was not his strongest work, but not because of its success in the competition. When Chadwick conducted the work with Walter Damrosch's New York Symphony in 1912, the reviewers there reacted much more supportively, and the Boston critics also softened their views upon its repeat performance there in 1924. At the heart of the critics' ambivalence seems to have been their difficulty in identifying its influences. The passing references to impressionism were inescapable and duly

Facing, **Example 3.10** Chadwick *Suite Symphonique*, third movement, mm. 196–99

The Second New England School and Their Contemporaries

noted, but the overall assessment was that the work reflected Chadwick's American character. The assessment was not so much due to quotations of American folk tunes but to something less tangible. It seems that the eclectic, mercurial nature of the work was perceived on some elemental level to be characteristically American.

CONCLUSION

Chadwick's three symphonies and three quasi-symphonies constitute the major American contribution to the symphonic repertoire before World War I. Taken as a whole, the critical reaction to these six works encapsulates the challenge faced by American composers in this era. Chadwick's works are imaginatively orchestrated, with touches of lighthearted humor and brilliant finales. Their eclecticism—variously incorporating Celtic-style melodies, allusions to American popular culture, Germanic heritage, and Impressionistic orchestration—can be heard as a reflection of the multifaceted American culture in which they were created. At the same time, their lack of organic unity made critics question their integrity as symphonic works. The generic association with the symphonic tradition led reviewers to demand a unity and seriousness to which Chadwick seldom aspired. Though "Jubilee" from the *Symphonic Sketches* has secured a place in the standard repertoire, Chadwick's other symphonic works have not appeared often on concert programs. The good news for twenty-first-century listeners is that all but the First Symphony are available on recordings, some of them quite good. Combined with the readily available recordings of his symphonic poems and orchestral overtures, they constitute a significant body of orchestral repertoire.

Amy Beach

The other member of the Second New England School who composed a symphony was Amy Beach (1867–1944), known during her lifetime as Mrs. H. H. A. Beach. Amy Marcy Cheney was a remarkably gifted prodigy whose parents secured early training in piano and composition but carefully protected her from scrutiny by limiting her public appearances. She made her debut shortly after her sixteenth birthday, playing Ignaz Moscheles's (1794–1870) Piano Concerto No. 2 in G Minor with Adolf Neuendorff's orchestra in Boston's Music Hall on October 24, 1883. She followed this with a solo recital on January 9, 1884, and several other solo performances; she made her debut with the Boston Symphony Orchestra on March 28, 1884, playing the Chopin Concerto in F Minor, Op. 21. In April of the following year, she played with the Theodore Thomas orchestra for the first time; at the first rehearsal, he famously started the last movement of the Mendelssohn Second Concerto in D Minor at a slower tempo out of consideration for her youth. She later recalled, "I did not know that he was sparing me, but I did know that the tempo dragged, and I swung the orchestra into time."[63] He never again made the mistake of underestimating her abilities.

At the same time that she burst onto the Boston scene as a performer, she began publishing songs. Her melodies were engaging, and several of her songs were very successful. Her musical career path was dramatically altered, however, when she married Dr. Henry Harris Aubrey Beach, a prominent Boston physician twice her age, a few months after her eighteenth birthday. He doted on her, and their marriage was by all accounts a happy one, but he had strong ideas about her career. He forbade her from pursuing a professional performing career, limiting her engagements to a few charity performances each year. He urged her to pursue composition as her primary occupation, but he convinced her to remain an autodidact so as

Table 3.4 The "Gaelic" Symphony of Amy Beach (1867–1944)

Title	Key	Date	Movements	Instrumentation	Comments
Symphony in E Minor, Op. 32, "Gaelic"	E minor	1894–96	1. Allegro con fuoco 6/8 (555 mm.) 2. Alla siciliana 12/8 (213 mm.) F major 3. Lento con molto espressione 6/4 (146 mm.) E minor 4. Allegro di molto ¢ (563 mm.)	Grand plus Picc., EH, Bclar., Tri.	Dedicated to Emil Paur. Premiered October 31, 1896, Boston Symphony Orchestra, conducted by Emil Paur. Published by Arthur P. Schmidt, 1897.

not to spoil her natural creativity with composition lessons. Her compositional style, formed through careful score study and concert attendance, is highly individual but not as varied as it might have been in other circumstances.

SYMPHONY IN E MINOR, OP. 32, "GAELIC"

Exactly one week after the *New York Herald* published Dvořák's famous pronouncements on the future of American music on May 21, 1893, the *Boston Herald* reprinted his article along with responses from ten of Boston's leading musicians.[64] Each took a different approach to the Bohemian's premature thoughts on his adopted home of eight months, ranging from Chadwick's curt dismissal to Paine's spirited defense of cosmopolitan style. The longest response came from the youngest musician, Amy Beach. She acknowledged Dvořák's underlying assumption, which was typical of late-nineteenth-century thinking, that nationalism was based on the folk music of the common people. But she took issue with his understanding of American folk music:

> Without the slightest desire to question the beauty of the negro melodies of which [Dvořák] speaks so highly, or to disparage them on account of their source, I cannot help feeling justified in the belief that they are not fully typical of our country. The African population of the United States is far too small for its songs to be considered "American." It represents only one factor in the composition of our nation. Moreover, it is not native American.... The Africans are no more native than the Italians, Swedes or Russians.
>
> Dr. Dvořák says: "The American musician understands these tunes ... because of their associations." This might be true of a musician born and brought up in the South.... But to those of us of the North and West there can be little, if any, "association" connected with negro melodies. In fact, excepting to those especially interested in folklore, only very few of the real negro melodies are even known. The songs with which we are familiar have been written by Stephen Foster and other song composers of our own race.... We of the North should be far more likely to be influenced by the old English, Scotch, or Irish songs, inherited with our literature from our ancestors.[65]

In late December 1893, Beach had the opportunity to hear Dvořák's "New World" Symphony in Boston. She heard it again in October 1894, and the entry in her notebook of musical impressions contains detailed observations on the structure, themes, and orchestration of the symphony, closing with this summary of her overall impression:

> The symphony as a whole made a far better impression on me than at its first performance last year. It is interesting throughout, the machinery of it admirably managed, the orchestral + harmonic coloring done by a master. It seems to me light in calibre, however, and to represent only the peaceful, sunny side of the negro character + life. Not for a moment does it suggest their sufferings, heartbreaks, *slavery*. It is all active, bright, cheery and domestic (the slow movet [*sic*] especially suggesting the home-life to me, with the baby being sung to sleep). From this point of view it is admirable, but there is much more that might have been added, of the dark, tragic side!! Dr. Dvorak [*sic*] is occasionally reminiscent of many composers, even Wagner, but much can be forgiven him for writing something interesting + short in the way of a Symphony.[66]

As she points out, Dvořák had limited experience of the tragic side of the African American experience, which restricted the emotional range of his composition. To her, the work lacked profundity and seriousness, traits that her Boston colleagues valued highly. By the time she wrote her evaluation of the "New World," Beach was already well underway with her own symphony, which may be surmised to be at least partly a response to it. Her work would share the tonic key of Dvořák's composition and reflect his call to make use of folk materials, but she chose a different folk source, and she strove to transcend what she heard as his lack of depth by expressing both the joys and sorrows of the Irish people. The second movement was the first to be finished, on March 22, 1894, and the third movement was added on November 11 of the same year. She completed the symphony in March 1896, and it premiered with the Boston Symphony Orchestra under the direction of Emil Paur on October 31, 1896.

Beach took seriously Dvořák's admonition to use folk music as a basis for American art music, but she turned for thematic material to a very different source than the one the Bohemian composer had advocated. She found her themes in a collection of Irish songs published in a Dublin magazine in 1841.[67] She inserted these tunes into the symphony in nearly complete form, making them stand out from the surrounding texture and calling attention to their difference. For whatever reason, Beach did not divulge that she had used actual folk tunes until after the initial performances, allowing reviewers to assume that the melodies were her own creations in the spirit of Gaelic folk songs.

The first movement, Allegro con fuoco, begins with a swirling introduction in the strings that rises from **pp** to a ***ff*** tutti before the arrival of the first theme of the sonata-allegro form. Adrienne Fried Block has observed that the introductory motive as well as P and S all derive from Beach's art song "Dark Is the Night!" (1890), a tempestuous evocation of a storm at sea. K, which appears in mm. 147–61 of the exposition and mm. 439–63 of the recapitulation, is an Irish tune entitled "Conchobhar ua Raghallaigh Cluann" (Connor O'Reilly of Clounish). This sprightly pentatonic tune, presented by solo flute, oboe, and English horn against a drone in the bassoon and low strings, contrasts starkly with the swirling chromatic lines of the rest of the movement.

The second movement is designated "Alla siciliana" in 12/8 meter. It begins with the simple melody "Goirtin Ornadh" (The Little Field of Barley), also from the 1841 collection, in an evocative scoring for wind choir. The bulk of the movement is a long central section in Allegro vivace tempo and 2/4 meter—a variant of "Goirtin Ornadh" that recalls the first movement with its energetic, swirling chromatic lines. The return of the Alla siciliana is accompanied by the Irish tune played by the English horn (calling to mind Dvořák's famous Largo) and then by the oboe; Beach scores it again for the wind choir, now with string accompaniment. A nineteen-measure coda brings back the Allegro vivace for a headlong rush to the double bar, recalling Chadwick's practice. Block has noted the similarity of this movement—a sort of reverse scherzo with the fast central section in duple meter framed by more relaxed outer sections—to Brahms's Symphony No. 2, Op. 73.[68] Sarah Gerk has called attention, however, to even more striking similarities to the second movement of the Camille Saint-Saëns (1835–1921) Violin Concerto No. 3, which Beach heard while she was writing her symphony. Both of these allusions demonstrate that the composer was thinking of much more than simply the Dvořák symphony as she worked.[69]

The third movement, Lento con molto espressione, is by far the most extended, necessitated by Beach's decision to develop two Irish themes—"Paisdin Fuinne" (The Lively Child) and "Cia an Bealach a Deachaidh Si" (Which Way Did She Go?)—extensively and combine them toward the end of the movement. Despite some lovely textures for solo winds, the thirteen-minute movement seems excessively long in the context of the rest of the symphony.

The Allegro di molto Finale introduces no folk tunes, but instead derives its thematic materials from those of the first movement, and thus ultimately from the "Dark Is the Night" song. She told a program annotator in 1917, "The finale tries to express the rough, primitive character of the Celtic people, their sturdy daily life, their passions and battles, and the elemental nature of their processes of thought and its resulting action."[70] Again in sonata form, the movement introduces a great variety of textures and moods from romantic solo lines to turbulent tuttis. The end of the movement features some of the most effective orchestral writing of the work as it builds to a dramatic brassy *fff* conclusion. Like so many other first-time symphonists, Beach could not resist the texture of punctuated chords over a timpani roll on the last page of the score.

Reaction to the premiere was extremely positive. Among the many instances of kudos was a handwritten note from Chadwick that Beach preserved in her autograph album: "I want you to know how much Mr. [Horatio] Parker and I enjoyed your symphony on Saturday evening. It is full of fine things, melodically, harmonically, and orchestrally, and mighty well built besides. I always feel a thrill of pride myself whenever I hear a fine work by any one of us, and as such you will have to be counted in, whether you will or not—one of the boys."[71]

The critical reaction mirrored Chadwick's personal note. Reviewers focused on the composer's gender, expressing surprise and pleasure that a woman could achieve a work of such strength, competence, and intellectual vigor. As the first symphony by a female composer that the critics had ever heard, it was subjected to a range of gendered criticisms, typified by Philip Hale's comment: "occasionally she is boisterous, but the boisterousness is healthy, not merely vulgar. The only trace of woman I can find in this symphony is this same boisterousness."[72] In an era when women were assumed to be intuitive creatures lacking the mental capacity to compose long complex works like symphonies, Beach's "Gaelic" Symphony was a revelation.

Entirely missing in the critical response was consideration of Beach's thematic choices and what her choice of Irish sources implied about her views on American nationalism. Block did an extensive survey of reviews of this work but could find only one—written in Kansas City in 1916—that responded to the nationalist content of the work in light of Dvořák's prescription for American music. The symphony was pathbreaking not only as an accomplishment by a female composer but also as an experiment in Americanism.

The last of the symphonies written by the composers of the Second New England School brings to a close an important chapter in American music history and set the stage for new directions in the twentieth century.

George Templeton Strong

No survey of late-nineteenth-century American symphonists would be complete without mention of George Templeton Strong (1856–1948). He was philosophically opposed to the composers of the Second New England School (which he called the "dryasdust school"), but his works frequently appeared on programs with theirs during the 1880s and 1890s. His closest aesthetic ally was Edward A. MacDowell (1860–1908), who did not complete any symphonies.

Strong was born to a wealthy family in New York City. His father, George Templeton Strong Sr. (1820–75), was an attorney and notable amateur musician and patron of the arts whose diaries of concert attendance constitute an important record of musical life in the city in the mid-nineteenth century.[73] The younger Strong chose to disregard his father's wishes by pursuing a career as a professional musician, leading to a rift that was never repaired. He studied violin and oboe, earning his living for a time as an oboist in New York. He enrolled in the Leipzig Conservatory in 1879 to study French horn and composition and remained in Europe for the rest of his life. He settled in Wiesbaden in the late 1880s, where he became close friends with Edward MacDowell. The two maintained an active correspondence after MacDowell moved to Boston in 1888, providing an enlightening and opinionated view of American musical life during the period. Strong lived in Switzerland from 1890 to his death in 1948 and left a prodigious body of musical compositions, most of them unpublished (table 3.5).

SYMPHONY NO. 1, "IN THE MOUNTAINS," OP. 14A

Strong's Symphony No. 1 in F Major, "In the Mountains" was written between 1882 and 1886. The full score of the first two movements has been lost, but the score of the last two movements and a four-hand piano reduction of the entire work survive. Its four movements are entitled as follows:

   I. "In the Afternoon"
   II. Adagio: "In the Gloaming"
   III. Allegro: "At Midnight—the Wild Hunt"
   IV. Allegro molto: "In the Morn"

The symphony was featured on the fifth and final concert of Frank Van der Stucken's (1858–1929) festival of American music in Chickering Hall, New York, on November 24, 1887.[74] The concert was reviewed in the major papers, giving a good sense of contemporary opinion of the work. Strong's effort was generally lauded by critics, with most pointing out the similarity of his work to European models. The review in the *American Art Journal* called attention to his melodic inspiration as a welcome antidote to recent German music. The *New York Sun* called the symphony "an encouraging work on the whole, well scored, and abounding in interesting melodies."[75] In a remarkable display of hyperbole, the *Musical Courier* called Strong's composition "on the whole, the most interesting that has yet been begotten by American musical brains."[76]

Perhaps most telling is the critique by the dean of American music critics, Henry E. Krehbiel, who found echoes in Strong's score of specific works by Richard Wagner and especially Joachim Raff. The structure and programmatic content, he pointed out, were derived from the latter's Symphony No. 3 in F Major, "Im Walde," Op. 153 (1869). He admitted that identifying the debts was something of a low blow, but he did so in the interest of the integrity of American music:

Table 3.5 The Symphonies of George Templeton Strong (1856–1948)

Title and date	Key	Movements	Instrumentation	Comments
Symphony No. 1 "In the Mountains," Op. 14a (1882–86)	F major	1. "In the Afternoon" 2. Adagio ("In the Gloaming") 3. Allegro ("At Midnight—the Wild Hunt") 4. Allegro molto ("In the Morn")		Premiered November 24, 1887, Festival of American Music in New York, conducted by Frank Van der Stucken. The full score of the first two movements is lost. A four-hand piano reduction of the entire work is extant.
Symphony No. 2, "Sintram: The Struggle of Man against Evil Powers," Op. 50 (1887–88)	G minor	1. Ziemlich langsam 4/2, 2/4—Rasch 3/4 (621 mm.) 2. Langsam 6/8 (240 mm.) E-flat major 3. Die drei entsetzlichen Gefährten: Tod, Teufel und Irrsinn (The Three Terrible Companions: Death, the Devil, and Insanity) (Sehr lebhaft) 3/8 (812 mm.) C minor 4. Kampf und Sieg (The Victorious Battle) (Rasch, Feierlich) 2/2 (851 mm.) G minor —> G major	Grand plus Picc., Bclar., EH, 1 Bssn., 1 Tpt., 1 Cbtuba	Dedicated to E. A. MacDowell. Movement 4 premiered April 12, 1892, Brooklyn Seidl Society, conducted by Anton Seidl. Entire work premiered March 4, 1893, New York Philharmonic Society, conducted by Anton Seidl. Published by Franz Jost, 1894.

It is to be expected that young composers will fall into the habit of copying the manner of the masters whom they admire before they develop an individual style of their own, but it would help them greatly if they would cultivate the lofty virtue of self-criticism until they were able after completion to prune their scores of every quotation direct or indirect which they are able to detect after a work has been long enough out of mind to make calm examination possible. For Mr. Strong's talent we have heretofore expressed much admiration. We believe that he will be a credit to the art of his native land, but before then he must become more original in his manner of expressing his musical thoughts. Nothing is more contemptible in musical criticism than the common penchant for hunting down reminiscences, but sometimes it becomes necessary to direct attention to borrowed ideas, and it can benefit the American movement if the men who stand for it now should be held to a strict accountability in the matter of meum and tuum.[77]

Krehbiel explicitly criticized the composer for quotations that were noted in passing by most of the other critics but ignored by none. A decade after Paine's First Symphony alluded so frankly to Beethoven's symphonies, critics were still uncomfortable with thematic references to European models in American works. As noted already, Christopher Reynolds has demonstrated that thematic allusions were pervasive in Romantic music and could serve a variety of functions in an artwork. For American critics, though, originality was the hallmark of compositional integrity, and they set a standard that was difficult if not impossible for American composers to achieve.[78]

SYMPHONY NO. 2 IN G MINOR, "SINTRAM: THE STRUGGLE OF MAN AGAINST EVIL POWERS," OP. 50

Strong's second symphony was an ambitious work lasting an hour in performance. He composed it in 1887–88 during the time that he was in daily contact with MacDowell in Wiesbaden. Heroic tales such as Norse mythology and Arthurian legends fascinated the two young composers, and their aesthetic ideals were strongly influenced by the music and philosophy of the New German School, particularly Liszt (whom both MacDowell and Strong met on several occasions) and Wagner. The last two movements of Strong's symphony contain programmatic titles after the model of those used by Liszt:

I. Ziemlich langsam—Rasch
II. Langsam
III. Die drei entsetzlichen Gefährten: Tod, Teufel und Irrsinn (Sehr lebhaft) ["The Three Terrible Companions: Death, the Devil, and Insanity"]
IV. Kampf und Sieg (Rasch, Feierlich) ["The Victorious Struggle"]

The Finale had its premiere at a concert of the Brooklyn Seidl Society under the baton of Anton Seidl on April 12, 1892; he conducted the entire work with the New York Philharmonic on March 4, 1893. It was heard once more on American soil in the nineteenth century when Frank Van der Stucken led a performance at the annual convention of the Music Teachers National Association in Cincinnati on June 21, 1899. Franz Jost of Leipzig published the 224-page score and parts in 1894.[79]

The work was inspired by Part II of Goethe's *Faust*, by an Albrecht Dürer woodcut titled *The Knight, Death and the Devil*, and by a Friedrich de La Motte-Fouqué story titled *Sintram and His Companions*, itself based on the woodcut. Strong directed that this quotation from *Faust* be included in concert programs when the symphony was performed:

> My weal I seek not in torpidity;
> Humanity's best part in awe doth lie;
> Howe'er the world the sentiment disown,
> Once seized, we deeply feel the vast unknown.

The programmatic content of the long, rambling musical composition deals with the abuse of power in society, derived from an allegorical tale of the triumph of Christianity over evil. Its four discrete scenes address themes of struggle, oppression, and defiance without giving a specific description of a series of events. The choice of larger-than-life battles among epic forces calls to mind the themes of Wagnerian operas. Even closer is the parallel to Gustav Mahler (1860–1911), who was writing his First Symphony at the same time: both works are an hour in length, and they feature similar titanic struggles. Mahler's symphony premiered unsuccessfully in Budapest in 1889 and was extensively revised before its next performance in Hamburg in 1893. There is no evidence that Strong knew Mahler's First Symphony when he composed "Sintram," and, at any rate, it premiered before Mahler's work reached its final form.

The reviewer for the *New York Times* aptly described the structure of the work as "simple in outline but complex in detail."[80] The first movement begins with a chorale theme intoned by the woodwind choir and interrupted by a turbulent theme in the strings, whose contrasting mood and orchestration are reminiscent of the overture to Wagner's *Tannhäuser*. These two ideas are extended, combined, and developed through a variety of permutations and tempo changes, always intense and serious, until the movement finally fades away into a soft, somber ending. The second movement begins with descending chromatic lines in the strings that again recall Wagner. The prevailing major tonality of the principal section contrasts with the first movement, and it also allows Strong to display his penchant for beautiful melodies and subtle orchestral mixtures. The contrasting B section of the second movement abandons the major tonality and grows to a level of intensity that continues the first movement's somber exploration of dark themes in minor keys. In this symphony, Strong often builds a long, gradual crescendo that he cuts off with a staccato chord at the moment of arrival. The second movement—both the shortest and most melodic of the four—ends in tranquility.

The orchestration of the third movement is impressive in its variety of moods and tone colors. Varied resources are used to explore programmatically the three terrible companions of the movement's title. After a brief opening fanfare, Death is represented through an extended chorale-like passage for low strings in C minor. This ominous theme gives way to an extended crescendo that sets up the Devil, whose jaunty, chromatic theme is played by solo bassoon accompanied by clarinets playing detached chords preceded by grace notes. The lineage of this passage can plausibly be traced to the final movement of Hector Berlioz's (1803–69) *Symphonie fantastique,* and it foreshadows Paul Dukas's (1865–1935) *Sorcerer's Apprentice*, which would not be completed until 1897. The Devil's theme cavorts through a series of chromatic modulations and orchestral color changes to a return of the Death theme, this time in low woodwinds. Insanity is introduced by solo English horn, gradually building up through the addition of more instruments to an extended contrapuntal passage uniting the three themes. The movement culminates with the stentorian restatement of the Death theme by the brass choir and accompanied by triple-tongued chords in the woodwinds and descending chromatic scales in the strings.

The fourth movement continues the theme of struggle, ending in a triumphant return of the opening chorale, which, as the *New York Times* reviewer noted, "always stands in music for the voice of the Protestant Church."[81] At eighteen minutes long, the progression from *Kampf* (struggle) to *Sieg* (triumph) proceeds in multiple waves, each starting softly and moving through long crescendos to fortissimo climaxes. The movement is dominated by the brass choir of three trumpets, three trombones, and contrabass tuba to a greater extent than any of the previous movements, calling to mind Wagnerian sonorities. Strong employs contrapuntal textures to enhance the crescendos, repeating motives and echoing them in different parts of the orchestra. Chromatic harmonies, frequent tempo changes, and kaleidoscopic timbral combinations all contribute to the impression of struggle. The final climactic crescendo culminates in a ***fff*** tutti that dissolves into a ***pp*** timpani roll giving way to low strings. The return of the chorale tune that follows is intoned first by the clarinets, French horns, and bassoons accompanied by pizzicato scales in the low strings, gradually adding more instruments and broadening the tempo until the symphony reaches its stately conclusion.

The critical reaction to this gargantuan work was extremely positive while acknowledging the somberness of the subject matter and the unremitting darkness of the orchestration. The *Chicago Tribune* called it "ultra-modern in its Wagnerian orchestral color, and Berlioz or

Strauss might have penned the last scherzo-like presto, but its themes are original and exceptionally well handled and developed."[82] Krehbiel, who had been so critical of Strong's first symphony five years earlier, was effusive: "The first movement is far and away the strongest part of the work, and it might fairly be questioned whether it has ever been equaled by an American symphonist in strength and fitness of idea and mastery of treatment. Mr. Strong's command of orchestral color is supreme, his thematic workmanship admirable and his part-writing, especially in the slow movement, worthy of the highest praise."[83]

Critics unanimously found the work too long. The otherwise glowing review in the *New York Times* stated it bluntly: "The symphony is certainly somber. Taking into consideration the unbroken gloom of the subject, which required dark harmonies and instrumentation from beginning to end, it would have been wise in the composer to shorten his symphony by 20 minutes. It is entirely too long, and it leaves the mind depressed."[84]

Strong moved to the United States for a year in 1891–92, and again briefly in the summer of 1896, but he returned to Switzerland each time, discouraged by musical conditions in the United States. After his second failed sojourn, which coincided with MacDowell's move from Boston to New York to accept a professorship at Columbia University, Strong abandoned music in favor of watercolor painting from 1897 to 1912 (hearing a performance of "Sintram" by the Lausanne Orchestra under Carl Ehrenberg persuaded him to return to composition). Coupled with MacDowell's mental breakdown in 1905 and death in 1908, Strong's withdrawal prompts speculation on the direction that American orchestral music might have taken in the hands of these two progressive composers. Their relatively modest impact left the Boston composers as the most prominent American orchestral composers until well into the twentieth century.

Edward A. MacDowell

This chapter concludes by turning to Edward MacDowell's own brief contribution to symphonic literature. This composer, who was born in New York in 1860 and died there in 1908, lived in Europe for twelve years, first as a student in Paris from 1876 to 1878 and then as a pupil of Joachim Raff and an aspiring professional in Frankfurt and Wiesbaden, Germany, from 1878 to 1888. A close friend of Strong, he was already well known when he returned to Boston in the fall of 1888. His reputation was cemented in the following years, and in 1896 the trustees of Columbia University identified him as the most prominent American composer and appointed him chair of their new music department. Conflicts with the administration led him to resign his position in 1904; he suffered a mental breakdown the next year and died on January 23, 1908.[85]

MacDowell was best known for his four piano sonatas, two piano concertos, and numerous short piano works. Nonetheless, he wrote four symphonic poems in the 1880s and two orchestral suites in the 1890s. Only the title page of a symphony from the 1880s survives, but he may have used the melodic materials from that work for his two-part composition *Die Sarazenen, Die schöne Aldâ*, Op. 30, two fragments after *The Song of Roland* (1886–90). Like his teacher Raff and his friend Strong, MacDowell resisted the notion of creating purely abstract orchestral compositions, preferring instead to include ample programmatic references after the pattern of Raff's mentor Franz Liszt. Of his entire orchestral output, only one work employs the formal procedures of a symphony (table 3.6).

Table 3.6 *Suite für grosses Orchester*, Op. 42, by Edward A. MacDowell (1860–1908)

Title and dates	Key	Movements	Instrumentation	Comments
Suite für grosses Orchester, Op. 42 (Original version, without Mvt. 3: 1888–91 Mvt. 3: 1893)	A minor	1. "In einem verwünschten Walde" (In a haunted forest) 6/8 (178 mm.) 2. "Sommer-Idylle" (Summer Idyll) 6/8 (53 mm.) A major 3. "Im October" (In October) 6/8, 3/4 (235 mm.) F major 4. "Gesang der Hirtin" (The shepherdess's song) 4/4 (66 mm.) C major 5. "Waldgeister" (Forest spirits) 2/4, 2/2 (314 mm.) A minor —> A major	Grand plus Picc., Tuba, and 1 extra Perc.	Premiered September 24, 1891, Worcester, Massachusetts Festival Orchestra, conducted by Carl Zerrahn. Published without Movement 3 by Arthur P. Schmidt, 1891. Movement 3 published by Schmidt, 1893.

SUITE FÜR GROSSES ORCHESTER, OP. 42

The first of MacDowell's two orchestral suites was published by Arthur P. Schmidt of Boston in 1891. In its broad outlines, the original version of this work resembles the traditional four-movement structure of a symphony: the opening movement in A minor consists of an introduction (Largamente, misterioso) followed by the movement proper (Allegro furioso), ending with a return to the opening tempo and thematic materials. The second movement in A major (Allegretto grazioso) moves in a slow 6/8 meter with minuet-like features. The third movement in C major carries the tempo marking Andantino, semplice, and the fourth movement (Molto allegro) has the characteristics of a rondo, beginning in the principal key of A minor and concluding in A major. The final movement contains a thematic reference to the first, effectively unifying the work as a whole.

The composer clearly did not wish to write a symphony, however, as the traditional broad symphonic outlines are undermined by the details. Despite the relatively traditional key scheme, there is much localized chromaticism, particularly in the two outer movements. Each movement carries a programmatic title in both German and English:

I. In einem verwünschten Walde (In a haunted forest)

II. Sommer-Idylle (Summer Idyll)

III. Gesang der Hirtin (The shepherdess' song)

IV. Waldgeister (Forest spirits)

As was his custom, MacDowell did not include a complete program but allowed the evocative titles to speak for themselves. It is noteworthy that, during an era of widespread Americanism in art music (seen most clearly in the Chadwick works discussed above), MacDowell eschewed any hint of American subject matter in this suite, opting instead for the universal themes of nature and pastoral scenes. The performance time of the entire work is under fifteen minutes, and the combination of attractive themes with light orchestration inspired the *New York Times* reviewer of the premiere performance to urge local conductors to add it to their repertoires. He especially liked the last movement, calling it "delightful in its airy piquancy and in the ingenuity of the instrumentation."[86]

The performance history of this work illustrates MacDowell's aversion to Americanism *per se*. The work was published before it premiered, and when the composer learned that its first performance was slated to be part of an all-American concert at the Worcester Festival in September 1891, he tried unsuccessfully to have it removed from the program. The organization performed it anyway, and MacDowell chose to boycott the premiere, although his wife Marian did attend. Chadwick described the success of the work in a letter to MacDowell:

> I have been trying to get around to telling you how much I enjoyed and admired your suite at Worcester. . . . It made everything else on the program sound <u>sick</u>! . . . What I particularly like about the whole thing is its conciseness and delicate touch—the purity of its color and freedom from stiff periods and cadences. All this is <u>not</u> modern German style and the Lord be praised if <u>some</u>body can get away from <u>that</u>. The little phrase for muted horns at the end of the A maj[or] movement is <u>lovely</u>—entirely successful. The work is full of striking effects of delicate color—and all so simple too![87]

MacDowell objected to the concept of American Composers' Concerts in principle (on the grounds that American compositions needed to be heard alongside works from the cosmopolitan European tradition and not in isolated programs only with other Americans), but he often benefited from the performance of his works on the same programs as less-inspired works by his compatriots.[88]

In 1892, MacDowell's suite was performed in Berlin, Dresden, Weimar, Leipzig, and Vienna as part of the same tour of American Composers' Concerts by the German-American conductor Franz Xavier Arens that featured Paine's Second Symphony. European critics consistently praised the suite, finding its cosmopolitan style to be simultaneously recognizable and original. Hans Paumgartner wrote, "A quality—and it is not one of the smallest—is possessed by MacDowell: he is interesting. Further, one can hear so much Wagner in the MacDowell suite without being allowed to blame him for plagiarism because of it."[89] The work enjoyed what Marian MacDowell called "a queer popularity in Germany for two or three years," with performances in Breslau, Cologne, and other German cities.[90]

Further undermining the symphonic outlines of the suite, MacDowell published in 1893 a supplementary movement called "In October" to be performed between the original second and third movements. This vigorous and brassy Allegro con brio is longer in performance than any of the original movements, containing numerous modulations to distant keys and changes of tempo and meter. Like the Finale, it contains thematic references to other movements in the suite. Its expansiveness militates against the conciseness that Chadwick admired about the suite in its original form, turning a gem of understatement into something more diffuse.

MacDowell's most admired orchestral composition was his Second ("Indian") Suite, Op. 48—his most celebrated foray into folkloric nationalism—premiered in 1896 and published by Breitkopf and Härtel in 1897. The work consists of five movements with titles evoking Native American scenes. Thematic materials for all but the fourth movement, "Dirge," were drawn from Theodore Baker's dissertation on the music of North American Indians.[91] The work has been extensively analyzed for its use of preexisting themes and for its influence on the Indianist movement in American composition, but its connections to the symphonic genre are even more tenuous than those of the First Suite.

Conclusion: American Symphonies in the Late Nineteenth Century

The period from 1870 to 1900 saw unprecedented economic growth accompanied by growing income inequality. These conditions were largely responsible for the era that has received the pejorative name the Gilded Age. A paradoxical result of the wealth and elitism that led to the creation of symphony orchestras throughout the country was greater access to symphonic music for persons of all classes. The new orchestras also provided a strong incentive for composers to write works in symphonic form. This confluence of events led to the creation of the repertoire discussed in this chapter.

American artists have been notoriously independent in their goals and methods, and, as in the antebellum period (see chapter 2 herein), the symphonies surveyed demonstrate the diversity of results. In the cosmopolitan symphonies of Paine, the Americanist quasi-symphonies of Chadwick, and the Wagnerian effusions of Strong, each composer approached the challenge of the genre in distinctive ways. A unifying theme throughout this body of work, however, is the relation of each composer to the European traditions of symphonic writing. Perhaps because symphonic writing was a recent phenomenon in America, perhaps because so many of the composers had studied in Europe, or perhaps because the repertoire played by American orchestras was almost exclusively European, the composers of the era and the critics who evaluated their works used the German repertoire as a measuring stick. Therefore, Paine wrote symphonies that contained no American references but were brimming with allusions to Beethoven, Schumann, and Raff. Chadwick followed this path in his first three symphonies but realized that the weight of generic expectations would not allow him to achieve all that he wanted. His three quasi-symphonies (and to a certain extent his Second Symphony) make reference to the tradition but move away from it. Beach's "Gaelic" Symphony is an individual response to Dvořák, but a response nonetheless. Strong wanted nothing to do with his more conservative compatriots, but he was unquestionably beholden to the aesthetics of the New German School. MacDowell chose not to publish a symphony, but his First Suite bears striking resemblance to a symphony in its original form. Each of these works is unique, many display inspiration and unimpeachable craftsmanship, and all of them deserve to be heard today. It remained for the new century, however, to produce American symphonic works that truly transcended the German tradition.

Bibliographic Overview

The cosmopolitan tradition in the United States has not been extensively discussed, although scores of most of the works in this chapter are available in PETRUCCI. Hughes/CONTEMPORARY provides a good introduction to critical opinion around 1900, and Bomberger/TIDAL WAVE discusses cosmopolitan music in the context of the American Composers' Concerts. Bomberger/GERMAN addresses the issue of European study by American musicians, and Bonds/AFTER BEETHOVEN and Reynolds/MOTIVES both discuss issues of influence germane to the American experience in the late nineteenth century. Dennison/BOSTON, Schnepel/GREAT, and Shadle/ORCHESTRATING provide insightful discussions of the critical reaction to American orchestral music. Howe/BOSTON SYMPHONY and Horowitz/MORAL provide good contextual background on music in Boston and specifically on the founding of the Boston Symphony Orchestra.

The scholarly literature on individual composers is extensive. John C. Schmidt's introduction to Paine/SYMPHONY and his biography of the composer (Schmidt/PAINE) give an excellent overview of Paine's symphonic works. Faucett/CHADWICK PRIDE and Yellin/CHADWICK are valuable studies of Chadwick and his symphonic works, and Faucett/CHADWICK SYMPHONIC gives exhaustive analyses of all his symphonic works. Block/BEACH, Block/DVORAK, and Gerk/AWAY are the best sources on Beach's symphony, and Block/BOSTON provides a valuable discussion of the Boston reaction to Dvořák's famous *New York Herald* article. For a sympathetic discussion of Dvořák's ideas on American music, see Beckerman/KREHBIEL. Loring/ROMANTIC-REALIST gives a detailed biography of Strong along with extensive excerpts from reviews of his "Sintram" Symphony, and Bomberger/MACDOWELL details his friendship with Edward MacDowell and its influence on his compositional style; the latter source examines MacDowell and his First Suite. For an overview of the era, see Tawa/AGE.

Notes

1. For a thorough examination of Thomas's commitment to orchestral works by American composers, see Brenda Nelson-Strauss, "Theodore Thomas and the Cultivation of American Music," in Spitzer/ORCHESTRAS, pp. 395–413.

2. Higginson's intentions were laid out in a "statement of purposes" from spring 1881, which is reprinted in Howe/BOSTON SYMPHONY, pp. 27–34.

3. Quoted in ibid., pp. 40–41.

4. The exception to Eurocentrism at the Boston Symphony Orchestra, of course, was the lengthy tenure of Japanese conductor Seiji Ozawa from 1973 to 2002.

5. Quoted in Henschel/MUSINGS, p. 286, and Howe/BOSTON SYMPHONY, p. 98. The Dvořák symphony in view is evidently the Sixth, which Henschel had conducted in the fall of 1883.

6. For a list of other proposed designations (the best known of which is "Boston Classicists"), see Charles S. Freeman's article "New England Composers" in *GDAM*.

7. Letter, E. A. MacDowell to George Templeton Strong, March 1, 1890, box 29/30, Edward and Marian MacDowell Collection, Library of Congress Music Division, Washington, DC [hereafter, MacDowell Collection].

8. To be fair, there *were* symphonies composed during this era by Niels Gade, Liszt, Robert Volkmann, Karl Goldmark, and others; Dahlhaus's point is that the cultural centrality of the symphony waned somewhat as the symphonic poem enjoyed its initial heyday of popularity.

9. Carl Dahlhaus, "The Second Age of the Symphony," in Dahlhaus/MUSIC, pp. 265–76.

10. The principal nonsymphonic works of the era are discussed in Yang/OVERTURES.

11. Quoted in Block/BOSTON, p. 11; the debate is further discussed in Block/DVORAK.

12. For a discussion of Dvořák's original article and Henry Krehbiel's promotion of the "New World" Symphony, see Beckerman/KREHBIEL.

13. For a summary of Dvořák's American years, his compositions from this time period, and their influence on future American music, see Beckerman/DVORAK and Beckerman/WORLDS. Shadle/NEW WORLD explores the racial politics surrounding the work's premiere and its subsequent reception history.

14. Schnepel/GREAT explores this paradox at length.

15. Hughes/CONTEMPORARY, pp. 145–46.

16. *Boston Herald*, April 26, 1896; quoted in Schmidt/PAINE, p. 197.

17. Quoted in Frank K. DeWald, liner notes to John Knowles Paine, Symphony No. 1, Ulster Orchestra, conducted by JoAnn Falletta, Naxos 8.559747 (2012).

18. "The Musical World: The Thomas Concert," *Boston Daily Globe*, January 27, 1876, p. 4.

19. Reynolds/MOTIVES, pp. 24–26.

20. Ibid., pp. 44–67.

21. For a discussion of Brahms's intentions in this regard, see "The Ideology of Genre: Brahms's First Symphony," ch. 5 of Bonds/AFTER BEETHOVEN, pp. 138–74.

22. Upton/SYMPHONIES, p. 202. The handwritten movement titles on the frontispiece of the autograph manuscript score, reproduced in Paine/SYMPHONY, plate 2, are almost identical to those in Upton.

23. Schmidt/PAINE, p. 351.

24. Quoted in Paine/SYMPHONY, p. ix.

25. [John Sullivan Dwight], "Mr. J. K. Paine's New Symphony," *Dwight's Journal of Music*, March 27, 1880, p. 54.

26. Quoted in Paine/SYMPHONY, p. ix.

27. Hughes/CONTEMPORARY, p. 150.

28. Bomberger/TIDAL WAVE, pp. 104–7.

29. N. F., "Konzert," *Dresdner Anzeiger*, March 21, 1892, p. 4.

30. "Kunst und Wissenschaft," *Dresdner Nachrichten*, March 21, 1892, p. 2.

31. According to Bill F. Faucett, "He changed the rhythmic profile of several melodies, added to its instrumentation, and significantly altered its form, all in an effort to make the work more recognizably 'American'" (Faucett/CHADWICK OVERTURES, p. ix).

32. Yellin/CHADWICK, p. 45.

33. For detailed discussions of Chadwick's conducting, see Faucett/CHADWICK PRIDE, pp. 77–79 and 125–54. On Chadwick's bitterness over his inability to reach the highest levels as a conductor, see Betz/CHADWICK, pp. 81–82.

34. Proteus [Louis C. Elson], "Music in Boston," *Church's Musical Visitor*, April 1882, p. 187; quoted in Faucett/CHADWICK PRIDE, p. 91.

35. Chadwick Memoirs, 1880–93, Spaulding Library, New England Conservatory; quoted in Faucett/CHADWICK PRIDE, p. 91.

36. Yellin/CHADWICK, p. 93.

37. [William F. Apthorp], *Boston Evening Transcript*, March 10, 1884, p. 1.

38. Yellin/PROSODIC, p. 449.

39. "The Eighth Symphony Concert," *Boston Post*, December 13, 1886, p. 5; quoted in Faucett/CHADWICK PRIDE, p. 109.

40. [William F. Apthorp], "Theatres and Concerts," *Boston Evening Transcript*, December 13, 1886, p. 1; quoted in Faucett/CHADWICK PRIDE, p. 111.

41. [William F. Apthorp], "Theatres and Concerts: Boston Symphony Orchestra," *Boston Evening Transcript*, December 27, 1887, p. 1.

42. "The Eighth Symphony Concert," *Boston Post*, December 13, 1886, p. 5; quoted in Faucett/CHADWICK PRIDE, p. 108.

43. Yellin/CHADWICK, p. 97.

44. *Musical Courier*, October 19, 1894, quoted in Faucett/CHADWICK SYMPHONIC, p. 79.

45. Ibid.

46. Ibid., p. 77. Chadwick himself freely acknowledged his debts to Brahms in this work.

47. Grant/MAESTROS, p. 79.

48. Louis C. Elson, "The Symphony," *Boston Daily Advertiser*, October 22, 1894, p. 4; quoted in Faucett/CHADWICK SYMPHONIC, pp. 80, 81.

49. Faucett/CHADWICK SYMPHONIC, pp. 85–86. The reviewer was Paul Zschörlich.
50. Debussy followed Chadwick's lead by subtitling his orchestral work *La mer*, completed in 1905, "Three Symphonic Sketches" (*trois esquisses symphoniques*).
51. Gilmore/HISTORY, p. 1.
52. Yellin/CHADWICK, p. 118.
53. Faucett/CHADWICK SYMPHONIC, p. 101 and Yellin/CHADWICK, p. 119.
54. Quoted in Faucett/CHADWICK PRIDE, p. 185.
55. Philip Hale, "Long Applause for Chadwick Sketches," *Boston Herald*, March 23, 1918, p. 16; quoted in Faucett/CHADWICK SYMPHONIC, p. 115.
56. H[enry] T. P[arker], "Mr. Chadwick as a True American Composer," *Boston Evening Transcript*, February 10, 1908, p. 13; quoted in Faucett/CHADWICK SYMPHONIC, p. 112.
57. Olin Downes, *Boston Post*, February 12, 1910, quoted in Faucett/CHADWICK SYMPHONIC, p. 135.
58. Quoted in Faucett/CHADWICK PRIDE, p. 217.
59. For a discussion of this aspect of the orchestration, described as "swirling melody, accompanied by the soft, staccato strings, and especially the combination of the harp and triangle," see Faucett/CHADWICK SYMPHONIC, p. 119.
60. R. R. G., "Music and Drama," *Boston Evening Transcript*, November 22, 1904, p. 15; quoted in Faucett/CHADWICK SYMPHONIC, p. 132. The symphony in question is probably No. 3, which appeared on the same program.
61. An extensive descriptive analysis of the work was published in Goepp/SYMPHONIES.
62. H[enry] T. P[arker], "The Symphony Concert," *Boston Evening Transcript*, April 14, 1911, p. 12; quoted in Faucett/CHADWICK SYMPHONIC, p. 156.
63. Quoted in Block/BEACH, p. 33.
64. Dvořák's original article appeared as "American Music: Dr. Dvořák Expresses Some Radical Opinions," *New York Herald*, May 21, 1893. The Boston response appeared as "American Music," *Boston Herald*, May 28, 1893.
65. "American Music," *Boston Herald*, May 28, 1893; quoted in Block/BOSTON, p. 11.
66. "Music Reviews," vol. 2, October 1894, pp. 33–34, box 4, folder 1, Amy Cheney Beach (Mrs. H. H. A. Beach) Papers, 1835–1956, MC 51, Milne Special Collections and Archives, University of New Hampshire Library, Durham, NH [hereafter, Beach Papers].
67. For extensive information on these tunes and their published source, see Block/DVORAK.
68. Block/BEACH, p. 89.
69. Gerk/AWAY, pp. 216–21.
70. Quoted in Block/DVORAK, p. 267.
71. Autograph Album, box 1, folder 19, Beach Papers; also quoted in Block/BEACH, p. 103.
72. Quoted in Block/BEACH, p. 103.
73. Lawrence/STRONG.
74. For a discussion of this festival, see chapter 4 of Bomberger/TIDAL WAVE.
75. "End of the American Series," *New York Sun*, November 25, 1887, p. 2.
76. "The American Concerts," *Musical Courier* 15, no. 22, November 30, 1887, p. 355.
77. [Henry Krehbiel], "The Last American Concert," *New York Daily Tribune*, November 25, 1887, p. 5.
78. For a discussion of allusion in its many forms during the Romantic Era, see Reynolds/MOTIVES; for a discussion of the role of American critics in shaping the discussion of originality in American symphonies, see Schnepel/GREAT.
79. The New York Philharmonic's copy of the full score is available in its Leon Levy Digital Archives: https://archives.nyphil.org/index.php/artifact/b49f5058-6843-46e2-bfd3-f306f9aceb61-0.1/fullview#page/1/mode/2up.

80. "A Week's Musical Topics," *New York Times*, March 5, 1893, p. 13.
81. Ibid.
82. "Lovers of Music Meet," *Chicago Tribune*, June 22, 1899, p. 8.
83. Quoted in Loring/ROMANTIC-REALIST, p. 178.
84. "Week's Musical Topics."
85. See chapter 19 of Bomberger/MACDOWELL for a discussion of MacDowell's mysterious illness, which appears to have been precipitated by bromism.
86. "Some Good Native Work: American Day at the Worcester Music Festival," *New York Times*, September 25, 1891, p. 2.
87. G. W. Chadwick, undated letter to MacDowell, "Wednesday" [September 30, 1891?], box 30/24, MacDowell Collection. Underlined words are in Chadwick's original.
88. For a discussion of MacDowell's uneasy relationship with the American Composers' Concert movement of the 1880s and 1890s, see chapter 9 of Bomberger/TIDAL WAVE.
89. Dr. h. p. [Hans Paumgartner], "Aufführung von Werken amerikanischer Componisten," *Wiener Zeitung* 154, July 7, 1892, pp. 2–3.
90. Marian MacDowell, typescript autobiography, 3:97, box 39/13, MacDowell Collection. For a discussion of the critical reaction in Breslau, see Bomberger/KINDNESS.
91. Baker/NORDAMERIKANISCHEN. For an English translation, see Baker/NORTH AMERICAN.

Bibliography

Baker/NORDAMERIKANISCHEN	Baker, Theodore. *Über die Musik der Nordamerikanischen Wilden*. Leipzig: Breitkopf and Härtel, 1882.
Baker/NORTH AMERICAN	Baker, Theodore. *On the Music of the North American Indians*. Translated by Ann Buckley. New York: Da Capo Press, 1977.
Beckerman/DVORAK	Beckerman, Michael. "Dvořák, Antonín." In *The Grove Dictionary of American Music*. 2nd ed. New York: Oxford, 2013, 3: pp. 56–60.
Beckerman/KREHBIEL	Beckerman, Michael. "Henry Krehbiel, Antonín Dvořák, and the Symphony 'From the New World.'" *Notes* 49, no. 2 (December 1992): pp. 447–73.
Beckerman/WORLDS	Beckerman, Michael. *New Worlds of Dvořák*. New York: W. W. Norton, 2003.
Betz/CHADWICK	Betz, Marianne. *George Whitefield Chadwick: An American Composer Revealed*. American Music and Musicians No. 1. Hillsdale, NY: Pendragon, 2015.
Block/BEACH	Block, Adrienne Fried. *Amy Beach, Passionate Victorian: The Life and Work of an American Composer*. New York: Oxford, 1998.
Block/BOSTON	Block, Adrienne Fried. "Boston Talks Back to Dvořák." *Institute for Studies in American Music Newsletter* 18, no. 2 (1989): pp. 10–11, 15.
Block/DVORAK	Block, Adrienne Fried. "Dvořák, Beach, and American Music." In *A Celebration of American Music: Words and Music in Honor of H. Wiley Hitchcock*. Edited by

	Richard Crawford, R. Allen Lott, and Carol J. Oja, pp. 256–80. Ann Arbor: University of Michigan Press, 1990.
Bomberger/GERMAN	Bomberger, E. Douglas. "The German Musical Training of American Students, 1850–1900." PhD diss., University of Maryland, 1991. UMI 92-25, 789.
Bomberger/KINDNESS	Bomberger, E. Douglas. "The Kindness of Strangers: Edward MacDowell and Breslau." *American Music* 32, no. 1 (Spring 2014): pp. 24–45.
Bomberger/MACDOWELL	Bomberger, E. Douglas. *MacDowell*. Master Musicians Series. New York: Oxford University Press, 2013.
Bomberger/TIDAL WAVE	Bomberger, E. Douglas. *"A Tidal Wave of Encouragement": American Composers' Concerts in the Gilded Age*. Westport, CT: Praeger, 2002.
Bonds/AFTER BEETHOVEN	Bonds, Mark Evan. *After Beethoven: Imperatives of Originality in the Symphony*. Cambridge, MA: Harvard University Press, 1996.
Dahlhaus/MUSIC	Dahlhaus, Carl. *Nineteenth-Century Music*. Translated by J. Bradford Robinson. Berkeley: University of California Press, 1989.
Dennison/BOSTON	Dennison, Sam. *American Orchestral Music, Late Nineteenth-Century Boston*. Boston: G. K. Hall, 1992.
Faucett/CHADWICK OVERTURES	Faucett, Bill F., ed. *George Whitefield Chadwick. Two Overtures: Rip Van Winkle (1878) and Adonais (1899)*. Recent Researches in American Music, vol. 55. Middleton, WI: A-R Editions, 2005.
Faucett/CHADWICK PRIDE	Faucett, Bill F. *George Whitefield Chadwick: The Life and Music of the Pride of New England*. Boston: Northeastern University Press, 2012.
Faucett/CHADWICK SYMPHONIC	Faucett, Bill F. *George Whitefield Chadwick: His Symphonic Works*. Composers of North America, No. 19. Lanham, MD: Scarecrow, 1996.
GDAM	*Grove Dictionary of American Music*, 2nd ed. Edited by Charles Hiroshi Garrett. 8 volumes. New York: Oxford University Press, 2013.
Gerk/AWAY	Gerk, Sarah Rebecca. "Away o'er the Ocean Go Journeymen, Cowboys, and Fiddlers: The Irish in Nineteenth-Century American Music." PhD diss., University of Michigan, 2014.
Gilmore/HISTORY	Gilmore, P[atrick] S. *History of the National Peace Jubilee and Great Musical Festival, Held in the City of Boston, June 1869*. Boston: self-published, 1871.
Goepp/SYMPHONIES	Goepp, Philip H. *Symphonies and Their Meaning, Third Series: Modern Symphonies*. Philadelphia and London: J. B. Lippincott, 1913.

Grant/MAESTROS	Grant, Mark N. *Maestros of the Pen: A History of Classical Music Criticism in America*. Boston: Northeastern University Press, 1998.
Henschel/MUSINGS	Henschel, George. *Musings and Memories of a Musician*. New York: Macmillan, 1919.
Horowitz/MORAL	Horowitz, Joseph. *Moral Fire: Musical Portraits from America's Fin de Siècle*. Berkeley, Los Angeles: University of California Press, 2012.
Howe/BOSTON SYMPHONY	Howe, M. A. DeWolfe. *The Boston Symphony Orchestra: An Historical Sketch*. Boston: Houghton Mifflin, 1914.
Hughes/CONTEMPORARY	Hughes, Rupert. *Contemporary American Composers*. Boston: L. C. Page, 1900.
Lawrence/STRONG	Lawrence, Vera Brodsky, ed. *Strong on Music: The New York Music Scene in the Days of George Templeton Strong, 1836–1862*. 3 vols. Chicago: University of Chicago Press, 1988–99.
Loring/ROMANTIC-REALIST	Loring, William C. Jr. *An American Romantic-Realist Abroad: Templeton Strong and His Music*. Composers of North America, No. 4. Lanham, MD: Scarecrow, 1996.
Paine/SYMPHONY	Paine, John Knowles. *Symphony No. 2 in A Major: Spring, op. 34*. Edited by John C. Schmidt. Middleton, WI: A-R Editions, 2010.
PETRUCCI	Petrucci Music Library: International Music Score Library Project, imslp.org.
Reynolds/MOTIVES	Reynolds, Christopher Alan. *Motives for Allusion: Context and Content in Nineteenth-Century Music*. Cambridge, MA: Harvard University Press, 2003.
Schmidt/PAINE	Schmidt, John C. *The Life and Works of John Knowles Paine*. Ann Arbor, MI: UMI Research Press, 1980.
Schnepel/GREAT	Schnepel, Julie. "The Critical Pursuit of the Great American Symphony, 1893–1950." PhD diss., Indiana University, 1995. UMI 96-08607.
Shadle/NEW WORLD	Shadle, Douglas. *Antonín Dvořák's New World Symphony*. New York: Oxford University Press, 2021.
Shadle/ORCHESTRATING	Shadle, Douglas. *Orchestrating the Nation: The Nineteenth-Century American Symphonic Enterprise*. New York: Oxford University Press, 2016.
Spitzer/ORCHESTRAS	Spitzer, John. *American Orchestras in the Nineteenth Century*. Chicago: University of Chicago Press, 2012.
Tawa/AGE	Tawa, Nicholas E. *The Coming of Age of American Art Music: New England's Classical Romanticists*. New York: Greenwood, 1991.
Upton/SYMPHONIES	Upton, George P. *The Standard Symphonies: Their History, Their Music, and Their Composers; A Handbook*. Chicago: McClurg, 1889.

Yang/OVERTURES	Yang, Hon-Lun Helan. "A Study of the Overtures and Symphonic Poems by American Composers of the Second New England School." PhD diss., Washington University of St. Louis, 1998.
Yellin/CHADWICK	Yellin, Victor Fell. *Chadwick: Yankee Composer*. Washington, DC: Smithsonian Institution Press, 1990.
Yellin/PROSODIC	Yellin, Victor Fell. "Prosodic Syncopation." In *A Celebration of American Music: Words and Music in Honor of H. Wiley Hitchcock*, edited by Richard Crawford, R. Allen Lott, and Carol J. Oja, pp. 449–59. Ann Arbor: University of Michigan Press, 1990.

CHAPTER FOUR

The Symphonic Works of Charles Ives

J. Peter Burkholder

Introduction

There is probably no more diverse a group of symphonic works than those by Charles Ives (1874–1954). The five completed works and one incomplete piece he called symphonies, shown in table 4.1, represent essentially six different conceptions of what a symphony is, ranging from a late Romantic cyclic work (Symphony No. 1) to a suite of four symphonic poems (*Holidays Symphony*) and from absolute music (Symphony No. 1) to characteristic symphonies suffused with American popular music (Symphony No. 2) or hymns (Symphony No. 3) and programmatic works evoking American holiday celebrations (*Holidays Symphony*), a spiritual journey (Symphony No. 4), and a contemplation of the cycles of the universe (*Universe Symphony*). In addition, he completed two three-movement suites of symphonic poems that he called orchestral sets and left sketches for a third, all shown in table 4.2. This chapter will treat all nine symphonic works but will focus primarily on the four numbered symphonies, for in those Ives most directly engaged with the symphonic tradition.[1]

The variety of Ives's symphonic works resulted in part from the diverse influences on his music and in part from his unusual circumstances as a professionally trained pianist, organist, and composer who made his living in the insurance business and thus could compose as he pleased. Born in Danbury, Connecticut, and educated at Yale in nearby New Haven, he grew up hearing, performing, and composing music in four very different traditions, which he then intertwined in his mature music.[2]

The first tradition was American popular music. Through his father George Ives, leader of Danbury's most prominent band, Ives learned the habits, sounds, and repertoire of nineteenth-century amateur bands, as well as songs of Stephen Foster (1826–64) and songs of the Civil War, in which George had served as a bandleader in the Union Army a decade before Charles was born. In his late teens and twenties, Ives encountered the up-to-date sounds of Tin Pan Alley and ragtime, as well as the strains of college and fraternity songs, and he composed marches, songs, and choral numbers in popular styles until graduating from Yale in 1898. All these familiar types from popular music ended up in his symphonic works. Sometimes he evokes them through timbre, texture, rhythm, or style, paralleling Mozart's use of topical allusions to eighteenth-century styles.[3] At other times these types are embodied in

Table 4.1 The Symphonies of Charles Ives (1874–1954)

Number and/or title	Key/Center	Dates	Movements	Instrumentation	Comments
No. 1	D minor	ca. 1897–ca. 1902	1. Allegro 3/4 (509 mm.) 2. Adagio molto 2/4 (113 mm.) F major 3. Scherzo: Vivace 3/8 (164 mm.) 4. Allegro molto C (4/4) (414 mm.) D major	Grand plus EH, Tuba, optional Flt. and Cbssn.	First performance: Washington, DC, on April 26, 1953, National Gallery Orchestra, conducted by Richard Bales. Published by Peer, edited by Roque Cordero (1971); critical edition by James B. Sinclair, published by Peer (1999).
No. 2	F major and A-flat major	?1899–?1902, ca. 1907–09	1. Andante moderato 3/4 (112 mm.) B minor/D major 2. Allegro molto C (4/4) (382 mm.) A-flat major 3. Adagio cantabile 3/4 (133 mm.) F major 4. Lento maestoso 3/2 (41 mm.) B minor 5. Allegro molto vivace C (4/4) (280 mm.) F major	Grand plus Picc., Cbssn., Tuba, SD, BD, Tri.	First performance: New York on February 22, 1951, New York Philharmonic, conducted by Leonard Bernstein. Published by Southern Music, edited by Henry Cowell and Lou Harrison (1951); critical edition by Jonathan Elkus, published by Peer (2007).
No. 3, *The Camp Meeting*	B-flat major	?1901–?04, ca. 1908–11	1. "Old Folks Gatherin'" (Andante maestoso—Andante con moto—Adagio cantabile) 3/2 (128 mm.) B-flat major [ends in F major] 2. "Children's Day" (Allegro moderato) C (4/4) (178 mm.) E-flat major 3. "Communion" (Largo) 6/8 (62 mm.) B-flat major	Flt., Ob., Clar., Bssn., 2 Hr., Trom., Bells, Strgs., optional Timp.	Awarded the Pulitzer Prize for Music in 1947. First performance: New York on April 5, 1946, by New York Little Symphony, conducted by Lou Harrison. Published by Arrow Music, edited by Lou Harrison (1947); revised edition by Henry Cowell, published by Associated Music (1964); critical edition by Kenneth Singleton, published by Associated Music (1990; 2nd ed., 2001).

No. 4	ca. 1912–18, ca. 1921–25	1. "Prelude" (Maestoso) 6/4 (41 mm.) 2. "Comedy" (Allegretto) 6/8 (238 mm.) 3. "Fugue" (Andante moderato) 4/2 (121 mm.) 4. "Finale" (Largo) 6/2 (90 mm.)	Grand plus Picc., Fl., Clar., Tsax, Barsax, 2 Hr., 4 Tpt., Cor., Trom., Tuba, Perc. (Bells, Tri., Indian Drum, SD, BD, Cym., 2 Gongs), Cel., Harp, Solo Pno., Quartertone Pno., Orch. Pno. (4-hands), Org., SATB mixed chorus, optional Ether Org. / Theremin, Xylo.	First performance: First two movements, New York, on January 29, 1927, by members of the New York Philharmonic, conducted by Eugene Goossens; complete work in New York on April 26, 1965, by American Symphony Orchestra, conducted by Leopold Stokowski, assisted by David Katz and José Serebrier. Mvt. 2 published in *New Music* (1929); full score published by Associated Music (1965); critical edition by William Brooks, James B. Sinclair, Kenneth Singleton, and Wayne Shirley, published by Associated Music (2011); performing edition by Thomas M. Brodhead, published by Associated Music (2020).
A Symphony: New England Holidays	assembled ca. 1917–19			First performance: Minneapolis on April 9, 1954, by Minneapolis Symphony Orchestra, conducted by Antal Dorati.
	?1909–13, ca. 1913–19, rev. ca. 1923–26	1. *Washington's Birthday* (Very slowly—Allegro—Andante) 4/4 (185 mm.)	Flt. (Picc.), Hr., Bells (or Pno.), Jew's harp (or 2 Clar.), Strgs., optional Bssn., Trom.	First performance: San Francisco on September 3, 1931, by New Music Society Orchestra, conducted by Nicolas Slonimsky. Published in *New Music* (1936); repr. Associated Music (1964); critical edition by James B. Sinclair, published by Associated Music (1991).

Table 4.1 *continued*

Number and/or title	Key/Center	Dates	Movements	Instrumentation	Comments
		?1912–13, ca. 1915–1920, rev. 1923–24	2. *Decoration Day* (Very slowly—Allegro) 4/4 (149 mm.)	Grand plus EH, Tuba, SD, BD, Cym., Glsp./Cel., Low bells/Chimes, optional Picc., E♭ Clar., Tpt.	First performance: Havana, Cuba, on December 27, 1931, by Orquesta Filarmónica de la Habana, conducted by Amadeo Roldán. Published in critical edition by James B. Sinclair, published by Peer (1989).
		?1911–13, ca. 1914–18, ca. 1919–23, rev. ca. 1930–31	3. *The Fourth of July* (Adagio molto—Allegro con spirito) 4/2 (122 mm.)	Grand plus Picc., 2–3 Fifes, Cbssn., Tpt, Cor, Tuba, SD, BD, Cym., Xylo., Bells (high, middle, low), Pno., optional Picc., Clar.	First performance: Paris on February 21, 1932, by Orchestre Symphonique de Paris, conducted by Nicolas Slonimsky. Published by Adler and New Music (1932); repr. Associated Music (1959); critical edition by Wayne D. Shirley, published by Associated Music (1992).

?1904, ca. 1913–19, rev. 1932–33	4. *Thanksgiving and Forefathers' Day* (Adagio maestoso—Adagio cantabile—Maestoso) 4/4 (279 mm.)	Grand plus Picc., Cbssn., Tpt., Tuba, Bells (high, medium, low), Chimes (church, low), Cel., Pno., optional Flt., Clar., Bssn., Hr., Tpt., Offstage ensemble [Cbssn., 4 Hr., Trom.], SSATTB chorus	First performance: Minneapolis on April 9, 1954, by Minneapolis Symphony Orchestra, conducted by Antal Dorati. Published in critical edition by Jonathan Elkus, published by Peer (1991).
Universe Symphony 1915–28	Prelude No. 1 4/2 (303 mm.) Prelude No. 2: "Birth of the Ocean Waters" (incomplete) Prelude No. 3 (lost) Section A: "Past: Formation of the Waters and Mountains," or "Formation and Chaos" (Largo) 4/4 (83 mm.) Section B: "Present: Earth, Evolution in Nature and Humanity" or "The Earth and Firmament" 4/2 (incomplete) Section C: "Future: Heaven, the Rise of All to the Spiritual" (incomplete)	Large orchestra divided into smaller ensembles, including a percussion ensemble	Incomplete; three performing versions. (1) Realization and completion by Larry Austin, first performance in Cincinnati on January 28, 1994, by Cincinnati Philharmonic Orchestra with the University of Cincinnati College-Conservatory of Music Percussion Ensemble and Chamber Choir, conducted by Gerhard Samuel. (2) Edition by David Porter of Prelude No. 1 and Section A with the Coda from Section C, first performance in Greeley, Colorado, on October 29, 1993, by University of Northern Colorado Symphony Orchestra, conducted by Kenneth Singleton. (3) Realization by Johnny Reinhard, first performance in New York on June 6, 1996, American Festival of Microtonal Music, conducted by Johnny Reinhard.

Table 4.2 The Orchestral Sets of Charles Ives

Number and/or title	Dates	Movements	Instrumentation	Comments
No. 1, *Three Places in New England*	ca. 1908–21, rev. 1929, rev. 1935	1. *The "St. Gaudens" in Boston Common (Col. Shaw and His Colored Regiment)* (Very slowly) 4/4 (83 mm.) 2. *Putnam's Camp, Redding, Connecticut* (Allegro) 4/4 (163 mm.) 3. *The Housatonic at Stockbridge* (Adagio molto) 4/4 (44 mm.)	Version 1 (full orchestra, original): Grand plus Flt. (Picc.), EH, Cbssn., Tuba, SD, BD, Cym., Gong Version 2 (chamber orchestra arr.): Flt., Ob., EH, Clar., Bssn., Hr., Tpt., Trom., Timp., SD, BD, Cym., Pno., Strgs., optional Picc., Hr., Tpt., Pno. Version 3 (chamber orchestra, 1935 pub.): Flt., Ob., EH, Clar., Bssn., Hr., 2 Tpt., 2 Trom., Tuba, Timp., SD, BD, Cym., Pno., Strgs., optional Picc., 3 Hr., 2 Tpt., Cel., Pno., Organ pedal, Theremin Version 4 (full orchestra, Sinclair edition): Grand plus Flt. (Picc.), EH, Cbssn., Tuba, SD, BD, Cym., Gong, Harp, Organ pedal, Pno. (Cel.), optional Harp	First performance: Version 2, New York City on January 10, 1931, Chamber Orchestra of Boston, conducted by Nicolas Slonimsky; Version 3: Boston on February 14, 1948, Boston Symphony Orchestra, conducted by Richard Burgin; Version 4, New Haven, Connecticut, on February 9, 1974, Yale Symphony Orchestra, conducted by John Mauceri; Version 1 (Mvts. 1 and 3), Greeley, Colorado, on October 29, 1993, University of Northern Colorado Symphony Orchestra, conducted by James Sinclair. Publications: Version 3, rev. by Ives, edited by Nicolas Slonimsky, published by C. C. Birchard (1935); Version 4 (Version 3, with full orchestration restored from Version 1), critical edition by James B. Sinclair, Mercury Music (1976, 2nd ed. 2008); Version 2 (reduction by Ives for Slonimsky's chamber orchestra), edited by James B. Sinclair, Mercury Music (1979).

No. 2	ca. 1909–1919, ca. 1923–1929	1. *An Elegy to Our Forefathers* (Very slowly) 4/4 (48 mm.) 2. *The Rockstrewn Hills Join in the People's Outdoor Meeting* (Allegro) 2/4 (183 mm.) 3. *From Hanover Square North, at the End of a Tragic Day, the Voice of the People Again Arose* (Very slowly—Andante maestoso) 2/4 (119 mm.)	2 Flt. (Picc.), 3 Clar., 2 Bssn., 2 Hr., 4 Tpt., 3 Trom., Tuba, Timp., SD, BD, Cym., Gongs, Tri., Chimes, Cel./Glsp., Low Bells, Zither, Accordions, 2 Harps, 2 Pno., Strgs., optional Unison chorus, Hr., Tpt., Trom., Harp, Org., 2 Theremins	First performance: Chicago on February 11, 1967, Chicago Symphony Orchestra, conducted by Morton Gould. Published in critical edition by James B. Sinclair, Peer (1999).
No. 3	ca. 1919–26	1. Andante moderato 9/4 (incomplete) 2. *An Afternoon, or During Camp Meetin' Week—One Secular Afternoon (In Bethel)* (Adagio molto) 3/2 (incomplete) 3. — 6/4 (incomplete)	2 Flt. (Picc.), Ob., 2 Clar., Bssn., Hr., Tpt., 3 Trom., Alto Hr., Timp., Low Bells, Chimes, Zither, Cel., Harp, Pno., Hand Organ, Org., Strgs. (instruments as named in sketches, possibly incomplete)	Incomplete; Mvts. 1 and 2 realized by David Porter, Mvt. 3 by Nors Josephson (unpublished); first performance of Mvt. 1, Fullerton, California, on March 16, 1978, California State University Orchestra, conducted by Keith Clark.

popular melodies borrowed or paraphrased as themes or quoted as fragments, often carrying specific associations.

A second tradition was American Protestant church music, encompassing traditional hymns, a newer repertory of gospel songs, and service music. Ives grew up attending Danbury's First Congregationalist Church, where the congregation sang many of the most widely known hymns of the nineteenth century. He also attended outdoor revival meetings, where his father sometimes accompanied group singing on his violin or cornet. As a youth, Ives studied piano and then organ with local teachers. He continued studying organ while at Yale, taking lessons with Dudley Buck, one of the leading American organists and church composers of the time, and with Harry Rowe Shelley. At the age of fourteen, Ives became a professional church organist, serving a series of Congregational, Baptist, Episcopal, and Presbyterian churches in Danbury, New Haven, Bloomfield (New Jersey), and New York for more than thirteen years. He played hymns in services and at revivals, and he also accompanied vocal solos, choral anthems, and psalms and canticles in Anglican chant—all genres in which he composed in the current late-nineteenth-century style until he left his last position as an organist in 1902. The hymns and gospel songs he learned as a churchgoer and organist appear in many of his symphonic works, with occasional hints of Anglican chant and choral anthems. Moreover, the textures, techniques, and tricks typical of organ music and organists pervade his orchestral scores, including fugal episodes, juxtaposed planes of sound, orchestration based on timbral contrasts, forms derived from organ improvisation, and special effects of distance and dynamics.[4]

The third tradition Ives absorbed was European classical music. Again he encountered this first through his father, who tutored him in music theory, counterpoint, and composition, introduced him to the preludes and fugues of Johann Sebastian Bach (1685–1750), and encouraged his first efforts in composition, such as a cornet duo modeled on the sextet from *Lucia di Lammermoor* by Gaetano Donizetti (1797–1848).[5] Ives played piano in recitals as a youth, but his deepest exposure to European classics in his teen years was as an organist, performing, among other works, Bach's "Dorian" Toccata and Fugue in D Minor, the organ sonatas and preludes of Felix Mendelssohn (1809–47), and transcriptions such as the *William Tell Overture* by Gioachino Rossini (1792–1868). In college, Ives received a thorough grounding in the classical tradition, studying harmony, counterpoint, instrumentation, and composition with Horatio Parker and hearing Parker's lectures on music history. Ives began his First Symphony as a senior thesis for Parker. Ives later promoted the idea that he had learned little from Parker and owed his training primarily to his father, but his assertion is clearly untrue; he worked very hard for Parker, and the rapid improvement in the quality of his music is apparent as much in the church music he was composing at the time as in the art songs and orchestral works he wrote under Parker and over the next few years.[6] Moreover, after college, Ives devoted himself to the creation of works in the classical tradition that Parker represented, abandoning popular genres and soon church music as well, and focusing instead on art songs, sonatas, chamber music, symphonies, and symphonic poems. This chapter can be written because Ives ultimately followed the path laid out for him by Parker, not the avenues available to him from his training in Danbury.

The final tradition, of which Ives is today regarded as the founder, was experimental music. From his teen years on, Ives sketched short pieces that tried out one or more new musical techniques, such as polytonality, whole-tone harmonies, novel chord structures, dissonant chords moving in parallel motion, new ways of creating a pitch center without traditional chord progressions, and layering of disparate material separated by rhythm and timbre. These pieces served as compositional exercises that demonstrated how such devices could be used, akin to the canons and fugues he wrote to learn counterpoint. Having tried them out in relatively short experimental works, he then adopted many of these novel techniques in his programmatic orchestral sets and late symphonies, using them for their rhetorical power and descriptive effect.[7]

The great diversity of Ives's symphonic music resulted in part from the varied experiences he gained from these four traditions. As we shall see, his First Symphony represents an almost pure expression of the classical tradition, his Second a mix of classical with American popular music and hymnody, his Third a blending of classical and church traditions, his *Universe Symphony* a culmination of the experimental tradition, and his Fourth Symphony, *Holidays Symphony*, and orchestral sets a combination of all four. No other composer had this diverse a background, nor this diverse an output. But Ives's isolation as a composer outside the music profession also affected his creative development.

By sending him to Yale, Ives's family seems to have intended for him a career not in music but in business, where the broad liberal arts education and the personal connections forged at a top Ivy League college would aid in his success. After he graduated, he moved to New York and took a job in an insurance agency in Manhattan. Although he invested more time and effort in his music courses than in others—and persisted in working as a church organist and choirmaster for another four years after graduation—he knew from Parker's instruction and example that no one could make a living in the United States solely as a composer of music in the classical tradition.[8] By the time he resigned his last church position in 1902, Ives had accepted that he could not emulate the three-legged career of his teacher, who supported his work as a composer through jobs as professor at Yale and as organist at a prestigious church in Boston. Instead, Ives abandoned music as a profession and committed himself to insurance. In January 1907, he founded his own agency in partnership with Julian S. Myrick, and two years later they cofounded an agency that became one of the largest, most successful, and most influential in the business. Ives was too shy to be a natural salesman, but he was a profound intellectual force, known for popularizing two of the most significant concepts in the history of insurance: the idea of estate planning—choosing the amount of life insurance to carry based on what one's family would need beyond existing assets should their breadwinner die—and training courses for agents, one of the ancestors of today's schools of business. By the time he retired in 1930, Ives was among the wealthiest Americans and was already using his financial resources to promote his music as well as that of several other American composers.

Publications and performances of his own music came in reverse chronological order, as is apparent from the premieres of the symphonic works. Since 1902, he had composed out of the public eye, despite his frequent attempts to interest musicians in performing his music and occasional private performances such as the premiere of his Violin Sonata No. 3 in 1917. In 1920–21, he self-published and distributed his Piano Sonata No. 2: *Concord, Mass., 1840–60* (known as the *Concord Sonata*), and in 1922 he published his collection of *114 Songs*, which included several songs arranged from as yet unperformed orchestral music. After these brought him a few musical allies, he naturally sought to get his most recent works played first. The first orchestral music to be performed in public was two movements from Symphony No. 4, completed by 1925, premiered in 1927, and favorably reviewed in the *New York Times*. Next were Orchestral Set No. 1: *Three Places in New England*, completed by 1921 and premiered in 1931; three movements from *A Symphony: New England Holidays*, composed in the 1910s, later revised, and premiered on separate concerts in 1931 and 1932; Symphony No. 3, completed by 1911 and premiered in 1946; Symphony No. 2, completed by 1909 and premiered in 1951; and Symphony No. 1, begun under Parker, completed by about 1902, and premiered in 1953, the year before Ives died.

To get a sense of how this antichronological series of premieres skewed opinions of Ives, one can imagine how Ludwig van Beethoven (1770–1827) would have been regarded had the Viennese public been introduced to him by hearing first his difficult and complex late quartets and piano sonatas, then his middle-period works such as the Third through Eighth Symphonies, and only then his early music that was so clearly indebted to Joseph Haydn (1732–1809) and Wolfgang Amadeus Mozart (1756–91). Ives's backward reception earned him a reputation as an ultramodernist, when even his most radical symphonic works draw on an essentially Romantic conception of music and its purpose. By going in chronological order, the following survey of his symphonic music seeks to recapture a sense of Ives as a Romantic composer, a follower of Beethoven and Johannes Brahms (1833–97), who gradually developed his own highly personal modernist idiom in order to convey what at heart is a Romantic experience through music.

Yet chronology is not straightforward for Ives. As noted in tables 4.1 and 4.2, Ives worked on each of his symphonic works over many years, so that the gestation of one piece often overlapped with several others. Because most of his works were not performed or published until years after completion, there is usually no independent verification of the dates Ives assigned to them on his manuscripts and in his work lists or other writings, which are often inconsistent. John Kirkpatrick, who created the first catalogue of Ives's music manuscripts in 1960, attempted to date every piece, drawing on both external and internal evidence, including manuscript dates, diaries, paper types, and handwriting.[9] For a generation, Kirkpatrick's were the accepted dates. After Maynard Solomon in 1987 accused Ives of dating many works too early in order to claim priority for his musical innovations, Gayle Sherwood Magee produced a revised chronology based on firmer dates for the music paper Ives used and for his handwriting. She demonstrated that her approach was accurate by showing how her new, slightly later dates for the choral works fit much more closely with Ives's church positions than did Kirkpatrick's—for instance, that Ives's Anglican service music was created during his year at an Episcopal church in New Haven and that choral anthems showing the specific influences of his teachers Dudley Buck and Horatio Parker were produced during or after his college years.[10] The dates given here reflect Magee's research and incorporate Ives's own testimony. In several cases, Ives asserted that an existing work or movement was adapted from an earlier one for which no sources remain, but without surviving manuscripts we cannot know what the earlier work was like or even whether the composer ever wrote it down. For all the uncertainty, the overall order in which Ives composed his symphonic works is clear, and a line of development can be discerned.

Another central issue in considering Ives's symphonic music is his reliance on musical borrowing. With the possible exception of the *Universe Symphony*, every symphonic work depends at least in part on reworking material borrowed from existing music, from a reliance on other symphonies as models for his first two symphonies to the use of themes and motives borrowed or paraphrased from popular songs, patriotic tunes, and hymns. How he used and reworked this material changed over time and from piece to piece. His sources and his methods of reworking are recurring topics throughout the following analyses.[11]

The Symphonies

SYMPHONY NO. 1 IN D MINOR

In his Symphony No. 1 in D Minor, Ives staked a claim to a place in the nineteenth-century symphonic tradition from Beethoven and Franz Schubert (1797–1828) through Antonín Dvořák (1841–1904) and Pyotr Ilyich Tchaikovsky (1840–93). He followed traditional late-nineteenth-century procedures and intensified them, suffusing the symphony with motivic fragmentation and development, developing variation, cyclic unification, contrapuntal combination of themes, and end-weighted form, including the gradual emergence of a climactic final theme. His mastery of craft is evident throughout, as he explores in a traditional context procedures that would become characteristic of his later music. It was his one symphonic exercise in absolute music, and it laid the foundation for all his later symphonic works.

According to Ives, he began composing his Symphony No. 1 at Yale under the guidance of Horatio Parker and submitted the second and fourth movements as his senior thesis. Parker typically kept student work, but these two movements are not in his collected papers; the second and fourth movements as we know them are apparently reconstructions or new versions Ives completed later. He claimed that parts of or early drafts for some movements were tried out by the Hyperion Theater Orchestra in New Haven in 1896–97, but those early versions do not survive. Ives recalled that Parker rejected his initial attempts at the first two movements but relented on the first movement (discussed later); Ives recast the rejected second movement as the opening section of the slow middle movement of his Symphony No. 2. Ives continued to work on the symphony after graduation, apparently completed it around 1902, and had the work professionally copied around 1908–10.[12]

On March 19, 1910, Walter Damrosch, a close friend of Parker's and a leading conductor in New York, directed a reading of the last three movements at a Saturday morning rehearsal of his New York Symphony Orchestra. As Ives wrote in his autobiographical recollections later published as *Memos*,

> He started with the second movement (adagio), an English horn tune over chords in the strings. When he heard the pretty little theme and the nice chords he called out "Charming!" When the second themes got going together, and the music got a little more involved (but not very involved), he acted somewhat put out, got mad, and said it couldn't be played without a great deal of rehearsing....
>
> So, after playing these three movements of Symphony No. 1, Wally turned to Mrs. Ives and said, "This instrumentation is remarkable, and the workmanship is admirable." But even at that, he said it is too difficult in places, and will take too much rehearsal time—for his pocketbook.[13]

The reading happened soon after Ives completed the Second Symphony and while he was working on the Third. It is one of the great "what ifs" of music history to wonder what might have happened had Ives secured performances around 1910 for this most Romantic symphony—and for the next two, so infused with American music—and won then the critical acclaim that came to him only decades later.

After Ives had made his reputation with other pieces, orchestras and conductors began to ask about the First Symphony in the 1940s, but the instrumental parts were not available until the Edwin A. Fleisher Collection prepared a set of parts under the Works Progress Administration Music Copying Project. The work was finally premiered on April 26, 1953, by the National Gallery Orchestra under conductor Richard Bales, at the opening concert of the

Table 4.3 Formal Plan of Ives's Symphony No. 1

Key:
+	two or more themes/motives superimposed in counterpoint
x	initial motive of a theme
~	figure drawn from a theme
M	cyclic melody (three phrases designated *m, n, o*)
WT	whole-tone progression of minor triads
dim	figure appears in diminution
aug	figure appears in augmentation
stretto	figure appears in stretto

I. ALLEGRO

Exposition

P			P			T								
a	*b*	*c*	*a*	*b*	*c*	*a*	*a+b+c*^{dim}	*d*	*e+c*^{dim}	*b*	*d*	*d+ax*	*e+a+c*^{dim}	*e+a*
1	10	18	26	34	42	50	72	75	83	88	91	94	98	102
d						mod		D♭	A		E♭		B	mod

S					S					codetta (K)			
f	*e*	*g*	*e*	*h*	*f*	*e*	*g*	*e*	*h*	*f*	*f+g+ex*	*g*^{stretto}	*c* :‖
112	127	131	135	137	143	158	162	166	168	174	184	201	224
F	B♭				F	B♭				F, mod			

Development

		+M*m*			+M*n*		+M*m*		+M*n*		+M*o*		
WT	WT+*fx*	WT+*fx*	*e*	*g*	*e*	*h*	*e*	*g*	*e*	*h*	*h+bx+~f*	WT+*a+f*	
228	236	242	249	255	259	263	265	270	274	278	280	285	304
on c♯		on g♯	c♯				D♭				mod		c♯

Recapitulation

P					T				S				
a	*b*	*c*	*a*	*a+b+c*^{dim}	*d*	*b*	*d*	*d+a*	*f*	*e*	*g*	*e*	*h*
325	333	341	349	371	374	376	379	382	397	412	416	420	422
d			mod						D		G		

Coda

		+M*mn*							
hx	*a+g*	+*ex*	*a+fx+g*^{dim}	*b*	*hx*	*ax*+WT	*a*	*g*^{dim}	*hx*	*ax*
427	433	439	441	449	457	484	490	499	501	508
mod						on d	d			

2. ADAGIO MOLTO

A							*B*			*A'*			
a	*b*	*c*	*a*	*d*	*d'*	*d''*+M*mn*	*d* ext	*e*	*d* ext	*a*+*d*	*b*+*b*^{dim}+*I/Pa*	*c*	*a*
1	9	17	25	33	41	49	57	65	77	81	89	97	104
F	C		F	d		D			mod	F	C		F

3. SCHERZO: VIVACE

Scherzo						*Trio*						*Scherzo da capo*		
A	*A'*	*B* (with ~*II/Ab'*)	*A*	*A*^{stretto}	‖:	*C* (~*II/Ab''*)	:‖:	*D*	:‖	*D*	*C*+M	M*x*		
1	20	38	70	89		95		111		132	136	158		
d	g	mod	d			F		mod			A♭	mod		

4. ALLEGRO MOLTO

Exposition

P			P			T			S			K					
a	*b*	*c*	*a*	*b*	*c*	*a*+*b*+~*c*	+*b*^{aug}	+M*x*	*d*	*d*+*II/Ab*	*d*+*II/Ab*+M*x*	*d'*	*e*+M*x'*	*e*+M*x'*	*f*	M*n*^{dim}
1	3	6	11	13	16	21	29	69	75	102	108	116	128	142	151	156
D						mod			A	D♭	D		A		mod	

Recapitulation

P			P			T						S			
a	*b*	*c*	*a*	*b*	*c*	*a*+*b*+~*c*	+*b*^{aug}	*I/Pa*	*a*+*b*^{aug}+*c*	+M*x*	*d*	*d*+*II/Ab*	*d*+*II/Ab*+M*x*		
163	165	168	173	175	178	183		191	219	226	234	240	267	273	
D						mod						D	G♭	G	

K							
d'	*e*+M*x'*	*d'*^{dim}	*I/Pab*+M	*e*^{dim}+M*x'*^{dim}	*f*	M*n*^{dim}	
281	287	291	295	304	316	321	
D	mod		D	mod			

Coda

	March									
~*b*+*c*	M^{dim}	*b'*	M^{dim}	*b'*	*g*	~M*o*	~*c*	M*x*+~*b*	*g*	*g*+M*x*+~*b*
326	336	342	356	362	376	380	383	386	392	398
	D									

Tenth American Music Festival at the National Gallery of Art in Washington, DC. The *Musical Courier* reviewer, James Deane, commented that the symphony "is striking, even if a bit long-winded, and its neglect seems unaccountable."[14] It was not published until 1971, the last of Ives's four numbered symphonies to appear.

As Thomas Willis wrote in the liner notes for the first recording of the First Symphony, released in 1966 by the Chicago Symphony Orchestra conducted by Morton Gould, in composing this piece, "Ives was doing his homework."[15] That is true not only because he started it under Parker's tutelage but also because, throughout the work, Ives engaged directly with several of the most prominent composers and symphonies of the nineteenth century, using them as models to learn his craft. The composition as a whole is modeled on Dvořák's *New World Symphony*, premiered in New York in December 1893, only a few years before Ives began composing his symphony. The theme, sound, and form of the slow movement are adapted from that of the *New World*, and all four movements draw formal and contrapuntal devices from Dvořák, including cyclic form, diminution and augmentation of themes, and contrapuntal combination of themes (including juxtaposing a theme with its own diminution). In addition, Ives drew on Schubert's *Unfinished Symphony*, Beethoven's Ninth Symphony, and Tchaikovsky's *Pathétique Symphony* for motives and procedures in the other movements, and more generally on techniques from Brahms and César Franck (1822–90)—two idols whose pictures he would later post in his music room.[16]

The formal plans of the movements are shown in table 4.3.[17] The symphony as a whole and all four movements individually are relatively simple and traditional in overall outline, featuring a fast sonata form, slow ternary form, scherzo and trio, and fast sonata form without development. Yet each movement is complex in detail, and all four are interrelated through cyclic procedures. Two themes, the opening idea in the first movement (*I/Pa*) and the second melodic unit in the second movement (*II/Ab*), are recalled in later movements. In addition, a melody (M) used as a countermelody in each of the first three movements, presented in relatively long notes like a cantus firmus, emerges as a major theme for the Finale, where it first appears in fragments, is later stated whole, and then comes into its own as the march theme in the coda, in rhythmic diminution. Thus the symphony is doubly cyclic: in the traditional sense of recollecting themes from earlier movements—a practice that goes back to Beethoven's Ninth Symphony—and in the more novel sense of forecasting later events.

In the first movement, the opening theme *P*, shown in example 4.1, is in three eight-bar units: *a*, a solo clarinet melody over undulating chords in the violas and pizzicato bass notes in the cellos; *b* (m. 10), a violin melody over the same accompaniment with flute punctuation, treated in sequence; and *c* (m. 18), a unison climbing sequence in the winds, punctuated by the strings. Each unit develops naturally from the preceding one, showing that Ives already understood the Brahmsian practice of developing variation: *b* varies the dotted rhythms, leaping fourths, rising stepwise motion, and falling stepwise close of *a*, and *c* treats in sequence the neighbor-note dotted figure from *b*. The motivic coherence of this melody is remarkable given that each unit derives from a different source: *a* from Schubert's *Unfinished Symphony* (see below), *b* from the hymn *The Shining Shore* by George F. Root (1820–95), and the neighbor-note figure in *b* and *c* from the gospel song *Beulah Land* by John R. Sweney (1837–99).[18] *P* is immediately repeated with altered orchestration, violins taking over the clarinet tune *a* and strings and winds switching roles in *c*. Such juxtapositions of contrasting timbres, simultaneously and in alternation, are typical of Ives's orchestration throughout the symphony, derived both from the symphonists he had studied and from the practice of organists in juxtaposing contrasting stops on different keyboards.

The Symphonic Works of Charles Ives

Example 4.1 "Symphony No. 1" by Charles Ives. Copyright © 1971 by Peer International Corporation. Copyright Renewed. Used by Permission. All Rights Reserved.

J. Peter Burkholder

Example 4.1 *continued*

As shown in table 4.3, the transition *T* (m. 50) at first focuses on *a*, then introduces two new lyrical ideas, *d* and *e*, and combines them contrapuntally with elements of *P* while exploring distant keys. The second theme *S* (m. 112) begins in the expected F major with a sprightly idea, *f*, marked by an octave leap, Scotch snaps, and running sixteenth notes. But the key is soon undermined: a varied repetition of *f* at m. 119 begins with a surprising swerve to G-flat major before restoring F major, and then the entire second half of the theme shifts to B-flat. For this second half of *S* (mm. 127–42), Ives expands the lyrical figure *e* from *T* into a full sixteen-measure melody by linking it with two new consequent phrases, *g* and *h*, in the pattern *e g e h*. This expanded melody adopts the character of a traditional second theme much more than *f*, which is more active than the first theme rather than more sedate. Thus, in this composite second theme the expected key is paired with an unexpected mood and the expected mood with an unexpected key. *S* repeats in full, confirming that both halves indeed belong to the theme. Ives brings the exposition to a close with a codetta (m. 174) that develops and contrapuntally combines elements of *S*, culminating in a three-part stretto on *g* between winds, brass, and strings. A closing tag borrowed from *c* effects a modulation back to D minor for the repetition of the exposition.

The development section, set primarily in C-sharp minor and its enharmonic parallel major D♭, focuses on *S* and introduces M, the cyclic theme that unites all four movements. The development opens in m. 228 with slowly changing chords in the winds that diminuendo to ***ppp*** and then mysteriously cadence in the distant key of C-sharp minor. A most unusual chord progression follows, a series of minor triads, each a measure long, the roots of which descend through the whole-tone scale on C♯ while the instrumental lines themselves rise, so that each successive triad is in a different inversion (c♯–b^6–a$^6_4$–g–f^6–e♭$^6_4$–c♯). This idea, designated WT (for whole-tone) in table 4.3, is first heard alone in second violins and violas and then repeated an octave higher in the flutes with the opening motive of *f*. It returns to the violins in m. 249, transposed up a fifth, with the opening motive of *f* now in the winds and a new idea in horn 1: the first phrase of M (*m*). As example 4.2a shows, the latter emerges almost imperceptibly from the chord progression. It begins by following the upper notes of the first three chords, and all its remaining notes are extracted from the chords. There follow two statements of the second half of *S*: in C-sharp minor at m. 255, accompanied by the second phrase of M (*n*) in horn 2 at m. 263, and then again in D-flat major at m. 270, with all of M now in violin 1, shown in example 4.2b.[19] The three-against-two rhythm at mm. 275–76 and 283–84 is the first hint in the symphony of superimposing different metric subdivisions, a technique that returns at times throughout the work and that Ives came to use frequently in his later symphonic music in ever more complex ways. The third phrase of M (*o*) at m. 285 is joined by fragments of *h* and of *b*, the first hint of *P* in the development. The opening ideas of the two main themes, *a* and *f*, return at m. 304 over the chord progression WT (and transposed variants), leading back to D minor and the recapitulation. Thus WT opens and closes the development, which is remarkable for its unusual key, significant new theme, and mostly serene atmosphere.

In the recapitulation (m. 325), *P*, *T*, and *S* (now in D major) are all abbreviated, eliminating the immediate repetition of *P* and *S* and omitting all passages with *e* in the transition. Ives's tendency to vary rather than repeat exactly is again evident in the presentation of *P*, now over a pizzicato walking bass. A lengthy coda (m. 427) provides more development and further thematic combinations, dwelling especially on *a* and *h*. A contrapuntal climax occurs in mm. 441–56, with *a* and *b* in the trumpets, the opening motive of *f* in the winds, *g* in triple diminution in the violins and violas, and M in cellos and trombones. Although the passage is notated

J. Peter Burkholder

a. First partial appearance (first movement)

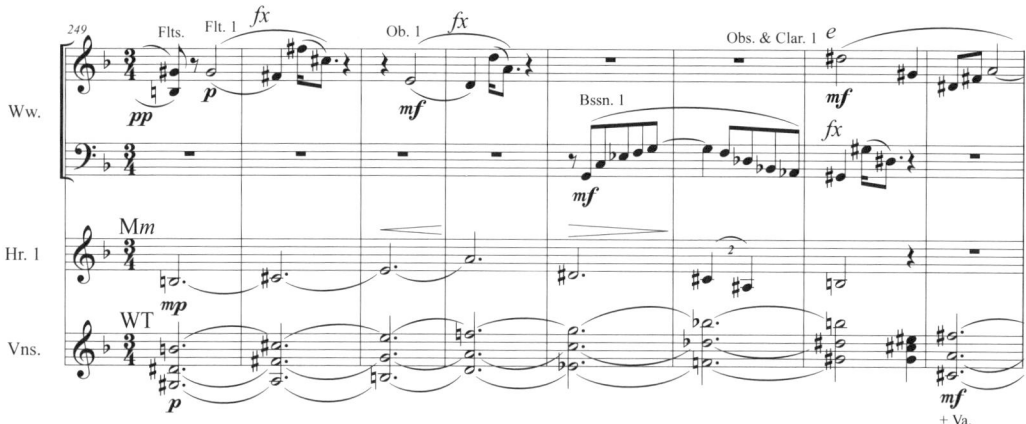

b. First complete appearance (first movement)

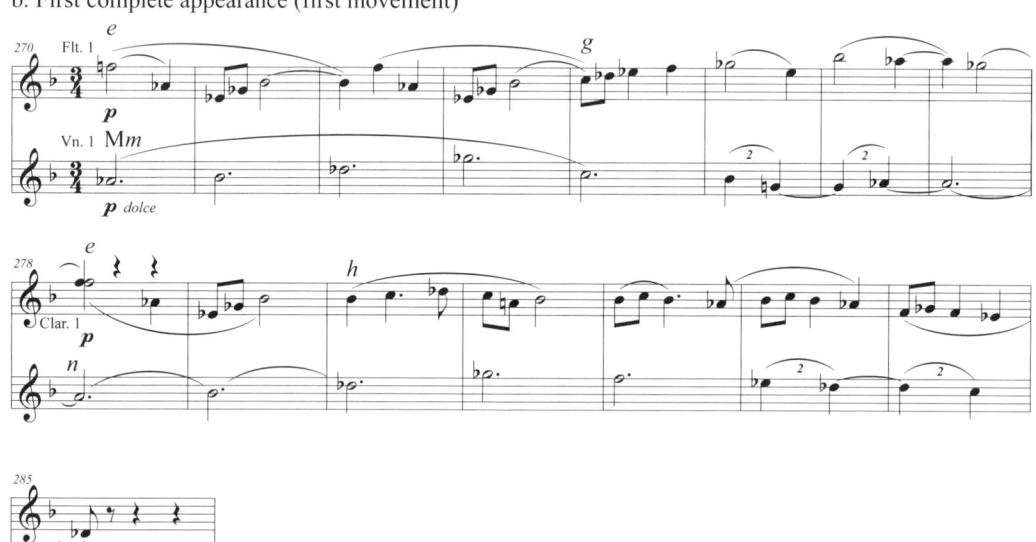

c. M in diminution as march theme in the finale

Example 4.2 Ives. Symphony No. 1, cyclic theme M: (a) First partial appearance (first movement, mm. 249–56); (b) First complete appearance (first movement, mm. 270–90); (c) M in diminution as march theme in Finale, mm. 336–42

in 3/4, in effect Ives superimposes three simultaneous meters: 9/8 for *g* in violins and violas, 2/4 for M in cellos and trombones, and 3/4 for all the other parts. The coda repeatedly returns to D minor or major, only to swerve away, until WT reappears (m. 484), transposed to begin and end on D minor, and the opening motives of *a* and *h* hammer away on the tonic.

Several unusual features of this movement have parallels in the first movement of Dvořák's *New World Symphony*: the appearance of part of *S* in the preceding transition, which is shortened in the recapitulation to remove these references; closing the exposition with a brief imitative passage on an element from the preceding theme; beginning the development with a diminuendo to very soft and with harmony based on symmetrical partitioning of the octave (the whole-tone-based chord sequence in Ives, an augmented triad in Dvořák); and, in the coda, presenting an important theme fragment in diminution and combining *P* in counterpoint with later themes. In every case, the Ives passage is more extensive and complex. The many similarities show that Ives borrowed procedures from Dvořák's first movement, often trying to outdo his prototype.

Another apparent model is the first movement of Schubert's *Unfinished Symphony*, which, like Ives's, is in minor mode, triple meter, and a similar allegro tempo; sets *P* in clarinet (doubled by oboe in Schubert's theme), introduced and accompanied by a vamp in the strings; immediately repeats both *P* and *S* in the exposition; has a long codetta that develops *S* rather than an independent closing theme; and ends the exposition with two three-part points of imitation on a portion of *S*.[20] Moreover, Ives's *a* and *h* both resemble motives in the *Unfinished Symphony*: the leaping fourths, dotted rhythms, rising stepwise motions, and overall shape of *a* resemble the opening phrase of Schubert's second theme, and the contour and rhythm of *h* echo the initial figure and part of his first theme.[21] The formal resemblances to Dvořák and Schubert and the motivic and stylistic echoes of the latter reveal Ives as a composer who wants us to hear this movement in relationship to his forebears, to recognize his command of his craft, and to mark how well he has built on tradition.

Ives recalled in his *Memos* that Parker objected to the opening theme of the first movement because of its harmonic explorations. The symphony "was supposed to be in D minor, but the first subject went through six or eight different keys, so Parker made me write another first movement. But it seemed no good to me, and I told him that I would much prefer to use the first draft. He smiled and let me do it, saying 'But you must promise to end in D minor.'"[22]

The first theme indeed begins and ends in D minor but includes phrases in A major (mm. 10–13) and C major (mm. 14–17), passing chords borrowed from other keys (mm. 6–8 and 19), and a long composing-out of a diminished seventh chord (mm. 20–25). As example 4.3 shows, the F^7, B minor, and C minor chords in mm. 6–8 are essentially nonfunctional chords that harmonize chromatic motion decorating a progression from A major to its dominant. Such chromatically generated successions of chords are found in the music of Fryderyk Chopin (1810–49), Franck, and other nineteenth-century composers; Ives may have learned this type of harmony from Franck (a fellow organist), who was famous for it. The move from A major to C major forecasts the overall move in the exposition from D minor to F major, for which keys A and C serve as dominants. The final segment of the theme, *c*, begins as if outlining the dominant minor ninth of C, which in m. 25 becomes the diminished seventh chord that resolves to A^7, the dominant of D minor. Thus, despite all the surface meanderings, the harmonies in mm. 6–25 simply serve to prolong the dominant.

This example illustrates Ives's harmonic practice throughout the symphony: the exploration of many subsidiary keys and distantly related harmonies as well as sudden changes of key, but

Example 4.3 Ives. Symphony No. 1/i, mm. 1–10, harmony in violas and cellos (notes in parentheses appear at repetition in mm. 26–34)

all within a relatively simple overarching structure. The same is true for the harmonic plan of the entire movement. Overall, the progression is simple and traditional: first theme in D minor and second theme in F, the relative major, recapitulated in D minor and D major, respectively. Yet half of S is in B-flat major, and the repetition of the first phrase begins in G-flat major; these subsidiary keys form a circle of major thirds with the tonic D. Meanwhile, there are references to A major in P and T and to D-flat major in T, and the development dwells on C-sharp minor and D-flat major; these keys of A and C-sharp/D-flat form a circle of major thirds with the contrasting key of F. Such key relationships, based on symmetrical partitioning of the octave, were pioneered by Schubert and used by many later Romantic composers, including Franz Liszt (1811–86) in his Piano Concerto No. 1 (which uses the B♭-D-F♯ circle), Brahms in his Piano Concerto No. 2 (which uses the F-A-D♭/C♯ circle in the first movement and B♭-D-G♭-B♭ between the outer and middle movements), and Franck in his Piano Quintet (using the same circles) and other works. Ives's usage here is subtler than theirs, but we will see in his Second Symphony a much more explicit use of a circle of thirds.

Between the relatively stable key areas indicated in table 4.3 are passages with rapidly changing keys, indicated as modulatory ("mod"). These fall in the expected places for sonata form: in transitions, extensions, and codas. But just as the relatively stable areas include chromatic juxtapositions and sudden changes of key, such as the unmediated shift from A major to C major amid the D-minor first theme (*Pb*) illustrated in example 4.1, these "modulatory" passages do as well. Often there is no modulation in the traditional sense of a gradual motion from one key to another, or of preparation for a change of key; Ives simply shifts to a new chord or key, using common tones or stepwise motion to create a sense of logical progression. The result is colorful and fresh, akin to the sudden harmonic shifts of Schubert and the chromatic harmony of Richard Wagner (1813–83), Franck, and Richard Strauss (1864–1949) but individual in many ways. As we will see, such harmonic practice is also characteristic of Ives's Second Symphony, and he extended it further in the Finale of the Third Symphony.

The second movement is closely modeled on the Largo from Dvořák's *New World Symphony*. Both are slow movements in modified ternary (*ABA'*) form, mostly soft, in a major key with the middle section in minor, and with a climax marked by the contrapuntal combination of first- and second-movement themes. Most significant, the opening theme in each is a largely pentatonic melody in English horn over sustained chords in muted strings, which returns in the same instrument at the end of *A* after interjections by strings and winds, and again in *A'* just after the climax of the movement. Ives's theme is paraphrased from Dvořák's, following a similar intervallic contour while avoiding any obvious motivic or rhythmic relationship, eliminating repetition, and making the phrasing irregular, resulting in a melody that sounds more like Brahms than Dvořák.[23]

Ives's *A* section is archlike in orchestration and form. It begins and ends with the eight-measure English horn tune in F major, labeled *a* in table 4.3 and shown on the top staff in example 4.4. This is closed by a full cadence and a pause, setting off the middle of the *A* section as a sixteen-measure period. The first phrase of the latter, *b* (m. 9), is a beautiful *con sordino* violin melody in C major accompanied by the strings, which is shown in example 4.5a and recalled in later movements as one of the three cyclic themes. After a half cadence, the next phrase, *c*, begins with winds alone playing a figure paraphrased from the middle of Dvořák's English horn theme and concludes with a full cadence on C in the strings, leading back to F major and the English horn tune. Frequent rests at the ends of phrases in *a* and *b* suggest a sense of breathless awe, before the momentum begins to build.

Example 4.4 Ives. Symphony No. 1/2, main ideas *a* (mm. 1–8) and *d* (mm. 33–40) compared

The main theme of the *B* section, *d* (m. 33), is a more active variant of *a*, transposed from F major to D minor. As shown by vertical alignment of the two themes in example 4.4, *d* follows the rising arpeggiation of *a* and borrows the motive that forms its peak (compare mm. 33–34 with mm. 2–4), decorates the rest of the melody in a higher register (compare mm. 35–36 with mm. 5–8), and then reworks the opening and closing portions of the melody again, creating a new climax (compare mm. 37–40 with mm. 2–8 and mm. 33–36). The subtle reshaping of *a* into *d*, easy to miss on first hearing, is typical of Ives's melodic reworkings throughout his symphonic works; he uses developing variation to create logical connections from one theme or moment to the next that are often easier to sense than they are to describe. The rest of the middle section is formed through such connections: *d* repeats in the winds, partly imitated in the violas (m. 41); it appears varied in D major in violins, with cyclic theme M as a countermelody in the horns (m. 49); this is followed by an extension based on the sighlike closing motive of *d* (m. 57); finally, a *stringendo* on this extension develops into a contrasting idea, *e*, that

a. First appearance (second movement)

b. Variant in third movement Scherzo

c. Variant in third movement Trio

Example 4.5 Ives. Symphony No. 1, cyclic theme *II/Ab*: (a) First appearance (second movement, mm. 9–12); (b) Variant in third movement Scherzo, mm. 42–44; (c) Variant in third movement Trio, mm. 95–102

accelerates and builds to a climax for strings alone and then calms as it returns to the closing motive of *d*.

With a sudden turn to *forte*, the A' section begins at m. 81 with a contrapuntal combination of *a* in the brass, harmonized in parallel thirds, and *d* in violins and violas, recast to work as a countermelody and somehow miraculously suggesting D minor against the powerful F major of the theme. When the violins take up *b* (m. 89), now ***ff*** and *tremolo*, they are joined by a double diminution of *b* in the upper winds and by *I/Pa*, which opened the first movement, in the horns. Here Ives reshapes *I/Pa* to work as a countermelody in C major and notates it in diminution so that it moves at roughly the same pace as before, in triplets that suggest a 6/8 meter against the reigning 2/4. After an intense climax on *c*, the opening English horn tune returns one last time, joined by two solo violins, to bring the movement to a quiet close.

The Scherzo that follows recalls another D minor scherzo, that of Beethoven's Ninth Symphony. After its initial *fortissimo* gestures, Beethoven's scherzo continues with imitative entries of a subject that drops an octave and then gradually rises (mostly stepwise) while outlining the tonic triad. Ives's Scherzo begins with imitative entries of a subject that traces the same contour, and in both scherzos the principal subject later returns in a stretto.[24] But as table 4.3 shows, Ives does not follow the traditional binary form of a minuet in either the Scherzo or the Trio. The Scherzo is in *AA'BA* form, in which *A* is a three-part canon on a sixteen-measure melody and *B* (m. 38) a contrasting section with short lyrical phrases in winds and violin 1 above a running staccato bass line in strings and bassoons that spins out a segment from the canon. The comic difficulty of this bassoon line should make this movement a required selection for orchestral bassoon auditions. The Trio begins as if in binary form, with two repeated strains *C* and *D*, but they have nothing in common: *C* (m. 95) is in F major with a flowing violin melody over light accompaniment, while *D* (m. 111) features streams of parallel thirds in mirror counterpoint between winds and strings and changes key constantly. Then *C* returns in the distant key of A-flat major, with cyclic theme M as a countermelody in the horns (m. 136), creating a kind of ternary form for the Trio. The Trio does not come to a close; instead, passing changes of key and a **_ff_** statement of the first motive of M lead back to the dominant of D minor and the reprise of the Scherzo.

In addition to M, both Scherzo and Trio make reference to cyclic theme *II/Ab*. In the *B* section of the Scherzo, the short lyrical phrases in violin 1 are adapted from *II/Ab*, as example 4.5b shows. The first strain of the Trio in example 4.5c is more distantly related, with multiple variants of the opening motive of *II/Ab* followed by a skipping version of its stepwise descent. (Vertical alignment of notes in example 4.5 shows the parallels.)

All the cyclic elements of the First Symphony culminate in the D-major Finale, a festive movement in full-blown Tchaikovsky mode. The most direct model is the third movement of the Russian composer's *Pathétique Symphony*, whose tempo (allegro molto vivace) and overall character are similar to Ives's Finale and whose march theme is echoed in a segment of Ives's first theme, motive *b* in in table 4.3. The overall forms of the two movements are also similar: Tchaikovsky's can be analyzed as *ABAB'* with coda and with the *B* section stated first in a contrasting key and then in the tonic, creating a shape resembling sonata form without development; Ives's is more overtly in the latter form, with clearly demarcated exposition, recapitulation, and coda, as table 4.3 shows. Sweeping scales in parallel octaves alternating between winds and strings in Ives's coda at Reh. X (mm. 330–35) echo the similar passage at Reh. X of the Tchaikovsky (mm. 221–28), and both passages lead to a marchlike melody over a stepwise descending bass line.[25]

In the Ives, the melody is cyclic theme M, transformed into a fast march (m. 336), as example 4.2c shows. The entire movement builds up to this march. The energetic opening theme *P*, presented twice in different scorings, consists of three segments that are then fragmented and placed in counterpoint with each other during *T* (m. 21); the middle segment, *b*, is highlighted in augmentation (mm. 29–40) and will later become part of the march theme in the coda. The first hint of M appears at mm. 69–70 in *T*, where its opening four notes—motive M*x* in table 4.3—are harmonized in a brass chorale. The second theme *S* (m. 75) by contrast is quiet and relaxed, with arching and angular lines, a turn figure, constantly shifting duple and triplet rhythms, and multiple contrapuntal lines over sustained notes in the bass. The layering of duple rhythms with half-note and quarter-note triplets produces a sense of multiple meters—2/2, 3/4, 4/4, and 6/4—that sometimes alternate and sometimes are superimposed, creating a supple, fluid, and airy texture. A countermelody to *S* (in bassoons at m. 75) shares the slow rhythm and rising contour of M*x* with altered intervals, and when cyclic theme *II/Ab* appears in the latter part of *S* (in violins at m. 102 and winds at m. 110), M*x* shows up as a countermelody in long values in the trombones (m. 108). *K* also includes references to M*x*, with two variants in long notes (respectively at m. 128 and at mm. 132 and 142) and a new thematic idea, *e*, whose first four notes are M*x* in retrograde (at mm. 130–31, 134–40, and 144–50). Ives always treats *e* in canon. This closing theme is modulatory and acts rather like a development, gradually intensifying through thematic combinations and cross-rhythms and culminating in a foretaste of the march theme at m. 156.

In the recapitulation, cyclic theme *I/Pa* returns as an interpolation in *T* (mm. 219–25), and *II/Ab* and M*x* appear as in the exposition. Ives intensifies *K* through diminutions and (as he did for *T*) expands it with an interpolation: a contrapuntal combination at m. 295 of cyclic theme *I/Pab* in the upper winds with cyclic theme M in brass and bassoon. This is another moment of metric superimposition, with *I/Pab* in quarter-note triplets (the equivalent of 6/4) against 4/4 in the other parts. When *K* ends, as before, with a foretaste of the march (m. 321), Ives dwells on a dotted neighbor-note figure from the march's second phrase; the alternation of this figure between violas (with horn) and the upper winds highlights the similar texture when we first heard this motive, as part of *I/Pb* (see example 4.1, mm. 12–23). The sweeping scales borrowed from the *Pathétique Symphony* (mm. 330–35) lead at m. 336 to the march theme, which begins as M in diminution and continues as a varied and extended form of *b* (m. 342). After the march theme repeats (m. 356), accompanied by triplets in the winds and culminating in a chorale-style ***fff*** climax (m. 373), the final allegro con fuoco (m. 376) introduces a new neighbor-note figure *g* and further fragments elements of the themes. Among other combinations, Ives shows that the rising motive M*x* fits in counterpoint with the descending motive from the end of *b* (mm. 386–91 and 398–403) and puts M*x* through three successive levels of diminution (at mm. 398–407), wringing every last drop of relatedness out of his material and saturating nearly every measure with thematic ideas.

In every movement, Ives designed his thematic material for contrapuntal combination. Both main themes of the Finale comprise a series of ideas that work in counterpoint with each other, points of imitation appear in every movement, the climax of each movement presents one or more themes simultaneously, and all the themes in the two outer movements (plus several in the middle movements) are at some point placed in counterpoint with one or more other themes. Ives's fundamentally polyphonic thinking arose naturally from his experience as an organist and from his studies with Parker. His practice in the First Symphony intensifies the contrapuntal combinations of themes he found in the *New World Symphony* and his other symphonic models. Such contrapuntal textures remained a characteristic of all his symphonic works, where simultaneous presentations of themes gradually grew to include simultaneous streams of different musical layers. The buildup to the Finale's coda as the culmination of the entire symphony is echoed in the Second Symphony, and the unveiling in the coda of a melody that has been foreshadowed since early in the movement anticipates Ives's practice of cumulative form in the Third Symphony and later compositions. The progress of this theme, shown in example 4.2—emerging in the first movement's development from the mysterious whole-tone-based chord progression, first presented complete as a countermelody to that movement's second theme, returning as a countermelody in the middle movements, appearing in the Finale in fragments, and culminating in the march theme—is an astonishing example of developing variation.

Throughout the symphony, Ives's craft is clear. His taste may sometimes be questioned—some reviewers of the first recording felt that the codas for the first movement and Finale go on too long—but Walter Damrosch was right to praise his workmanship, and the analysis here has shown that Ives is able to build climax upon climax in those codas by revealing yet unrealized potential in his themes. This is a composer with a command of the late-nineteenth-century conception of a symphony and a mastery of form, counterpoint, and development. He moves on to new conceptions in each later symphony, but he never loses that consummate craft.

Ives would never again write a purely absolute symphonic work. All his later orchestral works are characteristic or programmatic. But, in other ways, the First Symphony set the pattern for his later numbered symphonies, all of which are cyclic, are based in part on borrowed themes, and combine themes in counterpoint with each other.

SYMPHONY NO. 2

Having claimed a place in the lineage of symphonic composers with his Symphony No. 1, Ives sought in his next symphony to synthesize that tradition (and European art music more generally) with American popular music and Protestant church music, and thus to integrate his experience as an American who had grown up hearing and participating in all three traditions. The framework is a symphony in five movements marked by all the procedures we have seen in the First Symphony, from motivic fragmentation and development to cyclic unification, contrapuntal combination of themes, and end-weighted form. The content is a blend of American and European sounds: all the themes and many countermelodies are paraphrased from American popular songs, fiddle tunes, or hymns, while several transitions, including at least one in every movement, rework passages from Bach, Brahms, or Wagner. Whether or not listeners recognize the specific borrowings, they will hear the juxtapositions of musical topics, including evocations of familiar American and European styles. Throughout the work, Ives draws motivic connections between his borrowed materials, so that the symphony is thematically unified, each new idea proceeds logically from what precedes it, and the American and European sources are thoroughly integrated with each other and into the symphonic context. The result is a celebration of American music and of its place as part of a broader transatlantic musical world.[26]

According to Ives, he completed the symphony around 1902, drawing material from earlier works, all but one of them lost: the first movement (or perhaps the first two) from *Down East Overture* (1897–98), itself partly from an organ sonata of 1897; the slow third movement from the rejected slow movement for the First Symphony (ca. 1898), which survives in part, and a piece for string quartet played in a revival service at Center Church in New Haven (ca. 1897–98); the second theme of the Finale from a short piece called *The American Woods* (1889); and the second, fourth, and fifth movements from a set of overtures *In These United States*, composed between 1896 and 1898 for the Hyperion Theater Orchestra in New Haven, which included *Overture: Town, Gown and State* and perhaps *Down East Overture*.[27] But the sketches seem to suggest a different story. They include nearly every stage of composition from preliminary sketches to final drafts and show that Ives crossed off and replaced numerous rejected alternatives, including different initial ideas for the opening themes of the first and final movements. Looking over Ives's shoulder, we can see him invent and refine several of the themes, work out transitional and developmental passages, and figure out the continuity of each movement except the fourth, a varied reprise of the first. The changes we can see in the sketches reveal that none of the movements can have been based on the precise material or sequence of events of any earlier works, although a few themes that seem complete in their earliest sketch, such as the Finale's second theme, may have been taken from earlier pieces. Moreover, Gayle Sherwood Magee has determined that essentially all the surviving sketches and drafts for the symphony, except those directly derived from the rejected slow movement of the First Symphony, are written on paper not available before 1907, and in handwriting from circa 1907–9.[28] Assuming these dates are correct, the many changes in the sketches rule out the possibility that Ives could have drafted the complete symphony as we know it by 1902.

The symphony was certainly complete by about 1909–10, when Ives had a copyist make an ink score (mostly lost). As with the First Symphony, he tried to interest conductors in the piece, including Walter Damrosch. Ives wrote in *Memos* that in 1910 or 1911 he showed the first movement, which is scored almost entirely for string orchestra, to Edgar Stowell, a violinist with Damrosch's New York Symphony and orchestra director at the Third Street Music Settlement School, which served poor immigrant children; according to Ives, Stowell liked the movement and conducted it at a concert at the school.[29] Ives tried again around 1938, when he gave an emended photocopied score of the whole symphony to composer and conductor Bernard Herrmann, then the principal conductor of the CBS Symphony Orchestra, but no performance ensued. In 1943, the new conductor of the New York Philharmonic, Artur Rodzinski, asked to see some of Ives's orchestral music, and Ives drafted a letter offering to send him *Three Places in New England* or the Second Symphony. That same year, after Serge Koussevitzky, conductor of the Boston Symphony Orchestra, commissioned a patriotic piece from Roy Harris (1898–1979), Ives sketched a letter (probably never sent) offering Koussevitzky a suite of four patriotic movements including the Finale of the Second Symphony. In 1949, Ives showed his manuscript of the symphony to Henry Cowell (1897–1965), who prepared a score with Lou Harrison (1917–2003). The work was finally premiered on February 22, 1951, by the New York Philharmonic conducted by Leonard Bernstein (1918–90), and published later that year.[30]

We cannot know what Ives drew from the lost pieces he names as predecessors to the Second Symphony, since no scrap of them survives. But their titles reveal what was on his mind: representing the United States musically. This is the central goal of the Second, Third, and *Holidays* Symphonies, each of which approaches the task in a different way. In the Second Symphony, Ives draws on a wide array of mid- to late-nineteenth-century American sources—plantation songs, fiddle tunes, a patriotic song, a Civil War song, gospel songs, a college song, hymn tunes, a minstrel song, a marching band drum pattern, a parlor song, and a bugle call—and remakes them to fit beautifully within the framework of a traditional European symphony. As Magee aptly observes, "Raw-material melodies are extracted from their everyday musical contexts, smoothed out and regularized to suit the demands of their new environment. . . . Ives dresses them up in a new suit, combs their hair, and restricts their behavior to match the profile of a bona fide symphonic identity."[31] As we will see, his restylings are ingenious, transforming American vernacular tunes into symphonic themes and, often enough, into passages that literally echo the great composers of Europe.

If the Second Symphony was a product of the period roughly between 1907, when Ives began sketching in earnest, and about 1909–10, when he had it copied out in ink, its creation coincides with his engagement to Harmony Twichell in October 1907 and their marriage in June 1908. In correspondence during their engagement, Harmony praised the power of music to capture memories, and perhaps it was with this in mind that Ives turned to creating a symphony based on the music of his childhood.[32] Jonathan Elkus has suggested that the Second

Symphony was "Ives's wedding gift to his fiancée, Harmony Twichell, and her family." As Elkus has argued, that Ives was thinking in terms of overtures may explain the unusual shape of the symphony. Of its five movements, the first two and the last two form pairs in which a shorter slow movement serves as an introduction to a fast movement in sonata form—a format common to many nineteenth-century overtures. Elkus also points out that overtures were a part of popular entertainment in Ives's day, performed not only by symphony orchestras but by theater orchestras and in transcription by bands, pianists, and organists (including Ives himself).[33] The Second Symphony shares the same widely appealing character, and it has remained Ives's most popular symphony since its belated premiere.

Whatever its derivation, the Second Symphony is fully symphonic, continuing the traits of the First Symphony. Like the First, the Second is partly based on models: beyond the overtures suggested by Elkus, *Roman Carnival* by Hector Berlioz (1803–69) and the overture to *Zampa* by Ferdinand Hérold (1791–1833), the final two movements closely follow the form of the Finale of Brahms's First Symphony, and numerous passages throughout borrow from or echo other works by Brahms as well as by Bach, Wagner, Dvořák, and Tchaikovsky.[34] The formal plan of the symphony is shown in table 4.4, along with the sources for the various themes and other material. The two fast movements (the second and fifth) are in sonata form and the others in ternary or *ABABA* form. Yet—as in Ives's First Symphony—each movement has unique formal features, and all are interrelated through cyclic procedures: the first movement's second theme (*I/Bc*, m. 23) and second movement's two main themes (*II/Pa*, m. 1, and *II/Se*, m. 72) return in the Finale (at mm. 52 and 181); two ideas from the first movement (*I/Aa'*, m. 7, and *I/A'd*, m. 52) return in the middle section of the third (at m. 59), a passage that itself returns in the Finale (at m. 228); the fourth movement is a shorter variant of the first, with a new ending (*IV/g*, m. 37) that returns in the Finale just before the climax (at m. 246); and the Finale's second theme (m. 58) and climactic coda statement (m. 253) of the patriotic song *Columbia, the Gem of the Ocean* by Thomas A'Becket (1808–90) or David T. Shaw are both anticipated in the first movement (at mm. 33 and 67, respectively).

While the harmonic plan of the First Symphony's opening movement hints at circles of major thirds, the entire key scheme of the Second Symphony is based on a circle of minor thirds, B-D-F-A♭. The first and fourth movements begin in B minor and move to D major; the first ends in D, the fourth on the dominant of F, and both serve as slow introductions to the following fast movement. The sonata-form second movement is in A-flat major with *S* in F major, a recapitulation of both themes in F, and a coda in A-flat that states *S* and then both *P* and *S* in counterpoint, restoring the tonic. The central third movement is in F, and the Finale is in F with its second theme in A-flat, recapitulated in F. Thus F major is the ultimate key of the symphony, gradually coming to predominate over A-flat major, its opposite pole in the two fast movements, with B minor and D major as ancillary keys in the introductory movements. This same circle of minor thirds appears in two symphonies by Tchaikovsky, which most likely served as the closest models for Ives's key structure: in the first movement of Tchaikovsky's Fourth Symphony (f-A♭-B-d-f) and in the first theme of the opening movement of the *Pathétique* (b-d-f-a♭-b). This elaborate interlocking key structure, along with the cyclic elements, shows that Ives carefully planned the Second Symphony as a whole.

Ives's blend of European and American traditions is evident from the start. The first movement opens with a Baroque texture of strings alone, with a walking bass accompanying an arching melody joined at m. 7 by a slower-moving upper line. From its key and trio-sonata texture to the rising bass line and melodic shape, this theme, *a* in table 4.4, echoes the opening

Table 4.4 Formal Plan of Ives's Symphony No. 2

Key:

+	two or more themes/motives superimposed in counterpoint
x	initial motive of a theme
~	figure drawn from a theme
dim	figure appears in diminution
aug	figure appears in augmentation

1. ANDANTE MODERATO

A					A'				B'			A''				Coda
a	+a'	b(~a')	c	c+V/Sf	a	+a'	d	b	c+V/Njx	~c		a	b'	e	b'	ax
1	7	10	23	33	40	43	52	55	67	73		79	85	93	96	101
b		mod	A, mod	G, mod f♯		mod			D, mod	f♯ to V of b	b					D

Sources:

a	Foster, *Massa's in de Cold Ground* (plantation song); Bach, *The Well-Tempered Clavier* Book I, Prelude No. 24 in B Minor BWV 869
a', b	Foster, *Massa's in de Cold Ground*
c	*Pig Town Fling* (fiddle tune)
V/Sf	modeled on Foster, possibly *Old Black Joe* (parlor song)
V/Njx	A'Becket or Shaw, *Columbia, the Gem of the Ocean* (patriotic song)
B'~c	Brahms, Symphony No. 1 in C Minor, iv, mm. 273–78
e	Bach, Three-Part Invention (Sinfonia) in F Minor BWV 795, mm. 28–29

2. ALLEGRO MOLTO

Exposition														Development						
P					T					S	codetta					N				
a	a¹	a²	+b	a¹	a²ˣ	c	d	c+b	d+b	ax+~e	d	e	d+ex+f+b	g	g,b,f	b+aᵃᵘᵍ+f+e+g	bxᵈⁱᵐ+~b	b	i+f	~i
1	8	20	25	29	39	42	49	51	57	59	67	72	92	126	128	137	166	183	186	203
A♭		mod		A♭	ab/A♭		f/F					F	mod		mod	F		mod		V of F

Recapitulation

	P					*T*						*S*	codetta		*Coda* *S+N*	*P+S*				
a	*a²*	+*b*	*a¹*	*a*^(2x)	*c*		*d*	*c+b*	*d+b*	*ax+~e*	*d*	*e*	*d+ex+f+b*	*g,f*	*e+bx*	*a+e*	*b*	*t*^dim+*f*^dim	*bx+~e*	*ax*
212	219	231	236	240	248	251	258	260	266	268	276	281	301	325	329	340	353	355	367	373
F		mod		F		ab/Ab		f/F	mod			F			Ab		mod		Ab	

Sources:

a   Work, *Wake Nicodemus* (Civil War song)
c   Minor, *Bringing in the Sheaves* (gospel song)
e   *Where, O Where Are the Verdant Freshmen?* (college song)
g   Brahms, Symphony No. 3 in F Major, i, mm. 47–48
h   Mason, *Hamburg*; Mason, *Naomi* (hymn tunes)
i   Brahms, Symphony No. 1 in C Minor, i, mm. 181–83; *Street Beat* (drum pattern)

3. ADAGIO CANTABILE

Intro	*A*				*B*				*A'*				*Coda*	
	a	*b*	*c*	*c'*	*b*	*d*	*e*	*f(I/Aa' and I/A'd)*	*f'*	*c*	*c'*	*a*	*b*	*b'*	*~e+~b*
1	7	11	18	23	33	39	46	59	74	89	93	107	111	119	130
F	F		mod	F	F		Db	Bb		mod		F			

Sources:

ab   Sweney, *Beulah Land* (gospel song); Ward, *Materna* (hymn tune)
c'   Wagner, Prelude to *Tristan und Isolde*, mm. 20–22 and 61–63
d   Wagner, Prelude to *Tristan und Isolde*, mm. 39–40
e   Zeuner, *Missionary Chant*; Nettleton or Wyeth, *Nettleton* (hymn tunes)
f(I/Aa')   Foster, *Massa's in de Cold Ground*

4. LENTO MAESTOSO

Table 4.4 continued

A(I/A)			B(I/B')			A'(I/A")			Coda	
a	a+f	b	c+V/N/x	~c	b, a	a	b'	e	f'	g
1	3	10	17	23		29	32	34	36	37
b		mod	D, mod	f♯ to V of b		b		mod		V of F

Sources:

- a   Foster, *Massa's in de Cold Ground*; Brahms, Symphony No. 1, iv, 1–2
- f, f'   Brahms, "O Tod," mm. 29–30, from *Vier ernste Gesänge*
- b   Foster, *Massa's in de Cold Ground*
- c   *Pig Town Fling* (fiddle tune)
- V/N/x   A'Becket or Shaw, *Columbia, the Gem of the Ocean*
- B–c   Brahms, Symphony No. 1 in C Minor, iv, mm. 273–78
- e   Bach, Three-Part Invention (Sinfonia) in F Minor BWV 795, mm. 28–29
- g   Brahms, Symphony No. 1 in C Minor, iv, mm. 385–88

5. ALLEGRO MOLTO VIVACE

Exposition

P						T		S						
a	b	a¹	I/A"e	c	b, a	b+d	a+b	f+e	g(~I/Aa¹)+d	b	f+e	~g	f'+~g	g'
1	14	20	25	27	31	37	43	58	65	70	71	78	87	94	100
F							A♭, mod	A♭			C		f	G	mod

Recapitulation begins

P						T	
a	b	a¹	I/A"e	c	b, a	b+d	a+b
105	116	122	127	129	133	139	145
F							A♭

Development

	i	$ex(IIBc)+jx$	$+bx$	i	ax	$II/Pa^{dim}+II/Sex^{dim}$	e	$f+e$	$g+d$	h	$f+e$	$-g$	$f'+-g$	g'
	147	162	164	168	178	181	186	189	196	201	202	209	217	224
	mod					A♭, mod		F				A	d	G

Recapitulation continues   *S*

Coda

	$III/Bf(IIAa', I/A'd)$	$II/Pa+II/Pa^{dim}+d$	ext	$jx+-a$	IV/g	$+ax$	k	$j+a+e+II/Pax$	$-a, jx, ex$	$-g$	jx, k
	228	236	240	242	246	249	251	253	269		278
$II/A''e$	B♭	F	mod		V of F			F			

N+P

Sources:

- $a+b$ Foster, *Camptown Races* (minstrel show song), verse and refrain
- $II/A''e$ Bach, Three-Part Invention (Sinfonia) in F Minor BWV 795, mm. 28–29
- c Street Beat (drum pattern)
- d *Turkey in the Straw* (minstrel show song/fiddle tune)
- e *Pig Town Fling*; *Turkey in the Straw* (fiddle tunes)
- f modeled on Foster, possibly *Old Black Joe* (parlor song)
- g Foster, *Massa's in de Cold Ground*
- h Bayly, *Long, Long Ago* (parlor song)
- i Bach, *The Well-Tempered Clavier*, Book 1, Fugue No. 10 in E Minor BWV 855, mm. 13–17 and 22
- j A'Becket or Shaw, *Columbia, the Gem of the Ocean* (patriotic song), complete verse
- k *Reveille* (military call)

of the B-minor Prelude from Book 1 of Bach's *Well-Tempered Clavier*. But, as example 4.6a shows, the upper line at m. 7 (*a'*) is a phrase from the chorus of Stephen Foster's plantation song *Massa's in de Cold Ground*, and the melody throughout is paraphrased from that phrase, following its melodic contour with interpolations and changes of rhythm. (In this and other examples, melodic similarity is shown through vertical alignment of notes in the melodies being compared; material enclosed in brackets is repeated in the example to show further parallels.) The modulatory continuation *b* (m. 10) is suffused with scalar figuration, much of it based on the melodic contour of the Foster phrase *a'*, including the segment in the bottom staff of example 4.6a.[35] The *B* section at m. 23 (in A major) introduces the contrasting idea *c* in example 4.6b, drawn from the fiddle tune *Pig Town Fling*; violin 1 presents the opening figure, the viola overlaps with the next segment of the fiddle tune, and the neighbor-note motive from the tune (C♯-B-C♯-A) is developed in dialogue between the parts. This theme has quite a different character, representing a change of topic from Baroque to barn dance. Yet as the example shows, there is enough similarity of melodic contour to the Foster tune to make *c* seem like a logical variation of *a*, in a parallel to the developing variation of one theme into another seen in the First Symphony. Despite the thematic contrast, *c* maintains the sound of strings alone, which now evokes country fiddling rather than a Baroque orchestra.

As *c* is developed and modulates, the first phrase of the Finale's second theme (*V/Sf*, transformed into triple meter) appears in cellos and basses (m. 33), highlighted by the addition of bassoons, the first non-string instruments to appear in the symphony. In the Finale, *Pig Town Fling* will return as a countermelody to this second theme. The *A* section returns varied at m. 40 in the dominant minor F-sharp and again scored for strings alone, briefly interpolating a new idea *d* (mm. 52–54) that will play a more prominent role in the third movement. When the *B* section returns, now abbreviated and in D major (m. 67), *c* is accompanied in the horns (only the second non-string instruments to be heard) by the first phrase of *Columbia, the Gem of the Ocean*, which will be stated whole in the Finale's coda (*V/Nj*) with several countermelodies, including *Pig Town Fling*. By combining *Pig Town Fling* with the opening phrases of *V/S* and *V/N* in the first movement, then using it as a countermelody to these two themes in the Finale, Ives makes this symphony doubly cyclic in a similar way to the First Symphony, with thematic references used both to recollect themes from earlier movements and to forecast later events.

After the abbreviated reprise of *B*, the texture returns to strings alone, and an F♯ pedal point prepares the return of the opening material and key. Over this pedal point, the neighbor-note motive from *c* is treated in dialogue between the parts (m. 73) and develops into a passage paraphrased from a transition in Brahms's First Symphony Finale (compare mm. 76–78 to mm. 273–78 of the Brahms). The allusion emerges so naturally from the fiddle-tune material that it suggests Ives is making the point that the American and European traditions are not so different if a passage in the style of a Bach trio sonata can be based on a Stephen Foster melody and a fiddle tune can be transformed into an excerpt from a Brahms symphony. The varied reprise of *A* in the tonic (m. 79) includes another classical allusion: a new transition *e* (mm. 93–95) quotes an episode from Bach's Three-Part Invention in F Minor BWV 795 (mm. 28–29, transposed and immediately repeated in a rising sequence). Here and throughout the symphony, Ives borrows transitions and episodes from European masterworks such as these within his own transitional passages. By doing so, he emphasizes that European genres like symphonies and inventions *have* transitions and episodes between thematic statements—unlike the American popular songs, fiddle tunes, and hymns that serve as sources for his themes—and highlights his integration of European form with American thematic material.

a. *A* section theme (*a*) compared with part of Foster's *Massa's in de Cold Ground*

b. *B* section theme (*c*) with *Pig Town Fling* and *Massa's in de Cold Ground*

Example 4.6 "Symphony No. 2" by Charles Ives. Copyright © 1951 by Peer International Corporation. Copyright Renewed. Used by Permission. All Rights Reserved.

J. Peter Burkholder

After a climax, the coda (m. 101) restates *a* at its original pitch but reharmonized in D major and now in solo violin and viola over solo cello, emphasizing the trio-sonata texture. A solo oboe softly meditates on the first phrase of *a*, then leaps up to C, undermining the sense of closure. As it hangs in the air, it is suddenly joined *forte* by the clarinets and flutes in stating the first theme of the next movement in the new key of A-flat major. As fully formed and lengthy as the first movement is, this overlap links it to the second movement as a kind of prelude.

While the first movement themes were based on fragments of American tunes, those of the second movement illustrate Ives's ability to paraphrase longer segments or whole tunes to create shapely themes suitable for development in sonata form. The first theme *P* paraphrases the verse of *Wake Nicodemus*, an 1864 song by Henry Clay Work (1832–84) that celebrated the emancipation of enslaved African Americans in the rebel states. As example 4.7a shows, the song's first phrase features a single rhythm throughout, outlines the tonic triad with a few passing and neighbor tones, and ends on the tonic. This phrase repeats twice more in the verse's *AABA* form, and the *B* phrase keeps to the same rhythm. The song therefore is too repetitive, with too little variety in rhythm or harmony, to serve effectively as the opening theme for a symphonic movement.

In his paraphrase, Ives addresses these problems, as illustrated for the first period of *P* (*a* in table 4.4) in example 4.7a. He changes the initial descending gesture to provide more rhythmic variety, then immediately repeats it, varied, to mark it as a motive for later development. He continues to vary the rhythm in every bar, eliminating most instances of the dotted figure that suffused Work's song except for the downward stepwise motive at the beginning and the upward stepwise motive in m. 2 and at the end of the phrase. The latter he repeats in a sequence that descends by whole step, introducing colorful new harmonies and avoiding a close on the tonic. The repetition of the opening and closing dotted figures reveals them as related by inversion, so that the latter part of *a* seems to develop from the opening motive. Ives elaborates the turn-like contour that ends Work's first phrase, recasting it in a new rhythm at the end of his theme's first period (m. 7), and for good measure he adds another turn just before the peak of the phrase (m. 3).

The result is a Brahmsian theme with constant rhythmic and motivic variety, irregular phrasing, internal developing variation, and harmonic interest, which nonetheless preserves the pentatonic opening and sprightly rhythmic character of the original that make it sound American. Ives then derives the rest of *P* by varying this opening melody, creating four main phrases in the pattern $a\ a^1\ a^2\ a^1$ (with a brief recollection of a^2 as a closing tag). Since a^2 (m. 20) is much more distant from *a* than is a^1, Ives's entire first theme echoes the *AABA* form of Work's song, while at the same time it sounds like the whole first theme area emerges through a process of developing variation from the opening idea. At m. 25, the latter part of a^2 is joined in counterpoint by *b*, an octave leaping figure in an augmented dotted rhythm, which returns in later transitions and the development. In every respect from rhythm to form, Ives reworks his source into a first theme that strongly evokes its American origin while fitting like a native into a European-style symphonic movement.

Facing, **Example 4.7** Ives. Symphony No. 2/2, themes and their sources: (a) First period of first theme (*a*, mm. 1–7) compared with Work's *Wake Nicodemus*; (b) Second theme (*e*, mm. 72–89) compared with *Where, O Where Are the Verdant Freshmen?*

a. First period of first theme (*a*) compared with Work's *Wake Nicodemus*

b. Second theme (*e*) compared with *Where, O Where Are the Verdant Freshmen?*

On the other hand, *S* (m. 72) is much closer to its source, no doubt because the qualities characteristic of American popular songs—such as the simple harmonies, regular phrasing, and rhythmic repetitiveness we saw in *Wake Nicodemus*—are entirely appropriate for the restful interlude that a second theme so often represents. Example 4.7b shows how Ives derived *S* (motive *e* in table 4.4) from its source, the college song *Where, O Where Are the Verdant Freshmen?*—itself a retexting of the hymn *The Hebrew Children* by David Walker. Ives makes few changes in its initial presentation in F major: adding an upbeat figure that recalls *P*; changing the midpoint climax (m. 76) to create an inversion of the borrowed tune's opening motive; and altering the ends of the second and fourth phrases for greater elegance. But then he refashions the same source tune into a contrasting middle section (mm. 80–89), changing the repeated notes and skips of his source into undulating stepwise motion and transposing the second half down a fourth to set up a half cadence on the dominant. Simple as they are, these alterations change the character of the melody so much that it can be hard to recognize the middle section as a variant of the source despite the many shared notes, marked by crosses in example 4.7b. The first section of the theme then repeats to create a small ternary form for *S*, a contrast to the *AABA* song form of *P*. Ives heightens the contrast with *P* by slowing the rhythmic motion and tempo and scoring this theme in parallel thirds in oboes, violins, and flutes in turn. In mood, texture, key, and characteristic elements such as paired winds and drone fifths, *S* is a lovely evocation of the pastoral, which may arouse visions of a placid college campus for those who recognize the song on which it is based.

The transition between these two themes (*T*, mm. 42–71) is based on two ideas: *c*, a transitional theme paraphrased from the gospel song *Bringing in the Sheaves* by George A. Minor (1845–1904), and *d*, a linking figure. These ideas are stated first in A-flat minor/major (m. 42), then again in F minor/major (m. 51), where they are joined by *b*, the octave leaping figure first heard as a counterpoint to a^2. The dotted rhythm of *c* recalls that of *P* and of Work's original song, fragments of which can be found in *c*. These links backward in *c* are balanced by *d*, whose even quarter notes anticipate the rhythm of *S*. A more explicit look backward and forward occurs at m. 59, where the opening notes of *a* are developed in counterpoint with the viola countermelody from the beginning of *S*. As in the first movement of Ives's First Symphony, here an element of the second theme is anticipated in the preceding transition.

After *S*, there is no real closing theme but rather a modulatory and transitional codetta (m. 92), again as in the First Symphony's opening movement. Amid dialogue between *d*, elements of *e*, and *b*, a new idea *f* joins in (m. 97), spawned through developing variation from the descending skips of *d* and the rhythm of two eighths leading to a quarter note from *e*. The exposition closes with *g* (m. 126), a figure from the first movement of Brahms's Third Symphony (mm. 47–48) that Ives transposes and recasts from 9/4 into 4/4. In a later revision (observed in the first printed score and in most performances), Ives deleted the marked repeat of the exposition but kept *g* as a figure that demarcates the end of the exposition and recurs several times in the development.[36]

The end of the development is also marked by a figure borrowed from Brahms: *i*, from the first movement of Brahms's First Symphony (mm. 181–83), which Ives transposes and greatly extends to create his retransition (mm. 186–211). To build excitement, the bass drum and snare drum play a variant of the *Street Beat*, a standard march pattern for drums, creating yet another juxtaposition of European and American elements. With the Brahms figure in quarter-note triplets (the equivalent of 6/4) against 4/4 in the drums and horns, later joined by half-note triplets (the equivalent of 3/2, at m. 200) and half notes, Ives creates the sense of superimposed meters, as he had at several spots in the First Symphony.

Between these two Brahms references, the main event of the development is the appearance at m. 137 of a new theme *N* (motive *h*) in F major in the brass, in counterpoint with *a* in augmentation in violins and with other motives. *N* is presented in long notes, like a cantus firmus, and sounds like a hymn. Indeed, it combines two hymn tunes by Lowell Mason (1792–1872), with its first and third phrases from *Hamburg* ("When I survey the wond'rous cross") and the second and fourth from *Naomi*.[37]

The recapitulation at m. 212 follows the same course as the exposition, except that both *P* and *S* appear in F rather than in A-flat while *T* is stated at its original pitch. Then, in the coda at m. 329, the first phrase of *h* returns in A-flat in combination with *e*, followed at m. 340 by *a* in counterpoint with *e*. Thus the initial portions of all three themes, *P*, *S*, and *N*, appear in the coda in the tonic A-flat, resolving the appearances of these themes in F in the development and recapitulation. Moreover, since both *P* and *S* are used as countermelodies to *N*, and then to each other, Ives clearly planned them to fit together, as he had earlier designed several of the themes in the First Symphony to work in counterpoint with one another. A varied reprise of *i*, the closing passage of the development, at twice the speed and without the drums (m. 355), leads to a brief recollection of the opening ideas of *N* (accompanied by the middle section of *S*) and of *P*, and then a brilliant close. The strategy of achieving thematic climax through contrapuntal combination of themes is like that Ives used in the First Symphony.

The slow third movement features themes based on hymn tunes alongside bits of Wagner and reworkings of material from the first movement. It is in a large ternary form, with two contrasting elements in each section. After a brief introduction, the main theme of the *A* section appears in F at m. 7, a soft, pastoral melody that blends elements of two hymn tunes: it paraphrases most of the gospel song *Beulah Land* throughout segments *a* and *b* and works in part of the hymn tune *Materna* by Samuel A. Ward (1848–1903) at the melodic climax of *b* (in mm. 15–16).[38] A louder contrasting episode begins at m. 18, modulatory, chromatic, and based on a descending stepwise figure (*c*) that Ives develops and transforms into a motive from Wagner's Prelude to *Tristan und Isolde* (*c'* at m. 23, echoing mm. 20–22 and 61–63 of *Tristan*). A diminuendo and half cadence in F lead back to a reprise of the opening theme, without *a* and with a new conclusion (*d*) that closes with another brief quotation from *Tristan* (mm. 44–45, quoting mm. 39–40 of Wagner's prelude). The *B* section at m. 46 begins softly in D-flat with a theme (*e*) that combines two hymn tunes, joining motives from *Missionary Chant* ("Ye Christian heralds") by Charles Zeuner (1795–1857) to a complete though condensed paraphrase of *Nettleton* ("Come, Thou Fount of ev'ry blessing"), attributed to Asahel Nettleton (1783–1844) or John Wyeth (1770–1858). The loud second theme of this section (*f* at m. 59), in B-flat, draws on two motives from the first movement, I/A*a'* (the phrase from *Massa's in de Cold Ground*) and I/A*'d* (added at m. 65). After this theme repeats more quietly, the *A* section returns at m. 89 beginning with the contrasting episode *c*, lending an archlike shape to the movement. The coda at m. 119 varies *b* with some more-literal borrowing from *Beulah Land* and culminates in brief quotations from *Missionary Chant* and *Materna* (m. 130).

For those who recognize them, these direct borrowings at the end highlight the hymn-tune sources of the opening themes of the *A* and *B* sections and thus emphasize the contrast in mood and style between these soft, meditative themes and the louder, more active ideas that follow them within each section. But the closing quotations have misled many commentators and listeners who hear in them references Ives did not intend. The phrase from *Missionary Chant* coincidentally resembles the opening of Beethoven's Fifth Symphony, a similarity that Ives later punned on in his *Concord Sonata* but that is wholly irrelevant here. And *Materna* now carries associations that were in the future when Ives composed the Second Symphony. In his day, the tune was sung chiefly to the hymn text "O Mother Dear, Jerusalem," whose theme of longing for the Promised Land meshes perfectly with the words of *Beulah Land*, which speak of arriving there. But by the symphony's premiere in 1951, *Materna* was better known as the tune for Katherine Lee Bates's "America the Beautiful," with which it was first paired in print in 1910, after the symphony was finished and copied. Today audiences likely link the fragment Ives quotes in the third movement's opening theme and final measures with the phrase "And crown thy good with brotherhood" from the first verse of Bates's poem. But when Ives composed it, he would have expected them to connect it to the line "In thee no sorrow may be found," a message more in tune with the overall feeling of consolation and comfort suggested by his opening theme and the movement as a whole.

This example may serve to emphasize a crucial point about the borrowed material in this work: it is not necessary to recognize the specific popular melodies, hymn tunes, and passages from classical works in order to understand the symphony. Each movement is motivically coherent even for a listener who knows none of its sources for, as we have seen, Ives makes sure each idea develops naturally from what comes before. Far more important than naming the tunes as they go by—as one might do for the *Quodlibet* by Peter Schickele (b. 1935), where incongruous juxtapositions create humor—is hearing the contrasts of style, whether between Bachian counterpoint, Foster, fiddle style, and Brahmsian development in the first movement; jaunty and sentimental popular styles, hymn style, and (again) Brahms in the second; or hymnic consolation versus Wagnerian yearning in the third. Through these contrasts of style, exactly parallel to Mozart's many changes of musical topic, Ives delineates the structure of each movement and creates the expressive arc of the piece, with many dynamic changes of mood and surprising juxtapositions of American and European sounds.[39] For all these reasons, the symphony is comprehensible for listeners who do not catch a single reference.

At the same time, the music may carry more meaning for listeners who do recognize the borrowed tunes and passages, know their contexts, and bring their associations to bear in interpreting the music. The American tunes, the European works, and their associations were certainly important to Ives. Moreover, he was clearly concerned with the level of recognizability. His references to his sources vary from the overt to the disguised, catching our attention with gestures that sound familiar and inviting us to listen more closely and follow his thread as he varies and reworks that material into something new. The sketches show that in several places he changed his music to make its resemblance to his sources either more or less obvious, seeking the right balance, and he revised several passages to change nondescript figuration into a new allusion, saturating the symphony with borrowed material.[40] The process of gradual recognition—the interplay of the familiar with the new as Ives cites and transforms his sources—is part of what makes this music so appealing.

The fourth movement is an abbreviated reprise of the first. The return to B minor is startling after the serene F major close of the third movement, made more so by the loud dynamic, the stark opening statement of the first phrase of *a* in unaccompanied horns, and the addition at its repetition in m. 3 of a poignant new countermelody *f* in upper strings marked by a descending augmented triad and two downward leaps of diminished fifths. After an abbreviated presentation of the *A* section, Ives skips ahead (omitting mm. 20–66 of the first movement) to the statement of *B* in D major with fragments of *Columbia, the Gem of the Ocean* and Brahms's First Symphony (m. 17) and a shortened reprise of *A* in B minor (m. 29). Here the allusion to Bach's Three-Part Invention (*e*) leads to two more borrowings from Brahms: at mm. 36–37, a melodic fragment from the third of the *Vier ernste Gesänge* with two interlocked descending augmented triads (*f'*, clearly related to Ives's countermelody *f* from m. 3), and, at mm. 37–40, a climbing figure of rising fourths and falling thirds over a pedal point (*g*), from Brahms's First Symphony Finale (mm. 385–88), which serves as a grand dominant preparation for Ives's Finale.

The references to Brahms, and especially to his First Symphony, are clues to Ives's use of Brahms as a model. Ives originally conceived the present fourth and fifth movements as a single movement with a slow introduction, like the Finale of Brahms's First Symphony. The parallels are strong, from the shape of the opening horn melody in the slow introduction to the unusual form of the fast section, which, in both cases, can be understood as a sonata form with the development displaced to the middle of the recapitulation, after the first theme repeats in the tonic, as in a sonata-rondo. As a final signal, Ives repeats the passage from Brahms's Finale that he used at the end of the fourth movement in the middle of the coda of the fifth (m. 246), after other recollections and just before the climactic final return of the tonic, closely paralleling its position in Brahms's Finale.[41]

Yet the themes of Ives's fifth movement are American in source and sound, as in the other movements. The first theme group *P* in F major is drawn from Stephen Foster's minstrel show song *Camptown Races*, with an opening melody *a* rather distantly paraphrased from the song's verse and a contrasting idea *b* audibly based on the chorus.[42] A brief passage on *I/A''e*, the Bach Three-Part Invention, adds a cyclic link to the first movement; a march figure for winds and percussion (*c*), with a melody derived from mm. 3–4 of *a* over the *Street Beat* drum pattern, provides stylistic contrast; and a figure based on the verse of *Turkey in the Straw* (*d*) appears as a counterpoint to the last and most definitive statement of *b* at m. 37.

S (m. 58), in A-flat major, is a majestic melody passed between solo horns, in a small ternary form. The first period, *f*, sounds like a Stephen Foster tune, pentatonic and with a rhythm and contour reminiscent of his sentimental parlor song *Old Black Joe*. It is accompanied by *e*, a countermelody in the violins stitched together from fragments of fiddle tunes: the opening figure of *Pig Town Fling* (the source for *I/Bc*) and the chorus of *Turkey in the Straw*.[43] In conformance with Ives's consistent practice of anticipating the second theme in the preceding transition, portions of *e* appear at m. 52, a few measures before *S*. Motive *g*, the middle period of *S*, is derived in part from the same phrase of *Massa's in de Cold Ground* used in the first and third movements (*I/Aa'* and *III/Bf*) and features *d* (from the verse of *Turkey in the Straw*) as a countermelody, with a closing tag in the flute (*h*, mm. 70–71) from the rhythmically related popular song *Long, Long Ago* by Thomas Haynes Bayly (1797–1839). The combination of Foster-derived material in the horns with fiddle-tune countermelodies in the violins matches Ives's description of this passage in the first published score as "the part suggesting a Steve Foster tune, while over it the old farmers fiddled a barn dance with all its jigs, gallops and reels." After the ternary theme is over, a modulatory extension (m. 78) varies parts of both phrases and leads to the recapitulation of *P*.[44]

The recapitulation is fairly literal until the transition is unexpectedly interrupted by a new episode that serves as the movement's development, delayed until after the recapitulation has begun. The development begins at m. 147 with a sudden drop to ***pp*** and a passage (*i*) adapted from episodes from the E-minor fugue from Bach's *Well-Tempered Clavier*, Book 1 (mm. 13–14, 15–17, and 22). As usual, Ives makes the new element grow naturally out of what precedes it: its sixteenth-note figuration echoes that of *a*, *d*, and *e*, and Ives slyly changes Bach's arpeggiated figure into the opening motive of *b*, the chorus of *Camptown Races*. As in the opening theme of the first movement, here Bach and Foster meet on common ground. At m. 162, the opening phrase of *Columbia, the Gem of the Ocean* returns, combined with *Pig Town Fling* (the opening motive of *e*), as in the first and fourth movements, soon joined by the opening motive of *b*. After a varied repetition of *i* (m. 168), the opening motives of *II/P* and *II/S* appear in counterpoint (m. 181) in A-flat, recalling their joint appearance in that key in the second movement's coda. With an orchestral wave of the hand, Ives yanks the tonality back to F and returns to the recapitulation with *S* (m. 189), now with the main melody in a solo cello. His use of horn and solo cello for this theme shows his debt to late Romantic orchestration.[45]

The cyclic recollections—the first movement in the fourth movement and in both *V/P* and *V/S*, and the second movement in the development—culminate in the coda, which sums up the entire symphony. First (at m. 228) comes part of the middle section of the third movement, which was itself drawn from *II/A*; then *II/P* in counterpoint with itself in diminution (m. 236, paralleling the similar combination at m. 89 of the second movement of the First Symphony); and finally the Brahms dominant preparation from the end of the fourth movement (m. 246), which introduces quarter-note triplets in the horns that continue throughout the coming climax. But the linchpin is *Columbia, the Gem of the Ocean*, which emerges here as the climactic new theme for the coda (*N* and *j* in table 4.4), growing from fragments to a single whole statement in a manner that parallels the development of the march theme from cyclic theme M in the First Symphony. We first heard hints of *Columbia* in the first movement (m. 67), then a dotted leaping figure in the second movement (*II/Pb* at m. 25) that sounds like it could be related, then *Columbia* again in the fourth movement (m. 17). The sketches show that the opening theme of the Finale was designed from the start as a countermelody to *Columbia*, and one fragment of *Columbia* appears in counterpoint to it at its first presentation (mm. 11–12 in cellos, basses, and bassoons) as a hint of that future destiny.[46] Appearances of the opening motive of *Columbia* (*jx*) in counterpoint with *e* in the development (m. 162) and with a dotted motive from *a* in the coda (m. 242) prepare us for the Ivesian contrapuntal climax at m. 253, where *Columbia* appears complete and as loud as possible (marked *ffff*) in the trombones together with *a* complete in the upper strings, a variant of *e* in the winds (salted with elements of *d*), and the opening motive of *II/Pa* in the trumpets.

Ives reconsidered the end of the symphony more than any other passage, over a longer period. The sketches show that *e* was a later addition to this climax, and *II/Pa* later still; subsequently, Ives added the bugle call *Reveille* (*k* in table 4.4), which sounds in the trumpet at m. 251 and serves to announce the imminent climax. After the complete statement of *Columbia* with its attendant countermelodies *a* and *e*, a brief extension on motives from all three themes leads to a plagal cadence like that at the end of the First Symphony. This is where the piece ended in its 1908–10 score and ink copy. Much later, by 1938, Ives added the opening segment of *Columbia* in a new final score page. In a last revision for the 1951 score, Ives added *Reveille* to that and changed the final chord: from a sustained F major triad in the horns with concert F in all other instruments, to an accented eighth-note crunch with eleven of the twelve chromatic notes (missing only B), emphasizing the tonic F and its chromatic upper neighbor G♭.[47] In his premiere performance and subsequent recordings, Leonard Bernstein sustained this chord to stress the dissonances, and many other conductors have followed his lead. Yet doing so makes it sound like a raspberry. Ives clearly wanted the effect of a dissonant chord that sounds very briefly and stresses the tonic, a surprise but not a contradiction of all that came before. Indeed, it appears to be one last bit of Americana. Ives told Henry Cowell, who with Lou Harrison edited the score for the 1951 premiere and publication, that such a dissonance "was the formula for signifying the very end of the last dance of all: the players played any old note, good and loud, for the last chord."[48]

The blending of European and American music in the Second Symphony marked a new stage for Ives, uniting in a single work his experiences with the classical tradition, American popular music, and Protestant hymnody, and representing these American traditions through the international language of the symphony. Weaving together Bach and Stephen Foster in the first and last movements was a pairing particularly close to his heart. As Ives recalled in 1930, his father regarded the creations of both composers as "great music" and used them side by side in his teaching: "He started all the children of the family—and most of the children of the town for that matter—on Bach and Stephen Foster.... He put a love of music into the heart of many a boy who might have gone without it but for him."[49] The Second Symphony is Ives's earliest major piece to incorporate Foster tunes; later ones include the Fourth Symphony, *Holidays Symphony*, and Orchestral Sets Nos. 1 and 2.

Some of the Foster songs Ives uses—including *Massa's in de Cold Ground* and *Camptown Races*—were written for blackface minstrel shows, in which white performers blackened their faces and performed songs and skits that traded on racist stereotypes of African Americans. These songs can be disturbing to hear in Ives's music. Yet, in light of Ives's commitment to racial equality in his business and writings, the strong abolitionist current in his family, and his comments about Foster, he seems to have regarded the songs not as racist or offensive but as expressions of Foster's—and his own—sympathy for African Americans. When he wrote to Rodzinski and Koussevitzky in 1943, he described the Second Symphony's Finale, and especially its second theme modeled on *Old Black Joe*, as reflecting Foster's "sadness for slavery."[50] By including these Foster tunes—as well as the abolitionist song *Wake Nicodemus*, which hails "the great Jubilee" of emancipation and praises the enslaved African American named in its title as "the salt of the earth"—in his great synthesis of American and European traditions, Ives clearly meant to embrace African Americans as vital and necessary threads in the tapestry of American life and music.[51]

Ives did not attend the premiere of the Second Symphony, but his wife Harmony did. When it was broadcast on the radio ten days later, they both went over to the house of their country neighbors, the Ryders. As Luemily Ryder recalled, "Mr. Ives sat in the front room and listened as quietly as could be.... After it was over, I'm sure he was very much moved. He stood up, walked over to the fireplace, and spat! And then he walked out into the kitchen. Not a word. And he never said anything about it. I think he was pleased, but he was silent."[52] Harmony Ives wrote to Leonard Bernstein, "I have been familiar with [the Second Symphony]—in snatches—for forty years and more and to hear the whole performed at last was a big event in my life.... Mr. Ives heard the broadcast... and it took him back so to his father and his youth that he had tears in his eyes. You will be interested to know that his comment on the allegro movements was 'too slow'—otherwise he was satisfied. He thanks you from the bottom of his heart."[53]

The premiere was very well received and won Ives strongly positive reviews. Most, like Olin Downes in the *New York Times*, praised the work's originality, discussed its use of American tunes, and stressed how long it had waited to be played.

> It was reserved for Leonard Bernstein, to his eternal credit, to give the first performance anywhere in its entirety of the Second Symphony of Charles Ives, at the concert of the Philharmonic Symphony Orchestra last night in Carnegie Hall.
>
> It is not necessary to emphasize the fact that this symphony, an astonishing work today, was completed just fifty years ago, and that it has lain that long awaiting a public hearing, to prove the composer's originality. But it is testimony to Ives' complete conviction in his art, and audacity in expressing himself, to reflect upon the impression that this particular symphony, by no means the most daring of Ives' scores, would have made if it had been heard when it was completed at the beginning of the century....
>
> If the symphony were the work merely of a folk-lorist, if the score consisted only of references to old-time American tunes, it would have no particular individual or artistic significance. But these tunes, with their profound meanings to a creative artist, are matters of reference.[54]

Virgil Thomson, in the *New York Herald Tribune*, noted that the symphony centers on music, and therefore on the people who make and experience music.

> Charles Ives's Second Symphony, composed in the late 1890s [*recte* in the early 1900s] but never before performed in its entirety, is a five-movement rhapsodic meditation on American hymns of the nineteenth century, American dance ditties and football songs. It is essentially a landscape piece with people in it. The first movement gives us the lush Connecticut valley through a musical technique derived from the Bach choral-preludes. It is sustained, songful, organ-like, graciously contrapuntal, predominantly a piece for strings, with at the end a quotation from "Columbia, the Gem of the Ocean" to make the note of faith specific.
>
> From here on, song and dance material dominate.... Orchestrally, harmonically and melodically the symphony is both noble and plain. It speaks of American life with love and humor and deep faith. It is unquestionably an authentic work of art, both as structure and as composition.[55]

Although he had a hand in editing the symphony, Henry Cowell wrote about it for the *Musical Quarterly*. As might be expected from his own experimental proclivities, he regarded the piece as a forerunner to Ives's later, more modernist music.

> The work was a great success with the audience, and both Ives and Bernstein were eulogized by the press.
>
> The Second Symphony . . . contains only in the most embryonic state the unique outpouring of dissonances, rhythms, polyharmonies, etc., for which Ives has become especially known. Undoubtedly audiences are flattered by the discovery that they are able to enjoy such works as these, often without realizing that what they are listening to is not at all what they have been hearing about. The reception given to Ives's Symphony No. 2 was certainly helped, among slightly more knowing auditors who had braced themselves to hear unbearable dissonance, by the grand bagful of tunes in a familiar idiom that they were offered instead—tunes harmonized with only an occasional unexpected progression.
>
> The work is polyphonic much of the time, the polyphony formed of pieces of familiar tunes set against each other, in easily understandable association. The tunes are rarely sounded all the way through, and there is apt to be some distortion of rhythm. The melodic line often leads to some point not suggested in the original version. So in the fabric of sound familiar bits are frequently tossed to the surface and disappear again before one can recall just what they were. The impression of the work would doubtless be much more nostalgic if we knew the tunes still; but many of these are no longer remembered; even Ives has forgotten the names of most of them.
>
> The effectiveness of the Symphony No. 2 does not, however, rely only on nostalgic association. The tunes are often sprightly and attractive even if one has never heard them before, and they lead smoothly from one to another, with some unexpected key change and occasionally asymmetrical design. The underlying form is always easily discernable....

Without being as exploratory as his later works, it is nevertheless a finely wrought symphony, full of feeling and vitality, and there is no practical reason why it should not be frequently played and greatly enjoyed.[56]

In most respects, the Second Symphony continues the style and language of the First. Yet, by placing American music at the center, especially the diverse types of music he encountered in his youth, Ives began to establish an individual identity and set the stage for the orchestral works to come.

SYMPHONY NO. 3: *THE CAMP MEETING*

Ives's Symphony No. 3 is a little masterpiece, his most perfect meditation on nineteenth-century hymnody. It is his shortest symphony—only three movements, in the unusual arrangement slow-fast-slow, and about twenty-three minutes long—and his smallest, scored for chamber orchestra. It is also his first to carry a descriptive title, *The Camp Meeting*. Although it does not have a program, the symphony celebrates the spirit of the outdoor revival meetings Ives experienced as a youth, and all the themes are drawn from hymn tunes that he heard and sang there.[57]

In other respects, it builds on the achievements of his first two symphonies. Like its predecessors, the Third Symphony is tonal, with the two outer movements in B-flat major (although the first ends in F) and the middle one in E-flat. The middle movement is in ternary form, like the middle movements of the first two symphonies. The whole work features motivic fragmentation and development, developing variation, cyclic unification, harmonic explorations, contrapuntal climaxes, and the gradual emergence of a main theme from fragments, which we have seen in both prior symphonies, as well as the integration of American source material with European methods exemplified in the Second Symphony.

But in the outer movements, Ives takes this combination of elements in a new direction. Instead of reshaping American tunes into themes that fit neatly into sonata form, he treats American hymn tunes as themes in themselves. He presents them essentially whole near the end of the movement, where they are accompanied by countermelodies paraphrased from other hymn tunes, and precedes them with development that generates the themes and countermelodies from fragments. This approach means that Ives does not subordinate the American material to European form, as in the Second Symphony, but rather that he uses traditional symphonic techniques to generate the American tunes before our ears. The effect is cumulative, and because Ives used this format more than any other in his mature instrumental music, it can be regarded as a form, hence the name *cumulative form*.[58] Ives's approach resembles that of Jean Sibelius in symphonic works from around the same time, each working without knowledge of the other's music; both use a process of gradual revelation, although Ives consistently adopts a formal pattern focused on development and culminating presentation of the main theme (usually a borrowed melody), whereas Sibelius's structures are more varied.[59] In Ives's Third Symphony, the gathering of elements into a whole serves also as a musical metaphor for aspects of the religious experience and of the camp meeting itself.[60]

By his own account, Ives based each movement on a work for organ he composed and performed during services at Central Presbyterian Church in New York in his last year as organist there, 1901–2. This origin as service music—respectively a prelude, postlude, and piece for communion—would explain the presence of themes derived from hymn tunes in each movement as well as the organlike quality of some of the textures and orchestration.[61] Unfortunately, no such organ works survive; perhaps Ives improvised them or worked them out by memory and did not write them down. Ives gave various dates for the symphony in his annotations and work lists, ranging from 1901–4 to 1911, but he most consistently said it was completed between 1909 and 1911 and copied that year.[62] According to Gayle Sherwood Magee, the handwriting confirms a date of circa 1908–11, and all the extant sketches are on music paper that can be dated no earlier than 1907. The sketches include early and rejected versions for some of the themes themselves and for most of the musical fabric, suggesting that the movements we have are very different from whatever Ives may have improvised or composed before 1907.[63]

Like his earlier symphonies, the Third lay unperformed for decades. Ives wrote in *Memos* that Gustav Mahler (1860–1911), at the time the conductor of the New York Philharmonic, saw the work being copied in 1911 "and asked to have a copy—he was quite interested in it."[64] Had Mahler lived to conduct it in New York or Vienna, it might have won Ives recognition early in his compositional maturity. Ives sent an ink copy to Walter Damrosch in December 1911, but no reading or performance resulted, and Damrosch never returned the score.[65]

In the 1930s, Ives sent several photostated scores to Lou Harrison, including the pencil score of the Third Symphony. In 1945, when Harrison was invited to conduct part of a concert of the New York Little Symphony, he programmed the Third Symphony, had the score copied, produced the parts himself, and conducted the premiere on April 5, 1946, playing it twice on that concert. Players, audience, and reviewers were enthusiastic. It was performed again on May 11 by Edgar Schenkman and an orchestra of students from the Juilliard School of Music at an all-Ives concert at Columbia University, where it was warmly received by an audience that included Serge Koussevitzky, conductor of the Boston Symphony Orchestra, and Dimitri Mitropoulos, conductor of the Minneapolis Symphony Orchestra and future conductor of the New York Philharmonic. (Within the next eight years, these three major orchestras would premiere other works by Ives, although not under Koussevitzky or Mitropoulos.) Less than two months after the Columbia concert, the Third Symphony was played on the radio on July 3, conducted by Bernard Herrmann. This was more exposure in a short time than any Ives work had received. The symphony won a special citation from the New York Music Critics' Circle, it was published in March 1947, and in May 1947 it was awarded the Pulitzer Prize for music. In a characteristic gesture, Ives gave half the prize money to Harrison and the other half to another composer and friend, John J. Becker (1886–1961).[66] Mark Zobel has suggested that the very positive reception the Third Symphony received was due in part to timing; in the immediate aftermath of World War II, Americans yearned for a simpler pastoral past, which Ives captured through his reworkings of familiar hymn tunes in a modernist but still tonal language.[67]

Probably years after completing his pencil full score of the symphony, Ives inserted at certain places soft dissonant lines that added chromaticism or suggested another key, but later he crossed them out. In his *Memos* and letters to Lou Harrison and Bernard Herrmann, he called these soft dissonant lines "shadow parts." They were omitted from the 1947 score and thus were absent from all early performances but were included in the 1990 critical edition as performance options that may be played very softly or omitted at the discretion of the conductor.[68] Some of the shadow lines add chromatic motion snaking around voices in the counterpoint. Others imitate or parallel melodic lines in the main musical fabric, as at the end of the first movement, where a solo violin marked ***pppp*** plays part of the movement's countermelody in A-flat major, paralleling the flute's F major statement a major sixth below. The effect can be haunting, suggesting a fleeting memory, an echo, or one voice in the crowd at the revival reverently singing in the wrong key. Such shadow lines are frequent in the later symphonic works. Yet the heightened dissonance and polytonality they add are entirely out of character with the tonal and mostly triadic harmonic language of the Third Symphony. For that reason, these shadow parts are probably best omitted from performances of this work.

In the first movement, "Old Folks Gatherin'," the main theme (MT) is the hymn tune *Azmon*, arranged by Lowell Mason from a melody by Carl Gotthelf Gläser (1784–1829), and most often sung to these words by John Wesley:

> O for a thousand tongues to sing
> My great Redeemer's praise;
> The glories of my God and King,
> The triumphs of his grace!

Example 4.8a shows the full statement of this theme in violin 1 at m. 117, near the end of the movement. Above it, presented mostly in the flute with a brief bridging phrase in the oboe, is the countermelody (CM), paraphrased from the hymn tune *Erie* by Charles Converse (1832–1918) and recast to fit harmonically and contrapuntally with *Azmon*, while remaining in quadruple meter against the latter's triple meter.[69] Here Ives again creates the sense of superimposed meters, as in the previous symphonies, and the differences of meter and timbre emphasize the sense of separation between layers, an effect he used frequently in his later symphonies and orchestral sets. As the example shows, the beginning of CM closely follows the contour and rhythm of the first two phrases of *Erie*, but the paraphrase gradually becomes more distant from its source. Simply leaving off the opening note of the third phrase in the oboe makes it harder to recognize, and the melodic peak of CM in mm. 122–23 conflates elements from mm. 7–8 and 11–12 of the hymn tune to create a lovely melodic line whose relation to the source is even less obvious.

Yet the references are clear enough for a listener who knows both *Azmon* and *Erie* to hear how Ives weaves the two hymns together in counterpoint in this closing passage (mm. 117–28), suggesting a conjunction of their words as well as their melodies. *Erie* is usually sung to these words by Joseph Scriven:

> What a friend we have in Jesus
> All our sins and griefs to bear!
> What a privilege to carry
> Ev'rything to God in prayer!
> Oh, what peace we often forfeit,
> Oh, what needless pain we bear,
> All because we do not carry
> Ev'rything to God in prayer!

The combination of the two texts with the sense of drawing things together that is basic to cumulative form conveys the idea of "Old Folks Gatherin'" at the outdoor revival, coming together to sing praises, worship, pray, and bring their cares to God.[70]

Table 4.5 shows how the cumulative form in this movement falls into six large sections, each different in its presentation of thematic elements. The last section presents MT, complete for the first time and with CM (m. 117). Unlike the contrapuntal climaxes of the first two symphonies, this one is quiet, appropriate to the reverent atmosphere of a revival. The rest of the movement is like a sonata-form development, leading up to the complete statement of the themes.

At the outset, Andante maestoso, the violin 1 melody weaves together fragments of MT (mm. 0–1 and 5–6) and CM (mm. 2–3 and 5), like a distant hint of what is to come. Gradually, two countersubjects, CSa and CSb, emerge alongside fragments of MT. As example 4.8b

a. Culminating statement of MT *(Azmon)* and CM (based on *Erie*)

Example 4.8 Symphony No. 3: The Camp Meeting by Charles Ives. Copyright © 1947 (Renewed) by Associated Music Publishers, Inc. (BMI). International Copyright Secured. All Rights Reserved. Used by Permission.

b. Countersubjects derived in part from *Erie*

Example 4.8 *continued* (b) Countersubjects CSa (mm. 22–25) and CSb (mm. 38–40), derived in part from *Erie*

shows, these countersubjects are based on motives from *Erie*, the source for CM. In the second section, Andante con moto (m. 22), most of MT (mm. 1–6, all but the last phrase) is treated in fugato, joined first by CSa and then by both countersubjects. Already in the first two sections, the tendency to move from fragments to fuller statements through developing variation is clear.

The next section, marked Slower (m. 54), begins with a new theme, the first phrase of the hymn tune *Woodworth* ("Just as I am"), slightly varied in the horns under CSb in the strings; this is a foreshadowing of things to come, for *Woodworth* will become the main theme of the Finale. After this new idea is repeated, the development of fragments from MT and the two countersubjects continues. Then in the fourth section, marked Adagio cantabile and with a meter change to 4/2 (m. 75), Ives presents CM ***pp***, first in a distorted fragment in the oboe and then complete though somewhat varied in the flute (m. 78), with only a few hints of MT in the accompanying strings.

After a cadence on B-flat, development resumes in the fifth section (m. 88) with fragments of both themes and both countersubjects, beginning più mosso and later returning to 3/2 and Andante con moto. Most of the movement has centered on B-flat major, with excursions to other keys and to D Mixolydian and D Dorian in the third section, but a long pedal point on C at the end of the fifth section prepares a change to F major for the final section and the complete statement of MT with CM (m. 117). The movement closes in that key; the return to the tonic B-flat will have to wait until the symphony's Finale.

While the first movement is somewhat episodic, the third movement, "Communion," is more tightly developmental, focused on the main theme and principal countermelody throughout. Example 4.9 shows the culminating appearance of the two together in the final section. The main theme (MT) is *Woodworth*, anticipated in the first movement, with music by William B. Bradbury (1815–68) to words by Charlotte Elliott:

Table 4.5 Cumulative Form Movements in Ives's Symphony No. 3

1. OLD FOLKS GATHERIN' (ANDANTE MAESTOSO)
Main theme (MT): *Azmon*
Countermelody (CM): Paraphrased from *Erie*
Secondary ideas: Countersubject a (CSa): Derived in part from a segment of *Erie*
Countersubject b (CSb): Derived from a segment of *Erie*
Woodworth, first phrase

Sect.	Meas.	Music	Meter and tempo	Key
1	1	Mixture of MT, CM	3/2, Andante maestoso	B♭, many passing changes of key
	8	Fragments of MT with CSa and CSb		
2	22	MT mm. 1–6, fugato with CSa	Andante con moto	E♭, B♭, modulatory
	38	CSb enters, fugato continues		final statement on B♭
3	54	*Woodworth*, first phrase, with CSb	Slower	D Mixolydian
	60	Further development of fragments of MT, CSa, and CSb		modulatory, closing in D Dorian
4	75	**CM complete**, with a few MT fragments	4/2, Adagio cantabile	modulatory, ending in B♭
5	88	Development of fragments of CM, CSb, MT, and CSa	Più mosso	B♭, with passing changes of key
	101	Development continues	3/2, Andante con moto	B♭, modulating to F
6	117	**MT complete, with CM**	Largamente, Adagio cantabile	F

3. COMMUNION (LARGO)
Main theme (MT): *Woodworth*
Countermelody (CM): Paraphrased from *Azmon*
Secondary idea: Countersubject (CS) to CM: Original

Sect.	Meas.	Music	Key
1	1	Fragments of MT and CM	B♭, many passing changes of key
	12	First half of CM and CS, then continued development	F, modulating to B♭
2	20	**CM and CS complete**, with accompaniment as at m. 49	E♭
	25	MT fragments	modulatory, closing on F minor
3	29	Paraphrase of MT	modulatory
	37	Fragments of MT and CM, with varied reprise of mm. 1–3 at mm. 39–41	modulatory, closing on V of B♭
4	49	**MT complete, with CM and CS** and accompaniment	B♭
	57	Extension of MT and final cadence	C, B♭

Just as I am, without one plea,
But that Thy blood was shed for me,
And that Thou bidd'st me come to Thee,
O Lamb of God, I come! I come!

The countermelody (CM) is paraphrased from *Azmon*, the main theme of the first movement, creating a tight cyclic connection between the two cumulative-form movements. Indeed, the opening gesture of the Finale's countermelody is directly anticipated in the first movement (see violin 1, mm. 0–1, 75–76, and 78–79). As in that movement, the source for the Finale's countermelody is recast to fit harmonically and contrapuntally with the main theme. In addition, a countersubject (CS, not shown in the example) accompanies CM here and at two earlier appearances.

As table 4.5 shows, the movement falls essentially into four sections, within a weave of continual variation and development.

In the first section, set in a highly chromatic B-flat major with many brief modulations, fragments of MT and CM (sometimes chromatically altered) are developed in alternation. Example 4.10 shows this development, indicating notes from MT with crosses and notes from CM with circles. The cello introduces the first phrase of MT in B-flat in mm. 1–3, distended with chromatic interpolations, while the opening three notes are imitated in viola and violin 1. That same three-note motive recurs in m. 3, overlapping in viola, violin 1, and violin 2 in quick succession and tracing a whole-tone scale. Fragments from the second half of MT follow in violin 1 in mm. 4–5, including the melodic peak of the hymn in A major (alluded to earlier by violin 1 in m. 2, in G major). The winds interrupt with the first portion of CM in D-flat major in mm. 6–7. After a cadence, the opening returns, somewhat varied. Development continues, and, at mm. 12–14, the first halves of CM and CS appear in counterpoint.

In the second section at m. 20, CM in violin 1 and CS in clarinet are presented together with the viola figuration and bass line that will accompany them in the final section, all transposed to the subdominant E-flat major. Further development of fragments of MT leads to a cadence on F minor.

Here the third section begins with a paraphrase of MT, beginning in the horn (m. 29) and moving to violin 1 (m. 31) and violin 2 (m. 33). The melody is distorted by changing intervals so that it rises gradually in key, as if a crowd of singers growing in excitement were unable to keep from raising the pitch. The development continues, encompassing a varied reprise of the opening three measures of the movement at m. 39 and leading to a climax at m. 44 and a half cadence, ii^9-V in B-flat major, that repeats as the music grows gradually slower and softer.

The ritardando, diminuendo, and half cadence set up the return to B-flat for the quiet final section in example 4.9 (m. 49), where MT is presented by the cellos, doubled by a solo cello and flute an octave higher, with CM in violin 1 and CS in bassoon.[71] The hymn tune is almost complete, but Ives delays the final notes with a pause for breath and a musical parenthesis (mm. 57–59), repeating the third phrase of *Woodworth* in C major in ethereal high strings, then returning to B-flat for the final phrase in the violins and stating the last motive of the hymn tune, F-D, twice in the solo cello. This musical echo reminds those who know the hymn of the textual echo that ends each verse, "I come! I come!"

Above this ending, Ives writes another echo into the music: orchestral bells, softly alternating B minor and G-sharp minor triads three times, fading to nothing. Because of a comment by Henry Cowell that is included in the 1964 score, which suggests that Ives wanted the sound of church bells rather than orchestral bells, some performances and recordings use recorded

Example 4.9 Ives. Symphony No. 3/3, culminating statement at mm. 49–57 of MT (*Woodworth*) with CM (paraphrased from *Azmon*)

The Symphonic Works of Charles Ives

Example 4.10 Ives. Symphony No. 3/3, mm. 1–8

church bells at this point, often playing somewhat randomly. But the acoustical properties of church bells and the repeated minor third relationship between the two minor triads in the bells clarify Ives's intention. A church bell has a distinctive sound that emphasizes the notes of a minor triad, so that playing a minor triad on orchestral bells comes as close as possible to imitating that sound on orchestral instruments. If the parallel triads are played as directed, they will sound like church bells playing a repeated minor third, B-G♯—in other words, the last notes of the hymn, "I come," sounding up a tritone from the solo cello and rhythmically lagging a bit behind it. Ives often used distance of key as a metaphor for distance in space, so that the distance of a tritone, combined with the soft dynamic and difference in rhythm and timbre, creates a sound like that of church bells at a distance, ringing the last notes of the hymn. The effect is magical.

J. Peter Burkholder

Example 4.10 *continued*

The harmony in this movement is remarkable. Overall there is a simple plan, centering on the tonic in the first and final sections and on the subdominant in the second, while the third section begins and ends on the dominant and features rapid modulation in between, approximating a motion around the circle of fifths. But within this simple overarching structure, the chord-to-chord progressions vary from common practice to chromatic slippage. The opening of the movement in example 4.10 can serve as illustration. Between the initial gestures, which arpeggiate a tonic B♭-major triad in cellos, violas, and violin 1, and the ii$^6_5$ chord (decorated with appoggiaturas) on the third beat of m. 3 that marks the end of the first phrase, there is an astonishing succession of vertical sonorities that include (reading some notes enharmonically) F^2, $D♭^7$, $B♭^6_4$, C_6, c_6, G^6_4, b_6, C, E^2, $A♭^6_4$, E♭, e♭, b_6, C_6, and $B♭^6_4$. While some of these chords function in the key of B-flat, such as the c and E♭ chords in m. 2 that suggest a move toward the subdominant, most of these sonorities are simply the result of contrapuntal motion between the parts, which typically move by step, chromatically or diatonically. The passage is conceptually similar to the chromatic harmonies at the opening of Ives's First Symphony, shown in example 4.3, but it is more extensive and colorful. In the phrases that follow, the emphasis on A major in m. 5 (alternating with D) and on D-flat major (alternating with G-flat) in m. 6, leading to a registrally and rhythmically prominent F major triad on the fifth beat of m. 6 that prepares a return to the tonic B-flat, recalls the similar circles of major thirds in the First Symphony (A-D♭-F and D-G♭-B♭). Overall, the harmony is clearly tonal, while suggesting a freely flowing fantasy.

Between the two cumulative-form movements is a fast middle movement in ternary form, "Children's Day." Cumulative form, so apt for representing the sense of gathering in prayerful communion in the outer movements, would be less appropriate here for evoking the cheerful boisterousness of children at the camp meeting. The *A* section, Allegro moderato and in E-flat major, presents Lowell Mason's hymn tune *Naomi* like a cantus firmus in long notes in horns, bassoons, and pulsating violas, accompanied by cellos. Ives no doubt chose *Naomi* for this movement to create a motivic link to the outer movements. The first and third phrases of *Naomi* share an intervallic contour with the first phrase of *Woodworth*, quoted in the first movement and the main theme of the Finale; using numbers to indicate scale degrees and italics to indicate strong beats, these phrases all trace the melody *3*-3-*5*-4-*3*-2-*3*-4-*3*. Above the statement of *Naomi* unwinds a long theme *a* in the violins, spinning out motives from the first half of the verse of Mason's *Fountain* ("There is a fountain filled with blood"). As *Naomi* comes to an end in m. 27, theme *a* is taken over by cellos, violas, and bassoons, while the violins play the last phrase of *Naomi*. At m. 33 the key shifts to C major and a new thematic idea *b*, based on the end of *Fountain*'s verse (mm. 6–8), emerges in the cellos, violas, and bassoons. The new idea *b* is passed to the violins at m. 40, and the *A* section culminates with a crescendo, ritardando, and wedgelike expansion, the lower strings descending chromatically as the violins rise, to end on a climactic dominant of the dominant.

The *B* section begins at m. 50: soft, più allegro, and in the dominant key of B-flat, with theme *c* paraphrased from another Mason tune, *There Is a Happy Land*. The second half of the hymn tune (mm. 9–16) is paraphrased first, alternating between flute and violin 1 and then developed in a brief extension. The flute in m. 52 alters a segment of the hymn to resemble a motive heard in *Fountain* (m. 3) and in *Erie* (m. 1), creating a motivic link both to the *A* section of this movement and to the countermelody from the first movement. At mm. 59–62, the first half of *There Is a Happy Land* is paraphrased, shifting between D and F major. In mm. 62–66, a new element *d*, partly derived from the popular song *There's Music in the Air* by George F. Root, appears in dialogue between violins and winds. There follows a dotted march figure at m. 67, briefly interrupted by a fugato at mm. 71–74, that leads to a repetition of the *B* section so far (mm. 50–82). After the repetition comes a long developmental extension at m. 86 that combines the dotted march figure with theme *d* (at m. 88) and a new march tune (mm. 98–102). All these middle-section thematic ideas share a jaunty character that aptly captures the spirit of Children's Day at a revival.

The varied reprise of the *A* section comes in m. 120, prepared by another wedgelike expansion and rallentando. In a surprise, the reprise begins a tritone away from the tonic, on A major, but it slips back into E-flat midway through the cantus firmus statement of *Naomi* (m. 136). At m. 150, corresponding to where thematic idea *b* appeared in the *A* section, Ives instead combines elements of *a* and *b* into a complete paraphrase of *Fountain* with considerable variation and repetition (mm. 150–53 in low strings and brass, overlapping mm. 150–68 in violin 1). Beginning at a grand climax in m. 161, motives from the *B* section theme *c* join the counterpoint, creating a culminating combination of themes similar to what we have seen in several movements of the First and Second Symphonies. The pace gradually slows, the texture thins, and the movement ends quietly.

The fast ternary middle movement on paraphrased themes, in a style close to that of the Second Symphony, neatly balances the two slower outer movements in cumulative form. Together all three movements use the Romantic symphonic techniques Ives had honed in his two earlier symphonies, from developing variation to cyclic unification and contrapuntal combination of themes, to create a celebration of the hymns sung at camp meeting revivals and of the spirit Ives experienced there as a young man. The motivic links give the whole symphony a narrative arc, like a multimovement cumulative form, especially the gradual emergence of *Woodworth* from brief references in the first movement and (via its resemblance to *Naomi*) in the middle movement through gradual development in the third movement to the full statement at the end. This trajectory offers a musical parallel to a spiritual experience in which one grapples with an idea or feeling that only gradually becomes clear enough to articulate. For a listener who knows the hymns, that can be an explicit experience akin to worship, bringing one's praise and prayers and cares and very being into the presence of God, and ending with the simple affirmation "I come!" But even for a listener who has never heard the hymns, the symphony is comprehensible formally and thematically, and the process of gradual clarification can be felt and be emotionally affecting.[72]

Reviewing the 1946 premiere in the *New York Times*, Noel Straus noted the long wait between composition and first performance and praised the symphony's special qualities:

> That the symphony . . . had to wait forty years for its initial hearing is a sad commentary on the neglect that has been meted out to one of this country's most gifted composers throughout his long career. . . . Though the symphony represented Ives' methods of procedure before he had reached the maturity of his powers, it possessed a freshness of inspiration, a genuineness of feeling and an intense sincerity that lent it immediate appeal and manifested inborn talents of a high order.
>
> When Ives began the composition he was obviously more conservative in his approach than he became as the content grew. For of the three movements based on hymn tunes, the first, an Andante, moved the most warily along traditional lines. But in the central Allegro the composer showed greater daring in his harmonic texture, and in the final Largo he introduced passages of a boldness far ahead of their time.
>
> The symphony proved striking, too, because of its melodiousness, its natural contrapuntal skill and its raciness. It was music close to the soil and deeply felt. And if it was rather loose in its structural patterning, and too much alike in its scoring throughout, it was blest with a richness of orchestral sonorities that matched the richness of imagination abounding in every page of this youthful opus.[73]

SYMPHONY NO. 4

Of all Ives's completed symphonies, Symphony No. 4 was both the first and the last to premiere. Less than two years after its completion in around 1925, Eugene Goossens conducted the first two movements at Town Hall in New York on January 29, 1927, at a concert sponsored by the organization Pro Musica and played by members of the New York Philharmonic. The third movement followed on May 10, 1933, conducted by Bernard Herrmann in a concert of the New Chamber Orchestra at the New School Auditorium in New York. But a complete performance had to wait until April 26, 1965, more than a decade after the premieres of the other completed symphonies, in a Carnegie Hall concert by the American Symphony Orchestra conducted by Leopold Stokowski and assisted by David Katz and José Serebrier.[74]

Ives's music is so diverse that knowing one piece does not necessarily prepare one for another, and the gulf between Symphony No. 4 and its predecessors is especially wide. A listener who encounters Ives's four numbered symphonies in order would be surprised by the Fourth from its opening measures, shown in example 4.11. The modernist sound, chromaticism, dissonance, and multilayered textures are unlike anything in the first three. Many of the innovative techniques Ives had tried out in his experimental music find a home in this symphony,

The Symphonic Works of Charles Ives

Example 4.11 Symphony No. 4 by Charles Ives. Copyright © 1956 (Renewed) by Associated Music Publishers, Inc. (BMI). International Copyright Secured. All Rights Reserved. Used by Permission.

including polytonality, quarter-tones, dissonant chords that imitate drumbeats, and simultaneous streams of music in different meters and tempos.

The experience of listening to the Fourth Symphony is itself full of surprises, for each movement is scored for a different ensemble and moves in its own musical world. The first movement begins as if atonal, then settles into a mostly tonal hymn setting. The second constantly changes style, careering between moods from somber to comic, between soundscapes from hymns to a locomotive and a parade, and between textures from soft homophonic chords to multiple musical layers proceeding simultaneously in different meters and keys. The third movement is suddenly in a retrospective style, a fugue in C major that sounds foreign and completely unexpected in context. The Finale returns to a modernist sound, with more layers than ever, and then gradually clarifies into a cumulative form on a familiar hymn. The first two movements and Finale feature a solo piano and an orchestral piano (four hands at times), which disappear for the third movement, where an organ suddenly enters for the climax and conclusion; neither keyboard instrument plays a role in the previous symphonies.

Despite the Fourth Symphony's apparently radical differences from Ives's earlier symphonies, it demonstrates many continuous threads. The overall conception of the work is a Romantic symphony in four movements, with serious outer movements framing a kind of scherzo in the second movement and a slow third movement. As in his earlier symphonies, much of the thematic material is borrowed; indeed, more borrowed material appears in the Fourth Symphony than in any other Ives work. Also like the earlier symphonies, this one is cyclic, with thematic connections between the first and last movements, and end-weighted, with the most substantial and satisfying musical statement arriving only in the Finale. The fragmentation, juxtaposition, foreshadowing, and contrapuntal combination of musical material in this symphony build on procedures in his earlier ones. Similarly, the vertical combination of multiple streams of music builds on the counterpoint, layering, and effect of superimposing different subdivisions of the measure that we have seen in all three previous symphonies. There are borrowings from *Beulah Land*, as in the First and Second Symphonies; march episodes, fiddle tunes, Stephen Foster songs, and *Columbia, the Gem of the Ocean*, as in the Second Symphony; hymn tunes, as in the Second and Third; and a cumulative-form Finale on a hymn tune presaged in the first movement, as in the Third Symphony. Like the Second and Third Symphonies, each movement in the Fourth was adapted in part from previously existing music by Ives, although in this case many of those source works survive: for the first movement, the song *Watchman* (1913?), arranged from the middle section of the Finale of the First Violin Sonata (ca. 1909–12, revised 1917–25); for the second movement, the piano fantasy *The Celestial Railroad* (ca. 1921–25), itself about half drawn from excerpts from the "Hawthorne" movement of the *Concord Sonata* (ca. 1916–17); for the third movement, the opening fugue from String Quartet No. 1, which was adapted from an organ fugue he wrote for Horatio Parker (ca. 1897–98); and for part of the Finale, the closing passage from String Quartet No. 2 (ca. 1911–15), based on a lost *Memorial Slow March* from a decade earlier.[75]

Of Ives's four numbered symphonies, only this one has a program. That program explains everything else about the symphony, including the presence of hymn tunes, the variety of styles and performing forces, the choice of previous works Ives drew on, and the unusually long and convoluted gestation of the work.[76]

At its partial premiere in 1927, the program booklet included a note ostensibly written by Henry Bellamann but apparently in large part formulated by Ives.[77] Alongside information about Ives and some description of the orchestration and character of the music, the note outlines a program for the symphony. At the time, the fugue, now in third place, was second, before the current second movement.

> This symphony, the fourth, . . . consists of four movements—a Prelude, a majestic fugue, a third movement in comedy vein, and a finale of transcendental spiritual content.
>
> The aesthetic program of the work is that of many of the greatest literary and musical masterpieces of the world—the searching questions of What? and Why? which the spirit of man asks of life. This is particularly the sense of the prelude. The three succeeding movements are the diverse answers in which existence replies.
>
> One word should be spoken here of the peculiar place hymn tunes held in the consciousness of the old New Englanders of the country and the smaller towns. Religion was the only emotional outlet of these earlier Puritans, and hymns the only expression in art medium. All of the repressed humanity of those rock bound souls was poured into fervent renditions of them. Some of these hymns were fine, some very poor, and many were the worst of musical compositions, but we cannot take any account of the emotional workings of the mind and heart of the Puritan without an admission of these themes as vehicles.
>
> The texture of this symphony is threaded through with strands based on old hymns—not quotations from them, but thematic material derived from them. Most auditors will be surprised to discover that many of the hymn tunes are in a pentatonic scale (fourth and seventh either omitted or used sparingly on weaker accents). This characteristic makes it quite natural to interweave them, and is at the same time productive of atonal aspects of the musical development.
>
> The prelude is brief, and its brooding introspective measures have a searching wistful quality. It would seem to derive from the silence of a Sabbath hour when the soul, beset and weary of earthly vexations, turns toward the Infinite, toward life and in upon itself with questions of the ultimate meaning of existence.
>
> . . . The Fugue, omitted in this performance, is an expression of the reaction of life into formalism and ritualism.
>
> The succeeding movement [now the second movement], the one being played at this concert, is not a scherzo in any accepted sense of the word, but it is a comedy. It is comedy in the sense that Hawthorne's [short story *The*] *Celestial Railroad* is comedy. Indeed this work of Hawthorne's may be considered as a sort of incidental program in which an exciting, easy, and worldly progress through life is contrasted with the trials of the Pilgrims in their journey through the swamp. The occasional slow episodes—Pilgrims' hymns—are constantly crowded out and overwhelmed by the former. The dream, or fantasy, ends with an interruption of reality—the Fourth of July in Concord—brass bands, drum corps, etc. Here are old popular tunes, war songs, and the like.[78]

The published note does not give a program for the Finale, but the omission was apparently an editing error. When the second movement was published in the January 1929 issue of *New Music Quarterly*, Ives included an abbreviated note that ends with this paragraph: "The last movement is an apotheosis of the preceding content, in terms that have something to do with the reality of existence and its religious experience."[79]

In essence, the four movements of the symphony are in dialogue with each other. The first poses spiritual questions about "the ultimate meaning of existence" and the other three offer diverse replies. The second and third movements illustrate wrong paths: staking one's hopes on a too-easy trip through life and a false route to heaven, as satirized in Hawthorne's allegorical tale, or on "formalism and ritualism," represented by the tonal C-major fugue ("formalism") on a hymn-tune theme heard in church services ("ritualism"). The Finale presents a truer path, drawing "Nearer, my God, to Thee" through a cumulative form based on Lowell Mason's *Bethany*, the most familiar tune for that hymn text.

In a very real sense, the symphony was conceived not when the first notes were written for it but when Ives had the idea for the program and for weaving certain existing works into it: posing the questions through his song *Watchman*, using his piano fantasy *The Celestial Railroad* and his fugue for string quartet to embody the false answers, and reworking the closing passage of his Second String Quartet, a radiant combination of *Bethany* with other elements, as the culmination of the difficult but ultimately fulfilling journey toward transcendence and communion in the Finale. Since Ives composed *The Celestial Railroad* between 1921 and 1925, the conception of the symphony as we know it may be as late as then. According to Gayle Sherwood Magee's datings, all four movements were worked on and finalized between about 1921 and 1925. Ives traced the origins of the symphony to around 1910, and datable sketches are extant for the fugue from circa 1912–13 and for the other movements from circa 1915–18. Apparently Ives set out to write a fourth symphony soon after completing his Third, but the piece we have is a product of the early to mid-1920s, when Ives created the program and reworked whatever music he had composed earlier to include his orchestrated expansion of *The Celestial Railroad*.[80]

The brief first movement is in three sections, each roughly twice as long as the previous one and each serving in turn as a prelude to what comes next. The first section, shown in example 4.11, is only four measures long. Four layers of sound are juxtaposed: a *ff* unison melody in solo piano and low strings; dissonant chords in tremolo upper strings and piano; an atonal trumpet fanfare; and a very soft "Distant Choir" of four solo violins and harp playing fragments of *Bethany* with dissonant harmonies. The first three layers enter one by one, all loud—this is the only one of Ives's symphonic works to begin at a dynamic level above *p*—and piling on top of one another. They stop to reveal the Distant Choir sounding behind them, then the unison melody resumes to close this first section.

Such layering of elements and alternation of material become characteristic of the entire symphony. So do the techniques Ives uses to create the sense of multiple simultaneous streams of music, including differences of timbre, range, rhythm, meter, motive, pitch material, tonality or atonality, and dynamic level. The layering of contrasting motives and rhythms is rooted in Ives's love of counterpoint, as exemplified in all of his earlier symphonies. The differentiation of timbre and dynamic level is something he learned primarily from his experience as an organist alternating between Great and Swell manuals with contrasting stops. This includes the effect Nicolas Slonimsky called "sonic exuviation," shedding a loud shell of sound to expose soft music beneath, as when the main orchestra ceases at m. 3 and the Distant Choir is heard.[81] Ives uses this effect to suggest that the soft layer of music was sounding all along, unheard behind the louder sounds, and thus that we are in a vast expanse in which several streams of music, some close and others distant, are sounding simultaneously. Through musical means he conveys a sense of space, which is often made explicit in performance by placing the Distant Choir at the back of the stage, in the balcony, or offstage.[82]

Amid all this diversity and multidimensionality, Ives's practice of motivic variation is still evident. Horizontal brackets in example 4.11 show that the opening idea of a rising half step and minor third is echoed in inversion in the upper strings and in inversion, retrograde, and retrograde inversion in the closing melody.[83] The dotted scalar figure that ends the first measure reappears at the end of m. 4 and in inverted augmentation in a middle voice in m. 2. Moreover, the opening motive D-[E♭]-F♯-F♮-E is partly echoed in the trumpet call (D-F♯-F♮-[A]-E) and harp (F♯-F♮-E), with a similar dotted rhythm for the F♯-F♮ dyad in all three. Such subtle interrelating of material is present throughout the symphony in various ways. Here these moment-to-moment connections are not part of an overall developmental form, as in his earlier symphonies, but create a sense of continuity like that of an experience—or a dream.

This declamatory beginning, like an incantation, leads to the second section (mm. 5–16). Here a solo cello or violin spins out a melody that begins with the first phrase of *In the Sweet By-and-By* by James P. Webster (1819–75), one of the primarily pentatonic hymn tunes mentioned in the program, and then gradually becomes chromatic in a narrow range. The opening melody of the hymn carries the text "There's a land that is fairer than day," and thus quoting this phrase introduces the idea of the Promised Land. The solo melody is accompanied by subtly changing ostinatos in piano and pizzicato basses. Different parts divide the measure into two, three, five, six, or other equal subdivisions, heightening the separation between layers. The Distant Choir continues in its own meter and tempo, not coordinated with the main orchestra, and other layers gradually join in, notably the celesta playing fragments of *Bethany*.

The third and largest section (mm. 17–41) is an orchestral adaptation of Ives's song *Watchman*, based on Lowell Mason's hymn tune of the same name. A unison chorus and trumpet present the melody. Although Ives marks the voice part *ad lib.* and "(preferably without voices)," the meaning of the movement and thus of the whole symphony is clearer when the text is audible. Ives alters John Bowring's hymn text to end with a question and a call to see the star that promises the revelation of a new day. Originally the Christmas star in this Advent hymn, the star becomes in the symphony a sign of a search still underway, a goal in sight but not yet reached.

Bowring:	*Ives:*
Watchman, tell us of the night,	Watchman, tell us of the night,
What its signs of promise are.	What its signs of promise are.
Trav'ler, o'er yon mountain's height,	Trav'ler, o'er yon mountain's height,
See that glory-beaming star!	See that glory-beaming star!
Watchman, does its beauteous ray	Watchman, aught of joy or hope?
Aught of joy or hope foretell?	Trav'ler, Yes! Trav'ler, Yes!
Trav'ler, yes; it brings the day,	Trav'ler, Yes; it brings the day,
Promised day of Israel.	Promised day of Israel.
	Dost thou see its beauteous ray?
	Trav'ler, see!
	Oh, see its beauteous ray; See, see!

The piano and strings accompany the vocal melody, while other instruments add layers: *Street Beat* (a standard march pattern for drums) in the timpani; motives from *Bethany* and from the clock-chime tune *Westminster Chimes* in the celesta; a patchwork of phrases from several hymns in the flute, including bits of *Proprior Deo* (an English tune by Arthur Sullivan [1842–1900] that is also used for *Nearer, My God, to Thee*), *Something for Thee* (by Theodore Perkins [1831–1902]), *Bethany*, and *Crusader's Hymn*; and the Distant Choir continuing its ostinato based on *Bethany*, interrupted by increasingly long rests. Once again, layers are distinguished by rhythm: the string figurations divide the measure into three or nine beats against the 6/8 meter of the melody, the drums and flute have four beats per measure, the celesta is syncopated against the measure, and the Distant Choir continues its own meter and tempo. Both the flute and celesta parts exemplify the interweaving of pentatonic melodies described in the program note, capitalizing on resemblances in pitch contour and rhythm. All these added layers foreshadow the Finale, where *Bethany* becomes the theme of a cumulative form over a percussion ensemble suggesting a march with *Street Beat* and complementary patterns, and where *Proprior Deo*, *Something for Thee*, and *Westminster Chimes* again drift in, linked to *Bethany* by association and by motivic similarities. As the closing lines of Ives's text repeat in the chorus, which expands from unison to five parts, the opening phrase of *Bethany* sounds for the first time in the main orchestra (mm. 38–39 in violin 1, paralleled in the piano a fifth above). The conjunction of text and music suggests that *Bethany* and its opening words, "Nearer, my God, to Thee," are the "beauteous ray" the traveler sees and that nearness to God is the goal of the journey. The absence of *Bethany* in the next two movements marks those as false paths, and its return, development, and culminating statement in the Finale represent the promise fulfilled.

The first movement feels open-ended at its close because of the question and call that end Ives's text and because the melody and harmony do not come to rest on the tonic. The key is unclear at the outset; there are hints of D minor or major in the main orchestra clouded by fragments of *Bethany* in the Distant Choir in A, F, and E major. The second section begins with the solo cello in A major over a D pedal, and then moves toward D major. The third section has a key signature of D major, and the chorus sings in that key, but the accompanying parts suggest B minor, and the movement closes on a G major triad clouded with added tones. Together with *Bethany*, the key of D major will turn out to be the goal of the entire symphony, hinted at in the opening movement but withheld until the culmination in the Finale.

The second movement is the most famous, winning a reputation as the most complex orchestral work yet composed because of its many passages with two or more streams of music in contrasting rhythms and conflicting meters, often with nonsynchronous bar lines. Although the 1927 program note describes Hawthorne's "The Celestial Rail-Road" (1843), from *Mosses from an Old Manse*, as "a sort of incidental program" for the movement, the close relationship between short story and music was not fully understood until a 1994 article by Thomas M. Brodhead demonstrated that the movement closely follows the events in the story.[84] Hawthorne's allegorical tale is a satire, using the new technology of his era, the railroad, as a metaphor for nineteenth-century religious movements that promised an easy path to salvation, in contrast to the old-fashioned pilgrimage on foot (real or metaphorical) taken by earlier generations of faithful Christians. As Brodhead explains,

> The Hawthorne story is itself a comic trope on John Bunyan's *The Pilgrim's Progress*, in which a group of train passengers follow the route of Bunyan's Christian [the protagonist of Bunyan's allegorical book]. Like Bunyan's book, Hawthorne's tale begins with a nameless narrator who falls asleep and starts to dream. The narrator finds himself at a [railroad] depot in the City of Destruction, where he is befriended by a Mr. Smooth-it-away who escorts him aboard a waiting train. Once inside, the narrator learns that the locomotive speeds its passenger to the Celestial City in nineteenth-century comfort. The train then departs with its whistle blowing, passes through scenery known to readers of *The Pilgrim's Progress* (even stopping at the town of Vanity Fair [where wares suited to worldly tastes and delights are sold]), and finally comes to rest in Beulah Land [from which in Bunyan's book Heaven can be seen]. All the passengers leave the train and board a ferry that they are told will carry them across the River Jordan to the Celestial City. Once in the water, the narrator sees Mr. Smooth-it-away back on shore reverting to his true demonic form. The narrator realizes that all has been a hoax and leaps into the river to escape. The impact wakes the narrator and brings the story to a close.[85]

All these events have parallels in the music. Table 4.6 summarizes the musical characteristics and borrowed tunes Ives uses to represent each episode, including where and in what instruments each borrowing appears.[86]

As in the first movement, his use throughout of several simultaneous streams of music creates a multidimensional space that represents our experience of reality. Often the texture is a vast expansion of melody and accompaniment, with one or more prominent melodies over ostinatos (some remaining at pitch, others transposed at each reiteration) or figuration that repeats with variation. Such textures are intrinsically hierarchical, and Ives uses them to suggest how we perceive events around us. In life, some things are closer to us, others farther away. Ives manifests this both sonically through relative dynamic level and literally through prominence indicators, letters from A to G that mark the nearness or distance from the audience of each group of players.[87] Arranging the orchestra to realize Ives's intentions, however, requires such a large stage and number of players that few performances have attempted it. Among all these streams of music, some command our attention, while others are background, peripheral, or scarcely noticed. In other works, Ives uses this effect to suggest a real event or a memory, but here it conveys the seeming reality of the dream in Hawthorne's story. The multiple layers and meters on the first page inaugurate the dream, and in later sections the level of confusion and complexity shifts between relatively simple textures (such as m. 7), polyrhythmic passages with congruent bar lines but several different subdivisions of the measure and syncopated rhythmic groupings that cross beats and bar lines (as in mm. 62–74), fully polymetric passages with two or more conflicting meters (as in mm. 1–5 and 75–95), and passages in which distinct streams of music are actually in different tempos (as at mm. 43 and 122). In some performances, including the 1965 premiere of the complete symphony, the passages in conflicting meters and tempos have been led by two or more conductors, each charged with keeping together the players for an assigned stream.[88]

Specific elements of the program receive appropriate musical images. The "City of Destruction" (m. 7) is portrayed with soft quarter-tone harmonies in the strings, evoking a queasy not-quite-rightness.[89] The steam train is imitated literally, from the sounds of starting up and gradually increasing speed (mm. 19–37) to the whistle (high winds, mm. 34–35) and chugging steam (mm. 43–50). Ives emphasizes in his program note the contrast between the "exciting, easy, and worldly progress through life" and "the trials of the Pilgrims in their journey," and he makes this contrast vivid by juxtaposing the sounds of the train with the quiet trek of the pilgrims. We experience this both from the perspective of the pilgrims, as their soft hymns in the strings (m. 38) are suddenly overwhelmed by the noisy train as it passes and quickly recedes (mm. 43–51), and from the perspective of the passengers, who see the pilgrims out the window and then leave them behind (mm. 55–61). Mr. Smooth-it-away's mix of charm and deceptiveness is aptly captured by a diatonic melody that oozes into slippery repeating chromatic figures (mm. 119–21). The ease, comfort, and worldliness of Vanity Fair are evoked by a rhapsodic piano (from m. 122) that moves into ragtime (at m. 134), like a pianist in a tavern. Beulah Land and the Celestial City (mm. 181–83 and 190–97) are calm, in stark contrast to the fast and loud train. Both times, the train noises are cut off to reveal the quiet hymns of the pilgrims through sonic exuviation, which, as usual, creates the impression that the quieter layer had been sounding all along, unheard amid the ruckus. In the second of these soft passages, Ives adds a piano with undulating quarter-tone scales in the bass and a rippling chromatic ostinato in the treble with most notes a quarter-tone sharp relative to the rest of the orchestra. The wavelike motion suggests the river that separates the passengers from the Celestial City, while

Table 4.6 Ives's Symphony No. 4, Second Movement: Programmatic Structure

Reh.	Meas.	Episode	Music	Borrowings/reworkings (most prominent in boldface)
1	1	Opening, evocation of the dream	Multilayered, polymetric (5/8 vs. 6/8 [2/4] vs. 7/4 vs. unmetered), diverse figuration and dynamic levels	**Beulah Land** (Cb.), *God Be with You* (Bssn.)
1	6	Contemplation of the City of Destruction	Loud chords, tremolo strings	*Martyn* (Solo Pno.)
2	7	Contemplation of the City of Destruction	Soft quarter-tone harmonies in upper strings, thinly scored	*Martyn* (Vln. 1; Solo Pno. m. 13), **God Be with You** (Flt. m. 9), **Home! Sweet Home!** (Vln. 1 mm. 11–12), *Nettleton* (Solo Pno. and solo Vln. 1 m. 13)
3+2[a]	16	Send-off at the depot	Quarter-tone harmonies, parallel dissonant chords under melody	**God Be with You** (Flt. and Vln. 1)
4	19	The train ride begins	Imitation of steam train starting up, with low dissonant chords in parallel minor sevenths, percussion, gradual accelerando, increase in rhythmic density and dynamics, adding layers and instruments	*God Be with You* (Vln. 1 mm. 19–30)
6+2	34	The train's whistle	Imitation of whistle high Picc./Flt./Clar. as accelerando continues	
6+3	35	Full speed	Boisterous multilayered counterpoint, reaching a climax of density, dynamics, and tempo	**Tramp, Tramp, Tramp** (Trom.), *Throw Out the Life-Line* (low Strgs., Bssn. 1 and 2, and High Bells), **Marching Through Georgia** (Trom. m. 37)
7	38	The pilgrims make their way on foot	Suddenly soft (sonic exuviation) and Adagio, tunes in Strgs. with background filigree ostinatos, some quarter-tone harmonies	**In the Sweet By-and-By** (Vln. 1), *Nettleton* (solo Vln.)
8	43	The train roars by as the pilgrims continue	Divides into Upper Orchestra (Ww., Solo Pno., Timp.), Allegro and accelerando with loud ostinatos representing the train, vs. Lower Orchestra (Strgs., Perc.), continuing in Adagio with soft tunes and ostinatos representing the pilgrims	**In the Sweet By-and-By** (Vln. 1) and *Nettleton* (solo Vln.) continue; *Throw Out the Life-Line* (High Bells), *Beulah Land* (Flt.; Bssn. and Trom. mm. 47–50), *The Beautiful River* (Solo Pno. mm. 48–50)

9	52	The pilgrims trudge on	Pilgrims material continues; train figures gradually resume in low Strgs. at m. 53	*In the Sweet By-and-By* (Vln. 1), *Nettleton* (solo Vln.), and *Throw Out the Life-Line* (High Bells) continue
10	55	The train approaches again and leaves the pilgrims behind	Imitation of train through many overlapping dissonant ostinatos, accelerando	*In the Sweet By-and-By* (Vln. 1) continues; *Nettleton* (solo Vln. mm. 55–58; Low Bells mm. 57–63; Tpt. mm. 60–61; *Washington Post March* (Tuba mm. 56–59)
11+3	62	The train ride continues	Multiple layers of dissonant ostinatos, polyrhythmic, gradual accelerando, increase in rhythmic density and dynamics, adding layers and instruments	***Tramp, Tramp, Tramp*** (Trom. mm. 65–66), ***Marching Through Georgia*** (Trom. mm. 66–69), ***In the Sweet By-and-By*** (Trom. mm. 69–74), *Turkey in the Straw* (Vln. 1 mm. 72–74)
14	75		Multilayered, polymetric (3/16 vs. 6/8 [3/4] vs. 4/4), loud overlapping ostinatos	***Camptown Races*** (Solo Pno., Clar.), *Massa's in de Cold Ground* (Flt. begins m. 79)
15	81		Multilayered, polymetric (3/16 vs. 4/4), chromatic scales, syncopated chords, ostinatos, some quarter-tones	*Massa's in de Cold Ground* continues (Flt.); ***Hail! Columbia*** (Bssn. 1, Tpt. 1), *Beulah Land* (Cb. 1), *Throw Out the Life-Line* (High Bells mm. 84–85), *Old Black Joe* (Solo Pno. begins m. 84)
16	86		Multilayered, polymetric with changing meters in each layer, dissonant repeating figures and sequences, descending chromatic scale in bass	*Old Black Joe* continues (Solo Pno.), *Throw Out the Life-Line* (High Bells), *Nettleton* (Vln. 1)
17	89		Multilayered, polymetric (5/16 [2/4, 3/8] vs. 3/4), mostly tunes over percussion and reiterated F pedal	***In the Sweet By-and-By*** (Vln. 2, Clar., Tpt., Trom.), *Nettleton* (Vla., Vlc., Bssn.; High Bells mm. 93–95), *There Is a Happy Land* (Flt. mm. 89–93), *Westminster Chimes* (Cel. mm. 90–93)
18	96		Multilayered, polyrhythmic (4/4 with 3/8 groupings vs. three levels of triplets with eighth-note triplets in 7/8 groupings), tunes and ostinatos over alternating G# and G in bass	***Columbia, the Gem of the Ocean***, distorted (Tpt. 1, 2, and 3 with Clar. 1 and 2 in inversion), *Yankee Doodle* (Picc.), *Massa's in de Cold Ground* in canon at tritone (Bssn. 1 and 2 to m. 103 then unison mm. 104–5), *Beulah Land* (High Bells), *Street Beat* (Orch. Pno. 1, SD), *Throw Out the Life-Line* (Solo Pno. mm. 104–8), *Reveille* (Tpt. 3 mm. 105–6)

Table 4.6 continued

Reh.	Meas.	Episode	Music	Borrowings/reworkings (most prominent in boldface)
20	109		Multilayered, polyrhythmic (4/4; 4/4 with 5/16 groupings; 4/4 displaced by sixteenth and by eighth; eighth-note triplets, quintuplets, and septuplets; quarter-note sextuplets, some displaced by a quarter note; and quarter-note nonuplets at m. 111), tunes and ostinatos	**Columbia, the Gem of the Ocean**, distorted (Tpt. 1, 2, and 3 and Clar. 1 and 2; Picc. and Flt. mm. 112–13), *Beulah Land* (Solo Pno. and High Bells, blended with *The Beautiful River* at mm. 112–13), *Nettleton* (intervallic contour reflected in transpositions of ostinatos in Vln. 1 and 2)
21	114		Multilayered, polymetric (displaced 4/4 with 5/16 groupings and triplets in 5/4 groupings), thinner texture, tunes and ostinatos, ritardando and decrescendo	*The Beautiful River* continues (Solo Pno. and Orch. Pno. 1 mm. 114–15), **Columbia, the Gem of the Ocean** (Vlc. and Trom. mm. 115–16), *Throw Out the Life-Line* (Clar. mm. 116–18), *Throw Out the Life-Line* new variant (Bssn. 1 and 2)
22	119	Mr. Smooth-it-away	Softer, thinner, slower, chromatic repeating figures	none
23	122	A rest stop at Vanity Fair	Solo Pno., free fantasy, soft and Andante, with occasional percussion, over soft repeating figures in solo Vln. 2 (plus Bells) and solo Vla., each in its own tempo, meter, and rhythmic grouping	*In the Sweet By-and-By* (solo Vla.)
25+1	134		Quasi-ragtime Solo Pno. reinforced softly by Tpt., Strgs., and Perc., with Flt. 1 and 2 floating above	*In the Sweet By-and-By* (Flt. 1 and 2)
26	141	The train ride resumes	Multilayered, polyrhythmic, thicker texture, louder, Allegro, tunes and ostinatos	*In the Sweet By-and-By* (brass), **Theme from "The Alcotts"** (Solo Pno., Orch. Pno. 2, Vla., and Vlc. mm. 143–46)
27	146		Multilayered, polymetric, less dense, less loud, less fast, quasi-ragtime Solo Pno., varying figuration	*Pig Town Fling* (Bssn.), *Westminster Chimes* (High Bells mm. 149–51), *Long, Long Ago* (Cor. mm. 151–53, also Orch. Pno. 2)
28	154		Multilayered, polyrhythmic, thick, loud, a little faster, tunes and ostinatos	***Throw Out the Life-Line*** (Vln. 1 and 2 and High Bells, mm. 154–60; Tpt. 1, 2, and 3 mm. 161–64), *Nettleton* (Low Bells, plus High Bells 164–67), *Camptown Races* (Sax and Bssn. mm. 154–59) overlapping *Pig Town Fling* (Sax and Bssn. mm. 159–64), **Theme from "The Alcotts"** (Solo Pno. and Tpt. 3 mm. 164–67), *Massa's in de Cold Ground* (Flt. mm. 164–67)

30	167	Multilayered, syncopated, softer, less dense, slower, tune and ostinatos	***Throw Out the Life-Line*** (Vln. 1 and 2, Orch. Pno. 2, Flt.)
31	171	Multilayered, polyrhythmic (polymetric in Timp.), louder, faster, increasingly dense	Theme from "The Alcotts" (Tpt. 1, 2, and 3 mm. 173–78), *Beulah Land* (Trom. mm. 173–80), *Nettleton* (Bssn. 1 and Low Bells mm. 173–77, Vln. 1 and Orch. Pno. 1 mm. 173–80, intervallic contour reflected in transpositions of Clar. 1 ostinato mm. 173–80), *In the Sweet By-and-By* (Picc. and Flt. mm. 173–80, Solo Pno. mm. 174–80), *Massa's in de Cold Ground* (Cor. mm. 173–80), *Throw Out the Life-Life* (Tpt. 1, 2, and 3 mm. 178–80)
33	181	A glimpse out the window of the Celestial City and the pilgrims	Suddenly soft (sonic exuviation) and Adagio, thin texture, quiet hymn over soft ostinatos including Cel.	***Martyn*** (Solo Pno. and solo Vla. 1 and 2)
34	184	The final leg of the train ride and arrival	Peak of complexity and sound, multilayered, polyrhythmic (4/4 [3/2] with quintuplets, sextuplets, and septuplets against 3/8 groupings), tunes and ostinatos	***Beulah Land*** (Tpt. 3 and Trom.; also outlined by accented high notes in Vlc.), *In the Sweet By-and-By* (Picc., Flt., Clar., Orch. Pno. 1, and High Bells), *Massa's in de Cold Ground* (Cor. mm. 186–89), *Pig Town Fling* (Sax, mm. 186–88)
36	190	Arrival at Beulah Land and vision of the Celestial City across the water as the pilgrims enter it	Suddenly soft (sonic exuviation) and Largo, multilayered and polymetric, thin texture, two quiet hymns over soft ostinatos including quarter-tone Pno. and Cel.	***Beulah Land*** virtually complete and slightly varied (solo Vln. 1), ***Martyn*** (Solo Pno. and 2 solo Vla.)
38	198	The ferry bound for Hell/waking from the dream	Suddenly loud, fast, massive polymetric (2/4 vs. 7/4) and polyrhythmic dense texture, ostinatos, repeating figures, chromatic figuration, clusters in string glissandos	none

Table 4.6 continued

Reh.	Meas.	Episode	Music	Borrowings/reworkings (most prominent in boldface)
39	205	Back to reality: the Fourth of July in Concord	Multilayered, polymetric (4/4 [6/4 and 9/8] with several different groupings vs. 5/8), very loud, thick texture, march figures, tunes and ostinatos	*Throw Out the Life-Line* (Flt., Clar., and Vln. 2a), *Yankee Doodle* (Picc. and optional Xylo.), **Introduction from Country Band March** (Brass and Vln. 2b mm. 208–9)
40	210	Fourth of July Parade	As above with march tune prominent and other tunes overlaid	**Theme from Country Band March** (Brass), *Marching Through Georgia* (Picc., Flt., and Clar.), *Throw Out the Life-Line* (High Bells and Low Bells), *Turkey in the Straw* (Vla. and Bssn. followed in canon by Vln. and optional Xylo.), *Long, Long Ago* (Cor. mm. 211–25)
41	216		Stylized ragtime figuration, fewer layers with less rhythmic contrast between parts	none
42	219		Return to multilayered march, polyrhythmic gradually becoming polymetric, very loud, thick texture, march figures, ostinatos	*Marching Through Georgia* (Cor. and Tpt. 1), *Throw Out the Life-Line* (Picc., Flt., and Clar. 219–20), *Long, Long Ago* (Vlc. and Bssn. mm. 219–20), *St. Patrick's Day* (Vlc. and Bssn. mm. 221–24)
44	225		Faster, continuing multilayered polymetric march, imitating drum corps underneath tunes and ostinatos	**Street Beat** (Perc., solo Pno., and Vlc.), *Reveille* (Picc. and Flt.), *Long, Long Ago* (Cor. and optional Xylo.), *Camptown Races* (Bssn.), *Throw Out the Life-Line* (High Bells), *Nettleton* (Low Bells), *Garryown* (Vln. 1 and 2a and Vla. mm. 225–28), *St. Patrick's Day* (Vln. 1 and 2a and Vla. mm. 229–30), *Irish Washerwoman* (Vln. 1 and 2a and Vla. mm. 230–32)
46+2[a]	233		Almost homorhythmic	*Yankee Doodle* (tutti), *Nettleton* continues (Low Bells)
47	235		Return to multilayered, polymetric march figures, ostinatos, and tunes, ended by quick fade	*Marching Through Georgia* (Trom.), *Long, Long Ago* (Cor.), *Irish Washerwoman* (Vln. 1 and 2a and optional Xylo., *Nettleton* continues (Low Bells)

a. 3+2 means two measures after Rehearsal no. 3.

the quarter-tones again evoke a queasy sense that something is wrong. Then, in the opposite of sonic exuviation, suddenly loud ostinatos and string glissandos in clusters represent the narrator's shocking realization that he is on a ferry bound for hell (mm. 198–204). Rapid waves of motion suggest his efforts to escape and his plunge into the water. When he wakes to reality, Ives evokes "the Fourth of July in Concord—brass bands, drums corps, etc."—Ives's addition to Hawthorne's story—with march rhythms, drums, and the multilayered sounds of a crowd at a parade (m. 205).

The borrowed tunes enhance the program in various ways. Some, shown in bold in table 4.6, are the most prominent element in the texture, but others are woven into the background. Most appear only in fragments, and all are reworked, so that even a listener who knows them is likely to hear many only as wisps of familiar melody.

Most of the hymns are here because of their texts and associations. At the arrival in Beulah Land (m. 190) we hear almost the entire hymn *Beulah Land* in a solo violin, representing through its text and name both the goal of the train's journey and the vision of the Celestial City across the water. The tune is by John R. Sweney, and the words by Edgar P. Stites:

> I've reached the land of corn and wine,
> And all its riches freely mine
> Here shines undimmed one blissful day,
> For all my night has passed away.
>
> *Refrain:*
> O Beulah Land, sweet Beulah Land,
> As on thy highest mount I stand
> I look away across the sea,
> Where mansions are prepared for me,
> And view the shining glory-shore,
> My Heav'n, my home forevermore!

The first two phrases of the refrain are missing in Ives's rendition, and so are the last three notes, squelched by the eruption that represents the ferry to hell, truncating the final word and thus breaking the promise of an eternal home in heaven. Simultaneous with *Beulah Land*, we hear in the solo piano a variant of *Martyn*, a setting by Simeon B. Marsh (1798–1875) of a Charles Wesley text, which represents the pilgrims entering the Celestial City:

> Jesus, lover of my soul,
> Let me to Thy bosom fly,
> While the nearer waters roll,
> While the tempest still is high:
> Hide me, O my Savior, hide,
> Till the storm of life is past;
> Safe into the haven guide;
> O receive my soul at last.

Fragments of both *Beulah Land* and *Martyn* appear near the beginning, anticipating the goal of the journey, and recur occasionally throughout. Also identified with the pilgrims and their heavenly goal are *In the Sweet By-and-By* ("There's a land that is fairer than day, / . . . In the sweet by-and-by / We shall meet on that beautiful shore") and *Nettleton* ("Come, Thou Fount of ev'ry blessing"), heard together when we first encounter the pilgrims making their way on foot (m. 38) and interleaved periodically until we reach Beulah Land. During the stop at

Vanity Fair, *In the Sweet By-and-By* hovers in the background, perhaps as a reminder of the pilgrims and their goal the Celestial City, a place decidedly different from the fair of earthly delights. *The Beautiful River* ("Shall we gather at the river," mm. 48–50 and 112–13) by Robert Lowry (1826–99) and Mason's *There Is a Happy Land* (mm. 89–93) also offer visions of heaven. The send-off at the train depot (m. 16) is evoked by *God Be with You* ("God be with you till we meet again") by William G. Tomer (1833–96). The refrain of *Throw Out the Life-Line* ("Throw out the Life-Line! Someone is drifting away") by Edward S. Ufford (1851–1929) appears in varied chromatic form frequently during the train ride, perhaps as an ironic warning, and again when the narrator awakes from his dream (m. 205).

Snippets from secular tunes are interwoven as well. The Fourth of July parade (m. 205 to the end) is embodied by Ives's own *Country Band March* (discussed below with *Putnam's Camp*), the drummers' *Street Beat*, patriotic tunes *Yankee Doodle* and *Marching Through Georgia* (a Civil War song by Henry Clay Work), and the bugle call *Reveille*. Several fiddle tunes (*Turkey in the Straw*, *St. Patrick's Day*, *Garryowen*, and *Irish Washerwoman*) and popular songs (*Camptown Races* and *Long, Long Ago*) suggest further festivities of the day. Some of these also appear earlier during the train ride alongside other secular tunes (such as *Columbia, the Gem of the Ocean*, Stephen Foster's *Old Black Joe*, and the fiddle tune *Pig Town Fling*), perhaps suggesting the festive and not entirely religious mood of the passengers on the train. The encounter with the pilgrims is framed by loud trombone statements of phrases from the Civil War songs *Tramp, Tramp, Tramp* (George F. Root) and *Marching Through Georgia* (mm. 35–37 and 65–69) in parallel fifths and octaves, which may represent the train's passengers mocking the pilgrims' slow trudging on foot. (Ives was clearly unconcerned that when Hawthorne wrote his tale in 1843, the Civil War and these songs still lay in the future, as did most of the gospel songs he quotes elsewhere.) The chorus of *Massa's in de Cold Ground* may be a reminder of death.

Some fragments appear in part because their melodic contour resembles that of a tune already in the mix, as in the free association that is typical of dreams.[90] Just before the send-off (mm. 11–12), *Martyn* briefly morphs into a phrase from *Home! Sweet Home!* by Henry R. Bishop (1786–1855), and later *Beulah Land* blends with *The Beautiful River* (mm. 109–13). Both added tunes are appropriate to their programmatic contexts. *In the Sweet By-and-By* and *Nettleton* may have prompted Ives to include other pentatonic tunes with heavenly associations such as *There Is a Happy Land* and *Westminster Chimes* (mm. 90–93 and 149–51). The latter is also present in the symphony's first and last movements and so creates a subtle cyclic link, as does the sharing of *In the Sweet By-and-By* with the first movement and of *Martyn* with the Finale. Other melodic puns range farther afield and with less extramusical import, like the segments from the *Washington Post March* by John Philip Sousa (1854–1932) and from *Hail! Columbia* by Philip Phile (1734–93) that seem to develop from the chromatic neighbor-note motion in the variant of *Throw Out the Life-Line* (at mm. 56–59 and 81–86, respectively). Finally, some borrowed passages are parts of *The Celestial Railroad* that were taken directly from the "Hawthorne" movement of the *Concord Sonata* and thus contain its thematic elements and melodic borrowings, including the theme from the sonata's third movement, "The Alcotts" (mm. 165 and 173).

Capitalizing on melodic similarities to modulate from one borrowing to another is something we have seen before, as in the transformation in Ives's Second Symphony of *Pig Town Fling* into a passage from Brahms's First Symphony. But the use in this movement of borrowed materials in a symbolic and even allegorical manner based on their texts and associations is quite different from that in any of the earlier symphonies, where borrowed and paraphrased tunes were used primarily as themes or countermelodies. Yet the tunes that return often in various reworkings do give the movement thematic continuity, justifying the comment Ives and Bellamann make in their program note that "The texture of this symphony is threaded through with strands based on old hymns—not quotations from them, but thematic material derived from them."

The varying levels of prominence and recognizability of these tunes create a sense of dreamlike fluidity, coming in and out of focus. So do the subtle ways one tune connects to another melodically or seems to inspire another tune of the same type, whether hymn, fiddle tune, or secular song. As Ives composed, he added more borrowings, augmenting the piano fantasy *The Celestial Railroad* by interpolating episodes and including more layers and tunes at each stage from draft to short score to full score and later revisions. Both the compositional process and the final result illustrate Ives's technique of *collage*, in which fragments of borrowed melody are overlaid on a musical structure that is already coherent without them.[91] Here the central narrative thread is based in part on borrowed tunes that articulate important moments in the program, and further borrowings suggested by shared associations, similar genre, or melodic resemblance add to the dreamlike quality: a vast stream of consciousness in which images fly by, too fast to recognize all of them consciously, but all contributing to the overwhelming effect of the movement. Since recognizing everything is not the point—we cannot remember our dreams fully but know we have dreamed—much of the rhetorical effect of this movement still works for those who know few or none of the tunes, as many listeners can attest who learned these old hymns and songs only from studying Ives's use of them. Yet knowing the movement's roots in Hawthorne's tale "The Celestial Rail-Road" helps us understand how this dream about the danger of spiritual laziness fits into the programmatic arc of the symphony.

Ives knew that creating program music typically requires breaking the rules or confounding expectations, so that listeners have to interpret the unusual sounds they are hearing in terms of an extramusical program.[92] Discussing his *Yale-Princeton Football Game* (ca. 1899, revised ca. 1910–11), he wrote in *Memos* that when "one [is] using 'tones' to take off or picture a football game for instance, [how] natural it is to use sound and rhythm combinations that are quite apart from those that would be a 'regular music.' For instance, in picturing the excitement, sounds and songs across the field and grandstand, you could not do it with a nice fugue in C."[93] The extraordinarily unusual sounds, layerings, and juxtapositions in the first two movements of the Fourth Symphony exemplify this departure from "regular music" to embody a program and convey an experience.

But then Ives thwarts our expectations that he will continue in the same idiom, by presenting as his third movement "a nice fugue in C" on Lowell Mason's *Missionary Hymn* ("From Greenland's icy mountains"). What would have seemed "regular music" at the beginning of the symphony here sounds like a completely different world from what we have just been hearing. In context, it is a perfect "expression of the reaction of life into formalism and ritualism," combining the fugue as traditional form and compositional rite with the hymn as representation of collective church ritual rather than of the pilgrims' personal devotion. Even the notation suggests formalism and the ritual of academic exercises by using 4/2 meter, the theme marching *alla breve* in half notes, as in the learned *stile antico* and the classroom fugues of Ives's college days. The predominant texture of strings with only two solo winds, horn, and trombone (later joined by organ and a touch of timpani) also evokes an older style, like that of a Bach cantata.

There is a stark contrast between the inward-focused sentiment of hymns heard earlier in the symphony—the personal search for enlightenment in *Watchman* and the yearning for salvation in *Beulah Land* and *Martyn*—and the outward focus in *Missionary Hymn* on the corporate missionary work of the church. There is also a strong contrast in the mode of presentation. The first two movements feature mostly fragments of hymns, at various levels of recognizability, with a more complete statement of one hymn near the end. Here *Missionary Hymn* is presented phrase by phrase over the whole movement, paraphrased and treated in fugal counterpoint, as Bach treats chorales in some of his chorale cantatas, preludes, and fantasies.[94]

The hymn tune is in four phrases in the form AA'BA'': the first, second, and fourth phrases begin alike but have different endings, while the third phrase provides contrast and includes the melodic climax. Ives's fugal paraphrase expands on this form. The fugue subject, treated in the opening four-voice exposition (mm. 1–15), is the first phrase of the hymn, its final notes altered to allow fugal imitation and avoid closing on a cadence. The second phrase of the hymn is represented by later statements of the subject and by an imitative episode on a motive derived from the phrase's second half (mm. 22–26 and 51–54). After an extended modulatory episode, the hymn's contrasting third phrase marks the climactic return to the tonic (m. 83), briefly treated in imitation and emphasized by a long pedal point on C. The hymn's final phrase then appears near the end in augmentation, harmonized like a four-voice chorale (mm. 108–15).

Other borrowings enrich the allusions to fugues and hymnody. The episodes on the second half of the hymn's second phrase (mm. 22–26 and 51–54) are also direct echoes of an episode in Bach's "Dorian" Toccata and Fugue in D Minor BWV 538 (mm. 67–71).[95] At its second exposition (mm. 26–32), the fugue subject is joined by a countersubject, a phrase drawn from the late-eighteenth-century hymn *Coronation* ("All hail the power of Jesus' name") by Oliver Holden (1765–1844), which includes a turning motive featured in several episodes both as part of the countersubject (mm. 33–45) and independent of it (mm. 18–21, 50, and 69–76).

These borrowings from Bach and Holden were already in the fugue in its earlier form as the first movement of String Quartet No. 1. For the symphony movement, Ives added two hymns in the coda, the chorus of *Welcome Voice* by Lewis Hartsough (1828–1919) in the clarinet (mm. 110–16), followed by part of Mason's *Antioch* ("Joy to the world") in the trombone (mm. 115–19), and possibly others elsewhere (Handel's *Christmas* in the trombone at mm. 64–66 and a combination at mm. 88–91 of *Church Triumphant* by J. W. Elliott [1833–1915] in the clarinet with William Bradbury's *Brown* or Mason's *Lischer* in the flute). All these allusions fit the counterpoint smoothly, making them more like the borrowed countermelodies in the Second Symphony than like the added tunes in the collage in the previous movement. Ives also heightens the connection of this fugue to church services by introducing the organ, first at m. 45 as a brief echo of the previous measure and then from the climax in m. 83 through the end, and by altering the end of the movement so that it closes with a soft plagal cadence, like an "amen."

Another addition is less congruent with the original fugue: a 10-measure insertion (mm. 94–103) that reaches a height of nonfunctional dissonance and briefly stops harmonic motion in its tracks. This distorts the fugue, rather than enriching it; it wakes us up from our complacent listening to "regular music," reminds us of how different this movement is from its surroundings, and keeps the fugue in C major, however comfortable it may have been, from offering a satisfactory answer to the question posed in the symphony's first movement.

After the middle two movements offer false paths, the Finale, outlined in table 4.7, offers a truer one. The program note calls the movement "an apotheosis of the preceding content, in terms that have something to do with the reality of existence and its religious experience." In many ways it refers back to what has gone before, but it moves to a new conclusion. It invokes the first movement explicitly, citing and developing the opening of that movement in mm. 5–10, bringing back its Distant Choir, and meandering through several tonal centers to close in a serene D major, the key hinted at but not fully achieved in the first movement. This final movement is stylistically similar to the first two, yet its multilayered texture is integrated into a single unfolding process, gradually increasing in density and complexity, reaching a peak, and then fading away, without the startling juxtapositions of the second movement or the contrasting sections of the first. The sense of continuity is reinforced by the percussion battery—featuring drums, cymbals, and gongs, each playing a different figure that repeats in cycles of various lengths and may change after several cycles—that quietly begins the movement, undergirds it throughout, and is the last element to fade away. Thematically, the Finale draws on hymn tunes, as do all three preceding movements, and shares many of the same sources, including *Bethany*, *Proprior Deo*, and *Something for Thee* with the first movement; *Martyn*, *Nettleton*, and *There Is a Happy Land* with the second; and *Westminster Chimes* and *Street Beat* with both. In all these ways the Finale is a culmination, "an apotheosis of the preceding content."

But the fourth movement also offers the only satisfactory response to the questions raised in the first. It is a cumulative setting of *Bethany*, the hymn that was invoked in the first movement by the Distant Choir, focusing on its second half (mm. 9–16), shown in example 4.12. Since *Bethany* is in AA'BA' form, the second half includes the opening motivic material (mm. 13–16 parallel mm. 1–4 and 5–8), as well as the contrasting B phrase (mm. 9–12), while its text reiterates the poem's opening lines:

Nearer, my God, to Thee,	A (mm. 1–4)
Nearer to Thee!	
E'en tho' it be a cross	A' (mm. 5–8)
That raiseth me.	
Still all my song shall be,	B (mm. 9–12)
Nearer, my God, to Thee,	
Nearer, my God, to Thee,	A' (mm. 13–16)
Nearer to Thee!	

In programmatic terms, the gradual emergence of this hymn reveals that the goal of the yearning for joy and hope in the first movement is nearness to the divine, and the absence of this hymn in the two middle movements makes clear that the spiritual laziness and the faith in outward ritual that they embodied were not only unfulfilling but directed at the wrong goals.

As seen in table 4.7, the culminating statement of the complete second half of *Bethany* arrives at m. 72 with the return of the voices in the chorus, not heard since the first movement, coinciding with a V-I cadence in D major, the only such cadence in the Finale.[96] At the outset of the movement, the hymn is only in the extremes of the orchestra: low in the contrabasses in mm. 1–4 and high in the Distant Choir in mm. 6–7. It gradually comes into focus, moving from the extremes into the central register by m. 20 and from fragments and variants to more complete statements. The first half of the movement uses only the B phrase, until violin 2 introduces the motive that begins the other phrases at m. 47, and thereafter both are combined with each other and with other hymns. At m. 65, marked by the arrival on D major over descending whole-tone scales, is the contrapuntal climax of the movement, an almost

Example 4.12 Ives. Symphony No. 4/4, Theme A (mm. 50–58) and its sources.

full statement of the second half of *Bethany* accompanied by three principal countermelodies: the latter part of *Martyn* (mm. 11–20); the first phrase of *Bethany* elided with the second half of *Missionary Chant*; and a melody, called Theme A in the table and shown in example 4.12, that blends the B phrase from *Bethany* (mm. 9–12) with segments of *Westminster Chimes* and *Missionary Chant* by punning on their melodic similarities with *Bethany*. Like those in the cumulative-form movements of the Third Symphony, all three countermelodies are developed from fragments over the course of the movement, and *Missionary Chant* and Theme A appear complete in contrasting keys before their climactic appearance with the main theme in the tonic near the end: *Missionary Chant* at m. 40 in C major, and Theme A at m. 50 in A major.

Around this central thematic process Ives adds other hymns, suggested by melodic resemblance (including *Dorrnance* by Isaac Woodbury [1819–58], whose opening motive resembles that of *Missionary Chant*, and *Nettleton*, whose opening gesture is like that of *Bethany*) or textual or other association (like *Proprior Deo* and *There Is a Happy Land*). The melodic and other links, together with the multiple layers, lend this movement the texture of a collage and the feel of an inner experience, like the first and second movements, but without the great and sudden contrasts of the second movement. The consistency of tone throughout gives the Finale the feeling not of a dream but of religious revelation.

Even at the partial premiere of 1927, when the first two movements were played as the first orchestral music of Ives to be heard in a public concert, the symphony won the respect and

Table 4-7 Ives's Symphony No. 4, Finale: Cumulative Form and Principal Borrowed Tunes

Main theme: *Bethany* mm. 9–16
Other themes: *Missionary Chant Martyn* mm. 11–20
Theme A (composite of *Bethany* mm. 9–12, closing motive of *Westminster Chimes*, and *Missionary Chant* mm. 5–9)

Section	Measure	Music	Main key
1	1	Percussion battery begins, continues throughout (*Street Beat* in SD)	
		Bethany (Cb.)	implies E♭
	5	First movement mm. 1–4 recapitulated and developed, transposed then at pitch (at m. 8); includes *Bethany* in Distant Choir (mm. 6–7)	
2	11	*Dorrnance* punning with *Missionary Chant* and *Bethany* (Vln. 1 and 2, Distant Choir Vln. 1 and 2, Cel., and Ob.), *Bethany* (Flt. mm. 12–14)	B major over chromatic bass, then G pedal (m. 12)
	15	*Dorrnance* (Vln. 2)	B major over G pedal
	17	*Bethany* variants (Flt. and Vln. 1 and 2)	
3	20	Theme A elements (*Bethany* varied, Vln.1 and 2, Solo Pno., Tpt.)	modulatory
	24	Theme A elements continued (*Westminster Chimes* and *Missionary Chant*, Tpt. 1), *Martyn* (Clar. 1 and 2, Solo Pno., and Vln. 2), *Bethany* (Flt. and Ob.)	
	27	Theme A elements (*Bethany* and *Westminster Chimes*, Orch. Pno., Solo Pno., Tpt. 1, and Vln. 1 and 2)	
	29	*Martyn* (Vln. 1 and 3; Tpt. 1 m. 29)	
4	32	Theme A variant (Vln. 2, Solo Pno.; joined by Flt. 1 and 2 mm. 34-39; proper ending in Tpt. 1 and 2 mm. 37–39), *Bethany* (Distant Choir, Cel.), song of the thrush (Flt. 1 and 2 and Picc. mm. 32–33)	A♭ major over descending chromatic scales to m. 35, then D♭ pedal
5	40	***Missionary Chant* complete** (Hr., Tpt., and Vla. lower line, punning on *Dorrnance* in Tpt. mm. 41–43), *Bethany* variants (Vln. 1 and 2, Ob. 2, and High Bells), *Westminster Chimes* (High Bells and Cel. mm. 45–49)	C major, descending C scales
	47	*Missionary Chant* cadence elided with first half of *Azmon* (Hr. 1, Tpt., and Clar.) elided with first half of *Azmon* (Hr. 1, Tpt., and Vla. lower line), *Bethany* and *Missionary Chant* motives elided (Vln. 2, Flt., and Clar.)	

Table 4.7 continued

6	50	**Theme A complete** (Vla. upper line and Tpt. 1 and 2), *Missionary Chant* punning with *Dormance* (Vln. 2, Flt. 2, and Clar. 1 mm. 50–53), *Martyn* (Ob. and Clar. 2), *Bethany* variants (Low Bells, Flt. 1, and Distant Choir), *Nettleton* (Cel.), *Westminster Chimes* variants (High Bells mm. 50–55 and Picc. mm. 56–58), *Antioch* variant (Bssn. 2 mm. 50–53)	A major, descending A scales
	59	Theme A first half (Solo Pno. and High Bells), *Bethany* (Distant Choir Harp), ostinato on *Bethany* (Vln. 1 and 2, Ww., and Cel.)	mixed keys, chromatic chords
	64	*Westminster Chimes* (Solo Pno. and Distant Choir Harp), *Bethany* (Low Bells), song of the thrush (Picc., Flt., and Ob.)	
7	65	*Bethany* 9–15 (Vln. 1, lower line when divisi), **Martyn 11–20 complete** (Tpt. and Vln. 3 upper line), ***Bethany* 1–5 elided with *Missionary Chant*** 4–9 (Trom. 1 and Vln. 2 and 3 lower lines), **Theme A** first half (Vln. 1, upper line when divisi), *Proprior Deo/Something for Thee* blend (Cel. mm. 65–67), *Bethany* (Cel. mm. 67–71), *Westminster Chimes* (High Bells 1), *Westminster Chimes* and *Bethany* variants (Flt. and Vln. 2), *Bethany* elided with *Westminster Chimes* (Bssn. 1 and Ether Org.), *Bethany* ostinato (Low Bells), *There Is a Happy Land* (High Bells 2, Ob., and Clar.), *St. Hilda* (Hr.), *Dormance* (Picc.)	D major, descending whole-tone scales on D, closes on V of D
8	72	***Bethany* 9–16 complete** (Voices, Tpt., and Vln. 2), *Bethany* 1–6 (Flt. 1 mm. 72–77), **Theme A** first half (Vln. 1), *Bethany* elements, variants, and derived ostinatos (Clar., Trom. 1, Orch. Pno., Org., Low Bells, Solo Pno., Vln. 3, Vla., Vlc.; Flt. 2 76–78); *Bethany*/*Westminster Chimes* elements (Cel.), *Proprior Deo/Something for Thee* blend (Ob.), song of the thrush (Flt. 2 mm. 72–73)	D major, D pedal, descending whole-tone scales on D
	79	Coda, repeating figures from preceding	D major, D pedal, scales cease

interest of reviewers. Laurence Gilman wrote in the *New York Herald Tribune*, "This music is as indubitably American in impulse and spiritual texture as the prose of [eighteenth-century preacher and theologian] Jonathan Edwards; and, like the writing of that true artist and true mystic, it has at times an irresistible veracity and strength, and uncorrupted sincerity."[97] And Olin Downes wrote in the *New York Times*,

> There is something in this music: real vitality, real naivete and a superb self respect. The lachrymose hymn, reappearing in the fast movement, is jostled out of existence for periods, only to bob up here and there, as homely and persistent as Ned McCobb's daughter. And then Mr. Ives looses his rhythms. There is no apology about this, but a "gumption," as the New Englander would say, not derived from some "Sacre du printemps," or from anything but the conviction of a composer who has not the slightest idea of self-ridicule and who dares to jump with feet and hands and a reckless somersault or two on his way to his destination.
>
> And the picture of the Concord Fourth of July is really amusing, really evocative of the spirit of that time and day. Those were not safe and sane Fourths; they were Fourths that some survived, when patriotism was more than jingoism, and a stirring thought; when the nation was in its childhood and firecrackers took off the ear or put out an eye.
>
> The scrabble of war songs and brass band tunes that all the villages knew, the noise of the circus, the blare of the band, are in this eccentric symphony, with its holier-than-thou hymn tunes, its commotion, its rowdiness, blaze and blare. There is "kick" in the piece, regardless of the composer's philosophic or moral purpose, his scheme of rhythms, and all the rest. It is genuine, if it is not a masterpiece, and that is the important thing.[98]

On the other hand, the reception was not uniformly positive. When the second movement was published in 1929, the anonymous reviewer for the *Musical Courier* commented, "The reviewer does not pretend to be able to read this score and to form any mental picture of its sound, but his memory of it from the Pro Musica performance is that it was just simply awful, from beginning to end."[99]

A SYMPHONY: NEW ENGLAND HOLIDAYS

During the years he worked on the Fourth Symphony off and on, Ives was also composing numerous orchestral tone poems. Around 1917–19, he gathered four of them, each "based on something of the memory that a man has of his boy holidays," into *A Symphony: New England Holidays*, also known as *Holidays Symphony*.[100] This is music about how we Americans celebrate our distinctive holidays, and especially about how we use music in those celebrations, focusing on New England during Ives's youth in the 1880s. The first two movements are among Ives's most programmatic works, unfolding as a series of scenes described in a detailed narrative program; the other two are cumulative-form movements, shaped more by musical logic than by a program.

The four movements represent the cycle of seasons through musical pictures of uniquely American holidays celebrated at different times of the year: *Washington's Birthday* (February 22) for winter; *Decoration Day* (May 30, now known as Memorial Day) for spring; *The Fourth of July* for summer; and *Thanksgiving and Forefathers' Day* for autumn (Thanksgiving falling in November and Forefathers' Day on December 22). They also roughly follow the pattern for a four-movement symphony: serious three-part outer movements with a slow second movement and scherzolike third movement. When performed together, they have a symphonic logic, as a sequence of contrasting movements that culminates in the longest and most expansive movement and is thus end-weighted like Ives's other symphonies. They share common features, encompassing slow and fast sections, changes of meter and character, multiple musical layers, superimposition of contrasting meters and rhythmic subdivisions, ostinatos, shadow lines, noisy climaxes, sonic exuviations, soft endings, and representations of vernacular genres from quadrille and sentimental song in the first movement to marches and patriotic songs in the second and third and hymns in the last. Yet, in many ways, the four tone poems seem like separate works: each has a distinct compositional history, from initial drafts to final copy; they are scored for different ensembles (see table 4.1); they premiered at different times and places and are still more often performed individually than together; they are published separately, by two different publishers; and in contrast to Ives's numbered symphonies, no cyclic themes bind them together. In his *Memos*, Ives authorizes both conceptions: "although they were first called together a symphony, at the same time they are separate pieces and can be thought of and played as such—and also, and as naturally, be thought of and played as a whole."[101]

Washington's Birthday

Washington's Birthday is scored for the smallest orchestra of the four: just flute (doubling piccolo), horn, bells, Jew's harp, and about two dozen strings.[102] Ives usually dated the piece between 1909 and 1913, but the extant manuscripts suggest he completed the work somewhat later, then revised it and had it professionally copied around 1923–26. In *Memos*, he recalled trial performances in New York, in the back room of Tam's Copying Bureau in 1913 or 1914, at the Globe Theater in November 1914 and spring 1915, and at his house in 1918 or 1919, but no records or parts survive for such performances. The revised version was premiered on September 3, 1931, at a New Music Society concert in San Francisco by an orchestra conducted by Nicolas Slonimsky, and it was published in *New Music* five years later.[103]

The piece focuses on memories of the holiday as it was celebrated during Ives's boyhood in the 1870s and 1880s. The composer appended to the copyist's ink score a program that included quotations both from Henry David Thoreau's *Walden* and from John Greenleaf Whittier's poem *Snow-Bound: A Winter Idyl*:

"Cold and solitude," says Thoreau, "are friends of mine. Now is the time before the wind rises to go forth and see the snow on the trees."

And there is at times a bleakness, without stir but penetrating, in a New England midwinter, which settles down grimly when the day closes over the broken hills. In such a scene it is as though nature would but could not easily trace a certain beauty in the sombre landscape!—in the quiet but restless monotony! Would nature reflect the sternness of the Puritan's fibre or the self-sacrificing part of his ideals?

The older folks sit

the clean winged hearth about,
Shut in from all the world without,
Content to let the north wind roar
In baffled rage at pane and door.
—Whittier

But to the younger generation, a winter holiday means action!—and down through "Swamp Hollow" and over the hill road they go, afoot or in sleighs, through the drifting snow, to the barn dance at the Centre. The village band of fiddles, fife and horn keeps up an unending "breakdown" medley, and the young folks "salute their partners and balance corners" till midnight. As the party breaks up, the sentimental songs of those days are sung half in fun, half seriously, and with the inevitable "adieu to the ladies" the "social" gives way to the grey bleakness of the February night.[104]

Ives notes in his *Memos* that an audience needs to know the program in order to understand what the music is about, observing that the title alone might be misleading: "So if *Washington's Birthday* were put on a program with no program-[notes], the D.A.R. [Daughters of the American Revolution] would think it pretended to have something to do with Washington, or his birthday, or 'These United States'—or some speech by Senator Blowout!"[105]

The movement is in three sections, which respectively portray the winter landscape, the barn dance, and the sleigh ride home.[106] The slow first section conveys the cold bleakness of winter through soft dissonant chords in muted strings, at first tremolo as if shivering (mm. 1–6), then pulsing as if slowly warming up by the fire (mm. 8–14). The older folks sitting at home by the hearth are suggested by fragments of two old popular songs, Henry R. Bishop's *Home! Sweet Home!* (mm. 1–4 in violin 1) and Stephen Foster's *Old Folks at Home* (mm. 5 and 7–8 in horn and m. 15 in violin 1). The music moves now more quickly, now slowly again, always dissonant and mostly soft, evoking the "quiet but restless monotony" and the "certain beauty in the sombre landscape" under the muting effect of snow described in Ives's program. The parts are often rhythmically different, overlaying contrasting subdivisions, which mutes any sustained sense of meter and adds to the sense of stillness. The bells enter at m. 32, in a rhythm and meter independent from the rest of the orchestra, playing a repeating-note triadic figure ***ppp***, barely heard, like sparkles of light reflecting off the snow. At m. 48, the music grows more active and gradually louder and faster to capture the "action!" of the younger generation. The sleigh ride through hills and snowdrifts is depicted by rising and falling parallel dissonant chords in the strings and by glissandos in the contrabasses, and as we approach the barn dance we overhear coming from inside the strains of dance tunes in the flute (*Turkey in the Straw* and *Sailor's Hornpipe* in mm. 50–52) just before the sleigh slows to a stop.

The second section portrays the barn dance through its music, played by "the village band of fiddles, fife and horn" Ives mentions in the program. Mutes are now off, and the character and dynamic level change completely. Loud chords announce the key of D major and the fast duple meter of a quadrille (m. 56), leading to Ives's apparently original theme in the style of a fiddle tune (m. 60). Gradually a collage of phrases from other dance tunes surrounds it, including a swaying waltz a tritone away (mm. 65–72), *Sailor's Hornpipe* (mm. 80–84 and 89–91), *Camptown Races* (mm. 86–93), and *For He's a Jolly Good Fellow* (mm. 99–102). The rhythms grow ever more syncopated and then grind to a halt. Next, the fiddle tune *White Cockade* in A-flat major takes center stage, played by violins accompanied by the Jew's harp (at m. 109), and is joined by fragments of still more tunes, each rhythmically offset from the others, including *Turkey in the Straw* (mm. 112–14 and 126–45), *Massa's in de Cold Ground* (mm. 116–19), *Fisher's Hornpipe* (mm. 145–52), and *Money Musk* (mm. 153–61) in flute and piccolo, as well as Scotch and Irish tunes *Irish Washerwoman* (mm. 127–31), *The Campbells Are Coming* (mm. 134–40), *Garryowen* (mm. 141–45 and 149–50), and *Saint Patrick's Day* (mm. 145–49 and 150–52) in the horn.

While the main musical thread evokes the sound of the band, the swirl of added melody suggests other fiddle tunes and songs that would be heard at the dance. Ives wrote in *Memos* that, at barn dances, "In some parts of the hall a group would be dancing a polka, while in another a waltz, with perhaps a quadrille or lancers going on in the middle."[107] But the collage he creates in *Washington's Birthday* is not a realistic sound picture of two or more bands playing at once, because the added tunes are too fragmentary. Rather, the work seeks to capture the experience of a middle-aged man in the 1910s remembering the holidays of his youth and the role that music played in them, and the collage of added tunes represents the piling up of memories, as each tune suggests another with a similar rhythm, melodic contour, style, function, or set of associations. The tunes fly by in fragments, sometimes distorted, linked together in a wonderful musical analogy to how we remember.[108]

After the dance builds to a dissonant climax over a D pedal point, a sonic exuviation reveals a soft G major triad in the strings (m. 162). The sudden change signals the beginning of the final section, as the revelers head home after the dance. To represent singing "the sentimental songs of those days," the first violins play a G-major melody in four phrases that includes the most common clichés of nineteenth-century sentimental songs, with an initial motive that sounds like *Home! Sweet Home!* followed by lilting triplets, ornamental turns, circling figures, touches of chromaticism, dramatic leaps, appoggiaturas, Scotch snaps, and a closing climactic phrase that rises to the lowered seventh, falls back, then leaps up to a peak on the natural seventh and steps back down the scale. No nineteenth-century song has so many stereotypical gestures strung together, making Ives's tune both a gentle satire of and a multivalent reference to an entire genre of popular song—"half in fun, half seriously." The violin 1 melody is harmonized by the lower strings and doubled at the unison or in thirds by violin 2, later joined a sixth below by the horn. Meanwhile, in the background, at a much softer dynamic level, a muted solo violin spins out motives from the fiddle tunes *Pig Town Fling* and *Turkey in the Straw* in distant keys, mostly A-flat and B-flat major, and then disintegrates into fragments; its low notes are doubled by another solo violin playing pizzicato, later joined by bells, creating an ethereal effect. Here, as in other Ives works, the multiple conflicting streams of music represent simultaneous events: the G-major melody depicts the songs the partygoers sing on the way home, while the solo violin weaves around it memories of the barn dance and its music. Just as the main melody is about to cadence, the flute and violin softly play *Goodnight, Ladies* by Edwin P. Christy (1815–62) in F major (m. 178)—Ives's "adieu to the ladies"—and then soft dissonant tremolo chords like those of the very opening evoke "the grey bleakness of the February night."

Despite all the dissonance, the movement is based on a simple harmonic plan that reinforces the three-part structure. The first section hints at a center of G at the outset through fragments of melody and the initial drone bass note, but then it wanders, occasionally settling on E before moving on. The second section begins in a clear D major, shifts to A-flat major, then ends over a D pedal as the density, complexity, and dynamic level reach their peak. The final section is then in G major clouded with dissonance and polytonality until the closing measures, which recall some of the sonorities of the opening section, and the last bass note is G. The overall motion from G to its dominant and back is clear, as is the process of gradual clarification from apparent atonality to tonal function.

Decoration Day

The second movement, *Decoration Day*, is scored for full orchestra with added winds, brass, and percussion. Ives dated the piece 1912 or 1913, but the extant sketches are on music paper datable no earlier than 1915, and, as usual, he seems to have worked on it for several years. After completing the pencil full score, he arranged it for violin and piano around 1919, had orchestral parts ready for a read-through in 1920 by the National Symphony Orchestra under Paul Eisler, continued to revise it in the 1920s, and had it professionally copied by 1929. It was first performed at the Teatro Nacional in Havana on December 27, 1931, by the Orquesta Filarmónica de la Habana, conducted by Cuban composer Amadeo Roldán. It was not published until 1989, in a critical edition by James B. Sinclair.[109]

Of the four *Holidays* movements, *Decoration Day* is the most solemn, depicting early 1880s observances in Danbury, Connecticut, of the day for citizens to decorate with flowers the graves of the Union soldiers who had died in the Civil War.[110] As he did for *Washington's Birthday*, Ives added to the copyist's ink score a postface presenting the program:

> In the early morning the garden and woods about the village are the meeting places of those who, with tender memories and devoted hands, gather the flowers for the day's memorial. During the forenoon, as the people join each other on the [village] green, there is felt at times a fervency and intensity—a shadow, perhaps, of the fanatical harshness—reflecting old abolitionist days. It is a day, Thoreau suggests, when there is a pervading consciousness of "Nature's kinship with the lower order—man."
>
> After the town hall is filled with the spring's harvest of lilacs, daisies, and peonies, the parade is slowly formed on Main Street. First come the three marshals on plough horses (going sideways); then the warden and burgesses (in carriages!!), the village cornet band, the G.A.R. [local members of the Grand Army of the Republic, the Union veterans group] two by two, and the militia (Company G), while the volunteer fire brigade, drawing the decorated hose-cart with its jangling bells, brings up the rear—the inevitable swarm of small boys following. The march to Wooster Cemetery [outside Danbury] is a thing a boy never forgets. The roll of muffled drums and "Adeste fideles" answer for the dirge. A little girl on the fencepost waves to her father and wonders if he looked like that at Gettysburg.
>
> After the last grave is decorated, "Taps" sounds out through the pines and hickories, while a last hymn is sung. Then the ranks are formed again, and we all march back to town to a Yankee stimulant—Reeves's inspiring *Second Regiment [March]*—though to many a soldier the somber thoughts of the day underlie the tunes of the band. The march stops, and in the silence the shadow of the early morning flower-song rises over the town, and the sunset behind West Mountain breathes its benediction upon the day.[111]

The program reflected deep personal meanings for Ives. He was born just nine years after the war ended, so the Decoration Day celebrations during his youth must have been particularly poignant, as the people around him in Danbury remembered friends and family members who had served or died in the war. He conceived the piece during the fiftieth anniversary of the Civil War in 1911–15, when many Union veterans were still alive, and worked on it during World War I (1914–18), when descendants of Union and Confederate families went off side by side to fight in Europe and some of the divisions from the Civil War era seemed to be fading. But it was also a memorial for his father, who led "the village cornet band" in Danbury parades, played *Taps* for memorials at the cemetery, and had served in the Union army as a bandleader.[112] Both father and son considered the *Second Regiment Connecticut National Guard March* by David Wallis Reeves (1838–1900) their favorite march, and so its appearance here serves as an explicit emblem for Ives's father.

The movement closely follows the events outlined in Ives's program, although not every detail in the program has a parallel in the piece.[113] It opens ***ppp*** with muted strings playing a sustained G-sharp-major triad under a very slow B-major melody, almost every note of which is dissonant against the chord. The soft dynamic, motionless harmony, and slowly changing sweet dissonances create an effect like a misty dawn or the whispered beginning of a tale of long ago. An English horn introduces "the early morning flower-song" with a five-note motive (m. 5) that repeats alternately in violins (mm. 10, 14, 17, 21, 30, and 37) and flute (mm. 12, 20, and 34), each time leading to a different melodic continuation that weaves among several instruments over shifting harmonic background. The constant head-motive combined with endless variations of what follows aptly suggests many people pursuing a common purpose, each

Example 4.13 "Decoration Day" by Charles Ives. Copyright © 1962 by Peer International Corporation. Copyright Renewed. Used by Permission. All Rights Reserved.

person an individual with their own "tender memories and devoted hands," while the continuing soft dynamics and dissonances reflect the natural setting and their poignant thoughts as they gather flowers.

After a pause, the last appearances of the flower-gathering motive (mm. 37 and 39) initiate a new, slightly faster, and more diverse section representing people assembling on the green. Fragments of *Marching Through Georgia*, Henry Clay Work's song celebrating General William Tecumseh Sherman's 1864 march to capture Savannah for the Union, flit by in various instruments and keys (parts of the chorus in flute, bassoon, and violins, mm. 37–40, and of the verse in horn, flute, clarinet, and strings, mm. 39–46), symbolizing people's thoughts or conversations as they recall the war and the fight to free the slaves. A very quiet and sometimes changing ostinato in the bells, barely heard in the background of the next few scenes (mm. 39–145), may depict the firehose cart "with its jangling bells."[114] Soft, dissonant chords in the strings, half playing pizzicato and half arco with tremolos or with trills that glissando down a semitone (m. 50), imitate the "muffled drums."

The march to the cemetery (m. 54) features *Adeste fideles* in strings and horns (paralleled by soft offbeat dissonant flourishes in the flutes), its rhythm and contour clear but with some intervals altered. Best known as a Christmas song ("O come, all ye faithful"), the tune may seem an odd choice for "the village cornet band" to play on this occasion, but it was also sung

Example 4.13 *continued*

with other texts (such as "How firm a foundation" and "We gather, we gather") that would be appropriate for a memorial march in May. Woven between phrases of the hymn are fragments of two more Union songs, *Tenting on the Old Camp Ground* from 1864, a song by Walter Kittredge (1834–1905) expressing weariness of war and yearning for its end (mm. 61–64 and 68–69), and George F. Root's *The Battle Cry of Freedom*, a rallying cry from early in the war (mm. 65–68 in violin 1). These songs were among the best known of the Civil War, making them appropriate for the parade. Just as important, they perfectly capture the spectrum of conflicting emotions of the townspeople, from patriotic pride to sadness to hope.[115]

If the piece so far has evoked events through apt musical gestures and fragments of familiar tunes, the scenes at the cemetery and of the march back to town are as vivid as home videos, with two of the most precise programmatic quotations in Ives's output. Rather than depict the actual decorating of graves, Ives skips to the final moments of the memorial ceremony, shown in example 4.13. Here he combines *Taps* in an offstage (or muted) trumpet with the opening phrase of *Bethany* ("Nearer, my God, to Thee") played three times in tremolo violins. Both tunes are in F-sharp/G-flat major over a tremolo F♯ pedal point (mm. 74–81). *Bethany*, as a hymn often sung at memorial services, represents both the "last hymn" and the inner thoughts of the crowd, while the tremolos suggest people trembling with emotion as they hear the solitary bugle sounding *Taps*.

Dissonant chords in low strings imitate drums playing the *Street Beat* (m. 81), and the "march back to town" (mm. 89–145) includes the entire trio of Reeves's march in C major, the longest and most complete quotation in any Ives piece. Example 4.14 shows the beginning of the march. Since vivid memories are always better than the original, Ives livens up Reeves's march with enhancements, including running scales in trombones and tuba, doublings in strings and winds, added descants, and accented hemiolas on the repeat. Underlying the Reeves, and perhaps impossible to hear (though not to see or sense in live performance) amid its enthusiastic strains, are "the somber thoughts of the day," represented by *Taps* in low bells and solo viola, the opening notes of *Bethany* in two solo violins, and distorted fragments of *The Battle Hymn of the Republic* in oboes and clarinets (mm. 126–34).

When "the march stops," a sonic exuviation reveals the flower-gathering motive from the opening of the movement, in a similar scoring (mm. 146–48 repeat mm. 5–6 almost literally), suggesting that the silent thoughts of the townsfolk are still with the loved ones whose graves they have decorated—"in the silence the shadow of the early morning flower-song rises over the town." In the final measure an "amen" in divided upper strings, combined with the very soft opening motive of *Taps* in bells and solo viola, "breathes its benediction upon the day."

The harmonic plan for *Decoration Day* is less straightforward than that for *Washington's Birthday*, perhaps because the form is more episodic. Tritone, major-third, and whole-tone relationships are highlighted: tritones between the opening G-sharp-major triad and the subsequent D-major harmony under the English horn melody (m. 5) as well as between the F-sharp-major graveside ceremony with *Taps* and the C-major march back to town; major thirds between the D-major, F-sharp-major, and B-flat-major renditions of the flower-gathering motive; and whole tones between all these keys (C, D, F♯, G♯, and B♭), in the hints of D, C, and B-flat as keys in the dirge (mm. 54, 63, and 66), and melodically in the flower-gathering motive and the first three notes of *Bethany*. Brief references to B major at the outset and in the final "amen" provide a frame.

The Fourth of July

The Fourth of July is scored for large orchestra with added winds, brass, and percussion. Ives dated it 1911–13, but Gayle Sherwood Magee places the extant sketches around 1914, the score-sketch closer to 1919 (on paper that dates no earlier than 1917), and the full pencil score circa 1919–23, with subsequent revisions as late as 1930–31, when he had it professionally copied.[116] In composing the work, Ives incorporated passages from his song *Old Home Day* (?1913) and experimental concepts from several earlier pieces.[117] Perhaps ironically for a piece about the US celebrations of Independence Day, it had a European premiere: Nicolas Slonimsky conducted the first performance at the Salle Pleyel in Paris on February 21, 1932, with an orchestra comprising members of Orchestre Symphonique de Paris, and that same year it was published jointly by Edition Adler in Berlin and by New Music in San Francisco.

While the first two movements of the *Holidays Symphony* each depict a specific series of events described in their programs, *The Fourth of July* has only a general outline:

> It's a boy's 4th—no historical orations—no patriotic grandiloquences by "grown-ups"—no program in his yard! But he knows what he's celebrating—better than most of the county politicians. And he goes at it in his own way, with a patriotism nearer kin to nature than jingoism. His festivities start in the quiet of the midnight before, and grow raucous with the sun. Everybody

Example 4.14 Ives. *Decoration Day*, mm. 87–92

knows what it's like—if everybody doesn't—Cannon on the Green, Village Band on Main Street, fire crackers, shanks mixed on cornets, strings around big toes, torpedoes, Church bells, lost finger, fifes, clam-chowder, a prize-fight, drum-corps, burnt shins, parades (in and out of step), saloons all closed (more drunks than usual), baseball game (Danbury All-Stars vs. Beaver Brook Boys), pistols, mobbed umpire, *Red, White and Blue*, runaway horse—and the day ends with the sky-rocket over the Church steeple, just after the annual explosion sets the Town-Hall on fire. All this is not in the music—not now.[118]

Some elements of this description do appear in the music: the growth from a quiet beginning to a raucous climax; a pistol shot (m. 39); the village band playing *Columbia, the Gem of the Ocean* (also called *The Red, White and Blue*) with "shanks mixed on cornets" so that one or more players are in the wrong key; explosions (mm. 76–77 and 116–20); and a falling rocket at the end (mm. 121–22). Yet, for the most part, the piece is shaped not as a sequence of episodes corresponding to the program, but as a cumulative form enriched by a collage of tunes and sounds appropriate to the day, representing the memories of a middle-aged man recalling the Independence Days of his boyhood. In *Memos*, Ives called it "pure program music—it's also pure abstract music—'You pays your money, and you takes your choice.'"[119]

The overall form is charted in table 4.8, highlighting the thematic structure and significant events along with the tunes layered in collage.[120] The main theme (MT) is the verse of *Columbia, the Gem of the Ocean*, the same patriotic song used in the coda of the Second Symphony and in the second movement of the Fourth (mm. 99–114). The principal countermelody (CM) weaves together paraphrased portions of the verse and chorus of *The Battle Hymn of the Republic* and the second phrase from the chorus of *Marching Through Georgia* (at mm. 108–11).

The first section (mm. 1–44) presents fragments and paraphrases of MT. At the beginning, its first phrase, played ***pp*** in C-sharp minor over an F major triad (strings, mm. 1–3), creates the same types of dissonance and opening sonority as in *Decoration Day*, suggesting the boy's anticipation of the festivities "in the quiet of the midnight before." Next, the first phrase of MT sounds slowly in the bass (mm. 4–12), accompanied by quartal, quintal, and whole-tone chords derived from the opening melodic intervals of *Columbia*, which alternate perfect fourths and whole tones. In the background, marked ***ppp***, is a hazy chromatic figure in muted solo violins, dissonant and with constantly changing rhythmic subdivisions, that repeats every five measures through measure 63, like the haze of a long-ago memory. As the tempo gradually increases, fragments of MT appear at normal speed in upper winds and strings (mm. 16–25), followed by a paraphrase of its first two phrases with much repetition (flute and piccolo, mm. 28–36). These are framed by a cuckoo's call (piccolo, mm. 16 and 42) and punctuated by brief motives from bugle calls and two Civil War songs (see table 4.8); one of these, the first phrase from the chorus of *Marching Through Georgia*, anticipates the later appearance of that tune's second phrase in CM.

The middle section (mm. 44–79) continues the gradual increase in tempo and grows more complex, with more references to tunes appropriate for the holiday celebration. It falls into three subsections. The first features a theme adapted from the verse of Ives's song *Old Home Day* (OHD), which begins with an original melody in A minor (flute and clarinet, mm. 44–48) and continues by quoting the last phrase of the verse from *The Battle Hymn of the Republic* with a new closing tag (oboe, clarinet, and violin 1, mm. 49–53); this phrase from *The Battle Hymn* will later appear prominently in CM. Two hornpipes and the *Street Beat* sound quietly in the background, also anticipating things to come. The second subsection (m. 53) features loud, rapidly moving dissonant chords, each derived from stacking a single interval (fourths,

Table 4.8 Cumulative Form in *The Fourth of July* and *Thanksgiving*

THE FOURTH OF JULY

Main theme (MT): Verse of *Columbia, the Gem of the Ocean* (*The Red, White, and Blue*)
Countermelody (CM): Paraphrased from portions of *The Battle Hymn of the Republic*, with portion of *Marching Through Georgia*
Secondary idea: Verse of Ives's song *Old Home Day* (OHD)

Sect.	Meas.	Music	Tempo	Key/implied key of main melody
1	1	Fragments of MT	Adagio molto	C# minor over F major triad
	4	MT first phrase		B minor, C major
	12	Fragments of MT; also Cuckoo's call (Picc. m. 16), bugle calls (Clar. and Hr. mm. 26–27), *The Battle Cry of Freedom* (Vlc. m. 27)	Andante con moto, a little faster	mostly B major over C pedal
	28	Paraphrase of MT; also *Marching Through Georgia* (Tpt. mm. 34–36), Cuckoo's call (Picc. m. 42)	Allegretto, a little faster	A minor/major over C pedal
2	44	OHD (includes part of CM at mm. 49–52); also *Sailor's Hornpipe* (Ob. mm. 45–47), *Fisher's Hornpipe* (Flt. and Picc. mm. 49–51), Street Beat (BD and Timp. mm. 49–53)	Più allegretto	A minor/major
	53	Dissonant chords; also *The Battle Cry of Freedom* (Hr. mm. 53–54), Reveille (Hr. mm. 57–59 and Tpt. mm. 59–60), first phrases of CM (Flt. and Ob. mm. 60–63) and MT (Trom. mm. 62–63)	Più moto (at m. 55)	
	64	Fragments of OHD (Vn. 1 mm. 65–70 and 73–75 and Hr. mm. 70–73); also *Hail! Columbia* (Clar. and Bssn. mm. 64–65 and 73–74); fife tune (Fifes or Picc. mm. 66a–73a) from *White Cockade* (mm. 66a–69a), *Tramp, Tramp, Tramp* (mm. 68a–70a), and *The Girl I Left Behind Me* (mm. 70a–72a) over Street Beat (Timp., SD, Cym., BD, and Pno. mm. 66a–75); *London Bridge* (fragmented among Fifes/Picc., Flt., Ob., and Bssn. mm. 74–75)	Più moto (at m. 66a)	modulatory
	76	Explosion	Con furore	
	78	End of OHD	Meno mosso	
3	80	Fragments of MT in original and paraphrase; also *Hail! Columbia* (Hr. and Tpt. mm. 80–83, Vlc. 1 and Clar. 2 mm. 86–92), *Garryowen* (Xylo. and Pno. mm. 82–83 and 86–88), *Saint Patrick's Day* (Xylo. mm. 88–90 and 93–94. Tpt. m. 94), Reveille (Tpt. mm. 91–93), *Irish Washerwoman* (Tpt. mm. 95–96, Hr. 4 mm. 97–98); *Marching through Georgia* (Tpt. mm. 96–98); possible fragments of CM (upper Ww. mm. 96–98)	A tempo	A, B, B♭, and other keys

Table 4.8 *continued*

THE FOURTH OF JULY

Main theme (MT): Verse of *Columbia, the Gem of the Ocean* (*The Red, White, and Blue*)
Countermelody (CM): Paraphrased from portions of *The Battle Hymn of the Republic*, with portion of *Marching Through Georgia*
Secondary idea: Verse of Ives's song *Old Home Day* (OHD)

Sect.	Meas.	Music	Tempo	Key/implied key of main melody
		MT complete, with CM; also *Yankee Doodle* (Xylo. mm. 99–113, Bssn. mm. 101–07), *Street Beat* (Timp. mm. 99–100; SD, BD, and Cym. mm. 101–05), *Katy Darling* (Picc. mm. 99–109), *Dixie* fused with *Kingdom Coming* (Picc. mm. 109–14), *Assembly* (Ob. mm. 102 and 108–09, Clar. mm. 102–03 and 104, Vlc. 1 mm. 103 and 106), *The Star-Spangled Banner* (Brass and Bssn. mm. 114–15)	Quick-step: Allegro con spirito	B♭
	99			
	116	Explosion; *Yankee Doodle* (Cor. and Tpt., m. 118)	Allegro con fuoco	
	121	Falling rocket	Meno mosso	

THANKSGIVING AND FOREFATHERS' DAY

Main theme (MT): *Duke Street*, somewhat varied
Countermelody (CM): *Federal Street*, with mm. 9–12 replaced by mm. 9–12 of *Duke Street*
Secondary ideas: "Harvest Work Theme" (HWT)
Middle section, primary theme (MP); *Shining Shore*, slightly varied
Middle section, secondary theme (MS); paraphrase of *Shining Shore*

Sect.	Meas.	Music	Meter and tempo	Key
I	1	Opening ideas of CM, HWT, MP	4/4, Adagio maestoso	modulatory
	25	CM mm. 1–4, in imitation; shadow lines with fragments of other hymns (*Laban*, solo Vlns. mm. 29–35; *Bethany* blended with *Nettleton*, Flt. mm. 34–37; *Valentia*, Ob. mm. 42–44; *Arlington*, solo Vlas. 50–52; and perhaps others)	Poco adagio, Più mosso	
	51	MT fragments (mm. 1–4, 9–12), with CM mm. 1–4	Poco con spirito	mostly E♭
	69	CM, distorted paraphrase	A little faster	chromatic

	m.	Description	Tempo	Key
	88	HWT	Andante maestoso	
	98	*Duke Street* mm. 9–12 (part of MT and CM) paraphrase	Slow down	polytonal
	108	transition	Poco agitando	chromatic
	118	transition continues with MP mm. 1–8		A♭ over A pedal
2a	129	MP	3/4, Adagio cantabile, con moto	G
2b	153	MS (Vln. 1 at m. 155)	Più moto	G
	165	MS repeats; also shadow lines with paraphrased *Azmon* (Ob. 1 mm. 165–79, Ob. 2 mm. 172–79) and *In the Sweet By-and-By* (Ob. 2 mm. 165–72)	Allegro con moto	G
2a'	180	MP, modified and fragmented	Adagio con moto	G
3	210	transition, with HWT, CM mm. 1–4	Animando poco a poco	
	222	*Duke Street* mm. 9–12, HWT; CM mm. 1–4 paraphrase (Hr. mm. 230–35)	4/4, Andante con moto, ma maestoso (at m. 219)	E♭, B♭, modulatory
	244	**MT complete, with CM**, fragments of HWT	Maestoso	A
	259	extension on last phrase of CM		

tritones, fifths, minor sixths, and so on), creating a sudden burst of boisterousness. Around these chords Ives layers fragments of tunes with patriotic or military associations, including the first phrases of CM and MT, foreshadowing their later combination. The last subsection (m. 64) recalls fragments of the *Old Home Day* melody and overlays them with other tunes, including a fife-and-drum march stitched together from three tunes and metrically displaced from the rest of the orchestra like the "out of step" parade mentioned in Ives's program. An explosion—perhaps firing the "Cannon on the Green"—is suggested by a sudden loud dissonant chord covering the entire range of the orchestra followed by rapid, dissonant, and rhythmically variegated figuration in all instruments that gradually slows and diminuendos; this includes in the upper strings rising and falling waves of diatonic clusters in B-flat, B, and A major sounding all notes in each scale at once as they sweep up and down (mm. 76–77). The combination of sudden noise, rapidly changing sounds, and gradual decay in dynamics and density is an almost perfect musical evocation of an explosion and its aftermath.[121]

After fragments of MT in the first section and of CM in the second, the third section (mm. 80–122) leads up to their full presentation together, the formal and sonic climax of the movement. The first phrase of MT, in original and paraphrased forms, saturates the texture in various keys, along with fragments of *Hail! Columbia*, Irish dance tunes, hints of CM, and other patriotic songs (see table 4.8). Finally, as example 4.15 shows, MT appears complete and at full blast in trumpets and trombones in B-flat, combined with CM in flutes, oboes, clarinets, and cornet (mm. 99–114). Variants between the instruments playing both MT and CM suggest the sound of an amateur village band in which players make mistakes, get off the rhythm, or add improvised embellishments. Ives recreates the effect of "mixing shanks"—when, for example, in a passage for trumpets in B-flat one or more players have the wrong crook (or shank) in their instruments so that they are playing in a key other than B-flat—by including in the lines for trumpet and trombone notes that would be correct in a B-major rendition of MT and marking them at a lower dynamic level. Comparing the trombone and trumpet lines in example 4.15 shows that the notes marked *ff* in either part belong to MT in B-flat major while those marked *f* or *mf* are a semitone too high (and thus in B major), and the parts alternate who plays in the correct key. The result sounds like a band in which some players have the wrong crook and are thus sounding a half step sharp. The effect of a not-quite-together amateur band is augmented by cello 1, playing a variant of MT clouded by chromatic neighbor notes and different rhythms. The impression of a band playing is reinforced by a bass line harmonizing with MT and by *Street Beat* in drums and cymbals. The piano adds rhythmic patterns of dissonant chords that imitate drumming, an effect Ives invented in his youth and used in more than a dozen works.[122] To represent parts of the band getting out of step, some parts of the orchestra drop a beat here and there, shortening their measures from 4/4 to 7/8, and the bar lines get out of synchronization for a while (mm. 88–96 and 105–12) before coming back together.

Around the band playing *Columbia, the Gem of the Ocean* and *The Battle Hymn of the Republic* swirl other tunes appropriate to the Fourth of July, creating a collage: *Yankee Doodle* in xylophone and bassoon; a patchwork of popular songs in the piccolo (the sentimental *Katy Darling*, the minstrel song *Dixie* by Daniel Emmett [1815–1904], and the Union emancipation song *Kingdom Coming* by Henry Clay Work); and fragments of the bugle call *Assembly* in various instruments. Intensifying the tumult of sound are waves of diatonic clusters in the upper

Facing, Example 4.15 The Fourth of July by Charles Ives. Copyright © 1932 (Renewed) by Associated Music Publishers, Inc. (BMI). International Copyright Secured. All Rights Reserved. Used by Permission.

strings, like those in the earlier explosion at m. 76, simultaneously sounding all the notes in the principal key of B-flat major and in its chromatic upper and lower neighbor keys B and A major. As MT reaches a cadence, we hear the opening notes of *The Star-Spangled Banner* in the brass and bassoons (mm. 114–15). Then comes a brief pause, marked by a distant bell, and a final explosion, longer and louder than before, followed by a sonic exuviation and soft overlapping chromatic descending figures in solo violins, violas, and flute, depicting "the sky-rocket over the Church steeple, just after the annual explosion sets the Town-Hall on fire."

Such moments of "pure program music" punctuate a piece that is mostly "abstract music," organized by the gradual process of revealing the main theme and its countermelody and bringing them together, delineated by a three-part structure that focuses in turn on MT, on a contrasting theme (taken from *Old Home Day*) and CM, and then on the full presentation of MT and CM in counterpoint. The harmonic plan is one of gradual clarification, hinting at F major at the outset, presenting tune fragments in keys that surround B-flat chromatically (C-sharp, C, B, and A), and finally coming to focus on B-flat major while surrounding it with gyrating diatonic clusters of its chromatic neighbors B major and A major. The collage of tunes and other sounds from the cuckoo's call to the final rocket enhance the basic structure of the piece with more specific images, representing the memories of a middle-aged man remembering his boyhood holidays, as in the collage in *Washington's Birthday*.

Thanksgiving and Forefathers' Day

The final movement of the *Holidays Symphony*, *Thanksgiving and Forefathers' Day*, had the longest gestation. Ives said he based it on two organ works, a Prelude and Postlude he played at a Thanksgiving Day service in November 1897, his last year as organist at Center Church in New Haven. Only the first page of the Postlude survives, in a manuscript apparently dating from 1899 (perhaps a revision or fair copy), making it impossible to know past the opening measures how similar the organ works were to the orchestral movement. According to Ives's recollections, he composed *Thanksgiving* in 1904, adapting the Prelude for the middle section and the Postlude for the rest. Yet the extant sketches are from circa 1913–19, culminating in a score-sketch. Ives wrote out the full score during the winter of 1932–33, when he and his wife were vacationing in Taormina, Sicily. The piece was not played until the first performance of the entire *Holidays Symphony* on April 9, 1954 (less than six weeks before Ives's death on May 19), in Minneapolis, by the Minneapolis Symphony Orchestra under Antal Dorati. It was not published until the 1991 critical edition by Jonathan Elkus, almost a century after Ives created the organ pieces on which it was based.[123]

Thanksgiving and Forefathers' Day does not have a program, as the other three movements do, but rather evokes its two holidays and the Pilgrims they commemorate through musical and textual imagery. It opens with C major and D minor triads sounding together; Ives wrote in *Memos* that he intended this dissonant sonority "to represent the sternness and strength and austerity of the Puritan character, and it seemed to me that any of the major, minor, or diminished chords used alone gave too much a feeling of bodily ease, which the Puritan did not give in to."[124] Thanksgiving celebrates the first harvest of the Pilgrims, and Ives represents this aspect of the holiday with what he called the "Harvest Work Theme" on the Postlude manuscript and "a scything or reaping Harvest Theme" in *Memos*.[125] This theme features a repeating motive with a quarter or dotted-quarter note, quick neighbor-note motion in sixteenths, and a large leap, suggesting the sweeping notion of a scythe as it rocks back and forth between registers. Forefathers' Day, a regional New England holiday, marks the landing on December 21,

1620, of a group of Pilgrims from the *Mayflower* at the site that would become the Plymouth Colony. Ives's piece culminates at m. 244 with a choir singing a hymn appropriate to the day, slightly modified from the version that appeared in the hymnal Ives used at Yale. Leonard Bacon wrote the poem in 1833 for the 200th anniversary celebration of the founding of New Haven in 1838, and the tune is *Duke Street* by John Hatton (ca. 1710–93):

> God! Beneath Thy guiding hand,
> Our exiled fathers crossed the sea;
> And as they trod the wintry strand,
> With prayer and praise they worshipped Thee.[126]

Ives uses *The Shining Shore* by George F. Root as the main thematic source for the middle section, and it too has images appropriate to Forefathers' Day, speaking of the Promised Land in terms that can be read metaphorically to refer to the Pilgrims and their earthly voyage to another continent: "I, a pilgrim stranger"; "we stand on Jordan's strand"; "the shining shore / We may almost discover"; "and there's our home, / Forever, and forever." By focusing on these hymns, appropriate to a church service on Thanksgiving or Forefathers' Day, the movement also highlights the way Americans use music in their holiday observances, as the other movements do through their programs.

The movement combines cumulative form and ternary form. The first and third sections together comprise a cumulative form and surround a contrasting middle section, itself a small modified ternary form. Table 4.8 shows the structure.[127] The main theme (MT) is *Duke Street*, somewhat altered, and the countermelody (CM) is the rhythmically similar hymn *Federal Street* by Henry K. Oliver (1800–85), with its third phrase replaced by the third phrase of *Duke Street*. That phrase is shifted forward a measure in MT, resulting in a brief canon between MT and CM when they are combined (m. 244). In early sketches, *Federal Street* was the main theme; Ives inserted *Duke Street* as a countermelody in the score-sketch, and then he made it the most prominent line with the addition of the choir in the full score.[128] This compositional history explains why CM is less altered from its source than MT, the reverse of the usual situation as exemplified in the first and final movements of the Third Symphony and in *The Fourth of July*. The Harvest Work Theme (HWT) plays a secondary role in the outer sections. The middle section (mm. 129–209) has its own themes: *The Shining Shore*, slightly varied, as its cantabile primary theme (MP), and a spritely secondary theme (MS) paraphrased from the same hymn.

The first section presents fragments and paraphrases of the themes, as is typical for a cumulative form. It opens with a slow and majestic contrapuntal fantasia on the opening motives of CM, HWT, and MP, with dissonant harmonies (often sounding polytonal, like the opening chord) and contrasts between instrumental families that evoke an organlike texture. At m. 25, the first phrase of CM is treated in imitation and developed. In the background are phrases taken or adapted from other hymns in soft "shadow" lines, marked "Faintly, as choir practicing before church [as heard from] the distance." The density and intensity grow, leading to a slightly faster section developing fragments of MT and CM (m. 51) and a distorted paraphrase of CM in horns and trumpet over turbulent counterpoint in the other parts, featuring parallel dissonant chords and conflicting rhythms (m. 69). At the climax, the tempo slows for an extended majestic statement of HWT in upper strings, winds, and horns over parallel dissonant minor-minor-seventh chords in the lower instruments (m. 88). The tempo slows further, the music grows softer, and echoes of HWT continue as the lower instruments, still in their parallel chords and in long notes like a cantus firmus, trace the phrase of *Duke Street* shared by MT and CM (mm. 98–108). In the background, a flute quietly introduces a descending minor-third figure, picked up by bells at m. 102 and later by celesta throughout the middle section (from m. 128 through m. 208) and by strings at the beginning of the third section (mm. 206–18), like an echo of the descending minor third at the melodic peaks of *Duke Street* and of *The Shining Shore*. Through such a quiet gesture, Ives subtly weaves the contrasting parts of the form together by highlighting a scarcely noticed similarity between his source tunes.

A soft transition in two parts—chromatic undulations (m. 108) followed by an anticipation of MP in A-flat major over an A pedal and ostinatos in conflicting rhythms (m. 118)—leads to the middle section (m. 129). Here the texture thins, the tempo slows to adagio cantabile, the key clarifies to G major, and MP appears, slightly varied, divided between violin, flute, and oboe. The harmony is simple but still unorthodox, with alternating tonic and subdominant triads, pizzicato arpeggiating fifths (m. 138), and chromatically sliding parallel triads (m. 143). Suddenly louder string chords (m. 153) herald the more active contrasting theme, MS, presented first in violins over a bass ostinato and chugging chords and then reinforced with flutes, clarinets, and trumpets (at m. 165). The second time, Ives thickens the texture with more ostinatos and adds two more shadow lines in the oboes, variants of *Azmon* and *In the Sweet By-and-By* that are melodically related to *The Shining Shore* and thus to MS. Just as suddenly as it began, the louder and faster passage stops with a sonic exuviation, and we hear a varied and fragmented reprise of MP (m. 180).[129]

The third section begins with a transition (m. 210) that grows louder and more animated, reintroduces fragments of HWT and CM, and leads to a development of elements from all three themes of the first section: the phrase of *Duke Street* shared by MT and CM, HWT, and the first phrase of CM. From this emerges the climactic statement of MT in unison choir, trumpets, and bassoon 1 (m. 244), in a bright A major, with CM in the horns and trombone 1, fragments of HWT in the clarinet, and a descant in upper strings and winds. Meanwhile, in a "Church Bell Chorus," celesta and bells echo the minor-third figure from earlier, and church chimes play a change-ringing pattern in A major. The choir, doubled by trumpets and bassoon 1, repeats the last gesture of MT three times in overlapping waves, and the orchestra responds by restating the last phrase of CM several times over IV-I harmony, like a grand amen, as it fades to silence. The celesta minor-third figure gets the last word.

Suite and Symphony

A Symphony: New England Holidays is most easily understood as a suite of tone poems. All four movements include both slow sections and fast sections, changes of meter, and strong internal contrasts in character and style beyond those typical of a single symphony movement. These characteristics, along with their programs and descriptive titles, make them more like symphonic poems than like the movements of a traditional symphony. There is no key scheme or cyclic thematic link that binds them together. Each stands on its own and is most often performed separately. And a four-movement symphony that uses different instrumentation in each movement, including a full choir for just seventeen measures in the last movement, presents practical difficulties in performance.[130]

Yet there are still elements that resonate with symphonic tradition. These movements all continue the techniques of motivic fragmentation, developing variation, and contrapuntal combination of themes we have seen in every Ives symphony since the First. The first movement begins slow and moves to a faster section, like many opening movements from the eighteenth and nineteenth centuries. Although both middle movements build from slow, quiet material to a loud, fast march, *Decoration Day* is more somber and is slow for most of its length, allowing it to play the part of a slow movement. By contrast, *The Fourth of July* is shorter and more raucous and transgressive, suggesting the character of a scherzo. The last movement has a popular character and relatively simple texture, like many Haydn finales, especially in the middle section, and provides a weighty ending, like finales of nineteenth-century symphonies. The differences in form between each movement and the standard model have parallels in other symphonies, including Ives's. The strong contrasts between and within movements suggest "a world," akin to Gustav Mahler's vision of a symphony, and each movement paints a picture in sound of a holiday and a season in the New England of Ives's youth, giving the whole a unity of tone and subject.

It is typical of Ives to have things work in more than one way, as in his comment that *The Fourth of July* can be regarded as program music or as abstract music. In that sense, as in many others, the *Holidays Symphony* is characteristic.

UNIVERSE SYMPHONY

If the Fourth Symphony and *Holidays Symphony* stretch the parameters of the traditional symphony, the *Universe Symphony* bursts them. Although it is conceived as descriptive or programmatic music, as are all of Ives's symphonic works past the first two symphonies, and is composed for orchestra, it is in every other respect unlike any of Ives's earlier symphonies. Whereas they present a web of melodies supported by harmony and enriched by texture, the *Universe Symphony* has a relative dearth of melody and a focus instead on pitch, rhythm, and texture. It is pure systematic music, the culmination of all Ives's experiments in layers, chord structures, and metric subdivisions. To the extent that themes or motives are present, they are not developed but used symbolically to represent the Earth, clouds, or other images. None of the references to familiar music that are characteristic of all of Ives's other symphonies are present, other than what may be a fragment of *Bethany* in very long notes. If *Washington's Birthday* and *Decoration Day* describe landscapes, they are landscapes with people in them, and the people's activities are the focus. There are no people in the *Universe Symphony*, only a depiction of nature through the forces of generation.

The *Universe Symphony* has two faces, as vision and as realization. To some of his associates, Ives described it in terms so extravagant that it seemed more like a concept than a performable work. His secretary Christine Loring recalled that "it was to be played by two huge orchestras across from each other on mountaintops overlooking a valley." His copyist George Roberts said it was for "orchestras here and there on the hills, and different choruses all around the countryside." His biographers Henry and Sidney Cowell used similar terms: "Several different orchestras, with huge conclaves of singing men and women, are to be placed about in valleys, on hillsides, and on mountain tops."[131] But Ives also wrote at least thirty-four pages of sketches for an actual piece of music, radical in sound and form but nonetheless performable and intended for symphony orchestra. The piece suggested by the surviving sketches does not match the grandiose descriptions: there are no voices, and the music is far too subtle and complex—and often too quiet—to be heard well out of doors, much less from widely scattered groups of performers.[132] Like Ives's orchestral concert music that celebrates outdoor music making by bands or buglers, the *Universe Symphony* is to be played indoors and summon up visions of nature, Earth, and the universe.

Ives recalled that he conceived the work during a vacation in the Adirondacks in October 1915, no doubt inspired by the grandeur of the nearby mountains. The extant materials primarily date from 1915–16 for Section A and 1923–28 for the rest.[133] He described the piece in his work lists as "Prelude and sectional mvt. from a *Universe Symphony* (uncompleted), the underlying plan of which was a presentation and contemplation in tones, rather than in music (as such), of the mysterious creation of the earth and firmament, the evolution of all life in nature, in humanity, to the Divine."[134] The surviving sketches include notations toward two preludes (a third is referred to but not extant) and three sections, apparently envisioned as one continuous movement.

Roberts and the Cowells said that Ives never intended to finish the *Universe Symphony*, but what the composer writes about it in *Memos* suggests otherwise. He describes the piece in some detail; comments that "I had this fairly well sketched out, but not completed . . . but hope to finish it out completely this summer [of 1932]"; and adds that, "in case I don't get to finishing this, somebody might like to try to work out the idea, and the sketch that I've already done would make more sense to anybody looking at it with this explanation."[135]

His invitation has been taken up in recent decades by three musicians with different conceptions of the piece. Composer Larry Austin (1930–2018) was the first to try finishing the *Universe Symphony*, fleshing out Ives's sketches and supplementing them with original material. After two decades of work, his version was first performed on January 28, 1994, at the University of Cincinnati College-Conservatory of Music by the Cincinnati Philharmonic Orchestra and the College-Conservatory's Percussion Ensemble, conducted by Gerhard Samuel with six assistant conductors and computer-generated click tracks played through individual sets of headphones to keep everyone coordinated. It was released on CD later that year. A more modest edition by David Porter (1954–2010), a realization of only the most complete sketches (the first prelude and Section A) on commission by the Charles Ives Society, was performed a few months earlier, on October 29, 1993, at an Ives-Copland Festival in Greeley, Colorado, by the University of Northern Colorado Symphony Orchestra, conducted by Kenneth Singleton. On June 6, 1996, microtonal composer Johnny Reinhard (born 1956) conducted the premiere of his own completion of the *Universe Symphony* at the American Festival of Microtonal Music in New York. Arguing that the sketches were essentially complete but out of order, he rearranged the pages and, like Austin, provided solutions where the sketches lacked clarity. Unlike Austin, he insisted that the musicians execute their rhythms without a click track. A recording was released on CD in 2005.[136]

The sketches and three realizations show that the *Universe Symphony* would have been the culmination of Ives's experimental music, his most complex and complete systematic composition. There are multiple independent layers arranged in what Ives called "three fundamental orchestral groups: (1) the upper (clouds), (2) the lower (earth), [and] (3) the pulse (percussion). The lower group is divided into several orchestras (at least five); the upper group is divided into five groups of chordal counterpoint; the middle group [the pulse] comprises 18 different lines of percussion. At one time when the activity is at its height, there are 31 different lines of counterpoint."[137]

The first prelude features only the percussion, from drums and bells to tuned instruments such as piano and xylophone, plus piccolo. Austin calls this the "Life Pulse Prelude," extrapolating the name from Ives's comment that "The pulse of the universe's life beat was by the percussion orchestra, who play their movement first, all through, before any of the other orchestras play."[138] Ives had experimented in his chamber work *Scherzo: All the Way Around and Back* (ca. 1906) with superimposing rhythmic divisions based on the first six prime numbers, building up from one note per measure by adding subdivisions of 2, 3, 5, 7, and finally 11 equally spaced notes per measure, having all sound simultaneously at the peak, then reversing the process in a palindrome. The "Life Pulse Prelude" plays out in similar fashion, but at much greater length and intricacy, in a musical depiction of the deep underlying rhythms of life and the universe. A low bell sounds what Ives calls the "B.U." or "basic unit," a long note repeating every eight seconds or longer depending on the tempo.[139] One by one other instruments enter, playing different subdivisions of this basic unit, each articulating its own pulse as if in its own meter and tempo. The different pulses gradually stack up to include twenty simultaneous equal divisions of the basic unit in the ratios 1:2:3:4:5:6:7:8:9:10:11:12:13:14:17:19:22:23:29:31, which all coincide only on the opening beat of each basic unit.[140] The pulses comprise the first twelve prime numbers plus multiples of the first six primes, resulting in 190 discrete attack points between each toll of the bell and the next, an astonishingly complex texture that far exceeds the rhythmic and metric juxtapositions of even the Fourth Symphony.

In Austin's realization, the "Life Pulse Prelude" contains ten cycles.[141] The first cycle presents the contrasting rhythmic divisions and timbres in an additive manner, each giving its own pulse, building from the single bell to a wash of sound and then, as in *Scherzo: All the Way Around and Back*, dying back down in reverse order, creating a palindrome. After the first cycle, Ives varies the rhythms in some of the rhythmic layers, making the effect still more complex, and keeps some layers going into the next cycle, adding more each time until all the instruments play continuously from cycle 5 through cycle 8. The dense fabric of sound builds to a climax in cycle 7, a "free cadenza" that includes improvisation, each instrument maintaining its own pulse. Cycles 8 through 10 return to previous cycles in an abbreviated partial retrograde, ending with a cycle like the first, in which pulses alone pile on and then drop out again as everything dies back down to a single bell.[142]

The remaining portions of the work are similarly monumental. The one page of sketches for Prelude No. 2, "Birth of the Ocean Waters," depicts its subject with massive, widely spaced chords for two string orchestras, woodwinds, and brass.[143] Section A, "Past: Formation of the Waters and Mountains," is the most complete section of the piece, fully sketched with one missing page.[144] It features what Ives calls the "Earth Chord," a cyclic structure alternating tritones and perfect fourths, which he sustains throughout the section.[145] Meanwhile, spatially separated instrumental groups representing Earth and the Heavens present contrasting ideas in conflicting meters (including "rock formation" and "soil & vegetation" in the Earth group and "chordal cloud counterpoint" in four Heavens groups), all deployed over the "Life Pulse" percussion.

Sketches for Section B, "Present: Earth, Evolution in Nature and Humanity," are minimal, but cyclic structures and superimposed instrumental groups are again evident, including extensions of the Earth Chord that include all twelve notes of the chromatic scale scattered through various instruments. In this section, Ives introduces quarter-tones and just intonation alongside equal temperament, creating a mixture of primal pitch material that may represent the mix of elements in the Earth; certainly, the presence of pure intervals from the natural overtone series alongside the human-created equal-tempered and quarter-tone scales literally represents both nature and humanity.

Section C, "Future: Heaven, the Rise of All to the Spiritual," for which seven pages of fragmentary sketches survive, embodies Ives's ultimate striving for the sublime, representing heaven musically through a series of cyclically generated chords and the union of all life through a synthesis of tuning systems. David Porter has suggested that this final section is like a gigantic fugue in which the subsections of Section A all come together in a manner similar to that of the cumulative form of Ives's Third and Fourth Symphonies.[146]

The two "complete" realizations differ in their structure. Austin's realization begins with the Earth Chord, played by cellos and basses, and then superimposes the "Life Pulse Prelude," played by the percussion. At the seventh cycle of the prelude, the rest of the ensemble enters, divided into four "Heavens" orchestras of winds, strings, and light percussion and a "Rock formation orchestra" of brass. This large ensemble plays an introduction, followed by Section A superimposed over cycles 9–10 of the prelude. Then come Sections B and C, followed by a climactic coda that includes the Earth Chord and a varied repetition of cycle 10 of the prelude.[147] Reinhard arranges the material in a different way, with cycles 1–10 stretching over the entire piece:

    I. Fragment: Earth Alone
   II. Prelude No. 1: Pulse of the Cosmos (cycles 1–3)
  III. Section A: Wide Valleys and Clouds (begins at cycle 4)
  IV. Prelude No. 2: Birth of the Oceans (begins during cycle 6)
   V. Section B: Earth and the Firmament (begins during cycle 7)
 VI. Prelude No. 3: And Lo, Now It Is Night (begins during cycle 8)
VII. Section C: Earth Is of the Heavens (begins at cycle 9)

Reinhard deploys the players in three superimposed orchestras: "The Pulse of the Cosmos Orchestra" (percussion), "Earth Orchestra" (winds, brass, low strings, harp, piano, and organ), and "Heavens Orchestra" (flutes, clarinet, high strings, glockenspiel, and celesta).[148]

In both realizations, the whole work is shaped by gradual growth from near silence to a loud, dense, overwhelming climax, then a more rapid retreat to silence. Throughout, Ives grounds his music in cycles of both rhythm and pitch, reflecting the cycles of life, Earth, the planets, and the universe. The *Universe Symphony* thus represents a culmination for many of the techniques he had been exploring in his experimental music since his teens.

The effect of listening to such a piece is extraordinary. When the "basic unit" is being articulated by the low bell, one can focus on one of the divisions of that basic unit—such as the division into 11 equal parts marked by one percussion instrument, or into 13 equal parts marked by another—counting off the beats, and all the other rhythms will sound like syncopations against it. On a second hearing, one can focus on a different subdivision, and it will sound like there is a different primary beat and a different tempo; what was background now becomes foreground and vice versa.[149] Which is figure, and which is ground, can change with your perspective. This multivalence is quite different from the layered textures in Ives's other works, such as the *Holidays Symphony* and the Fourth Symphony, where he almost always clearly establishes which is the most prominent line and what the various levels of background are. In such pieces, Ives is trying to capture the experience of one individual, who sees and hears the events from a particular vantage point. By contrast, the *Universe Symphony* is an experience of transcendence, a glimpse into the cycles of nature, that is meant to be seen and heard from many perspectives.

In a review of Austin's realization, Richard Taruskin aptly characterized the *Universe Symphony* as a work "directly in the line of European symphonic transcendentalism," attempting "to give through musical tones an intimation of the sublime." The line begins with Haydn's oratorio *The Creation* and includes Beethoven's Ninth Symphony, Wagner's *Ring* (especially the opening of *Das Rheingold*), Mahler's *Song of the Earth*, and two unfinished works that were almost exact contemporaries of the *Universe Symphony*: *Mysterium* by Alexander Scriabin

(1872–1915) and *Die Jakobsleiter* by Arnold Schoenberg (1874–1951).[150] The cyclic procedures that Ives uses in the symphony grew out of his experimental strand, but the impulse that led him to compose it has roots in the Romantic tradition of aspiring to the sublime. At the same time, as Taruskin wrote in previewing the premiere of Reinhard's realization, "Ives's omnivorous 'Universe,' at least as mediated by Mr. Reinhard, foreshadows today's musical scene in all its polymorphous perversity, its rejection of stingy theorizing, and its reopening to universal possibility."[151] Thus Ives's *Universe* looks simultaneously to the past and to the future.

What ultimately most differentiates the *Universe Symphony* from Ives's other mature symphonic works is precisely its emphasis on the universal. In his other symphonies, from the Second to the *Holidays Symphony*, he relied on "local color" that, in his conception, was "a true pigment of the universal color," capable of carrying a universal message through an authentic expression of the particulars of one group's or even one person's experiences.[152] Here the entire universe is his subject, and it can be portrayed as the experience of no one person or group.

The Orchestral Sets

Ives's three orchestral sets are not symphonies but suites of symphonic poems, with three in each set. The first two sets have a similar sequence of movements, in the pattern slow-fast-slow (like the Third Symphony) and with parallel subjects and tone: a memorial elegy that starts soft, swells to a climax, and fades away; a scherzo that celebrates Ives's memories of outdoor music making; and a re-creation of a recent personal experience of overhearing a hymn tune outdoors (one along a rural river and the other in the middle of the city), with murmuring dissonant ostinatos suggesting the background noises and helping to create a three-dimensional soundscape. Although the movements in each set apparently were first conceived independently of each other, they are rarely performed separately, as movements in the *Holidays Symphony* or in the suite *Má vlast* by Bedřich Smetana (1824–84) often are; Ives's orchestral sets are almost always played *as* sets. He sketched his Third Orchestral Set along similar lines but did not finish it. A realization of the sketches has recently been recorded, making this the last multimovement symphonic work by Ives to appear.

ORCHESTRAL SET NO. 1: *THREE PLACES IN NEW ENGLAND*

Orchestral Set No. 1, better known by its alternate title *Three Places in New England*, is one of Ives's most famous works and among the handful that established his reputation.[153] Each movement celebrates a place but is also linked with people Ives associated with that place. In the *Holidays Symphony*, he evoked familiar music to represent the people and their actions in the scenes he was depicting, whether singing, dancing, or playing in bands. Here, such references again represent people and what they do but also embody the places themselves.

Table 4.2 shows four versions of the set. Ives assembled the set in the late 1910s from pieces with separate origins and scored it for full orchestra (version 1). He then revised it and rescored it for chamber orchestra in 1929 (version 2) so that Nicolas Slonimsky could perform it with the Chamber Orchestra of Boston, made up of players from the Boston Symphony Orchestra. After a private hearing in New York in February 1930, they premiered the work at New York's Town Hall on January 10, 1931; this was only the second Ives symphonic work to be given a public professional performance, four years after the first two movements of the Fourth Symphony. They played it again in Boston on January 25, in Havana on March 18, and in Paris on June 6, the first performances of Ives's orchestral music in Latin America and Europe. Ives subsequently revised the chamber orchestra score for publication in 1935 by C. C. Birchard (version 3). This version was first performed on January 14, 1948, by the Boston Symphony Orchestra, conducted by their associate conductor Richard Burgin, at Boston's Symphony Hall; it had to wait for its premiere until Ives was better established as an orchestral composer, having won the Pulitzer Prize in 1947 for his Third Symphony. In 1974, James B. Sinclair reconstituted the full orchestration (version 4), drawing on Ives's original for the scoring and on the published version for continuity. It was published in 1976, followed by a critical edition of the first chamber orchestra version in 1979.[154] Versions 3 and 4 are most often performed; versions 1 and 2 are rarely played but have been recorded.

The "St. Gaudens" in Boston Common

The "St. Gaudens" in Boston Common (Col. Shaw and His Colored Regiment) commemorates the monument at the northeast corner of Boston Common, facing the statehouse across the street, designed by Augustus Saint-Gaudens and dedicated in 1897. The monument honors one of the first regiments of African American soldiers in the Union Army during the Civil War, the 54th Regiment Massachusetts Volunteer Infantry, and their white commander, Colonel Robert Gould Shaw, born in Boston to an abolitionist family. Ives said he began work on the piece in 1911–12, the fiftieth anniversary of the outbreak of the Civil War, although the surviving sketches and score-sketch are on paper datable no earlier than 1914 or 1915, and the full score dates to around 1919–21.[155] Ives had a personal connection to the subject not only through his father, who had served in the war, but through earlier generations of Iveses who were strong abolitionists.[156]

Formed in March 1863, the 54th Regiment trained during the spring, marched through Boston in May, traveled south, and on July 18 led the assault on Fort Wagner in South Carolina, in which Shaw died and almost half his men were killed, wounded, or captured. Ives suggests this series of events in the movement, which seems to form out of fragments, coalesces into a march (m. 35), builds to a loud passage that may represent the battle, and after the climax (m. 63) quickly fades to a quiet close.[157] The music also reflects the look of Saint-Gaudens's bronze, which depicts the regiment from the side, as if we were watching the soldiers marching in ranks with Shaw on horseback beside them, nearest to us. Shaw and the closest men are in fully rounded sculpture, soldiers just behind them in high relief, and those furthest from the viewer etched in bas relief or outline, fading into the flat surface behind them. In the same way, Ives varies the prominence of the layers in his music, setting some into relief by making them more audible or recognizable than others, while others recede into the hazy background.

The main melody in violin 1 is a patchwork of motives from Stephen Foster's parlor song *Old Black Joe*, his plantation song *Massa's in de Cold Ground*, and Henry Clay Work's Civil War song *Marching Through Georgia*. In this melody, Ives exploits motives the three tunes share—falling and rising minor thirds, and a major second followed by a minor third in the same direction—to create an almost seamless flow through overlap and subtle variation. The individual tunes are effaced, blended into a long-breathed, meandering melody that evokes the common style of pentatonic tunes shared by American songwriters in the mid-nineteenth century.[158] Another Civil War song that features the same motives, George F. Root's *The Battle Cry of Freedom*, plays a secondary role in the piece.

At the outset, the first violin melody unfolds over a bass ostinato of a rising minor third, derived from the source tunes, in an uneven rhythm that suggests a slow trudge. Then, at mm. 24–27, the ostinato stops and the violins paraphrase the first half of the chorus of *Old Black*

Joe ("I'm coming, I'm coming, for my head is bending low"). Recognizable fragments of the four source tunes also pop up from time to time in other instruments throughout the first section. The march at m. 35 is conveyed by *Street Beat* in the drums, which continues to the end of the piece; a more regular bass ostinato based on the falling major second and minor third from the source tunes; and a paraphrase in the violins of the first half of the chorus of *Marching Through Georgia* ("Hurrah! Hurrah! we bring the Jubilee! Hurrah! Hurrah! the flag that makes you free!"). After a brief episode in ragtime rhythms (m. 42), the next section (m. 48) builds to a climax, developing motives from *Marching Through Georgia* in upper winds and strings (especially the rising figure at "So we sang the chorus"). As the music swells to a peak of dynamics and density, Ives adds a countermelody based on the chorus of *The Battle Cry of Freedom* (at the words "The Union forever, Hurrah, boys, hurrah!") in mm. 58–62 in the trombone (piano in versions 2 and 3). The final section recalls previous material in reverse order, creating a kind of arch form. At m. 66, the march returns, now with most of the chorus of *The Battle Cry of Freedom* in the flute as a countermelody to the chorus of *Marching Through Georgia* in the first violins, sounding like the final contrapuntal combination of themes in a cumulative-form movement. Fragments of the verse of *Marching Through Georgia* (horn and clarinet, mm. 71–72) and of *Massa's in de Cold Ground* (violin 1, mm. 72–73) lead to material from the opening measures and a gradual diminuendo to silence.

All the source tunes are motivically interrelated, so that the movement is coherent even for a listener who recognizes none of the source melodies. These interrelationships show Ives's continual interest in motivic links and developing variation, which we have seen since his First Symphony, and his ability to weave multiple borrowed tunes into a unified tapestry by exploiting their common elements. For a listener who does recognize the songs or styles he borrows, there are further layers of meaning, as he represents the Black soldiers through ragtime style and Foster's songs, and their role in the 54th Regiment through songs about the Union military campaign. And if one knows the words for the songs, the segments Ives quotes most overtly are directly appropriate to the story told in Saint-Gaudens's sculpture and in this movement: "I'm coming, I'm coming"; "Hurrah! Hurrah! we bring the Jubilee!"; "The Union forever, Hurrah, boys, hurrah!"; "Hear dat mournful sound; All de darkeys am a-weeping."

The last text, from *Massa's in de Cold Ground*, may provoke a shudder today at Foster's depiction of slaves mourning their master, and perhaps a feeling of regret that Ives chose to represent the brave free men of the regiment, and the feelings they had for their commander, through songs created by a white composer for the entertainment of white audiences that embodied stereotypes of African Americans, rather than using their own songs. But his sincere admiration for the regiment's soldiers is evident, not only in the elegiac music, but also in the poem he crafted to accompany it and had printed in the score as a preface to this movement:

> Moving—Marching—Faces of Souls!
> Marked with generations of pain,
> Part-freers of a Destiny,
> Slowly, restlessly—swaying us on with you
> Towards other Freedom!
> The man on horseback, carved from
> A native quarry of the world Liberty
> And from what your country was made.
> You images of a Divine Law

> Carved in the shadow of a saddened heart—
> Never light abandoned—
> Of an age and of a nation.
> Above and beyond that compelling mass
> Rises the drum-beat of the common-heart
> In the silence of a strange and
> Sounding afterglow
> Moving—Marching—Faces of Souls![159]

As in the *Holidays Symphony*, the tonal plans in *Three Places in New England* are simple in overall structure even if complex in detail. *The "St. Gaudens" in Boston Common* starts and ends with an A-C ostinato in the bass, hinting at an A minor center, while the tune segments above it imply rapidly fluctuating keys (mm. 1–23, 63–65, and 76–end). The march sections have an E-E-D-B bass ostinato that leads back to A (mm. 35–41 and 66–72), suggesting a dominant-to-tonic resolution, while *Marching Through Georgia* above it is mostly in D major. The timpani's *Street Beat* is on A (m. 35 to end), which is also the apparent tone center of the ragtime section (mm. 42–52). The climax (mm. 53–63) includes three successively more emphatic cadences, each created through simultaneous rising and falling stepwise motions in an expanding wedge. These close respectively on E, A, and C, closely related tone centers that outline an A minor triad. Altogether, the music projects A minor, overlaid with tunes in other keys.

Putnam's Camp

The second movement, *Putnam's Camp, Redding, Connecticut*, commemorates the Revolutionary War through a sound picture of a place near Ives's summer home in West Redding, Connecticut. As the composer wrote in a program note published with the score,

> Near Redding Center, Conn., is a small park preserved as a Revolutionary Memorial; for here General Israel Putnam's soldiers had their winter quarters in 1778–1779. Long rows of stone camp fire-places still remain to stir a child's imagination. The hardships which the soldiers endured and the agitation of a few hot-heads to break camp and march to the Hartford Assembly for relief, is a part of Redding history.
> Once upon a "4th of July," some time ago, so the story goes, a child went there on a picnic, held under the auspices of the First Church and the Village Cornet Band. Wandering away from the rest of the children past the camp ground into the woods, he hopes to catch a glimpse of some of the old soldiers. As he rests on the hillside of laurels and hickories, the tunes of the band and the songs of the children grow fainter and fainter;—when—"mirabile dictu"—over the trees on the crest of the hill he sees a tall woman standing. She reminds him of a picture he has of the Goddess of Liberty,—but her face is sorrowful—she is pleading with the soldiers not to forget their "cause" and the great sacrifices they have made for it. But they march out of camp with fife and drum to a popular tune of the day. Suddenly a new national note is heard. Putnam is coming over the hills from the center,—the soldiers turn back and cheer. The little boy awakes, he hears the children's songs and runs down past the monument to "listen to the band" and join in the games and dances.
> The repertoire of national airs at that time was meagre. Most of them were of English origin. It is a curious fact that a tune very popular with the American soldiers was "The British Grenadiers." A captain in one of Putnam's regiments put it to words, which were sung for the first time in 1779 at a patriotic meeting in the Congregational Church in Redding Center; the text is both ardent and moving.[160]

In this piece, there are two levels of memory, and two functions for the place named in the title. In the middle of the movement, it is recalled, through a child's imagination, as a site where Revolutionary War soldiers camped and a potentially disastrous failure of morale was averted. The outer sections convey memories of the place as a park, a site of public celebration more than a century after the soldiers broke camp, framing the child's dream vision of the late eighteenth century with an adult's recollections of his childhood experiences at a picnic in the late nineteenth century.

Ives's movement embodies this program in specific musical terms. There are three main sections, depicting in turn the village band playing at the park, a dream sequence with a vision of soldiers marching, and a sudden return to the band concert and reality. *The British Grenadiers* appears first in fragments and then gradually comes together as the principal countermelody to the main theme. Ives took the outer sections from an earlier piece called *Country Band March* (composed between ca. 1905 and ca. 1914), a whimsical and fond look at the foibles of an amateur band, and the middle section from *Overture and March "1776"* (ca. 1903–7), first conceived as the overture for an opera about the Revolutionary War. He then combined elements of both source pieces in a raucous closing passage. Ives dated *Putnam's Camp* 1912, although, as in the case of *The "St. Gaudens" in Boston Common*, the surviving sketches apparently date from circa 1914 to circa 1921.[161]

The movement starts with a blast, a loud dissonant chord (a typically Ivesian combination of two augmented triads joined by a diminished triad) that marches in parallel motion down by half steps and then by whole steps. From this the band emerges, playing a brief introduction and then the opening strain of a march in B-flat (m. 6).[162] The marks of amateur performance are everywhere, including dropped or added beats, wrong notes, missed cues, and improvised solos. The wind instruments overlay phrases from *The British Grenadiers* (mm. 14–17) and a military call (bassoon, mm. 19–20), and, at a varied repetition of the march tune (m. 27), Ives piles on a collage of snippets from marches, popular songs, and patriotic tunes appropriate to a Fourth of July celebration: *Street Beat* (bass and snare drums); John Philip Sousa's *Semper fideles* (tuba) and *Liberty Bell March* (viola, clarinet 2, and oboes); Foster's *Massa's in de Cold Ground* (flutes and clarinet 1); the fiddle tune *Arkansas Traveler* (trumpets); *Marching Through Georgia* (verse in flute 1 and clarinet 1, mm. 30–31, and chorus in violins and violas, mm. 31–34 and 36); *The Battle Cry of Freedom* (trumpet 1 and trombone 1, mm. 32–34); and *Yankee Doodle* (mm. 34–35, divided between trumpet, piccolo, and strings).[163] After a climax comes a softer theme in C major, sounding like a contrasting trio strain in a march (m. 37), with bits of *Marching Through Georgia* thrown in (verse in flute, m. 47, chorus in violins, mm. 43–44 and 47–50). No band sounds like this, but Ives captures the memory of an amateur band concert by exaggerating its mistakes and high spirits and by adding to the march a collage of other tunes the band might play at such a celebration. As the first section draws to a close, the band music quiets and slows in gradually descending chromatic harmonies, as if fading into the distance as the child walks away from the picnic (mm. 50–63).

A soft dissonant chord sustained in strings and arpeggiated in the piano (m. 64) signals the dream or vision in the middle section of the movement. The pleas of Liberty are suggested by an oboe melody (m. 67), the soldiers by two groups of instruments marching to the rhythm of the *Street Beat* in different tempos. Strings present the pattern in the foreground every two measures (m. 65), and other instruments—piano, snare drum, bassoon, and viola 2—state it every measure and a half (m. 68), quietly, as if at a distance, joined by the trumpet playing snippets of *The British Grenadiers*.[164] As the tempo gradually increases and the distant march continues, in violin 1 (mm. 74–77) and winds (mm. 80–81) we hear bits of melody paraphrased from the post-Revolutionary patriotic song *Hail! Columbia* (1798, with words by Joseph Hopkinson and music from Philip Phile's 1793 *The President's March*). The distant marchers stop, and the chromatic harmony continues over a pulsing E♭ in the bass. Then "suddenly, a new national note is heard": a jaunty melody in the brass (m. 89), echoed by the strings and joined by phrases from *The British Grenadiers* in the flute (mm. 91–97), representing Putnam coming over the hill and back to camp. *Hail! Columbia* returns, louder than ever (mm. 103–8, trumpets), over a pulsing D pedal, and the dissonances, rhythmic density, and dynamic level swell to a peak as the soldiers cheer (mm. 107–13).

A sonic exuviation (m. 114) brings us suddenly back to the strain that suggested the trio of the march, now in G, as the child awakes and again hears the band. Ragtime syncopations lead to a new dissonant climax in pulsing syncopated chords (m. 124) and a return to the march theme (m. 126), now in A-flat with a countermelody in the winds assembled from bits of *The British Grenadiers*, later taken up by the trumpet first in fragments (mm. 130–33) and then in a more direct statement (mm. 134–37). A final reprise of the march theme (m. 144) with snippets of *The British Grenadiers* (violin 1, mm. 144–45 and 148–55), *Marching Through Georgia* (flute, m. 147), and a bugle call (trumpet, 154–56) leads to a climactic swirl of dissonance, the opening notes of *The Star-Spangled Banner* (tutti, mm. 162–63), and a final ***ffff*** yawp.

The Housatonic at Stockbridge

The last movement, *The Housatonic at Stockbridge*, had two inspirations, a personal experience and a poem. Ives wrote in *Memos* that he was spurred to write it by a walk along the river with his wife Harmony in the summer of 1908, soon after their marriage: "We walked in the meadows along the river, and heard the distant singing from the church across the river. The mist had not entirely left the river bed, and the colors, the running water, the banks and elm trees were something that one would always remember. Robert Underwood Johnson, in his poem, *The Housatonic at Stockbridge*, paints this scene beautifully."[165]

Ives found "To the Housatonic at Stockbridge" in a collection of Johnson's *Poems* published that same year, 1908. He combined poem and scene in an orchestral song without words, capturing the mists, trees, and currents in the water through several layers of ostinatos over slowly moving harmonies, and representing "the distant singing from the church across the river" (not mentioned in the poem) in the principal melody, paraphrased from a hymn tune to fit words excerpted from Johnson's poem. From an initial 1908 sketch for instruments, he created a draft for voice and piano by circa 1914, elaborated the orchestral version circa 1913–19, scored the piece circa 1919, and adapted it in 1921 as a song that he published the next year in his collection *114 Songs*.[166]

The opening orchestral texture is extraordinary. In a slow quadruple meter, six layers appear in different registers, dynamic levels, relative speeds, and rhythmic groupings, creating a wash of sound that evokes the mists and rippling water. In the foreground, marked between ***p*** and ***mp***, basses and second cellos sustain an open fifth C♯–G♯ in repeated whole notes while first cellos play a slow C-sharp major baritone-register melody above them, moving mostly in half notes. An octave higher, ***pp*** and muted, first violas play an ostinato, seven quarter notes long, that moves in waves through the chromatic notes between E and C♯ in a repeating pattern of triplet quarter and triplet eighth notes. Next higher and softer is violin 4, ***ppp*** and muted, with a chromatic sixteenth-note figure that repeats, transposed and slightly varied, every three eighth notes. In the far background, higher and softer still (***pppp*** and muted), are violins 2 and 3, playing diatonic tremolo eighths, and violin 1, with a chromatic undulating figure in a rhythm of ten sixteenths (a decatuplet) in the time of each three-eighth-note grouping below. The figures in violins 1, 2, and 3 all repeat, varied, every three eighth notes, transposed up or down in lockstep with violin 4. All the upper layers are dissonant against each other and against the C-sharp major music below, setting each layer on a different musical plane. There is no better example in the literature of how to create the effect of space and depth through layering, and the linking of higher register with softer dynamic level and greater activity perfectly evokes the deep and slowly moving river, its gentle surface currents, and the lighter wisps of mist and more quickly fluttering leaves above the water.

Over this bed of sound enters the main melody of the movement in an alto range, **mp** to **mf**, alternating between horn and English horn, doubled by second violas. This extraordinarily beautiful melody is paraphrased from the pentatonic hymn tune *Dorrnance*, evoking the hymn singing from the church across the river, but reshaped to fit the words Ives selected from Johnson's ode to the Housatonic River.

Ives whittled down Johnson's sixty-six lines in four stanzas to these fourteen:

> Contented river! in thy dreamy realm—
> The cloudy willow and the plumy elm: . . .
>
> Thou beautiful! From every dreamy hill
> What eye but wanders with thee at thy will, . . .
>
> Contented river! and yet over-shy
> To mask thy beauty from the eager eye;
> Hast thou a thought to hide from field and town?
> In some deep current of the sunlit brown . . .
>
> Ah! there's a restive ripple, and the swift
> Red leaves—September's firstlings—faster drift; . . .
> Wouldst thou away, dear stream? Come, whisper near!
> I also of much resting have a fear;
> Let me tomorrow thy companion be
> By fall and shallow to the adventurous sea![167]

Each of Ives's brief stanzas is set to a different paraphrase of the hymn tune, and the opening cello line paraphrases the last four measures of the tune.[168] Thus, the shape of the whole movement parallels a congregation singing a hymn with four verses after the organ plays the hymn's closing phrase as an introduction to give them the pitch. The first stanza (m. 7) is closest to the hymn in contour, in D-flat major over supporting tonal harmony in the lower strings and low brass (enharmonically in C-sharp major). Each later stanza of Ives's melody is more distant from the hymn than the previous one: more complex, with more omissions, more internal variation and repetition, and—in the last two verses—added notes, often chromatic and scalar in contrast to the pentatonic hymn tune. Each stanza also becomes more harmonically adventurous, evoking the increasingly restive river as it heads toward the sea. The second stanza (m. 15) alternates D-flat with D major. The third (m. 23), with the melody now in unison violins, is in E major over C-sharp minor/major harmonies and a more varied background with harps, celesta, and winds. The last stanza (m. 33), mostly in horn and trumpet (sometimes in parallel fourths), modulates quickly through several keys as the other instruments grow ever more active, chromatic, and dissonant, capturing the growing restlessness of the river and building to a huge climax. After a sonic exuviation we hear the quiet, muted strings play one last statement of the melody's opening motive in E major, harmonized with a C♯ minor seventh and a F♯ major ninth chord. This brief wisp of music reminds us of the hymn heard over the river and hints at an amen progression, unifying the entire scene through a sense that to experience nature is itself to experience the divine. The final hymn fragment and chord progression also restore a sense of tonal hearing after the preceding chromaticism without providing a real cadence, producing an open ending that by this time was typical for Ives.

Reviews

A perceptive review by Stephen Somervel in the *Boston Herald* of the Boston premiere called *Three Places in New England*

> modern in the exact manner of those painters whose canvases—so redolent of this chaotic age—are a patchwork of jagged fragments overlapping, dovetailing, with an added complexity which painting cannot rival, namely that of a bewilderingly crowded simultaneity, an extraordinary contrapuntal freedom. This is especially true of the second of the pieces, in which the American village band is not so much parodied as portrayed in a jumble of fragments and splinters of popular band tunes, dancing in an all-pervading cacophony that somehow does not seem meaningless. In the first of the pieces, inspired by the Boston Common memorial to Col. Shaw and his colored regiment, the obscure and brooding suggestion of Negro tunes is mournfully punctuated by a muffled drum-beat.[169]

Paul Le Flem, reviewing Slonimsky's Paris concert in *Comoedia*, wrote that Ives

> seems to have created for himself, before the *Rite of Spring*, a style whose audacities place its author among the pioneers. Compared to his compatriots, he appears to be the most spontaneously gifted musician, whose savage daring, though sometimes awkward, is never in contradiction with the aspirations of his feeling. . . .
>
> Charles Ives's *Three Places in New England* is by turns humorous, with an amiable sincerity, and at other times a little heavy. He is as knowledgeable as his colleagues and manipulates polytonality without letting it blow up in his hands. But he knows how to add to his craft something sensitive, fresh, and alive which is not a mere extravagance. There is an infinite sweetness in the first movement, in which a quiet distress emerges from a tranquil harmonic background. *The Village March* [*Putnam's Camp*], whose rhythm is curiously displaced due to a late eighth-note, builds up energy and does not eschew the common vulgarity of a popular waltz. As for the last movement, at the opening the polytonal divisions of the muted violins leave room for a theme of adorable freshness, evoking large spaces, but he does not delay in enriching his sonorities. Then there is a change of mood and all of the cacophony suddenly dives into a final and brief pianissimo.[170]

ORCHESTRAL SET NO. 2

Orchestral Set No. 2 has never been as widely performed and recorded as *Three Places in New England*. There are logistical reasons for this, for the set requires a large orchestra with the addition of a zither, an organ, accordions, and (briefly) an offstage choir. There are also historical reasons, as *Three Places in New England* was his first complete multimovement orchestral piece to be performed and published, and it helped to make his reputation. But the lesser prominence of the Second Orchestral Set no doubt is also due to its lack of a catchy title. If Ives had called it *The Power of Music* or *The Voice of the People*, perhaps it would be more widely known. Certainly, its final movement, which Ives called "one of the best that I've done," deserves to be heard more often.[171] Composed and scored between 1909 and 1929 and professionally copied around 1930, the set was not played until 1967, by the Chicago Symphony Orchestra under Morton Gould, and not published until 1999, the last of Ives's completed symphonic works to be premiered and printed.[172]

An Elegy to Our Forefathers

Ives composed the first movement, *An Elegy to Our Forefathers*, between 1909 and 1916 and orchestrated it between 1923 and 1929. He had earlier considered calling it *Overture to Stephen Foster* or *An Elegy for Stephen Foster*, and it is imbued with the spirit of Foster in his most solemn and sentimental mood.[173] In sound, sources, and effect, it closely resembles *The "St. Gaudens" in Boston Common*. In a single unbroken gesture, the music begins softly, builds in volume and density, and then gradually fades away, like a procession that appears in the distance, slowly approaches, passes nearby, and moves on. Interlocking ostinatos in cycles of different length create a bed of sound that suggests at once a very slow march and a continuous flow: a bass ostinato of a falling and rising minor third (D♭-B♭-D♭) in irregular rhythm, repeating every six beats; a bass drum and gong pattern, repeating every ten beats; and then more active figurations in cellos, piano, triangle, violas, and harp until all the notes of the chromatic scale except A and C are in constant circulation.

Laid on top are three almost continuous strands of melody. First to enter and last to exit—but also the softest of the three—is the zither, playing a patchwork of two Foster tunes in E major, harmonized with quartal chords that rise and fall with the melody.[174] The chorus of *Old Black Joe* ("I'm coming, I'm coming, for my head is bending low," m. 3) gradually blends into the opening of the verse of *Massa's in de Cold Ground* (mm. 13–21), and then the latter's complete chorus (mm. 21–31) leads back to the first half of the chorus of *Old Black Joe* (mm. 37–40). Both are mostly pentatonic melodies that rise to the upper octave and descend by step, a resemblance Ives exploits to interweave them. At the dynamic crest (mm. 20–29) the zither part adds two countermelodies in D-flat major below, both based on hymns: the opening of *Nettleton* (another mostly pentatonic tune with similar melodic gestures) and a meandering figure paraphrased from *Throw Out the Life-Line*.

The second strand to enter, and the most prominent of the three, is the movement's principal melody, in violins and trumpets and in D-flat major (mm. 13–35). It is based not on a Foster tune but on the chorus of William Bradbury's *Jesus Loves Me*, which is also pentatonic, begins with the same melodic contour as the chorus of *Old Black Joe* (5-3-5-6-8, in a different rhythm) and ends with the same melodic gesture as *Massa's in de Cold Ground* (1-3-2-1). Thus the salute to Stephen Foster embraces an entire style of nineteenth-century American melody that blends the pentatonic frame of Scotch and Irish folk songs with the smooth sentimentality of parlor songs and can be heard across genres from plantation songs to hymns. As he does for the zither line, Ives mixes in other tunes: what may be the opening of the spiritual *Nobody Knows the Trouble I've Seen* in C major (m. 15, trombone and violin 1), and a bit of *Massa's in de Cold Ground* in G major (mm. 19–21, violin 1 and bells).

Finally, the flute, doubled by part of the violins, adds a descant (mm. 19–34), mostly based on *Massa's in de Cold Ground* (changing keys from D-flat to G to C major), with a few quick bugle call figures thrown in (m. 20, in C-flat, B-flat, A, and F). The fanfares mark the moment where the texture reaches its greatest complexity, with the addition of the flute descant and the zither's countermelodies. The music swells to a dynamic high point (m. 25) and slightly faster tempo, although there is never a real sense of climax. As the principal tune in violin 1 and trumpet 1 comes to a cadence (m. 31), the music begins gradually to grow calmer and slower. At the end, in a kind of coda (m. 37), the strings sustain and embellish a D♭-major triad, the zither plays its chorus of *Old Black Joe* in E major (still harmonized by quartal chords), the overlapping ostinatos simplify and adjust to repeating regularly every measure, and the bells and harp add the opening of the chorus of *Massa's in de Cold Ground* in G major as a new offbeat ostinato. The bass ostinato changes from D♭-B♭-D♭ to D♭-B♭-E♭♭, with an option to play the last note a quarter-tone lower, which adds a dark neighbor tone to the tonic D♭. Gradually, each layer fades and disintegrates into two- or three-note repeating figures, leaving faint sparks of dissonance against the sustained D♭-major triad. The continuous bass ostinato, D-flat-major main melody, and closing triad all create a sense of harmonic stasis combined with gradual clarification as the other voices enter, swell, and disappear. The movement offers a stunning demonstration of how tonal and polytonal elements, and diatonic and chromatic material, can combine to create a powerful emotional effect.

Ives is often most closely identified with his rambunctious side, as found in pieces like *Putnam's Camp* and *The Fourth of July*. Yet the quiet Ives represented by *An Elegy to Our Forefathers* is just as original, compelling, and characteristic, and this movement is utterly hypnotic and mesmerizing. In its own way, *Elegy* is as complex as the Fourth Symphony in its rhythm, texture, and sound while conveying a very different feeling.

The Rockstrewn Hills

Ives derived the second movement, *The Rockstrewn Hills Join in the People's Outdoor Meeting*, from the first three of his four *Ragtime Dances* for theater orchestra, especially the third. According to Ives, he began improvising and composing pieces based on ragtime rhythms during his college years, created the *Ragtime Dances* for piano in 1902–4, and scored them in 1911. Yet the surviving sketches are all on music paper not available before 1912; perhaps Ives developed versions by memory at the keyboard before working them out on paper. According to Gayle Sherwood Magee, this movement was sketched circa 1914–19, the score-sketch is from around 1923, and the full score was made between 1923 and 1929.[175]

Like the *Ragtime Dances*, *The Rockstrewn Hills* draws on the rhythmic character of ragtime, sometimes by echoing typical ragtime figuration but more often by extrapolating the ideas of syncopation and of metric conflict to create complex rhythmic patterns. Although ragtime is a secular tradition, Ives's main thematic material is drawn from three gospel songs, reflecting his combination of American popular music and Protestant church music within the European classical genre of the orchestral tone poem. The gospel songs represent the outdoor revival in Ives's title, and the jolts and bumps of the ragtime rhythms and metric shifts may suggest both the fervency of the people and the rocky landscape around them.

Each of the three source hymns is in verse-refrain form, and *The Rockstrewn Hills*, like every movement of the *Ragtime Dances*, reflects that form: a "verse" based primarily on George A. Minor's *Bringing in the Sheaves*, combined with elements from the verse of *Happy Day*, is followed by a much shorter refrain (which Ives calls "Chorus") that states the refrain of Lewis Hartsough's *Welcome Voice* ("I am coming Lord!"), slightly varied (mm. 172–83). The verse section is primarily in 2/4, like most ragtime, and the refrain is in 3/4 to suit the hymn. *The Rockstrewn Hills* is unlike the *Ragtime Dances* in that its refrain melody also appears in the verse section, at first in varied fragments and then progressively more complete, giving the movement the shape of cumulative form. All three hymns are melodically related, each ending both verse and refrain with the same cadential figure (2-1-3-2-1); in addition, the first two share a prominent rising figure (5-1-2-3) that appears twice at the beginning of *Happy Day* ("O happy day that fixed my choice") and three times in *Bringing in the Sheaves*, including near the end of both verse and refrain, at the words "We will come rejoicing." Moreover, the two principal tunes, *Bringing in the Sheaves* and the refrain of *Welcome Voice*, both begin with a strong I-IV progression that Ives emphasizes in this movement. As he did in other symphonic works based on multiple borrowings, Ives exploits the similarities between his source melodies to create a motivically coherent movement that evokes other music for listeners who are familiar with the hymns.

A brief, lumbering introduction alternates bass notes and chords in a repeated I^9-IV^9 progression in A major, overlaid with hints of *Welcome Voice* in the winds in other keys (mm. 4–5 and 9). Then a paraphrase of the verse of *Bringing in the Sheaves* appears in a chromatically decorated E major (m. 11), combining syncopations that suggest ragtime together with added beats and shifts to triplets and triple meter. There follows a kind of developmental section (m. 35) that meanders through many keys while alternating stylized ragtime figurations with variations of fragments from *Bringing in the Sheaves*, including the chorus as well as the verse. Two more extended paraphrases of the verse (mm. 77–87 and 88–103) lead to a climax, then a quieter contrasting section (m. 103) and a varied recollection of the opening introduction, back in A major (m. 117). Through all this, variants of *Welcome Voice* continue to appear: at first decorated with the dotted neighbor-tone figure it will feature in the chorus (mm. 18–19 and 23–25 in winds and 25–27, 32, and 39–42 in violins); then stated more plainly (mm. 48–50 in violins); more extended and varied (mm. 77–82 in trumpet), perhaps hinting at *The Girl I Left behind Me*; and finally unadorned as the leading line in violin 1 in A major (mm. 127–32), with *Rock-a-bye Baby* as countermelody in winds and piano. A varied reprise of the opening E-major paraphrase of *Bringing in the Sheaves* (m. 137) culminates in the most direct borrowing from that hymn's chorus (at m. 148, again with a variant of *Welcome Voice* in the winds). After an extended cadence and a repeated, chromatically and rhythmically salted dominant seventh chord on E, the climax of the movement (the "Chorus") arrives with the refrain of *Welcome Voice* in A major (m. 172) over ragtime-inspired ostinatos, which fade and slow to a quiet close.[176]

From Hanover Square North

The Finale bears the longest title Ives ever gave anything: *From Hanover Square North, at the End of a Tragic Day, the Voice of the People Again Arose*. According to Ives, it memorializes his experience on Friday afternoon, May 7, 1915, the day the *Lusitania* was sunk by a German torpedo, when people's feelings about this national tragedy, the loss of life, and the threat of war were distilled through group singing. He was heading home from work in downtown Manhattan, taking the northbound elevated train from Hanover Square Station.

> As I came on the platform, there was quite a crowd waiting for the trains, which had been blocked lower down, and while waiting there, a hand-organ or hurdy-gurdy was playing in the street below. Some workmen sitting on the side of the tracks began to whistle the tune, and others began to sing or hum the refrain. A workman with a shovel over his shoulder came on the platform and joined in the chorus, and the next man, a Wall Street banker with white spats and a cane, joined in it, and finally it seemed to me that everybody was singing this tune, and they didn't seem to be singing in fun, but as a natural outlet for what their feelings had been going through all day long. There was a feeling of dignity all through this. The hand-organ man seemed to sense this and wheeled the organ nearer the platform and kept it up fortissimo and the

chorus sounded out as though every man in New York must be joining in it. Then the first train came in and everyone crowded in, and the song gradually died out, but the effect on the crowd still showed. Almost nobody talked—the people acted as though they might be coming out of a church service. In going uptown, occasionally little groups would start singing or humming the tune.

Now what was the tune? It wasn't a Broadway hit, it wasn't a musical comedy air, it wasn't a waltz tune or a dance tune or an opera tune or a classical tune, or a tune that all of them probably knew. It was only the refrain of an old Gospel Hymn that had stirred many people of past generations. It was nothing but—*In the Sweet Bye and Bye*. It wasn't a tune written to be sold, or written by a professor of music—but by a man who was but giving out an experience.

The third movement is based on this, fundamentally, and comes from that "L" station. It has its secondary themes [and] rhythms, but widely related, and its general make-up would reflect the sense of many people living, working, and occasionally going through the same deep experience, together. It would give the ever changing multitudinous feeling of life that one senses in the city.[177]

Ives recalled that the piece was completed and scored by fall 1915, although the sketches suggest he continued work for the next few years, completing the score-sketch around 1919 and the full score by 1929.[178]

In the Sweet By-and-By was the perfect song for the occasion, a gospel hymn offering reassurance about the afterlife whose hopeful refrain and central image—"In the sweet by-and-by, We shall meet on that beautiful shore"—must have resonated with the crowd grieving for innocent lives lost at sea just miles from the Irish shoreline. And cumulative form, which Ives had used in the Third Symphony and several other works, was the perfect form for a symphonic movement based on this event, for its process of developing from fragments and paraphrases toward a complete theme parallels the sense Ives describes of many voices gradually coming together into a definitive statement. Table 4.9 shows the structure of the movement. Its seven continuous sections are delineated by the thematic process and by a series of pedal points that help to give the piece harmonic shape, moving from a center on D minor/major for the first five sections to F major for the last two. Unlike other cumulative-form movements we have seen, there is no countermelody, as none would be appropriate to the event.

Before *In the Sweet By-and-By* first appears, an introduction scored for an offstage ensemble (Distant Choir) sets the scene, evoking city sounds and the day's mournful mood. The murmur of traffic and other urban noises is suggested by interwoven, chromatically tinged ostinatos in solo muted strings, piano, harp, and chimes that continue with subtle changes throughout the movement; most emphasize notes from the chords of D minor/major or F major, but any sense of key is blurred by persistent chromatic neighbor tones and the endlessly cycling haze of sound. A unison chorus intones the opening words of the Anglican Te Deum using a variant of the Gregorian psalm tone in the Hypodorian mode: "We praise Thee O God. We acknowledge Thee to be the Lord. All the Earth doth worship Thee." The recitation on F and cadences on D foretell the pitch centers to come while establishing D minor as the local key. A muted horn, metrically displaced, softly plays a sorrowful melody in D major, emphasizing the semitones F♯–G and F♯–E♯ to heighten the sense of grief and hint at alternating D major and minor. This tune is melodically related to *In the Sweet By-and-By* in both form (AABB) and contour and may be a paraphrase of it, a heartbroken counterpart to the brightly optimistic hymn.

The second section begins at m. 20 as the horn melody comes to a close and the low strings of the main orchestra enter over the continuing ostinatos of the Distant Choir. First the

Table 4.9 Cumulative Form in *From Hanover Square North*

Main theme (MT): *In the Sweet By-and-By*

Sect.	Meas.	Music	Pedal point	Key/implied keys of main melodies
1	1	*Te Deum* (unison chorus), distant Hr. melody first half; Distant Choir (offstage ensemble) plays softly throughout movement		D minor/major
	12	Distant Hr. melody second half		
2	20	MT verse opening phrase, varied (Vlc., Clar.)	D	B♭ major
	28	Paraphrase of MT verse opening phrase (Hr.)	D	B♭ major
	33	MT verse, varied (Vla./Vlc., Clar., Pno.)	D	B♭+A♭, then F+A♭+D
3	40	MT verse spun out (Vln. 1 and 2, Vla., Vlc., Clar. 1 and 2, Pno.)	C	D+A♭+B♭
	45	Same	B♭	D+A♭+B♭
4	56	Varied paraphrase of MT verse opening phrase (Hr., Pno.)	A	D
	62	MT verse spun out (Vln. 1 and 2, Hr., Pno.)	A	D+F+A♭
5	68	Refrain of MT, almost complete (Vln. 1 and 2, Tpt.)	D	D+F
6	83	Refrain of MT in imitation (Vln. 1 and 2, Flt.), with *Massa's in de Cold Ground* (Vla.)	F	D+F (*Massa* in B♭)
	96	Cadence and extension	C	F
7	102	**Refrain of MT with harmonization** (Tutti)	F	F+B
	109	Fragments of MT (Vln.) and fade	F	F+B♭

cellos and then a clarinet state the opening phrase of *In the Sweet By-and-By*, rhythmically augmented and slightly varied, in B-flat over a tremolo D in the basses. The dotted rhythm characteristic of the hymn is missing from its usual positions, displaced to m. 24 in piano and cellos. A more remote paraphrase of the same phrase appears in the orchestral horn (m. 28), suffused with dotted figures and flavored with the repeated notes and half-steps of the distant horn melody. Then variants of the whole hymn verse, still augmented and rhythmically altered, appear in viola and cello (in B-flat modulating to F), clarinet (B-flat modulating to D), and piano (in A-flat). As the melodic contour lengthens, gradually the hymn becomes more recognizable. In the third section (m. 40), the bass tremolo descends through C and B♭ while the violins spin out a long variant of the hymn verse in D, intertwining with other variants in A-flat (clarinet 1 and piano) and B-flat (clarinet 2, violas, and cellos). When the bass reaches A to mark the fourth section (m. 56), the dynamics rise to *f* and the orchestral horn, joined by piano, plays a variant of its earlier paraphrase, followed by more spinning out of the verse with violins in D, horn in F, and piano in A-flat. The coexistence of different versions of the hymn, in different keys, rhythms, and timbres, suggests the many voices in the crowd, singing together but not quite in unison.

The remaining three sections focus on the refrain of the hymn and evoke the gradual coming together of the crowd. The bass tremolo drops to D (m. 68), and the violins sing out most of the hymn's refrain in D major, close to its original rhythm but rhythmically augmented with added dotted figures punctuating the long notes. Meanwhile, the trumpet plays a rhythmic variant of the refrain in F. Then the pedal point rises to F (m. 83), which becomes the new tonal center. Here in the sixth section the violins again play the refrain in D, this time completing it, while the flute follows a measure behind in F. Meanwhile, softer and in B-flat, violas play the "Down in de cornfield" phrase from *Massa's in de Cold Ground*, which Ives also used in Symphony No. 2, Symphony No. 4, *Washington's Birthday, The "St. Gaudens" in Boston Common, Putnam's Camp, An Elegy to Our Forefathers*, and *The Rockstrewn Hills*. Certainly, the idea of a "mournful sound" is appropriate here. But because of how often Ives borrows this tune—always including this particular phrase, and usually only this phrase—it is closely identified with him. It seems plausible that he included it here as a sign that he was present on the elevated train platform.

An extension (m. 96) with ostinatos circling *poco agitando* over a C pedal builds momentum and leads to the final section (m. 102), the full-throated, climactic presentation of the refrain of *In the Sweet By-and-By* in F major in most of the orchestra. It is embellished with slightly off-key interjections, layered with background ostinatos, and combined with metrically offset renditions of the hymn by one or more accordions in F major and by flutes and clarinet in B major, a paraphrase of *Ewing* ("Jerusalem, the golden") by Alexander Ewing (1830–95) in the organ, and a snippet of *My Old Kentucky Home* (cello, mm. 108–9). After the complete statement, the orchestra suddenly quiets (m. 109), parts of the refrain repeat in violin 2 (in F) and high in violin 1 (in B-flat), and the music fades with gradually disintegrating repeating figures over an F-major triad, evoking the crowd dispersing while quietly humming bits of the hymn.

The layering of multiple strands of music, the many ostinatos, the use of a hymn tune as a theme, the overlay of different variants in different keys, the cumulative form—all neatly portray the incident Ives describes, using tools he had perfected over the years, as if that event on the elevated train platform encapsulated everything he was prepared to do. The music does not represent every detail in his program, but it captures the spirit of strangers joining in communion through song on a tragic day, by means of a musical structure that would make perfect sense even if Ives had never explained what inspired it. No wonder he thought it was one of the best things he had ever done.

Although Ives gave it no overarching title, the Second Orchestral Set is as unified in theme as the First. Whereas the three movements of Orchestral Set No. 1 are all about places, those of No. 2 are ultimately about the power of music, and especially of song, to move our emotions and stir our souls: the feelings and memories evoked by nineteenth-century songs and hymns, the spirit of awe and celebration generated by the singing at an outdoor revival, and the way joining in song can draw people together and express common feelings. It is a fitting capstone to Ives's career-long celebration of his musical roots through his symphonic works.

ORCHESTRAL SET NO. 3

In the fall of 1918, Ives had a health crisis that he described as a heart attack but was in fact a diagnosis of diabetes. At that time diabetes was a virtual death sentence, giving him a life expectancy of five to fifteen years at most, and the only remedy was a starvation diet very low in carbohydrates. Before he began taking insulin in 1930, Ives dropped from 160 to 110 pounds, with profound effects on his health and vigor.[179] In the aftermath of the diagnosis, face to face with his mortality, Ives set out to complete and get into print and performance the major works he had composed or sketched over the previous decade, starting with the *Concord*

Sonata and *114 Songs* and continuing with Symphony No. 4, the *Holidays Symphony*, and the first two orchestral sets.

The only orchestral work Ives began after his diagnosis was his Third Orchestral Set, whose three movements he conceived and partially sketched in 1919. He seems to have interrupted work on it for a few years, picked it up again around 1925–26, and then left it unfinished. As his wife Harmony told John Kirkpatrick, soon after they had moved into a new house in 1926, "he came downstairs one day and with tears in his eyes said that he couldn't seem to compose any more—nothing would go well, nothing sounded right."[180] He added a few notations to the sketches over the next twenty-five years but never completed it, apparently dissatisfied. In his 1980 MA thesis, David Porter transcribed the sketches and produced a realization of the first movement, for which Ives had finished sketches of each section and a partial score-sketch.[181] In 2008, a complete realization of the first two movements by Porter and the third movement by Nors Josephson was released on CD, but the score remains unpublished.[182]

Ives planned Orchestral Set No. 3 along the same lines as the earlier orchestral sets, with two slow movements around a central fast movement. All feature the multiple borrowing, multiple layers, and dissonant harmonic language characteristic of the other orchestral sets, but only the second movement carries a title. The first movement is the most finished in the sketches, laid out in five sections, all more or less complete even where it remained for Porter to fully work out the texture and scoring. It is a collage-like movement based on portions of eight hymns, of which *The Shining Shore* is most prominent, and has an arc of gradually increasing and then decreasing density and dynamic level, a pattern akin to that of the first movements of the other two sets.[183] The second movement, *An Afternoon* or *During Camp Meetin' Week—One Secular Afternoon (in Bethel)*, is another collage, borrowing almost two dozen tunes, more secular than sacred. It begins with hymn fragments, evoking the spirit of an outdoor revival with music softer and more dissonant than the middle movement of the Second Orchestral Set. Then it switches tone entirely, with active dissonant ostinatos in the strings (modeled on those from Ives's *Yale-Princeton Football Game*); a flurry of popular tunes that ends with a bit of *Alexander* (as paraphrased in Ives's Study No. 20 for piano), a ragtime song by Harry Von Tilzer (1872–1946); and then a band playing the verse of *Columbia, the Gem of the Ocean* twice (in passages adapted respectively from the trio of Ives's *Overture and March "1776"* and from an early version of *The Fourth of July*) with a collage of other tunes between and around the two renditions. The sketches for the third movement are more fragmentary than those for the other two but are skillfully woven together in the realization by Josephson, who added relatively few notes. The most remarkable part of the movement is its soft, slowly developing opening, with a delicious use of the harp under sustained high notes. From this texture emerge more than half a dozen hymn fragments, mostly Ives favorites such as *Woodworth* and *The Shining Shore*, and a section based on a theme from his *Robert Browning Overture*.

In its fully realized form, the Third Orchestral Set has its charms, including some extraordinary moments and sounds, but it is no rival to the other orchestral sets or to the symphonies. The passages and themes recycled from earlier Ives pieces, along with the many echoes of earlier sounds and techniques, suggest that the composer was running out of ideas. In a letter to Nicolas Slonimsky, Harmony Ives wrote, "It wasn't lack of audience & appreciation that made Mr. Ives stop composing. It just happened—the War & the complete breakdown in health. He had worked tremendously hard in his quarry all those years & exhausted the vein I suppose. I am always hoping he may open a new vein & he may—His ideas are by no means exhausted, but there are the physical disabilities to be contended with."[184]

Her hope that he would find a new vein of rich ore in his quarry went unrealized. But we can be grateful for what he had found in his earlier explorations, and for the consummate craft with which he shaped that ore into works we treasure.

Conclusion

Because most of Ives's symphonic works lay unperformed for years, their greatest influence was felt not by the next generation, that of Aaron Copland (1900–90) and Roy Harris, but by those who came to maturity from the 1940s to the 1980s. And because Ives's music came to light in reverse chronological order, his deep roots in the European symphonic tradition and his mastery of traditional compositional craft were not immediately recognized; the highly individual flavor of his music made it seem that he was a wholly original American voice. John Cage (1912–92) observed in 1964 that "Ives's relevance increases as time goes on. . . . And now that we have a music that doesn't depend on European musical history, Ives seems like the beginning of it."[185]

By example, Ives gave composers who encountered his music permission to try something new: to combine American vernacular idioms with European art traditions, as Leonard Bernstein did in his symphonies and operas; to create music whose metrically independent layers could sometimes overwhelm the listener, as Karlheinz Stockhausen (1928–2007) did in *Gruppen* and other works; to break the rules and violate the expectations of the European tradition, as Cage and the postwar avant-garde did, and as Frank Zappa (1940–93) and other younger avant-garde composers continued to do well into the 1980s. But by then music historians were tracing his roots back to common practice and began to see even his most radical works, like the Fourth Symphony, as personal extensions of the Romantic impulse—bursting boundaries, yes, but bursting out of a traditional symphonic frame. Composers in recent decades, such as John Corigliano (b. 1938) in his Symphony No. 1 and *The Ghosts of Versailles*, John Adams (b. 1947) in *On the Transmigration of Souls* and *My Father Knew Charles Ives*, and Mohammed Fairouz (b. 1985) in his Symphony No. 4 *In the Shadow of No Towers*, have found inspiration in Ives's combination of disparate elements side by side or layer on layer, including tonal materials and familiar sounds as part of the mix.[186] Cage's comment that "the music we are writing now influences the way in which we hear and appreciate the music of Ives more than that the music of Ives influences us to do what we do" rings true as much for recent composers as for Cage's cohort in the 1960s.[187] Ives's synthesis of all the traditions he knew as a youth and young man into something wholly individual and new now seems like what most musicians do today, including John Adams and John Zorn (b. 1953), Jason Moran (b. 1975) and Esperanza Spalding (b. 1984), and Radiohead and Beyoncé (b. 1981). Viewed from our eclectic present, Ives feels like a fellow spirit.

Bibliographic Overview

Although now widely recognized as the greatest American composer in the classical tradition born before 1900, Ives has been a controversial figure since his music began to reach the public and invite commentary in the 1920s. Overviews of Ives published in his lifetime include Cowell/CHARLES E IVES and several collected in Burkholder/IVES AND HIS WORLD, pp. 361–442. Paul/IVES IN THE MIRROR traces his reception, showing that different images of Ives emerged from each era, in part reflecting the concerns of that time and of individual advocates and scholars. The changes in perception of Ives are also reflected in the biographies: advocacy in the first biography, Cowell and Cowell/CHARLES IVES, published the year after Ives's death; deconstruction of "the Ives Legend" in Rossiter/IVES; the psychoanalytical approach of Feder/IVES; and the sympathetic account in Swafford/IVES, now the standard biography.[188] The issues of dating have been discussed in this chapter; Magee/IVES RECONSIDERED is the first biography to use the revised chronology, also reflected in the brief overviews in Burkholder/GROVE and Burkholder/LISTENING. Each biography has brought forward much new information and new interpretations. The latest is Budiansky/MAD MUSIC, which rejects the revised chronology while clarifying aspects of Ives's health and personal life.

Ives's writings are collected in Ives/ESSAYS and Ives/MEMOS, and selected letters appear in Ives/CORRESPONDENCE, which is organized thematically. The Charles Ives Society has been sponsoring critical editions since 1973, but no collected works edition is in progress. The definitive catalog of his music is Sinclair/CATALOGUE, although the older Kirkpatrick/CATALOGUE contains much useful information about individual manuscripts. Ives's papers other than music manuscripts are catalogued in Perlis/CHARLES IVES PAPERS. Reminiscences of Ives are gathered in the masterful oral history Perlis/IVES REMEMBERED. The most up-to-date bibliography of research on Ives is Magee/RESEARCH. Burk/OMNIBUS includes useful lists of performances, a bibliography, a discography, and other items. Burkholder/IVES AND HIS WORLD includes correspondence, reviews, and profiles from his lifetime, as well as newer essays, and Lambert/IVES STUDIES includes several significant essays.

Much of the literature on Ives has examined general issues that cross genres and are relevant to the symphonic works. Burkholder/IDEAS traces the development of the ideas in Ives/ESSAYS, why those ideas were important to him, and who were his important influences in music and thought. Perry/IVES links Ives to trends in American aesthetics and philosophy, including Transcendentalism, realism, revivalism, the social gospel, and pragmatism. Hertz/ANGELS explores how Ives absorbed Ralph Waldo Emerson's influence and used it in part to deflect the potentially overwhelming influence of Claude Debussy (1862–1918). Marc Johnson/YANKEE REALISM deepens his connection to realism, pragmatism, and progressivism. Another kind of influence is baseball, and Timothy Johnson/BASEBALL explores what baseball meant to Ives and how he used it as an inspiration for new musical procedures. Horowitz/MORAL FIRE positions Ives among other Americans in the late nineteenth and early twentieth centuries who saw music as a moral force. Horowitz/DVOŘÁK'S PROPHECY compares Ives to Mark Twain and sees him as part of a multiracial tradition in American classical music stemming from Dvořák.

The musical traditions Ives drew from are outlined in Burkholder/TRADITIONS. Elkus/BAND TRADITION looks at the American band tradition and its influence on Ives's music. Burkholder/ORGANIST shows the significant, lifelong influence of Ives's career as an organist on his music, in both obvious and unexpected ways. The essays in Block and Burkholder/CLASSICAL argue that Ives's music is rooted in the European tradition and that it parallels music of his European contemporaries in significant ways. Nicholls/EXPERIMENTAL and Shultis/SILENCING place him at the head of the American experimental tradition.

Analytical studies have taken a variety of approaches. Burkholder/LISTENING is a general introduction for nonspecialists with descriptive analyses of about forty pieces, including the five completed symphonies and two completed orchestral sets. Burkholder/ALL MADE is a detailed study of how Ives borrowed and reworked existing music throughout his career, from the traditional practices he learned as a youth to the extraordinary techniques he developed in his mature music, such as cumulative form and collage. All the tunes Ives borrowed are assembled in Henderson/TUNEBOOK. Rathert/SEEN AND UNSEEN examines Ives's aesthetics in relation to Samuel Coleridge and the Transcendentalists and applies them to analyses of Ives's music. Starr/UNION OF DIVERSITIES shows how Ives constructs form by juxtaposing heterogeneous musical styles, and Burkholder/TOPICS places this approach in the tradition of musical topics. Lambert/MUSIC offers an excellent theoretical discussion of Ives's characteristic musical procedures. McDonald/TIME'S ARROW shows how Ives manipulated time in his music, as does Thurmaier/TIME.

No general monograph on Ives's symphonic music has appeared, but several dissertations have contributed insights. Eiseman/SYMPHONIC TRADITION places Ives's first two symphonies in the European symphonic tradition. Magers/ASPECTS describes the thematic and formal structures of the four numbered symphonies, and Badolato/SYMPHONIES provides an overview. Roller/ANALYSIS examines movements from the First, Third, and Fourth Symphonies using linear and set-theory analysis. Rathert/ZUR ENTWICKLUNG and Lück/VISIONEN offer brief overviews of Ives's development as a symphonist.

The most extensive studies in print of Ives's First and Second Symphonies are in Burkholder/ALL MADE, pp. 88–136. Elkus/SECOND SYMPHONY links the Second Symphony to nineteenth-century overtures. Zobel/MUSIC and Zobel/THIRD SYMPHONY place the Third Symphony in context with a focus on the musical borrowings and overall meaning. Gail/FOURTH SYMPHONY is a significant and comprehensive study of the sources of the Fourth Symphony along with extensive analysis and interpretation. Jacko/CONTEXT examines context and performance issues for the Fourth Symphony. Brodhead/PREFACES provides much useful background on the Fourth Symphony along with clarifications of notation and performance issues in the context of Brodhead's performance edition of the piece, based on the critical edition, Ives/SYMPHONY. Glarner/INVESTIGATION offers an in-depth theoretical analysis of the Fourth Symphony; shorter analytical studies include Brooks/UNITY, Cyr/INTERVALLIC, and Janicka-Słysz/IV SYMFONIA. Magers/OPTIMISM, Rathert/SYMPHONIE NR. 4, Gail/4. SYMPHONIE, and Browning/INTERDISCIPLINARITY address issues of meaning, and Brodhead/CELESTIAL, Lipkis/ASPECTS, and Rathert/SEEN AND UNSEEN examine the Fourth Symphony alongside other works by Ives.

Two studies consider *A Symphony: New England Holidays* as a complete work: Thurmaier/TIME focuses on manipulations of temporal processes with evidence from the sketches, and Kramer/POLITICS OF MEMORY attempts a political interpretation. Other scholarly articles focus on individual movements. Crane/JEW'S HARP considers the unusual inclusion of a Jew's harp in *Washington's Birthday*. Feder/DECORATION DAY examines the biographical implications of the second movement. Maisel/FOURTH and Nelson/BEYOND analyze *The Fourth of July* through Schenkerian and philosophical lenses respectively, and Shirley/SECOND OF JULY compares the final version to the score-sketch.

Most publications on the unfinished *Universe Symphony* focus on its various realizations by David Porter (1993), Larry Austin (1994), and Johnny Reinhard (1996). Richard Taruskin briefly considers the latter two realizations in Taruskin/UNIVERSE. Austin details his own process in Austin/PRELUDE and Austin/UNIVERSE, and Reinhard explains his approach in the unpublished Reinhard/IVES UNIVERSE. Zachary Lyman's detailed study, Lyman/DUALITY, compares all three realizations, and he has also published his interviews with Austin and Reinhard in Lyman/COMPLETING and Lyman/REALIZING, respectively. Other studies of the *Universe Symphony* include Rathert/PAYSAGE, which interprets the work as conveying both Romantic and modern sensibilities, and Lambert/IVES'S UNIVERSE, which places it alongside other musical works that have aimed to represent the cosmos.

Orchestral Set No. 1: *Three Places in New England* has been the subject of a DMA dissertation, Stein/MUSICAL LANGUAGE. Other studies have looked at individual movements: the first in Josephson/INITIAL SKETCHES and Von Glahn Cooney/NEW SOURCES and the second in Von Glahn Cooney/SENSE OF PLACE and Kramer/MUSICAL TIME. Rathert briefly considers Orchestral Set No. 2 in Rathert/AURATISCHE FORM, and Von Glahn examines and compares the finales of the two sets in Von Glahn/FROM COUNTRY TO CITY. Magee/EVERY places the Finale of Orchestral Set No. 2 in historical context. The incomplete Orchestral Set No. 3 is the subject of a master's thesis, Porter/THIRD ORCHESTRAL SET.

Notes

1. Ives also composed several overtures, notably the Overture in G Minor (ca. 1899), *Overture and March "1776"* (?1903–4, ca. 1909–10), *Emerson Overture* for Piano and Orchestra (ca. 1910–14, rev. ca. 1920–21), and *Robert Browning Overture* (ca. 1912–14, rev. ca. 1936–42); numerous short orchestral works, including the famous tone poems *The Unanswered Question* (1908, rev. ca. 1930–35) and *Central Park in the Dark* (?1906, ca. 1909, rev. ca. 1936); and eleven sets for chamber or theater orchestra. Only the symphonies and sets for full orchestra will be considered here. Unless otherwise noted, dates used in this chapter are based on those in Burkholder/GROVE and Sinclair/CATALOGUE.

2. This and the following paragraphs summarize Burkholder/TRADITIONS; see the footnotes there for further relevant literature.

3. For topics, their application to Ives, and a comparison to Mozart, see Burkholder/TOPICS.

4. See Burkholder/ORGANIST for the influence of Ives's experience as an organist on his music. Rossiter/IVES, Osborne/ORGANIST, and Swafford/IVES offer the best published accounts of his career as a church organist.

5. Burkholder/ALL MADE, pp. 17–20.

6. On Ives and Parker, see Ives/MEMOS, pp. 39, 48–52, 115–16, 180–84, and 257–58; Burkholder/IDEAS, pp. 58–66; Sherwood/REDATING; Burkholder/IVES AND YALE; and Magee/IVES RECONSIDERED, pp. 38–66.

7. Burkholder/IDEAS, pp. 45–50, introduced the term "experimental music" for Ives's sketches and short pieces that try out new musical ideas and argued that Ives always maintained a distinction between such experiments, which were generally private compositional exercises, and his public concert music, which in later years often absorbed the techniques tried out in earlier short pieces. Nicholls/EXPERIMENTAL and Shultis/SILENCING place Ives at the beginning of a tradition of American experimental music that includes Henry Cowell, John Cage, and others. But Lambert/MUSIC, pp. 1–22, argues that this trend in Ives's music is better called "systematic" than experimental.

8. Burkholder/IDEAS, p. 80.

9. Kirkpatrick/CATALOGUE.

10. Solomon questioned Ives's dates in Solomon/VERACITY. Three years later, Carol K. Baron defended Ives's dates on the basis of a detailed study of his handwriting (Baron/DATING). In the mid-1990s, Gayle Sherwood (later Gayle Sherwood Magee and Gayle Magee) devised a rigorous approach for dating the music paper Ives used and combined those dates with more specific dates for the handwriting to produce her new chronology, focusing initially on the choral works in Sherwood/CHORAL WORKS, Sherwood/QUESTIONS, and Sherwood/REDATING. Her revised dates for the manuscripts of Ives's other music, including his symphonic works, have not been published separately but are presented in the endnotes to Burkholder/ALL MADE and incorporated into Magee/

IVES RECONSIDERED, Sinclair/CATALOGUE, and Burkholder/GROVE, whose list of Ives's works is jointly credited to Sinclair, Magee, and Burkholder. Magee's dates may not be the final word, but they are the best available at present.

11. For a thorough study of borrowing and reworking in the symphonies, orchestral sets, and other Ives works, see Burkholder/ALL MADE, whose analyses contribute substantially to those given here. The melodies Ives borrowed are helpfully collected in Henderson/TUNEBOOK, and audio examples of most of them are available on the website of the Charles Ives Society at charlesives.org/borrowed-tunes.

12. Sinclair/CATALOGUE, pp. 3–5; Burkholder/ALL MADE, pp. 89 and 441n2; Magee/IVES RECONSIDERED, p. 60.

13. Ives/MEMOS, pp. 51 and 86–87. Editorial brackets (enclosing the editor's insertions) and italic parentheses (enclosing Ives's later additions) omitted. Ives's reference to "the pretty little theme and the nice chords" shows contempt, not for his own symphony, but for Damrosch's musical taste; the latter's preference for the simple opening theme over the relatively complex counterpoint of the middle section was evidently the opposite of Ives's own view of the movement and apparently bruised Ives's pride in his craftsmanship.

14. Deane/PREMIERES.

15. Quoted in Burkholder/ALL MADE, p. 89.

16. Burkholder/ALL MADE, pp. 89–102. See Perlis/IVES REMEMBERED, p. 90, for a photograph of the doors of Ives's studio, with photos of Franck and Brahms surrounded by other memorabilia.

17. The analyses given here expand on those in Burkholder/ALL MADE, pp. 89–102, and Burkholder/LISTENING, pp. 63–71. For other views and analyses of the First Symphony, see Eiseman/SYMPHONIC TRADITION, pp. 149–54; Magers/ASPECTS, pp. 28–79; and Badolato/SYMPHONIES, pp. 10–62. Roller/ANALYSIS, pp. 34–75, offers a Schenkerian analysis of the second movement. Table 4.3 and table 4.4 (for the Second Symphony) adopt the analytical symbols used in previous volumes of this series, except that motivic material is assigned lowercase letters sequentially throughout each movement, rather than starting over for each major section, in order to clarify and highlight the progress of individual motives, the interrelatedness of themes, and their contrapuntal combinations.

18. See the discussion and examples in Burkholder/ALL MADE, pp. 98–101. Horatio Parker initially objected to this first theme and to Ives's hymn-based first try at a slow movement, suggesting that Ives may have originally intended to base his First Symphony on hymns and Parker steered him away from doing so. All of Ives's later numbered symphonies include themes derived from hymn tunes, but this is the only theme in the First Symphony to draw on an American melody.

19. Example 4.2b omits the accompanying chords. In m. 274, Ives changes the first note of motive *g* from D♭ to C in order to harmonize better with M; the repeated eighth-note figure is a marker of *g* everywhere else in the movement, but the change here reveals a subtle similarity to the fifth and sixth measures of *a* (see mm. 6–7 in example 4.1).

20. In A. Peter Brown's analysis of Schubert's movement in this series, volume 2, pp. 623–28, the threefold point of imitation at m. 94 is labeled *1K(S)*. A similar analysis would be appropriate for Ives's exposition, reading the "codetta" in table 4.3 as a transition or extension leading to a closing theme at m. 201. The stretto on *g*, however, is too greatly changed in the recapitulation to regard it as a closing theme there. Instead, the analysis in table 4.3 emphasizes the parallels between a developmental codetta for the exposition and a developmental coda for the movement.

21. See the demonstration in Burkholder/ALL MADE, pp. 98–99.

22. Ives/MEMOS, p. 51. The alternate version of the first movement does not survive.

23. For a full analysis of the theme and its relationship to Dvořák's, see Burkholder/ALL MADE, pp. 90–94.

24. See the comparison of Ives's melody with Beethoven's in ibid., pp. 97–98. Dvořák's *New World* scherzo also starts with imitative entries, and it includes a reference to a theme from the first movement in a transition, as does Ives's.

25. See Burkholder/ALL MADE, pp. 95–97.

26. This paragraph and the analysis below draw primarily on ibid., pp. 102–36, and Burkholder/LISTENING, pp. 126–38. For alternate formal analyses of the Second Symphony, see Magers/ASPECTS, pp. 80–142, and Badolato/SYMPHONIES, pp. 63–112. For thematic unification, see Eiseman/SYMPHONIC TRADITION, pp. 154–87. Earlier studies of the borrowed material include Charles/BORROWED, Sterne/QUOTATIONS, and Burkholder/QUOTATION, all superseded by Burkholder/ALL MADE.

27. Ives/MEMOS, pp. 51–52; Sinclair/CATALOGUE, p. 8; Elkus/SECOND SYMPHONY, pp. 320–21. There are contradictions here; the first movement, supposedly based on *Down East Overture*, has the same themes and several of the same transitional passages as the fourth movement, supposedly based on *Overture: Town, Gown and State*.

28. Burkholder/GROVE. In Burkholder/ALL MADE, pp. 103 and 443n20, Magee described the first movement sketches as on unidentified paper in a hand from ca. 1902–7, but by the time of the *Grove* work list she was able to date the paper more precisely at ca. 1907.

29. Ives/MEMOS, p. 87.

30. Sinclair/CATALOGUE, pp. 8–10; Ives/CORRESPONDENCE, pp. 293–97. Aaron Copland had tried in 1934 to interest Koussevitzky in performing one of Ives's orchestral works, but nothing came of it; Ives/CORRESPONDENCE, p. 223.

31. Magee/IVES RECONSIDERED, p. 88.

32. Burkholder/IDEAS, pp. 96–97.

33. Elkus/SECOND SYMPHONY, quoting note 11 on p. 327.

34. Ibid.; Burkholder/ALL MADE, pp. 126–33.

35. Burkholder/ALL MADE, pp. 105–7, demonstrates that in an earlier sketch the opening theme was derived from the hymn tune *Nettleton* and led smoothly into the current passage at mm. 10ff. As a result, figures derived from *Nettleton* are woven into the counterpoint in *b*, but they are unlikely to be heard as such without the more obvious and prominent paraphrase of *Nettleton* that began that sketch.

36. Burkholder/ALL MADE, p. 127, points out the parallel roles this figure plays in the Ives and Brahms symphonies, suggesting the latter is a formal model as well. Charles/BORROWED, p. 106, suggests that the opening motive of Ives's movement (*Pa*) echoes the opening motive of Brahms's; the closest resemblance is the varied repetition of *a* in Ives's development at mm. 149–50 in the violins.

37. Mason had adapted *Hamburg* from a Gregorian chant and *Naomi* from a tune by Johann Naegeli. See Henderson/TUNEBOOK, pp. 45–46 and 61.

38. See the examples and discussion in Burkholder/ALL MADE, pp. 111–14.

39. See Burkholder/TOPICS.

40. See the discussion of the sketches in Burkholder/ALL MADE, pp. 105–7, 111–14, 118–19, 120–24, 126–27, and 128–29.

41. Ibid., pp. 132–33.

42. See ibid., pp. 115–20, for the derivation of this theme from *Camptown Races*, and pp. 130–31, for a possible reference in the first measure of *Pa* to the scherzo theme of Tchaikovsky's Fourth Symphony, whose first movement's key scheme and cyclic form were models for Ives in this symphony.

43. One motive in *e* (m. 60), taken from *Turkey in the Straw*, resembles a motive in the second theme of the first movement of Dvořák's *New World Symphony*, hinting at other parallels with that symphony (ibid., pp. 130–31).

44. The modulatory extension at m. 78 may also draw on *Antioch* ("Joy to the World"), adapted from Handel by Lowell Mason (ibid., pp. 123–24).

45. For the relationship between Ives's orchestrations and the European symphonic tradition, see Eiseman/SYMPHONIC TRADITION, pp. 231–39.

46. Burkholder/ALL MADE, pp. 118–19.

47. See the discussion and facsimiles in Magee/IVES RECONSIDERED, pp. 175–80.

48. Cowell/CHRONICLE, p. 402; reprinted in Burkholder/IVES AND HIS WORLD, p. 358.

49. Ives/MEMOS, p. 237.

50. Ives/CORRESPONDENCE, pp. 294–95.

51. On blackface minstrelsy, Foster, and Ives, see Burkholder/LISTENING, pp. 141–43.

52. Interview with Will and Luemily Ryder, in Perlis/IVES REMEMBERED, p. 98.

53. Ives/CORRESPONDENCE, p. 357.

54. Olin Downes, "Symphony by Ives is Played in Full: Bernstein Leads Philharmonic in Composer's 2d, Heard in Entirety for First Time," *New York Times*, February 23, 1951, p. 33; excerpted in Burkholder/IVES AND HIS WORLD, pp. 352–53.

55. Virgil Thomson, "Music: From the Heart," *New York Herald Tribune*, February 23, 1951, p. 16; excerpted in Burkholder/IVES AND HIS WORLD, pp. 353–54.

56. Cowell/CHRONICLE. Reprinted in Burkholder/IVES AND HIS WORLD, pp. 355–58.

57. The discussion here of the Third Symphony draws primarily on Burkholder/ALL MADE, pp. 137–54 and 238–40, and Burkholder/LISTENING, pp. 149–58. For alternate overviews and analyses, see Magers/ASPECTS, pp. 143–92, Badolato/SYMPHONIES, pp. 113–51, Roller/ANALYSIS, pp. 76–149 (on the third movement), Zobel/MUSIC, and especially Zobel/THIRD SYMPHONY.

58. The comprehensive overview of cumulative form in music by Ives and other composers is Burkholder/ALL MADE, pp. 137–266. See also Zobel/THIRD SYMPHONY, pp. 37–50.

59. See James Hepokoski's discussion of "teleological genesis" in Hepokoski/SIBELIUS, especially pp. 26–27 and 58–84, and Burkholder/ALL MADE, pp. 231, 465n30, and 469n70.

60. For an examination of Christian symbolism in the Third Symphony, see Zobel/MUSIC and Zobel/THIRD SYMPHONY, pp. 69–80.

61. See Burkholder/ORGANIST, pp. 259–60, 273–76, and 301–8. According to Sinclair/CATALOGUE, p. 12, a brief sketch survives for a potential fourth movement, but this sketch is in a very different style from the other movements. See also the discussion below of the Third Orchestral Set.

62. Sinclair/CATALOGUE, pp. 12–14.

63. On the dates, see Burkholder/ALL MADE, pp. 143, 450n5, 451n8, and 151, for the first and third movements and pp. 238 and 466n41 for the second, which may have been begun in 1907, earlier than the other two. In Magee/IVES RECONSIDERED, p. 97, Magee suggests an even later date, saying that the symphony "was begun probably around 1910–11."

64. Ives/MEMOS, p. 121.

65. Ives/CORRESPONDENCE, pp. 54–56.

66. Sinclair/CATALOGUE, pp. 13–14 and 683; Swafford/IVES, pp. 421–22.

67. Zobel/THIRD SYMPHONY, especially pp. 30–36. See the similar comment in Magee/IVES RECONSIDERED, p. 170.

68. Sinclair/CATALOGUE, p. 14; Ives/MEMOS, p. 55; and Singleton/PREFACE, pp. iv and ix.

69. The accompanying parts are omitted in examples 4.8 and 4.9 in order to highlight the contrapuntal combinations of themes in the Third Symphony.

70. Magee/IVES RECONSIDERED, pp. 94–99, links this movement to the Iveses' mourning after Harmony's failed (perhaps ectopic) pregnancy and resulting emergency hysterectomy in 1909 made it impossible for her to bear children. While the mood of the symphony is certainly more solemn and less rambunctious than the Second, the central part of Magee's argument (p. 98) relies on a little-used text for *Azmon* (one that changes Wesley's words "praise" to "worth" and "triumphs of his grace" to "triumph of his birth") and on an alternate text for the same tune that was not written until 1909 ("We bear the strain of earthly care," by Ozora S. Davis). Both texts were likely unknown to Ives.

71. The flute differs slightly in rhythm from the cello line, perhaps hinting at the heterophony of hymn singing at a camp-meeting revival. The flute is in its lowest register, omitting the low B♭s that lie outside its range and two of the low Cs. The flute is marked at a dynamic level lower than the cellos, suggesting that its primary function (and perhaps that of the solo cello) is to reinforce the first harmonic of the cellos.

72. Zobel/THIRD SYMPHONY, pp. 37–49, argues that the three movements "outline a narrative in which the camp meeting worshippers of Ives's memory move from being 'old folks' weary and broken down by life, to congregants in a childlike state of innocence, to the faithful at peace and in ultimate communion with God" (quoting p. 37).

73. Noel Straus, "Symphony by Ives in World Premiere: Composer's Third Featured by Little Symphony Here, with Harrison on Podium," *New York Times*, April 6, 1946, p. 10; excerpted in Burkholder/IVES AND HIS WORLD, pp. 338–39.

74. Sinclair/CATALOGUE, pp. 18–19.

75. Ibid., p. 19. For an exhaustive examination of the sources for the Fourth Symphony, see Gail/FOURTH SYMPHONY, pp. 1: 19-271. The dates given here are those in Burkholder/GROVE; Sinclair and Gail offer slightly different dates.

76. The interpretation that follows draws on Burkholder/ALL MADE, pp. 389–410, and Burkholder/LISTENING, pp. 257–69. The most thorough analysis and interpretation of the symphony is Gail/FOURTH SYMPHONY, pp. 1: 273-548. For alternate overviews, see Swafford/IVES, pp. 349–65; Magers/ASPECTS, pp. 193–266; Badolato/SYMPHONIES, pp. 152–208; Rathert/SEEN AND UNSEEN, pp. 209–46; Jacko/CONTEXT; and, for the first movement, Brooks/UNITY. The complexity of the Fourth Symphony has engendered a variety of analytical approaches. Gail/4. SYMPHONIE discusses how the second movement can be interpreted in terms of purely musical, programmatic, political, psychological, religious, existential, and artistic-historical expressions. This complexity is mirrored in the variety of theoretical approaches. For example, Glarner/INVESTIGATION focuses on sound density and texture; Rathert/SYMPHONIE NR. 4 and Cyr/INTERVALLIC examine the motivic and formal characteristics; Roller/ANALYSIS, pp. 150–207, analyzes the first movement using Schenkerian and set theory; Lipkis/ASPECTS analyses a sense of postmodern time in the fourth movement; Browning/INTERDISCIPLINARITY relates Ives's symphony to other artistic impulses to transcend generic conventions; and Magers/OPTIMISM explores the musical development of the written program.

77. See Bellamann/MOVEMENTS, p. xiii, n1.

78. Bellamann/MOVEMENTS. Reprinted in Brodhead/PREFACES, pp. xxvi-xxvii.

79. Charles E. Ives, *The Fourth Symphony for Large Orchestra*, in *New Music* 2, no. 2 (January 1929): p. ii; reprinted in Gail/FOURTH SYMPHONY, p. 8, and in Brodhead/PREFACES, p. xxvii, n2. In Ives/MEMOS, p. 66, Ives attributes the sentence to "Mr. Bellamann's program notes," meaning the notes for the 1927 concert.

80. Sinclair/CATALOGUE, p. 221, dates *The Celestial Railroad* in summer 1925, no sooner than 1921; Brodhead/CELESTIAL, pp. 394–410 and 415–19, dates it 1921–23. Gayle Sherwood Magee's initial dates for this and the symphony movements appear in Burkholder/ALL MADE, pp. 490–91n56 and 500n61, and her revised dates in Burkholder/GROVE. For Ives's own dates, see Sinclair/CATALOGUE, p. 18.

81. On sonic exuviation and its origins in organ music, see Burkholder/ORGANIST, pp. 276–82. Nicolas Slonimsky coined the term, defined in Slonimsky/MUSIC, p. 1171.

82. See also Glarner/INVESTIGATION for Ives's uses of texture here and throughout.

83. Swafford/IVES, p. 351, calls the rising half step and minor third the *Urmotiv*, labels the three-note motive of two descending whole steps that begins *Bethany* the "lyric motive," and argues that these are the two primary melodic motives that unify the whole symphony, including most of the borrowed tunes. Much of his analysis is in his endnotes, pp. 491n1–96n41.

84. Brodhead/CELESTIAL. Earlier discussions of the movement in relation to Hawthorne's story are in Magers/ASPECTS, pp. 338–49; Magers/OPTIMISM, pp. 76–80; Feder/IVES, pp. 277–78; and Rathert/SEEN AND UNSEEN, pp. 94–106.

85. Brodhead/CELESTIAL, pp. 389–90.

86. Table 4.6 follows the rehearsal numbers and measure numbers of the 2011 critical edition; those in other editions differ. The code "3+2" in the rehearsal number column means "two measures after rehearsal 3." The table is based in part on table 10.1 in Burkholder/ALL MADE, pp. 393–99. The latter offers more detail, including which borrowed material is shared with *The Celestial Railroad*, which episodes in the symphony were interpolated into the piano piece, which borrowings appear in layers added to the symphony, and which borrowings were added only at the time of Ives's autograph score or even later. Both tables ultimately depend on the parallels between story, piano piece, and symphony movement described in Brodhead/CELESTIAL and in Gann/CONCORD, pp. 134–56, which also clarifies the relationship between *The Celestial Railroad* and the "Hawthorne" movement of the *Concord Sonata*. For more on the borrowed material, see Thomas M. Brodhead's color-coded analysis of borrowings, on a DVD included with Ives/SYMPHONY, and Gail/FOURTH SYMPHONY.

87. See Ives's "Conductor's Note" in Ives/SYMPHONY, pp. xxv–xxix (reprinted in Brodhead/PREFACES, pp. xxvii–xxxiii), James Sinclair's explanation in Ives/SYMPHONY, pp. xxiii–xxiv, and Brodhead/PREFACES, pp. xxxiv–xxxv.

88. See Brodhead/PREFACES, p. xl, for a list of places assistant conductors can be useful.

89. The first and most frequent chord of this passage (m. 7) is the same as that in "Chorale," the third of Ives's *Three Quarter-tone Pieces* for two pianos, composed 1923–24 and premiered in February 1925, but there appears to be no other material shared with that piece.

90. See also Cyr/INTERVALLIC for intervallic similarities between borrowed tunes.

91. For the definition of collage and a discussion of its functions, see Burkholder/ALL MADE, pp. 376 and 379–81. For identification of tunes that were added in later stages of composition, see table 10.1 in Burkholder/ALL MADE, pp. 393–99.

92. See Burkholder/RULE-BREAKING, especially pp. 376–82.

93. Ives/MEMOS, p. 40. For a description of *Yale-Princeton Football Game*, see Burkholder/LISTENING, pp. 93–96.

94. For the analysis that follows, see Burkholder/ALL MADE, pp. 70–73 and 402.

95. Burkholder/ORGANIST, pp. 290–92.

96. Table 4.7 is based on table 10.2 in Burkholder/ALL MADE, pp. 403–5.

97. Lawrence Gilman, "Music: A New Opera, a New Symphony, and a New Debussy Fragment," *New York Herald Tribune*, January 31, 1927, p. 11; excerpted in Burkholder/IVES AND HIS WORLD, pp. 295–96, quoting from p. 296.

98. Olin Downes, "Music: Pro-Musica Society," *New York Times*, January 30, 1927, sec. 1, p. 28; excerpted in Burkholder/IVES AND HIS WORLD, pp. 293–95, quoting from p. 295. *Ned McCobb's Daughter* was a play by Sidney Howard then playing on Broadway, in which the titular heroine's faithful persistence brings her faithless husband and his brother, both criminals, to justice. Downes's comparison is apt.

99. "Recent Publications: New Music, January, 1929," *Musical Courier* 98, no. 10, March 7, 1929, p. 46; reprinted in Burkholder/IVES AND HIS WORLD, pp. 296–97, quoting from p. 297.

100. Ives/MEMOS, p. 95. For extensive discussion of the symphony in relation to issues of time, memory, and compositional process, see Thurmaier/TIME. Kramer/POLITICS OF MEMORY reads the piece in political terms (less convincingly).

101. Ives/MEMOS, p. 94. Editorial italic parentheses, indicating a later insertion, have been omitted. On his manuscripts and work lists, Ives waffled on whether it was a symphony or not, calling it sometimes "Holidays Symphony" or "4th Symphony," at other times "1st Orchestral Set" or "Set of Pieces for Orchestra," and in one case "IV Symphony (or Set for Orchestra #1)"; at times he also

avoided the question of genre entirely, using titles such as "New England Holidays" (Sinclair/CATALOGUE, p. 20).

102. For Ives's facility in scoring for the Jew's harp and certain performance challenges, see Crane/JEW'S HARP.

103. Ives/MEMOS, pp. 97–99; Sinclair/CATALOGUE, pp. 22–23; Burkholder/ALL MADE, pp. 497–98n42.

104. Ives/WASHINGTON'S BIRTHDAY, p. 31, emended by reference to the version in Ives/MEMOS, pp. 96–97n1, which includes the phrase "half in fun, half seriously" and differs in some punctuation. Ives rearranges two lines of the Whittier poem, where this section begins "Shut in from all the world without,/ We sat the clean-winged hearth about,/ Content to let the north-wind roar / In baffled rage at pane and door."

105. Ives/MEMOS, p. 98.

106. The following analysis draws on Burkholder/ALL MADE, pp. 383–85, and Burkholder/LISTENING, pp. 176–81. For a detailed discussion of the movement and Ives's sketches for it, see Thurmaier/TIME, pp. 83–116.

107. Ives/MEMOS, p. 97.

108. On collage as a representation of memories, see Burkholder/ALL MADE, pp. 380–81.

109. Sinclair/CATALOGUE, pp. 24–26; Burkholder/ALL MADE, p. 486n14.

110. Decoration Day was established in 1868 by the Grand Army of the Republic, an association of Union veterans. It was later made a federal holiday, renamed Memorial Day, and broadened to honor all who died while serving in any branch of the US military in any era.

111. Ives/DECORATION DAY, p. 33.

112. Feder/DECORATION DAY and Feder/IVES, pp. 237–43 (also see pp. 31–43 on George Ives's Civil War service). Magee/IVES RECONSIDERED, p. 126, links the whole *Holidays Symphony* to remembrances of the Civil War and to the ongoing World War I.

113. The following analysis draws on Burkholder/ALL MADE, pp. 345–46, and Burkholder/LISTENING, pp. 181–85. For other analyses, see Feder/DECORATION DAY, which focuses on the programmatic aspects, and Thurmaier/TIME, pp. 117–56, which examines the sketches and issues of time.

114. Another possible interpretation is that the bell figure, joined in unison by an extra violin in mm. 47–80, adds a sonic blur that reinforces the idea of scenes remembered from the past, like gauze over a movie lens or sepia color in a photograph. This may explain why the bell figure continues throughout the scene at the cemetery, when the firehose cart would likely not be moving and its bells not jangling—or perhaps they are still jangling in the breeze.

115. Several scholars have suggested other possible borrowings in *Decoration Day*, summarized in Burkholder/ALL MADE, pp. 486n16 and 486–87n17. See also Thurmaier/TIME for suggestions that the opening melody foreshadows *Adeste fideles* (pp. 126–27) and that the flower-gathering melody is related to *Marching Through Georgia* (pp. 138 and 141–42).

116. Sinclair/CATALOGUE, pp. 26–28; Burkholder/ALL MADE, p. 495n21.

117. Shirley/PREFACE, p. iv.

118. This is the longer version of the postface, printed in Ives/MEMOS, p. 104n1.

119. Ibid., p. 104. In ibid, p. 104n3, Kirkpatrick says Ives is quoting the end of chapter 28 from Mark Twain's *Huckleberry Finn* (1884), although the phrase appeared in print as early as 1846; see Burkholder/LISTENING, p. 304n26.

120. The table and the following analysis draw primarily on Burkholder/ALL MADE, pp. 376–82, and Burkholder/LISTENING, pp. 185–89. For other analyses, see Maisel/FOURTH; Nelson/BEYOND; Shirley/SECOND OF JULY; and Thurmaier/TIME, pp. 157–97. The latter two also examine Ives's process of composition.

121. On compositional procedures that produce both explosions in *The Fourth of July*, see Ives/MEMOS, pp. 104–6, and Thurmaier/TIME, pp. 172–86.

122. Ives/MEMOS, p. 42.

123. Ibid., p. 95; Sinclair/CATALOGUE, pp. 30–31; Burkholder/ALL MADE, p. 456n50; Burkholder/GROVE.

124. Ives/MEMOS, p. 39.

125. Burkholder/ALL MADE, p. 185; Ives/MEMOS, p. 39.

126. For the Yale hymnal, see Burkholder/ALL MADE, pp. 185 and 456n52. Ives alters both the text and the rhythm of the melody; Bacon's original read "O God, beneath Thy guiding hand / Our exiled fathers crossed the sea; / And when they trod the wintry strand, / With prayer and psalm they worshipped Thee." The choir is marked "optional" to make the piece performable by orchestras when no choir is available, but the choir's material clearly marks the culmination of Ives's piece, and what it sings is doubled by trumpets and bassoon 1 to make sure the hymn remains prominent even if the chorus is omitted.

127. This analysis is based in part on Burkholder/ALL MADE, pp. 168–69 and 185–86, and Burkholder/LISTENING, pp. 190–93. See also Thurmaier/TIME, pp. 83–85 and 198–222, which discusses aspects of the sketches.

128. Burkholder/ALL MADE, p. 186. The text Ives associated with *Federal Street* is by Isaac Watts: "Come, dearest Lord, descend and dwell / By faith and love in every breast; / Then shall we know and taste and feel / The joys that cannot be expressed." This combination of tune and text is found on a page from the hymnal used at the Central Presbyterian Church in New York while Ives was organist there in 1900–1902, on which Ives sketched *The Shining Shore* in counterpoint with it, a combination that does not occur in the final piece. For this sketch, see Thurmaier/TIME, pp. 83–85. This text does not seem to relate directly to Thanksgiving or Forefathers' Day, and so the ultimate recasting of *Duke Street* as the main theme rather than the countermelody makes sense. But the compositional process revealed in the sketches helps to explain why *Federal Street* and *The Shining Shore* are so prominent in the first section of the movement.

129. Measures 153–79 sound like an insertion because they were; the music originally moved from m. 152 to m. 180 without a break, and the intervening measures were added in the score-sketch (Burkholder/ALL MADE, pp. 185 and 456n51).

130. No doubt the impracticality is what prompted Ives to mark the mixed chorus in *Thanksgiving* as optional, and it is sometimes performed without voices, although the unexpected entrance of the choir is a stunning effect that clearly was part of Ives's concept for the piece.

131. Perlis/IVES REMEMBERED, pp. 117 and 188; Cowell and Cowell/CHARLES IVES, p. 201.

132. Austin/UNIVERSE, pp. 183–85, notes that a chorus is mentioned on some sketch pages, but no music is sketched for it. Austin calculates that about 214 instrumentalists are required for the piece and notes that the division into multiple "orchestras" or "groups" is for groups of like instruments rather than separate symphony orchestras. For facsimiles of sixteen of the sketch pages, see ibid., pp. 217–32.

133. Sinclair/CATALOGUE, pp. 34–35 and 36–37. On the *Universe Symphony* and the Adirondack Mountains, see Tucker/ADIRONDACKS, especially pp. 185–89.

134. Ives/MEMOS, p. 163.

135. Perlis/IVES REMEMBERED, p. 188; Cowell and Cowell/CHARLES IVES, p. 126; Sinclair/CATALOGUE, p. 36; Ives/MEMOS, pp. 106–8.

136. Sinclair/CATALOGUE, p. 35; Austin/PRELUDE; Austin/UNIVERSE; Reinhard/IVES UNIVERSE; Lyman/COMPLETING; Lyman/REALIZING. Lyman/DUALITY compares the three realizations. Austin's realization is on the CD Charles Ives, *Universe Symphony, Orchestral Set No. 2, The Unanswered Question*, Cincinnati Philharmonic Orchestra, C.C.M. Percussion Ensemble, and C.C.M. Chamber Choir, conducted by Gerhard Samuel (Baton Rouge, LA: Centaur CRC

2205, 1994); Reinhard's is on the CD Charles Ives, *Universe Symphony*, realized by Johnny Reinhard, AFMM Orchestra, conducted by Johnny Reinhard (New York: Stereo Society SS007, 2005).

137. Manuscript comment, quoted in Sinclair/CATALOGUE, p. 37. The number of layers varies between the sketches, and also in the three realizations.

138. Ives/MEMOS, p. 107.

139. Ives's sketches appear to conflict on the precise duration of the basic unit. Austin's realization puts each unit at eight seconds, Porter's at ten, and Reinhard's at sixteen (Lyman/DUALITY, p. 196). Ives does not define his abbreviation "B.U."; it probably means "basic unit," but David Porter suggests that it could also mean "battery unit" or "bell unit" (ibid., p. 332).

140. The order of entry is 1, 2, 3, 6, 12, 4, 9, 8, 5, 10, 7, 14, 11, 13, 17, 22, 19, 23, 29, and 31, so that the prime numbers enter in order from lowest to highest, followed—at times quite closely—by their multiples. Austin/UNIVERSE, p. 195, figure 8.2, charts the individual instruments and their effective meters and tempos.

141. As noted below, in Austin's realization of the full *Universe Symphony*, the last four cycles of the "Life Force Prelude" overlap with an introduction and Section A. Reinhard realizes the ten cycles in a similar way but spreads them over the entire symphony.

142. Austin/PRELUDE, p. 65; Austin/UNIVERSE, pp. 192–97, especially figures 8.1–3; Lyman/DUALITY, p. 332.

143. Austin/UNIVERSE, pp. 185–86, suggests this is not a separate prelude but an early sketch for the symphony. Reinhard's realization includes it as a prelude between Sections A and B.

144. Ives numbered pages 1–10 of the Section A sketches, but page 8 is lost (Sinclair/CATALOGUE, p. 34; Austin/UNIVERSE, p. 198).

145. In Austin's realization, the Earth Chord appears first, alone, and is sustained throughout the "Life Pulse Prelude." An "Introduction" (from Prelude No. 2) appears over cycles 7 and 8 of the "Life Pulse Prelude," and Section A, "Past," over cycles 9 and 10. For this disposition, see the chart in Austin/UNIVERSE, p. 211, figure 8.4.

146. Lyman/DUALITY, p. 336. For descriptions of the sketches for sections A, B, and C and of Austin's realization, see Austin/UNIVERSE, pp. 198–216. Reinhard/IVES UNIVERSE likewise offers detailed descriptions of the sketches and how they relate to his realization. Both also include facsimiles.

147. See Austin/UNIVERSE, pp. 210–13.

148. Reinhard/IVES UNIVERSE.

149. See Ives's comments on such changing focus in Ives/MEMOS, pp. 106 and 125.

150. Taruskin/UNIVERSE, pp. 53–54. Taruskin's chapter combines two articles originally published in the *New York Times*, his 1994 review of the recording of Austin's version and his 1996 preview for the first performance of Reinhard's.

151. Ibid., p. 59. For other reflections on the work's meanings, see Lambert/IVES'S UNIVERSE and Rathert/PAYSAGE.

152. Ives/ESSAYS, pp. 77–81, quoting p. 81.

153. Stein/MUSICAL LANGUAGE is the only extended study of the entire piece. The following discussion draws in part on Burkholder/LISTENING, pp. 195–209. In a memo probably written after it was published in 1935, Ives wrote he would prefer to title the work *A New England Symphony* (Sinclair/CATALOGUE, p. 42), showing that at least once he thought of it as a symphony rather than as a suite. Of course, using that title would create confusion with *A Symphony: New England Holidays*. As we saw earlier, at times he thought of the latter as a set rather than a symphony.

154. Sinclair/CATALOGUE, pp. 40–42. For the performances, see also Ives/MEMOS, pp. 333–34. The only previous performance of Ives's music in Europe was apparently Oskar Ziegler's performance of *The Alcotts* at Salzburg on July 31, 1928. At the time when Slonimsky premiered *Three Places in New England*, he was secretary to Boston Symphony Orchestra conductor Serge Koussevitzky, and in 1948

Richard Burgin was associate conductor under Koussevitzky; the latter's role, if any, in either performance is unknown.

155. Sinclair/CATALOGUE, p. 40; Magee's dates from Burkholder/ALL MADE, p. 481n33; Burkholder/GROVE. Josephson/INITIAL SKETCHES examines the sketches for this movement, highlighting its continuity and harmonic characteristics.

156. Burkholder/IDEAS, pp. 33–36 and 99–100. Von Glahn Cooney/NEW SOURCES gives a masterful account of the meanings of and cultural contexts for this movement, based in part on Ives's familiarity with writings about the war and the Shaw monument.

157. See the program suggested by Von Glahn Cooney/NEW SOURCES, pp. 28–42, and the description in Burkholder/LISTENING, pp. 198–202.

158. Burkholder/ALL MADE, example 8.3 on p. 318, shows how Ives stitches the tune fragments together. Henderson/TUNEBOOK, p. 34, suggests that the horn at mm. 56–57 quotes the African American spiritual *Deep River* (mm. 7–8, which shares the same motives as the other tunes Ives uses), but it is not clear that Ives knew this tune.

159. Ives/THREE PLACES, p. 1. See Von Glahn Cooney/NEW SOURCES for possible literary influences on Ives's poem.

160. Ives/THREE PLACES, 20; original punctuation. For the text of the song Ives refers to here, see Ives/MEMOS, pp. 84–85.

161. For the relationships between *Putnam's Camp* and its source pieces, see Burkholder/ALL MADE, pp. 386–89; Sinclair/COUNTRY BAND TABLE; and Sinclair/OVERTURE TABLE. The overture is the only extant music Ives sketched for an opera to be based on a verse play by Ives's uncle Lyman Brewster, *Major John Andre*, printed in Ives/MEMOS, pp. 281–317. For the dates, see Sinclair/CATALOGUE, p. 40; Magee's dates from Burkholder/ALL MADE, p. 499n56; and Burkholder/GROVE. For analyses of the movement, see Von Glahn Cooney/SENSE OF PLACE and Burkholder/LISTENING, pp. 202–6.

162. This is the introduction and march theme Ives later borrowed in the second movement of the Fourth Symphony at mm. 208ff, as discussed earlier and shown in table 4.6. Ives also used this passage in several other works, including *The Celestial Railroad* (the source for the symphony movement), the "Hawthorne" movement of the *Concord Sonata* (the main source for *The Celestial Railroad*), and the song *He Is There!* (later revised as *They Are There!*), making it the passage he most often borrowed from himself. In each of these pieces, it conveys the sound of an amateur band, evoking a Fourth of July celebration (as in *Putnam's Camp*), a parade (as in "Hawthorne"), or both.

163. The instruments named here and throughout the description of this and the following movement play these parts in version 4; other versions differ in instrumentation.

164. As he recollected in Perlis/IVES REMEMBERED, p. 148, Nicolas Slonimsky renotated this passage in version 3 (with Ives's permission) using nonsynchronous bar lines to reflect the way he conducted the strings' march with his right hand and the other march group with his left hand, "so four bars of my left hand equaled three bars of my right hand." Sinclair restored Ives's original notation in his edition of version 4.

165. Ives/MEMOS, p. 87.

166. For the dates, see Sinclair/CATALOGUE, pp. 40 and 399, and Magee's dates in Burkholder/ALL MADE, pp. 482–83n50. Von Glahn/FROM COUNTRY TO CITY, pp. 64–90, analyzes this movement in relation to other literary and artistic celebrations of the Housatonic, including an engraving showing the Housatonic with a church in the distance, a setting that closely parallels the scene Ives describes. The following draws on Von Glahn's analysis and on Burkholder/ALL MADE, pp. 327–30, and Burkholder/LISTENING, pp. 206–9.

167. This is the text of the song; Ives includes additional lines from Johnson's poem as a preface before the first page of the orchestral score. In both, he changed Johnson's "field or town" to "field and

town." See Von Glahn/FROM COUNTRY TO CITY, p. 289n33, for other changes in the original copy of the orchestral score.

168. For the paraphrase, see Burkholder/ALL MADE, pp. 327–30, especially example 8.6. To accommodate Johnson's poetry, Ives adds a pickup note at the beginning of each phrase, making the opening motive sound like *Missionary Chant*; in contrast to his treatment in the Fourth Symphony, however, where Ives puns at length on these two similar hymns, there is no further trace of *Missionary Chant* in this movement. The melody in the orchestral movement lacks the words but is otherwise almost identical to the vocal melody in the song, showing that Ives shaped the melody to fit the text. Michael Tilson Thomas added a chorus singing the words to his performance of this movement with the San Francisco Symphony on the CD *Charles Ives: An American Journey* (New York: 2002, RCA Victor 09026-63703-2); the effect is marvelous, but such a performance was not sanctioned by Ives and is as radical as it would be to add a voice and words to the portions of Mahler's First Symphony that were borrowed from his *Lieder eines fahrenden Gesellen*.

169. Stephen Somervel, "Music: Chamber Orchestra of Boston," *Boston Herald*, January 26, 1931, p. 12; excerpted in Burkholder/IVES AND HIS WORLD, p. 299.

170. Translated in Burkholder/IVES AND HIS WORLD, pp. 301–2.

171. Ives/MEMOS, p. 92. In typical Ives fashion, he takes it back as soon as he says it: "that's not the same as saying that it's any too good."

172. Sinclair/CATALOGUE, pp. 45–46.

173. Ives dated the movement variously between 1909 and 1915. According to Gayle Sherwood Magee, the extant sketches and score sketch are from circa 1914 and the full score between 1923 and 1929 (Sinclair/CATALOGUE, p. 45; Burkholder/ALL MADE, p. 481n31; Burkholder/GROVE). On the title, see Ives/MEMOS, p. 91, and Sinclair/CATALOGUE, p. 43. The following discussion is based in part on the analysis in Burkholder/ALL MADE, pp. 316–17.

174. The zither is hard to hear, and Ives suggests solo strings as a substitute. The zither, however, is a magical sound, unusual in an orchestral context, and balance issues can be resolved through sensitive amplification.

175. Sinclair/CATALOGUE, pp. 45–46; Magee's dates are from Burkholder/ALL MADE, p. 461n94. Movements 1, 2, and 4 of the *Ragtime Dances* ended up in the First Piano Sonata, and the orchestral *Ragtime Dances* have been reconstructed and edited by James B. Sinclair. For brief analyses of all the works related to *Ragtime Dances*, see Burkholder/ALL MADE, pp. 212–14.

176. Brief fragments of two other tunes appear, *Yankee Doodle* in the flute at mm. 43–46 and *Massa's in de Cold Ground* in trumpet 1 at m. 153–54; the resemblances may be coincidental or may serve to suggest the high spirits of the revival.

177. Ives/MEMOS, pp. 92–93. Italic parentheses inserted by the editor to indicate later insertions have been deleted. Magee/EVERY illuminates the impact of the sinking on New York, Ives, and the insurance business.

178. Magee's dating from Burkholder/ALL MADE, p. 471n83. The following analysis draws on Burkholder/ALL MADE, pp. 262–66; Von Glahn/FROM COUNTRY TO CITY, pp. 90–109; and Burkholder/LISTENING, pp. 210–15.

179. Budiansky/MAD MUSIC, pp. 171–76.

180. Kirkpatrick in Perlis/IVES REMEMBERED, p. 224.

181. Porter/THIRD ORCHESTRAL SET is the definitive study. See also Sinclair/CATALOGUE, pp. 47–49.

182. Charles Ives, *The Three Orchestral Sets*, Malmö Symphony Orchestra and Chamber Chorus conducted by James Sinclair (Hong Kong: Naxos 8.559353, 2008).

183. According to Ives, this movement was partly based on a rejected fourth movement for the Third Symphony (Sinclair/CATALOGUE, pp. 48–49 and 12–13), although the sketch he identifies as that rejected movement is in a style completely different from that of the rest of that symphony.

184. Letter from Harmony Ives to Nicolas Slonimsky, July 6, 1936, in Ives/CORRESPONDENCE, p. 128.
185. Cage/TWO STATEMENTS, p. 38.
186. The symphonies of Corigliano and Fairouz, as well as selected works by Adams, are discussed in chapter 9.
187. Cage/TWO STATEMENTS, p. 41.
188. All these are addressed in Paul/IVES IN THE MIRROR, who summarizes "The Ives Legend" on p. 3.

Bibliography

Austin/PRELUDE	Austin, Larry. "Charles Ives's Life Pulse Prelude for Percussion Orchestra: A Realization for Modern Performance from Sketches for His *Universe Symphony*." *Percussive Notes* 23, no. 6 (1985): pp. 58–84.
Austin/UNIVERSE	Austin, Larry. "The Realization and First Complete Performances of Ives's *Universe Symphony*." In *Ives Studies*, edited by Philip Lambert, pp. 179–232. Cambridge: Cambridge University Press, 1997.
Badolato/SYMPHONIES	Badolato, James Vincent. "The Four Symphonies of Charles Ives: A Critical, Analytical Study of the Musical Style of Charles Ives." PhD diss., Catholic University of America, 1978.
Baron/DATING	Baron, Carol K. "Dating Charles Ives's Music: Facts and Fictions." *Perspectives of New Music* 28, no. 1 (Winter 1990): pp. 20–56.
Bellamann/MOVEMENTS	Bellamann, Henry. "Two Movements from a Symphony." Reprinted in Charles E. Ives, *Symphony No. 4*, edited by James B. Sinclair, William Brooks, Kenneth Singleton, and Wayne D. Shirley, p. xiii. New York: Associated Music, 2011.
Block and Burkholder/CLASSICAL	Block, Geoffrey, and J. Peter Burkholder, eds. *Charles Ives and the Classical Tradition*. New Haven, CT: Yale University Press, 1996.
Brodhead/CELESTIAL	Brodhead, Thomas M. "Ives's *Celestial Railroad* and His Fourth Symphony." *American Music* 12 (Winter 1994): pp. 389–424.
Brodhead/PREFACES	Brodhead, Thomas M. Prefaces to *Symphony No. 4: Charles Ives Society Performance Edition*, by Charles E. Ives, pp. v–xliii. Edited by Thomas M. Brodhead. New York: Associated Music, 2020.
Brooks/UNITY	Brooks, William. "Unity and Diversity in Charles Ives's Fourth Symphony." *Yearbook for Inter-American Musical Research* 10 (1974): pp. 5–49.
Browning/INTERDISCIPLINARITY	Browning, J. Robert. "'My God, What Has Sound Got to Do with Music?!': Interdisciplinarity in Eliot and Ives." In *T. S. Eliot's Orchestra: Critical Essays on

	Poetry and Music, edited by John Xiros Cooper, pp. 195–213. New York: General Music, 2000.
Budiansky/MAD MUSIC	Budiansky, Stephen. *Mad Music: Charles Ives, the Nostalgic Rebel*. Lebanon, NH: ForeEdge, 2014.
Burk/OMNIBUS	Burk, James Mack. *A Charles Ives Omnibus*. Hillsdale, NY: Pendragon, 2008.
Burkholder/ALL MADE	Burkholder, J. Peter. *All Made of Tunes: Charles Ives and the Uses of Musical Borrowing*. New Haven, CT: Yale University Press, 1995.
Burkholder/GROVE	Burkholder, J. Peter. "Ives, Charles (Edward)." In *The Grove Dictionary of American Music*, 2nd ed., edited by Charles Hiroshi Garrett, vol. 4, pp. 378–406. New York: Oxford University Press, 2013. In *Grove Music Online* at www.oxfordmusiconline.com/grovemusic.
Burkholder/IDEAS	Burkholder, J. Peter. *Charles Ives: The Ideas Behind the Music*. New Haven, CT: Yale University Press, 1985.
Burkholder/IVES AND HIS WORLD	Burkholder, J. Peter, ed. *Charles Ives and His World*. Princeton, NJ: Princeton University Press, 1996.
Burkholder/IVES AND YALE	Burkholder, J. Peter. "Ives and Yale: The Enduring Influence of a College Experience." *College Music Symposium* 39 (1999): pp. 27–42.
Burkholder/LISTENING	Burkholder, J. Peter. *Listening to Charles Ives: Variations on His America*. Lanham, MD: Amadeus/Rowman and Littlefield, 2021.
Burkholder/ORGANIST	Burkholder, J. Peter. "The Organist in Ives." *Journal of the American Musicological Society* 55 (Summer 2002): pp. 255–310.
Burkholder/QUOTATION	Burkholder, J. Peter. "'Quotation' and Paraphrase in Ives's Second Symphony." *19th-Century Music* 11 (Summer 1987): pp. 3–25.
Burkholder/RULE-BREAKING	Burkholder, J. Peter. "Rule-Breaking as a Rhetorical Sign." In *Festa Musicologica: Essays in Honor of George J. Buelow*, edited by Thomas J. Mathiesen and Benito V. Rivera, pp. 369–89. New York: Pendragon, 1995.
Burkholder/TOPICS	Burkholder, J. Peter. "Stylistic Heterogeneity and Topics in the Music of Charles Ives." *Journal of Musicological Research* 31 (2012): pp. 166–99.
Burkholder/TRADITIONS	Burkholder, J. Peter. "Ives and the Four Musical Traditions." In *Charles Ives and His World*, edited by J. Peter Burkholder, pp. 3–34. Princeton, NJ: Princeton University Press, 1996.
Cage/TWO STATEMENTS	Cage, John. "Two Statements on Ives." In *A Year from Monday*, pp. 36–42. Middletown, CT: Wesleyan University Press, 1967.
Charles/BORROWED	Charles, Sydney Robinson. "The Use of Borrowed Materials in Ives's Second Symphony." *Music Review* 28 (May 1967): pp. 102–11.

Cowell/CHARLES E IVES	Cowell, Henry. "Charles E. Ives." In *American Composers on American Music*, edited by Henry Cowell, pp. 128–45. Stanford, CA: Stanford University Press, 1933.
Cowell/CHRONICLE	Cowell, Henry. Note on Ives's Second Symphony, in "Current Chronicle." *Musical Quarterly* 37 (July 1951): pp. 399–402.
Cowell and Cowell/CHARLES IVES	Cowell, Henry, and Sidney Cowell. *Charles Ives and His Music*. Rev. ed. New York: Oxford University Press, 1969.
Crane/JEW'S HARP	Crane, Frederick. "How Should the Jew's Harp Part of 'Washington's Birthday' Be Played?" *Vierundzwanzigstejahrsschrift der Internationalen Maultrommelvirtuosengenossenschaft* 1 (1982): pp. 49–57.
Cyr/INTERVALLIC	Cyr, Gordon. "Intervallic Structural Elements in Ives's Fourth Symphony." *Perspectives of New Music* 9, no. 2, and 10, no. 1 (Spring/Summer–Fall/Winter 1971): pp. 291–303.
Deane/PREMIERES	Deane, James G. "Capital's U.S. Fete Includes Fifteen Premieres." *Musical Courier* 147, July 1953, p. 29.
Eiseman/SYMPHONIC TRADITION	Eiseman, David. "Charles Ives and the European Symphonic Tradition: A Historical Reappraisal." PhD diss., University of Illinois at Urbana-Champaign, 1972.
Elkus/BAND TRADITION	Elkus, Jonathan. *Charles Ives and the American Band Tradition: A Centennial Tribute*. Exeter, UK: American Arts Documentation Centre, University of Exeter, 1974.
Elkus/SECOND SYMPHONY	Elkus, Jonathan. "Ives's Second Symphony as Two Cyclic Overtures with an Unrealized Debt to Berlioz: A Wind Band Perspective on the 'Overture Habit.'" In *Kongressberichte Bad Waltersdorf/Steiermark 2000, Lana/Südtirol 2002*, edited by Bernhard Habla, pp. 317–34. Alta Musica: Eine Publikation der Internationalen Gesellschaft zur Erforschung und Förderung der Blasmusik, no. 24. Tutzing, Germany: Hans Schneider, 2003.
Feder/DECORATION DAY	Feder, Stuart. "Decoration Day: A Boyhood Memory of Charles Ives." *Musical Quarterly* 66 (April 1980): pp. 234–61.
Feder/IVES	Feder, Stuart. *Charles Ives, "My Father's Song": A Psychoanalytic Biography*. New Haven, CT: Yale University Press, 1992.
Gail/4. SYMPHONIE	Gail, Dorothea. "Die 4. Symphonie von Charles Ives: Hermeneutik zwischen Programmatik und absoluter Musik." In *Charles Ives*, edited by Ulrich Tadday, pp. 73–87. Musik-Konzepte n.s. 123. Munich: Text und Kritik, 2004.

Gail/FOURTH SYMPHONY	Gail, Dorothea. *Charles E. Ives' Fourth Symphony: Quellen—Analyse—Deutung*. 3 vols. Hofheim, Germany: Wolke, 2009.
Gann/CONCORD	Gann, Kyle. *Charles Ives's "Concord": Essays after a Sonata*. Urbana: University of Illinois Press, 2017.
Glarner/INVESTIGATION	Glarner, Robert Lewis. "An Investigation into the Relationship of Instrumental Density and Dynamics of the Fourth Symphony by Charles Ives." PhD diss., University of Arizona, 1993.
Henderson/TUNEBOOK	Henderson, Clayton. *The Charles Ives Tunebook*. 2nd ed. Bloomington: Indiana University Press, 2008.
Hepokoski/SIBELIUS	Hepokoski, James. *Sibelius: Symphony No. 5*. Cambridge: Cambridge University Press, 1993.
Hertz/ANGELS	Hertz, David Michael. *Angels of Reality: Emersonian Unfoldings in Wright, Stevens, and Ives*. Carbondale and Edwardsville: Southern Illinois University Press, 1993.
Horowitz/DVOŘÁK'S PROPHECY	Horowitz, Joseph. *Dvořák's Prophecy: and the Vexed Fate of Black Classical Music*. New York: W. W. Norton, 2022.
Horowitz/MORAL FIRE	Horowitz, Joseph. *Moral Fire: Musical Portraits from America's Fin de Siècle*. Berkeley: University of California Press, 2012.
Ives/CORRESPONDENCE	Ives, Charles. *Selected Correspondence of Charles Ives*. Edited by Tom C. Owens. Berkeley: University of California Press, 2007.
Ives/DECORATION DAY	Ives, Charles E. *Decoration Day*. Edited by James B. Sinclair. New York: Peer International, 1989.
Ives/ESSAYS	Ives, Charles. *Essays Before a Sonata, The Majority, and Other Writings*. Edited by Howard Boatwright. New York: W. W. Norton, 1970.
Ives/MEMOS	Ives, Charles. *Memos*. Edited and with appendices by John Kirkpatrick. New York: W. W. Norton, 1972.
Ives/SYMPHONY	Ives, Charles E. *Symphony No. 4*. Edited by James B. Sinclair, William Brooks, Kenneth Singleton, and Wayne D. Shirley. New York: Associated Music, 2011.
Ives/THREE PLACES	Ives, Charles E. *Three Places in New England*. Boston: C. C. Birchard, 1935.
Ives/WASHINGTON'S BIRTHDAY	Ives, Charles E. *Washington's Birthday*. Edited by James B. Sinclair. New York: Associated Music, 1991.
Jacko/CONTEXT	Jacko, Michael Alexander. "Context, Ideology, and Performance in Charles Ives's Symphony No. 4." DMA diss., University of Maryland, 2014.
Janicka-Słysz/IV SYMFONIA	Janicka-Słysz, Małgorzata. "IV Symfonia Charlesa Edwarda Ivesa [Charles Ives's Fourth Symphony]." *Zeszyty naukowe: akademia muzyczna im. stanisława moniuszki w Gdańsku, Poland* 27 (1988): pp. 75–94.

Johnson/BASEBALL	Johnson, Timothy. *Baseball and the Music of Charles Ives: A Proving Ground.* Lanham, MD: Scarecrow, 2004.
Johnson/YANKEE REALISM	Johnson, Marc E. "Charles Ives's (Utopian, Pragmatist, Nostalgic, Progressive, Romantic, Modernist) Yankee Realism." *American Music* 20 (Summer 2002): pp. 188–231.
Josephson/INITIAL SKETCHES	Josephson, Nors S. "The Initial Sketches for Ives's 'St. Gaudens in Boston Common.'" *Soundings* 12 (1984–85): pp. 46–63.
Kirkpatrick/CATALOGUE	Kirkpatrick, John. *A Temporary Mimeographed Catalogue of the Music Manuscripts and Related Materials of Charles Edward Ives.* New Haven, CT: Yale Music Library, 1960.
Kramer/MUSICAL TIME	Kramer, Jonathan D. "Postmodern Concepts of Musical Time." *Indiana Theory Review* 17, no. 2 (Fall 1996): pp. 21–61.
Kramer/POLITICS OF MEMORY	Kramer, Lawrence. "Music and the Politics of Memory: Charles Ives's *A Symphony: New England Holidays.*" *Journal of the Society for American Music* 2 (November 2008): pp. 459–75.
Lambert/IVES STUDIES	Lambert, Philip, ed. *Ives Studies.* Cambridge: Cambridge University Press, 1997.
Lambert/IVES'S UNIVERSE	Lambert, Philip. "Ives's Universe." In *Ives Studies*, edited by Philip Lambert, pp. 233–59. Cambridge: Cambridge University Press, 1997.
Lambert/MUSIC	Lambert, Philip. *The Music of Charles Ives.* New Haven, CT: Yale University Press, 1997.
Lipkis/ASPECTS	Lipkis, Laurence Alan. "Aspects of Temporality in Debussy's 'Jeux' and Ives' 'Symphony No. 4,' Fourth Movement." PhD diss., University of California, Santa Barbara, 1984.
Lück/VISIONEN	Lück, Hartmut. "Visionen einer anderen Wirklichkeit: Die symphonischen Werk von Charles Ives." In *Charles Ives, 1874–1954: Amerikanischer Pionier der neuen Musik*, edited by Hanns-Werner Heister, pp. 123–37. Trier, Germany: Wissenschaftlicher Verlag Trier, 2004.
Lyman/COMPLETING	Lyman, Zachary. "Completing Ives's *Universe Symphony*: An Interview with Larry Austin." *American Music* 26 (Winter 2008): pp. 442–73.
Lyman/DUALITY	Lyman, Zachary T. "Duality and Process in 'The Greatest Legend of American Music': A Comparative Study of Realizations and Completions of Charles Ives's *Universe Symphony* by Larry Austin, David Porter, and Johnny Reinhard." DMA diss., University of Iowa, 2007.

Lyman/REALIZING	Lyman, Zachary. "Realizing Ives's *Universe Symphony*: An Interview with Johnny Reinhard." *American Music* 28 (Winter 2010): pp. 459–80.
Magee/EVERY	Magee, Gayle. "'Every Man in New York': Charles Ives and the First World War." In *Over Here, Over There: Transatlantic Conversations on the Music of World War I*, edited by William Brooks, Christina Bashford, and Gayle Magee, pp. 37–57. Urbana: University of Illinois Press, 2019.
Magee/IVES RECONSIDERED	Magee, Gayle Sherwood. *Charles Ives Reconsidered*. Urbana: University of Illinois Press, 2008.
Magee/RESEARCH	Magee, Gayle Sherwood. *Charles Ives: A Research and Information Guide*. New York: Routledge, 2010.
Magers/ASPECTS	Magers, Roy Vernon. "Aspects of Form in the Symphonies of Charles Ives." PhD diss., Indiana University, 1975.
Magers/OPTIMISM	Magers, Roy V. "Charles Ives's Optimism: or, The Program's Progress." In *Music in American Society 1776–1976: From Puritan Hymn to Synthesizer*, edited by George McCue, pp. 73–86. New Brunswick, NJ: Transaction, 1977.
Maisel/FOURTH	Maisel, Arthur. "*The Fourth of July* by Charles Ives: Mixed Harmonic Criteria in a Twentieth-Century Classic." *Theory and Practice* 6, no. 1 (August 1981): pp. 3–32.
McDonald/TIME'S ARROW	McDonald, Matthew. *Breaking Time's Arrow: Experiment and Expression in the Music of Charles Ives*. Bloomington: Indiana University Press, 2014.
Nelson/BEYOND	Nelson, Mark D. "Beyond Mimesis: Transcendentalism and Processes of Analogy in Charles Ives' *The Fourth of July*." *Perspectives of New Music* 22, no. 1–2 (Fall/Winter 1983–Spring/Summer 1984): pp. 353–84.
Nicholls/EXPERIMENTAL	Nicholls, David. *American Experimental Music, 1890–1940*. Cambridge: Cambridge University Press, 1990.
Osborne/ORGANIST	Osborne, William. "Charles Ives the Organist." *American Organist* 24, no. 7 (July 1990): pp. 58–64.
Paul/IVES IN THE MIRROR	Paul, David C. *Charles Ives in the Mirror: American Histories of an Iconic Composer*. Urbana: University of Illinois Press, 2013.
Perlis/CHARLES IVES PAPERS	Perlis, Vivian, comp. *Charles Ives Papers*. Yale University Music Library Archival Collection Mss. 14. New Haven, CT: Yale University Music Library, 1983.
Perlis/IVES REMEMBERED	Perlis, Vivian. *Charles Ives Remembered: An Oral History*. New Haven, CT: Yale University Press, 1974.
Perry/IVES	Perry, Rosalie Sandra. *Charles Ives and the American Mind*. Kent, OH: Kent State University Press, 1974.

Porter/THIRD ORCHESTRAL SET	Porter, David. "The Third Orchestral Set of Charles Edward Ives." MA thesis, California State University, Fullerton, 1980.
Rathert/AURATISCHE FORM	Rathert, Wolfgang. "Auratische Form und Lebenswirklichkeit—zu Charles Ives' Orchestral Set No. 2 (1909–19)." In *Charles Ives, 1874–1954: Amerikanischer Pionier der neuen Musik*, edited by Hanns-Werner Heister, pp. 138–48. Trier, Germany: Wissenschaftlicher Verlag Trier, 2004.
Rathert/PAYSAGE	Rathert, Wolfgang. "Paysage imaginaire et perception totale: l'idée et la forme de la symphonie *Universe*." *Contrechamps* 7 (1986): pp. 129–54.
Rathert/SEEN AND UNSEEN	Rathert, Wolfgang. "*The Seen and Unseen*": Studien zum Werk von Charles Ives. Berliner musikwissenschaftliche Arbeiten 38. Munich: Emil Katzbichler, 1991.
Rathert/SYMPHONIE NR. 4	Rathert, Wolfgang. "Charles Ives: Symphonie Nr. 4, 1911–1916." *Neuland* 3 (1982–83): pp. 226–41.
Rathert/ZUR ENTWICKLUNG	Rathert, Wolfgang. "Zur Entwicklung des symphonischen Werkes von Charles Ives." In *Bericht über das Internationale Symposion "Charles Ives und die amerikanische Musiktradition bis zur Gegenwart" Köln 1988*, edited by Klaus Wolfgang Niemöller, pp. 53–70. Kölner Beiträge zur Musikforschung 164. Regensburg, Germany: Gustav Bosse, 1990.
Reinhard/IVES UNIVERSE	Reinhard, Johnny. "The Ives Universe: A Symphonic Odyssey." Unpublished manuscript, 2003.
Roller/ANALYSIS	Roller, Jonathan. "An Analysis of Selected Movements from the Symphonies of Charles Ives Using Linear and Set Theoretical Analytical Models." PhD diss., University of Kentucky, 1995.
Rossiter/IVES	Rossiter, Frank R. *Charles Ives and His America*. New York: Liveright, 1975.
Sherwood/CHORAL WORKS	Sherwood, Gayle Dawn. "The Choral Works of Charles Ives: Chronology, Style, Reception." PhD diss., Yale University, 1995.
Sherwood/QUESTIONS	Sherwood, Gayle. "Questions and Veracities: Reassessing the Chronology of Ives's Choral Works." *Musical Quarterly* 78 (Fall 1994): pp. 429–47.
Sherwood/REDATING	Sherwood, Gayle. "Redating Ives's Choral Sources." In *Ives Studies*, edited by Philip Lambert, pp. 77–101. Cambridge: Cambridge University Press, 1997.
Shirley/PREFACE	Shirley, Wayne D. Preface to *The Fourth of July*, by Charles Ives, pp. iii–vii. Edited by Wayne D. Shirley. New York: Associated Music, 1992.
Shirley/SECOND OF JULY	Shirley, Wayne D. "'The Second of July': A Charles Ives Draft Considered as an Independent Work." In

	A Celebration of American Music: Words and Music in Honor of H. Wiley Hitchcock, edited by Richard Crawford, R. Allen Lott, and Carol J. Oja, pp. 391–404. Ann Arbor: University of Michigan Press, 1990.
Shultis/SILENCING	Shultis, Christopher. *Silencing the Sounded Self: John Cage and the American Experimental Tradition*. Hanover, NH: University Press of New England, 2013.
Sinclair/CATALOGUE	Sinclair, James B. *A Descriptive Catalogue of the Music of Charles Ives*. New Haven, CT: Yale University Press, 1999.
Sinclair/COUNTRY BAND TABLE	Sinclair, James B. "Table of Correlative Measures." In *"Country Band" March*, by Charles E. Ives, pp. iii–iv. Edited by James B. Sinclair. Bryn Mawr, PA: Merion Music, 1976.
Sinclair/OVERTURE TABLE	Sinclair, James B. "Table of Correlative Measures." In *Overture and March "1776,"* by Charles E. Ives, p. 34. Edited by James B. Sinclair. Bryn Mawr, PA: Merion Music, 1976.
Singleton/PREFACE	Singleton, Kenneth. Preface to *Symphony No. 3: "The Camp Meeting,"* by Charles Ives, pp. i–xi. Edited by Kenneth Singleton. New York: Associated Music, 1990.
Slonimsky/MUSIC	Slonimsky, Nicolas. *Music since 1900*. 5th ed. New York: Schirmer, 1994.
Solomon/VERACITY	Solomon, Maynard. "Charles Ives: Some Questions of Veracity." *Journal of the American Musicological Society* 40 (Fall 1987): pp. 443–70.
Starr/UNION OF DIVERSITIES	Starr, Larry. *A Union of Diversities: Style in the Music of Charles Ives*. New York: Schirmer, 1992.
Stein/MUSICAL LANGUAGE	Stein, Alan. "The Musical Language of Charles Ives' *Three Places in New England*." DMA diss., University of Illinois at Urbana-Champaign, 1975.
Sterne/QUOTATIONS	Sterne, Colin. "The Quotations in Charles Ives's Second Symphony." *Music and Letters* 52 (January 1971): pp. 39–45.
Swafford/IVES	Swafford, Jan. *Charles Ives: A Life with Music*. New York: W. W. Norton, 1996.
Taruskin/UNIVERSE	Taruskin, Richard. "Two Stabs at the Universe." In *The Danger of Music and Other Anti-utopian Essays*, pp. 51–59. Berkeley: University of California Press, 2009.
Thurmaier/TIME	Thurmaier, David P. "Time and Compositional Process in Charles Ives's *Holidays Symphony*." PhD diss., Indiana University, 2006.
Tucker/ADIRONDACKS	Tucker, Mark. "Of Men and Mountains: Ives in the Adirondacks." In *Charles Ives and His World*, edited by J. Peter Burkholder, pp. 161–96. Princeton, NJ: Princeton University Press, 1996.

Von Glahn/FROM COUNTRY TO CITY	Von Glahn, Denise. "From Country to City in the Music of Charles Ives." In *The Sounds of Place: Music and the American Cultural Landscape*, pp. 64–109. Boston: Northeastern University Press, 2003.
Von Glahn Cooney/NEW SOURCES	Von Glahn Cooney, Denise. "New Sources for *The 'St. Gaudens' in Boston Common (Colonel Robert Gould Shaw and His Colored Regiment)*." *Musical Quarterly* 81 (Spring 1997): pp. 13–50.
Von Glahn Cooney/SENSE OF PLACE	Von Glahn Cooney, Denise. "A Sense of Place: Charles Ives and 'Putnam's Camp, Redding, Connecticut.'" *American Music* 14 (Fall 1996): pp. 276–312.
Zobel/MUSIC	Zobel, Mark A. "'Music Close to the Soil and Deeply Felt': The Use of American Hymn Tunes in Charles Ives's Third Symphony." PhD diss., University of Colorado at Boulder, 2005.
Zobel/THIRD SYMPHONY	Zobel, Mark. *The Third Symphony of Charles Ives*. CMS Sourcebooks in American Music, no. 6. Hillsdale, NY: Pendragon, 2009.

CHAPTER FIVE

From 1920 to 1950 in the United States

THE SYMPHONY IN A WORLD UPENDED

Susan Key, with Drew Massey[1]

Symphonic activity in the United States from 1920 to 1950, initially rooted in established (albeit recently established) orchestral and academic institutions, quickly reflected the impact of economic, political, and technological developments that threatened to undermine both those institutions and the cultural alliances that supported them. At the same time that the rise of mass media radically altered patterns of musical consumption and dissemination, world events initiated new ways of thinking about music's social role and expressive purposes. Successive political and economic crises—World War I, the Russian Revolution, the Great Depression, the rise of fascism, and finally World War II—led to a moment that George Antheil starkly recalled as a time "when the entire future of the world hung in balance."[2] Absorbing the resulting cultural turmoil into musical expression was neither smooth nor homogeneous. Fittingly, the era produced symphonic music that was by turns grandiose and homespun, idealistic and ironic, conventional and ultramodern.

Undergirding the growth of symphonic music in this volatile environment was a steadily maturing musical infrastructure encompassing performance, pedagogy, and commentary. Essential to the search for the "Great American Symphony" was the establishment of the "Great American Symphony Orchestra." To the ensembles in the East and Midwest described by Douglas Bomberger in chapter 3 were added those in San Francisco (1911), Cleveland (1918), and Los Angeles (1919). The new orchestras needed a supply of capable instrumentalists; initially dominated by Europeans, burgeoning university music programs trained aspiring performers and eventually composers. Although the conductors continued to be overwhelmingly European, their repertoire was not one-dimensional. Leopold Stokowski (1882–1977) had been in the United States since 1909, and his unique programming blend of the popular and the avant-garde included many American works. Serge Koussevitzky (1874–1951), who arrived in 1924 and took US citizenship in 1941, championed the work of American composers in a way that Aaron Copland (1900–1990) deemed "unprecedented and irreplaceable."[3] An additional outgrowth of the enriched concert activity was the founding of musical journals: *Etude* (1883), *Musical Courier* (1880), *Musical America* (1898), and *Modern Music* (1924), all of which provided visibility and a lively critical outlet.[4]

Even while these developments fostered a sense of American achievement, they reflected evolving allegiances to European models. Through the first quarter of the century, both music and musical institutions were shaped primarily by Germany; as Douglas Bomberger writes in chapter 3 of this volume, "Perhaps because symphonic writing was a recent phenomenon in America, perhaps because so many of the composers had studied in Europe, or perhaps because the repertoire played by American orchestras was almost exclusively European, the composers of the era and the critics who evaluated their works used the German repertoire as a measuring stick."[5] By contrast, the generation of the 1920s and 30s, which came of age in the shadow of World War I, turned away from the German models that had shaped their forebears; they looked toward other sources of influence and training, both in Europe—especially France and Italy—and at home in the United States. Factors both political (anti-German sentiment stimulated by World War I) and aesthetic (compelling stylistic innovations making headlines in France) contributed to the phenomenon. Enriching and complicating international relationships was the wave of émigré composers who entered the country as refugees from totalitarian regimes and often stayed to attain US citizenship and establish careers. In their capacities as composers and teachers, they contributed both new repertoire and stylistic stimuli to their new institutions.

Both homegrown and émigré activity weakened the hegemony of the institutions and networks of patronage that the Eastern Seaboard had enjoyed up to that point. Although virtually all the composers considered in this chapter built at least part of their careers in New York or Boston, the collective imagination increasingly looked west, both to a burgeoning concert life there and to opportunities provided by the new film industry. And while émigré contributions to film and Broadway garnered more public attention than their contributions to the concert stage, they were also responsible for memorable symphonies.

Amplifying the impact of these demographic and cultural changes was the growth of radio broadcasting. Shortly after the first public broadcasts in 1920 came the boom of 1922, when sales of sets, parts, and accessories totaled $60 million—a figure that had grown to more than $800 million (nearly $14 billion in today's dollars) by the time the stock market crashed in October 1929. As the Great Depression transformed American lifestyles during the next decade, so did the new medium, as both rural and urban dwellers welcomed radio into their most intimate domestic settings. Americans turned to radio for sports, news, and drama—and above all for music. As an early program director stated, "The basis of radio programs has established itself: it is music."[6] Networks consolidated and extended radio's reach: the National Broadcasting Company (NBC) in 1926, the Columbia Broadcasting System (CBS) in 1927, and the Mutual Broadcasting System in 1934. Their establishment brought about a merging of resources that allowed for large-scale cultural efforts; most pertinently for this chapter, the networks established extensive music departments and in-house orchestras that reached an audience far beyond their civic counterparts.

As a result of these developments, the 1930s saw an increase in the number of serious music broadcasts, and, although European music still dominated, the native presence was significant and included many works by the symphonists considered in this chapter. Scattered prizes and competitions sponsored by the networks benefited American composers, for example, the 1932 NBC Orchestral Awards (for works not exceeding twelve minutes) and the Columbia Composer's Commissions (for works not exceeding 40 minutes), instituted in 1937 and 1938. Aaron Copland, Roy Harris, Robert Russell Bennett, Walter Piston, Howard Hanson, Marc Blitzstein, Jerome Moross, Leo Sowerby, William Grant Still, and Carlos Chávez all received commissions from CBS. NBC broadcast portions of Hanson's Festivals of American Music. William Levi Dawson's *Negro Folk Symphony* was broadcast to great acclaim. Regular broadcasts of the New York Philharmonic and the Philadelphia Orchestra often featured composers serving as commentators.[7]

Extending the media's efforts to reach a significant audience were those of the Federal Music Project (FMP). The project supported a range of musical styles, but the largest beneficiaries were orchestras. Its director, Nikolai Sokoloff, favored classical music, although many concert orchestras played popular music as well. The emphasis on American musicians—both performers and composers—was a major factor addressing unemployment in that sector. Symphonies written by Ernst Bacon and Robert Whitney and other compositions by James P. Johnson, William Schuman, and David Diamond were promoted by the FMP.[8] Another initiative of the FMP was the Composers' Forum Laboratory, in which new works were previewed and followed by composer discussions with the audience. Successful works were performed by FMP orchestras across the country; a study notes that "by April 1939 the project's orchestras had performed 6,722 American compositions," including works by Howard Hanson, Virgil Thomson, and Frederick Jacobi.[9] It is difficult to assess the long-term impact of the program, but for younger composers getting started (such as Schuman and Diamond), the career boost was significant.

The steadily increasing quality of American musical life bolstered the country's self-image, and the worth of the music and musical institutions was understood both as a reflection of and contribution to the nation's democratic ideals. In the nineteenth century, John Sullivan Dwight had already articulated the link: "we as a democratic people, a great mixed people of all races, overrunning a vast continent, need music even more than others. . . . The hard-working, jaded millions need expansion, need the rejuvenating, the ennobling experience of JOY."[10] Henry Higginson's embrace of "practical idealism" motivated his establishment of the Boston Symphony Orchestra; he offered low-priced tickets to attract working people.[11] The orchestras founded in the ensuing decades initiated education and outreach concerts from their beginnings, further conflating the highest musical expression with the most sacred national ideals.

Naturally, radio also built on the already established connection between musical institutions and US democracy. In a 1939 speech, CBS's Davidson Taylor reiterated the responsibility and opportunity of writing for a mass audience: "It seems to me that the chief advantage of writing music for radio is social. The availability and amiability of such an enormous audience should tend to increase the dignity of the composer's position, both in his own eyes, as a custodian of revelations, and in the eyes of the community which is willing to hearken to him. . . . it seems to me that a composer has more obligation to speak earnestly to a large community of listeners than he has to speak earnestly to a prince and his court."[12]

Taylor's differentiation between the role of the composer in contemporary life and the servant of the prince and his court reflected the heightened social consciousness about the plight of common people hard hit by the Depression—a phenomenon that shaped both institutional and artistic priorities. Composers as diverse as Aaron Copland, Roy Harris, George Antheil, William Grant Still, and Florence Price, as well as Swiss émigré Ernest Bloch, created symphonies of possibility, intended to celebrate the open-ended vision the United States offered. In this effort, many turned to civic and artistic US heroes (especially Abraham Lincoln and Walt Whitman) for subject matter and to its vernacular styles for a populist musical expression of national ideals—thus redefining greatness as rooted in everyday people. As Copland expressed it, "The need to communicate one's music to the widest possible audience is no mere opportunism. It comes from the healthy desire in every artist to find his deepest feelings reflected in his fellow-man. It is not without its political implications also, for it takes its source partly from that same need to reaffirm the democratic ideal that already fills our literature and our stage."[13]

Copland also acknowledged the connection between the private aesthetic ideal and broader public relevance: "Any composer who ignores the potential mass listener of the future is simply not aware of the time in which he is living. The new radio and phonograph audience . . . is a challenge to every contemporary composer. I visualize a music which is profound in content, simple in expression, and understandable to all."[14]

The decades after World War I thus seemed perfect for the American symphony both as an artistic genre and as an institution—a moment that offered potential for realizing the grand vision of artistic greatness that sprang from and expressed democratic appeal. A 1930 journalist expressed a common optimism: thanks to radio, "there will be more composers, and more interest in composers and their work."[15] Composer Marc Blitzstein proclaimed, "The great mass of people enter at last the field of serious music."[16] Yet, while the genre's expansive and idealistic vision suited the American ethos, its European-derived vocabulary made a poor aural match for the American experience. The postwar ideal of the Great American Symphony demanded something new of composers: music that expressed a transcendent American vision in everyday, democratic language.

In its attempt to understand how, or even if, a symphony that reflected the received understanding of greatness could speak with a distinctively American voice, the musical community of the United States continued the dialogue spurred by Antonín Dvořák's charge to base an American style on Native American and African American idioms. In the 1930s, what had begun as an assumption that white composers might look to African American sources acquired a new reality as four Black symphonists—all directly inspired by Dvořák—emerged to put his idea into practice in works that combined personal, ethnic, and national expressions.

Dvořák's artistic counsel received far from universal acceptance, however. As Bomberger states in chapter 3 of this volume, "American composers of the late nineteenth century found themselves in a double bind: if they wrote music in cosmopolitan style, they could be accused of blindly following German models with no originality of their own; if their music was based on American folk materials, they could be dismissed as provincial or accused of choosing the wrong source material because of America's lack of cultural homogeneity."[17]

Randall Thompson echoed this sentiment in 1932: "When viewed from a distance, the procession of the world's composers resembles a vast spectrum in which one color blends imperceptibly into the next. But if an American composer ventures to join the procession, he is caught in the act and disqualified. On one hand, he is condemned if his work reveals a similarity to that of any other American. . . . And on the other: woe to the American composer who exhibits any kinship with the musical lights of Europe!"[18] The terms of this conversation remained stubbornly durable through midcentury even as composers, critics, and educators grappled with the conversation's relevance to the world around them.

The attempt to reconcile artistic vision, vocabulary, and mission resulted in diverse and sometimes contradictory stylistic currents. An especially dissonant note in the optimism about the potential of the new mass media was the disturbing tendency of the new mass audience to prefer "jazz"—a term used indiscriminately at the time to refer to contemporary popular music.[19] Leonard Liebling expressed a combination of hope and despair when he acknowledged "the opportunity [radio] affords embryo composers in obscure localities. . . . If it starts only one American composer on the road to great achievement, the loudspeaker may be forgiven for some of its abominable sins in jazz."[20] When asked whether there was a prejudice against his music because of its popular orientation, Morton Gould responded, "Absolutely. My friends were snobs. It gave me a kind of unique experience, but it established prejudices that were hard to overcome. [In my efforts in popular music] I was broadcasting to millions of people, versus symphonic works to hundreds. The disparity created a kind of stigma."[21] As will be seen in this chapter, even many of the composers who consciously cultivated an American voice looked to rural folk idioms that more easily fit into a romantic conception of pure musical sources than did the new commercial genres.

In spite of the establishment's dismissive attitude toward contemporary popular music, it inspired a number of stylistic responses among the symphonists considered in this chapter—from a bit of local color to a more systematic musical influence. Moreover, it served as the vehicle for a new hybrid orchestral style explored by arguably the most important American composer of the era: George Gershwin's *Rhapsody in Blue* was followed four years later by the symphonic composition *An American in Paris*.[22] Such works stimulated an even more thoroughgoing integration of the popular music of Harlem into traditional concert genres; this style, explored especially by James P. Johnson and Duke Ellington, has been termed "concert jazz." As John Howland notes, "The hybrid symphonic jazz sound developed an unusual cultural breadth that spanned the concert hall, jazz and dance bands, radio orchestras, Tin Pan Alley, Broadway musical theater, the variety prologue shows of the deluxe movie palaces, and certain genres of film music of the late 1920s and 1930s."[23] Favorite genres for the new style included symphonies and especially symphonic poems or similar descriptive works. As Bomberger points out in chapter 3 of this volume, both Europeans and Americans were building on the genre of the symphonic poem during the late nineteenth century, and the radio outlet only added to the genre's attractiveness; indeed, some of the multimovement works discussed in this chapter, such as Johnson's *Harlem Symphony*, could equally be described as sets of symphonic poems.

Another point of tension in this era was the growing polarization between "moderns" and "music appreciators": while some within the modernist community of the 1920s, motivated by the Depression, modified their language to reach a wider audience, others largely ignored the challenge of reconciling their ideological commitment to the broad dissemination of new music with a compositional idiom that appealed only to a small audience. This conflict also affected émigré composers such as Ernest Bloch, whose grand symphony *America*—which climaxed in an audience chorale—became an important element in undermining his reputation as a modernist.[24] Composers in this chapter, most prominently Hanson and Thompson, were articulate about such pressures. As Hanson put it, The composer "must be atonal, pantonal, polytonal, cereal-rolled oats or puffed wheat—duodecaphonic, octadaphonic or pentadaphonic or perhaps electrophonic; music, concrete, or cement. Honesty is not easy and often is indulged in with the greatest economy."[25]

The outbreak of World War II in Europe and the subsequent attack on Pearl Harbor intensified a sense of artistic urgency and need for clarity, and a number of symphonies examined in this chapter were either a direct or indirect response to the war. Writing in 1943, Douglas Moore reported not just an increase in activity but in enthusiasm: "Audiences were quicker to respond to our native music . . . with the increase of national pride which has followed automatically in the wake of the war."[26] The impact of Dmitri Shostakovich's (1906–75) 1941 *Leningrad Symphony* underscored the genre as the most appropriate for the historical moment. As Annegret Fauser puts it, the symphony was "the crowning genre of musical Americana during World War II . . . because—rather than in spite—of its universalist pedigree.[27]

Composers, critics, and educators thus found themselves divided on three fronts: over the definition of greatness, over the desirability of composing for a mass audience, and over what deserved to be celebrated as American. By the end of the period, even those who celebrated the mass audience were faced with the cultural contradictions that slowly but inexorably emerged, and the post-1945 era saw the dialogue about the "Great American Symphony" and the mass audience gradually abandoned by the intellectual and artistic community. But, through the war years, the quest for the elusive iconic symphonic statement was still part of the fluid mix of philosophy and practicality in the contemporary environment, and until midcentury the idea of its achievement remained a pervasive, if elusive, hope.

～

This chapter considers twenty composers whose bodies of symphonies ranked among the most prominent efforts in the genre between 1920 and 1950.[28] Because the symphony still represented the pinnacle of instrumental composition, they were affiliated with the leading concert and academic institutions and the foremost stylistic trends of the time (Romanticism, Neoclassicism, "Americana," and Modernism). They are grouped in three major sections: (1) American symphonists who studied in Europe, (2) American composers who studied in the United States, and (3) symphonists who immigrated to the United States.

The organization of the chapter requires some explanation, as it differs from the more typical organization based on style. For this group of American composers, however, such an approach would obscure rather than illuminate. Because so many of them were stylistically eclectic, such a scheme would mean that a single composer's symphonies would appear in multiple sections, which would depart from the approach taken by this series. Moreover, eclecticism itself provides insight into the many influences, both homegrown and from abroad, that the composers encountered and is best untangled from a straightforward geographic perspective. There remain significant overlaps within the categories: many composers, like Samuel Barber, who trained abroad, studied in the United States first, and many American-based figures, such as William Grant Still, also took lessons with émigré Europeans. Nonetheless, the distinctions are useful for illuminating the ways in which American musical culture was evolving.

While it remained the widespread practice for composers in the generation that came of age in the 1920s to go to Europe for study, these artists, as earlier noted, generally turned away from Germany and mostly migrated to two centers established nearly simultaneously in 1921: the American Conservatory in Fontainebleau, France, and the newly created music program at the American Academy in Rome (some composers studied elsewhere in Europe, but the most significant overseas-trained symphonists attended one of these two institutions).

The European-trained cohort would come to occupy the majority of leadership positions within the classical music institutions of the country, but American-educated composers on the periphery of these establishments nonetheless made major contributions to the symphonic repertoire. The standouts among them are four Black symphonists (William Grant Still, Florence Price, William Levi Dawson, and James P. Johnson), the modernist-turned-Hollywood composer George Antheil, and the idiosyncratic Henry Cowell.

The third section focuses on émigré composers and their important contributors to the symphonic repertoire. Many of their works also played an important role in shaping academic and concert life in the period covered in the present chapter. The chapter will close with "brief mentions" of fifty-one composers whose symphonic works have fallen out of favor but enjoyed at least a brief period of recognition and respect. To be sure, the list points to the ephemeral nature of fame, but it also says something about the stranglehold that the major universities and symphonic institutions had on the music that Americans continued to hear after a work enjoyed a first blush of enthusiasm.

No single chapter can do justice to the sweep of the American symphony from 1920 to 1950, and many composers who were heard frequently at the time have necessarily been left out of the present account. Julie Schnepel's index of American symphonies performed between 1893 and 1950 points to other composers who moved in this musical world during the 1930s and 1940s. The brief mentions include many works worthy of more attention in all three categories: European-trained, American-trained, and émigrés. Taken together, the following pages reflect a much more diverse musical landscape than is generally provided by standard surveys. We hope that music directors and academics will find both new repertoires to program and new scholarly topics that will contribute to a fuller understanding of this vital cultural era.

European-Trained Composers: The *Boulangerie*

The importance of Nadia Boulanger (1887–1979) to music pedagogy, especially for twentieth-century American composers, is well documented. The daughter of a Prix de Rome winner, she studied at the Paris Conservatoire and placed second in that competition in 1908 before eventually abandoning composition in favor of teaching. (Her younger sister, Lili, won the Prix de Rome in 1913; she died prematurely in 1918.) In 1921, Nadia's discovery by a trio of young Americans—Melville Smith, Aaron Copland, and Virgil Thomson—led to a steady stream of aspiring composers coming from across the Atlantic. She also spent time in the United States during World War II, teaching at Wellesley College, Radcliffe College, Peabody Conservatory, and the Juilliard School, and she also conducted the Boston Symphony Orchestra, the Philadelphia Orchestra, and the New York Philharmonic.[29] Her influence has persisted beyond her death through the composition and teaching careers of her many distinguished alumni, a list that includes, in addition to the composers discussed later, Elliott Carter, Ingolf Dahl, David Diamond, Thea Musgrave, Astor Piazzolla, Quincy Porter, Louise Talma, and Philip Glass.[30]

Much has been written about Boulanger's unique pedagogical approach. As Leon Botstein has observed, "What made Boulanger a great and magnetic teacher not only for a cadre of famous composers but for many other distinguished musicians who studied with her was less the imposition of an aesthetic than the transmission of discipline and the encouragement of individuality."[31] As Virgil Thomson put it, "Her teaching of the musical techniques is . . . full of rigor, while her toleration of expressive and stylistic variety in composition is virtually infinite."[32] Walter Piston recalled that "she never taught composers particular styles, but rather she influenced them to find their own."[33]

It was important to the evolution of American music during this period that Boulanger was also supportive of the discussion of what made a specifically "American" sound. Thomson recalled that her message to Americans was "that they would find no model in Western Europe for their growing pains, and very little sympathy," comparing their situation to that of Russia in the mid-nineteenth century.[34] Accordingly, she encouraged her students to take advantage of the jazz and popular music–infused soundscape of postwar France.[35] Although the four major American symphonists whom she trained (discussed here in alphabetical order) were stylistically diverse, each benefited from her insistence on exacting standards as a path toward individual creativity.

MARC BLITZSTEIN: THE *AIRBORNE* SYMPHONY

Marc Blitzstein (1905–64) composed only a single symphony, the *Airborne* (table 5.1). It is arguably more oratorio than symphony, to judge by its instrumentation: thirteen winds, eleven brass, timpani, percussion, harp, piano, strings, speaker (whom Blitzstein calls the monitor), baritone and tenor soloists, and all-male chorus. The work lasts almost an hour in performance, with spoken and sung texts permeating the work. Despite its exceptional characteristics, it also represents a prime illustration of the drive to create a public pronouncement through a large symphonic work.

Using music to create public commentary was a longtime concern of Blitzstein's. After studies at the Curtis Institute of Music and then in Europe with Boulanger and Arnold Schoenberg (1874–1951), he settled in New York in the mid-1930s and immersed himself in both music and politics, eventually joining the Communist Party. As he recalled in an interview with the *Daily Worker*, "I realized that this world I never made needed change and, as an artist, I could use my music as a weapon in that struggle."[36] His 1937 pro-labor musical play *The Cradle*

Table 5.1 The *Airborne Symphony* of Marc Blitzstein (1905–64)[a]

Date	Movements	Instrumentation	Comments
1943–44	Part I[b] 1. Theory of Flight 2. Ballad of History and Mythology 3. Kitty Hawk 4. The Airborne Part II[b] 5. The Enemy 6. Threat and Approach 7. Ballad of the Cities 8. Morning Poem Part III[b] 9. The Ballad of Hurry-Up 10. Night Music: Ballad of the Bombardier 11. Chorus of the Rendezvous Epilogue 12. The Open Sky	Grand + Flt. (doubling Picc.), Ob. (doubling EH), Clar. (doubling Bclar.), Cbssn., Tpt., Tuba, Perc. (BD, SD, Cym., Tam-tam, Xylo., Chimes in C and D-flat, Ratchet, Sleigh-bells, Tri., Wood Block, Tamb., Wind Machine), Harp, Pno. Cel. Speaker ("Monitor"), Tenor solo, Baritone solo, TTBB Chorus	While serving in the military, Blitzstein proposed the symphony to the Army Air Force in late 1942. First performance: April 1, 1946, by the New York City Symphony, conducted by Leonard Bernstein, with Orson Welles as the Monitor, and Charles Holland and Walter Scheff singing the tenor and baritone solos, respectively. Published by Warner/Chappell; materials on rental from European American Music. Text by the composer. Blitzstein variously labeled the work as a "lyric symphony" or "ballad symphony"; he also accepted "dramatic cantata," "oratorio," "dramatic suite," and "tone poem."

a. The autograph is digitized on the New York Philharmonic Archives website (http://archives.nyphil.org/index.php/artifact/143f37c1-a9aa-4529-87a8-d742f0986039/fullview#page/1/mode/2up), but only vol. 1 (parts I and II) is available.

b. In unpublished notes, Blitzstein names the three parts "Air Age," "Air Threat," and "Air Force."

Will Rock attracted notoriety when the Works Progress Administration canceled the premiere over concerns that its biting commentary would further aggravate political tensions. As with a number of his ideological colleagues, the outbreak of the war shifted Blitzstein's attention from domestic to international struggles, and he felt the magnitude of the situation required music capable of grand statements. As he wrote to David Diamond, "Of course symphonies must be written now."[37] Fittingly, the *Airborne* combines urgent social commentary with the *gravitas* of a symphony.

Blitzstein joined the military in 1942, and he lent his talents to a number of musical and dramatic projects. He proposed the *Airborne* to his superiors in the Army Air Force in December 1942, and his project was approved the following month. He was relieved of almost all other duties, and although he initially thought the work would take about six months to write, he did not announce its completion until April 17, 1944.[38]

The *Airborne* follows the 1920s tradition of dramatic concert works with a spoken narrator (such as Arthur Honegger's 1921 *Le Roi David* and Igor Stravinsky's 1927 *Oedipus Rex*, as well as Copland's recently debuted *A Lincoln Portrait*), but it relies on a structure beholden to no single genre. Blitzstein called it a "lyric symphony" or a "ballad symphony," but he also entertained describing it as a "dramatic cantata," "oratorio," "dramatic suite," or "tone poem." He wrote the text himself, naming poets Genevieve Taggard and W. H. Auden as two of his influences.[39]

The timing of *Airborne* coincided with another change of aesthetic orientation, as biographer Howard Pollack notes: "The early 1940s [was] a turning point for the composer in terms not only of an increasingly populist outlook, but relatedly, a more wholehearted embrace of various kinds of folk music. As such, he approached attitudes held for several years by some musical friends on the left, although his special attachment to Soviet and African-American music represented a point of difference from, say, Thomson or Copland, who seemed more attracted to Anglo-American and Latin-American folklore."[40]

Blitzstein considered that the chorus might be "composed equally of white and black singers" and he wanted a "negro voice" for the tenor solo.[41] The monitor is specified as tenor or baritone.

The symphony is divided into twelve movements, which the composer grouped into three large sections with an epilogue.[42] In unpublished notes, Blitzstein titled the sections "Air Age," "Air Threat," and "Air Force," and they follow a basic thematic outline of celebrating the early history and development of flight, its destructive potential in war, the life of pilots, and the push toward victory.[43] Blitzstein's panorama, ranging from mythology and primitive human history to contemporary experience, offers a musical analogue to the large murals (often supported by the Works Progress Administration) created in the 1930s and '40s that addressed various aspects of technology within the huge sweep of human experience.[44]

Within the twelve movements, Blitzstein circulates through many instrumental and vocal combinations as well as musical styles, creating a kind of musico-dramatic kaleidoscope. For example, the full ensemble of orchestra, chorus, soloists, and narrator employed in "Ballad of the Cities" is immediately followed by "Morning Poem," in which the narrator recites a text without any accompaniment. In the third movement, "Kitty Hawk," Blitzstein makes an interesting decision to introduce the crucial moment of flight with the simple words "There you go"; the flight itself is depicted musically, with light woodwinds building to grand dissonant statements, and it ends with the text of the matter-of-fact telegram from Orville Wright to his father announcing the brothers' achievement. The narrator also employs a variety of paces, rhetorical tones, and narrative stances vis-à-vis the audience, at times speaking in first person and directly addressing the audience ("you and I").

The variety of aesthetic choices reveals Blitzstein's fluency in moving between multiple registers and genres both musically and dramaturgically. Incongruous on the surface as a symphony, it reveals a deeper truth about the way music and text can weave together; the ultimate effect is that of unstaged theater akin to the radio dramas of the era, and in fact the *Airborne* libretto was included in the 1947 volume *Radio's Best Plays*. Blitzstein had worked in radio, and in fact he conceived of the piece early on as "a concert-work, but one adaptable for radio—or even film production."[45]

Supporting the variety of dramatic shapes is an analogous musical eclecticism, harnessing both vernacular and cultivated idioms to achieve maximum effect. The vocal writing is largely quite simple, perhaps to allow amateur choruses to sing (this also makes words quite clear). The large orchestra includes such special instruments as a wind machine, ratchet, and sleigh bells. A lush Hollywood style is used for large climaxes.

In their evocation of vernacular idioms, several moments stand out. The blues- and folk-inflected solo tenor melody of the second movement, "Ballad of History and Mythology," is accompanied by jaunty woodwind syncopations. The reference is still more explicit when recalling that Blitzstein envisioned a Black singer as the soloist. Similarly, the "Ballad of Hurry-Up" unmistakably relies on a variety of Americanisms: the barbershop quartet, the Tin Pan Alley song, phrases such as "the side is retired." For its part, the movement "Night Music: Ballad of the Bombardier," draws on the lyrical conventions of 1940s musical theater, including intimate vocal passages accompanied by piano.

At the same time, there are moments when Blitzstein cultivates learned styles. He makes extensive use of solo wind counterpoint, including early in the first movement. In the fifth movement, "The Enemy," he creates a playfully ironic mismatch between the bouncing orchestra and the stern narrator, whose rhythmic speaking over Stravinskyan winds seems almost like a reimagining of that composer's *Histoire du soldat* or even Prokofiev's *Peter and the Wolf*. Similarly, the freely dissonant counterpoint in this movement is followed by the *Sturm und Drang* of "Threat and Approach." Blitzstein had Beethoven's String Quartet in C-sharp Minor, Op. 131, in mind—a "long pattern that repeats towards the end, gaining excitement, before Grave."[46] There are echoes of Shostakovich in the jagged wind insertions and asymmetrical melodic patterns, contrasted with a more lyrical section.

The last movement, "The Open Sky," begins with the chorus intoning "Glory" twice before being joined by the orchestra and then the narrator lauding "victory"—all suggesting that the piece will have a triumphant ending. Yet a pastoral interlude leads in a different direction, and soon the narrator introduces a note of ambiguity: "Whose victory" and "not without warning." The ambivalence was deliberate: "I have taken a risk in the ending of the Airborne. Most symphonies, you know, end on a single note, maybe triumph, maybe tragedy. But a symphony about our times cannot have that luxury—you cannot do that and be honest with yourself. No victory is unqualified victory, no glory is unqualified glory. So the Airborne ends in conflict. There is a great paean of triumph over the enemy, sung by the chorus, but a single voice—the narrator—begins to jab in the note of warning! Warning!"[47]

Leonard Bernstein conducted the premiere of the *Airborne* on April 1, 1946, with the New York City Symphony; Orson Welles was the narrator, and Charles Holland and Walter Scheff sang the tenor and baritone solos, respectively. Heard only a year after V-E Day and less than eight months after V-J Day, the piece spurred a "frenzied ovation."[48] The critical response was largely positive, and some writers even heard in the work a path forward to a new synthesis for the Great American Symphony. The composer Wallingford Riegger (1885–1961)—himself a symphonist in the serial style—wrote that Blitzstein "has found a common denominator between the 'highbrow' and 'lowbrow' . . . and with unerring good taste has avoided any impression of incongruity."[49] Harold Clurman echoed this sentiment: "Should this piece prove ephemeral[,] . . . it is still important as a pioneer piece for those ultimate syntheses which will one day come, perhaps through another generation of artists. There is an aliveness here certainly which didn't obtain in the more 'dignified' academic American music of yesteryear."[50]

Although the work received several performances after its premiere—exhaustively catalogued in Pollack's biography—later critics tended to find the work somewhat embarrassing. Donal Henahan, writing for the *New York Times*, groused that "it drapes itself clumsily over some of the worst poesy ever committed to paper"; Bernard Holland thought it was "closer to Norman Rockwell than to Beethoven's Ninth."[51] Pollack considers these criticisms unfair, and asks us to consider the composer's goals when appraising the work: "Blitzstein did not write the piece so much in order to 'rally the folks back home' as to be performed and heard by military personnel in the field of operations. And if he wanted to amuse the 'kids' in the air force with 'Ballad of History and Mythology' and 'Ballad of Hurry-Up,' or tug at their heartstrings with 'Morning Poem' and 'Ballad of the Bombardier,' he also meant the *Airborne* as a sort of learning piece."[52]

In mounting such a response to critics of the *Airborne Symphony*, Pollack underscores again the dilemma faced in evaluating topical compositions: he invites us to consider the material in its historical context while at the same time tacitly acknowledging that the milieu is comparatively foreign to the twenty-first century concertgoing public. Nonetheless, the work can still find relevance for today's ensembles, as its social commentary and focus on the devastating effects of war could definitely resonate with modern audiences.[53]

AARON COPLAND

The three symphonies of Aaron Copland (1900–1990) rank among his most important works, and a lengthy bibliography attests to the centrality of their role, along with his other orchestral compositions, in defining his presence among American composers in the twentieth century.[54] (table 5.2) Despite his long career, all his symphonies are concentrated in the period under consideration here: the First Symphony dates from 1924 (rev. 1928), the Second or *Short Symphony* from 1931–33, and the Third Symphony from 1944–45.[55] The three exemplify crucial moments in the evolution of his style, from the early influences of popular styles and jazz as well as Stravinsky to a leaner, high modernist style, and then to populism. Yet what is most striking when the works are juxtaposed is the underlying stylistic consistency: repetitious, even obsessive, rhythmic patterns; spare textures; distinct articulations highlighted by percussion; and melodic and harmonic material built on open fourths and fifths. These features give Copland's musical voice its distinctive lean, distilled, and tightly constructed quality.

Symphony for Organ and Orchestra / First Symphony

Copland's First Symphony originated as a Symphony for Organ and Orchestra, written in 1924. That piece, his first large-scale orchestral work, marked a turning point for the young composer, as it established Copland's relationship with Serge Koussevitzky. Nadia Boulanger organized the meeting between conductor and composer in Paris in 1923. Copland remembered the encounter vividly, twenty years later:

Table 5.2 The Symphonies of Aaron Copland (1900–1990)

Title and date	Movements	Instrumentation	Comments
Symphony for Organ and Orchestra/First Symphony (1924, rescored 1928)	1. Prelude: Andante 6/8 (91 mm.) 2. Scherzo: Allegro molto—Moderato 3/4 (295 mm.) 3. Finale: Lento; Allegro moderato 4/4 (266 mm.) (Measure numbers based on the score of the First Symphony)	Symphony for Organ and Orchestra: Grand + Picc., EH, Bclar., Cbssn., Tpt., Tuba, Perc. (Xylo, Cym., Wood Block, BD, SD, Tamb.), 2 Harps, Cel., Org. First Symphony: Grand + Picc., EH, Bclar., Cbssn., Asax., 4 Hr., 3 Tpt., Perc. (Glsp., Xylo., Cym., Tam-tam, Wood Block, BD, SD, Tamb.), Pno., 2 Harps	Written at the encouragement of Serge Koussevitzky and Nadia Boulanger (who would play the organ). Dedicated to Nadia Boulanger "with admiration, A. C. (1924)." First performance: January 11, 1925, by the New York Symphony Orchestra, conducted by Walter Damrosch. Second performance with Koussevitzky and the Boston Symphony Orchestra followed on February 20. Score published by Cos Cob, 1931; distributed by Boosey and Hawkes. In 1928, Copland rescored the symphony for full orchestra without organ, replacing it with additional instruments. He renamed the work First Symphony. Premiere: Berlin, December 1931, by the Berlin Symphony Orchestra, conducted by Ernest Ansermet. Score published by Cos Cob, 1931; distributed by Boosey & Hawkes.
Dance Symphony (1929)	1. Introduction: Lento—Molto allegro—Adagio molto C (202 mm.) 2. Andante moderato 3/4 (132 mm.) 3. Allegro vivo 5/4 (314 mm.)	Grand + Picc., EH, D Clar., Bclar., Cbssn., Tpt., Cor., Tuba, Perc. (Xylo., Cym., Tam-tam, Tri., Wood Block, Whip, BD, SD, Tamb., Rattle), 2 Harps, Pno., Cel.	Created as a submission for a $25,000 competition, sponsored by RCA Victor, for a new symphonic work; Copland split the award with three other entrants. Dedicated to Harold Clurman. First performance: April 15, 1931, by the Philadelphia Orchestra, conducted by Leopold Stokowski. Score published by Cos Cob, 1931; distributed by Boosey & Hawkes. Not a true symphony, but a set of three dances (with some newly written passages) taken from the unperformed ballet *Grohg* (1922–25).

Short Symphony (Symphony No. 2, 1933)	1. ♩ = 144 C (179 mm.) 2. ♩ = ca. 44 2/2 (95 mm.) 3. ♩ = 144 (preciso e ritmico) 2/4 (236 mm.)	2 Flt. (1 doubling Alto Flt.), Picc., 2 Ob., EH (doubling Heckelphone ad lib.), Bclar., Cbssn., 4 Hr., 2 Tpt., Pno., Strgs.	Dedicated to Carlos Chávez. First performance: November 23, 1934, in Mexico City by the Orquesta Sinfónica Nacional de México, conducted by Chávez. Score published by Boosey & Hawkes, 1955. Because of its rhythmic difficulties, the symphony received few performances and Copland rescored it in 1937 as a sextet for clarinet, piano, and string quartet.
Third Symphony (1944–46)	1. Molto moderato C (180 mm.) 2. Allegro molto ₵ (352 mm.) 3. Andantino quasi allegretto 5/4 (234 mm.) 4. Molto deliberato (Fanfare)—Allegro risoluto C (388 mm.)	Grand + Flt., Picc., EH, E♭Bclar., Bclar., Cbssn., Tpt., Tuba, Perc. (Glsp., Tubular Bells, Xylo., Anvil, Tam-tam, Tri., Claves, Wood Block, Whip, BD, SD, Tenor Drum, Rattle), 2 Harps, Cel., Pno.	Commissioned by the Koussevitzky Music Foundation and dedicated "to the memory of my dear friend Natalie Koussevitzky." New York Music Critics' Circle Award for best new orchestral work of the 1946–47 concert season. First performance: October 18, 1946, by the Boston Symphony Orchestra, conducted by Serge Koussevitzky. Score published by Boosey & Hawkes, 1947.

Mademoiselle Boulanger, knowing the Russian conductor's interest in new creative talents of all countries, took it for granted that he would want to meet a young composer from the country he was about to visit for the first time. That she was entirely correct in her assumption was immediately evident from the interest he showed in the orchestral score under my arm. It was a *Cortège Macabre*, an excerpt from a ballet I had been working on under the guidance of Mademoiselle Boulanger. With all the assurance of youth—I was twenty-two years old at the time—I played it for him. Without hesitation he promised to perform the piece during his first season at Boston.[56]

Koussevitzky commissioned the symphony as a work Boulanger could play as soloist in an upcoming tour of the United States. It was Walter Damrosch, however, conducting the New York Philharmonic with Boulanger at the organ, who introduced the piece—and the twenty-three-year-old Copland as a symphonist.[57] (Koussevitzky conducted it the following month, again featuring Boulanger at the organ.)

The work elicited strong reactions. After the performance, Damrosch memorably addressed the audience: "If a gifted young man can write a symphony like this at the age of 23, within five years he will be ready to commit murder!"[58] On the other hand, Virgil Thomson reportedly wept when hearing the symphony, calling it "exactly the American piece several of us would have given anything to write and that I was overjoyed someone had written."[59] In 1928, addressing the narrow performance opportunities for a symphony featuring an organ, Copland rescored the work and renamed it First Symphony. The revisions primarily involve orchestration: to replace the organ he added an alto saxophone, more brass, percussion, and piano.[60] The symphony is a good example of Copland's first stylistic period, with diverse influences, including Stravinsky, American popular and jazz styles, and a Debussy-like chord parallelism.

The first of the three movements begins with a slow, contemplative melody in the flute. The winds are largely responsible for developing the material in the opening, with the undulating strings (especially the lower strings) providing a minimal accompaniment. The uneasy dissonance in the winds lays the ground for the forceful Scherzo, with its driving ostinatos and rapid shifts of textures and accents. Copland called the movement jazzy and said that it pointed to his later more "American" style.[61] The eerie middle section, with the English horn and alto saxophone introducing a more lyrical line over muted strings, reveals the inventiveness of Copland as an orchestrator even early in his career. Although the third movement begins with a plaintive viola solo that expands into a full brass hymn, it proves to be but an introduction for a sharp, modernist Finale, made all the more dramatic by its decisive use of pairs of thirty-second notes to shape the line.

Short Symphony (Symphony No. 2)

The three movements of Copland's *Short Symphony*, played without a break, last a mere 15 minutes in performance. It premiered in Mexico City in 1934, conducted by its dedicatee, his close friend Carlos Chávez. As the composer said, he wrote the work "at intervals between 1931 and 1933 in a variety of places from Morocco to Mexico"; the influence of Latin American music is especially notable.[62] And yet its tight construction is signature Copland; as Chávez noted, "The dialectic of this music, it is to say, its movement, the way each and every note comes out from the other as the only natural and logical possible one is simply unprecedented in the whole history of music."[63]

The *Short Symphony* uses a somewhat more modest orchestra than the First Symphony does: it does include a heckelphone (as well as bass clarinet and double bassoon), and a piano, but gone are the saxophone, the extended percussion complement, most of the brass, and the harps.[64] The limited timbral palette puts more focus on the melodic process; as Copland explained, "all melodic figures result from a nine-note sequence—a kind of row—from the opening two bars."[65] Permutations of the motive outlined by the first five notes unify the first movement across a series of quick tempo and meter changes; shifting and suggestive tonal play is mirrored in shifting and suggestive rhythmic play. The second movement, *Lento* (played *attacca*), opens with a kind of distorted blues introduced by alto flute. Metric shifts result in a kind of suspended animation before giving way to a hymn. Arthur Berger opined that this movement had "the spaciousness that has been associated . . . with the American landscape."[66] The quick Finale (also *attacca*) weaves together brief motives subjected to overlapping imitative bursts both between solo instruments and between fuller sections; their constant shifting emphasizes Copland's fluid transparency of orchestration and texture. The highly syncopated rhythmic language reminds the listener of the composer's recent excursions to Mexico.

The symphony's rhythmic difficulties made for a sparse performance history that continues to this day; Copland called the work one of his "neglected children." Stokowski, who conducted the American premiere with NBC Symphony Orchestra in 1944 (ten years after its first performance in Mexico), noted that "It is still a difficult work to perform, and even more so to interpret."[67] Copland revised the work as a sextet in 1937, but the difficulties of performing it even for a small ensemble caused the delay of a projected radio broadcast of the work.[68]

Third Symphony

Copland's Third Symphony (1944–45) was the most extended and serious statement among his symphonies, although other orchestral works (*Fanfare for the Common Man* and the ballet suites) continue to enjoy a broader audience today. Copland described it as his "first proper full-scale symphony."[69] He took on this ambitious project after a decade of works in the populist and accessible idiom that he had adopted in response to the Depression and the audience created by mass media: these include shorter orchestral works like *El Salón México* (1936); the ballets *Billy the Kid* (1938), *Rodeo* (1942), and *Appalachian Spring* (1944); film scores (*Our Town*, 1940); and nationalist works like *A Lincoln Portrait* (1942).

At the same time that Copland desired to reach a much broader audience, a variety of voices from within the musical establishment were trying to lure him back to weightier works. In 1939, David Diamond scathingly wrote him, "By having sold out to the mongrel commercialists half-way already, the danger is going to be wider for you, and I beg you dear Aaron, don't sell out yet, hang on to a more vital, inventive, and more creative impulse when it comes."[70] Arthur Berger wrote with a similar complaint: "What I expect next is to see you try some of the larger symphonic proportions, à la Shostakovich. . . . To me the important thing is not the sum or extent of one's achievements, but *the* achievement. And I would like to see you now write *the* big work: a concerto or cantata or symphony."[71] And just as Copland was beginning his Third Symphony, he received a letter from Samuel Barber: "I hope you will knuckle down to a good symphony. We deserve it of you, and your career is all set for it." Copland dryly noted that his friends "had no way of knowing that I had been working on such a composition for some time. I did not want to announce my intentions until I was clear in my own mind what the piece would become."[72]

With the Third Symphony, Copland tried his "darndest to write a symphony in the grand style."[73] Koussevitzky premiered the work with the Boston Symphony Orchestra—an ensemble Copland knew well—on October 18, 1946, and it featured the largest orchestra of any of the three symphonies: fourteen winds, eleven brass, timpani, four percussionists, two harps, celesta, piano, and strings. In the percussion section, the use of wood block, claves, and xylophone is carried over from his earlier "jazzy" period, but now the composer employed them within a more traditionally orchestral format.

The work is free of specific extramusical allusions. Copland noted in his autobiography that "if I forced myself, I could invent an ideological basis for the Third Symphony. But if I did, I'd be bluffing—or at any rate adding something ex post facto, something that might or might not be true but that played no role at the moment of creation."[74] At the same time, he conceded that the symphony was designed to reflect a mood of postwar celebration, which he indicated musically by incorporating the *Fanfare for the Common Man* into the Finale. As he put it, "I used this opportunity to carry the *Fanfare* material further and to satisfy my desire to give the *Third Symphony* an affirmative tone. After all, it was a wartime piece—or more accurately, an end-of-war piece—intended to reflect the euphoric spirit of the country at the time."[75] By employing the *Fanfare* in his symphony, Copland manages to balance programmatic and absolute modes of musical representation. At the same time, he avoided the use of self-consciously American sources; in his program notes for the premiere, Copland stated, "Any reference to jazz or folk material in this work was purely unconscious."[76]

Copland described the symphony as having "the general form of an arch, in which the central portion, that is the second-movement scherzo, is the most animated, and the final movement is an extended coda, presenting a broadened version of the opening material."[77] The work opens with I/A, a typical Copland melody: broad, stately, with prominent leaps of fourths and fifths, phrasing that stretches over the bar line, and smooth rhythms (example 5.1). This passage exemplifies some of the remarkable features that Howard Pollack has noted about the symphony: "The Third presents long themes that, to an extraordinary degree, keep their shape, the score moving from one long theme to another. . . . At times, especially when the themes are augmented, it takes pages and pages of orchestral score—perhaps a minute or two of music—to get from the beginning of a particular theme to its end. Such intensely thematic writing gives the Third an astounding breadth and monumentality."[78] Darius Milhaud referred to the "melancholy simplicity of its themes."[79] The initial sighing motive expands into a slow hymn, gradually transitioning into a more martial theme on trombones before returning to the opening mood.

Example 5.1 Copland, Symphony No. 3 opening theme

The interior movements are a scherzo and a set of variations, exemplifying what Pollack has called the "dialectical" quality of the Third Symphony, its dramatic tensions between extremes. The Scherzo is brass-heavy, with a kind of rambunctiousness reminiscent of Sergei Prokofiev (1891–1953; e.g., in the ballet *Chout*); its theme is derived from a discarded sketch for *Fanfare for the Common Man*.[80] The trio is gentle, focusing on winds, with a canonic passage on its theme. As Copland says, the return to the Scherzo theme is not literal; rather, it "returns in a somewhat disguised form in the solo piano" before making a full restatement in the orchestra.

Copland describes the third movement, which reduces the brass section to solo horn and trumpet, as "the freest of all in formal structure. Although it is built up sectionally, the various sections are intended to emerge one from the other in continuous flow, somewhat in the manner of a closely-knit series of variations."[81] The opening section is built on the trombone theme from Movement I; a new melody on the flute serves as the basis of ensuing variation-like sequences, principally in the winds and strings. Arthur Berger notes that "one of its transformations exemplifies a typically Coplandesque, jerky device of extending an incisive figure to form an ever longer phrase on each repetition."[82] The initial evocative atmosphere returns before leading without a break into the Finale.

The last movement again clearly exemplifies the dialectical tendency of the symphony. The fanfare begins in the flute before being given its statement with the full force of brass and percussion. This is followed by an energetic *P* introduced by the oboe; its running sixteenth notes elaborate an underlying structure of fourths and fifths. Copland describes the unfolding of the Finale: "One curious feature of the movement consists in the fact that the second theme is to be found embedded in the development section instead of being in its customary place. The development, as such, concerns itself with the fanfare and first theme fragments. A shrill *tutti* chord, with flutter-tongued brass and piccolos, brings the development to a close."[83] *P* returns in the piccolo and flute. A coloristic passage for wind choir, harp, and keyboards at m. 103 recalls the sound world of the First Symphony. At the beginning of the coda, *S* is heard in the trombone in even rhythms, accompanied by the fanfare over more fourths and fifths and against strident accents in winds, strings, and percussion (including claves and an anvil). Beginning at Reh. 121, *I/A* merges with the fanfare to lead to the symphony's triumphant conclusion.

Arthur Berger's 1948 analysis is notable for the way its rhetorical style captures the feel of what he calls "the longest and most panoramic of the movements." After describing the way the fanfare gives way to "a syncopated new theme" and "the development of a Latin-American dance rhythm," he goes on with the following description:

> the dance becoming ever more frenzied, like the indulgences around the golden calf (to pick a random analogy for this eminently pictorial episode), precipitously interrupted, when it seems impossible for the abandon to become any more extreme, by an explosive, chastising chord oddly mixing steely percussiveness and gloomy hollowness, and leaving destruction and annihilation in its wake; a lonely note, haltingly reiterated high up (piccolo) between reiterations of the chord, materializing into a return of the pastoral warblings which had opened the allegro, except that now these create a new hurdy-gurdy effect serving as a counterpoint to the subdued version of the fanfare and later to the opening theme of the symphony (violins).[84]

Koussevitzky was enthusiastic: "There is no doubt about it—[Copland's Third] is the greatest American symphony. It goes from the heart to the heart."[85] Nevertheless, after its premiere, Copland made a number of cuts in the Finale in consultation with both Koussevitzky and Leonard Bernstein (1918–90), who found the work not only too long but too "grandiose."[86] Bernstein's critique is a shadow that has haunted Copland's Third Symphony, despite its many successes and status as one of the most—if not the most—frequently performed and recorded American symphonies in the repertoire. An often cited review in *Time* accused Copland of having "a kind of popularity that seemed to keep him too busy to be a great composer."[87]

Another critic sneered, "You might title the Symphony Shostakovich in the Appalachians."[88] Still, the reception of Copland's Third Symphony shows that it did manage to achieve a symbolic significance that went beyond its allegedly nonprogrammatic origins. As William Austin noted, "nothing can persuade a listener to enjoy the piece if he is altogether out of sympathy with its rather New-Dealish spirit of hopeful resolution and neighborliness. But if one can entertain such a spirit for a moment, Copland offers him a priceless opportunity to enter into it more deeply."[89]

Although the work lacks the overt technical difficulties of the *Short Symphony*, it is still challenging to pull off; the slowly developing themes and transparent textures require an ensemble with impeccable intonation and phrasing. Moreover, the style is rooted in a specific cultural moment. In 1946, Arthur Berger could, without irony or ridicule, describe the Scherzo's brass writing as "signature music for a newsreel or March of Time film."[90] It is this association—a particularly American style of optimistic and grandiose pronouncement—that at once lends the piece its authenticity and also points to its vulnerability.

It became virtually a ritual in late-twentieth-century writing about Copland for critics to nod thoughtfully about how unlikely a candidate he was—a gay Jewish kid from Brooklyn, born into a modestly musical and working-class family—to lead the charge for the Great American Symphony. Michael Tilson Thomas wondered about the process by which "somebody who is a young, wild-eyed radical maverick composer gradually becomes a symbol of every conceivable solid American family value and ultimately the patriarch—the musical father—of the nation."[91] But such comments seem to merely perpetuate the very system they challenge: symphonists in the United States during this period had wildly different biographies, and the fact that Copland realized one of the fullest articulations of the Great American Symphony should not be discounted because of his background. If anything, the composers that we hold up as most emblematic in this search tended to have remarkably diverse upbringings and biographies. In fact, it shows America as the land of opportunity—just as anyone can grow up to be president, anyone from anywhere or any background in the country can grow up to be the voice of a time, place, and genre.

ROY HARRIS

Few composers enjoy such a succinctly stated origin legend: "Born in a log cabin on Lincoln's birthday in Lincoln County, Oklahoma."[92] As Beth Levy has explained, the frontier mythology that surrounded Roy Harris (1898–1979) remained unsullied by his subsequent relocation to California as a boy, his studies with Arthur Farwell at Berkeley and (after a stint as a dairy truck driver) with Boulanger in France, and his widely diverse positions as a university professor all around the nation (Juilliard, Westminster Choir College, Princeton, Cornell, Colorado College, University of Utah, Peabody College for Teachers, Southern Illinois University, Indiana University, UCLA, California State University Los Angeles).[93] During his studies with Boulanger (1926–29), he rebelled against her systematic approach to the point that she described him as her "autodidact." John Tasker Howard, controversially dubbing him the "white hope of American music," described the composer as "untouched by the artificial refinements of Europe or even the stultifying commercialism of cosmopolitan New York; a prophet from the Southwest who thought in terms of our raciest folk tunes."[94]

One with such a biography seemed predestined to look afresh at the highest of instrumental genres, and indeed Harris was one of the most prolific symphonists considered in this chapter—fourteen completed works as well as several unnumbered or unfinished ones. (A

Table 5.3 The Symphonies of Roy Harris (1898–1979)[a]

Title	Movements	Instrumentation	Comments
Symphony—Our Heritage (1925, rev. 1926)			Projected symphony, of which Harris completed only the Andante, which became his first orchestral work. That movement premiered in 1926 with the Eastman-Rochester Orchestra, conducted by Howard Hanson.
Symphony—American Portrait 1929 (1929)	1. "Initiative" 2. "Expectation" 3. "Speed" 4. "Collective Force"		Harris's first completed symphony, intended to convey "the [four] dominant characteristics of the American people." Subsequently withdrawn by the composer, who incorporated some of the materials into the First and Second Symphonies.
Symphony 1933 (First Symphony, 1933)	1. Allegro 2. Andante 3. Maestoso		Written at the invitation of Serge Koussevitzky. Material was drawn and extensively reworked from preexistent pieces, including the "Collective Force" Finale of *American Portrait 1929* (in the Maestoso) as well as three other chamber and orchestral compositions. First performance: January 26, 1934, by the Boston Symphony Orchestra, conducted by Koussevitzky; 1934 recording with that ensemble at Carnegie Hall was the first for an American symphony. Unpublished.
Symphony No. 2 (1934)	1. Con bravura 2. Molto cantabile 3. Maestoso		The Finale reworks the last movement of his First String Quartet (1929). First performance: February 28, 1936, by the Boston Symphony Orchestra, conducted by Richard Burgin. Unpublished. Harris later dismissed the work as a "failure" with "only one good movement, the second." In 2002, David Alan Miller revised the score, restoring cuts Harris had made, and recorded the work with the Albany Symphony Orchestra (TROY 515).

Table 5.3 *continued*

Title	Movements	Instrumentation	Comments
Symphony No. 3 (1938, rev. 1940)	One continuous movement (C, 703 mm.), in an arch design outlined by the composer as follows: Section I. Tragic (mm. 1–56) Section II. Lyric (mm. 57–208) Section III. Pastoral (mm. 209–415) Section IV. Fugue—dramatic (mm. 416–566) Section V. Dramatic-tragic (mm. 567–703)	Grand + Flt., Ob., Clar., Tpt., 2 Tubas, Timp., Perc. (Vbp., Xylo.).	By far Harris's most acclaimed work and for many years one of the most widely admired American symphonies. First performance: February 24, 1939, by the Boston Symphony Orchestra, conducted by Serge Koussevitzky. Score published by G. Schirmer, 1939 and 1940.
American Symphony—1938 (1938)	1. Furiously 2/2 (379 mm.) 2. "Sad Song" C (123 mm.)	Flt., 3 Clar., 1 Bclar., 2 Asax., 1 Tsax., 3 Tpt., 4 Trom., Timp., Xylo., Pno., Cb.	Originally intended as his Fourth Symphony, written for the Tommy Dorsey Band. Harris composed the first and second movements but abandoned the symphony "because the band had no rehearsal time to devote to a new project" (according to his note in the manuscript). He incorporated some material into the *Folk-Song Symphony*. Reconstructed by Brian Lamb from manuscript parts in the Library of Congress and the personal collection of Dan Stehman. For more, see Lamb/AMERICAN SYMPHONY.

Work	Movements	Instrumentation	Notes
Folk-Song Symphony (Symphony No. 4, 1940, rev. 1942)	1. "The Girl I Left behind Me" ¢ (244 mm.) 2. "Western Cowboy" C (253 mm.) 3. "Interlude: Dance Tunes for Strings and Percussion" 4. "Mountaineer Love Song" C (128 mm.) 5. "Interlude: Dance Tunes for Full Orchestra" 6. "Negro Fantasy" 3/4 (185 mm.) 7. "Welcome Party" ("When Johnny Comes Marching Home") 6/8 (159 mm.)	Grand + Flt., Ob., 2 Clar., Bssn., Tpt., Tuba, Perc., Pno. SATB Chorus	Different sources, including from Harris's lifetime, render the title variously as *Folksong*, *Folk Song*, and *Folk-Song*. The published scores indicate *Folk-Song*. Composed on a commission by Howard Hanson for a work for chorus and orchestra. Materials are drawn from the anthologies *Cowboy Songs and Other Frontier Ballads* (John and Alan Lomax) and *The American Songbag* (Carl Sandburg). First performance: April 26, 1940, at the American Spring Festival at the Eastman School of Music, conducted by Hanson (first version, without the instrumental interludes and with the first and last movements reversed). Second version (including instrumental interludes and outer movements in present order) first performed on December 26, 1940, by the Cleveland Orchestra, conducted by Artur Rodzinski. Each choral movement published in vocal score as individual octavo by G. Schirmer, 1940 (orchestral score available as rental from Associated Music).
Symphony No. 5 (1942, rev. 1945–46)	1. Prelude (♩. = 66) 6/8 (233 mm.) 2. Chorale (♩. = 46) 4/4 (235 mm.) 3. Fugue (Appassionato, ♩. = 72) 6/4 (308 mm.)	Grand + Flt. (doubling Picc.), Ob., E♭ Clar. (optional), Bclar., Tsax, Bssn., 4 Hr., Tpt., Btuba, Perc. (Military Drums, Chimes, Vbp.), Harp, Pno.	Commissioned by Serge Koussevitzky in 1940. War symphony controversially dedicated to "the heroic and freedom-loving people of our great Ally, the Union of Soviet Socialist Republics." First performance: February 26, 1943, by the Boston Symphony Orchestra under Koussevitzky. Score published by Mills, 1961.

Table 5.3 *continued*

Title	Movements	Instrumentation	Comments
Symphony No. 6 "Gettysburg" (1943–44)	I. Awakening ("Fourscore and seven years ago . . .") II. Conflict ("Now we are engaged in a great civil war . . .") III. Dedication ("We are met on a great battlefield of that war . . .") IV. Affirmation ("that we here highly resolve that these dead shall not have died in vain . . .")	Grand + Flt., Ob., Clar., Tsax., Bssn., 4 Hr., 2 Tpt., Trom., 3 Tubas, Perc., Harp, Pno.	Commissioned by the Blue Network (forerunner of the American Broadcasting Corporation) for a symphony about Abraham Lincoln. Each movement is inspired by a phrase from Lincoln's Gettysburg Address. Dedicated to "the Armed Forces of Our Nation." First performance: April 14, 1944, by the Boston Symphony Orchestra, conducted by Serge Koussevitzky. Rental score available from Associated Music.
Symphony for Band "West Point" (1952)	In one movement.	Picc., 2 Flt., Ob., EH, E♭ Clar., 4 Clar., E♭ Aclar., Bclar., Cbclar., Sopsax., E♭ Asax., Tsax., E♭ Barsax, 3 Cor., 4 Hr., 3 Trom., 2 Euph., 2 Tubas, Cb., Timp., 4 Perc. (BD, Chimes, Crash Cym., SD), Harp	Commissioned by West Point Band conductor Francis Resta to commemorate the 150th Anniversary of West Point. First performance: West Point Band, May 30, 1952. Unpublished; manuscript housed at the library of the West Point Band at the US Military Academy at West Point.
Symphony No. 7 (1952, rev. through 1955)	In one movement 3/2 (624 mm.)	Grand + Flt., Ob., Clar., Bssn., Tpt., Tuba, Perc. (Xylo., Large and Small SD, Large and Small Military Drums, BD, Cym., Chimes, Vbp.), Harp	Commissioned by the Koussevitzky Music Foundation in 1946 but not begun until 1951. Dedicated to the memory of Serge and Natalie Koussevitzky. Harris described the work as "in one sense a dance symphony [and] in another sense a study in harmonic and melodic rhythmic [*sic*] variations." First performance: November 20, 1952, by the Chicago Symphony Orchestra, conducted by Rafael Kubelik. Score published by Associated Music, 1956.

Symphony No. 8, "San Francisco Symphony" (1961–62)	In one movement, comprising five interconnected parts, named by the composer as follows: Part I: "Childhood and Youth" Part II: "Renunciation" Part III: "The Building of the Chapel" Part IV: "The Joy of Pantheistic Beauty as a Gift of God" Part V: "Ecstasy after the Premonition of Death"	Grand + Picc., EH, Bclar, Cbssn., Tpt, Tuba, Perc., Harp, Pno.	Commissioned by the San Francisco Symphony to celebrate the fiftieth anniversary of its founding. Each section depicts specific periods or events in the life of St. Francis of Assisi, the patron saint of the city. Some musical materials borrowed from his cantata *Canticle of the Sun* (1960). The piano and trumpet play important soloistic roles. First performance: January 17, 1962, by the San Francisco Symphony, conducted by Enrique Jordá, with Johana Harris as soloist. Rental score available from Associated Music.
Symphony No. 9 (1962)	1. Prelude: "We the People" 3/2 6/4 (243 mm.) 2. Chorale: " . . . to form a more perfect Union" 4/2 (198 mm.) 3. Contrapuntal structures: "to promote the general welfare" 4/2 (292 mm.) Part I: "Of Life immense in passion, pulse, power" Part II: "Cheerful for freest action formed" Part III: "The Modern Man I Sing"	Grand + Picc., Flt., EH, Bclar, 2 Bssn. (4 doubling Cbssn.), 4 Hrn., Tpt., C Tpt., Btrom., Barhr., Tuba, Perc. (Chimes, Vbp., Cym., Tamb., 2 SD [large and small], 2 Large Military Drums, BD), Harp, Pno.	Commissioned by Eugene Ormandy and the Philadelphia Orchestra. Dedicated to the city of Philadelphia, "the cradle of American democracy." Each movement bears a subtitle taken from the Preamble to the US Constitution. The final movement is subdivided into three sections carrying titles from the "Inscription" of Walt Whitman's *Leaves of Grass*. First performance: January 18, 1963, by the Philadelphia Orchestra led by Ormandy. Score published by Associated Music, 1966.
Symphony No. 10, "Abraham Lincoln Symphony" (1965)	1. "Lonesome Boy" 2. "The Young Wrestler" 3. "Abraham Lincoln's Conviction" 4. "Civil War—Brother against Brother" 5. "Praise and Thanksgiving for Peace"	Brass, Perc., 2 Pno. SATB Chorus	Written to commemorate the 100th anniversary of Abraham Lincoln's assassination. According to Harris, the work explores "two moods from the youth of Lincoln and three moods expressing his profound concern for the destiny of our democratic institutions." The third and fourth movements set writings by Lincoln; Harris wrote the rest of the texts. First performance: April 14, 1965. Rental score available from Associated Music.

Table 5.3 *continued*

Title	Movements	Instrumentation	Comments
Symphony No. 11 (1967)	In one movement, divided into two parts 12/8 (457 mm.)	Grand + Picc., Flt., Ob., EH, Clar., Bclar., 2 Bssn. (4 doubles Cbssn.), 2 Hr., 2 Tpt., Trom. (doubling Btrom.), Tuba, Barhr., Perc. (Small, Medium, Large, and Military SD, BD, Cym., Chimes, 2 Vbp., Gong), Harp, Pno., Cel.	Commissioned by the New York Philharmonic to celebrate its 125th anniversary. Dedicated to Johana Harris. First performance: January 8, 1968, by the New York Philharmonic, conducted by the composer. Score published by Associated Music, 1967.
Symphony No. 12, "Père Marquette Symphony" (1967–69)	Five movements in two divisions. Part I: "The Old World" IA. "The Early Life of Marquette" IB. "Marquette's Initiation into the Priesthood of the Society of Jesus" [setting of the Credo] Part II: "The New World" IIA: "The Moods of the Wilderness" IIB: "The Preachments of Marquette to the Indians": [setting of John 1:1–14, in Latin] IIC: "Père Marquette's Death in the Wilderness" [setting of the Sanctus]	Grand + Picc., EH, Bclar., 2 Bssn. (4 doubling Cbssn.), Hr., C Tpt., Tuba, Barhr., Perc. (Glsp., Vbp., Xylo.). Tenor / Speaker.	Commissioned for the opening ceremony of a five-year celebration of the 300th anniversary of Father Jacques Marquette's exploration of the American Midwest. A portion of the score premiered in 1968 for the celebration. First performance of the full score: November 8, 1969, by the Milwaukee Symphony, conducted by the composer. Rental score available from Associated Music. A symphony-cantata with texts drawn from the Bible and from the Ordinary of the Mass.

Bicentennial Symphony 1976 (Symphony No. 13, 1975)	1. Introduction; "Preamble to the Constitution" 2. "Freedom versus Slavery" 3. "Civil War: Brothers Kill Brothers" 4. "Emancipation Proclamation" 5. "Freedom"	For six-part chorus and orchestra with solo voices and speakers,	Commissioned by California State University, Los Angeles. Written for performance in Washington, DC, as part of the US Bicentennial celebrations. Texts taken from the Constitution and the Gettysburg Address, as well as original words by Harris. Originally labeled Symphony No. 14 by the composer out of superstition over the number 13, but posthumously renumbered Symphony No. 13 with the approval of Harris's widow. First performance: February 10, 1976, by the National Symphony Orchestra, conducted by Antal Dorati. Rental score available from Associated Music.

a. Scores for a number of Harris's symphonies are unpublished or very difficult to obtain; as a result, some entries lack measure numbers, instrumentation details, and publication dates. Most of his manuscripts are preserved in the Library of Congress. This table does not include the *Symphony for Voices* (1935), a setting of Walt Whitman texts for unaccompanied SATB chorus. Besides the fragmentary works listed, several others appear to be lost (if they were ever completed), including a Choral Symphony (1936), a Symphony for High School Orchestra (1937), and a *Walt Whitman Symphony* for baritone solo, chorus, and orchestra (1955–58).

fifteenth, the Symphony for Voices of 1935, sets poetry of Walt Whitman to music for unaccompanied chorus). Because of his supposed status as a composer who could represent the nation's heartland, Harris retains a symbolic importance in the role that westward expansion had in the dialogue about the Great American Symphony (see table 5.3).

Early efforts included an unfinished work (*Our Heritage*, ca. 1925) and the completed but withdrawn *Symphony—American Portrait 1929*. Responding to Koussevitzky's request that Harris provide the conductor with a "big symphony from the Vest," the First Symphony (*Symphony 1933*) brought him acclaim and holds the distinction of being the first American symphony to be recorded (by the Boston Symphony and Koussevitzky); it reworks passages of *American Portrait* and several other preexistent works into an original structure that points the way to Harris's mature style.[95] The next year, Harris completed his Second Symphony for the Boston Symphony. For whatever reason, Koussevitzky and Harris had a falling out and the conductor declined to lead its premiere in 1936, giving the baton to his assistant conductor Richard Burgin; the composer, for his part, chose not to attend. The symphony quickly fell into obscurity and Harris labeled it a "failure."[96]

Third Symphony in One Movement

Harris's Third Symphony (1938) was perhaps the most performed American symphony of the 1940s, widely recognized as vying with the Thirds of Copland and Schuman for the most celebrated work in the national canon.[97] Commissioned by Hans Kindler for the National Symphony Orchestra, it received its premiere under Koussevitzky on February 24, 1939 (Harris's rift with the conductor evidently had been resolved). The music reflects Harris's desire to develop a sound that could be objectively described as American without making appeals to vernacular elements. He was not opposed to such idioms, as subsequent compositions would demonstrate, but he wanted to craft a sonic identity that was in his mind intrinsic to the national character.[98] Wherever it was played, the critics congratulated Harris for achieving his goal.[99] Copland spoke on Harris's project: "What [Harris] writes is music of real sweep and breadth, with power and emotional depth such as only a generously built country could produce. It is American in rhythm, especially in the fast parts, with a jerky, nervous quality that is peculiarly our own. It is crude and unabashed at times, with occasional blobs and yawps of sound that Whitman would have approved of."[100] (Copland's invocation of Whitman is significant, as the critics pointed to Whitman's poetry as the paragon of great American literature—the "'supreme spokesman' [who] expressed, as did no other American poet, what America meant to an American."[101])

In spite of its wide-ranging emotional canvas (see Harris's descriptive titles in the discussions that follow), the work is not monumental but compact: a single-movement work lasting eighteen minutes in performance. Nor did this experiment prove unique: the Seventh, Eighth, and Eleventh Symphonies, as well as the Symphony for Band, were also to consist of one movement. Dan Stehman concludes that "His idiosyncratic handling of the one-movement type is perhaps his most significant contribution to the history of the genre."[102] The central quality of the Third, in fact, is the way Harris marshals musical elements to exert a substantial, expansive impact within the compressed structure, beginning with the sizable orchestral forces: eleven winds, twelve brass, an extended percussion battery, and strings.

Harris's melodic approach—long, asymmetrical, relatively conjunct, and freely spun-out themes, often with modal inflections—likewise contributes to the impact of the work and earned praise from contemporaries. As Walter Piston noted, "the continual change in length of the rhythmic units making up a melodic line imparts a sense of wandering and seeking which may account in part for the attempts to describe Harris's music in terms of the great open spaces of the West."[103] Copland was similarly admiring, writing that the composer's "melodic gift is his most striking characteristic. His music comes closest to a distinctively American *melos* of anything yet done. . . . Celtic folksongs and Protestant hymns are its basis, but they have been completely reworked, lengthened, malleated."[104] Harris himself called his melodic approach "autogenetic" (self-generating), a term defined by his student Sidney Thurber Cox as "expand[ing] and extend[ing] the possibilities inherent in the original germ."[105]

The way Harris's melodies interact with his harmonic and rhythmic procedures also contributes to his signature style. He likes to begin with perfect intervals, move progressively to denser harmonies, and then return to perfect intervals. In conjunction with the similarly organically evolving melodic material, this technique brings melodic and harmonic material together into a weblike texture that makes the counterpoint less obvious to the ear. Although he tends to favor uniform note values in primary themes, with rhythmic variety provided by short accompanying or contrapuntal motives, the rhythmic phrasing is often asymmetrical. This feature became a defining feature of his "American" sound; as Harris himself wrote, "Our rhythmic impulses are fundamentally different from . . . Europeans; and from this unique rhythmic sense are generated different melodic and form values. Our sense of rhythm is less symmetrical than the European rhythmic sense. European musicians are trained to think of rhythm in its largest common denominator, while we are born with a feeling for its smallest units."[106] Taken together, the fusion of these elements creates a style that is at once compact and meandering, particularly suited to a one-movement format even in major symphonic works.

Harris provided a detailed outline of the Third Symphony, which falls into five sections connected without a break:

Section I: Tragic—low string sonorities

Section II: Lyric—strings, horn, woodwinds

Section III: Pastoral—woodwinds, with a polytonal string background

Section IV: Fugue—dramatic

  A. Brass and percussion predominating

  B. Canonic development of materials from Section II constituting background for further development of the fugue

  C. Brass climax, rhythmic motive derived from fugue subject

Section V: Dramatic—tragic

  A. Restatement of violin theme of Section I; *tutti* strings in canon with *tutti* woodwinds against brass and percussion developing rhythmic ideas from climax of Section IV

  B. Coda—development of materials from Sections I and II over pedal timpani.[107]

The five sections fall into three larger units (not so marked by the composer): the first and second sections constitute a kind of introduction and thematic exposition, the third an interior dance-like section, and the fourth and fifth an energetic finale with coda.

As his outline shows, the work's emotional trajectory follows an arch, with the subdued beginning gradually brightening but then ending darkly—a mood that, according to Harris,

Example 5.2 Harris, Symphony No. 3 opening

reflects the political atmosphere of the late 1930s.[108] The relationship of timbre and mood could also be described as "autogenetic," for the sections evolve in a series of subtle transitions from darker to brighter tone colors. The orchestration reveals distinctive traits throughout: brief splashes of brass and percussion as well as antiphonal exchanges between families. It also shows the importance of timbre in Harris's mind, as he tends "to formulate melodies, motives, and figuration in terms of specific instruments or instrumental choirs."[109]

A, the first phrase group in Section I (Con moto ♩ = 84) (example 5.2) is a distinctive example of a Harris autogenetic melody. Triadic with modal touches, the harmony unfolds in a progression from unison to perfect intervals to thirds within a narrow tonal range. Only cellos and violas are heard for most of the section, though the bass clarinet and bassoon join in after a cadence on a B-major chord. The use of regular note values moving in asymmetrical groupings throws the intervallic and harmonic relationships into sharper relief. Harris lends some variety to the monochromatic orchestration through diverse articulations, including pizzicato. Brass chords usher in a passage (m. 57; ♩ = 72–80) in which *B*, a broad and rather slow-moving theme, is developed in counterpoint, its overlapping phrases recalling Renaissance polyphony. Section II (m. 152) is built on a more angular theme (*C*) in strings and winds. The lyricism is dark and intense, and the harmonies more triadic.

In Section III (m. 209; Poco più mosso; ♩ = 96–104), Harris subtly brightens the color through the woodwinds; the folkish theme features the pastoral timbres of the English horn, oboe, and clarinet over polytonal string arpeggiations, which give way to increasingly active antiphonal exchanges between winds and brass. The passage is a good example of Harris's asymmetrical rhythm and extroverted treatment of the brass: Dan Stehman describes it as "the first fully realized example of the sort of sound and texture he employed subsequently to represent an open-air, nature ambience." It also demonstrates Harris's approach to harmony: "the lower foundation members are always major, while the upper members fluctuate between major and minor and appear in constantly changing relationships to the lower members to form a shifting spectrum of colors and intensities."[110]

Bright and brash brass and percussion dominate Section IV (m. 416; ♩ = 112). The fugal subject has a character different from that of the preceding themes; instead of a long-breathed and freely unfolding melody, it is short and harmonically closed (each of the three phrases ends on D major); rhythmically sharp—the time signature is designated as 3/2 6/4 meter—it includes frequent hemiolas. Canonic treatment of materials from Section II constitutes a background for further development of the fugue. The section illustrates Harris's remark (quoted earlier) about focusing on the "smallest units of rhythm." The overall effect is Coplandesque and decidedly the most vernacular-sounding passage of the symphony.

Section V (m. 554; Con moto ° = 66–72) features a restatement of *A*. The "Dramatic" passage is based on *B* in canon in strings and winds while brass and timpani play an insistent eighth-note motive derived from the fugue subject. The "Tragic" Coda (m. 634, Meno mosso, pesante, 4 after Reh. 63) develops fragments of *B* and *C* over a pedal D in the timpani. It ends with a large statement of the tonic triad G minor, which Harris has withheld until now, making Sections IV and V into a giant V-i (D major–G minor), a large structural motion that gives the symphony a feeling of breadth in spite of its compact design. Originally, the symphony ended more abruptly, but Harris added a more extended coda after complaints at the premiere that the ending sounded anticlimactic; the revision, as Peter Korn describes it, highlights "Harris's acknowledged debt to the grand symphonic tradition.[111]

Although the work does not have the sweep of Copland's Third, its qualities—"clarity of form, directness of expression, and eloquence"—quickly gave it iconic stature.[112] A respectable though not unqualified critical success at its premiere, the revised work quickly won unprecedented fame for an American symphony, receiving at least twenty-six performances before 1950, and with all of the major American orchestras of the period (Boston, New York, Chicago, Philadelphia, Cleveland).[113] Critics raved about its distinctive individual voice: decades later, William Schuman, who went on to study with Harris, observed that "For me the sounds were like no others I had ever heard—his whole 'autogenetic' concept of form, the free and strong orchestration, the extraordinary beauty and sweep of the melodic material."[114] It quickly became a critical trope to equate the qualities Schuman cites, as well as Harris's idiosyncratic rhythms—in other words, the "abstract" national sound that the composer sought—with the open spaces and rugged pioneer spirit of the American Midwest.[115] For some time afterward, Harris's Third Symphony was regularly singled out as the most significant symphony by any American composer, even (whether the phrase was invoked or not) the work that most closely approached the fabled Great American Symphony.[116] Even listening to the work today, one cannot help but be struck by the way Harris compresses so much space and intensity into a single movement.

Fourth and Fifth Symphonies

Harris's symphonies from this point on alternate between purely abstract works that incorporate a more intangible American style (e.g., Symphonies 5, 7, 9) and symphonies that have national titles or incorporate American vernacular idioms (e.g., Symphonies 4, 6, 10). Although Harris's seven-movement *Folk-Song Symphony* for Chorus and Orchestra was composed shortly after the Third (between 1940 and 1942), its turn to vernacular sources reflected the altered wartime context. He derived much of the material from an uncompleted American symphony intended for the Tommy Dorsey band.[117] Harris sets seven folk songs in it, and yet the work rises above a purely Americana sound. As the composer stated, "Certain ways of musical treatment of folk songs seemed to me more natural than others; the harmony should be clear in texture and intent, confirming the cadence and the sentiment of the melody; the rhythmic patterns should be complementary to the melodic phrases and the orchestration should be unobscured and direct."[118]

The first movement sets "The Girl I Left behind Me," and the second ("The Western Cowboy") is primarily based on "O Bury Me Not on the Lone Prairie" with a short transition to "Streets of Laredo" before a final reprise of "O Bury Me Not." "Interlude—Dance Tunes for strings and percussion," a newly composed passage, follows. The fourth movement ("Mountaineer Love Song") is based on "He's Gone Away." This is followed by another original "Interlude—Dance Tunes for orchestra." The sixth movement ("Negro Fantasy") is based on "De trumpet sounds"; more than half the movement is an extended orchestral fantasy, almost like a tone poem. The Finale is based on a tune Harris used repeatedly, "When Johnny Comes Marching Home" (most notably in his *When Johnny Comes Marching Home—an American Overture* of 1934).

Harris's three-movement Fifth Symphony also claims our attention for its illumination of the politics of the 1940s. Drawing on public sentiment during the war, the work honored the Soviet Union: "As an American citizen I am proud to dedicate my Fifth Symphony to the heroic and freedom-loving people of our great Ally, the Union of Soviet Socialist Republics, as a tribute to their strength in war, their staunch idealism for World peace, their ability to cope with stark materialistic problems of world order without losing a passionate belief in the fundamental importance of the arts."[119] The premiere in Boston on February 26, 1943, included the "Internationale"; the performance was broadcast worldwide.[120]

Although the musical language resembles that of the Third Symphony, the first movement uses a lighter, more classically driven phrase structure. The beginning—a spritely dance-like idea introduced by horns and joined by strings—is certainly unexpected for a grand wartime statement, and the frequent syncopation and rhythmic changes continue the movement's quirky, tongue-in-cheek quality, emphasized by the sudden brass fanfare after Reh. 14—one of the few moments in which a conspicuously Americanist gesture crops up. The second movement demonstrates the most *gravitas*: it begins with a steady dirge in the timpani and lower strings, which is then gradually transformed into a slightly faster section before settling into a broad, hymnlike ending. The rhythmic weight of the opening section stands in maximum possible contrast to the lilt of the first movement. In the third movement, Harris returns to off-balance rhythms; the scoring, which treats the orchestra almost like a series of interlocking chamber groups, emphasizes the rhythmic disjunctions. For example, at Reh. 21, we hear rapidly alternating sets of performing forces, always deployed with restraint; by Reh. 30 the movement has settled into a martial finale.

The symphony received mixed reviews both for its musical content and its cultural associations. The American pianist and editor John Kirkpatrick wrote to Harris that "the soul doesn't seem to be in a state of action . . . and the vertical chord-sequences absorb all the polyphonic strains in a kind of immense, static basket-weave."[121] Harris's unabashed (and naïve) admiration of Stalin's USSR was viewed with suspicion by some as soon as the symphony premiered; during the Cold War, the association undermined the symphony's viability as a piece to program in America. The composer's at times almost jingoistic fanaticism did not go over well with his colleagues: as early as 1940, Virgil Thomson presciently, if hyperbolically, observed that "no composer in the world, not even in Italy or Germany, makes such shameless use of patriotic feeling to advertise his product."[122]

Sixth and Seventh Symphonies

Commissioned for radio broadcast, Harris's Symphony No. 6, "Gettysburg," was also a war symphony (composed in 1943–44), but here he turned toward a homespun patriotism. As Harris put it, "In Lincoln's Gettysburg speech I find a classic expression of that great cycle which always attends any progress in intellectual or spiritual growth of people."[123] Although purely instrumental, each movement is prefaced in the score by lines from Lincoln's Gettysburg Address: *Awakening* ("Fourscore and seven years ago"); *Conflict* ("Now we are engaged in a great civil war"); *Dedication* ("We are met on a great battlefield of that war"); *Affirmation* ("that we here highly resolve that these dead shall not have died in vain"). The piece has an attractive emotional quality and succeeds in capturing the overall change in mood of the Lincoln address. Dedicated to "the Armed Forces of Our Nation," the piece premiered under Koussevitzky and the Boston Symphony Orchestra.[124]

Harris's one-movement Seventh Symphony was commissioned by Koussevitzky, but the work did not premiere until 1952, after the conductor's death. Harris revised the work twice; its final version was published in 1956. For the 1955 revision, the composer described the symphony as follows:

> The work was conceived as a dynamic form with an uninterrupted time span of 20 minutes. In one sense it is a dance symphony; in another sense it is a study in harmonic and melodic rhythmic variation. The first half is a passacaglia with five variations. The second half is divided into three sections—contrapuntal variations in asymmetrical rhythms; contrapuntal variations in symmetrical meters; and further statement and development of the preceding two sections, wherein the original passacaglia theme is restated in large augmentation and orchestration, while ornamentation develops the melodic and rhythmic materials of the second section. A final variation of the rhythmic materials of the work serves as the coda.[125]

Harris adds that the first half is "contemplative and traditional" and the second "an expression of merry-making America." The orchestration includes a large percussion complement, with vibraphone; the composer uses both solo and antiphonal textures to great effect throughout the symphony. A somber march opens the work, with the passacaglia theme introduced in the strings. The brighter second half features more transparent harmony and orchestration. Harris sustains the intensity throughout the distinct moods; Stehman notes the composer's achievement in "unifying his diverse, and essentially unrelated, thematic materials in such a way that the listener perceives a logical, unbroken, and inevitable sense of flow and continuity from beginning to end."[126]

Later Symphonies

From this point on, Harris's symphonic output becomes much more variable in quality. As Tawa describes it, "beginning in the 1950s, Harris was under frequent censure for writing too much, too hurriedly, and for being too welcoming of weak ideas. Self-criticism was not his forte."[127] Works included the Symphony for Band, "West Point" (1952), commissioned by the US Military Academy. The Symphony No. 8, "San Francisco" (1962), unfolds in one movement divided into five sections; Harris based it on the life of St. Francis.[128] The Ninth (1962), commissioned by the Philadelphia Orchestra Association, was premiered by that ensemble under Eugene Ormandy in 1963. Although not programmatic, the composer prefaces each movement with a quote from the Preamble to the Constitution: I. *Prelude*: "We the People"; II. *Chorale*: "to form a more perfect union"; and III. *Contrapuntal Structures*: "to promote the general welfare." Harris designates the three sections of the last movement with quotes from

Walt Whitman: (1) "Of Life immense in passion, pulse, power"; (2) "Cheerful for freest action formed"; (3) "The Modern Man I Sing."

The Tenth Symphony, "Abraham Lincoln" (1965), features the unusual scoring of high school chorus, speaker, brass, two amplified pianos, and percussion. Harris himself conducted the premiere of Symphony No. 11, another one-movement work composed in 1967 in honor of the New York Philharmonic's hundred twenty-fifth anniversary. No. 12, "Père Marquette" (1968, rev. 1969), scored for tenor soloist, speaker, and orchestra, honors Father Jacques Marquette, a Jesuit missionary and explorer who with Louis Joliet explored and mapped the upper Mississippi River in 1673 (Marquette University in Milwaukee commissioned the work). The *Bicentennial Symphony* was Harris's last; it premiered in Washington, DC, in February 1976. After an introduction, "Revolution for Freedom," come five movements: (I) "Preamble to the Constitution," (II) "Freedom versus Slavery 1976," (III) "Civil War, brothers kill brothers," (IV) "Emancipation Proclamation," and (V) "Freedom." In addition to quoting passages from the Constitution, the Gettysburg Address, and the Emancipation Proclamation, this choral symphony sets texts by the composer protesting the nation's poor record of race relations. The critics lacerated the work: writing in the *Washington Post*, Paul Hume damned it as "a caricature of music, a parody of Abraham Lincoln's message and a travesty of all it sets out to do."[129]

Harris was a man of both vision and ambition, and his symphonies played a central role in coalescing judgment about what constituted Americanness and (briefly) greatness. He also left a legacy as a teacher; significant students include William Schuman and Peter Schickele. Yet tastes changed after the 1940s, and the music of Roy Harris has largely been consigned to the narrow niche of midcentury Americana. Beth Levy's broad assessment of his career shows its general arc: "It would take a special kind of man to undertake this messianic mission [of realizing America's musical destiny]: together, Harris and his critics made sure he fit the bill. They were successful during the 1930s. But in the end, the critical conviction required to sustain this mythmaking enterprise faltered."[130]

Nonetheless, one may ask how much of this "critical conviction" is in reality the result of lingering aesthetic prejudices that have consigned the American sounds of midcentury to a kind of Americana cliché that falls outside our ideas of greatness.

WALTER PISTON

Walter Piston (1894–1976) has come to serve as a symbol of the ongoing importance of formal mastery during this period's heady mix of innovation and populism. After training first as an engineer and then as a visual artist, Piston enrolled at Harvard in 1919 to study music, graduating in 1924 at the age of 30. His earliest works date from the period immediately after that, when he studied composition in Paris with Nadia Boulanger and Paul Dukas and violin with George Enescu, but he wrote most of his major works during his professorial tenure at Harvard (1926–1960) and after.

Piston was an exacting craftsman, and his music—not surprising for a teacher who wrote important books on harmony, analysis, counterpoint, and orchestration—reflects a deep knowledge of traditional forms and techniques such as fugue, canon, sonata, and rondo. Howard Pollack described Piston's synthesis of classical control of line and clarity of form and technique with late-nineteenth-century Romantic expressiveness as a "conservative modernist style" all his own.[131] Piston taught many composers at Harvard, including Leonard Bernstein, who spoke admiringly of Piston's "non-pedantic approach to such academic subjects as fugue."[132] Another student, Elliott Carter, was even more forceful about Piston's talents in an article from 1946:

> Through the years when the "avant-garde" moderns were busy exploring fantastic new sounds and sequences, often under the inspiration of literary and theatrical ideas, through the early thirties when a new wave of nationalism and populism started many into thinking that the concert hall with its museum atmosphere was finished as a place for living new music, down to the present more conservative situation, Piston went his own way. He stood firmly on his own chosen ground, building up a style that is a synthesis of most of the important characteristics of contemporary music and assimilating into his own manner the various changes as they came along. As a result of this tireless concentration combined with rich native musical gifts, his works have a uniform excellence that seems destined to give them an important position in the musical repertory.[133]

While he supported American musical culture, Piston had no use for the attempt to create a distinctively national style. As he put it, "The self-conscious striving for nationalism gets in the way of the establishment of a strong American school of composition and even of significant individual expression. If composers will increasingly strive to project themselves in the art of music and will follow only those paths of expression which seem to them the true way, the matter of a national school will take care of itself. The composer cannot afford the wild-goose chase of trying to be more American than he is."[134] Although Piston was certainly not considered an Americanist, his works reveal an occasional disciplined rambunctiousness through jerky syncopations and allusions to American dances.

Piston's eight symphonies represent the apex of his output, displaying his musical imagination in its most concentrated form (table 5.4). Each symphony is compact and relatively brief—No. 3 is the longest at circa 35 minutes—and consists of three or four movements. The movement structures are generally clear, though not necessarily strictly traditional. Although his overall style is less romantic than Howard Hanson's or Samuel Barber's, expressivity is central to his aesthetic, particularly in the pensive, often intense, slow movements that can stand in stark contrast to the rhythmically active outer movements. Piston shows a fondness for extended syncopated themes that, if not usually as memorable as Hanson's or Barber's, are still often quite lyrical. His orchestration generally emphasizes clarity of sound, though the texture can be rhythmically and harmonically complex. Layered syncopated material often creates a kind of rhythmic ambiguity in which the underlying meter is obscured in favor of asymmetrical pulses.

Piston wrote four symphonies for the Boston Symphony Orchestra (Nos. 1 and 3 for Koussevitzky, No. 6 for Charles Munch, No. 8 for Erich Leinsdorf), an example of the way a composer can identify strongly with a particular orchestra beyond economic patronage. As he put it, "I have always composed music from the point of view of the performers. I love instruments, and I value the cooperation of the performers."[135]

Symphony No. 1

In contrast to Hanson, Copland, and Barber, all of whom wrote their first symphonies in their early to mid-twenties, Piston did not create his first until 1937, when he was past 40. The three-movement work, a commission from the League of Composers, premiered with the composer leading the Boston Symphony Orchestra on April 8, 1938. Its instrumentation is compact, with

Table 5.4 The Symphonies of Walter Piston (1894–1976)

Title and date	Movements	Instrumentation	Comments
Symphony No. 1 (1937)	1. Andantino quasi-allegro—Allegro 4/4 (320 mm.) 2. Adagio 6/8 (156 mm.) 3. Allegro con fuoco 2/2 (342 mm.)	Grand + Flt, Ob., Clar., Bssn., Tpt., Tuba	First performance: April 8, 1938, by the Boston Symphony Orchestra, conducted by the composer. Score published by G. Schirmer, 1945.
Sinfonietta for Chamber Orchestra (1940–41)	1. Allegro grazioso 4/4 (211 mm.) 2. Adagio 6/8 (60 mm.) 3. Allegro vivo 6/8 (261 mm.)	2 Flt, 2 Ob, 2 Clar, 2 Bssn., 2 Hr, Strgs.	Dedicated to Bernard Zighera, the harpist of the Boston Symphony Orchestra. First performance: March 10, 1941, by the Boston Symphony Orchestra, conducted by Zighera. Score published by Boosey & Hawkes, 1942.
Symphony No. 2 (1943)	1. Moderato 6/4 (285 mm.) 2. Adagio 8/8 (72 mm.) 3. Allegro ₵ (290 mm.)	Grand + Flt, Ob., Clar., Bssn., 2 Tpt., Tuba, Perc. (Tamb., Tri., SD, BD, Cym.)	Commissioned by the Alice M. Ditson Fund of Columbia University. New York Music Critics' Circle Award for best new orchestral work of the 1944–45 concert season. First performance: March 5, 1944, by the National Symphony Orchestra, conducted by Hans Kindler. Holograph score published by Associated Music, 1944.
Symphony No. 3 (1947)	1. Andantino 5/4 (125 mm.) 2. Sarabande 2/4 (372 mm.) 3. Intermezzo 4/4 (86 mm.) 4. Passacaglia and Fugue 3/4 (278 mm.)	Grand + Picc., EH, Bclar., Cbssn., Tpt., Tuba, Perc. (Glsp., Xylo., Cym., BD, SD, Tamb.), 2 Harps	Commissioned by the Koussevitzky Music Foundation. Dedicated to the memory of Natalie Koussevitzky. Awarded the Pulitzer Prize of 1947. First performance: January 9, 1948, by the Boston Symphony Orchestra, conducted by Serge Koussevitzky. Score published by Boosey & Hawkes, 1951.
Symphony No. 4 (1950)	1. Piacevole ₵ (238 mm.) 2. Ballando 3/4 (248 mm.) 3. Contemplativo 12/8 (52 mm.) 4. Energico 6/8 (247 mm.)	Grand + Flt, Ob., Clar., Bssn., Tpt., Tuba, Perc. (Tri., Wood Blocks, SD, Cym., BD), 2 Harps	Commissioned by the University of Minnesota for its centennial celebration in 1951. First performance: March 30, 1951, by the Minnesota Symphony Orchestra, conducted by Antal Dorati. Score published by Associated Music, 1953.

Symphony No. 5 (1954)	1. Lento—Allegro con spirito 6/8 (295 mm.) 2. Adagio 4/4 (70 mm.) 3. Allegro lieto C (164 mm.)	Grand + Flt., Ob., Clar., Bssn., Tpt., Tuba, Perc. (SD, BD, Cym.), 2 Harps	Commissioned by the Juilliard School of Music in celebration of its 50th anniversary. First performance: February 24, 1956, by the Juilliard Orchestra, conducted by Jean Morel. Holograph score published by Associated Music, 1956.
Symphony No. 6 (1955)	1. Fluendo espressivo 3/4 (251 mm.) 2. Leggerissimo vivace 2/4 (252 mm.) 3. Adagio sereno 3/4 (136 mm.) 4. Allegro energico ¢ (206 mm.)	Grand + Flt., Ob., Clar., Bssn., Tpt., Tuba, Perc. (BD, Tri, SD, Military Drum, Tamb, Tam-tam, Cym.), 2 Harps	Commissioned by the Boston Symphony Orchestra in celebration of its 75th anniversary. Dedicated to the memory of Serge and Natalie Koussevitzky. First performance: November 25, 1955, by the Boston Symphony Orchestra, conducted by Charles Munch. Holograph score published by Associated Music, 1957.
Symphony No. 7 (1960)	1. Con moto 3/4 (322 mm.) 2. Adagio pastorale 6/8 (77 mm.) 3. Allegro festevole 2/4 (288 mm.)	Grand + Flt., Ob., Clar., Bssn., Tpt., Tuba, Perc. (BD, Cym., Tri, SD, Tamb., Tam-tam, Wood Blocks), 2 Harps	Commissioned by the Philadelphia Orchestra Association. Dedicated to Eugene Ormandy. Winner of the Pulitzer Prize, 1961. First performance: February 10, 1961, by the Philadelphia Orchestra, conducted by Ormandy. Holograph score published by Associated Music, 1961.
Symphony No. 8 (1965)	1. Moderato mosso 6/8 (93 mm.) 2. Lento assai 4/4 (105 mm.) 3. Allegro marcato 6/8 (235 mm.)	Grand + Flt., Ob., Clar., Bssn., Tpt., Tuba, Perc. (Tri, Cym., Suspended Cym., Tam-tam, Tamb., SD, BD), 2 Harps	Commissioned by Erich Leinsdorf and the Boston Symphony Orchestra. Dedicated to Leinsdorf. First performance: March 31, 1965, by the Boston Symphony Orchestra, conducted by Leinsdorf. Holograph score published by Associated Music, 1966.

eleven winds, ten brass, strings, timpani, and percussion. Although almost identical to the scoring of Hanson's *Nordic Symphony* (save that he omits the harp and adds an English horn), Piston creates a much more austere and lean sound world. In its combination of energetic, motorized objective outer movements with a strongly brooding and impassioned subjective slow movement, it recalls the music of Albert Roussel (1869–1937), whose own brand of Romantic neoclassicism Piston admired.[136]

The first-movement sonata is marked by abrupt changes of section and character. In the expansive introduction, a soft timpani roll sets the stage for an enigmatic *O*, an ostinato in pizzicato cellos and basses that to greater or lesser degrees will generate much of the thematic material of the symphony; four measures later a bassoon solo overlaps it. A balanced and elegant violin melody enters; it builds to a climax that sets up the dramatic *P* (Allegro, m. 28), in which harsh eighth notes end with a more lyrical exclamation. Several driving theme groups in staccato eighths are presented until a somewhat more relaxed *S* appears in legato divisi strings. Following a short fugato, we find ourselves in the recapitulation, which closes with a rescored *S* gliding to a halt with the strings on C. The ostinato returns at the end in augmentation (quarter notes instead of eighths).

The second movement, an Adagio in ABA form, opens with a solo English horn; flutes, clarinets, bass clarinet, and two horns join it in a solemn chorale that gradually expands to include the strings. Except for the horns, the brass does not play in this movement, and the prominence of the woodwinds (especially the low winds) gives it an atmospheric quality, most notably in the "curiously exotic and static B section."[137] The return of *A* is immediately followed by a flute melody (m. 66), which inches its way above the treble staff. At the *poco stringendo* (m. 95) the flute introduces a rhapsodic, cadenza-like passage, and we hear *A* one last time in the English horn, as a reminiscence. Much of the movement is spare in texture, but climaxes are dense, with many passages of close counterpoint.

Following classical conventions, the third movement is a swift rondo (Allegro con fuoco); the main theme is an inversion of *I/O*, stated in a decisive C minor. A notable feature of the movement is the contrast between eighth-note figurations of *I/O* and the bold brass of the episodes. In m. 61, the low brass states a melody with multiple repeated notes; the second episode features an obsessive viola repeating an E against the cellos; the third episode again highlights the brass, now speaking out as a full-throated unit. The contrast between the nimble ritornellos and the declamatory episodes reaches its apotheosis with a series of massive dissonant chords blasted out by the brass. The work ends on a C-major harmony.

In spite of relatively positive critical reaction—Arthur Berger called it a "solid work."[138]—the symphony did not elicit the enthusiastic audience response later accorded to the Third Symphonies of Harris and Copland. Even given its wide emotional range, it was perhaps seen as out of step with the more grandiose ambitions of the Great American Symphony.

Symphony No. 2

Piston's second symphony was commissioned by Columbia University and premiered in March 1944 with the National Symphony Orchestra under Hans Kindler. At first despondent about the war and unable to compose, he found encouragement and renewed strength from servicemen. As he wrote to Arthur Berger in 1942, "As a composer, I had a slump for the first year of the war, feeling that writing music was about the most futile occupation. What got me out of it chiefly was getting letters from men in the armed forces who said they hoped I was keeping on composing because that was one of the things they were out there for. I have now completely recovered a sense that it is important and . . . I am now on my second symphony."[139]

Although not explicitly topical, the emotional arc of the new symphony reflected, according to Tawa, "Piston's personal commentary, indirect as it may have been, on the war."[140] The work enjoyed great critical acclaim and won the New York Music Critics' Circle Award of 1944.

Piston wrote his own account of the work:

> The first movement (*Moderato*) is based on two themes, one given out at the opening of the movement by violas and cellos, legato and flowing, the other first played by the oboe, accompanied by clarinets and bassoons, staccato and rhythmic. The first of these themes receives the principal development, and the movement ends with a canonic statement of the melody by the brass choir, *pianissimo*.
>
> The second movement (*Adagio*) is a quiet lyrical development of the motive announced at the beginning by the bassoon and the melody played by the clarinet, accompanied by muted strings. The movement is continuous rather than sectional in form.
>
> The Finale (*Allegro*) is compounded of three themes: the first vigorous and rhythmic, played by cellos and horns; the second march-like, by clarinets and bassoons; and the third, of more songful character, first heard on English horn and clarinet.[141]

The first-movement themes are a study in contrast: P, a sinewy 6/4 in A minor with César-Franck-like chromatic contours, versus a lively C-major syncopated S with percussion that suggests the sound of a hoedown (Piston played in dance bands in his youth and had recently written the lighthearted ballet *The Incredible Flutist*). The second movement, in G major, features an elegiac mood, a long spinning out of a spacious, long-breathed melody.[142] The third movement alternates three vigorous dance-like themes. It ends in A minor, but without a sense of tragedy.

Symphony No. 3

Piston's Third Symphony (1947) was commissioned by the Koussevitzky Music Foundation—as were Copland's Third and Harris's Seventh—and, like most works funded by the foundation, it bore a dedication to the memory of Serge Koussevitzky's wife Natalie, who had died in 1942. Koussevitzky premiered and recorded the symphony with the Boston Symphony Orchestra, and it won the Pulitzer Prize of 1948. Piston again provided program notes:

> I. *Allegro* 5/4—based on three thematic elements: the first heard as a melody for the oboe; the second, more somber in character, played on the bassoon, clarinets and English horn; the third, soft chords for brass. These ideas are developed singly and in combinations to form a prelude-like movement. Tonality C.
>
> II. *Allegro* 2/4—a scherzo in three-part form. The theme, stated by violas and bassoons, is treated in contrapuntal imitative fashion. The middle part is marked by a melody for flute, accompanied by clarinets and harps. Tonality F.
>
> III. *Adagio* 4/4—the movement has four large and closely connected sections, or rather "phrases" of musical development. The first of these is the statement of strings of the theme, which is in three parts (part one by violins, part two by violas, part three by all except basses). The second section is a variation of the theme, with woodwinds and harps predominating. The third section, starting with basses and celli, builds up to the climax of the movement, and the final section returns to the original form of the theme, played by solo viola, the closing cadence recalling the variation by clarinet and bassoon. Tonality G.

IV. *Allegro* 4/4—a three-part form similar to that of a sonata form movement. There are two themes, the first being developed fugily [*sic*] in the middle section. The second theme is march-like, first heard in oboes and bassoons, over a staccato bass, and later played by full brass at the climax of the movement. Tonality C.[143]

It is somewhat unusual that the first movement's "prelude-like" elements are all introduced in the winds or brass; it builds to a resolute end in C major. The second movement (in F) is a lively scherzo, syncopated and jerky in rhythm. The Adagio is in a variation form emphasizing the strings; its powerful climax exhibits the expressive quality that Piston is capable of achieving. The sunny fourth movement moves back to the home key, with a syncopated *P* followed by a march-like *S*.

Symphony No. 4

Piston received the commission to write his Fourth Symphony (1950) from the University of Minnesota to mark its centenary; Antal Dorati conducted the premiere with the Minnesota Symphony Orchestra on March 30, 1951. The work contrasts with the decidedly Neoclassical writing of the First Symphony. As Piston wrote to Donald Ferguson to describe his more romantic approach: "I am at a total loss to know what to write about my symphony. It is not intended to convey other than musical thoughts, although I think you will agree that this leaves more freedom to the listener to bring to the music what he will. . . . I feel this symphony is melodic and expressive and perhaps nearer than my other works to the problem of balance between expression and formal design. It should not prove complex to the listener in any way."[144]

The symphony is in four movements: *Piacevole, Ballando, Contemplativo,* and *Energico.* It calls for twelve winds (from piccolo to contrabassoon), eleven brass, timpani, percussion, two harps, and strings, representing a larger orchestral complement than the First Symphony.

The gentle and restrained first movement (*Piacevole*) is convincing evidence of Piston's balance of formal design and expression. The opening violin melody, *P*, plainly stated in C major, spins out against a sparse but syncopated accompaniment. In his analysis of this work, William Austin notes that "All the aspects of this theme—its long, singing line, its lively variety of rhythm, its clear, fresh sonorities, its gently fluctuating dynamics, its contrapuntal vitality, and above all its smooth but unconventional harmony—show the same character that Piston shows as an occasional conductor of his own music."[145]

S features a chromatic and dissonant duet between clarinet and bassoon. Piston's treatment creates the effect of a loose rondo form, with excursions away from and back to the eminently recognizable *P*, instead of the organic development of two opposing ideas. At m. 103, Austin describes "a long span recapitulating, developing, and answering the first theme." The bassoon leads a charge toward *S* (mm. 190–99) and then *P* returns, succinctly and without fanfare, to end the movement.

Ballando is a distorted dance, with a swiftly changing metrical structure that moves unpredictably between five, six, and seven eighth notes to the bar. Yet its form is essentially transparent. After the first theme *A*, with its marked rhythmic snap (example 5.3)—especially

Facing, Example 5.3 Piston, Symphony No. 4, II, *II/P*

noticeable in m. 27, when the percussion enters—the cellos introduce *B*, a legato but no less energetic theme in m. 49. After a return of *A* in m. 74, Piston somewhat uncharacteristically shifts focus abruptly to new material at m. 115, a passage of flashy violin writing that strongly suggests American folk fiddling (example 5.4). *A* comes back once more in the flute, and the lyrical *B* returns in slightly modified form; as in the first movement, a brief statement of *A* brings thematic closure. The movement therefore combines two kinds of nationalistic elements, American-style syncopation (*A*) and folk-dance rhythm (*B*), and it offers a compelling example of how to incorporate such idioms into the texture without making an explicit or even

Example 5.4 Piston, Symphony No. 4, II, fiddle-style writing

implicit extrageneric reference.

The third movement, *Contemplativo*, is the only pensive passage in the symphony; its melancholic F minor stands in strong contrast to the bright C major and A major that came before. Written in a languid 12/8, its metrical stability is balanced against the eerie woodwind melody of the opening; only at m. 12 do we have a decisive establishment of the key with the introduction of a lyrical melody in the violins. Piston spins out this melody like a continuous thought, building to an intense climax for full orchestra followed by the brass choir.

The final movement (*Energico*) fully embraces sonata form, despite its compact proportions. Written in a driving and syncopated 6/8, it returns to a major key (B-flat). *P* harnesses the growling energy of the low violin, juxtaposing it with a more elegant *S* introduced by the oboe in m. 44. The development is as compact as it is forceful: after only 42 measures Piston brings in the recapitulation, making the Finale the most concise of the four movements.

Fifth and Sixth Symphonies

Piston composed his Fifth Symphony (1954) for the fiftieth anniversary of the Juilliard School of Music. The first movement, in E minor, begins with a haunting slow introduction before leading into a sonata-allegro form. Dissonant passages, albeit with clear melodic lines, recall some of the astringency of Symphony No. 1. The introduction returns as coda. The second movement, an Adagio in A major, begins with a twelve-note row, the intervals related to motives from the first movement. The primary theme of the movement, which Piston subjects to continuous variations, is diatonic but relates to the motives of the first movement. The textures are spare except at the climax. The third movement, Allegro lieto, is a rondo with driving rhythms similar to those of the *Ballando* from Symphony No. 4. Its C-major refrain spans two octaves in jagged fourths. The syncopations lend a typically American spaciousness.

To celebrate the seventy-fifth season of the Boston Symphony Orchestra, Piston created the Sixth Symphony (1955); since the Koussevitzky Music Foundation commissioned the work (as it had Symphony No. 3), the composer dedicated it to the memory of Serge and Natalie Koussevitzky. The work shows Piston's familiarity with specific players in the Boston ensemble: "While writing my sixth Symphony, I came to realize that this was a rather special situation in that I was writing for one designated orchestra, one that I had grown up with, and that I knew intimately. Each note set down sounded in the mind with extraordinary clarity, as though played immediately by those who were to perform the work. On several occasions it seemed as though the melodies were being written by the instruments themselves as I followed along. I refrained from playing even a single note of this symphony on the piano."[146]

In this work, Piston includes a larger percussion battery than in his previous symphonies. The first movement (Fluendo espressivo, A minor) begins with *P*, a flowing string theme with some chromatic twists; initiated by the harp, *S* changes wind colors. Separate instrumental families are showcased. The Scherzo, Leggerissimo vivace (D major), is set in motion by percussion; not American this time, the movement represents Piston's version of Mendelssohnian elfin music—fast, mostly soft, with staccato strings and winds. The third movement (Adagio sereno, F-sharp minor) begins with a theme in the solo cello; the ABABA form alternates strings and winds, reaching a passionate climax in the second B. In the final A, the cello plays the BACH motive, probably as a tribute to conductor Charles Munch's enthusiasm for that composer. The last movement (Allegro energico, A major) is one of Piston's best airy finales with a catchy main tune treated with American exuberance and folk-sounding syncopations. A fugal passage in the middle and a jubilant ending lend structural clarity.

Seventh and Eighth Symphonies

Piston's last two symphonies are more experimental in form and harmony. He composed the three-movement Symphony No. 7 in 1960 for the Philadelphia Orchestra and conductor Eugene Ormandy; again, he wrote the work with the specific orchestra in mind. A fine composition with many of the characteristics observed in the earlier symphonies, it won the Pulitzer Prize in 1961. Similar in mood and approach to the *Three New England Sketches* (1959), Pollack says it could be described as Piston's *Pastoral Symphony*.[147] Noting its "defiance of systems of harmonic control in favor of a liberated melodic impulse," composer and Piston student Clifford Taylor emphasized Piston's ongoing ability to mine new directions in what was essentially a tonal language: "Piston's employment of clearly traditional contexts and materials in pursuing this policy has been a remarkable demonstration of how, without abandoning its familiar guises, an art can manifest wholly new aesthetic impulses such as we have experienced in this century, which in effect alter its traditional definition."[148]

Piston composed his final symphony, the three-movement Eighth, for Erich Leinsdorf and the Boston Symphony Orchestra in 1965. As he had done in the second movement of the Fifth Symphony, he employs a twelve-note theme in the first movement (Moderato mosso); he accompanies it with six-note chords that form another aggregate. The movement is not rigorously serial, however. Reaching an anguished climax, it ends in a mood of ambivalence. Piston sets the second movement (Lento assai) as a theme and variations. The Finale (Allegro marcato), a rhythmically propulsive binary movement, ends with a short coda brought to a close with a timpani solo; not as dark as the first two movements, the symphony still ends in a more ambivalent mood than does its predecessors. Pollack described the "murky and surreal details that overwhelm the formal design."[149]

Tawa described Piston's contribution to the symphonic repertoire as "masterly," and the recognition Piston received for his symphonies indicates an admiration that lasted for most of his career: a New York Music Critics' Circle award (Second Symphony), a Naumburg Recording Award (Fourth Symphony), and two Pulitzer Prizes (Third and Seventh Symphonies). Conventional wisdom has seized on his prominent academic career and an expertly crafted musical language more conventional that of the other members of the Boulangerie to dismiss his music glibly as Neoclassical—meaning, in this context, unexpressive—while overlooking the restrained but strong Romantic feeling within. Perhaps his "conservative modernist" language became a victim of an age that conflated grandiosity and emotion. At any rate, Piston's symphonic achievement—in addition to his other orchestral and chamber works—urgently demands fuller exposure, with Symphonies 2, 4, and 6 being good places to start.

VIRGIL THOMSON

The version of modernism embraced by Virgil Thomson (1896–1989) drew on the expansive and populist dimensions of the search for a distinctively American symphonic style. In contrast to the harsh, alienating stance of such American ultramodernists as Charles Ives (at times), Carl Ruggles, Ruth Crawford Seeger, and Leo Ornstein, Thomson's modernism was refined and restrained. Although his best-known contributions are his operatic collaborations with Gertrude Stein (*Four Saints in Three Acts* and *The Mother of Us All*, premiering in 1934 and 1947 respectively), his three symphonies—*Symphony on a Hymn Tune* (1926–28), Symphony No. 2 (1931, rev. 1941), and the Third Symphony (1972)—all reflect an ongoing interest in experimenting with alternatives to the dominant modernist aesthetic (table 5.5).

Symphony on a Hymn Tune

Thomson wrote *Symphony on a Hymn Tune* early in his sojourn in Paris, where he lived from 1925 to 1940. At the time, he was one of the most visible members of the Boulangerie, and it was in this context that he found a level of creative freedom. "America was impatient with us, trying always to take us in hand and make us a success, or else squeezing us dry for exhibiting in an institution. . . . As Gertrude Stein was to observe, 'It was not so much what France gave you as what she did not take away.'"[150] What France gave Thomson was a distinctive approach to Modernism that distorted conventional forms while leaving their overall legibility intact (Erik Satie, 1866–1925, was a strong inspiration). The composer began work on *Symphony on a Hymn Tune* during the end of his studies with Boulanger but never showed it to her, perhaps understanding how much it flouted the compositional training he was receiving.[151]

Thomson described the work succinctly: "It is a set of variations on the hymn 'How Firm a Foundation'; each movement consists of a further set of variations tightened-up in various ways, the first in the manner of a sonata, the second as a Bach chorale-prelude, the third as a passacaglia. The fourth is twice tightened-up, once as a fugato, once as a rondo."[152]

As Michael Meckna has noted, *Symphony on a Hymn Tune* also relies highly on the hymn "Jesus Loves Me," which permeates the work almost as much as "How Firm a Foundation." As a (nonbelieving) Southern Baptist brought up in midwestern Kansas City, these melodies were as much a part of his formation as the hymns popular in New England were for Ives. But while Ives similarly quotes hymns in his Third Symphony and Henry Cowell alludes to hymn style (as well as the fuguing tune) in his Fourth Symphony, Thomson takes his two melodies, strips them of their cultural or religious associations, and treats them in a highly abstract and decontextualized manner that approaches satire.

Thomson's distortions are evident in multiple musical parameters. Although the harmonic language in this symphony is clearly less challenging than that of his Modernist colleagues, odd juxtapositions abound. Sometimes they result from rhythmic manipulation, such as unusual meters (4½ / 4), multimeter, and cross-rhythms. Distinctive thematic processes contribute as well: rather than conventional development or organic elaboration, Thomson places bits and pieces of themes in odd combinations, which leads Meckna to describe the composer's

Table 5.5 The Symphonies of Virgil Thomson (1896–1989)

Title and date	Movements	Instrumentation	Comments
Symphony on a Hymn Tune (1926–28)	1. Introduction and Allegro 4/4 (253 mm.) 2. Andante cantabile 3/4 (93 mm.) 3. Allegretto 4/4 (180 mm.) 4. Alla breve 4/4 (200 mm.)	Grand + Picc., Cbssn., Tuba, Perc. (SD, Rattle, Tamb., Tri, Cym., Tam-tam, BD)	The tune in question is "How Firm a Foundation" (John Rippon, 1787); "Jesus Loves Me" (William Bradbury, 1862) also appears prominently. First performance: February 22, 1945, by the New York Philharmonic-Symphony Society, conducted by the composer. Score published by Southern Music, 1954. Arranged in 1928 for piano four-hands by John Kirkpatrick.
Symphony No. 2 in C Major (1931, rev. 1941)	1. Allegro militaire ¢ (249 mm.) 2. Andante 3/4 (152 mm.) 3. Allegro ¢ (264 mm.)	Grand + Flt. (Flt. 2–3 doubling Picc.), EH, Clar. (doubling Bclar.), Bssn. (doubling Cbssn.), Tuba, Perc. (SD, BD, Cym., Chime in low G, Tam-tam)	Orchestral arrangement of the Piano Sonata No. 1 (1929). First performance: November 17, 1941, by the Seattle Symphony, conducted by Thomas Beecham. Score published by Leeds Music/MCA Music, 1954.
Symphony No. 3 (1972)	1. Swinging 6/8 (114 mm.) 2. Tempo di Valzer 3/4 (207 mm.) 3. Adagio sostenuto 4/4 (63 mm.) 4. Allegretto 4/4 (99 mm.)	Grand + Perc. (Gong, Glsp., Cym., Tam-tam, BD, SD, Tamb., Field Drum), Harp.	Orchestral arrangement of String Quartet No. 2 (1931). First performance: December 26, 1976, by the American Symphony Orchestra, conducted by Kazuyoshi Akiyama. Score published by Boosey & Hawkes, 1974.

Example 5.5 Thomson, *Symphony on a Hymn Tune*, combination of hymn tunes "How Firm a Foundation" (trumpet) and "Jesus Loves Me" (violins and winds)

process as a "collage."[153] He uses harmonic procedures to suggest religious connotations: the tritone relationship of key centers that recurs throughout the symphony implies a struggle between good and evil, while simultaneous parallel fifths in the lower voices and parallel thirds in the upper voices evoke Roman Catholic and Protestant traditions.[154] He also makes use of unusual timbral combinations such as horn and violas in the second movement and piccolo and tuba in the fourth movement.

The work begins with a passage featuring parallel fifths in brass and woodwinds that ends on E-flat. "How Firm a Foundation" immediately follows in A major, thus establishing the tritone. This straightforward string statement of the hymn tune is mirrored in the woodwinds over a descending bass line that creates dissonance. He then subjects the tune to character variations, such as a waltz onto which he imposes "Jesus Loves Me" bitonally (example 5.5). Some passages display dissonant counterpoint and others strong syncopations. An extended group cadenza closes the first movement, introduced with a trombone solo—perhaps a nod to the instrument's religious associations?—onto which Thomson layers passages in the piccolo, cello, and violin.

The second movement features running triplets and variations on a melody derived from "How Firm a Foundation"; the third follows with a passacaglia based on the bass line of the tune.[155] Thomson's satire comes through at the end, as the movement's "firm foundation" of A major is challenged by a B-flat on trombone, piccolo, and flute.

The Finale turns the theme into a folk-style ground, to which he adds "For He's a Jolly Good Fellow." Both hymn tunes are stated fully before a series of emphatic chords lead to a closing A-major harmony. Although whimsical in effect, the ending does not maintain the interest of the rest of the piece. As John Cage put it, "One wonders . . . whether the *Symphony on a Hymn Tune* has ever been properly concluded. The emphatic ending in the published version suggests the substitution of strength and loudness for conviction. The final pages are introduced in the same manner as the astounding cadenza of the first movement, but the expected passage revealing new elements does not occur."[156]

Although finished in 1928, the *Symphony on a Hymn Tune* did not premiere until 1945. Thomson felt the work was misunderstood, for which he blamed Koussevitzky. According to Thomson, the conductor responded positively to the first three movements but urged him to replace the Finale, saying "I could never play my audience that"; Thomson merely "thanked him for his graciousness and left."[157] In his autobiography, the composer wrote, "Once I got mad at him for telling me how not to try to write a piece. I even, on account of his discouragement, held back performance of the piece. Then twelve years later it started being played. That was my *Symphony on a Hymn Tune*."[158] The work finally debuted in February 1945, when the New York Philharmonic played it under the composer's baton.

Second and Third Symphonies

Thomson created two more symphonies, but both are orchestral arrangements of preexistent solo and chamber works. Despite their nonsymphonic origins, both pieces exhibit the approach to large-scale instrumental music that Thomson had set in motion with the *Symphony on a Hymn Tune*: clear orchestration, legible if distorted forms, diatonic but nonfunctional harmony, and a commitment to an aloof accessibility that made his works simultaneously charming and mysterious.

The Second Symphony (1931, rev. 1941) began life as a piano sonata. As he described the work,

> My Second Symphony is cyclic in thematic content and asymmetrical in form. Its opening measures are the motif, the germ from which the whole is developed. Its forward progress is continuous, moreover, no section and almost no phrase being repeated exactly. Its structure is that of an open curve.
>
> The first and third movements are squarely in C major, the second in A flat. The tunes are all diatonic, and so is the harmony. Tonalities are sharply juxtaposed, rather than superimposed.

Instrumentation "by threes" has facilitated the scoring of unrelated chords in contrasting colors. The expressive character of this symphony is predominantly lyrical. Dancing and jollity, however, are rarely absent from its thought; and the military suggestions of horn and trumpet, of marching and of drums, are a constant recurring presence both as background and as foreground.[159]

The Third Symphony (1972) originated as the composer's Second String Quartet from four decades earlier. Butterworth notes that it is "neoclassical in manner" and observes, "There is an easy-going, unchallenging air to the whole work, especially in the two short middle movements, a waltz and a relatively somber tango. That the score sounds like a *bone fide* orchestral piece is credit to the composer's skill in instrumentation."[160]

European-Trained Composers: The American Academy in Rome

The second major European center of activity for aspiring American composers was the American Academy in Rome, which established a composition prize in 1921. Musical fellows were not obliged to follow a prescribed course, but they were required to compose a certain amount. A number studied with Ottorino Respighi, who arranged for their works to be played by the Augusteo Orchestra.[161]

The contrast between the Rome Academy and the Boulangerie is both geographical and aesthetic. Carol Oja notes the academy's fundamentally conservative orientation, in contrast with Boulanger's stylistic openness: "While the American Academy in Rome emerged as an important mechanism for transnational interaction after World War I, the degree to which its elders clung to the past—to the known and the comfortably established—was remarkable."[162] Felix Lamond, an organist and professor at Columbia Teachers' College, who became "professor in charge of music" at the academy, expressed the attitude this way: "A week devoted to ultra-modern music gave us the power to distinguish styles and form judgments as to its value and merits. We returned to Rome more than ever impressed with the fact that classical composition must be the foundation on which we must build."[163]

Characteristically, composers trained at the Rome Academy generally took a more traditional approach to the symphony, and upon their return to the United States, most settled into roles at prominent musical institutions (as did some members of the Boulangerie, especially Piston). Even so, there were individual stylistic differences: Samuel Barber and Howard Hanson leaned toward a purer European aesthetic, while Randall Thompson and Leo Sowerby experimented with a combination of vernacular and modernist elements. And, although the classical training might have implied a compositional emphasis on the symphony, Hanson was the only real symphonist in this group; the others built their reputations primarily on vocal, choral, and nonsymphonic orchestral genres.

SAMUEL BARBER

Samuel Barber (1910–81) stands out as a somewhat perplexing figure in the symphonic repertoire of this period. His music has achieved a lasting position both in the United States and abroad: his *Adagio for Strings* is one of the few twentieth-century compositions that has achieved the status of a pop classic, and his Violin Concerto, songs, and piano works continue to be programmed far more than the works of any of the other composers discussed in this chapter except Copland. His early mastery—he wrote most of his famous orchestral pieces in his twenties—and popular successes allowed him the freedom to compose without the

Table 5.6 The Symphonies of Samuel Barber (1910–81)

Title and date	Movements	Instrumentation	Comments
Symphony No. 1 (in One Movement), Op. 9 (1936, rev. 1942)	In one movement, divided into four sections: 1. Allegro ma non troppo 6/4 (mm. 1–137) 2. Allegro molto 6/8 (mm. 138–437) 3. Andante tranquillo C (mm. 438–518) 4. Con moto 3/4 (mm. 519–620)	Grand + Picc., EH, Bclar, Cbssn., Tpt, Tuba, Perc. (Cym., BD), Harp	Composed in Rome during Barber's first year at the American Academy. Dedicated to Gian-Carlo Menotti. Modeled on Sibelius's Seventh Symphony. Barber's 1942 revision replaced the original Scherzo with a more extended one. First performance: December 13, 1936, by the Augusteo Orchestra, conducted by Bernardino Molinari. First American performance: January 21, 1937, by the Cleveland Orchestra, conducted by Rudolph Ringwall. First performance of revised version: February 18, 1944, by the Philadelphia Orchestra, conducted by Bruno Walter. Score published by G. Schirmer, 1943.
Symphony No. 2, Op. 19 (1943, rev. 1947)	1. Allegro ma non troppo 3/4 (481 mm.) 2. Andante, un poco mosso 5/4 (83 mm.) 3. Presto—Allegro risoluto 3/4 (527 mm.)	Grand + Picc., EH, E♭Clar., Bclar., Cbssn., Tpt., Tuba, Perc. (Cym., SD, BD, Wood Blocks), Pno.	Commissioned by the US Army Air Force, to which the symphony is dedicated. Written to express "the mood, the adventure, the vivid action of the individual flying man." The original version of the second movement included an electric tone generator to simulate the sound of a radio beam; Barber replaced it with an E♭ clarinet in the 1947 revision. First performance: March 3, 1944, by the Boston Symphony Orchestra, conducted by Serge Koussevitzky. Score published by G. Schirmer, 1950. Barber destroyed both the score and parts in 1964; he retained only the second movement, which he rescored very slightly and issued as an independent symphonic poem, *Night Flight* (1964). A surviving set of parts was found after Barber's death, and in 1990 Schirmer republished the work.

constraints of teaching or administration. Nevertheless, while his two symphonies stand as fully realized works, they are somewhat peripheral to the appreciation of Barber today (table 5.6).

Despite—or perhaps because of—his public successes, Barber's more iconoclastic contemporaries remained nonplussed by his steadfastly lyrical, romantic, and cosmopolitan style. ("Skyscrapers, subways, and train lights play no part in the music I write," he asserted in 1935.)[164] As the introduction to this chapter discussed, American composers faced a dilemma reconciling the competing demands of modernism and populism. Barber's admiration of Jean Sibelius figures into the way this dilemma played out for him; by the 1940s, Sibelius was a target for more overtly progressive composers, and Barber's association with him was interpreted as a sign of weakness. Those influenced by Sibelius, Copland wrote, "are composers who feel lost in the mazes of the contemporary idiom. Sibelius is a refuge to them, since he proves conclusively that a composer need merely treat the materials of music in his own way in order to transfuse the commonest chord or theme with meaning. In that sense his influence has been a salutary one. But insofar as his followers use him as justification for escaping the problems of their own time and place, their work is certain to awaken nothing but echoes of a past era."[165]

Copland was not alone in his skepticism of composers drawn to a neoromantic style. Critic Ashley Pettis expressed the same concerns to a larger audience in a letter to the *New York Times*. Pettis applauded the promise that broadcasts of new music by prominent figures such as Arturo Toscanini held, but he but bemoaned Toscanini's choice of Barber:

> Potentially it is an event of great significance and might easily have an enormous influence upon our musical life, both in acquainting a wide public with the fact that there are serious, contemporary works and to provide fresh impetus and incentive to our musicians. . . . One listened in vain for evidences of youthful vigor, freshness or fire, for use of a contemporary idiom . . . Mr. Barber's was . . . utterly anachronistic as the utterance of a young man of 28, A.D. 1938. . . . Such a choice by the great musical Messiah in our midst can only have a retarding influence on the advance of our creative musicians. They realize only too well that they have small chance of performance by the greatest musical organizations and conductors . . . unless they write music for people who listen with ears of the nineteenth and early twentieth centuries at latest—whose criteria are that "new" music shall have the familiar melodic, harmonic and rhythmic characteristics of the past.[166]

Pettis's letter provoked a number of responses; one from Roy Harris was more philosophical, describing the "cultural storm" between the "venerable" patrons of the European traditions and the "vulnerable" young composers. In the final analysis, wrote Harris, "Time, who is no respecter of persons, will call his own court of appraisal to order and render final judgment on what is offered. No amount of wish-thinking on the part of either party will alter the real stature of what we do."[167]

First Symphony (in One Movement)

Barber's First Symphony (1936, rev. 1942) was situated squarely in these cultural crosshairs. He began the work the summer before he left for Rome, and it received its first performance in that city.[168] Howard Pollack has argued persuasively for its affinities with Sibelius's Seventh Symphony: both are in one movement, and Barber wrote an analysis of the older composer's work around the same time he was working on the symphony.[169] Additional affinities with the Finnish composer include a propensity for darker tone colors, modal inflections, and sustained rolls in timpani and bass drum. Barber's highly lyrical style is his own, but, like Sibelius's, it exhibits a propensity for motives built from an initial melodic "germ."

In order to structure this one-movement work, Barber relied on a hybrid form. On the one hand, the symphony is made up of four sections that follow the typical layout of the movements of a symphony: Allegro ma non troppo, Scherzo, Andante tranquillo, and a concluding passacaglia. At the same time, since the end of the symphony recalls the material from the beginning, it can also be seen as an extended one-movement sonata form. The composer's note explains this interrelationship:

> The form is a synthetic treatment of the four-movement classical symphony. It is based on three themes of the initial *Allegro ma non troppo*, which retain throughout the work their fundamental character. The *Allegro ma non troppo* opens with the usual exposition of a main theme, a more lyrical second theme, and a closing theme. After a brief development of the three themes, instead of the customary recapitulation, the theme in diminution forms the basis of a scherzo section (*vivace*). The second theme (oboe over muted strings) then appears in augmentation, in an extended *Andante tranquillo*. An intense crescendo introduces the finale, which is a short passacaglia based on the first theme (introduced by violoncelli and contrabass), over which, together with figures from other themes, the closing theme is woven, thus serving as a recapitulation for the entire symphony.[170]

At the beginning, little would indicate that we are experiencing anything other than a more-or-less conventional sonata exposition. We hear a clearly articulated, angular, dotted-rhythm *P* in muted strings and winds in E minor (example 5.6), followed by the more conjunct *S* (suggesting B minor) introduced in the English horn and viola. High woodwinds and strings state a third theme, *K* (2 before Reh. 6). The development is primarily based on *P*. At Reh. 12 the trombone intones a variation of *P* under more active strings and woodwinds—a striking passage with both textural interest and structural significance, as it foreshadows the passacaglia theme of the final section. The formal twist comes at the end of the development, when an Allegro molto in 6/8 (4 after Reh. 15) hails the arrival of a Scherzo rather than a recapitulation.

Example 5.6 Barber, Symphony No. 1, opening

In the Scherzo, Barber develops a motoric rhythmic drive, beginning in the strings and then expanding to the whole orchestra; shifting accents between groups of twos and threes enhance the effect. The theme is a variant of I/P in diminution. We have moved into a B-flat major tonality, with wild chromatic modulations followed by a contrasting, though no less animated, section in F before returning to the full-throated drive of the beginning of the Scherzo. A strident horn melody indicates a devastating climax on C. Through a deft modulation led by the bassoon, Barber situates us in the C-sharp minor embrace of the slow section.

Led by the oboe, this Andante tranquillo is as lyrical as the Scherzo is unforgiving. The melody is an extension of I/S, presented in long, languid oboe lines over a slowly undulating muted string accompaniment. A trio of cellos presents an alternating idea that unfolds into searing string writing—a fine example of Barber's lyricism at its most intense—before resolving to E minor. In a subtler nod to the nineteenth century, the symphony closes with a passacaglia in E minor, with its six-measure ground melody based on *I/P* (example 5.7). The allusion to the Finale of Brahms's Fourth Symphony is tangible (Barber strongly admired Brahms): not only do the two movements share the key, but Barber subjects his theme to 12 strict variations, with some of the variations grouped into larger sets (e.g., variations 4–6) while others remain freestanding. Material from earlier in the symphony—most prominently *I/K*—is freely juxtaposed, bringing the work to both a tonal and thematic conclusion with timpani rolls and stentorian brass declamations.

Example 5.7 Barber, Symphony No. 1, passacaglia theme (bass line, 1 before Reh. 42)

The symphony received performances on both sides of the Atlantic. Its premiere in Rome on December 13, 1936, was met with a cool response from the Italian listeners: "at the time it was thought too dark-toned, too Nordic and Sibelian."[171] Audiences in the United States reacted much more enthusiastically to performances by the Cleveland Orchestra and Rudolph Ringwall in January 1937 and by the New York Philharmonic under Artur Rodzinski in New York two months later. *NewYork Herald Tribune* critic Francis Perkins praised the work's "clearly defined musical ideas of considerable cogency in an instrumental garb wrought with unusual mastery."[172] That summer, under Rodzinski, it became the first American work performed at the Salzburg Festival; David Ewen praised his "facility in self-expression, his extraordinary gift in formulating his copious ideas into a coherent and integrated pattern . . . his capacity for writing a line of melody, and his instinct for harmony and orchestration."[173]

Symphony No. 2

Barber's Second Symphony (1944, rev. 1947) was a war symphony, premiered just a month after George Antheil's Fourth (discussed later), on March 3, 1944, with Koussevitzky conducting the Boston Symphony Orchestra. Like Blitzstein, Barber served in the air force during World War II and wrote the symphony in honor of that service, working on it full-time while living at home.[174] Although the symphony was commissioned by the air force and was understood to represent it—the work initially bore the subtitle "Airborne"—Barber insisted that it did not have a particular program. In a letter to his uncle Sidney Homer, he said, "The first movement tries to express the dynamism and excitement of flying—and ends way up 50,000 feet! The second is a lonely sort of folk-song melody for English horn, against backgrounds of string-clouds. It might be called solo flight at night. Otherwise there is no program."[175] Even so, as Nathan Broder pointed out, "an imaginative listener . . . could easily find in it the reaction of a poet thrust into a world of war machines."[176]

The work's three movements called for 13 woodwinds, 11 brass, 3 percussionists, piano, and strings, a scoring similar to that of the First Symphony except for the piano replacing the harp. When Barber played a draft for his superior officer, he was concerned that it would be found insufficiently popular in style. He need not have worried: "'Well, corporal, it's not quite what we expected from you. Since the air force uses all sorts of the most modern technical devices, I hope you'll write this symphony in quarter-tones. But do what you can, do what you can, corporal.'"[177] In response, he added an electric tone generator in the second movement to suggest the sound of radio beams used to direct night flyers.

Barber became dissatisfied with the work as time went on. He revised it substantially in 1947, replacing the tone generator with an E-flat clarinet and dropping the title "Airborne." In 1964, he destroyed the score and published parts, preserving only the second movement as a tone poem entitled *Night Flight*. Fortunately, a copy of the parts was found in a warehouse in 1984, three years after Barber's death, and it formed the basis of a reconstructed version.

The opening of the first movement (Allegro ma non troppo) fearlessly declares its departure from what might be expected of a composer so frequently described as lyrical, with strident major seconds in the winds accosting the listener in the very first bar; they accompany a jagged, descending double-dotted *P* (the most recognizable melody in the movement), which bears a faint resemblance to *I/P* of the First Symphony (example 5.8.) The effect, as Walter Simmons describes it, is "a harsher, more athletic, and more extroverted type of expression" than that encountered in his previous works.[178] Yet, at the same time, it follows a lucid developmental plan. After this lumbering, dissonant opening, the meter changes to 3/8 for quick transitional material (Reh. 3) followed by a more characteristic singing *S* led by the oboe (Reh. 9). The development begins at Reh. 17, opening with a pensive focus on B as its tonal center. A more agitated section begins at Reh. 20. Its rapidly alternating blocks of performing forces, emphasizing woodwinds and shifting accents, recalls Stravinsky. By Reh. 27, the striking *P* has returned for the recapitulation.

In ternary form, the 5/4 second movement (Andante un poco mosso), in A minor, features the English horn singing softly over subdued divisi strings and piano. Tightly constructed chromatic turns give the otherwise serene surface a notable pathos. The movement builds to a dissonant climax at Reh. 6; the horns step in to resolve it and return the work from the distant E-flat minor of the middle section to the safety of the original key signature.

The third movement (Presto) contrasts a rapid, freely moving (*senza battuta*) eighth-note figure with dissonant arrival chords. A second theme introduces a stern chromatic descending figure. As in the first movement, the performing forces are broken up into discrete units, often rapidly alternating among one another and moving more as a sequence of episodes than by development; a short fugato in the strings uses the descending chromatic figure as its basis. By Reh. 24, the brass has joined in, stating a version of the initial eighth-note theme in augmentation. At Reh. 27 the complete *senza battuta* passage returns, and the recapitulation seems to be moving at full steam until a bold pedal on F-sharp interrupts the action for a meandering string interlude. Just as abruptly as the reverie begins, it is over, with the brass leading the charge to the devastating closing bars on a picardy F-sharp.

Tawa describes Barber's Second Symphony as "ambivalent." Barber's own decision to destroy the score—which Pollack attributes to a combination of aesthetic dissatisfaction with the work, rejection of its distasteful association with war propaganda, and frustration over a lack of performances—indicates that the composer was the first to experience any ambivalence. In a 1948 overview of Barber's music, Nathan Broder noted that "at the first performance of the Second Symphony some listeners expressed distrustful surprise at what they regarded as a sudden change in Barber's style."[179] Both Tawa and Pollack, however, would have history vindicate Barber's work: Tawa detected a consensus in the 1980s that the Second Symphony "deserves to be ranked with the best symphonies that Americans had produced" and Pollack

Susan Key, with Drew Massey

***Above and facing*, Example 5.8** Barber, Symphony No. 2, I/P (mm. 1–8)

From 1920 to 1950 in the United States

361

argues that it "stands up well as an ambitious and distinctive contribution to the American symphonic repertory."[180]

It is perhaps surprising that Barber's two symphonies are not characteristic either in the context of his own *oeuvre* or within the larger trends of American music at the time. Nevertheless, they are an important reminder that composers did not pursue a single aesthetic agenda between the Depression and World War II and that even the creative life of a single individual could reflect competing aesthetic and topical issues.

HOWARD HANSON

Few composers in this chapter made their presence felt in as many spheres as Howard Hanson (1896–1981). Not only were his seven symphonies central to the genre, he was also an active champion of American music as conductor, educator, and administrator (table 5.7). Born in Nebraska to a family of Swedish descent, he studied at Luther College, with additional studies at the Institute of Musical Art (a precursor to the Juilliard School) and Northwestern University. He taught at the College of the Pacific from 1916 to 1919, becoming dean of that school's Conservatory of Fine Arts in 1919 at age 23. As the second recipient of the Rome Prize in music, he spent three years there (1921–24), studying with Ottorino Respighi (1879–1936).[181] Upon his return to the United States, he became director of the Eastman School of Music (at 28), a position that he used to great effect during his 40-year tenure to promote contemporary American music. He organized the American Composers Orchestral Concerts and annual Festivals of American Music. In 1939, he cofounded the American Music Center, whose mission it was to disseminate information about compositions from the United States.[182]

Along with Respighi, Hanson claimed Grieg and Sibelius as his greatest musical influences. As a composer, he was an unabashed Romantic, at odds with contemporary Neoclassical and atonal schools. This aesthetic orientation was infused with a deep spirituality that dated back to childhood: "I was very much interested in religion, I think too much so, really. . . . But on the other hand, I remember playing basketball in high school and playing games and being a good bicycle rider and having a good time."[183] Randall Thompson noted the "mystical elements" in Hanson's style as well as its expansive vision: "The music of Howard Hanson combines elements of austerity and introspection with those of a sweeping and optimistic democracy."[184]

Hanson's music features beautiful, broad lyric themes, often in legato strings, written in chromatic harmonies with lush orchestration strongly influenced by the sound worlds of Sibelius and Respighi (as well as Respighi's teacher, Nikolai Rimsky-Korsakov [1844–1908]): "My love for big luxurious orchestral sonorities was undoubtedly influenced by Respighi."[185] The scoring is similar in the symphonies: pairs of winds, four horns, three trumpets and trombones, a tuba, strings, harp, and timpani with a small percussion battery. His instrumental combinations often make the sonority seem bigger than one might expect from the size of the ensemble. There are many passages of extended tertian harmonies, chord parallelism, and triads with added tones; modal counterpoint; and final cadences that end on inversions rather than root-position chords. He is fond of quintuple meters and compound meters with syncopations and hemiolas, rhythmic asymmetries perhaps influenced by his love of Gregorian chant. Hanson's forms tend to be sectional but developmental, with new themes often derived from previous ones. Transitions often come quickly and abruptly, with the result that Hanson's symphonies can feel episodic, juxtaposing tableaux of sound instead of following coherent formal structures. While less effective at the conventional thematic development of a

Table 5.7 The Symphonies of Howard Hanson (1896–1981)

Title and date	Movements	Instrumentation	Comments
Symphony No. 1 in E Minor, "Nordic" (1922)	1. Andante solenne; Allegro con forza 5/4 (240 mm.) 2. Andante teneramente, con semplicità 3/4 (78 mm.) 3. Allegro con fuoco ¢ (184 mm.)	Grand + Flt. (doubling Picc.), Bssn. (doubling Cbssn.), Tuba, Perc. (Cym., BD), Harp	Composed in Rome. Dedicated to Felix Lamond. Second movement inscribed to his mother, third movement to his father. "Sings of the solemnity, austerity, and grandeur of the North, of its restless surging and strife, of its sombreness and melancholy" (Hanson). First performance: May 30, 1923, by the Augusteo Orchestra, conducted by the composer. First American performance: March 19, 1924, by the Rochester Philharmonic Orchestra, again conducted by the composer. Score published as Vol. 1 of Publications of the Department of Music of the American Academy of Rome (Leipzig, Ger.: C.G. Röder), 1929; available from Carl Fischer.
Symphony No. 2, "Romantic" (1929)	1. Adagio; Allegro moderato C (333 mm.) 2. Andante con tenerezza C (85 mm.) 3. Allegro con brio 2/4 (183 mm.)	Grand + Flt. (doubling Picc.), Ob. (doubling EH), Tpt, Tuba, Perc. (Drums, Cym.), Harp	Commissioned by the Boston Symphony Orchestra to commemorate the 50th anniversary of its founding. Hanson's goal: "to create a work that was young in spirit, lyrical and romantic in temperament, and simple and direct in expression." First performance: November 28, 1930, by the Boston Symphony Orchestra, conducted by Serge Koussevitzky. Score published by Carl Fischer, 1932.
Symphony No. III (1936–37)	1. Andante lamentando—Agitato 5/4 (282 mm.) 2. Andante tranquillo C (151 mm.) 3. Tempo scherzando 3/8 (477 mm.) 4. Largamente e pesante C (237 mm.)	Grand + Flt. (doubling Picc.), Ob. (doubling EH), Clar. (doubling Bclar.), Bssn. (doubling Cbssn.), Tpt., Tuba	Commissioned by the Columbia Broadcasting System and written to commemorate the 300th anniversary of the first Swedish settlement in Delaware in 1638. Dedicated to Serge Koussevitzky. First performance of Movements I–III: September 19, 1937, in a radio broadcast by the NBC Symphony Orchestra, conducted by the composer. Hanson and the NBC Orchestra presented the complete work—again on the radio—on March 26, 1938. First concert performance: November 3, 1939, by the Boston Symphony Orchestra, conducted by Koussevitzky. Score published by the Eastman School of Music, 1941; available from Carl Fischer.

Table 5-7 *continued*

Title and date	Movements	Instrumentation	Comments
Symphony No. IV "Requiem," Op. 34 (1943)	1. "Kyrie" (Andante inquieto) 12/8 (165 mm.) 2. "Requiescat" (Largo) C (54 mm.) 3. "Dies irae" (Presto) 2/8 (258 mm.) 4. "Lux aeterna" (Largo pastorale) 3/4 (102 mm.)	Grand + Flt. (doubling Picc.), Bssn. (doubling Cbssn.), Tuba, Perc. (SD, Xylo.), Harp	"In memory of my beloved father." Winner of the first Pulitzer Prize for music, 1944. First performance: December 3, 1943, by the Boston Symphony Orchestra, conducted by the composer. Holograph score published by Eastman School of Music, 1945; available from Carl Fischer.
Symphony No. V, "Sinfonia sacra" (1954)	In one movement with three distinct sections C (311 mm.)	Grand + Flt. (doubling Picc.), Ob. (doubling EH), Tpt., Tuba, Perc. (Gong, Suspended Cym., Cym., Xylo., SD), Harp	Inspired by the account of Christ's resurrection in the Gospel of John. First performance: February 18, 1955, by the Philadelphia Orchestra, conducted by Eugene Ormandy. Holograph score published by Eastman School of Music, 1955; available from Carl Fischer.
Symphony No. 6 (1967)	1. Andante C (42 mm.) 2. Allegro scherzando 12/8 (169 mm.) 3. Adagio ¢ (100 mm.) 4. Allegro assai 12/8 (77 mm.) 5. Adagio ¢ (63 mm.) 6. Allegro ¢ (120 mm.)	Grand + Flt. (doubling Picc.), EH, Cbssn., Tpt., Tuba, Perc. (SD, Tri.).	Commissioned by the New York Philharmonic to commemorate its 125th anniversary. Dedicated to the New York Philharmonic and Leonard Bernstein. First performance: February 26, 1968, by the New York Philharmonic, conducted by the composer. Score published by Carl Fischer, 1968.
Symphony No. 7, "A Sea Symphony" (1977)	1. "Lo, the Unbounded Sea" (Largamente) C (127 mm.) 2. "The Untold Want" (Adagio) C (51 mm.) 3. "Joy, Shipmate, Joy!" (Allegro molto—Molto meno mosso) 3/4 (114 mm.)	Grand + Flt. (doubling Picc.), Ob. (doubling EH), Clar. (doubling Bclar.), Bssn. (doubling Cbssn.), Tpt., Tuba, Perc. (Suspended Cym., Tubular Bells, Xylo.), Pno., Harp., SATB Chorus	"To Joseph Maddy and the National Music Camp of Interlochen [Michigan] on its 50th anniversary." Short choral symphony based on texts by Walt Whitman. First performance: August 7, 1977, by the Interlochen International Youth Orchestra and Choir, conducted by the composer. Holograph score published by Carl Fischer, 1977.

classical symphony, he excels in lyrical warmth and intensity, driving rhythm, and a beautiful command of orchestral sound.

Symphony No. 1 in E Minor, "Nordic"

Hanson competed his First Symphony, subtitled "Nordic," in 1922 while at the American Academy in Rome. He conducted its first performance in Rome a year later, and it helped to secure his position as head of the Eastman School. In three movements, Hanson dedicated the complete work to Felix Lamond (as noted earlier, a pivotal figure in the creation of the Rome Prize) and the second and third movements individually to his mother and father. It has no specific program, but parts of the work evoke the spirit of Nordic epics, not unlike Sibelius's *En saga*, especially in the third movement's battle music and central heroic dirge. Hanson described the symphony as music that "sings of the solemnity, austerity and grandeur of the North, of its restless surging and strife, of its somberness and melancholy."[186]

Like Barber, Hanson achieved orchestral maturity early. The gestural language of the symphony is sweeping and rhapsodic: his characteristic sound, melodic style, and approach to rhythm are already present. As he often does, Hanson employs cyclic construction, as the principal theme of Movement I (a Dorian melody in 5/4) becomes the source of much of the work's thematic material. Asymmetrical phrase structures and rhythmic counterpoint create a musical energy that combines forward momentum and deferral simultaneously; it eventually reaches a point of saturation rather than sharp climax, then relaxes and builds again—a musical embodiment of the Nordic "surging and strife" he wished to capture.

After a harmonically ambiguous opening, the second movement eventually settles in F major; a descending sequence of woodwinds in thirds recurs throughout. The Finale opens with a feint toward B minor in the initial theme, its martial character tempered by asymmetrical accents. It unfolds in an intelligible ABA form (distinguishing this movement from its more formally diffuse predecessors). A pair of flutes reprise the descending pattern from the second movement—an obvious nod to his mother within the "father" movement. A Swedish folk tune, "Magdalena stod i grönan lund," serves as one of the main themes.[187] He treats all the material with his signature textural complexity and contrapuntal conversation, conveyed by the kind of opulent orchestration that became his hallmark (example 5.9).

At letter Q, marked "Finale," the low strings introduce a marchlike theme (though in 5/4) back in E minor. The fact that the symphony bears a key in its title (E minor—also, coincidentally or not, the key of Sibelius's first symphony) indicates an allegiance to the historical tradition of tonally driven forms, but Hanson's harmonic language is so free with extended tertians and other colorations that the tonality feels far from settled for most of the work. Even so, the symphony keeps a sense of momentum throughout its nearly 30 minutes.

Symphony No. 2, "Romantic"

Hanson's best-known symphony (1930), in D-flat major, has become one of the most popular American symphonies of the 1920–50 period. To celebrate the fiftieth anniversary of the Boston Symphony Orchestra, Koussevitzky commissioned works from a number of prominent composers; in addition to Hanson's symphony, the anniversary commission gave us Arthur Honegger's Symphony No. 1, Albert Roussel's Symphony No. 3, the first version of Sergei Prokofiev's Symphony No. 4, and, most notably, Igor Stravinsky's *Symphony of Psalms*. Responding to the prevailing anti-Romantic sentiment of the interwar period, Hanson designed his symphony in part as a polemic statement, as its deliberately provocative subtitle indicates: "The

Susan Key, with Drew Massey

Above and facing, **Example 5.9** Hanson, Symphony No. 1, III mm. 45–53

From 1920 to 1950 in the United States

Susan Key, with Drew Massey

Example 5.9 *continued*

symphony represents for me my escape from the rather bitter type of modern musical realism which occupies so large a place in contemporary thoughts. Much contemporary music seems to me to be showing a tendency to become entirely too cerebral. I do not believe that music is primarily a matter of intellect, but rather a manifestation of the emotions. I have, therefore, aimed in this symphony to create a work that was young in spirit, lyrical and romantic in temperament, and simple and direct in expression."[188]

Although inferior in construction to the "Nordic" Symphony—the episodic and static tendencies noted in that composition are particularly pronounced here—the strong profile of the themes and skillful handling of atmosphere have proven durable.

The first of the three movements, in sonata form, is the longest and introduces much of the material that will shape the entire work, beginning with a rising motive whose profile is reversed in *P*, announced by a horn fanfare. Hanson's technique of shortening the last measure of a melodic phrase infuses even a wide-spaced and slow-moving theme with a sense of forward momentum. *S* (Reh. F) has acquired a life of its own as the so-called "Interlochen" theme, played annually at the close of the summer music camp at the Interlochen Center for the Arts in Michigan (example 5.10).

Example 5.10 Hanson, Symphony No. 2, I/S

The second movement, Andante con tenerezza, repeats the technique of shortening the end of the phrase, as Hanson reduces the last measure of the four-measure phrase from 4/4 to 2/4. The extremely colorful third movement has a particularly Respighian opening. *P* is introduced by four horns, and *S* first by cellos and then by English horn. An atmospheric interlude for woodwinds is harmonically ambiguous, leading into the development (at Reh. G), which features the unusual combination of a horn fanfare over pizzicato string accompaniment; as it evolves, offbeat accents and prominent percussion hint at a sense of "primitivism." The music reaches a climax with the reprise of *I/P*—building to another sweeping arrival point with *I/S*. The strong profiles of both first-movement themes create a recapitulatory effect, emphasizing the cyclical nature of the work.

Symphony No. 3

The "Romantic" Symphony, which helped solidify Hanson's reputation as one of the leading symphonists in the United States, was followed in 1937–38 by the Third Symphony, generally considered his most important contribution to the genre. Commissioned by the Columbia Broadcasting System in 1936, Hanson explained in the program note that he wrote it "in commemoration of the 300th Anniversary of the first Swedish settlement on the shores of Delaware in 1638." It has its inspiration in the composer's "reverence for the spiritual contribution that has been made to America by that sturdy race of northern pioneers . . . who were in later centuries also to constitute such a mighty force in the conquering of the West."[189] The work

Above and facing, **Example 5.11** Hanson, Symphony No. 3, III. mm. 202–19

is in four movements (the previous symphonies were in three) and lasts about 36 minutes in performance. Hanson scored it for his usual complement of twelve winds, eleven brass, timpani, and strings. The music was not consciously conceived to fit the broadcast medium; as CBS executive Goddard Lieberson stated, the symphony was a "straight piece of music with no particular significance for radio production."[190] Hanson made his attitude clear: "If music sounds well on the ordinary concert stage, then it should sound all right when broadcast. Of course, some instruments are better or worse than others from the 'mike' standpoint, but those inequalities are the problem of the sound-engineer, not that of the composer, who should write as he feels."[191]

Three movements were completed in time for the CBS broadcast; the full symphony was broadcast on March 15, 1938, by the NBC Symphony Orchestra. Both performances featured the composer as conductor. Although the piece has not enjoyed the success of Hanson's Second Symphony, it continues to receive performances.

The influence of Nordic composers is especially strong in this work, as the composer acknowledged: "There is much Sibelius influence there, because I was steeped in Sibelius at that time."[192] The impact of the Finnish master is especially evident in much of the writing for

From 1920 to 1950 in the United States

winds, especially the low winds; in addition, like Sibelius's Fifth Symphony, the first movement begins with a slower section that transitions into a scherzo.

As in his First Symphony, thematic unfolding is quite brisk, creating a constantly shifting musical surface. The opening establishes an A-minor drone on the timpani against a slow, wandering eighth-note line in the strings in 5/4. In quick succession follows a contrasting tune in the first violin (Reh. 2), a second theme in the winds in 4/4 (Reh. 5), a chorale-like theme in the brass and timpani (Reh. 9), and transitional material in the winds (Reh. 11). While this rapid presentation of material is disorienting at first—each musical segment is so self-contained that the movement seems to operate more as a medley than as a symphonic developmental process—the structure is gradually clarified over the course of the piece. In addition, these segments (especially the chorale) set out some of the substance for material in later movements. The transition leads to a passionate scherzo (Reh. 15), mostly in 5/8, the highly subdivided theme of which appears at Reh. 17. At Reh. 27, Hanson combines this melody with the earlier chorale melody, the latter eventual triumphing (Reh. 31). The permeable borders of this movement are further underscored with Hanson's choice to end in A major in first inversion rather than root position, as if to communicate a hopeful yet incomplete thought.

The second movement, Andante tranquillo, features one of those expansive lyrical melodies at which Hanson excelled, as a floating, contemplative wind passage cedes to a G major string chorale (Reh. 2). Reh. 4 introduces a more dramatic idea that recalls the opening movement with its steady quarter-note timpani, this time on E. Hanson subjects both ideas to more sustained melodic development in the agitated middle section. This movement is the beginning of a more overt tonal signaling in the symphony as well; for example, the clear arrival of G major (Reh. 14) is followed immediately by the closing on E minor.

The third movement, Tempo scherzando, opens with a timpani solo, with a quick opening figure that forms the background for much of the movement. The brass and winds sound an ominous cadential gesture that appears at various spots, while the oboe and clarinet introduce the principal theme, a pentatonic melody somewhat reminiscent of the Scherzo of Dvořák's "New World" Symphony. Hanson's gifts for rhythmic invention are on full display in this movement, especially after Reh. 15, when the introduction of hemiolas begin to destabilize the motoric rhythmic drive (example 5.11).

The Finale begins with the cadential gesture of Movement III sounded menacingly by the full orchestra. It further establishes the cyclical nature of this symphony with a return of the low, plodding 5/4 tune with which the work opened, this time with the timpani droning on F-sharp rather than A. The cellos state the central motive (Reh. 5), which becomes more dramatic as the tempo picks up; a fanfare derived from the motive appears in the brass at Reh. 14. As in the first movement, however, the Finale prominently employs first-inversion tonics where we might expect more conclusive root positions, as in the D-major arrival of the final section in Reh. 28. A long span of increasing tension culminates in the reprise of the lyrical melody of Movement II and the chorale from Movement I (Reh. 27–28); with the return of these themes, the symphony ends on a joyous note.

Later Symphonies

Hanson's fourth and fifth symphonies explore more explicitly spiritual dimensions. Written in memory of his father, the Fourth Symphony, "Requiem" (1943), won the Pulitzer Prize in 1944 and remained the composer's favorite among his symphonies.[193] Hanson inscribed each movement with the name of a part of the Requiem mass: Kyrie, Requiescat, Dies irae, and Lux aeterna. The first movement presents the principal theme in horns and trombone over throbbing strings (marked "Kyrie eleison" in score); it features rhythmic subtleties and a timbral palette featuring alternations between orchestral families. An emphatic coda is marked "Christe eleison." The second movement is a threnody dominated by a lyrical cello melody somewhat suggestive of Sibelius (e.g., the second movement of his Third Symphony). The very short third movement features notable ostinatos in timpani and snare drum as well as a prominent xylophone; it demonstrates Hanson's ability to create maximum impact with spare orchestral forces. The melody is full of quick triplet subdivisions—again, an effect that recalls Sibelius. The fourth movement goes from luminescent to agitated and finally peaceful, ending on a first-inversion C-major chord. Primarily a sequence of moods, the work is nonetheless very effective.

Hanson wrote the Fifth Symphony (1954) for Eugene Ormandy and the Philadelphia Orchestra; subtitled "Sinfonia sacra," it underscores the composer's commitment to plumbing spiritual depths in his music. A compact 15-minute one-movement symphony in three sections inspired by the account of the Resurrection in the Gospel of John, it features striking counterpoint, especially in the first section.

The Sixth Symphony, composed in 1968 for Leonard Bernstein and the New York Philharmonic, employs an experimental form: six short movements and connected *attacca*, all linked by a three-note figure heard at the outset, which the composer described as "one three-tone chord, the perfect fifth with a major second on top of it [C-G-A] with all of its variations, permutations and extensions."[194] The symphony demonstrates Hanson's increasing engagement with theory that resulted from his work on *Harmonic Materials of Modern Music* (1960)[195]; as he noted, "you can't be working as intensively as I was for forty years on that theory without being automatically influenced. And I was always fascinated by how much logic there is in musical progression."[196]

Hanson wrote this of the work: "Most of my symphonies are essentially cyclic in construction. The Sixth, in contrast, is held together by a very simple three-note 'motto,' which, I think, unifies the entire structure.

"The first movement asks the question. The second and fourth movements are rather sardonic *scherzi*, surrounding the third movement which is quiet and contemplative. Since the fifth movement, a kind of improvisatory *parlando*, leads without a pause into the dynamic finale, the slow movement becomes a kind of keystone of the architectonic 'arch' of the six movements—a small, intimate soul surviving in the framework of cynicism and strife."[197]

The opening C-G-A motive produces more dissonance as the work progresses. It is energetic and lyrical, with leaner textures than those of the earlier symphonies. As Frank Lehman notes, "I think the symphony should serve as a reminder that sophistication of composition or theory does not need to equal 'difficult' or 'abstract' music. If this work is successful, it is because Hanson is able to translate a tiny mote of musical data into a succession of vividly different symphonic moods. Their brevity insures that the Sixth Symphony is never heard to be *heavy*, tasting more like a well thought out menu of little dishes that together make for a satisfying meal."[198]

Hanson's last symphony ("A Sea Symphony," 1977) is a short choral work that sets three sections from Walt Whitman's *Leaves of Grass*. He wrote it for the fiftieth anniversary of the National Music Camp at Interlochen, Michigan, which, for many years, as noted, has ended its concerts with *I/S* of the "Romantic" Symphony.

Like Barber, who died the same year (1981), Hanson was rejected as an anachronism by many of his contemporaries; but he has since returned to favor, especially on recordings. And, to be sure, his work as a champion of other composers' music as a conductor, teacher, and administrator would have assured his status as a central figure in American symphonic history even if he had not been an active composer.

In her review of a recording of several Hanson symphonies from the early 1990s, Edith Borroff points to a paradox: in terms of expression, the compositions "comprise a journey of the spirit [and] a total and heartfelt commitment to Romanticism"; but with regard to technique, "Hanson was anti-Romantic (and truly American) in structuring his works with texture, rather than theme."[199] While one might question Borroff's decisive divide between Romanticism and Americanism in view of the success of melodists like Barber during the same time, her insight into Hanson's sound world—that his musical structures are built principally out of striking washes of sound rather than motivic integration and development—is apt.

Borroff's comment underscores the way Hanson forged a monumentality on different terms than those of his colleagues. It was a world of sound that he sought to create rather than a logical process of thematic and tonal development. In many ways, his aesthetic was more akin to that of film composers such as Erich Wolfgang Korngold (1897–1957) than to his contemporaries in the concert world. And, indeed, Hanson's music has been used for films; the Second Symphony appears in the film *Alien* and provided a model for John Williams in composing for *E.T.*[200] It is fair to ask whether Hanson's name would have endured as more than an occasional curiosity had musical culture allowed for more engagement between the world of film and that of the university and concert hall.

LEO SOWERBY[201]

Organist and composer Leo Sowerby (1895–1968) belonged to what Carol J. Oja calls the "forgotten vanguard" of the 1920s, a group that included fellow Rome Prize recipients Howard Hanson and Randall Thompson.[202] Early audiences and critics like Oscar Sonneck found Sowerby's music highly dissonant and even jarring, but, by the 1950s, his version of Modernism was no longer current; even Ned Rorem (1923–2022), himself no avant-garde artist, would call Sowerby's works "stuffy."[203] Part of the reason for the eclipse of Sowerby's compositional reputation (he remained a respected pedagogue) may be that his orchestral style remained consistent amid the changing tastes of the times. While his compositions continued to find favor among church musicians, his orchestral works came to be heard as aesthetically retrograde, and his symphonies received little critical attention. Despite the championship of the conductors Frederick Stock and Serge Koussevitzky, few performances and fewer recordings appeared. His obituary in the *Chicago Tribune* mentions only his choral music and 1946 Pulitzer Prize (for the cantata *Canticle of the Sun*) and that the Chicago Symphony Orchestra frequently performed his works.[204]

Born in Grand Rapids, Michigan, and educated in Chicago, earning a Master of Music from the American Conservatory in Hammond, Indiana (1918), Sowerby generally operated far outside the East Coast orbit. During World War I, he served in the army as a bandmaster. Afterward, he focused on religious music, both choral and instrumental, as well as works for organ. In 1921, he was the first musician awarded a fellowship at the American Academy in Rome, which enabled him to spend three years studying and composing in Italy. He was elected to the National Institute of Arts and Letters in 1935 and was also the first American named as a Fellow of the Royal School of Church Music in London. He spent most of his career in Chicago, teaching composition at the American Conservatory (1925–62) and working as organist and choirmaster at the Episcopal Cathedral of Saint James (1927–62); there he found enthusiastic support from Frederick Stock and the Chicago Symphony Orchestra. In his final years, he became the founding director of the College of Church Musicians at the National Cathedral in Washington, DC (1962–68).[205]

Sowerby composed five symphonies and a few orchestral poems and suites (table 5.8). The symphonies cover a long chronological span with generous periods between: Nos. 1 and 2 (1921, 1927), Nos. 3 and 4 (1939–40, 1944–47), and No. 5 (1964). He also wrote his Symphony in G (1932), in which, following Charles-Marie Widor and Louis Vierne in France, Sowerby adheres to traditional sonata-cycle patterns while substituting the solo organ for traditional orchestral forces.

Sowerby's compositional style was more strongly marked by the Americanist trends of the 1920–50 period than by any of the divergent modernisms of the midcentury. In addition to European influences, Sowerby drew on American folk song as well as blues and popular styles.[206] He favored Baroque forms like the passacaglia, chaconne, canon, and fugue, likely

Table 5.8 The Symphonies of Leo Sowerby (1895–1968)[a]

Title and date	Movements	Instrumentation	Comments
Symphony No. 1 in E Minor (1920–21)			First performance: April 7, 1922, by the Chicago Symphony Orchestra, conducted by Frederick Stock. Unpublished.
Psalm Symphony (1923–24)		For SATB Chorus, Orchestra, and Organ	Not performed or published.
Symphony No. 2 in B Minor (1926–27)	1. Sonatina: Sprightly 2. Recitative: Very slowly 3. Fugue: Not fast, with dignity		First performance: March 29, 1929, by the Chicago Symphony Orchestra, conducted by Frederick Stock. Score published by Theodore Presser, supported by the Leo Sowerby Foundation, 1994. Recorded by the Chicago Sinfonietta, conducted by Paul Freeman (Cedille 90000 039).
Symphony No. 3 in F-sharp Minor (1939–40)			Written for the 50th anniversary of the Chicago Symphony Orchestra and dedicated to Dr. Frederick Stock and the CSO. First performance: March 6, 1941, by the Chicago Symphony Orchestra, conducted by Stock. Archival broadcast of performance by the Chicago Philharmonic Orchestra conducted by Henry Weber is available on YouTube. Unpublished.
Symphony No. 4 in B (1944–47)			First performance: January 7, 1949, by the Boston Symphony Orchestra, conducted by Serge Koussevitzky. Unpublished.
Symphony No. 5 (1964)			Commissioned by Eugene Ormandy, but apparently never delivered or performed. Unpublished.

a. Sowerby's best-known symphony, in G (1932), is for solo organ. The orchestral scores—all but one unpublished—are not easily accessible, and therefore most movement and instrumentation information is absent from this table.

a result of his study of the organ repertoire. He hews closely to the late nineteenth century in terms of harmonic language, orchestration, and an inspiration from vernacular sources. His style invites comparison with Paul Creston (1906–85), also an organist and another outsider to the modernist trends of his day (the 1950s and 1960s); Creston, however, more consistently pursued the symphony and other orchestral works throughout his career.[207] Two of Sowerby's more frequently recorded orchestral works, the tone poem *Prairie* (1929) and *Suite, From the Northland* (1923), blend folklike melodies, lush orchestral sonorities, and episodic or quasi-narrative forms. Sowerby also tried his hand at symphonic jazz with two works for Paul Whiteman, *Synconata* ("syncopation" + "sonata," 1924) and *Monotony* (1925);[208] these works are closer to the modernist trends of the moment and to other Whiteman commissions than they are to his orchestral style before or after. Raymond Durward Jones writes, "If there is not a cloud of mystery hanging over his music, it does at least arouse curiosity, since it will not conveniently fit into any of the slots or analytical pigeon holes where music is supposed to fit. His music is new in concept but not avant garde nor revolutionary. It is extremely (maybe excessively) dissonant but always tonal. Sowerby's roots remain in traditional Romanticism. Dissonance sometimes comes very close to bi-tonality, or perhaps it is only the superimposition of tonalities, but there was never a negation of tonality."[209]

Reacting to a quip by Oscar Sonneck, who sarcastically identified the three B's as "Bach, Beethoven and SowerB!"—the play on *sour* referring to the composer's occasionally dissonant harmonic vocabulary—Burnet C. Tuthill defended Sowerby's works as the furthest thing from slavish imitation of Brahms. He acknowledged several similarities, however, in their melodic and harmonic styles, as well as "in their fundamental respect for, and use of, the long established forms and the contrapuntal technique of which both are masters"; further, he noted an occasional similarity of "rhythmic treatment," by which he meant syncopation, hemiola, and other manners of beat displacement.[210]

Sowerby's Symphony No. 1, finished during his time at the American Academy in Rome, was first performed by the Chicago Symphony Orchestra under Frederick Stock on April 7, 1922. The Symphony No. 2 in B Minor premiered on March 29, 1929 (also with Stock and the CSO), and it remains his only commercially recorded orchestral symphony. The Second Symphony captures many of Sowerby's key traits: his distinctive melodic style, the influence of the American vernacular, his preference for late-Romantic harmony, and his Classicism.

The first movement takes the form of a sonatina, with two contrasting ideas and a brief developmental section that features some thorny harmonies while retaining a sense of tonal grounding. The retransition and the end of the recapitulation feature rushing glissandi from the strings and harp that give the climax a glittering, almost cinematic feel, while the brief, somber codetta returns the listener to the shadier B minor. According to Burnet Tuthill, the melodic style alternates between two categories: tunes that are "closely knit in form and have a rhythmic verve and snap . . . akin to folk or popular music and have a quality that definitely marks them as American"; and melodies "of a contrasting type" that are freer in construction, "even meandering."[211] Although Sowerby labels the music "sprightly," on the whole it tends toward a rhythmic insistence and level of dissonance that might better be described as "intense."

The second movement, "Recitative: Very slowly," features the second type of Sowerby melody; it opens with a plaintive horn solo, featuring some wide leaps, but expands gradually through repetitions of similar motivic cells. The harmonic ambiguity, rhythmic flexibility, and freely moving line all evoke a sense of recitative. Twice the string section responds to the solo horn with quiet, diffuse sonorities, largely consonant but seemingly unanchored. The third solo statement leads to a duet between the English horn and the clarinet, gradually joined by the full woodwind section. There are moments of harmonic clarity and tunefulness as the movement builds from a muted pastoral sound through an utterly Romantic textural and dynamic crescendo. The solo horn heralds the entrance of the brass section, which works its way to a chorale-like statement at the height of the movement. In a mirror image, the texture returns to woodwind solos, then a section for solo flute that mimics the opening horn line over a pizzicato walking bass in low strings. The last sounds heard are a fading horn solo over a quiet timpani roll, making the movement essentially one large hairpin gesture. The third movement, a fugue, is typical of Sowerby's dedication to contrapuntal forms and ends in a triumphal march, replete with thundering timpani, full brass, and clamoring triangle. The turn toward a radiant B major inscribes the whole of the symphony as a traditional tragic-to-transcendent arc.

Sowerby's Third Symphony premiered with the Chicago Symphony Orchestra under Stock, and Serge Koussevitzky and the Boston Symphony Orchestra gave the first hearing of the Fourth. The Fifth Symphony was solicited by Eugene Ormandy but Sowerby apparently never delivered it.[212] Sowerby's symphonies were largely ignored after their premieres, although a few conductors did manage to keep some of his other orchestral works alive. In 1956, Robert Whitney and the Louisville Orchestra recorded the tone poem *All on a Summer's Day* (1954). In that work, the preoccupation with fugal writing continues, as does the recourse to a tonal center. The lush string section, sweeps of the harp, and trilling flutes are all standard indicators of orchestral warmth, and the tuneful trumpet solo is chromatic but still balanced. Chugging basses and syncopated string and woodwind lines add a restless energy while the occasional invocation of folksy pentatonicism keeps the whole rooted in a presumed midwestern atmosphere. Dean Dixon recorded *Prairie* and *Suite, From the Northland* with the Wiener Symphoniker in the 1960s, and Paul Freeman recorded the Second Symphony and several other orchestral works in the 1990s. Portions of the "forgotten vanguard" have been recovered, but Sowerby's place in the narrative of the American symphonic tradition has not. Nevertheless, his works have continued to be appreciated by organists and choral musicians throughout the twentieth century.

RANDALL THOMPSON

Randall Thompson (1899–1984) combined a compositional commitment to conservatism—he once declared that "conventions are precisely what we need"[213]—with a long and varied career in academe. A Harvard alumnus, he returned to teach there for seventeen years (1948–65); before then, he held positions at Wellesley (1927–29); the University of California–Berkeley (1937–39), Curtis (1939–41, as director), the University of Virginia (1941–46, as director of the School of Fine Art), and Princeton (1946–48). He also wrote a 1935 Carnegie Foundation–funded report for the Association of American Colleges that presented a comprehensive review of the way that music education was conducted in the United States. His three symphonies stand at the center of the efforts to cultivate an American symphonic sound from within the walls of the university (table 5.9).

This strong academic connection might suggest a composer whose approach was theoretical and abstract, and whose style was oriented more toward peers than toward the general public. On the contrary, Thompson envisioned a musical language that would be more humanistic in practice and more fully integrated into the lives of his fellow Americans: "A composer's first

Table 5.9 The Symphonies of Randall Thompson (1899–1984)

Title and date	Movements	Instrumentation	Comments
Symphony No. 1 (1929)	1. Allegro brioso 3/2 (268 mm.) 2. — 6/8 (69 mm.) 3. — 3/4 (490 mm.)	Grand + Flt. (doubling Picc.), Ob. (doubling EH), Clar. (doubling Bclar.), Bssn. (doubling Cbssn.), 2 C Tpt., Tuba, Perc. (SD, BD, Cym., Tamb., Tri.), Org., Harp	Dedicated to Howard Hanson. Music based on two settings of odes by Horace for baritone, chorus, and orchestra (1925): *Poscimur*, the source for the first movement, and *Vides ut alta*, the source for the second and third movements. First performance: February 20, 1930, by the Eastman Rochester Orchestra, conducted by Hanson. Score published by Eastman School of Music of the University of Rochester (distributed by C. C. Birchard), 1931.
Symphony No. 2 (1931)	1. Allegro 2/4 (282 mm.) 2. Largo 4/4 (52 mm.) 3. Vivace—Capriccioso—Tempo I 3/4 + 2/2 (273 mm.) 4. Andante moderato—Allegro con spirito 4/4 (305 mm.)	Grand + Flt. (doubling Picc.), Ob. (doubling EH), Clar., Bssn., Tpt., Tuba, Cym.	Commissioned by the Alice M. Ditson Fund of Columbia University. Dedicated to M.W.T. (Thompson's wife). First performance: March 24, 1932, by the Eastman Rochester Orchestra, conducted by Howard Hanson at an American Composers' Concert. Score published by Eastman School of Music (distributed by Carl Fischer), 1932.
Symphony No. 3 (1947–49)	1. Largo elegiaco 2. Allegro appassionato 3. Lento tranquillo 4. Allegro vivace	Grand + Flt. (doubling Picc.), Ob. (doubling EH), Clar., Bssn. (doubling Cbssn.), Tpt., Tuba, Perc.	First performance: May 15, 1949, by the CBS Symphony Orchestra, conducted by Thor Johnson, at the Fifth Annual Festival of Contemporary Music at Columbia University. Rental score available from Carl Fischer.

responsibility is, and always will be, to write music that will reach and move the hearts of his listeners in his own day."[214] He lamented the myopic practice of concentrating on performance training to the exclusion of the liberal arts, writing that "we flood the country annually with virtuosi, far in excess of the demand for them."[215] And, like his fellow academic Hanson, he railed against the modernist pressures to conform to a more dissonant and abstruse style.

Thompson's invocation of "listeners in his own day" as the composer's primary target raises the question of durability as the chief marker of greatness, as those who promoted the Great American Symphony insisted: in other words, should the prime directive of the composer have been to create an artwork for the ages? While most of their symphonies were not explicitly topical (save during World War II) or intended for a specific purpose in the manner of *Gebrauchsmusik*, most mid-century American composers sensed that the critical imperative to create a permanent museum of transcendent musical masterworks could be at odds with the equally strong compositional obligation to communicate with the contemporary American public.[216]

Thompson's aesthetic influences were diverse. After postcollegiate studies with Ernest Bloch in New York City, he won a three-year Prix de Rome fellowship, which he described in glowing terms: "Since I first went to Rome in 1922, Italian culture, the Italian people and the Italian language have been the strongest single influence on my intellectual and artistic development as a person and as a composer. So true is this that I cannot imagine what my life would be without all the bonds that bind me in loyalty and devotion to Italy and to my Italian friends."[217] His love of the human voice resulted in a number of classic choral works, and a corresponding sense of lyricism pervades his symphonies. Further from the classical mainstream, but equally important for his career, was his experience in New York after returning from Rome, where he worked as a Broadway pianist and composer. As he wrote to Felix Lamond the year after his return from Rome, "I wrote music all last year—mostly songs and music for the theatre—but I felt that I was in the thick of it so I was happy."[218]

Thompson's First and Second Symphonies were both published in 1931–32. Like some other composers from this time, Thompson deployed a language of folk music without using actual quotations. His themes are derived from a number of styles of American popular music but developed with considerable sophistication using the nonvernacular "American" traits of inventive and complex rhythmic and metric manipulations, harmonic twists, and the orchestration by alternating families also observed in the music of Roy Harris and others.

First Symphony

The First Symphony (1929) originated as two settings of odes by Horace, *Poscimur* and *Vides ut alta*, composed for baritone, chorus, and orchestra in 1925: *Poscimur* became the source of the first movement and *Vides ut alta* the second and third (the three movements follow without a break). Thompson's score includes a prominent organ and harp, but the orchestra, bolstered by a significant percussion battery (timpani, snare and bass drums, cymbals, tambourine, and triangle), avoids a conventional religious sound. The opening features syncopations alternating with a bluesy clarinet solo before reaching a dramatic cadence on B-flat major just before Reh. 4. The bassoon then takes over the solo role, alternating with more lyrical orchestral passages.

Until Reh. 90, the highly episodic music moves in short declamatory motives full of changing meters, probably to reflect the original text. The declamatory quality undercuts the success of the movement; Elliot Forbes observed that "despite its exuberance, the music seems to suffer from the lack of text; for the changes of mood seem arbitrary rather than inevitable, and the melodic material does not have the contour and directness that characterize so much of his music."²¹⁹ The timbres, along with imaginative and effective counterpoint, result in an effect closer to a piece of night music than a symphonic movement.

At the same time, as Forbes notes, Thompson employs a language of seemingly endless deferral of harmonic implications redolent of Richard Wagner (1813–83). One example occurs in Reh. 44–47 of the first movement, where Thompson seems to delight in moving through many strategies to avoid resolution. The First Symphony is also a good example of Thompson's sometimes obstinately crude developmental techniques—which we might interpret as a way to make the folk idiom go beneath the surface of the thematic material and permeate the musical form—such as in Reh. 108–9 of the third movement, which features rather awkward repeated figures as a means of building tension.

Second Symphony

Forbes pinpoints Thompson's Second Symphony (1931), written during a Guggenheim Fellowship, as one his first mature works to represent "the composer's real language and style."²²⁰ Howard Hanson conducted its premiere in 1932, and the symphony enjoyed a strong reception in both the United States and Europe. It features a thoroughgoing modal language (which was hinted at in the First Symphony) and a much more forceful exploration of novel rhythmic textures. In the composer's own description, "it is based on no program either literary or spiritual. It is not cyclical. I wanted to write four contrasting movements, separate and distinct, which together should convey a sense of balance and completeness."²²¹

Rhythm more than pitch defines the syncopated, jazzy *P* sounded out by the horns and trumpets. The motive yields many permutations; at one point, an inversion of *P* accompanies *S*. The slower development focuses on the winds. The rhythmic momentum returns forcefully in the modified and expanded recapitulation (Reh. 21).

The slow movement begins with a plaintive hymn in the strings; at the same time, Thompson colors it with chromatic inner voices to achieve a distinct "eclectic" character (to borrow one of his own characterizations of the impulses present in the American music of his day). As Quincy Porter put it, the movement features "a melody just around the corner from the typical popular song and the harmonies that accompany it, exquisitely worked out, are just outside the window of the barber shop."²²² The final cadenza places a blue note (lowered seventh) in the horn on the concluding C-major harmony. Thompson addressed this quality of the work: "If there is 'jazz' in my music, it is not because I tried to put jazz into it, but because I am using the dialect most natural to me as a result of the environment in which I grew up."²²³

Perhaps the most striking part of Thompson's Second Symphony is the third movement, a scherzo dominated by a lurching syncopated melody in 7/4, which he treats in a kaleidoscope of changing accents (example 5.12). A sustained tone in the English horn takes us to the witty

Example 5.12 Thompson, Symphony No. 2, III low strings opening

middle section, marked *Capriccioso*, in which Dvořákian wind passages alternate with Impressionistic chord streams in the strings. This, combined with its G-minor modality (which moves from there to D to C minor and back to G minor, maintaining a closely related key structure), contributes a dark energy to the work.

The last movement begins with a hymnlike introduction in winds with light Scotch-snap rhythms. The strings take over at the Allegro con spirito (Reh. 65), at which the Scotch-snap rhythms turn into ragtime. There is a perky interlude starting off in the winds (Reh. 69). With each return, the hymn takes on more of the character of vaudeville or musical theater, including barn-dance strings and jazzy trombone effects.[224]

Critics generally liked the work and commented favorably on its popular character and the American qualities of the melodic and rhythmic language. It received 19 performances by major orchestras between 1933 and 1950 and was described as "one of the most popular symphonies by an American composer."[225]

Third Symphony

Thompson said that his Third Symphony, written in 1947–49, expressed the collective postwar mood. He provided a succinct analysis:

> The first movement (in A minor, common time) is in sonata form, with only one principle [*sic*] theme and one principal rhythm. The prevailing mood is one of sadness. The second movement (in D minor, alla breve) is full of action and defiance. The form is a modified rondo in which the final statement of the principal theme is presented more slowly. Allusions to the theme of contrast, also greatly augmented, bring the movement to a desolate conclusion. The third movement (in F major, with lowered seventh, in three-half time) is introduced by a phrase in the horn which later grows into a melody. The principal theme is song-like, and its three presentations are set off by plaintive passages in the woodwinds alone. The Finale (in A major, six-eight time) is in sonata form, and all the material is cheerful. There is no apotheosis of themes nor any heroic peroration. The serious and even tragic elements of the earlier movements are dispelled in exuberance.[226]

The greater degree of dissonance and extended harmonic techniques encountered in this symphony compared to its predecessors—including bitonal passages in the first movement—were perhaps responsible for the muted reaction to this work.

Frederic Wilson notes that "Thompson has been largely dismissed in academic circles as an amateurs' composer, but this categorization belies the technical challenges present in many of his works."[227] And, although Thompson's choral works such as *Alleluia* and *The Peaceable Kingdom*, are more ordinarily encountered on contemporary concert programs, his symphonies equally deserve to be recognized for a musical idiom that was at once elevated and vernacular.

American-Trained Composers

It is a testament to the energetic *fin de siècle* efforts on behalf of the American musical infrastructure (described in chapter 3) that, by the end of World War I, a composer could receive all his or her training in the United States. Even so, the term "American-trained" needs some qualification, as many of the composition programs in American institutions were dominated by European émigrés or European-trained Americans. Of the symphonists discussed in this section, George Antheil studied with émigré Ernest Bloch, Florence Price with the European-trained George Whitefield Chadwick, William Grant Still with Chadwick and émigré Edgard Varèse, William Levi Dawson with émigrés Felix Borowski and Adolph Weidig, and James

P. Johnson with Italian émigré Bruto Giannini, who also taught Scott Joplin. Henry Cowell alone possesses an exclusively all-American pedigree; as is fitting, he is also unchallenged in his maverick status among American symphonic composers of this period. In sum, this American-trained cohort is distinguished more for what their output says about the enhanced musical culture in the United States than by any stylistic commonalities.

One of the most notable aspects of the American symphony in the 1930s is the emergence and acceptance of symphonies written by Black composers. Antonín Dvořák's well-publicized comments about the importance of African American music had clearly resonated with a generation of aspiring Black composers who harbored idealistic beliefs about the universal appeal of both the sources and their suitability for elaboration in a classical work. The outstanding Black symphonists discussed in this section—William Levi Dawson, Florence Price, and William Grant Still—all had premieres with distinguished orchestras (the Philadelphia Orchestra, the Chicago Symphony Orchestra, and the Eastman-Rochester Symphony Orchestra, respectively), with the genuine and enthusiastic support of their conductors Leopold Stokowski, Frederick Stock, and Howard Hanson. Less prominent, but still notable, was the championing of James P. Johnson's *Harlem Symphony* by conductor Paul Kosok and the Brooklyn Civic Orchestra. By and large, although critics also welcomed these works, they expressed ambivalence over the presence of popular styles readily identified with African American culture in symphonies (regardless of the composer's race). As Julie Schnepel notes, "Although some critics did bring their condescending attitudes toward jazz, the blues, or popular musics into their reviews of American symphonies, they actually only rarely did more than mention the existence of these idioms in the work being reviewed. . . . By far critics preferred the expression of Americanism in the form of mood, spirit, temperament, or atmosphere. More 'tangible' types of expression were likely to be exposed as 'tricks' or superficial attempts to sound American."[228]

The new visibility of African American symphonic composers reflected a multifaceted range of artistic activity. Both New York and Chicago boasted centers of "African American Renaissance"; along with the well-known Harlem Renaissance, Black writers and artists were cultivating a new consciousness in Chicago during the 1930s and 1940s, a kind of midwestern alternative to Harlem. While less prominent than the Harlem Renaissance, the Chicago Black Renaissance was centered in a South Side neighborhood known as Bronzeville; as Rae Linda Brown notes, the area "had a cultural vitality in the 1920s and 1930s that was generated by the black elite located in that city. There were regular gatherings of artists where musicians, writers, and visual artists could assemble to support each other."[229] Outside the scope of this chapter, but important to note, are the tensions that existed between the more literary-oriented musicians and those who worked in popular genres. Alain Locke and the other theorists of the New Negro movement wanted a cultivation of "higher works" infused with folk sources rather than popular idioms (and held up Still, Price, and Dawson as their ideals), whereas Johnson and Duke Ellington were more drawn to the current styles of Harlem (ragtime, stride, theatrical and dance-band music).[230] In this way, W. E. B. Du Bois's concept of "double consciousness" might be extended to a "triple consciousness," as African Americans attempted to reconcile Classical, Black, and American within individual artistic voices.

In spite of the thorough—and mostly traditional—musical pedagogy that the American-trained composers received, their careers provide a contrast to the European-trained cohort in their tendency to fall outside major institutional boundaries. After earning reputations as ultramodernists, both George Antheil and William Grant Still settled in Hollywood, moving between film and symphonic composition.[231] For various personal reasons, Cowell, Dawson, Johnson, and Price lived and worked away from the most visible symphonic outlets. None of the composers found a niche in the country's most prominent compositional training institutions. Their absence suggests that programming and hiring policies at performing and academic institutions continued to favor those with European training, and that the surest pathways to employment originated in Paris and Rome.

GEORGE ANTHEIL

George Antheil (1900–1959) is most frequently remembered for the image he presented in his autobiography *The Bad Boy of Music* (1945): a rogue genius, in the mold of Henry Cowell, and a virtuoso pianist who fought tooth and nail to establish a brutal modernist sound with works like *Ballet mécanique* (1925). Although not European trained, he studied with Constantine von Sternberg in Philadelphia (1916–19) and Ernest Bloch in New York City (1919–21, overlapping in Bloch's studio with Randall Thompson and Roger Sessions). The patronage of Philadelphia philanthropist Mary Louise Curtis Bok allowed him freedom to travel; he departed for Berlin and Paris in 1922, where he garnered a great deal of mostly negative publicity and earned himself the "bad boy" moniker for his ultramodern experiments.

Antheil relocated to Hollywood in 1936, writing music for films and television. He wrote six numbered symphonies, the last four of which date from his time on the West Coast (table 5.10), a period that coincided with a change in his aesthetics. He turned his back on Parisian frivolity and Neoclassicism ("a great stylist period, where style was everything and content nothing—insofar as human meaning is concerned"), as well as his "bad boy" ultramodernism, in favor of a more conservative and accessible style.[232] At the same time, he retained a distinctive modular technique that strung blocks of sound together with minimal transition, as in a mosaic—a process he had created in his European works but now refined with lessons he learned from his cinematic scores. These blocks not infrequently make audible references to the sound worlds, and sometimes even to actual themes, of symphonists Antheil admired (more than one critic accused Antheil of musical "kleptomania"[233]). All this he ties together with an effusion of melody and a boundless energy that is sometimes unrelenting but almost always infectious.

Early Symphonies

Antheil's history with the symphony is complicated: as we will see, along with the six numbered symphonies, he wrote several without numbers, and their positions in his *oeuvre* are not always clear; in addition, he renumbered some symphonies and replaced others, without necessarily discarding the withdrawn work. He composed his first symphony in 1920–22 and revised it in 1923, at which time he subtitled it "Zingareska" for reasons he did not explain. The symphony dates from his studies with Ernest Bloch, but its layered textures and multimeters owe more to the spirit of Les Six and Stravinsky; echoes of *Petrushka* come through especially clearly in the last movement (also notable are the eccentric movement titles, rife with misspellings and curious juxtapositions). The next symphonic efforts date from his years in Europe. Inspired by Stravinsky's *Symphonies of Wind Instruments* (1920), he composed the Symphony for Five Instruments in 1923 as a three-movement chamber work for flute, bassoon, trumpet, trombone, and viola. He wrote two symphonies in 1925–26. The one-movement *Jazz Symphony* was originally commissioned for the famous Paul Whiteman Carnegie Hall concert that introduced *Rhapsody in Blue*, but it was not finished in time. It premiered instead at that venue

Table 5.10 The Symphonies of George Antheil (1900–59)[a]

Title and date	Movements	Instrumentation	Comments
Symphonie No. 1, "Zingareska" (1920–22, rev. 1923)	1. Innocènte 2. Vivo, alla zinaresco, poi "ragtime" 3. Doloroso elevatò 4. Ragtime: Faces: Ada[b]	Grand + Flt. (doubling Picc.), Ob. (doubling EH), Clar. (doubling Bclar.), Cbssn., Tpt., Tuba, Perc. (SD, Cym., BD, Tam-tam), 2 Harps, Cel.	"For the happiness of Mary Louise Bok" (the composer's patron). Subtitle added for 1923 revision. First performance (first two movements only): November 30, 1922, by the Berlin Philharmonic, conducted by Rudolf Schulz-Dornburg. First full performance: 2000, with the Frankfurt Radio Orchestra conducted by Hugh Wolff. Holograph score published by G. Schirmer, 1999.
Symphony for Five Instruments: Quintette for Flute, Bassoon, Trumpet, Trombone, and Viola (1922; second version, 1923)	1922 version 1. Allegro 2. All*tto* [sic] 3. Finale: Grand galop 4. Allegro barbaro 1923 version[c] 1. Allegro 2. Lento 3. Presto	Flt., Bssn., Tpt. Trom. Va.	"For my faithful friend, Mary Louise Bok." Antheil and his wife later referred to this work as the "Joke" Quintet. 1922 version (Berlin) apparently unperformed and unpublished. 1923 version (Paris). First performance: October 16, 1926, at the Salle Gaveau, Paris. Preceded by two private salon performances in January 1924 and June 1926. Published by Weintraub, 1923.
A Jazz Symphony (1925, rev. 1955)	In one movement. 1925 version: 4/4 (510 mm.) 1955 version: 4/4 (371 mm.)	1925 version: 4 Sax. and 2 Clar. (three players alternating between these instruments), 2 Ob., 3 Tpt., 3 Trom., Tuba, 2 Banjos, 2 Pno., Piano soloist, Perc. (Xylo., Glsp., Steamboat Whistle, Drum Set), Strgs. 1955 version: Flt., 3 Clar., 3 Tpt., 3 Trom., Timp., 2 stands of Vln. 1, 1 stand of Vln. 2, Vla., Vlc., Cb.	Commissioned by Paul Whiteman. Dedicated to Evelyn Friede. First performance of 1925 version: April 10, 1927, by W. C. Handy's Orchestra, conducted by Allie Ross, with the composer as soloist. First performance of 1955 version: December 14, 1960, by the Orchestra of America, conducted by Richard Korn. 1925 version published by Weintraub, 1978 (distributed by G. Schirmer). Rental score of 1955 version available from Weintraub. Holograph of 1925 version also labels the work "Concertino in three parts with solo piano."

Work	Movements	Instrumentation	Notes
Symphonie en fa pour grand orchestra [sic] (1925–26)	1. Lento 2. Allegro vivace 3. Andante 4. Allegro	Grand + 2 Picc., Ob., 4 Hr., 2 Tpt., Trom., Perc.	"For Mary Louise Bok." First performance: June 19, 1926, by an ensemble conducted by Vladimir Golschmann at the Théâtre des Champs-Élysées in Paris. Published by G. Schirmer but listed as unavailable.
Second Symphony (1931–38, rev. 1943)		Grand + 2 Flt. (4 doubling Picc.), EH, Bclar, Cbssn., Tpt., Tuba, Perc., Pno., Banjo.	Withdrawn. Third movement performed separately as *Archipelago* (*Rhumba*) in 1935.
Second [deleted] Symphony; Third Symphony, "American" (1936–41, rewritten 1946)	1941 version: 1. "New York" 2. "New Orleans" 3. "San Antonio" 4. "Los Angeles" 1946 version: 1. Allegro 2/4 (329 mm.) 2. Andante 3/4 (157 mm.) 3. "The Golden Spike" 4/4 (166 mm.) 4. "Back to Baltimore" 3/4 (324 mm.)	Grand + Tpt., Tuba, Perc. (Cym., Trap Set, Glsp., Tamb., BD, Tri., Xylo.)	"For Peter Richard Antheil" (the composer's young son). Originally intended to replace the withdrawn Second Symphony (and numbered as such), the first version of this work reflects the impressions of the cross-country trip the Antheils took in 1936 when moving from New York to Hollywood. The 1946 version replaces the place names as well as much of the music; Antheil renumbered it as the Third Symphony and gave it the subtitle "American" ("It is the America of the future, bold, fearless, new, and coming from the very breath of the new continent"). First performance (*The Golden Spike* only): November 28, 1945, by the National Symphony Orchestra, Washington, DC, conducted by Hans Kindler. First complete performance: 2004, by the Frankfurt Radio Symphony, conducted by Hugh Wolff. 1946 version published by G. Schirmer, 1980.
Fourth Symphony, "1942" (1942)	1. Moderato 4/4 (316 mm.) 2. Allegro C (211 mm.) 3. Scherzo: Presto 3/4 (208 mm.) 4. Allegro non troppo 2/4 (286 mm.)	Grand + Flt. (doubling Picc.), Ob. (doubling EH), Bclar, Cbssn., Tpt., Tuba, Perc. (Gong, Vbp., Xylo., Cym., Tri., Castanets, Wood Block, BD, SD, Tamb.), Harp, Pno.	"To Böski, my wife." First performance (radio broadcast): February 13, 1944, by the NBC Symphony Orchestra, conducted by Leopold Stokowski. First concert performance on January 7, 1945, by the National Symphony Orchestra, conducted by Hans Kindler. Score published by Boosey & Hawkes, 1947.

Table 5.10 continued

Title and date	Movements	Instrumentation	Comments
Fifth [deleted] Symphony, "Tragic" (1945–46)	1. Adagio 2. Presto 3. Largo: expressivo 4. Largo: molto expressivo	Grand + Flt. (doubling Picc.), Picc., EH, Bclar., Cbssn., Tpt, Tuba, Perc., Harp	"To my brother, Henry, Jr." (a diplomat who died in the Soviet invasion of Estonia in 1940). Antheil originally intended the work to serve as "some kind of a dirge for all the young war dead." Fully composed but then withdrawn and replaced with a completely new Fifth Symphony, "Joyous."
Fifth Symphony, "Joyous" (1947–48)	1. Allegro 4/4 (344 mm.) 2. Adagio molto 6/8 (129 mm.) 3. Allegretto maestoso—Allegro giocoso 2/4 (332 mm.)	Grand + Picc., EH, Bclar., Cbssn., Tpt., Tuba, Perc. (SD, Tamb, Wood Block, Tam-tam, Tri., Cym., BD, Glsp.), Pno.	Commissioned by Eugene Ormandy. Dedicated to Noma Rathner. In contrast to the discarded Fifth Symphony, this work, according to the composer, "is very joyous, full of glee." First performance: December 31, 1948, by the Philadelphia Orchestra, conducted by Ormandy. Score published by Leeds Music, 1950.
Sixth Symphony, "after Delacroix" (1947–48, rev. 1949–50)	1. Allegro molto marcato 4/4 (256 mm.) 2. Larghetto 3/4 (205 mm.) 3. Allegro 4/4 (294 mm.)	Grand + Picc., EH, Bclar., Cbssn., Tpt., Tuba, Perc. (Cym., Military Drum, Tri., Gong, SD, BD, Xylo., Glsp., Tamb, Wood Block), Pno.	First movement inspired by Eugene Delacroix's painting *Liberty Leading the People* (1830). A portion of the first movement originated as an unpublished concert overture entitled *Heroes of Today* (1945). First performance: February 10, 1949, by the San Francisco Orchestra, conducted by Pierre Monteux. Score published by Weintraub Music, 1954.
Seventh Symphony (1953–54)			Antheil sketched out the first movement and part of the second for this projected work.

a. Many of Antheil's symphonies exist in multiple and profoundly different versions, bear alternate titles and occasionally quirky movement names, or were later renumbered or discarded. Much of the confusion is disentangled in Appendix A of Whitesitt/ANTHEIL, pp. 225–39.
b. Movement titles are given as they appear in the manuscript.
c. 1923 version omits 1922 Mvts. 2 and 4; 1923 Mvt. 2 is newly composed.

in 1927 with W. C. Handy's (1873–1958) orchestra. The composer recalled that "The 'Jazz Symphonietta' [sic] was, after the finale of my First Symphony, my second attempt at symphonic synthesis of jazz; but its poor first reception that evening precluded further performance. Still, it is rather a historic work, after a fashion; it was certainly one of the first authentic attempts to synthesize one of our most difficult national mediums."[234] In contrast, the *Symphonie en fa* represents a turn toward Neoclassicism, again influenced by Stravinsky. The Second Symphony (1931–38, rev. 1943) was withdrawn by the composer; he later published the third movement separately as *Archipelago (Rhumba)*.[235]

Third Symphony, "American"

In 1936, Antheil had returned permanently to the United States to pursue a career in film composition in Hollywood. At that time, he began an extensive period of study of Beethoven, Gustav Mahler (1860–1911), Sibelius, Shostakovich, and Prokofiev and subjected himself to a thorough self-analysis of his "composing faults."[236] In his autobiography, he described how he repudiated his earlier "effete" style and found himself drawn more and more to the traditional symphony; as he told Aaron Copland one evening, "I feel that the symphonic form is still the most important phase of music and that it is being neglected. Nobody writes symphonies any more, only long pieces which, because they are appropriately long, they call symphonies for lack of a better name. But they are not symphonies."[237]

The last line was directed in part toward Harris's Third Symphony, the "structural methods" of which he dismissed as "primitive, naïve—and whatever else one may call a symphony, one cannot call the most advanced form of musical composition naïve."[238] As Antheil developed his new symphonic language, he conceived of an alternative vision of the American sound: instead of the rural and pastoral Midwest ideal of Harris or Copland, Antheil would project an America of skyscrapers and steel focused on forward progress—an urban style that would soon be cultivated in New York–based composers like William Schuman and Leonard Bernstein.[239]

Marking the turning point from ultramodernism to a new and more accessible film-inspired style, the Third Symphony has a characteristically tangled history.[240] Originally the work was intended to replace the withdrawn Second Symphony. Antheil began it during a cross-country trip with his wife and drew inspiration for the four movements from specific locations: New York, New Orleans, San Antonio, and Los Angeles. As he wrote to his patron Mary Louise Bok in 1938, "It is an American symphony, but it does not pull out all the old darky stops and tremolos. It is the America of the future, bold, fearless, new, and coming from the very breath of the new continent." He went on to describe the influence of his film composition: "The movies . . . have taught me (a) how to write quickly and surely; (b) how to write melodies that all people all over the earth understand; (c) good showmanship and actual continuous contact with a large-scale public."[241] Antheil's goals were ambitious: the new work "was to be the vehicle through which he would demonstrate his mastery of formal elements and express the spirit of the American people. He also hoped that it would be a popular success in the United States, repair his damaged reputation, and definitively establish him as leader of the new generation of American composers."[242]

Antheil composed the bulk of the work between 1936 and 1939, finishing it in 1941. His efforts to secure a performance in 1943 failed. The adverse feedback from conductors, coupled with his own discontent, led him to rewrite the composition completely; he renumbered the result as the Third Symphony and gave it the subtitle "American." In this version, Antheil replaces the original place names with tempo designations for the first two movements and new titles for the last two that bear no relation to the original locales of San Antonio and Los Angeles. He hoped that Hans Kindler and the National Symphony Orchestra would premiere the work in 1945 but, in the event, they performed only the third movement, "The Golden Spike"—which was all Antheil ever heard of the symphony.[243]

Despite the absence of descriptive titles in the first two movements, this symphony, more than Antheil's subsequent ones, resembles a suite of symphonic poems. The first movement, Allegro, begins with a brisk fanfare followed by a lyrical motive in strings; in characteristic style, there are abrupt contrasts of melody, harmony, and timbre throughout, evoking the pace and diversity of its original New York inspiration (to whatever degree of it remains in the final version). The second, Andante, also reveals the composer's penchant for block construction; traded back and forth are a brass chorale, a sweeping string melody, a steady but spritely march primarily in the woodwinds, and a Latin-derived syncopated theme. The third movement, "The Golden Spike"—based on Antheil's unused music for the Cecil B. DeMille film *Union Pacific* (1939)—features a distinctively Americana sound of a syncopated dance and transparent textures in alternation with a direct quote (heard three times) of the opening of the Finale of Sibelius's Fifth Symphony.[244] The final Presto, "Back to Baltimore," uses swirling winds and percussion to animate angular melodies reminiscent of Prokofiev as it builds to a triumphant climax.

Symphony No. 4, "1942"

Antheil's Fourth Symphony, premiered by Leopold Stokowski and the NBC Symphony Orchestra on February 13, 1944, was one of many efforts by Americans to contribute to wartime expression. As the composer described it, "The Fourth Symphony was written . . . during a period in which I was one of the assistant editors of the [Los Angeles] *Daily News*. . . . It was my particular job to analyze the war news from day to day; and it is entirely possible that my various frames of mind during this all-important period . . . influenced to some degree my composition. I suppose that a particularly imaginative commentator could trace the whole history of the war during this period in my symphony."[245]

Even as each movement reflects a different perspective on the conflict, it is not explicitly programmatic.[246] The overall plan is conventional: three movements in sonata form and a third-movement scherzo. The formal clarity and the approach to motivic structure and development represents a conscious attempt on Antheil's part to correct what he viewed as his weak handling of planning and structure.[247] Although the movements are in sonata form, his signature block technique creates a kind of narrative tension that is original and not dependent on conventional harmonic relationships. Linda Whitesitt describes Antheil's use of harmony as "nonarchitectonic."[248] There is also something Ivesian in the way the motives appear and disappear within the texture.

The opening measures lay out a series of intense and memorable gestures in unison brass and piano—a condensed version of Antheil's larger block construction (example 5.13). Each is a version of either a fanfare or a march, thus infusing the movement with the atmosphere of war. They unfold in the following sequence: a two-measure block, a four-measure block, and a final (seventh) measure in 3/2 that interrupts the pattern and leads with a flourish into *P*, an inversion of the opening idea in lower strings and piano (now transmuted from a fanfare into a march) juxtaposed with bits and pieces of the second idea, also in various inversions. The treatment of the winds here unmistakably invokes Shostakovich. Both the sequence of gestures and the immediate turn to variation operate as a set of building blocks that will recur throughout

Example 5.13 Antheil, Symphony No. 4, I opening

Susan Key, with Drew Massey

Example 5.13 *continued*

the symphony. At Reh. 3, there is a sudden change to a hushed chorale in bassoons and brass, which yields to a ghostly march rhythm in cellos and bass, layered by P on piccolo solo and drum in a brighter tempo—another Shostakovich-derived moment, both in timbre and in intervallic construction. The orchestration—with relatively short sections of distinctive instrumental combinations (at one point a trio of bassoon, contrabassoon, and tuba)—underscores the block construction of the thematic material. An extended development section weaves together fragments of the various motives; the movement ends with a tapped-out rhythm in wood block over low strings and woodwinds, eventually fading to a bass line marked in the score "barely audible."

The second movement (Allegro) was inspired by Antheil's reaction to the news of wartime massacres in Eastern Europe; its string writing recalls Sibelius in its juxtaposition of a broadly flowing melody over undulating patterns. There is a keening, nearly human, vocal quality to the melodic gestures of both P and S, which Antheil gives to various woodwinds and strings. The development includes Antheil's typically sudden metrical and harmonic changes that plunge us into new worlds: after an augmented version of P—now in the piccolo over the rumbling strings—the texture shifts to a sentimental and melancholy tune on clarinet and viola with bassoon and harp accompaniment. This section evokes the lost innocence of small-town life, recalling not only Antheil's study of Mahler but his experience as a film composer. This tune undergoes subtle transformations and is punctuated by an inverted version of I/P on piccolo and piano, which gives the passage an unsettled quality. As the transformations continue, I/P weaves itself into the fabric of the melody. After a distorted recapitulation, the opening gestures of the first movement suddenly returns in their original form (Reh. 63, marked *agitato* [almost as in beginning]) and ushers in a concluding section where bits and pieces of the thematic material from both movements are tossed back and forth in a succession of mood changes.

The final two movements are considerably shorter. In the Scherzo, Antheil expresses "a brutal joke, the joke of war";[249] the themes have a distorted Shostakovich-like quality exaggerated by unexpected percussion timbres and jazzy effects in the brass. The Trio is fugal: working with a version of I/P, it is at one point interrupted by the second movement's sentimental interlude, as well as by various bits of first-movement material. The Finale (Allegro non troppo) uses a series of marches to capture the sense of victory not yet achieved but within sight; according to Antheil, the movement, "written after the turn of the tide at Stalingrad and our landings in Morocco, heralds victory."[250] Although in sonata form, its block structure, quotations from earlier movements, and frequent changes of mood seem more like a series of film sequences with marching forces streaming in from multiple directions; as the material varies themes from the preceding three movements, it feels like both summation and fulfilment.

Stokowski's "most magnificent premiere" of the piece was nationally broadcast on NBC Radio—which is how Antheil heard it, from his home in California—and received a great welcome from the critics. The composer attended a subsequent hearing—"an absolutely superlative performance, one which I shall remember forever"—in January 1945 by the National Symphony Orchestra under Hans Kindler (played three times, in Washington, DC, and Baltimore); the critics again reacted enthusiastically, and the composer recalled reading the rapturous reviews with "utter disbelief."[251]

While comparisons with Shostakovich's Seventh Symphony are inevitable, in light of the numerous and conspicuous similarities in motivic style and sound, Antheil's piece is thoroughly American in its exuberance, its cinematic quality, its marches, and its brassy sound overlaid with vibraphone, wood blocks, tambourine, and piano. Erich Leinsdorf noted its "brilliant orchestration" and observed that "The communicative power of this music is great. It succeeds where Mahler has failed and Shostakovich is failing in his later symphonies: it is democratic music. No elaborate analysis is needed to comprehend this music. Yet it does not carry the tag 'Made for popular enjoyment at all costs.'"[252] Also significant is the relative economy of scale: it is less than half of the length of the Russian composer's work. While that fact might create a less monumental effect, it perhaps reflects the American experience of the war and thus reflects Antheil's goal: "an honest attempt to make a modern symphony that is truly symphonic, expressive, significant of the age in which it is written."[253]

Symphony No. 5, "Joyous"

The story of Antheil's Fifth Symphony is even more complicated than that of the Third. In the case of the latter, Antheil thoroughly rewrote the work, changed its numerical designation from Second to Third, and altered its programmatic intent (without clarifying at first that he had done so). With the Fifth Symphony, however, the composer created two separate compositions with the same number. Between 1943 and 1946, he composed what he called a symphony for the war dead—which included his younger brother Henry, a US diplomat who died when the Soviets shot down his plane in 1940 as it left Estonia for Finland (the occupation of the Baltic nation was underway). This funereal symphony would have been his fourth in number, but he broke off work on it to compose the completely unrelated "1942" Symphony. Afterward, he returned to the memorial composition and completed it in 1945–46, designating it his Fifth Symphony with the subtitle "Tragic." In his autobiography, which closes at this point, he stated that "Into this new symphony I have put, without shame, all of my tears, my anger. It is the best music of which I have been, so far, capable."[254]

When Eugene Ormandy commissioned Antheil for a new symphony in 1947, the composer was embarking on what he called a "new direction," one in which he pledged "to disassociate myself from the now passé modern schools of the last half century, and create a music for myself and those around me which has no fear of developed melody, real development itself, tonality, or understandable form."[255] Withdrawing the as-yet-unperformed and unpublished "Tragic" Symphony, he proceeded to write a new one that bore the same number but offered totally different content: the new work was light, relatively brief (three movements; 20 minutes), and expressed a celebratory spirit—hence its subtitle "Joyous."[256]

In a letter to the expatriate conductor F. Charles Adler, who recorded the work in 1952, Antheil explained his course reversal (the awkward spelling is his):

> Of recent years I have felt that the trend of the American symphony was too much towards the tragic, the bleak. The general tendency was to regard a new American symphony in the light of it's "deep-frowningness." People tended, generally, to judge a symphony's worth by either it's dismal outlook on life, or it length, or it's scholasticism. . . .
>
> I therefore attempted—and, I believe, carried out successfully—what I wanted to call my "Joyous Symphony," which is the subtitle of the Fifth. Although some critics have unjustly called the work derivative in style, particularly parts of the first movement, it is written in a style which I have used, and developed, since 1928. . . . It will be discovered that I have used precisely the style, the various mannerisms (particularly including the peculiar "boogie-woogie"-like basses of the first movement) in the overture of my first opera, "Transatlantic." . . . Indeed, I even roused several motives from this early overture in the Fifth Symphony.[257]

From 1920 to 1950 in the United States

Example 5.14 Antheil, Symphony No. 5, I opening (mm. 1–9)

In their introductory note to the score, the publishers explained that the symphony "signals a return to an earlier mood, a happy and optimistic one, thus being radically different from his Third and Fourth Symphonies."[258] As he had to the Fourth Symphony, Virgil Thomson reacted with enthusiasm to the premiere of the "Joyous" with Ormandy and the Philadelphia Orchestra in 1948; he declared it the apotheosis of Antheil's Romantic language.[259]

The first movement, Allegro, begins with a bustling syncopated theme in the trumpets over an offbeat accompaniment (example 5.14). Although Antheil described the form as sonata-allegro in his letter to Adler, the effect is essentially episodic, presenting a variety of contrasting thematic materials in a virtually uninterrupted eighth-note pulse that lends unity despite abrupt changes of meter and melodic contour in the development. This rhythmic drive—syncopated lines over the "boogie-woogie bass"—creates an altogether different sensation than the more pastorally driven symphonies of Thompson or Thomson. While unambiguously based on the motorized sound world of the second and fourth movements of Prokofiev's Fifth Symphony (1944)—to the point that one understands again why Antheil's detractors, to his

Susan Key, with Drew Massey

Example 5.14 *continued*

Example 5.15 Antheil, Symphony No. 5, II, mm. 15–21

deep annoyance, repeatedly charged him with derivativeness—there is yet something distinctively American in its sense of rapid, driving, forward motion. Antheil portrays an America that is going to achieve its destiny through industry rather than nature. He pointed to the "trace of our popular music and bands of this 1920–45 era, with their wild breaks, their particular American style."[260]

The second movement (Adagio molto) offers a particularly fine example of the kind of melodic profile that suggests a national sound yet distinguishes itself from both folk-driven idioms and Harris's brand of nonvernacular Americanism. In this case, film composition seems to be Antheil's likely groundwork, all the more in that the movement evoked, in Antheil's words, "things remembered at youthful campfires, when I was a boy-scout on the upper Delaware." A moody, harmonically evasive opening in 6/8 shortly gives way to a gentle string melody in duple meter and B-flat major (example 5.15). Antheil described the structure as "partially song-form, yet with development throughout." Modal shifts provide subtle contrasts, while the composer's fertile imagination for variation keeps the listener's interest throughout.

The Finale, Allegretto giocoso, "tends toward the rondo, yet being sonata-allegro in basic form." Breathlessly syncopated, almost circus-like, it returns to the relentless eighth-note pulse and Prokofievian atmosphere of the first movement, though with some moments of repose not found there. Antheil described it as "less folk-songy . . . a synthesis . . . as it should be."

The composer concluded, "We Americans are a fun loving people. Of all the peoples in the world, we are more quickly able to laugh at ourselves, appreciate a good joke. That there is at least one 'Joyous' American symphony, of the present day, should not be totally out of place. I feel, here, I have written an American symphony of our time, and place." Later that year, he wrote to Adler: "THE FIFTH SYMPHONY IS MY FAVORITE SYMPHONY OF ALL MY SYMPHONIES. Honest."[261]

Sixth Symphony

While the Fifth Symphony was well received, critics reacted with less enthusiasm to the Sixth Symphony, which the San Francisco Symphony premiered under Pierre Monteux on February 10, 1949. The first movement was inspired by painter Eugène Delacroix's *Liberty Leading the People* (1830); Antheil expressed his music's connection with "the smoke of battle, courage, despair, and hope, all marching into the future"; he describes the last movement as "the triumph of joy and optimism over despair, war, annihilation . . . the natural follow-up to the courage and hope-against-hope mood of the first movement."[262]

The publication of the score in 1955 received a scathing review from Robert Sabin: "It is in the finale that we suffer most heavily from the composer's tendency to spin out and repeat his ideas with more bustling energy than logic or organic development. It goes through its paces very smartly, but it has the empty vehemence of a campaign speech. There was a time when all symphonists were supposed to write in the grand manner, but today we do not demand ponderosity. Antheil's ideas in this Sixth Symphony fail to bear the strain he puts upon them."[263] Sabin's comments may ring true to some listeners, but they are also a historical artifact of their own, an indication of the changing tastes among critics about what an American symphony "ought" to do.

Throughout his own stylistic journey, and in spite of the vagaries of musical fashion, Antheil retained a sense of the genre's traditional largeness of purpose. In 1948, he wrote, "I believe, first of all, that the symphony of all times and periods is a spiritual as well as an abstract musical canvas, and that any 'symphony' written to present purely abstract musical values is a misnomer. In other words, I believe that every symphony ever written could be subtitled 'The Life of Man' as seen by the composer of that particular period while writing that particular symphony. It is like a great novel which shows some complete large section of life, and has some deep spiritual moving comment upon it."[264]

After his return to America and change of style from a rabble-rousing "bad boy" modernist to a convinced adherent of symphonic tradition, Antheil had developed a markedly individual vision of the American symphony. His freely eclectic—or, to borrow Leinsdorf's term (cited earlier), "democratic"—style combining clearly audible influences from celebrated present and past European masters with American rhythms; his modular construction, borrowed from or at least reinforced by the Hollywood film industry; his advocacy of a symphonic sound that celebrated the present and future of the nation instead of the past (as embodied in the midwestern prairie style, at least according to Antheil); and his conception of the symphony as a "great novel" in tones, which glorified Romantic expressiveness over Neoclassical abstraction—all this argued for an alternative path to a viable (and "great") American symphonic style in the 1940s.

HENRY COWELL

The all-embracing musical enthusiasms and idiosyncratic imagination of Henry Cowell (1897–1965) obscured the conventional cultural fault line between the rustic simplicity of folk music and the sophisticated cosmopolitanism of twentieth-century modernism. Although rightly celebrated as an ultramodernist icon, the deepest wellspring of his inspiration lay in sources further afield both chronologically and geographically. As biographer Joel Sachs puts it, "The biggest surprise, as Henry Cowell's music and ideas become better known, is that his dedication to world music constituted far more of his creative life than his more celebrated ultramodernism."[265] While many of his contemporaries used folk or vernacular sources to achieve accessibility or an identifiable national identity, Cowell was primarily interested in such sources for their *musical* qualities, and he extrapolated from them diverse and sometimes incongruous artistic results that defy categorization. As he said in 1955, "I want to live in the *whole world* of music! . . . I have never deliberately concerned myself with developing a distinctive 'personal' style, but only with the excitement and pleasure of writing music as beautifully, as warmly, and as interestingly as I can."[266]

Cowell's early years immersed him in environments perfectly suited to stimulating a wide-ranging interest in music and ideas. Born in Menlo Park, California, he later moved with his mother to San Francisco, where he particularly enjoyed Chinese music; as he recalled, "The Chinese found out many centuries ago that . . . banging noises have musical value and enjoyment-giving possibilities."[267] From his father he inherited a knowledge and love of Irish music. Charles Seeger helped him begin study at Berkeley in the fall of 1914, followed in 1916 by several months in New York at the Institute of Musical Art. Upon returning to California, he lived in the theosophical community of Halcyon (led by the poet John Varian)—a relationship that continued into the 1920s.[268]

Studies in Europe on a Guggenheim Fellowship in 1931 deepened his exposure to "the whole world of music": "By the time Cowell went to Germany, the [Berlin Phonogramm-Archiv] had become the world's preeminent archive of recordings of indigenous musics from around the world. Cowell had the opportunity there to study Indian and Indonesian music with noted specialists, and to listen critically to numerous recordings in the collection. He reported excitedly on his sonic journey around the world in letters to his family, [Charles] Ives, and Carlos Chávez."[269]

Table 5.11 The Symphonies of Henry Cowell (1897–1965)[a]

Title and date	Movements	Instrumentation	Comments
Symphony No. 1 in B Minor (1915–18, scored 1921–22, rev. 1940)	1. Allegro moderato—Allegro molto—Presto—Tempo I 2. Presto 3. Moderato con moto		Dedicated to the composer's father. Not performed or published.
Symphony No. 2, "Anthropos" (1938)	1. "Repose" (Largo—Sostenuto) 5/2 (48 mm.) 2. "Activity" (Poco presto) 11/8 (90 mm.) 3. "Repression" (Molto espressivo) 3/4 (188 mm.) 4. "Liberation (Liberty Hornpipe)" (Allegro vivace) 4/4 (12/8) (147 mm.)	2 Flt., 3 Ob., 3 Clar., 3 Bssn., 2 Hr., 2 Tpt., 1 Trom., Tuba, Timp., Perc. (2 Wood Blocks, 2 Dragonmouths, 2 Tom-toms, 2 Medium Gongs, 2 Low Gongs, SD, BD, Glsp., Xylo.), Strgs.	According to Sidney Cowell, the symphony is meant to depict "the life of man." First performance: March 9, 1941, by the New York Civic (WPA) Orchestra, conducted by the composer. Holograph score published by Peters, 1953.
Gaelic Symphony (Symphony No. 3 for Band and Strings, 1942)	1. Maestoso C (142 mm.) 2. Andante cantabile C (94 mm.) 3. Allegretto con moto 6/8 (132 mm.) 4. Allegro ¢ (188 mm.)	Grand + Flt., Ob., 2 Clar., Bssn. and 1 additional Bssn. ad lib., 4 Sax., Tpt., Euph., Tuba, Perc.	First performance (Movement I only): July 24, 1942, by the Ernest Williams Symphony Orchestra and Band, conducted by Ernest Williams (no record exists of a performance of the complete work.) Unpublished; digitized holograph score available online, https://www.wisemusicclassical.com/work/27046/Symphony-No-3-Gaelic-Henry-Cowell/
Symphony No. 4 (Short Symphony, 1946)	1. "Hymn" (Allegro—Meno mosso [Andante]—Allegro) C (148 mm.) 2. "Ballad" (Andante) 4/4 (66 mm.) 3. "Dance (Vivace) 12/8 (111 mm.) 4. "Introduction and Fuguing" Tune (Allegro con brio—Moderato con moto) 3/4 (202 mm.)	Grand + Flt., Ob., Clar., Bssn., Tpt., Tuba, Timp., Perc. (Tom-tom, Wood Blocks, Cym., SD, BD, Chimes, Xylo.), Harp	Written for and dedicated to Serge Koussevitzky. Principal melody of last movement borrowed from *Hymn and Fuguing Tune No. 6* (1946). First performance: October 24, 1947, by the Boston Symphony Orchestra, conducted by Richard Burgin (Koussevitzky was indisposed). Score published by Associated Music, 1948.

Table 5.11 *continued*

Title and date	Movements	Instrumentation	Comments
Symphony No. 5 (1948)	1. Con moto 2/4 (188 mm.) 2. Andante 4/4 (133 mm.) 3. Presto 6/8 (194 mm.) 4. Largo sostenuto, quasi andante C (134 mm.)	Grand + Flt, Ob., Clar., Bssn., Tpt., Tuba, Timp., Perc. (Xylo., Bells, Chimes, SD, 2 Tom-toms, Cym.), Pno.	First performance: January 5, 1949, by the National Symphony Orchestra, Washington, DC, conducted by Hans Kindler. Holograph score published by Associated Music, 1948.
Symphony No. 6 (1951–52)	1. Allegro 4/4 (173 mm.) 2. Andante 4/4 (123 mm.) 3. Allegro 6/8 (235 mm.) 4. Allegro moderato 3/4 (158 mm.)	Grand + Flt, Ob., Clar., Bssn., Tpt., Tuba, Timp., Perc. (Xylo., Bells, Chimes, SD, BD, Tom-tom, Cym.)	The entire symphony is generated from a single theme. First performance: November 14, 1955, by the Houston Symphony Orchestra, conducted by Leopold Stokowski. Material on rental from Peters.
Symphony No. 7 for Small Orchestra (1952)	1. Maestoso—Allegro—Più mosso—Tempo I 2/2 (156 mm.) 2. Andante 4/4 (113 m.) 3. Presto 6/8 (200 mm.) 4. Maestoso—Vigoroso—Maestoso 4/4 (187 mm.)	2 Flt., Ob. (doubling EH), 2 Clar. (doubling Bclar.), Bssn., 2 Hr., B♭ Tpt, Trom., Timp., Perc. (Bells, Xylo., Cym.), Pno., Strgs.	First performance: November 25, 1952, in the Auditorium of Peabody Conservatory by the Little Orchestra of Baltimore, conducted by Reginald Stewart. Holograph material on rental from Associated Music.
Symphony No. 8 for Orchestra, Chorus, and Optional Contralto Solo (1952)	1. Con moto—Lento (tempo di blues)—Poco più mosso—Andante—Allegro—Meno mosso 2/4 (435 mm.) 2. Andante—Allegretto—Meno mosso—Allegretto 3/4 (144 mm.) 3. Allegro moderato—Più mosso—Vivace—Più mosso—Meno mosso—Allegro molto 6/8 (435 mm.) 4. Con moto—Allegro molto—Allegro—Larghetto 2/2 (167 mm.)	Grand + Flt, Clar., Tpt., Tuba, 4 Timp., Perc. (Cym., Tom-toms [or Hindu tablas or congas if available], SD, BD, Cuban maracas with rattles, Brazilian maracas, Claves, Wood Block, Castanets, Xylo.), Pno. SSATBB Chorus, optional Mezzo or Contralto soloist	Written for Wilmington College (Ohio) and the Society of Friends. In the first three movements, the chorus vocalizes on syllables. In the final movement, it sings the hymn "Behold, a Voice Angelic Sounds," to the tune *Majesty New*, from p. 33 of *Sacred Melodeon* by J. Dalbey Jr., and J. B. Peat (1858). First performance: March 1, 1953, at Wilmington College, as part of its Sixth International Folk Festival. The ensemble was to be the All-Ohio High School Orchestra and Chorus, conducted by Thor Johnson, but logistical problems necessitated a much smaller ensemble. In conjunction with the Festival, the College awarded Cowell an honorary doctorate. Unpublished.

Symphony No. 9 (1953)	1. Largo 3/2 (57 mm.) 2. Allegro C (181 mm.) 3. Allegretto quasi andante 3/4 (152 mm.) 4. Presto 6/8 (108 mm.) 5. Allegro C (200 mm.)	Full + 2 Trom., Perc., Pno. (or Harp)	Commissioned by and dedicated to Otto Karp and the Green Bay Symphony Orchestra (Wisconsin). Movement 1 is a slightly shortened version of the Hymn from the *Hymn and Fuguing Tune No. 9* for cello and piano (1950, arranged for orchestra in 1953). First performance: March 14, 1954, by the Green Bay Symphony Orchestra, conducted by Ralph Holder. Holograph score published by Associated Music, 1953.
Symphony No. 10 (1953)	1. "Hymn" (Largo) 3/2 (58 mm.) 2. "Fuguing Tune" (Allegro) 4/4 (102 mm.) 3. "Comallye" (Andante con moto) 3/4 (128 mm.) 4. "Jig" (Allegro) 12/8 (61 mm.) 5. "Intermezzo" (Allegretto quasi andante) 3/4 (120 mm.) 6. "Fuguing Tune" (Maestoso) 4/4 (195 mm.)	Full	Commissioned by F. Charles Adler and the Vienna Symphony Chamber Orchestra. Dedication: "Dem Kammerorchester der Wiener Symphoniker und Herrn F. C. Adler für die 1953 Israel-Tour gewidmet." The tour apparently never took place and the symphony was not heard until it was recorded in 1955 by the Vienna Orchestral Society under Adler (Unicorn Records, UNLP 1045, released in 1957). Movements 1 and 2 are arrangements of the string orchestra version of *Hymn and Fuguing Tune No. 5* (1946). Movements 5 and 6 are orchestrations of the *Hymn, Chorale, and Fuguing Tune No. 8* (1947; the "Chorale and Fuguing Tune" are combined in Movement 6). First concert performance: February 24, 1957, by the City Symphony of New York, conducted by Franz Bibo. Holograph materials available on rental from Associated Music.

Table 5.11 *continued*

Title and date	Movements	Instrumentation	Comments
Symphony No. 11, "Seven Rituals of Music" (1953)	1. Andantino ("Music for a Child Asleep") 4/4 (83 mm.) 2. Allegro ("The Ritual of Work") 4/4 (104 mm.) 3. Lento ("The Ritual of Love") 4/4 (50 mm.) 4. Presto ("The Ritual of Dance and Play") 6/8 (160 mm.) 5. Adagio ("The Ritual of Magic and Mystery") 4/4 (65 mm.) 6. Vivace ("The Ritual of Preparation for War") 5/4 (44 mm.) 7. Andante ("The Ritual of Death") 4/4 (53 mm.)	Grand + Tpt., Tuba, 2 pair Timp., Perc. (Xylo., Cym., 4 Small Suspended Cym., Large Suspended Cym., 4 "Different-size" Bowls, 4 Tom-toms or Bongos, Anvil, BD, 2 Wood Blocks, Bells, Glsp.), Pno. (doubling Cel.), Harp (ad lib.)	Commissioned by the Louisville Symphony Orchestra. Subject concerns "seven rituals of music in the life of men from birth to death" (Cowell). First performance: May 29, 1954, by the Louisville Symphony Orchestra, conducted by Robert Whitney. Score published by Associated Music, 1957.
Symphony No. 12 (1955–56)	1. Andante C (85 mm.) 2. Allegro C (116 mm.) 3. Presto 2/4 (159 mm.) 4. Maestoso—Allegro molto—Maestoso—Allegro molto C (102 mm.)	Grand + Flt., Clar, Tpt., Tuba, Perc. (Xylo., Glsp., 2 Anvils, SD, 2 Bongos or Tom-toms, Cym.), Cel., Pno.	Written for Leopold Stokowski. First performance: March 28, 1960, by the Houston Symphony Orchestra, conducted by Stokowski. Score published by Associated Music, 1960.
Symphony No. 13, "Madras" (1956–58)	1. "Alapna" (Andante rubato 2/4 (178 mm.) 2. "Tala Adi" (Allegretto) 16/4 (105 mm.) 3. Allegro 3/4 + 2/4 (71 mm.) 4. Andante 3/4 (103 mm.) 5. Allegro 7/8 (2/4 + 1 ½/4) (121 mm.)	Full (without Tpt.) + Timp. (4 hand or 2 pedal), Perc. (High and Low Gongs, Tabla or Tuned Tom-toms, Jalatarang, Glsp., Xylo.), Cel.	Dedicated to the Madras Musical Academy, India. First performance: March 3, 1959, by the Little Orchestra Society of New York, conducted by Thomas Scherman in Madras as part of an Asian tour. The concert was broadcast on All-India Radio. First US performance: October 19, 1959, by the same ensemble. Holograph score published by Peters, 1969.

Symphony No. 14 (1959–60)	1. Adagio—Allegro 3/4 (268 mm.) 2. Andante C (123 mm.) 3. Vivace 6/8 (240 mm.) 4. Allegro ¢ (259 mm.)	Grand + Flt., Ob., Clar., Tpt., Tuba, Perc. (Xylo., Vbp., Glsp., 5 Bongos or Tom-toms, 8 tuned High Drums or 8 Graduated Tom-toms, 5 Temple Blocks or Wood Blocks, Large Cym., 3 Small Suspended Cym., BD, 1 Medium SD, 1 High SD, 3 Muted Gongs, 5 Porcelain Bowls, Low Metal Sheet, 5 Graduated Metal Sounds), Cel., Pno.	Commissioned by the Serge Koussevitzky Music Foundation in the Library of Congress and dedicated to the memory of Serge and Natalie Koussevitzky. First performance: April 27, 1961, by the Eastman-Rochester Philharmonic Orchestra, conducted by Howard Hanson, in Washington, DC, as part of the Second Inter-American Music Festival. Materials on rental from Associated Music.
Symphony No. 15, "Thesis" (1960)	Movement I 1. Largo 5/4 (30 mm.) 2. Andante C (46 mm.) 3. Presto 5/4 (57 mm.) 4. Allegretto 5/2 (13 mm.) 5. Allegro—Recapitulation (Largo—Allegretto—Presto—Andante—Allegro) 7/8 (208 mm.) Movement II 6. Moderato C (102 mm.)	Grand + Flt., Ob., Clar., Tpt., Tuba, Perc. (5 Metal Pieces, 5 Tom-toms, Gong, Cym., BD, Xylo., Tam-tam), Cel.	Commissioned by BMI to celebrate its 20th anniversary. "Written for Carl Haverlin and Broadcast Music, Inc., 1960." Movements 1–4 are arrangements of sections of Cowell's String Quartet No. 3 ("Mosaic Quartet," 1935); Movement 6 is an arrangement of his Movement for String Quartet (1928). Cowell did not explain the meaning of the subtitle "Thesis." First performance: October 7, 1961, by the Louisville Symphony Orchestra, conducted by Robert Whitney. Score published by Associated Music, 1962.

Table 5.11 *continued*

Title and date	Movements	Instrumentation	Comments
Symphony No. 16, "Icelandic" (1962)	1. Moderato con moto—Poco più mosso C (98 mm.) 2. Allegro 4/4 (200 mm.) 3. Adagio cantabile 3/2 (83 mm.) 4. Vivace—Più mosso 2/4 (155 mm.) 5. Maestoso—Molto vivace—Lento—Allegro 4/4 (236 mm.)	Grand + Tuba, Perc. (6 "Different-sized" Drums without snares, Gong, Cym., Xylo, 6 Pieces of Ringing Metal), Harp	Commissioned by the government of Iceland for the ceremonies dedicating a new University of Iceland Auditorium in Reykjavik. "For the Iceland Symphony Orchestra, with William Strickland." In this work Cowell draws on Icelandic traditional melodies, modes (Lydian), and performance styles. First performance: March 21, 1963, by the Iceland Symphony Orchestra, conducted by Strickland, in the University Auditorium. Materials on rental from Associated Music, 1963.
Symphony No. 17, "Lancaster" (1963)	1. Moderato—Allegro—Allegro—Allegro—Allegro—Maestoso 3/4 (260 mm.) 2. Andante vigoroso 3/4 (45 mm.) 3. Drone and Ground: Maestoso 3/4 (130 mm.) 4. Presto 6/8 (171 mm.) 5. Allegro—Maestoso—Allegro—Allegro—Allargando ¢ (190 mm.)	Grand + Tuba, Perc. (BD, 5 Small Drums, SD, Cym., 5 Metal Sounds, Gong, Glsp., 5 Temple Blocks)	Written at the invitation of the city of Lancaster, Pennsylvania, for a celebration of Cowell's career. The second section of Movement 1 incorporates and develops the fuguing tune of the *Hymn and Fuguing Tune No. 15-B* (1963). First performance (of Movement 1, as *Lancaster Overture*): February 5, 1963, by the Lancaster Symphony Orchestra, conducted by Louis Vyner. The full symphony apparently still awaits a performance. Holograph materials on rental from Associated Music.
Symphony No. 18 (1963–64)	1. Moderato C (145 mm.) 2. Allegro—Meno—Allegro—Tempo II—Tempo I—Più mosso—Meno mosso Tempo II—Più mosso—Vivo 6/8 (213 mm.) 3. Con moto quasi andante C (114 mm.) 4. Presto 9/8 (164 mm.) 5. Moderato con brio—Presto—Moderato—Moderato con brio ¢ (237 mm.)	Grand + Flt, Ob., Clar, Bssn., Tpt., Tuba, Perc. (Xylo., Glsp., 5 Medium Drums, 5 Ringing Metal Sounds, 4 Temple Blocks, SD, Crash Cym., Pair Finger Cym. or Small High Cym.), Cel.	Not as yet performed. Holograph score published by Peters, 1977.

Symphony No. 19 (1964–65)	1. Allegro moderato 3/2 (165 mm.) 2. Andante C (126 mm.) 3. Vivace 12/8 (165 mm.) 4. Andante ¢ (58 mm.) 5. Allegro—Vivace—Tempo I C (255 mm.)	Grand + Flt, Ob., Clar., Bssn., Tpt., Tuba, Perc. (Xylo., Mrb., Vbp., Glsp., 7 Tuned Drums, 5 Tom-toms, SD, BD, 5 Metal Sounds, 3 Gongs, Cym., 3 Tri., 7 Untuned Porcelain Bowls, 2 Wood Blocks), Pno.	"Dedicated to the Doctors and Nurses of Brooklyn Jewish Hospital, without Whom This Music Would Never Have Been Written." Cowell had been a patient in the hospital from mid-October to mid-December 1964. The program for the first performance states that the work was "Especially written for and dedicated to the [Nashville] Orchestra on the Occasion of Its 20th Anniversary Season." First performance: October 18, 1965, by the Nashville Symphony, conducted by Willis Page. Materials on rental from Associated Music, 1967.
Symphony No. 20 (1965)	1. Allegro moderato 4/4 (47 mm.) 2. Allegro 3/4 (172 mm.) 3. Lento 3/2 (62 mm.) 4. Allegro 5/4 (101 mm.)	Grand + Flt, Ob., Clar., Bssn., Tpt., Tuba, Perc. (5 Tom-toms, 5 Metal Sounds, 2 SD, Xylo.), Pno., Cel.	According to his wife, Cowell started to compose the work on March 15; he worked until June 4, when a major stroke incapacitated him, and he left the fourth movement incomplete. Lou Harrison reconstructed the first ten measures of the opening movement and completed the last fifteen measures of the fourth movement according to Cowell's instructions. The composer planned to close the symphony with a fifth-movement Hymn and Fuguing Tune but left no sketches for it. Awaits first performance. Holograph score published by Peters, 1968.
Symphony No. 21 (1965)			Assorted sketches, presumably from April and June 1965.

a. Most of the information for this table is drawn from William Lichtenwanger, *The Music of Henry Cowell: A Descriptive Catalog*, I.S.A.M. Monographs No. 23 (Brooklyn, NY: Institute for Studies in American Music, Conservatory of Music, Brooklyn College of the City University of New York, 1986), which is reprinted on the Henry Cowell website, http://www.henrycowell.org/.

Cowell was an energetic presence in multiple facets of American musical life on both coasts. As a young composer and performer he burst forcefully onto the scene by radically experimenting with coaxing new sounds from the piano, as in the tone clusters of the thunderously dissonant *Tides of Manaunaun* (ca. 1917) or playing the strings inside the piano in *The Banshee* (1925). In 1925, he established the New Music Society of California and the quarterly journal *New Music*, which published scores of contemporary music; in 1934, he founded New Music Quarterly Recordings. His efforts promoted the emergence of California as a center of musical experimentation. While living in New York, he served as president of the Pan American Association of Composers (1929–33). A 1933 book of essays, *American Composers on American Music*, included essays by fellow composers on each other's music. *New Musical Resources*, his attempt to categorize his theories about music, was first written in 1919 and revised in 1929.

Cowell began composing for orchestra relatively early, with the 1928 Sinfonietta for chamber orchestra (an arrangement of an earlier string quintet) and *Synchrony* (1929–30), a single-movement composition for large orchestra originally conceived as a dance piece for Martha Graham.[270] Although he continued to compose during his well-documented imprisonment at San Quentin from 1936 to 1940, the conviction resulted in an isolation from which it was difficult for Cowell to emerge even after his release and subsequent pardon in 1942.[271] Cowell's symphonic output is lopsided chronologically: his 21 symphonies—more than any other composer considered in this chapter—cluster significantly toward the end of his career (table 5.11). He was one of the few ultramodernists from the 1920s who wrote numbered symphonies to begin with (Ives was a notable colleague on this front), and even as his language became simpler in some ways, it still drew on the sliding tones and polymetric intricacies that figure in some of his earlier works.

To generalize about Cowell's symphonies is difficult, as he took an extremely eclectic approach to the genre, not only from work to work but even within a single one. As Hugo Weisgall put it, "Each work, often each movement, can be regarded as an enthusiastic synthesis of some musical experience Cowell has just undergone, written with a great sense of immediacy."[272] Some symphonies (e.g., No. 4) draw on a kind of vernacular Americana through forms such as the fuguing tune, the jig, and the ballad. Some apply his pre-1936 experimental piano techniques to the orchestra (Nos. 11, 15). Others evoke non-American Western or non-Western cultures (India in No. 13, Iceland in No. 16). Some are original, and others (such as Nos. 9, 10, and 15) are revisions of earlier works. Cowell's later symphonies are decidedly unconventional and often feature unusual proportions.

Within this stylistic diversity, Weisgall notes two principal tendencies: first, a "consistent use of chromatic dissonant material, usually expressed polyphonically; the other is a broad extension of modal principles, frequently utilizing 'exotic' scales, rhythmic forms, and instruments."[273] Equally salient throughout this body of work is Cowell's somewhat surprising fondness for large Romantic gestures, as when the tone clusters and dissonance are swept into a grand climax on a major chord. Three symphonies—the Fourth ("Short," 1946), Eleventh ("Seven Rituals of Music," 1953) and Fifteenth ("Thesis," 1960)—are examined here to show the diversity of Cowell's sound world as his interest in the symphony expanded.

Fourth Symphony, "Short"

There is nothing unusually short about Cowell's Fourth Symphony, which, at roughly twenty minutes in length, is comparable to most of his other symphonies. Written during the "especially productive" summer of 1946, it premiered on October 24, 1947, with the Boston

Symphony Orchestra.[274] It stands apart from the other two Cowell symphonies considered here for several reasons. One is its avowedly "Americana" language: as the anonymous introductory note to the score explains, "Since 1941 Cowell has been engaged in the composition of a series of works which are a modern development from the style of certain American 'Primitive' composers at the end of the Eighteenth Century."[275] Accordingly, the rhythms are straightforward, without the jazzy syncopations of so many works of the era, although the large wind section, harp, and multiple percussion (including chimes, xylophone, tom-tom, and wood blocks) lend the piece a modern flair.

The introductory note provides a short description of each movement: "The First movement of the short symphony presents without preliminary the melodic material on which the entire composition is based. The movement consists of three contrasting hymn-like tunes. The first is in chorale or psalm-tune style, with variations; next comes a flowing Andante melody, and last an energetic Modal melody more strictly in the shaped-note hymn tradition than the first two. Each of these is repeated, with extended melodic development."[276]

The structural similarity of the tunes as well as the lack of true development contribute to some structural awkwardness, as Irving Fine pointed out in a review of a Howard Hanson-led recording some years later.[277]

The introductory note says the following about the second and third movements:

> Adhering to symphonic convention, the next two movements are in song form and in dance form. The Second Movement is built on a melody of the unaccompanied narrative ballad character, set in a tonal atmosphere suggestive of a backwoods landscape rather than a literal instrumental accompaniment. The Dance Movement, an elaborately developed jig melody, has a strong Irish flavor which gives a striking family resemblance to the tunes played for square dancing or for solo jig competitions among loggers from Maine to Washington, across the Northern United States. This is a type of tune that turns up frequently in the compositions of Henry Cowell; due perhaps to his Irish parentage, it is a kind of lively music that appeals to him particularly.[278]

Although the moods of these interior movements represent a study in contrast, they share Cowell's ingenious interplay of orchestration and motivic counterpoint. The theme of the second movement, introduced in the flutes, becomes an accompaniment figure at Letter A. Rather than being "suggestive of a backwoods landscape," reviewer Irving Fine thought the melody ventured "perilously close to the banality of certain types of film music."[279] In the third movement, the jig is tossed back and forth across instruments in a way that plays against the monochromatic nature of the melody; as Fine describes it, the music "bubbles along with Mendelssohnian spontaneity and finesse."[280]

The last movement of Cowell's Fourth Symphony sets it apart from other symphonies of the time, in that it consists of an introduction, fuguing tune and coda. Cowell wrote some eighteen works entitled "Hymn and Fuguing Tune" between 1944 and 1964, and they exemplify the radical simplification of his style that can be heard after his release from San Quentin; the Finale for the *Short Symphony* follows the same pattern. As the introductory note puts it, "The fullest development of the thematic material has been reserved for this movement. The fuguing tune is a development from the famous William Billings style, with the addition of occasional dissonant notes, retaining, however, the plainness of form and the polyphonic vigor of the style."[281] As in traditional fuguing tunes, the initial point of imitation is followed by free counterpoint. One of the hymns from the first movement makes an appearance, and the piece concludes on open fifth, as does much tunesmith and shape-note music.

Reception was generally positive. In a 1949 review of a recording by the Eastman-Rochester Symphony Orchestra, Weldon Hart emphasized the skillful use of tone color: "The *Short Symphony* is orchestrated with an obvious knowledge of what sounds best with the least trouble, and I am sure that anyone with conducting experience will be tempted, on examining this score, to grab a baton and rush out to conduct the nearest orchestra in these big, sonorous effects."[282] Despite his reservations, Fine concluded that the work was "a consistently musical and effective score by a genuinely gifted and thoroughly professional composer."[283] Unlike Antheil, Cowell creates an American sound in this symphony not by looking into the future but by reaching back into the nation's musical past, though his approach to eclecticism is equally individual and distinct.

Eleventh Symphony, "Seven Rituals of Music"

Cowell's Eleventh Symphony (1953) was commissioned by the Louisville Orchestra, an especially important patron in the 1950–70 period.[284] The work is in seven extraordinarily brief movements, with only one lasting longer than four minutes. As a result, it is more a series of miniatures than a study in thematic development. The first six movements depict what Cowell describes as the rituals of music in the life of a man: birth, work, love, dance, magic, and combat; the final movement, on funereal rituals, accordingly sums up the work by recalling (not transforming) the material introduced in the first six, like a musical eulogy. The orchestration features a large percussion battery, including anvil, glass and porcelain bowls, and piano. The subject offers full scope for many of the musical ideas Cowell had been developing for decades: through the imagined rituals in the symphony, he combines folk gestures (Movement IV), ultramodernism ("sliding tones," Movements III and V), non-Western textures (Movement II), and even grand Romantic gestures (Finale).

The score includes an outline and brief descriptions of each movement:

I
The Symphony opens gently (*Andantino*) with music for a child asleep, and grows into a celebration of youth and strength. Before the movement ends there is a moment's premonition of grief, foreshadowing the lament with which the symphony closes.
II
The second movement is a busy one (*Allegro*), featuring percussion. This is music for the ritual of work, and it hints at struggle and violence to come.
III
The third movement (*Lento*) is a song for the ritual of love, with its premonition of magic.
IV
The fourth movement (*Presto*) is music for the ritual of dance and play, with some reminiscence of the music for work.
V
The fifth movement (*Adagio*) is for the ritual of magic and the mystical imagination, with some remembrance of the music for the magic of love.
VI
The sixth movement (*Vivace*) is for the ritual dance that prepares man for struggle and combat; it includes man's work.
VII
The introduction to the last movement (*Andante*) is a fugal exposition of the themes of the preceding six movements; it leads into the music for the ritual of death, which begins as a lament and grows in intensity until the symphony comes to an end.[285]

From 1920 to 1950 in the United States

Example 5.16 Cowell, Symphony No. 11, I, opening (mm. 1–6)

*glissandi in artificial harmonics, played freely, rubato

Example 5.17 Cowell, Symphony No. 11, V, mm. 13–16

The haunting atmosphere of the first movement is created by dissonant chromatic contrapuntal lines beginning with a pair of flutes (example 5.16). Melodic fragments drift in and out of the texture, traded between the cellos, English horn, muted trumpets and, eventually, trombones. In the second movement, a gamelan-like texture accompanies a syncopated pentatonic tune. There is prominent percussion (including xylophone, timpani, "four bowls of different sizes," tom-toms, and large and small cymbals); toward the end of the movement, the rapid figures in xylophone and piano recall the mechanized rhythmic complexities of Cowell's contemporary Conlon Nancarrow (1912–97). The third movement is coloristic, featuring one of Cowell's innovations, a technique he called "sliding tones," essentially slow-moving glissandi (the composer defined them as "ever-changing values of pitch instead of steady pitches").[286] In this case, the sliding tones move over a very chromatic accompaniment. Bells and celesta offer the "premonition of magic." In contrast, the next movement uses multisectional form to evoke "dance and play": for the former, a jiglike theme decorated with wood block accents and for the latter a middle section that recalls the gamelan textures of Movement II, combined with a rhythm that evokes American popular culture. The melody then returns to the dance, harking back to the Americana style of the Fourth Symphony.

Sliding tones evoke the "magic and the mystical imagination" of the fifth movement. He divides the movement into three sections: the first (mm. 1–10) features slides in thirds in the strings. The second section (mm. 13–23) contains, as Nancy Rao puts it, "tiers of slides," some of which also incorporate harmonics in the strings along with flute, celesta, and harp, to create a particularly otherworldly effect (example 5.17).[287] In the third section, Cowell recombines elements of the previous textures to create a massive, undulating sound that adds more percussion and covers more than four octaves. (The flute passages heard throughout this movement bring to mind the flute-manipulated electronic music of Otto Luening [1900–1996], as in *Fantasy in Space* of 1952.) The sixth movement moves in 5/4 meter with anvil and bass drum; the melody has a generally pentatonic shape. The last movement's fugal exposition recalls all preceding themes and leads to a modal theme accompanied by dyads before the lament climaxes on a strong major chord, bringing this fascinating work to an end.

Fifteenth Symphony, "Thesis"

Cowell's Fifteenth Symphony (1960) has proportions similar to those in the Eleventh but a completely different genesis: its movements combine orchestrations of two earlier chamber works, the *Mosaic Quartet* (1935) and *Movement for String Quartet* (1928). Cowell offered this description: "There is no extra-musical program. The form is unusual: five tiny movements; a choral-like introduction, an impassioned melody, a scherzo, a longer quiet melody, an irregular-rhythm dance which leads into a recapitulation of these elements in one movement, and at the end a sonata-form movement based on an extension of the primary motiv [*sic*] (a descending whole followed by a half step), which is the mainstay of all movements. As the last movement is in sonata form, I decided to call it my 15th Symphony."[288]

Cowell's casual approach to symphonic form and nomenclature adumbrates the equally nonchalant attitude of his younger contemporary, Alan Hovhaness (1911–2000), whose music he supported.[289] He does not explain the meaning of his subtitle "Thesis."

There are six movements, the first four of which draw from the *Mosaic Quartet*. The work opens with a pandiatonic hymn in 5/4, the angular lines of its dissonant accompaniment somewhat recalling Stravinsky. The second movement, based on the third movement of the *Mosaic Quartet*, again makes use of sliding tones; here, they sound like distant sirens overlaying an impassioned melody in 4/4 in cellos. The instrumental colors are particularly striking, both in timbral choices (strings, clarinets, and bassoons) and in their manipulation, as when the sliding tones stagger (some voices slide, others sustain a tone) between violins and violas.

The third movement, taken from the fourth movement of the *Mosaic Quartet*, is a Scherzo in 5/4. The 13-measure fourth movement, based on the second movement of the *Mosaic Quartet*, closes with polymetric writing (voices moving in different meters simultaneously, although all of them are notated in 5/2); Cowell first began to explore this technique in his well-known treatise *New Musical Resources* (1930).[290] The fifth movement, the only newly written one, presents a dance in an irregular 7/8 in the A section; the musical material gives Cowell an opportunity to display his interest in dissonant counterpoint. The B section recapitulates previous movements.[291] The last movement, which draws from the *Movement for String Quartet*, is a sonata form based on an extension of a primary motive made of descending whole and half steps.

Music critic Alfred Frankenstein wrote of the piece that it "as a whole is one of the strongest, most eloquent, and powerful in Cowell's huge list, and is a crushing reply to those who would write him off as one of the conservative elder statesmen of modern American music."[292] In contrast, Robert Goss described it as "a mildly successful piece in a clearly traditional vein."[293] Perhaps Richard Franko Goldman summed it up best in saying that the symphony "is full of apparent contradictions. It seems both of our time and remote from it. Compared to the music being written on the advanced frontiers, it is curiously innocent and removed; yet compared with the more academic writing of the sixties, it seems as fresh as spring flowers."[294]

Cowell continued to contribute to the genre with his "Icelandic" Symphony (1962), which, as Sachs points out, "used the basic property of Icelandic 'double-singing,' with its parallel fifths and cross-relations, as a tool to steer his material toward a kind of atonality and then back again."[295] He wrote his last three symphonies while in failing health.

As a whole, Cowell's works stand apart in the context of the midcentury American symphony. Like Antheil's, they are self-consciously eclectic, but they borrow from a wider array of sources: non-Western styles and textures, experimental techniques, and Americana all combine in a seemingly random mix that can strike the listener as a particularly interesting type of sensory kaleidoscope that one might encounter in a visit to an aural museum. Weisgall observed that, "Quite apart from a remarkable fecundity and exuberance, Cowell seems always to have been temperamentally incapable of excluding from the corpus of his work anything offered by his creative mind. His is a nature that accepts wholeheartedly; he does not easily reject anything, whether in himself or others."[296] As Cowell himself put it, "If a man has a distinctive personality of his own, I don't see how he can keep out of his music. And if he hasn't, how can he put it in?"[297] In their exceptionally wide-ranging diversity of materials, Cowell's symphonies serve as a clear antecedent to the works of Lou Harrison (1917–2003; a student and protégé) and of works of the twenty-first-century postmodernists.[298]

Cowell's approach to composition challenges the idea of a masterwork, and certainly there is no Great American Symphony in his output (nor did he attempt one). Cowell's symphonies have not found much of a place in American orchestral programming. As Sachs notes, "his insistent exploration of new ideas, his refusal to create a single compositional persona, had their liabilities. Such multisided minds also can sometimes produce music that does not seem fully ripened."[299] Yet, if his imagination seemed ill-suited to the confines of the weightiest and most traditional of genres, the results remain perennially interesting, and Cowell's open-ended approach inspired some of the most fruitful experiments within modernism, looking beyond to postmodernism.

Susan Key, with Drew Massey

WILLIAM LEVI DAWSON[300]

Of the four symphonies by Black composers that made their first appearance during the 1930s, Dawson's is perhaps the least well known. William Grant Still's *Afro-American Symphony* premiered in 1931 by the Rochester Philharmonic Orchestra; Florence Price's Symphony No. 1 was first heard in 1933 with the Chicago Symphony Orchestra; William Levi Dawson's *Negro Folk Symphony* premiered in 1934 with the Philadelphia Orchestra, and James P. Johnson's *Harlem Symphony* was first performed in 1937 by the New York Negro Symphony Orchestra (see table 5.12). In its day, however, the work was a cultural sensation; Gwynne Kuhner Brown explains that the work was "the most prominent and prestigious in terms of conductor, orchestra venue, and size of audience; moreover, the tumultuous approbation the Negro Folk Symphony received from critics and audiences alike set it apart—not only from contemporaneous works by African Americans, but also from most new classical music of the period."[301] Like Still, Price, and Johnson, Dawson (1899–1990) was inspired by Dvořák's advocacy for African American music as a central element in the American voice. And, like them, he sought to use the symphonic genre to create an expression of the Black experience that was both authentic and uplifting.

Dawson's musical training began in his native Alabama; at the age of 13 he left home to attend the Tuskegee Institute, where he studied various instruments, singing, and composition. He then earned his bachelor of music from the Horner Institute of Fine Arts in Kansas City, Missouri, followed by a master's degree in composition from the American Conservatory of Music in Chicago in 1927, where he encountered Dvořák's compositions and learned about the Bohemian master's advocacy of Black music.[302] Chicago's importance as a hub of African American culture also shaped Dawson's aesthetic direction. He played an active role in the city's musical life for the next three years in both jazz and classical environments and won two Wanamaker prizes for musical composition.[303] In spite of these successes, he was lured away in 1930 to become director of the School of Music at the Tuskegee Institute, where composing took a back seat to his activities as an educator, conductor, and arranger. He worked on his symphony over a span of some five years, completing it in 1932.[304]

Table 5.12 The *Negro Folk Symphony* of William Levi Dawson (1899–1990)

Title	Movements	Instrumentation	Comments
Negro Folk Symphony (1928–32)	1. "(The Bond of Africa)" 4/4 (537 mm.) 2. "(Hope in the Night)" 4/4 (260 mm.) 3. "(O, Le' Me Shine, Shine like a Morning Star)" ₵ (497 mm.)	Grand + Picc., EH, Bclar., Cbssn., Tuba, Perc. (Gong, Chimes, African Clave [Adawura], Tri., Tenor Drum, SD, Xylo., Cym., BD), Harp	Dawson added the movement titles at the request of conductor Leopold Stokowski. First performance: November 14, 1934, by the Philadelphia Orchestra, conducted by Stokowski. Dawson revised the symphony in 1952 after a visit to West Africa, incorporating African-influenced rhythms. Score published by Shawnee, 1963.

On a trip to New York City with his Tuskegee Institute choir in the winter of 1932–33, Dawson met Leopold Stokowski, who was intrigued to learn that the young choir director had completed a symphony. Dawson sent the score to Stokowski, who premiered the work with the Philadelphia Orchestra in that city in November 1934 and reprised it at Carnegie Hall only days later; the second performance was followed in July 1935 by another Philadelphia Orchestra performance led by William Van Den Burg. Inspired by a trip to Africa, Dawson revised the piece in 1952 to enhance the role of percussion. The revisions stimulated a few more performances and a recording by Stokowski and the American Symphony Orchestra.[305]

The score Dawson submitted to Stokowski bore no programmatic titles, but the conductor sent a telegram shortly before the performance asking for them ("Feel that individual title such as allegro adagio meaningless"). Dawson thereupon provided the movement names. The question remains whether he would have done so without the conductor's prompting, and to what extent the after-the-fact names altered his and his listeners' perceptions of the music.[306]

Dawson wrote an extended description of the symphony for the Philadelphia Orchestra program book in which he laid out his creative approach, emphasizing both the personal and communal importance of the material:

> This Symphony is based entirely upon Negro folk-music. The themes are taken from what are popularly known as Negro spirituals, and the practiced ear will recognize the recurrence of characteristic themes throughout the composition.
>
> This folk-music springs spontaneously from the life of the Negro people as freely today as at any time in the past, though the modes and forms of the present day are sometimes vastly different from the older creations.
>
> In this composition the composer has employed three themes taken from typical melodies over which he has brooded since childhood, having learned them at his mother's knee.[307]

Dawson describes the first movement as follows:

> FIRST MOVEMENT—"THE BOND OF AFRICA"
> The introduction (Adagio, E-flat major, 4-4 time) opens with a "Leading Motive" played by the first horn, which is symbolic of the link uniting Africa and her rich heritage with her descendants in America. It is pentatonic, and shows itself in numerous guises, forms, and circumstances throughout the entire composition.
> The chief theme of the main movement (Allegro con brio, E-flat major, 2-2 time) is given to the first horn, first B-flat clarinet, and E-flat clarinet, with a tremolo on the higher strings. Afte7r a few measures of contrasting material, this theme is sung by the full orchestra. A transitional passage based on the "Leading Motive" leads to the second theme, presented by the first oboe, and based on the Negro melody:
> Oh, m' litt'l' soul gwine-a shine, shine,
> Oh, m' litt'l' soul gwine-a shine lik' a star.[308]
> After the woodwinds have sung this theme, a new idea appears in the strings. It suggests the rhythmical clapping of the hands and patting of the feet, and is immediately taken up by the full orchestra.
> The development begins (Adagio, 4-4 time) with the "Leading Motive" in the trombones (in A flat minor), and a working-out of the principal theme. This is followed by further elaboration of the principal theme. A section is now devoted to a working-out of the second theme, after which another section is devoted to the principal theme. Finally, the full orchestra gives out a new version of the "Leading Motive," and gradually leads into the Recapitulation. Except for changes in the instrumentation, and a few abbreviations, this division is the same as before. A short coda brings the movement to a close.[309]

Example 5.18 Dawson, *Negro Folk Symphony*, "leading motive"

The pensive "leading motive" that dominates the Introduction gives the piece symbolic meaning through its interjections at highly fraught times in the symphony (example 5.18). After its first iteration, a woodwind phrase uses the Scotch snap rhythm of the motive in a kind of "call and response" that evokes African American music. As Brown points out, "Even these first measures reveal this to be a work at least as concerned with rhythm and tone color as with pitch-related processes."[310] The "leading motive" is repeated in the English horn before the exposition introduces *P* and *S*, both developed as the composer describes. The movement impresses through its vivacious energy, catchy themes (such as *S*), and its very skillful scoring, which includes numerous solos (especially winds), as well as the use of tremolos for added color.

The second movement, although not based on a specific spiritual, is infused with the mood and shape of that genre. Dawson's notes lay out the images evoked:

> SECOND MOVEMENT—"HOPE IN THE NIGHT"
>
> This movement opens (Andante, 4-4) with three strokes from the gong, intended to suggest the Trinity, who guides forever the destiny of man. The strings, playing pizzicato, provide a monotonous background, creating the atmosphere of the humdrum life of a people whose bodies were baked by the sun and lashed with the whip for two hundred and fifty years; whose lives were proscribed before they were born. The English horn sings a melody that describes the characteristics, hopes, and longings of a Folk held in darkness. After a climax, this division is followed by one conceived in a happier mood. The children, unmindful of the heavy cadences of despair, sing and play; but even in their world of innocence, there is a little wail, a brief note of sorrow. After much development of the theme of the children, and a cry from the strings, muted brasses, and trilling woodwinds, there is a return of the previous material. This in turn is succeeded by another outburst, in which the "Leading Motive" is given out by the full orchestra. The movement closes with slow crescendoes and decrescendoes after each of three mysterious sounds from the gong and other percussion instruments.[311]

Dawson assigns the mournful melody, which shares a clear kinship with the leading motive, to the English horn; whether intentionally or not, his choice of timbre inevitably invokes the Largo of Dvořák's "New World" Symphony. The interjection of the leading motive at the climax creates an effect not unlike that of "Fate" motive in the last movement of the Fourth Symphony of Tchaikovsky—another important nationalist figure. The ending stays in a series of tonic chords with variations of tone color, punctuated by the "mysterious sounds" from harp, gong, chimes, timpani, and triangle. This striking passage illustrates Dawson's command of tone color not only as an absolute musical element but also as a symbolic echo of the opening of the movement (example 5.19).

Dawson's description of his third movement again points to the ways in which he drew from spirituals:

From 1920 to 1950 in the United States

Example 5.19 Dawson, *Negro Folk Symphony*, II, mm. 238–48

THIRD MOVEMENT—"O LEM-ME SHINE"

The third movement begins (Allegro con brio, E-flat major, 2-2) with four introductory measures in the strings, which precede the entrance of the principal theme. This movement is based on two Negro melodies. For the first time the composer has used the melody:

O lem-me shine, O lem-me shine,
O lem-me shine, shine lik' a mornin' star![312]

This theme, after being given out by the woodwinds, is followed by related material, which in turn is succeeded by a return of the principal theme. A short episode leads to the second theme in G major, which is stated by the first oboe, and immediately taken up by the full orchestra. This is the second of the two Negro melodies used in this movement—"Hallelujah, Lord, I been down into the sea." The development begins with the principal theme of the movement in the first clarinet, above a tremolo on the lower strings, and is taken up respectively by the first oboe, first flute, and first horn. A new picture of the second theme, combined with the principal theme of the first movement, is now presented, and fragments of ideas from the codetta of the third movement are made use of. The principal theme is now given out by the brasses and woodwinds in augmentation. This section, after rising to a great climax, descends slowly to the Recapitulation. A coda is built on the two themes of the movement, and is brought to a close as the brasses exhibit in bold relief the principal theme, "O lem-me shine lik' a mornin' star."[313]

The introduction of *P* is by way of "call and response" between oboe, bassoon, and clarinet, with the response phrase answering on the dominant. The prominence of a minor third and the Scotch snap creates a family resemblance to themes in earlier movements, which offers Dawson scope for flexibility in handling thematic material while remaining coherent. Johnson notes that Dawson follows a "continuous process of variation and development" rather than strict formal procedures, going on to note that "the close relationship and deep affinities of the thematic material both within and across the movements yield what is at once a dense yet highly unified whole."[314]

The work was received enthusiastically at its performances in November 1934 with Stokowski and the Philadelphia Orchestra, especially the striking second movement. As reported in the *New York Times*, "The custom of no applause during a symphony gave way after the second movement to a spontaneous outburst that brought the orchestra to its feet, and at the end the enthusiasm was so great that Mr. Dawson was called to the stage repeatedly to bow his acknowledgements."[315]

Alain Locke noted the work's significance as a marker for Black achievement in that Dawson seemed to have resolved any inherent tension between racial identity and symphonic tradition: "It is classic in form but Negro in substance, it shows mastery or near-mastery of the terrific resources of the modern orchestra, it builds on to the classic tradition with enough 'modernism' to save it from being purely academic, and with enough originality to save it from the blight of imitation, and more than all else it is unimpeachably Negro."[316] A CBS broadcast of the work on November 16 prompted nationwide commendation and pride, especially within the African American community.[317]

The following years saw occasional interest expressed by a variety of orchestras and conductors, but most of the time inquiries resulted in dead ends. Even the brief revival of interest after the composer's revision and Stokowski's recording failed to stimulate regular ongoing performances. (Part of the reason, at least at first, was the difficulty in securing the score and parts.[318]) As John Andrew Johnson puts it, the symphony became "an often-cited, prominent example or historical relic, rather than a living work of art."[319] It would be misleading to ascribe the neglect solely to racial prejudice, as the same situation often befell white composers (e.g., Roy Harris) who sought to synthesize folk materials with symphonic tradition. In Dawson's case, the result is a symphonic repertoire deprived not only of worthwhile music but also a uniquely American midcentury voice.

JAMES PRICE JOHNSON

James P. Johnson (1894–1955) offers one of many dispiriting examples of careers stunted by cultural prejudices and practices. Earlier in the century Scott Joplin (1868–1917) was crushed by the experience of trying to stage his opera *Treemonisha*. Johnson, the pianist who carried Joplin's ragtime style forward into stride, similarly struggled to find a way to use popular music as a vehicle to create larger forms such as the symphony, tone poem, concerto, chamber work, choral work, ballet, or opera. In addition to Joplin, Johnson's most direct musical influence was George Gershwin, whom he met in 1920 and with whom he felt an immediate aesthetic affinity: "Like myself, he wanted to write [blues] on a higher level. We had lots of talks about our ambitions to do great music on American themes."[320]

Johnson's family moved to Jersey City in 1902 and then to the Hell's Kitchen neighborhood of Manhattan in 1908. There he met and found increasing success within the lively ragtime scene in the city, working in small clubs and cabarets. Along with Luckey Roberts (1887–1968) and Willie "The Lion" Smith (1893–1973), Johnson developed the stride piano style. His *Carolina Shout*, recorded in 1921, became an instant classic of the genre.[321]

Along with his popular music pursuits, Johnson studied classical music with Italian émigré Bruto Giannini: Giannini used to "teach me my harmony and counterpoint for just a dollar a lesson. He taught me for four years. I had to throw away my fingering and learn to put the right finger on the right note. I was on Bach, and double thirds need good fingering."[322] Johnson included additional classical studies in a 1942 overview of his career, mentioning specifically E. A. Jackson (a pupil of Percy Goetschius [1853–1943]) and Mr. Markham, a Royal Fellow from Royal College, London.[323]

Gershwin's *Rhapsody in Blue* was a model for Johnson's first extended symphonic work, *Yamekraw*, composed in 1927 and premiered by W. C. Handy at Carnegie Hall in a 1928 concert tracing "the evolution of Negro music."[324] Influenced in part by conversations with Will Marion Cook, the work depicts a Gullah settlement on the coast of Georgia.[325] Originally composed and published for piano solo and later orchestrated by William Grant Still, it is an early example of Johnson's facility for incorporating all manner of African American styles, both rural and urban, in a kind of musical kaleidoscope. Howland describes it thus: "*Yamekraw*'s thematic materials were by no means Dvořák-prescribed melodic borrowings from the 'primitive' folk music of Gullah and Geechee communities. Nor were these materials employed within a high-art context governed by New Negro ideologies concerning the mastery of classical form and technique. [His approach] is filtered through the same sophisticated relation that existed between 1920s black musical theater and the Harlem stride idiom, on the one hand, and the source materials of these traditions, on the other, in ragtime and nineteenth-century brass band, dance, folk, and black religious music."[326] *Yamekraw* was adapted as the basis for two 1930s short films, for 1938 performances by the American Negro Ballet, and for Orson Welles's 1939 *Macbeth*.[327]

Harlem Symphony

The distinction between using ethnic sources as the basis for thematic material within a conventional symphonic idiom and manipulating those materials according to authentic popular

Table 5.13 The Symphonies of James Price Johnson (1894–1955)

Title and date	Movements	Instrumentation	Comments
Harlem Symphony (1932)	1. Maestoso—Allegro moderato—Andante grandioso: "A Subway Journey—Pennsylvania Station. 110th St., Jewish Neighborhood; 116th St., Spanish Neighborhood, 125th St. Shopping District . . . (Lady Shoppers Gossiping); 135th St., Negro Neighborhood; 7th Ave. Promenade" 2. Andante espressivo—"Song of Harlem" 3. Allegro con brio—"The Night Club" 4. Largo—Allegro—"In a Baptist Mission"	"Revised" version premiered in 1937: 1 Flt., 1 Ob., 1 Clar., 1 Bssn., 4 Sax., 3 Tpt., 2 Trom., Drum, Gui., Strgs., Bass (or Tuba), Pno. "Original" version performed in 1939 and 1945: Grand + Clar., Tpt. (or Cor.), Tuba, Perc.	The symphony exists in two manuscripts: a version for full orchestra in the Johnson family archives and a "revised" version for theater ensemble at the Jazz Institute Archive at Rutgers University. According to Howland/CONCERT JAZZ (p. 221), the orchestral score was Johnson's preferred version. First performance of Mvts. I and II: in the revised version, as part of the inaugural concert of the American Negro Ballet company and New York Negro Symphony Orchestra on November 21, 1937. First performance of the full symphony (original version): March 11, 1939, by the Brooklyn Civic Orchestra conducted by Paul Kosok. The second movement was transcribed for piano solo by Domenico Savino (presumably with Johnson's approval) and published in 1944 by Robbins Music under the title "April in Harlem." Otherwise unpublished.
Symphony in Brown (1935?)			Composed about 1935 according to Johnson, but it apparently is unfinished.

practice is important to keep in mind when approaching Johnson's 1932 *Harlem Symphony* (table 5.13). While the movements create the veneer of a conventional sonata cycle (a first-movement "statement," a lyrical second, a dancelike third, and a concluding apotheosis), the work can seem more like a series of episodes—and even within the episodes, a sense of rapidly changing vignettes. It is decidedly theatrical and even cinematic in its evocation of programmatic and semiprogrammatic scenes.

Popular influence is apparent on several fronts: Johnson's melodic language recalls "old Hollywood" scores, and his use of close brass and woodwind harmonies suggest the sound of the swing band. In addition, he often achieves traditional classical shifts—such as the move to a different key for a new theme—through jazz-based techniques such as the quick solo "break" within a jazz band. As Johnson stated, "From listening to classical records and concerts . . . I would learn concert effects and build them into blues and rags. . . . I'd make an abrupt change like I heard Beethoven do in a sonata."[328] In this way the two styles are fused more closely than in the works of Price or Dawson, which are more clearly in a conservative symphonic idiom but with themes that draw on folk traditions.

Formal analysis of individual movements can be tricky, both because of the ways in which Johnson's contemporary popular techniques obscured traditional formal structures and because of discrepancies among the two existing autograph scores (the symphony remains unpublished).[329] The first movement, "A Subway Journey," is intended to evoke a "programmatic travelogue through Harlem."[330] After a declamatory beginning, the jaunty *P*, with its back-and-forth chromatic figures, suggests the train leaving Penn Station; in the score the composer marked "train effect—wire brushes."[331] The second part of *P* features a soulful horn solo intended to suggest "110th St. Jewish Neighborhood" before we reboard the train. Clarinet arpeggios provide a transition to *S* ("116th St. Spanish Neighborhood"), scored for clarinet trio with accompanying wood blocks; the opening syncopated rhythmic gesture and half-step melodic movement tie it closely to *P*. The development section ("125th St. Shopping District") features a lighthearted dotted-note theme—also interspersed with clarinet interpolations—marked "lady shoppers gossiping." A variation of *S* decorated by swirling piccolo phrases ("135th St. Negro Neighborhood") ends with a bus horn effect in the trombones, leading to the recapitulation labeled "7th Ave. Promenade." Descending parallel chords bring us back to *S* in the original key, nicely answered by ascending parallel chords that in turn return us to the introductory music, now functioning as a coda. The ethnic touches within the scenes are lightly drawn, and the family resemblance between the themes result in the movement feeling integrated.[332]

The second movement, "Song of Harlem," paints a portrait of a romantic drama.[333] The first theme, presented in the oboe over pizzicato strings and guitar, suggests the blues with its lowered third, but he avoids the conventional 12-bar structure that William Grant Still used in the primary theme for his *Afro-American Symphony* (discussion follows). The second theme, "Harlem Love Song," answers the forlorn mood with a lush, sweeping string melody, harmonized with the added fifths, sevenths, and ninths of popular practice. The contrast between the two themes, and the extended transition passages between them, evoke the emotional ups and downs of a love story. Gann calls this a "sonata without development, as the recapitulation of the second theme is in the tonic key."[334]

The third movement, "The Night Club," is a series of dances that functions as a symphonic scherzo. The opening returns to the mood and rhythmic drive of the first movement, yet here the percussion effects evoke the shuffling of feet and the snapping of fingers. The limits of

Western classical analysis become apparent in this movement. The score labels the movement "3 Part Song Form / 2 Trios," but that designation fails to capture the way that Johnson creates a fluid series of dances with internal variations of repeated themes, decorated by Dixieland-style counterpoint, and separated by transitions featuring vivid instrumental effects—in one case, glissandi traded between winds and strings that suggest a dance twirl. The sum total is much more freewheeling than the clear divisions in a traditional minuet, in which the formal outlines of the dance are foregrounded.

The fourth movement, "Baptist Mission," is a set of variations on the spiritual "I Want Jesus to Walk with Me." Unlike the variations in Thomson's *Symphony on a Hymn Tune*, Johnson never abstracts the melody but rather uses it to build an increasingly intense scene. The movement begins with a slow, subdued statement of the spiritual and then introduces an ostinato pattern that underlies the first five variations. A horn solo in variation 1 suggests a single worshipper. It is followed by a livelier variation in strings with woodwind interjections. Muted trumpet and clarinet in the third variation introduce a jazzier feel, while the fourth builds the texture with woodwind arpeggios that suggest congregational swaying. That gives way to an even jazzier variation with trumpet syncopations. The sixth variation, "The Prayer," begins with a sequence of calls and responses among winds, and it features the phrase "Let My People Go" from the spiritual "Go Down, Moses." The energy builds for the last variation, and the piece ends with a series of modulations that make their way back to G minor before a final surprise ending on G major.

Years passed between the completion of the symphony and its 1937 premiere (of the first two movements) at a performance of the American Negro Ballet company; the occasion also marked the debut of the New York Negro Symphony Orchestra. The next few years brought relatively wide exposure of the full symphony, both in concerts and broadcasts.[335] After 1945, though, the piece fell into obscurity before conductor Marin Alsop rediscovered and championed the work in the 1990s. Like Dawson's *Negro Folk Symphony*, Johnson's *Harlem Symphony* richly deserves to be more than an occasional curiosity on concert programs.

Johnson maintained his ambitions as a composer of concert music; his efforts included an unfinished *Symphony in Brown* and *De Organizer*, a one-act opera with libretto by Langston Hughes.[336] He twice applied unsuccessfully for a Guggenheim Fellowship in 1937 and 1942.[337] He maintained an active presence in clubs and broadcast venues until a serious stroke in 1951 ended his career.

FLORENCE PRICE[338]

In a 1943 letter to Serge Koussevitzky—one of seven she would write the conductor, in a vain attempt to interest him in her music—Florence Beatrice Price (1887–1953) led off with what she later called "the worst": "Mr. dear Dr. Koussevitzky, To begin with I have two handicaps—those of sex and race. I am a woman; and I have some Negro blood in my veins."[339] Price persevered through those professional handicaps and personal challenges to build a successful compositional career. Although best known for her vocal music, she also wrote for orchestra (symphonies, concertos, and other works) and became the first Black woman to have a composition performed by a major symphony orchestra.

Price (born Florence Smith) grew up in Little Rock, Arkansas, when it was a hub of African American social activity, and Blacks in the middle class could enjoy comparative prosperity in the post-Reconstruction South. Her family's circle of friends included William Grant Still. In

Table 5.14 The Symphonies of Florence Price (1887–1953)

Title and date	Movements	Instrumentation	Comments
Symphony No. 1 in E Minor (1932)	1. Allegro ma non troppo 4/4 (300 mm.) 2. Largo, maestoso 3/2 (266 mm.) 3. Juba 4/8 (190 mm.) 4. Finale 6/8 (324 mm.)	Grand + Picc., Perc. (BD, Cym., Crash Cym., Cathedral Chimes, Tri., Large and Small African Drums, Bells, Wind Whistle), Cel.	First Prize, Rodman Wanamaker Competition, 1932. The first symphony by a Black woman to be performed by a major orchestra. First performance: June 15, 1933, by the Chicago Symphony Orchestra, conducted by Frederick Stock. Score published by G. Schirmer, 2018 (reprint of the edition in Brown and Shirley/PRICE).
Symphony No. 2 in G Minor (1930s)			Apparently completed, but lost or destroyed; only one page survives, dated "193–."
Symphony No. 3 in C Minor (1940)	1. Andante 4/4 (253 mm.) 2. Andante ma non troppo 3/4 (140 mm.) 3. Juba 4/8 (195 mm.) 4. Scherzo: Finale 6/8 (242 mm.)	Grand + Flt, Picc., EH, Bclar, Tpt., Tuba, Perc. (Tamb., SD, Cym., BD, Tri., Crash Cym., Wood Block, Sand Paper, Castanets, Slapstick, Gong, Orchestral Bells, Xylo.), Harp	First performance: November 6, 1940, by the Michigan WPA Symphony Orchestra, conducted by Valter Poole. Score published by G. Schirmer, 2018 (reprint of the edition in Brown and Shirley/PRICE).
Symphony No. 4 in D Minor (1945)	1. Tempo moderato 4/4 (280 mm.) 2. Andante cantabile 4/4 (117 mm.) 3. Juba 4/8 (183 mm.) 4. Scherzo 6/8 (305 mm.)	Grand + Flt, Picc., EH, Bclar, Tpt., Btrom, Tuba, Perc. (Cym., SD, BD, Tri., Tamb., Tam-tam, Wood Block, Chinese Drum, Indian Drum, Wire Brush, Small Crash Cym., Sand Paper, Gong, Orchestral Bells), Harp, Cel.	Thought lost for many years but rediscovered in 2009. First performance: May 12, 2018, by the Fort Smith Symphony (Arkansas), conducted by John Jeter. Score available through G. Schirmer.

1903, she began studies in the New England Conservatory, where she focused on organ performance, piano teaching, and—eventually—composition with George Whitefield Chadwick. After graduation, she taught in Little Rock and Atlanta before returning to Little Rock in 1912 to marry and start a family.

Her first husband, attorney Thomas Jewell Price, faced a slowdown in work after the implementation of Jim Crow laws throughout the South at the end of the nineteenth century. As a result of increasing racial violence in Little Rock, the family moved to Chicago in 1927, part of the Great Migration of African Americans from the South to the North in the first part of the twentieth century. Price became engaged in the city's Black musical scene, working through the Chicago Music Association and the National Association of Negro Musicians. As Rae Linda Brown notes, "During the 1930s, hardly a week went by without some mention of Price's performances in the local or national edition of [the Black newspaper] *Chicago Defender*."[340] Price received a Wanamaker Prize in 1932 for her first symphony. She was active in the Chicago Club of Women Organists, the members of which worked in classical ensembles, radio, theater, and churches.[341] She and Thomas Price divorced in 1931; after a brief second marriage ended in 1934, Price lived with a series of friends, including Estelle Bonds (mother of composer Margaret Bonds), through whom she met poets Countee Cullen and Langston Hughes. She continued to gain recognition in the United States and Europe until her sudden hospitalization and death in 1953.

Price wrote four symphonies (table 5.14). Except for a single page, the Second is lost, and, for many years, the Fourth was thought to have suffered the same fate. In a story almost too good to be true, a cache of the composer's manuscripts and personal documents was discovered by a couple preparing to renovate an abandoned and severely dilapidated house outside St. Anne, Illinois, which had served as Price's summer home.[342] Among the works retrieved were two violin concertos and the Fourth Symphony, which received its premiere in May 2018. The following discussion will deal with the First and Third Symphonies, with brief comments on the Fourth.

Symphony No. 1 in E Minor

Commentators have noted the influence of Dvořák's "New World" Symphony (as well as the music of Samuel Coleridge-Taylor) on Price's First Symphony in E minor (1931–32), premiered in 1933 by Frederick Stock and the Chicago Symphony Orchestra. Not only is Price's work in the same key but her core orchestral instrumentation resembles his: pairs of woodwinds, four horns, two trumpets, three trombones, tuba, timpani, percussion, and strings. The most noteworthy departure from the standard symphonic complement was in her choice of percussion instruments, including "large and small African drums" and a "Wind Whistle," used to striking effect in the third movement.

Both temporal and emotional weight lie in the first two movements. The first is almost statuesque in its classical proportions. *P* relies on a pentatonic scale, imprinting it with an unmistakable atmosphere of Americana (and Dvořákiana); Price harmonizes it with almost transparently spare string writing. The theme builds to a strong tutti restatement. *T* (m. 50) is similarly austere and direct, built from trading wind solos. The slower *S* (m. 71), in the relative G major, showcases the French horn in another gapped-scale theme. A rhythmically square chromatic descending line in m. 105 introduces *K*. The exposition repeats. The development inverts *P* and *S* and puts the material through a series of harmonic journeys before arriving at the retransition in m. 223. When the recapitulation begins in m. 231, Price marks the tempo

From 1920 to 1950 in the United States

Example 5.20 Price, Symphony No. 1, II, mm. 92–94

as "Andante maestoso," broadening the already expansive line of *P* with a tremolo countermelody.

The second movement is an expressive Largo in E major—the choice of tempo again recalling the "New World" Symphony. It begins with a slow hymn in the brass and African drum featuring call-and-response between the various performing forces. Price sets the short B section in the relative minor (m. 44). The hymn returns at m. 63; beginning at m. 90, it goes through a series of remarkable modulatory distortions (example 5.20). The combination of sophisticated Wagnerian harmony with the direct appeal of the hymn—Price was a noted composer of church music—is a consistent feature of her language and gives her music a distinctive sound.[343] Although technically in ABA form, to describe the movement thus obscures the rhapsodic extension of the second A section, which becomes so expansive that it nearly eclipses the rest of the movement. It ends with a restatement of the hymn over a gurgling clarinet obbligato and cathedral bells.

As Still did in the *Afro-American Symphony*, Price employs a distinctive vernacular genre for the Scherzo. She chooses a Juba (also known as "Pattin' Juba"), an antebellum dance imported to the United States by enslaved peoples from West Africa. It is a quick-tempo dance that in its original form relied heavily on body percussion: claps, stomps, and slapping of the chest, arms, and legs. It often involved singing, and, when available, accompaniment on banjo and fiddle. The Juba came to have an important role in public life as well, with its incorporation into minstrel shows in the nineteenth century. In many ways, the Juba resembles later forms like the cakewalk and classic ragtime with a stride bass and rapid, syncopated melodic material, all taking place in clearly articulated sections of 16 bars; the sound resembles that of a theater orchestra. For Price, this movement was also an occasion to use some of the more exotic effects in her orchestration: for example, the Wind Whistle creates a sense of the whooping calls that one might have expected during an actual Juba dance.

The Finale is surprisingly compact in comparison with the proportions of the first and second movements. It is basically a rondo in E minor, with its dancelike main theme a driving triplet figure first articulated by the violins, flute, and oboe. Rhythmically and melodically, it evokes an Irish dance or a sea shanty, thus distinguishing it from the syncopation of the Juba dance. The opening figure recurs at mm. 65 and 166, and by m. 295 it forms the basis of a coda that drives the symphony to its forceful conclusion. Contrast is provided in more lyrical sections featuring solo winds.

Public reaction to the symphony was enthusiastic: "Price, elegantly dressed in a long white gown, was recalled to the stage again and again and acknowledged the enthusiastic applause." Reviews were laudatory in both the black and white press: African American writers focused on the symbolism of the event ("there was a feeling of awe as the Chicago Symphony Orchestra, an aggregation of master musicians of the white race . . . swung in to the beautiful, harmonious strains of a composition by a Race woman") while white critics celebrated the music ("It is a faultless work . . . that speaks its own message with restraint but yet with passion. Miss Price's symphony is worthy of a place in the repertory").[344] On the other hand, Alain Locke—known popularly as the dean of the Harlem Renaissance—expressed disappointment at the absence of folk theme quotations, a blues progression, or other overt racial markers (he ignored the Juba, perhaps because Price did not incorporate an actual dance melody). In his book *The Negro and His Music* (1936), Locke implicitly criticized Price's symphony for being, in his opinion, no different from any other (white) symphony: "In the straight classical idiom and form, Mrs. Price's work vindicates the Negro composer's right, at choice, to go up Parnassus by the broad high road of classicism rather than the narrower, more hazardous, but often more rewarding path of racialism. At the pinnacle, the paths converge, and the attainment becomes, in the last analysis, neither racial nor national, but universal music."[345]

Third Symphony in C Minor

Commissioned by the Federal Music Project, Price's Third Symphony received its first performance with the Detroit Civic Orchestra in November 1940. In a letter to Michigan Works Progress Administration (WPA) orchestra administrator Frederick Schwass, Price describes her approach to the issue of musical identity in this work:

> The Symphony No. 3 in C Minor was composed in the late summer of 1938, laid aside for a year and then revised. It is intended to be Negroid in character and expression. In it no attempt, however, has been made to project Negro music solely in the purely traditional manner. None of the themes are adaptations or derivations of folk songs.
>
> The intention behind the writing of this work was a not too deliberate attempt to picture a cross section of present-day Negro life and thought with its heritage of that which is past, paralleled or influenced by concepts of the present day.[346]

Price's description of "present-day Negro life and thought" is important in her evolving aesthetic. As Rae Linda Brown points out, Price "turned away from the compositional procedures she had used in the past; she no longer composed melodies and rhythms closely aligned with African-American spirituals and black folk dance."[347] Yet *pace* Locke, this did not mean that

Price rejected her cultural heritage; rather, much as Harris and Antheil had done, she sought to create a more generalized but recognizably American sound (or African American sound in her case) that revealed its identity without recourse to quotations. This larger tapestry, built of a contemporary rather than nostalgic employment of ethnic materials, took the form of melding urban and rural sources, as she explained in a 1941 letter to Serge Koussevitzky: "I tried to portray a cross section of Negro life and psychology as it is today, influenced by urban life north of the Mason and Dixon line. It is not 'program' music. I merely had in mind the life and music of the Negro of today and for that reason treated my themes in a manner different from what I would have done if I had centered my attention upon the religious themes of antebellum days, or yet the rag-time and jazz which followed; rather a fusion of these, colored by present cultural influences."[348]

Price's First and Third Symphonies are similar in certain respects. Both consist of the conventional four movements, the first two significantly longer than the others. Both feature strong themes and effective scoring, including extensive use of solo winds. Markedly different in the later symphony is the more thoroughgoing developmental language. The clear, classical proportions of the thematic sections in the First Symphony have been exchanged for a more fantasia-like development of ideas, with numerous stops and starts that give the movements a somewhat episodic structure. Along with the solo wind passages that characterized the First Symphony, we hear frequent uses of alternating choirs.

The work is more complex right from the beginning. An eighteen-measure Andante introduction, scored for brass and woodwinds and featuring chromatic chords in the winds, includes a fair amount of passing dissonance that signals that this is no purely folksy work. The tempo changes to Allegro and *P* is introduced through a dialogue between strings. While not as obviously ethnic as *1/P* of the First Symphony, it does make use of pentatonic shapes, syncopation, and brief moments of call and response between and within instrumental choirs. A false second theme (m. 45) moves to G minor before yielding to the more lyrical *S* in E-flat major (mm. 78–87), which hints at Dvořák but develops a bluesy extension on trombone (example 5.21). There is an extended transitional section after *S*, which in a way justifies the comparatively brief development section. After the recapitulation, a 41-measure coda presents the themes in augmentation and diminution in four contrasting episodes.

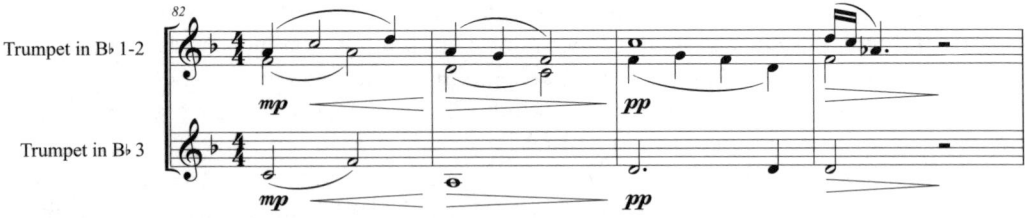

Example 5.21 Price, Symphony No. 3, I, mm. 82–85

The second movement, Andante ma non troppo, is in ABA (A♭-G-A♭) form, yet the number of melodies—two themes in the A section—and the recognizable profile of the opening motive combine to create a formal structure that Rae Linda Brown calls "quasi-rondo."[349] The movement features some polytonality, especially in the B section, as well as moments of Impressionistic scoring. A striking example occurs early in the B section, when the violins answer the lyrical theme with eerie parallel harmonies and whole-tone scales.[350] The movement ends with a hymn, emphasized by a closing drawn-out plagal cadence.

As in the First Symphony, the E-flat major Scherzo is a rondo based on a Juba dance; here it is more complex, with unequal phrases and cross-rhythms. The dance also has a more sophisticated melodic and harmonic language: a lowered third in the theme and a jazzy harmonic progression combine to integrate the urban blues into the rural juba; in addition, Price modulates freely to distant keys. The B section includes castanets and a more complex texture with multiple percussion layers. After a brief reprise of A, a quiet episode in the C section features trumpets with tin mutes and a Latin *habanera* rhythm followed by bluesy interjections in the woodwinds and strings; the effect resembles the Spanish tinge (a passage of Afro-Cuban rhythm) that "Jelly Roll" Morton (1890–1941) considered essential for blues and jazz and that appears in works like his "New Orleans Blues" and W. C. Handy's "St. Louis Blues."[351] The final reprise of A changes the meter from the prevailing 4/8 to 2/4. The scoring includes much percussion and unique effects such as an episode for flute and xylophone.

A jig in sonata form, the fourth movement recalls the Finale of the First Symphony in style and form; its triplets are equally driving but more tightly constructed. It features numerous antiphonal passages between strings and winds. As in the third movement, Price's melodic language updates a basic folk outline; here, *P* incorporates the seventh of the scale; as Brown notes, it "gives the otherwise ordinary figure much-needed flavor."[352] *S* (m. 22) is introduced by the English horn and trombone; a chromatic accompaniment figure in the bassoons creates some dissonance and emphasizes the modal ambiguity of the theme. The use of chromaticism remains a consistent feature during the development and lends depth and piquancy as both themes are fragmented, combined, and recombined. An extended coda ends with a dramatically slower six-measure series of alternating C major/C minor chords with chromatic violin underlay, concluding in intense repeated C minor chords; the ending of this symphony thus displays a *gravitas* lacking in the First.

In 2018, the Fort Smith (Arkansas) Symphony, under the direction of John Jeter, premiered and recorded the recently discovered Fourth Symphony (1945), edited from the manuscript by composer Miho Sasaki. According to Jeter, the work represents a logical continuation of Price's style. It is in four movements. The first, as in the other symphonies, is a big and "almost Wagnerian" movement; the main theme bears a resemblance to the spiritual "Wade in the Water." The second movement is a Dvořákian lullaby with variations, though in places it "goes into a jazz direction." Once more the dance movement is a Juba, though "more sophisticated, urban, and complex" than the parallel movements in the earlier symphonies.[353] The fourth movement, a scherzo in 6/8, wanders into a kind of improvisatory dissonance, which Jeter attributes to Price's background as an organist.[354]

Critical reception for Price's music tended to be favorable, but, as her letters to Koussevitzky indicate, she understood and articulated the particular dilemmas that a female Black composer confronted. Like much of the midcentury symphonic repertoire discussed in this chapter, her works have until recently been mostly overlooked as regular features on concert programs. Happily, however, the recent publications and recordings are reigniting interest in Price's works as more than historical curiosities.

WILLIAM GRANT STILL

William Grant Still (1895–1978) is often called the dean of African American composers—a moniker that speaks to the way his racial identity was easily absorbed into existing institutional structures. His reputation is based primarily on the *Afro-American Symphony*, which in 1931 became the first symphony by a Black composer to be performed by a major American orchestra (the Rochester Philharmonic under Howard Hanson). Yet Still's *oeuvre*—including his symphonies—has much more to offer, both as artistic achievement and as historical record, than such a single-minded focus might suggest. He was one of the few artists who bridged the relatively independent creative worlds of Greenwich Village and Harlem in the 1920s, and New York and Hollywood afterward. In all, he wrote five symphonies, each with a subtitle: "Afro-American," "Song of a New Race" (No. 2, 1947), "Western Hemisphere" (No. 5, 1945, rev. 1970), "Autochthonous" (No. 4, 1947), and "The Sunday Symphony" (No. 3, 1958) (see table 5.15).

Born in Mississippi, Still moved to Ohio to attend Wilberforce University in 1911. After several years working in Dayton and Columbus, during which time he also worked as an arranger for W. C. Handy, Still moved to New York in 1919, living and working in Harlem in both art and popular music venues.[355] At the same time that he became increasingly known for his arranging skills in the black jazz and musical theater worlds, he took composition lessons both with George Whitefield Chadwick (as had Florence Price fifteen years earlier) and with the ultramodernist Edgard Varèse (1883–1965). After winning a Guggenheim in 1934, Still left New York and resettled in Los Angeles, where he composed for film and television and wrote several operas. His popularity dwindled in the 1950s and 1960s, until a resurgence of interest in his work emerged in the years surrounding his centennial.[356]

Still's work in the 1920s, after his studies with Varèse, reflected the ultramodern style of the time, combining new approaches to timbre and harmony with elements of jazz. In 1925, the International Composers' Guild presented his now lost *From the Land of Dreams* for winds, strings, percussion, and three female voices (used instrumentally). Music critic Paul Rosenfeld wrote that "the use of jazz motives in the last section of [this] work is more genuinely musical than any to which they have been put, by Milhaud, Gershwin, or anyone else."[357] Olin Downes, being somewhat nonplussed by the same work, wrote in a contrasting, conservative light, "Still knows the rollicking and often original and entertaining music performed at negro revues. But Mr. Varese [*sic*], Mr. Still's teacher, has driven all that out of him. Is Mr. Still unaware that the cheapest melody in the revues he has orchestrated has more originality and inspiration in it than the curious noises he has manufactured? . . . This is music unprofitable to compose or listen to."[358]

Still came to agree: "It is not Still but Varèse who speaks in *From the Land of Dreams*. The realization of this fact enabled me to see that it was necessary for me to find an idiom that would be modern but not so much so that it would fail to be recognized at once as Negroid."[359] His multifaceted training and experience prompted a self-conscious contemplation of his musical language and sparked a multiyear transition to a style that was at once more traditionally symphonic and ethnically infused. For the League of Composers, Still composed *Levee Land* (1925), which premiered in Aeolian Hall on an International Composers Guild concert featuring Broadway star Florence Mills. The work is often cited as an example of Still's incorporation of African American elements into a dissonant, modernist musical context. He uses the voice of a "backslider" (a singer recounting that she once had religion but then lost it, explicitly blaming jazz). Still recalled that "*Levee Land* was a step nearer the idiom I was seeking, yet it was still too extreme."[360]

Catherine Parsons Smith explains the composer's dilemma this way: "Still came to understand that (1) he wanted to write concert music whose African American character was clearly

Table 5.15 The Symphonies of William Grant Still (1895–1978)

Title and date	Movements	Instrumentation	Comments
Afro-American Symphony (Symphony No. 1; 1930, rev. 1969–70)	1. Moderato assai ("Longing") C (136 mm.) 2. Adagio ("Sorrow") C (74 mm.) 3. Animato ("Humor") C (100 mm.) 4. Lento, con risoluzione ("Aspiration") 3/4 (219 mm.)	Grand + Flt., EH, 2 Clar., Tpt., Tuba, Perc. (Vbp., Tri., Wire Brush, Cym., Small Cym., SD, BD, Gong, Bells), Harp, Cel., Banjo	"With humble thanks to God, the source of inspiration." Originally dedicated to Irving Schwerké, but the dedication was not retained in the 1935 publication or in the subsequent revisions. It was the first symphony by a Black American composer to be performed by a leading orchestra. Each movement is preceded by a poem by Paul Laurence Dunbar. First performance: October 28, 1931, by the Rochester Philharmonic, conducted by Howard Hanson, as part of the American Composers' Concerts. Published by J. Fischer and Bros., 1935; revised edition by G. Schirmer/Novello, 1970.
Symphony No. 2 in G Minor, "Song of a New Race" (1937)	1. Slowly 12/8 (156 mm.) 2. Slowly and deeply expressive 4/4 (138 mm.) 3. Moderately fast ₵ (164 mm.) 4. Moderately slow 4/4 (135 mm.)	Grand + Flt. (doubling Picc.), EH, 2 Clar., Tpt., Tuba, Perc. (SD, BD, Small and Large Suspended Cym., Crash Cym., Vbp.), Harp, Cel.	Dedicated to Kosabel Morse Jones. Still regarded this work as the third member of a trilogy about the Black experience in the United States. The orchestral suite *Africa* (1928) portrays the ancestral continent; the *Afro-American Symphony* describes "the American colored man of yesteryear, not far removed from slavery"; and the present work depicts "American colored man of today; in so many instances a totally new individual produced through the fusion of white, Indian, and Negro bloods." First performance: December 10, 1937, by the Philadelphia Orchestra, conducted by Leopold Stokowski. Score published by WGS Music, 2000.
Symphony No. 3, "The Sunday Symphony" (1958)	1. Moderately ("The Awakening") C—2/4 (204 mm.) 2. Very slowly ("Prayer") C (79 mm.) 3. Gaily ("Relaxation") 2/4 (72 mm.) 4. Resolutely ("Day's End—and a New Beginning") ₵ (71 mm.)	Grand + Flt. (doubling Picc.), EH, Clar., Tpt., Tuba, Perc. (Bells, Tri., Tamb, SD, Small, Medium, and Large Tom-toms, Suspended Cym., Cym.), Harp, Cel.	Dedicated to the composer's friend Christian Dupriez. Depicts a day in the life of a devout worshipper. Still wrote this symphony to replace the withdrawn Symphony No. 3 (which he later revised as Symphony No. 5). First performance: February 12, 1984, by the North Arkansas Symphony, conducted by Carlton Woods. Materials on rental from Carl Fischer.

Symphony No. 4, "Autochthonous" (1947)	1. Moderately ("The spirit of optimism and energy") 4/4 (181 mm.) 2. Slowly ("Pensive, later animated in a folksy way") 4/4 (121 mm.) 3. With a Graceful Lilt ("Humorous") ₵ (112 mm.) 4. Slowly and Reverently ("Love of Mankind") 4/4 (209 mm.) Movement subtitles are by Still.	Grand + Flt. (doubling Picc.), EH, Clar., Cbssn., Tpt., Tuba, Perc. (Glsp., Chime, Tri., Wire Brush, Drums, Military Drum, Cym, Gong), Harp, Cel.	Dedicated to Maurice Kessler, Still's teacher at Oberlin. Intended to represent "the spirit of the American people." First performance: March 18, 1951, by the Oklahoma City Symphony Orchestra, conducted by Victor Alessandro. Materials on rental from Carl Fischer.
Symphony No. 5, "Western Hemisphere" (1945, rev. 1970)	1. Briskly ("The vigorous, life-sustaining forces of the Hemisphere") 4/4 (105 mm.) 2. Slowly, and with Utmost Grace ("The natural beauties of the Hemisphere") 4/4 (97 mm.) 3. Energetically ("The nervous energy of the Hemisphere") 9/8 (118 mm.) 4. Moderately ("The overshadowing spirit of kindness and justice in the Hemisphere") 4/4 (165 mm.) Movement subtitles are by the composer's wife, Verna Arvey.	Grand + Flt. (doubling Picc.), EH, Clar., Tpt., Tuba, Perc. (Bells, Chime, Mrb., SD, Cym., Large Suspended Cym., Small Draped Cym.), Harp, Cel.	Originally Still's Third Symphony, but the composer withdrew it and wrote "The Sunday Symphony" in its place. He revised the score in 1970 and released it as his Fifth Symphony. First performance: November 9, 1970, by the Oberlin College Orchestra, conducted by Robert Baustian, as part of a celebration of the composer's 75th birthday. Score published by WGS Music, n.d.

recognizable to white audiences and (2) a "serious" African American style could not, by its nature, use much of the ultramodern dissonance to which Varèse had introduced him and at the same time reach the audience with which he sought to communicate."[361]

Looking back with the benefit of hindsight, Still summarized his creative goals as they stood in 1930: "After this period [of composing 'ultramodern' music], I felt that I wanted for a while to devote myself to writing racial music. And here, because of my own racial background, a great many people decided that I ought to confine myself to that sort of music. In that too, I disagreed. I was glad to write Negro music then, and I still do it when I feel so inclined, for I have a great love and respect for the idiom. But it has certainly not been the *only* musical idiom to attract me."[362]

The result of Still's contemplations was his First Symphony, the *Afro-American*: a consciously "racial" work that melded indigenous idioms with symphonic tradition. But while his First and Second Symphonies (and the Third, to a lesser extent) embrace their African American identity, the Fourth and Fifth branch out to embrace other cultures as well.

Symphony No. 1, Afro-American Symphony

The *Afro-American Symphony* (1930), then, marks a turning point for Still personally and for the greater public dialogue about American—and African American—identity within the genre. Still was clear about his aims: "I knew I wanted to write a symphony; I knew that it had to be an *American* work; and I wanted to demonstrate how the *Blues*, so often considered a lowly expression, could be elevated to the highest musical level."[363] While the notion of "elevating" African American material might seem condescending today, Still's remarks reveal his sincere opinion that the symphony genre represented "the highest musical level" and his desire to achieve both racial authenticity and aesthetic transformation.

The *Afro-American Symphony* is in four movements, with eleven woodwinds, eleven brass, strings, three percussionists, celeste, harp, and tenor banjo; only the banjo forms a marked departure from other instruments in use during the period. In his "Note on the *Afro-American Symphony*," the composer suggested that the movements respectively correspond to "Longing," "Sorrow," "Humor," and Aspiration."[364] While not suggesting programmatic content, the semidescriptive epigrams at least imply an emotive tone. To press the point further, Still included in the published score four poetic fragments by Paul Laurence Dunbar (1872–1906). The first three are written in dialect; the last is not:

> I. Moderato assai
> "All my life long twell de night has pas'
> Let de wo'k come ez it will,
> So dat I fin' you, my honey at las',
> Somewhaih des ovah de hill."
>
> II. Adagio
> "It's moughty tiahsome layin' 'roun'
> Dis sorrer-laden earfly groun',
> An' oftimes I thinks, thinks I
> 'Twould be a sweet t'ing des to die
> An' go 'long home."
>
> III. Animato
> "An' we'll sout ouah halleluyahs,
> On dat might reck'nin day."

IV. Lento, con rizoluzione
"Be proud, my Race, in mind and soul.
Thy name is writ on Glory's scroll
In characters of fire.
High 'mid the clouds of Fame's bright sky
Thy banner's blazoned folds now fly,
And truth shall lift them higher."

The symphony follows a straightforward formal plan with a sonata-form movement, slow movement, quick third movement, and finale.[365] The opening movement rapidly establishes the vernacular languages that will permeate the work. After a short invocation on English horn, *P* is an original 12-bar blues melody in A-flat major presented twice, both iterations in standard call-and-response style (the first given by muted trumpet answered by horns, the second by clarinet answered by frisky countermotives in the woodwinds). At Reh. 5, a variation of *P* leads into *S*, an oboe melody over harp chords decorated with a flute filigree. According to the composer, this melody is in the style of a spiritual, a short ABA structure in G major in which Still moves both melodically and texturally from earthier blues and spiritual roots into a "sweet jazz" style. The somewhat rhapsodic development is based entirely on *P*. At Reh. 11, the recapitulation starts with *S* in the strings in A-flat minor rather than major. *P* returns in swing rhythm: Still directs that the dotted eighth-sixteenths be performed as triplet quarter-eighths. The modular return of material in African American idioms (blues, spirituals) and the call-and-response instrumentation infuse the classical sonata form with the ongoing, improvisatory feel of Black vernacular. A short coda features a descending *P* in the bass clarinet that sputters to a last **pp**; offbeat vibraphone interjections color the final chord.

The second movement opens with a blues-laden theme marked doloroso: first a duet between the flute and oboe, it gradually incorporates interjections from solo violin and viola, clarinets, English horn, and bassoons, which is freely developed against an increasingly chromatic harmony (example 5.22). Still's experience as an arranger is strongly in evidence in this expressive movement. *S* is introduced on flute; because it shares the distinctive opening rhythmic gesture of the first theme, it does not establish the classic tension between the two themes and thus the movement feels more like an ongoing conversation—an effect amplified by the back-and-forth nature of the orchestration.

Example 5.22 Still, Symphony No. 1, *II/P* (Reh. 15)

For his Scherzo, Still employs a distinctively Black vernacular genre: a ring shout in duple meter, evoking a genre that Black composers drew on to depict moments of jubilation, as in Scott Joplin's ring chorus from *Treemonisha*. The clear resemblance of the flute melody to Gershwin's "I Got Rhythm" (five before Reh. 23) has inspired much commentary; it remains unclear whether the resemblance is coincidental, and if not, which composer created it first.[366]

The scoring prominently features the banjo and quickly dampened small cymbals. Harmonically, too, Still reaches into the popular toolbox, as he employs secondary dominants in a jazzy vein.[367] The coda includes a reference to *I/P*.

Still makes the unusual choice to end the symphony with a predominantly slow movement. The tone is in keeping with the aspirational (rather than melancholy) tenor of Dunbar's poetry. The change from ethnic dialect to high-flown language creates a not-so-subtle implication that an evolution toward elevated rhetorical expression by African Americans would in turn create elevated social standing. Still describes the music as "largely a retrospective viewing of the earlier movements with the exception of its principal theme."[368] As befits the chosen Dunbar text, the form is relatively rhapsodic, with an exposition of two themes, a Vivace section that elaborates on both, and then a closing Maestoso. *IV/S* is a variation of *I/P*, the blues theme from the first movement. Warm lyricism alternates with bluesy touches; Slattery notes the frequent use of chords with both major and minor thirds.[369] The muscular, rhythmic ending is in F minor.

The symphony received a warm welcome when Howard Hanson premiered it with the Rochester Philharmonic on October 28, 1931. One critical voice complained about the generally rhapsodic approaches to the sonata-form movements (as opposed to a more conspicuously disciplined formal approach); as a result, he pronounced the work "not cyclical or symphonic in the accepted sense. . . . [It] would be more acceptable had it been called a suite."[370] Nevertheless, the symphony went on to enjoy numerous performances throughout the United States in the 1930s. Hanson took the work with him on a tour of Europe, and when he conducted the Scherzo in Berlin with the Berlin Philharmonic in early 1933, the audience demanded an encore; this proved to Hanson that "music which has its roots deep in the human heart is the most personal, the most national, and also, the most universal."[371]

The *Afro-American Symphony* appeared at the same moment that some of the most significant ultramodernist works emerged from New York in 1930 and 1931, such as Aaron Copland's *Piano Variations*, Ruth Crawford's *String Quartet 1931*, and Edgard Varèse's *Ionisation*. Carol Oja writes that "Still's *Afro-American Symphony* has been seen as part of a separate story from these other landmark works of the early 1930s. Yet it, like them, was a product of the vigorous young composers' movement of the previous decade, a movement that brought figures such as Copland, Henry Cowell, and Virgil Thomson their first public recognition. Still rose to prominence alongside them. Yet like most artistic figures in Harlem, he was forced to straddle two distinct yet intersecting worlds, one black and the other white."[372]

This sometimes uncomfortable artistic coexistence colored the perception of Still's music in the years surrounding the composition of the *Afro-American Symphony*. In 1933, Henry Cowell noted this split personality when he wrote that "William Grant Still, Negro, uses his people's themes and feelings as a base for his music, which is otherwise in modern style with some rather vague European influence. Perhaps he possesses the beginnings of a genuine new style. At present, however, his works are unformed and contain many crudities."[373]

Still's later symphonies continue the style of the *Afro-American*, though the specific ethnic references gradually broaden from his own race to a more all-embracing cultural focus. Like the earlier symphony, they follow the four-movement classical structure, with a free approach to individual movement forms. They were designed as abstract pieces, with programs added after the fact. They continue to demonstrate expert orchestration: warm string writing, much focus on solo instruments (especially winds), and some popular touches such as trumpets with mute and cymbals that evoke jazz or club bands. Still's gift for lyricism with vernacular elements (blue notes, pentatonic melodies) comes through, no doubt honed by his work in film.

The scherzos continue to draw on particular urban African American inflections: ragtime, jazz, and Big Band.

Symphony No. 2 and No. 3

Still composed his Symphony No. 2 in G Minor ("Song of a New Race") in 1937. He considered it the third of a trilogy, following *Africa* (1928) and the *Afro-American Symphony*: the new work represented "an extension or evolution of [the *Afro-American Symphony*, which] represented the Negro of days not far removed from the Civil War. The Symphony in G Minor represents the American colored man of today; in so many instances a totally new individual produced through the fusion of white, Indian, and Negro bloods."[374] It was premiered by Leopold Stokowski and Philadelphia Orchestra in 1937. In the first movement, the lilting, pastoral *P* bears some resemblances to *IV/P* of the *Afro-American*. The second movement is deeply expressive, in sharp contrast to the third movement, a moderately fast cakewalk with jazzy inflections. As in the preceding symphony, the work ends somewhat unconventionally with a moderately slow finale.

The Third Symphony ("The Sunday Symphony," 1958) was never performed in Still's lifetime, premiering only in 1984. In 1945 he released a symphony called "Western Hemisphere" as his third symphony; but he subsequently withdrew the piece for revision and composed the "Sunday Symphony" in its place (the new version of the "Western Hemisphere" Symphony would appear in 1970 as Symphony No. 5). According to the composer, the "Sunday Symphony" expresses a day in the life of a devout worshipper. The first movement, "Awakening," features an energetic, catchy tune. The second, "Prayer," features a Dvořákian melody in English horn slightly altered by blue notes. The third, "Relaxation," is a delightful scherzo with tambourine and triangle. The fourth, "Day's End and a New Beginning," features elements typical of African American worship: pentatonic themes, modal harmonies, and extensive call-and-response effects.

Symphony No. 4, "Autochthonous"

Composed in 1947, Still's Symphony No. 4 premiered in 1951 with Victor Alessandro and the Oklahoma Symphony Orchestra. According to program notes by the composer and his wife Verna Arvey, the somewhat cumbersome title means "indigenous," chosen to represent "the spirit of the American people" as well as "the fusion of musical cultures in North America."[375] The composition is tonal (D minor/major) and Neoromantic, but it uses a harmonic vocabulary that goes beyond the earlier symphonies to include quartal chords and polychords.[376] As in his first symphony, classical forms are treated with some improvisational freedom.

According to Still and Arvey's note, the first movement "exemplifies the feeling of optimism and energy: the American ability to 'get things done.'" The form is a modified sonata-allegro with two themes, variations on both, and a coda. An introductory motive sets the "indigenous" tone in both rhythmic and melodic profiles. *P*, which marks a strong contrast with the introductory motive, is given out by the strings; as in the *Afro-American Symphony*, it recurs in subsequent movements. Its recognizable "short-long" rhythms serve as both a point of aural reference for the listener and a formal unifying gesture. *S* is related to the introductory motive.

Still goes on to describe the second movement as "more pensive, then, in the 'second subject,' animated in a folky way." The pensive mood begins immediately, with a series of woodwind chords that are dissonant and harmonically ambiguous. Both the introductory idea and the much brisker *S* are related to *I/P*. All the thematic ideas undergo transformation; a return to the pensive mood makes this movement feel more like an ABA form than a conventional sonata-allegro. Harp and celeste give the last chords an ethereal quality.

The brief third movement is "humorous and unmistakably typical of our country and its rhythms." It is a jazz scherzo, recalling the style of what were called the big bands. The opening with wire brush on military drum underlays a jaunty clarinet motive before yielding to *P,* which evokes the film sound of westerns and reminds us that Still was living in Los Angeles and working in that industry. *S* is another variant of *I/P*.

The fourth movement, a modified rondo, expresses "the warmth and spiritual side of the American people—their love of mankind." *P* alternates with episodes drawn from thematic transformations of *I/P*. Frequent textural and harmonic changes reinforce the episodic nature of the Finale. As Paul Slattery notes, as a result of more adventurous harmonic language, "the tension-release cycle has a greater range of extremes."[377] Chimes and a brass chorale provide a conventionally uplifting ending.

Symphony No. 5, "The Western Hemisphere"

In Still's Fifth Symphony, "The Western Hemisphere" (1945, rev. 1970), he again turns to a semiprogrammatic intersection of cultural and natural landscapes. Brief first and third movements are followed by more substantial movements. Still wrote the following prefatory note to the score:

> One day in eternity has come to its close. A mighty civilization has begun, come to a climax, and declined. In the darkness, the past is swept away. When the new day dawns, the lands of the Western Hemisphere are raised from the bosom of the Atlantic. They are endowed by the Great Intelligence who created them and who controls their destiny with virtues unlike any that have gone before: qualities which will find counterparts in the characters of the men who will inhabit them eventually, and who will make them the abode of freedoms, of friendship, of the sharing of resources and achievements of the mind and of the spirit. These are our fellow-Americans in Latin America, Canada, and the islands of the Western Seas, who are today working with us to convert our ideals into realities.[378]

Verna Arvey created descriptive subtitles for each movement. The opening of the first ("The vigorous, life-sustaining forces of the Hemisphere") is striking: a melodically restless motive becomes increasingly chromatic over an unchanging but similarly restless harmony. Throughout the movement, rhythmic impulses—especially offbeats—prevail, thus providing a sense of forward motion. The second movement, marked "slowly, and with utmost grace," celebrates "the natural beauties of the Hemisphere." Tonic beats on harp and marimba impart both stability and momentum to a graceful string melody. Masterful orchestration employs rotating instrumental colors to create constantly shifting lights and shadows. The third movement—"the nervous energy of the Hemisphere"—returns to the rhythmic energy of the first movement, its two-note motive charging to a final minor chord. The Finale depicts "the overshadowing spirit of kindness and justice in the Hemisphere," with a lively theme building to a triumphant climax. As in the Fourth Symphony, Still's use of chimes at the end contributes to a sense of spirituality.

All Still's symphonies create an optimistic picture of America and the American spirit. In no way blind to the racial issues in America, as his choral work *And They Lynched Him on a Tree* (1940) attests, his music nonetheless projects a conviction that progress is possible. And, as the later symphonies demonstrate, Still's racial focus broadened to a more universal idealism: "If I have a wish to express, it would be that my music may serve a purpose larger than mere music. If it will help in some way to bring about better interracial understanding in America and in other countries, then I will feel that the work is justified. . . . We are all human beings, citizens, children of God. We need to learn more about each other so that we all may live together in peace and mutual appreciation. Can music help accomplish this? I believe it can."[379]

Howard Hanson summed up the nature of Still's contributions: "William Grant Still's place in music history as the dean of America's Negro composers is assured. It is a proud distinction, but it is not enough. For Still is, above all, an American composer, interpreting the spiritual values of his own land through his own brand of personal genius."[380]

Émigrés

From colonial days Americans turned to Europeans—both visitors and émigrés—to help build a musical infrastructure worthy of new-world cultural ambitions. As chapter 3 discussed, the last quarter of the nineteenth century saw the expansion of both institutional and human capacity. The nascent national autonomy would be complicated, however, by twentieth-century world affairs: as a result of the Russian Revolution and the rise of Nazi Germany, the number of émigré musicians entering the United States actually increased during the decades before midcentury.[381] Along with a host of lesser names came composers at the highest level of international reputation: Igor Stravinsky, Arnold Schoenberg, Béla Bartók (1881–1945), Paul Hindemith (1895–1963), Darius Milhaud, and Bohuslav Martinů. Amplifying the impact of sheer numbers was an impressive geographical reach, as they settled not only in New York but also New England, Oregon, southern California, and points between. In addition to their high-profile careers, émigrés made a long-term impact because many shaped the next generation of American composers through their work at universities, in film, and on Broadway.

Whether spurred by economic opportunity, political oppression, or conscience, each émigré faced the twin challenges of loss and reinvention: "They all had to abandon their homes, their positions, their countries, their friends, their business, their fortunes. They all had to go abroad, try to start life anew, and generally at a much lower level of living, of influence, of esteem; many even had to change their occupation and to suffer humiliation."[382] Layered onto these struggles was the ambivalent reception by Americans who expressed concern that these Europeans would eclipse homegrown talent on concert programs and thus set back the progress made in building a national musical identity. Yet the underrepresentation of American music, especially on symphonic programs, was not the product of a simple "us versus them" scenario; rather, as Ernst Krenek reflected two decades later, it mirrored the tension between modern music and more accessible styles discussed in the introduction to this chapter: "American composers may well have been justified in their grievances. Still, their colleagues that emigrated from Europe were scarcely able to convince them that conductors were disposed not so much against modern American music as against modern music in general. In place of Piston and Harris it was not Schoenberg or Bartók that got played, but Brahms and Tschaikovsky. Yet the prevailing mood of the time darkened the facts of the case and one tended to look upon the European exodus with more scruples than it deserved."[383]

Each émigré of course brought an individual musical style to the United States and, once here, faced the challenge of navigating the process of artistic growth under far different circumstances. As Reinhold Brinkmann observes, "The central problem was to keep a balance between the preservation of an artistic identity based on the European tradition and the necessary adaptation to the new cultural and professional situation in America."[384] The academics were, naturally, more oriented toward traditional genres such as the symphony, but symphonies by film composers—many of whom, like Erich Wolfgang Korngold, had abandoned established careers in chamber and orchestral music—are also notable legacies of the era. They made Hollywood a major world cultural center ("Weimar on the Pacific," in Ehrhard Bahr's phrase) and through their dominance of the film music industry were creating an American voice that reached millions.[385] Indeed, émigrés writing for the silver screen were responsible not only for the majority of symphonic music heard in the United States but also for shaping the sound that came to identify the nation, both at home and to the rest of the world. In addition to Korngold, notable figures include Max Steiner (1888–1971), Miklós Rózsa (1907–95), Ernst Toch (1887–1964), and Franz Waxman (1906–67).

It is difficult to generalize about the impact of the United States on émigré composers because of their number and variety. They came at different points in their careers, with different aesthetic goals, and found themselves in different institutional contexts. Some composers, like Milhaud and Martinů, wrote their first symphonies either just before or shortly after arriving in the United States, and so there is not a natural point of comparison between their earlier and émigré styles.

Critic Albert Goldberg ran a feature in the *Los Angeles Times* attempting to answer the very question of émigré influence by inviting the composers themselves to comment.[386] Contributors included Arnold Schoenberg, Igor Stravinsky, Mario Castelnuovo-Tedesco, Ernst Krenek, Eugene Zador, Miklós Rózsa, and Eric Zeisl. Most composers denied a specific influence even while acknowledging the impossibility of giving an unambiguous answer. Krenek commented in a separate article:

> There were composers who even before their emigration leaned to the moderate center and conformed to the line of tradition. Hence one might hardly notice that those pieces of theirs written in America had for their authors men who had been transplanted to an entirely different environment. Composers like Hindemith and Martinů belong to this group. Hindemith's music, above all, exhibits an attitude of busy-ness, firm structures based on traditional learning, thus easily perceivable, obviousness of form and content, and practicality of execution as well. These traits bring it within reach of a public which is far less inclined to contemplation than to being busily occupied, a public that does not fancy speculation, but wants to know what the matter is. As a result of its Puritan heritage, it is inclined to consider those things that are less entertaining as serious and weighty.[387]

The end of World War II brought relief to the émigrés, of course, but also moments of indecision: should they stay, return, or live between two worlds? The choices were personally and professionally fraught, for these composers realized that the world they would return to bore little resemblance to the one they had left. Whatever their decisions, their presence during this crucial period represents an important cultural and compositional legacy in the history of American music, including the American symphony.

The composers discussed in the following pages are those whose symphonies were most prominent in both quantity and quality. They are discussed in alphabetical order. (See table 5.16 for selected symphonies by notable émigrés.)

Table 5.16 Symphonies Written in America by Eight Notable Émigrés

Ernest Bloch (1880–1959) moved to America in 1916
    America: An Epic Rhapsody (1927)
    Sinfonia breve (1952)
    Symphony for Trombone and Orchestra (1954)
    Symphony in E-flat (1954–55)

Igor Stravinsky (1882–1971) moved to America in 1939
    Symphony in C (1939–40): wrote first two movements in Europe, the last two in the United States
    Symphony in Three Movements (1942–45)

Ernst Toch (1887–1964) moved to America in 1935
    Symphony No. 1, Op. 72 (1950)
    Symphony No. 2, Op. 73 (1951)
    Symphony No. 3, Op. 75 (1955). Pulitzer Prize, 1956
    Symphony No. 4, Op. 80 (1957)
    Symphony No. 5, "Jeptha," Op. 89 (1963)
    Symphony No. 6 (1963)
    Symphony No. 7 (1964)

Bohuslav Martinů (1890–1959) in America from 1941 to 1953
    Symphony No. 1 (1942), dedicated to the memory of Natalie Koussevitzky
    Symphony No. 2 (1943)
    Symphony No. 3 (1945)
    Symphony No. 4 (1945)
    Symphony No. 5 (1946)
    Symphony No. 6, *Fantaisies symphoniques* (1953)

Darius Milhaud (1892–1974) in America from 1940 to 1947, then between America and France from 1947 to 1971
    Symphony No. 1, Op. 210 (1939), written just before his emigration for the Chicago Symphony Orchestra's 50th anniversary
    Symphony No. 2, Op. 247 (1944)
    Symphony No. 3 "Te Deum," Op. 271 (1947)
    Symphony No. 4, *Composée à l'occasion de Centenaire de la Révolution de 1848*, Op. 281 (1947)
    Symphony No. 5, Op. 322 (1953)
    Symphony No. 6, Op. 343 (1955), commissioned for the 75th anniversary of the Boston Symphony Orchestra and dedicated to the memory of Serge and Natalie Koussevitzky
    Symphony No. 7, Op. 344 (1955)
    Symphony No. 8, "Rhodanienne," Op. 362 (1957), commissioned by the University of California-Berkeley
    Symphony No. 9, Op. 380 (1959)
    Symphony No. 10, Op. 382 (1960)
    Symphony No. 11, "Romantique," Op. 384 (1960), commissioned by the Dallas Public Library and Dallas Symphony
    Symphony No. 12, "Rurale," Op. 399 (1961), commissioned by the University of California–Davis

Paul Hindemith (1895–1963) in America from 1940 to 1953
    Symphony in E-flat (1940–41)
    Symphonia serena (1946)
    Die Harmonie der Welt Symphony (1951)
    Symphony in B-flat for Concert Band (1951)
    Pittsburgh Symphony (1958), written after his return to Europe for the Pittsburgh Symphony

Erich Wolfgang Korngold (1897–1957) moved to America in 1934
    Symphony in F-sharp Major, Op. 40 (1952)

Ernst Krenek (1900–91) moved to America in 1938
    Symphony No. 4, Op. 113 (1947)
    Symphony No. 5, Op. 119 (1949)
    Symphony "Pallas Athene," Op. 137 (1954)

Susan Key, with Drew Massey

ERNEST BLOCH

The reputation of Ernest Bloch (1880–1959) now rests primarily on his so-called Jewish works, but his entire symphonic output—both the full-scale symphonies discussed in this chapter and several notable symphonic poems—is highly varied and interesting. An early émigré (he came to the United States in 1916, with his family following the next year), he distinguished himself as an educator in the United States, holding teaching posts at David Mannes School of Music in New York and the Julius Hartt School of Music in Hartford, Connecticut, before receiving an invitation to become the founding director of the Cleveland Institute of Music in 1920. He worked in Cleveland until 1925, when he was recruited by the San Francisco Conservatory. In 1930, a trust fund set up by the Rose and Jacob Stern family allowed him to compose full-time. The Blochs returned to Europe in 1930 before the political atmosphere prompted their return to the United States in 1939. They retired to the small town of Agate Beach, Oregon; from 1941 to 1952, Ernest taught at the University of California–Berkeley.

Bloch's symphonic output represents three distinct phases of his life. He had already written two symphonies, the First in C-sharp Minor (1901–3) and the *Israel Symphony* (1912–16), before coming to the United States. He wrote *America* during his time in San Francisco, and his last three symphonies date from the years in Agate Beach.

America: An Epic Rhapsody for Orchestra

In 1927, the journal *Musical America* sponsored a competition for the best symphonic work on an American theme by an American composer; of the 92 entries, Bloch's *America: An Epic Rhapsody for Orchestra* was unanimously selected the winner of the $3,000 prize (he had become a US citizen in 1924). The three-movement work for chorus and orchestra, including celeste and two harps, was performed simultaneously in New York, Boston, Philadelphia, Chicago, and San Francisco on December 21, 1928.

On the title page is a dedication reflecting Bloch's idealistic goals (the format and capitalizations are the composer's):[388]

> **America**
> An epic Rhapsody in three parts for orchestra
> This Symphony has been written in love for this country
> In reverence to its Past—In faith in its Future
> It is dedicated
> To the memory of Abraham Lincoln
> And
> Walt Whitman
> Whose vision has upheld its inspiration

The Ideals of America are imperishable. They embody the future credo of all mankind: a Union, in common purpose and under willingly accepted guidance, of widely diversified races, ultimately to become one race, strong and great. But, as Walt Whitman has said: "To hold men together by paper and seal or by compulsion, is of no account. That only holds men together which aggregates all in a living principle, as the hold of the limbs of the body or the fibres of plants."

Though this Symphony is not dependant [*sic*] on a program, the composer wants to emphasize that he has been inspired by this very Ideal.

The *Anthem*, which concludes the work, as its apotheosis, symbolizes the Destiny, the Mission of America. The Symphony is entirely built upon it. From the first bars it appears, in root, dimly, slowly taking shape; rising, falling, developing, and finally asserting itself victoriously in its complete and decisive form.

It is the hope of the composer that this Anthem will become known and beloved, that the audience will rise to sing it, becoming thus an active and enthusiastic part of the work and its message of faith and hope.

The first movement is *1620—the Soil—the Indians—(England)—the Mayflower—the Landing of the Pilgrims*. Here Bloch depicts the early history of the country, using native American melodies (based on the research of Frances Densmore), hymns, and martial music. The second movement, *1861–1865—Hours of Joy—Hours of Sorrow*, evokes the Civil War through "Old Folks at Home" and other period music. The last movement, *1926 . . . the Present—the Future (Anthem)*, brings the work into the modern era. Urban sounds lead to "the inevitable collapse" before ending with a hymn intended for audience participation:

> America! America!
> Thy name is in my heart.
> My love for thee arouses me
> To nobler thoughts and deeds.
> Our fathers built up a nation
> To give us justice and peace
> Towards higher aims,
> Towards greater goals,
> Towards freedom of all mankind.
> We still are here America
> To stand by thee,
> To give to thee our strength,
> Our hearts and our lives!

The style of *America* is certainly different from Bloch's contemporary works, drawing on familiar ethnic clichés and a kind of monumental and pictorial style that strikes the modern ear as hopelessly dated. Yet, as David Kushner observes, "Contrapuntal skills acquired in the composer's youth are now evidenced in the masterful combination of folk songs, and the orchestral brilliance manifested in the 'Jewish Cycle' comes to the fore in a totally new environment. The perfect fourth 'calls,' a shofar-like reference in the context of the 'Cycle,' are here a clarion call to fellow Americans. . . . In short, characteristics which had been assigned narrowly to Jewish sources become Blochian traits when observed in compositions far removed stylistically from those with specific Hebraic content."[389]

Bloch himself reflected on the style he adopted for this work as well as his 1929 tone poem *Helvetia* (an homage to his native Switzerland): "It is evident that 'Helvetia' and 'America' required a style that matched the subject I was interpreting. A style clearly diatonic and tonal, stirring and traditional. . . . In each of these works, I have set free a different part of my personality. In 'Helvetia' and 'America' the subject being more 'localized,' this personality appears less 'picaresque' or 'original' as they say, 'modern' to those who judge by the surface."[390]

Whatever the justification, many of Bloch's contemporaries found the work embarrassingly naïve and backward-looking. Irving Weil dismissed it as "imitative" and Paul Rosenfeld as "cheap"; meanwhile, since Bloch knew "stupid music from good," Alfred Frankenstein questioned whether "something in the music life of America stifles the creation of genuine music among us."[391] The consistent criticism from modernists led Bloch's student Randall Thompson to observe that

> Ernest Bloch's *America* [combines] jazz, spirituals, folk-songs, and a hymn, with an abstract and idealistic expression of our spirit. Why this stirring work has not received the whole-hearted endorsement of the intelligentsia it is not difficult to explain. Our musical Solons say to themselves, "We enjoy it, but would it go in Europe?" It might not. But when shall we stop seeking the European stamp of approval? Does Europe await our endorsement of things European? The European yardstick is no measure for the things we do, and we shall never achieve artistic autonomy so long as we employ a foreign unit of measure. It constitutes a tyranny of opinion under which we struggle to please Europe but only succeed in displeasing and aping it.[392]

The tide of critical opinion has never moved back toward *America*, and, as a result, the symphony has enjoyed more attention as a cultural phenomenon than as a living musical artwork.

Late Symphonies

Bloch's *Sinfonia breve*, composed in 1952, premiered in London the following April with Sir Malcolm Sargent and the BBC Orchestra. Henry Cowell noted the way the work brought together Bloch's various aesthetic impulses: "20th-century tonal materials are integrated with his sense of Baroque form and movement . . . [and] with his characteristically sustained rhapsodic and flowing music."[393] A dissonant declamatory introduction gives way to an Allegro. The second movement, Andante, employs a twelve-tone theme, but, as Cowell described it, the row "is warm and expressive, with a certain suggestion of the Hebrew melos."[394] The Scherzo features jagged, syncopated motives punctuated with sudden and unexpected tempo and mood changes. The Finale wraps up the work with an impressive—even visionary—rapture that belies the implicit inconsequentiality of its title.

The Symphony for Trombone and Orchestra (1954), premiered in Houston in April 1956, was inspired by the Juilliard trombonist Davis Shuman. The work is not quite symphony, not quite concerto. As composer and critic Paul Chihara described it,

> Its overall structure suggests a single extended arc. It begins as a lament, progresses as an heroic struggle and ends, Calmo, in resignation. The first and last movements are relatively short and serve as introduction and conclusion to the massive middle movement which is in the expanded sonata-allegro tradition of Beethoven. There is much unrest in this movement, in which conflicting themes and moods are juxtaposed and transformed in skillful counterpoint. The final movement (Allegro deciso) begins with an orchestral outburst, as though the despair in the opening movements was returning. But by degrees the pain subsides; previous materials return in transformed, less threatening colors; and the symphony concludes quietly."[395]

The Symphony in E-flat (1955–56) premiered in London in February 1956 with Efrem Kurtz and the Royal Philharmonic Orchestra. A four-note motive unifies the work: heard at the beginning and in a variety of manifestations throughout the four movements, it gives the symphony a taut energy. In the second-movement Allegro, Bloch expands the four-note motive into a twelve-tone theme. The third movement is a brooding Andante; its opening theme recalls the second thematic variation of the opening motive. The fourth movement, Allegro deciso, recalls themes from earlier in the piece.

Bloch's long tenure in the United States is remarkable for his influence as a pedagogue: his students included several composers studied in this chapter, as well as one of the most prominent postwar symphonists. As Robert Strassburg notes, "Bloch directly influenced the lives and careers of hundreds of music students. He taught an entire generation of America's most talented composers, among them Roger Sessions, Douglas Moore, Bernard Rogers, Randall Thompson, Quincy Porter, Ernst Bacon, Theodore Chanler, Herbert Elwell, George Antheil,

Henry Cowell, Mark Brunswick, Isadore Freed, Frederick Jacobi, Ethel Leginska and Leon Kirchner."[396] In its geographic reach, musical contributions, and generational influence, Bloch left an important cultural and compositional legacy in the history of American music.

PAUL HINDEMITH

Paul Hindemith (1895–1963) was a reluctant émigré. The essentially apolitical composer's association with Jewish performers and his modernist idiom made him an outcast to the Nazis, who branded much of his music of the 1920s as "cultural Bolshevism." Matters came to a head in 1934, when Wilhelm Furtwängler's proposed performance of the opera *Mathis der Maler* was prohibited by the authorities. Furtwängler wrote open letters to the newspapers, but his efforts to stir a public controversy were ineffective, and Hindemith resigned his teaching post at the Berlin Academy of Music the following year. His reputation as a "decadent" artist—he figured in the 1938 *Entartete Musik* Exhibition—combined with his wife's Jewish heritage, spurred the Hindemiths to leave Germany for Switzerland in 1938. Concert tours in the United States in 1937, 1938, and 1939 were followed by emigration in 1940.

Hindemith had a deep and lasting influence on the teaching of music in America, beginning with lectures and classes at the University of Buffalo; Wells College in Aurora, New York; and Cornell College before assuming a long-term professorship at Yale. There he was a key figure in the reorganization of the school's music curriculum, particularly strengthening the role of music theory. He also taught two summers at the Tanglewood music center in Western Massachusetts, where one of his students was Lukas Foss. He took US citizenship in 1946 but returned to Europe in 1953, settling in Switzerland.

Hindemith wrote six major symphonies during his career: of these, only the first and last (the *Mathis der Maler* Symphony and the *Pittsburgh Symphony*) were composed outside the United States. One of his most popular orchestral works, the *Symphonic Metamorphosis on Themes by Carl Maria von Weber* (1943), also dates from his American years.

Hindemith began the Symphony in E-flat at Tanglewood in the summer of 1940 and finished it in December of that year. The work was originally intended for the Boston Symphony Orchestra (BSO), but Serge Koussevitzky canceled the premiere, saying that the time to prepare was inadequate; the symphony was eventually performed by Dimitri Mitropoulos and the Minneapolis Symphony Orchestra in November 1941. (In spite of some ruffled feathers over the cancelation, Koussevitzky did perform the piece in January 1942.[397])

Beyond the title, the work shows many markers of the Austro-Germanic tradition: four movements, the first beginning with a heroic brass signal, the second darkly lyrical, the third a sprightly Scherzo and Trio, the Finale a march and a contrasting intermezzo section that builds to a glorious ending on a major chord. Although the BSO did not premiere the work, Hindemith's experience with the orchestra at Tanglewood evidently inspired the composition, and the virtuosic solo and sectional wind writing throughout suggests that he had the sound of that ensemble in mind.[398]

As its name suggests, the *Symphonia serena* (1946) reflects a lighter postwar mood. The work was commissioned by Dallas Symphony Orchestra and premiered in February 1947 under the direction of Antal Dorati. The opening movement is captioned "Moderately fast." The second, for winds alone and marked "Geschwindmarsch by Beethoven," paraphrases that composer's "Yorck'sche Marsch." The third movement, "Colloquy," is scored for strings. Hindemith explores the section in imaginative textures, including solos for both onstage and offstage violins; later the call and response is from offstage to onstage viola. The Finale, "Gay," reunites the entire ensemble. Contrapuntal manipulation of thematic material is elaborate, even phantasmagoric at points, but never thick. It has the resolute ending but none of the serious weight of the Symphony in E-flat.

As with the *Mathis der Maler* Symphony, Hindemith based his *Die Harmonie der Welt* Symphony (1951) on music from his opera of the same name; an interesting note is that he finished the symphony a decade before the opera. The composer described it this way: "The three movements are pieces of music from an opera adapted for concert performance. They are about the life and work of Johannes Kepler, the contemporary events that encouraged or hindered him, and the search for the harmony that doubtless rules the Universe." Each movement is titled according to the categorizations of Boethius: *musica instrumentalis, musica humana,* and *musica mundana.*

The first movement suggests the cosmic proportions of the subject, beginning with dramatic brass gestures that yield to a succession of moods—mysterious, portentous, lyrical, and sprightly—before ending with the intensity of the opening. The second movement features angular, sweeping string passages punctuated by bright spots of woodwind color. A gathering orchestral climax is interrupted by an extended flute solo. A coda for strings and glockenspiel unites the human with the ethereal. The third movement is a passacaglia, which begins with dark colors, gradually grows livelier, and is interrupted by another flute solo before ending in a ringing E major.

In the same year that *Die Harmonie der Welt* premiered, Hindemith received a commission from the United States Army Band; the resultant Symphony in B-flat for Band received its first performance in April 1951 in Washington, DC, with the composer at the podium. The scoring takes advantage of the brightness and idiomatic sound of the wind ensemble; his handling of textures among the idiosyncratic wind voices is of particular interest. The first of the three movements is marked "Moderately fast, with vigor." The second uses an animated middle section to set off the moody reflections of the outer sections. The final movement, called "Fugue," actually includes two fugues. Luther Noss describes the piece as "a masterpiece of its genre."[399] On the other hand, noting the difficulty of timbral balance, particularly at the extremes of register, Richard Franko Goldman complained that it "sounds very much like a poorly done transcription; the virtues of 'original' band music are by no means made apparent, and one is tempted to think that a good arrangement of either the E-flat Symphony or the *Symphonic Dances* might achieve a more satisfactory result."[400] Nonetheless, the work remains a staple of the wind ensemble repertoire today.

Although Hindemith had left the United States by this time, he wrote the 1958 *Pittsburgh Symphony* in response to a request from the Pittsburgh Symphony Orchestra's music director William Steinberg for a celebration of the city's two hundredth anniversary. The musical sources are eclectic, including both a quote from Webern and the song "Pittsburgh's a Great Old Town." The program book for the Pittsburgh Symphony premiere quoted Frederick Dorian: "The Dutch are very familiar to me; their German dialect is almost the same as that of my old home. . . . And their lieder are those which to this very day are sung in the country-side where they once originated. I did not want to omit setting a tonal monument—in a musical piece addressing the inhabitants of Pennsylvania—to this very blend of the early American colonial scene with the southern German language and with the southern German style of life."[401]

The first movement is a Molto energico. The second begins with a march, followed by variations on a Pennsylvania Dutch tune. In the finale, Ostinato, Hindemith works with an eight-note series before reaching a climax and turning to the "Pittsburgh's a Great Old Town" melody. Gunther Schuller panned the piece in terms similar to those used against Bloch's *America*: "The inclusion of a Pennsylvania Dutch 'ditty' in the second movement (scored in minor ninths!) is already fairly trying, but the ultimate in paucity of imagination and tastelessness is achieved as the work ends on the banal strains of 'Pittsburgh Is a Great Old Town.'"[402]

Hindemith's American years must be considered a success in all aspects of his teaching, conducting, and especially composing. As Noss notes, "Hindemith received more commissions during this period than any other contemporary composer living in this country, whether native, foreign, or naturalized."[403] Yet his stint was not without ambivalence toward the country, its culture, and its aesthetic values. Kim Kowalke has noted that "Hindemith's attitudes toward his experience in the United States—before, during, and after World War II—were, in fact, always deeply conflicted"; he cites the composer's disdain for "the sentimental display of an overwhelming and nationwide feeling of artistic inferiority compensated for by loudness"—even as he, like so many Americans, chose the poetry of Walt Whitman for a major postwar work.[404] Hindemith's ambivalence captures the unstable combination of challenges and opportunities shared by all the émigrés during this era.

BOHUSLAV MARTINŮ

The Czech composer Bohuslav Martinů (1890–1959), who had been living in Paris since 1923, fled the German invasion of France and arrived in New York in the spring of 1941. He was not impressed: "Believe me, New York's endless avenues and streets are not exactly the best source of inspiration. . . . They fall in on you, hold you fast so escape is impossible."[405] Nonetheless, he slowly learned English, found a musical network, and developed his compositional skills here. Martinů moved to the United States at a relatively advanced age and began symphonic composition only then. Earlier European efforts include an unfinished symphonic sketch from 1912 and a one-movement work from 1928 initially titled *La Symphonie*. (He changed the title to *Allegro symphonique* and then in 1930 to *La Rhapsodie*.) Although it is impossible to say whether turning to the symphony was a direct result of exposure to American culture, the composer expressed a shift away from focusing on technique toward freer expression: "My work is developing and getting air—sometimes I can let myself go. I don't know whether this is a good thing but it certainly is a fact."[406]

Beethoven and Brahms served as models for Martinů's symphonic writing; as he put it, "the large proportions, the expansive form of the symphony necessarily force the composer to put himself on a high plane."[407] Even so, the "expansive forms" are built from very simple materials; and the "large proportions" are often created through repetition and manipulation of short motives. His structures tend to be sectional, with divisions articulated by the orchestration. Passages are atmospheric but never murky; the more animated passages often feature high woodwinds, especially the flute, either as a solo or in small groups; strings are usually in choirs. As Michael Crump points out, his orchestration produces "a sense of dynamism, of growth throughout each section . . . encouraged by an increasingly weighty presentation, often culminating in the deployment of the brass and percussion."[408] The harmony also works in tandem with this increasing weight from tonal ambiguity toward resolution.

Early Symphonies

Martinů's Symphony No. 1, commissioned by Koussevitzky in honor of his late wife Natalie, premiered in November 1942 in Boston. According to the composer, the First Symphony of

Brahms was his model: "I have tried to find new sound combinations and to elicit from the orchestra a unified sonority in spite of the polyphonic working which the score contains. It is not the sonority of impressionism, nor is there the search for color, which rather is integral in the writing, and the formal structure, the character of the work is calm and lyric."[409]

In the first movement, he quotes a favorite Bohemian hymn: "Holy Wenceslas, do not let us perish." Folk songs similarly form important material in the Finale.

Symphony No. 2 premiered in October of the following year with Erich Leinsdorf and the Cleveland Orchestra. It is shorter and more folklike than the First. Martinů again used the description "calm and lyric" for the music.[410]

Although the first two symphonies date from the war as well, the Third through Fifth are specifically considered Martinů's wartime symphonies. Symphony No. 3, composed while the composer and his wife vacationed near Ridgefield, Connecticut, premiered in October 1945 with the Boston Symphony. Martinů lamented having to "drag it out of myself."[411] The music possibly "reflects Martinů's sense of desolation during the early months of 1944. . . . [He] seems to be communing with himself on the fate of Czechoslovakia, and he bases his first movement on a three-note motif which is not far removed from two works bearing the epithet 'pathétique'—Beethoven's Piano Sonata, Opus 13, and Tchaikovsky's Sixth Symphony."[412]

Martinů began Symphony No. 4 in April 1945, and it premiered under Ormandy and the Philadelphia Orchestra in November of that year. By that time the war was coming to an end, and the optimistic mood was reflected in a work that was more lyrical, with a triumphant ending.[413]

Symphony No. 5

Composed in 1946 in New York but dedicated to the Czech Philharmonic, Symphony No. 5 was the last of the cluster of wartime symphonies. The work is in three movements, with the middle one serving as both slow movement and scherzo. The composer referred to its "more modern, better structure" as opposed to the "old symphony form."[414]

The structure of the first movement is A B A B Coda. An opening Adagio begins with an atmosphere that, in Crump's words, "would not be out of place in the score of a Hitchcock thriller."[415] The harmonic ambiguity is created with a pair of tritones (B-natural to F and B-flat to E). The mood is intensified as staccato woodwinds and pizzicato strings uneasily manipulate the intervals from the opening. This moves seamlessly into the Allegro, which settles into B-flat major as it unfolds a series of short motives presented in syncopated dialogue between woodwinds and layers in the strings, brass, and piano. A more lyrical section that follows recalls Aaron Copland at one point in its combination of texture, syncopation, and motives built on open intervals (Reh. 90; example 5.23). Shortly afterward, the second Adagio recalls the opening motives in somewhat altered form. The second Allegro expands on its previous material before yielding to a relatively brief coda that adds the weight of the brass for a dramatic conclusion. Crump sums up the achievement of this movement thus: the composer "has embraced extremes of exhilaration and disquietude, united them through the simplest of intervallic and rhythmic devices, and enclosed the whole in one of his most precisely measured forms."[416]

The Larghetto creates a kind of perky, urbane, almost French sound. Its form is a free rondo, but the lack of a classically compact and memorable theme gives it the feel of a series of excursions in which the extroverted mood is alleviated occasionally by introspective moments. Long and distinctive transition passages create a lot of busyness. While the basic meter and

From 1920 to 1950 in the United States

Example 5.23 Martinů, Symphony No. 5, I, mm. 86–95

metronome marking remain the same, Martinů varies the note values to give the impression of speeding up and slowing down.[417] The opening theme is most distinctive for the effect of reiterated sixteenth notes layering over a bar of eighth-note syncopations dependent on half steps (example 5.24). The B section features an extended and wandering flute solo, while C provides the most serene music of the entire movement, as a lyrical trumpet duet overlays orchestration that once again could be described as Coplandesque. The Coda (m. 183) returns to the rhythmic energy of the A section, punctuated by a slower-moving trumpet melody. The ending is truly remarkable: cellos imitate the trumpet melody in three iterations with successively longer note values, the last overlaid by delicate woodwind intonations of the movement's distinctive sixteenth-note rhythm. It is both a summation and a transcendence.

After the individual wind colors at the end of the Larghetto, the string-based opening of the Finale draws the listener into a more contemplative atmosphere. A three-note motive forms the basis of the opening Lento; its permutations unfold over a series of subtly shifting harmonies.[418] Eventually a horn echoes the motive; three measures later, oboes, clarinets, and bassoons overlay it with harmonic color. The form duplicates that of the first movement: A B A B Coda. The succeeding Allegro includes more motivic manipulation before presenting a warm, slightly off-kilter melody that simultaneously hints at American and Czech folk dances. The

Example 5.24 Martinů, Symphony No. 5, II opening

prominent use of a rhythm from the first movement of Beethoven's Seventh Symphony adds both musical substance and an extramusical nod. The second A reiterates the skillful motivic counterpoint but in a lighter mood; the second B begins with a new woodwind theme that emphasizes the familiarity of the Beethoven dotted rhythm when it makes its appearance 20 measures later. The Coda ratchets up the musical tension with the Beethoven rhythm gathering steam till the dramatic end on a unison D. In this movement, the composer creates a musical kaleidoscope to achieve what biographer Brian Large dubs "the most convincing finale of the symphonies."[419]

Symphony No 6

Symphony No. 6, *Fantaisies symphoniques* (1953), was the last of Martinů's efforts in the genre. Written in New York and Paris, it was dedicated to conductor Charles Munch in celebration of the Boston Symphony's seventy-fifth anniversary. Michael Steinberg recalls that the origin of the work lay in the composer's fascination with Hector Berlioz (1803–69), which suggested the idea of writing a *Nouvelle Symphonie fantastique*.[420] Although he abandoned that ambitious title in favor of the simpler *Fantaisies symphoniques,* the character of that work retains its inspiration.

> There is one reason for this work which is clear and certain for me: I wished to write something for Charles Munch. I am impressed and I like his spontaneous approach to the music where music takes shape in a free way, flowing and freely following its movements. An almost imperceptible slowing down or rushing up gives the melody a sudden life. So I had the intention to write for him a symphony which I would call "Fantastic," and I started my idea in a big way, putting three pianos in a very big orchestra. This was already fantastic enough, and during work I came down to earth. I saw it was not a symphony but something which I mentioned before, connected with Munch's conception and conducting. I abandoned the title and finally I abandoned also my three pianos, being suddenly frightened by these three big instruments on stage.
>
> I called the three movements "Fantasies," which they really are. One little fantasy of mine is that I used a few bars quotation from another piece, from my opera *Juliet*, which, to my mind, fitted perfectly well. That is of the nature of fantasy.[421]

The work's three movements are of roughly equal length. As the composer noted, they do not create a conventional symphonic flow but are fantasylike. In place of clearly delineated structures based on themes or harmonies, all the movements combine and recombine three basic kinds of material: highly mysterious and atmospheric music; lush romantic passages in the major with a folklike flavor, and marchlike sections often featuring brass fanfares. The inventive manipulation of these basic moods gives the piece an aesthetic unity even as the fantasy-like series of impressions gives it an almost cinematic quality.

Michael Crump argues that the work is Martinů's "supreme artistic testament, and deserves a place among the very greatest pieces of orchestral music of the twentieth century."[422] Of all the émigré symphonies discussed in this section, Martinů's—especially the last two—are the most unjustly neglected.

DARIUS MILHAUD

When Marseille-born Darius Milhaud (1892–1974) arrived in the United States, he already had a reputation and connections in the United States as a result of concert tours in 1919 and 1922. The music he heard during these travels—particularly jazz—impressed him and became a well-documented influence on his compositions of the 1920s. His music had been played in concerts of the International Composers' Guild, the League of Composers, and the Copland-Sessions concerts. The German invasion of France forced the Jewish composer and his wife to flee to the United States in 1940, where he was warmly welcomed and provided a position at Mills College in California.[423] Like a number of his émigré colleagues, Milhaud became an important educator; his students included Steve Reich, Dave Brubeck, and Burt Bacharach. After World War II ended, Milhaud divided his time between France and the United States; he continued to teach at Mills until 1971.[424]

Between 1917 and 1923, Milhaud had already composed six so-called "little symphonies"—*petit* both in their chamber scorings and very short durations (none of these three-movement works exceeds seven minutes, and several are less than four). But it was just before his emigration in 1940 that he began what would become a corpus of twelve full-length orchestral symphonies. The symphonies occupy more than two decades of Milhaud's career. Although each is an autonomous work, they share some common qualities:

> The first movements generally consist of an exposition of several successive ideas; these ideas are then reworked according to various contrapuntal formulas and are finally restated as in the opening section, only in a different sequence and often with an exchange of tonalities. The slow movements are frequently in three-part "song form"; the scherzo is replaced by an interplay of contrasting material, either capricious or mysterious in mood; the final movement tends to be a fugato or free fugue. The movements rarely receive classic tempo designations, but are instead suggestive of moods: Pastorale, Mystérieux, Avec sérénité, Tumultueux. Sometimes mood and tempo designations are combined: Vif et cinglant, Lent et doux, Joyeux et robuste.[425]

Milhaud's diverse stylistic influences, his frequent use of polytonality, and his tendency to emphasize atmosphere over development often makes the overall effect disjointed. He composed many film scores in the 1930s, and a scenic quality carries over to the symphonies.

Symphony No. 1 was commissioned by the Chicago Symphony Orchestra as part of their fiftieth anniversary season. Milhaud began writing it in the fall of 1939, just after the start of World War II in Europe, while he was still in France. He was suffering from rheumatoid arthritis and distress about the international situation, writing "I am in a mental daze, without reaction. I can only think about all of these young people who defend us and die every day." Yet the commission brought him some relief: "I felt incapable of getting to work, yet I had to deliver a work for the Chicago orchestra's anniversary. The idea that it would be the only French composition on the program shook me from inactivity, and I started my First Symphony."[426] He finished the work in France in December, and it premiered in Chicago the following October.

Wartime worries and the deaths of both parents did not slow down Milhaud's creative output during his time in the United States; he composed chamber and orchestral works, ballets, and vocal works. He finished Symphony No. 2 in November 1944; it premiered with the Boston Symphony Orchestra in December 1946 under Milhaud's direction.

The composer wrote Symphony No. 3, "Te Deum," for chorus and orchestra to celebrate the end of the war; he completed it at Mills in the fall of 1946. His only vocal symphony, it brings in a mixed chorus and soloists in the last movement to sing the "Te Deum" text. The first performance was in Paris in October 1947; Milhaud conducted the American premiere with the San Francisco Symphony in March 1949.

Symphony No. 4, *Composée à l'occasion de Centenaire de la Révolution de 1848* (1947), originated as a commission from the French Ministry of Education. Milhaud worked on it on board ship for his first visit home since coming to the United States, finishing it in France. At its American premiere in Los Angeles in 1949, critic Albert Goldberg wrote that "It is not the composer's most serious work, but in the long run it is apt to prove to be one of the most attractive."[427]

A five-year break from composing symphonies followed before Milhaud wrote Symphony No. 5 (1953) on a commission from Italian radio. Commissioned for the seventy-fifth anniversary of the Boston Symphony Orchestra, Milhaud dedicated Symphony No. 6 (1955) to the memory of Serge and Natalie Koussevitzky, and Charles Munch premiered it in October of that year. The critical response was more negative than for earlier works, particularly pointing to its inconsistent level of quality.[428] Symphony No. 7 (1955) followed immediately upon the completion of No. 6; commissioned by Belgian Radio, it premiered with the L'Orchestre de l'Institut National Radiodiffusion-Belge conducted by Franz André in September 1955.[429]

Milhaud composed Symphony No. 8, "Rhodanienne," in spring 1957 on a commission from the University of California–Berkeley, for the dedication of Alfred Hertz Memorial Hall; it premiered with the San Francisco Symphony, conducted by Enrique Jordá. The work is a portrait of the Rhône River: the first movement depicts the birth of the river; in the second, "the Rhône crosses Lake Geneva"; the third is titled "Through the Rhône Valley"; and in the fourth, the river reaches the Mediterranean.[430]

Milhaud composed his next three symphonies (Nos. 9, 10, and 11) during a six-month stay in Paris between 1959 and 1960. No. 11 originated as a commission from the Dallas Public Library and Dallas Symphony as part of a Composers' Conference that featured Milhaud as both speaker and moderator. It premiered with Dallas Symphony Orchestra conducted by Paul Kletzki. The composer called it "Romantique," though the name does not appear in the published version.[431] Milhaud's twelfth and last symphony, subtitled "Rurale," dates from the summer of 1961. A commission from University of California–Davis, it premiered with the San Francisco Symphony under Enrique Jordá in February 1962.

In a 1970 interview, Milhaud lamented the relative lack of exposure his symphonies received: "I am stuck with the conductors with *Création du Monde*, *Suite française* and *Suite provençale*. I have written twelve symphonies. They are played a little bit, of course, but not to the extent of the three works I just mentioned."[432] The intervening decades have not redressed their obscurity. The abiding problem is that, in spite of beautiful moments, the whole of each symphony does not equal the sum of the parts. As critic Martin Anderson puts it, "his use of polytonality works against the development of genuinely symphonic drama: if you constantly throw in keys with no apparent relation to what is being heard, you will necessarily deprive yourself of the long-term generative power of tonal tension. The result sounds somewhat like running on the spot."[433]

The very qualities that undermine Milhaud's symphonies within the genre suggest that they could profitably be mined for performance in various contexts. It would be interesting to extract individual movements for concert programs; Milhaud's sense of mood and color would also lend itself to adaptation for film scores.

IGOR STRAVINSKY

The biography of Stravinsky (1882–1971) is already well documented elsewhere. After leaving Russia, he lived in France and Switzerland before emigrating to the United States in 1939, settling in Los Angeles, and becoming a US citizen in 1945. He tried several times to work in the film industry but never could agree on terms, for reasons either of compensation or artistic vision.[434] The composer and his wife Vera became part of an elite cultural circle that included many émigré musicians, writers, and artists, and his music figured prominently in the iconic "Evenings on the Roof" concerts. Ironically, although he lived near the other towering figure in twentieth-century music, Arnold Schoenberg, the two were at aesthetic odds, with the result that the southern California musical community was divided. Leon Kirchner recalled the "rival gangs that roamed the beaches and canyons of Santa Monica. . . . They veered off like two opposing forces. . . . Neither group looked at the other."[435]

Stravinsky composed an early symphony, the Symphony in E-flat (1905–7), during his studies with Nikolai Rimsky-Korsakov. The *Symphonies of Wind Instruments*, composed in 1920 in memory of Claude Debussy (1862–1918) and reorchestrated in 1947, is a one-movement work in which the composer invokes the original meaning of symphony, a "sounding together." His two remaining symphonies are connected to his early American years.

Symphony in C

The Symphony in C premiered in November 1940 with the Chicago Symphony Orchestra under the composer's baton. The piece shows Stravinsky's geographic reach in the late 1930s: he began the first movement in 1938 in Paris and completed it, along with the second, in the Sancellemoz sanatorium in Switzerland; he wrote the third in Cambridge, Massachusetts; and the fourth emanated from his new home in Beverly Hills in 1940.[436] The result is that, as the composer himself suggested, the work divides into a "European" half for the first two movements and an "American" half for the rest.[437] Stravinsky wrote this work during a particularly unhappy period: in quick succession (November 1938 to June 1939), he lost his daughter, wife, and mother; the period in Switzerland was spent in the sanatorium where his wife had died, as the composer and two of his surviving children were themselves under treatment for tuberculosis; and he departed for America in September 1939. But it was also the period of Stravinskyan Neoclassicism in which he was at pains to insist that music was incapable of expressing any emotions or feelings, conscious or unconscious. Thus he asserted the following about the Symphony in C: "It is no exaggeration to say that [after his daughter's death] I myself survived only through my work on the symphony in C—though, I hasten to add that I did not seek to overcome my personal grief by 'expressing' or 'portraying' it in music, and the listener in search of that kind of exploitation will search in vain, not only here but everywhere in my art."[438]

Stravinsky called the score "unmysterious" and "easy to follow at all levels and in all its relationships."[439] He invoked Haydn as his model along with the first symphonies of Beethoven and Tchaikovsky. In consistency with his Neoclassical tendencies, he outwardly follows eighteenth-century practice in instrumentation and proportions but reinterprets them by applying his own approaches to rhythm and harmony—as in the title of the symphony, which intentionally lacks a modal designation.

The first movement, Moderato alla breve, is in a clearly defined sonata form. P is a wide-ranging melody on the oboe that rests securely in C major. S, introduced by oboe and bassoon, modulates to the subdominant. Signature Stravinskian touches include ostinatos, extensive use of both solo and sectional winds, dry staccato articulations, and textures that are full and sometimes layered but never muddy. Within a stable 2/2 meter—the first time in mature Stravinsky that a movement remains in a single meter (the subsequent ones do not)—varying articulations and rhythmic groupings create a sense of durational asymmetry. As composer and music theorist Edward T. Cone (1917–2004) points out, the formal structure is nearly a perfect arch, as balanced as his eighteenth-century models, yet it serves his own twentieth-century purpose:

> The typical classical balance, even when apparently rigid, controlled contrasting events moving at varying speeds, so that the listener's experience usually belied the exact parallel of the time-spans and defeated most attempts to measure one against the other. Stravinsky's sections—rhythmically persistent, harmonically static, melodically circular—not only invite the hearer to make the comparisons leading to just such measurement, but also reward him for doing so. Far from exploiting the sonata form as the traditional vehicle for realizing the musical or dramatic potentialities of tonal conflict and progression, he adapts it to his own perennial purpose: the articulated division of a uniform temporal flow.[440]

The beginning of the second movement (Larghetto concertante) recalls the woodwind counterpoint of the *Symphony of Psalms:* the oboe begins the melody, but the violins soon absorb it into a more complex texture.[441] Stunning instrumental effects are dominated by woodwinds but with effective string touches, for example, the use of three violas as an ever-so-brief interlude between woodwind sections (m. 79). A middle section is more agitated.

The third movement, Allegretto, is a minisuite with minuet, passepied, and fugue. Here Stravinsky achieves rhythmic asymmetry through constant metric changes. The fourth movement (Largo, tempo giusto, alla breve) opens with a brief introduction. Bassoons create a "growly" effect with ambiguous part writing; the accompaniment of cornets and trombones further clouds the melodic material. The introduction then leads to a stylized march: although it stays in the same register, the crisp rhythms create an utter contrast in their transparency and rhythmic clarity. The music gathers steam and intensity—interrupted momentarily by a brief largo chorale for bassoons and cornets (Reh. 162) before drawing back to reveal a final section that is all about pretending to yield to the pull of C. The ending is a remarkable series of shifting harmonies which again gives out the opening motive and culminates on a ghostly bitonal (C/G) chord.

Choreographer Martha Graham (1894–1991) chose the first three movements as the music for her 1987 ballet *Persephone*.

Symphony in Three Movements

If the Symphony in C reflects Stravinsky's experience of living between worlds, the Symphony in Three Movements (commissioned and premiered by the New York Philharmonic on December 28, 1945) is unimaginable apart from his newfound American identity. Conceding extramusical inspiration on this occasion, the composer described it as a "war symphony," one that also forms part of his long and complicated history with the film industry.

> It was written under the sign of [world events]. It both does and does not "express my feelings" about them, but I prefer to say only that, without participation of what I think of as my will, they excited my musical imagination. And the events that thus activated me were not general, or ideological, or specific: each episode in the Symphony is linked in my imagination with a concrete impression, very often cinematographic in origin, of the war. . . . The beginning of [the third movement] is partly, and in some—to me wholly inexplicable—way, a musical reaction to the newsreels and documentaries that I had seen of goose-stepping soldiers. The square march-beat, the brass-band instrumentation, the grotesque *crescendo* in the tuba—these are all related to those repellent pictures.[442]

The first movement (Overture: Allegro) is the longest and follows a loose three-part form; the longer and polyphonic middle section builds on the motives introduced in the first section, while the short final section brings back material from both its predecessors. "The wonderful achievement of the first movement is the fact that, in spite of its continuous free evolution, the intentional absence of both thematic development and striking melodic interest, it creates a break-less and tight structural whole."[443] The melodic second movement (Andante: Interlude) adapts music Stravinsky originally composed for the film *The Song of Bernadette*; the film is based on a popular 1941 novel by fellow expatriate Franz Werfel (1890–1945), inspired by the life of Saint Bernadette Soubirous (1844–79), whose story he learned while hiding from the Nazis in Lourdes, France. Stravinsky's music was never used—Alfred Newman (1900–1970) composed the score and won an Oscar for it—but the sense of setting, character, and atmosphere remains in the Stravinsky work. The third movement (Con moto) is highly polyphonic, with fugal sections.

Aspects of the piece recall the *Rite* period, most prominently its repeated chords with asymmetrical pounding accents. Once again, Stravinsky confused the critics, who had questioned his turn to Neoclassicism and who now confronted a seeming return to Primitivism.

> Like many of the greatest works of art, the Symphony in Three Movements is a work of synthesis. True, it recaptures the Scythian fury of *The Rite of Spring*, but in no sense is it a revisionist score. Like all Stravinsky's main works of the thirties and early forties, it channels energy into counterpoint, a kind of writing where the individual parts enjoy a certain autonomy but within which what might be called socially defined limits. . . . The symphony finale, with its dazzling fugal and imitative exchanges, breathes a refinement that civilizes the ferocity, without in any way drawing its sting. It is neoclassicism without fancy dress and come of age.[444]

When asked whether the work represented a new phase, Stravinsky answered, "I cannot answer that question. I do not have any ultimate viewpoint of composition and when I write my next symphony it will then be an expression of my will at that moment. And what that will is going to be I do not know now. I wish people would let me have the privilege of being at least a little bit unconscious. It is so nice sometimes to go blind, just with the *feeling* for the right thing!"[445]

Although two decades of productivity remained, there would be no "next symphony." Nor was there a definable "American Stravinsky." As Hermann Danuser reflects, "Stravinsky, regardless how his American period is viewed, can serve as an example of a composer bound to an ideal of autonomy, one that grounded him artistically throughout the various periods, countries, and stylistic phases of his life: Russian, French, American; or Russian folk-like, (neo) classical, serial."[446] Nonetheless, Stravinsky's two "American" symphonies have earned a secure place in the history of the genre.

Conclusion

Despite—and occasionally because of—economic and political crises, the stars were aligned after World War I for a golden age of the symphony in the United States, as performing art institutions, academe, and the film industry combined to provide the jobs and expertise to put the United States at the center of the international musical map. The quantity and quality of works described in this chapter provide ample evidence that, in one way, the potential of this combination was fulfilled: a multitude of excellent symphonies—including important expressions of courage and hope during a dark historical hour—were created and made accessible to an increasingly broad audience through both live and broadcast performances.

It is puzzling and frustrating, then, to realize that two generations have passed with little or no critical attention to these works beyond scattered performances and historical publications. As Brian Hart notes in chapter 1 of this volume, "Despite its largeness and high quality, much of the symphonic repertoire of the United States has generally been regarded as little more than a postscript to the history of the genre." In fact, statistics from the League of American Orchestras demonstrate that the top ten most frequently performed composers by American orchestras are all European.[447]

Both aesthetic and economic factors have contributed to the neglect. Stylistically, the pressure to create the Great American Symphony resulted in works in which a monumental quality often coexisted uneasily with ethnic or topical references. Bloch's *America* and Blitzstein's

Airborne are the two most obvious examples, with Copland's Third Symphony the clearest exception. Many of the identity symphonies—those works with specific folk and ethnic references—now seem naïve, such as Harris's *Folk-Song Symphony* or Hindemith's *Pittsburgh Symphony*. In the end, the search for greatness in the American symphony probably hindered its development: it remained an ideal type, more aimed for in theory than realized in sound. (In view of the parallels with the search for the Great American Novel, it is interesting to contemplate how American writers were perceived as more successful in realizing their ambition to merge a large transcendent vision with a vernacular voice, beginning in 1885 with Mark Twain's *Adventures of Huckleberry Finn*.)

The realities of concert design and marketing have also worked against the inclusion of multimovement symphonies outside the European canon. Stubborn tokenism in programming has generally meant that only one American or modern work appears on a program. To fill this slot, symphonic poems or shorter works are preferable to season planners, as they often have descriptive titles that are attractive to the potential ticket buyer—or at the very least a patron who, with greater or lesser grace, will tolerate a shorter unfamiliar work in order to hear a favorite Beethoven symphony. Even American-composed concertos are more likely to appear than symphonies because they have individual champions: the soloist serves as a headliner and the audience is motivated to purchase a ticket more for the performer than for the particular composition. From its premiere, Korngold's Violin Concerto was championed by the popular violinist Jascha Heifetz (1901–87), for example, and the work remains a frequent offering. In contrast, symphonies need a more collective advocacy.

An interesting irony in an era concerned with the broad dissemination of symphonic music is that "the masses" experienced high-quality symphonic music most regularly through film. Indeed, the influence of film scores far exceeded that of their composers' concert music. That this medium was never celebrated as a cultural benefit the way radio had been reflected the deep divide between film and concert composition. As Copland commented, "I was puzzled at why film composers were so isolated from the rest of the music world! In 1939 there were four major figures—Erich Korngold, Max Steiner, Alfred Newman, and Herbert Stothart [1885–1949]—and these men were not known outside of Hollywood."[448] As a result, the loss to the genre includes both native-born Americans such as Newman and Stothart and numerous Europeans, including Steiner, Franz Waxman, and Mario Castelnuovo-Tedesco (1895–1968).

It is certainly true that composing for film inevitably required a composer to give up a measure of artistic control. As Copland noted in 1941, "The man who insists on complete self-expression had better stay home and write symphonies. He will never be happy in Hollywood."[449] And yet, as works by Stravinsky, Antheil, and Korngold discussed in this chapter show, music originally conceived for film can be successfully adapted for use as concert music.

Some crossover has occurred from concert stage to sound stage. Antheil and Still wrote symphonies along with film and television scores. Thomson's *The Plow That Broke the Plains* (1936) pioneered an Americana style suitable to its subject and influenced Copland's well-regarded film scores, such as *Of Mice and Men* (1939), *Our Town* (1940), *The North Star* (1943), *The Red Pony* (1948), the Oscar-winning *The Heiress* (1949), and *Something Wild* (1961). Even émigré luminaries Stravinsky and Schoenberg made overtures to the studios.[450]

Contrarily, few film composers crossed over to symphonic music. Obviously, one factor is the greater economic reward from film composition. Yet there was also a bias toward abstract music, with the symphony as the standard bearer and film music considered second-class rather than an interesting alternative. And yet composers for centuries had been composing occasional music, incidental music, and opera along with symphonic music. Moreover, the kind of large-conception narrative drama required for successful film composition might very well have been seen as a natural fit for symphonists.

More than anything, the symphonies considered here were written during a time of enormous upheaval in the United States, and they are musical emblems of that period. They were public statements written for a country looking to find a viable concert music tradition, and, in this sense, regardless of their individual successes or failures, as a repertoire they have an enduring place in the history of American music. That their contributions to symphonic life in this country have largely faded away is a consequence of a cultural biases that have persisted both in programming decisions and in musicological analyses. The technological developments that allow for enhanced musical access and dissemination, combined with an increasing appetite for multimedia experimentation by orchestras, will provide some of these works the revivals they so richly deserve.

Brief Mentions

American symphonic activity during the period between 1920 and 1950 was both diverse and wide-ranging, and it included far more composers than have been covered thus far. The following list includes additional figures who composed one or more symphonies during this time. Those marked with a plus sign (+) had a symphony performed by at least one of the five major American orchestras (Boston, Chicago, Cleveland, New York, Philadelphia), and for that reason the composition belongs to Julie Schnepel's "core repertoire of American symphonies" between 1920 and 1950.[451] In other cases, one or more of a composer's symphonies resulted from a prominent commission or received a prestigious award. Finally, some composers are mentioned who achieved greatest fame in other genres, especially film music.[452]

Ernst Lecher Bacon (1898–1990) composed four symphonies. Symphony No. 1 (1930) won the 1932 Pulitzer Fellowship (forerunner of the Pulitzer Prize) and premiered with the San Francisco Symphony in 1934. His Symphony No. 2 from 1937 was first heard with the Illinois Symphony Orchestra in Chicago in 1940. The third symphony, the *Great River Symphony* (1957), presents a musical panorama of the Rio Grande for narrator and orchestra; the Dallas Symphony Orchestra performed it in 1957. Symphony No. 4 was projected to be five movements, but Bacon did not complete it. In addition to composing, he was prominent in performing, teaching, conducting, and administration. He overlapped with Ernest Bloch at the San Francisco Conservatory, headed the San Francisco WPA, and founded the Carmel Bach Festival.

+ Robert Russell Bennett (1894–1981), who studied with Nadia Boulanger from 1926 to 1929, was best known as a Broadway orchestrator. His symphony *Uke* received an honorable mention in the *Musical America* contest won by Ernest Bloch's *America* (discussed earlier).[453] *Abraham Lincoln: A Likeness in Symphony Form* (1929) shared a composition prize from RCA Victor with Bloch's *Helvetia*, Copland's *Dance Symphony*, and Louis Gruenberg's first symphony. He also composed a *Symphony in D for the Dodgers* (1941, commissioned by WOR radio) and *Four Freedoms—a Symphony after Four Paintings by Norman Rockwell* (1943); these works reflected the composer's sense that his generation was "beginning to put our real America into music."[454] Other works include an early Symphony (1926), *Symphony on College Themes* (No. 4, n.d.), *A Sym-*

phonic Story of Jerome Kern (1946), *A Symphonic Picture of Carousel* (1946), *A Commemoration Symphony* (1960, based on songs by Stephen Foster), and the Symphony No. 7 (1962).

+ Nikolai Berezowski (1900–1953) emigrated to the United States from Russia in 1920. His career as a violinist included stints with the New York Philharmonic and the Coolidge String Quartet; as a conductor, his most prominent engagement was with CBS radio. Koussevitzky frequently performed his symphonies. No. 1 (1931) was premiered by the Boston Symphony Orchestra with the composer conducting; No. 2 (1934) premiered with Koussevitzky leading the BSO; No. 3 (1937) was premiered by José Iturbi and the Rochester Philharmonic and also was performed on CBS conducted by Howard Barlow in 1940; No. 4 (1943) was commissioned by the Koussevitzky Foundation and premiered by Koussevitzky and the BSO. Berezowski's Sinfonietta (1932) won a prize in an NBC composition contest.

+ Felix Borowski (1872–1956) was born in England and emigrated to the United States in 1896, settling in Chicago, where he taught composer Silvestre Revueltas (1899–1940) at Chicago Musical College. He wrote three symphonies, in D Minor (1932), E Minor (1933), and G Major (1937).

+ Charles Wakefield Cadman (1881–1946) was prominent in the Indianist movement and in the founding of the Hollywood Bowl. His Symphony in E Minor, "Pennsylvania" (1939), premiered on March 4, 1940, with the Los Angeles Philharmonic under Albert Coates as part of a national broadcast.

+ John Alden Carpenter (1876–1951), a prominent Chicago businessman, studied in Rome with Edward Elgar. His Symphony No. 1, "Sermons in Stones," premiered in Norfolk, Connecticut, in 1917; he extensively revised the work for the fiftieth anniversary of the Chicago Symphony Orchestra, which performed it on October 24, 1940. After hearing the work, Bruno Walter premiered Carpenter's Second Symphony with the New York Philharmonic in 1942; he revised it too five years later.[455]

+ Frederick Converse (1871–1940) studied with Joseph Rheinberger in Munich. His symphonies include works in C Minor (1919), E Minor (1923), F Major (1934), and F Minor (1940). During a seven-year career at the New England Conservatory and Harvard University, he taught, among others, Florence Price and Alan Hovhaness.

+ Eric DeLamarter (1880–1953) was a Chicago-based organist, composer, and critic. He composed three symphonies: No. 1 (1914); No. 2, "After Walt Whitman" (1925); and No. 3 in E (1931).

+ Marcel Dick (1898–1991), a Hungarian émigré, taught at the Cleveland Institute of Music. His Symphony No. 1 (1948), supposedly the first full-length twelve-tone symphony, was first performed by the Cleveland Orchestra under the direction of Dimitri Mitropoulos and reviewed by *Cleveland News* music critic Elmore Bacon, who praised Dick's "magical gift for orchestration."[456]

+ Vladimir Dukelsky (1903–69) was best known for his popular music under the name Vernon Duke. He emigrated from Russia to the United States in 1921, where he composed two symphonies: No. 1 in F (1927–28) and No. 2 in D-flat (1928–30). Koussevitzky premiered the latter with the BSO.

Hanns Eisler (1898–1962) emigrated to the United States in 1938 after five years of exile from Nazi Germany in Europe and Mexico. He composed for film, including the Oscar-nominated score for *Hangmen Also Die!* (1943). His Chamber Symphony (1940; German title: *Kammer-Symphonie*) was adapted for the film *White Flood* (1940). He was deported in 1948 after being accused of Communist activities, eventually settling in East Berlin, where he composed the national anthem for East Germany.

Edward Kennedy ("Duke") Ellington (1899–1974), a seminal figure in the history of jazz, deserves mention in this volume for his large-scale works of concert jazz and other jazz-infused orchestral compositions. Early efforts include *Creole Rhapsody* (1931), *Reminiscing in Tempo* (1935), and a score for the 1935 film *Symphony in Black*. *Black, Brown and Beige* (1943) was intended, in the composer's words, to be "an immortal symphony" commemorating the "hisstory of his race."[457] It was followed by a series of extended concert works performed at Carnegie Hall, for example, *New World a-Comin'* (1943), *Blutopia* (1944), *Deep South Suite* (1946), *Liberian Suite* (1947), *Symphomaniac* (1948), *The Tattooed Bride* (1948), and *A Tone Parallel to Harlem* (1950). Some additional notable works are *Night Creature* (1955), *Non-violent Integration* (1964; originally composed in 1949 as *Grand Slam Jam*), and *Celebration* (1972).

Anis Fuleihan (1900–1970), a Cypriot émigré, wrote two symphonies, No. 1 (1936) and No. 2 (1962). After a dissonant early style, he lived in the Near East from 1925 to 1928 and absorbed influences from that area.

+ Eugene Goossens (1893–1962) is best known as a conductor of the Rochester and Cincinnati Symphony Orchestras. He composed two symphonies, No. 1 (1939–40) and No. 2 (1945).

Morton Gould (1913–96) achieved the most fame for shorter descriptive orchestral works. His symphonies include four numbered works: No. 1 (1943), No. 2, "On Marching Tunes" (1944), No. 3 (1947, rev. 1948), and No. 4 for band (1952). Gould also composed *Little Symphony* (1936), *Symphony of Spirituals* (1976), and *Centennial Symphony for Band* (1983).

Louis Gruenberg (1884–1964) emigrated from Russia to the United States as an infant. Best known for his 1933 opera *The Emperor Jones*, he completed four symphonies and left two unfinished. The First (1919, rev. 1928) shared a composition prize sponsored by RCA Victor with Bennett's *Abraham Lincoln: A Likeness in Symphony Form*, Bloch's *Helvetia*, and Copland's *Dance Symphony*; Koussevitzky premiered it in 1933. The Second Symphony dated from 1941 (rev. 1959, 1963), the Third from 1941–42 (rev. 1964), and the Fourth from 1946 (rev. 1964).

+ Henry Kimball Hadley (1871–1937) was well known as a conductor: his positions included the Mainz Stadttheater, Seattle Symphony, San Francisco Symphony (he was the founding music director in 1911), the New York Philharmonic (associate conductor, 1920–27), and the Manhattan Symphony Orchestra, an ensemble devoted to the promotion of American compositions, for which Hadley was a tireless advocate. He wrote five symphonies: No. 1, "Youth and Life" (1897), performed by the Pittsburgh Symphony Orchestra under Victor Herbert; No. 2, "The Four Seasons" (1899), performed in 1900 by the Boston Symphony Orchestra and later awarded the Paderewski

Prize; No. 3 (1906), premiered by the Berlin Philharmonic Orchestra under Hadley's baton; No. 4, "North, East, South, and West" (1910); and No. 5, "Connecticut" (1935). He also composed numerous symphonic poems. All the works show the influence of Chadwick, with whom he studied. Hadley also spent time in Hollywood working on the synchronization of film and music.

+ Bernard Herrmann (1911–75), a highly acclaimed film composer (his scores include *Citizen Kane, Vertigo, Psycho, North by Northwest,* and *Taxi Driver*), also composed works for orchestra, chamber orchestra, and the stage. His Symphony (1941) was premiered by Howard Barlow and the New York Philharmonic in November 1942.

+ Edward Burlingame Hill (1872–1960) studied with John Knowles Paine and George Whitefield Chadwick; he later took lessons with Charles-Marie Widor in Paris. As a teacher at Harvard, he taught Virgil Thomson, Elliott Carter, and Leonard Bernstein. He wrote four symphonies (No. 1, 1927; No. 2 in C, 1929; No. 3 in G, 1936; No. 4 in E flat, 1940) as well as many programmatic orchestral works. Koussevitzky premiered the first three symphonies with the BSO.

+ Werner Josten (1885–1963) emigrated from Germany to the United States in 1920 to teach at Smith College in Massachusetts; he became a US citizen in 1933. His most popular work was a symphonic poem, *Jungle*, premiered by Koussevitzky in 1929 and played by various ensembles, such as Stokowski and the Philadelphia Orchestra. His Symphony in F (1936) was premiered by the Boston Symphony Orchestra with Josten conducting; in 1938, the work was awarded a Juilliard Publication Award.

Erich Wolfgang Korngold (1897–1957), born in Vienna, wrote early ballet, theater, and instrumental scores that garnered international attention. He came to the United States in 1938 and took US citizenship in 1943. He became a leading composer for the cinema, pioneering the symphonic film score and winning two Oscars for *Anthony Adverse* (1936) and *The Adventures of Robin Hood* (1938). His symphonic output includes an early Sinfonietta and a Symphonic Serenade for Strings in B-flat (1947). He dedicated the Symphony in F-sharp Major, Op. 40 (1947–1952, premiered 1954), to the memory of Franklin D. Roosevelt. He adapted some of its thematic material from his music for the film *The Private Lives of Elizabeth and Essex* (1939).

+ Ernst Krenek (1900–1991) emigrated to the United States in 1938 and became a US citizen in 1945. His European output includes Symphony No. 1, Op. 7 (1921); Symphony No. 2, Op. 12 (1922); Symphony No. 3, Op. 16 (1922); the Symphony for Winds and Percussion, Op. 34 (1925); and the Little Symphony, Op. 58 (1928). He composed no further symphonies until after World War II. He explained the hiatus this way:

> My main interest was devoted to the form of the symphony, and in this I can see a certain symptom of being conscious of historical continuity. . . . First I wrote no less than three symphonies at the age of twenty-three and each one of them has, in my opinion, retained to this day some elements of vitality. The fact that I did not approach the problem of the symphony for another twenty years should, however, indicate that I was not quite convinced of the validity of the project. When I took it up again in the 1940s, I found the results rather disappointing. My only comfort is that nobody else has succeeded any better in continuing the great symphonic tradition.[458]

The "rather disappointing" results included three works: Symphony No. 4, Op. 113 (1947), Symphony No. 5, Op. 119 (completed in Albuquerque in 1949), and the Symphony "Pallas Athene," Op. 137 (1954), based on his opera of the same name.[459] By the time of these later symphonies, Krenek had adopted twelve-tone procedures in his writing.

+ Normand Lockwood (1906–2002) studied with Ottorino Respighi at the American Academy in Rome and with Nadia Boulanger in Paris. His Symphony "A Year's Chronicle" (1934) was followed by *Symphonic Sequences* (1965), Symphony for String Orchestra (1975), Symphony (1979), Symphony in Four Movements and Coda (1993), and *Symphonic Interlude* (1995).

+ Nikolai Lopatnikoff (1903–76) left Russia with his family in 1918, eventually emigrating to the United States in 1939. Koussevitzky premiered several of his compositions, including Symphony No. 2. He wrote four symphonies: No. 1, Op. 12 (1928), No. 2, Op. 24 (1938–39; withdrawn), No. 3, Op. 35 (1953–54), and No. 4, Op. 46 (1970–71).

+ Arthur Vincent Lourié (1891–1966) studied at the St. Petersburg Conservatory before striking out on his own to explore avant-garde and futurist techniques. Both his symphonies precede his 1941 move to the United States: No. 1 *Sinfonia dialectica* (1930) and No. 2, subtitled "Kormtchaia") (1939); Koussevitzky premiered the latter with the Boston Symphony Orchestra in November 1942.

+ Daniel Gregory Mason (1873–1953), best known for his work in music criticism and music appreciation, studied in the United States with John Knowles Paine and George Whitefield Chadwick and in Paris with Vincent d'Indy. His symphonic efforts include Symphony No. 1 in C Minor (1913–14), Symphony No. 2 in A Major (1928–29), and Symphony No. 3, "A Lincoln Symphony" (1935–36). A stylistic conservative, he nonetheless was a champion of American composition and a well-known author on musical subjects.

+ Harl McDonald (1899–1955) followed studies at University of California–Berkeley and University of Redlands (California) with lessons at the Leipzig Conservatory. He taught at the University of Pennsylvania (1926–46) and also served as general manager of the Philadelphia Orchestra (1939–55). His symphonies all had programmatic titles: No. 1, "The Santa Fe Trail" (1933); No. 2, "The Rhumba" (1934); No. 3, "Lamentations of Fu Hsuan" (1935); and No. 4, "Festival of the Workers" (1935).

+ Douglas Moore (1893–1969) studied in Paris with Vincent d'Indy, followed by a year of lessons with Ernest Bloch in Cleveland. He was a prominent pedagogue and administrator (at Columbia University) and critic. He is best known for his opera *The Ballad of Baby Doe* (1956). He composed two symphonies, *A Symphony of Autumn* (1930) and Symphony No. 2 in A (1945). The latter, which Tawa describes as "an extraordinary affirmation of postwar faith in what America stood for and demonstrates trust in events still to come," premiered in Paris and was subsequently performed by the Los Angeles Philharmonic, NBC Orchestra, and the New York Philharmonic.[460]

Jerome Moross (1913–83) is known for his contributions to art music, theater, and film. "In 1934 CBS commissioned Moross to compose a work to be broadcast on *American School of the Air: Folk Music of America*. John Lomax, who produced the show, suggested an arrangement of the tune 'Midnight Special,' which Moross completed, giving it the title

Ramble on a Hobo Tune. Eventually this work became the basis for Moross's first (and only) Symphony (1940–42), premiered by the Seattle Symphony Orchestra in 1943, directed by Sir Thomas Beecham. Lawrence Morton, who reviewed the work, called it an "an attractive piece, a cheerful commentary upon some of the simple pleasures of American life." Morton goes on to list those pleasures: the drugstore soda, a colorful sunset, cool sheets at bedtime, the appreciation of one's congressman and "being grateful for the Red Cross."[461]

+ Arne Oldberg (1874–1962) studied with Josef Rheinberger in Munich. He taught at Northwestern University for more than 40 years; his pupils included Howard Hanson. He wrote at least six symphonies; two, Symphony in F Minor, Op. 23, and C Minor, Op. 34, took national composition prizes.[462]

+ Quincy Porter (1897–1966) studied composition at Yale with Horatio Parker and David Stanley Smith before taking lessons in Paris with Vincent d'Indy and in New York and Cleveland with Ernest Bloch. He taught at Vassar College, the New England Conservatory, and Yale, and he received honors such as the Elizabeth Sprague Coolidge Medal and election to the National Institute of Arts and Letters. He is most celebrated for concertos and for chamber music (especially nine string quartets), but he also composed two symphonies: No. 1 in 1934 and No. 2 in 1962.

John Powell (1882–1963) studied in Vienna with Theodor Leschetizky and Karel Navrátil. An avowed white supremacist, he nonetheless incorporated both Anglo- and African American folk sources in his compositions, which were heard frequently on national radio broadcasts. His Symphony in A, "Virginia Symphony" (1945, rev. 1951), incorporates modal Anglo-American melodies within a lush romantic style.

+ Gardner Read (1913–2005) studied composition with Bernard Rogers and Howard Hanson at the Eastman School of Music. During a 1939 stint in Europe, he studied with Ildebrando Pizzetti and met Jean Sibelius. In 1941, he had lessons with Aaron Copland at Tanglewood. His Symphony No. 1 (1937) received first prize in the New York Philharmonic-Symphony Society's American Composers' Contest. His Symphony No. 2 (1943) received first prize in the Paderewski Fund Competition; Read conducted its premiere with the Boston Symphony Orchestra. He also composed many descriptive pieces for orchestra.

+ Lazare Saminsky (1882–1959) studied with Nikolai Rimsky-Korsakov in his native Russia before emigrating to the United States in 1920. Symphonies comprise No. 1, subtitled "Of the Great Rivers" (1914); No. 2, *Symphonie des sommets* (1918); No. 3, subtitled "Symphony of the Seas" (1924); No. 4 (1927); and No. 5, *Jerusalem, City of Solomon and Christ*, for chorus and orchestra (1932).

+ Robert L. Sanders (1906–74) was a Fellow at the American Academy in Rome from 1925 to 1929. His Little Symphony No. 1 (1936–37) received a prize from the New York Philharmonic; he composed two other Little Symphonies (No. 2 in 1953 and No. 3 in 1963). He also wrote a Symphony for Concert Band in 1942–43 and Symphony in A in 1954–55.

+ Arnold Schoenberg (1874–1951) emigrated to the United States in 1933 and took US citizenship in 1941. He composed no full-scale symphonies but deserves mention because of his prominent position in American musical life. His Second Chamber

Symphony, Op. 38 (1939, begun in 1906), marked a change back toward tonality in some of his compositions. He arranged his First Chamber Symphony (1906) for full orchestra in 1935 (as Op. 9B). His Suite for String Orchestra (1934) was the first work he composed in the United States.

+ Tibor Serly (1901–78) emigrated from Hungary with his family in 1905 but returned to Budapest to study with Hungarian composer Zoltán Kodály (1882–1967) in the 1920s. He established himself in the United States as a composer, performer, and educator and was a major support for Béla Bartók in the country (he orchestrated the last 17 measures of Bartók's Third Piano Concerto and constructed the Viola Concerto from the composer's sketches). His symphonic output consists of Symphony No. 1 (1931), No. 2 (for wind, brass, and percussion, 1932), Symphonic Variations for Audience and Orchestra (1956), String Symphony (1956–58), and Symphony in Four Cycles (strings, 1960).

+ Harold Shapero (1920–2013) studied with Nicolas Slonimsky, Ernst Krenek, Walter Piston, Paul Hindemith, and Nadia Boulanger between 1937 and 1943. His music of the 1940s recalled the forms, phrase structure, and harmonic rhythm of the Classical and early Romantic eras. He modeled his Symphony for Classical Orchestra (1947)—which resulted from a 1945 commission by the Koussevitzky Music Foundation—on the works of Beethoven. Leonard Bernstein premiered the symphony in 1948 with the Boston Symphony Orchestra and recorded it with the Columbia Symphony Orchestra in 1954. Music critic Alan Rich called it "the greatest American symphony."[463]

+ Arthur Shepherd (1880–1958) studied at the New England Conservatory with Percy Goetschius and George Whitefield Chadwick. "Neither nationalist nor iconoclast, Shepherd remained a stubborn traditionalist of original bent."[464] His Symphony No. 1, "Horizons," dates from 1927; Symphony No. 2 in D Minor from 1938. Shepherd conducted the latter with the Boston Symphony Orchestra in 1940.

+ Elie Siegmeister (1909–91), who studied with Boulanger from 1927 to 1931, wrote works incorporating folk themes, and most of his large orchestral works are descriptive. In addition to vocal and stage works (including nine operas), he wrote thirty-seven orchestral works, nine of which were symphonies: Symphony No. 1 (1947, rev. 1972), Symphony No. 2 (1950, rev. 1971), Symphony No. 3 (in One Movement) (1957), Symphony No. 4 (1967–70), Symphony No. 5, "Visions of Time" (1971–75), Symphony No. 6 (1983), Symphony No. 7 (1980s), Symphony No. 8 (1989), and Symphony No. 9, "Figures in the Wind" (1990). According to musicologist James Cassaro, these works, "especially the third and fourth, show a mastery of form in which the musical architecture is masked by fantastical and improvisatory effects."[465]

+ David Stanley Smith (1877–1949) studied with Horatio Parker at Yale, where he later taught theory; he also studied in Europe with Ludwig Thuille in Munich and Charles-Marie Widor in Paris. He composed four symphonies (F Minor, 1910; D Major, 1917; C Minor, 1928; D Minor, 1937); he conducted the Boston Symphony Orchestra in the premiere of the latter in 1939.

+ Howard Swanson (1907–78), an African American, received a Rosenwald Fellowship to study with Nadia Boulanger from 1938 to 1941. His Short Symphony (1948) premiered in 1950 with the New York Philharmonic under Dimitri Mitropoulos and was honored as "the most interesting composition of the season" by the New York Music Critics'

Circle in 1952.⁴⁶⁶ His style is essentially Neoclassical with the subtle influence of Black folk idioms.

Ernst Toch (1887–1964), a prominent member of the musical avant-garde in Germany in the 1920s, came to the United States in 1935 and became a US citizen in 1940. He composed for film both in Europe and America; of his 16 scores for Hollywood, three earned Academy Award nominations. Despite this success, he was disillusioned by the obstacles he encountered in securing performances of his concert music. In his later years, he devoted himself to composing symphonies, of which he wrote seven between 1950 and 1964: No. 1 (1951–52), No. 2 (1953), No. 3 (1955), No. 4 (1957), No. 5 (1961–62), No. 6 (1963), and No. 7 (1964). These works largely follow a traditional late Romantic style. The Third Symphony, premiered by the Pittsburgh Symphony Orchestra on December 2, 1955, won the Pulitzer Prize for Music in 1956.

+ David Van Vactor (1906–94) studied at Northwestern University (B.M., 1928; M.M., 1935), the Vienna Music Academy (1928–29), the École Normale, Paris (1931), and the Paris Conservatoire (1931); his teachers included Paul Dukas and Franz Schmidt. He composed seven symphonies. The Symphony No. 1 in D Minor (1936) won a prize of $1,000 in a 1938 competition sponsored by the New York Philharmonic Symphony Orchestra. The later symphonies include No. 2, "Music for the Marines" (1943), No. 3 in C Major (1958), No. 4, "Walden" for chorus and orchestra (1969), No. 5 (1975), No. 6 for band or orchestra (1980), and No. 7 (1982); he also composed a *Sinfonia breve* for small orchestra (1964).

+ Charles Vardell (1893–1962) wrote his *Carolinian Symphony* while in residence at the Eastman School of Music during the 1937–38 academic year. It premiered in April 1938 at the Festival of American Music and was performed by the Philadelphia Orchestra in 1940.⁴⁶⁷

+ Constant Vauclain (1908–2003) was a composer and theorist. His Symphony in One Movement dates from 1947; it is unclear how many other symphonies he composed.⁴⁶⁸

+ Bernard Wagenaar (1894–1971) came to the United States from the Netherlands in 1920 and became a US citizen in 1927. He taught for 43 years at the Juilliard School, where his pupils included William Schuman and Elie Siegmeister. He wrote four symphonies (1926, 1930, 1936 and 1946) and a number of other Neoclassical orchestral, vocal, and chamber music. Willem Mengelberg premiered Symphony No. 1 with the New York Philharmonic in 1928 and Arturo Toscanini performed his Second Symphony with the same ensemble.

+ Robert E. Ward (1917–2013) studied at the Eastman School of Music with Howard Hanson and Bernard Rogers and with Frederick Jacobi at the Juilliard School. Most famous for his opera *The Crucible* (1961), he composed numerous works for large ensemble, including seven symphonies (1941, 1947, 1950, 1958, 1976, 1988, and 1993). The Fifth, *Canticles of America*, a bicentennial work, sets texts of Walt Whitman and Henry Wadsworth Longfellow for soprano, baritone, narrator, chorus, and orchestra.

+ Jaromír Weinberger (1896–1967) studied at the Prague Conservatory and the Leipzig Conservatory. He achieved his greatest fame with the opera *Švanda dudák* (*Schwanda the Bagpiper*) in 1926. Emigrating to the United States in 1939, he became a US citizen in 1948. His *Lincolnova symfonie* (*Lincoln Symphony*) dates from 1941.

- + Emerson Whithorne (1884–1958) composed two symphonies (1929, 1935). The First was premiered by the Cleveland Orchestra in 1934. The Second (1935), also introduced by the Cleveland Orchestra, won a Juilliard School competition for the publication of American orchestral works in 1939.
- Meredith Willson (1902–84) attended Juilliard and played flute in John Philip Sousa's band before moving to San Francisco to work in radio. Although best known for his work in musical theater (especially *The Music Man* of 1957) and film scoring (*The Great Dictator*, 1940), his two symphonies—No. 1 in F Minor, "A Symphony of San Francisco" (1934–36), and No. 2 in E Minor, "Missions of California" (1963–64)—both celebrated his adopted state.

Bibliographic Overview

As Brian Hart has pointed out in chapter 1, there are few comprehensive sources for information on the symphony in the United States during the years covered in this chapter. Korn/SYMPHONY is a useful chapter from Robert Simpson's *The Symphony*. Butterworth/SYMPHONY and Tawa/GREAT are more complete surveys, although the quality is uneven in both. Steinberg/SYMPHONY includes essays on symphonies by Copland, Hanson, Martinů, Piston, and Stravinsky.

The issue of American identity, a lively source of debate during the era, has prompted scholarly commentary as well. Zuck/AMERICANISM looks at the evolution of attitudes toward both the cultural and musical issues of identity from the early nineteenth through the mid-twentieth century; although there are too many gaps to be completely satisfactory, Zuck includes an in-depth consideration of Harris's Third Symphony. Levy/FRONTIER and Levy/WHITE HOPE offer excellent analyses of the role of the West in defining musical identity during the era. The impact of World War II on music in the United States is covered in Fauser/WAR. Schnepel/GREAT is the most valuable source for considering the interrelationship of "Americanness" and "greatness."

As noted in chapter 1, the European centers of training for American composers shifted after World War I from Germany to France and Italy. Brody/AMERICAN ACADEMY, a book of essays, considers the cultural and musical issues in the American Academy in Rome. Simmons/WILDERNESS considers the Neoromantics, including Rome Prize alumni Hanson and Barber as well as Bloch. Although no such equivalent source is available for Nadia Boulanger's center, her influence as a pedagogue is discussed in Thomson/GREATEST; her influence on specific works is considered in Fauser/COPLAND AND BOULANGER and Francis/BOULANGER.

The way African American identity infused the work of three major symphonists has been the topic of significant scholarly activity. Studies on William Grant Still include a number of essays in Haas/FUSION, Smith/STILL, and Murchison/POETICS; Oja/STILL looks specifically at the *Afro-American Symphony*. Johnson/DAWSON and Brown/DAWSON present in-depth research on Dawson's *Negro Folk Symphony*. Brown and Shirley/PRICE and Brown/HEART are indispensable for studies of the First and Third symphonies of Florence Price. (At the time of writing, Douglas Shadle and Samantha Ege are preparing a volume on Price for the Master Musicians Series, published by Oxford University Press.) Brown/HARLEM presents invaluable information on all three of these composers. Howland/CONCERT JAZZ is an important source for James P. Johnson's *Harlem Symphony*, as well as other works of symphonic jazz by Johnson and Duke Ellington.

Composers of the era were keenly interested in each other's work, and their writing is a valuable source of information both about the music itself and about broader cultural issues relevant to the symphony; important sources are the *Musical Quarterly* and *Modern Music*. Cowell/COMPOSERS and Copland/OUR NEW are similarly valuable contemporary sources. Useful autobiographical materials are Antheil/BAD; Copland and Perlis/1900-1942 and SINCE 1943; and Thomson/THOMSON. Cowell and Nicholls/RESOURCES points to the new ways of thinking about musical materials that would be explored more fully in the decades after World War II.

Some scholarly literature provides treatments of the émigré experience from both cultural and musical perspectives: Crawford/WINDFALL, Danuser/EXILE, and Bahr/WEIMAR deal with the numerous émigrés fleeing Nazism. Maher/MILHAUD and Noss/HINDEMITH both focus on the way emigration to the United States affected particular composers' identities. Walsh/STRAVINSKY is the most useful source on the composer's life in the United States. "Life and works" examples are Strassburg/BLOCH, Crump/MARTINŮ, Large/MARTINŮ, and Rybka/MARTINŮ. Swickard/MILHAUD is a detailed examination of all the composer's symphonies. Émigrés who made careers in the film industry shaped symphonic music if not symphonies during this era; Kalinak/WEST and Karlin/MOVIES along with contemporary commentary by Antheil and Copland help us understand more about the relationship between that industry and concert and institutional life.

Many of the composers discussed in this chapter have at least one monograph devoted to their life and music, with discussion of the symphonies. Howard Pollack's published biographies Pollack/BLITZSTEIN, Pollack/COPLAND, and Pollack/PISTON (the latter based on his dissertation) are indispensable. Other biographies of note are Sachs/COWELL, Dickinson/BARBER, Heyman/BARBER, Broder/BARBER, Hoover and Cage/THOMSON, and Whitesitt/ANTHEIL. More analytical approaches to certain composers' works are taken in Cohen/HANSON, Slattery/STILL, and Stehman/SYMPHONIES.

Sources for the more obscure of the "brief mentions" include *Grove Music Online* as well as Reis/COMPOSERS and the American Supplement of the 1939 *Grove Dictionary of Musicians*.

Notes

1. Drew Massey wrote the initial draft of this chapter; shortly thereafter, personal obligations forced him to withdraw from the project, and Susan Key graciously agreed to take over. While much information from Massey's draft is retained, the content of this chapter—the organization, historical perspective, and most of the analytical commentary—is fully hers. I created the composer tables for this chapter [Editor].

2. Quoted in Whitesitt/ANTHEIL, p. 145.

3. Copland/KOUSSEVITZKY, p. 255.

4. As John Howland points out, even *Metronome* (1881) and *Down Beat* (1934) included coverage of symphonic music, especially when it drew on distinctively "American" styles (Howland/CONCERT JAZZ, p. 241).

5. See chapter 3, p. 167.

6. Fred Smith, WLW program director. Quoted in Lichty and Topping/SOURCE BOOK, p. 295.

7. Aaron Copland, for example, was featured on the 1936–37 CBS program "Modern Masters."

8. See statistics in Cornelius B. Canon, "The Federal Music Project of the Works Progress Administration: Music in a Democracy," PhD diss., University of Minnesota, 1963. Proquest #6307915.

9. Bindas/FMP, p. 66.

10. John Sullivan Dwight, "Music a Means of Culture," *Atlantic*, September 1870, p. 326.

11. *Life and Letters of Henry Lee Higginson*, vol. 2 (Boston: Atlantic Monthly Press, 1921), p. 395.

12. Davidson Taylor, "Music Written for Radio." Papers read by members of the American Musicological Society at the Annual Meeting, 1939, pp. 251–66. JSTOR, http://www.jstor.org/stable/43873179. Accessed February 24, 2023.

13. Aaron Copland, "The Musical Scene Changes," *Twice a Year*, Fall–Winter 1940, p. 343.

14. Aaron Copland, "What Do I Think of Radio and Records?," *Musical Courier*, December 1, 1940, p. 5.

15. "The New NBC Artists Service," *Musical Courier*, February 22, 1930, p. 36.

16. Marc Blitzstein, "Coming—the Mass Audience!," *Modern Music*, May–June 1936, p. 25.

17. Chapter 3, p. 125. For a full discussion, see Schnepel/GREAT. As Douglas Shadle explains in Shadle/NEW WORLD, the debate over using Black folk materials in particular was often racially motivated.

18. Thompson/CONTEMPORARY, p. 16.

19. While primary sources in this chapter refer to "jazz" as an umbrella term for popular styles, I will use it only for those styles we would recognize as part of a true jazz tradition.

20. Leonard Liebling, "Variations," *Musical Courier*, January 21, 1933, 17.

21. Telephone interview by the author with Morton Gould, October 22, 1993.

22. I am grateful to Mark Clague for pointing out in a conversation that Gershwin's radio success with *An American in Paris* was both artistic and economic; he was paid the astronomical sum of $5,000 for the broadcast premiere. See Clague/HARMONIZING.

23. Howland/CONCERT JAZZ, p. 2. While the serious music community largely looked down on their efforts, these composers were attacked from the other direction as well, as jazz aficionados deplored what they decried as the lack of jazz authenticity. See the extended discussion in Howland/CONCERT JAZZ.

24. See the essay on Bloch later in the present chapter for a fuller discussion of this issue.

25. Howard Hanson, "Cultivating a Climate for Creativity," *Music Educators Journal* 46, no. 6 (June–July 1960): p. 29. Also see Howland/CONCERT JAZZ, pp. 242–43, for the way in which polarization affected the reception of hybrid styles.

26. Quoted in Tawa/GREAT, p. 86.

27. Fauser/WAR, p. 255.

28. Also to this period belong the earliest, and sometimes the most prominent, symphonies by Roger Sessions, Paul Creston, William Schuman, David Diamond, Vincent Persichetti, and Leonard Bernstein; but, because their most important work with the genre—compositional or promotional—occurred between 1950 and 1970, and they will be covered in chapter 6.

29. Caroline Potter, "Nadia Boulanger," in *Grove Music Online*.

30. See chapter 6 of this volume for the symphonic contributions of Diamond and chapter 9 for the works of Carter and Glass.

31. Leon Botstein, essay written for the American Symphony Orchestra concert "Nadia Boulanger: Teacher of the Century," performed on May 13, 1998, at Avery Fisher Hall at Lincoln Center, https://www.leonbotstein.com/blog/nadia-boulager-teacher-of-the-century.

32. Thomson/GREATEST, p. 43.

33. Piston/CONVERSATION, p. 7.

34. Thomson/GREATEST, p. 43.

35. See a full discussion in Fauser/COPLAND AND BOULANGER.

36. Pollack/BLITZSTEIN, p. 73.

37. Fauser/WAR, p. 262.

38. Pollack/BLITZSTEIN, pp. 282–83. Pollack includes an extended description of the symphony. Samuel Barber also wrote his Second Symphony on the subject of the Air Force, which he began the following year.

39. Ibid., p. 289.

40. Ibid., p. 259.

41. Ibid., p. 284.

42. The score to the first half of the *Airborne Symphony* is available online at http://archives.nyphil.org/index.php/artifact/143f37c1-a9aa-4529-87a8-d742f0986039/fullview#page/6/mode/1up.

43. Pollack/BLITZSTEIN, p. 286.

44. See, for example, Helen Lundeberg's *History of Transportation*, https://www.inglewoodpublicart.org/projects/the-history-of-transportation/.

45. Pollack/BLITZSTEIN, p. 282.

46. Ibid., p. 285.

47. Quoted from the analysis published on the Marc Blitzstein website, http://www.marcblitzstein.com/pages/music/intros/airborne.htm.

48. Pollack/BLITZSTEIN, p. 290. While the postwar euphoria might have dampened the immediate impact of the "warning" with which the *Airborne* ended, it did inspire folksinger Lee Hays's "The Hammer Song," and thus might be said to have had a crossover impact on the next generation (p. 291).

49. Quoted in ibid., p. 291.

50. Quoted in ibid.

51. Quoted in ibid., p. 293.

52. Ibid., p. 293.

53. The full piece was performed in San Francisco in 2016 by Curious Flights under the baton of Alasdair Neale. While noting the score's difficulties, artistic director Brenden Guy said that musicians and audience alike appreciated the work's eclecticism and dramatic impact (telephone interview with the author, June 3, 2017). These characteristics also suggest that the piece presents an opportunity for multimedia presentation, as Irving Kolodin suggested in a 1966 review (Pollack/BLITZSTEIN, p. 292). In today's media environment, this could be done with sophisticated tools using a mixture of period and contemporary visual material. In particular, the "Ballad of the Cities" movement could profitably be singled out for such treatment.

54. For an overview, see Robertson and Armstrong/COPLAND.

55. The *Dance Symphony* of 1929 is not discussed here because, as Copland stated, it was not a "symphony in the traditional sense," the music being extracted from his unperformed ballet *Grohg* (1925; Copland and Perlis/1900-1942, p. 163). Nonetheless, it is of some significance to the history of symphonic work in America, as it shared the prestigious $25,000 RCA Victor Prize in 1929 with compositions by Robert Russell Bennett, Louis Gruenberg, and Ernest Bloch.

56. Tawa/GREAT, p. 7.

57. Ibid., p. 172.

58. Copland and Perlis/1900-1942, p. 104. Copland understood the remark as Damrosch's "way of smoothing the ruffled feathers of his conservative Sunday afternoon ladies faced with modern American music" (ibid.).

59. Butterworth/SYMPHONY, p. 50.

60. Copland and Perlis/1900-1942, p. 108.

61. Butterworth/SYMPHONY, p. 51.

62. Copland and Perlis/1900-1942, p. 208.

63. Pollack/COPLAND, p. 221. Similar words have been used to describe the slightly earlier Piano Variations of 1930.

64. Perhaps inspired by the *Short Symphony*, Chávez used a heckelphone in his First Symphony of 1934 (*Sinfonía de Antígona*). See chapter 8 of this volume for a discussion of Chávez's six symphonies.

65. Copland and Perlis/1900-1942, p. 209.

66. Berger/COPLAND, p. 442.

67. Both Copland's and Stokowski's descriptions are quoted in Copland and Perlis/1900-1942, p. 212.

68. William Fineshriber Jr. to Aaron Copland, May 1, 1941, box 335, folder 8, Aaron Copland Collection, Library of Congress. According to Pollack, the sextet was first performed in 1939 (Pollack/COPLAND, p. 290).

69. Crist/SKETCH TO SCORE, p. 377.

70. Ibid., p. 378.

71. Ibid., p. 379.

72. Copland and Perlis/SINCE 1943, p. 64.

73. Pollack/COPLAND, p. 410.

74. Program notes quoted in Crist/RECEPTION, p. 254; see also Copland and Perlis/SINCE 1943, p. 67.

75. Copland and Perlis/SINCE 1943, p. 68.

76. Crist/RECEPTION, p. 254; Copland and Perlis/SINCE 1943, p. 67.

77. Copland and Perlis/SINCE 1943, p. 67.

78. Pollack/COPLAND, p. 412.

79. Crist/SKETCH TO SCORE, p. 390.

80. For a thorough compositional history, see ibid.

81. Crist/RECEPTION, p. 255.

82. Berger/SYMPHONY, p. 25.

83. Crist/RECEPTION, p. 256.

84. Berger/SYMPHONY, p. 27.

85. Copland and Perlis/SINCE 1943, p. 68.

86. Crist/SKETCH TO SCORE, p. 398. After a few performances, Bernstein took it on himself to make what he called a sizable cut near the end; Copland was annoyed at first but came to agree that shortening the Finale improved the work (Copland and Perlis/SINCE 1943, p. 71).

87. Quoted in Crist/RECEPTION, p. 237.

88. From a 1946 review by Warren Storey Smith for the *Boston Post*. Quoted in ibid., p. 237.

89. Quoted in Pollack/COPLAND, p. 411.

90. Berger/SYMPHONY, p. 24.

91. Key and Rothe/MAVERICKS, p. 47.

92. Levy/FRONTIER, p. 227.

93. See the full chronology in Stehman/PIONEER.

94. Quoted in Levy/WHITE HOPE, pp. 131–32.

95. Quote from Schnepel/GREAT, p. 509. For an analysis, see Robertson/SYMPHONIES I and Stehman/PIONEER, pp. 52–57.

96. Stehman/PIONEER, p. 58.

97. Schnepel/GREAT, p. 513.

98. For an extended discussion of Harris's attitudes to Americanism, see Zuck/AMERICANISM, pp. 235–43.

99. Schnepel/GREAT, pp. 513, 516.

100. Copland/OUR NEW, pp. 119–20.

101. Schnepel/GREAT, p. 241.

102. Stehman/PIONEER, p. 68.

103. Quoted in Levy/FRONTIER, p. 246.

104. Quoted in ibid., pp. 246–47.
105. Quoted in ibid., p. 247.
106. Roy Harris, "Problems of American Composers," in Cowell/COMPOSERS, p. 151.
107. Stehman/PIONEER, pp. 64–65. Also see discussion in Tawa/GREAT, p. 57.
108. Quoted in Perlis and Van Cleve/VOICES, p. 345.
109. Stehman/PIONEER, p. 67.
110. Ibid., pp. 66, 69.
111. Korn/SYMPHONY, p. 251.
112. Stehman/SYMPHONIES, p. 256.
113. Schnepel/GREAT, p. 513.
114. Quoted in Butterworth/SYMPHONY, p. 84.
115. See examples in Schnepel/GREAT, pp. 513–22. There were also occasional reservations about the one-movement form, especially in the original version with the overly brief ending.
116. Tawa/GREAT, p. 57. For example, Virgil Thomson in 1970: this symphony "remains to this day America's most convincing product in that form" (quoted in Schnepel/GREAT, p. 522).
117. See Lamb/AMERICAN SYMPHONY, pp. 1–4.
118. Stehman/PIONEER, p. 72.
119. Tawa/GREAT, p. 61.
120. Fauser/WAR, p. 260.
121. Quoted in Massey/KIRKPATRICK, p. 37.
122. Quoted in Tawa/GREAT, p. 62. The composer's notorious vanity also alienated fellow musicians: Copland tartly observed in 1930 that he "wish[ed] I only knew him thru his music" (Pollack/COPLAND, p. 170).
123. Robertson/SYMPHONIES I, p. 13.
124. See Fauser/WAR, pp. 251–55, for more on this work.
125. Stehman/SYMPHONIES, p. 545.
126. Ibid., p. 546. Stehman finds the Seventh to be perhaps Harris's finest symphony (Stehman/PIONEER, p. 100).
127. Tawa/GREAT, p. 63.
128. Stehman/PIONEER considers the *San Francisco* the most successful of the later symphonies (p. 114). He regards all the subsequent works as uneven, though having impressive moments—except for the *Bicentennial*, "the least substantial of all Harris's symphonies in musical invention" (p. 146).
129. Quoted in Robertson/SYMPHONIES II, p. 27.
130. Levy/FRONTIER, p. 228.
131. Howard Pollack, "Walter Piston," *Grove Music Online*.
132. Quoted in ibid.
133. Elliott Carter, "Walter Piston," *Musical Quarterly* 32, no. 3 (July 1946): p. 354.
134. Butterworth/SYMPHONY, p. 69.
135. Ibid., p. 67.
136. Pollack/PISTON, p. 175.
137. Ibid., pp. 47–48.
138. Ibid., pp. 48–49.
139. Tawa/GREAT, p. 124.
140. Ibid., p. 125.
141. Butterworth/SYMPHONY, pp. 68–69.
142. Bernstein conducted this movement as a memorial to Piston when he died in 1976.
143. Butterworth/SYMPHONY, pp. 69–70.
144. Pollack/PISTON, p. 111.

145. William Austin, "Piston's Fourth Symphony: An Analysis," *Music Review* 16, no. 2 (May 1955): p. 121.
146. Butterworth/SYMPHONY, p. 72.
147. Pollack/PISTON, p. 133.
148. Clifford Taylor, "Walter Piston: For His Seventieth Birthday," *Perspective of New Music* 3, no. 1 (Fall–Winter 1964): p. 114.
149. Pollack/PISTON, p. 141.
150. Meckna/SACRED, p. 466.
151. Thomson/THOMSON, p. 76.
152. Quoted in Michael Meckna, Review of *Symphony on a Hymn Tune* and Symphony No. 2, *American Music* 18, no. 3 (Fall 2000): pp. 338–40.
153. For a detailed analysis of *Symphony on a Hymn Tune*, see Meckna/SACRED.
154. Both harmonic techniques are noted by John Cage in his discussion of the piece (Hoover and Cage/THOMSON, pp. 154–55).
155. Cage calls this "not a passacaglia" but an ostinato (ibid., p. 156).
156. Ibid.
157. Ibid., p. 131.
158. Thomson/THOMSON p. 72.
159. Quoted in Butterworth/SYMPHONY, p. 62.
160. Ibid., p. 63.
161. For a comprehensive history, see Olmstead/ROME PRIZE.
162. Oja/ROME PRIZE, p. 161.
163. Ibid., p. 159.
164. Heyman/BARBER, p. 130.
165. Quoted in Pollack/SIBELIUS, p. 184.
166. Ashley Pettis, letter to the music editor, *New York Times*, November 13, 1938, p. 8x.
167. Roy Harris, letter to the music editor, *New York Times,* November 27, 1938, p. 6x.
168. As he did with many of his works, Barber revised the score in 1942, replacing the Scherzo and lightening the texture. See Butterworth/SYMPHONY, p. 109.
169. For details, see Pollack/SIBELIUS.
170. Heyman/BARBER, p. 140.
171. Barber, speaking in 1949, quoted in Heyman/BARBER, p. 143.
172. Ibid.
173. Dickinson/BARBER, p. 16.
174. Fauser/WAR, p. 23.
175. Heyman/BARBER, p. 223.
176. Broder/BARBER, p. 81.
177. James Fassett interview with the composer in Dickinson/BARBER, p. 36.
178. Simmons/WILDERNESS, p. 284.
179. Nathan Broder, "The Music of Samuel Barber," *Musical Quarterly* 34, no. 3 (July 1948): p. 331.
180. Tawa/GREAT, pp. 129–35; Pollack, Review of Barber's Second Symphony in *Notes* 47, no. 3 (March 1991): p. 958.
181. See the discussion in Oja/ROME PRIZE.
182. His cofounders were Marion Bauer, Aaron Copland, Harrison Kerr, Otto Luening, and Quincy Porter. For an introduction to the American Music Center, see Harrison Kerr, "The American Music Center," *Notes* 1, no. 3 (June 1944): pp. 34–41.
183. Williams/HANSON, p. 21.
184. Thompson/CONTEMPORARY, p. 13.
185. Simmons/WILDERNESS, p. 119.

186. Butterworth/SYMPHONY, p. 76.
187. Matthew Robert Bishop, "Patriotism, Nationalism, and Heritage in the Orchestral Music of Howard Hanson" (MA thesis, Florida State University, 2013).
188. Butterworth/SYMPHONY, p. 79.
189. Howard Hanson, Introduction to the Third Symphony (Rochester, NY: Eastman School of Music, 1941).
190. Goddard Lieberson, "Over the Air," *Modern Music* 15, no. 1 (November–December 1937): p. 53.
191. Quoted in Frederick William Westphal, "Music in Radio Broadcasting" (PhD diss., Eastman School of Music, 1948), p. 238. The others tapped for these inaugural "Columbia Composers Commissions" were Aaron Copland, Louis Gruenberg, Walter Piston, Roy Harris, and William Grant Still.
192. Williams/HANSON, p. 19.
193. Simmons/WILDERNESS, p. 133.
194. Cohen/HANSON, pp. 120, 105.
195. Hanson/HARMONIC.
196. Cohen/HANSON, p. 105.
197. Quoted in Butterworth/SYMPHONY, p. 81.
198. Frank Lehman, "Neo-Romantic Minority Report—Hanson's 6th," *Unsung Symphonies* blogspot, September 29, 2010, http://unsungsymphonies.blogspot.com/2010/09/middle-america-has-given-us-two-great.html.
199. Edith Borroff, Record Review of Howard Hanson's symphonies, *American Music* 10, no. 3 (Fall 1992): p. 387. The recordings include Symphonies 1, 2, 3, and 6.
200. Karlin/MOVIES, p. 6.
201. The section on Sowerby is substantially based on an initial draft by Katie Baber.
202. Oja/ROME PRIZE, p. 196.
203. Francis Crociata, "Leo Sowerby: The Crucial Piece of the Puzzle at Last," liner notes to the recording Sowerby: Symphony No. 2, Cedille Records CDR039, conducted by Paul Freeman, *DRAM* online, http://www.dramonline.org/albums/sowerby-symphony-no-2/notes.
204. *Chicago Tribune*, July 9, 1968, p. 12.
205. J. M., Leo Sowerby obituary, *Musical Times* 109, no. 1507 (September 1968): p. 842; Ronald Stalford and Michael Meckna, "Leo Sowerby," *Grove Music Online*.
206. Stalford and Meckna, "Sowerby."
207. See chapter 6 for Creston's symphonies.
208. Olmstead notes that by 1925 Whiteman had played *Synconata* about 90 times (Olmstead/ROME PRIZE, p. 16).
209. Raymond Durward Jones, "Leo Sowerby: His Life and His Choral Music" (PhD diss., University of Iowa, 1973), p. iv.
210. Tuthill/SOWERBY, p. 249.
211. Ibid., pp. 252–54.
212. Crociata, "Leo Sowerby."
213. Thompson/CONTEMPORARY, p. 10.
214. From Thompson's inaugural address at Princeton University, 1946, quoted in Forbes/THOMPSON, p. 1.
215. Thompson/CONTEMPORARY, p. 17. The tendency in midcentury America to value the virtuoso performer (or conductor) over the composer is a running theme in Horowitz/EXILE.
216. See the discussion of prevailing critical assumptions about timelessness in Schnepel/GREAT, pp. 70–71.
217. Randall Thompson to Alfredo Trinchieri, 13 June 1959, quoted in Schmidt and Schmidt/THOMPSON, p. 3.

218. Quoted in Schmidt/TUNESMITH, p. 306.
219. Forbes/THOMPSON, p. 3.
220. Ibid., p. 2.
221. Quoted in Tawa/GREAT, p. 64.
222. Quincy Porter, "American Composers, XVIII: Randall Thompson," *Modern Music* 19 (1942): p. 239.
223. Quoted in Schnepel/GREAT, p. 490.
224. See Schmidt/TUNESMITH for more detail on Thompson's experience with these styles.
225. See a full discussion of critical reaction in Schnepel/GREAT, pp. 481–93.
226. Quoted in Tawa/SYMPHONY, p. 169.
227. Frederic Wilson, "Randall Thompson," *Grove Music Online*.
228. Schnepel/GREAT, p. 446.
229. Brown/HARLEM, p. 76.
230. Howland/CONCERT JAZZ, pp. 54–57.
231. Like Antheil and Still, a number of film composers contributed symphonic works—either full symphonies or shorter one-movement works—that played an important part in what Americans heard in concert halls and on the radio. A list of these composers will be found at the end of this chapter. For more, see my own research about music on Depression-era radio (Margaret Susan Key, "'Sweet Melody over Silent Wave': Depression-Era Radio and the American Composer," PhD diss., University of Maryland at College Park, 1995), as well as the list of the core repertoire of American symphonies in Schnepel/GREAT.
232. Antheil/BAD, p. 356.
233. In his autobiography, Antheil noted that some of the passages in his Fourth Symphony that reminded critics of recent Shostakovich symphonies actually originated in the last act of his 1928 opera *Transatlantic*. He added, "In any case, I am not going to change *my* style to please said critics: finders is keepers [*sic*]" (ibid., p. 221).
234. Ibid., p. 194. Antheil revised the work in 1955 and both versions now receive performances.
235. Parts of the piece remain in manuscript while other parts were incorporated into the Third Symphony. For a detailed history, see Statham/ANTHEIL, pp. 7–12.
236. Quoted in Whitesitt/ANTHEIL, p. 149.
237. Antheil/BAD, p. 252.
238. Ibid., pp. 323–24. Copland responded that Harris's symphony "often sounds like Sibelius to me, at least in construction, quite too much so, in fact." Still, he liked the work because, whatever its structural debts, the content was completely individual and original.
239. See chapter 6 of this volume for a discussion of these composers and their urban style.
240. For a comprehensive discussion, see Statham/ANTHEIL.
241. Ibid., p. 6.
242. Ibid., p. 5.
243. Ibid., p. 16.
244. Antheil drafted a score for the film about the completion of the Transcontinental Railroad, but DeMille disliked what he heard and replaced the composer (Kalinak/WEST, p. 210).
245. Unpublished typescript quoted in a review by Mauro Piccinini of *George Antheil: Symphonies and Other Works* (3 CDs), in *American Music* 22, no. 1 (Spring 2004): p. 200.
246. Tawa/GREAT, p. 95.
247. Whitesitt/ANTHEIL, p. 149.
248. Ibid., p. 150.
249. Antheil, quoted in Whitesitt/ANTHEIL, p. 145.
250. Ibid., p. 145.
251. Antheil/BAD, pp. 340–41, 345.

252. Leinsdorf, review in *Notes*, 2nd ser. 2, no. 3 (June 1945): pp. 174–75.
253. Whitesitt/ANTHEIL, p. 145.
254. Antheil/BAD, p. 346.
255. Whitesitt/ANTHEIL, p. 153.
256. For a history of the two versions, see Whitesitt/ANTHEIL, pp. 152-3.
257. Letter to F. Charles Adler, August 22, 1952. Copy in George Antheil Collection, Stanford University Library Box 1 Folder 1.
258. Publisher's note, Antheil, Symphony No. 5 (New York: Leeds Music Corporation, 1950).
259. Linda Whitesitt, Charles Amirkhanian, and Susan C. Cook, "George Antheil" *Grove Music Online*. See chapter 1, p. 23, of the present volume for Thomson's enthusiastic reaction to the Fourth Symphony.
260. Letter to F. Charles Adler, August 22, 1952. George Antheil Collection, Stanford University Library, Box 1 Folder 1. The descriptive quotes about the piece in the following two paragraphs also come from this letter.
261. Letter to F. Charles Adler, December 1952. The capitalization is Antheil's.
262. Whitesitt/ANTHEIL, pp. 156–60.
263. Robert Sabin, review of Antheil, Sixth Symphony, *Notes* 2nd ser. 13, no. 1 (December 1955): p. 146.
264. Statham/ANTHEIL, p. 16.
265. Sachs/COWELL, p. 512.
266. Weisgall/COWELL, p. 498.
267. Hicks/COWELL, p. 429.
268. For a full account of this important facet of Cowell's development, see Johnson/COWELL.
269. Miller/COWELL AND CAGE, p. 55.
270. Weisgall/COWELL, p. 492.
271. On the incident, see Michael Hicks, "The Imprisonment of Henry Cowell," *Journal of the American Musicological Society* 44, no. 1 (Spring 1991): pp. 92–119. Cowell's imprisonment on a morals charge in 1936 damaged his formerly warm relationship with Charles Ives, though perhaps not to the degree often assumed (Leta Miller and Rob Collins, "The Cowell-Ives Relationship: A New Look at Cowell's Prison Years," *American Music* 23, no. 4 [Winter 2005]: pp. 473–92).
272. Weisgall/COWELL, p. 485.
273. Ibid., p. 490.
274. Sachs/COWELL, p. 401.
275. Introductory note to Henry Cowell, Symphony 4 (New York: Associated Music, 1948).
276. Ibid.
277. Fine/COWELL, pp. 312–13.
278. Introductory note.
279. Fine/COWELL, p. 313.
280. Ibid.
281. Introductory note.
282. Weldon Hart, review in *Notes* 6, no. 2 (March 1949): p. 323.
283. Fine/COWELL, p. 313.
284. For more on the Louisville Orchestra and its patronage of the American symphony, see chapter 6 in this volume.
285. Henry Cowell, Symphony No. 11 musical score (New York: Associated Music, 1955), p. 2.
286. Quoted in Rao/COWELL, p. 283.
287. Ibid., p. 301.
288. Composer note, https://www.wisemusicclassical.com/work/27042/Symphony-No-15-Thesis--Henry-Cowell/.

289. See his review of Hovhaness's 24-movement Symphony No. 9, "St. Vartan," *Musical Quarterly* 37 (July 1951): pp. 396–99. That work and two other symphonies by Hovhaness are examined in chapter 6 in this volume.

290. See the discussion of polymeters in Cowell and Nicholls/RESOURCES, pp. 66–72.

291. See the analytical chart in Spilker/NEW ORDER, pp. 198–99.

292. Quoted in Sachs/COWELL, p. 476.

293. Goss, review in *Notes* 22, no. 1 (Autumn 1965): p. 824.

294. Goldman/COWELL, p. 23.

295. Sachs/COWELL, p. 476.

296. Weisgall/COWELL, p. 489.

297. Quoted in ibid., p. 498.

298. For details on the symphonies of Harrison and the postmodernists, see chapter 9 in this volume.

299. Sachs/COWELL, p. 512.

300. I am especially indebted to Gwynne Kuhner Brown for sharing her research on Dawson with me; this essay is largely based on her article Brown/DAWSON. More information and analysis about the symphony can be found in Johnson/DAWSON. The latter source includes a detailed analysis of the original version of the work. Both authors theorize about the cultural and aesthetic factors that prevented Dawson's symphony from entering the repertoire in the way that Still's *Afro-American Symphony* did.

301. Brown/DAWSON, p. 434.

302. Johnson/DAWSON, p. 46.

303. Brown/DAWSON, p. 435. The prize was one of many arts patronage efforts by businessman Rodman Wanamaker.

304. Johnson/DAWSON, p. 47.

305. A detailed chronology is in Brown/HARLEM, p. 76. The revision was published in 1963 and is the version performed today. Stokowski's 1963 recording was on Decca Gold Label Stereo DL 710077.

306. Brown/DAWSON, pp. 437–38.

307. Program Notes on *Negro Folk Symphony* from Philadelphia Orchestra Concert at Carnegie Hall, November 20, 1934. Quoted in ibid., p. 453.

308. A transcription of this spiritual credited to John W. Work's *American Negro Songs* appears in Farrah/SEMIOTIC. Farrah analyzes the original version of the symphony.

309. Program Notes on *Negro Folk Symphony* from Philadelphia Orchestra Concert at Carnegie Hall, November 20, 1934. Quoted in Brown/DAWSON, p. 453.

310. Brown/DAWSON, p. 450.

311. Program Notes on *Negro Folk Symphony* from Philadelphia Orchestra Concert at Carnegie Hall, November 20, 1934. Quoted in Brown/DAWSON, p. 453.

312. Abromeit/SPIRITUALS points to Ballanta-Taylor's *Saint Helena Island Spirituals* (1925) for the source of this spiritual. I am indebted to Gwynne Kuhner Brown for directing me to this source. "Hallelujah, Lord" Dawson pulls from the first of the Johnson brothers' books of *American Negro Spirituals* (also 1925).

313. Program Notes on *Negro Folk Symphony* from Philadelphia Orchestra Concert at Carnegie Hall, November 20, 1934. Quoted in Brown/DAWSON, p. 454.

314. Johnson/DAWSON, p. 48.

315. Quoted in Brown/DAWSON, p. 433.

316. Alain Locke, "Toward a Critique of Negro Music," *Opportunity* (December 1934): p. 385; quoted in ibid., p. 442.

317. Brown/DAWSON, pp. 440–41.

318. Ibid., pp. 444–47.

319. Johnson/DAWSON, p. 48.
320. Howland/CONCERT JAZZ, p. 65. Another factor in Johnson's desire to elevate Black music derived from his friendship with Dvořák student Will Marion Cook (1869–1944; ibid., p. 57).
321. Ibid., pp. 24–25.
322. Quoted in Marcello Piras, "Garibaldi to Syncopation: Bruto Giannini and the Curious Case of Scott Joplin's *Magnetic Rag*," *Journal of Jazz Studies* vol. 9, no. 2 (Winter 2013): pp. 107–77. This article provides a fascinating in-depth study of Bruto Giannini, who also taught Scott Joplin. Howland also notes that Johnson apparently studied at the Conservatory of Musical Art in New York. Howland/CONCERT JAZZ, p. 24.
323. Howland/CONCERT JAZZ, pp. 208–9.
324. Howland also mentions an even earlier *Symphonic Dance: Carolina Shout*, though that work does not appear in Johnson's own list of symphonic works (ibid., pp. 64–65).
325. The Gullah culture is popularly known through Dubose Heyward's 1925 novel *Porgy* and its subsequent incarnations as a Broadway play (1927) and Gershwin's opera *Porgy and Bess* (1935).
326. Howland/CONCERT JAZZ, pp. 79–80.
327. Ibid., p. 47.
328. Tom Davin, "Conversations with James P Johnson," *Jazz Review* 2, no. 6 (July 1959): p. 12.
329. Both Howland and Kyle Gann provide detailed analyses of the work; the differences between the two, especially in the first movement, reflect these analytical challenges (Howland/CONCERT JAZZ, pp. 220–39; Kyle Gann's is online at Kyle Gann, "James P. Johnson: Harlem Symphony (1932)," https://www.kylegann.com/JohnsonHarlem.html).
330. Scott Brown, quoted in Howland/CONCERT JAZZ, p. 222.
331. Ibid., p. 230.
332. Rather than a loose sonata form, Howland describes this movement as a loose set of variations separated by interludes (ibid., pp. 231–35).
333. Presumably with the composer's approval, Domenico Savino arranged this movement for solo piano, and Robbins Music published it in 1944 under the title "April in Harlem: A Modern Composition for Piano." The 1945 Carnegie Hall performance of the *Harlem Symphony* adopted "April in Harlem" as the title for the second movement.
334. Gann, "James P. Johnson."
335. See details in Howland/CONCERT JAZZ, p. 212.
336. Ibid., p. 245.
337. Winners of the Guggenheim mentioned in this chapter include George Antheil, Ernst Bacon, Samuel Barber, Robert Russell Bennett, Marc Blitzstein, Aaron Copland, Henry Cowell, Roy Harris, Bohuslav Martinů, Walter Piston, Harold Shapero, William Grant Still, Virgil Thomson, and Randall Thompson. A comprehensive list is available at https://www.gf.org/fellows/.
338. Much of what follows is a distillation of Rae Linda Brown's biographical and analytical essay "Lifting the Veil: The Symphonies of Florence B. Price," in Brown and Shirley/PRICE, pp. xv–lii.
339. Ibid., p. xxxv.
340. Ibid., p. xxv.
341. Jackson/PRICE, p. 40.
342. Alex Ross, "The Rediscovery of Florence Price," *New Yorker*, February 5, 2018.
343. Another example of this hybrid musical surface can be found in the *Five Folksongs in Counterpoint* for string quartet (1951), which combines the vernacular melodies (two spirituals and three folk songs of various ethnic and racial origins) with European techniques of intricate counterpoint and late Romantic chromatic harmonies.
344. Brown and Shirley/PRICE, pp. xl–xlii.
345. Ibid., p. xvl.
346. Ibid., p. xlix.

347. Ibid., p. xlix.
348. Ibid., p. lii.
349. Ibid., p. l.
350. The first two-measure gesture of the B theme resembles Stephen Foster's 1851 minstrel song "Old Folks at Home." Rae Linda Brown states that the gesture "suggest[s] popular music" (ibid.); she does not mention Foster, but, on account of the enduring popularity of his song, it is hard to believe that the similarity is purely coincidental.
351. Gioia/JAZZ, p. 6.
352. Brown and Shirley/PRICE, p. li.
353. In his liner notes for the recording (Price First and Fourth Symphonies, Naxos 8.559827, released 2019), Douglas Shadle likens the musical language of its middle section to the "jungle sounds" of "Duke" Ellington's band.
354. All quotes are from a telephone interview with John Jeter, July 5, 2018.
355. Murchison/POETICS, p. 47. Still orchestrated James P. Johnson's *Yamekraw* for piano and orchestra, in which version the work premiered in a concert given by W. C. Handy at Carnegie Hall in 1928 (Johnson's pupil Thomas "Fats" Waller [1904–43] was the pianist, as the composer was unable to attend).
356. Gayle Murchison and Catherine Parsons Smith, "William Grant Still," *Grove Music Online*.
357. Quoted in Oja/STILL, p. 152.
358. Downes, quoted in ibid., p. 153.
359. Catherine Parsons Smith, "Personal Notes," in Smith/STILL, p. 223. Online version at https://publishing.cdlib.org/ucpressebooks/view?docId=ft1h4nb0g0&chunk.id=d0e7410&brand=ucpress.
360. Quoted in ibid., p. 224.
361. Smith/STILL, p. 71.
362. Oja/STILL, p. 154. Bracketed emendations are Oja's.
363. Haas/FUSION, p. 11.
364. Quoted in Oja/STILL, pp. 159–60.
365. A more detailed analysis is in Slattery/STILL.
366. See discussion in Smith/STILL, pp. 136–44.
367. Slattery/STILL, p. 123.
368. Ibid., p. 128.
369. Ibid., p. 127.
370. Emanuel Balaban, quoted in Schnepel/GREAT, p. 436. As the analysis indicates, Balaban erred in declaring the symphony was not cyclic.
371. Hanson quoted in the preface to Haas/FUSION, p. ix.
372. Oja/STILL, p. 146.
373. From Cowell/COMPOSERS. Quoted in Oja/STILL, p. 164.
374. Smith/STILL, pp. 322–23.
375. Quoted in Slattery/STILL, p. 130. All quotations from the composer's program notes in this section come from Slattery/STILL.
376. See detailed analysis in ibid., pp. 130–40.
377. Ibid., p. 139.
378. Quoted in David Ciucevich Jr., liner notes to the recording of Still's Fourth and Fifth Symphonies (Naxos 8.559603, 2009), p. 4.
379. Quoted in Kushner/STILL, pp. 34–35.
380. Haas/FUSION, p. ix.
381. More than 1,500 arrived between 1933 and 1944 alone. For more detail, see Peter Gay, "'We Miss our Jews': The Musical Migration from Nazi Germany," in Brinkmann and Wolff/PARADISE, p. 21.

382. Arnold Schoenberg, "On Artists and Collaboration" in *Modern Music* 22, no. 1 (November–December 1944): p. 4.

383. Krenek/INFLUENCE, p. 113. The original article (in German) appeared in 1959.

384. Reinhold Brinkmann, "Reading a Letter" in Brinkmann and Wolff/PARADISE, p. 9.

385. Bahr/WEIMAR and Crawford/WINDFALL.

386. Goldberg, "The Transplanted Composer," Sounding Board, *Los Angeles Times*, May 14, 21, and 28, 1950. See also Eric Zeisl, "The Reception of Austrian Composers in Los Angeles," http://www.zeisl.com/essays-and-articles/the-reception-of-austrian-composers-in-los-angeles.htm.

387. Krenek/INFLUENCE, p. 115.

388. See the detailed history and description in Móricz/BIRTH.

389. Kushner/BLOCH, p. 83.

390. From program notes for the Boston Symphony Orchestra, 1938–39, pp. 28–31. Quoted in Strassburg/BLOCH. Emphasis in the original.

391. Quotes from Brotman/BLOCK, pp. 436–37.

392. Thompson/CONTEMPORARY, p. 12.

393. Cowell/CHRONICLE, p. 237.

394. Ibid, p. 239.

395. Quoted in Suzanne Bloch, *Ernest Bloch: Creative Spirit: A Program Source Book* (New York: Jewish Music Council, 1976), p. 95.

396. Strassburg/BLOCH, p. 80. The symphonies of Roger Sessions are covered in chapter 6 of this volume.

397. Noss/HINDEMITH, p. 113.

398. Ibid., p. 116.

399. Ibid., p. 137.

400. Richard Franko Goldman, review of a recording by Eastman Symphonic Wind Ensemble in *Musical Quarterly* 44, no. 1 (January 1958): p. 127.

401. Quoted from Frederick Dorian, "Chronicle," *Musical Quarterly* 45, no. 4 (October 1959): pp. 524–25.

402. Gunther Schuller, review in *Notes* 19, no. 1 (December 1961): p. 143.

403. Noss/HINDEMITH, p. 155.

404. Kowalke/HINDEMITH, p. 168.

405. Large/MARTINŮ, p. 82.

406. Šafránek/MARTINŮ, p. 13.

407. Evans/MARTINŮ, p. 19.

408. Crump/MARTINŮ, p. 370.

409. Quoted in Rybka/MARTINŮ, p. 125. The grammar and punctuation are Martinů's.

410. Ibid., p. 132.

411. Ibid., p. 137.

412. Large/MARTINŮ, p. 91.

413. Rybka/MARTINŮ, p. 140.

414. Šafránek/MARTINŮ, p. 14.

415. Crump/MARTINŮ, p. 321.

416. Ibid., p. 332.

417. Ibid., pp. 332–33.

418. A more detailed analysis is in ibid., pp. 341–43.

419. Large/MARTINŮ, p. 93. Martinů had previously invoked the famous opening of Beethoven's Fifth Symphony at the climax of his deeply moving threnody *Memorial to Lidice* (1943).

420. Steinberg/SYMPHONY, p. 366.

421. Quoted in ibid., p. 372. In a footnote, Steinberg also mentions that "The *Fantaisies symphoniques* turned out to be Martinů's only symphony without a piano in the orchestra. He used to say that the reason he started using the piano in his orchestral scores was that he had not learned to figure out the complicated transpositions that writing for the harp required."
422. Crump/MARTINŮ, p. 408.
423. Reis/COMPOSERS, CONDUCTORS, pp. 182–86.
424. See the extended discussion in Maher/MILHAUD.
425. Collaer/MILHAUD, p. 217. For a detailed analysis of all twelve symphonies, see Swickard/MILHAUD.
426. Maher/MILHAUD, p. 46.
427. Quoted in Swickard/MILHAUD, p. 96.
428. Ibid., p. 112.
429. Collaer/MILHAUD, p. 220.
430. Ibid., p. 220
431. Ibid., p. 159.
432. Milhaud and Breitrose/CONVERSATIONS, p. 56.
433. Martin Anderson, review of various Milhaud works, *Tempo* 198 (October 1996): p. 52.
434. See the chapter on "Stravinsky in Hollywood" in Crawford/WINDFALL pp. 222–42.
435. Quoted in ibid., p. 232. Schoenberg and Stravinsky themselves studiously avoided meeting while they were both resident in California.
436. See the detailed chronology in Francis/BOULANGER.
437. Stravinsky wrote in 1962 that some details in the last two movements "would not have come to my ears in Europe" and "would not have occurred to me before I had known the neon glitter of the California boulevards from a speeding automobile" (Steinberg/SYMPHONY, p. 616).
438. Quoted in ibid.
439. Quoted in ibid., p. 617.
440. Cone/CONVENTION, p. 295.
441. Elmer Schönberger and Louis Andriessen, "The Utopian Unison" in Pasler/CONFRONTING, pp. 208–9.
442. Stravinsky and Craft/DIALOGUES, pp. 50–51.
443. Dahl/STRAVINSKY, pp. 160–61.
444. Walsh/STRAVINSKY, pp. 186–87.
445. Dahl/STRAVINSKY, p. 165.
446. Danuser/EXILE, p. 161.
447. In spite of this fact, the League's 2022 Orchestra Repertoire Report does show that progress is being made in repertoire diversity. https://americanorchestras.org/2022-orchestra-repertoire-report/.
448. Copland and Perlis/1900–1942, p. 300. Also see Bick/MICE. Bick also discusses the influence of Virgil Thomson and Copland on Hollywood film music.
449. Copland/SECOND THOUGHTS, p. 141.
450. Crawford/WINDFALL. Also see Feisst/SCHOENBERG.
451. Schnepel/GREAT, pp. 345–47.
452. Unless otherwise noted, the information in this section is from *Grove Music Online*.
453. *New York Times*, June 8, 1928, p. 36.
454. Quoted in a recording review by Noah Andre Trudeau, *American Music* 18, no. 3 (Autumn 2000): pp. 320–22. Information about the other symphonies is from Roy Benton Hawkins, "The Life and Work of Robert Russell Bennett" (PhD diss., Texas Tech University, 1989).
455. See Howard Pollack, *Skyscraper Lullaby: The Life and Music of John Alden Carpenter* (Washington and London: Smithsonian Institution Press, 1995), as well as Tawa/GREAT, PP. 72–80.

456. Wilma Salisbury, "Marcel Dick," Cleveland Arts Prize biographical essay, retrieved January 15, 2023, http://www.clevelandartsprize.org/awardees/marcel_dick.html. There is no entry on Dick in *Grove Music Online*.
457. Howland/CONCERT JAZZ, p. 180.
458. Krenek/CIRCLING, p. 22.
459. Stewart/KRENEK.
460. Tawa/GREAT, p. 155; see Tawa for more on the Symphony in A.
461. Lawrence Morton, "Jerome Moross: Young Man Goes Native." *Modern Music* Vol. 22 No. 2 (January-February 1945), 113–14.
462. Reference to composition prizes are from Grove 1939; reference to multiple symphonies are from the biographical essay by Beth Levy in *Grove Music Online*.
463. Quoted in Anthony Tommasini, "A Work Twice Lost, Now Twice Found?," *New York Times*, February 21, 1999, Section 2, p. 44.
464. Biographical essay in *Grove Music Online* by Richard Loucks, revised by Graydon Beeks.
465. Biographical essay in *Grove Music Online* by James P. Cassaro.
466. John Haag, "Howard Swanson," *New Georgia Encyclopedia*, last modified November 14, 2013, http://www.georgiaencyclopedia.org/articles/arts-culture/howard-swanson-1907-1978.
467. Anna Withers Bair, "Charles Gildersleeve Powell," *Dictionary of North Carolina Biography*, last modified January 1, 1996, edited by William S. Powell, https://www.ncpedia.org/biography/vardell-charles. According to Reis/COMPOSERS, the symphony was broadcast on NBC and the Mutual Broadcasting System. There is no entry in *Grove Music Online* on Vardell.
468. A brief biography of Vauclain appears on the website of researcher Tobias Broeker https://www.tobias-broeker.de/newpage83ac97eb. There is no entry in *Grove Music Online* for Vauclain.

Bibliography

Abromeit/SPIRITUALS	Abromeit, Kathleen A. *Spirituals: A Multidisciplinary Bibliography for Research and Performance*. Middleton, WI: Music Library Association and A-R Editions, 2015.
Antheil/BAD	Antheil, George. *Bad Boy of Music*. New York: Da Capo, 1981 (originally published 1945).
Bahr/WEIMAR	Bahr, Ehrhard. *Weimar on the Pacific: German Exile Culture in Los Angeles and the Crisis of Modernism*. Berkeley: University of California Press, 2008.
Berger/COPLAND	Berger, Arthur. "The Music of Aaron Copland." *Musical Quarterly* 31, no. 4 (October 1945): pp. 420–27.
Berger/SYMPHONY	Berger, Arthur. "The Third Symphony of Aaron Copland." *Tempo* 9 (Autumn 1948): pp. 20–27.
Bick/MICE	Bick, Sally. "'Of Mice and Men': Copland, Hollywood, and American Musical Modernism." *American Music* 23, no. 4 (Winter 2005): pp. 426–72.
Bindas/FMP	Bindas, Kenneth J. *All of This Music Belongs to the Nation: The WPA's Federal Music Project and American Society*. Knoxville: University of Tennessee Press, 1996.
Bomberger/1917	Bomberger, E. Douglas. *Making Music American: 1917 and the Transformation of Culture*. New York: Oxford University Press, 2018.

Brinkmann and Wolff/PARADISE	Brinkmann, Reinhold, and Christoph Wolff, eds. *Driven into Paradise: The Musical Migration from Nazi Germany to the United States.* Berkeley: University of California Press, 1999.
Broder/BARBER	Broder, Nathan. *Samuel Barber.* Westport, CT: Greenwood, 1985.
Brody/AMERICAN ACADEMY	Brody, Martin, ed. *Music and Musical Composition at the American Academy in Rome.* Rochester, NY: Boydell and Brewer, 2014.
Brotman/BLOCK	Brotman, Charles. "The Winner Loses: Ernest Bloch and His *America*," *American Music* 16, no. 4 (Winter 1998): pp. 417–47.
Brown/DAWSON	Brown, Gwynne Kuhner. "Whatever Happened to William Dawson's *Negro Folk Symphony*?" *Journal of the Society for American Music* 6, no. 4 (2012): pp. 433–56.
Brown/HARLEM	Brown, Rae Linda. "William Grant Still, Florence Price, and William Dawson: Echoes of the Harlem Renaissance." In *Black Music in the Harlem Renaissance: A Collection of Essays*, edited by Samuel A. Floyd Jr., pp. 71–86. New York: Greenwood, 1990.
Brown/HEART	Brown, Rae Linda. *The Heart of a Woman: The Life and Work of Florence B. Price.* Edited and with a foreword by Guthrie P. Ramsey Jr. and an afterword by Carlene J. Brown. Urbana: University of Illinois Press, 2020.
Brown and Shirley/PRICE	Brown, Rae Linda, and Wayne Shirley, eds. *Florence Price, Symphonies Nos. 1 and 3.* Music of the United States of America, vol. 19. Middleton, WI: A-R Editions, 2008.
Butterworth/SYMPHONY	Butterworth, Neil. *The American Symphony.* Brookfield, VT: Ashgate, 1998.
Clague/HARMONIZING	Clague, Marc. "Harmonizing Music and Money: Gershwin's Economic Strategies from 'Swanee' to *An American in Paris*." In *The Cambridge Companion to Gershwin*, edited by Anna Harwell Celenza, pp. 130–52. Cambridge: Cambridge University Press, 2019.
Cohen/HANSON	Cohen, Allen. *Howard Hanson in Theory and Practice.* Westport, CT: Praeger, 2004.
Collaer/MILHAUD	Collaer, Paul. *Darius Milhaud.* Translated and edited by Jane Hohfeld Galante. San Francisco: San Francisco Press, 1988.
Cone/CONVENTION	Cone, Edward T. "The Uses of Convention: Stravinsky and His Models." *Musical Quarterly* 48, no. 3, *Special Issue for Igor Stravinsky on His 80th Anniversary* (July 1962), pp. 287–99.

Copland/KOUSSEVITZKY   Copland, Aaron. "Serge Koussevitzky and the American Composer." *Musical Quarterly* 30 (1944): pp. 255–69.

Copland/OUR NEW   Copland, Aaron. *Our New Music: Leading Composers in Europe and America*. New York: McGraw-Hill, 1941.

Copland/SECOND THOUGHTS   Copland, Aaron. "Second Thoughts on Hollywood." *Modern Music* 17 (March-April 1940), pp. 141–42.

Copland and Perlis/1900–1942   Copland, Aaron, and Vivian Perlis. *Copland: 1900–1942*. New York: St. Martin's/Marek, 1984.

Copland and Perlis/SINCE 1943   Copland, Aaron, and Vivian Perlis. *Copland since 1943*. New York: St. Martin's, 1989.

Cowell/CHRONICLE   Cowell, Henry. "Current Chronicle." *Musical Quarterly* 40, no. 2 (April 1954): p. 235–43.

Cowell/COMPOSERS   Cowell, Henry, ed. *American Composers on American Music*. New York: Frederick Ungar, 1962.

Cowell and Nicholls/RESOURCES   Cowell, Henry, and David Nicholls. *New Musical Resources*. Cambridge: Cambridge University Press, 1996.

Crawford/WINDFALL   Crawford, Dorothy Lamb. *A Windfall of Musicians: Hitler's Émigrés and Exiles in Southern California*. New Haven, CT: Yale University Press, 2009.

Crist/RECEPTION   Crist, Elizabeth Bergman. "The Reception History of Aaron Copland's Third Symphony." *Musical Quarterly* 85, no. 2 (Summer 2001): pp. 232–63.

Crist/SKETCH TO SCORE   Crist, Elizabeth Bergman. "Aaron Copland's Third Symphony from Sketch to Score." *Journal of Musicology* 18, no. 3 (Summer 2001): pp. 377–405.

Crump/MARTINŮ   Crump, Michael. *Martinů and the Symphony*. London: Toccata, 2010.

Dahl/STRAVINSKY   Dahl, Ingolf. "Stravinsky in 1946." *Modern Music* 23, no. 3 (July 1946): pp. 159–65.

Danuser/EXILE   Danuser, Hermann. "Composers in Exile: The Question of Musical Identity." In Brinkmann and Wolff/PARADISE, pp. 155–71.

Dickinson/BARBER   Dickinson, Peter, ed. *Samuel Barber Remembered: A Centenary Tribute*. Rochester, NY: University of Rochester Press, 2010.

Evans/MARTINŮ   Evans, Peter. "Martinů the Symphonist." *Tempo* 55–56 (Autumn–Winter 1960): pp. 19–26 and 31–33.

Farrah/SEMIOTIC   Farrah, Scott David "'Signifyin(g)': A Semiotic Analysis of Symphonic Works by William Grant Still, William Levi Dawson, and Florence B. Price." PhD diss., Florida State University, 2007.

Fauser/COPLAND AND BOULANGER   Fauser, Annegret. "Aaron Copland, Nadia Boulanger, and the Making of an 'American' Composer." *Musical Quarterly* 89, no. 4 (Winter 2006): pp. 524–54.

Fauser/WAR	Fauser, Annegret. *Sounds of War: Music in the United States during World War II*. New York: Oxford University Press, 2013.
Feisst/SCHOENBERG	Feisst, Sabine M. "Arnold Schoenberg and the Cinematic Art." *Musical Quarterly* 83, no. 1 (Spring 1999): pp. 93–113.
Fine/COWELL	Fine, Irving. Review of a recording by the Eastman-Rochester Symphony Orchestra of Cowell's Symphony No. 4. *Musical Quarterly* 40, no. 2 (April 1954): pp. 312–13.
Forbes/THOMPSON	Forbes, Elliot. "The Music of Randall Thompson." *Musical Quarterly* 35, no. 1 (January 1949): pp. 1–25.
Francis/BOULANGER	Francis, Kimberly. "A Most Unsuccessful Project: Nadia Boulanger, Igor Stravinsky, and the Symphony in C, 1939–45." *Musical Quarterly* 94, nos. 1–2 (Spring–Summer 2011): pp. 234–70.
Gioia/JAZZ	Ted Gioia, *The History of Jazz*. New York: Oxford University Press, 1997.
Goldman/COWELL	Goldman, Richard Franko. "Henry Cowell (1897–1965): A Memoir and an Appreciation." *Perspectives of New Music* 4, no. 2 (Spring–Summer 1966): pp. 23–28.
Haas/FUSION	Haas, Robert Bartlett, ed. *William Grant Still and the Fusion of Cultures in American Music*. Los Angeles: Black Sparrow, 1972.
Hanson/HARMONIC	Hanson, Howard. *Harmonic Materials of Modern Music: Resources of the Tempered Scale*. Appleton-Century-Crofts, 1960.
Heyman/BARBER	Heyman, Barbara B. *Samuel Barber: The Composer and His Music*. Oxford: Oxford University Press, 1994.
Hicks/COWELL	Hicks, Michael. "Cowell's Clusters." *Musical Quarterly* 77, no. 3 (Autumn 1993): pp. 428–58.
Hoover and Cage/THOMSON	Hoover, Katherine, and John Cage. *Virgil Thomson*. New York: Sagamore, 1959.
Horowitz/EXILE	Horowitz, Joseph. *Artists in Exile: How Refugees from Twentieth-Century War and Revolution Transformed the American Performing Arts*. New York: Harper Perennial, 2008.
Howland/CONCERT JAZZ	Howland, John. *Ellington Uptown: Duke Ellington, James P. Johnson, and the Birth of Concert Jazz*. Ann Arbor: University of Michigan Press, 2009.
Jackson/PRICE	Jackson, Barbara Garvey. "Florence Price, Composer." *Black Perspective in Music* 5, no. 1 (Spring 1977): p. 40.
Johnson/COWELL	Johnson, Steven. "Henry Cowell, John Varian, and Halcyon." *American Music* 11, no. 1 (Spring 1993): pp. 1–27.

Johnson/DAWSON	Johnson, John Andrew. "William Dawson, 'The New Negro,' and His Folk Idiom." *Black Music Research Journal* 19, no. 1 (Spring 1999): pp. 43–60.
Kalinak/WEST	Kalinak, Kathryn. *How the West Was Sung: Music in the Westerns of John Ford*. Berkeley: University of California Press, 2007.
Karlin/MOVIES	Karlin, Fred. *Listening to the Movies: The Film Lover's Guide to Film Music*. Belmont, CA: Schirmer Cenage Learning, 1994.
Key and Rothe/MAVERICKS	Key, Susan, and Larry Rothe. *American Mavericks: Musical Visionaries, Pioneers, Iconoclasts*. Berkeley: University of California Press, 2001.
Korn/SYMPHONY	Korn, Peter Jona. "The Symphony in America." In *The Symphony*, edited by Robert Simpson, pp. 243–67. Vol. 2 of *Elgar to the Present Day*. Middlesex, UK: Penguin, 1967.
Kowalke/HINDEMITH	Kowalke, Kim H. "For Those We Love: Hindemith, Whitman, and 'An American Requiem.'" *Journal of the American Musicological Society* 50, no. 1 (Spring 1997), pp. 133–74.
Krenek/CIRCLING	Krenek, Ernst. "Circling My Horizon." In *Horizons Circled: Reflections on My Music*, 17–97. Berkeley: University of California Press, 1974.
Krenek/INFLUENCE	Krenek, Ernst. "America's Influence on Its Émigré Composers." Translated by Don Harrán, *Perspectives of New Music* 8, no. 2 (Spring–Summer 1970): pp. 112–17.
Kushner/BLOCH	Kushner, David Z. "Ernest Bloch: A Retrospective on the Centenary of His Birth," *College Music Symposium* 20, no. 2 (Fall 1980): pp. 77–86.
Kushner/STILL	Kushner, David Z. "The Multifaceted Nationalism of William Grant Still." *American Music Teacher* 52, no. 1 (August–September 2002): pp. 32–35.
Lamb/AMERICAN SYMPHONY	Lamb, Brian. "Roy Harris' *American Symphony–1938*: A Perspective on Its Historical Significance and Autogenetic Elements with a Performance of a Reconstructed Modern Wind Ensemble Edition." DMA diss., University of North Texas, 2001.
Large/MARTINŮ	Large, Brian. *Martinů*. New York: Holmes and Meier, 1976.
Levy/FRONTIER	Levy, Beth. *Frontier Figures: American Music and the Mythology of the American West*. Berkeley: University of California Press, 2012.
Levy/WHITE HOPE	Levy, Beth. "'The White Hope of American Music.' or, How Roy Harris Became Western." *American Music* 19, no. 2 (Summer 2001): pp. 131–67.

Lichty and Topping/SOURCE BOOK	Lichty, Lawrence W., and Malachi C. Topping, *American Broadcasting: A Source Book on the History of Radio and Television*. New York: Hastings House, 1975.
Maher/MILHAUD	Maher, Erin K. "Darius Milhaud in the United States, 1940–71: Transatlantic Constructions of Musical Identity." PhD diss., University of North Carolina at Chapel Hill, 2016.
Massey/KIRKPATRICK	Massey, Drew. *John Kirkpatrick, American Music, and the Printed Page*. Rochester, NY: Rochester University Press, 2013.
Meckna/SACRED	Meckna, Michael. "Sacred and Secular America: Virgil Thomson's *Symphony on a Hymn Tune*." *American Music* 8, no. 4 (Winter 1990): pp. 465–76.
Milhaud and Breitrose/CONVERSATION	Milhaud, Darius, and Henry Breitrose. "Conversation with Milhaud." *Music Educators Journal* 56, no. 7 (March 1970, pp. 54–56.
Miller/COWELL AND CAGE	Miller, Leta. "Henry Cowell and John Cage: Intersections and Influences, 1933–1941." *Journal of the American Musicological Society* 59, no. 1 (Spring 2006): pp. 47–112.
Móricz/BIRTH	Móricz, Klára, "The Birth of a Nation and the Limits of the Human Universal in Ernest Bloch's *America*." *American Music* 29, no. 2 (Summer 2011): pp. 168–202.
Murchison/POETICS	Murchison, Gayle. "'Dean of Afro-American Composers' or 'Harlem Renaissance Man': The New Negro and the Musical Poetics of William Grant Still." *Arkansas Historical Quarterly* 53, no. 1 (Spring 1994): pp. 42–74.
Noss/HINDEMITH	Noss, Luther. *Paul Hindemith in the United States*. Urbana: University of Illinois Press, 1989.
Oja/ROME PRIZE	Oja, Carol. "'Picked Young Men,' Facilitating Women, and Emerging Composers: Establishing an American Prix de Rome." In Brody/AMERICAN ACADEMY, pp. 159–94.
Oja/STILL	Oja, Carol. "'New Music' and the 'New Negro': The Background of William Grant Still's *Afro-American Symphony*." *Black Music Research Journal* 12, no. 2 (Fall 1992): pp. 145–69.
Olmstead/ROME PRIZE	Olmstead, Andrea. "The Rome Prize from Leo Sowerby to David Diamond." In Brody/AMERICAN ACADEMY, pp. 13–41.
Pasler/CONFRONTING	Pasler, Jann, ed. *Confronting Stravinsky*. Berkeley: University of California Press, 1986,
Perlis and Van Cleve/VOICES	Perlis, Vivian, and Libby Van Cleve. *Composers' Voices from Ives to Ellington*. New Haven, CT: Yale University Press, 2005.

Piston/CONVERSATION	Piston, Walter. "Conversation with Walter Piston." Interview by Peter Westergaard. *Perspectives of New Music* 7, no. 1 (Autumn–Winter 1968): pp. 3–17.
Pollack/BLITZSTEIN	Pollack, Howard. *Marc Blitzstein*. Oxford: Oxford University Press, 2012.
Pollack/COPLAND	Pollack, Howard. *Aaron Copland: The Life and Work of an Uncommon Man*. Urbana: University of Illinois Press, 1999.
Pollack/PISTON	Pollack, Howard. *Walter Piston*. Ann Arbor, MI: UMI Research Press, 1981.
Pollack/SIBELIUS	Pollack, Howard. "Samuel Barber, Jean Sibelius, and the Making of an American Romantic." *Musical Quarterly* 84, no. 2 (Summer 2000): pp. 175–205.
Rao/COWELL	Rao, Nancy. "Cowell's Sliding Tone and the American Ultramodernist Tradition." *American Music* 23, no. 3 (Autumn 2005): pp. 281–323.
Reis/COMPOSERS	Reis, Claire. *Composers in America*. Rev. ed. New York: Macmillan, 1947.
Reis/COMPOSERS, CONDUCTORS	Reis, Claire. *Composers, Conductors and Critics*. New York: Oxford University Press, 1955.
Robertson/SYMPHONIES I	Robertson, Malcolm D. "Roy Harris's Symphonies: an Introduction (I)." *Tempo* 207 (December 1998): pp. 9–14.
Robertson/SYMPHONIES II	Robertson, Malcolm D. "Roy Harris's Symphonies: an Introduction (II)." *Tempo* 214 (October 2000): pp. 20–27.
Robertson and Armstrong/COPLAND	Robertson, Marta, and Robin Armstrong. *Aaron Copland: A Guide to Research*. New York: Routledge, 2001.
Rybka/MARTINŮ	Rybka, R. James. *Bohuslav Martinů: The Compulsion to Compose*. Lanham, MD: Scarecrow, 2011.
Sachs/COWELL	Sachs, Joel. *Henry Cowell: A Man Made of Music*. New York: Oxford University Press, 2012.
Šafránek/MARTINŮ	Šafránek, Miloš. "Martinů's Musical Development." *Tempo* 72 (Spring 1965): p. 13.
Schmidt/TUNESMITH	Schmidt, Carl B. "The Unknown Randall Thomson: 'Honeytonk Tunesmith, Broadway Ivory-Tickler.'" *American Music* 27, no. 3 (Fall 2009): pp. 302–26.
Schmidt and Schmidt/THOMPSON	Schmidt, Carl B., and Elizabeth K. Schmidt. *The Music of Randall Thompson (1899–1984): A Documented Catalogue*. Fenton, MO: E. C. Schirmer, 2014.
Schnepel/GREAT	Schnepel, Julie. "The Critical Pursuit of the Great American Symphony: 1893–1950." PhD diss., Indiana University, 1995.
Shadle/NEW WORLD	Shadle, Douglas. *Antonín Dvořák's New World Symphony*. Oxford Keynotes Series. New York: Oxford University Press, 2021.

Simmons/WILDERNESS	Simmons, Walter. *Voices in the Wilderness*. Lanham, MD: Scarecrow, 2004.
Slattery/STILL	Slattery, Paul. "A Comprehensive Study of the *Afro-American Symphony*." In Haas/FUSION, pp. 101–43.
Smith/STILL	Smith, Catherine Parsons. *William Grant Still: A Study in Contradictions*. Berkeley: University of California Press, 2000.
Spilker/NEW ORDER	Spilker, John. "'Substituting a New Order': Dissonant Counterpoint, Henry Cowell, and the Network of Ultra-Modern Composers." PhD diss., Florida State University, 2010.
Statham/ANTHEIL	Statham, Sabra. "'Back to Baltimore': George Antheil's Symphonic Excursion from European Modernism to American Postmodernism." *Musical Times* 153, no. 1921 (Winter 2012): pp. 3–16.
Stehman/PIONEER	Stehman, Dan. *Roy Harris: An American Musical Pioneer*. Boston: Twayne, 1984.
Stehman/SYMPHONIES	Stehman, Dan. "The Symphonies of Roy Harris: An Analytical Study of the Linear Materials and of Related Works." PhD diss., University of Southern California, 1973.
Steinberg/SYMPHONY	Steinberg, Michael. *The Symphony*. Oxford: Oxford University Press, 1995.
Stewart/KRENEK	Stewart, John L. *Ernst Krenek: The Man and His Music*. Berkeley: University of California Press, 1991.
Strassburg/BLOCH	Strassburg, Robert. *Ernest Bloch: A Voice in the Wilderness*. Typescript printed at California State University, Los Angeles, 1977.
Stravinsky and Craft/DIALOGUES	Stravinsky, Igor, and Robert Craft. *Dialogues*. Berkeley: University of California Press, 1962.
Swickard/MILHAUD	Swickard, Ralph James. "The Symphonies of Darius Milhaud: An Historical Perspective and Critical Study of Their Music, Content, Style, and Form." PhD diss., University of California at Los Angeles, 1973.
Tawa/GREAT	Tawa, Nicholas. *The Great American Symphony: Music, the Depression, and War*. Bloomington: Indiana University Press, 2009.
Thompson/CONTEMPORARY	Thompson, Randall. "The Contemporary Scene in American Music." *Musical Quarterly* 18, no. 1 (January 1932): pp. 9–17.
Thomson/GREATEST	Thomson, Virgil. "'Greatest Music Teacher' at 75." *Music Educators Journal* 49, no. 1 (September–October 1962): pp. 42–44.
Thomson/THOMSON	Thomson, Virgil. *Virgil Thomson: An Autobiography*. New York: E. P. Dutton, 1966.

Tuthill/SOWERBY	Tuthill, Burnet C. "Leo Sowerby." *Musical Quarterly*, 24, no. 3 (July 1938): pp. 249–64.
Walsh/STRAVINSKY	Walsh, Stephen. *Stravinsky: The Second Exile: France and America, 1934–1971*. New York: Alfred A. Knopf, 2006.
Weisgall/COWELL	Weisgall, Hugo. "The Music of Henry Cowell." *Musical Quarterly* 45, no. 4 (October 1959): pp. 484–507.
Whitesitt/ANTHEIL	Whitesitt, Linda. *The Life and Music of George Antheil*. Ann Arbor, MI: UMI Research Press, 1981.
Williams/HANSON	Williams, David Russell. "Howard Hanson (1896–1981)." *Perspectives of New Music* 20, nos. 1–2 (Autumn 1981–Summer 1982): pp. 12–25.
Zuck/AMERICANISM	Zuck, Barbara A. *A History of Musical Americanism*. Ann Arbor, MI: UMI Research Press, 1980.

CHAPTER SIX

Forgotten Modernisms

THE SYMPHONY IN THE UNITED STATES FROM 1950 TO 1970

Katherine Baber[1]

As often as the idea of "the Great American Symphony" is invoked, it is hardly ever used according to the sense in which it was originally meant. When Leonard Bernstein used the phrase in the title of an essay, he meant it to be interrogatory rather than inspiring or teleological: "Whatever Occurred to the Great American Symphony?" In that essay, included in *The Joy of Music*, which topped best-seller lists during the 1959 holiday season, Bernstein expressed his doubts about the longevity of the genre and its relevance to American culture. When addressing the American Symphony Orchestra League in 1980, Bernstein remained hopeful about the future of the symphony orchestra but not about the symphony as a genre. Whereas in 1959 he had wondered whether it was possible for an "abstract" American symphony to emerge out of American theater music as the classical symphony had from opera and *Singspiel*, he now viewed the whole symphonic tradition as having ended abruptly in 1945: "It is as though that apocalyptic bomb had demolished not only Hiroshima but, as a side effect, the whole tonal symphonic concept as well."[2] Leaving aside the provocative analogy and his refusal to uncouple the symphony from tonal tradition, narratives of American musical history often read similarly to Bernstein's version of events. He had, in that sense, a gravitational pull on our understanding of the American symphony, both during his lifetime as a conductor, composer, and public intellectual with a large audience, and after in terms of how his prolific comments have influenced those writing the history.

The 1950s and 1960s tend to be cast as a tipping point or precipice. One regularly reads about the splintering of American art music into the warring stylistic factions of Schoenberg versus Stravinsky—"Us" versus "Them." These were also the last decades in which "high art" and "classical music" had an aura of glamour, particularly in New York City: photojournalism captured Jacqueline Kennedy's attendance at various performances, along with other members of the political and social elite—a latter-day version of the scenes at the opera house in Edith Wharton's *The Age of Innocence* (1920). America at midcentury saw the creation of Lincoln Center (1962) and the Kennedy Center for the Performing Arts (1971) and the rise to prominence of new orchestral powerhouses like the Louisville Symphony Orchestra and the National Symphony Orchestra. But these decades also marked the beginning of the financial decline of arts institutions, the retreat of composers into the academy, and the increasing marginalization of classical music. Histories by Richard Crawford, Charles Hamm, Joseph

Horowitz, and Nicholas Tawa generally agree that this was a period of decline or at least reconfiguration.[3] In this sense, Bernstein once again seems to have anticipated them, calling on American orchestras to reinvent themselves, not just as custodians of tradition but as proving grounds for whatever comes next: "The so-called 'symphony orchestra' has developed an added function, distinct from its identity as a museum, and that is to provide the fertile soil in which new kinds of orchestral music can be cultivated."[4] In many ways this is still the project of American orchestras today, but it was a transformation already underway in the postwar decades. Along with shifts in the performance and economics of classical music, the genre of the symphony underwent multiple transformations as well.

Funding and performing midcentury American symphonic works would present new challenges and opportunities. There were still foundations and societies that continued in an older mode of philanthropic patronage and corporate funding. The Naumburg Foundation and Rockefeller Foundation, as well as the societies of the oldest orchestras like the Boston Symphony Orchestra (BSO) and New York Philharmonic, could be counted on to fund commissions. They depended, though, on the mediation of conductors like Serge Koussevitzky, Eugene Ormandy, Antal Dorati, and Leonard Bernstein to choose which young American composers received the commissions. Even after his death in 1951, Serge Koussevitzky's Music Foundation continued the work that he had begun during his tenure at the Boston Symphony Orchestra. Although, as we will see, the narrative of the postwar retreat of composition into the academy is exaggerated, universities did their share of commissioning new works, including several of the symphonies discussed in this chapter. Companies like Ford or Coca-Cola, however, could not put their name on a symphony, so corporate support often came in oblique ways. Without the Ford Foundation's support for the Omnibus television programs, Bernstein could never have reached as wide an audience as he did, but it did not fund the writing of any of his symphonies. More importantly, though, support now became a part of government and privately funded grants, like the $500,000 grant in 1953 from the Rockefeller Foundation to the Louisville Symphony Orchestra for the purpose of commissioning, premiering, and recording new works. That ensemble accordingly premiered and recorded a number of symphonies from the mid-twentieth century and beyond.

Whatever the symphony lacked in the potential financial success enjoyed by musical theater or opera, it compensated for in cultural prestige. Government support for the arts had reached its zenith in the New Deal, an era of support for creative activity that many of the composers of the 1950s and 1960s could remember vividly. Funding remained available during the Cold War but was awarded more for performances and tours than for sabbaticals to write a symphony. But from 1954 to 1963, composers like Virgil Thomson, Howard Hanson, and William Schuman had the opportunity, through the Music Advisory Panel of the American National Theater and Academy, to advise the State Department on which musicians and works to send abroad as proof of American cultural vitality. Some, like Bernstein and Aaron Copland, went to Latin America, Europe, the Middle East, and the USSR. The American government may have done nothing to help Schuman write his Symphony No. 6, but it was heard in South America in 1958 because of federal support and the music panel's programming advice to Bernstein and the New York Philharmonic. To an extent, these highly politicized presentations did represent a new reality at home in that American music and American conductors were increasingly prominent in the nation's symphonic institutions, due in large part to the initiative of figures like Koussevitzky, Charles Munch, Bernstein, and Schuman.

During the 1950s and 1960s, the center of gravity shifted in the symphonic world of the United States toward American conductors and away from the corridors between Boston and Philadelphia, Cleveland and Chicago. Although they had existed for decades, other orchestras across the country attained new prominence and made a point of fostering living American composers. The New Orleans Symphony and Seattle Symphony Orchestra welcomed Alan Hovhaness, and the latter ensemble has recorded the symphonies of a number of twentieth-century American composers, including Hanson, Walter Piston, Paul Creston, Schuman, David Diamond, Hovhaness, and Peter Mennin.[5] The San Francisco Symphony, St. Louis Symphony Orchestra, National Symphony Orchestra, Dallas Symphony Orchestra, Houston Symphony Orchestra, Minneapolis Symphony Orchestra, and Louisville Symphony Orchestra were all moving into new halls, commissioning new works, and performing and recording new symphonies that might have otherwise remained isolated on the East Coast. The Los Angeles Symphony Orchestra had a particularly wide reach since it began offering summer concerts in 1922 at the Hollywood Bowl with its 18,000-seat capacity. Municipal support and cooperation proved vital to the success of these institutions, and many of these orchestras would be the ones to initiate a new round of "outreach" programs. Again, Louisville is an excellent example—the boost from the Rockefeller Foundation was important, but equally crucial was the central place of the orchestra in the city's cultural life as encouraged by Mayor Charles Farnsley and conductor Robert Whitney.

That the innovations of Louisville's orchestra were fostered by an American conductor shows a midcentury shift away from the preeminence of European émigrés in American culture (though they certainly remained significant). Leonard Bernstein's appointment as the first American-born conductor of the New York Philharmonic in 1958 is generally understood as the turning point—and he certainly did as much as anyone, even Koussevitzky, to advocate for American symphonists. There were others, however, including Thomas Schippers in New York, Chicago, and Cincinnati; Leonard Slatkin in Saint Louis and later the National Symphony Orchestra; and Walter Hendl, who took over for the Hungarian-born Antal Dorati in the leadership of the Dallas Symphony Orchestra. However, this expansion of orchestral activity and the energy lent by new voices and new ideas did not guarantee stability or satisfaction. In 1966, the Ford Foundation had granted $80.2 million to American orchestras, but they were required to raise matching funds, which meant increasing revenue from subscriptions and ticket sales. Concert seasons were extended, largely through educational programs and pops concerts that were often underrehearsed. The budgets of orchestras expanded dramatically, but this was mostly due to newly required marketing divisions.[6] The alliance between the corporate and symphonic worlds did not make a good fit, and musicians—performers, conductors, and composers alike—were often caught in the middle.

Despite existing narratives that cast this as an era of sharp divides—native composers competing with émigrés, nationalist versus cosmopolitan works, absolute versus programmatic symphonies, and serialists versus tonalists—American symphonists frequently occupied an aesthetic middle ground. Many of the composers included in this chapter emerged out of the orbit of Copland, Thomson, and Roy Harris. In their early works, Schuman, Bernstein, Vincent Persichetti, Mennin, and Diamond all show traces of a populist, neotonal version of American modernism. Although he was to drift farther than them from it, Roger Sessions also began with a language similar to Copland's early style. The two cooperated on the landmark Copland-Sessions concerts (1928–31) and would remain friendly throughout their careers.

Schuman, Bernstein, Persichetti, and Diamond would all pursue versions of the "Great American Symphony." On the other hand, Sessions, Creston, Mennin, and Julia Perry (at first) were less comfortable with the nationalist ideal and with Copland's explicit Americanness; they were cosmopolitan—that is, European—and critics understood them as such. Notably, both Diamond and Perry had extended midcareer sojourns in Italy. Of the midcentury symphonists, Hovhaness differed the most from his contemporaries: he had no institutional affiliations, embraced various non-Western as well as European influences, and developed a highly idiosyncratic approach to the symphony, which in his hands encompassed whatever thematic materials, structures, and narrative or philosophical ideas he wanted to work with at the moment.

In terms of American musical nationalism, the place of Black musics had shifted by midcentury. To greater and lesser degrees, Schuman, Bernstein, and Perry all noticeably incorporated blues- and jazz-derived vocabulary in their symphonies. But the notion of "symphonic jazz" of the type produced by James P. Johnson, "Duke" Ellington, or George Gershwin became increasingly fraught, not least because jazz musicians made increasingly liberal use of European modernist techniques in their compositions. The harmonic choices and performance practices of bebop musicians broke down the supposed barriers between jazz and modernist "high art." And when composers like Mary Lou Williams looked to blend jazz with European forms or genres, the symphony was no longer the touchstone. Gunther Schuller coined the term *third stream* in 1957 to attempt to capture the fusion of traditions that was underway, but even among works that appeared in this vein, like his own *Journey into Jazz* (1962) or Concertino for Jazz Quartet and Orchestra (1959), the scope was not symphonic. Various permutations of "jazz with strings" continued to appear, but the idea of jazz as something that could be "transformed" in a symphony context fell away with the leveling of jazz and classical music as artistic spheres.

Hovhaness and Bernstein consistently employed extramusical points of reference in their symphonies. Though not as often, Perry, Sessions, Schuman, Diamond, and Mennin also composed symphonies that contained programmatic references, set a text, engaged in musical portraiture, or grappled with philosophical or political issues through music. Persichetti referenced vocal styles like the hymn or chorale as well as "found" sounds such as the bells of Rome; nevertheless, his symphonies are hardly programmatic. Rather than observing a chasm between absolute and programmatic works, these composers moved along a continuum, never staying firmly at one pole or another.

The distance between serialism and neotonality in the midcentury symphony is not as wide as often assumed, as the works covered in this chapter will show. Sessions is the only symphonist considered at length here who consciously identified himself as a serialist (Wallingford Riegger was another), but he applied the method in his own way. His student Diamond did not begin adopting twelve-tone procedures until long after his studies concluded, and by his own admission, he did so after the manner of Berg (i.e., with tonal references) instead of Schoenberg. During and after her extended apprenticeship with Luigi Dallapiccola, Perry adapted twelve-tone and serial procedures freely, incorporating them as transformational tools in her own harmonic and rhythmic language. Taking an ecumenical approach to counterpoint and harmony, Persichetti insisted that every composer ought to be familiar with Schoenberg's method as one of the many techniques in the compositional toolbox. Schuman, Bernstein, and (less often) Mennin also experimented with rows, mostly restricting themselves to twelve-tone "themes" that do not generally determine the work's overall structure. Hovhaness, meanwhile, looked to other cultures for nontonal approaches to pitch organization. Bernstein might have tried to cast Stravinsky and his partisans (himself included) as the tonal saviors of modern music, but his own works and those of his contemporaries speak to a more nuanced dialogue between serialism and the many atonal and neotonal styles at play in the United States.

Roger Sessions

The work of Roger Sessions (1896–1985) forms a bridge between the generation of Copland and Harris and that of Schuman, Diamond, and Bernstein. While he began his career as a tonal modernist, and like others of the period studied extensively in Europe, his style ultimately gravitated toward twelve-tone serialism and other strains of postwar atonality. Sessions was a prodigy, graduating from Harvard with his bachelor of arts in 1915 and from Yale with a bachelor of music in 1917. At Yale he took lessons with Horatio Parker and went on to study with Ernest Bloch in New York in 1919, later holding a position as his assistant at the Cleveland Institute (1921–25). He taught at various colleges and universities, most notably Princeton (1936–45; 1953–65), the University of California at Berkeley (1945–53 and 1966–67 as Bloch Professor), and at Juilliard (1966–83). He gave the Norton lectures at Harvard in 1968–69. Between 1925 and 1933, Sessions remained in Europe, supported by two Guggenheim Fellowships (to study in Paris and Florence), a Carnegie grant (Berlin), and a three-year Rome Prize (1931–33). Fluent in French, German, Italian, and Russian, he corresponded with figures like Stravinsky, Koussevitzky, and Dallapiccola in their native languages. His cosmopolitanism and firsthand experience with the rise of fascism in Italy and Germany helped shape his left-leaning politics and a worldview that would occasionally produce pointedly political works like the Sixth, Seventh, and Eighth Symphonies.

By the numbers, both of his students and his symphonies, Sessions was one of the most influential figures examined in this chapter. Of his students, Diamond, John Harbison, and Ellen Taaffe Zwilich are significant symphonists, with David Del Tredici, Andrew Imbrie, and Conlon Nancarrow among other notables. Most of Sessions's symphonies date from the 1950s and 1960s. Although he continued composing to the end of his life, he produced only one symphony after 1970. Sessions received many honors: elected to both the American Academy of Arts and Letters (1953) and the American Academy of Arts and Sciences (1961), he also received the Gold Medal of the former (1961); other awards included a MacDowell Medal (1968), the Brandeis Creative Arts Award (1958), and two Pulitzer Prizes (Special citation, 1974, and Concerto for Orchestra, 1982). Despite such recognition, his critical and public reception (as well as his legacy) were heavily influenced by the narrative of serialism as "academic," and he was therefore regarded as reclusive, serious, and unapproachable.

Sessions occupied as much of the center of America's musical world as Copland, with whom he collaborated in the Copland-Sessions concerts of 1928–31, yet by comparison his works were seldom performed and frequently received with critical hostility. Sessions's friend Alfredo Casella described his music as *nato difficile* (born difficult).[7] His tendency to miss deadlines—which alienated erstwhile patrons like Koussevitzky—and dismissal of reviewers' opinions likely did nothing to help: "I am convinced that every mature or really talented composer, however much he may be momentarily pleased by a 'good' criticism or irritated by a 'bad' one, will and must remain—through the strength of his creative impulse and for the good of his art—fundamentally indifferent to it."[8] While Sessions began his career as a French-influenced Neoclassic composer, he shifted toward serialism in the 1950s. The degree of dissonance in his

Table 6.1 The Symphonies of Roger Sessions (1896–1985)

Title	Movements	Instrumentation	Comments
Symphony No. 1 in E Minor (1926–27)	1. Giusto 2/4 (6/8) (319 mm.) 2. Largo 4/2 (107 mm.) 3. Allegro vivace 2/4 (333 mm.)	Grand plus Flt. (doubling Picc.), Ob. (doubling EH), E♭ Clar., Bclar., Bssn. (doubling Cbssn.), 2 Tpt., Tuba, Perc. (Xylo., Chimes, Cym., Suspended Cym., BD, Tri., Tamb., 2 Chinese Drums, 2 SD), Pno.	Dedicated to the memory of the composer's father, who died while Sessions was writing the slow movement. First performance: April 22, 1927, by the Boston Symphony Orchestra, conducted by Serge Koussevitzky. Score published by Cos Cob (large score) and Arrow Music (small score), both 1929.
Symphony No. 2 (1944–46)	1. Molto agitato; Tranquillo e misterioso 4/4 (212 mm.) 2. Allegretto capriccioso 2/4 (64 mm.) 3. Adagio, tranquillo ed espressivo 5/4 (86 mm.) 4. Allegramente 5/4 (185 mm.)	Grand plus Picc., EH, Bclar, Tpt., Tuba, Perc. (Xylo., Tam-tam, Tri., Tamb., SD, BD, Tenor Drum, Cym., Suspended Cym.), Pno.	Commissioned by the Alice M. Ditson Fund of Columbia University. "To the memory of Franklin Delano Roosevelt" (who died while Sessions was writing the third movement). First performance: January 9, 1947, by the San Francisco Orchestra, conducted by Pierre Monteux. Winner of the 1949 Walter W. Naumburg Foundation American Composition Award. Score published by G. Schirmer, 1949.
Symphony No. 3 (1957)	1. Allegro grazioso 6/8 (152 mm.) 2. Allegro, un poco ruvido 4/4 (183 mm.) 3. Andante sostenuto 5/4 (120 mm.) 4. Allegro con fuoco 2/2 (330 mm.)	Grand plus 2 Picc., EH, E♭ Clar, Bclar., Cbssn., Tuba, Perc. (Xylo., Tam-tam, Tamb., SD, Field Drum, Cym., Suspended Cym., BD, Temple Blocks, Tri., Vbp., Wood Block, Tambour de Provence, Chinese Drum), Harp, Cel.	Commissioned by the Boston Symphony Orchestra for its 75th anniversary. Dedicated to the memory of Serge and Natalie Koussevitzky. First performance: December 6, 1957, by the Boston Symphony Orchestra, conducted by Charles Munch. Score published by Edward B. Marks, 1962.
Symphony No. 4 (1958)	1. Burlesque: Allegro giocoso 4/4 (153 mm.) 2. Elegy: Adagio 2/4 (192 mm.) 3. Pastorale: Andante tranquillo e grazioso un poco idolente 6/8 (137 mm.)	Grand plus Picc., EH, Aclar., Bclar., Cbssn., Tpt., Tuba, Perc. (Xylo., Vbp., Wood Block, Tamb., BD, Ratchet, Cym., Suspended Cym., Tambour de Provence, Chinese Drum), Harp, Pno. doubling Cel.	Commissioned by the Minneapolis Symphony Orchestra in celebration of the centennial of the State of Minnesota. "To my wife." First performance: January 2, 1960, by the Minneapolis Symphony Orchestra, conducted by Antal Dorati. Score published by Edward B. Marks, 1963.

Table 6.1 continued

Title	Movements	Instrumentation	Comments
Symphony No. 5 (1964)	1. Tranquillo 3/4 (139 mm.) 2. Lento 4/4 (56 mm.) 3. Allegro deciso 7/4 (85 mm.) Mvts. played without pause.	Grand plus Flt. (doubling Aflt.; Flt. 2 doubles Picc.), EH, E♭ Clar., Bclar., Cbssn., Tuba, Perc. (Xylo., Mrb., Vbp., Suspended Cym., Tri., Cym., Tamb., Tenor Drum, SD, Wood Block, Whip, Maracas, Tam-tam, BD, Tambour de Provence, Chinese Drum), Harp, Pno., Cel.	Commissioned by Eugene Ormandy and dedicated to the conductor ("a 1963–64 Eugene Ormandy commission"). First performance: February 7, 1964, by the Philadelphia Orchestra, conducted by Ormandy. Score published by Edward B. Marks, 1971.
Symphony No. 6 (1966)	1. Allegro 3/4 (162 mm.) 2. Adagio e tranquillo 4/4 (58 mm.) 3. Allegro moderato 5/8 (162 mm.)	Grand plus Picc., EH, E♭ Clar., Bclar., Cbssn., Tuba, Perc. (Xylo., Mrb., Glsp., Vbp., SD, Field Drum, Tenor Drum, Tamb., Claves, Tri., Cym., Suspended Cym., BD, Maracas, Güiro, Whip, Chinese Drum, Tambour de Provence, 2 Tam-tams), Harp, Pno.	Commissioned by the New Jersey Symphony in celebration of the 300th anniversary of the state of New Jersey. Sessions later described this work as the first of a trilogy of symphonies written in response to current events, especially the Vietnam War. First performance (the first two movements only): November 19, 1966, by the New Jersey Symphony, conducted by Kenneth Schermerhorn (the first full performance took place that fall). Not heard again until 1977, with the Juilliard Orchestra, conducted by José Serebrier; Sessions considered this the true premiere, as the New Jersey rendition he found "unrecognizable as my music, except for a bass clarinet solo." Score published by Merion Music (Theodore Presser), 1975.
Symphony No. 7 (1966–67)	1. Allegro con fuoco 4/4 (245 mm.) 2. Lento e dolce 4/4 (66 mm.) 3. Allegro misurato 4/4 (166 mm.)	Grand plus Picc., EH, E♭ Clar., Bclar., Cbssn., Tpt., Tuba, Perc. (Xylo., Mrb., Glsp., Vbp., Whip, Tamb., SD, Wood Block, Field Drum, Maracas, Cym., Suspended Cym., BD, Tam-tam, Chinese Drum, Tambour de Provence), Harp, Pno.	Commissioned by the University of Michigan in commemoration of its sesquicentennial. The second symphony inspired by his opposition to the Vietnam War; also reflects the composer's reaction to reading the French erotic horror novel *The Story of O*. Sessions's favorite of his symphonies. First performance: October 1, 1967, by the Chicago Symphony Orchestra, conducted by Jean Martinon, to whom Sessions dedicated the work. Score published by Merion Music (Theodore Presser), 1977.

Symphony No. 8 (1968)	1. Adagio e mesto 4/4 (mm. 1–77) 2. Allegro con brio 4/4 (mm. 78–271) Mvts. played without pause.	Grand plus Aflt., Picc., EH, E♭ Clar., Bclar., Bssn., Cbssn., Tpt., Trom., Tuba, Harp, Pno.	Commissioned by the New York Philharmonic for its 125th anniversary. Dedicated to the composer's daughter Elizabeth. Final member of Sessions's Vietnam War trilogy. He said that this symphony, unlike its predecessors, represented resignation rather than anger. First performance: May 2, 1968, by the New York Philharmonic, conducted by William Steinberg. Score published by Edward B. Marks, 1973.
Symphony No. 9 (1975–78)	1. Allegro 5/4 (217 mm.) 2. Con movimento adagio 4/4 (87 mm.) 3. Allegro vivace 5/4 (210 mm.) Mvts. 2–3 played without pause.	Grand plus Picc., EH, E♭ Clar., Bclar., Cbssn., 2 Tpt., Tuba, Perc. (SD, Güiro, Tamb., Xylo., Maracas, Whip, Field Drum, Cym., Suspended Cym., Mrb., Vbp., Chimes, Tri., Wood Block, Tenor Drum, BD, Glsp., Chinese Drum, Rattle, 3 Tam-tams, Tambour de Provence), Harp, Pno.	Commissioned by the Syracuse Symphony Orchestra. Dedicated to Frederik Prausnitz. First performance: January 17, 1980, by the Syracuse Symphony, conducted by Christopher Keene. Score published by Merion Music (Theodore Presser), 1984.

music did not change markedly—the First Symphony was already heard as quite discordant by many critics and audience members—and his interest in serial methods was a logical outgrowth of his abiding interest in counterpoint.

Unlike his lifelong friend Copland, Sessions adamantly insisted that his works were not in any way specifically American.[9] He, like his student Diamond after him, adopted a conspicuously cosmopolitan approach to composition, which his extended periods of residency in Europe can only have reinforced. The consistent influence of Stravinsky shows in his favoring of polymeter, ostinati, layered textures, and general rhythmic complexity, as well as in his unique blend of Neoclassic style and serial principles. Elliott Carter, whose symphonic writing betrays Sessions's influence, described him as "one of the very last composers to have formed his outlook in the pre-first-world-war time and to have held to the standards of that period—as did Stravinsky, Bartók, and Schoenberg," a figure who carved his own path with a special "integrity as a man and a musician."[10] At the same time, Sessions shared with Copland the teaching of Nadia Boulanger, and each in his own way absorbed and reinterpreted her *grande ligne* in his melodic writing.

Jazz and other popular styles impact only Sessions's early works, and their presence is less an overt Americanism than a source for rhythmic variety and an additional ingredient in a generally cosmopolitan style. When asked about the influence of jazz on his early works, particularly the First Symphony, Sessions acknowledged that he "heard a lot of it," but so did many European composers—in fact, upon his return to the United States in 1933, the popular music he heard reminded him of Ravel.[11] The application of jazz idioms is one of the few traits he shared with Copland; notably, both composers largely turned away from jazz after the 1920s.

In terms of structure, most of Sessions's symphonies stick to schemes of three or four movements with the predictable alternation of tempos and characters; only the two-part Symphony No. 8 stands significantly apart in this respect (table 6.1). Modifications to the sonata principle abound, and scherzos are by turns boisterous, mischievous, or even violent. Although he tends to prefer large orchestras that feature unusual timbral choices or combinations, the scorings generally differ little from those of his contemporaries. It is his harmonic vocabulary, and in particular the use of modified serial procedures, that sets Sessions apart from the mainstream of symphonic tradition.

SYMPHONY NO. 1

The performance of the Symphony No. 1 in 1927, by the Boston Symphony Orchestra under Serge Koussevitzky, was effectively Sessions's introduction to the public. The work already exhibits many of the traits that would become central to his symphonic style, albeit in an explicitly tonal framework that he would soon abandon. Andrea Olmstead notes the long phrases juxtaposed with dense polyphony, the high level of dissonance, colorful orchestration, and a tendency toward rhythmic and contrapuntal complexity.[12] Sessions began the first movement while studying with Nadia Boulanger in the winter of 1926–27; his father died on January 5, 1927, hence the dedication to his memory.[13] The first and third movements are modified sonata-allegro forms and the second movement is an ABA, with the B section taking shape as a trio for woodwinds.[14] Olmstead describes the second movement as "a long cantilena much like that of a Bach aria."[15] Sessions himself acknowledged that composer's influence ("perhaps consciously modeled on Bach, a little") and added that the last movement was "somewhat consciously modeled on Mozart"—"ridiculous" aims both, since "Bach and Mozart are quite impossible to imitate."[16] While the literal repetition of the second and closing themes in the recapitulation of the first movement are rare in Sessions's music, the Boulanger-influenced long lines, use of ostinato, pandiatonicism, and "rootless diatonic sonorities" of the third movement are all typical features.[17]

By and large, the audience did not respond enthusiastically to the new symphony, but it did find sympathetic reviews. Paul Rosenfeld felt that the work showed "notable talent and not a little promise." Roy D. Welch's review in *Modern Music* was favorable, even if the music struck him as "stark, almost grim in its restraint." While noting that this was a first symphony, he expressed a hope that the thirty-one-year-old composer would seek a style "more rounded-out, more expansive, more tender than the first symphony" but also asserted that "whatever he says will command attention."[18] Welch certainly turned out to be right in that Sessions's style quickly evolved, albeit hardly in a "tender" manner: as Olmstead notes, the stylistic difference between first and second symphonies is greater than between any of the others.[19]

SYMPHONY NO. 2

The Second Symphony (1946) was the last Sessions wrote before his turn to twelve-tone serialism in the 1950s, and the composer recognized it as a pivotal creation: "I feel the Second Symphony as a point towards which I had been moving in a number of previous works . . . and on which forms, as it were, a point of departure for the music I have written since."[20] Both the First and Second Symphonies share Neoclassical features with the music of Stravinsky and the French-influenced American composers of the *Boulangerie*, but the Second also finds Sessions turning away from sonata form and clearly delineated key areas: the D minor at the beginning is merely a starting point and the D-major conclusion is just as incidental. We also hear Sessions the internationalist reacting to contemporary domestic politics in much the same way he would later do in the Sixth, Seventh, and Eighth Symphonies. He likened the climactic passage in the Finale to the atomic bombing of Japan.[21] He dedicated the work to the memory of Franklin Delano Roosevelt, who died as Sessions was finishing the third movement: "In a very real sense I think a great many people, including myself, felt the death of Roosevelt as a kind of personal loss."[22] Shortly before completing the symphony, Sessions suffered another personal loss in the death of his mother.

Commissioned by the Alice M. Ditson Fund of Columbia University and premiered by the San Francisco Symphony Orchestra on January 9, 1947, with Pierre Monteux conducting, the symphony received what Sessions remembered as an "excellent" performance. He similarly praised its New York premiere under Dimitri Mitropoulos on January 12, 1950.[23] The work won the first American Composition Award offered by the Naumburg Foundation for the 1949–50 season and was recorded by Mitropoulos and the New York Philharmonic under the auspices of the foundation.[24]

The first movement breaks away from Sessions's Neoclassical vein and moves toward the atonal and aggregate-based writing that would characterize his embrace of serialism. Taking D minor as a starting point, the first movement ranges widely in terms of harmonic language before returning to D in a perfunctory fashion in the final bars. The form is a symmetrical ABABA based on the contrast in character between the Molto agitato (mm. 1–54, 76–143, 164–212) and Tranquillo passages (mm. 55–75, 144–63). Each section is further distinguished by differences in instrumentation: a tighter and somewhat percussive combination of muted trumpets, stopped horn, piano and xylophone, horns and trombones, doubled woodwinds, and high string lines versus the softer and darker writing for muted strings, solo flute, and other woodwinds. These two sound palettes are combined in the final A section (mm. 194–212).[25]

A referential sonority unifies the movement; first appearing in the woodwinds and horns in m. 1, it heralds the beginning of each section.[26] The sonority reads at first as a Mm7 chord on G, plus a major ninth. Each iteration alters the extended tertian chord slightly, introducing a modal ambiguity typical of Sessions's harmonic language during this period: for example, in m. 55 the sonority appears on E-flat with a lowered third (G-flat in the third horn) but it retains the identifying major ninth high in the voicing (F in flutes and oboes); in m. 78, at the return to the A section, it settles on a G Mm7+9, but introduces E a minor third below, offering the possibility of an extended sonority based on an Emm7 chord. As a referential sonority, it remains recognizable—particularly given its consistent orchestration—but refuses to confirm any particular key.

Apparently following the analysis of British composer John Veale, Olmstead locates three other recurring ideas in the first section.[27] In mm. 3–6, the horn and trumpet present a pair of brief, fanfare-like ideas. The horns state a second theme in a chorale-like fashion in mm. 10–11, featuring a dotted rhythm and arpeggiations that suggest another fanfare. The oboe theme in mm. 16–20, which opens with a striking pair of major sixth leaps, also seems to conjure the heroic. The Tranquillo sections focus on longer solo lines in the violin and woodwinds. Each section features what Olmstead calls "imaginative" recurrences, recalling material from earlier sections not in the same order but in a "random, dreamlike manner" and combining thematic ideas previously stated sequentially in counterpoint.[28] In contrast to the forceful cast of the opening, the final A section fades out of existence: the winding string accompaniment at play since the beginning continues **pp** in a muted solo viola as other ideas fragment and fade away and the movement ends with pizzicato strings on D.

The second-movement scherzo, mostly in F major, is brief (under two minutes) and basically monothematic, a slightly off-kilter march with occasional metrical irregularity. Sessions thought of the movement as an intermezzo rather than a "full-fledged scherzo."[29] First presented in the oboe and English horn in mm. 1–4 (example 6.1), the theme comes in two halves: a roly-poly triadic arpeggiation followed by a staccato repeated-note idea that appears to be momentarily "stuck."

Example 6.1 Sessions, Symphony No. 2, mvt. 2, first theme (mm. 1–4)

The similarities to the scherzo of Shostakovich's Fifth Symphony, frequently performed in the United States during World War II, are striking: both composers replace the conventional scherzo with a march which is antiheroic in tone and seems to stutter. After this puckish interlude, the symphony proceeds without pause into the Adagio, another quasi-tonal movement that begins in B-flat minor, explores A-flat minor, F-sharp major and minor, E-flat minor, and D major, and ends in B-flat minor.[30] Three long-breathed themes are gradually developed throughout this movement: mm. 1–10 in the violas, mm. 10–16 in the solo oboe, and mm. 31–34 in the solo clarinet.[31] The brief excursion to D major (mm. 73–78) anticipates the last movement, but the key is sounded in the trumpet amid such grinding dissonance that it is hardly recognizable. In this movement Sessions's contrapuntal techniques are on full display.

The final movement again plays with classical principles, combining sonata and rondo forms (ABACADBA) and clearly articulating D major while preserving a fair degree of dissonance. By beginning and ending in that key, the symphony traces the traditional tragic-to-triumphant *topos* that features so strongly in symphonic tradition. The rondo theme falls through a major triad on D and introduces the galloping rhythmic motto that pervades the movement. Otherwise, the A section (mm. 1–22, 50–76, 99–129, 159–85) is a cluster of fanfare and marchlike figures with rushing scales as occasional accompaniment. The B sections (mm. 23–49, 137–58) introduce an almost heroic figure in the English horn and clarinet accompanied by triplet figures that gradually gain momentum while the brass interject with repeated-note figures. In both instances, however, the B section yields, *morendo*, to the A section. Together, the second A and C sections (mm. 76–98) constitute a development. Section D is little more than a detour or transition (mm. 130–36) in the wake of the climactic "atomic bomb," as Sessions put it, of the third A section (mm. 99–129); together with the second iteration of B, the D section allows the dust to settle before building through the final statement of the rondo theme (mm. 159–85) to what would be a stirring finish were it not for the *subito piano* hesitation of mm. 183–84. Like Bernstein in the last movement of his Second Symphony (*The Age of Anxiety*), Sessions seems reluctant to write a fully triumphal finale, and he is even more hesitant than Bernstein to settle on a program.

Juxtaposed with the clear tonal areas outlined in each movement of the symphony, Olmstead finds a shift toward serial procedure. While little of the thematic or harmonic structure is recognizably twelve-tone, she finds a "row" at the beginning of each movement.[32] In the opening movement, the first 14 notes of the violin accompaniment encompass all 12 pitches of the chromatic scale. The same motive then appears in inversion in mm. 13–14. In the second movement, mm. 1–4, the total texture of oboe, English horn, and cello "implies" a row, as does the viola melody in mm. 1–10 of the third movement. The fourth movement states all 12 tones by the end of the first measure in the flute, bassoons, trumpet, and piano.

At the same time, moves to the aggregate and functional rows are quite different: an aggregate neither ordains an order of the 12 pitches nor yields row permutations or other structural techniques, and the viola melody of the third movement reads as highly chromatic rather than serial. As Joseph Straus has pointed out, aggregate harmonies and melodies, as well as serial procedures with rows of fewer than 12 tones, were common in American ultramodernist works from the 1920s on, so it would be difficult to identify the precise inspiration for such processes in Sessions's transitional works.[33] Likewise, the use of inversion is as much an outgrowth of his long-standing interest in counterpoint and structural coherence as of his growing familiarity with Schoenberg's works and writings.[34]

Straus observes that Sessions's first comments on Schoenberg's method, in two essays in *Modern Music* (1933 and 1937), expressed reservations about what he perceived as a doctrinaire system. Sessions would seem to agree with Straus that his shift toward serialism was organic.[35] Even as late as the Fourth Symphony, he calls the presence of the row "tenuous."[36] Of the composers discussed in this chapter, he certainly would become the most prominent and thorough in his use of twelve-tone techniques, but his approach was never legalistic—an attitude he passed on to his students, including Diamond. Perhaps Stravinsky's nonorthodox treatment of tone rows, not to mention Schoenberg's own relatively casual approach to his system (for the purposes of expression), inspired Sessions's stance. Whatever the case, as with many American composers of twelve-tone music, serialism was not necessarily the defining factor of his highly personal style.

While the award from the Naumburg Foundation did bestow a seal of approval, critical reactions to both the San Francisco and New York performances and recording of the Second Symphony were mixed. Marjory M. Fisher's review in *Musical America* was thoroughly negative, and even Diamond expressed reservations.[37] Howard Taubman, however, found the symphony reflective of a "mellowing and deepening of his [Sessions's] artistic point of view" as opposed to his earlier works, which tended to be "grim and uncompromising": "One finds this score readily accessible after several hearings. Its design is big and integrated, but it never loses sight of the essential requirement of all good music that it must say something to the heart. Here is deep feeling, not only in the grave, lofty and restrained slow movement, but in places of the first. There is also a new note of lightness and perkiness, reminiscent in spirit of Prokofieff, perhaps, but in an idiom that is Mr. Sessions's own."[38] He asked the reader to "give it a chance." By contrast, Olin Downes applauded the principle of the Naumburg award and the opportunity that subsidizing a recording offered to study a complicated work at greater leisure, but he found the symphony "too long and artificial in its method to constitute living music." However "carefully worked out," in the end the work simply "does not communicate."[39]

THIRD, FOURTH, AND FIFTH SYMPHONIES

In the following decades, Sessions's symphonies often suffered from subpar performances: the composer remembered the premieres of the Third Symphony as "bad" and the Sixth as "a total loss."[40] At the same time, despite repeated complaints about his "intellectual" and hard-to-understand music, he steadily gained critical acclaim.

Although Sessions had become estranged from Koussevitzky in 1936, when chronic delays in finishing the score and disputes over soloists led to the cancellation of the premiere of his Violin Concerto, he maintained a relationship with the Boston Symphony Orchestra, which commissioned the Symphony No. 3 for its seventy-fifth anniversary; it premiered under Charles Munch in 1957.[41] This is the first symphony in which Sessions employs a twelve-tone row (oboe, mm. 27–31), albeit thematically rather than structurally. The first movement is governed by another modified sonata form.[42]

Like its predecessor, the opening movement of the Fourth Symphony (1958) integrates a row with sonata form.[43] The Fourth also resulted from a commission, this time for the celebration of the Minnesota Centennial; beyond that initial function, Dimitri Mitropoulos was looking for a short work that he could perform often.[44] The central movement had begun as an elegy for Sessions's brother John, who had died from tubercular meningitis in 1948. Olmstead describes the symphony as a poem to nature "in the widest and deepest sense."[45] Sessions concurred: "I thought of it as a pastoral symphony . . . there's certainly a storm in the middle of the first movement [and] there are episodes in the last movement especially where there are sort of rustlings and chirpings."[46] Natural sounds also infiltrate the first movement: the song of an ovenbird at its opening and whip-poor-will at its end.[47] A violin solo in the coda of the first movement parodies a passage from his Second Symphony.[48] Sessions only realized the scope of the work afterward: "Why not call it a symphony? I hadn't thought of the movements as differing in terms of tempo, but of character and mood. Actually, they are different in tempo."[49] The Fourth Symphony marks the move toward a structural, though flexible, use of the twelve-tone system.

Sessions composed his Symphony No. 5 (1960–64) while he completed his opera *Montezuma*, which had been almost 30 years in the making. In this opera, he developed and refined a highly individual sound world comprised of (in Olmstead's words) "the strident sonority of violins in their highest register refusing octave doubling; the blurred warmth of the brass interweaving in a dense counterpoint that cannot be untangled; the black laughter of woodwinds, which breaks off into florid bel canto-like solos of intense expression played by piccolo, alto flute, bass clarinet, even contrabassoon; the brittle foreground of xylophone and marimba; and the ominous drums and maracas."[50] Such scoring finds its way into the later symphonies, starting with the Fifth. Again, a row helps organize it, especially the first movement.[51] More significant, though, is that the work concludes with what Olmstead calls the "Sessions ending": sustaining a low pitch while the melodic material peters out above it.[52] This type of close will recur in the Eighth Symphony, where it assumes quasi-programmatic significance.

THE WAR TRILOGY: SYMPHONY NOS. 6, 7, AND 8

The New Jersey Symphony Orchestra commissioned the Symphony No. 6 in celebration of the three hundredth anniversary of statehood. That ensemble under Kenneth Schermerhorn premiered the work for the anniversary celebration in January 1966, in a partial performance (Sessions had not completed the Finale); it premiered the full symphony on November 19, but hearing it gave the composer no pleasure ("unrecognizable as my music, except for a bass clarinet solo"[53]). Still, even in January the work was hailed as "dashing, bracing, almost always at high tension, complex but always extremely clear."[54] The second (and much better) performance of the complete symphony took place 10 years later, on March 4, 1977, with the Juilliard Orchestra conducted by José Serebrier.[55] After this, the symphony languished for years.[56] Its fate resembled that of many Sessions works: the difficulty of the music led to deficient performances and a subsequent lack of attention. Formally, the row [G—C♯—D—C—A♭—B—B♭—E—D♯—A—F—F♯] is treated freely but permeates more of the symphony than had been typical to this point.[57]

Sessions conceived of the Sixth Symphony as a sequel to the Fifth, but it soon took on a different meaning. As he composed his next symphony in mid-1967 (on commission by the University of Michigan for its sesquicentennial), Sessions was feeling deep distress about the seemingly intractable war in Vietnam, and he came to view the Sixth, Seventh, and Eighth Symphonies (all written between 1966 and 1968) as a trilogy reflecting on the war. The Symphony No. 7 was further inspired by the dark novel *The Story of O* (1954) by Pauline Réage, the pen name of French writer and translator Anne Desclos.[58] Sessions dedicated the symphony to Jean Martinon, who conducted the premiere with the Chicago Symphony Orchestra on October 1, 1967, in Ann Arbor.

Given its association with a violent work of fiction and a real-life conflict, it is difficult not to hear the Seventh Symphony in a narrative or pictorial fashion, even in the absence of a program. Each of the three movements, however, takes a clear and almost Neoclassic form that is perceptible without any extramusical references; similarly, the twelve-tone organization functions independently of any possible narrative.

The first movement is a large-scale arch with a central contrasting section (mm. 90–157) and a brief coda (mm. 240–45). There is symmetry, too, in the deployment of the row. The first presentation of its prime form appears within the first five measures, spread throughout the orchestral texture: [G—E♭—D♭—F—E—B—C—A—D—G♯—F♯—B♭—C♯]. This Webern-like pointillism reappears throughout the movement, alongside clear echoes of Schoenberg. The row then appears in retrograde at the end of the movement, a mirror version that parallels the A-B-A construction of the whole. This clarity of form serves to contain and order the stylistic content, which is severe, dissonant, and occasionally violent. The first 30 measures demonstrate the tendency toward extremes that characterizes the whole movement. Abrupt strikes from snare drum, field drum, and even a whip (m. 6) punctuate an orchestral texture that juxtaposes narrow oscillations and the lower ranges of the oboes, English horn, clarinets, and bass clarinet (mm. 6–10) with angular lines in the extreme upper ranges of the flute and violin sections (mm. 12–14). The section culminates in what sounds like a scream from the flute and piccolo (m. 29).

In the Tranquillo passage that follows (m. 42), the combination of solo alto flute with marimba and harp maintains the sound palette developed for *Montezuma*, while the sul ponticello tremolos from viola and violin 2 with melodic lines in the clarinet and bass clarinet briefly recall the sound world of Schoenberg's *Pierrot lunaire*.[59] The chamber music texture continues until the *poco animando* in m. 55, after which the rest of the orchestra begins to intrude and bring back the disjunct contours and *Klangfarben*-like distribution of thematic ideas that characterized the opening. The B section is perhaps even more violent, apart from brief moments of respite in mm. 120–25 and in the transition back to the A section (mm. 150–57). The coda (mm. 240–45) is nothing other than a final series of sforzando blows from nearly every section of the orchestra in turn.

In a rather traditional point of contrast, the second movement proceeds Lento e dolce, albeit in Sessions's dissonant counterpoint. The form is a classic, well-proportioned rounded binary. The A section (mm. 1–24) contains two key pieces of thematic material: the viola soli in mm. 1–4 (*a*) and the solo flute line in mm. 7–11 (*b*). The B section (mm. 25–45) begins "quasi recitativo," with a speechlike if somewhat awkward line in the oboes and English horn. This new thematic material is occasionally juxtaposed with an accompanimental figure from A, as in mm. 47–48 when the oboes take up one of the string lines that originally accompanied *b*. A brief transition (mm. 52–53) leads to a varied reprise of A (mm. 54–66). The themes return in reverse order: *b* in mm. 53–54, before Sessions splinters it among the rest of the woodwinds; and *a*, first in inversion (mm. 59–62 in the violins) and then in its original form (mm. 62–64), moving from alto flute to bass clarinet and finally bassoon.

Throughout this movement, the voices seem to float freely among one another, often in extreme ranges. For example, an ethereally high and smoothly contoured descent in the string section (mm. 22–24) leads to the more disjunct unison B theme, with the oboes low enough in their range that they seem to groan (mm. 25–29). They are accompanied by a similarly dark line of tremolos in the lower register of the clarinet section (mm. 27–31). Meanwhile, the strings and flutes continue with their more placid, higher-voiced lines. As opposed to the stridency of the first movement, the total effect of Sessions's careful orchestration is a dreamlike sense of disassociation.

Sessions describes the third and final movement as "a kind of scherzo with dark rumblings underneath" and overall "rather grim" and "most brutal," except for the ending.[60] Considering the severity of the first movement, this statement is striking; perhaps the composer was thinking of the Finale's restless pace. As he suggested, the movement takes the ABA form of a scherzo and trio with an epilogue. While Sessions makes only occasional use of compound or triple rhythms, the general level of activity and mischievously shifting meters do conjure up the typical personality of a scherzo. The central contrasting section (mm. 35–85, Allegretto, un poco scherzando) even features the lighter texture and shift in orchestration, featuring woodwinds and horns, found in traditional trios. Still, the atmosphere is anything but pastoral. Both A sections (mm. 1–34 and mm. 86–139) begin with an eighth-note ostinato in the strings, staccato horn section, and piano, with occasional punctuation by xylophone. In the second iteration at m. 86, the strings are martellato, and the ostinato expands to the harp as well, making its return even dryer and more percussive. In both cases the thematic material—consisting of sustained altissimo, initiated by prodigious leaps upward (of a seventh or more)—is equally strident. This passage, along with the other thematic material of the movement, is based on the prime form of the row: [G—E♭—F—E—B—C—A—D—G♯—F♯—B♭—C♯], and its combinatorial inversion, I^{11}: [F♯—B♭—A♭—A—D—C♯—E—B—F—G—E♭—C].[61] Together, the first halves of each row complete the aggregate, as do the second halves, which ensures a certain amount of dissonance as well as a symmetry that mirrors the otherwise Neoclassic features of the symphony as a whole.

Rather than driving toward the end of the movement, the second A section seems to stall in mm. 130–39. While the rest of the orchestra, including piano, harp, and percussion, articulates a final series of sforzando blows, the horn section provides another ostinato, but it gradually slows. The loss of momentum is achieved not through a tempo shift—in fact, Sessions takes care to reiterate the tempo marking in m. 133—but through a change in meter (the orchestra changes from its 2/4 to adopt the 6/8 of the horns) and in the notated rhythms. This is, in effect, a brief instance of metric modulation, usually associated with Elliott Carter. Though Sessions did not employ this technique regularly, the two composers' shared interest in rhythmic variety and complexity is evident.

After this striking transition, the epilogue (mm. 140–66) continues in a dramatically different vein from the rest of the movement. The trumpets, trombones, tuba, percussion, and piano drop out and the texture becomes increasingly thinner and darker. Of the flutes, only the alto continues past m. 152, and the oboes and clarinets exit in mm. 161–62. At the same time, we hear the retrograde version of the prime row—the mirror image of the pitch material at the opening of the movement, although radically different in orchestration and thematic character. The last four notes are introduced in mm. 162–63 and then sustained: E in horn 1, F in the timpani, E-flat in the bass, and G in the English horn. Rearticulations in alto flute, horn 2, and horn 3 make the sostenuto harmony pulsate gently, as does the gradually slowing ostinato in the timpani (again through changes in rhythm rather than tempo). Like the thinning of the orchestral texture, the slowing of the timpani is a powerful gesture, significantly similar to the slowing of a heartbeat. Sessions admired his own achievement in this epilogue: "If I may say so, that's about the best ending I ever wrote. Or one of them. It's quite unusual."[62] He regarded this symphony as his personal favorite.

The Symphony No. 7 encapsulates many of the distinctive traits of Sessions's orchestral writing. The wide array of percussion, preference for darker woodwind timbres like the English horn and clarinet, and high-flying string lines are typical of his scorings. The dense counterpoint and metric irregularities are hallmarks of Sessions's "difficult" style. His tendency toward sudden alterations of mood and tempo—whether through abrupt juxtapositions of agitated and tranquillo passages or through unexpected depletions of rhythmic energy and thinning orchestral texture—is also on display. In the case of the Symphony No. 7, this last trait has potential programmatic bearing.

The violence and sheer kinetic energy of Movements 1 and 3, which dissipate in a final quiet passage (a common musical signifier for death), fit both extramusical inspirations for the work. The resonances with warfare are obvious, and if we hear the epilogue as "funereal," it conjures the visual images of death so prevalent for the American public during the Vietnam War: whether photographs of destruction abroad or of soldiers' coffins at Dover Air Force Base, they lent urgency to the anti-war protests with which Sessions's Sixth, Seventh, and Eighth Symphonies aligned. In another, more clearly narrative vein, all three movements trace the arc of *The Story of O*, a novel concerning sadomasochism in which a young woman (known to the reader only as O) is repeatedly whipped, beaten, and sexually used by her lover and his circle of fellow practitioners. Having fully submitted to such treatment, O is eventually abandoned, after which one version of the published epilogue has her asking for, and receiving, permission to commit suicide. Given the prominent percussion—including the whipcrack in the first movement—the physicality and violence of the first and third movements is not difficult to associate with an imagined world of sadomasochism. The disassociation in the second movement makes perhaps even more sense in the context of O's psychology and her submission—the physical violence of the world around her recedes in favor of an inner world, as trysts with her lover or with others trigger periods of intense self-reflection. And the oddity of the epilogue—its suddenness and relative peacefulness—is an especially disturbing vision of death in the form of a suicide as release.

The *Chicago Daily News* compared the symphony, curiously, to the poetry of Robert Frost—an Americanist framing at odds with Sessions's internationalism and with the partial inspiration for this work in a piece of French literature: "His writing is all bone and muscle, without an ounce of spare flesh, and its meaning is always uncompromisingly evident."[63] Leighton Kerner later wrote in *Musical America* that the Seventh Symphony confirmed Sessions as "the greatest symphonist since Mahler." Kerner's is a more communicative Sessions: "Music meets its audience more than halfway when it's this directly powerful, as in the symphony's outer movements, this dazzlingly orchestrated throughout, and this diaphanous and lyrical, albeit atonally so, in its middle movement and in the ghostly chiaroscuro of the finale's epilogue."[64]

The Symphony No. 8, composed in just four months in 1968, conveys a sense of weariness and resignation about the war.[65] The work was commissioned by the New York Philharmonic for its one hundred twenty-fifth anniversary, near the end of Bernstein's tenure as music director. Although Bernstein surely agreed with Sessions's anti-war stance, Michael Steinberg directed the premiere. The two-movement form is unusual for Sessions and perhaps a secondary indicator of his exhaustion then. The Adagio e mesto manages to convey both lugubriousness and agitation across its three sections. The reappearance of two-note and four-note rhythmic figures lend the movement a dirgelike cast, occasionally interrupted by dissonant and strident outbursts from the woodwinds and brass. The second movement features more rhythmic flexibility—what Sessions called "a kind of prose rhythm in a way."[66] The controlling row [E—F—G—B♭—F♯—B—C—A—C♯—D♯—D—G♯] appears at the beginning in the violins accompanied by maracas that conjure, in the composer's words, a "snake in the underbrush."[67] The rest of the work makes prominent use of inversion, fragmentation, and other principles associated with twelve-tone serialism, but which also reach back to Sessions's fascination with Baroque counterpoint.

The critical reaction to the work reflects Sessions's reception throughout his career, ranging from a sense of pro forma admiration to outright dislike. Winthrop Sargeant in the *New*

Yorker witheringly recapitulated the by-now standard narrative of academism and deliberate disregard for the audience: "From his throne in Princeton, he reigns over the fashions taught at countless university music departments, where tyro composers learn to compose more or less like him. His own pupils are ubiquitous. Just how much all this has to do with the American musical public is a debatable point. I have never heard any concertgoer express an anguished hunger that nothing but one of Mr. Sessions' symphonies could satisfy. His realm is the college composition classes of America, and these have somehow become divorced from the needs of people who go to hear music."[68]

Sargeant also noted, quite correctly, that by 1968 this sort of modernism was no longer the vanguard: "Of course, the avant-garde is way out there ahead of Mr. Sessions. He is the stalwart conservative of modernism. But if you want to hear music pretty much as Schoenberg began composing about half a century ago, Mr. Sessions is your man." The complaint over the death of a listenable tradition was by no means unique, though Sargeant was unusually caustic: "While listening to the symphony, I did some thinking, and came to the conclusion that there are two possible diagnoses for the kind of music Mr. Sessions composes. Either it is a passing disease from which we shall one day recover or music is dead and Mr. Sessions is one of its most enthusiastic pallbearers." The supposedly fatal disconnect between twelve-tone serialism (or other types of modernism) and listenability, an American voice, or the symphonic tradition is, of course, a myth. Sessions seems also to have come to view the symphony as something of a myth, and it is worth noting that after 1968 he wrote several more large works for orchestra but only labeled one of them a symphony. Still, the view of Sessions as a highly skilled but also hard-edged and academic composer persisted. Harold C. Schonberg called the Eighth Symphony a "severe, dissonant, unmelodic piece, beautifully scored and organized"; Sessions was "one of the best academic composers of America" and accordingly "there is little in this score that rises above eclectic academism."[69] Sessions had earned critical respect but often not affection.

SYMPHONY NO. 9

The Symphony No. 9 (1975–78) is an appropriately monumental end to Sessions's symphonic corpus, although he would go on to complete the Pulitzer Prize–winning Concerto for Orchestra in 1981. The symphony employs two tone rows: [A—B♭—E♭—F—D—C♯—G♯—B—G—F♯—C—E], and [A—G—F—F♯—D—A♭—B♭—D—B—E♭—E—C♯]. As in the final movement of Symphony No. 7, the first row is combinatorial in that its second hexachord is an inversion of the first—an unusual tack for Sessions given his preference for a flexible treatment of the row. The first movement features a sonata-like return to its opening material, although it ends rather suddenly with what Olmstead, somewhat at a loss, calls an "unresolved-question conclusion."[70] Though it is by no means "tender," the second movement (Con movimento adagio) demonstrates that Sessions can write plaintively and with open emotion, while its scherzando middle section displays the contrapuntal flair and sense of dark humor or mischief found throughout his works. The mournful trombone solo of the opening returns to close the movement, providing the only satisfying ending in the work.

The Allegro vivace propels the work toward its end "with a defiant cadence, a sudden bang," in Olmstead's phrase.[71] However, the sudden pullback before the end and the rhythmic displacement of the final exclamation make the conclusion seem frustratingly abrupt. Perhaps the key to this ending lies in the famous William Blake poem that, according to Sessions, inspired the symphony:

> Tyger, Tyger burning bright
> In the forests of the night
> What immortal hand or eye
> Could frame thy fearful symmetry?

By casting the symphony as oppositions of mood, style, and technique, might Sessions be playing with his own "fearful symmetry"? Olmstead suggests that the abrupt ending relates to Blake's profound question: "Did He who made the lamb make thee?"[72] She also connects the leitmotivic use of a syncopated major second in the first and third movements with the sound of "tiger" as pronounced in American English, making it a sort of Wagnerian meditation on the nature of the fabled cat.[73] Further influence of Wagner, as well as Bach's *Fortspinnung*, can be heard in the long-breathed melodic writing as well as the continuity produced by overlapping phrases, endlessly cresting and then lulling.

Nevertheless, in the Ninth Symphony, as always, Sessions obeys the logic of no one but himself. About a year after its premiere, he saw no need to apologize for the arc of his compositional style: "I suppose there's always the assumption that if I like it, some day others will, too. If you don't like your own music you can be sure no one else will. You have to work on the idea that public taste will catch up to what composers are doing. That's the way it's been in the history of music so far."[74] Sessions's consistency and rigor, even in the face of lifelong criticism, is the hallmark of his career.

Ironically, another constant was Sessions's ambivalence about the symphony genre. Despite being one of the more prolific symphonists of the mid-twentieth century, he remained leery of the label. His symphonies have much in common with his operatic writing, and he often employed narrative totems like novels and poems; the last three symphonies in particular list toward multimovement tone poems. While programmatic symphonies had a long and storied history by this point, one can see in his responses to critics and peers that his resistance to the genre ran deeper than a need for drama and narrative. When Dallapiccola expressed his admiration for the Fourth Symphony, Sessions responded, "I'm not sure it *is* a symphony . . . I still don't know exactly what a symphony is."[75] In this sense—as well as his having found a middle way between the paths of Stravinsky and Schoenberg—Sessions captured the tensions of his era.

Paul Creston

Like Hovhaness, Paul Creston (born Giuseppe Guttoveggio, 1906–85) operated outside the circle of East Coast, conservatory-trained composers who were his contemporaries as symphonists. Creston was self-taught in theory and composition, although he did take lessons from organists Gaston Dethier and Pietro Yon, and he sent some of his early pieces to Henry Cowell, who championed the younger composer's music.[76] His compositional models included Baroque, Romantic, and Impressionist figures: J. S. Bach, Domenico Scarlatti, Frédéric Chopin, Claude Debussy, and Maurice Ravel.[77] His musical language thus stood apart from the Neoclassicism of Boulanger's circle as well as from atonal and serialist modernism; the former he could coexist with, as they shared a neotonal harmonic language (however different in style), but the latter eventually eclipsed him.

Creston was among the most widely performed and critically acclaimed American composers in the 1940s and 50s but was passed over during the 1960s, by which time his works sounded distinctly out of date. Nonetheless, Creston's career was successful: he served as organist at St. Malachy's Church in New York City before turning to composition in the early 1930s. He was

Table 6.2 The Symphonies of Paul Creston (1906–85)

Title	Movements	Instrumentation	Comments
Symphony No. 1, Op. 20 (1940)	1. With Majesty 5/4 (158 mm.) 2. With Humor 3/4 (309 mm.) 3. With Serenity 6/8 (113 mm.) 4. With Gaiety 2/4 (277 mm.)	Grand plus Flt. (doubling Picc.), Tuba	First performance: February 22, 1941, by the NYA Symphony Orchestra (Brooklyn), conducted by Fritz Mahler. Awarded the New York Music Critics' Circle Award of 1943 as well as first prize in the 1952 Paris International Referendum. Score published by G. Schirmer, 1940 (composer's holograph).
Symphony No. 2, Op. 35 (1944)	Four movements in two parts. I. Introduction & Song 1. Introduction 12/8 (mm. 1–49) 2. Song 4/4 (mm. 50–172) II. Interlude & Dance 1. Interlude 3/4 (mm. 1–44) 2. Dance 3/4 (mm. 45–370)	Grand plus Picc., Flt., EH, Bclar., Cbssn., Tpt., Tuba, Perc. (Tamb., Tri, Xylo, Tam-tam, SD, Cym., Suspended Cym., BD, Tom-tom), Pno.	Dedicated "to Dr. William Filler in profound gratitude." Described by composer as the "apotheosis of the two foundations of music: song and dance." First performance: February 15, 1945, by the New York Philharmonic, conducted by Artur Rodzinski. Score published by G. Schirmer, 1954.
Symphony No. 3, "Three Mysteries," Op. 48 (1950)	1. Nativity 9/8 (310 mm.) 2. Crucifixion 3/4 (153 mm.) 3. Resurrection 4/4 (316 mm.)	Grand plus Flt. (1 doubling Picc.), EH, Bclar, Cbssn., Tpt., Tuba, Harp.	"Dedicated to the Worcester Music Festival, 1950, in memory of Aldus C. Higgins." Each movement reflects images (specified by the composer) associated with the title of that movement. Incorporates seven Gregorian chant melodies. First performance: October 27, 1950, by the Philadelphia Orchestra, conducted by Eugene Ormandy. Score published by Shawnee, 1957 (composer's holograph).
Symphony No. 4, Op. 52 (1951)	1. Maestoso—Allegro 4/4 (216 mm.) 2. Andante pastorale 9/8 (104 mm.) 3. Allegretto giocoso 3/4 (230 mm.) 4. Vivace saltellante 6/8 (391 mm.)	Grand plus Flt. (doubling Picc.), Tuba	Creston's favorite of his symphonies. Commissioned by Viola V. Malkin in memory of Joseph D. Malkin. First performance: January 30, 1952, by the National Symphony Orchestra, conducted by Howard Mitchell. Score published by Shawnee (G. Schirmer), 1961 (composer's holograph).

Table 6.2 *continued*

Title	Movements	Instrumentation	Comments
Symphony No. 5, Op. 64 (1955)	1. Con moto 2. Largo 3. Maestoso—Allegro		Commissioned by the National Symphony Orchestra in celebration of its 25th anniversary. First performance: April 4, 1956, by the National Symphony Orchestra, conducted by Howard Mitchell. Unpublished. Manuscript located in the Paul Creston Collection in the LaBudde Special Collections of the Library of the University of Missouri-Kansas City.
Symphony No. 6 for Organ and Orchestra, Op. 118 (1981)	In one movement (352 mm.)	Grand plus Perc. (BD, Cym., Tamb., Tenor Drum, Suspended Cym., Xylo., Gong), Org.	Commissioned by the 1982 American Guild of Organists. First performance: June 28, 1982, by the National Symphony Orchestra, conducted by Philip Brunelle with James Moeser, organ. Score published by G. Schirmer, 1984.

awarded a Guggenheim Fellowship in 1938 and his First Symphony received the Music Critics' Circle Award in 1943. There was no shortage of commissions, and his symphonies were premiered by first-rank orchestras. Creston also served as professor and composer-in-residence at Central Washington State College (1968–75) and authored two textbooks, *Principles of Rhythm* (1964) and *Rational Metric Notation* (1979), the product of his thoroughgoing study of four centuries of rhythmic practice.[78] Like William Schuman, Vincent Persichetti, and Peter Mennin, he also held prominent leadership positions as president of the National Association for American Composers and Conductors (1956–60) and director of the American Society of Composers, Authors, and Publishers (1960–68).

Creston's interest in rhythm, as evidenced in his pedagogical publications, extended to his compositional style. At its root, this fascination with rhythm grew out of his conviction that the fundamental sources of all music were song and dance.[79] He often employed syncopated and other kinds of energetic rhythms, which only coincidentally sounded like jazz or other popular styles of American dance music. As Creston famously declared, "I make no special effort to be American in my music. I work to be my true self, which is American by birth, Italian by parentage, and cosmopolitan by choice."[80] Creston seems to have defined "dance" ecumenically, as it could encompass popular or folklike vivacity, balletic grace, and Baroque tradition. Comparing Creston's rhythmic profile to Stravinsky and Ravel, Tawa points out that he often still subordinated it to a melodic line.[81] At the same time, despite the presence of generative repeated patterns and free-flowing metrical plays that create a feel of timelessness, seldom do we find Stravinsky's layered, multimetrical ostinati. Indeed, such a construction would undermine the kind of flowing melodies and rich homophonic textures Creston preferred.

Like his rhythmic language, the points of inspiration for Creston's "song" ranged widely: everything from the smooth, ametrical flow of plainchant to the casual grace of Tin Pan Alley and Broadway love songs appears in his symphonies. These melodies are typically supported in a rather conventional manner, often with lush, extended tertian sonorities; the result is more "neo-Romantic" in sound than anything written by Diamond, who often bore that label. His tendency to use tonal or modal vocabulary (or a combination thereof) without confirming a tonal center allies him more closely to Debussy and "Impressionist" harmony than to his American neotonal contemporaries. The thickness of his orchestration—Creston often doubles lines rather than leaving solo instruments exposed—means that his sound has solidity but lacks the more hard-edged "force" of works from the same period by Schuman, Diamond, or Mennin.

Although he wrote only six symphonies, Creston clearly invested the genre with some weight (table 6.2). As with Mennin, the occasional extramusical point of reference is incidental and ultimately subordinated to "absolute" formal and stylistic procedures. Creston's symphonies occasionally turned toward the Baroque, adopting two-movement structures built on strong contrasts, but at times he also developed material in a free-form manner. Creston's compositions, including symphonies, were designed to be openly emotional without being programmatic and to speak in terms understandable to a general audience. His self-analysis strikes a posture strikingly similar to Mennin's: "My philosophic approach to composition is abstract. I am preoccupied with matters of melodic design, harmonic coloring, rhythmic pulse, and formal progression; not with imitations of nature or narrations of fairy tales or propounding of sociological ideologies."[82] His contention notwithstanding, Creston had an interest in mysticism not unlike Hovhaness's, and his music often seems to have a meditative or spiritual meaning. Tawa's label of Creston's symphonies as "self-reliant," meaning autonomous and abstract, is therefore misleading: as opposed to the open programmaticism of Bernstein and Hovhaness, Creston's symphonies, like those of many of his contemporaries, negotiated a middle ground between the absolute and the programmatic.[83]

SYMPHONY NO. 1

Creston's first two symphonies proved the viability of his approach. In 1943 he won the Music Critics' Circle Award for his Symphony No. 1, which had been premiered in 1941 by the NYA Symphony Orchestra, conducted by Fritz Mahler. That this symphony won the prize for the most outstanding composition heard in New York that season over Copland's *Lincoln Portrait* as well as works by Schuman and Morton Gould attests to Creston's high profile at the time.[84] Creston's First Symphony (1940) is his most traditional in the sense that it conforms to the expected four-part plan: each compact movement stays in character, progressing from the "majesty" of the opening sonata to the "humor" of the scherzo, the "serenity" of the slow movement, and finally the "gaiety" of the rondo finale (Walter Simmons identifies these four characters as the "primary aspects" of Creston's "musical personality" as well as essential elements of his compositional style). The work is neotonal, managing to avoid trite tonal formulas without resorting to excessive dissonance. Simmons calls the first movement "a proudly Whitmanesque assertion of self" and notes the rhythmic play typical of Creston that gives the second movement its "off-kilter" character. The third movement recalls the Gregorian chant movement of his String Quartet (1936) while also looking ahead to some aspects of his Third Symphony with what Simmons calls "a fusion of sensual and spiritual yearning."[85] Indeed, the long string lines alternate between the narrow range and meditative atmosphere of chant and the lilting rhythms and sweeping arcs of the lush orchestral scores in films of the day. Similarly, the Trio of the Scherzo recalls the glamour and romance of Hollywood's Golden Age. As might be expected of a neophyte symphonist (but which would continue to be typical of Creston), the energetic Finale is largely homophonic. Near-constant running and skipping figures in the strings and woodwinds are juxtaposed with bolder, syncopated passages in the brass, leavened by occasional moments of lyricism. Overall, the work is promising but also predictable.

SYMPHONY NO. 2

Just three years later, Symphony No. 2 (1944) became what Creston called "an apotheosis of the two foundations of all music: song and dance."[86] The work unfolds in two movements devoted to each of these musical pillars: Introduction and Song, and Interlude and Dance. The opening Introduction slowly unfurls a melody in the cello section that gradually expands, in mostly stepwise and triadic fashion, to incorporate all 12 tones within the implied tonality of F Phrygian. The texture builds from this ground up—viola, violin 2, and then violin 1, each with its own theme—to create what Simmons calls a "cumulative ground bass."[87] The 12/8 meter and contrasting accents of each line obscure any sense of metrical grounding; Creston relies on the string section to anchor the work as a variety of other gliding, chromatic lines are introduced in the winds that sustain a "smooth dissonance."[88] This unusual structure perhaps explains why the Introduction is quite short, concluding with a unison tutti statement of the opening theme (mm. 42–46), followed by a brief coda (mm. 47–49).

In contrast to the complexities of the Introduction, the "Song" takes its inspiration from plainspoken folk song and the subtle sophistication of Richard Rodgers. Much of the "neo-Romanticism" of Creston's music stems from the sweeping melodies of the midcentury American ballad, which, as Allen Forte notes, typically features careful attention to the upper and lower extremities of a given melody, as well as to the more obvious appoggiaturas and suspensions that can add a plaintive note.[89] Like these popular melodies, those of Creston are strongly shaped by the assimilation of blue notes, borrowings from the parallel mode, and unstable or yearning sonorities like diminished sevenths or augmented sixth chords (i.e., the Tristan chord).[90] The "Song" theme, which Creston treats to a series of variations, is a case in point. While essentially a triadic rendering in D-flat major of the opening cello theme from the Introduction, its character shifts gradually to incorporate blue notes: the apex C at the end of m. 53 slips to C-flat (♭7) at the end of m. 55, and A-flat slips to G-natural (♭5) in mm. 56–57. Particularly when rendered by the flute (mm. 50–58) and oboe (mm. 59–68), the melody sounds more bittersweet than bluesy—an example of the kind of assimilation Forte describes. The gentle oscillating accompaniment that begins in the woodwinds and then travels to the strings also suits the ballad-like vocality of the theme. Occasional sumptuous touches in the orchestration—for example, the rippling piano motive and fluttering of the flutes that accompany the solo horn variation of the "Song" (mm. 77–84)—bend even further toward Broadway or Hollywood film scores.

The movement continues to build in texture and volume to a passionate tutti statement of the theme in mm. 132–52, followed by another reflective coda (similar to the end of the Introduction) in which the "Song" theme appears one more time in the oboe (mm. 156–72). This Americanized vernacular provides a contrast to the chromatic introductory theme as well as to the plainchants from which Creston draws in works like the Third Symphony.

The brief Interlude that begins the second movement (mm. 1–44) is also based on a transformation of the introductory theme; it vacillates between agitation and mystery. The shift in character is mostly due to the "aggressive and defiant" rhythmic alteration of the theme and the addition of an "ominous" oscillating ostinato based on the accompanimental motive from the "song."[91] A muted variant of the principal theme appears in the solo flute (mm. 25–34). This Interlude is even briefer than the Introduction and is essentially an extended transition into the second movement.

Triggered by a unison statement of the "aggressive" main theme as it first appeared in the Interlude (mm. 39–44), the "Dance" bursts forth with a fortissimo passage that settles into a taut staccato groove from m. 52, over which brass and woodwind solos leap and twirl. This section is the only one in the symphony that falls obviously into a particular meter, staying in 3/4 throughout with a constant syncopated ostinato (3+2+3+2+2) in the background.[92] As the movement spins on, layers accumulate in a series of textural waves. Syncopated brass lines add an unmistakably American flavor to the whole, and churning string lines create a sense of urgency while occasional ritardandi allow for broader gestures that conjure more expansive choreography, like limbs flung wide. The blues implications of the "Song" are fulfilled here, particularly in the brass—for example, the muted trumpet solo in mm. 61–71. Simmons asserts that these passages "clearly resemble" jazz improvisation, but compared to Bernstein (e.g., *Prelude, Fugue and Riffs* and the Second Symphony) or even Copland, jazz influences in Creston's work are quite restrained, more like those of Harris or Sessions.[93] The momentum dissipates almost completely in mm. 252–80, with shuddering tremolos from the woodwinds while the strings create an unexpectedly ominous atmosphere. It builds again in a contrapuntal passage for strings alone that recalls the Introduction (m. 281); this fades briefly in a unison passage before the entrance of staccato woodwinds in m. 310 heralds the final burst of energy that drives the symphony to its end. A transformation of the "Song" theme soars in the high strings (mm. 318–32) over interlocking ostinati and is then joined by the woodwinds (mm. 333–50). This last melodic turn is rooted in E-flat minor, but in a final surprise, the work as a whole closes abruptly in G-flat major.[94]

Creston's Second Symphony premiered on February 15, 1945, with the New York Philharmonic under Artur Rodzinski, alongside Thomson's *Symphony on a Hymn Tune* (1928). Noting its formal integration and the composer's claim to achieve an "apotheosis" in the work, Olin Downes's review observed "a symbolic and a musical relation between the themes and their unfoldment." His verdict: "The Introduction, for the strings alone, is serious; the mood is more lyrical, gay and romantic as the work proceeds. There is much variety of orchestral coloring, as well as of rhythmic effect. Fine workmanship is evident throughout. . . . Whether in following a fixed structural idea Mr. Creston has helped or hindered himself is a thing better to be decided after longer acquaintance with the composition."[95] Downes thus finds in the work more promise than greatness achieved. Having the benefit of that "longer acquaintance," on the other hand, Simmons praises the Second Symphony—"perhaps Creston's most distinctive, most representative, and . . . greatest work"—for its "rich elaboration and thorough integration of a personal and original aesthetic concept into a cohesive work of great appeal . . . a major landmark of American Neo-Romanticism and one of the most significant American symphonies of the 1940s."[96]

SYMPHONY NO. 3, "THE THREE MYSTERIES"

The Third Symphony (1950) takes on a drastically different character, tending toward the meditative and spiritual rather than the embodied vitality of the Second Symphony. Subtitled "The Three Mysteries"—the Nativity, Crucifixion, and Resurrection—the symphony draws deeply on Creston's Catholic heritage while avoiding any specific narrative. He indicates as much in the Preface to the score: "Though it derives its inspiration from [these biblical events], historic and mystic, the work is a musical parallel of inherent emotional reactions rather than a narrative or painting, these emotions being sometimes of the spectators of the first enactment of the drama and sometimes of the spectators of the annual re-enactment. The programmatic content, such as there may be, also justifies the utilization of Gregorian Chant in a non-liturgical aspect."[97] Plainchant melodies, then, represented another kind of "song" for Creston; he quotes or alludes to seven of them in this symphony, all of which he identifies in the Preface.

Although the first movement is intended to paint an "innocent and blissful" picture (Tawa's phrase), it opens with an oddly dissonant and disorienting passage for the strings.[98] Perhaps it reflects the darkness of the world before the coming of Christ; whatever the case, the harp soon sweeps the mood away (m. 20) and the movement then opens onto a pastoral series of horn and woodwind solos that could reasonably be called "innocent," with harmony that is certainly tonal and "blissful." The horn line quotes *Puer natus est nobis* (A Boy Is Born for Us), the introductory chant for the Mass for Christmas Day. As the movement continues to develop the chant melody, it becomes increasingly festive, with a lilting 9/8 dance. At m. 131 the pastoral section turns more peaceful and reflective, with a Poco meno mosso shift to 3/4 as a series of sweet woodwind melodies unfold over a drone. Together, the winds paraphrase the opening of the Gloria from the *Missa Deus sempiterne* and the accompaniment in open fourths, fifths, and octaves recalls early polyphony. This respite then gives way to a new dance in a lively 2/4, based again on *Puer natus* (m. 182). This section features more counterpoint than before: strings, winds, and brass layer their own motives upon each other as the movement rushes gaily forward. It ends with a triumphant-sounding march and glistening D-major chord, complete with a crescendo and harp glissando that lend it a cinematic flourish.

The second movement features two plainchant melodies over a ground bass: the first, *Pater, si non potest hic calix* (Father, if this Cup cannot Pass Away; a Palm Sunday chant), is heard from a mournful cello (m. 1) and the second, the *Stabat Mater* sequence, in the English horn (m. 27). Again, the open-voiced accompaniment to the cello conjures up an ancient, churchly atmosphere before ominous punctuations from the timpani and horns and turbulence in the strings disrupt it. The movement settles again into meditation for the entrance of the English horn. Below this Good Friday melody, a passacaglia over a four-measure descending chromatic ground bass likely references famous settings of the *Crucifixus*, especially in Bach's Mass in B Minor (mm. 23–66). The movement as a whole is intensely contrapuntal, and the development continues as the bass rises a step in m. 51 and the theme migrates to the winds. From m. 80 the movement takes on the character of a limping, forced march in 3/4 that grows in agitation and dissonance. A suspended string tremolo (mm. 118–26) slows the momentum of the march as the solo bassoon reprises the *Stabat Mater* (m. 130); it is accompanied by pulsing half-step "sigh" figures, a long-standing signifier of pain, here intensified in dissonant layers of woodwinds and strings. As the movement fades, we hear both melodies one final time, played in counterpoint by muted solo viola (*Stabat Mater*) and solo cello (*Pater, si no potest*) both high in their range—a striking timbre and a haunting gesture.

According to Tawa, "The last movement aims at dignified magnificence in delivering its message of affirmation" with modal harmonies that "generate an ancient ambience" and takes the listener "to a moment beyond time and place."[99] The use of divisi strings in harmonics helps achieve an almost vaporous texture at the outset while the cellos and basses unfold a hymnlike melody, paraphrased from the chant *Angelus Domini descendit de caelo* (An Angel of God Descended from Heaven), but reminiscent of the initial presentation of the *Ode to Joy* in Beethoven's Ninth Symphony. A horn chorale (mm. 12–17) and solo trumpet (mm. 18–20) quietly present the next chant, *Christus resurgens ex mortuis* (Christ Is Risen from the Dead)—a fitting choice as the two timbres often represent "heralds" of triumph, worldly or otherworldly. The clarinet joins in m. 22 with the third and final chant, *Victimae paschali laudes* (Praise to the Passover Victim, the sequence from the Easter Mass), here heard in a lively 2/4 but tinged with melancholy due to the Dorian setting of the original chant. What ensues is a dancing celebration, at first tentative and then with growing enthusiasm, conveying the joy of the miracle. All three chants are developed as the music grows steadily more syncopated and energetic, ending in a chorale for brass and winds over churning sixteenth notes in the strings.

Henry Cowell captured the essence of the symphony well, particularly its unusual blend of traditions and styles: "Gregorian melody served up with romantic passion, sometimes with impressionistic instrumentation, with 20th-century dissonance and rhythm; now and again atonal implications are found cheek-by-jowl with the ecclesiastical modes." Unfortunately, as Cowell also points out, the opinions expressed after the concert proved that "the result of Creston's insistence on going his own way is that his combination of extremes has been decried as so shocking as to be almost a violation of elementary musical decency." Cowell's defense of the work is succinct and almost Neoclassical in its justification, as he reminded readers "that plainsong, in various periods of musical history, has been treated in non-liturgical music in the style of the period without offending the sensibilities of its auditors."[100] Simmons, likewise, holds up the work as an example of the seriousness and ambition of which Neoromantic works were capable.[101] While unique in conception, the Third Symphony well demonstrates Creston's developed compositional voice.

FOURTH AND FIFTH SYMPHONIES

The Fourth and Fifth Symphonies continue in a similar vein, offering striking details within fundamentally conventional frameworks. While much lighter in tone than the Third Symphony or even the Fifth, the Symphony No. 4 (1951)—the composer's personal favorite—maintains his typical formal and technical precision.[102] Like the First Symphony, it follows the traditional four-movement plan with a sonata-allegro first movement and a gentle pastorale in ABA form in the second movement, followed by a scherzo and a rondo finale. Each movement displays Creston's penchant for rhythmic play and ostinati, carefully crafted melody, and contrapuntal texture. All three combine in the coda of the first movement, in which an appealingly syncopated line for the brass soars over churning string and woodwind figures. The second movement, built around a three-note motif and a lilting siciliana figure, is simple but striking, with an interlude build on a subtractive ostinato (4+3+2).[103] In a series of woodwind and horn solos, the rather plain melody becomes an arabesque, with swirling figurations that still sway in time to the movement's grounding rhythm. Creston's penchant for unusual rhythmic schemes is tempered in this work and more approachably danceable—the Scherzo and Finale operate on this principle. Likewise, his interest in counterpoint is simplified, and what remains in the foreground is the appealing "song." Overall, the symphony has an almost cinematic sweep: Simmons identifies its sound as the sort of "mood" music offered on radio and television in the late 1940s and early 1950s—what some critics derided as a "pops concert" tone. Whatever the source, one might align this symphony with the sort of middlebrow culture then in ascendance since it is, in Simmons's estimation, both a "fully elaborated symphony" and "readily accessible to even the least sophisticated listener."[104] The work premiered with the National Symphony Orchestra under Howard Mitchell in January 1952.

Three years later, the same orchestra commissioned Creston to write a new symphony for its twenty-fifth anniversary.[105] Instead of celebrating, however, the Fifth Symphony (1955) is engulfed in turmoil, achieving its tragic-to-triumphant arc only in the last moments. In his program note, Creston revealed that the "keynote of the emotional basis of this symphony is intensity, and the feeling is generally one of spiritual conflicts which are not resolved until the final movement." As usual, Creston makes efficient use of generative material, employing three "rhythmically patterned themes" that evolve over the course of the work. The first two, one "aggressive and defiant" (*I/P*) and the other (*I/S*) "lyric and impassioned," appear in the first movement. The third, a "tender and poignant" theme played by the flute, first appears as *II/S* and from that point on becomes the primary focus of the symphony.[106]

The opening of the first-movement sonata is striking, with basses and cellos presenting *P*, which has a *Fortspinnung* character, joined in counterpoint with the violas and then the violins, each layer moving faster than the other. The rhythmic energy here is agitated and spastic, too off-kilter to be danceable. The only contrast to the agitation is the "wailing" *S*, an inversion of the first theme.[107] The second movement, likewise, builds from the ground up with another restless bass line. *II/S* is not as clear in its direction as some of his other melodies; indeed, the movement as a whole is tonally ambiguous, especially when compared with its counterpart in the Fourth—that is, until the movement ends with a quiet English horn solo and some Debussyesque parallelism and oscillation in the strings, as the harmonic confusion dissolves into a luminous Picardy third. The minor mode returns in the third movement, in which a turbulent opening gives way to the purposeful stride of a walking bass. The triumphant turn in this work is hammered home multiple times in a series of climaxes that Simmons accurately describes as "unconvincingly bombastic."[108] Even so, the Fifth Symphony, together with the Fourth, is exemplary of the key aspects of Creston's style, albeit in contrasting emotional tones.

SYMPHONY NO. 6

The American Guild of Organists commissioned Creston in 1981 to compose a work for organ and orchestra, and the resulting Symphony No. 6 premiered in June 1982 with the National Symphony Orchestra; Philip Brunelle conducted and James Moeser was the soloist.[109] And the organ does indeed take the role of soloist, as much of the work lists closer to the concerto than to the symphony. Camille Saint-Saëns's Symphony No. 3 in C Minor, the "Organ" Symphony (1886), is an obvious model. In his efforts to "renew" the symphonic form and modernize the orchestral palette, Saint-Saëns incorporated the organ, as well as the piano and newer valved horns and trumpets.[110] Creston would have unavoidably been reminded of Saint-Saëns's work, although the influence manifests itself more in structure than in the role for the organ. It was Saint-Saëns's stated goal to trim away "needless repetition," and to do so he condensed the four movements of the symphony into two divisions.[111] However, while the resulting work is concise and formally integrated, his rigorous use of cyclic processes and thematic transformation, which for contemporary critics tied the work to the symphonic poem, do mean that repetition plays a crucial role.[112] In a similar way, Creston makes use of two germinal motives to create almost all the material of his single-movement work. Additionally, Saint-Saëns's use of fugal passages and chorale-like textures in the strings and brass (particularly in the Finale) ground his work in genres and techniques that permeated the organ repertoire. Creston also produced an "Organ" Symphony rooted in the instrument's repertoire, although the Sixth does not draw as much inspiration from liturgical genres as does his "Three Mysteries."

Although Creston was undoubtedly inspired by Saint-Saëns in combining the organ with orchestral forces, Copland's Symphony for Organ and Orchestra (1925) is the more proximate model and perhaps the stronger influence, both in its concision (its three movements are brief, approximately 25 minutes in full) and in the way that he uses the organ as a soloistic force throughout. Copland's work treats the organist as a concert soloist: after a brief introduction, the instrument takes over the primary material for the first movement, as expected in a concerto, whereas Saint-Saëns leaves the thematic labor to the orchestra (in fact, the organ appears only in the second and fourth movements). The reflective cadenza and virtuosic passages in Copland's second movement also draw from the concerto genre, although he does use the organ in its more traditional roles as a ground bass and voice of chorales. However, there is generally more focus on call-and-response than on counterpoint in Copland's symphony, except in the opening of the third movement. Overall, Creston adopts more of the American precedent in his choice of a more condensed formal structure and the soloistic treatment of the organ while also retaining his interest in counterpoint. Samuel Barber's First Symphony of 1936 provides a third prototype: both works share the one-movement structure of roughly 20 minutes, the four sections of which correspond to conventional symphonic movements.[113]

The thematic transformation that customarily drives his symphonic works is present here as well. The first two themes of the first section provide the material for the rest of the work. *P* appears in the organ (mm. 1–4) and is repeated before being taken up (in part) by the strings and flutes (m. 10). Despite the *Maestoso* indication, the theme has a flashy, *Fortspinnung*-like character. *S*, introduced at the Andante (m. 14) by the violins and violas, is more sweeping and romantic in tone.[114] Although formally it works like a truncated sonata form, in character the first section more resembles an organ prelude—a chance for some flashy demonstration of technique and impressive contrasts.

The transition to the second section begins in m. 86 with a tempo shift to Allegretto and a curious move from 4/4 to 9/12, which Creston (or his editors) later amended to a more traditional 9/8. Simmons notes that a favorite rhythmic ostinato appears in this section—an irregular 2+2+2+3 pattern (e.g., timpani and percussion, mm. 99–110)—and grounds the lilting of the strings and the seemingly improvisational virtuoso demonstrations of the organ. A lyrical theme, heard first in the violin 1 in m. 113, provides something like the lightness of a Trio. Indeed, the section does form a miniature ABA.

Another transition occurs in m. 153, with the return of 4/4 and of *I/S* in unison strings (a tempo). The third section then settles into an Andante "slow movement." A prominent four-note motive (E♭—G—D♭—B♭) is drawn from *I/P* and serves as the thematic subject of the rest of the symphony.[115] After the organ's extended meditation on *P*, the strings and woodwinds return to *S*, eventually rejoined by the organ imitating flutes and strings to accompany a solo horn version of *S* (mm. 199–206). Another passage for organ alone bookends the section (mm. 213–32), winding down with a peaceful reiteration of the four-note theme.

Creston begins the Finale with another of his bottom-up constructions, starting with a motive in the cellos—a version of the four-note motive from the third section, with the opening major third altered to a major second (m. 233). The cellos then play out a *Fortspinnung* line similar to that of the organ at the opening of the work. The violas enter next (m. 238), followed by violin 2 (m. 243) and violin 1 (m. 248), each presenting their own ideas, drawn from a theme or accompaniment pattern heard earlier in the work—a contrapuntal display worthy of Bach or Telemann. The rest of the movement continues in this vein, with a cyclical recall of almost all material heard throughout the three prior sections, but with a focus on the four-note motive from *I/P* as well as *I/S*. The latter theme, as Simmons puts it, gradually "comes to the fore to lead a grand apotheosis."[116]

Simmons includes the Sixth Symphony among Creston's "festive and virtuosic" works, and it is certainly both. At the same time, he finds the work routine compared to the earlier symphonies (a fault that in his opinion mars many of Creston's late works).[117] But while certainly full of his typical style traits (use of ground bass and counterpoint, traditional forms and references to older genres such as organ preludes and chorales, and the favoring of ostinato and rhythmic and metrical oddities), one could equally argue that the Sixth Symphony represents a daring fusion of prior models—the modernism of Copland, the virtuosic bravado of the organ tradition since Buxtehude, late Baroque counterpoint, and the lushness and orchestral sensitivity of Saint-Saëns—all in a radically condensed "Americanized" version of the conventional four-movement symphony. In the end, it seems that Creston used the symphony to moderate and control a diversity of ideas—a sort of container for his cosmopolitan diversity.

Creston's works never attained the critical stature of many of his contemporaries, nor have they remained available in the way that even many of Hovhaness's have (largely thanks to the latter founding his own recording label)—though, as of this writing, all the symphonies except the Sixth are available in commercial recordings. This tepid reaction to his neotonal and openly appealing style, when paired with the frequent rejection of the modernist standard-bearer Roger Sessions, illustrates the double bind faced by composers at midcentury. In hewing to the tonal tradition, Creston would never be sufficiently modern; on the other hand, in pursuing atonal and twelve-tone formal innovations, Sessions was branded as inaccessible. In addition, both composers were avowed cosmopolitans who avoided musical nationalism and so their works sit uneasily in many narratives of American music, whereas Schuman and Bernstein are more likely to be included alongside earlier symphonists like Harris and Copland.

William Schuman

William Schuman (1910–92) exerted tremendous influence on American musical culture in the 1950s and 60s: as president of the Juilliard School (1945–62) and then Lincoln Center (1962–68); as a member of the Music Advisory Panel to President Dwight D. Eisenhower's Cultural Presentations Program (1954–60) and an artistic ambassador for the State Department and the United Nations Educational, Scientific and Cultural Organization; as chair of the Koussevitzky Music Foundation (to 1983) and director of the Naumburg Foundation (1957–62); and as chair of the Norlin Foundation and the MacDowell Colony (1970s). Biographers Steve Swayne and Joseph Polisi describe a skilled leader and negotiator who logged many hours in service to the institutions for which he worked, and though not all his initiatives succeeded, the international reputation of Juilliard and the ongoing work of Lincoln Center are the products of his vision and organizational acumen. One of his guiding principles was to maintain and promote the ideal of symphonic music in the United States. The 10 symphonies he wrote over the course of his career stand as the counterpart to his work as an administrator, advocate, and educator (table 6.3).

Schuman shares notable stylistic traits with his similarly multifaceted friend and colleague Leonard Bernstein. Both belonged to the generation of American composers after Roy Harris and Aaron Copland who pursued a range of neotonal, atonal, and serial approaches (others included Lukas Foss, David Diamond, and George Rochberg). They sought to create an explicitly American symphonic language; cultivated a distinctly "urban" voice (as opposed to the "cowboy" compositions of Harris or the more generally pastoral tone of Copland), of New York in particular; engaged with materials as diverse as jazz and twelve-tone serialism; and shared an interest in music for the stage. (In Schuman's case this last trait manifested itself in ballets for choreographers Antony Tudor and Martha Graham, the score for the film *The Earth Is Born*, and the opera *Casey at the Bat*). Schuman and Bernstein, along with David Diamond and Virgil Thomson, shared a fondness for musical portraiture.

On the other end of the spectrum, Schuman also shares some stylistic characteristics with Sessions: both began their careers as neotonalists close to Copland's circle and went on to adopt highly chromatic musical languages, eventually pursuing their own unique treatments of twelve-tone technique within the symphonic genre (although Schuman came to serialism later). In addition, both maintained a constant interest in counterpoint. One could never confuse the two composers, however. Schuman consistently used triadic vocabulary and maintained different preferences in terms of orchestration, often featuring instrumental choirs in contrapuntal dialogue as well as attentive and knowledgeable writing for strings (Schuman trained as a violinist). Schuman and Sessions share an interest in the sounds made possible by an expanded percussion battery and a large brass section, from the bright and sharp to the forceful or even violent. In terms of form and character, he ranged more widely than his contemporaries—producing symphonies of one to four movements and displaying an unusual preference for slow first movements. Forms like fugue and passacaglia abound. Schuman also maintained an affection for Tin Pan Alley song and musical theater throughout his life, and he sometimes displayed his flair for a well-turned melody. Moreover, Schuman was quite clear

Table 6.3 The Symphonies of William Schuman (1910–92)

Title	Movements	Instrumentation	Comments
Symphony No. 1 (1935)	1. Allegro risoluto 2. Allegretto 3. Adagio	Chamber group of 18 musicians.	Finale an adaptation of an unfinished *Choreographic Poem* for seven instruments. First performance: October 21, 1936, by the Gotham Symphony Orchestra, conducted by Jules Werner, as part of a Composers' Forum-Laboratory Concert sponsored by the Federal Music Project. Withdrawn after this performance.
Symphony No. 2 (1937)	In one movement.		Awarded first prize from the Composers' Committee to Aid Spanish Democracy. First performance: March 25, 1938, by the Greenwich Orchestra, conducted by Edgar Schenkman. Other performances: September 11, 1938, with the CBS Symphony Orchestra, led by Howard Barlow (the radio broadcast of this performance is available on YouTube); February 17–18, 1939, with the Boston Symphony Orchestra and Serge Koussevitzky; and March 1940, with Harold Barlow conducting the Baltimore Symphony Orchestra. Withdrawn after the Baltimore performance.
Symphony No. 3 (1941)	Four movements in two parts. Part I: 1. Passacaglia 3/4 (mm. 1–145) 2. Fugue 4/4 (mm. 146–382) Part II 1. Chorale 4/4 (mm. 1–141) 2. Toccata ℓ (mm. 142–428)	Grand plus Picc., EH, E♭ Clar, Bclar, 2 Tpt, Trom, Tuba, Perc. (BD, Cym., SD, Xylo.) Optional but "very desirable" additional instruments: Flt., doubling second Picc.; Ob., Clar; Bssn.; Cbssn.; 4 Hn.; Pno. The parts for optional winds and piano are notated in the score, but it is unclear when or how often the extra horns are to play.	Dedicated to Serge Koussevitzky. First performance: October 17, 1941, by the Boston Symphony Orchestra, conducted by Koussevitzky. Awarded the first New York Music Critics' Circle Award, 1941. Score published by G. Schirmer, 1942.

Work	Movements	Instrumentation	Notes
Symphony No. 4 (1941)	1. ♩ = 72 6/4 (254 mm.) 2. Tenderly, simply C (99 mm.) 3. ♩ = 144 C (291 mm.)	Grand plus Flt. (doubling Picc.), Ob, EH, Clar., E♭ Clar, B♭clar, Bssn., Cbssn., Tpt., Tuba, Perc. (SD, Cym., BD, Glsp., Xylo.)	Finale borrows material from the Finale of the Third String Quartet (1939). First performance: January 22–24, 1942, by the Cleveland Orchestra, conducted by Artur Rodzinski. Score published by G. Schirmer, 1950.
Symphony for Strings (Symphony No. 5) (1943)	1. Molto agitato ed energico 6/4 (161 mm.) 2. Larghissimo 3/2 (96 mm.) 3. Presto ¢ (385 mm.)	Strgs.	Commissioned by the Koussevitzky Music Foundation. Dedicated to the memory of Natalie Koussevitzky. First performance: November 12, 1943, by the Boston Symphony Orchestra, conducted by Serge Koussevitzky. Score published by G. Schirmer, 1943.
Symphony No. 6 in One Movement (1948)	One movement 3/2 (714 mm.)	Grand plus Flt. (doubling Picc.), EH, B♭clar, Cbssn., Tpt., Tuba, Perc. (SD, Glsp., Cym., Suspended Cym., BD)	Commissioned by the Dallas Symphony League. First performance: February 27, 1949, by the Dallas Symphony Orchestra, conducted by Antal Dorati. Score published by G. Schirmer, 1952.
Symphony No. 7 (1960)	1. Largo assai 3/4 (120 mm.) 2. Vigoroso 4/4 (104 mm.) 3. Cantabile intensamente 5/4 (74 mm.) 4. Scherzando brioso 4/4 (235 mm.) Mvts. played without pause.	Grand plus Flt. (Flts. 2–3 double two Picc.), EH, B♭clar, Cbssn., Tpt., Tuba, Perc. (BD, Chimes, Glsp., SD, Suspended Cym., Wood Block, Xylo.), Pno. Optional additional winds: Flt, Ob, Clar, E♭ Clar, Bssn, 2 Hr, Tpt, Tenor Tuba	Commissioned by the Serge Koussevitzky Foundation in the Library of Congress for the 75th anniversary of the Boston Symphony Orchestra. Dedicated to the memory of Serge and Natalie Koussevitzky. An adaptation and enlargement of a work originally commissioned by the Philadelphia Orchestra but then withdrawn by Schuman. First performance: October 21–22, 1960, by the Boston Symphony Orchestra, conducted by Charles Munch. Score published by Merion Music, 1962.

Table 6.3 *continued*

Title	Movements	Instrumentation	Comments
Symphony No. 8 (1962)	1. Lento sostenuto–Pressante vigoroso—Lento 4/4 (161 mm.) 2. Largo–Tempo più mosso 4/4 (206 mm.) 3. Presto—Prestissimo 3/2 (494 mm.)	Grand plus 2 Flt. (doubling Picc. 1–2), Bclar., Cbssn., 2 Hr., 2 Tpt., Trom., Tuba, Timp., Perc. (SD, BD, Cym., Tam-tam, Wood Block, Chimes, Glsp., Vbp., Xylo., 2 Suspended Cym.), 2 Harps, Pno. Optional additional instruments: Ob., Clar., Bssn.	Commissioned by the New York Philharmonic to celebrate its move from Carnegie Hall to Lincoln Center. Finale reworks the last movement of his Fourth String Quartet (1950). First performance: October 4, 1962, by the New York Philharmonic, conducted by Leonard Bernstein. Score published by Merion Music, 1964.
Symphony No. 9, "Le fosse ardeatine" (1968)	In one movement 3/2 (629 mm.), divided into three sections: Anteludium (1–109) Offertorium (110–535) Postludium (536–629) Section divisions are not indicated in the score but can be discerned from the composer's program note.	Grand plus Flt. (doubles Picc.), EH, Bclar., Cbssn., 2 Tpt., Tuba, Perc. (Tubular bells, Xylo., Suspended Cym., SD, Tenor Drum, Tam-tam, BD, Cym.), Pno.	"Commissioned by friends of Alexander Hilsburg, in his memory." Inspired by Schuman's visit to the Ardeatine Caves outside Rome, site of an infamous 1944 Nazi massacre of 335 Italians. Though it is not programmatic, the composer intended the work as a memorial ("Whatever future my symphony may have, whenever it is performed, audiences will remember"). First performance: January 10, 1969, by the Philadelphia Orchestra, conducted by Eugene Ormandy. Score published by Merion Music, 1971.
Symphony No. 10, "American Muse" (1975)	1. Con fuoco 3/4 (228 mm.) 2. Larghissimo 4/2 (124 mm.) 3. Presto; Andantino; Leggero; Pesante; Presto possibile ¢ (528 mm.)	Grand plus Flt. (Flt. 2–3 doubling Picc. 1–2), EH, Eb Clar., Bclar., Cbssn., 2 Hn., 2 Tpt., Tuba, Perc. (Xylo., Glsp., SD, Cym., BD, Tam-tam, Tubular bells, Suspended Cym., Vbp., Crotales), Harp, Pno. (doubling Cel.) Optional additional instruments: Flt., Ob., Clar., Bssn.	Commissioned by the National Symphony Orchestra for the American Bicentennial. First movement revises his *Prelude for a Great Occasion* of 1974. First performance: April 6, 1976, by the National Symphony Orchestra, conducted by Antal Dorati. Holograph score published by Merion Music, 1977.

FIRST AND SECOND SYMPHONIES

Schuman's first two symphonies emerged from a similar political and aesthetic milieu as works by Harris, Thomson, and Copland. Not only did he, like them, study in Europe—at the Mozarteum in Salzburg in the summer of 1935, where he studied conducting with Bernhard Paumgartner and attended numerous operatic and orchestral performances at the Salzburg Festival—but he returned with the same urgent conviction that American composers must find their own compositional voice. Although Schuman shared the left-leaning perspective of Copland, Thomson, and Marc Blitzstein, as well as Bernstein, Sessions, and European émigrés like Kurt Weill, Steve Swayne notes that he was generally reserved in his public rhetoric and often refrained from overt political statements or patriotism of the "flag waving" kind.[118] However, as his later work with the State Department's Music Advisory Panel demonstrates, he certainly shared their conviction that government support for the arts was essential. The early stages of his own career clearly benefited from such support.

Schuman began composing the First Symphony (1935) during his summer in Salzburg and finished it in the United States that December; it premiered the next year under the auspices of President Franklin Delano Roosevelt's Works Project Administration, a New Deal program that funded the work of many American artists during the late 1930s and early 1940s. Through its artistic subdivision the Federal Music Project, the Works Project Administration sponsored the New York City Composers' Forum-Laboratory as a venue for the performance of new works and conversations between composers and audiences. On October 21, 1936, Schuman's First Symphony premiered alongside his *Canonic Choruses* and First String Quartet, with Jules Werner conducting. Schuman would go on to write the Second Symphony (composed in November–December 1937) for another concert at the Composers' Forum-Laboratory and it premiered on May 25, 1938, with the Greenwich Orchestra under the direction of Edgar Schenkman.[119] The Second Symphony was awarded first prize by the Composers' Committee to Aid Spanish Democracy, which was adjudicated by Copland, Harris, Sessions, and Bernard Wagenaar. It received two further hearings in short order.[120] Schuman withdrew both works, probably on account of their variable receptions. Changes in America's political landscape may have further prompted Schuman to reject the Second Symphony. Although anti-fascist, Schuman was not a communist, and as the cause of Spanish democracy and supporting organizations like the Aid Committee drifted in the direction of communism, the composer perhaps became less inclined to remind people of its association with his symphony.[121] As much of his writing and public remarks attest, he continued to view democracy as essential to citizens and artists. Inspired, in part, by the ideas of John Dewey, Schuman saw musical (artistic) experience as drawing musicians and audiences together in a fundamentally optimistic kind of populism that also motivated his work as an educator.[122]

While the First and Second Symphonies show Schuman embedded in the political and artistic world of the late 1930s, stylistically they illustrate practices that would continue to define his orchestral output. The First Symphony did not carry an evocative title, but Schuman's program note indicated that he hoped this concert piece "may also serve as a setting for a choreographic composition."[123] It was public knowledge that Schuman had adapted the last movement from an unfinished chamber work for seven instruments called *Choreographic Poem*. Although in this case the prospective staging never materialized, he would go on to score several dance works, and kinetic energy motivates many of his subsequent works. The tendency to adapt existing material—his own and others'—to suit new purposes remained a part of Schuman's compositional approach. As Swayne notes, Schuman generally avoided revising a published piece, but he would often either recast all or part of an existing piece in a new medium or rework an unfinished or withdrawn piece into an entirely new work.[124] The Seventh Symphony would likewise emerge out of a withheld commission and bear traces of its original purpose. Schuman's sense of economy was already in place before his successes in the 1940s and would remain a hallmark of his work as a whole.

The Second Symphony captured the emergent traits that would go on to define Schuman's symphonies, as well as some of his formative influences: rhythmic vitality, careful attention to orchestration, an interest in counterpoint, and a general aura of intensity that characterized most of his music and was particularly apparent in his symphonies. Schuman's program note for the Boston Symphony describes a work built around layers of ostinati, the contrapuntal development of a single theme—the opening melody in the first half of the work, its transition, and of one of the ostinati in the second half—and a nearly constant articulation of the pitch C in the brass (stated first in alternating trumpets and then in four horns): "Throughout the piece the sound of C is stated or implied."[125] Indeed, it was the insistence of that pitch that drew the attention of the critics, who at all three of its earliest performances—by the Greenwich Orchestra under Schenkman, the CBS Orchestra under Howard Barlow, and the Boston Symphony Orchestra under Serge Koussevitzky—found the work polytonal or simply highly dissonant and pronounced it an interesting technical experiment, forceful in presentation, but ultimately unrewarding.[126]

On February 17 and 18, 1939, the Boston Symphony Orchestra included the work on a program that juxtaposed Schuman's symphony with Sibelius's Third Symphony and Beethoven's Third Piano Concerto—all three works sharing the tonic of C. Typical of the reviews, Warren Storey Smith of the *Boston Post* stated that the repeated C "at first arrests and then irritates the listening ear," adding that the orchestration exacerbated the annoyance: "When in the course of the single movement this pedal tone, mostly carried by a trumpet, is dropped, the listener experiences a blessed sense of relief, as when a dentist removes his drill, and the music for a moment seems actually to get somewhere."[127] Alexander Williams of the *Boston Herald*, for whom the work "sounds like fury," questioned the genre designation:

> We have become so loose in the application of our musical terms that Mr. Schuman has probably as much right to call his work a symphony as other composers have to use the word concerto with such abandon. Somehow one thinks of a symphony as a more important work than this piece. Symphonies always abound in contrast, and of that quality Mr. Schuman's score is singularly barren. It may be too much to say that this music was written solely to demonstrate the structural possibilities of the one note idea, but it is hard to see any other artistic justification for it.[128]

Williams frames his evaluation of the work relative to the value of a symphony—the work ought to be "important." Though he did not invoke symphonic standards directly, Smith lamented that Schuman had substituted a "process" for "ideas and thoughts," locating the worth of a symphony in the originality of its germinal material. On the other hand, Moses Smith's more tempered review praised the symphony's "muscular drive as well as intellectual conviction," reprising the question of significance and adding the masculine descriptors that would long adhere to Schuman's symphonies.[129] In general, critics acknowledged Schuman's contrapuntal ingenuity and the intensity, but a single choice in his orchestration—the incessant C in the brass—seems to have obscured all else. Among the other features of the Second Symphony that now appear prescient, one might have noted his tendency to build textures from the bottom up: the germinal melody is introduced by the low strings, bassoons, bass clarinet, and bass trombone; and the accumulated ostinati begin with the double basses and only gradually drift upward in the texture.

The single-movement form of the work went largely unremarked, but it reveals some of Schuman's early influences. In this case, the most obvious is Sibelius's Seventh Symphony, also in C and in one movement. As noted in the introduction and in chapter 4, this 1924 work served as an important model for many American composers. For Bernstein, then in his senior year at Harvard, the similarities to Sibelius were apparent before rehearsals with the BSO even began. Sent to meet Schuman at the train station, he managed to persuade the older composer (after a few beers) to let him borrow a copy of the score to study. After a night spent studying, he awoke long enough the next morning to slur "Seeeebeeeelius!"[130] (Bernstein is more coherent in biographer Humphrey Burton's account, asserting "You like Sibelius," before returning to slumber.[131]) This marked the first meeting of lifelong friends and mutual advocates. Bernstein's initial assessment is accurate enough: Sibelius's work begins with an ascending line in the low strings and features insistent, sustained tones in the horn section—gestures strikingly similar to Schuman's preferences for lower, darker timbres (like the bass clarinet) and drones.

Concluding that these are "surface level similarities," Swayne rightly focuses on the comparison with Roy Harris's one-movement Third Symphony, also premiered by the BSO during the 1938–39 season.[132] Given that Schuman had begun studying with Harris in October 1936 and would continue to do so throughout the composition of the Second Symphony, it is difficult to tell who made the decision to compose a single-movement symphony first.[133] There are many similarities in terms of form and style between Harris's and Schuman's works in the late 1930s and early 1940s, as we will see below. The much remarked-upon counterpoint of the Second Symphony, a trait that Schuman would retain and refine over the course of his symphonic output, was more likely the product of his earlier studies with Charles Haubiel (1932–34).

SYMPHONY NO. 3

The premiere of his *American Festival Overture* later that year, on October 6, 1939, again with Koussevitzky and the BSO, was much more enthusiastically received than the Second Symphony and proved that Schuman could marshal his intensity to excite an audience. Bernstein's repeated performances and recording of the work would help make it a twentieth-century orchestra standard. Schuman's next two symphonies followed in short order, with the Third completed in January 1941 and the Fourth in August. The reception of the Third Symphony established Schuman as a "serious" American composer and a critical success. Its creation was supported by a Guggenheim Fellowship for 1940–41, although Schuman maintained half of his workload at Sarah Lawrence College, where he taught composition and briefly assumed directorship of the college choir, and choral writing for instruments would become a hallmark of his sound.[134]

What he had been perceived to lack to this point was melodic interest—a criticism he would never completely overcome—and he wrote Serge Koussevitzky in November 1940 of his desire to feature more melody in the Third Symphony (and to express his appreciation for the conductor's championing of his music): "In this new work I feel that the melodic writing is sustained. It is my fervent hope, and I must confess my belief, that this work will justify your faith in my progress. For these reasons I am taking the liberty of dedicating my first composition to you and your orchestra."[135] The Boston Symphony Orchestra premiered the Third

Symphony on October 17, 1941, alongside Mozart's "Haffner" Symphony and Tchaikovsky's "Pathétique." In subsequent years, the work would often be programmed with other famous "Thirds" including those of Harris and Copland—both of which Koussevitzky also premiered.

The similarities to Harris's Third are clear, particularly given the prominence of a forceful chorale in both works. Harris's melodic writing is more influenced by the American vernacular—the open plains as opposed to Schuman's urban soundscapes; however, he did pass on the concept of "autogenesis" to his student. Although vaguely defined at best, this organic approach to form, in which each phrase and section grows out of the opening "seed motif," bears a striking resemblance both to Brahms's "developing variation" (as conceptualized by Schoenberg, now resident in the US) and Bernstein's "melodic concatenation" as it would feature in his Second Symphony. Theorist Richard Pye sees the autogenetic concept worked out most clearly in the Symphony No. 6.[136] However, one can detect something of Harris's formal principles in the Third Symphony in the transformation of the passacaglia theme of the first movement throughout the rest of the work.

Overall, the Third Symphony demonstrates Schuman's continued interest in contrapuntal forms, rhythmic variety, a use of ostinato admittedly similar to Stravinsky's, and an approach to orchestration influenced by his ongoing immersion in choral music. Taking shape as four movements in two parts, the Third Symphony revitalizes traditional forms as contrasting pairs: the serene austerity of the Passacaglia versus a vigorous, brassy Fugue; and the stately and occasionally imposing Chorale juxtaposed with the almost nervous kinetic energy of the Toccata, propelled by its snare drum ostinato.

The first movement opens with the triple-time passacaglia theme, which begins with a striking octave leap, presented in strict canon in the viola section (mm. 1–7), then violin 2 (mm. 8–14), cellos (mm. 15–21), and violin 1 (mm. 22–28). (See example 6.2.) Each entrance begins a half step higher, rising from E to G, which ensures that this could not be mistaken for any Baroque passacaglia. The string section then provides a pizzicato accompaniment and a spinning out of the theme while a series of woodwind choirs present the passacaglia theme anew. Again, we see that Schuman, like Creston, tends to build from the bottom up. This passage begins with the bass clarinet, bassoons, and contrabassoon in unison (with double bass) beginning on A-flat (m. 29); they then join the steadily churning strings as the horn section enters in unison beginning on A (m. 36). The upper woodwinds, including piccolo and E♭ soprano clarinet, state the theme with a more strident unison statement beginning on B-flat (m. 43). A second section begins at m. 50 with a shift to a triplet accompaniment in the strings as two trumpets and two trombones state the passacaglia theme on F. A series of sforzando blasts from the trumpet, trombone, and horn sections initiates the transition (mm. 63–73). The transition, based on intervals from the second half of the passacaglia theme, picks up pace (Vigoroso) in m. 80 before settling into the next section (m. 87) with a metrical shift to 3/2 (quarter note = half note).

The new section begins with a sotto voce accompaniment featuring rapid scalar figures in the cellos (eventually joined by the violas and basses) over which a much slower dolce melody, also related to the passacaglia theme, unfolds in violin 1 and 2 (m. 91). The effect here is similar to *IV/S* of Sibelius's Second Symphony, in which a soft, rumbling line in the cellos accompanies a chorale passed among the woodwinds. By way of transition, Schuman gradually decreases the durations of the melody until m. 121, where the meter shifts to 6/4 (quarter note = quarter note) and the strings begin overlapping statements of an agitated dotted-note figure (drawn from the second half of the passacaglia theme with its descending third expanded to

Forgotten Modernisms

Example 6.2 Schuman, Symphony No. 3, mvt. 1, passacaglia theme (mm. 1–28)

Example 6.2 *continued*

a descending fifth). This rhythmically intense accompaniment propels the music forward into the Fugue (m. 146) while the trombone choir summarizes the passacaglia theme in augmentation.

The Fugue opens with the seven-voice exposition of a subject in 4/4 and with a different rhythmic profile from the passacaglia but built out of intervals drawn from it. The subject begins with an octave descent (as opposed to the rising octave of the passacaglia) before continuing in a similarly angular contour that emphasizes the same intervals of the third, fourth, fifth, and octave (see example 6.3). Each entry of the fugue subject moves by semitone from B-flat through E, thus completing the progression begun in the passacaglia (E through B-flat). The combinations of instruments that make up each fugal "voice" display Schuman's ingenuity: pizzicato violas and cellos reinforce the unison horn section (m. 146) before yielding to the more homogenous violin section (m. 150) and viola/cello (m. 157). Next comes a series of contrasts between higher and lower as well as darker and brighter registers: tuba and contrabass (m. 165) followed by woodwinds (m. 172), then a passage for brass choir, moving from the trombones (m. 180) to the trumpets (187). Each entrance except for the opening horns is followed by a three-bar codetta, making this an unusually prolix exposition, reminiscent of Hindemith with its densely woven textures and contrary motion.

Example 6.3 Schuman, Symphony No. 3, mvt. 1, fugue subject, horns in F (mm. 146–50)

A four-part stretto canon in the trumpet choir begins the first episode (m. 195) that evolves out of the opening three notes of the fugue subject. A transitional section for the woodwinds and horns (m. 210) introduces the first variation of the fugue subject. The term *variation*, drawn from John N. Burk's program notes for the BSO, is apt given that all returns to the fugal subject bear little resemblance to the traditional second or third expositions. The English horn presents a syncopated and filled-in version of the theme in eighth notes instead of the original quarter-note pace (m. 220) before yielding to the bassoon accompanied by a countermelody in the oboe (m. 225). Flute and bass clarinet follow (m. 231) in another ingenious combination typical of Schuman's orchestration habits (he often featured bass clarinet either alone or in surprising combinations). Solo clarinet filters in last (m. 237) before the woodwind section is joined by the strings with quicker figurations derived from the woodwind's theme that hurry the transition forward (m. 248). The entrance of the timpani (m. 273) heralds a new variation of the fugue subject in the horns (m. 285) over an agitated rhythmic figure in the strings. The horns are joined by trombones and bass clarinet, bassoons, and contrabassoon (m. 293) and then the upper woodwinds (m. 301) in another low-to-high layering of timbres. The addition of the brighter trumpets to the brass choir brings this section to a climax in m. 309.

The final section of the Fugue revolves around an E-flat pedal point in the contrabassoon, third and fourth trombones, and contrabasses (m. 319). The string section and woodwinds trade one-measure statements of the fugue subject, transformed here by fragmentation and diminution. The trombones (m. 327) and then the horns (m. 330) join with a countermelody, which is an augmented version of the passacaglia theme. A final coda for brass choir (m. 351), propelled by a marchlike version of the fugue theme in the contrabasses and trombones brings the movement to a sonorous close. Schuman uses a similar gesture in "Chester" from his *New England Triptych* (1956), one of his more popular works, and this tendency toward the grandiose and forceful is part of what makes his music so appealing. Far more integral to Schuman's style, however, is that many of the passages in the Fugue are for one instrument family alone (e.g., winds in mm. 220–47 or strings in mm. 49–90 of the next movement) or for one timbre alone in divisi choirs (e.g., trumpets, mm. 195–207, or the cellos in mm. 261–81 of the last

Example 6.4 Schuman, Symphony No. 3, mvt. 2, chorale theme, solo trumpet in C, mm. 21–31

movement) or even one section in unison (e.g., horns, mm. 285–317), with or without accompaniment. Often these instrumental "choirs" alternate statements, as they do in mm. 320–50 of the Fugue.

The Chorale, like the fugue subject, is a variation on the passacaglia theme (see example 6.4). An Andantino introduction for divisi cellos and violas precedes the presentation of the choral melody in the solo trumpet (m. 22). The melody is tranquil but wide-ranging, with frequent leaps of an octave or more, and it ends in a prominent modal cadence (♭7-1). Joseph Polisi compares this melody to the inquisitive trumpet solo from Ives's *Unanswered Question* and to Copland's writing for the instrument.[137] There is indeed a similarity to the trumpet solo and ensuing duet in Copland's score for Irwin Shaw's play *Quiet City* (1939), except that Schuman pairs the trumpet with a countermelody in solo flute rather than English horn, and the instruments play in sequence rather than in dialogue. After this duet, Schuman weaves the chorale throughout the string section, sometimes augmenting or extending it, as the counterpoint builds to a ***fff*** tutti statement of the melody in strings and winds except for the horn section (m. 91). The arc of this opening is reminiscent of the beginning of the third movement ("Communion") of Ives's Third Symphony.

After a swift diminuendo (mm. 104–05), the chorale then passes from choir to choir: beginning with distant-sounding horns with hands in bells (m. 111), it migrates to muted strings (m. 126) and a muted trumpet duet (m. 128), dissolving into the opening divisi texture of cellos and violas, this time limned by the oboe and English horn. Schuman would later incorporate the chorale melody into his opera *Casey at the Bat* (1953).[138] In the version at hand, the chorale showcases Schuman's much-admired orchestration and reflects Harris's autogenesis process— or at least a more broadly organic approach to composition—as it is devoted entirely to the gradual transformation of a single melody, itself derived from the first movement's passacaglia.

The snare drum solo at the beginning of the Toccata announces its character as a virtuosic piece worthy of the Baroque, by way of an obvious Stravinskian influence in the insistence of the ostinato. With the driving rhythmic profile of the toccata theme laid out, the pitch material enters by way of a florid bass clarinet solo (m. 156), the flawless performance of which earned the bass clarinetist Rosario Mazzeo the composer's permanent admiration. (Indeed, Schuman had Mazzeo in mind when he incorporated a similarly challenging duet for soprano and bass clarinets into the first movement of the Seventh Symphony.[139]) The rest of the woodwinds develop the melody contrapuntally, accompanied by the insistent snare drum ostinato. A brass choir joins the texture (m. 203) before the ostinato passes to timpani (m. 208) under a sustained wind choir. The melody fades back to woodwind counterpoint and dissolves into a fragmented statement in the cellos (m. 244) before the snare drum gradually ceases its tapping.

What follows is a cadenza for strings (mm. 244–311), beginning with the cellos and building upward through violas and violins. This passage is indeed virtuosic—both for each section and the conductor—and at times terrifying (divisi violins at ***fff*** soaring over a rumbling contrabass tremolo in mm. 286–91), and nearly every critic remarked upon it after the premiere. Schuman apparently thought the transitional cadenza successful, since he repeated the effect in the Seventh Symphony. (He also clearly found interest in writing for strings alone, as in the third movement of the Seventh, an "aria" for strings, or the whole of the Fifth Symphony.) After their cadenza, the strings introduce their own ostinato, taking over the motoric role from the percussion. A series of imposing choral statements—sometimes grouping larger sections of the orchestra and sometimes placing individual sections in near-chaotic dialogue—further develop the toccata theme as ever-greater rhythmic activity and thicker textures drive the work to its conclusion. The percussion section returns, with rim shots from the snare drum (m. 373), and the piano adds resonance to the incessant ostinato.

Both then and now, it is possible to hear the Third Symphony in relation to World War II, although the United States would not formally enter the conflict until after the work's premiere. Reviews repeatedly invoke the creative "exhaustion" of European composers compared to Schuman's vitality and his mastery of counterpoint and orchestration. Writing of the premiere, Leonard Liebling referred to 1941 as a "banner season" for American works and placed it within an implicitly wartime context: "Whether brought about by the current wave of nationalism in the United States, or by sudden personal conviction on the part of conductors, the fact remains that the tendency is both timely and useful, for Europe has stopped sending us its former generous supply (numerically) of symphonic novelties. Our American composers have amply demonstrated their high command of orchestral technic [sic], if not of high melodic creativeness, but that seems to be the general style of the music of the present period. In that field, modern Americans operate as skillfully and successfully as their European colleagues.[140]"

Responding to the first performance in New York, Olin Downes praised Schuman while calling on American composers to stop "aping Europe's product."

> It is true that the cerebral element is omni-present in Mr. Schumann's [sic] score, and that he cultivates what are essentially the methods of the contrapuntalists of Europe of the eighteenth century and earlier; and that for ourselves, we believe these methods will presently be outmoded and superseded by something freer and more direct in approach when our composers have really gotten out from under the still binding influence of foreign cultures. We don't believe, either, that Mr. Schumann will follow the path he now pursues when another decade has passed. . . .
>
> And, furthermore, while contrapuntal technique, and the cerebral element, are much to the fore in this piece, there is also present the lyrical substance. There are vistas of harmonic as well as linear beauty. The old forms of canon, fughetta, passacaglia, toccata and whatever else you please of the ancient machinery of composition, are handled with exceptional and exhilarating flexibility. And there is laughter in it, too. And a technical advance over all recent scores of Mr. Schumann that we have heard, which goes very far toward setting him free.[141]

At least by Downes's estimation, Schuman appears to have achieved some of the melodic interest he had promised to Koussevitzky. While counterpoint remains a defining feature of his music, critics generally received the work as interesting rather than dry and even as evidence of a sense of humor. According to Downes: "When Mr. Schumann's [sic] snare drum begins wickedly tapping the measure for what we can only term an intentionally insulting adoption of the toccata idea of more majestic times, and when he uses a fly-hitter or a baseball bat or some other contraption for rhythmic purposes as he nears his climax, it has the air of a form of bastinado applied by the Davidsbuendler to the more protuberant parts of the Philistines."[142] This impression of humor (albeit rather dark) has receded somewhat with the passage of time. Nicholas Tawa hears only the strength of the work in the face of adversity: "It sounds like a giant flexing his muscles, like an America ready to cope no matter what. The symphony is muscular and potent. Its gestures are given kinetic force and impress the listener deeply. The score's projection of authority and strength may possibly be Schuman's unconscious response to the enemy forces clamoring at the American gates."[143] This kind of projection onto the work is encouraged by historical retrospection, but it does find its parallels in contemporary reviews. At the very least, Schuman was explicitly identified as an American composer and one likely to lead a young generation out from under the influence of Europe.

Nationalism aside, the critical reception to the music was enthusiastic. Alexander Williams, who, as we have seen, rejected the Second Symphony out of hand, felt obliged to issue a retraction:

> Somewhat to our embarrassment, in light of the quality of this new symphony, we appear to have rather high-handedly dismissed the former in these columns two years ago. Doubtless we should now hear in it many virtues which were obtusely hidden from us at the time.
>
> We should like to pass this off by now saying that "Mr. Schuman has found his feet"; but clearly any composer who can write so well-knit and powerful a symphony as this must have had his feet somewhere near the ground in his earlier work. The new symphony requires pretty close attention on the listener's part, but, granted that, interest should not falter for an instant.[144]

Writing of a 1951 reprise of the work by the Philadelphia Orchestra under Eugene Ormandy, Virgil Thomson asserted that while no work was perfect, Schuman's Third was distinguished by its wealth of character: "That character, in Schuman's case, is hard to put the finger on; but it is there. It is there in a certain matchless exuberance. It is there in the brightness of the orchestral sound. It is there in the sustained seriousness of the intent, of the composer's need to project a genuinely personal attitude toward life and music. The work has, in consequence, nobility, power and distinction. I have known it for ten years and always remembered it with pleasure. Rehearing it brings no disappointment."[145] In just two years Schuman had managed to win over even the staunchest critics, as confirmed when the work won the first New York Music Critics' Circle Award. Perhaps even more remarkable, though, was that critical consensus about the merits of the symphony aligned so clearly with Schuman's goal: to write a work of significant melodic interest while continuing to play with counterpoint and experimental orchestration. The Third Symphony features several devices that would appear in later symphonies, including the focus on bass clarinet and other darker timbres, a preference for slower or broader tempos (including slow first movements), an emphasis on continuity between movements, and the unexpected use of a cadenza as a transitional gesture.

SYMPHONY NO. 4

Compared with the Third Symphony, the Fourth remains less known and successful. Though not a return to the disastrous premiere of the Second Symphony, the audience reaction was unenthusiastic and the critical reaction varied from cool to dismissive. Arthur Loesser's assessment was the most diplomatic—"an essay in pure design"—and does indicate something of the work's character. The Fourth Symphony is contrapuntally complex and its themes are subjected to thorough development, but it lacks the integration of the Third Symphony and its forceful, even heroic, cast. Many hallmarks of Schuman's style are still present: the use of "choirs"; the focus in the first movement on brass and bold use of percussion; alternately bouncy, agitated, or driving rhythms; virtuosic passages for woodwind sections and soloists in the Finale and the sensitive writing for cantabile strings in the interior movement. Walter Simmons's evaluation of the Finale summarizes the work's deficiencies as a whole: "episodic, rambling, and discursive, with a sense of being 'forced' through developmental procedures as a matter of course, rather than conviction."[146]

Again locating the work within a wartime context, as the Fourth was premiered by the Cleveland Orchestra six weeks after the bombing of Pearl Harbor, Tawa calls the work "gloomy, fervid, and astringent."[147] The Third Symphony had a longer gestation than the Fourth and Swayne suggests that Schuman felt some pressure to finish another work before the end of his Guggenheim Fellowship.[148] Taking the germinal material for the Finale from the third movement of the Third String Quartet might then have been a matter of expediency, although such self-borrowing was hardly rare for him. Either way, the difference in time spent on the composition seems evident.

SYMPHONY NO. 5

The Fifth Symphony was commissioned by the Koussevitzky Music Foundation and was accordingly dedicated to the memory of the conductor's second wife, Natalie. Serge Koussevitzky premiered the work with the Boston Symphony Orchestra on November 12, 1943. Avoiding the connotations of a heroic or monumental Fifth Symphony (especially in the context of ongoing global conflict), Schuman opted to name the work Symphony for Strings. As a violin player himself, Schuman had already proved himself particularly skilled and innovative in his use of the string section, and many of the key traits of his writing are present in this work: frequent divisi; interesting juxtapositions of pizzicato, arco, and strumming; and a tendency to treat each section as fully independent, whether in relation to the rest of the strings or to the orchestra as a whole. The "strumming" gesture in particular often appears in somber or dirge-like moments, as in the second movements of the Third and Fifth Symphonies.[149] The Symphony for Strings also demonstrates that the "forceful" or "muscular" nature of Schuman's music did not solely reside in his use of brass and percussion. The first movement in particular draws much of its force from ostinati, syncopation, and an overall rhythmic profile that is unmistakably Schuman's own. Even the more introspective or serene second-movement Larghissimo features a passage (mm. 58–73) in which the polyphonic complexity that characterizes both the movement and the symphony as a whole is further intensified by having sections of the orchestra (i.e., violin 1 and cellos versus violin 2 and violas) move at a different pace or with a different degree of rhythmic activity before culminating in a climactic rhythmic unison. The third movement (Presto) is another witty Finale, featuring a division between pizzicato and arco strings, as well as an entirely pizzicato passage that, as Polisi notes, is a parody of the third movement of Tchaikovsky's Fourth Symphony.[150] As ever, Schuman is willing to demonstrate his awareness of European tradition—its symphonic models and contrapuntal forms—but not his fidelity.

SYMPHONY NO. 6

The Sixth Symphony (1948) was commissioned and premiered by the Dallas Symphony Orchestra under Antal Dorati, who in his joining the orchestra had insisted that it commission one new work a year; this was the third and last under his leadership, which lasted only from 1945 to 1949.[151] This work inaugurates what has been called Schuman's middle-period style. There is no longer any apparent influence from Roy Harris, though his mentor's ideas had marked Schuman's music indelibly (as Schuman would always readily admit), and the degree of dissonance reaches its height in these works from 1945 onward. Simmons compares this independent Schuman style to the International Style in modern architecture: "bold, urbane, and confident, with clashing metallic sonorities, hard-edged planes of sound, and nervous, tightly coiled rhythms."[152] What had always been a high degree of contrapuntal interest crystallized into the multilayered sound described by Simmons, Polisi, and Swayne alike. Swayne compares the Sixth's emotional tone to Bernstein's contemporaneous Symphony No. 2: *The Age of Anxiety* (1949), in that it is not victorious or heroic like Copland's Third. Both works reject what Bernstein called the symphony in the "Koussevitzky manner": "full of climaxes, orchestrated to the hilt, eloquent, evocative, moody, brilliant, and on a very grand scale."[153] The Sixth also departs from precedent: over the course of its single movement, it compasses a greater expressive range than the previous symphonies and continues to demonstrate Schuman's willingness to follow a single line (e.g., mm. 325–402 in first violins), but without the contrapuntal insistence of the earlier works, though counterpoint is not entirely absent. Overall, the Sixth Symphony's differences are of degree rather than kind.

It was during this middle period, after the Sixth Symphony, that Schuman began to investigate Schoenberg's twelve-tone method. Although it is difficult to say exactly what he thought about Schoenberg, George Rochberg sent him *The Hexachord and Its Relation to the Twelve-Tone Row*, which he had published in 1955. Schuman requested a study copy of the complete works of Webern around this time.[154] Twelve-tone music was also infiltrating his immediate sound world: Luigi Dallapiccola was in residence at Queens College in 1956–57 and Juilliard premiered his *Cinque canti* on February 1, 1957. And Schuman's friend Leonard Bernstein incorporated a twelve-tone fugue into the song "Cool" in his wildly successful *West Side Story* (1957). Like Bernstein, Schuman could afford to experiment at this point in his career, as he was receiving steady commissions. His engagement with new musical materials, however, was just beginning.

SYMPHONY NO. 7

The Seventh Symphony (1960) began as a work of smaller scope—"between 8 and 14 minutes in length"—commissioned by the Philadelphia Orchestra on New Year's Eve 1958 and intended to serve as an "opener, a symphonic poem, or a closing number" for the anniversary gala of the Academy of Music (the orchestra's administrative branch) on January 23, 1960.[155] Schuman had drafted a Fanfare (Vigoroso), Aria (Cantabile intensamente), and Dance (Scherzando brioso) intended to showcase the Philadelphia sound, particularly in the strings-only cantabile movement.[156] A dispute between Schuman's publisher, Theodore Presser, and the management of the orchestra over the performance fee led the composer to withdraw the work and recast it as a symphony for the Boston Symphony Orchestra's seventy-fifth anniversary, commissioned by the Serge Koussevitzky Foundation in the Library of Congress and dedicated to the memory of the conductor and his wife Natalie. To create a first movement to precede the existing *Celebration Concertante*, Schuman repurposed part of a film score, *The Earth Is Born*, and a twelve-tone exercise for piano that he had begun in November 1959.[157]

The first movement, although the last written, introduces the material and the moods to come. Polisi calls both the first and third movements "a mammoth wall of sound" against which the shorter, quicker movements seem light by comparison.[158] Composed of thickly scored, highly dissonant polychords, the opening of the Largo seems to stutter; sustained tutti chords interspersed with dotted and double-dotted figures never allow the movement to gain momentum. Though the introduction of a solo trumpet (m. 15) offers the possibility of a stately fanfare, the rhythmic hesitancy seems more ponderous than triumphant. (The true fanfare will arrive only in the second-movement Vigoroso with a flurry of trumpet, trombone, and horn calls). Simmons notes that the trumpet solo also introduces the central intervallic material for the work as a whole: a major third followed by a major fifth.[159] Before the trumpet, however, the cellos present an espressivo melody that encompasses all 12 tones (mm. 8–12), which is a more lyric version of the rhythmic and thickly chordal statement of the row in mm. 1–8. As Swayne indicates, this row was the genesis of the first movement.[160] Schuman then explores the possibilities of this row and the rhythmic figures of the introduction through his trademark instrumental choirs. The texture and volume gradually build in a series of waves, the last of which dissipates suddenly in m. 75 as the cellos return with a transformation of the opening row (transposed down a major second from A-flat to F-sharp).

A bass clarinet solo built out of the same third-plus-fifth gesture as the earlier trumpet solo (this time a minor third) unfolds over a **pp** chorus of strings (m. 80). The bass clarinet is then joined by soprano B♭ clarinet in a blistering duo cadenza that serves as a transition between the first and second movements. As Swayne notes, the inclusion of a feature for Boston's bass clarinetist, Rosario Mazzeo, was likely intended to obscure the work's earlier incarnation as a commission for the Philadelphia Orchestra, just as the incorporation of the fanfare motive served to make this added first movement more of a piece with the three that follow.[161] This remarkable section features hexachordal sonorities and inversion to create extended mirrorlike passages between the two clarinets (mm. 97–100 and 109–20), the last of which leads directly into the second movement. Call-and-response statements between the two instruments frequently complete the aggregate. Overall, the twelve-tone row is treated as thematic material rather than as a harmonic foundation, though the grinding, dissonant chords featured throughout the movement occasionally encompass all 12 tones. Still, serially derived procedures, like retrograde and inversion, permeate the work and were perhaps an intuitive choice for a composer who remained interested in contrapuntal procedures.

The second movement is comprised almost entirely of statements of the initial motto of a major third plus a perfect fifth (the "Fanfare" of the *Celebration Concertante*). Something of Schuman's interest in twelve-tone technique appears here as well, for within the first 30 measures of the movement, this motto is heard in inversion (m. 4), retrograde (m. 20), and retrograde inversion (fragmented, mm. 28–31). The antiphonal exchanges rotate through various choirs and sections of the orchestra, adapting the melodic contour with a variety of triplet and dotted rhythms and syncopations that all generate the impression of significant physical effort. A thundering timpani solo, also composed out of the opening motto, enters in m. 64 and, along with the rest of the large percussion battery, helps propel the movement toward its climax (mm. 90–98). The large sonority in m. 98, founded on the dissonant major seventh span of the opening motto and its interior intervals, dissipates quickly—just as the first movement did at its height in m. 75—and the bass clarinet and solo oboe restate an augmented, espressivo version of the motto, fading from **mf** to **p**. After only a slight pause, the fanfare yields to the third-movement "Aria."

Despite the contrast in character, the Cantabile intensamente, for strings alone, evolves directly out of the intervals of the second-movement motto, resulting in an opening that is sonorous and triadic but not explicitly tonal. What follows is a gradual accumulation of dissonance on the way to what Simmons calls "an almost unprecedented level of agonizing intensity."[162] The struggle of the fanfare reappears at first as a sweetly triadic melody (e.g., mm. 1–6 in violin 1) but is then transformed into a series of searching or yearning gestures as Schuman leans into rising half-step motions in addition to the wider rising fifth and seventh of the motto. The familiarity of this expressive content also yields a more traditional ABA form, well suited to his point of reference, an aria, and also recalls the part forms of the traditional symphonic Andante.

The A section (mm. 1–20) features two related ideas. The first, the aforementioned *cantabile dolce* passage (*a*) explores the intervals of the third, fifth, and seventh, often filled in chromatically, in a free contrapuntal texture for violins 1 and 2, viola, and cello (mm. 1–14); it gradually yields to a homophonic statement in which the contrabasses enter (pizzicato as opposed to the arco of the other sections) that initiates a *sonoro molto* section (*b*) with greater chromaticism and volume (mm. 15–20). The B section that follows (mm. 20–49) provides contrast with its greater degree of rhythmic activity and predominantly homophonic texture. As the two larger groupings of upper and lower strings (divisi) are pitted against one another, there is a further increase in volume and dissonance. The A section (mm. 50–74) emerges from the sudden decay of the B material, this time with the *a* and *b* ideas reversed to form a symmetrical arch. A fragment of the cantabile melody in the first violin returns an octave higher (m. 55 violin 1) and is then transformed and extended. The movement fades away (morendo) with one final statement of the motto: a rising major seventh in violin 1 and cello, a retrograde version of the fanfare in the violin 2, and sustained tones a major second apart from the violas and basses. This hushed dissonance (***ppp***) is superseded by a positively traditional E-minor sonority in the woodwinds and piano as the Scherzando brioso takes off.

A scherzo in mixed meter, alternating 4/4 and 3/4 at first regularly and then at unpredictable intervals, the Finale is an off-kilter "Dance," as Schuman first characterized it in the context of the original *Celebration Concertante*. Most of the material, again distributed largely in terms of orchestral choirs, is derived from the second movement's fanfare, and its derivation is particularly clear in a duet for solo horn and trumpet (m. 56). A more lyrical melody in 3/4, presented by the string section in m. 107 with syncopated interjections from the woodwinds, provides a point of contrast. However, Schuman sets the unison melody a half step apart between the first and second violins, blurring what would have been a series of parallel 6/3 triads. It is as if we are hearing a waltz through the aural equivalent of a funhouse mirror. While Schuman's music is often forthright or "muscular," there is a sense of humor at work both here and in the Finale of the Third Symphony. What follows is a gradual interleaving of this waltz melody with the more agitated material of the opening before the Finale builds to a clangorous ending on E-flat major in what Simmons calls an "incongruously triumphant peroration."[163] This typically loud but atypically consonant ending makes sense both in the original context of the *Celebration Concertante* and Philadelphia's Academy of Music gala, and in its final purpose of celebrating the seventy-fifth anniversary of the Boston Symphony Orchestra, an organization with which Schuman had a long professional relationship as well as a deep personal connection through Serge Koussevitzky.

The reception of the Seventh Symphony proves that Schuman was able to use the twelve-tone system while still "sounding like himself." None of the reviewers seem to have been aware of his use of serial technique, and John Burk's program notes do not comment on the presence of a row. Until Swayne's analysis, there was no discussion of the impact of the twelve-tone technique on this symphony.[164] The comparison between the Schuman of the Seventh Symphony and his earlier symphonic self was aided and abetted by the revival of the Third Symphony by Leonard Bernstein and the New York Philharmonic at Schuman's fiftieth birthday concert on October 13, 1960, just a few months after the premiere of the Seventh.

SYMPHONY NO. 8

The Philharmonic gave Schuman another boost with the commission of the Eighth Symphony, which celebrated the move in 1962 from Carnegie Hall to the new Lincoln Center, an occasion that also produced Copland's first twelve-tone orchestral work, *Connotations*. The urgent nature of the commission (as well as the time it took for Schuman to complete a previous commitment, *A Song of Orpheus*) perhaps necessitated the reworking of the last movement of his Fourth String Quartet (1950) as a symphonic finale—although, as we have seen, repurposing earlier works was common practice for Schuman. More importantly, the lesson of the Seventh and Eighth Symphonies is that by the 1960s, serialism was just "one of the tools in Schuman's compositional toolbox."[165] The symphony opens with a major-minor triad and then, in a solo horn melody (m. 25), works through 11 of the 12 chromatic tones before allowing any to repeat.

The first two movements, both slow, are typical of his level of intensity, which, combined with the more strident tone and greater dissonance, makes for a compelling experience. The lively rhythms of the third movement, where some of Harris's influence still shows, and the lighter, virtuosic play among instruments provides a welcome contrast. The cadenza for bassoon and bass clarinet once again shows Schuman's preference for darker, resonant timbres even in a scherzo-like atmosphere.

Schuman's Eighth Symphony opened the long-delayed Philharmonic Hall at Lincoln Center on October 4, 1962, with Bernstein conducting in a moment that must have been deeply satisfying for both men, the director of the New York Philharmonic and the head of Lincoln Center, respectively. The new symphony was preceded (fittingly) by Beethoven's *Consecration of the House* Overture and the Adagio from the Notturno for Strings and Harp by Irving Fine, who had died two months earlier. Ross Parmenter contrasted the "charm and considerable melancholy beauty" of the Fine with the "tragic and intense" Schuman symphony. He also noted that, despite the contrast in tempo between the first two movements and the Finale, the work as a whole "hangs together remarkably well," as if all three movements are "dominated by a single broad-arched, rather mournful melody." Although he praised it as "unfailingly expressive" and demonstrating mastery in terms of orchestration, he noted that "its applause did not call for more than three bows."[166] A review as lukewarm as the audience reception appeared in the *Musical Quarterly*, by Richard Franko Goldman: "Technically, the Eighth reveals little change from Schuman's other works of recent years. The basic harmonic trademark is still the major-minor triad in wide-open position; the melodies are still more notable as 'tunes' than as themes or motifs; and the rhythmic bounce and restlessness, the energetic punctuation of brass and percussion are still stylistically characteristic. In the Eighth Symphony, one feels this latter element of the Schuman style to be more of an overlay than it has appeared to be previously."[167] With the benefit of hindsight, it may simply be that Schuman's work did not conform to the sentiments expected on the occasion. Instead of offering a celebratory composition, or even a solemn and majestic one, Schuman proceeded along the stylistic path he was already on, experimenting with more strident dissonance and twelve-tone language as they might fit with his own compositional voice. In this sense, his approach was similar to Copland's in *Connotations*; as a result, both works received less than enthusiastic welcomes, even from friends like Bernstein (he never programmed the Eighth Symphony again and publicly dismissed Copland's experiments with twelve-tone system).

SYMPHONY NO. 9, "LE FOSSE ARDEATINE"

In comparison to his other symphonic works, the Symphony No. 9 "Le fosse ardeatine," begun after a trip to Europe to promote the Lincoln Center Festival, is far more of an anomaly. Schuman's hosts in Rome, Hugo and Nathalie Weisgall (the former a composer-in-residence at the American Academy in Rome), had taken him to see the monument to the 1944 Nazi massacre of 335 Italians at the Ardeatine Caves outside Rome. After inquiry and correspondence with Nathalie about the nature of the massacre and the monument, Schuman produced an unusually extensive set of program notes. Although the programmaticism of the work makes it distinctive, in terms of its harmonic vocabulary it is of a piece with the Seventh and Eighth Symphonies. Swayne notes that the melody of the first section traces all 12 tones in its first nine measures; that the whole is underpinned by "subterranean serial passages"; and that the final chord of the work is, lifting a phrase from Whitman, a "barbaric fortissimo yawp that contains all 12 notes of the chromatic scale, as though in that one chord Schuman exorcised once and for all the serial daemon that possessed his works for a decade."[168] Schuman would never return to this level of engagement with twelve-tone music in his symphonies, nor would he pursue such a dissonant harmonic vocabulary again.

Like the Eighth Symphony, the Ninth has a tripartite division—Anteludium, Offertorium, and Postludium—though they flow together as part of one continuous movement. As usual, the family divisions of instruments form the core of the orchestration. Solos for bass clarinet and timpani add to the shadowy moments and ominous character of the work. The thick counterpoint—for example, as the Anteludium builds in layers—is perhaps less typical of Schuman but contributes to the overall intensity. The tricky passagework and challenging syncopations, however, are wholly typical of Schuman's writing, and here they add turbulence and keep the weight of the work from becoming turgid. The combination of the pathos of the inspirational event, Schuman's eloquent program note, and the force of his music make for a powerful work. In February 2019, Riccardo Muti and the Chicago Symphony Orchestra commemorated the seventy-fifth anniversary of the massacre by programming Schuman's Ninth Symphony, the performance of which was accompanied by an extended essay in the program booklet (including appreciative letters from the president of Italy and the Italian ambassador) and an exhibit detailing the history of the atrocity. As the moving written and visual displays—not to mention the impressive performance—made clear, Schuman succeeded in his stated goal of keeping the memory of the event and its victims alive: "Whatever future my symphony may have, whenever it is performed, audiences will remember."

SYMPHONY NO. 10, "AMERICAN MUSE"

The Symphony No. 10 "American Muse" strikes a more optimistic tone, perhaps because it began life as a *Prelude for a Great Occasion* in 1974, for the dedication of the Hirschorn Museum and Sculpture Garden of the Smithsonian Institution. The *Prelude* ends in E-flat major, as does the Tenth Symphony, leading Swayne to call it a "warm up" for the larger work. Schuman had already announced that he was planning on writing the Tenth and calling it "American Muse."[169] Composition of the larger work was funded by a $20,000 grant from the National Symphony Orchestra in advance of the nation's bicentennial, and it premiered on April 6, 1976, with Antal Dorati conducting. The abundance of brass fanfares and relative plain-spokenness of the work suited the occasion, leading John Rockwell to call it "blissfully old-fashioned."[170] Indeed, Schuman had moved away from his experiments with atonality and serialism, although there is still plenty of dissonance in the work—here reflecting the conflict that brought the United States into being and, in the Larghissimo slow movement, the yearning that sustains it.

In another three-movement structure—the layout for all Schuman's symphonies from the Fourth on, excepting only the Sixth and Seventh—he traces the tragic-to-triumphant course traced in many symphonies since Beethoven. However, the "triumph" is characteristically deferred. The Con fuoco, with its alarums and emphasis on brass and percussion, casts Schuman's typical major-minor sonorities and other harmonic ambiguities, as well as his rhythmic complexity, into a metaphorical struggle. Only a brief, somewhat sudden turn to the major mode at the end of the movement offers hope. The Larghissimo alternates between plaintive and strident, with only a passage for trumpet and flute in the middle leaning toward the aspirational. Schuman's preference for long lines helps the movement hang together even as the tonal ambiguity persists until another, rather abrupt, clearing into the major with a luminous string texture. The Presto begins furtively, with pizzicato strings and burbling staccato woodwinds. The movement is weighed down, however, slowing to Andantino and then Pesante before returning to the Presto, which finally works itself up into the sort of victorious tone that one might have expected to occupy more space in this symphony. Still, even as it propels itself forward, fragments of hymn- or anthemlike tunes are perceived through a dissonant foreground (not unlike Ives's treatment of similar material). Overall, the work seems more a reflection of how far and through what struggles the country has come—and yet faces—than a less-complicated, star-spangled approach to the bicentennial.

Although not the Americana of Harris or Copland, it is fitting that Schuman's final symphonic work would address directly his career-long dedication to American music. More so than any other figure in this chapter, except perhaps Bernstein, Schuman sustained the American symphonic world through the mid-twentieth century. Not only did he produce several symphonies of consistent quality, as did Sessions, he also fostered the efforts of other American composers through his work as president of Juilliard and then Lincoln Center and at the head of funding organizations like the Koussevitzky and Naumburg Foundations. He also traversed multiple stylistic realms within midcentury modernism without losing his own compositional voice, which is rooted in the music of American voices from decades and centuries past. His 10 symphonies capture the breadth of midcentury harmonic language and the distinctly American vein of symphonic composition that continued from the early twentieth century.

Alan Hovhaness

Although he was born in Boston and received a similar music education to Leonard Bernstein, Alan Hovhaness (1911–2000) was socially and stylistically removed from the other composers in this chapter. Born Alan Hovhaness Chakmakjian to an Armenian father and a Scottish mother, he later shortened his name to Alan Hovhaness. After piano lessons with Heinrich Gebhard (also Bernstein's teacher), Hovhaness studied with Frederick S. Converse at the New England Conservatory from 1932 to 1934 and began learning about Indian music at a time when Uday Shankar's dance company was touring the United States regularly. (Bernstein also remarked on his encounters with their music during these tours.) During the 1930s, he played piano for social gatherings of the Greek, Arab, and Armenian communities in Boston, earning enough to make a living. He also worked as a jazz arranger for a Works Progress Administration program and as an organist in an Armenian church.[171] Hovhaness studied at the Berkshire Music Center at Tanglewood (Koussevitzky's brainchild) with Bohuslav Martinů. His work was roundly criticized by others of the Koussevitzky circle, notably Copland and Bernstein, though the conductor himself supported it. Shortly thereafter, in 1940, Hovhaness destroyed all the music he had written to that point, including an early symphony. He went on to teach at the Boston Conservatory (1948–51), worked for three years at the summer school of the Eastman Conservatory in the mid-fifties, and then served as composer-in-residence with the Seattle Symphony Orchestra from 1966 to the end of his career; the latter position is a potent example of the shift in influence away from East Coast conservatories and orchestras during this period.

Hovhaness never attained the international profile of Bernstein and Roger Sessions, or the kind of domestic prominence achieved through long association with a particular institution like William Schuman, Vincent Persichetti, or Peter Mennin. Nonetheless, Hovhaness's works were often well received by audiences and have received sustained support from particular communities. His early career was launched with a series of concerts in Boston in 1944, sponsored by Armenian organizations, and in New York there were annual concerts with an Armenian student group, beginning with an evening at Town Hall in June 1945, which Lou Harrison attended (with John Cage) as reviewer for the *New York Herald Tribune.* Harrison described the scene in the lobby as "the closest I've ever been to one of those renowned artistic riots." He blamed the furor on a conflict between the "Chromaticists and the Americanists," both of whom objected to the fact that "here came a man from Boston whose obviously beautiful and fine music had nothing to do with either camp and was, in fact, its own very wonderful thing to begin with."[172] Hovhaness was dismissed by both sides of the traditional atonal-tonal split. Given their shared interest in Eastern sources of musical inspiration, it is unsurprising that Harrison wrote glowingly of Hovhaness, as did Cage in the June 1947 issue of *Modern Music*.[173] Harrison also eloquently captures the lack of "camp" affiliation that may explain Hovhaness's relatively low profile in scholarly writings and on orchestra programs today. When Hovhaness does appear in historical narratives of the twentieth century, the evaluation tends to range from damning with faint praise to absolutely scorching.

Although the more prominent composers of the midcentury were already disparate in terms of compositional approach—compare, for example, Copland, Thomson, Harris, and Barber—Hovhaness's musical language followed a completely idiosyncratic path. Schuman, Bernstein, and Diamond, who remained essentially tonal composers, absorbed some of the harmonic and structural vocabulary of twelve-tone serialism; Hovhaness's works, by contrast, do not even meet the minimum complexity requirements of 1950s and 60s modernism. Harrison perceptively asserts that Hovhaness's style originates from outside the language of either the tonal or atonal traditions. Neil Butterworth notes that he "explored the inner spiritual world of ritual repetition and rapt serenity."[174] Some degree of meditative intent and occasionally mesmerizing processes do permeate most of Hovhaness's works. As many commentators have observed, Hovhaness's works tend to sound very similar; according to conductor Dennis Russell Davies, this consistency is the result of "the authenticity of a voice that he's pursued for a lifetime."[175] The idea of a pursuit is useful, for despite the parallels there are subtle shifts in his style over the decades, largely the result of seeking out and absorbing new musical cultures—a lifelong process one can easily track through his symphonies.

Some elements of Hovhaness's earliest works persist throughout his career. First, he took an interest in contrapuntal procedures of the Renaissance and Baroque eras, and his works often feature polymodal canons, fugues—including double and even quadruple fugues—and other richly contrapuntal structures (often with strict isorhythmic patterns), though typically without tonal progressions.[176] He called the polyphonic tradition running from the Renaissance to Bach and Handel the "one great unique culture" of the West.[177] Second, Hovhaness began his compositional career, like others of his generation, in the late 1940s, with a harmonic vocabulary steeped in late Romanticism, and he held to aspects of it throughout his career.[178] Finally, his attraction to rhythmic complexity and ostinati led to an interest in creating an unmetered

Table 6.4 The Symphonies of Alan Hovhaness (1911–2000)[a]

Title	Movements	Instrumentation	Comments
"Sunset" Symphony (1932)	3 movements		First movement performed at New England Conservatory of Music in 1932; awarded the Samuel Endicott Prize of the school's composition department. Hovhaness withdrew the symphony and later recast this movement as the first movement of his Eleventh Symphony. By 1942, Hovhaness had apparently written as many as seven symphonies; in addition to the "Sunset," the manuscripts of Symphonies 2 (1942) and 4 (n.d.) survive, all unpublished.
Exile Symphony (Symphony No. 1), Op. 17 #2 (1937)	1. Lament 2. Conflict 3. Triumph For the 1961 publication, the titles were replaced by tempo markings: 1. Allegretto 2. Presto 3. Finale In a 1970 revision, Hovhaness replaced Mvt. 2 and rescored passages of the outer movements: 1. Allegretto 2. Grazioso 3. Finale	Grand plus Tpt., Tuba, Harp	Hovhaness's first acknowledged symphony, dedicated to Sir Francis Bacon, his favorite philosopher. Title refers to the forced dispersion of Armenians (including his father's family) during the Armenian Genocide of 1914–23. First performance: 1939, by the BBC Orchestra, conducted by Leslie Heward. First American performance: 1942, by the NBC Orchestra, under Leopold Stokowski. Score published as "Symphony No. 1," Op. 17, by Whitman Blake Music Publisher, 1938 and by C. F. Peters, 1961; published as *Exile Symphony* (Symphony No. 1), Op. 17 #2, by C. F. Peters, 1972. Short analysis in Athens/HOVHANESS, pp. 26–30.

Table 6.4 *continued*

Title	Movements	Instrumentation	Comments
Mysterious Mountain (Symphony No. 2), Op. 132 (1955)	1. Andante con moto 2. Double Fugue: Moderato maestoso—Allegro vivo 3. Andante espressivo: Con moto	Grand plus Flt, Ob., Clar., Bssn., Hr., Tpt., Tuba, Harp, Cel.	Dedicated to Leopold Stokowski, who conducted the first performance with the Houston Symphony on October 31, 1955; the premiere was broadcast on NBC Radio. The title was an afterthought, as was the opus number (which Stokowski chose, somewhat at random). Score published by AMP, 1958. Analysis in this chapter, as well as Athens/HOVHANESS, pp. 122–26.
Symphony No. 3, Op. 148 (1956)	1. Andante maestoso—Presto 2. Andante 3. Allegro molto	Grand plus Flt, Ob., Clar., Bssn., Hr., Tpt., Tuba, Tam-tam, BD, Harp, Cel.	Hovhaness called this symphony, one of his personal favorites, "a tribute to Mozartian classical sonata form." Commissioned by Leopold Stokowski. First performance: October 1956, by the Symphony of the Air, conducted by Stokowski. Holograph score published by C. F. Peters, 1958.
Symphony No. 4 for Wind Orchestra, Op. 165 (1958)	1. Andante (Hymn & Fugue) 2. Allegro (Dance—Trio—Dance) 3. Andante espressivo (Hymn & Fugue)	Wind ensemble: 3(or 6) Flt., 2(6) Ob., 1(2) EH, 2(6) Clar., Bclar., 2(6) Bssn., Cbssn., 4(6) Hr., 2(6) Tpt., 3(6) Trom., Tuba, Perc. (Timp., Giant Tam-tam, Glsp., BD, Mrb, Xylo., Chimes, Vbp. Gong), Harp	Commissioned by American Wind Symphony Orchestra of Pittsburgh. Dedicated to William P. Snyder III. First performance by American Wind Symphony Orchestra, conducted by Robert Boudreau. Score published by C. F. Peters, 1958.
Symphony No. 5, "Short Symphony," Op. 170 (1953, rev. 1963)	1. Adagio 2. Andante 3. Canon in 24 Voices	Grand plus EH, Tpt, Tuba, Tam-tam, Glsp., Harp, Cel.	Short work (movements are four, five, and two minutes, respectively written between Symphonies 9 and 13 and before No. 2. Dedicated to Edgar and Dori Curtis and the Scottish BBC. First performance: July 16, 1953, by the Scottish BBC Glasgow, conducted by Edgar Curtis. Score published by C. F. Peters, 1963.

Symphony No. 6, "Celestial Gate," Op. 173 (1959)	In one movement	Chamber Orchestra: 1 Flt., 1 Ob., 1 Clar., 1 Bssn., 1 Hr., 1 Tpt., Timp, Chimes, Harp, Strgs.	Inspired by the work of Greek mystic painter Herman di Giovanno ("my spiritual teacher who opened the gate to the spiritual dimension"). Commissioned by Edward B. Benjamin.

Holograph score published by C. F. Peters, 1960.

Short analysis in Athens/HOVHANESS, pp. 144–49. |
| Symphony No. 7 for Wind Orchestra, "Nanga Parvat," Op. 178 (1959) | 1. Con ferocita [sic]
2. March
3. Sunset | Wind ensemble: 3(6) Flt., 2(6) Ob., EH, 2(6) Clar., Bclar., 2(6) Bssn., Cbssn., 4(6) Hr., 2(6) Tpt., 3(6) Trom. (Trom. 3 and/or 6 doubling Btrom.), Tuba, Timp., Perc. (Giant Tam-tam or Deep Balinese Gong, SD without snares or a Small Chinese Drum, Tenor Drum or a Large Chinese Drum, Glsp., Vbp., BD, Chimes), Harp | Title ("Without Trees") refers to a mountain in Kashmir. Composer describes the scene as "serene, majestic, aloof, terrible in storm, forever frozen in treeless snow."

Commissioned by the Edgar J. Kaufmann Charitable Foundation. First performance: Summer 1960, by the American Wind Symphony Orchestra of Pittsburgh, conducted by Robert Boudreau.

Score published by C. F. Peters, 1960. |
| Symphony No. 8, "Arjuna," Op. 179 (1947) | In one movement | 1 Flt., 1 Ob. (doubling EH), 1 Clar., 1 Bssn., 1 Hr., Timp., Pno., Strgs. | Dedicated to Handel Manuel and the Madras Musical Association.

Originally conceived as a double concerto for piano, timpani, and small orchestra of winds and strings entitled "Ardos," after an Armenian mountain. Retitled "Arjuna," after a hero in the *Bhagavad Gita*, and performed (with the timpani replaced by a *mridangam*) on February 1, 1960, at the Madras Music Festival, India.

Score published by C. F. Peters, 1960. |

Table 6.4 *continued*

Title	Movements	Instrumentation	Comments
Symphony No. 9, "Saint Vartan," Op. 80/180 (1949–50)	Arranged in 24 short movements ("steps"), divided into two larger parts: Part I 1. Yerk [Armenian song] 2. Tapor [Armenian procession] 3. Aria 4. Aria 5. Aria 6. Bar [canonic dance] 7. Tapor 8. Bar 9. Bar 10. Estampie 11. Bar 12. Bar 13. Aria 14. Lament (Death of Vartan) 15. Estampie Part II 16. Yerk (To Sensual Love) 17. Aria (To Sacred Love) 18. Estampie 19. Bar 20. Aria 21. Bar 22. Bar 23. Bar 24. Estampie	Asax., 1 Hr., 4 Tpt., 1 Trom., Timp., Perc. (Cym., SD, Gong, Tam-tam, Vbp.), Pno., Strgs.	Dedicated to Herman di Giovanno. Symphony commemorates the 1500th anniversary of the death in battle of St. Vartan Mamikonian (AD 451). First performance: March 11, 1951, by the New York Philharmonic, conducted by the composer. Score published by Peer, 1964. Analysis in this chapter.

Symphony No. 10, "Vahaken," Op. 184 (1944, rev. 1965)	1. Andante; Allegro 2. Intermezzo (Allegretto) 3. Andante; Allegro	1 Flt., 1 Ob. (doubling EH), 1 Clar., 1 Bssn., 1 Hr., 1 Tpt., 1 Trom. Timp., Perc. (Xylo., Chimes, Optional BD), Harp, Strgs.	Named after the Armenian pagan god Vahagn. As with many of Hovhaness's works of this period, Armenian and Indian idioms are combined. First performance: February 7, 1947, by members of the New York Philharmonic at Carnegie Hall, sponsored by the Friends of Armenian Music. Score published by C. F. Peters, 1960.
Symphony No. 11, "All Men Are Brothers," Op. 186 (1960, rev. 1969)	1. Andante appassionato 2. Allegro maestoso 3. Andante con nobilita [*sic*]	Grand plus Flt. (doubling Picc.), EH, Bclar., Cbssn., Tpt., Tuba, Perc. (Giant Tam-tam, Cym., Chimes, Vbp.), Harp	Commissioned for the 20th anniversary of the New Orleans Philharmonic. The composer's goal was to "express a positive faith in universal cosmic love as the only possible ultimate goal for man and nature." Mvt. I uses material from the first movement of the 1932 "Sunset" Symphony; Mvt. II uses material from the 1940s. First performance: March 21, 1961, by the New Orleans Philharmonic, conducted by Frederick Fennell. "Completely new version" of 1969 premiered by the same orchestra under Werner Torkanowsky. Score of the "new version" published by C. F. Peters, 1969. Short analysis in Athens/HOVHANESS, pp. 204–07.
Symphony No. 12, Op. 188 (1960)	1. Andante 2. The Lord Is My Shepherd 3. Bird of Dawn 4. He Leadeth Me	1 Flt., 2 Tpt., Timp., 2 Perc., Harp, Strgs., Recording of a mountain waterfall, SATB Chorus	Setting of Psalm 23. Score published by C. F. Peters, 1961.
Symphony No. 13 (in one movement), "Ardent Song," Op. 190 (1953)	In one movement	1 Flt., 1 Ob. (doubling EH), 1 Clar., 1 Bssn., 1 Hr., Timp., Perc. (Xylo, Glsp., Chimes, BD, Giant Tam-tam), Harp, Strgs.	Revision of 1945 ballet *Ardent Song*, written for Martha Graham. Holograph score published by C. F. Peters, 1960.

Table 6.4 continued

Title	Movements	Instrumentation	Comments
Symphony No. 14 for Wind Orchestra, "Ararat," Op. 194 (1960)	1. ♩ = 60 2. ♩ = around 60 3. Maestoso (♩ = 84)	5 Flt. (2 doubling Picc.), 3 Ob., 6 Clar., 3 Bssn., 6 Hr., 6 Tpt., 6 Trom., Tuba, 5 Timp., Perc. (6 Chimes, BD)	"Wild fierceness of volcanic earthquake and avalanche-shaken mountains, wrought stones, caves, rocks sculptured by tornadoes inspired this symphony of rough-hewn sounds" (Hovhaness). Commissioned by Miles T. Epling. Holograph score published by C. F. Peters, 1961.
Symphony No. 15, "Silver Pilgrimage," Op. 199 (1962)	1. Mount Ravana 2. Marava Princess 3. River of Meditation 4. Heroic Gates of Peace	Grand plus Tpt., 3 Perc. (BD, Tam-tam, Chimes), Harp	Inspired by the novel *Silver Pilgrimage* by Indian author and jurist Madhavaiah Anantanarayanan. Mvt. 4 reworks *Tapor*, Op. 14 (1948). Commissioned by the Watermull Foundation. "Dedicated to G.J. Watermull by his family with love and appreciation." Written for the Louisville Orchestra. First performance in 1962 at the Festival of Music and Art by the Honolulu Symphony Orchestra, conducted by George Barite. Score published by C. F. Peters, 1963. Short analysis in Athens/HOVHANESS, pp. 155–61.
Symphony No. 16, "Kayagum," Op. 202 (1962)	1. Possibly ♩ = 80 2. Possibly ♩ = 88 3. Possibly ♩ = 96 4. Senza misura; Possibly ♩ = 126 5. Possibly ♩ = 92	Timp., Perc., Harp, Strgs., 6 Korean instruments: *kayagum* (12 strings, similar to *koto*), *janggo* (rod drum with 2 sticks), *juago* (hanging drum), 3 *pyeonjong* (bronze bells) The Perc. and Harp substitute for the Korean instruments if needed: the Timp. for the *janggo*, the BD for the *juago*, the Vbp. for the *pyeonjong*, and the Harp for the *kayagum*.	Written after a period of study in Japan and Korea. "This symphony is inspired by the beauty of Korean mountains, the sublimity of Korean traditional music, the wisdom and nobility of Korean people." Hovhaness cited specifically the influence of a Korean landscape painting as well as the sounds of Korean music. First performance in Seoul, conducted by the composer, and broadcast on South Korean radio. Score published by C. F. Peters, 1963.

Work	Movements	Instrumentation	Notes
Symphony for Metal Orchestra (Symphony No. 17), Op. 203 (1963)	1. Andante 2. Largo 3. Allegro 4. Adagio	6 Flt., 3 Trom., Glsp., 2 Vbp., Chimes, Giant Tam-tam	Commissioned for performance at a metallurgical convention; as a result, Hovhaness employs only metallic instruments. The trombones and percussion suggest the sound of ceremonial *gagaku* music of Japan and Korea, while the flutes imitate the *shō*, a Japanese mouth organ. First performance on October 23, 1963, by members of the Cleveland Orchestra, conducted by Louis Lane. Score published by C. F. Peters, 1963.
Circe (Symphony No. 18), Op. 204a (1963)	In one movement	Grand (except only 2 Hr.) plus Tuba, 2 Perc., Harp, Cel.	Essentially reproduces a ballet written for the Martha Graham Dance Company, with an expanded scoring. Score published by C. F. Peters, 1963.
Symphony No. 19, "Vishnu," Op. 217 (1966)	In one movement	Grand plus Flt., Ob., Clar., Bssn., Tpt., Tuba, Perc. (BD, Tam-tam, Glsp., Vbp., Chimes), 2 Harps, Cel. Optional: second Chimes and Vbp.	Originally conceived as a tone poem entitled *To Vishnu* (the Hindu solar god). The work represents Hovhaness's most radical experiments with *senza misura* passages, which he described as "controlled chaos." Commissioned by the New York Philharmonic for its 1967 Promenade season. First performance: June 2, 1967, by the New York Philharmonic, conducted by André Kostelanetz, who—much to the composer's dismay—drastically cut the score from 30 minutes to 11. Score published by C. F. Peters, 1967. Analysis in this chapter, as well as Athens/HOVHANESS, pp. 179–86.

Table 6.4 *continued*

Title	Movements	Instrumentation	Comments
Symphony No. 20, "Three Journeys to a Holy Mountain," Op. 223 (1968)	1. Andante espressivo 2. Allegro moderato 3. Andante maestoso	Full band: 8 Flt, Picc., 2 Ob., EH, 12 Clar. (in 3 groups of 4), 2 E♭ Clar., 2 E♭ Aclar., 2 Bcl., Cbclar., 2 Bssn., 2 E♭ Asax., 1 Tsax., Barsax, 4 Hr., 6 Cor. or Tpt. (including baritone treble and bass clefs), 9 Trom. (in 3 groups of 3), 6 Tuba or Btrom., Cb, Timp, Giant Tam-tam, BD, Cym., Large Chimes, Vbp.	First performance: Ithaca High School Concert Band, conducted by Ronald Socciareli, 1969. Score published by C. F. Peters, 1969.
Symphony No. 21, "Etchmiadzin," Op. 234 (1968)	1. Andante maestoso 2. Pavana 3. Introduzione, Largo, Maestoso	2 Tpt. (can use 2 Clar. instead), Timp, Large Chimes, Giant Tam-tam, Strgs.	"This Symphony celebrates the heroic spiritual victory of the bells of Etchmiadzin. Etchmiadzin is the religious capital of Armenia. Above the cathedral-monastery tower the two mountain peaks of Ararat" (from the score). Commissioned by Haik Kavookjian to honor His Holiness Vaskan I, Catholicos of All Armenians (i.e., leader of the Armenian Apostolic Church). Score published by C. F. Peters, 1978.
Symphony No. 22, "City of Light," Op. 236 (1970)	1. Allegro moderato 2. Angel of Light: Largo 3. Allegretto grazioso 4. Finale: Largo maestoso	Grand plus Flt. (doubling Picc.), Clar. (doubling Bclar.), Bssn. (doubling Cbssn.), Tpt., Tuba, 3 Perc. (Vbp, Glsp., Tam-tam, Chimes), Harp	Commissioned by the Birmingham (Alabama) Symphony Orchestra in celebration of the centennial of the city. The title refers not to Birmingham but to "a million lights, an imaginary city." Fugal finale adapted from the withdrawn Symphony No. 2 of 1942. Score published by C. F. Peters, 1971.

Symphony No. 23, "Ani," Op. 249 (1972)	1. Adagio legato espressivo 2. Allegro grazioso 3. Adagio con molto espressione	For large band with antiphonal brass choir II *ad lib.*: 7 Flt., Picc., 2 Ob., 2 Eb Clar., 2 Eb Aclar., 2 Bclar., 2 Bssn., Eb Asax., 1 Tsax., Eb Barsax., 8 Cor. (in 2 groups of 4), 8 Hr. (2 groups of 4), Barhr. (treble clef), 2 Barhr. (bass clef), 18 Trom. (3 groups of 6), 4 Tuba, Cb, Timp., Tam-tam, BD, Glsp., Mrb., Vbp., Xylo., Chimes	Named after the ancient capital of Armenia (known as a "city of a thousand and one cathedrals"), now a ghost town within Turkey. Commissioned by Lawrence Sobol for the Smithtown (New York) Central High School Symphonic Band. First performance: May 13, 1972, by the Smithtown Central High School Symphonic Band, conducted by Sobol. Score published by C. F. Peters, 1972.
Symphony No. 24, "Majnun," Op. 273 (1973)	Nine sections in two parts: Part I 1. Majnun 2. Letters in the Sand 3. The Distracted Lover Part II 4. The Sword-Wind 5. Majnun Answered 6. The Beloved 7. The Celestial Beloved 8. Majnun's Love Song 9. The Mysterious Beloved	Tpt., Vln., Strgs. Tenor solo, SATB Choir	Symphony-cantata setting passages of Jami's epic Persian poem *Salaman and Absal* (15th c.), as translated in 1856 by Edward Fitzgerald. The poem tells the love story of Majnun and Layla. Commissioned by the International Center for Arid and Semi-Arid Land Studies for Focus on the Arts Series at Texas Tech University (Lubbock). First performance: January 25, 1974, in Lubbock, with the orchestra conducted by the composer. Score published by AMP, 1978.
Symphony No. 25, "Odysseus," Op. 275 (1973)	In one movement	1 Flt. (doubles Picc.), 1 Ob., 1 Clar., 1 Hr., 1 Tpt., 1 Trom., Tuba, Timp., Perc. (BD, Tamb., Tam-tam, Vbp., Chimes), Strgs.	Quasi-symphonic poem evoking the trials of Odysseus as he returns to Penelope. First performance: a concert in London conducted by Hovhaness. Score published by Peer, 1975.

Table 6.4 continued

Title	Movements	Instrumentation	Comments
Symphony No. 26, Op. 280 (1975)	4 movements	Grand plus Flt., Tpt., Tuba, Perc., Harp	First performance: October 24, 1975, in San Jose, California, with the composer conducting. Score published by Peer, 1976.
Symphony No. 27, Op. 285 (1976)	6 movements	Small orchestra: 1 Flt., 1 Ob., 1 Hr., 1 Tpt., Timp., Perc., Strgs.	Commissioned by the Armenian Symphonic Music Association of Los Angeles. First performance (along with Symphony No. 28): April 23, 1977, at the Armenian Symphonic Music Association's Commemorative Concert at the Dorothy Chandler Pavilion of the Los Angeles Music Center; the pickup instrumentalists (many of them members of the Los Angeles Philharmonic) conducted by Hovhaness. Facsimile of the holograph published in 1976 by Fujihara, the composer's private label, which releases all the published symphonies from this point forward except for Symphonies 29 and 50.
Symphony No. 28, Op. 286 (1976)	5 movements	Chamber orchestra of 1 Flt., EH, 1 Tpt., Timp., Strgs.	Dedicated to the memory of the composer's Armenian grandmother. He called this work a "love symphony" to Hinako Fujihara, who would soon become his wife. First performance (along with Symphony No. 27): April 23, 1977, at the Armenian Symphonic Music Association's Commemorative Concert at the Dorothy Chandler Pavilion of the Los Angeles Music Center; the pickup instrumentalists (many of them members of the Los Angeles Philharmonic) conducted by Hovhaness. Facsimile of the holograph published by Fujihara, 1976.

Symphony No. 29, Op. 289 (1976)	1. Andante religioso 2. Adagio espressivo 3. Lento—Allegro moderato—Presto 4. Finale	Barhr. and Grand plus Flt., Tpt., Tuba, Perc. (Tenor Drum, Vbp., Large BD, Large Chimes, Tamb, Giant Tam-tam), Harp	Commissioned by Henry Charles Smith and the C. G. Conn Corporation. First performance: September 1976, by the Minnesota Orchestra. Hovhaness later arranged the work for band. Holograph score published by Alexander Broude, 1978.
Symphony No. 30, Op. 293 (1952–76)		1 Flt., 1 Ob., 1 Tpt., Strgs.	Facsimile of the holograph published by Fujihara, 1976.
Symphony No. 31, Op. 294 (1976–77)	1. Andante molto cantando 2. Presto 3. Lento 4. Fuga. Presto ma non troppo 5. Allegro vivace 6. Andante con molto espressione 7. Fuga. Presto	Strgs.	Facsimile of the holograph published by Fujihara, 1977.
Symphony No. 32, "The Broken Wings," Op. 296 (1977)		1 Flt., 1 Ob., 1 Clar., 1 Hr., 1 Tpt., Perc., Strgs.	Facsimile of the holograph published by Fujihara, 1977.
Symphony No. 33, Op. 307 (1977)		1 Flt., 1 Clar. (doubling Bclar.), 1 Tpt., 1 Trom., Perc., Strgs.	Facsimile of the holograph published by Fujihara, 1977.
Symphony No. 34, Op. 310 (1977)	1. Largo, cadenza 2. Andante 3. Scherzo 4. Andante maestoso	Btrom., Strgs.	Essentially a concerto for bass trombone, commissioned by trombonist David Taylor. First performance: January 17, 1980. Score published by Fujihara.

Table 6.4 *continued*

Title	Movements	Instrumentation	Comments
Symphony No. 35, Op. 311 (1978)		Two orchestras. Orch. 1: instruments for Korean *aak* (ceremonial court music): *sogeum* (small flute), *daegeum* (large flute), *piri* (oboe), *haegeum* (fiddle), *kayagum* (zither) ad lib., *komungo* (zither) ad lib., *ajaeng* (wide zither), *yanggeum* (hammered dulcimer), *juago* (hanging drum), *pyeongyeong* (tuned stone chimes), *pyeongjong* (bronze bells). Orch. 2: Grand plus Flt., Ob. (doubling EH), Clar. (doubling Bclar.), Bssn. (doubling Cbssn.), Tpt., 2 Tuba, Perc., Harp	Commissioned by the Korean government for the opening of the Seoul Art Centre on June 9, 1978. Facsimile of the holograph published by Fujihara, 1978.
Symphony No. 36, Op. 312 (1978)	3 movements	Flt. and Grand plus Flt., Ob. (doubling EH), Clar. (doubling Bclar.), Bssn. (doubling Cbssn.), Tpt., Tuba, Perc., Harp	Commissioned by flutist Jean-Pierre Rampal. First performance: January 16, 1979, with Rampal and the National Symphony Orchestra, conducted by Mstislav Rostropovich. Score published by Fujihara.
Symphony No. 37, Op. 313 (1978)		Grand plus Tpt., Tuba, BD, Harp	Score published by Fujihara.
Symphony No. 38, Op. 314 (1978)	1. Allegretto—Presto—Allegretto 2. Andante—Allegretto—Appassionato—Presto 3. Allegro maestoso—Andante 4. Lullaby: Allegretto—Andante 5. Andante maestoso	1 Flt., 1 Tpt., Strgs. Soprano soloist	Written for the composer's wife Hinako Fujihara, a coloratura soprano. Texts drawn from various sources. Facsimile of the holograph published by Fujihara, 1978.

Symphony No. 39, Op. 321 (1979)	1. Adagio 2. Allegro 3. Andante 4. Allegro	Gui. and Grand plus Flt., Ob., Tpt., Tuba, Perc., Harp	Commissioned by the National Symphony Orchestra and first performed by that ensemble in January 1979, under conductor Mstislav Rostropovich. Score published by Fujihara.
Symphony No. 40, Op. 324 (1979–80)	1. Andante espressivo 2. Largo 3. Allegretto maestoso—Allegro	Brass quintet (1 Hr., 2 Tpt., 1 Trom., Tuba), Timp., Strgs.	The original Symphony No. 40 was lost when his briefcase containing the only copy of the completed manuscript was stolen. Hovhaness said he could not re-create the work, so he replaced it with a new symphony written in February 1980. Holograph score published by Fujihara, 1983.
Symphony No. 41, Op. 330 (1979)		Brass quartet (1 Hr., 2 Tpt., 1 Trom.), Strgs.	Score published by Fujihara.
Symphony No. 42, Op. 332 (1979)		1 Flt., 1 Tpt., 1 Trom., Strgs.	Score published by Fujihara.
Symphony No. 43, Op. 334 (1979)	1. Largo—Arioso (Oboe and Strings) 2. Presto—Canon (Timpani and Strings) 3. Christmas Vision: Vision of Infinite Compassion (Oboe and Strings) 4. Allegro—Canon (Timpani and Strings) 5. Aria (Oboe and Strings) 6. Fuga (Trumpet, Timpani, and Strings)	1 Ob., 1 Tpt., Timp., Strgs.	First performance: August 31, 1980, by the Cabrillo Festival Orchestra, conducted by the composer. Holograph score published by Fujihara, 1980.
Symphony No. 44, Op. 339 (1980)		1 Flt., 1 Ob., 1 Tpt., Timp., Perc., Strgs.	Score published by Fujihara.

Table 6.4 continued

Title	Movements	Instrumentation	Comments
Symphony No. 45, Op. 342 (1954)	3 movements	2 Pno. and Grand plus Perc.	Apparently the same work as a quasi-concerto grosso for two pianos written in 1954 and originally entitled Concerto No. 10, Op. 123 #3; it is not clear if Hovhaness made any revisions to the unperformed concerto before recasting it as Symphony No. 45. Score published by Fujihara.
Symphony No. 46, "To the Green Mountains," Op. 347 (1980)	1. Prelude 2. Aria, Hymn, and Fugue 3. River and Forest Music 4. Mountain Thunderstorm and Thanksgiving Music	Grand plus Flt., Tpt., Tuba, Perc. (Giant Tam-tam, Vbp., BD, Chimes), Harp	Written for the Vermont Symphony Orchestra and first played by that ensemble on May 2, 1981. Holograph score published by Fujihara, 1981.
Symphony No. 47, "Walla Walla, Land of Many Waters," Op. 348 (1980)	1. Fantasy "Journey to Walla Walla" 2. Cantata "Land of Many Waters" 3. Love Song 4. Finale	Grand plus Flt., Ob., Tpt., Tuba, Perc., Harp. Coloratura soprano soloist	Commissioned by the Walla Walla Symphony to celebrate its diamond jubilee. Text for second movement combines words by John Muir and Hinako Fujihara (Hovhaness's wife). First performance in Walla Walla on November 24, 1981. Score published by Fujihara.
Symphony No. 48, "Vision of Andromeda," Op. 355 (1981)	1. Andante 2. Fugue: Allegro 3. Andante—Allegro moderato 4. Largo solenne—Allegro maestoso—Andante maestoso espressivo	Grand plus Flt., Tpt., Tuba, Perc., Harp	First performance: June 21, 1982, by the Minnesota Symphony Orchestra, conducted by Leonard Slatkin, as part of Minnesota Sommerfest. Score published by Fujihara.
Symphony No. 49, "Christmas Symphony," Op. 356 (1981)	1. Celestial Prophecy 2. The Angel 3. Pastoral 4. The Star, "Watchman Tell Us of the Night"	Strgs.	Score published by Fujihara, 1985.

Symphony No. 50, "Mount St. Helens," Op. 360 (1981–82)	1. Andante 2. Spirit Lake: Allegro 3. Volcano: Adagio—Allegro	Grand plus Flt., Ob. (doubling EH), Tpt., Tuba, Perc., Harp	Commissioned by C. F. Peters, which published most of Hovhaness's music between 1958–72. First performance: March 2, 1984, by the San Jose Symphony, conducted by George Cleve. Score published by C. F. Peters, 1982. The best known of Hovhaness's later symphonies. Short analysis in Athens/HOVHANESS, pp. 222–27.
Symphony No. 51, Op. 364 (1982)		1 Tpt., Strgs.	Unpublished.
Symphony No. 52, "Journey to Vega," Op. 372 (1983)		1 Flt., 1 Ob., 1 Clar., 1 Bssn., 2 Hr., 2 Tpt., 1 Trom., Tuba, Timp., Strgs. (or String Quintet)	Unpublished.
Symphony No. 53, "Star Dawn," Op. 377 (1983)	1. Maestoso sostenuto 2. Moderato sostenuto con molto espressione	Wind band: 1 Flt. (doubling Picc.), 1 Ob., EH, Sop. Clar., E♭ Clar., E♭ Aclar., Bclar., Cbclar., 1 Bssn., Cbssn., 2 E♭ Asax., Tsax., E♭ Barsax., 4 Hr., 5 C Tpt., 3 Trom., 2 Barhr., Tuba, Timp., Perc. (2 Vbp., Glsp., Chimes, BD, Tam-tam)	Title taken from a line by Dante. The work evokes space travel: a journey from Earth in Mvt. 1, and the arrival of humans on a distant planet in Mvt. 2. Dedicated to Charles D. Yates and the San Diego State University Wind Ensemble. First performance: February 1990, at Carnegie Hall, by the Yale University Concert Band, conducted by Thomas Duffy. Score published by Fujihara.
Symphony No. 54, Op. 378 (1983)		Grand plus Tpt., Tuba	Score published by Fujihara.
Symphony No. 55, Op. 379 (1983)		Grand plus Flt., Tpt., Tuba, Perc., Harp, Pno.	Score published by Fujihara.
Symphony No. 56, Op. 380 (1983)		Grand plus Flt., Tpt., Tuba, Perc., Pno.	Score published by Fujihara.

Table 6.4 *continued*

Title	Movements	Instrumentation	Comments
Symphony No. 57, "Cold Mountain," Op. 381 (1983)	1. Andante misterioso 2. Andante espressivo 3. Allegro assai 4. Andante—Allegro 5. Allegretto maestoso 6. Moderato—Andante 7. Moderato maestoso—Adagio espressivo 8. Moderato 9. Allegro 10. Allegro 11. Allegro 12. Allegro 13. Adagio 14. Adagio espressivo—Andante 15. Andante misterioso	Clar., Strgs. (or String Quintet). Tenor (or Soprano) soloist	Setting of poems by Han-Shan (*ca.* 9th c.), translated from the Chinese by Burton Watson. Intended for a tenor soloist but a soprano may substitute. "Dedicated to The Grossmann Family of East Madison, New Hampshire." Holograph score published by Fujihara, 1985.
Symphony No. 58, "Symphony sacra," Op. 389 (1985)		1 Flt., 1 Hr., 1 Tpt., Timp., Chimes, Harp, Strgs. Soprano and Baritone soloists, SATB Chorus	Text arranged by Joseph F. McCall. First performance: November 10, 1985, in Valparaiso, Indiana. Unpublished.
Symphony No. 59, Op. 395 (1985)		Grand plus Flt., Tpt., Tuba, Perc., Harp	First performance: January 28, 1985, in Bellevue, Washington. Score published by Fujihara.

Symphony No. 60, "To the Appalachian Mountains," Op. 396 (1985)	1. Adagio doloroso 2. Allegro 3. Senza misura: Adagio 4. Finale: Andante—Allegro	Grand plus Flt., Tpt., Tuba, Perc., Harp

Loosely draws upon the idioms of Appalachian music and shape-note hymnody.

Commissioned by Martin Marietta Energy Systems, Inc., in recognition of "Homecoming '86," a celebration of the cultural heritage of the State of Tennessee.

First performance: April 24, 1986, in Knoxville, Tennessee.

Unpublished.

Symphony No. 61, Op. 397 (1986)		Grand plus Picc., Flt., Tpt., Tuba, Perc., Harp

First performance: October 4, 1986, in Boise, Idaho.

Unpublished.

Symphony No. 62, "Oh, Let Not Man Forget These Words Divine," Op. 402 (1987–88)		Tpt., Strgs. Baritone soloist

Text by Sir Francis Bacon.

Score published by Fujihara.

Symphony No. 63, "Loon Lake," Op. 411 (1988, rev. 1991)	1. Prelude: Largo solenne—Andante pastorale 2. Andante misterioso—Maestoso—Presto—Allegro	Picc., 1 Flt., 1 Ob., EH, 2 Clar., 2 Bssn., 2 Hr., 2 Tpt., 1 Trom., Timp., Chimes, Harp, Strgs.

Commissioned by the New Hampshire Music Festival and the Loon Preservation Society.

First performance: August 18, 1988, by the New Hampshire Music Festival Orchestra, conducted by Thomas Nee. Hovhaness later revised the ending, and the new version premiered during the New Hampshire Festival on July 2, 1991.

Score published by Fujihara.

Symphony No. 64, "Agiochook," Op. 422 (1991)		Tpt., Strgs.

Score published by Fujihara.

Symphony No. 65, "Artstakh," Op. 427 (1991)		Grand plus Flt., Tpt., Tuba, Perc., Harp

First performance: October 6, 1991, by the American Composers Orchestra, conducted by the composer. The occasion was a concert at Carnegie Hall celebrating Hovhaness's 80th birthday.

Score published by Fujihara.

Table 6.4 continued

Title	Movements	Instrumentation	Comments
Symphony No. 66, "Hymn to Glacier Peak," Op. 428 (1992)	1. Andante maestoso 2. Andante espressivo, "Love Song to Hinako" 3. Largo maestoso, "Prelude and Fugue"	Grand plus Flt., Tpt., Tuba, Perc., Harp	Commissioned by the Seattle Youth Symphony. First performance: May 10, 1992, by the Seattle Youth Symphony, conducted by Reuben Gurevich. Score published by Fujihara. Short analysis in Athens/HOVHANESS, pp. 231–33.
Symphony No. 67, "Hymn to the Mountains," Op. 429 (1992)		Grand plus Flt., Tpt., Tuba, Perc., Harp	Score published by Fujihara.

a. Much of the material in this table draws upon the descriptions in the detailed (but incomplete) website http://www.hovhaness.com/Symphonies_Hovhaness.html; additional information comes from one of the few scholarly sources on the composer, Niccolo Davis Athens's doctoral thesis "The Music of Alan Hovhaness" (DMA diss., Cornell University, 2016). By his own admission, Hovhaness was an extremely lax cataloguer of his compositions until about 1960, and the numbering of the first 13 symphonies does not reflect the order of composition. Scores for many later symphonies, especially those published by Fujihara Music Co. (the composer's private company) proved impossible to obtain; multiple entries, therefore, lack movement titles (or even the number of movements), percussion instrumentation, or dates of first performance or publication. Meters and measure numbers are not given in this table.

or "timeless" space. Many works feature passages that are quasi-aleatoric or *senza misura*, with all or part of the orchestra playing with specified pitches *ad libitum* and without coordination.

Hovhaness's interest in modal musics focused first on ancient Armenian chant, inspired in large part by his study of the music of the priest and composer Komitas Vardapet (1869–1935).[179] Musics of South and East Asia influenced Hovhaness's stylistic evolution in the 1950s; in 1953 he received the first of two successive Guggenheim Fellowships and then in 1959 he was awarded a Fulbright to study Karnatic music in South India. He also visited Japan for the first time during this period and returned in 1962–63 to study gagaku (ceremonial court music), learning a few of the key instruments in that orchestral ensemble such as the *hichiriki* (a flute) and the *shō* (a mouth organ).[180] The 1960s were marked by a particularly strong interest in the music of Japan and Korea; after 1970, he returned to Western influences.

Once an influence entered Hovhaness's stylistic world, it never really departed, and so techniques and processes—modal melodies, imitative counterpoint, impressionistic chord streams, bitonal passages, and ostinati, set in gradually unfolding and meditative forms—accrue over the course of his development. With regard to the symphony, Hovhaness stands out for his very free conceptualization of the genre: a catchall name for any large-scale composition for orchestra, wind ensemble, or other body, and of any length, number of movements, or purpose—a vessel for bringing together selected Western traditions with idioms as disparate as Armenian modes, Indian rhythmic and melodic formulas, and timbres of East Asian ensembles. The idiosyncrasy of Hovhaness's attitude is evident in the sheer number of symphonies—67—and also the wide range of instrumentations—for example, a "metal orchestra" (Symphony No. 17) and "Korean orchestra" (Symphony No. 16).

Given the (very American) diversity of stylistic influences, variety of orchestral models, and general flexibility of his formal approach, it becomes clear that Hovhaness's understanding of the symphony bears little relation to Euro-American visions of the genre and is indeed antithetical to the nineteenth-century Western notion of symphony as transcendent masterwork. Hovhaness's principal debt to the Romantic tradition is in the extramusical inspiration of his symphonies: many carry an evocative title, if not a specific program. Subjects frequently involve the natural world: six symphonies mention *mountain* in their title and others refer to various landscapes and natural phenomena. Even at the level of structure and style, his works seem to mimic natural processes such as waves or the ebb and flow of a tide. Only occasionally is this landscape encoded as specifically American—Symphony No. 50, "Mount St. Helens," is a famous example—and even then he often turns to the native place names. More atypically, the Symphony No. 18, "Circe," started out as a ballet, commissioned and choreographed by Martha Graham. Others feature solo instruments in the manner of a concerto grosso. Hovhaness's approach to the symphony is perhaps closest to Bernstein, then, in that he consistently challenged assumptions about what the symphony meant (table 6.4).

The 1950s and 60s were a period of professional success and expanding musical vocabulary for Hovhaness, as well as the beginning of his sustained engagement with the symphonic medium. Rather than attempt to survey all the symphonies—a near-impossible task at any rate, as many are virtually inaccessible—we will focus on three representative works from these two decades that demonstrate significant aspects of his evolving style—the contrapuntal legacy of the Western tradition merged with music of Armenia and South and East Asia—as well as the stark differences in instrumentation and formal organization possible in Hovhaness's versions of the symphony.

SYMPHONY NO. 9, "ST. VARTAN"

The "Saint Vartan" Symphony, Op. 180 (1950; also catalogued as Op. 80) premiered in Carnegie Hall alongside Hovhaness's *Janabar*, Op. 81, a five-movement suite for chamber orchestra, on March 11, 1951.[181] The orchestra consisted of members of the New York Philharmonic, with the composer conducting. Both are concertante works, the former scored for brass, percussion, and string orchestra and the latter for violin, trumpet, piano, and strings. Whereas the programmatic implication of *Janabar* is vaguer—the title means "journey" in Armenian—the invocation of Saint Vartan carries a great deal of specific meaning. The concert was given for the benefit of the Armenian Cathedral and Cultural Center Project and, according to the archive at Carnegie Hall, "marked the 1500th anniversary of the Holy Wars of Vartan." Saint Vartan (Vardan Mamikonian) was an Armenian military commander who fought against the Persian Sassanid dynasty and was slain at the Battle of Avarayr (ca. June 2, 451). He was remembered as a martyr in the defense of Christianity (the Persians had attempted to impose Zoroastrianism on the Armenians) and was later canonized and enshrined as a folk hero. Vartan was particularly important as a symbol under the repression of the Ottoman Turks and, after the 1915 Armenian Genocide, he became a significant cultural figure for the diaspora, of which Hovhaness's father was a member. Fittingly, the work draws deeply on the composer's study of Armenian music.

Over the course of a 40-minute span consisting of 24 sections grouped into two unequal parts (see table 6.4), the symphony explores dance and song in a startling array of variations. Some sections explicitly reference Western European traditions, like the estampie and aria, while others invoke Armenian traditions, like the *yerk* (song) and *tapor* (a procession around the church). In the movements intended to conjure songs, the brass instruments (including alto saxophone) take the role of a voice filled with the modal inflections characteristic of Armenian church music and folk song; the strings provide accompaniments that typically feature ostinati and drones, both traits associated with self-accompanied Armenian poet-singers (*gusan*).[182] The processional *tapor* sometimes invokes a richly ornamented chant (no. 2) and sometimes a march (no. 7). Occasionally the accompaniments will use *senza misura* passages—which Hovhaness calls "spirit sounds"—in order to allow some freedom for the "vocal" lines.[183] Other than an epic atmosphere conveyed through a wide range of mood, tempo, and thematic materials, the only direct reference to any narrative event is the "Lament" for the death of Vartan (no. 14). The harmonic material effectively evokes the difference of this Christian tradition (although the use of tam-tam, gong, and cymbals can be heard as self-exoticizing), while the emphasis on brass soloists and antiphonal call-and-responses fits neatly with the framework of a heroic narrative.

In its conception, this symphony is more like a series of short character pieces than the formally integrated work prized by most midcentury composers. The two *yerks*, six arias, two *tapors*, nine *bars* (dances), four estampies, and the central lament are arranged in a seemingly random order. (*Janabar* features a similar, though much briefer, medley of *yerk*, *tapor*, and Western genres like the toccata and fantasy.) There is plenty of complexity—canons in stretto, a polytonal estampie in no. 18, abundant layered textures, and isorhythmic patterning in no. 22—but teleological development is absent. Movements often start and end abruptly, as does the symphony as a whole, but the sheer variety of tone color in the careful orchestration holds one's attention. No. 14, the lament for trombone and piano, is notable in both its bitonality and the one appearance of the piano. Likewise, no. 16, a *yerk* subtitled "sensual love," is unique within the symphony in its use of the solo alto saxophone, which spins out a highly ornamented cadenza, joined eventually by timpani and vibraphone to form an unusual trio. In this early symphony—chronologically the third of the numbered corpus—Hovhaness is already emptying the symphony of its conventional expectations and reconceiving the work to suit whatever material he is handling at the time.

The premiere received a favorable response. Lou Harrison admired it, as did the *Times* reviewer, who praised it as "completely original in conception" and singled out Hovhaness's attention to contrasts in orchestration, tempo, and character that helped the symphony "avoid the monotony which might result from insistent rhythms and oft-repeated tunes."[184] Although he would eventually leave behind overt references to specific types of Armenian music, the modal vocabulary and textures of his ethnic heritage would permeate the rest of his works. The "Saint Vartan" also demonstrates his tendency to blend non-Western traditions with those aspects of common-practice music that he appreciated.

SYMPHONY NO. 2, *MYSTERIOUS MOUNTAIN*

Along with Serge Koussevitzky, Leopold Stokowski was an early advocate for Hovhaness's music. For an inaugural concert with the Houston Symphony, Stokowski asked Hovhaness for a fanfare, and the composer responded with a short piece for brass addressed to a "mysterious mountain." Stokowski was interested enough to request a larger work, which became the Symphony No. 2: *Mysterious Mountain*, Op. 132 (1955).[185] This three-movement symphony employs the instrumentation standard since the nineteenth century, but with a special emphasis on harp and celesta that recalls Béla Bartók's (1881–1945) *Music for Strings, Percussion and Celesta* (1936). In general, the orchestration is impressionist, with streams of chords from the strings and colorful, improvisatory touches in the woodwinds. Like Schuman, Hovhaness often handles the instruments within their families, a consistent feature of his scoring.

While the first and third movements are clearly inspired by his interest in music of the medieval and early modern periods, the second movement is a thoroughgoing double fugue that leaves no doubt as to Hovhaness's careful study of Renaissance and Baroque models. The structures of the outer movements are open-ended part forms that grow in textural and harmonic density as well as volume, creating a series of slow-moving waves. Additionally, both movements draw on chant-like modal melodies, spiced with bitonality and with an ametric feel achieved through the manipulation of 10/4 or 7/4 time signatures. Long periods of harmonic stasis reinforce this sense of timelessness, with unexpected progressions providing momentum into cadence points. Overall, the effect often feels cinematic in a way that anticipates exoticist film epics of the era like *Ben-Hur* (1959) and *Lawrence of Arabia* (1962).

The opening Andante begins with a dignified chorale in the low woodwinds and divisi strings that vacillates between E minor and G major. The repetition of the rhythm [♩-♩-♩-♩.-♪-♩-°] in the string section functions not unlike a talea (the repeated rhythmic pattern that serves as the foundation for an isorhythmic work) and creates a meditative atmosphere. Once the brass join in m. 4, the texture and volume swell toward a blatant V^7-I motion from an Emm7 to a throaty A-major chord (mm. 10–11). As the wave crests, though, it drops to a functionally inexplicable E-flat major triad. The harmonic language here is typical of the rest of the movement: despite a handful of recognizably tonal gestures, the whole is governed by smooth voice leading and the melodic formulas typical of modal music. The gesture of mm. 10–11 is repeated, sotto voce, by the string section in mm. 12–14, before the beginning of the middle section (mm. 15–56). The 10/4 meter and bitonal organization of this opening section combine to create an appropriately "mysterious" atmosphere.

The central portion of the movement functions around a series of intoned statements from the woodwinds, beginning in the oboe at m. 18, with a line that centers around repeated articulations of B-natural, while occasionally indulging in flurries of ornamentation. The second oboe provides an antiphonal response in mm. 23–25, extended by the English horn in mm. 25–28. The clarinets then reiterate a similar pattern, again centering on B-natural. This all takes place over a slow-moving modal chorale that rises and falls so gradually as to function more like a drone than a countermelody. The shift in meter from 10/4 to an alternation between 4/4 and 3/4 further suspends the texture, allowing the chanting of the woodwinds to float freely. The effect is not unlike the Armenian musics evoked in the "St. Vartan" Symphony, particularly the passages suggesting the *gusan* or *vipasan* (lyric and epic songs of the Armenian poet-singers, often self-accompanied with string drones). The celesta provides ornamentation with alternately triadic and quintal arpeggiations while the harp adds another layer of modal mysticism centered on E-flat.

The final passage (mm. 57–94) combines features of both sections. In conjunction with a metrical shift back to 10/4, the strings return to a 3+3+4 pattern and a chorale that resembles the opening section, except that it is now based on a tetrachordal formula that evokes the harmonic organization of much Armenian music.[186] A trumpet solo adopts the repeated B-natural of the woodwind solos in the central portion of the movement and the harp and celesta continue their accompanimental figures. The whole texture builds to a homophonic passage for the full orchestra beginning in m. 84; a sonorous finish on a G-major triad settles the harmonic ambiguity, although in a somewhat arbitrary fashion.

The second movement presents two alternatives for the dominant character of a fugue: dignity and solemnity in the opening Moderato maestoso and perpetuum mobile in the Allegro vivo. Compared to the free-floating sense of the first movement, the processional 2/2 statement of the first fugal subject seems rather sober as it unfolds through a divisi string section. (See example 6.5.)

The first subject unfolds in A minor (with a lowered seventh scale degree) in the upper half of the first violins and violas, receiving a real answer in E from the other half of those sections. The third and fourth voices of the fugue, in the second violins, cellos, and basses, follow the same tonal pattern. This first half of the movement is restricted to the woodwinds and strings, except for the entrance of the horn section in m. 117 that, in another example of textural accretion, helps the movement swell toward its *attacca* transition into the Allegro vivo (m. 131). The second fugue subject in D minor (also with lowered seventh) beginning in the second violins with its repetitive rhythms, scalar figures, and bariolage, recalls Vivaldi by way of Bach (see example 6.6).

The tonal answer on A appears in the first violins, with the subject-answer repeated in the violas and cellos/basses to create a second four-voice fugue. That the ensuing episodes and expositions remain confined to the strings, drawing on their idiomatic techniques, emphasizes the resemblances to Baroque contrapuntal genres. The horns present a hymnlike countersubject centered on A in m. 171, later taken up by trumpets (m. 181) and trombone (m. 192). The movement climaxes in a forte chordal passage for the whole orchestra with a melodic statement passed among the brass section; it derives from the subject of the first fugue, beginning with the stepwise ascent from the third note. Once again, the movement ends with a G-major

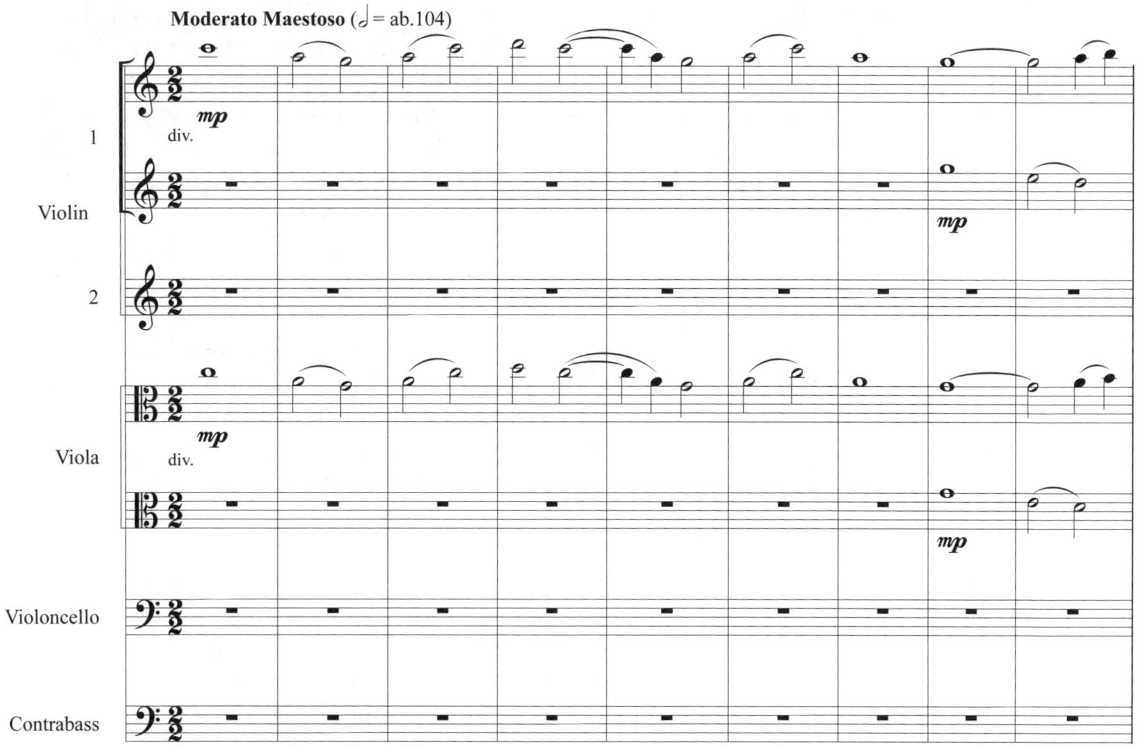

Forgotten Modernisms

Example 6.5 Hovhaness, Symphony No. 2, mvt. 2, first fugue subject (mm. 1–8)

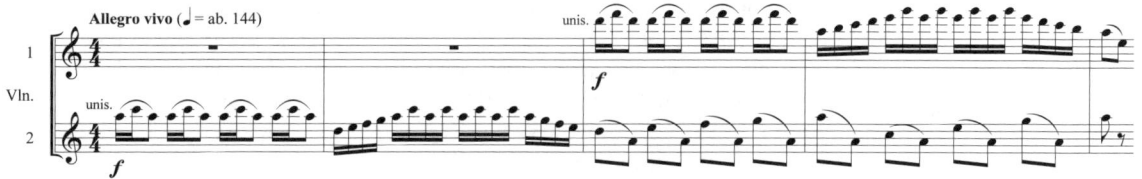

Example 6.6 Hovhaness, Symphony No. 2, mvt. 2, second fugue subject (mm. 131–35)

chord, which seems arbitrary in the context of the possible tonal centers offered by the two fugues.

Returning to the mood of the first movement, the Finale begins with a chant-like statement on a G-major chord, although in this case it is magnified by its presentation in the horn section, followed by low brass. This is clearly the "short fanfare" with which Hovhaness began, although the meditative mood makes for a more somber invocation. The 7/4 of the opening makes the passage feel unmetered as in the plainchant traditions of both the Eastern and Western churches, while the chorale-like texture recalls his favored Renaissance. The beginning of the con moto section (m. 6), however, sets up a groove in the harp and string section over which extremely slow and narrow lines spin out six statements of the same material. The upper voices seem to float free from the substratum, not only on account of their relatively static character but also because the horns (and eventually the rest of the wind section) alternate 3/4 and 4/4 against the 9/8 and 12/8 of the strings—a juxtaposition of compound and duple meters that allows for a sense of rhythmic intensity while remaining timeless. Overall, the Finale forms a series of dynamic and textural waves, accompanied by brief recollections of material from earlier movements, ending with a solid wall of G major; it leaves the audience in no doubt as to the tonal orientation of the work while simultaneously avoiding much of the vocabulary associated with the eighteenth- or nineteenth-century symphony.

From its premiere, *Mysterious Mountain* has been one of Hovhaness's best-received works, largely eclipsing his other compositions. Although most critics praised it, the composer much preferred other works, such as Symphony No. 19, "Vishnu." Of *Mysterious Mountain* he said, "My feelings are mixed—I am happy it is popular but I have written much better music and it is a very impersonal work, in which I omit my deeper searching."[187] Eventually he came to actually dislike the piece ("now I cannot bear to hear it"), to the point that he had to leave the hall whenever it was performed.[188] At the same time, he was also undeniably moved by the metaphysical content of the work, which he attributed to a dream state.

SYMPHONY NO. 19, "VISHNU"

Dedicated to the New York Philharmonic, and premiered by them under André Kostelanetz on June 2, 1967, the "Vishnu" Symphony reflects Hovhaness's study of South and East Asian musics in the 1950s and 1960s; he melds those techniques with previously discussed aspects of his style. More a tone poem than a symphony by Hovhaness's own admission, the single thirty-minute movement represents Vishnu, a solar god of the Hindu tradition in an "abstraction of the circulation of divine energy throughout the universe." In his program for the premiere, Edward Downes points to rotations and spiral motions in the music; he quotes Hovhaness, who directs the listener to the following:

> Wild, but controlled, chaos bursts out in brass and percussion in free, rhythmless passages, followed by bells. This might possibly symbolize the explosions which take place in the central core of giant galaxies of stars and planetary systems. Free passages of controlled chaos follow and act as preludes and interludes between phrases of an unfolding giant melody of adoration to the immensity and sublimity of limitless stellar universes. Bells and trumpets reach a climax of wild, free sounds circling like orbits of fire. A solemn, cosmic love song vanishes amid high, free, rhythmless gliding orbits of sounds in flutes and harps.[189]

This description aligns with the traits Hovhaness considers central to Asian musics: the long melodic line; complex canons; microtonal pitch content; a concept of "timespace" that allows for passages of "no rhythm, anti-rhythm, rhythmlessness"; and a highly developed "sense of sound and silence."[190] All abound in "Vishnu."

The structure of the single-movement work alternates between unmetered and metered sections (compare the beginning to Reh. 13, for example). The "timeless" passages make extensive use of *senza misura* and short melodic and rhythmic formulas derived from Indian ragas and talas; the effect resembles Witold Lutosławski's "aleatoric counterpoint," in which exact notes and rhythm are indicated, but the coordination is *ad libitum*. Hovhaness gives only approximate timings for each section and indications of crescendos and decrescendos; the rhythmic and melodic formulas vary in each passage. At times, the metered Largo passages take the form of melodies over a dissonant drone in the strings, often with glissandi, which are as close to microtones as Hovhaness could get the New York Philharmonic to produce; in other instances, they simply float strange, dissonant chords, whispered by divisi strings. In either type of passage there can be timelessness or great contrapuntal interest, and sometimes they coexist.

Although Hovhaness employs no "foreign" instruments, he focuses more than ever on expanded percussion and he uses glissandi and other techniques to simulate non-Western sounds on wind and brass instruments, especially flute and trombone. The stately "giant melody" unfolds for the first time in Reh. 46, and the string melody that follows at Reh. 52 recalls the dances from "St. Vartan." In the treatment of the orchestra as families of instruments and its focus on the strings, "Vishnu" has much in common with *Mysterious Mountain*. The central section between Reh. 64 and 78 comprises a "noble and heroic" Andante in 7/4, with what we might hear as stanzas of the "giant melody" interrupted by *senza misura* "interludes." From Reh. 80 the Largo modal melody—Hovhaness's "solemn, cosmic love song," heard mostly in the woodwinds—seems to move away from the listener in a slow, nearly timeless, 12/8 procession.

Raymond Ericson reported a favorable response in the *New York Times*, although there appears to be a disconnect between the composer's estimate of the time (30 minutes) and Ericson's (10 minutes), a difference that can be attributed to extensive cuts made by Kostelanetz, much to Hovhaness's disappointment.[191] Ericson called the work "hypnotic"—a description that fits with Hovhaness's evidently meditative, cosmological approach to this symphony.

Although critics and audiences were seldom hostile to his music, Hovhaness depended on self-promotion: in 1965 he founded his own record label (Poseidon Records), as well as his own publishing firm (Fujihara Music Company), which published almost all his music from the late 1970s forward, including most of the last 35 symphonies; he also enjoyed the support of more "off-beat" orchestras like the Louisville Orchestra and the Seattle Symphony. In Seattle he found an organization that, inspired by its locale in the Pacific Northwest, was in tune with his aesthetic of naturalism and independence of spirit. In a post-minimalist world, and with the popularity of environmental composers like John Luther Adams, it is also possible that Hovhaness's works, visionary as they are—in all senses of the word—will enjoy a newfound respect.

David Diamond

Like Leonard Bernstein and William Schuman, David Diamond (1915–2005) belonged to the group of younger composers mentored by Aaron Copland and based in New York City. However, Diamond began his musical training at the Cleveland Institute of Music with André de Ribaupierre, a famous violin pedagogue, before moving on to the Eastman School and then to the New School of Music in New York, where he studied with Roger Sessions and Paul Boepple. Like Copland, Virgil Thomson, Schuman, and many other American composers during the interwar period, Diamond spent much time in Europe. Supported by an Elfrida Whiteman Scholarship and the first of three Guggenheim Fellowships, Diamond was able to study with Nadia Boulanger in Paris and to meet Maurice Ravel (his favorite composer), Darius Milhaud, and Albert Roussel.[192]

Diamond shared the left-leaning convictions of the New York composers. Schuman largely kept his political beliefs to himself, but Diamond and Bernstein were vocal enough to invite government scrutiny. In 1956, while performing in the pit orchestra for Bernstein's *Candide* (a coded critique of McCarthyism and America's Cold War jingoism), Diamond was called to testify before the House Committee on Un-American Activities, as Copland had been. Close friends from the 1940s, Bernstein and Diamond's relationship extended beyond political affinity, as the two shared some romantic sentiment (although apparently no physical relationship).[193] Bernstein would champion Diamond's works during his directorship of the New York Philharmonic.

Both because of his dislike of McCarthy's America and his desire (shared with Roger Sessions) to look beyond America's musical scene, Diamond spent a considerable portion of his career abroad. Despite his political stances, he managed to secure government support. In 1951 he was awarded a one-year Fulbright professorship at the University of Rome, after which he was signed to an exclusive contract by Peermusic Classical, an independent publisher specializing in contemporary music, and this enabled him to move the next year to Florence, where he lived until 1965. He returned to the United States only briefly—during his mother's final illness in 1956 (when he had the unfortunate encounter with HUAC), and to assume the Slee professorship at the University of Buffalo in 1961 and 1963. Diamond returned to a "revival" of his music and to high-profile teaching positions at the Manhattan School of Music (1966–67) and the Juilliard School of Music (1973–86). He also held several composer-in-residence positions, including with the Seattle Symphony Orchestra (like Hovhaness) and a fellowship at the American Academy in Rome (1971). He continued to teach at Juilliard even after his retirement, only giving up his studio in 1997.

Diamond resisted categorization throughout his career. Many of his early (pre-1950) works—including the first four symphonies—tend to employ tonal or modal language, with widely voiced triads that some hear as American; a number of compositions are also "consciously French in style," influenced by Ravel and Satie.[194] Diamond favored symphonies of two or three movements built with clear and simple structures—modified sonata forms, scherzos and trios, large-scale binary and ternary forms—although his expansive lyricism sometimes means a movement will sprawl. Canons, fugal passages, and other imitative textures are common; according to Mary Wallace Davidson, these have much to do with Diamond's desire to be comprehensible to an audience.[195] A tendency toward syncopation and other forms of rhythmic displacement gives the early symphonies a feeling of exuberance that, when taken together with his largely diatonic harmonic choices, contributes to the perception of Diamond as "American" (table 6.5).

Diamond's orchestra leans heavily on the brass section in various configurations for a sense of boldness, but he is equally capable of sensitive writing for the strings and occasionally turns toward thinner textures. His close attention to timbre sometimes yields surprising combinations of instruments in smaller, chamber-like ensembles. For example, the choice to add a solo trumpet obbligato to a violin melody in Movements I and II of the First Symphony points to the brilliant orchestrations to come. Likewise, adding trumpet to the woodwind choir (instead of horn) as he does in the second movement yields a striking and altogether individual sound. Schuman, too, was fond of separating the orchestra into choirs, but no listener could confuse their two timbral profiles.

Scholars like Davidson and Victoria Kimberling have tended to hear the melodic, harmonic, and formal approaches in Diamond's early works as a variant of French Neoclassicism. Virgil Thomson, on the other hand, considered him "neo-Romantic."[196] Either way, the focus is on his lyricism, which became increasingly chromatic through the 1950s and '60s. What Thomson heard as Romanticism, including some expressive chromaticism, would eventually turn toward a dissonance that others would identify as Schoenbergian. Diamond would not call his music twelve-tone but, as the analysis of the Eighth Symphony below will show, he

Table 6.5 The Symphonies of David Diamond (1915–2005)

Title	Movements	Instrumentation	Comments
Symphony No. 1 (1940–41)	1. Allegro moderato con energia 4/4 (246 mm.) 2. Andante maestoso 4/4 (114 mm.) 3. Maestoso—Adagio—Allegro vivo 3/4 (218 mm.)	Grand plus Flt. (doubling Picc.), EH, Bclar, Cbssn., Tpt, Tuba, Perc. (Tubular bells, BD, Cym.)	Dedicated to Katherine Anne Porter. First performance: December 21, 1941, by the New York Philharmonic Symphony Society, conducted by Dimitri Mitropoulos. Score published by Southern Music Publishing Co. (Peer), 1969.
Symphony No. 2 (1942–43)	1. Adagio funèbre 4/4 (231 mm.) 2. Allegro vivo 3/4 (479 mm.) 3. Andante espressivo quasi Adagio 3/4 (225 mm.) 4. Allegro vigoroso 4/4 (327 mm.)	Grand plus Flt. (doubling Picc.), EH, Bclar, Cbssn., Tpt, Tuba, Perc. (Glsp., Xylo., SD, Tri., BD, Cym., Deep Gong)	First performance: October 22, 1944, by the Boston Symphony Orchestra, conducted by Serge Koussevitzky. Holograph score published by Southern Music Publishing Co. (Peer), 1978.
Symphony No. 3 (1945)	1. Allegro deciso 4/4 (334 mm.) 2. Andante 6/8 (106 mm.) → 3. Allegro vivo 4/4 (218 mm.) 4. Adagio assai 4/4 (77 mm.)	Grand plus Flt. (doubling Picc.), EH, Bclar, Cbssn., 2 Tpt., Tuba, Perc. (Xylo., Tri., Cym., SD, Tenor Drum, BD), Harp, Pno.	"To my Mother and Father." First performance: November 3, 1950, by the Boston Symphony Orchestra, conducted by Charles Munch. Holograph score published by Southern Music Publishing Co. (Peer), 1969.
Symphony No. 4 (1945)	1. Allegretto ¢ (170 mm.) 2. Adagio 3/4 (93 mm.) 3. Allegro 4/4 (230 mm.)	Grand plus 2 Flt., 2 Ob., 2 Clar., 2 Bssn., 2 Hr., Tpt, Tuba, Xylo., 2 Harps, Pno. Reduced version available: 1 Flt., 1 Ob., 1 Clar., 1 Bssn, all else same	Diamond originally provided a program (later withdrawn) by which the symphony reflected philosopher Gustav Fechner's ideas about the cycle of life and death. Commissioned by the Koussevitzky Music Foundation. Dedicated to the memory of Natalie Koussevitzky. First performance: January 23, 1948, by the Boston Symphony Orchestra, conducted by Leonard Bernstein. Reduced orchestra version published by G. Schirmer, 1949.

Table 6.5 *continued*

Title	Movements	Instrumentation	Comments
Symphony No. 5 for Large Orchestra (1951–64)	1. Adagio (3/4)—Allegro energico (6/4) (325 mm.) 2. Andante—Fuga: Allegretto ℓ (230 mm.)	Grand plus Picc., EH, E♭ Clar., Cbssn., Tpt., D Tpt., Tuba, Timp., Perc. (SD, Tenor Drum, Xylo., Glsp., Cym.), Pno., Org.	Begun in 1951 but finished after completing the Eighth Symphony. Dedicated to Leonard Bernstein. First performance: April 28, 1966, by the New York Philharmonic, conducted by Bernstein. Score published by Southern Music Publishing Co. (Peer), 1968.
Symphony No. 6 (1954)	1. Introduzione: Adagio—Allegro, fortemente mosso 3/4 (273 mm.) 2. Adagio 3/4 (132 mm.) 3. Deciso; poco Allegro 3/4 (227 mm.)	Grand plus Picc., EH, E♭ Clar., Bclar., Cbssn., Tpt., Tuba, Timp., Perc. (BD, Chimes, Glsp., Tam-tam, Suspended Cym., Tenor Drum, Xylo., Gavel, Snap), Pno.	"To Charles Münch and the Boston Symphony." First performance: March 8, 1957, by the Boston Symphony Orchestra, conducted by Charles Munch.[1] Score published by Harms, 1955.
Symphony No. 7 (1959)	1. Andante—Allegro ma non troppo 4/4 (173 mm.) 2. Andante 4/4 (101 mm.) 3. Allegro moderato 4/4 (228 mm.)	Grand plus Picc., EH, Bclar., Cbssn., Tpt., D Tpt., Perc. (SD, Tenor Drum, BD, Gong, Xylo., 2 Cym., Suspended Cym.), Harp, Pno.	Dedicated to Ciro Cuomo. First performance: January 26, 1962, by the Philadelphia Orchestra, conducted by Eugene Ormandy. Score published by Southern Music Publishing Co. (Peer), 1963.
Symphony No. 8 for Large Orchestra (1960)	1. Moderato—Adagio—Allegro vivo 4/4 (448 mm.) 2. Theme (Adagio)—Variations—Double Fugue 3/4 (345 mm.)	Grand plus Picc., EH, E♭ Clar., Bclar., Cbssn., D Tpt., F Tpt., Tuba, Perc. (SD, Tenor Drum, BD, Xylo, Vbp., Glsp., Tri., Gong, Cym.), Harp, Pno.	Dedicated to Aaron Copland for his 60th birthday. First performance: October 27, 1961, by the New York Philharmonic, conducted by Leonard Bernstein. Score published by Southern Music Publishing Co. (Peer), 1964.

Work	Movements	Instrumentation	Notes
To Music: Choral Symphony (1967)	1. Invocation to Music: Allegro agitato 4/4 (131 mm.) 2. Symphonic Affirmation 3. Dedication: Adagio con grand' espressione 3/4 (150 mm.)	Grand + Picc., EH, E♭ Picc. Clar., A Clar., Bclar., Picc., D. Tpt., Tuba, Perc. (BD, SD, Tenor Drum, Cym., Large Gong, Tri., Gavel, Wood Block, Xyl., Glsp.), Harp, Pno. Tenor and Baritone Soloists, SATB Chorus	First movement sets a poem by John Masefield and the third a poem by Henry Wadsworth Longfellow (the second movement is an orchestral interlude). Commissioned by the Thorne Music Fund for a work for soloists, chorus, and orchestra to celebrate the Golden Anniversary of the Manhattan School of Music. Dedicated to Ann and Francis Thorne. First performance: January 31, 1970, for the dedication of the John C. Borden Auditorium, by the orchestra of the Manhattan School of Music, conducted by the composer. Vocal score (first and third movements only) published by Southern Music Publishing Co. (Peer), 1969.
Symphony No. 9 (1977–85)	Two movements	Grand + Baritone soloist	Dedicated to the memory of Dimitri Mitropoulos. Texts by Michelangelo. First performance: November 17, 1985, by the American Composer Orchestra (David Arnold, baritone), conducted by Leonard Bernstein. Unpublished.
Symphony No. 10 (1985–2000)	Four movements	Grand plus Org.	Finished after completing Symphony No. 11. First performance: July 1, 2000, by the Seattle Symphony, conducted by Gerard Schwarz (Caroll Terry, organ), as part of a week-long dedication of the Watjen organ in the Seattle Symphony's Benaroya Hall. Unpublished.

Table 6.5 *continued*

Title	Movements	Instrumentation	Comments
Symphony No. 11 (1989–91)	1. Moderato ma deciso; Allegro moderato 3/4 (308 mm.) 2. Adagio assai e molto cantabile 4/4 (167 mm.) 3. Allegro scherzoso all burla 2/4 (192 mm.) 4. Allegro moderato; Più mosso 2/4 (1129 mm.)	Grand plus Flt. (Flt. 2 and 3 doubling Picc. 1 and 2), EH, E♭ Clar., Bclar., Cbssn., Picc. Tpt., Bass Tpt., Tpt., Tuba, Timp., Perc. (Tenor Drum, SD, BD, Cym., Antique Cym., Glsp., Xylo., Tamb., Gong, Tri., Tubular Bells), Pno. (doubling Cel.), Harp.	Commissioned by the Philharmonic Symphony Society of New York for its 150th anniversary. First performance: December 3, 1992, by the New York Philharmonic, conducted by Kurt Masur. Holograph score published by Peer (Hal Leonard), 2016. Holograph of Adagio movement also published separately by Peer, 2001.

1. The Alsatian conductor was born with the name Münch, but he generally omitted the umlaut during his years in the United States. Both spellings are common.

engaged more with the process than he would admit.[197] His approach is free enough: it hardly resembles Sessions's twelve-tone symphonies, let alone the works of the Second Viennese School (except perhaps Berg) or postwar serialists like Milton Babbitt. Still, the turn toward a more dissonant harmonic vocabulary meant that audiences who had enjoyed his earlier works did not confer the same favor on those of the 1960s. Some critics responded coldly as well, despite the heralded "revival" of his music after his long absence from the United States.

FIRST, SECOND, AND THIRD SYMPHONIES

Written between 1941 and 1945, his first four symphonies show Diamond under the influence of Copland, Harris, and Thomson amid the vogue for a particular kind of modern Americana: robust and rhythmically vital, both rural and urban in its landscapes, neotonal, and often populist in its implied politics. He completed the Symphony No. 1 (1941) during a residence at the Artist's Colony at Yaddo, a personal haunt of Copland's. Perhaps unsurprisingly, this is the Diamond symphony that most resembles Copland, who was emerging as the acknowledged father figure of the following generation. The work was premiered by the New York Philharmonic on December 21, 1941, under Dimitri Mitropoulos. It, together with his String Quartet No. 1, won Diamond the Prix de Rome in 1941. It also received a nomination for the first New York Music Critic's Circle Award, which ultimately went to Schuman's Third Symphony. Reviewer Noel Straus called the symphony "ultramodern"—a misnomer by today's understanding of the term—and oddly remarked on its "jagged" melodic outlines (the Adagio is quite lyrical, though perhaps his description is accurate enough for the first and third movements). Still, Straus captures something of the resonance between Diamond's early symphonies and those of his contemporaries in that "all of its three movements were propelled by an extraordinary muscularity"—*muscularity*, *vigor*, and *strength* being terms frequently applied to Harris and Schuman.[198] On the other hand, the wide-ranging (rather than "jagged") lyricism and diatonic or modal harmonies betray the influence of Copland.

Diamond's focus on melody crystallized in the Second Symphony (1942), even as his Allegro movements continued to display propulsive energy. Thomson first applied the label "neo-Romantic" to Diamond in reviewing this symphony, which he praised for its lyricism and "elegance."[199] The warm, string-dominated writing, most apparent in the first and third movements, is perhaps what inspired Thomson's description. It is reasonable to attribute the first movement (Adagio *funèbre*) to the traumas of World War II, but the *marcia funèbre* was also a Romantic trope to which Diamond returned in other works. Some of the stridency in the first movement seems reminiscent of Shostakovich while the orchestration of the second movement (Allegro vivo) echoes Schuman's tendency to write for instrumental choirs. Diamond's lyricism, however, is smoother than either of theirs.

The turbulence of the second-movement Scherzo is balanced by the lush yet plaintive third movement (Andante espressivo, quasi adagio). Had Diamond ended the symphony here, it would have made a fitting bookend to the first movement, for they are roughly of equal length and, where the opening is uniformly somber, the third movement at times transcends its sadness with sonorous brass chorales, shining chord streams in the strings, and soaring lines for solo trumpet and colla parte violins. Instead, in keeping with his Neoclassic roots and the tradition of the common-practice symphony, he ends with a raucous dance that can easily be heard as a bit of Coplandesque Americana: the same syncopated rhythmic vitality, evocations of fiddling, and folksy lyricism typical of *Rodeo* or *Appalachian Spring* are on display here.

The premiere on October 22, 1944, with the Boston Symphony Orchestra under Serge Koussevitzky was warmly received by a wartime audience eager for more music in the vital and distinctly American vein Diamond and others were mining. The Boston critics, however, thought the work prolix.[200] The same could be said of the last movement of Symphony No. 1: following an expansive second movement, its prefatory Maestoso and Adagio sections delay the onset of the Finale perhaps a bit too long.

Diamond completed both his Third and Fourth Symphonies in 1945 and they share quite similar stylistic profiles. Still neotonal, both reach at times toward highly chromatic and even twelve-tone vocabulary, albeit in subtle and often unnoticed ways (the themes remain dependent on triads). Much about both symphonies hews to Thomson's "neo-Romantic" ideal as well as to the exuberance and "muscularity" of his first two symphonies. Diamond's own commentary reveals an awareness of twelve-tone method: "two 'motival' themes link together the entire symphony cyclically, appearing in their disguised forms (transposition, retrograde, etc.) completely or in fragments" (see example 6.7).[201] The Third Symphony did not premiere until November 3, 1950, with Charles Munch and the Boston Symphony Orchestra.

Example 6.7 Diamond, Symphony No. 3, "motival themes"

In the Third Symphony, an ostinato for timpani, low strings, and piano—used for its percussive force rather than harmonic capabilities—drives much of the first movement. The brass lead for much of the movement with syncopated punches and bravura lines. The second movement features Diamond's melodic sensitivity: the presentation of the modal melody in flute (rather low in its range), with pointillistic accompaniment from piano and harp, is remarkable and rather Neoclassic in its clarity of texture. In contrast, the lush lines of the central section are more Romantic in their timbre and expressive register. Details of orchestration—like the combination of divisi strings with alternating harp and piano (mm. 44–59) or the quintet of oboe, clarinet, bass clarinet, bassoon, and harp at m. 65—are part of what make Diamond's slow movements hypnotic. Furthering the effect of this Andante is the structure of simple imitative passages that have the mesmerizing character of a round. Diamond had achieved this effect with greater economy in his best-loved work, *Rounds for String Orchestra* (1944), which Mitropoulos, Koussevitzky, Bernstein, Copland, and Thomson all admired.

The Scherzo returns to Diamond's more exuberant tone and has a propulsive rhythm and degree of open space reminiscent of the Finale of the Second Symphony. The opening of the Finale, Adagio assai, moves through a triad, making the cyclical structure (based on the "motival themes") perfectly clear to the audience. The orchestration for violas, outlined by harp, is yet another brilliant timbral turn. This Finale can be heard either as restful or meandering;

whichever way, it denies the general character of a "Koussevitzky Finale," but that is perhaps to be expected for a symphony written during the last days of World War II.

SYMPHONY NO. 4

While the Third Symphony is, overall, comparatively more Neoclassic, Thomson's "neo-Romantic" label seems apt for the Fourth Symphony (1945). Again Diamond employs classical forms, but with an emphasis on the development sections (particularly in the first movement) that recalls Beethoven. This trait, when combined with his usual sensitive and openly emotional melodic writing, as well as the use of tropes such as the *marcia funèbre*, brings this work closer to Romantic sensibilities than his previous symphonies. But the solemnity is not purely for historicist purposes: the Fourth Symphony was commissioned by Koussevitzky Music Foundation and dedicated "to the memory of Natalie Koussevitzky—*Magni Nominis Umbra*" ("the shadow of a great name"; it is not clear whether the "great name" denotes her or her husband). Koussevitzky was to conduct the premiere with the Boston Symphony Orchestra, but he became ill and Bernstein took the podium on January 22, 1948. Given the latter's commitment to tonality as a central compositional principle, one can see in the Fourth Symphony why he embraced Diamond's music.

The first movement follows a clear sonata form with the standard tonal procedures. Diamond's capacity for long-lined melodic writing is apparent in P, the first half of which (Pa) appears in the clarinet, bass clarinet, violin 2, and cello and is clearly in A minor. The accompaniment of falling minor triads in the first clarinet, harps, first violin, and viola reinforces the tonal sense of the movement. Pb begins in m. 15 in the violin and viola sections and is accompanied by what Diamond calls a "cortège-like" rhythm in the bassoons; both the smooth, mostly stepwise melody and its supporting rhythm reappear throughout the movement, sometimes separately. After a brief T (mm. 23–31) the solo oboe presents S in dotted rhythms (mm. 32–47) over a pizzicato walking bass in the lower strings; at first the sprightliness of the tune might seem at odds with the D-minor tonality and the relatively solemn six-part horn chorale that accompanies it (mm. 36–47), but it works somehow as a sober but not lugubrious sort of march.

The development begins with a reappearance of the cortège rhythm in the trumpets (m. 47) and explores fragmentations and transformations of both P and S. There is a false recapitulation at m. 105, in which the bass clarinet, bassoons, and low strings present Pa over the cortège rhythm in trumpets and trombones while S appears in the flutes and oboes joined by clarinets. This counterpoint between P and S builds throughout the whole orchestra before reaching a climax in m. 131 with the appearance of the falling minor triads of the opening in the upper woodwinds and strings, juxtaposed with the cortège rhythm in the trumpets and P in the horns. The true recapitulation occurs after the decrescendo that dissolves this climax (m. 136), with the entrance of P in solo trumpet at ***mp*** and its original accompaniment of falling triads in clarinets, bassoons, and harps, all at their original pitch level. S is heard in the brief codetta (mm. 155–70), first in solo flute and bassoon over chorale-like strings, then with the flute continuing over the cortège rhythm in bassoons; thus, all the significant material—P, S, and funereal rhythm—returns to the initial pitch level and (roughly) the original instrumentation.

The second movement takes the part form often found in interior slow movements of Romantic symphonies, though its language has more in common with Neoclassic practice. There are clear pitch centers but functionality is blurred, as opposed to the focused tonality of the first movement. The opening melody of the introduction—a chorale-like passage for brass and bassoons, could be in either G major or B minor, and that modal ambiguity characterizes the rest of the movement. As the introduction comes to a close with a woodwind chorale, what Diamond calls the exposition (Andante con moto, m. 12) offers F as its central pitch. Much of the "cantilena melody" (*1A*) that begins in the violas in measure 16 seems to unfold in F minor, although functionality is difficult to hear (beyond the clear articulation of C as a secondary pitch), and the section closes with a Phrygian cadence (mm. 34–35). *2A* begins in three clarinets, followed by the violins; strings and winds then fragment the theme and elaborate it contrapuntally through closely overlapping partial statements of both halves, sometimes only a measure apart.

This development leads eventually to a reprise of *1A* (beginning with its third note) laid on top of a chorale texture for the whole orchestra (m. 59). A transitional section follows this sonorous climax as the English horn and first violins spin out another statement of *2A* (mm. 65–71). As the coda begins (Tempo dell' Andante, mm. 72–93), three clarinets intone the chorale theme that began the movement, in a manner that closely mimics the sound of the organ (mm. 72–76); four trumpets elaborate in their own chorus. The shift from a darker, hollow woodwind timbre to brighter sounds (kept restrained with the ***p*** dynamic and the indication *espressivo supplichevole*) continues on to harps and piano as strings maintain the chorale. Two final scalar fragments in the solo oboe and clarinet drift upward from A to E and B to F-sharp over a D-A-B sonority in the strings, strongly implying B minor but without the sense of a functional conclusion. The ending is nonetheless peaceful and an emotional foil to the boisterous Finale that follows.

Combining properties of sonata form and rondo, the refrain of the last movement bursts forth from the horns, trombones, and bassoons at the outset, joined by trumpets in the second measure; perhaps it is the brashness of this theme—enhanced by its staccato repetitions, syncopated punctuations, and sixteenth-note accompaniment that alternately repeats notes and oscillates on a half step—that led Diamond to state that the movement has an "American feeling." Further, when played by the lower strings in mm. 2–3, this material sounds quite like rural fiddling, an effect the composer had honed in the Second and Third Symphonies. Points of contrast appear through chorales for brass (mm. 31–34), woodwinds (mm. 50–52), and strings (mm. 80–83).

B (mm. 38–82) begins with a melody in the flute and violins that is more lyrical in character, though built out of the stepwise motion prominent in *A*. The violins introduce truly contrasting material in m. 47 that yields to more triadic transformations of the theme in mm. 53 and 67. The more plainspoken melodies here—in contrast to the long-line melodies of the Boulangerie in the second movement—as well as the pluralistic range of styles and thematic material might have represented a further "American" element to Diamond. After a return of *A* (mm. 83–98), *C* strips down the texture to percussion, harps, piano, and low strings before introducing a new theme, striking with its broader triplet rhythms (mm. 99–180). This section also manipulates thematic material and accompaniment figures of *A* and *B*, in the manner of a development. A presentation of the refrain in the timpani introduces the final *A* (mm. 181–233), which also incorporates *B* and *C* (mm. 186, 208); the propulsive material from the beginning of the work remains dominant in the manner of a rousing rondo finish.

Although Diamond later disavowed it, a program lies behind this symphony and arguably explains some of his compositional choices. In m. 56 of the Finale, for example, he introduces a quick rhythmic patter in the tenor drum that he calls "a Mercury-like, sometimes elfish intrusion." The figure reappears in m. 62 in the timpani and m. 66 in tenor drum, before going silent for most of *B* (except for a brief muttering in m. 82). When the "elf" is heard in the snare drum in m. 156, it heralds the return to *A*, at which point its entrances come closer and closer together, helping to propel the work toward its hectic finish. As Diamond put it, "What seemed earthbound at the start of the movement, at the end is released." The movement concludes in something like A major, replete with Diamond's trademark widely spaced triads during the windup for a strident unison "yip" on A. In the shift from A minor to A major, the symphony traces the "tragic to triumphant" outline familiar from Beethoven's symphonies onward.

According to Diamond, the darkness-to-light trajectory in this symphony reflected the philosophy of Gustav Fechner (1801–1887), who argued that death was another form of birth.[202] Thus, one can locate the "cortège-like" rhythm and other funereal ideas in the first movement, the meditative chorale and supplicating cantilena of the second movement, and the vigorous "rebirth" of A minor as A major in the Finale, within a particular conceptual—and unabashedly Romantic—context. Fechner's work was available to American readers from 1904 when Mary C. Wadsworth's English translation of the *Büchlein vom Leben nach dem Tode* (*The Little Book of Life after Death*, 1836) was published with a foreword from noted American philosopher William James. This program also makes sense in the context of the Koussevitzky commission and its required dedication to Natalie, who had died in 1942. Whatever they might have thought of the program of the symphony, the unabashed theatricality and emotionalism of the work appealed to its first audiences.

Critical reception seems to have benefited from an energetic performance by Bernstein, although aesthetic evaluations were more divided. Writing in *Musical America*, Cecil Smith praised Diamond's concision but questioned the wisdom of the program: "Scarcely more than 20 minutes in length, the symphony achieves concentrated economy in the setting forth and evolving of its materials without destroying a sense of structural amplitude seldom achieved nowadays even in much longer works. . . . It is open to question whether Mr. Diamond helped matters by suggesting that the symphony deals successively with continual sleep, the alternation between sleeping and waking, and eternal waking. But at least this metaphysical description gives an impression of the seriousness of the music, which must be considered one of the most impressive American works in symphonic form."[203]

In the *Musical Courier*, Jules Wolffers devoted most of his time to praising Bernstein's work on the podium. The work he found much less impressive: "glib, clever and flashy, with effective treatment covering a multitude of musical platitudes." Wolffers, too, was frustrated by the vagueness of the program. He responded to Diamond's caveat-cum-invitation ("More than this I cannot interpret for the listener. The rest he must ask of himself") with sarcasm: "I, for one, refuse to ask of myself."[204] One can see why Diamond ultimately withdrew the program.

Ironically, the work likely appealed to Bernstein because of its theatricality, which found a counterpart in his own symphonies. Moreover, the heroic finish was a trait common to what Bernstein called a symphony "in the Koussevitzky manner"; although he would shortly abandon the style himself with his own deliberately anticlimactic Symphony No. 2, he retained an affection for Diamond's most Neoromantic symphony.[205] Bernstein programmed the Fourth Symphony on his inaugural 1957–58 season with the New York Philharmonic as part of what would be an ongoing advocacy for American composers, with Diamond a special favorite. He also recorded the work with the ensemble, praising Diamond from the liner notes: "His music restates, in his own terms, the most lasting aesthetic values."[206]

SYMPHONIES 5, 6, AND 7

The Fifth Symphony, which Diamond began in 1951 but finished in 1964 (after the Eighth Symphony), spans a shift in his style away from the obvious Neoclassic influence of Copland and his circle toward a more highly chromatic vocabulary. The Sixth, Seventh, and Eighth Symphonies continue in this vein, but the Fifth awkwardly straddles the distance between this new chromatic, even twelve-tone, language and an eventual return to elements of his earlier style. Although not explicitly twelve-tone, the astringent Sixth Symphony (1954) nonetheless bore the burden of critics' distaste for serialism in their symphonies. Writing for the *New Yorker*, Winthrop Sargeant painted Diamond with the same brush that he had Sessions: "It is a style that is apparently looked upon with favor by the small but powerful group of composer-politicians who are in control. . . . It is also, I am afraid, a style that is rapidly reducing the art of symphonic composition to the status of an unimportant and irresponsible little private hobby."[207]

He went on to declare that the Sixth Symphony is "not only not a symphony: it is not, even by the most generous definition, music." Although Sargeant tended toward the conservative, Kimberling aptly summarizes the rest of the reviews when she says they "criticized the work for being noisy, artificial and lacking originality" (for his part, Diamond considered it his most "mature and dramatic" work yet).[208] The Seventh Symphony hardly fared any better. Composed nearly side by side in 1959 and 1960, respectively, the Symphonies Nos. 7 and 8 share a similar scope and highly chromatic vocabulary. We will focus on the latter.

SYMPHONY NO. 8

Diamond composed the two-movement Eighth Symphony (1960) toward the end of his residency in Florence, Italy. Although he had intended to have the work ready earlier, he finished the Eighth Symphony one day after Aaron Copland's sixtieth birthday, on November 15, 1960, and dedicated the work to him. It was fittingly premiered by his fellow Copland devotee Bernstein and the New York Philharmonic on October 27, 1961. Bernstein presented Diamond's symphony with Satie's *Parade*, Fauré's Ballade for Piano and Orchestra in F-sharp Major, Op. 19 and Saint-Saëns's Piano Concerto No. 4 in C Minor, Op. 44 as part of a series of concerts he called "The Gallic Approach." Bernstein was certainly thinking of Diamond's earlier works, rather than the quasi-serialist symphonies he had written in Italy, but Diamond always held an affection for French music and his time in Paris. Edward Downes's program notes for the premiere mention Stravinsky as the most prominent composer to "assimilate the Gallic approach," and Stravinsky's evolution makes for an apt comparison here, as Diamond likewise had absorbed both French Neoclassicism and the twelve-tone technique.

The first movement begins with a tutti fanfare con forza that states five notes of the chromatic scale; its rhythmic nature is contradicted in the second measure with the entrance of a lyrical clarinet solo that completes the rest of the aggregate. The rhythmic profile and melodic contour of the clarinet's pattern is then rephrased as the beginning of a twelve-tone row in the solo horn (m. 4) that repositions the opening five notes of the fanfare as the last five of the row. The overall cast of the melody is sensitive and perhaps yearning. The row itself has what Downes described as "a strongly tonal feeling."[209] Given Diamond's admission that Berg served as his serialist role model, using a row with tonal implications makes sense.[210] Not unlike the row of Berg's Violin Concerto (1935), which unfolds at first as a series of ascending thirds, Diamond's opens with a descending third and goes on to emphasize the fourth and fifth: [F-D-G-C-A-G#-B-F#-E-D#-A#-C#]. (See example 6.8 for the horn row.) The rising perfect fourth between G and C is adapted at the end of the introduction in the low strings and timpani (mm. 19–22) in a gesture that strongly connotes a V-I cadence.

Example 6.8 Diamond, Symphony No. 8, mvt. 1, twelve-tone row in solo horn in F (mm. 4–8)

According to Diamond, the movement takes on a "extended free sonata-allegro structure" with the exposition beginning in measure 23 as the tempo shifts from Moderato to Allegro vivo. The P^{11} version of the row (beginning on E) appears in the woodwinds and piano with occasional coloration from trumpets, xylophone, and violins. In this iteration the row takes a jaunty, syncopated character, proper for a sonata-form P in the tradition of Haydn and Mozart. After a brief transition (mm. 43–45), a solo clarinet presents the lyrical S, accompanied by pizzicato strings, which works its way through a triad and then a minor seventh. Its overall contour is the inverse of P. The string accompaniment combines fragments of the row before revealing a nearly complete statement in the violas (now arco) beginning in measure 63. The string section presents a freely contrapuntal passage that bears an intervallic similarity to the rows both of P and of S (mm. 70–84). The horns join the counterpoint in m. 74, and eventually woodwinds and the trumpets enter to bring S to an *allargando* culmination in mm. 85–86. The fanfare of m. 1—that is, the final pentachord of the row—reappears in m. 87, initiating K.

The lengthy development proves worthy of a post-Beethovenian symphony, perhaps showing the composer's continued preference for the Neoromantic despite his radical shift toward the atonal. It begins in m. 104 with a statement of the row in its P^{11} form, mimicking the presentation of P in the tonic that often heralds the development in a classic-era symphonic sonata form. As Downes points out, Diamond will subject the row to fragmentation, sequence, and other traditional manipulative strategies—another instance of Diamond blurring the boundaries between serial and tonal techniques.[211]

Diamond eschews a traditional recapitulation in favor of interweaving fragments of P and S. There is, however, a full presentation of the P row, buried in the tutti passage, which contributes to a sense of culmination (meno mosso, mm. 353–78). (See example 6.9: first violin line, mm. 353–58.) Both P and S are technically atonal while keeping a strong tonal cast. The resulting melodic language is highly chromatic but not overwhelmingly dissonant and, when combined with sonata-form procedures, is as coherent and expressive as it is unabashedly modern.

Example 6.9 Diamond, Symphony No. 8, mvt. 1, twelve-tone row in violin 1 mm. 353–358

The second movement combines serialist and other post-tonal languages with preclassic procedures in a move reminiscent of Stravinsky's works from the 1950s like the *Canticum sacrum* (1955). Formally, it consists of a theme and variations (mm. 1–198) followed by a double fugue (mm. 199–332) and codetta (mm. 333–345). The theme, presented in the first violin (m. 3) is 40 measures long—a post-tonal *Fortspinnung*—and all the variations are continuous. Though the melody is necessarily quite repetitious (see the serial principle of nonrepetition), it features some of the same intervals as the twelve-tone row of I/P, particularly at its opening where it falls in a similar contour and at roughly the same pitch level (see example 6.10: violin 1 melody mm. 3–9). Diamond's writing here for the strings is as warm as in any of his other symphonies, proving that, as with Stravinsky, serial language could be compatible with a variety of styles.

Example 6.10 Diamond, Symphony No. 8, mvt. 2, violin 1 melody, mm. 3–9 (compare pitches E, C#, F#, and B in mm. 4-6 with beginning of I/P, Ex. 6.9)

The first variation takes the form of a serene but stately canon at the octave between the first violins and the cellos (one measure behind). The rest of the strings as well as oboes, clarinets, and bass clarinet provide two-note accompanimental gestures that alternately rise and fall through intervals common to the theme: descending and rising thirds, falling fifths and fourths, and rising and falling half steps. The winds continue this gentle accompaniment as rhythmically agitated thematic material migrates from violas (m. 64) to solo flute (m. 65), bassoon (m. 67), and E-flat clarinet (m. 71). The imitative entrances continue but the strictness of the canon eventually breaks down.

Variations 2 and 3, bridged by a piccolo solo, form a pair that follows a single trajectory toward a ***fff*** tutti statement (mm. 87–90). Variation 4 momentarily winds down the energy accumulated over the course of the preceding variations. Diamond presents the theme in Webernian *Klangfarbenmelodie* among the woodwinds and strings; the second half of the variation builds up the energy again. Variation 5 features antiphonal statements between choirs of woodwinds, strings, and brass, with the sharper sound of the brass section often serving as punctuation. This variation generates a tension gradually released in a series of ***p*** and ***pp*** woodwind and horn solos over a contrapuntal string texture (mm. 130–35).

In a surprising turn, Variation 6 creates an ethereal atmosphere reminiscent of Bartók's "night music." Rolled extended tertian chords from the harp and piano, the use of harmonics in the strings, and the soft dynamics seem a world away from the rest of the movement, which abounds in dry attacks, contrapuntal tension, and rhythmic intensity. The quiet horn section, sounding *a lontano*, precedes a call-and-answer between solo horn and piccolo trumpet. All take place over slowly unspooling counterpoint in the strings. Variation 7 (m. 161) recapitulates the canon of the first variation in a move plausibly drawn from earlier mergers of variations with sonata and other forms, as in the Finale of Brahms's Fourth Symphony. This final variation builds to a highly contrapuntal tutti climax in m. 194 that proceeds directly into the fugue (m. 199).

The first subject of this double fugue is the twelve-tone row from the first movement, this time given a marchlike cast in *alla breve* time. The quasi-martial character is reinforced by the scoring for trumpets (and violin 2) with punctuation from the timpani. Whether Diamond is thinking of it, the combination of stile antico counterpoint with a military topic would not be out of place in the finale of a classic symphony. The fugal entrances occur about two measures apart; the second voice, in horns and violas, enters with a pickup to m. 201, and the cellos come in on the second beat of the next measure. Recalling the *Klangfarben* passages of Variation 4, the statements of the subject do not always finish in the same "voice" that they begin. The second subject emerges at **mp** in the wake of a boisterous tutti statement of a fragment of the first subject in mm. 224–25. What this sonic exuviation reveals is a melody in the first violin that transforms *I/S*. (See example 6.11: vln. 1 melody in m. 225–35.) The second violin follows with a positively tonal entrance a fourth up (m. 229) with a countermelody in the cellos.

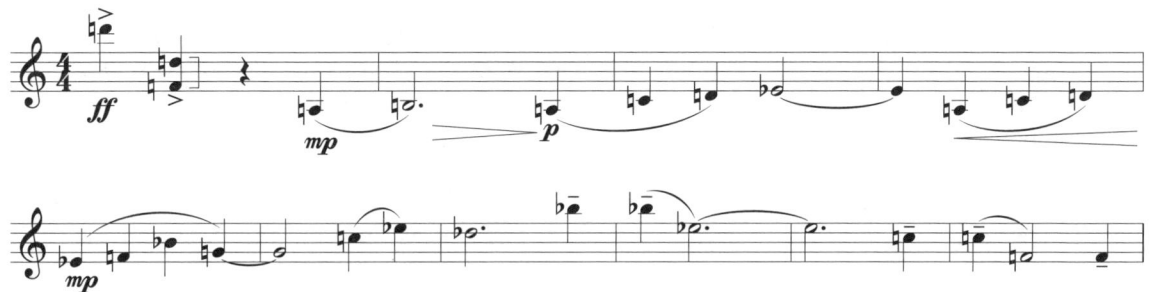

Example 6.11 Diamond, Symphony No. 8, mvt. 2, violin 1 melody, m. 225–235

Throughout this impressive contrapuntal display, Diamond runs the gamut of fugal techniques—inversion, stretto, fragmentation—while also recalling thematic material from the first movement. A brief codetta (mm. 333–45) recalls the fanfare of the first movement before rushing to a blazing finish on a polychord that implies either G or A-flat as a center—a gesture characteristic of much of Diamond's earlier, more strongly tonal or modal writing. The symphony is remarkable for its cyclical integration and economy of material, as well as the ability to blend twelve-tone technique with expressive melodic writing and organizational principles from the tonal tradition. In many ways the Eighth Symphony epitomizes Diamond's symphonic writing up through the 1960s, while the Fifth Symphony, begun before Symphonies Nos. 6–8 but finished four years after the Eighth, is more of a return to an earlier style.

The 1965 premiere heralded what Richard D. Freed would call the "rediscovery" of Diamond's music.[212] Robert Sabin revealed in *Musical America* that he "awaited its premiere with gloomy forebodings, since I have heartily disliked nearly all of Mr. Diamond's output during the past decade or so." However, "[a] delightful surprise awaited me. The work held me first note to last. It seemed inspired, coherent, fascinatingly knit and altogether compelling. It is strongly contrapuntal. The two massive movements are interrelated through the use of a 12-tone row, but the treatment is very free and tonal centers are constantly established. In the variations and double fugue of the second movement, Mr. Diamond's life-long devotion to classic forms bears rich fruit. They are both masterly in design and completely original in style. Mr. Bernstein conducted the work as if he had written it."[213]

But skeptics remained. Harold C. Schonberg wrote tersely in the *New York Times*: "The work is in two movements; runs about thirty minutes; is dissonant; busy; complicated; highly rhythmic; melodically dry; has twelve-tone aspects; snarling brasses; makes plenty of noise; has a slow movement with determinedly melodic figurations that sound more calculated than natural. Routine modernism, with everything evolved from everything else. That is, it starts with a tone row and the row forms the basis of the entire work. What else? Plenty of energy coupled to almost a total lack of charm or relaxation: neuroticism unreined."[214]

Bernstein, too, seemed to prefer the Fifth Symphony, "his finest and most concentrated symphonic work to date. But even more important, I find it to be a work that revives one's hopes for the symphonic form."[215] Dedicated to Bernstein, the Fifth—said by Diamond to be inspired by the ancient play *Oedipus Rex*—was slightly less dissonant and retained the tonal vocabulary, sensitive orchestration, and the melodic flair for which Diamond had earlier been known. Looking back, the composer regarded it as one of his "favorite works . . . [with] the most perfect fugue I ever wrote for an orchestral work."[216] Together, the Eighth and Fifth Symphonies constitute, if not an apotheosis, at least a turning point. Regardless of fluctuations in individual opinion, Diamond was now recognized as an indisputably significant American composer.

SYMPHONIES 9, 10, AND 11

In 1967 Diamond received a commission from the Thorne Music Fund for a work for soloists, chorus, and orchestra to celebrate the golden anniversary of the Manhattan School of Music.[217] That commission yielded the Choral Symphony, which Diamond did not include among his numbered symphonies; indeed, the work is really more of an oratorio, based on Masefield's poem "To Music" in the first movement and Henry Wadsworth Longfellow's "Dedication" in the third, with an orchestral interlude as the second movement. The work was performed on January 31, 1970, at the dedication concert of the John C. Borden Auditorium at the Manhattan School, with the composer conducting.[218]

The Ninth Symphony (1985)—premiered by the American Composers Orchestra under Bernstein—had almost as torturous a gestation as the Fifth Symphony, again perhaps because of its dedication to the memory of a man important to Diamond: Dimitri Mitropoulos. Between 1977 and 1979 he tried to finish the work but did not do so until 1985.[219] Scored for baritone and orchestra, it returns somewhat to the Neoromantic attitude of Diamond's early style, while keeping his later chromatic vocabulary—the typical procedure for works written from the 1970s on. According to Bernard Holland, at its premiere, "the dark, baritonal, deeply Romantic quality from a large assembly of instruments" was received "warmly" by the audience.[220] Based on texts by Michelangelo, the symphony unfolds a transcendent narrative not unlike that of the discarded program of the Fourth Symphony. The first half of the work is "turbulent and roiled" as Michelangelo rages against the slow ruin of old age, whereas the second half is "calmer, more welcoming, sometimes funny, sinking finally into a hoarseness and then sleep."[221] It is hard not to read this work as a meditation by the 70-year-old composer (and the 67-year-old conductor, for that matter) on his own mortality through the medium of what amounts to a Mahlerian orchestral song cycle. Gustav Mahler was far more Bernstein's bailiwick than Diamond's, but the latter's characteristic lyricism serves the texts well.[222]

The Symphony No. 10, begun in 1985, was finished in 2000, after the Symphony No. 11, making Diamond the only composer featured in this chapter to have completed a symphony in the twenty-first century. The Tenth Symphony is also, like Paul Creston's Symphony No. 6, a relatively rare symphony with organ. Premiered by the Seattle Symphony, with Gerard Schwarz conducting, in July 2000, the symphony served as part of a week-long dedication of the newly installed Watjen Organ in the two-year-old Benaroya Hall. Like Saint-Saëns, however, Diamond hardly wrote an "organ symphony" as such—the instrument in question does not appear until the scherzo-like third movement, where it is only present for a brief, scampering passage in counterpoint to the strings and brass. Virtuosic passages for the organ, however, intercut the whole of the Finale, contributing to its jubilant sound. Most often, however, the organ performs with the orchestra, whether in a chorale-like texture in combination with an orchestral "choir," in quick flurries of call-and-response, or in florid counterpoint. Overall, though, this was a deeply traditional symphony for the new millennium.

Commissioned for the one hundred fiftieth anniversary of the New York Philharmonic, and premiered under Kurt Masur, the Eleventh Symphony (1992) sprawls over four movements. One can still hear Diamond's natural lyricism in the second movement's elegy for strings. Alex Ross noted the intricacy of its structure, including the cyclical treatment of themes. The work is thoroughgoing and weighty. Ross's comparison to Bruckner is apt: "In the best tradition of Schubert and Bruckner, the structure is capped with a finale that throws out a superfluity of themes and goes on way too long. Mr. Diamond's familiar acerbic harmonies and terse lyricism held sway, giving the piece a somewhat antique sound throughout. But the confidence and conviction of the voice were unmistakable and, in the end, rather impressive."[223] Like many of the composers in this chapter, Diamond struggled against the hypermodernist headwinds of the midcentury, but he lived long enough that the developments of postmodernism, particularly the return to tonal vocabulary in minimalism, made for a much warmer welcome for his late works. Conductors, critics, and fellow composers continued to respect his symphonies, and, after his death, he was memorialized as an "intensely lyrical composer," the label that best suits his 11 symphonies.

Vincent Persichetti

Along with Peter Mennin and William Schuman, Vincent Persichetti (1915–87) exerted influence from the center of the Juilliard School. Schuman appointed him to the faculty in 1947, and he became head of the composition department in 1963 under Mennin's presidency. Persichetti had overseen theory and composition at the Philadelphia Conservatory (1941–47). Like Leonard Bernstein, Persichetti studied conducting with Fritz Reiner at the Curtis Institute and took lessons in piano with Olga Samaroff and in composition with Paul Nordoff at the Philadelphia Conservatory. A native of Philadelphia, he had begun studies in piano, organ, and double bass from the age of five. In both his compositions and his teaching, Persichetti kept an open attitude toward technique and style, even in the postwar era of sharp partisan

Table 6.6 The Symphonies of Vincent Persichetti (1915–87)

Title	Movements	Instrumentation	Comments
First Symphony, Op. 18 (1942)		Grand plus Ob., Bssn., Tpt., Tuba, BD	Performed once on October 21, 1947, at an informal concert of the Eastman-Rochester Symposium Orchestra, conducted by Howard Hanson. Withdrawn.
Second Symphony, Op. 19 (1942)		Grand plus Ob., Bssn., Pno.	Never performed; withdrawn.
Third Symphony, Op. 30 (1942–46)	1. Somber 4/4 (99 mm.) 2. Spirited 3/4 (372 mm.) 3. Singing 3/4 (174 mm.) 4. Fast and Brilliant 12/8 (325 mm.)	Grand plus Flt., Ob., Clar., Bssn., Tpt., Tuba, Perc. (SD, Cym., BD), Pno.	First performance: November 21, 1947, by the Philadelphia Orchestra, conducted by Eugene Ormandy. Score published by Elkan-Vogel (Theodore Presser), 2016.
Fourth Symphony, Op. 51 (1951)	1. Adagio—Allegro 4/4 (326 mm.) 2. Andante 2/4 (184 mm.) 3. Allegretto 3/4 (150 mm.) 4. Presto 2/4 (498 mm.)	Grand plus Flt., Ob., Clar., Tuba	First performance: December 17, 1954, by the Philadelphia Orchestra, conducted by Eugene Ormandy. Holograph score published by Elkan-Vogel, 1958.
Symphony for Strings in One Movement (Symphony No. 5), Op. 61 (1953)	In one movement 4/4 (695 mm.)	Strgs.	Commissioned by the Louisville Philharmonic Society. First performance: August 28, 1954, by the Louisville Symphony Orchestra, conducted by Robert Whitney. Holograph score published by Elkan-Vogel, 1955.

Work	Movements	Instrumentation	Notes
Symphony for Band (Symphony No. 6), Op. 69 (1956)	1. Adagio—Allegro 4/4 (292 mm.) 2. Adagio sostenuto 3/2 (57 mm.) 3. Allegretto 6/8 (126 mm.) 4. Vivace ¢ (297 mm.)	Wind ensemble: 2 Flt., Picc., 2 Ob., 3 Clar., E♭ Clar., Aclar., Bclar., 2 Bssn., 2 Asax., Tsax., Barsax., 4 Hrn., 2 Tpt., 3 Cor., 3 Trom., 2 Euph., Tuba, Timp., Perc. (2 Suspended Cym., 3 SD, Tamb., Tom-tom, Tri., BD, Tenor Drum, Sizzle Cym., Xylo.)	Commissioned by Washington University, St. Louis. First performance: April 16, 1956, by the Washington University Band, conducted by Clark Mitze at the MENC National Convention, St. Louis. Holograph score published by Elkan-Vogel, 1958.
Seventh Symphony, "Liturgical," Op. 80 (1958)	In one movement divided into five sections: Lento 4/4 (mm. 1–195) Allegro 2/4 (mm. 196–479) Andante 3/2 (mm. 480–585) Vivace ¢ (mm. 586–974) Adagio ¢ (mm. 975–1005)	Grand plus 2 Flt., Ob., 2 Clar., Bssn., Tpt., Tuba, Perc. (BD, Tenor Drum, Chimes, 3 SD, 2 Suspended Cym.)	Most of the thematic material is drawn from melodies in Persichetti's *Hymns and Responses for the Church Year*. Commissioned by the St. Louis Symphony Society for its eightieth anniversary in 1959. First performance: October 24, 1959, by the St. Louis Symphony Orchestra conducted by Edouard van Remoortel. Holograph score published by Elkan-Vogel, 1959.
Eighth Symphony, Op. 106 (1967)	1. Adagio—Allegro grazioso 4/4 (484 mm.) 2. Andante sostenuto 4/4 (92 mm.) 3. Allegretto 3/4 (232 mm.) 4. Vivace 2/4 (540 mm.)	Grand plus Flt., Ob., Clar., Tuba, Perc. (BD, SD, Tenor Drum, Sizzle Cym., Suspended Cym.), Harp	Commissioned by Baldwin-Wallace Conservatory. First performance: October 29, 1967, by the Baldwin-Wallace Orchestra, conducted by George Poinar. Holograph score published by Elkan-Vogel, 1967.
Sinfonia: Janiculum (Symphony No. 9), Op. 113 (1970)	In one movement, four sections (Misterioso—Allegro articolato—Cantabile—Vivace) 4/4 (452 mm.)	Grand plus EH, E♭ Clar., Bclar., Cbssn., Tpt., Tuba, Perc. (Timbales, SD, Suspended Cym., Tam-tam, Tenor Drum, BD with head up, Glsp., Xylo., Chimes), Harp	Composed while in Rome on a Guggenheim Fellowship; stayed at the Villa Aurelia (site of the American Academy in Rome), on top of the Janiculum hill. Work supposedly inspired not only by the landscape but by the figure of the two-faced Janus and a meditation on life's questions inspired by the god. Commissioned by the Hilsberg Estate for the Philadelphia Orchestra. First performance: March 5, 1971, by the Philadelphia Orchestra, conducted by Eugene Ormandy. Holograph score published by Elkan-Vogel, 1972.

divides between aesthetic camps. His *Twentieth Century Harmony* (1961) covers all the techniques available to composers in the mid-twentieth century from traditional counterpoint to twelve-tone serialism and various neotonal approaches. Persichetti considered the sum of these advances the new "common practice" for twentieth-century composers.[224] Just as his compositions reflect his comprehensive knowledge of the most recent and historical repertoires, so also the profiles of his students—from Philip Glass or Steve Reich to Lowell Liebermann and Leo Brouwer—reflect his advocacy of stylistic diversity.

Persichetti's ecumenicism perhaps most resembles Bernstein's. So, less happily, did his critical reception, as reviewers generally found his music derivative—skillfully and intelligently made, but little more than a patchwork of others' languages. Walter Simmons notes the influence of Stravinsky, Bartók, Hindemith, Harris, and Copland, channeled through "an almost childlike sense of mischief and a pervasive geniality of spirit, reveling in the joy of pure, abstract creativity while remaining in full control of whatever dynamic conflicts may be present within the music."[225] Persichetti's harmony can utilize twelve-tone techniques adroitly but tends above all toward Neoclassicism with a preference for pandiatonic, quartal, and polytonal harmonies unfolding in contrapuntal textures. He often cast large sections or even whole movements of a work in a lively, syncopated duple meter—a stylistic trademark that Simmons labels the "Persichetti 2/4."[226]

Persichetti composed in a wide range of genres: while best known for keyboard music—sonatas, sonatinas, and pedagogical pieces for organ, harpsichord, and especially piano—as well as for band compositions, he wrote nine symphonies throughout his career. The two most famous, the Fifth and Sixth, are for specialized ensembles (strings and winds, respectively), while the others employ the full orchestra, with a sizable percussion battery in the last three symphonies. Although he spent most of his career in New York City, the Philadelphia-born Persichetti kept a connection to his hometown through his relationship with Eugene Ormandy and the Philadelphia Orchestra: Symphonies Nos. 3, 4, and 9 all premiered there under Ormandy's baton (table 6.6).

THE FIRST FOUR SYMPHONIES

Persichetti wrote his first two symphonies in 1942 and they remain unpublished. The Symphony No. 1 was heard only once, in 1947, in an informal reading by the Eastman-Rochester Symposium, with Howard Hanson conducting. The Symphony No. 2 was never performed, although Persichetti did play it at the piano for Roy Harris, with whom he briefly studied in 1943; its apparently modest dimensions prompted Harris to make the memorable (if not especially enlightening) remark that "a symphony should be like a billboard!"[227] According to the composer's wife, Dorothea, Persichetti planned to rescore the symphony for chamber orchestra, but it is not known if he ever did.[228]

Persichetti began his Symphony No. 3 (1946) in the same year as these two ill-fated works, but its destiny proved much happier. As his first symphony written after his lessons with Harris, this work reflects the older composer's influence in what Simmons calls its "large-boned, assertive grandeur."[229] In addition, while Persichetti's composition consists of four separate movements, they bear emotionally generic titles that recall those of the sections of Harris's Third Symphony. The first, *Somber*, is full of pathos, beginning with a stark fanfare for percussion and brass, followed by tortured chromatic lines in the strings and muttering woodwinds. The intervals of a contrasting theme seem derived from the *Dies irae*, first heard clearly in the horn section. A mournful trumpet solo (based on the opening melody of the strings) takes up the central portion of the movement and adds a martial tone to the prevailing melancholy, proper to Persichetti's description of the work as a "war symphony."[230]

The second movement, *Spirited*, features the piano prominently (as does the Finale), and the pastoral melody, woodwind solos, and lightly scored strings fit the character of a Scherzo. As Simmons notes, the pandiatonic harmony here (in contrast to the dense chromaticism of the first movement) nods in the direction of Copland.[231] The third movement, *Singing*, opens with an English horn solo over luminous muted strings, one of the most striking examples of Persichetti's prowess in orchestration; it is neatly bookended by the quiet coda at the end of the movement, with an oboe solo against a similar background. The movement builds to what Simmons calls a "climax of considerable strength," although the strident orchestration for percussion and brass makes it seem like more of an interruption than a continuation of the gentler dissonances in the contrapuntal web of strings and woodwinds.[232]

The *Fast and Brilliant* Finale moves to a "triumphant peroration" in its return to the martial overtones of the first movement, and this resonates with works of Harris and Schuman from the time.[233] However, certain facets of the orchestration, as well as the return of the *Dies irae*–like motive of the first movement combined with the prevailing demonic energy, recall the "Dream of a Witches' Sabbath" from Hector Berlioz's *Symphonie fantastique* (1830). Whole families of instruments are on display, with brilliant solos passing from clarinet to bass clarinet, or from contrabassoon back up to bassoon. Persichetti employs extended techniques and a range of articulations, and the enlarged percussion section figures prominently, including fleet solos for piano and timpani. Simmons refers to this symphony as an "isolated work of heroic virility" that has more in common with the music of Schuman and other contemporaries than it does with the rest of his own output.[234] At the same time, Persichetti builds the work with the finely honed counterpoint and orchestration found in his later symphonies.

Although its 1947 premiere with the Philadelphia Orchestra under Eugene Ormandy received a warm audience response, reviewers reacted tepidly, and the Third Symphony has received few performances. The critics reacted with like ambivalence to the Fourth Symphony (1951), although in this case a high-quality recording that followed shortly after (again with the Philadelphia Orchestra and Ormandy) helped the work's long-term reputation.

Whereas Simmons hears the legacy of Persichetti's teacher Harris in the Third, he finds the Fourth a mature work attesting to a "far more individual compositional persona."[235] When taken together, these two symphonies illustrate the contrasting "graceful" and "gritty" characters Persichetti identified in his musical personality.[236] While the Third Symphony featured some of his densest and most dissonant writing, in the Fourth Persichetti clarifies his harmonic language. It suggests a Neoclassicism reminiscent of Haydn and Mozart and points the way to the symphonies to follow. In terms of form, the Fourth hews closely to Viennese models, with a sonata-allegro first movement, rondo Andante, an Allegretto intermezzo, and a Presto Finale, with its "brilliant whirlwind" of perpetual motion and recall of most of the thematic material from the rest of the work.[237] The character of each movement—whether the gentleness of the Andante or the playfulness of the Allegro—plus the more triadic tonal language could all be called "graceful." Over the course of his first decade of symphonic compositions, as shown by the Third and Fourth Symphonies, Persichetti worked out crucial matters of technique and explored the emotional spectrum possible in the genre, finding his own voice by the beginning of the 1950s. As with the Third Symphony, reviewers received the Fourth Symphony with apathy: Olin Downes and others found fault with what Simmons hears as "straightforward, unpretentious" musical intentions.[238]

Katherine Baber

SYMPHONY NO. 5 FOR STRINGS

As a pair, the Symphony No. 5 for String Orchestra and the Symphony No. 6 for Band broadly represent Persichetti's style and reflect midcentury trends in commissioning symphonic works. The Louisville Philharmonic Society commissioned and premiered the Fifth Symphony under Robert Whitney on August 28, 1954. Aided by a $500,000 grant from the Rockefeller Foundation, the Louisville Philharmonic Orchestra embarked upon an ambitious series of commissions, many of which were then recorded by the orchestra's record label First Edition Recordings, founded in 1947 and the first of its kind. Persichetti's symphony thus benefited from the collusion of a new form of corporate sponsorship and philanthropy in conjunction with the expansion of the American symphonic world beyond the Boston–New York–Philadelphia axis.

The Symphony No. 5 gives full evidence of Persichetti's eclectic language, as well as his awareness of contemporaneous models both in medium (string symphony) and structure (single-movement work).[239] According to the composer's liner note for the recording, the work divided into five continuous sections, although Dorothea Persichetti's own analysis argued for six.[240] Like Schuman, Diamond, and Bernstein, Persichetti sought to infuse aspects of twelve-tone language into his otherwise non-serial writing: the opening viola theme demonstrates this merger, as it includes all the chromatic tones; the rest of the work evolves out of this thematic material. Two motifs provide the developmental impetus: the falling seventh followed by an ascending tritone (*a*) and the falling third (*b*) (mm. 1–2, 4–5 in example 6.12).[241] Persichetti's thematic material leans both toward the tonal tradition, with the minor and major thirds, and away from it, with the major and minor sevenths obscuring any notion of a single tonal center. The presence of the tritone also guarantees a certain degree of dissonance.

Example 6.12 Persichetti, Symphony No. 5, viola theme (mm. 1–19)

Forgotten Modernisms

In terms of character, the theme clearly reflects the doloroso and *fervente* markings Persichetti assigns it (the same could be said for the rest of the first section as a whole). As the violas reach their peak on C, the cellos and double basses join with **ff** chords that punctuate the line (m. 16) and then growl their way down to a sustained E/F♯ (m. 20); over this the violins enter in the altissimo with a melody derived from the viola theme (m. 21). The rest of the orchestra produces "slashing contrapuntal lines" (Simmons) that eventually yield to a transition by the solo violin (mm. 26–28), joined by a solo second violin in a duet (mm. 29–33). This passage, marked *Piacevole* (m. 29), releases some of the tension and explores the *a* motif, at first in more serene counterpoint, then in a stretto passage (mm. 46–61). The stretto grows in agitation to an *intenso* statement by the whole orchestra in block chords that brings the first section to an emphatic close on a grinding dissonance—an extended tertian chord that encompasses both the major/minor thirds and major/minor sevenths of the opening theme (mm. 65–67; see example 6.13).

Example 6.13 Persichetti, Symphony No. 5, strings, mm. 65–67

The second section (mm. 68–245) expels this tension in a frenetic duple-meter passage, a typical "Persichetti 2/4," although the occasional tremolos and frequent repeated-note figures make for a more agitated version of this type. This section focuses on the *b* motif, in counterpoint with *a*, and features a con fuoco restatement of the opening theme (m. 198) now nearly unrecognizable for its transformation in character. Another transitional violin solo (mm. 234–51) bridges the second and third sections. Entering **mp** against the **fff** din in the rest of the strings, the soloist hovers serenely as fragmented statements of *a* peter out, leaving a brief *liberamente* measure for just the solo violin over a solo cello drone.

The third and fourth sections (mm. 247–315, 316–411) provide contrast with their relatively calm and diatonic character. The third begins with an Adagio serena in which Persichetti explores the tonal possibilities of the *a* motif, deemphasizing the tritone, and presents the *b* motif in a more melodic fashion. A passage for five solo strings (four violins and a viola; mm. 268–85) conjures the conversational sound of a string quartet, after which the Andante affettuoso (m. 239) introduces a comparatively sweet triadic melody with accompaniment. The Meno mosso (m. 305) unwinds even further, with a sparse texture of hesitant falling thirds and fourths, first in the cellos, then in a solo violin, answered with soft chords. This section ends with a Lento (mm. 312–15) that almost completely halts the forward motion of the piece with a ***ppp*** version of the triadic melody in a homophonic texture.

A third and final transition for solo violin begins the next section (m. 316), which features lucid *b*-derived counterpoint among four solo violins, two solo violas, and solo cello. Both *a* and *b* blend into the diatonic and chorale-like Tranquillo (m. 329). Persichetti marked the beginning of the fifth section at the Allegro agitato in m. 412, which begins with another "Persichetti 2/4."[242] This final section of the work returns to a darker atmosphere, by turns agitated, tense, and severe.[243] Despite the considerable harmonic ambiguity, however, the symphony rushes to a vigorous close in C major.

The Fifth Symphony is clearly neotonal in its harmonic structure and quite varied in terms of its stylistic profile and possible models. There are American predecessors like Harris and Schuman for the severe tone and single-movement form. Additionally, the amorphous interior structure and the scoring for strings alone harkens back to the earliest symphonies by Giovanni Battista Sammartini and others that predate the standardization of the structure.[244] Throughout the work, Persichetti explores the different timbres possible in a string orchestra, whether through range or through special effects like mutes and *senza vibrato* passages.

As we have seen, Persichetti's symphonies often received indifferent reviews, although audiences reacted favorably; along with Sessions and Mennin, Persichetti suffered from an "academic" reputation (their disparate styles notwithstanding). Three months after its August 1954 premiere, the Louisville Symphony Orchestra recorded the Fifth Symphony; that recording, as well as another performance in 1959 by Ormandy with the Philadelphia Orchestra, introduced the work to a wider audience. Arthur Berger, writing in the *Saturday Review*, equivocated: "What it lacks in stylistic distinction it makes up in vital musicianship. Persichetti is headed in the direction of the ranks of our best American composers."[245] After the Philadelphia performance, Max de Schaunsee noted the audience's favorable reaction to a work that was "remarkably serious" and "often beautiful and moving."[246]

SYMPHONY FOR BAND (SYMPHONY NO. 6)

While the Fifth Symphony arose as a traditional orchestral commission, the Symphony No. 6 demonstrates the rise of collegiate wind ensembles as sponsoring organizations (the final chapter will cover several more symphonies for wind ensemble). The Symphony No. 6 originated as a commission for an eight-minute work from Clark Mitze, director of bands at Washington University, St. Louis. After Persichetti informed Mitze that the short work had "gotten out of hand," both sides agreed on a symphony for band following along the line of Hindemith's Symphony in B-flat (1951). Mitze and his Washington University wind ensemble premiered the resulting four-movement work at the April 1956 meeting of the Music Educators National Conference (now the National Association for Music Education).

In contrast to its more experimental and neotonal predecessor, the Sixth Symphony is protoypically Neoclassic in structure and style. The first movement follows a loose sonata-allegro form, with its primary and secondary themes derived from gestures in the slow "Haydnesque" introduction.[247] As in the Fifth Symphony, those themes can be distilled to distinctive intervallic motifs: *a*, a falling fifth and a rising sixth in the horn; *b*, a stepwise ascent, then descent; and *c*, rising thirds. Motive *a* serves as a kind of fanfare to precede *b* (mm. 3–4 in the bass clarinet, bassoon, baritone saxophone, euphonium, and tuba), which will transform into *P* once the Allegro begins (mm. 25–33). The arpeggiation of motif *c* (mm. 8–9 in solo horn and mm. 16–17 in the brass section) provides the contrasting upward trajectory of *S* (appearing in mm. 74 and 90–93); the syncopated and jazzy demeanor of this *c*-based theme strongly contrasts with the *b*-derived *P*. Beginning in m. 120, the development works over *P* and *S* and then *P* again; for most of this section, the energy level is less than it was in the exposition. The thirty-second-note patter in the snare drum and timpani heard in the introduction serves to unify the work as sixteenth notes in the body of the sonata form; at the end, they help propel the movement to its *lunga* ending with an extended tertian sonority revolving around F.

The interior movements revisit the common forms and styles of classic symphonies. The Adagio sostentuto is a chorale based on the hymn "Round Me Falls the Night," which Persichetti borrowed from his own *Hymns and Responses for the Church Year*.[248] Given his thorough approach to counterpoint as an educator, Persichetti likely made himself familiar with earlier arrangements of the tune (also known as *Thuringia*) as a chorale by J. S. Bach and as an English anthem. Dividing the ensemble into various brass and wind choirs (as well as intriguing combinations thereof) again recalls a defining trait of William Schuman's symphonies. The modal harmony with a clear center on E also follows in the Neoclassical vein. The third movement is a simple intermezzo based on two contrasting ideas: a vaguely Celtic-sounding folk song set as a 6/8 gigue, first presented by solo clarinet with accompanying choir (mm. 1–8), and a 2/4 marchlike idea with a syncopated twist at its end (mm. 27–40), perhaps a foreshadowing of the "Persichetti 2/4" to come in the Finale. Although the movement is not a typical minuet or scherzo and trio, the first theme has the pastoral character of many trios and the march has something of the mischievousness of a scherzo.

The Finale summarizes many of Persichetti's distinctive traits. His tendencies toward formal cohesion and thoroughgoing development are on full display. He develops themes from each movement, including all three basic motifs laid out in the slow introduction of the first movement. The Neoclassic character of the whole is affirmed with a quick, somewhat hectic march cast in rondo form. This allegiance to the Viennese classical tradition sets Persichetti apart from the French-influenced Neoclassicism of the Boulangerie, as heard in the symphonies by Sessions, Diamond, and Bernstein. The orchestration and surprising changes in dynamics, on the other hand, resemble Schuman's brassy and percussive bravura. (Some of the latter is attributable to conductor Frederick Fennell, who persuaded Persichetti to give the percussion a larger role when he prepared the published version of the work in 1958.) At the same time, Persichetti has a lighter hand than Schuman: this work achieves an almost airy quality in the scoring, seldom using the tutti ensemble.

The reaction to the Symphony for Band (No. 6) followed a similar course to that of the Fifth. While the members of the MENC were enthusiastic and the work has had a long and frequent performance history among wind ensembles, critics had little positive to say after its New York premiere in August 1956, with Persichetti conducting the Goldman Band. Those comments that are favorable pay tribute more to Persichetti's reputation as a learned musician than to the thematic or emotional success of his music. Edward Downes called the work "inviting" and noted its contemporary feel with "jaunty rhythms not unrelated to jazz" and its "beguiling melodic flow" in the slow movement. He also praised Persichetti's skill at thematic development and orchestration.[249] The review in the *New York Herald Tribune*, however, was dismissive: "What its creator is trying to say is anybody's guess. And it is quite possible that he isn't trying to say anything special at all, but merely making what turned out to be fairly palatable music, which he apparently does easily enough."[250]

SYMPHONIES 7, 8, AND 9

Despite the lack of critical acclaim, Persichetti was still a widely respected composer who had no shortage of commissions and awards. He received three Guggenheim Fellowships as well as grants from the National Foundation on the Arts and the Humanities and the National Institute of Arts and Letters. Each of his last three symphonies resulted from commissions from performing or educational institutions.

The St. Louis Symphony Orchestra commissioned Persichetti's Seventh Symphony to mark its eightieth anniversary. The one-movement work in five continuous sections draws all its thematic material from 15 selections in *Hymns and Responses for the Church Year*; accordingly, Persichetti subtitled the symphony "Liturgical." Simmons praises its compositional virtuosity in motivic development and counterpoint as well as the effective treatment of modal and diatonic hymn sources in an essentially atonal context; Schuman's influence is particularly strong in its harmonic language (nontonal triads) and scoring ("chattering winds"). On the debit side, Simmons notes a somewhat detached character emotionally—a liability critics observed in his late symphonies in general.[251]

While the "Liturgical" Symphony has links to the Symphony for Strings, the Eighth, composed on a commission by Baldwin Wallace Conservatory in Ohio, returns to the Neoclassicism of Symphonies 4 and 6 while keeping the impersonal character of No. 7. Because of the latter, Simmons finds it one of Persichetti's less successful symphonies, as "the austerity of the harmonic language . . . seems at odds with its intended expressive effect."[252]

By contrast, the Ninth Symphony ranks as Persichetti's "most complex and challenging."[253] It resulted from a commission by the Philadelphia Orchestra for a work in memory of concertmaster Alexander Hilsberg. At the time, Persichetti was living in Rome on the second of his Guggenheim Fellowships; he stayed at the Villa Aurelia (now the site of the American Academy in Rome), on the summit of the Janiculum Hill, where he could hear the church bells of the city. The composer entitled the work *Sinfonia Janiculum*.

Annotator John Briggs argues for a philosophical interpretation of the symphony, by which it represents "a meditation in music on the meaning of existence"; the subtitle refers not only to Janiculum Hill but to its namesake, the Roman deity Janus, whose dual faces symbolize every aspect of life.[254] (It is not clear whether this interpretation is his or the composer's.) Like the "Liturgical" Symphony, the *Janiculum* is in a single movement, unfolding this time in four continuous sections; although the prevailing language is atonal, the symphony is anchored on E.

Sinfonia Janiculum premiered on March 5, 1971, with Eugene Ormandy conducting the Philadelphia Orchestra. As usual, the critical response was mixed: praised for craftsmanship, faulted for lacking expression. The same ensemble recorded the work later that year and released it on an LP with Schuman's "Le fosse ardeatine"—two American Ninth Symphonies similarly inspired by the Eternal City but from profoundly different motivations, as we have seen.[255]

In his position at the Juilliard School, Persichetti did as much to shape the sound of American composition as did his colleagues Schuman and Mennin, as heard in the stylistic diversity of his many students and in the continued usefulness of *Twentieth-Century Harmony* as a point of reference. Among the world of collegiate and professional wind ensembles, Persichetti is respected alongside Hindemith and Grainger for his contributions to the literature, not only in the Sixth Symphony but in other works as well, especially the *Divertimento* of 1950. If the rest of his symphonic works are perceived as less worthy now, perhaps that has more to do with modern attitudes toward the stylistic and critical currents of the midcentury than it does with Persichetti's skill or taste as a composer. Like many of the composers from this era, his music is due for reconsideration.

Leonard Bernstein

With only three symphonies to his credit, Leonard Bernstein (1918–90) is certainly not a prolific symphonist. However, he profoundly shaped the American symphonic world as a conductor, educator, and advocate. Bernstein famously boosted Gustav Mahler to a new prominence, starting with a cycle of all the symphonic works given during his first season as music director of the New York Philharmonic (1959–69; laureate conductor, 1969–90); he also programmed the symphonies of Carl Nielsen with relative frequency, fixing them in the ears and minds of American audiences and musicians. But, most importantly for our purposes, he continued the work that his mentor Serge Koussevitzky had begun in terms of promoting American symphonic works. Joseph Horowitz credits Bernstein with a "necessary corrective" to the Philharmonic's Eurocentric and somewhat conservative programming and highlights the ways in which his administrative decisions were part of a larger quest for identity—personal and national—a quest made possible through his "singular powers of advocacy" and "powers of inquiry."[256] In pursuing symphonic composition, despite his preference for theatrical works and mixed performing forces, Bernstein was essentially putting into action the progressive ideals that guided his programming and that he preached from the podium.

Over the course of the postwar decades, however, Bernstein seemed ambivalent about the fate of the symphony as a genre. His invocation of the phrase "Great American Symphony" was, in fact, quite pessimistic. He asserts in that essay, imagined as a dialogue between himself and (tellingly) a "Broadway Producer," that "Haydn and Mozart and Brahms surely didn't write their symphonies in a vacuum; their symphonies were expected of them. Nobody today really expects a symphony of anybody. Our American composers have an obligation to the theater, which is alive and which needs them."[257] Of course, Bernstein penned this essay during a period in which he was experiencing success as a theater composer, and to a certain extent his remarks on musical issues always bent toward his current projects. Although he did increasingly program American and twentieth-century symphonic works as a conductor, his ambivalence remained. Even after writing his own rather well-received Third Symphony, his remarks to the press in April 1965 on a series of twentieth-century symphonies echo his earlier estimation: "Symphonies would now seem to be sports of a kind, appearing intermittently, and evermore rarely. It also follows that the symphony orchestra, by the same token, would become a kind of museum of the past—if we regard the symphony orchestra as a natural externalization of this symphonic growth over a century and a half. It then follows that conductors would become curators, and the whole institution of symphonic concerts a phenomenon inevitably cut off from the mainstream of contemporary composition."²⁵⁸ Withholding a final opinion, he muses that it "seems to me natural and important that the New York Philharmonic should, at this mid-century point, cast a reflective look over the whole symphonic progress of our century, and give our thinking public a chance to decide for themselves the validity of this concept." By this time his own symphonies had already shown his ambivalence with the "symphonic concept," but by 1980 he was cautiously optimistic about the fate of the institution of the symphony orchestra and symphonic music, and he was willing to preserve the genre through performance of existing works as "museum" pieces; at the same time, he conceded that in moving forward, other forms would be vital:

> What, may I ask, is wrong with a museum—especially one in which we are dealing not with paintings and statues but with live bodies, great performing artists, breathing and recreating our priceless symphonic heritage, with a director who is no mere curator, but a veritable high priest in this sanctuary? Of *course* this symphonic *Gestalt* is a museum, and we should be proud and grateful for it. In other words, the so-called "symphony orchestra" has developed an added function, distinct from its identity as a museum, and that is to provide the fertile soil in which new kinds of orchestral music can be cultivated. And here is where the problems begin to come clear: this new rich area seems to demand different schedules, different approaches, even, at times, different personnel from those serving at the altar of Brahms.²⁵⁹

Bernstein was always a keen observer of musical culture, but by this point his attitude was relatively conservative compared to younger composers. He seems almost to be stepping out of the way of compositional evolution. Given his infamous tussle with the younger, forward-thinking Glenn Gould, and his evident distaste for modernist music from Anton Webern to Pierre Boulez, this is the most accepting one could expect him to be.

In terms of his personal conception of the symphonic form, Bernstein was highly idiosyncratic, though obviously influenced by his idols Beethoven and Mahler (table 6.7). Of the three, the Symphony No. 1 *Jeremiah* is the closest to any traditional notion of a symphonic work. The mezzo-soprano soloist in the final movement ("Lamentation") recalls Mahler's Fourth Symphony, which features a soprano soloist in the Finale ("Das himmlische Leben"); both movements were written as orchestral songs prior to the rest of the symphonic works that ultimately encompassed them. The Symphony No. 2 *The Age of Anxiety*, composed after the poem by W. H. Auden, is perhaps the most hybridized of the three, incorporating traits of the program symphony and symphonic poem, but featuring the pianist so centrally as to almost be a concerto. The Symphony No. 3 *Kaddish*, with its combination of vocal soloists, choral forces, and orchestra, might better be described as an oratorio, if not for the prominence of Beethoven's Ninth Symphony and Mahler's Second Symphony in Bernstein's musical world. He repeatedly conducted both works—Mahler's Second served as a go-to piece for significant occasions—and discussed them in his educational programs. Though it occurred well after the composition of his Third Symphony, Bernstein's performance of Beethoven's Ninth Symphony with British, Russian, German, French, and American musicians after the fall of the Berlin Wall in 1989 was a high-water mark in its ongoing performance history. His retexting of the "Ode to Joy" as the "Ode to Freedom" (swapping "Freude" for "Freiheit") further enshrined Schiller's text and Beethoven's melody in the modern political consciousness. The material for Bernstein's own choral symphony, however, was more personal than universal, as were the themes of the rest of his symphonic works.

All three of Bernstein's symphonies are programmatic—dealing with Jewish themes (either explicitly or by implication) or a more general search for faith—and rooted in song in some

Table 6.7 The Symphonies of Leonard Bernstein (1918–90)

Title	Movements	Instrumentation	Comments
Jeremiah: Symphony No. 1 (1942)	Three movements, played *attacca*. 1. Prophecy: Largamente 5/4 (90 mm.) 2. Profanation: Vivace con brio 6/8 (322 mm.) 3. Lamentation: Lento 3/4 (133 mm.)	Grand plus Flt. (doubling Picc.), EH, E♭ Clar. (doubling Bclar.), Cbssn., Tpt., Tuba, 3 Timp., Perc. (BD, Cym., SD, Tri., Wood Block, Maracas on Timp.), Pno. Mezzo-soprano solo	"For my Father." Source of text in Mvt. 3: verses, sung in Hebrew, from the Book of Lamentations, traditionally attributed to the prophet Jeremiah (1:1–3, 8; 4:14–15; 5:20–21). First performance: January 28, 1944, Syria Mosque, Pittsburgh, by the Pittsburgh Symphony Orchestra, conducted by the composer, with Jennie Tourel, mezzo-soprano. First New York performance on March 29, 1944, by the New York Philharmonic, again with Bernstein and Tourel. New York Music Critics' Circle Award, 1944. Score published by Boosey & Hawkes, 1943.
The Age of Anxiety, Symphony No. 2 for Piano and Orchestra (after W. H. Auden) (1949, rev. 1965)	Six movements grouped into two parts; movements within each part are played *attacca*. PART I 1. The Prologue C (mm. 1–21) 2. The Seven Ages (Variations I to VII) 3/2 C (mm. 22–267) 3. The Seven Stages (Variations VIII to XIV) 3/2 (mm. 268–631) PART II 4. The Dirge 3/2 (mm. 1–79) 5. The Masque 2/4 (12/16) (mm. 80–273) 6. The Epilogue 2/4 (mm. 274–372)	Grand plus Picc., EH, Bclar., Cbssn., Tpt., Tuba, 3 Timp., Perc. (BD, Cym., Suspended Cym., SD, Tenor Drum, Tri., Tam-tam, Glsp., Xylo., Chimes, Temple Blocks, Set), 2 Harp (Harp 2 optional), Cel. (doubling Pianino), Pno. solo	A symphonic meditation upon W. H. Auden's narrative poem *The Age of Anxiety*. Dedication: "For Serge Koussevitzky, in tribute" (the conductor was about to retire). First performance: April 8, 1949, by the Boston Symphony Orchestra, conducted by Koussevitzky, with Bernstein at the piano. Score published by G. Schirmer, 1950. The revised version (with changes primarily to the Epilogue) published by Boosey & Hawkes, 1993.

Table 6.7 continued

Title	Movements	Instrumentation	Comments
Kaddish: Symphony No. 3 (1963, rev. 1977)	Seven movements grouped into three parts, performed without pause. Movement I 1. Invocation 6/4 (mm. 1–29) 2. Kaddish 1 6/4 (mm. 30–169) Movement II 3. Din-Torah 6/4 (mm. 1–91) 4. Kaddish 2 5/8 (mm. 92–240) Movement III 5. Scherzo 3/4 (mm. 1–251) 6. Kaddish 3 3/4 (mm. 252–377) 7. Finale 6/4 (mm. 378–695)	Grand plus 2 Flt. (Flt. 3 doubles Aflt., Flt. 4 doubles Picc.), EH, E♭ Clar, Bclar., Cbssn., Tpt., Tuba, Asax, 6 Timp., Perc. (BD, Cym., SD, Tenor Drum, Field Drum, Tri., Tamb., Tam-tam, Glsp., Xylo., Vbp., Chimes, Crotales, Wood Block, Temple Block, Whip, Ratchet, Israeli Hand Drum, Sand Blocks, 3 Bongos, Rasp, 2 Suspended Cym., Finger Cym. Maracas, Maraca played on Timp.), Harp, Cel. (doubling Pno.). Speaker, Soprano soloist, SATB Chorus, Boys' Chorus	The Kaddish prayer is sung in Hebrew and Aramaic, while the spoken text (written by Bernstein) is in English. He originally conceived the speaker as a female role, but in 1977, as part of an extensive revision of both the music and the text, he recast the role for either a woman or a man. Commissioned by the Koussevitzky Music Foundation and the Boston Symphony Orchestra, in celebration of its 75th anniversary. Dedicated "to the beloved memory of John F. Kennedy," whose assassination occurred as Bernstein was orchestrating the Finale. First performance: December 10, 1963, in Tel Aviv, with the Israel Philharmonic Orchestra, conducted by Bernstein, with Hannah Rovina as speaker and Jennie Tourel as soprano soloist. First American performance: January 31, 1964, with the Boston Symphony Orchestra, conducted by Charles Munch, with Felicia Montealegre, speaker, and Jennie Tourel, soprano. Vocal score prepared by Abraham Kaplan and Ruth Mense, published by Amberson Enterprises (G. Schirmer), 1965. The revised score published by Boosey & Hawkes, 1985. With the approval of the Bernstein estate, Samuel Pisar created an alternate version of the text that focuses on the Holocaust (Pisar was a survivor), which premiered in 2003.

way. The first movement of the *Jeremiah* Symphony to take shape was the Finale, "Lamentation," which in the summer of 1939 Bernstein simply called a "Hebrew song." Then in 1942 the New England Conservatory hosted a competition, chaired by Serge Koussevitzky, that motivated Bernstein to complete the work by year's end, adding the first two movements, "Prophecy" and "Profanation." The "soul" of the symphony, though, is the song (transposed in its revision from soprano to mezzo-soprano), set to text from the Book of Lamentations by the prophet Jeremiah.

The Second Symphony, too, emerged from the drafting of a lamentation; he composed "The Dirge" (the beginning of the second movement) during a two-month stay in Israel in the fall of 1948, at a time in which the Israeli army was making territorial gains in the Negev Desert. Bernstein rushed to orchestrate the movement so that it could be performed at a fundraising concert marking the first anniversary of the UN partition resolution, which had divided Mandatory Palestine into Arab and Jewish territories after the end of British colonialism.[260] Bernstein borrowed his own blues song "Ain't Got No Tears" (cut from *On the Town*) for the "Masque," where it is more nostalgic than lamenting. Although it is not as explicitly biblical or Jewish as the other two symphonies, the program that took shape around the "Dirge"—based on Auden's long poem *The Age of Anxiety*—dealt with questions of identity and featured a character, Rosetta, who (to readers of the poem) was recognizably Jewish and recited at one point the "Sh'ma Yisrael" prayer. In his preface to the symphony Bernstein described the concluding "Epilogue" as a rediscovery of faith in the face of modern isolation and loneliness but does not allow that the symphonic program confirms that faith: "The way is open; but, at the conclusion, is still stretching long before him [the piano-protagonist]." Bernstein expressed as much ambivalence about symphonic programmaticism as he did about the symphonic genre overall, and he insisted that any pictorial similarities to Auden's poem were entirely "unconscious." At the same time, he conceded that "if the charge of 'theatricality' in a symphonic work is a valid one, I am willing to plead guilty. I have a suspicion that every work I write, for whatever medium, is really theater music in some way, and nothing has convinced me more than these new discoveries of the unconscious hand that has been at work all along in *The Age of Anxiety*."[261]

The Third Symphony embraces programmaticism with an implicit narrative arc for the speaker as she argues with God; the score includes extended passages of melodrama. Bernstein's affinity for song asserts itself as well, with the second recitation of the Kaddish prayer taking the form of a lullaby for the soprano soloist, similar in its emotional tone to the "Lamentation" of *Jeremiah*. Unlike the first two symphonies, however, the *Kaddish* Symphony seems to affirm faith, even if its tone is more defiant than hopeful. Certainly, Bernstein is embracing an overtly Jewish identity in this work, even as he continues to express himself, at least in part, with an American vocabulary.

In whatever genre he worked—or, more accurately, in whatever genre he chose to redefine—Bernstein was aggressively polystylistic in a way that prefigured part of the postmodern aesthetic. This tendency is perhaps most apparent in the symphonies, where historical and contemporary models crowd close. Along with all the prophets and father figures in the programs for these works, the influence of Aaron Copland is readily apparent in Bernstein's expansive melodic language and neotonal approach. In terms of harmonic ambiguity, one can also hear shades of Wagner and Debussy. Regarding gesture and orchestration, Shostakovich and Prokofiev are never far from the scene. Bernstein also explicitly compared his own use of American popular song and jazz styles to Gershwin—a connection reiterated in reviews of his

Second Symphony. The instrumentation for all three symphonies is rather large and features a diversity of percussion, with the most Mahlerian in scale being the Third Symphony. As with Mahler, though, the orchestration often features chamber ensembles alongside weightier configurations, and one is left with the impression that the goal of the larger orchestra was flexibility, particularly in terms of imitating a variety of popular and classical styles.

Listening across Bernstein's works in several genres, it becomes apparent that this stylistic range is often deployed in terms of meaningful associations: atonality, serialism, and other forms of modernism frequently stand for chaos or violence, whereas the blues and various jazz styles are invoked for a range of dramatic and political purposes.[262] References to Jewish liturgical music can be heard in many of Bernstein's works; some of these Jack Gottlieb has traced as "symbols of faith," and they are crucial to interpreting the three symphonies.[263] In conjunction with this stylistic play, however, Bernstein is also clearly concerned with formal unity, a point stressed in his writings from the collection of essays and television scripts in *The Joy of Music* to the Harvard lectures recorded in *The Unanswered Question*. Beethoven is most frequently invoked as the model for motivic and harmonic integration—the "must-ness" of each note within a larger scheme—principles Bernstein applies both to theatrical and symphonic works.[264] Throughout the theater works, Bernstein makes use of what Helen Smith calls "intervallic composition" and a range of contrapuntal techniques that serve to emphasize development, another of Bernstein's dearly held musical values.[265] Mahler seems another likely source for this intensity of motivic (self-)reference in Bernstein's symphonic works, whether within a single symphony or across multiple works. Finally, Bernstein was adamant about the value of tonality as an "innate" force of musical unity (however modernized or reconfigured), without which all meaning was lost. This is not to say that he did not write long stretches of atonal music, particularly in larger works like the Second and Third Symphonies, nor that he avoided twelve-tone organization—he did, in fact, use rows to organize multiple theatrical scenes and symphonic movements—but that the return to the tonal world was always necessary and, in the case of the symphonies, often a meaningful gesture within the context of an implied or explicit narrative.

JEREMIAH: SYMPHONY NO. 1

The *Jeremiah* Symphony was an early career success that helped to catapult Bernstein to national fame—one important facet of the public image of a *Wunderkind* conductor-composer. Premiered on January 28, 1944, by the Pittsburgh Symphony Orchestra under Bernstein's direction, the work was warmly received, although its reception was folded into the rising-star narrative prevalent after his conducting debut with the New York Philharmonic on November 13, 1943. Although Bernstein did not win the 1943 competition for which he had hastily completed the work, both Fritz Reiner and Koussevitzky admired it; according to Bernstein, the latter hailed the work as "great Jewish music."[266] Bernstein led the work with the Boston Symphony Orchestra three weeks later, and the critical reaction to both performances was favorable, apart from Virgil Thomson's skepticism: "It is not a masterpiece by any means, but it has solid orchestral qualities and a certain charm that should give it a temporary popularity."[267] Temporary or not, it received four more performances in March and April with the New York Philharmonic under Bernstein's baton and it won that year's New York Music Critic's Circle Award. The First Symphony remains one of Bernstein's most frequently performed orchestral works and is generally the most respected of his symphonies.

Jeremiah presents Bernstein much more clearly as a Jewish American than any of his other works of the period, and the dedication to his father, Samuel J. Bernstein, calls out its relationship to the composer's heritage. According to Bernstein: "The symphony does not make use to any great extent of actual Hebrew thematic material. The first theme of the scherzo is paraphrased from a traditional Hebrew chant, and the opening phrase of the vocal part in the 'Lamentation' is based on a liturgical cadence still sung today in commemoration of the destruction of Jerusalem by Babylon. Other remembrances of Hebrew liturgical music are a matter of emotional quality, rather than of the notes themselves."[268] Jack Gottlieb, however, has located references to several specific cantillation formulas and key motives that can be traced across many of Bernstein's other works: according to him, the opening of the first movement is derived from the *Amidah* ("standing" prayers) of the High Holy Day liturgy, a fixed benediction heard at all Sabbath or holiday services; along with the *Yigdal* hymn and the "Sh'ma Yisrael" prayer, it constitutes one of the most commonly heard combinations of words and music in Jewish congregations.[269] Bernstein noted, however, that "the first movement ('Prophecy') aims only to parallel in feeling the intensity of the prophet's pleas with his people." Although Gottlieb may have erred in calling it a quotation, then, the opening motive does have a recitational character, and it provides the material for the rest of the movement in a thematic working out that would be typical of the rest of Bernstein's symphonies (example 6.14). The prevalence of open fourths and fifths in the melodic lines and the breadth of rhythm also point toward Aaron Copland, whom Bernstein viewed as something of a musical prophet.[270]

Example 6.14 Bernstein, Symphony No. 1, mvt. 1, opening theme (mm. 1–4)

The Scherzo, "Profanation," was meant to "give a general sense of the destruction and chaos brought on by the pagan corruption within the priesthood and the people." Gottlieb finds material based on formulas for chanting the Torah, particularly the *Haftara* portion—motives well-known to Bernstein, as to any Jewish youth, from the Bar Mitzvah.[271] Again, the reference may not be as specific as Gottlieb assumes, but the character of the recitational formulas is easily called up by one as familiar with the tradition as Bernstein. The most salient feature of the second movement, however, is its jazz-derived rhythmic profile, which Bernstein and many listeners acknowledged. Here, it seems to stand for a worldly or pagan enthusiasm that leads to destruction. This sort of wild, multimeter dance would reappear many times in Bernstein's works, including the Third Symphony and *Mass*, where the implied pagan zeal is similar. In each of these cases, the asymmetries of Stravinsky's rhythms, particularly in *Rite of Spring* (also evoking a pagan ritual), are an obvious touchstone and one Bernstein would go on to discuss at length in his Charles Eliot Norton Lectures at Harvard (1973).

Bernstein allowed that the vocal third movement—a setting of Lamentations 1:1–3, 1:8, 4:14–15, and 5:20–21 (in the original Hebrew) for mezzo-soprano—was "a more literary conception": "It is the cry of Jeremiah, as he mourns his beloved Jerusalem, ruined, pillaged, and dishonored after his desperate efforts to save it." The prominent perfect fourths, present since the beginning of the work, still abound in the melodic contours, but by the end of the movement, the descending fourth of the opening horn call has been transmuted to a descending major sixth, which then descends stepwise to complete the octave. The symphony closes on an extended tertian sonority on E, resolving the tension between E and E-flat presented in the opening chords of the first movement. Given that Bernstein composed the last movement first, the way in which he managed harmonic and thematic unity is striking and, as it would turn out, typical of his symphonic writing.

The ambiguity of key is also characteristic of Gustav Mahler, whose *Das Lied von der Erde* served as a possible model for Bernstein. The idea of an orchestral song, to which Bernstein would return in his Third Symphony, clearly comes from Mahler's orchestral song cycles, as do some of the musical details. Bernstein was not yet a well-known conductor of Mahler's works, but his mentor, Bruno Walter, was the Austrian composer's protégé and had led the first (posthumous) performances of *Das Lied* and the Ninth Symphony. We can see points of inspiration in the declamatory vocal line—descended from Wagner, whose works Mahler had conducted—the instrumental lament in the middle of the movement, and the subdued epilogue for strings and winds. The latter two traits appear also in the final movement of *Das Lied von der Erde*, "Der Abschied" (Farewell)—also for mezzo-soprano—which resonates with Bernstein's "literary conception" of the movement as a "farewell" to Jerusalem.

THE AGE OF ANXIETY: SYMPHONY NO. 2 FOR PIANO AND ORCHESTRA (AFTER W. H. AUDEN)

Bernstein's Second Symphony (1949) engages in another exploration of identity and draws together several texts and experiences that he found meaningful. Among the inspirational fragments Bernstein assembles in this symphony, Auden's sprawling metaphysical poem is certainly one of the most significant. During the summer of 1947, Bernstein read *The Age of Anxiety*, which depicts an existential encounter between four individuals in New York City during wartime: Rosetta, Quant, Emble, and Malin, who represent Carl Jung's fourfold division of the psyche (Feeling, Intuition, Sensation, and Thought, respectively).[272] Malin and Rosetta also represent Christian and Jewish perspectives. Auden's narrative unfolds over the course of a single evening. The four individuals meet in a bar in The Prologue, converse in a series of metaphysical wanderings through The Seven Ages and The Seven Stages of Man, before departing in a taxi in The Dirge, heading to a party at Rosetta's apartment in The Masque, and then dispersing during The Epilogue. This "baroque eclogue"—which vacillates between English pastoral settings and urban American ones—is a psychological journey in which the four characters confront their own isolation. For both Auden and Bernstein, Hitler's Germany cast a long shadow over the postwar world, encapsulated in the notion of an age of anxiety.[273]

Bernstein's two-part symphony in six movements follows Auden's plan closely:

Part I:
The Prologue (Lento moderato)
The Seven Ages (Variations 1–7)
The Seven Stages (Variations 8–14)

Part II:
The Dirge (Largo)
The Masque (Extremely fast)
The Epilogue (Adagio; Andante; Con moto)

"The Prologue" opens with a "lonely improvisation by two clarinets" followed by a series of descending scales in the woodwinds that, according to Bernstein, "acts as a bridge into the realm of the unconscious." This first movement also constitutes one of the many chamber ensembles to appear throughout the symphony: just woodwinds, harp, timpani, piano, and low strings. In turn, the piano solo—which Bernstein characterizes as the "piano-protagonist," implying a first-person narrative as opposed to Auden's omniscient third person—bridges "The Prologue" and the following movements. To convey the metaphysical peregrinations of "The Seven Ages" and "The Seven Stages," he constructs two series of variations (14 in total). These variations feature what Gottlieb calls "melodic concatenation," in which, rather than superficially recasting the same theme in different contexts, every variation's subsequent theme evolves gradually from the preceding one.[274]

To mirror the physical and emotional journey of Part II, he elides the three final movements, as he did the Prologue and variations, though each movement contrasts quite strongly in terms of thematic context and mood. Throughout the symphony, character and emotional tone may shift dramatically, but there is no true ceasing of momentum other than the pause between the last of "The Seven Stages" and "The Dirge." The second half of the symphony begins, according to Bernstein, "in a harmonic way, [with] a twelve-tone row out which the main theme evolves." This gesture encompasses the aggregate but does not provide a serial organization for the work, as he would later do in the Third Symphony.

A contrasting section of "almost Brahmsian romanticism" follows this dense chromatic opening. Drafted first in Israel, "The Dirge" came to symbolize for Bernstein the mourning for the loss of the "'colossal Dad,' the great leader who can always give the right orders, find the right solution, shoulder the mass responsibility, and satisfy the universal need for a father-symbol." In retrospect, we can see Bernstein pondering narrative and emotional territory similar to that in the speaker's text in the Third Symphony. Various father figures are possible—Bernstein's own father, Franklin Delano Roosevelt, Koussevitzky, Copland (all of whom except Roosevelt were still living)—but the specifics matter less than the metaphorical language. It is also worth noting that Bernstein conceived "The Dirge" literally as "sung by the four as they sit in a cab en route to the girl's apartment." Even with no vocalist at hand, Bernstein is thinking in terms of song, or perhaps more generally in terms of a theatrical scene. He had, after all, written a number sung in a taxicab for *On the Town*, although the comedy of the scene and the brashness of the taxi driver, Hildy Esterhazy, are of a totally different mood than that in Auden's taxi ride.

The following "Masque" is also songful, derived from the blues number "Ain't Got No Tears" (accompanied by another chamber orchestra, including percussion configured to imitate trap set). Here again, Bernstein invokes jazz, this time a "fantastic piano-jazz" that is meant to sound "by turns nervous, sentimental, self-satisfied, vociferous"—one of many shades for this style of music in Bernstein's palette. Eventually, the music spins out of control (as it does in *Jeremiah*'s "Profanation") and "four bars of hectic jazz" mark the transition to "The Epilogue." While this passage shares some characteristics with Bernstein's earlier impressions of jazz piano improvisation, as in the ballet *Fancy Free* and musical *On the Town* (both from 1944)—an impression largely based on the language of stride piano and boogie-woogie—the profile here has more to do with the angular lines and off-kilter interjections of percussion found in the nascent bebop style. In the wake of this orchestral outburst, a pianino continues the piano-jazz of "The Masque," which continues to sound faintly into the beginning of the "The Epilogue." For Bernstein, this sonic exuviation effected "a kind of separation of the self from the guilt of escapist living," which allowed the protagonist "to examine what is left beneath the emptiness" in "The Epilogue."

As the music winds down, a trumpet solo states a motive built out of a descending perfect fourth (recalling "Prophecy"), a theme that Bernstein here calls "something pure" and eventually identifies as the "newly-recognized faith." This profoundly affective musical moment coincides with Rosetta's soliloquy and recitation of the Jewish prayer "Sh'ma Yisrael" in Auden's poem. Besides being an American symphony, then, *The Age of Anxiety* also addresses Jewish identity, whether geographic, religious, or cultural. The coincidence of this reading with the specifically American styles at play in the work, most significantly the jazz of "The Masque," suggests the search on a more personal level to define a Jewish American identity. Whether the search is successful is called into question by Bernstein's revision of the Finale. In the first version of "The Epilogue" Bernstein left the piano-protagonist behind to observe an extended orchestral meditation on the trumpet's theme, before joining perfunctorily with a single chord. In 1965, after the composition of the Third Symphony, he revised "The Epilogue" to include the pianist, giving the soloist a series of meditative cadenzas spread across the movement as well as a role in punctuating the final chord. The expanded role of the piano soloist in the revised version of the symphony holds out more hope for reconciliation between individual (the piano-protagonist) and community (the orchestra) than did the more open-ended finale of the 1949 version or the denouement of Auden's poem.

The Age of Anxiety premiered on April 8, 1949, with Bernstein as piano soloist and Koussevitzky conducting the Boston Symphony Orchestra. Bernstein dedicated the work to the conductor, with whom he had often corresponded during its composition. The first New York performance, with Bernstein conducting the New York Philharmonic, took place on February 23, 1950, with Lukas Foss as soloist (Bernstein had mentioned him in his notes during the composition of the work). The revised version premiered with the New York Philharmonic again on July 15, 1965. The initial reception of the work was less than enthusiastic, and many critics found the work derivative, reaffirming the assumption that composer-conductors like Bernstein and Mahler tended to be second-rate composers. According to Jules Wolffers of *The Jewish Advocate*, "The work has no originality of style—it is a composite of Mahler, Copland, Broadway, Hollywood, Schoenberg and the dive around the corner."[275] Others heard Rachmaninoff, Berlioz, and Liszt as well, and Virgil Thomson declared it a rehash of Strauss's *Death and Transfiguration* over which "floats an intangible shadow of Mahler."[276] A decade after its premiere, Russian audiences were described as "picking out passages . . . that reminded them of Gershwin, Shostakovich, and Prokofieff."[277] Hints of this bias would only become more prevalent, even in Bernstein's own remarks, the longer he remained a conductor. While the polystylism in this work is intense even by Bernstein's standards, it serves a narrative purpose—something that seems to have been missed in the critical reception.

The work has been revived in recent years and a few interesting scholarly interpretations have emerged. In David Schiller's analysis, the Symphony No. 2 is a more cryptic work than the other two symphonies, which we might attribute to its emergence from a transitional period: Schiller notes that Bernstein was "moving not only from city to city, but also from assimilation to Zionism."[278] Schiller also highlights the Jewish presence embodied in Rosetta and connects her monologue in the poem to Gottlieb's identification of a Tetragrammaton cipher in the score. Gottlieb asserts that Bernstein outlines the Hebrew letters for the name of God—YHVH—with the pitches D♭-A-D♭-A in the trumpet solo in mm. 13–19 of "The Epilogue."[279] Schiller understands the Jewish question in the Second Symphony to be quite literally encrypted and dependent on motivic symbols and corresponding Kabbalistic points of reference (Kabbalah is a mystic Jewish tradition). Schiller's focus on the interplay of Jewish liturgical music and theological concepts within the Western classical framework, as well as on the question of assimilation, is common in the field of Jewish music studies. However, the stylistic play of the work as a whole—in consonance with the program though not dependent on it—can still be interpreted as Jewish discourse even though the jazz of "The Masque" does not "sound Jewish."

On the other hand, the Symphony No. 2 was partially composed in the United States and premiered in an American context. And as often as Bernstein mentioned Israel during this period, he was usually speaking to Americans, whether Jewish or gentile. Even the prospect of writing a symphony seemed, in a fraught way, to be an American endeavor. Whether Bernstein intended to contribute to the Great American Symphony with this work is open to debate. Philip Gentry convincingly interprets this work as an ironic reversal of Copland's Popular Front musical rhetoric, and as an ironic engagement with the concept of the "Great American Symphony," which reflects the growing anxieties of the early McCarthy era by denying a triumphal finale.[280] One can also hear the work in conversation with Marc Blitzstein's *Airborne* Symphony (1946), which Bernstein premiered during his first season with the New York City Symphony Orchestra on April 1, 1946.[281] Blitzstein's symphony, which follows a three-part program in 12 sections, may have given Bernstein the permission to let *The Age of Anxiety* sprawl in a similar way. Like all three of the symphonies, *The Age of Anxiety* is inescapably, although not exclusively, American.

KADDISH: SYMPHONY NO. 3

In a fitting turn that brought Bernstein back to his roots—religious, familial, and professional—the Symphony No. 3 *Kaddish* (1963) fulfilled a joint commission from the Boston Symphony Orchestra and the Koussevitzky Foundation in 1955, for the orchestra's seventy-fifth anniversary. Work on the symphony took place between conducting engagements in 1961–63, including a summer spent at the MacDowell Colony in 1962. Conducting commitments and overlapping collaborative work on what would become two landmarks of American musical theater—*Candide* (1956) and *West Side Story* (1957)—explain Bernstein's belated start. Shortly after the premiere of *West Side Story*, he was named the first American-born director of the New York Philharmonic; his tenure began with the 1958–59 season and included two highly successful international tours with the group.

Kaddish was the first major work Bernstein completed when he returned to composition and the process finished with what Jack Gottlieb describes as "a hectic three-week orchestration period" in November 1963. Gottlieb rendered some assistance in orchestrating the Scherzo with a "road map" from Bernstein.[282] This process mirrored his close direction of orchestration in the theater works, as noted by frequent collaborators like Sid Ramin and Irwin Kostal and borne out in the sketch materials for works from *On the Town* through *West Side Story*. On November 22, 1963, President John F. Kennedy was assassinated and the completed symphony that would have been a celebration of a premiere American performing institution, as well as an homage to a revered musician and mentor, became a memorial for a beloved national figure and a friend of the Bernsteins. However, while the symphony ultimately bore the dedication "to the beloved memory of John F. Kennedy," an even more personal loss would accrue to it. Like the Symphony No. 2, the *Kaddish Symphony* seems to have been influenced by Bernstein's friend and much-admired fellow composer, Marc Blitzstein, whose *Airborne*

Symphony also used a narrator, vocal soloists, and chorus (although all male). Not long after the premiere of *Kaddish* in Israel, Bernstein learned of Blitzstein's violent death on January 22, 1964 (he was murdered by three sailors outside a bar in Martinique), an event that undoubtedly colored the subsequent American premiere.

With the permission of the BSO, the Third Symphony premiered in Tel Aviv on December 10, 1963, with the Israel Philharmonic under Bernstein's direction; Jennie Tourel served as soprano soloist and the actress Hannah Rovina as speaker. Bernstein's longtime friend and associate Abraham Kaplan directed the choruses, and Dan Miron translated the English portions of the text into Hebrew. The American premiere took place in Boston on January 31, 1964, with the composer's wife, Felicia Montealegre, as speaker, followed by a performance in New York shortly after. Bernstein later revised the work, most notably making the text suitable for either a male or female speaker, and the premiere of the revised version took place in Mainz, Germany, on August 25, 1977, during a tour of the Israel Philharmonic. Samuel Pisar, a Holocaust survivor who had discussed the work at length with Bernstein at the time of its composition, made a posthumous revision of the text. This version, which stands as an alternate accepted by the composer's estate, centered more explicitly on the Holocaust and the voices of the victims, while still offering hope for reconciliation; it was premiered by the Chicago Symphony Orchestra on August 1, 2003, with Pisar himself as speaker. Whereas the 1977 revision had simply anonymized the gender of the speaker and focused on remediating the text in the face of its most common criticisms (mostly toning down clichés), Pisar's text faces more squarely the realities of the Holocaust. Pisar's version realizes some of what Bernstein evidently felt unqualified to do in his text, but it also shifts the focus from the composer's worries about the imminent violence of the nuclear age.

The continuing fluctuation of the symphony's form after its 1963 premiere can be traced back to its genesis and Bernstein's ongoing search for answers to existential questions. The earliest writings that point toward *Kaddish* are undated but shed light on a point prior to Bernstein's having settled on a genre for the work. At the top of a page he writes "A Boston Mass" (presumably referencing the BSO commission) but then lists a host of other possibilities for the form of the work: a cantata, the S. Ansky play *The Dybbuk*, a "straight symph (BSO?)" possibly to include material from the "Cool" scherzo of *West Side Story*, and a "big opera."[283] Bernstein would eventually explore all these options, although the *Mass* (1971) would not be for Boston, and the Third Symphony would combine elements of the "straight" version of the genre with the cantata. He also wrote the score for Jerome Robbins's ballet *Dybbuk* (1974), and at the end of his life he was still exploring the possibilities of writing an opera that would contemplate the Holocaust and the widest possible scope of Jewish experience (Pisar was one of the many writers with whom Bernstein consulted).

In the early 1960s, though, Bernstein was concerned with broader existential questions: "I want answers. About me and where I am; about why all this exists around me, or why I exist in it (if indeed either is true); about talent and space and *real* human motives."[284] To that end he first proposed to himself a "lamentation on Hebrew-Yiddish materials that move me." The "lamentation," of course, harkens back to the Finale of the *Jeremiah Symphony*, dedicated to his father, and among the list of possible topics that follow (all framed as questions) is "Guilt toward my father?"—an interpretation borne out by the text and pursued by many writers. Bernstein continues reflecting on his family background, asking "What are the 'Jewish roots' I long for?" He considers nostalgia for his youth and his first cultural experiences, highlighting the works of Solomon Braslovsky as "the first real music I heard." His list also raises the question whether Jewishness as a "larger identity" is a race, a creed, or simply faith in a supernatural force. The reference to Braslovsky, the music director and organist of the congregation Mishkan Tefila, where Bernstein's family had attended services, also draws the quest for identity back to his youth and to Boston.

In his search for texts for this cantata-symphony, Bernstein considered the Hebrew hymn *Yigdal*, the story of Judith, the writings of Yiddish author Sholem Aleichem, and biblical sources like the psalms and the Song of Songs. In the summer of 1960 he drafted a scenario called "Call Me Moses," which featured a mix of biblical and modern settings.[285] Eventually, he settled on his own transliteration of the Kaddish prayer and English-language text, the latter having been from the beginning intended for a speaker with the Yiddish or Hebrew set for a singer.[286] According to Gottlieb, he also spent considerable time working with the poetry of Robert Lowell and Frederick Seidel before drafting his own English text for the speaker, although he did retain thematic material similar to the third of Lowell's *Three Poems for Kaddish* (1979).[287]

Given the overt references to nuclear destruction in the speaker's text, it would also be hard to ignore the significance of Lowell's *Fall 1961*. Its apocalyptic reference to the moon—"Our end drifts nearer/the moon lifts/radiant with terror"—is echoed in Bernstein's meditation as he set out to write the Third Symphony, which revolves around the endless poetic interpretations of the moon:

> It is easy to say: "The Russians took photos of the other side of the moon—so what? It is still beautiful; I prefer to have it be a heavenly light, Diana, chaste, Pierrot, green cheese." But no— there must be answers. They are right to photograph it; and such things must continue a millionfold. The moonlight on this palm will always move me, no matter what I know about it. Beauty is mysterious because it elicits aesthetic responses, not because (necessarily) it is unknown in its origins or manifestations. The mystery is why we respond, why the moonlight is moving;—not why it exists.[288]

Taken together, the weight of the questions Bernstein poses, the significance of the commission to his own "Jewish roots" in Boston, his esteem for Koussevitzky (who was of Jewish heritage), and Bernstein's intertextual inspirations led not only to a tangled drafting process but also to endless tinkering and revisions to the text and, necessarily, to the music.

Kaddish also has several musical models as well, both obvious and subtle. Mahler's symphonies loom largest among the former. Even more than the "Resurrection" (or Beethoven's Ninth), Mahler's Third Symphony with boys' and women's choirs and alto soloist resonates with Bernstein's Third. The "visions of heaven" offered by the speaker of *Kaddish* echo the childlike vision of heaven presented by the soprano soloist in the Finale of Mahler's Fourth Symphony (which itself shares the melody of the boys' chorus in the Third Symphony)—a passage that Bernstein famously explained during a Young People's Concert "Who Is Gustav Mahler?" (1960). The sheet on which Bernstein scrawled his first thoughts about genre also includes the note "pop tune like Trunkene im Frühling with changing keys at cadences"—a reference to the fifth movement of *Das Lied von der Erde*, another Mahler work that both he and his mentors, Walter and Koussevitzky, conducted relatively often in the United States.[289] Bernstein elsewhere described *Das Lied von der Erde* as a "farewell" to tonality, and the torturous journey through several cadences in "wrong" keys during *Kaddish*, before reaching the goal of G major, seems to bear out this initial thought.[290] The recurring "Kaddish tune," first introduced by the alto saxophone, can perhaps be heard as "pop" in this sense. Finally, the allegorical role of the speaker, who names herself "Havazélet ha-Sharón" (the Rose of Sharon) and "daughter of Zion," parallels the roles assigned to the SATB soloists in Part II of Mahler's Eighth Symphony. Although inspired by Goethe's *Faust*, the figures in Mahler's work emerge from a similar biblical imagination as Bernstein's "defiant daughter," who comes from the Song of Songs.

Because of the liturgical overtones of *Kaddish*, Ernest Bloch's *Sacred Service* (1934) is another possible model. Indeed, Bernstein conducted this work in April 1960, with his friend Rabbi Judah Cahn reading the part of the minister—this perhaps inspired the concept of a work for speaker as well as chorus and soloists. The concert, which also included Pergolesi's *Stabat Mater* in honor of the two hundred fiftieth anniversary of that composer's birth, was part of a three-concert series on "Twentieth-Century Problems in Music." This series formed a substratum to the 1959–60 Mahler cycle, and in addition to many parallels to that composer's works, the "Search for God" Bernstein proposes for the Pergolesi-Bloch program bears directly on *Kaddish*. In his preconcert remarks on the Bloch, he raises some of the same questions he would address in the Third Symphony: "Great music has for so long now been allied with matters religious and spiritual, in the larger sense, that it is almost impossible to conceive of music as pure entertainment. And yet the composer of today lives in what is usually deplored as a 'materialistic society.' Where, then, is he to find his spiritual incentive? Yet, somehow he does find it, in himself; no great composer can function apart from his deepest spirituality. . . . But how can we account for this reconciliation between the contemporary artist and the age of rationalism in which he lives?"[291] The similarities here to the ruminations in his notes before the Third Symphony, particularly the tension between rationalism and matters of faith (and aesthetics), are clear. At the time, he turned to a lengthy quotation from Albert Einstein for answers, and in Einstein's phrasing we can see the beginnings of Bernstein's own response: "You will hardly find one among the profounder sort of scientific minds without a peculiar religious feeling of his own. But it is different from the religion of the naïve man. For the latter, God is a being from whose care one hopes to benefit and whose punishment one fears; a sublimation of a feeling similar to that of a child for its father, a being to whom one stands to some extent in a personal relation, however deeply it may be tinged with awe."[292] In the text of the Third Symphony, Bernstein constructs an explicit father-child relationship between God and the "Rose of Sharon," and the narrative of the whole traces the arc from a "naïve" relationship (which also mentions punishment) to a "personal relation" in which the speaker alternately expresses tenderness and awe.

In terms of structure, there are yet further models, including other tripartite works. Although there are seven named movements, Kaddish III and the Finale are explicitly grouped as one movement, with the Finale performed *attaca subito,* making for six movements in essence, not unlike both Mahler's Third Symphony and *Das Lied von der Erde*. Most analysts acknowledge Bernstein's own understanding of the work as "A Threefold Kaddish," as he inscribed on the cover page of the final sketch (given to Jack Gottlieb). Bernstein's notes also address the import of this structure: "three reasons for saying Kaddish"; "three ways to say Kaddish"; and labels for the three parts as "Reader's Kaddish," "Rabbi's Kaddish," and "Mourner's Kaddish." These labels acknowledge the different occasions on which the Kaddish prayer is recited: a half or whole Kaddish is routinely said between or after prayers by the leader ("reader's Kaddish"); a slightly different version is recited at the end of a lesson by the rabbi ("rabbi's Kaddish"); and the Kaddish is also recited in the 11 months following a relative's passing and afterward on the Yahrzeit, or the anniversary of the person's death ("mourner's Kaddish"). In each case there must be a minyan, the traditional quorum of 10 men (or persons). None of these ideas are necessarily inconsistent with Bernstein's other note that this would be a "Kaddish for Us All," as in each case the text of the prayer differs only slightly and keeps the basic function of a Kaddish as a prayer that sanctifies the name of God, affirms the Lord's power, and asks for collective redemption.

Although he crossed out the words, Bernstein had also proposed three purposes for the work: 1. To Avert the Evil Day, 2. To Comfort God, and 3. To Affirm Life. One can still see something of these themes in the final symphony, particularly in the lullaby "to comfort God" heard in Kaddish II. As if following Bernstein's cue, Karen Rasmussen proposes an organization based on three rhetorical theses. The first thesis is that "The Omnipotent God's Creation Warrants Faith" (Invocation, Kaddish I, and Din-Torah). The second thesis is that "The Compassionate Father's Promise of Salvation Warrants Faith" (Kaddish 2 and Scherzo) and the final thesis is that "Humanity and God in a Process of Continuous Recreation Warrants Faith" (Kaddish 3 and Finale).[293] Schiller agrees but follows Gottlieb's grouping of the movements, which is the structure affirmed in the published score:

Part I: Invocation and Kaddish I
Part II: Din-Torah and Kaddish II
Part III: Scherzo and Kaddish III—Finale

However one groups these movements, there is also a structural difference built on the linguistic content of the text: the Aramaic of the Kaddish prayer is given to the soprano soloist and choirs, and the vernacular text is reserved for the speaker.

In terms of musical structure, Schiller also notes similarities between Bernstein's manipulation of the two twelve-tone rows that form part of the structure of the Third Symphony and Alban Berg's approach to the twelve-tone system. The first row, like that of Diamond's Eighth Symphony, is strongly indebted to the Austrian composer's Violin Concerto; with its opening series of thirds, Bernstein's row mimics Berg's even more closely.[294] On a thematic level, similarities have also been noted to Copland's melodic language in *Appalachian Spring* (Gottlieb) as well as the Third Symphony (Bernard); for his part, Schiller hears Copland's Piano Variations in Bernstein's handling of rhythm in both *The Age of Anxiety* and *Kaddish*.[295] It bears considering, then, that Copland's Third Symphony—which Bernstein had conducted several times, including with the Israel Philharmonic—is also tripartite, the last section encompassing both slow third movement and Finale. Finally, the cyclical elements that lend cohesion to Bernstein's work (beyond the relation between music and text) have many antecedents, from Beethoven—whom Bernstein credited with the highest level of musical unity—to Mahler and then to Copland's Third Symphony. More importantly, they form a crucial part of his own answer to the symphonic question.

In terms of the question of faith, however, Bernstein's Third Symphony offers no more certainty than his Second Symphony. While the Kaddish prayer sanctifies the Lord's name and asks for peace, the speaker's text does virtually the exact opposite. The daughter speaks to her father in a familiar, at times even disrespectful, tone as she questions if, by allowing the degree of earthly conflict and violence we experience, God has honored his covenant with humanity. More than this, she challenges his authority by convening a Din-Torah—a trial by Jewish law. Gottlieb's comments on the 1977 revised edition of the symphony shed light on Bernstein's reasoning in terms of the relationship to God as experienced by Jewish people, with reference points from ancient figures to modern philosophers: "Such 'blasphemy' has a Biblical precedent in the story of Job, and also has its roots in the folk tradition, as in the legend of Rabbi Levi Yitzhok of Berditchev. Bernstein strongly felt the peculiar Jewishness of this 'I-Thou' relationship in the whole mythic concept of the Jew's love of God. From Moses to the Hasidic sect, there is a deep personal intimacy that allows things to be said to God that are almost inconceivable in another religion."[296] Indeed, the Din-Torah has been an important part of the relationship between the Jewish people and God in the twentieth century. While *The Age of Anxiety* referenced the Holocaust obliquely, Bernstein faces it directly by invoking Jewish legal tradition to bring God to account for the destruction of human life, both in the past and in the potential future of a nuclear Holocaust or in threats to the nation of Israel. Although stories of rabbis putting God on trial while in concentration camps (and finding him guilty) persist, Bernstein was aware how potentially shocking his text might be in the postwar period.[297] Before the premiere in Tel Aviv he sent the text to Abe Cohen (manager of Israel Philharmonic), who conferred with an authority on Hebrew literature and philosophy; his "unqualified opinion" was that there should be "no hesitation whatsoever, as there were many precedents of this type of poem in Jewish and Hebrew literature."[298] Indeed, the speaker's text was hardly remarked upon in the Israeli press, as opposed to the more fraught reception at the US premiere. After all, the text ultimately seeks to reaffirm faith, or at least "Bernstein's conviction that human beings as creators, as artists, as dreamers—as, therefore divine manifestations—could be immortal."[299]

Part I unfurls the textual and musical themes that will move the rest of the symphony forward. In the Invocation the speaker expresses the desire to pray to a "lonely, disappointed Father" while doubting the ability to complete that Kaddish: "Is my end a minute away? An hour? Is there even time to consider the question?" The suddenness of the implied stop ("it could be here, while we are singing") invokes the nuclear fears of the Cold War era and of an embattled Israel, while the fear that "there may be no one to say it after me" describes the kind of generational disruption that characterized the Holocaust. And as a dialogue between generations, one might also hear this fear within the context of Bernstein's personal relationship with God and his own father, an interpretation that Gottlieb, Schiller, biographer Joan Peyser, and one of the later speakers, Michael Wager, have all offered.[300]

Aleatoric humming from the two choruses accompanies the speaker's opening declaration—"I want to pray"—followed closely by the unfolding of the head motif that will permeate the rest of the work: a rising minor second followed by a rising minor sixth, later extended with minor seventh leaps (mm. 2–4).[301] Schiller notes the similarity to the opening of Wagner's *Tristan und Isolde*, and given Bernstein's fascination with motivic integration—or what Helen Smith calls "intervallic composition"—this seems reasonable.[302] Following Smith's analysis, through the prevalence of the minor seventh we can hear resonances with the score for *Candide*. Contrapuntal treatment of the head motif follows in the strings, before the alto saxophone presents the melody Gottlieb calls the "Kaddish tune" (m. 15), juxtaposed with expansive statements of the head motif in the upper woodwinds. As the speaker continues the Invocation, the orchestra quietly meditates on these two segments of thematic material. Various permutations of the head motif continue under the speaker's exclamation "MAGNIFIED . . . AND SANCTIFIED . . . BE THE GREAT NAME . . . AMEN," that prefaces the first Kaddish, at which point a sudden accelerando and crescendo push into the "Wild!" Allegro molto that begins the Kaddish I proper.

The tempo change from a deliberate Adagio in 6/4 to the vigor of the Allegro molto, which alternates between 7/8 and 3/4, coincides with the first appearance of the Kaddish I row, accompanied by material derived from the head motif. This is also the *P* of what Schiller identifies as a loose sonata form. The opening of Kaddish I continues the typical slow introduction begun in the Invocation (mm. 25–31) before the *1T* area introduces the first twelve-tone row of the work (mm. 32–56). (Because they together constitute a cohesive form, the Invocation and Kaddish I are numbered continuously.) The first seven notes of Row I (example 6.15a, in strings and some winds) consist mostly of minor thirds that, in the row's prime form, hint at a tonal center of G minor. The latter half of the row begins with a sequential tetrachord composed of two overlapping tritones separated by a half step (C-B-F♯-F), a tetrachord that appears in numerous twentieth-century works. The last four pitches, however, belong to G-flat major and the row ends with a perfect fifth.[303] The basic thematic and harmonic material of Kaddish I, then, embodies the tension between tonality and atonality that figures so prominently both in Bernstein's writings, particularly *The Unanswered Question*, and in his music.

The rest of *1T* is rounded out with presentations of Row I on B-flat (m. 42) and E (m. 52) before the transition moves forward (mm. 57–75) with bold statements, both in the orchestra and chorus, of a minor-seventh fanfare drawn from the extension of the head motif. The most prominent accompanimental figure in this section is a descending scale (mostly A major) in the contrabassoon and basses, which contrasts strongly with the upward arc of the minor sevenths. This struggle between upward and downward motion mirrors the similar strategy of the first movement of Mahler's Second Symphony. The "Kaddish tune" appears as *2T* (mm. 76–91), then in counterpoint with the head motif as the *CT* (mm. 92–99). A relatively brief developmental section begins with Row I on B-flat (m. 100) and then on E (m. 110) and continues with more permutations of the head motif. An Adagio come prima (m. 132–34) recalls the presentation of the head motif in the Invocation, before yielding to another exploration of the "Kaddish tune" in m. 135. A perfunctory recapitulation (mm. 151–64) returns to the prime version of Row I and finishes with an un-earned cadence on G. There is a great deal of forward momentum, and a strident F♯-G leading-tone motion overrides the row's finish in G-flat. Not for lack of force, the conclusion rings false, and accordingly the speaker's next monologue calls the Creator to account for promises broken and the falsity of his "bargain with Man." In its exhilaration, we hear ecstasy tinged with blasphemy. As Schiller points out, Kaddish I in its rhythm and tempo resembles the "jazzy" second movement of *Jeremiah*, "Profanation," with its multimeter and asymmetrical rhythms. So far, Bernstein's Kaddish is "ambiguous—part profanation, part prayer. But clearly it is not the 'gallant Yit-gadal' [the first words of the Kaddish prayer] that the narrator had hoped to sing."[304]

Part II continues with the Din-Torah, which gives the balance of material to the speaker rather than the chorus, as befitting the tone of accusation. A Din-Torah is a trial by biblical law and the speaker becomes the prosecutor in this scene. According to Schiller, "The specific legal principle that has been violated is the most important principle of all, *pikuah nefesh*, regard for human life."[305] The grounds for the speaker's accusation are various: the Holocaust of man's "new-found fire" could be the nuclear version or the crematoria of the death camps (Pisar would choose the latter). Both were on the public's mind in 1963, as Adolf Eichmann, the architect of Hitler's "final solution," had been captured and tried in Israel in 1960–61, and October 1962 brought nuclear fears to a peak with the Cuban missile crisis.[306] The Din-Torah thus abounds with musical signifiers that Bernstein associated with disorder, destruction, and chaos. Opening with a passage for resonant and wooden percussion reminiscent of Varèse—timpani, wood blocks, temple blocks, field drum, cymbal, tam-tam, bass drum, and rasp—the tenors and basses of the choir softly hum the "Kaddish tune" in C-sharp minor on "Amen." As the speaker's agitation grows, so does the texture, expanding to include the rest of the choir and the low strings; they finish the "Kaddish tune" just as the speaker finishes her questions and lays out her accusation: "Your bargain is tin!"

She asks defiantly, "And where is faith now—yours or mine?" as the orchestra crescendos into an atonal interlude that features the minor seventh leaps of the head motif, cast now as a shofar call, different from the descending perfect fourth of *Jeremiah* but no less prophetic. (The shofar may be overused as a point of reference in analyses of Bernstein and other Jewish composers. In this case, however, the wide leaps in the three-note fanfare, plus the dissonance in this gesture, caused by overlapping "near-misses" of an octave, do approximate the sound of an untempered instrument meant to be heard over long distances.) In m. 25 Bernstein introduces Row II (see example 6.15b), which according to Schiller "refers back to and extends the atonal gesture" in the middle of Row I.[307] The percussion section intrudes violently again (m. 34) before a choral interlude (mm. 40–84) accompanied by the percussive and orchestral gestures built from the tritones of the two rows and minor seventh leap of the head motif.

Example 6.15a Bernstein, Symphony No. 3, Row I, strings, mm. 32–35

Beginning in m. 48, a swinging passage for woodwinds, low strings, and percussion configured to imitate a trap set introduces a rhythm Bernstein marks as both "jazzy" and "grotesque" and is gesturally similar to "Cool" from *West Side Story*—the song Bernstein mentioned in his earliest meditations on the Third Symphony. Given that in this earlier instance, jazz (specifically bebop and other postwar styles) underscores the violence the Jets seek to repress, the appearance of a "jazzy" section here similarly serves as a marker of disorder by emphasizing the disruption and the violence invoked in the speaker's text: "And now he [Man] runs free—free to play with his new-found fire, avid for death, voluptuous, complete and final death."[308] It is precisely this fracturing of Man (the masculine) from his Godly half—"I am that part of Man You made to suggest immortality . . . the part that refuses death, that insists on You"—embodied by the female narrator that poses an existential threat. (Like Schiller, I interpret the

Forgotten Modernisms

Example 6.15b Bernstein, Symphony No. 3, Row II, strings, mm. 25–26

original text rather than the revision, although the points here hold true with a narrator of either gender.) The passage then deteriorates into a choral cadenza composed of eight different ostinati—one of which is the "jazzy" rhythm—which creates a haunting Babel. As the speaker says, "Chaos is catching." The emphasis on the tritone interval in both Rows I and II recalls the score for *West Side Story* as well, and not surprisingly, this tritone provides continuity between the Din-Torah and the following Kaddish II.

The second iteration of the Kaddish prayer is led by the soprano soloist, recalling the responsorial nature of the prayer when recited by a congregation, as the speaker attempts to reconcile with God. Over the fading choral ostinati at the end of the Din-Torah, she begs: "Forgive me father. I was mad with fever" and attributes to God a very human vulnerability— "You too are vulnerable . . . tender, fallible"—which precipitates the form of the next movement. Cued by the speaker—"If could comfort You, hold You against me, rock You and rock You into sleep"—Kaddish II is a lullaby, with a gently oscillating accompaniment in 5/8 provided by the harp and strings and accented by celesta and upper woodwinds. The melody of this "Yit'gadal" first traces a stepwise course up a tritone before converting the gesture into a

603

diatonic melody that outlines major and minor sixths and finishes with a rising perfect fourth that earns a peaceful "Amen" from the choir (mm. 17–19). The B section (mm. 40–104) picks up momentum in 5/16 and introduces occasional biting chords against the melody, which preserves the perfect fourth and major and minor sixth intervals—when expressed harmonically rather than melodically, the modal tension between the sixths generates some of this dissonance. The A section returns (mm. 105–50) to wind down the movement, with the lullaby melody once again suggesting a cadence in G major. In the final peroration, however, the D-G yields to a cadence on a shimmering C-major chord with added ninths, a movement from tonic to subdominant that according to Schiller is an attempt to adhere to symphonic norms.[309] Indeed, the gentleness of the movement is similar to many symphonic Adagios and the *völkisch* overtones of the melody again conjure Mahler. However, the attempt at reconciliation between daughter (the speaker), now appearing as mother (the soprano soloist), and God as father-child figure is not to last.

Part III opens with a Scherzo for the speaker and orchestra and takes an ironic tone found in many similar movements by Mahler. In fact, the orchestration of the opening (for piccolo, E♭ clarinet, and pizzicato strings) and the prominent glissandi and flutter tonguing recall the shrillness and tongue-in-cheek character of the Scherzo in Mahler's Second Symphony. A passage of *Klangfarbenmelodie* for the string section (mm. 43–65) draws on orchestration techniques more closely associated with atonal modernism, and when coupled with the contrapuntal play in the winds, serves to disorient the listener. All this seems to contradict the imagery of the speaker's text that, with its lambs frisking and wheat rippling, echoes the childlike vision of heaven in the text from *Des Knaben Wunderhorn* employed in Mahler's Fourth Symphony. As the speaker says, "Something is wrong"; that "something" is expressed through the turn toward atonality and, eventually, back to Row I (m. 78). Schiller describes the setting of the row as a "stilted and mechanical" ostinato; it reflects the falseness of this vision of heaven by highlighting the artificiality of the twelve-tone method as form without meaningful content; as the speaker says, in this space is a "sterile," false vision of the Kingdom of Heaven, in which there is "nothing to know" and "nowhere to go."[310]

The "Kaddish tune" also returns in m. 158 as if to herald the speaker's new covenant, in which she invites God to "behold my Kingdom of Earth!" and points out the rainbow in the sky that she has created for him to signify their new covenant. The speaker exhorts God to believe, but its fugal treatment generates tension rather than joy as the speaker declares, "MAGNIFIED . . . AND SANCTIFIED . . . BE THE GREAT NAME OF MAN!" The speaker is at her boldest here, supplanting God's divinity with the power and force that humankind has acquired. There is much to provide wonder among the works of humanity, but there is also the potential for violence. As foreshadowed by the artificiality of the twelve-tone music, this covenant too proves false and the music breaks forth into a "Wild!" passage (m. 173) that heralds the return of Row I in its prime form (m. 181)—the quintessence of the man-made.

As Gottlieb states, the Scherzo is the "crux" of the symphony: almost all its principal material appears here, and it propels the listener toward a joyous transformation of Row I into a diatonic melody in G-flat major cued by the word "Believe!" (mm. 222–37). The minor seventh of the head motif features prominently in the melody as well, and it does indeed receive a magnificent fugal treatment that expands and warms the texture in woodwinds and strings as the boys' choir rises to burst forth with the final Kaddish. We do seem to receive, in a clearly tonal G-flat major, our "gallant Yit'gadal" as a soaring trumpet line takes up the "Believe" melody. Schiller cautions against reading this as the fulfillment of the symphonic plan, though, as

G-flat major is not the "right" key—it should be G major.³¹¹ In addition, Row I interrupts m. 15 of Kaddish III, as does the speaker, without allowing the choir to finish any more than the first line of the prayer. The dream is not over—"Don't waken yet!" urges the speaker, who offers to help God suffer the pains of that wakening and continues to promise heaven on earth, "just as you planned." With eyes open, a new covenant could still be the way forward, perhaps more on equal terms, with neither man nor God supreme. As she says in the Finale: "We can still be immortal, You and I, bound by our rainbow."

A variation of the "Kaddish tune" winds down the texture and volume of the interruption (m. 38) and the woodwinds play a frisky melody full of playful leaps (mm. 47–57), before the "Believe" melody returns (m. 58). At this point, the boys' choir is allowed to continue with the prayer, cued by the speaker: "The voices of Your children call from corner to corner, chanting Your praises." The "Believe" melody is ushered in by the trumpet at m. 55 as if from a distance, yielding in m. 58 to a chamber orchestra of winds and piano. Occurring in the subdominant C major this time, the melody fades rather than grows as a soft, five-part divisi in the strings diffuses the texture and the boys' choir skips toward the end of the first section of the prayer, just before the congregational response. Although the boys' line cadences sweetly in F major, as Schiller points out, "the response, and the acceptance and reconciliation it symbolizes, is withheld."³¹² True reconstruction of the relationship with this God and father figure must take place outside the dreamworld, as acknowledged by the speaker at the end of Kaddish III: "We must wake up now; and the dawn is chilly."

Continuing *attaca subito*, the Finale jars the listener with a *Schrekensfanfare* worthy of Beethoven or Mahler; it initiates a cyclical recollection of the Din-Torah (mm. 1–5). Other material returns as well, from Row II to the "Kaddish tune" and the rising sixth of the head motif.³¹³ A **pp** trumpet solo that begins with a descending perfect fourth (m. 14) recalls the "faith" motive from the Epilogue of Symphony No. 2, while descending obbligato lines from the woodwinds, many of which reiterate the perfect fourth interval, help wind down the tension. The speaker returns at m. 27 over a **pp** vamp based on the "Believe" melody in divisi strings. As the speaker vows that she and God are "one, after all" and "together we suffer, together we exist, and forever will recreate each other," the horns state the "Believe" melody as if it is a *lontano* call. In response, both choirs and the soprano soloist burst into a fugue based on Row II but transformed in F Lydian and built around the descending perfect fourth interval that Gottlieb hears as a symbol of faith and that Smith tracks through almost all Bernstein's works in the form of the *Urmotiv*.³¹⁴

A second exposition (m. 90) provides the opportunity to revel in the material, which is presented as a joyous, multimeter dance, a sound Bernstein would return to in *Mass*. In the first version of the symphony, between "V'imru:" ("let us say") and the harmonic goal of G major, Bernstein inserted two chromatic glissandi on the word *Amen*, the second of which ended on an unpitched syllable.³¹⁵ This was perhaps intended to recall the ambiguity of the hummed opening, and its revisions, like the changes to the Finale of *The Age of Anxiety*, may signal greater certainty or optimism. In either version, however, the symphony ends with a dramatic gesture: the soprano soloist enters on a "clear and luminous" G (m. 168) as the boys' choir and then SATB choir enter top to bottom creating an expansive G-E dyad. On the second syllable of the "Amen," the sonority shifts to an F-major chord with an added major sixth (m. 174), resolving the minor sixth head motif upward, while the woodwinds, pitched percussion, harp, piano, and strings reiterate the descending perfect-fourth "faith" motive. The rest of the orchestra then joins with a dramatic **sfffz** G-major chord with a few spare pitches (E and A) that complicate the sonority just enough to make it brilliant but not trite. Whereas the Second Symphony had questioned the possibility of recovering faith, the Third Symphony seems to confirm its existence threefold, provided the nature of that belief expands to include faith in humanity as much as in God.

The reception of the premiere in Tel Aviv was almost as joyous as the performance by Bernstein and the Israel Philharmonic. Multiple reports describe the tumult both onstage and in the audience, and most of the reviews were positive. Many critics mentioned the significance of Bernstein choosing to premiere the work in Israel while also acknowledging its deep ties to America via the dedication to John F. Kennedy and the Boston commission. By 1963, Bernstein had been in close association with Israel and its orchestra for nearly 15 years, and although he had turned down directorship of the orchestra, he remained a favorite of the musicians and audiences. In July 1967 he would return to lead the Israel Philharmonic in a concert on Mount Scopus to celebrate the end of the Six-Day War earlier that summer and the liberation of Jerusalem, cementing two decades of his close ties to what he called a "land of miracles"; that concert, not surprisingly, featured Mahler's Second Symphony. Earlier, Israeli audiences had reacted positively to his *Jeremiah Symphony*, and he had composed significant portions of the Symphony No. 2 while in Israel. A review in *Ha'aretz* captures the admiration expressed by many: Bernstein's performance as conductor and his worth as a composer are praised as "two aspects of a great musical genius" possessed of "dynamic power that has no equal in the music of our time." Like others, this reviewer compared Bernstein to Mahler in a manner intended to be flattering and that highlighted their shared Jewish heritage:

> This work is a sort of musical drama, a vocal symphony on the eternal problem of the opposite poles: man and his God. The work is impressive because of the giant personnel involved in its performance: a mixed choir, a children's choir, a speaker, a singer and an orchestra in Mahlerian proportions. You can't avoid comparison between Bernstein and Mahler: two great conductors, a metaphysical subject in the center of their spiritual world, complete mastery of the art of musical composition and understanding of the Jewish temperament . . . a deeply impressive work whose language is not avant-garde yet reflects our times faithfully.[316]

For the reviewer, and likely for much of the audience, "a Jewish-Hebrew religious thread winds throughout this universal music, together with some American tones." Perhaps surprisingly, the spoken text produced little reaction other than an occasional recognition of its engaging with the storied Jewish tradition of arguing with God:

> [T]his composition speaks, in its own language, of the problems of faith and existence in our time which literature, religion and philosophy are discussing nowadays in their language. This work is another chapter of the Psalms; a continuation of "Your memory is not in death . . ." and in "Not the dead will praise the Lord . . ."; a link in the long chain of "those who cry from the depths," of those whose dialogues between man and his maker from Eben-Gevirol's "Thou art too righteous, O God, that I quarrel with Thee, but I will chastise thee" to his "I will flee from Thee to Thee," —to the famous "Din Torah" of Rabbi Levi Yitschak of Berditchev.[317]

The one negative Israeli reaction on record expressed frustration with the pictorialism or melodrama of the orchestral accompaniment for the speaker:

> The choir rises to powerful heights and then slowly dies out, really dies . . . what a fantastic effect . . . Effect? Suddenly all I hear is effects . . . the words he has put in her [the speaker's] mouth are moving, but not as moving as he thinks. Whoever advised him to write a modern sequel to Job did not do him a good service . . . Effects, effects . . . Divine harp, the violins, the heavens open,

then back to hell with drums and trumpets. Stormy waves, the tremendous Orchestra is working with extraordinary efficiency. I try to concentrate on the music and cannot because the music is painting pictures. Now I know what's lacking—a film: Marlon Brando "On the Water Front," or Jerome Robbins' dancers. The music is not for its own sake; it accompanies a show that does not exist. Unless we count Rowina all in black and Tourel all in gold and the white Zadikoff children and the chief dancer on the podium, as a show.[318]

The reviewer concedes that his represents a "minority opinion," although it anticipated many critics' objections in America when the symphony premiered there two months later. American audiences were readied for a great event by reports of the Tel Aviv concert in the *New York Times*, *Variety*, and Jewish periodicals like *American Jewish World* (Minneapolis) and the *Jewish Chronicle* (London).

Most reviews of the American premiere begin with a primer on the Kaddish prayer and its liturgical context—a gesture that was unnecessary for audiences in Israel. Many also hailed Bernstein as the "prodigal son" returned to Boston, and the audience seems to have warmly welcomed him back. Like the Israeli reviewer, American critics noted the similarities to Mahler's symphonies; comparisons to Britten, Stravinsky, Debussy, Ravel, and Strauss were also made, though not with the same dismissiveness that characterized the reception of the Second Symphony. Indeed, Harold Rogers in the *Christian Science Monitor* noted: "It is a mature piece of composition; the eclectic lines, if any, are blurred: it represents the composer at his most serious and at his finest. . . . Mr. Bernstein has called upon the ancient and the modern in music to match the ancient Kaddish and his modern interpretation of it. He has successfully brought these disparate elements into a unified whole."[319] With respect to genre, several critics noted the theatrical bent of the work and the elements drawn from the oratorio and (not mentioned in Israel) the Requiem. Robert Taylor welcomed the stylistic and generic cross-pollination, hailing the work as "genius," although he began with a backhanded compliment:

So long has Mr. Bernstein occupied the role of the flawed genius that his triumph must be regarded as the release of a talent freed from the lashings of its own facility. . . . The tri-partite design is fundamentally narrative, with the narrator imploring, exhorting, and addressing God in terms of profound intimacy. The score comments on the emotional surge, which rushes from anger to humility to exaltation; and at times, molded to the natural inflections of spoken English, becomes the chief agent of a dramatic soliloquy. Mr. Bernstein's stylistic garb is often eclectic, but he brings an overwhelming rhythmic invention, vivid and evocative orchestration and a spacing of sonorities to his writing, attaining an idiomatic warmth. Stravinsky, Strauss and Mahler color various passages; and in a section describing the pastoral glories of paradise the parallel to the Wunderhorn movement of Mahler's Fourth is evident. The closest relationship, however, is more to the tumult and the bedizened vitality of such a work as Walton's "Belshazzar's Feast."[320]

On the other hand, this programmatic overriding of the symphonic model led to some of the most strident criticism. Michael Steinberg decried the "unashamed vulgarity" of the work and protested that "it is so strongly derivative, that the hearing of it becomes as much as anything a strain on one's credulity." He noted the ambition of the work but implied that Bernstein had overreached his abilities and propriety with the text: "The idea is splendidly imaginative, and it is tempting to think of what a poet like Auden might have made of it. But Bernstein as a writer of words has only fluency at his command, and that fluency produces a lava-flow of clichés wherein a few cozy intimacies (speaker to God, 'We'll make it a sort of holiday') are contrasted against the tinny rhetoric of Norman Corwin's radio plays from the forties."[321] When he tells us that "as a composer of music, Bernstein's bent is principally theatrical," we are not meant to read it as a compliment. Steinberg was perhaps the bellwether critic, for the reception of the symphony in New York in April was decidedly less warm than in Boston. Ross Parmenter had praised the work at first in Boston, particularly for the evocativeness of the orchestral music; but on second hearing, he found the "swelling movie-music" of the "Believe" passage unconvincing, the work more derivative, and the lullaby of Kaddish II "pretty, but thin."[322] Both in Israel and America, the same essential musical qualities of the work—its mixture of styles and symphonic models, play with the conventions of the genre, and its drama—could turn a listener on or off.

The response to its theological aspects, on the other hand, could not have been more starkly different. At least two American critics responded quite negatively to the "blasphemy" in Bernstein's text. The author of the music column in *Time* implied that Bernstein's "chutzpah" was the source of his aesthetic undoing:

> Because his concentration span is short to the point of dilettantism, he achieves with all his battalions of singers and musicians only the affectation of beauty. Worse, his metaphysics overwhelms his music—the orchestra does little more than italicize the words of the speaker, and the emotional flow of the music follows the text almost sheepishly. The despair he portrays is only the despair of the prideful; drama is merely melodrama. Bernstein is a man of both cheek and genius; and in this case, the composer in him has been no more than the advocate of the showman, the charmer, the chap in the chukka boots shouting down from the balcony.[323]

The charge of showmanship was nothing new, but its linkage here to a particularly Jewish attitude and Bernstein's metaphysical view belongs to a centuries-long vein of anti-Semitic criticism, the likes of which Mahler experienced as well. It could also be that the reaction betrays some anxiety about the nascent "Death of God" theology as discussed by J. J. Altizer, Paul van Buren, and Charles Hamilton, although the movement did not come to larger public awareness until later in 1965.

Joseph McLellan, writing for *The Pilot* (the official paper of the Archdiocese of Boston) started out in a more conciliatory tone, evidently grateful for the resurgence of religiously themed music and Bernstein's transposition of the traditional prayer to a "modern, humanistic context." He also seems pleased both by the accessibility and programmaticism of the music: "The composer of 'West Side Story' knows how to please an audience without compromising musical quality." He further recognizes in Bernstein's text affinities with other writers who have addressed God, including the "familiar, derogatory, even vulgar tones" that recall William Blake and the "self-conscious folksiness" of Carl Sandburg. In the end, though, McLellan is obliged to come down on the side of Christian piety: "[Bernstein's theology] is at best a half truth. Certainly men do make gods in their own image; they always have and they do today. But this idolatry has nothing to do with the Creator revealed long ago to the Jews and Christians. In the terms presented by this composition, what Mr. Bernstein offers to be worshipped is evidently the artistic and altruistic potential of humankind. This is symbolized both by the speaker and by the being to whom she speaks, and while it is a fine thing in itself it makes a fairly shabby god."[324] These starkly contradictory national responses call into question for whom Bernstein was writing this symphony. He could not have anticipated Kennedy's death when he composed it, but later he willingly discussed the association of the work in his mind with the slain president. Because of the commission, he was certainly thinking of his mentor Koussevitzky and his hometown of Boston, like the way Copland's shadow fell over the *Jeremiah Symphony*. All three were "father figures," either to the nation or to Bernstein.

However, the struggle with a father figure in his text is drawn, at least in part, from his relationship with his own father—the Kabbalistic overtones of the text were something we know he associated with the elder Bernstein. While he took his family to a conservative synagogue with a distinctly American character, Samuel Bernstein had grown up in a Chasidic family that had produced several rabbis, and he kept an interest in those mystic traditions. Speaking in honor of his father's birthday in 1963, Bernstein applied the male-female duality described in the Kabbalah between Chachmah (wisdom) and Binah (understanding) to his own mother and father.[325] In that speech he also outlined the dynamic that is central to the speaker's text: "Every son, at one point or another, defies his father, fights him, departs from him, only to return to him—if he is lucky—closer and more secure than before. Again we see clearly the parallel with God: Moses protesting God, arguing, fighting to change God's mind. So the child defies the father; and something of that defiance remains through his life."[326] In this earlier description of the relationship between humankind and God, and between children and parents, Bernstein assumes a male perspective, although he also understood the necessity of both genders to keep balance. This may be why Bernstein ultimately decided to leave the matter of the speaker's gender indeterminate in *Kaddish*.

In terms of performers, Bernstein's written thoughts and testimonies from others show that, from the beginning, he conceived of Jennie Tourel as the soloist and his wife, Felicia (a professional actress), as the speaker. Abraham Kaplan's chorus was also likely on Bernstein's mind—he later incorporated bits of a work he wrote for the chorus into *Mass*. In terms of intended audience, the trouble Bernstein took to negotiate with the BSO for an Israeli premiere shows that he felt strongly about the work as a communion with his adopted country. However, the stylistic vocabulary draws deeply on American music from within and without the concert hall. In the end, taking the first-person speaker at face value perhaps tells us all we need to know, which is that it is a work of deeply personal motivations. Bernstein wrote this symphony for himself and in his own voice.

For Bernstein, the symphony was a genre that bridged his work as a conductor and as a composer. Often this led to the criticism of these works as derivative of the music he conducted, a dubious honor he shared with his symphonic idol, Gustav Mahler. Eventually, Bernstein embraced this dual role, particularly in his writings and public statements around the Mahler centenary in 1960.[327] Similarly, he defended his tendency to borrow from the music of others and highlighted the eclecticism of composers he admired, like Stravinsky. Given his preference for genre bending—whether in the tragic musical comedy of *West Side Story* or the amorphousness of *Mass*—he might have abandoned the symphony all together. Instead, he used the symphonic format to explore a stunning breadth of emotions and to grapple with existential questions, particularly the question of faith, whether understood in a specifically Jewish or more ecumenical way. While he loved writing for the Broadway stage, scoring for what are still some of the largest pit orchestras, the symphony provided him a larger canvass and a more varied orchestral palette. And as someone whose mentors repeatedly urged him to pick a career, writing a symphony may still have seemed like a signal achievement. For his efforts as both conductor and composer, the American symphony, in no small degree, owes its persistence at midcentury to Bernstein.

Peter Mennin

Peter Mennin (1923–83) had much in common with William Schuman and Vincent Persichetti, both in terms of their professional circles and their musical styles. Mennin succeeded Schuman as president of Juilliard in 1962 and held the post until his death in 1983. He began his musical education at Oberlin Conservatory, studying with Normand Lockwood, and finished his bachelors at Eastman after returning from military service during World War II. He also earned his MA and PhD (1947) from Eastman, where he studied with Howard Hanson and Bernard Rogers. Schuman appointed Mennin to the composition faculty of the Juilliard School quickly thereafter, in the same year that Persichetti joined. (In a further entwining of their careers, Mennin promoted Persichetti to head of the composition department during his own tenure as president.) Mennin briefly departed Juilliard to serve as director of the Peabody Conservatory (1958–62), until he was hired back as the school's president.

Despite following parallel and sometimes interweaving paths as administrators and composers, Mennin and Schuman had a contentious personal relationship. During his presidency Mennin largely excluded his predecessor from the affairs of the school, yet he continued Schuman's management patterns, appointing faculty in an ecumenical manner—hiring many composers whose styles were different from his own—and further expanding the school, as befitting its central location at Lincoln Center (the move to which Mennin oversaw), with the addition of the Theater Center in 1968, the American Opera Center in 1970, and a permanent conducting program in 1972. Although Mennin was not as prolific as Schuman had been during his presidency, he still received commissions from the Coolidge Foundation, the Cleveland Orchestra, the National Symphony Orchestra, and the New York Philharmonic. He received numerous awards, including Guggenheim Fellowships (1949 and 1957) and the Naumburg Award (1952). He was later president of the Naumburg Foundation from 1964 to 1971 (when Schuman engineered his removal), as well as a member of the Composers Forum; the Koussevitzky Foundation; the American Society of Composers, Authors, and Publishers; and the National Institute of Arts and Letters. As Schuman had done, he served as an adviser to the government on the State Department Advisory Committee on the Arts.

Mennin's compositional style manages to compass both a boundless energy and a thoroughgoing, almost sober approach to counterpoint. There is also remarkable consistency from one work to another, which some critics found tiresome.[328] Like Schuman and Persichetti, Simmons sees Mennin as a "modern traditionalist": committed neither to (Neo-)romantic self-expression nor Neoclassical simplicity; favoring a highly chromatic and dissonant idiom that did not exclude tonality; and fundamentally cosmopolitan in orientation.[329] Specifically, Mennin shared the dedicated interest in counterpoint that animated Schuman and—despite the radically different harmonic language—Sessions; however, whereas Schuman and Sessions approached counterpoint from a broadly Neoclassic perspective, Mennin was influenced by his study of Renaissance polyphony.[330] His use of "bottom up" structures like ground bass, canon, ostinato, and cantus firmus show this influence, as does what Simmons describes as "a continuous unfolding of polyphonic lines through imitative counterpoint, rather than the more conventional dialectical opposition and integration of contrasting themes."[331] Mennin also favored large genres and abstract forms; in terms of regular engagement with the genre, he is more of a traditional "symphonist" than any of the other American composers at midcentury. His own comments show that he valued the genre both for its scope and for the

Table 6.8 The Symphonies of Peter Mennin (1923–83)

Title	Movements	Instrumentation	Comments
Symphony No. 1 (1941)			Withdrawn.
Symphony No. 2 (1944)	1. Allegro deciso 2. Andante moderato 3. Allegro vigoroso	Grand plus Flt. (doubling Picc.), EH, Tpt., Tuba, Perc.	First performance: March 27, 1945 (first movement only), by the New York Philharmonic, conducted by Leonard Bernstein; November 27, 1945 (the complete symphony), at the Eastman School of Music. The first movement (entitled "Symphonic Allegro") won the Gershwin Memorial Award, while the entire symphony received the Joseph H. Bearns Prize of Columbia University. Score published in 1945 by Carl Fischer. Mennin withdrew the symphony but lifted the ban shortly before his death.
Symphony No. 3 (1946)	1. Allegro robusto 3/2 (199 mm.) 2. Andante moderato 4/4 (111 mm.) 3. Allegro assai 2/2 (506 mm.)	Grand plus Flt. (doubling Picc.), Tpt., Tuba, Timp., Perc. (SD, Suspended Cym., BD)	First performance: February 27, 1947, by the New York Philharmonic, conducted by Walter Hendl. Score published by Hargail Music, 1948.
Symphony No. 4, "The Cycle" (1947–48)	1. Allegro energico 2/4 (324 mm.) 2. Andante arioso 3/4 (123 mm.) 3. Pronunziato: Allegro deciso 3/2 (475 mm.)	Grand plus Flt. (doubling Picc.), Tpt., Tuba, Perc.	Text by the composer, a philosophical rumination on the life cycle. Commissioned by Collegiate Chorale. First performance: March 18, 1949, by the New York Philharmonic and Collegiate Chorale, conducted by Robert Shaw. Vocal score published by Carl Fischer, 1949.
Symphony No. 5 (1950)	1. Con sdegno (or Con vigore) 3/4 (185 mm.) 2. Canto 4/4 (128 mm.) 3. Allegro tempestuoso 2/4 (496 mm.)	Grand plus Picc., Tpt., Tuba, Perc. (Suspended Cym., SD, BD)	Commissioned by Dallas Symphony Orchestra. First performance: April 2, 1950, by the Dallas Symphony Orchestra, conducted by Walter Hendl. Holograph score published by Independent Music Publisher (Theodore Presser), 1950.

Table 6.8 The Symphonies of Peter Mennin (1923–83)

Title	Movements	Instrumentation	Comments
Symphony No. 6 (1953)	1. Maestoso—Allegro 4/4 (336 mm.) 2. Grave 4/4 (111 mm.) 3. Allegro vivace 9/8 (459 mm.)	Grand plus Picc., EH, Bclar., Tuba, 2 Timp, Perc. (BD, Cym., Suspended Cym., SD)	Commissioned by Louisville Symphony Orchestra. First performance: November 18, 1953, by the Louisville Symphony Orchestra, conducted by Robert Whitney. Score published by Carl Fischer, 1956.
Symphony No. 7, "Variation-Symphony" (1964)	One movement in five sections: Adagio 4/4 (mm. 1–105)— Allegro 2/2 (mm. 106–384)— Andante 5/4 (mm. 385–598)— Moderato 3/4 (mm. 599–717)— Allegro vivace 4/4 (mm. 718–802)	Grand plus Picc., EH, Bclar., Cbssn., Tpt, Tuba, 2 Timp.	Commissioned by George Szell and the Cleveland Orchestra. First performance: January 23, 1964, by the Cleveland Orchestra under Szell. Score published by Carl Fischer, 1967.
Symphony No. 8 (1973)	1. *In principio*: Sostenuto 4/4 (92 mm.) 2. *Dies irae*: Allegro con moto 2/4 (139 mm.) 3. *De profundis clamavi*: Adagio 4/4 (103 mm.) 4. *Laudate Dominum*: Allegro vivace 2/4 (437 mm.)	Grand plus Flt. (doubling Picc.), EH, Bclar, Cbssn., Tpt, Tuba, 3 Timp., Perc. (SD, Tenor Drum, Cym., BD, Bongos, Timbales, Temple Blocks, Chimes, Vbp., Mrb., 2 Suspended Cym., 2 Tam-tams)	First and last movements are revised versions of a two-movement *Sinfonia* Mennin wrote in 1970 and then withdrew. First performance: November 21, 1974, by the New York Philharmonic, conducted by Daniel Barenboim. Score published by Carl Fischer, 1978.
Symphony No. 9 (1981)	1. Lento, non troppo 2. Adagio arioso 3. Presto tumultuoso	Grand plus Flt. (doubling Picc.), EH, Bclar, Cbssn., Tpt, Tuba, 2 Timp, Perc. (BD, Cym., Tom-tom, Tam-tam, Chimes, 2 Suspended Cym.)	Originally subtitled *Sinfonia capricciosa*. Commissioned by the National Symphony Orchestra for its fiftieth anniversary. First performance: March 10, 1981, by the National Symphony Orchestra, conducted by Mstislav Rostropovich. Score published by Carl Fischer, 1982.

discipline that pursuing the symphonic ideal required: "I love to write a symphony. I need to write in large forms; I like a big canvas. A symphony is not something that can be tossed off over a weekend. It is cultivated by those who believe in it."[332] His compositional output bears him out: of his 30-odd completed works, nine are symphonies—almost a third of his output (table 6.8).

Mennin eschewed Romanticism or any extroverted emotionalism but did seek to "depict an intense inner drama through thoroughly abstract means."[333] His attitude toward extramusical or programmatic points of reference was ambivalent; even when dealing with a text, as in the Fourth Symphony, or with specific narratives or philosophical concepts as in the Concertato, *Moby Dick* (1952), he tended to approach them "from a lofty, somewhat depersonalized perspective."[334] The Eighth Symphony, discussed at length below, is a case in point. Simmons and Butterworth both hear Mennin's awareness of Schuman in the occasionally lush writing for strings, the tendency to separate the orchestra into choirs, the fragmentary and syncopated interjections from brass and woodwinds, and the long lyrical line (although Diamond's lyricism is another valid point of reference).[335] Like Sessions and Creston, Mennin took an essentially internationalist approach: Simmons compares his "unswerving quest to pursue and refine a particularly focused expressive goal" to Anton Bruckner, his "contrapuntal energy" to Paul Hindemith, and the "lofty grandeur" of some passages to the symphonies of Ralph Vaughan Williams.[336] At the same time, the high rhythmic energy of his music, including its occasional jazzlike syncopations, can be seen as an "American" trait. Indeed, the relentless intensity affected the reception of his earliest symphonies, according to whether the reviewer found it invigorating or exhausting.

Mennin withdrew his First Symphony, but his Symphony No. 2 (1945) was quite successful, winning the first Gershwin Memorial Award for the performance of the first movement only (at Eastman, by the New York Philharmonic under Leonard Bernstein) and the Joseph H. Bearns Prize at Columbia University for the whole symphony.[337] For whatever reason, Mennin withdrew this work as well, though he lifted the ban on performances near the end of his life.

SYMPHONY NO. 3

In 1946 Mennin completed his Third Symphony, premiered on February 27, 1947, by the New York Philharmonic (in New York City this time), with Walter Hendl conducting; a grant from the Naumburg Foundation would soon fund its recording by the New York Philharmonic under Dimitri Mitropoulos. Mennin was still technically a student, but Virgil Thomson gushed: "Here, with little warning, was a fully-fledged symphonic composer in his early twenties."[338]

The Third Symphony is still clearly in a neotonal world, but there are hints in the chromatic melodic writing of the more dissonant counterpoint yet to come. The first movement, Allegro robusto, stretches out a long-breathed string line that twists and bends chromatically but is hardly dissonant. The rhythmic syncopation of this theme gives it some sense of urgency despite the smooth contour. In his review of the work, Henry Cowell noted similarities to the first movement of Beethoven's Fifth Symphony; both themes begin with a repetition of three notes, but Beethoven's falls by a major third (G-E♭) and Mennin's rises by a minor third (C-E♭). Comparing the two movements, Cowell hears Mennin's as the more interesting: "Both begin in C minor, but Mennin takes us through a rapid series of new tonalities as his melodic line is developed. These details would hardly be worth comment if it were not for the fact that, in spite of the strong similarity between the two motives, Mennin's has natural possibilities of development not open to Beethoven."[339] Presumably Cowell is referencing the expanded harmonic possibilities available since Beethoven's time, even to those not committed to serial procedures. He also notes that the harmonic language revolves around an alternation between major and minor thirds, a procedure Mennin would revisit in the Symphony No. 8.

The pursuit of a Beethovenian "heroic" tone might also explain the jarring rhythmic interjections from the brass; a churning double-bass ostinato also gives Mennin's first movement its restlessness. As is common in his symphonic works, though, the momentum built up throughout the movement fades at the end to quiet stillness. Built around a melody introduced in the violas and cellos with a countermelody from the oboe, the second-movement Andante moderato is highly contrapuntal, as are many of Mennin's slow movements. The movement is once again highly chromatic but in a gentle way and fades to a major sonority at its conclusion.

The Finale, Allegro assai, begins with an ostinato in the low strings, over which the solo bassoon presents a theme and the rest of the woodwind sections work antiphonally. The form is a series of elaborations of the bassoon melody, with only the occasional contrast. The theme migrates from section to section with frequent strident interjections from the brass. Sometimes the melody is treated in imitation (as in the string passage at m. 258), sometimes it takes the form of a chorale, and sometimes it appears with a countermelody or as part of a call-and-response between sections. This monothematic movement could be heard as monotonous—a frequent criticism leveled at Mennin's music.[340] On the other hand, it represents a modernist revision of the cantus-firmus form and is far more energetic than the typical Renaissance or Baroque counterparts. Indeed, most of Mennin's symphonies revive older contrapuntal forms and structures, from ground bass to fugue (presumably the Chaconne of Brahms's Fourth Symphony provided a model), while pursuing a different sort of expressive language than the Neoclassicism of Hindemith, Stravinsky, or Copland. Cowell and others heard promise in the work: "The general impression is of a conservative, delicately original work, musical, feelingful, performable, enjoyable."[341]

SYMPHONY NO. 4, "THE CYCLE"

At the time he joined the Juilliard faculty (at age 24), Mennin began his Fourth Symphony (1947–48). It premiered on March 18, 1949, with members of the New York Philharmonic under Robert Shaw and the singers of the Collegiate Chorale, which had commissioned the work. This symphony is unique among Mennin's symphonies in that it bears a descriptive subtitle and sets a text. The poem, written by the composer, presents his fatalistic philosophy of existence in a rather terse fashion. The first movement, Allegro energico, presents symbols of eternity such as the ocean, time, and emotion; the following Andante amoroso is a stately movement focusing on finite humanity; and the third movement, Pronunziato: Allegro deciso, lays out the eternal cycle of disintegration and rebirth.[342] Characteristically he treats the text and its philosophical implications in a relatively dispassionate manner: the music often seems like an autonomous instrumental work with the frequently homophonic voices as another line in the texture. Mennin sets the first movement in the Locrian mode, while the finale moves with the same rhythmic vigor of the preceding symphony.

"The Cycle" elicited opposing reactions. Cecil Smith expressed doubt that any choral symphony, even Beethoven's, has been wholly successful—Stravinsky's *Symphony of Psalms* comes closest, in his opinion, to balancing the demands of symphonic and choral writing. Smith holds up Vaughan Williams's *A Sea Symphony* and Holst's *First Choral Symphony* as examples of the pitfalls, the two composers having "wound up by making rhapsodic settings of Whitman and Keats that cannot be considered true symphonies at all." Neither has Mennin composed a symphony but rather juxtaposed choral and symphonic forces in a fashion that "does not achieve a unity." Smith also dismissed Mennin's poetry.[343]

While equally scornful of the text ("without literary value"), Thomson reacted enthusiastically, though not uncritically, to the music of the symphony and particularly to the composer's skill at integrating voices and instruments: "I don't think I have ever heard a choral symphony in which the forces were so well equilibrated in the whole expressive achievement. He has really composed them as cooperating towards a single end. . . . He has resolved a hitherto unsolved problem, and created by that fact, a musical work of genuine originality."[344]

In Simmons's opinion, the principal value of this work is that through his own words the highly reticent composer gives us "some insight into the emerging character of [his] expressive language . . . the cosmic fatalism he was striving to suggest in much, if not all, of his work to follow."[345]

Regardless of one's opinion on their success, Mennin's early achievements cannot be dismissed. Between 1945 and 1948, he had finished one symphony per year, and together the New York Philharmonic and Thomson had practically anointed him as the future of American symphonic music; the latter wrote at the end of the aforementioned review, "He is twenty-five years old. Draw your own conclusions about his future."[346]

SYMPHONY NO. 5

After the success of these early symphonies, commissions followed in short order and from some of the same sources that were reinvigorating symphonic composition more broadly. The Dallas Symphony Orchestra commissioned the Symphony No. 5 and premiered it on April 2, 1950, with Hendl conducting. The work was subsequently taken up by both Charles Munch and Pierre Monteux; the latter led performances in Boston, New York, and San Francisco, and he also took the work on tours in Europe and South America.[347]

As one progresses through Mennin's symphonic output, one finds few stylistic shifts; instead, there is a continuous process of intensification that, in the Fifth and Sixth Symphonies, takes on "a new grimness and sobriety, while the contrapuntal activity became almost compulsive in its unremitting agitation and frenzy." Mennin retains the discipline and "clear musical logic" that characterized the earlier works, while also articulating "a bold vision and wild, massive forces in ceaseless turbulence and violent conflict, escalating in intensity toward cataclysmic explosions of almost manic brutality."[348] In terms of harmonic language, both symphonies make use of modal melodies and feature thoroughgoing counterpoint. Furthermore, although the Fifth Symphony is more insistently dissonant, both works depend largely on pandiatonic and triadic vocabulary: quartal sonorities, polychords, and extended tertian chords. Both are triptychs, which was Mennin's preferred structure.

Each movement of the Fifth Symphony is a thematically integrated unit with extensive contrapuntal development, even in the slow second movement. The opening Con vigore revolves around three motifs: a fanfare introduced by the woodwinds, a wedge-shaped extended sequence stated for tutti orchestra, and a syncopated call from the horn section. Despite its grounding in traditional contrapuntal procedures, the character of the movement can be heard as American in its syncopations and other rhythmic irregularities that at times obscure the 3/4 meter.[349] The *Canto* begins with a plaintive oboe solo floating over sustained chords in the strings, in a texture and timbre not unlike the *Singing* third movement of Persichetti's Third Symphony. The Finale, Allegro tempestuoso, is like the first movement in determination and agitation. It revolves around two closely related motives, both in Locrian mode, which are driven relentlessly forward by "syncopated rhythms, rushing patterns, and various canonic devices."[350] A beautiful imitative passage for strings lets the movement pause for breath, before scurrying wind figures and ominous bass drum and timpani resurface to drive the movement toward its decisive conclusion.

The critical reaction, both to the Dallas premiere and to the subsequent performance in New York by the Boston Symphony Orchestra with Charles Munch, was by turns reserved and optimistic. Critics like Jay S. Harrison, Howard Taubman, and Arthur Berger generally agreed that the symphony was fully developed and Mennin was a "real composer," in the sense that he had pursued the symphonic genre with dedication and some originality.[351] Cowell was the most perceptive, highlighting the work's thematic integration and consistency of style: "One is left with an impression of greater cohesion than is to be found in most other contemporary symphonies." He praised Mennin's dedication to "long-limbed" melodic lines and grasped the composer's harmonic third way between serialism and tonality: "One gathers that neither key, mode, nor atonality is a main point of interest to the composer, whose style draws on all these elements without seeming to care particularly about any of them."[352]

SYMPHONY NO. 6

While the Sixth Symphony (1953) has much in common with the Fifth, Simmons distinguishes it in terms of level of intensity: here Mennin's symphonic writing passes from "assertive" to "manic and driven." The rhythmic profile is even more irregular, and the consequences of his contrapuntal elaborations, while still rooted in triadic structures, are more severely dissonant.[353] The first movement opens with an unsettling Maestoso introduction that lays out three related motifs that reappear throughout the work. Opening with strings alone, it layers in the shadowy lower registers of clarinet and bassoon and culminates with discordant brass, heralding an uncertain fanfare. The ensuing Allegro is nearly monothematic, determinedly exploring an irregular line unfurled in hushed but urgent tones by the strings. As is becoming Mennin's custom, the movement unfolds in a series of waves of "ever-increasing intensity" that set P in counterpoint with the briefer motifs of the introduction.[354] Another emerging habit is that the second movement (Grave) is lyrical but solemn, a reflective moment between the intensity of the outer movements. Most of the material derives from the motifs of the first movement. In like fashion, the concluding Allegro vivace takes up a variant of I/P and develops it in "whirlwind fashion."[355] Although different in character—one the traditional interior slow movement and the other combining Scherzo and Finale—both the second and third movements build gradually, but determinedly, to a climax. Whereas the second movement returns briefly to the somber, restrained mood of its beginning, the end of the third movement pushes through tenaciously and even violently to reach a stunning conclusion on a Picardy third in A major.

The Symphony No. 6 was commissioned by the Louisville Symphony Orchestra and premiered on November 17, 1953, under Robert Whitney, who in his way did as much to champion American symphonic composition as Koussevitzky, Ormandy, or Bernstein. By this point, the reaction of critics was turning from appreciation to something more uncertain. Reviewers acknowledged the composer's impressive achievement of six symphonies composed by age 31 but viewed his move toward an "expressive extremism" with discomfort.[356] Although the Louisville Symphony recorded the Sixth in 1954, no other recording would appear for more than 40 years, and the work was seldom programmed. Still, while the Sixth Symphony may have made disquieted listeners, by the early 1950s, Mennin was widely regarded as a major symphonic composer in a way that many contemporaries like Bernstein and Diamond were not.[357]

SYMPHONY NO. 7, "VARIATION-SYMPHONY"

There was a nine-year gap between the Sixth Symphony and the Seventh as Mennin explored other genres such as concertos and took on his first administrative post at Peabody in 1958. When the Symphony No. 7, "Variation-Symphony," premiered on January 23, 1963, with George Szell leading the Cleveland Orchestra, a new version of Mennin as symphonist emerged. (That orchestra commissioned the work, and Szell—a friend and supporter of the composer—personally provided the funding.) His extended hiatus from symphonic writing wrought notable shifts in his language. As Butterworth describes it, "Gone are the mannerisms, motor rhythms for pages at a time and over-repetitions of figures. The harmonic language is now less tonal with more complex contrapuntal writing."[358] The one-movement structure is a radical departure for Mennin, who had previously only composed tripartite symphonies in fast-slow-fast divisions; accordingly, his penchant for violent outer movements framing a quiet one is telescoped into a single unit consisting of constantly shifting moods. (As the composer wrote, "In my work there has always been some element of violence and the element of contrast. Here they come out with a vengeance."[359]) His abiding interest in ground bass and cantus firmus techniques serve the needs of a "Variation-Symphony" well.

In this work Mennin, like Schuman, Diamond, Persichetti, and Bernstein, adopted twelve-tone materials without committing to Schoenberg's approach. The principal theme from which the symphony evolves embraces all 12 notes (with some repetitions): [F♯-E♭-D-C-E-C♯-F-E-C-A♭-A-B-B♭-D-D♭]. Mennin divides the work into five continuous sections, each with its own contrasting character, freely developing motivic fragments derived from the principal theme. In the opening Adagio, he introduces the theme in the cellos and basses, fragments it, and plays with the various motifs. While the Allegro is a fierce scherzo, the Andante is calm and lyrical. The fourth section, Moderato, develops the main theme in the manner of a passacaglia. Finally, the concluding Allegro vivace works over the various motifs heard to this point, building in intensity and contrapuntal density. As opposed to Mennin's normal practice of ending his symphony with a major triad (no matter how turbulent the preceding material), this one concludes on an open fifth.[360]

After the premiere in Cleveland, Szell conducted the work in New York, both with his own orchestra and two months later with the New York Philharmonic. Initial reactions were guarded at best, but with time the symphony has grown in esteem. Both Simmons and Butterworth consider it his finest symphony; the latter describes the "Variation-Symphony" as "a closely argued work of massive integrity."[361]

SYMPHONY NO. 8

Mennin was appointed as Juilliard's president shortly before the premiere of the Symphony No. 7, and another decade-long gap ensued before the premiere of the Eighth Symphony, with Daniel Barenboim leading the New York Philharmonic on November 21, 1974. Like its predecessor, the Eighth at first appears exceptional in Mennin's symphonic output, but on closer examination it combines long-standing traits of his compositional style with an embrace of recent trends from outside his stylistic world.

For a composer who rejected Romantic expressiveness in general and programmaticism in particular, the evocative titles and biblical references for each movement seem unusual (see

Table 6.9 Mennin's Concert Note for the Eighth Symphony

The Eighth Symphony . . . is in four separate movements yet connected with an underlying musical idea. Whereas the Seventh Symphony was an extensive symphonic essay based on one large idea and conception that was severe in mood and highly unified in structure and technical makeup, the thrust of the Eighth Symphony has a diversity and contrast of musical ideas and of moods, texture, and instrumental relationships, not only between movements, but also within them. . . . Each of the four movements was stimulated emotionally by Biblical texts. These emotional-musical reactions are not programmatic in nature. On the contrary, each movement is a personal musical response that unfolds along purely musical lines. The texts allied to each of the movements are:

  I. In the beginning . . . Genesis (*In principio* . . .)
 II. Day of wrath . . . Zephaniah (*Dies Irae* . . .)
III. Out of the depths . . . Psalm 130 (*De Profundis Clamavi* . . .)
IV. Praise ye the Lord . . . Psalm 150 (*Laudate Dominum* . . .)

  I. Sostenuto. The Symphony opens with slow suspended sonorities based on grouping of notes which later unfold melodically. In its gradual exposition there is a feeling of suspension of meter which basically characterizes this movement. The interplay of thematic sonorities and textures develops and the musical ideas are proclaimed in various orchestral settings. The movement ends with a new feeling of the suspension of meter as it began.

 II. Allegro con moto. The movement contains strong contrasts of clearly defined musical ideas, from the opening virtuosic flourish in the strings, to the concluding, fanciful close. Much use of the percussion section is made, along with orchestral outbursts based on clearly defined musical motifs developed antiphonally a linerally [*sic*].

III. Adagio. This movement displays the composer's abiding interest in the long, singing melodic line. The purpose in this section is direct and simple: to sing out its ideas expressively and clearly. The melodic lines and sonorities are contrasting transmutations from the opening movement.

IV. Allegro vivace. Though the Finale introduces several transformed motivic fragments from earlier movements, the effect of suspension of time-element [*sic*] is presented in a more dramatic way than in the opening movement. New musical ideas are introduced and emphasized in the brass section, making highly virtuoso demands of each player. There follows a gradual gathering of musical ideas and forces which develop to a climactic conclusion.

Source: Mennin/EIGHTH

table 6.9). Only the Fourth Symphony made such extramusical references, and it did so in the framework of a choral symphony. On a more basic level, the four-movement structure represents another departure from Mennin's typical three-movement format. The composition originated as a two-section orchestral *Sinfonia* (1970), which he withdrew and reconfigured as the first and fourth movements of the Eighth Symphony.[362] Other aspects of the work are fully consistent with Mennin's style: the emphasis on counterpoint—particularly stricter fugal techniques and ostinati—as well as the somewhat belabored slow movements and the general intensity of expressiveness. The level of dissonance, too, reflects Mennin's long-term development toward "more chromatic lines, more dissonant harmonies, more irregular rhythm."[363]

There is evidence of Schuman's influence as well. Despite the men's personal hostilities, they were well aware of each other's works and (along with Persichetti) shared key style traits that characterize a "modern traditionalist." In the Eighth Symphony the attentive writing for the string section is like—and perhaps even surpasses—Schuman's, and the sudden F-major ending of the fourth movement recalls the older composer's tendency to end a work with a major triad, whether its pitch organization was neotonal, atonal, or twelve-tone. Throughout his symphonies, Mennin remained open to new ideas and trends, as with the expanded percussion featured in the second and fourth movements of the Eighth Symphony—although, unlike most of his contemporary symphonists, he never incorporated the piano into his orchestra. Most striking, however, is that Mennin's contrapuntal intensity yields music that sounds at times like the cluster styles of György Ligeti and Krzysztof Penderecki. Whether coincidentally or deliberately, the Eighth Symphony demonstrates an awareness of the most recent developments in international modernism as well as the American symphonic world.

The first movement encapsulates both the new and the typical for Mennin. He again explores the twelve-tone technique in an oblique way. The dissonant opening hexachord in the strings revolves mostly around major and minor thirds but produces an unsettling sonority, as they form members of an augmented triad [D-B♭-G♭] and diminished triad [E♭-A-C], respectively. When the woodwinds enter with their own hexachord in m. 5, Mennin preserves the focus on thirds with a second-inversion minor triad in the clarinets and a first-inversion major seventh chord in the flutes (minus the fifth, D, which remains sustained in the basses). This new hexachord [A♭-D♭-E-B-F-G] is the combinatorial answer to the first hexachord, completing the aggregate in the first five measures of the movement. These "thematic sonorities," as Mennin calls them, go on to unfold linearly throughout the movement—perhaps an outworking of the title, "In the beginning."[364]

The first motivic material of the movement, heard in the horns in mm. 27–29, is built from both major and minor thirds. The answering lines from the woodwinds in mm. 30–37 employ thirds both linearly and vertically, moving in parallel thirds and fifths. The orchestration in this A section (mm. 1–38) recalls Penderecki's string clusters in its use of *divisi*: *a 5* in the first violins, *a 4* in the second violins, and *a 4* or *a 8* in the cellos. At the same time, Mennin's treatment of the individual lines, especially when coupled with dramatic crescendi and decrescendi as in mm. 15–21, results in a vibrating, even shuddering, texture more strongly reminiscent of Ligeti's technique. Section B (mm. 39–48) features the same third-based motives and textures, while maintaining a high level of dissonance. The passage builds through a stretto of quick figuration in the strings and later the woodwinds; its effect is not quite as intense as Ligeti's micropolyphony, but the sound is similar.

The wave crests at the beginning of Section C (mm. 49–57), which consists primarily of a furious thirty-second-note ostinato in the strings and woodwinds, over which the bassoons and brass present a sinister but oddly chorale-like melody. Like the motivic material of the other sections, it revolves around a series of major and minor thirds, hence its ability to evoke a tonal/modal genre amid a highly dissonant passage. By creating a "row" in the first two sonorities of the work that is built out of thirds (with the attendant tonal associations), and then drawing his thematic material out of that, Mennin pursues a strategy similar to Berg's in the Violin Concerto (1935)—or, more proximately, to Diamond's and Bernstein's in the Eighth Symphony (1960) and *Kaddish* Symphony (1963), respectively, themselves modeled on the Austrian work.

The following D section (mm. 58–75) begins with a pointillistic texture that is less *Klangfarbenmelodie* than the constant susurration of a basically static sonority. The overlapping articulations in the brass and woodwinds—not quite stretto but similar in intensification—build from m. 63 to the ***fff*** tutti cluster chord in m. 69. This section resembles B in its emphasis on parallel thirds in the texture and the overlapping statements. The wavelike structure of each section—both in textural thickness and dynamics—reflects the opening passage of the Book of Genesis, specifically the water imagery of the second verse: "And the earth was without form, and void; and darkness was upon the face of the deep. And the Spirit of God moved upon the face of the waters." On the other hand, given that this movement, originating in the withdrawn *Sinfonia*, predates the symphony and its extramusical references, it is more likely that the structure Mennin had created reminded him of the biblical passage—a process that would be more in keeping with his attitude toward musical creation and inspiration.

The denouement in mm. 76–92 is essentially a condensed version of the A section, returning the music to its static, third-based chords at their original soft dynamic. The notable change is that the melodic material in the cellos (mm. 76–81), though it begins like the melody in m. 27 for the horns, rises through a major instead of a minor third and then continues upward instead of drifting back down, still using thirds as the significant interval. Though by no means a triumphal transformation à la the first movement of Beethoven's Third Symphony, this gesture does leave the way open for further events (as does the *In principio* title).

Mennin begins the second movement with a gesture that neatly subverts conventions for setting the *Dies irae*. Though this movement is based on a passage from the book of Zephaniah and not the chant from the Requiem Mass, Verdi's famous "Dies irae" is the most obvious point of comparison, and Mennin's take maintains a similar level of chaotic energy.[365] The movement begins with a two-measure ***ff*** flurry of activity in the winds and strings. The percussion battery creeps in between ***p*** and ***mf***, setting up an ostinato in the timpani, bongos, temple blocks, cymbal, and bass drum that creates a tension no less ominous than Verdi's thunderclaps. This ostinato, in fact, serves as the primary thematic material for a sort of sonata form based on homogeneity between ideas rather than strong contrasts. Like the first movement, each section unfolds as a series of dynamic and textural waves.

Over the percussive ostinato, *P* (mm. 1–20) is a series of static chords in the woodwinds and brass that gradually build in thickness and volume. The section essentially starts over with *T* (mm. 21–32), which follows another wavelike build of texture and volume. The wave crests with the beginning of *S* (mm. 33–64), a second ostinato—a constant sextuplet rhythm distributed over long, contrapuntal lines that still incorporate triadic figures—which begins in the strings before shifting to the woodwinds. The constantly overlapping entrances push the section relentlessly forward, while the horns and strings take over the role of sustaining sonorities (also largely triadic). As at the end of the first movement, the growth typically proceeds from the bottom upward (as at m. 67 and m. 180), in a way similar to Schuman. The marimba and vibraphone punctuate the ostinato, but the suspended cymbals add a shiver to the sustained lines. A final stretto in the string section (essentially *K*, mm. 65–78) continues the triadic material and pushes the section to its climax, as if this were an exposition in a fugue rather than a sonata form.

A brief return to the first ostinato heralds the development section (mm. 79–121), which features contrapuntal interplay between a new *Klangfarbenmelodie* in the strings, syncopated lines in the brass, and material drawn from both the first and second thematic ostinati (as opposed to the "thematic sonorities" of the first movement). After a short grand pause, a passage consisting of sustained chords, constantly rearticulated by choirs made up of high or low strings, low brass, horns and trumpets, and high or low woodwinds, functions as a retransition (mm. 122–48). The exclusive focus on timbral shifts in this passage and the absence of any ostinato contrast sharply with the contrapuntal *perpetuum mobile* of the rest of the movement, making the return of the first ostinato—and thus the beginning of the recapitulation (mm. 149–99)—that much more apparent. Both *P* and *S* are condensed before the coda (mm. 200–38), in which several iterations of the B-A-C-H motive are heard in the tubular bells; the rest of the orchestra gradually fades away as a new **pp** ostinato in the percussion propels the movement to its close, at least rhythmically. This is a rather sudden turn for a movement that announced itself so ferociously, but the final murmurs of the string section create an expectant silence that makes the beginning of the third movement all the more effective.

Beginning with only a high C con sordino in the first violins, joined by a high B-flat in m. 3, the Adagio "De Profundis Clamavi" seems to call out from the heights rather than the depths, although the general impression of distance is effective. The highly chromatic counterpoint in the rest of the muted string section, however, is certainly plaintive enough. Each of the melodic lines in this homorhythmic texture revolves around major and minor thirds while sounding anything but tonal. The same is true of the interjections from the clarinet section (mm. 3 and 5) and then the rest of the woodwinds (from m. 6). The shivering sound of the muted string section is likely why Simmons hears this movement as having an "icy beauty."[366] Mennin's writing for strings in this movement rivals Schuman's with its attention to timbre and the intensely contrapuntal writing for many divisi subsections. The rest of this part form gradually transforms the initial melodic idea while introducing new themes that bear a genetic resemblance to one another—all chromatic but still focusing on thirds or sixths.

The melody first heard in the violins in mm. 2–3 and then continued after a half rest in mm. 4–5 (example 6.16) migrates to a choir of trumpets and trombones in m. 20 and returns in its string chorale guise in m. 47, now without mutes.

Ex 6.16 Mennin, Symphony No. 8, "De Profundis Clamavi," first theme, violin 2, mm. 2–5

This might be perceived as the primary material for the movement, except that it fades in prominence as one of the alternate themes, heard first in the flute in m. 23 and quickly followed by the violas and cellos in m. 27, assumes the place of a recapitulation in m. 63 (see example 6.17).

Example 6.17 Mennin, Symphony No. 8, "De Profundis Clamavi," second theme, solo flute, mm. 23–26

Vaguely similar countermelodies appear throughout the movement: examples include the line in the first violins in m. 9 and the trumpet and trombone duet in m. 13. The point of greatest contrast occurs in mm. 37–46 with a three-voice fugue on a subject that begins with a rising minor sixth—a change from the other thematic ideas in this movement, which typically begin with a rising half step despite being based on thirds. The opening chorale reasserts itself at m. 47. The new section beginning in m. 54 features a theme in the bassoons, cellos, and contrabasses that opens with the drop of a whole step—the first time a theme has begun with a descent. As usual, the accompanying chords in the low brass and trumpets are composed of thirds, but their voicing makes them unsettling, as does the agitation of the dotted rhythms. Another wave builds as the woodwinds join these chords with overlapping articulations that increase in frequency, creating a kind of stretto. Screeching glissandi in the strings punctuate the texture from m. 58 until its abrupt end in m. 63, followed by the sonic exuviation of the theme in the violas and cellos (recalled from m. 23), accompanied by soft chords in the strings. As has every movement so far, the Adagio fades gradually to silence.

Originally the second half of the *Sinfonia*, the Allegro vivace "Laudate Dominum" summarizes the contrapuntal techniques employed throughout the work so far and provides a stirring if not exactly joyous finish. According to Simmons, the movement "conveys a tremendous sense of agitation, its unremitting tension and explosions of violence seemingly at odds with its rubric, Laudate Dominum."[367] However, a closer look at Psalm 150 shows Mennin's orchestral meditation to be more in keeping with the biblical text than Simmons supposes, although the composer does not explicitly evoke the psalm beyond the movement title. The psalmist exhorts the reader to praise God for his "mighty acts" and "greatness" and to use all the audible forces available for such adoration: trumpet (shofar), psaltery, harp, timbrels, stringed instruments, organs, and cymbals (high and low). One is urged to dance as well. Nowhere is sweetness or harmony invoked—rather a festival of noise, which this movement certainly embodies. The choice of "Laudate Dominum" as a name for this (preexisting) movement and a cap for the symphony does make logical and expressive sense.

Mennin describes the Finale as a cyclical recall of motives from prior movements and an intensification of the character of the whole; in particular, "the effect of suspension of time-element [*sic*] is presented in a more dramatic way than in the opening movement."[368] To highlight this similarity, the Finale begins like the first movement, with soft, sustained string chords, although it is more quickly interrupted by punctuation from the woodwinds and brass, as well as the strings' own glissando (m. 6). Although the movement goes on to have a greater degree of rhythmic and metric complexity than any of the others, the "suspension" begins again as stasis. By m. 37 the percussion has begun to interject, and in m. 59 Mennin launches a variation on the ostinato that accompanied *II/P. II/S* recurs as well in the form of the agitated triplet lines in the strings in m. 117, although the precise contour is modified. As this second thematic ostinato murmurs along at **pp**, the stretto-like overlapping of divisi string lines comes close once again to Ligeti.

Although it is difficult to hear any of the expressive content of the Adagio in this hectic movement, the intricate counterpoint, as in the fugal texture that thickens gradually between m. 164 and m. 192, recalls the textures of that movement. Mennin introduces a sixteenth-note ostinato in m. 194, first on a static sonority in the strings and then in the woodwinds followed by the brass, before adding to this constant propulsive foundation a winding, chromatic contour that outlines both major and minor thirds (m. 210). While the pulse remains nearly constant until the end of the movement, churning away in the string section, Mennin obscures any sense of meter by introducing compound rhythms, syncopations, hemiolas, and other rhythmic irregularities in the winds and brass. Overall, the formal process is an open-ended series of waves, as in the first movement, although coming at a faster pace here. (There are four such waves in mm. 193–370 and four more in mm. 388–453.) A brief section of contrast in mm. 371–87 returns to the homophonic texture of the first movement and features a chorale-like melody in the first violins that echoes themes from both the first and third movements. The texture builds again and the sixteenth-note ostinato returns, rushing toward a sudden end on F major, confirmed not by tonal function but by sheer force of will: Mennin sustains the chord from m. 431 until the end 22 measures later.

The reaction to the premiere of the Eighth Symphony was divided, throwing into sharper relief some of the internal contradictions of Mennin's style as it evolved, as well as its elements of continuity. Harold Schonberg in the *New York Times* was indifferent: "Everything sounds a little secondhand; the symphony does not really say very much." Oddly, he claimed that the work had an air of "nostalgia, of a sort." He heard the "busy-busy style of the prewar international school" of which Mennin had been a part, along with Harris, Copland, Schuman, and others. It is true that the second and fourth movements feature the sort of perpetuum mobile and "impulsive rhythmic patterns" that had characterized Mennin's earlier symphonies, and that the third movement is "an adagio that is typical of Mr. Mennin's melodic style," with "long-breathed" lines that Schonberg finds "curiously uncommunicative." Mennin's approach to the program is similarly characteristic in that the titles and the texts they invoke are, as Schonberg perceived, "clues to the emotional nature of the music rather than an attempt to tell a story."[369] These continuities with Mennin's earlier works are all apparent enough, but Schonberg seems not to have heard the incredible shift toward dissonance and even twelve-tone structure in the harmonic language.

Harriet Johnson is perhaps more accurate in her assessment of the music as "loud, dissonant, unrelenting and ultimately bombastic."[370] Accusations of monotony also seem to stick when listening to the Symphony No. 8, in which Mennin draws everything out of two third-based sonorities in the first movement. In some ways, this reaction is analogous to the alleged "impotence" of Brahms in the Fourth Symphony—which also belabors the third as an organizing interval across all the movements.[371] What is striking about Mennin's achievement, though, is that he has managed to unify the work via the interval of the third without it sounding remotely tonal. Reviewing a 1989 recording of the work by the Columbus Symphony Orchestra under Christian Badea, Edith Borroff is perceptive concerning the place of the Eighth Symphony in Mennin's evolution as a composer; it represents "an expansion of orchestral language in both internal and external facets—in both idea and the statement of idea, form, and orchestration."[372]

SYMPHONY NO. 9

The Symphony No. 9 (1981) continued to explore the new harmonic realm the Eighth Symphony had opened. Commissioned by the National Symphony Orchestra for its fiftieth anniversary celebrations, the Ninth Symphony premiered in the Kennedy Center for the Arts with Mstislav Rostropovich conducting. The work originally carried a subtitle, *Sinfonia capricciosa*, but the composer retracted it and simply described the symphony as "dramatic."[373] In this work, Mennin returns to his favored three-movement format. What Mennin calls the "brooding" quality of the first movement Lento, non troppo recalls the opening of the Seventh Symphony, as does some of the motivic contours. The open lyricism of the Adagio arioso, however, is something not heard from Mennin since the Third Symphony. The brief finale, Presto tumultuoso, is as wild as anything in the Sixth Symphony, and, like that symphony, it ends on a suddenly clear tonic, this time in a forceful unison. The Ninth Symphony, then, might be heard as a summary of the composer's symphonic efforts, something only made possible by his gradual evolution from work to work.

By and large, Mennin's music has not shared in the posthumous revival that many other composers in this chapter have enjoyed (limited as some may be). His reputation, fostered by recurring critical complaints about the astringency and relentlessness of his music, coupled with the highly private composer's refusal to promote himself, has inhibited his exposure in the concert hall and to an extent on recordings (though all the works from Symphony No. 3 on have been recorded at least once, especially the Seventh). Mennin was, in a sense, caught between two worlds: because he rejected Romantic expression, he removed his symphonies from the nineteenth-century tradition that many listeners still hear as the heart of symphonic experience; but equally aloof from the avant-garde and uncommitted either to serialism or to tonality, preferring instead to devote himself to contrapuntal explorations inspired by music from the Renaissance forward, he could still be labeled "traditionalist." Nevertheless, Mennin's symphonies belong just as firmly to midcentury tradition, and their energetic rhythms and polyphonic mastery give them a distinctive and distinguished place in the American tradition. As David Wright perceptively commented in program notes for an all-Mennin concert at the Juilliard School: "You can talk about the wild visions of Ruggles and Varèse, or about the big-sky sound of Harris and Schuman, but for sheer propulsive force channeled through tightly-wound counterpoint there is nothing like an allegro by Mennin. Even his slow movements, pretty as their melodies are, are intensely worked, almost impatient in their urge to get on with it. If you want to hear how a composer steeped in classical technique expresses the 'on the go' spirit of America in the mid-20th century, Mennin's music does the job."[374]

Julia Perry

Julia Perry (1924–79) charted much the same course in her early musical career as did many of the composers of her generation, including other symphonists featured in this chapter. After earning a bachelor's and master's of music at Westminster Choir College, she studied choral conducting with Hugh Ross at the Berkshire Music Festival at Tanglewood in the summer of 1949; she returned there in 1951 to study with Luigi Dallapiccola, following him that fall to Italy to continue studies in Florence. She received performances of her *Stabat Mater* (1951); *Short Piece for Orchestra* (1952); and various songs in Milan, Turin, and Salzburg before continuing on to France to study with Nadia Boulanger at the American Conservatory in Fontainebleau in the summer of 1952. While there she claimed the Prix Fontainebleau with her Viola Sonata.[375] Although many of the foremost American composers before and after her were members of the Boulangerie, her style was much more heavily influenced by her time with Dallapiccola. Like Diamond, she spent many years in Europe, particularly in Italy, rather than making her career through American institutions. She also received two Guggenheim Fellowships (1953 and 1956), and in ways similar to Copland, Bernstein, and Schuman, she became part of American postwar cultural diplomacy. At the behest of the US Information Service she toured several European cities in 1957, lecturing on music and conducting orchestras, including the BBC Orchestra and the Vienna Philharmonic.[376] She also spent two summers at the MacDowell Colony (1954 and 1959) as part of a gradual return to full-time residence in the United States by 1961. As Helen Walker-Hill notes, "More than most other black women composers, Perry pursued her career in a largely white musical world."[377] Although she began her career with several well-received solo vocal and choral works, most notably her *Stabat Mater*, she was also committed to writing in large-scale symphonic forms—a province still dominated by white male composers.

However, Perry also shared many experiences with other African American classical musicians. Perry's family members were part of the Black intelligentsia that W. E. B. Du Bois called "the talented tenth": her father was a physician and amateur pianist and her mother was a schoolteacher. Perry and her four sisters took violin and voice lessons and had the benefit of being schooled in an Ohio neighborhood near the University of Akron with what Walker-Hill describes as "a cordial racial atmosphere."[378] That Perry would claim in 1949 that she had "enjoyed remarkable freedom from prejudice and misunderstanding" is, as Walker-Hill notes, an attitude absorbed from the Black upper middle class. As a result of this class distinction, she likely could avoid many instances of public bias or embarrassment, but she also would have learned not to speak about "the hurts and humiliations they were unable to avoid, especially to white Americans."[379] Similar to many Black musicians, her training and career involved mostly white teachers and colleagues. She first studied with Mabel Todd, who had been a student of John Finley Williamson at Westminster College, and during Perry's own time at Westminster, Adele Addison and Lillian Hall were the only other Black students.[380]

The most supportive of Perry's white colleagues were often European rather than American. In this she was not alone: it is part of a pattern that Kira Thurman has traced across the careers of multiple generations of Black musicians from the turn of the twentieth century through Perry's own postwar period. Regarding Central European teachers working with Black students in the United States, Thurman posits that "the transnational nature of their relationship might have permitted German teachers to imagine how their students could build careers for themselves that were not limited to the United States. These teachers' backgrounds, in other words, freed them from seeing Black lives and potential careers solely through the lens of American race relations."[381] The same might be said of Henry Switten—Perry's composition teacher at Westminster and later her colleague when she joined the faculty at the Hampton Institute (1948–49)—who was French-born and trained.[382] Most consequential, however, was the friendship and advocacy of young Italian conductor Piero Bellugi, whom she met in 1950 at International House in New York City; he convinced his former teacher Dallapiccola to accept Perry as a student at Tanglewood.[383] As Thurman notes, the vaunted universalism of classical music sometimes worked in favor of Black musicians' inclusion. Some institutions, like Westminster, admitted them at a time when they were still excluded in many educational settings, and individual teachers took on Black students, "thus practicing the gospel of musical universalism they themselves preached."[384]

This is not to say, however, that Perry did not face challenges on account of her race or that her time in Europe was free of racialized perceptions. Although she studied and worked busily in New York from the fall of 1949 through 1951, Perry was not formally enrolled at any institution there: rather, she studied voice independently with Eugenia Giannini Gregory, who was on the faculty at Curtis; took conducting classes with Emanuel Balaban at the Extension Division of Juilliard; and served as an assistant coach in the Columbia University Opera Workshop.[385] On the one hand, Perry might have been working out a way to pursue her multiple interests in singing, composing, and conducting—but on the other, these provided pathways into prestigious musical and educational spheres without a formal institutional connection. In Europe, Italian audiences and critics enthusiastically received Perry, and by all accounts she integrated well, quickly becoming fluent in Italian. However, even among European friends, her relationships were not colorblind. While she stayed in Florence, Bellugi's family members took to calling her "Giuliettina Nera," which, although clearly meant affectionately, nonetheless marked her racially.[386] In Italy she also befriended the white journalist Patricia Sides, with whom she later became an artistic collaborator; Sides recalls Perry joking that in the United States their friendship would shock southern sensibilities.[387] In 1949 Perry had claimed that "music is an all-embracing, universal language" and that it had a "unifying effect on the peoples of the world" for whom it served as "a common meeting ground."[388] As Walker-Hill states, "According to the facade presented by the musical establishment at that time, race and gender were irrelevant to musical excellence," and as a result "Perry would not have asserted her identity as a woman composer or a Negro composer."[389] However, she was clearly aware of the role her race played in others' perceptions, even in Europe, and she certainly faced challenges specific to both her race and her gender in the course of her career.

In an analogue to her personal history, her musical style seems to face toward a "universal" midcentury modernist style and to specifically Black musical materials and experiences. Although she had written a few early vocal works that drew on the spiritual, by the 1950s, Perry's music had moved, according to Walker-Hill, into "the mainstream of contemporary European compositional techniques. She had left what traces her music had of Negro idioms behind her, and had gained entrance into the most prominent musical circles."[390] Indeed, among the composers in this chapter, the depth of her engagement with serialism is second only to Roger Sessions. At the same time, she also shared a neotonal harmonic language with the likes of Schuman, Diamond, and Bernstein. She was, in other words, wholly typical of her generation—somewhere between European and American modernism, between atonality and serialism on one side and neotonality and Neoclassicism on the other.

After Perry returned to the US, her political and aesthetic attitudes shifted. During the final years of her European residency, the civil rights movement gained momentum. At the same time, as Walker-Hill notes, her initial fame as a gifted young composer was beginning to fade: "All she had striven for—the approval of the white mainstream—was under question."[391] From 1966 on, she increasingly made overt references to race in music as well as poetry. She incorporated Negro folk songs in *Module for Orchestra* (1967–75) and the Symphony No. 5 "Integration" (1966–67) and references to Black popular music, such as rhythm and blues, in *A Suite Symphony* (late 1960s) and the Symphony No. 10, *Soul Symphony* (1972).[392] In this second phase of her compositional style, Perry shared an aesthetic position with other Black women composers, although she dedicated more of her time to writing in symphonic genres than others.

Among the "forgotten modernisms" of the 1960s was the emergence of early postmodernist styles, as seen in works like Bernstein's *Kaddish Symphony*. And distinct from these is what Tammy Kernodle identifies as a specifically Black postmodernism that first appeared in the works of Black women composers, "whose eclectic representations of sonic Blackness and narratives of protest and resistance redefined the cultural context of the Black concert milieu in the decade following World War II."[393] Although Perry did not return to the spiritual as a generative force or engage with the Black church or historically Black colleges and universities, as did Undine Smith Moore or Margaret Bonds, she did challenge some of the meta-narratives about American music and modernism that Kernodle identifies. Foremost among these was the narrative of race formed during the Harlem Renaissance—the New Negro movement, which "concentrated upon the concept of a national Black culture that coupled mastery of European

Table 6.10 The Symphonies of Julia Perry (1924–79)[a]

Title	Movements	Instrumentation	Comments
Symphony in One Movement for Violas and String Basses (Symphony No. 1) (1961)	One movement in three continuous sections 1. Allegro 4/4 (83 mm.) 2. ——— (42 mm.) 3. Presto (75 mm.)	At least 2 Vla. and 2 Cb.	Dedicated to sculptor Henry Moore. Digitized copy of score available at Julia Perry Working Group, ed. Kendra Preston Leonard (https://hcommons.org/groups/julia-perry-working-group/documents/).
Symphony No. 2 (1962)	Three movements	Large orchestra	
Symphony No. 3 (1962, rev. 1970)	Three movements	Large orchestra	
Symphony No. 4 (1964–68)	1. Moderate 6/4 (168 mm.) 2. Fast 7/8 (90 mm.) 3. Very slow 5/4 (46 mm.)	Grand plus Flt. (doubling Picc.), Bclar, B♭ Sopsax., B♭ Tsax, Barhr., Bssn., Perc. (Tri., SD, BD, Cym., Suspended Cym., Tamb., Cowbell, Vbp.), Pno. (doubling Cel.), Harp	Perry referred to this work at one point as *The Selfish Giant Symphony* (after an opera of that name, though Walker-Hill finds no musical connections to it) and at another as "Choreographic Symphony." Parts survive incomplete: those for Tsax., Bssn., and BD are missing for some or all movements. A digitized copy of a reconstruction of the score by Helen Walker-Hill and Christopher Hahn is available at Julia Perry Working Group, ed. Kendra Preston Leonard (https://hcommons.org/groups/julia-perry-working-group/documents/).
Symphony No. 5, "Integration" (1966–67)	1. Slow, desolate 2. Very fast	Ob., Asax., 6 Brass, Timp., Perc. (including Mrb.), Pno., Harp, Strgs.	Lost (?)
Symphony No. 6 for Winds (1966)	1. Moderately Fast 2. Fast 3. Very Slow 4. Fast—Very Fast—Fast	3 Flt. (doubling Picc.), 2 Ob., EH, E♭ Clar., 3 Clar., Bclar., 3 Bssn., B♭ Sopsax, E♭ Asax., B♭ Tsax., E♭ Barsax., 4 Hr., 3 Tpt., 3 Cor., 4 Trom., 2 Btrom., 2 Euph., 3 Tuba, Timp., Perc.	Holograph score published by Carl Fischer, 1968.

Table 6.10 *continued*

Title	Movements	Instrumentation	Comments
Symphony No. 7, "Symphony U.S.A." (1967)	Five short movements	Chorus and small orchestra	Lost (?)
Symphony No. 8 (1968–69)			Lost (?)
Symphony No. 9 (= *A Suite Symphony*?) (1965–70)			Lost (?); may be the same work as *A Suite Symphony*.
A Suite Symphony (= Symphony No. 9?) (ca. 1969)	1. Bass-Amplification in "Rock and Roll" Style (Rather slow) 4/4 (55 mm.) 2. Wagon Train and Indians after Sundown (Moderate) 9/8 (55 mm.) 3. Global Warfare (Moderate) 3/4 (53 mm.) 4. Sonic "E" in Space (Moderate) 2/4 (34 mm.) 5. Slums (Rather slow) 4/4 (61 mm.) 6. Rhythm and Blues (Rather fast) 4/4 (78 mm.) 7. Coal-Miners Sealed in a Condemned Coal Mine (Very slow) 7/4 (18 mm.)	2 Flt, 2 Clar, B♭ Sopsax., B♭ Tsax., 2 Bssn., 2 Hr., 2 Tpt, 2 Trom. (1 tenor, 1 bass), Timp., Perc. (Vbp., Xylo., Suspended Cym., Tam-tam [high], Conga, 4 Temple Blocks, Casaba, BD, Marching Bells, Steel Plate, SD, Tri., Gong, Whip), Harmonica, Pno., Strgs.	In letters to Dominique-René de Lerma in the 1970s, Perry described the work as a five-movement symphony and separated out *Global Warfare* and *Slums* as independent "short oeuvres" for orchestra (Walker-Hill/SPIRITUALS, p. 135 n90). Holograph score (with *Global Warfare* and *Slums*) published by Peermusic. Digitized copy of score available at Julia Perry Working Group, ed. Kendra Preston Leonard (https://hcommons.org/groups/julia-perry-working-group/documents/).

Work	Movements	Instrumentation	Notes
Symphony No. 10, *Soul Symphony* (1972)	1. Moderate 4/4 (121 mm.) 2. Perpetual repetition 4/4 (52 mm.) 3. Very slow 6/4 (36 mm.) 4. Raucous 4/4 (129 mm.)	Grand (2 Hr. and 2 Trom. only) plus 2 Picc., B♭ Tsax, Barhr., Perc. (Tri., SD, Scraper, Timbales, Wood Block, Ratchet, Crash Cym., Suspended Cym., Xylo., Cowbell, Vbp., Slapstick), Pno. (doubling Cel.), Harp. Baritone soloist	Digitized copy of score edited by Helen Walker-Hill and Christopher Hahn available at Julia Perry Working Group, ed. Kendra Preston Leonard (https://hcommons.org/groups/julia-perry-working-group/documents/).
Marching Band Symphony (1972)	1. Marching Band Salute 2. Venus Moon 3. Fireworks on Mars 4. Theme, Variations, and Finale	Concert Band	See below under Symphony No. 11 and *Space Symphony*.
Symphony No. 11 (= *Space Symphony*?) (1972)	Four movements	Concert band	Lost (?); may be the same work as *Space Symphony*.
Symphony No. 12 (1973)	Two movements	3 Clar., 3 Tpt, Perc., Strgs.	Also titled *Simple Symphony* or *Children's Symphony*.
Space Symphony (= *Marching Band Symphony*?) (1975)	Four movements	Concert band	May be the same work as *Marching Band Symphony* or a reworking of Symphony No. 11.
Symphony No. 13 for Wind Quintet (1976)	1. Moderate 4/4 (39 mm.) 2. Fast 5/4 (42 mm.) 3. Slow 6/8 (51 mm.) 4. Fast 4/4 (57 mm.)	Flt., Ob., Clar., E♭ Asax., Bssn.	Same work as "*Quartette*" for Wind Quintette (1963), with minor revisions in the last two movements. Digitized copy of score edited by Helen Walker-Hill and Christopher Hahn available at Julia Perry Working Group, ed. Kendra Preston Leonard (https://hcommons.org/groups/julia-perry-working-group/documents/).

a. The material in this table draws upon the descriptions in Walker-Hill/SPIRITUALS, with scoring and measure details taken from scores available through the Julia Perry Working Group, ed. Kendra Preston Leonard (https://hcommons.org/groups/julia-perry-working-group/documents/). Only Symphony No. 6 has been commercially published (Peermusic released a holograph copy of *A Suite Symphony*, but it is available only through the Working Group site), and most have never received a performance. Daunting logistical challenges confront the Perry scholar. Five symphonies—Nos. 5, 7, 8, 9, and 11—appear to be lost; Perry habitually revised and renamed compositions, however, so at least some of the missing works (especially 9 and 11) may exist under other titles. Some symphonies such as No. 4 lack one or more instrumental parts. Finally, in her later years, Perry suffered a series of debilitating strokes, and her handwriting on scores after 1971 becomes increasingly difficult, if not impossible, to decipher.

form with representations of an African mood and spirit (rhythms, blue tonality)."[394] In line with Alain Locke's version of Black modernity, this metanarrative perpetuated "a type of compositional homogeneity" that emphasized European Romanticism; marginalized Black vernacular musics like jazz, blues, and gospel; and was overwhelmingly masculine.[395] The works of William Grant Still and Florence Price were typical of this modernist vein.

In turning to folk song, rhythm and blues, rock and roll, and soul music, Perry rejected Locke's framework. Similarly, she rejected the overwhelming tendency of American modernism, as embodied by Roger Sessions or Milton Babbitt, to avoid a specifically American sound; she kept up experimentation with modernist techniques while integrating Black vernacular music and other identifiably American and popular sounds. She also experimented with a wide diversity of ensembles for the symphonies: scorings include four or more lower strings (No. 1); full orchestra with saxophones, varied percussion, and harmonica (*A Suite Symphony*); wind ensemble (No. 6 and *Space Symphony*); and wind quintet (No. 13).

Operating without the affiliation of a university or major symphony orchestra, Perry represented a generation of Black women composers who "questioned the meta-narrative of nationalism and the centralization of the concert hall."[396] It is not surprising, then, that her works from the 1960s on garnered fewer performances, recordings, and publications compared with her earlier works that conformed more closely to mainstream expectations—those of female composers, in her focus on vocal music and shorter forms, and those of Black composers, in her judicious use of the spiritual.

Unfortunately, it is precisely these later works that encompass the majority of Perry's symphonies (table 6.10), which she wrote between 1961 and 1976. Apart from her early success with *A Short Piece for Orchestra* (1952), almost all her other orchestral pieces, including her symphonies, have gone unperformed and unpublished. Although some works like *Homage to Vivaldi* (1959) attained some success and exist as rental parts, most survive only as manuscripts spread across multiple archives. Some symphonies, for example No. 4, lack one or more instrumental parts. Worse, up to five symphonies (Nos. 5, 7, 8, 9, and 11) appear to be lost entirely, at least in that form; as the table shows, however, Perry sometimes reworked and retitled pieces, and one or two of the missing symphonies may exist, at least to some degree, in other incarnations. After suffering the first of several debilitating strokes in 1970, her handwriting became increasingly hard to decipher, adding illegibility to the obstacles facing the Perry scholar. The challenges in identifying and accessing most of Perry's orchestral music mean that facilitating performances and accurately assessing her achievement as a symphonist remain difficult. Nonetheless, from the published research of Walker-Hill, and the small number of published scores, we can glean some significant facets of her orchestral style and general compositional approach.[397]

A SHORT PIECE FOR ORCHESTRA

Perry's first orchestral work (1952) serves to represent both her approach to the symphonic medium and the first phase of her compositional style. It is also the first work to appear after she began studying with Dallapiccola, and as such it was influenced by his lyrical approach to twelve-tone language: "his emphasis on motivic unity, rich orchestration, and expressive melodic lines combined with austere contemporary practices."[398] In particular, *A Short Piece for Orchestra* features an "economy of thematic material" and the use of pitch cells to generate cohesion, as well as a creative and varied use of the orchestral palette.[399] Overall the work is intensely polyrhythmic, including several passages of quickly shifting meters. Perry's preference for hemiola and syncopation is clear in those sections where the meter does settle into the predominant 3/4. In terms of harmonic language, the work is highly dissonant but nonetheless tonal, beginning and ending with a clear declaration of D as the pitch center, despite whatever ambiguities may surround it.

Although Perry would embrace serialist techniques for organizing not only pitch but also rhythm, dynamics, and timbre, the organization principle here is not a twelve-tone row. Walker-Hill identifies an organic development based on three interrelated generating cells. All three motives appear within the first five measures: a group of half steps, both rising and descending; a chord structure of two minor thirds plus a fourth; and a melodic contour of a rising half step and fifth, plus descending half step and fourth.[400] In terms of form, Michelle Edwards and Walker-Hill agree on a modified rondo: A–B–A1–C–A2–D–A3.[401] The refrains tend to shift meters more frequently than the contrasting episodes, and the melodic contours are as jagged as the rhythmic profile. Although not twelve-tone in its organization, the processes used to transform the germinal motives of the A section are derived from serialism.

In the opening fanfares we hear Perry's tendency to oppose blocks of timbre: a quick alarm from flutes, oboes, clarinets, muted horn, and low strings versus the aggressive quarter-note stomping of bassoons, horns, trombones, and violins. The B section is a languid Andante (mm. 32–66), beginning with a wide-ranging, highly chromatic melody from the flute, which then passes to the oboes and eventually clarinet and horn. The section might be described as a post-tonal take on the pastorale until short, agitated motives adapted from the A section begin to intrude from the low strings up through the texture (m. 43). Fragments of the chromatic melody return once more in the solo violin (m. 54) and a dissonant string halo (mm. 58–66) surrounds the gradual acceleration back into the A2 section (mm. 67–93). The C section (mm. 94–130) is marked Meno mosso but retains the propulsive energy of the refrains. Much of the material in this contrapuntal texture is derived from the second cell with its minor thirds and fourth. After a modified refrain (mm. 131–56) the D section provides the strongest contrast with a cooling off of energy. Marked Molto lento, it settles into the longest uninterrupted stretch of 3/4, although the persistent hemiola in the strings keeps the section floating free. The slow pulsing of sustained string chords begins with octaves before gradually filling in the triad, after which Perry introduces persistent dissonances: an A against B in the violins, E against F and F-sharp against E in the violas. Overall, the pace is glacial as is the frosty timbre: muted strings and French horn, flute, harp, and celesta. By dint of repetition, B is the pitch center of this section, although at m. 194 the refrain suddenly returns, rending the static atmosphere and briefly but firmly asserting D as the true harmonic center of the work.

Early performances of the work reflect something essential about the first half of Perry's career, in that it was heard most often outside the United States. It was premiered as a piece for chamber orchestra by the Turin Symphony Orchestra under Dean Dixon in 1952 and was likely heard on Perry's later European tours sponsored by the State Department. The US premiere took place in 1955 with the Little Orchestra Society, conducted by Thomas Scherman. William Steinberg performed it with the Pittsburgh Symphony Orchestra on its tour of Europe in 1964 and with the New York Philharmonic at home in 1965. It was recorded by the Imperial Philharmonic Orchestra of Tokyo under William Strickland and released by Composers Recordings Inc. in 1961.[402] The reception was mostly favorable, with Ross Parmenter remarking that it "perhaps could have been longer to its own advantage, for Miss Perry is both gifted and individual in her style."[403] Although Harold Schonberg of the *New York Times* expressed disappointment, the 1961 recording received enthusiastic reviews in *Hi Fidelity* and

American Record Guide.[404] *A Short Piece for Orchestra* has gone on to have one of the more robust performance histories of Perry's works, alongside the *Stabat Mater*.

SYMPHONY NO. 10, *SOUL SYMPHONY*

In many ways, the Symphony No. 10 (1972) encapsulates the changes Perry's politics and musical style underwent in the 1960s. When she returned from Italy in February 1959, she brought with her a new orchestral work, the *Requiem for Orchestra*, later known and published as *Homage to Vivaldi*. Premiered at a Music in the Making Concert at the Cooper Union, conducted by Howard Shanet, it anticipated some of the developments to come.[405] Although based on themes by Vivaldi, which make its motoric ostinatos a natural choice, the degree to which it relies on rhythmic energy more than melodic interest becomes a hallmark of Perry's later style. Starting in the 1960s, she began to refer to movements as "Speeds" and to indicate tempos and dynamics with English words and abbreviations.[406] For example, the Symphony No. 4 (1964–68) consists of three speeds: Moderate, Fast, Very Slow.

The tripartite organization of Symphony No. 4, along with the reinterpreted Italian Baroque stylistic allusions in *Homage to Vivaldi*, suggest the influence of Neoclassicism. Stravinsky might provide a useful model, not just in terms of preclassic musical references, but in the deliberately static quality of the symphony. Walker-Hill notes the avoidance of progression, the obstinate repetition, and the continued use of small pitch cells.[407] The primacy of timbre and rhythmic interest over melody are also shared traits with the Neoclassic Stravinsky of the *Symphony of Psalms* and Symphony in C.

In the mid-1960s, Perry returned to Black musics as touchstones for her symphonic writing. The *Module for Orchestra* (1965–75) comprised 20 variations on a "Negro folk song" and the Fifth Symphony (1966–67) was tellingly subtitled "Integration."[408] We can only guess about the musical content of the latter since the score is lost, but it most likely bridged the space between the Symphony No. 4 and later works that drew quite explicitly on Black musics, like *A Suite Symphony* (1969) and the Tenth Symphony. What distinguishes the latter two works from *Module for Orchestra* and Perry's early spiritual-inspired vocal works is the type of vernacular music she references. Starting in 1969, in a move that distinguished her from other Black women composers like Moore and Bonds, as well as from white men like Bernstein, Perry turned to "contemporary urban genres."[409] Her choice is all the more striking given the Black bourgeois influence of her upbringing, which shunned "popular" musics, whether ragtime, jazz, blues, or boogie-woogie. The Symphony No. 10 is the work of a singular composer, forging a path not traveled by any other symphonist of any race in this period—a path taken up only by later generations, as in the blues- and jazz-infused symphonies of Wynton Marsalis.[410]

Although Walker-Hill sees a "radical departure in aesthetic philosophy" in the *Soul Symphony* in terms of accessibility, many of the characteristics noted above remain: melodies of short motivic cells, repeated patterns, and priority given to rhythm. She also uses some serial techniques. And as in the *Short Piece for Orchestra*, contrasting timbral groups help to delineate formal sections. What separates this piece from her previous output is the minimal degree of dissonance, with harmonic emphasis given to extended tertian chords and modal sonorities of jazz.[411] Rather than see this as a departure, it might be heard as a distillation of the essential traits of Perry's compositional style with a substitution of Black musical harmonies for modernist dissonance.

The tempo indications distinguishing each of the four speeds seem to conform to conventional expectations for a four-movement symphony: "Robust" (bold opening movement),

"Perpetual repetition" (fast scherzo-like movement), "Very slow" (contrasting slow movement), and "Raucous" (lively finale). However, we might also read her choice to reject formal expectations within movements—in terms of meter, for example, "Perpetual repetition" is no scherzo and trio—and to name movements and dynamics with English markers as decolonizing moves. The first movement also eschews the developmental character of a sonata form, instead featuring three contrasting themes that remain relatively unchanged. The first is a fanfare of two-note phrases in rising thirds that spell out a seventh chord (a signature harmony for Perry). The second theme, which Walker-Hill describes as a "jazzy, blueslike riff in eighth notes," is treated in call-and-response fashion.[412] Both themes have a steady, four-on-the-floor character in terms of meter, but the third theme is in 13/8 meter and consists of short rising and falling fragments of the chromatic scale; the third theme is handled like a refrain between variations on the first two themes.[413] In this new symphonic context, the contrast in timbre between groups of instruments, combined with the frequent use of call-and-response, shares traits with jazz orchestration, as does the overlapping texture and increasing rhythmic activity in the drive toward the end of the movement (what would be called a "shout chorus" in a jazz arrangement).

The second speed is based on the "jazzy" second theme of the first movement, lending some cohesion between movements. The earlier rhythmic insistence of this motive now becomes a true ostinato that is passed between sections of the orchestra eight times. Perry later subjects the motive to serial procedures—retrograde, inversion, and retrograde inversion. A contrasting theme breaks up the rhythmic monotony with a combination of 4/4 and 5/4 meters. The latter half of this contrasting theme is subjected to augmentation in the coda, gradually lengthening the motive if not actually slowing the tempo in order to transition to the next speed.[414]

In the third speed, "Very slow," we encounter a more experimental take on the materials: Perry handles them in a way similar to minimalism, which had come to prominence in the 1960s.[415] At only 36 measures, it is also strikingly brief and its spare texture sets it apart from the more robust and layered movements on either side. Similar versions of a triadic melody that rises and falls over four measures appear successively in clarinet, bassoon, tenor saxophone, trumpet with straight mute, a bass-baritone vocalist singing falsetto, and string bass. Between each statement, the harp slowly repeats unison notes, alternating between G and D. Walker-Hill identifies a point of reference for the melismatic style and slow tempo in long-meter gospel hymns.[416] The oscillation of the harmony between G and D might also point to the spiritual, whereas the two "stanzas" of three statements might passingly indicate the blues. We might even hear the meditative sense of the movement as predicting the "holy minimalism" or "spiritual minimalism" of Arvo Pärt and John Tavener. Indeed, from the late 1950s friends had noticed changes in Perry's attitude, notably a fervent interest in religion and St. Catherine of Siena, as well as her increasing reticence in social interactions. In 1970 she had suffered a stroke and her right hand was paralyzed.[417] It is entirely possible that this movement reflects those changes to her spiritual outlook or a response to her struggles.

The fourth speed, "Raucous," broadly conforms to the expectations of a vigorous, triumphant symphonic finale, but in a way inspired by Black popular music more than Haydn or Beethoven. It begins with a boisterous tutti, which then alternates with three contrasting themes differentiated by timbre. Walker-Hill identifies the vocabulary of the three contrasting themes with jazz: lowered thirds and fifths, prominent triplet rhythms, and syncopations.[418] However, these traits are most typical of the blues, which had been revived and reconfigured after the war as part of the jump, rhythm and blues, and rock and roll styles. Combined with the four-on-the-floor meter and the prominent backbeats in the percussion (configured to sound like a trap set), the inspiration here is more likely rock or rhythm and blues than it is the postbop jazz styles of the 1960s and early 1970s.

In the *Soul Symphony*, Perry made what may have been her final attempt to work out the dichotomy inherent in many of her works from the late 1960s on: the divide between the aesthetic and formal imperatives of the European symphonic model and the aesthetic and ideals of Black musics. Olly Wilson identified this opposition as the defining characteristic of Black orchestral composers from the early twentieth century on and connected it to W. E. B. Du Bois's concept of the "double-consciousness" as experienced by African Americans.[419] In other words, Black Americans are forced to perceive themselves according to the standards of white society: "One ever feels his two-ness—an American, a Negro; two souls, two thoughts, two unreconciled strivings; two warring ideals in one dark body, whose dogged strength alone keeps it from being torn asunder."[420] Wilson sees this dynamic reflected in two general tendencies in the orchestral music of Black composers: sometimes their works are indistinguishable from those of non-Black composers and are thus broadly typical of their time, while other compositions bear traits "clearly derived from traditional African American musical practices."[421] Most of Perry's symphonies fall into the latter category, while most of her music from the 1950s does, indeed, reflect mainstream Euro-American modernism.

Walker-Hill offers an evenhanded assessment of Perry's career and her significance in the history of American music: "She drew on the strengths and musical traditions of her African American heritage, competed successfully in the white mainstream musical world, and gained an international reputation as a composer of undisputed talent and skill in an eclectic twentieth-century musical language. This achievement was not only impressive but also subversive, a challenge to the status quo without being intentionally political."[422] However, as Wilson and Kernodle have shown, her very existence as a Black woman modernist and her attempts to integrate the various facets of her musical and personal experiences are unavoidably political. Likewise—with all the daunting practical challenges involved in accessing or even recovering many of her symphonies duly noted—the ensuing neglect even of those works that are readily accessible must be understood within the musical politics of American concert halls, orchestral institutions, and recording companies in the late twentieth century. The supposed "universal" values and the meritocracy of classical music, as shown by Thurman, helped some African American artists to succeed in garnering instruction, funding, performance opportunities, and critical attention. However, the colorblind attitude that emerged in American musical institutions, as in other facets of American society in the late twentieth century, will not help recover works like Perry's symphonies that challenge the dominant narratives of modernism and nationalism at midcentury.

Conclusion

Together these composers span generations and they share significant traits and circumstances with the composers active in the 1930s and 1940s, as well as those who rose to prominence in the 1970s. Looking back, each was as profoundly affected by the central conflict of World War II as were Harris, Copland, Sowerby, and others discussed in chapter 5, and the earliest symphonic works of most of the composers at hand were heard in the same stylistic and critical milieu as those older figures. Looking forward, Hovhaness, Bernstein, Persichetti, and Mennin take a nondoctrinaire attitude toward style that could arguably be called postmodern. In a related vein, the choices of "traditional modernists" like Schuman, Persichetti, Mennin, and Perry (in her early works) showed that relentless forward motion is not the only music-historical trajectory. This is crucial when considering a time period that, in existing narratives, is dominated by the avant-garde and academic serialism and subscribes so strongly to concepts of progress and antithetical dualities. In response to the postwar modernist turn toward serialism, composers like Schuman, Sessions, Diamond, Bernstein, Mennin, and Perry proved that serialism need not be dogmatic and that tonal and twelve-tone techniques could coexist in a given work. In particular, Perry's music proves that the integration of serialism, dissonance, and intense counterpoint with Neoclassical or neotonal language, as well as an embrace of one's heritage through vernacular and popular musics, could be part of a viable path toward an American symphony.

The harsh lesson for these composers was that although there was little place for the nineteenth century in the artistic circles of postwar modernism, audiences still listened with the same ears conditioned by Beethoven, Brahms, Franck, Tchaikovsky, and Dvořák. Particularly when working within the symphonic tradition, if one does not embrace the nineteenth century and its Romantic or nationalist visions of the symphony—as do Bernstein, Diamond, Schuman, and Mennin at various moments, albeit in their own ways—one must sometimes look a good deal further back, as do most of these composers in some way. The reception of Roger Sessions's symphonies demonstrated that atonal and serial modernisms presented their own problems in relation to the symphonic model, even if only in the ears of critics and audience listeners. Although not as rigorously, Diamond, Schuman, Mennin, Bernstein, and Perry all explored ways of incorporating post-Schoenberg vocabulary into their personal styles and approaches to the symphonic genre and took varying degrees of criticism for the dissonance of their music. Although it would take decades for musicological scholarship to break down the stereotype of an unbridgeable gulf between European-oriented serialists, on the one hand, and Americanist tonal composers, on the other, several composers discussed in this chapter spent their careers pointing the way.[423] They almost immediately were submerged by dualistic narratives and remain a largely forgotten vanguard in American music.

In terms of the promotion and distribution of these works, traditional models of patronage coexisted with government funding and new sources of private wealth like the Norlin Foundation. Dependence on the goodwill of eminent conductors like Serge Koussevitzky coexisted with the programming innovations of the Louisville Orchestra and American upstarts like Robert Whitney, as well as independent record labels like Hovhaness's Poseidon Records and Harry Partch's Gate 5 Records. Further, while the frequent accusatory trope of the composers' retreat to the academy was at least partly true, it not only enabled "academic serialism" but the rise of the wind ensemble as both a symphonic medium and a commissioning organization—perhaps the only true uniquely American phenomenon discussed in this volume. The symphony at midcentury, for each of these composers, points both backward and forward, outward and inward. To the extent that the works in this chapter are symphonies between worlds—neither fully removed from the European tradition nor fully committed to it, neither exclusively serialist nor completely disinterested in its vocabulary and procedures—they are perhaps fittingly understood as American symphonies.

Brief Mentions

As we have seen, American symphonic activity during the period between 1950 and 1970 was no less diverse and wide-ranging than in the previous decades, and contributors to the genre numbered far more composers than have been covered thus far in this chapter. The following list includes additional figures who composed one or more symphonies during this time. Among the entries are listed all composers not covered elsewhere who had symphonies premiered or performed by Serge Koussevitzky or received commissions from the Koussevitzky Music Foundation (see tables 1.1 and 1.2 in chapter 1). Unless otherwise noted, the information in this section is drawn from Grove Music Online.

Born in Siberia, **Aaron Avshalomov** (1894–1965) lived and worked in China for 30 years before emigrating to the United States in 1947. He wrote three symphonies. The first, in C Minor (1938–39), dates from his years in Shanghai. Koussevitzky commissioned the Second in E Minor (1949), and the Koussevitzky Music Foundation commissioned the Third Symphony (1953).

Irwin Bazelon (1922–95) was born in Evanston, Illinois. His teachers included Darius Milhaud at Mills College (1946–48). Settling in New York, he completed 10 symphonies between 1961 and 1992, which are noted for spare textures highlighting counterpoint in striking timbral combinations, free serialism, and jazz idioms. They include No. 1 (1961); No. 2, "Testament to a Big City" (1961); No. 3, scored for brass, percussion, piano, and string sextet (1962); No. 4 (1965); No. 5 (1967); No. 6 (1969); No. 7 in Two Parts "Ballet for Orchestra" (1980); No. 8 for strings (1986); No. 8 ½ (1988); No. 9 "Sunday Silence" (1992). A Symphony No. 10 (1992–95) was unfinished at his death, but one movement has been performed.

Warren Benson (1924–2005) became a distinguished professor of composition at Ithaca College (1953–67) and the Eastman School of Music (1967–93). Essentially self-taught, he specialized in music for percussion and wind ensembles, for which he wrote two symphonies: Symphony for Drums and Wind Orchestra (1962), which features four sets of timpani and five solo percussionists, and Symphony No. 2, "Lost Songs" (1983).

Easley Blackwood Jr. (1933–2023) studied with Olivier Messiaen, Paul Hindemith, and Nadia Boulanger; he taught theory and composition at the University of Chicago from 1958 to 1997. His musical style went through several sharply different phases. The Neoclassical First Symphony (1955), written during his studies with Boulanger, premiered with the Boston Symphony Orchestra under Richard Burgin in 1958 and was later recorded by that ensemble under Charles Munch. The next three symphonies increasingly incorporate serial techniques; the Second (1960) premiered with George Szell and the Cleveland Orchestra, the Third (1964) with Jean Martinon and members of the Chicago Symphony Orchestra, and the Fourth (1977, written for the Illinois Sesquicentennial), again with the Chicago Symphony Orchestra, under Georg Solti. After a period of experimentation with microtones, Blackwood turned to a Neoromantic language. The composer described the Fifth Symphony (1990), commissioned by the Chicago Symphony Orchestra to celebrate its centennial, as "the kind of symphony Sibelius might have written had he experimented with the modernist techniques that attracted composers like Casella and Szymanowski."[424]

John Barnes Chance (1932–72) wrote music that is tonal, rhythmically inventive, and sensitively orchestrated. He composed two symphonies. The First (1956), for orchestra, served as his master's thesis for the University of Texas, Austin. The Second (1972), for winds and percussion (his best-known medium), revolves around a four-note motto clearly derived from Dmitri Shostakovich's DSCH (D-E♭-C-B in German musical notation) "signature"; Chance completed this work just before his early death in a domestic accident.

Frank Erickson (1923–96), a student of Mario Castelnuovo-Tedesco and Halsey Stevens, composed and arranged music for band (including Carlos Chávez's *Sinfonía India* in 1971). His compositions include three wind symphonies (1954, 1959, and 1984).

Irving Fine (1914–62) studied composition with Edward Burlingame Hill, Walter Piston, and Nadia Boulanger, and conducting with Koussevitzky. Commissioned by and dedicated to Charles Munch and the Boston Symphony Orchestra, his three-movement Symphony (1962) merges Stravinskian elements, serial techniques, intricate contrapuntal textures, and colorful orchestration with a distinctive lyricism. The symphony is Fine's most substantial composition but also his last: the composer died of a coronary thrombosis five months after its premiere.

Ross Lee Finney (1906–97) studied composition with Nadia Boulanger and Edward Burlingame Hill; he also had lessons with Roger Sessions and with Alban Berg in Vienna. He taught composition at the University of Michigan in Ann Arbor from 1949 to 1974; his pupils included George Crumb. During the war years, Finney wrote in a folk-influenced American style; works include his 1942 Symphony No.1 (*Communiqué 1943*). Later he adopted a rigorous but lyrical and tonally oriented twelve-tone language. Symphony No. 2 (1958), commissioned by the Koussevitzky Music Foundation, premiered with the Philadelphia Orchestra under Eugene Ormandy. The same forces also gave the first performance of Symphony No. 3 (1960), which Finney wrote during a residency at the American Academy in Rome; it is similarly twelve-tone though more lyrical. His final symphony, No. 4 (1972), commissioned by the Baltimore Symphony Orchestra, includes passages of indeterminate notation.

Nicolas Flagello (1928–94) studied composition with Vittorio Giannini and conducting with Jonel Perlea at the Manhattan School of Music; he in turn taught both subjects there from 1950 to 1977. Through a Fulbright Fellowship he continued his studies at the Accademia di S Cecilia, Rome in 1956. His works combine expressive melody and harmonic richness with concise structure and colorful instrumentation. He wrote two symphonies: the First for full orchestra (1968), and the Second, "Symphony of the Winds," for wind ensemble (1970). According to Simmons, the First "exemplifies the Neo-Romantic paradigm of the symphony as quintessential medium for the representation of serious emotional crisis. . . . along with the Symphony No. 7 of Peter Mennin, it may be the greatest of all American traditionalist symphonies."[425]

The family of **Lukas Foss** (1922–2009) emigrated from Berlin to the United States in 1937. He studied composition with Rosario Scalero and Randall Thompson as well as conducting with Fritz Reiner and Serge Koussevitzky; he also had lessons for a year with Paul Hindemith at Yale University. In 1950–51 he was a fellow of the American Academy in Rome. A successful composer-conductor, he wrote four symphonies that bookend his career. The music from 1944 to 1960 is predominantly Neoclassical and includes the Symphony in G (1944), championed by Leonard Bernstein, and the *Symphony of Chorales* (1956–58), commissioned by the Koussevitzky Music Foundation and based on four Bach chorales. He explored various experimental techniques in the 1960s and 70s but later returned to traditional genres. Symphony No. 3, "Symphony of Sorrows" (1991) includes an elegy for Anne Frank as well as a meditation on T. S. Eliot's poem *The Waste Land*. The fourth symphony, subtitled "Windows to the Past" (1995), quotes pieces from the composer's earlier years and evokes the worlds of Ives and Copland.

Vittorio Giannini (1903–66), like his student Nicolas Flagello, belongs to the "modern Romantic tradition" that put priority upon Italianate lyricism, tonal orientation, and at times intense emotion.[426] The Philadelphia-born composer studied in Milan and at Juilliard, received numerous honors, and held several prominent teaching positions; in addition to Flagello, his pupils included John Corigliano and Adolphus Hailstork. His output includes seven symphonies (the first two unnumbered), of which the best known by far is Symphony No. 3 for band

(1958); the others include a Symphony "In memoriam Theodore Roosevelt" (1935); Symphony, "IBM" (1939); Symphony No. 1, "Sinfonia" (1950); Symphony No. 2 (1955); Symphony No. 4 (1960); and Symphony No. 5 (1965). Simmons considers Symphonies 1, 4, and 5 to be the most accomplished.[427]

Don Gillis (1912–78) studied music at Texas Christian University and North Texas State University. Most of his compositions are based on American subject matter and incorporate popular source materials, including jazz. He wrote 11 symphonies between 1939 and 1967, all with descriptive and sometimes whimsical titles. They include Symphony No. 1, *An American Symphony* (1939–40); Symphony No. 2, *Symphony of Faith* (1940); Symphony No. 3, *A Symphony for Free Men* (1940–41); Symphony No. 4, *The Pioneers* (1943); Symphony No. 5, *In Memoriam* (1944–45); his best-known work, the Symphony No. 5½, *A Symphony for Fun* (1945–47, performed by Toscanini); Symphony No. 6, *Mid-Century USA* (1947); Symphony No. 7, *Saga of the Prairie School* (1948); Symphony No. 8, *A Dance Symphony* (1950); Symphony No. 9, *Star-Spangled Symphony* (1951); and Symphony No. X, *Big D(allas)* (1967).

Robert Kurka (1921–57) died from leukemia before completing the orchestration of his best-known work, the opera *The Good Soldier Schweik*, based on a classic (and ironically equally unfinished) Czech novel; Hershey Kay arranged the rest of the opera. James Wierzbicki describes his music as "neo-classical in style and influenced by the folk music of the former Czechoslovakia . . . [and] characterized by its use of repeated melodic and rhythmic motifs, the appearance of dissonant elements within a tonal structure and an energetic rhythmic drive."[428] These traits appear in his Symphony No. 1, Op. 17 (1951) and especially his highly regarded Symphony No. 2, Op. 24 (1952).

The family of **Benjamin Lees** (1924–2010) emigrated to the United States from Russia by way of China (where he was born); he studied at the University of Southern California with Halsey Stevens and privately with George Antheil. He composed the first of five symphonies in 1953 and the second (perhaps his most respected) in 1958. His Third Symphony dates from 1968. He set the expansive Symphony No. 4, "Memorial Candles" (1985) for mezzo-soprano, solo violin, and orchestra; written to commemorate the fortieth anniversary of the Holocaust, it sets poems of Nelly Sachs. His final symphony, "Kalmar Nyckel" (1986), was commissioned by the foundation of that name for the 350th anniversary of the founding of New Sweden (a Swedish colony along the Delaware River). Lees's idiom is traditional, with influences of Prokofiev and Bartók as well as Antheil; his music is noted for extended tonality with semitonal inflections, active and often irregular rhythms, and secure command of orchestral technique and form.

Hall Overton (1920–72) was a successful composer of concert music and opera as well as a respected jazz pianist and arranger. He studied at Juilliard (where he later taught) with Vincent Persichetti and also took private lessons with Wallingford Riegger and Darius Milhaud. His concert music was deeply though not overtly influenced by jazz. He wrote two symphonies: the first, for strings, resulted from a Koussevitzky Music Foundation commission (1955); the second (1962) unfolds in one short movement.

Daniel Pinkham (1923–2006) studied composition with Walter Piston and Aaron Copland at Harvard University; with Paul Hindemith, Arthur Honegger, and Samuel Barber at Tanglewood; and privately with Nadia Boulanger. He enjoyed a successful career as a composer, organist and harpsichordist, and teacher at Harvard and later the New England Conservatory. While most celebrated for sacred choral and organ music, his prolific output includes four symphonies. Symphony No. 1 dates from 1961 and No. 2 from 1962; in this period, he experimented with integrating twelve-tone and tonal languages. Symphony No. 3 dates from 1985–86, and No. 4 from 1990.

H(erbert) Owen Reed (1910–2014) received his PhD in 1939 from the Eastman School of Music, where he studied with Howard Hanson and Bernard Rogers; his Symphony No. 1 appeared in the same year. He took lessons with Bohuslav Martinů, Aaron Copland, and Leonard Bernstein at Tanglewood in 1942, and with Roy Harris during the summer of 1947. His best-known and most influential composition is *La fiesta Mexicana* of 1949, which he subtitled "Mexican Folk Song Symphony for Band." The composer spent six months in Mexico in 1948–49, and the three-movement work draws upon a number of Mexican folk and popular melodies.

Wallingford Riegger (1885–1961) became a prominent member of the 1920s ultramodernist generation alongside Henry Cowell, Carl Ruggles, and Edgard Varèse. He became one of the first American composers to adopt twelve-tone language, albeit freely and with occasional tonal references. He wrote a number of pieces in the 1930s for the pioneers of modern abstract dance, including Martha Graham; the slow movements of his third and fourth symphonies incorporate passages from these dance scores. His music is generally characterized by forceful rhythms and imitative contrapuntal processes such as canon, fugue, and passacaglia. Riegger wrote his first symphony in 1944 and his second (for school orchestra) in 1945; he later withdrew both. The Symphony No. 3 (1946–47), however, brought him wide recognition both in the United States and Europe: commissioned by the Alice M. Ditson Fund of Columbia University, it won the New York Music Critics' Circle Award in 1948 and a Naumburg Foundation Recording Award. His final symphony (1956), commissioned by the Fromm Music Foundation of Chicago, blends serialism with tonality.

While justly celebrated for his vocal music, especially his almost 400 art songs, **Ned Rorem** (1923–2022) also created many instrumental works. Growing up in Chicago, he studied music theory with Leo Sowerby; he attended the Curtis Institute but left to become secretary and music copyist to Virgil Thomson. He studied composition with Copland in 1946 and 1947 at Tanglewood, and with Arthur Honegger in Paris in 1949. Like Francis Poulenc, to whom he has often been compared (by Thomson among others), his music is fundamentally but nonfunctionally diatonic, though Rorem included passages of polytonality and modified serialism. During the 1950s, he composed three symphonies for full orchestra: No. 1 (1950), which dates from his time with Honegger; No. 2 (1956); and No. 3 (1957–58), which Bernstein premiered with the New York Philharmonic. In addition, he composed a Sinfonia for wind ensemble in 1957 (he arranged the Scherzo from the Symphony No. 3 for wind ensemble as well in 2002). Finally, he composed a String Symphony in 1985.

William Russo (1928–2003) was a prominent composer, jazz musician, and teacher; he was trombonist and composer-arranger for the Stan Kenton Orchestra from 1950 to 1954; between 1953 and 1957 he studied privately with John J. Becker and Karel Jirák in Chicago. In 1957 he composed his Symphony No. 1. The next year he wrote Symphony No. 2, "Titans," on a commission from the Koussevitzky Music Foundation; it premiered with Leonard Bernstein and the New York Philharmonic (the work features a prominent role for solo trumpet). His music is noted for distinctive melody as well as the colorful scoring and lively rhythms of jazz.

Gunther Schuller (1925–2015), born in New York to German émigrés, started his career as a member of the Metropolitan Opera Orchestra from 1945 to 1959, serving as principal hornist for nine years. An influential teacher, writer, and administrator, his compositional interests lay in assimilating twelve-tone writing and modern jazz; he famously coined such hybrid works "third stream." His prolific output (which features over 20 concertos) includes two symphonies, neither of which are third stream. Symphony for Brass and Percussion (1950) consists of four movements, each of which represents a different aspect of brass playing; Dimitri Mitropoulos and the New York Philharmonic performed it in New York as well as at the Salzburg Festival in 1957. He composed a Symphony for full orchestra in 1965 on commission from the Fine Arts Department of the Dallas Public Library for the Dallas Symphony Orchestra. The composer described it as "a four-movement symphony which, though employing very advanced compositional techniques, allows for the return to formal procedures used by Bach, Beethoven, and others without being aesthetically in discrepancy with them."[429]

Leo Smit (1921–99) was closely associated with Stravinsky and Copland; he recorded the latter's complete piano music. Though his most important works are theatrical or vocal (including six song cycles to Emily Dickinson's poetry), Smit composed three symphonies. The Neoclassical Symphony No. 1 (1955) resulted from a 1951 Koussevitzky Music Foundation commission; Charles Munch premiered it with the Boston Symphony Orchestra in 1957. Symphony No. 2 dates from 1965 and the much later Symphony No. 3 from 1981.

Halsey Stevens (1908–89) was a prominent musicologist as well as composer; his biography of Béla Bartók remains a standard reference. His prolific output includes three symphonies composed in close proximity: Symphony No. 1 (1945, rev. 1950) became the best known; it was followed by his Second and Third Symphonies in 1945 and 1946, respectively. Eleven years later he composed a *Sinfonia breve* (1957). The music is tonal, with vigorous rhythms, distinctive melodies, and inventive timbral combinations.

Alexander Tcherepnin (1899–1977) spent his early years in Russia, where as part of a musical family he encountered Rimsky-Korsakov, Stravinsky, and Prokofiev. The family emigrated to Paris after the Russian Revolution; there Tcherepnin wrote his Symphony No. 1 in E Major (1927), which features a Scherzo scored exclusively for unpitched percussion (four years before Edgard Varèse's *Ionisation*). From 1948 to 1964, he taught at DePaul University (his students included Gloria Coates); during that time he composed three more symphonies. No. 2 in E-flat Major (1947–51) premiered with the Chicago Symphony Orchestra under Rafael Kubelik in 1951. No. 3 in F-sharp Major (1952), commissioned by Patricia and M. Martin Gordon of Chicago, premiered with the Indianapolis Symphony Orchestra under Fabien Sevitzky in 1955. A 1951 Koussevitzky Music Foundation grant led to the creation of his final symphony, No. 4 in E Major (1956–57), widely regarded as his best; Charles Munch premiered it with the Boston Symphony Orchestra. Tcherepnin's works are notable for their use of various synthetic scales, contrapuntal textures, and an emphasis on percussion. At his death in 1977 he was working on two symphonies, one of which was intended for percussion alone.

Lester Trimble (1923–86) received early encouragement in composition from Arnold Schoenberg and studied with Milhaud and Copland at Tanglewood and with Boulanger, Milhaud, and Honegger in Paris. Leonard Bernstein appointed him composer-in-residence with the New York Philharmonic in 1967–68. He composed three symphonies: Symphony in Two Movements (1951); Second Symphony (1968), commissioned by the Koussevitzky Music Foundation; and "The Tricentennial" (1984–85), commissioned to commemorate the three hundredth anniversary of the city of Albany. His works are marked by harmonic intensity, distinctive melodies, and a concern with close-knit thematic organization.

John Vincent (1902–77) studied with Frederick Converse and George Whitefield Chadwick and later with Walter Piston and Nadia Boulanger. He succeeded Schoenberg as professor of composition at UCLA (1946–69). His music is strongly rhythmic and lyrical, making use of what he called "paratonality," the predominance of diatonicism within polytonal or even atonal material. His Symphony in D, subtitled *A Festive Piece in One Movement* (1954, rev. 1956), became his best-known work. In 1960 he composed a chamber work entitled *Consort*, which he arranged into his Symphony No. 2 in 1976. (A *Folk Song Symphony* of 1931 is lost.)

Richard Yardumian (1917–85), like Alan Hovhaness, drew upon music of his Armenian heritage but also upon an eclectic array of other sources, including Appalachian ballads and the music of Debussy; he created a system of 12 notes based on superimposed thirds built from alternate black and white notes of the keyboard. He enjoyed a close relationship with the Philadelphia Orchestra from 1951 to 1964, and the orchestra gave almost one hundred performances and made four recordings of his music. These recordings include two symphonies. The first, "Noah" (1950, rev. 1961), is a programmatic work depicting the biblical Flood and the departure from the Ark. Symphony No. 2, "Psalms," sets various passages from that book for mezzo-soprano or baritone and orchestra; Yardumian completed the first movement in 1947, the second in 1964.

Bibliographic Overview

Annegret Fauser's astute observation that the primacy of the symphonic genre is built into the American vernacular—that American audiences go "to the symphony" rather than to orchestral concerts—can be true of narratives of American music as well.[430] One consequence of this tendency to privilege the "symphonic," however, is that analyses of the symphonic repertoire are often diffused throughout histories of classical music in the United States. The symphony as a genre is nearly always present but seldom the focus—as opposed to the prominent books focused exclusively on opera in America (whether the production and reception of European operas and operettas, or operas and other forms of musical theater written by Americans). Further, the postwar conceptions of the symphony as derivative and ill-suited to democratic and populist sentiment—a stark change from John Sullivan Dwight's nineteenth-century assertion that Beethoven's symphonies represented a musical metaphor for democratic ideals—have led to its decentering in America's musical life, or at least that is how the story is often told.[431] As a result, when historical overviews like Horowitz/CLASSICAL reach the 1950s and 60s, they often center their narrative on the dissolution of classical music and the retreat of composition to the academy.[432]

In turn, this master-narrative reinforces another trope in histories of the postwar period: the Manichean divide between the avant-garde and American populism. Witness the *Cambridge History of Twentieth-Century Music*, which divides the period from 1945 through the 1960s into two chapters: one by David Osmond-Smith on "the international avant-garde" and another by Arnold Whittall on the more accessible "moderate mainstream"; most of the symphonic examples, of course, appear in the latter chapter. Similarly, the *Cambridge History of American Music* separates "tonal traditions" of the twentieth century (1920–60 by Larry Starr and 1960 onward by Jonathan Bernard) from Stephen Peles's chapter on "serialism and complexity" and David Nicholls's on "avant-garde and experimental music." Even within his own chapter, Bernard/TONAL divides the array of post-1960 symphonic styles into the "old guard" who never abandoned tonality; "converts" from serialism to tonality; minimalists; and finally, "new and newer Romantics," who hover off to the side. Although not focused on symphonic or even orchestral writing *per se*, Straus/TWELVE-TONE is an important corrective to these narrative tendencies that have obscured how complex the web of stylistic and personal affiliations of the postwar period could be for American composers. Straus does offer the occasional analytical detail regarding Sessions's symphonic works, but overall the book is more helpful in shedding light on the "myths" that shaped the reception of midcentury symphonists, particularly Sessions and Diamond.

Tawa/GREAT, with its focus on 18 symphonists active during the Depression and World War II, is emblematic of the tendency to view these decades as a golden age in American classical music and the period afterward as a retreat: anything beyond the late 1940s is designated "the symphony in the leanest years."[433] However, since many composers active in the 1950s and 60s came of age and wrote their early works during the 1940s, Tawa provides a good deal of coverage for Bernstein, Creston, Diamond, Mennin, Schuman, and Sessions, with passing mention of Hovhaness. There is a good deal of musical description, although the analyses rarely penetrate below the surface and include no musical examples. The evocative titles for each chapter may entice the reader but do a disservice to the internal variety of a given composer's style. Schuman's "muscular symphony" and Sessions's "knotty symphony" are particularly unhelpful labels, although they do have their roots in the reception of these composer's works. Tawa does provide an important contextual background and framework for the flourishing of the symphony from the 1920s through the 1960s and is a rare text that considers midcentury symphonists side by side.

Other vital sources for description and analyses of these symphonies are the program notes preserved in the digital archives of the Boston Symphony Orchestra and New York Philharmonic. In particular, John N. Burk writing for the BSO provides a similar type of description to Tawa in his notes for the premieres of several of the symphonies included here. Composers themselves often contributed to or wrote these program notes, so in the absence of access to interviews, sketches, and other primary sources, they can provide a window onto a symphonist's thinking about the work at hand and even the genre in general.

The work of musicologist Andrea Olmstead is vital to any understanding of Roger Sessions's music. Olmstead/BIOGRAPHY provides a comprehensive survey of his works. She devotes a fair amount of consideration to Sessions's symphonic writing but more as exemplars of his style and technique than as an engagement with the genre and its import. Her extensive interviews with the composer, Olmstead/CONVERSATIONS, are perhaps more helpful in decoding his symphonies, most crucially in teasing out programmatic and other intertextual references. As a composer who wrote many texted works and two operas, Sessions's symphonic works, even those without explicit programs or evocative titles, abound with literary references. The interviews also help nuance Sessions's position among other composers of his day, particularly in terms of the presumed divide between serialists like himself and those of the "Stravinsky camp." His remarks also occasionally touch on his attitude toward the symphony as a genre.

Like Diamond and Barber, both Creston's initial reception and subsequent historiographic treatment have been deeply affected by the (neo-)Romantic label. Butterworth/SYMPHONY and Simmons/VOICES are both emblematic of this trend. Although Butterworth traces the interesting rhythmic elements that connect Creston to several other American symphonists like Bernstein, Harris, Sessions, and Schuman, as well as to the shared legacy of Stravinsky, he also takes Creston's stated interest in melody as evidence of his emotional intensity that wells up from a "warm Romantic vein."[434] Creston did posit song and dance as "the two foundations of all music," but from his perspective "song" embraced Gregorian chant and Renaissance polyphony as well as Romantic lyricism.

Simmons seizes upon Creston's privileging of melody in order to include him in what was already a broad definition of a "Neo-Romantic ideal," in which "expression of emotion, depiction of drama, and evocation of mood" are coequal to "formal coherence, developmental rigor, and structural economy."[435] Simmons's definition also presumes a relative conservatism, particularly concerning tonality, at which point most of the composers in this chapter could plausibly bear the label. Tawa/GREAT provides a useful counterpoint: whereas Butterworth and Simmons see the program of Creston's Third Symphony as evidence of his latent Romanticism, Tawa connects its Catholic mysticism and the evident interest in modal harmonies to the influence of Messiaen and Hovhaness's similar interest in the spiritual and cosmic.[436] Creston also has much in common with those of his slightly older generation, including Sessions and Leo Sowerby (see chapter 5), so the Neoromantic label obscures more than it reveals. Repeated references to Creston's autodidact compositional studies—Tawa unhelpfully names his chapter "The Self-Reliant Symphony"—also discounts the significance of his training as an organist, which is important to his Sixth Symphony.

Three significant studies of Schuman were published within as many years: two biographies, Polisi/MUSE (2008) and Swayne/ORPHEUS (2011), and Simmons/STEEL (2011). Swayne offers more in-depth examination of Schuman's compositional style than Polisi, making it more valuable to anyone interested in his contributions to the symphonic repertoire; Swayne gives a particularly penetrating analysis of the Seventh Symphony. As the successor of Schuman and Mennin to the presidency of Juilliard, and with close ties to Schuman and his family, Polisi has a vested interest in promoting the composer, which can skew a biography; on the other hand, as Schuman's handpicked successor, he has the advantages of proximity, access, and institutional knowledge.

Like Swayne, Simmons offers much in the way of musical analysis, and his placement side by side with Persichetti and Mennin offers a useful comparison of all three composers' styles, enmeshed as they are in a shared context. Simmons categorizes Schuman's works into early, middle, and late periods, locating the celebrated Sixth Symphony as the culmination of the middle period, which on the whole he describes in ways that echo both Beethoven's heroic middle period and tragic vein. Simmons also views this period as Schuman's heroic "emancipation from the dominating influence of Harris."[437] This is an overused historiographic trope, and by beginning the late period—which Simmons otherwise casts as mannerist, self-indulgent, or redundant—with the works in which Schuman begins to play with serialist and atonal ideas (namely, the Seventh, Eighth, and Ninth Symphonies), he reinforces the myth of serialism as inaccessible, decadent, or strange, which Straus has tried to combat. Swayne's is, on the whole, the most balanced treatment of Schuman and his works, using the composer's institutional affiliations, artistic collaborations, and commissions as signposts rather than markers for artificial stylistic periods. Butterworth rightly describes Schuman as a "cornerstone of mid-century symphonic achievement."[438]

Despite their contributions to the symphony, Diamond and Hovhaness remain marginal figures in narratives of American music. This is particularly surprising for Diamond, who traveled personally and professionally in the same circle of gay composers as Bernstein, Copland, Marc Blitzstein, Paul Bowles, and Ned Rorem, all of whom helped define American music in the twentieth century. Although the most prolific symphonist of the group, his bibliography features only one major monograph: Kimberling/DIAMOND, a bio-bibliography.

Likewise, Hovhaness is sidelined in existing histories, if not outright denigrated. Butterworth is rather more fair than Bernard and most others: "To appreciate his world, it is necessary to shed most of one's preconceived ideas of twentieth-century music and accept him on his own mystical terms."[439] However, his portioning of Hovhaness with composers of "eastern influences" is problematic because it downplays his interest in natural phenomenon and spirituality in favor of the exoticism of his Armenian heritage and presumes the primacy of Western tradition in twentieth-century practice. One might argue that Hovhaness's works go the furthest in decentering the European-ness and Western-ness of the symphony as a genre—a precursor to the developments in the post-1970 period, which would make him influencer rather than influenced. The best source on Hovhaness's symphonies is located on The Alan Hovhaness Website; the section http://www.hovhaness.com/Symphonies_Hovhaness.html includes detailed information on many of the works; gaps remain, however, and virtually no information is available on symphonies the site does not cover (even from the composer's private company Fujihara)—as the incomplete entries in table 6.4 illustrate. One of the few scholarly sources on the composer is Athens/HOVHANESS, a doctoral thesis from Cornell University.

The indispensable source on Julia Perry is Walker-Hill/SPIRITUALS, which provides a comprehensive overview, works list (to the degree it can currently be reconstructed), and discography.

Persichetti and Mennin are often grouped together with Schuman as a "Juilliard school." The assessment in Simmons/STEEL that they share a loosely articulated aesthetic viewpoint as "modern traditionalists" is more useful, even though it exposes as many differences as it does similarities. Broadly, they all retain tonality as a part of their compositional toolbox, despite greatly varying degrees of dissonance and approaches to counterpoint. However, Simmons casts Persichetti as the eclectic and Mennin as the more rigorous traditionalist. His portrayal of Mennin—determined to "develop abstract ideas logically and coherently . . . as if from a lofty, somewhat depersonalized perspective"—unfortunately echoes early opinions of the composer as highly competent but fundamentally uninspired.[440] At the same time, Simmons has rescued each composer from his reputation as primarily an excellent teacher (Persichetti) and administrator (Mennin). Persichetti in particular comes in for something of a postmodernist redemption as a composer for his "conception of a broad working vocabulary, or 'common practice,' based on a fluent integration of the myriad materials and techniques that appeared during the twentieth century. This all-encompassing embrace set him apart from his peers at a time when partisan antagonism divided American concert music into rival stylistic camps."[441] The role he assigns Persichetti is one that might be attributed to all the figures in this chapter, for upon closer inspection, as with Howard Hanson and Walter Piston, none belong wholly to any one of the several different "camps" that the historiography has given.

If Simmons seems reluctant to let go of the picture of a stylistically divided, aesthetically antagonistic midcentury, it is perhaps because a figure more prominent than any of the Juilliard school was reinforcing the idea even during the period itself. Bernstein produced his own bibliography filled with books of essays; television scripts; a series of lectures at Harvard; and articles in journals, magazines, and newspapers. He is especially famous for his ability to explain the works of other composers in compelling and accessible detail, as in the televised Young People's Concerts. In doing so, however, he also reveals much about his own music and aesthetics, and he was quite clear in thinking that American composers were divided into camps, and he knew to which one he belonged—the tonal one. About one thing he was less clear, and this was the question of genre—particularly of the value of the symphony. Perhaps for this reason, despite the volume of scholarship on Bernstein's multifaceted career, studies of his compositional style often neglect his symphonies in favor of the stage works, even as many trumpet the "symphonic" scope of his writing for other genres. There are a few exceptions, most notably Schiller/JEWISH, in which the author reads the Third Symphony in great detail, from small motivic cells through larger formal and programmatic considerations, in order to demonstrate how Bernstein responded to the Holocaust through his music. There are also shorter discussions of the First and Second Symphonies and the ways in which they may (or may not) be heard as Jewish works. Gentry/ANXIETY explores how Bernstein's Second Symphony took shape during the McCarthy era and in conversation with Copland's Third Symphony and the idea of the triumphal American symphony in the "Koussevitzky manner." Baber/JAZZ reads the Second Symphony as a working out of a specifically Jewish American identity, an interpretation supported by a narrative and topical analysis, particularly of the role of bebop as a distinct jazz style.

Notes

1. Pandemic-related administrative responsibilities made it impossible for Dr. Baber to complete the final revisions suggested by the anonymous reader (except for the sections on Schuman and Bernstein, as well as the introduction and conclusion); at her request, I revised the remainder of the chapter and created the composer tables as well as the Brief Mentions. [Editor]
2. Bernstein/ADDRESS. Also published in *High Fidelity* as "I vill not stop to vork until it vill not be more beautiful!"
3. Crawford/MUSICAL LIFE; Hamm/MUSIC; Horowitz/CLASSICAL; Tawa/GREAT.
4. Bernstein/ADDRESS.
5. See chapter 1, table 1.3 for a list of these and many other recordings of American symphonies.
6. Horowitz/CLASSICAL, pp. 483–84.
7. Sessions/DIFFICULT.
8. Sessions/IMMATURITY.
9. Olmstead/SESSIONS.
10. Quoted in Olmstead/BIOGRAPHY, p. 208.
11. Olmstead/CONVERSATIONS, p. 23.
12. Olmstead/SESSIONS.
13. Olmstead/BIOGRAPHY, p. 207.
14. Olmstead/MUSIC, p. 52.
15. Olmstead/BIOGRAPHY, p. 214.
16. Quoted in Olmstead/MUSIC, p. 51.
17. Ibid., p. 52.
18. Roy D. Welch, "A Symphony Introduces Roger Sessions," *Modern Music* 4, no. 4 (May–June 1927): p. 30.
19. Olmstead/MUSIC, p. 52.
20. Roger Sessions, Program Note, Symphony No. 2, New York Philharmonic, January 12, 1950.
21. Olmstead/BIOGRAPHY, p. 273.
22. Quoted in Olmstead/MUSIC, p. 76. Sessions's was not the only symphony to memorialize Roosevelt; the president is a likely candidate for the "father figure" mourned in the dirge of Bernstein's Second Symphony (1949).
23. Olmstead/CONVERSATIONS, p. 40.

24. Taubman/RECORDS.
25. Olmstead/MUSIC, p. 77.
26. Ibid.
27. Olmstead/CONVERSATIONS, p. 77, citing John Veale as quoted by Herbert F. Peyser in New York Philharmonic Program Note, January 12, 1950.
28. Olmstead/MUSIC, p. 77.
29. Ibid.
30. Ibid., p. 78.
31. Ibid.
32. Ibid.
33. Straus/TWELVE-TONE, pp. x–xxi.
34. Ibid., p. 66.
35. Ibid., p. 70.
36. Olmstead/CONVERSATIONS, p. 34.
37. Marjory M. Fisher, "Sessions Symphony Has Premiere," *Musical America*, January 25, 1947; David Diamond, "Roger Sessions: Symphony No. 2," *Notes*, June 7, 1950, pp. 438–39.
38. Taubman/RECORDS.
39. Olin Downes, "Corigliano Soloist for Philharmonic: Violinist Heard in Concerto by Elgar—Sessions Symphony Featured on Program," *New York Times*, January 13, 1950.
40. Olmstead/CONVERSATIONS, pp. 40–41.
41. Olmstead/BIOGRAPHY, p. 249.
42. Olmstead/MUSIC, p. 113.
43. Ibid., p. 118.
44. Ibid., p. 116.
45. Ibid., p. 118.
46. Quoted in Olmstead/BIOGRAPHY, p. 322.
47. Olmstead/MUSIC, p. 117.
48. Ibid., p. 118.
49. Quoted in ibid., p. 117.
50. Ibid., p. 141.
51. Ibid., p. 140.
52. Ibid. Earlier this distinctive gesture had appeared in *Montezuma* as well as the first two movements of the Third Symphony (Olmstead/BIOGRAPHY, p. 357).
53. Ibid., p. 145.
54. Theodore Strongin, "Symphony Given Jersey Premiere: Sessions Is First Composer to Receive State Grant," *New York Times*, January 20, 1966.
55. Olmstead/MUSIC, p. 144.
56. Ibid., p. 145.
57. Ibid.
58. Ibid., 147. Sessions apparently encountered the novel through its first English-language edition, published in 1965.
59. Olmstead/MUSIC, p. 139.
60. Quoted in ibid., p. 148.
61. Ibid., p. 149.
62. Quoted in ibid., p. 148.
63. Quoted in Olmstead/BIOGRAPHY, p. 361.
64. Quoted in ibid., p. 359.
65. Ibid., p. 149.

66. Ibid., p. 150.
67. Ibid., p. 151.
68. Winthrop Sargeant, "Musical Events: Is Music Dead?" *New Yorker*, May 11, 1968, p. 140.
69. Harold C. Schonberg, "Steinberg Leads Philharmonic in New Sessions Work, 'Scheherazade' is After on the Program," *New York Times*, May 3, 1968.
70. Olmstead/MUSIC, p. 176.
71. Ibid.
72. Olmstead/BIOGRAPHY, p. 364.
73. Ibid.
74. John Rockwell, "Roger Sessions, Nearing 85, Is Still a Maverick Composer," *New York Times*, March 22, 1981.
75. Olmstead/MUSIC, p. 117.
76. Tawa/GREAT, p. 186.
77. Ibid., p. 185.
78. Simmons/VOICES, p. 199.
79. Ibid., p. 202.
80. Ibid. Creston made this statement in a letter to Henry Cowell.
81. Tawa/GREAT, p. 187.
82. Simmons/VOICES, p. 202. This is from the same letter to Cowell.
83. Tawa/GREAT, p. 184.
84. Simmons/VOICES, p. 195.
85. Ibid, p. 213.
86. Ibid., p. 231.
87. Ibid.
88. Ibid.
89. Forte/BALLAD, pp. 15–16.
90. Ibid., pp. 8–12.
91. Simmons/VOICES, p. 232.
92. Ibid.
93. Ibid.
94. Ibid., p. 233.
95. Olin Downes, "Rodzinski Offers Creston Symphony," *New York Times*, February 16, 1945.
96. Simmons/VOICES, pp. 231, 233.
97. Quoted in Butterworth/SYMPHONY, p. 135.
98. Tawa/GREAT, p. 189.
99. Ibid., p. 190.
100. Henry Cowell, "Review: Creston Symphony No. 3," *Musical Quarterly* 37 (January 1951): pp. 78–79.
101. Simmons/VOICES, p. 216.
102. Ibid., p. 226.
103. Ibid.
104. Ibid.
105. Ibid., p. 217.
106. Program note, quoted in ibid., p. 218. Creston indicated that a personal crisis lay behind the work but would not elaborate.
107. Ibid.
108. Ibid.
109. Ibid., p. 226.

110. Hart/FRENCH, p. 565.
111. Ibid.
112. Ibid., p. 570.
113. See chapter 5 for more on the symphonies of Copland and Barber.
114. Simmons/VOICES, p. 227.
115. Ibid.
116. Ibid.
117. Ibid.
118. Swayne/ORPHEUS, pp. 130–31, 163.
119. Ibid., p. 88.
120. Ibid., p. 90.
121. Ibid., p. 92.
122. Ibid., pp. 83, 131–40.
123. Ibid., p. 73.
124. Ibid., p. 75.
125. William Schuman, quoted by John N. Burk, Symphony No. 2 Program Note, Boston Symphony Orchestra, February 17 and 18, 1939.
126. As of this writing, the radio broadcast of the CBS performance can be heard on YouTube.
127. Warren Storey Smith, "Myra Hess Soloist at Symphony: Work by Schuman Is Received Rather Coldly," *Boston Post*, February 18, 1939.
128. Alexander Williams, "Music: Symphony Concert," *Boston Herald*, February 18, 1939.
129. Moses Smith, "Symphony Concert: Miss Hess as Soloist, and 100 Men to Follow," *Boston Transcript*, February 18, 1930. The critic praised Koussevitzky for "disclosing to Boston audiences a genuine American talent."
130. Swayne/ORPHEUS, p. 114.
131. Burton/BERNSTEIN, p. 43.
132. Swayne/ORPHEUS, p. 102.
133. Ibid.
134. Ibid., p. 120.
135. Quoted in ibid., p. 119.
136. Pye/INSIDE, p. 69.
137. Polisi/MUSE, p. 386.
138. Ibid.
139. Swayne/ORPHEUS, p. 119.
140. Leonard Liebling, "Boston Forces Give American Novelty," *Musical Courier*, December 1, 1941. Similarly, after the performance of the symphony at the New York Critics' Circle Concerts in May 1942, Olin Downes reiterated the need for American composers to free themselves from tradition:

> Why young Americans think that musical salvation lies in these directions we don't know. That a modern European, who in a sense is not only a great craftsman but fundamentally an epigone, like Paul Hindemith, should resort to these efforts to find the spring of musical youth and rejuvenate an ancient culture is more than understandable. It is inevitable, with Europe at the end of its creative rope, as at the present day. The phoenix has yet to arise from those ashes. But what are we—we Americans—waiting for? What have we to do with these 'sere remains of foreign harvests'? Or are we, like the European artists, exhausted and afraid?

Olin Downes, "Impressions of Two Programs of Music by American Composers," *New York Times*, May 17, 1942.
141. Olin Downes, "Boston Orchestra Offers New Work: Third Symphony of William Schuman Called Best Number by Young American," *New York Times*, November 23, 1941.

142. Ibid.
143. Tawa/GREAT, p. 67.
144. Alexander Williams, "Symphony Concert," *Boston Herald*, October 18, 1941.
145. Virgil Thomson, *New York Herald Tribune*, March 14, 1951.
146. Simmons/STEEL, p. 70.
147. Tawa/GREAT, p. 70.
148. Swayne/ORPHEUS, p. 150.
149. Simmons/STEEL, p. 69.
150. Polisi/MUSE, p. 388.
151. Swayne/ORPHEUS, p. 230.
152. Simmons/STEEL, pp. 75–76.
153. Bernstein, quoted in Gentry/ANXIETY, p. 316.
154. Swayne/ORPHEUS, p. 318.
155. Eugene Ormandy quoted in ibid., p. 238.
156. Ibid., p. 239.
157. Ibid., pp. 319–20.
158. Polisi/MUSE, p. 197.
159. Simmons/STEEL, p. 110.
160. Swayne/ORPHEUS, p. 319.
161. Ibid., p. 320.
162. Simmons/STEEL, p. 110.
163. Ibid.
164. Swayne/PUZZLING.
165. Swayne/ORPHEUS, p. 323.
166. Ross Parmenter, "Season Is Opened by Philharmonic," *New York Times*, October 5, 1962.
167. Richard Franko Goldman, "Current Chronicle: New York," *Musical Quarterly* 49, no. 1 (January 1963): p. 92.
168. Swayne/ORPHEUS, pp. 399–400.
169. Swayne/ORPHEUS, pp. 463–65.
170. John Rockwell, "Music: Schuman by Skrowaczewski," *New York Times*, April 22, 1979.
171. Kostelanetz/HOVHANESS, p. 15.
172. Ibid., p. 16.
173. Ibid.
174. Butterworth/SYMPHONY, p. 148.
175. Kostelanetz/HOVHANESS, p. 17.
176. Rosner and Wolverton/HOVHANESS.
177. Hovhaness/THOUGHTS, p. 368.
178. Rosner and Wolverton/HOVHANESS.
179. Ibid.
180. Kostelanetz/HOVHANESS, p. 16.
181. The numbering of Hovhaness's early symphonies reflects their order of publication rather than chronology. Thus, the "St. Vartan" Symphony predates Symphony No. 2, *Mysterious Mountain*, by five years but was published after the latter work.
182. Housepian/ARMENIA, pp. 732–33.
183. Hovhaness/THOUGHTS, p. 369.
184. N. S., "Hovhaness Works in Premiere Here," *New York Times*, March 12, 1951.
185. Kostelanetz/HOVHANESS, p. 16.
186. Housepian/ARMENIA, p. 727.

187. "All About 'Mysterious Mountain,'" http://www.hovhaness.com/hovhaness-mysterious-mountain.html#background, accessed December 22, 2018.

188. Ibid. In this way, Hovhaness found common ground with Rachmaninoff, Stravinsky, Schoenberg, Barber, and others who found a popular early work overshadowing their more mature products.

189. Edward Downes, Program Note, New York Philharmonic, June 2, 1967.

190. Hovhaness/THOUGHTS, p. 369.

191. "Alan Hovhaness Symphonies, Part 3," http://www.hovhaness.com/Sym_15_30.html, accessed December 22, 2018.

192. Davidson/DIAMOND.

193. David Diamond to Leonard Bernstein (November 5, 1940), in Simeone/BERNSTEIN LETTERS, p. 59.

194. Davidson/DIAMOND.

195. Ibid.

196. Thomson/ELEGANCE.

197. Kimberling/DIAMOND, p. 30.

198. Noel Straus, "Huberman Soloist at Carnegie Hall: Polish Violinist Plays Joachim Cadenza in Beethoven Concerto at Concert," *New York Times*, December 22, 1941.

199. Thomson/ELEGANCE.

200. William Blair, "Report from Boston," *New York Times*, October 22, 1944. Quoted in Kimberling/DIAMOND, p. 11.

201. John N. Burk, Program Note, Boston Symphony Orchestra, November 3, 1950, http://collections.bso.org/digital/, accessed December 15, 2018.

202. Diamond's original program note states that "the entire symphony was created with the idea of life and death—Fechner's theories of life and death as (I) a continual sleep, (II) the alternation between sleeping and waking, and (III) eternal waking, Birth being the passing from I to II and Death the transition from II to III." Reprinted in Kimberling/DIAMOND, p. 24.

203. Cecil Smith, "Diamond Symphony Given Premiere: Leonard Bernstein Leads Boston Symphony in Presentation of New Work," *Musical America*, February 1948, p. 375.

204. Jules Wolffers, "Boston: Two Native Scores Bow," *Musical Courier* 137 (February 15, 1948): p. 51.

205. Bernstein, "Concert talk or lecture" [Copland Third Symphony] (October 1948), Box 71, Folder 49, Leonard Bernstein Collection, Library of Congress.

206. Bernstein, quoted in Kimberling/DIAMOND, p. 19.

207. Winthrop Sargeant, "Musical Events: A Neglected Tradition," *New Yorker*, March 30, 1957.

208. Kimberling/DIAMOND, pp. 40–41. See pp. 38–39 for his analysis of the symphony.

209. Edward Downes, Program Note, New York Philharmonic, October 27, 1961.

210. Kimberling/DIAMOND, p. 30.

211. Edward Downes, Program Note, New York Philharmonic, October 27, 1961.

212. Ibid., p. 64.

213. Robert Sabin, "Bernstein Introduces Diamond Eighth," *Musical America*, December 1961.

214. Harold C. Schonberg, "Diamond's 8th Symphony Has Premiere," *New York Times*, October 28, 1961.

215. "The Discovery of David Diamond," *Rochester Democrat and Chronicle*, February 27, 1966. Quoted in Kimberling/DIAMOND, p. 63.

216. Kimberling/DIAMOND, pp. 58–59. See pp. 58–63 for his analysis (with examples).

217. Ibid., p. 68.

218. Ibid.

219. Ibid., p. 49.

220. Bernard Holland, "Concert: Bernstein Leads Debut of Diamond's Ninth," *New York Times*, November 18, 1985.

221. Ibid.
222. See Kimberling/DIAMOND, pp. 50–52, for his program note as well as the texts.
223. Alex Ross, "Diamond's 11th Symphony," *New York Times*, December 7, 1992.
224. Simmons/STEEL, p. 193.
225. Ibid., p. 194.
226. Ibid., p. 195.
227. Quoted in ibid.
228. Ibid.
229. Ibid., p. 239.
230. Ibid., p. 238.
231. Ibid., p. 239.
232. Ibid.
233. Ibid.
234. Ibid.
235. Ibid., p. 240.
236. Simmons/PERSICHETTI.
237. Simmons/STEEL, p. 241.
238. Ibid., p. 242.
239. String antecedents from the Americas include Schuman's Symphony for Strings (1943) and Diamond's *Rounds for String Orchestra* (1944), as well as Carlos Chávez's Symphony No. 5 (1953). Symphonies in one or two movements became increasingly prevalent at midcentury, in the wake of Harris's works and in an era that repudiated any notion of a formal symphonic standard. See chapter 1 for more on the highly varied structures of American symphonies in the twentieth and twenty-first centuries.
240. Persichetti met his future wife, Dorothea (1919–87), when they were fellow piano students at the Philadelphia Conservatory; they married in 1941. She completed a Doctor of Musical Arts document on his music in 1960, in which she analyzed the Fifth Symphony and many other compositions; Simmons freely cites this unpublished monograph ("Vincent Persichetti's Music," in the Persichetti Archive of the New York Public Library) as a principal source for his own observations. Simmons/STEEL, pp. 176, 185.
241. Ibid., p. 243. Bernstein likewise unified his stage and concert works through referential intervals, such as the tritone in *West Side Story*.
242. Ibid., p. 244. Dorothea Persichetti regarded the Tranquillo as the beginning of the fourth section, with the fifth beginning at the Molto appassionato in m. 377. Both divisions track to clearly perceptible changes in character.
243. Ibid. Dorothea located the beginning of a sixth section at the Severamente (m. 582) where *a* returns.
244. See Churgin/SAMMARTINI for a discussion of Sammartini's symphonies of the 1730s for strings (and continuo), many movements of which tread the ground between ritornello and sonata-allegro structures.
245. Quoted in Simmons/STEEL, p. 245.
246. Ibid.
247. Ibid.
248. Ibid. Persichetti composed *Hymns and Responses* as a modern hymnal for ecumenical use; the music sets both traditional devotional texts and secular poetry. He published the first volume in 1955; he started to prepare a second volume near the end of his life, and it appeared posthumously in 1991. Ibid., pp. 249, 299–301.
249. Quoted in ibid., p. 248.
250. Quoted in ibid., p. 249.

251. Ibid., pp. 250–51.
252. Ibid., p. 253.
253. Ibid., p. 254.
254. Briggs's commentary is quoted in ibid., p. 254.
255. Ibid., pp. 255–56.
256. Horowitz/DIRECTOR, p. 136.
257. Bernstein/GREAT, p. 42.
258. Bernstein, Press conference remarks on 20th c. symphony series with New York Philharmonic (April 27, 1965), Box 82, Folder 18, Leonard Bernstein Collection, Library of Congress.
259. Bernstein/FINDINGS, pp. 347–48.
260. Burton/BERNSTEIN, p. 185.
261. Bernstein/ANXIETY.
262. For more, see Baber/JAZZ.
263. See Gottlieb/FAITH.
264. Giger/JOY, p. 312.
265. Smith/PLACE, p. 15.
266. Burton/BERNSTEIN, p. 107.
267. Ibid., p. 124.
268. Bernstein/JEREMIAH.
269. Gottlieb/FAITH.
270. On his seventieth birthday, Bernstein described his lifelong friend in an explicitly Hebraic way, as "a cross between Walt Whitman and an Old Testament prophet, bearded and patriarchal." Bernstein/FINDINGS, p. 286.
271. Gottlieb/JEREMIAH, p. iv.
272. Callan/ALLEGORY, p. 155.
273. Baber/JAZZ, pp. 117–18.
274. Gottlieb/MUSIC, pp. 208–14.
275. Obviously Wolffers is focusing on "The Masque" when he alludes to Hollywood and "the dive." Jules Wolffers, "Music in Review," *Jewish Advocate*, April 14, 1949.
276. For references to Rachmaninoff, Schoenberg, Mahler, and Copland, see Anonymous, "Age of Anxiety: New Bernstein Symphony Heard in Boston," *New York Herald Tribune*, April 9, 1949. For Berlioz and Liszt, see L. A. Sloper, "Composer Is Piano Soloist at Premiere of Symphony," *Christian Science Monitor*, April 9, 1949, p. 7. For Strauss, see Thomson/ANXIETY.
277. Max Frankel, "Bernstein Work Heard in Moscow," *New York Times*, August 24, 1959, p. 16.
278. Schiller/JEWISH, p. 131.
279. Ibid., p. 139.
280. Gentry/ANXIETY, pp. 326–27. For further discussion of Copland's style as influenced by American populism and the expectations of symphonic conductors like Serge Koussevitzky, see chapter 5.
281. For a discussion of the *Airborne Symphony*, see chapter 5.
282. Gottlieb/WORKING, p. 123.
283. Leonard Bernstein, undated musing, early 1960s, Box 78, Folder 1, LBC.
284. Ibid. Bernstein's emphasis.
285. Bernstein, "Call Me Moses" [silent home movie: scene outlines and title list] (Summer 1960), Box 71, Folder 18, LBC.
286. Bernstein, Notes for speaker's text and transliterations of the Kaddish prayer, Box 78, Folders 1 and 24, LBC.
287. Gottlieb/WORKING, p. 127.

288. Box 78, Folder 1, LBC.
289. Ibid.
290. *The Little Drummer Boy: An Essay on Gustav Mahler by and with Leonard Bernstein* DVD (Philips, 1985, reissued 2007).
291. Bernstein, "On Bloch, Sacred Service," Thursday evening preview talk (April 7, 1960), Box 78, Folder 10, LBC.
292. Ibid.
293. Rasmussen/KADDISH, pp. 155, 158, 160.
294. Schiller/JEWISH, pp. 151–52.
295. Ibid., pp. 164–65.
296. Gottlieb/PREFACE.
297. Jenni Frazer, "Wiesel: Yes, We Really Did Put God on Trial," *Jewish Chronicle*, September 19, 2008, accessed January 1, 2019.
298. Burton/BERNSTEIN, p. 338.
299. Gottlieb/PREFACE.
300. Gottlieb/WORKING, p. 128.
301. Schiller/JEWISH, p. 148.
302. Smith/PLACE, p. 15.
303. Schiller/JEWISH, p. 152.
304. Ibid., p. 153.
305. Ibid., p. 154.
306. Ibid.
307. Ibid., p. 155.
308. Baber/JAZZ, p. 194.
309. Schiller/JEWISH, p. 157.
310. Ibid., p. 158.
311. Ibid., p. 160.
312. Ibid., p. 161.
313. Ibid.
314. Gottlieb/SYMBOLS, p. 290; Smith/PLACE, p. 18.
315. Schiller/JEWISH, p. 163.
316. Anonymous, *Ha'aretz*, December 11, 1963.
317. *La Merchav*, December 13, 1963.
318. Anonymous, "'Kaddish,' a Minority Opinion," *Ha'aretz*, December 16, 1963.
319. Harold Rogers, "Bernstein's 'Kaddish' in U.S. Premiere," *Christian Science Monitor*, February 1, 1964.
320. Robert Taylor, "'Kaddish' Reveals Bernstein Genius," *Boston Herald*, February 1, 1964.
321. Michael Steinberg, "Bernstein's 'Kaddish' Has Premiere Here," *Morning Globe*, February 1, 1964.
322. Ross Parmenter, "Leonard Bernstein's Kaddish," *New York Times*, April 10, 1964.
323. Anonymous, *Time* magazine, February 7, 1964; a clipping in the scrapbook in the Leonard Bernstein Collection: Box SB 56, Vol. 51. January 31, 1964–April 21, 1964, microfilm, reel 28.
324. Joseph McLellan, "Leonard Bernstein's Requiem for Mankind," *Pilot*, February 8, 1964.
325. Bernstein, "Tribute to S. J .B." (January 1, 1963) in Bernstein/FINDINGS, p. 176.
326. Ibid.
327. Baber/MIRROR, p. 23.
328. Simmons/STEEL, p. 345.
329. Ibid., pp. 8–9.

330. Ibid., p. 346.
331. Ibid.
332. Quoted in ibid., p. 345.
333. Ibid., p. 347.
334. Ibid., pp. 346–47.
335. Butterworth/SYMPHONY, p. 158.
336. Simmons/STEEL, pp. 345–46.
337. Butterworth/SYMPHONY, p. 157.
338. Ibid., p. 156.
339. Cowell/MENNIN NO. 3, p. 328.
340. Simmons/STEEL, p. 347.
341. Cowell/MENNIN NO. 3, p. 328.
342. Simmons/STEEL, pp. 356–57.
343. Smith/MENNIN, p. 488.
344. Quoted in Simmons/STEEL, p. 358.
345. Ibid., pp. 356–57.
346. Ibid., p. 358.
347. Butterworth/SYMPHONY, p. 157.
348. Simmons/MENNIN 5, p. 5.
349. Simmons/STEEL, p. 362.
350. Ibid., p. 363.
351. Ibid., pp. 363–64.
352. Quoted in ibid., p. 364.
353. Ibid., p. 372.
354. Ibid., p. 373.
355. Ibid.
356. See excerpts from reviews by Olin Downes, Paul Henry Lang, and Irving Kolodin in ibid., pp. 374–75.
357. For example: "Mennin is a symphonist by nature and intent, and his ideas fall naturally into large units, both as to structure and musical content." Walter Hendl, "Music of Peter Mennin," quoted in ibid., p. 377.
358. Butterworth/SYMPHONY, p. 157.
359. Mennin's liner notes for the first recording, quoted in Simmons/STEEL, p. 386.
360. Ibid., pp. 385–86.
361. Butterworth/SYMPHONY, p. 158.
362. Ibid.
363. Ibid., p. 345.
364. Mennin/EIGHTH.
365. Zephaniah, one of the so-called minor prophets in the Hebrew Scriptures, devotes much of his short book to the coming day of judgment (the "Day of the LORD"). Mennin may have in mind passages like 1:15, "That day will be a day of wrath—a day of distress and anguish, a day of trouble and ruin, a day of darkness and gloom, a day of clouds and blackness" (English Standard Version).
366. Simmons/STEEL, p. 394.
367. Ibid., p. 394.
368. Mennin/EIGHTH.
369. Harold C. Schonberg, "A New Mennin: Philharmonic Offers Symphony No. 8," *New York Times*, November 22, 1974.
370. Quoted in Simmons/STEEL, p. 395.

371. A reference to Hugo Wolf's famously withering review of the Fourth Symphony, quoted in Brown/BRAHMS, p. 100.
372. Borroff/MENNIN 8, p. 330.
373. Simmons/STEEL, p. 398.
374. Quoted in ibid., pp. 406–07.
375. Walker-Hill/SPIRITUALS, p. 94. The work is unfortunately lost.
376. Ibid., p. 101.
377. Ibid., p. 106.
378. Ibid., p. 97.
379. Ibid., p. 107.
380. Ibid., p. 106.
381. Thurman/SINGING, p. 29.
382. Anonymous, "HI Choir Unit at Rutgers in Concert Tour," *Daily Press,* Newport News, Virginia (February 26, 1950), p. 10.
383. Walker-Hill/SPIRITUALS, p. 99.
384. Thurman/SINGING, pp. 30–31.
385. Walker-Hill/SPIRITUALS, p. 99.
386. Ibid., p. 100.
387. Quoted (from interview) in ibid., p. 107.
388. Quoted in ibid., p. 96.
389. Ibid., p. 107.
390. Ibid.
391. Ibid., p. 108.
392. Ibid.
393. Kernodle/ENTER, p. 771.
394. Ibid.
395. Ibid.
396. Ibid., p. 772.
397. Walker-Hill/SPIRITUALS, p. 115. In addition to the few commercially available scores, engraved scores compiled by Helen Walker-Hill and Christopher Hahn and accompanying MIDI recordings are available the Center for Black Music Research in Chicago and American Music Research Center at the University of Colorado Boulder. The Julia Perry Working Group at the Humanities Commons, moderated by Kendra Leonard, has also made some liner notes and scores available digitally, including those for Symphonies 1, 4 (with missing parts reconstructed), 10, 13, and *A Suite Symphony.*
398. Ibid., p. 112.
399. Ibid., p. 117.
400. Ibid.
401. Ibid.
402. Ibid., p. 116. The recording is available through New World Records and Spotify.
403. Quoted in ibid.
404. Ibid.
405. Ibid., p. 113.
406. Ibid., p. 114.
407. Ibid., p. 119.
408. Ibid., p. 115.
409. Ibid., p. 115.
410. See chapter 9 for a discussion of Marsalis's symphonies.

411. Walker-Hill/SPIRITUALS, p. 120.
412. Ibid.
413. Ibid., p. 121.
414. Ibid.
415. Ibid.
416. Ibid.
417. Ibid., p. 102.
418. Ibid., p. 122.
419. Wilson/COMPOSER, p. 29.
420. W. E. B. Du Bois, *The Souls of Black Folk* (1903; reprint New York: Oxford University Press, 2007), p. 8.
421. Wilson/COMPOSER, p. 31.
422. Walker-Hill/SPIRITUALS, p. 97.
423. For an overview of this trend in the reception of twelve-tone music in the United States, see Straus/REVISIONIST.
424. Butterworth/SYMPHONY, p. 174.
425. Simmons/VOICES, p. 377.
426. Walter Simmons, "Vittorio Giannini," https://www-oxfordmusiconline-com.auth.lib.niu.edu/grovemusic/view/10.1093/gmo/9781561592630.001.0001/omo-9781561592630-e-0000011077?rskey=bGX7Ku.
427. Simmons/VOICES, p. 161.
428. James Wierzbicki, "Robert Kurka," https://www-oxfordmusiconline-com.auth.lib.niu.edu/grovemusic/view/10.1093/gmo/9781561592630.001.0001/omo-9781561592630-e-0000015691?rskey=BfITrX.
429. Butterworth/SYMPHONY, p. 104.
430. Fauser/SOUNDS, p. 256.
431. See chapters 1 and 2 for more on Dwight's concept of the symphony and its place in American music.
432. Bernstein's description of the course of American music at midcentury also reflects the historiography of the period: that "the whole notion of the symphonic form is a German notion" and so the path to a distinctly American opera runs through musical comedy (the American *Singspiel*)— "developing *Pal Joey* into whatever American music is going to become"; Bernstein/GREAT, p. 46. Midcentury musicologists such as Czech immigrant Paul Nettl reinforced the Germanocentric orientation. According to his son Bruno (an esteemed ethnomusicologist), Paul held that "music in its loftiest sense is essentially a German product. . . . Thus teaching Americans about music meant, ipso facto, teaching them about German music . . . [and] striving to present a portrait of European erudition that his students were supposed to admire but could never hope to achieve." Quoted in Horowitz/EXILE, p. 214.
433. Tawa/GREAT, p. 205.
434. Butterworth/SYMPHONY, p. 135.
435. Simmons/VOICES, p. 11.
436. Tawa/GREAT, p. 187.
437. Simmons/STEEL, p. 80.
438. Butterworth/SYMPHONY, p. 131.
439. Ibid., pp. 151–52.
440. Simmons/STEEL, pp. 346–47.
441. Ibid., pp. 193–94.

Bibliography

Anonymous. "Age of Anxiety: New Bernstein Symphony Heard in Boston." *New York Herald Tribune*, April 9, 1949.

Anonymous. "The Discovery of David Diamond." *Rochester Democrat and Chronicle*, February 27, 1966.

Anonymous. "'Kaddish,' a Minority Opinion." *Ha'aretz*, December 16, 1963.

Athens/HOVHANESS — Athens, Niccolo Davis. "The Music of Alan Hovhaness." DMA diss., Cornell University, 2016.

Baber/JAZZ — Baber, Katherine. *Leonard Bernstein and the Language of Jazz*. Champaign-Urbana: University of Illinois Press, 2018.

Baber/MIRROR — Baber, Katherine. "Mahler in the Mirror: Bernstein, Mahler, and Music Criticism in the United States and Austria." *Anklänge* (Universität für Musik und darstellende Kunst, 2015): pp. 15–40.

Bernard/TONAL — Bernard, Jonathan W. "Tonal Traditions in Art Music since 1960." In *The Cambridge History of American Music*, edited by David Nicholls, pp. 535–66. Cambridge: Cambridge University Press, 1998.

Bernstein/ADDRESS — Bernstein, Leonard. Speech to the American Symphony Orchestra League, June 16–17, 1980, Box 93, Folder 4, LBC.

Bernstein/ANXIETY — Bernstein, Leonard. Preface, Symphony No. 2: *The Age of Anxiety*. London: Boosey & Hawkes, 1993.

Bernstein, Leonard. "Call Me Moses" [silent home movie: scene outlines and title list] (Summer 1960), Box 71, Folder 18, Leonard Bernstein Collection, Library of Congress.

Bernstein, Leonard. "Concert talk or lecture" [Copland Third Symphony] (October 1948), Box 71, Folder 49, LBC.

Bernstein/FINDINGS — Bernstein, Leonard. *Findings*. New York: Simon and Schuster, 1982.

Bernstein/GREAT — Bernstein, Leonard. "Whatever Happened to that Great American Symphony?" In *The Joy of Music*, pp. 40–51. New York: Simon and Schuster, 1980.

Bernstein/JEREMIAH — Bernstein, Leonard. Program Note, Symphony No. 1: *Jeremiah*. London: Boosey & Hawkes, 1992.

Bernstein, Leonard. *The Little Drummer Boy: An Essay on Gustav Mahler (1860–1911) by and with Leonard Bernstein*. Philips, 1985; reissued, 2007.

Bernstein, Leonard. Notes for speaker's text and transliterations of the Kaddish prayer, Box 78, Folders 1 and 24, LBC.

Bernstein, Leonard. "On Bloch, Sacred Service," Thursday evening preview talk (April 7, 1960), Box 78, Folder 10, LBC.

Bernstein, Leonard.	Press conference remarks on 20th c. symphony series with New York Philharmonic (April 27, 1965), Box 82, Folder 18, LBC.
Bernstein, Leonard.	Undated musing, early 1960s, Box 78, Folder 1, LBC.
Blair, William.	"Report from Boston [Diamond Symphony No. 2]." *New York Times*, October 22, 1944.
Borroff/MENNIN 8	Borroff, Edith. Review: Peter Mennin, Symphony No. 8. *American Music* 9 (Autumn 1991): pp. 330–31.
Brown/BRAHMS	Brown, A. Peter. "The Symphonies of Johannes Brahms." In *The Symphonic Repertoire*. Vol. 4: *The Second Golden Age of the Viennese Symphony: Brahms, Bruckner, Dvořák, Mahler, and Selected Contemporaries*, edited by A. Peter Brown, pp. 35–124. Bloomington: Indiana University Press, 2003.
Burk, John N.	Program Note, Boston Symphony Orchestra [Schuman Symphony No. 2]. February 17 and 18, 1939.
Burk, John N.	Program Note, Boston Symphony Orchestra [Diamond Symphony No. 3]. November 3, 1950.
Burton/BERNSTEIN	Burton, Humphrey. *Leonard Bernstein*. New York: Doubleday, 1994.
Butterworth/SYMPHONY	Butterworth, Neil. *The American Symphony*. Aldershot: Ashgate, 1998.
Callan/ALLEGORY	Callan, Edward. "Allegory in Auden's *The Age of Anxiety*." *Twentieth Century Literature* 10 (1965): pp. 155–65.
Churgin/SAMMARTINI.	Churgin, Bathia. "Giovanni Battista Sammartini." In *The Symphonic Repertoire*. Vol. 1: *The Eighteenth-Century Symphony*, edited by Mary Sue Morrow and Bathia Churgin, pp. 146–69. Bloomington: Indiana University Press, 2012.
Copland/SCHOOL	Copland, Aaron. "The New 'School' of American Composers." *New York Magazine*, March 14, 1948.
Cowell/MENNIN NO. 3	Cowell, Henry. Review of Peter Mennin, Symphony No. 3. *Notes* 6 (March 1949): p. 328.
Crawford/MUSICAL LIFE	Crawford, Richard. *America's Musical Life: A History*. New York: W. W. Norton, 2001.
Davidson/DIAMOND	Davidson, Mary Wallace. "David Diamond." *Oxford Music Online*, https://www-oxfordmusiconline-com.auth.lib.niu.edu/grovemusic/view/10.1093/gmo/9781561592630.001.0001/omo-9781561592630-e-0000007718?rskey=eX9vUX.
Diamond/SESSIONS	Diamond, David. "Roger Sessions: Symphony No. 2." *Notes* 7 (June 7, 1950): pp. 438–39.
Downes, Edward.	Program Note for [Alan Hovhaness's] *Vishnu*. New York Philharmonic, June 2, 1967.
Downes, Edward.	Program Note [Diamond Symphony No. 8]. New York Philharmonic. October 27, 1971.

Downes, Olin.	"Boston Orchestra Offers New Work: Third Symphony of William Schuman Called Best Number by Young American." *New York Times*, November 23, 1941.
Downes, Olin.	"Corigliano Soloist for Philharmonic: Violinist Heard in Concerto by Elgar—Sessions Symphony Featured on Program." *New York Times*, January 13, 1950.
Downes, Olin.	"Impressions of Two Programs of Music by American Composers." *New York Times*, May 17, 1942.
Downes, Olin.	"Rodzinski Offers Creston Symphony," *New York Times*, February 16, 1945.
Fauser/SOUNDS	Fauser, Annegret. *Sounds of War: Music in the United States during World War II*. New York: Oxford University Press, 2013.
Fisher, Marjory M.	"Sessions Symphony Has Premiere." *Musical America*, January 25, 1947.
Forte/BALLAD	Forte, Allen. *The American Popular Ballad of the Golden Era: 1924–1950*. Princeton, NJ: Princeton University Press, 1995.
Frankel, Max.	"Bernstein Work Heard in Moscow." *New York Times*, August 24, 1959, p. 16.
Frazer, Jenni.	"Wiesel: Yes, We Really Did Put God on Trial." *Jewish Chronicle*, September 19, 2008, accessed January 1, 2019.
Gentry/ANXIETY	Gentry, Philip. "Leonard Bernstein's *The Age of Anxiety*: A Great American Symphony during McCarthyism." *American Music* 29, no. 3 (Fall 2011): pp. 308–31.
Giger/JOY	Giger, Andreas. "Bernstein's *The Joy of Music* as Aesthetic Credo." *Journal of the Society for American Music* 3, no. 3 (August 2009): pp. 311–39.
Gottlieb/FAITH	Gottlieb, Jack. "Symbols of Faith in the Music of Leonard Bernstein." *Musical Quarterly* 66 (April 1980): pp. 287–95.
Gottlieb/JEREMIAH	Gottlieb, Jack. Prefatory Note, Symphony No. 1, *Jeremiah*. London: Boosey & Hawkes, 1992.
Gottlieb/MUSIC	Gottlieb, Jack. "The Music of Leonard Bernstein: A Study of Melodic Manipulations." DMA diss., University of Illinois Urbana-Champaign, 1964.
Gottlieb/PREFACE	Gottlieb, Jack. Preface, Symphony No. 3: *Kaddish*. London: Boosey & Hawkes, 2002.
Gottlieb/WORKING	Gottlieb, Jack. *Working with Bernstein*. Milwaukee, WI: Amadeus, 2010.
Hamm/MUSIC	Hamm, Charles. *Music in the New World*. New York: W. W. Norton, 1983.
Hart/FRENCH	Hart, Brian. "The French Symphony after Berlioz: From the Second Empire to the First World War." In

	The Symphonic Repertoire, Vol. 3, Part B: *The European Symphony, from ca. 1800 to ca. 1930: Great Britain, Russia, and France*, edited by A. Peter Brown with Brian Hart, pp. 527–755. Bloomington: Indiana University Press, 2007.
Holland, Bernard.	"Concert: Bernstein Leads Debut of Diamond's Ninth." *New York Times*, November 18, 1985.
Horowitz/CLASSICAL	Horowitz, Joseph. *Classical Music in America: A History of Its Rise and Fall*. New York: W. W. Norton, 2005.
Horowitz/DIRECTOR	Horowitz, Joseph. "As Music Director: A Quest for Meaning and Identity." In *Leonard Bernstein: American Original*, pp. 135–51. New York: Philharmonic-Symphony Society of New York, 2008.
Horowitz/EXILE	Horowitz, Joseph. *Artists in Exile: How Refugees from Twentieth-Century War and Revolution Transformed the American Performing Arts*. New York: Harper Perennial, 2008.
Housepian/ARMENIA	Housepian, Ari, ed. "Music of Armenia." *Garland Encyclopedia of World Music*. Vol. 6, *The Middle East*, edited by Virginia Danielson, Scott Marcus, and Dwight Reynolds, pp. 723–38. New York: Routledge, 2002.
Hovhaness/THOUGHTS	Hovhaness, Alan. "Thoughts on East-West Music in Honor of Dr. Lee Hye-ku, Great Scholar of Korea." In *Essays in Ethnomusicology: A Birthday Offering for Lee Hye-Ku*, pp. 367–70. [Seoul?] Korean Musicological Society, 1969.
Kernodle/ENTER	Kernodle, Tammy L. "'When and Where I Enter': Black Women Composers and the Advancement of a Black Postmodern Concert Aesthetic in Cold War-Era America" in Colloquy: Shadow Culture Narratives: Race, Gender, and American Music Historiography, *Journal of the American Musicological Society* 37, no. 3 (Fall 2022): pp. 770–78.
Kimberling/DIAMOND	Kimberling, Victoria J. *David Diamond: A Bio-Bibliography*. Metuchen, NJ: Scarecrow, 1987.
Kostelanetz/HOVHANESS	Kostelanetz, Richard. "Remembering Alan Hovhaness: Making the Right Connections." *21st Century Music* 7 (September 2000): pp. 15–18.
Liebling, Leonard.	"Boston Forces Give American Novelty." *Musical Courier*, December 1, 1941.
McLellan, Joseph.	"Leonard Bernstein's Requiem for Mankind." *Pilot*, February 8, 1964.
Mennin/EIGHTH	Mennin, Peter. Program Note, Symphony No. 8, New York Philharmonic, November 21, 1974.
N. S.,	"Hovhaness Works in Premiere Here." *New York Times*, March 12, 1951.

Olmstead/BIOGRAPHY	Olmstead, Andrea. *Roger Sessions: A Biography*. New York: Routledge, 2008.
Olmstead/CONVERSATIONS	Olmstead, Andrea. *Conversations with Roger Sessions*. Boston: Northeastern University Press, 1987.
Olmstead/MUSIC	Olmstead, Andrea. *Roger Sessions and His Music*. Ann Arbor, MI: UMI Research Press, 1985.
Olmstead/SESSIONS	Olmstead, Andrea. "Sessions, Roger." *Oxford Music Online*. https://www-oxfordmusiconline-com.auth.lib.niu.edu/grovemusic/view/10.1093/gmo/9781561592630.001.0001/omo-9781561592630-e-0000025507?rskey=qKur1X&result=1.
Parmenter, Ross.	"Leonard Bernstein's Kaddish." *New York Times*, April 10, 1964.
Parmenter, Ross.	"Season Is Opened by Philharmonic." *New York Times*, October 5, 1962.
Polisi/MUSE	Polisi, Joseph W. *American Muse: The Life and Times of William Schuman*. Milwaukee, WI: Amadeus, 2008.
Pye/INSIDE	Pye, Richard. "'Asking about the Inside': Schoenberg's 'Idea' in the Music of Roy Harris and William Schuman." *Music Analysis* 19 (March 2000): pp. 69–98.
Rasmussen/KADDISH	Rasmussen, Karen. "Transcendence in Leonard Bernstein's Kaddish Symphony." *Quarterly Journal of Speech* 80 (May 1994): pp. 150–73.
Rockwell, John.	"Music: Schuman by Skrowaczewski." *New York Times*, April 22, 1979.
Rockwell, John.	"Roger Sessions, Nearing 85, Is Still a Maverick Composer." *New York Times*, March 22, 1981.
Rogers, Harold.	"Bernstein's 'Kaddish' in U.S. Premiere." *Christian Science Monitor*, February 1, 1964.
Rosner and Wolverton/HOVHANESS	Rosner, Arnold, and Vance Wolverton. "Alan Hovhaness." *Oxford Music Online*. https://www-oxfordmusiconline-com.auth.lib.niu.edu/grovemusic/view/10.1093/gmo/9781561592630.001.0001/omo-9781561592630-e-0000013420?rskey=WoN2JN&result=1.
Ross, Alex.	"Diamond's 11th Symphony." *New York Times*, December 7, 1992.
Sabin, Robert.	"Bernstein Introduces Diamond Eighth." *Musical America*, December 1961.
Sargeant, Winthrop.	"Musical Events: A Neglected Tradition." *New Yorker*, March 30, 1957, pp. 87–89.
Sargeant, Winthrop.	"Musical Events: Is Music Dead?" *New Yorker*, May 11, 1968, pp. 140–43.
Schiller/JEWISH	Schiller, David M. *Bloch, Schoenberg, and Bernstein: Assimilating Jewish Music*. London: Oxford University Press, 2003.

Schonberg, Harold C.	"A New Mennin: Philharmonic Offers Symphony No. 8." *New York Times*, November 22, 1974.
Schonberg, Harold C.	"Diamond's 8th Symphony Has Premiere." *New York Times*, October 28, 1961.
Schonberg, Harold C.	"Steinberg Leads Philharmonic in New Sessions Work, 'Scheherazade' Is After on the Program." *New York Times*, May 3, 1968.
Sessions/DIFFICULT	Sessions, Roger. "How a 'Difficult' Composer Gets That Way." *New York Times*, January 8, 1950.
Sessions/IMMATURITY	Sessions, Roger. "Composer's Concern with Journalistic Criticism a Sign of His Immaturity." *New York Times*, March 11, 1934.
Simeone/BERNSTEIN LETTERS	Simeone, Nigel, ed. *The Leonard Bernstein Letters*. New Haven, CT: Yale University Press, 2015.
Simmons/CRESTON	Simmons, Walter. "Paul Creston." *Oxford Music Online*. https://www-oxfordmusiconline-com.auth.lib.niu.edu/grovemusic/view/10.1093/gmo/9781561592630.001.0001/omo-9781561592630-e-0000006817?rskey=qIWtkU&result=1.
Simmons/MENNIN 5	Simmons, Walter. Liner Note: Peter Mennin: Symphonies Nos. 5 and 6, Albany Symphony Orchestra. Albany Records, Troy 260, 1997.
Simmons/PERSICHETTI	Simmons, Walter. "Vincent Persichetti." *Oxford Music Online*. https://www-oxfordmusiconline-com.auth.lib.niu.edu/grovemusic/view/10.1093/gmo/9781561592630.001.0001/omo-9781561592630-e-0000021384?rskey=pLYk87&result=1.
Simmons/STEEL	Simmons, Walter. *The Music of William Schuman, Vincent Persichetti, and Peter Mennin: Voices of Stone and Steel*. Lanham, MD: Scarecrow, 2011.
Simmons/VOICES	Simmons, Walter. *Voices in the Wilderness: Six American Neo-Romantic Composers*. Lanham, MD: Scarecrow, 2006.
Sloper, L. A.	"Composer Is Piano Soloist at Premiere of Symphony." *Christian Science Monitor*, April 9, 1949, p. 7.
Smith, Cecil.	"Diamond Symphony Given Premiere: Leonard Bernstein Leads Boston Symphony in Presentation of New Work." *Musical America*, February 1948, p. 375.
Smith/MENNIN	Smith, Cecil. Review of Peter Mennin, Symphony No. 4. *Notes* 6 (June 1949): pp. 487–89.
Smith/PLACE	Smith, Helen. *There's a Place for Us: The Musical Theatre Works of Leonard Bernstein*. London: Ashgate, 2011.
Smith, Moses.	"Symphony Concert: Miss Hess as Soloist, and 100 Men to Follow." *Boston Transcript*, February 18, 1930.

Smith, Warren Storey.	"Myra Hess Soloist at Symphony: Work by Schuman Is Received Rather Coldly." *Boston Post*, February 18, 1939.
Starr/IVES	Starr, Larry. *A Union of Diversities: Style in the Music of Charles Ives*. New York: Schirmer, 1992.
Steinberg, Michael.	"Bernstein's 'Kaddish' Has Premiere Here." *Morning Globe*, February 1, 1964.
Straus/REVISIONIST	Straus, Joseph N. "A Revisionist History of Twelve-Tone Serialism in American Music." *Journal of the Society for American Music* 2 (2008): pp. 355–95.
Straus/TWELVE-TONE	Straus, Joseph N. *Twelve-Tone Music in America*. Cambridge: Cambridge University Press, 2009.
Straus, Noel.	"Huberman Soloist at Carnegie Hall: Polish Violinist Plays Joachim Cadenza in Beethoven Concerto at Concert." *New York Times*, December 22, 1941.
Strongin, Theodore.	"Symphony Given Jersey Premiere: Sessions Is First Composer to Receive State Grant." *New York Times*, January 20, 1966.
Swayne/ORPHEUS	Swayne, Steven. *Orpheus in Manhattan: William Schuman and the Shaping of America's Musical Life*. New York: Oxford University Press, 2011.
Swayne/PUZZLING	Swayne, Steven. "William Schuman's Puzzling Seventh Symphony." AMS-Library of Congress Lecture, March 25, 2010.
Taubman/RECORDS	Taubman, Howard. "Records: Sessions Second Symphony Played by Philharmonic under Mitropoulos as Naumburg Award." *New York Times*, July 2, 1950.
Tawa/GREAT	Tawa, Nicholas. *The Great American Symphony: Music, the Depression, and War*. Bloomington: Indiana University Press, 2009.
Taylor, Robert.	"'Kaddish' Reveals Bernstein Genius." *Boston Herald*, February 1, 1964.
Thomson/AMERICAN	Thomson, Virgil. "On Being American" (originally published January 25, 1948). In *Music Right and Left*. New York: Greenwood Press, 1951.
Thomson/ANXIETY	Thomson, Virgil. "Music [Bernstein *Age of Anxiety*]." *New York Herald Tribune*, February 24, 1950.
Thomson/ELEGANCE	Thomson, Virgil. "The Sincerity of Elegance." *New York Herald Tribune*, February 5, 1946.
Thurman/SINGING	Thurman, Kira. *Singing Like Germans: Black Musicians in the Land of Bach, Beethoven, and Brahms*. Ithaca, NY: Cornell University Press, 2021.
Walker-Hill/SPIRITUALS	Walker-Hill, Helen. *From Spirituals to Symphonies: African-American Women Composers and Their Music*. Westport, CT: Greenwood, 2002.

Welch, Roy D.	"A Symphony Introduces Roger Sessions." *Modern Music* 4 (May–June 1927): pp. 27–30.
Williams, Alexander.	"Music: Symphony Concert." *Boston Herald*, February 18, 1939.
Williams, Alexander.	"Symphony Concert." *Boston Herald*, October 18, 1941.
Wilson/COMPOSER	Wilson, Olly. "The Black American Composer and the Orchestra in the Twentieth Century," *Black Perspective in Music* 14, no. 1 (Winter 1986): pp. 26–34.
Wolffers, Jules.	"Boston: New Scores Have Hearing." *Musical Courier* 137 (February 1, 1948): p. 13.
Wolffers, Jules.	"Boston: Two Native Scores Bow [Diamond Fourth Symphony, Shapero Symphony]." *Musical Courier* 137 (February 15, 1948): p. 51.
Wolffers, Jules.	"Music in Review." *Jewish Advocate*, April 14, 1949.

CHAPTER SEVEN

The Symphony in South America

Carol A. Hess

Introduction

In the mid-1940s, composer Alberto Ginastera returned to his native Argentina from a stint as a Guggenheim fellow in the United States. He enthused to his compatriots about many things, including the abundance of symphony orchestras. In an article, he noted some two hundred orchestras "distributed throughout the entire country [that] form a solid base through which the activities of composers, performers, and publishers are affirmed."[1] In light of ever-shrinking budgets for the arts in the United States, Ginastera's words may strike us as nothing short of fantastic. Likely he was comparing the US orchestral scene to that of South America. To be sure, Ginastera hailed from a country that has long prided itself on culture—including orchestral culture—thanks, in part, to the Teatro Colón, the acoustically perfect Beaux Arts–style performance space and, since 1908, the principal venue in Buenos Aires for classical music. Ginastera himself composed fifteen-odd orchestral works, excluding film scores and incidental music. Many more South American composers have confronted obstacles such as lack of infrastructure, scant government or private support, or the absence of a ticket-buying public. Whereas Argentina, Brazil, and Chile have boasted several symphonic composers, other countries have far fewer. Yet as discussed below, orchestral music has sustained itself under some surprising circumstances. Further, if we expand our definition of "symphonic music" to include the colonial-period music of cathedrals and other ecclesiastical establishments—all part of European evangelization—our understanding is enhanced from both a historical and aesthetic point of view.

Music's power in spreading Christianity has come under scrutiny in recent years, mainly with respect to erasure of native traditions and abuse of political power.[2] However hegemonic evangelization may seem to us today, it is a fact that in Latin America the ensemble we nowadays recognize as an orchestra began in cathedrals, churches, and missions. From the early eighteenth century, orchestras of string and wind instruments, often with Native performers, were part of ordinary life, whether in the Jesuit missions in Bolivia and Paraguay or Franciscan missions in Bolivia; likewise, enslaved (or formerly enslaved) Africans made music in Minas Geraís (Brazil) and other parts of South America, often playing European-style instruments they had built themselves. Besides masses and motets, the villancico was a favorite genre.[3]

Many villancicos have continuo parts for harp or organ only. But others call for *corneta* (cornett), *chirimía* (shawm), *bajón* (similar to the bassoon), *sacabuche* (sackbut/trombone), trumpet, organ, *violón* (viol) and other stringed instruments, including double bass and harp—such that by the eighteenth century, the Latin American villancico, like its counterparts in Spain and Portugal, was accompanied by an orchestra. A variety of styles, some with popular dance elements or with metric structures associated with a particular group or region, afforded villancico composers a wealth of creativity. Also, some villancicos were composed in indigenous languages, just as the *negrito*, a subgenre of the villancico, presumably imitated African speech patterns.

Outside of religious observance, instrumental music marked civic ceremonies and other events, a dimension of South American music making that scholars have tended to overlook until recently.[4] Such music offers clues to social structures. A fiesta, for example, can spatially and musically situate ethnic and social groups—Europeans, *criollos* (people born in Spanish America but whose parents were of Spanish heritage), Native Americans, Africans, whether urban or rural—marking the differences between them while also obscuring the boundaries through the act of performance.[5] Tied to these phenomena is the very definition of *concert*. If at one time the term simply meant adding voices over plainsong, a dictionary of 1793 defined it as the act in which a "multitude of musicians" sang or played instruments.[6] Amid a growing print culture, instrumental music circulated among secular music academies, philharmonic societies, professional and nonprofessional orchestras, and opera companies. Without this foundation, Ginastera, Villa-Lobos, Chávez, Revueltas, and many other composers from Latin America would simply not have written the music we admire today.

Several other factors should also be kept in mind. First, the proper role of European influence has been an ongoing subject of debate. At various points, South American composers have either been drawn to the Western canon, widely considered "universal," or have resisted European hegemony, often through musical nationalism.[7] Although most composers began their musical studies in local conservatories, many studied abroad, often in France thanks to long-standing attachments to Gallic culture. As discussed below, Vincent d'Indy's *Cours de composition musicale*, which emphasized form and unity, influenced South American symphonic composition to no small degree. (Others trained in Brussels or London; a few studied in Spain.) Composers opting for nationalism, on the other hand, sought a native voice free of European influence. They often availed themselves of the folk traditions of their respective countries, to which folklorists had devoted themselves from the 1920s on.[8] With either approach, the question of modernism loomed. As in the United States, many South American composers recognized that they were pursuing "modernism on the periphery,"[9] skirting the fraught and ill-defined relationship between the local and the global. However alluring globalization might be, with its promise of liberal democracy and rationalism, it can exact a heavy price, with national or regional identity usually a casualty.[10] Such tensions ebb and flow in tandem with political and cultural phenomena, such as immigration during the Spanish Civil War and World War II, which impacted musical life in South America.

The second factor is the United States, sometimes dubbed the "Colossus of the North" in the often-charged language of North-South relations. Since the era of the Monroe Doctrine, US invasions and occupations of the region have poisoned North-South relations just as genuine attempts at goodwill hinted at rapport. One such moment for the latter was the Good Neighbor policy, a series of cultural exchange programs crafted by President Franklin D. Roosevelt's administration to help unite the Americas against European fascism in the 1930s and 40s. Several Latin American composers visited the United States, whether through private or public funds, and US musicians visited Latin America.[11] Among the latter were Aaron Copland, who made a nine-country cultural diplomacy tour in 1941, and the Russian émigré Nicolas Slonimsky, dispatched that same year by the philanthropist Edwin Adler Fleisher to undertake what Slonimsky called a "Latin American fishing trip," gathering scores by Latin American composers.[12] The hundreds of orchestral compositions Slonimsky obtained remain at the Free Library of Philadelphia for use by scholars and performers. Slonimsky also wrote a still-useful book on his findings.[13]

Good Neighborly sentiment survived World War II, and in 1946, several South American composers of orchestral music studied at the Berkshire Music Center (Tanglewood): Juan Orrego-Salas and Claudio Spies (Chile), Héctor Tosar (Uruguay), Antonio Estévez (Venezuela); and Ginastera; the Brazilian conductor Eleazar de Carvahlo worked there with Serge Koussevitzky, director of the Boston Symphony Orchestra.[14] During the Cold War, South American composers studying in the United States included Edgar Valcárcel (Peru), León Schidlowsky (Chile), and Mario Davidovsky (Argentina). Performance opportunities included the Washington, DC–based series of Inter-American Music Festivals, which began in 1958 and showcased numerous symphonic works. The Louisville Orchestra commissioned several Latin American works in its midcentury campaign to promote new music. All the while, however, political tensions mounted as the United States, motivated by anticommunist zeal, returned to the hated practice of interventionism. Any number of South American composers wrote programmatic works in defiance of US imperialism.

In sum, Latin Americans wrote abundantly for orchestra, with the mid-twentieth century something of a "golden age." Since the 1960s, composers have increasingly bypassed orchestral music, devoting themselves to electroacoustic composition and multimedia like their international counterparts. Yet many exceptions exist, including into the present. As explored below, this repertory is stylistically much richer than is often recognized. Although identity-conscious works such as Ginastera's *Estancia* may remain the most frequently performed on concert programs (often under the rubric of a themed concert titled *Latin Holiday* or *¡Fiesta!*), a much ampler picture emerges when we consider late-romantic, Neoclassical, atonal, serial, and eclectic styles in South American orchestral music. While some composers did pursue folkloric gestures—what the Cuban composer Aurelio de la Vega scathingly branded "maracas and drums" style—others favored identity-neutral, cosmopolitan styles, which they considered just as legitimate.[15]

In studying South American instrumental music, fascinating possibilities for future research emerge. Although Nadia Boulanger's influence on US composers is widely recognized, several South Americans studied with her as well: Astor Piazzolla, Rodolfo Arizaga, and Miguel Ángel Rondano (Argentina); Cláudio Santoro (Brazil); Jorge Urrutia Blondel (Chile); Rodolfo Holzmann (Peru); Jaime Mendoza-Nava (Bolivia); Gerardo Guevara (Ecuador); and Adolfo Mejía and Francisco Zumaqué (Colombia).[16] Only recently have scholars begun to consider immigration and classical music in South America, whether through the experience of European Jewish musicians who fled Hitler for Argentina or that of the Jewish composer Erich Eisner in Bolivia.[17] Likewise, the stories of Spanish expatriates to South America, unwelcome in Spain after Franco's victory, have yet to be told, as is true of numerous women composers.

The main point I wish to make in this essay is that South American orchestral music extends far beyond the handful of works we hear in concert and on recordings. These works, moreover, are not confined to Brazil and Argentina. To that end, I begin our discussion with the small nation of Uruguay, known for its government's generous support for the arts, followed by Paraguay, Argentina, Brazil, Chile, Peru, Bolivia, Ecuador, Colombia, and Venezuela.

Uruguay

In 1516, when Juan de Solís arrived in what is now Uruguay, he encountered the Charrúa and the Guaraní natives. After incursions by Magellan and Cabot, Jesuits and Franciscans established settlements, the Spanish increasing their presence from around 1620 under the threat of Portuguese domination. Few missions (*reducciones*) existed during this time, and many Indigenous peoples died from European diseases. In 1726, the Spanish founded Montevideo. Musical life was less vibrant in Uruguay than elsewhere in this relatively poor region, but after the expulsion of the Jesuits in 1767, musicians from elsewhere came to the area, initiating a long history of immigration in Uruguay's history. In 1793, the Casa de Comedias theater was erected.[18] Much has been made of Uruguay's status as a "white republic": Slonimsky calls it "white man's land."[19] In fact, in 1800 approximately one-third of the population of around thirty thousand were enslaved Africans, and Black and mixed-race individuals took a role in church music. Slavery was abolished in 1842, but, faced with discrimination and other obstacles, the Afro-Uruguayan population decreased to the point that by 2011 it totaled only 4.6 percent. Musical assertions of Afro-Uruguayan identity were preserved, however, as in *candombe*, a genre that inspired later symphonic composers such as Miguel del Águila (b. 1957).

In 1811, the quest for independence began and in 1830 the constitution was ratified. Two composers who came of age at this time were Antonio Cayetano Barros, who wrote an Italianate *Grand Symphonie*, and Jacinta Furriol, whose *Contradanza de los militares y empelados* was performed in 1833. In 1856, the Teatro Solís opened its doors, the oldest such theater in the Americas. (The Academy of Music in Philadelphia opened the following year.[20]) For over 150 years the Solís has welcomed a host of international musical personalities to Montevideo such as Camille Saint-Saëns, who conducted his *Rapsodie d'Auvergne* there in 1916, and Toscanini, who appeared there for the first time in 1930—both wildly applauded in this cosmopolitan city whose large immigrant population appreciated classical music.[21]

Uruguay's first professional orchestra, the Sociedad Filarmónica, was founded in 1868 by Luigi Preti-Bonati, an immigrant from Toulouse, with its inaugural concert featuring Beethoven's *Eroica* Symphony.[22] One of the first Uruguayans to compose orchestral music was León Ribeiro (1854–1931), whose first symphony premiered in 1886, albeit in nearby Buenos Aires. Three years later, a concert exclusively of his works was presented in Montevideo, featuring the premieres of his second and fourth symphonies. Luis Sambucetti (1860–1926), son of the concert master of the Sociedad Filarmónica, studied in Montevideo and France; he is credited with introducing French impressionist works to Montevideo. Some scholars consider his *Suite d'orchestre* (1898) the first significant orchestral work by an Uruguayan composer. Another figure was Carlos Pedrell (1878–1941), nephew of the Catalan musicologist, critic, and composer Felipe Pedrell, whose staunch support for musical nationalism held sway in some Latin American musical circles. The younger Pedrell worked with his uncle and then with d'Indy at the Schola Cantorum. His symphonic works include a *Catalan Overture*, undated but perhaps a souvenir of his studies with his uncle. Alfonso Broqua (1876–1946) studied with d'Indy at the Schola Cantorum and wrote some orchestral music.

Eduardo Fabini (1882–1950) began as a violinist but studied composition with August de Boeck in Brussels from 1900 to 1903. He is credited with forging a nationalist style in Uruguay,

Table 7.1 Symphonic Music from Uruguay and Paraguay

Uruguay

León Ribeiro (1854–1931). Four symphonies (by 1889).
Alfonso Broqua (1876–1946). *Impresiones sinfónicas* (1912); *Noche campera* (1931); *Poema de las Lomas* (1937).
Eduardo Fabini (1882–1950). *Campo* (1913); *La isla de los ceibos* (1924–26); *Melga sinfónica* (1931); *Patria vieja* (perf. 1931); *Tristes* (perf. 1931); *Mburucuyá* (1933).
Benone Calcavecchia (1886–1953). *Uruguay* (1931); *Impresiones de 1930* (1931); *Preludio* (1931).
Luis Cluzeau Mortet (1889–1957). *Llanuras* (1932); *Soledad campestre* (1936); Concerto for String Orchestra (perf. 1936); *Rancherío* (1940); *Sinfonía Artigas* (1951).
Vicente Ascone (1897–1979). *Suite uruguaya* (perf. 1931); *Paraná guazú* (perf. 1931); *Farsa sentimental y grotesca* (1931); *Cantos del atardecer* (perf. 1935); *Nocturno native* (perf. 1935); *Tres danzas* (perf. 1936).
Héctor Tosar (1923–2002). Symphony No. 1 (1945); Symphony for Strings (1950); Sinfonía concertante for piano and orchestra (1957).
León Biriotti (1929–2020). Concertino (strings, 1960); *Sinfonía Ana Frank* (strings, 1964); Symphony No. 2 (1965); Symphony No. 3: In memoriam Lauro Ayestarán (1968); Symphony No. 4 (1969); *Espectros* (1970); *Soles* (1974); Symphony No. 6 (1991); Symphony No. 7 "Jerusalem" (1996); Sinfonietta (1997).
Antonio Mastrogiovanni (1936–2010). *Introducción, passacaglia y danza* (1963); Sinfonía da camara (1966); *Sequencial* I (1971); *La leyenda de la kena* (1980); *Omaggio* (1987).
José Serebrier (b. 1938). *Leyenda de Faust* (1956); *Elegía* (string orchestra, 1952); Symphony No. 1 (1956); *Partita para orquesta* (Symphony No. 2) (1958); Fantasia (string orchestra, 1960); *Colores mágicos* (chamber orchestra, lighting effects, 1971); *Winterreise* (1999); Symphony No. 3 (Symphonie mistique, 2003).

Paraguay

Florentín Giménez (1925–2021) . . . *Minas-kué* (1968); *El río de la esperanza* (1969); *Suite campiña* (1974); *Suite Arasy* (1976–78); *Ciclo* (1979); Symphony-ballet No. 4 in G Major (*Sortilegio*) (1988–90); *Fantasía Étnica* (1990); Symphony No. 5 in F Minor (*Ritual*) (with piano, 1991–92); Symphony No. 7 in D Major (*Nitsuga*) (1994); Symphony No. 8 in G Minor (*Aldeana*) (2003–04); Symphony No. 9 (Choral) in G Major (*Gestas de nuestra historia*) (2016).

---

most evident in his symphonic poem *Campo*, a thematically varied and free-form work that premiered in Montevideo in 1922. (Richard Strauss conducted it with the Vienna Philharmonic in Buenos Aires and it was also performed by the Syracuse Symphony under Vladimir Shavitch.) The second of Fabini's three symphonic poems, the impressionist *La isla de los ceibos* (The Island of the Coral Trees) of 1924–26, was recorded by RCA Victor. His half-dozen orchestral works are listed in table 7.1. Ramón Rodríguez Socas (1886–1957), who studied at the Conservatorio La Lira in Montevideo and then in Italy, composed three orchestral works: *Undinas*, *Afrodita*, *Bolero*, and *Obertura Andina*.[23]

Uruguay's long tradition of social welfare, public education, and strong central government bore fruit in musical circles in 1931, when the state-funded SODRE (Servicio Oficial de Difusión Radio Eléctrica) was established, along with a symphony orchestra known as the OSSODRE (Orquesta Sinfónica del Servicio Oficial de Difusión Radio Eléctrica). Eventually the SODRE came to support a chamber orchestra, a chorus, a ballet company, a record library, a theater, radio broadcasting, and a television channel.[24] Visiting conductors of the

Carol A. Hess

OSSODRE included Copland, Erich Kleiber, Paul Hindemith, Igor Stravinsky, and Albert Wolff. The first regular music director was Lamberto Baldi (1895–1979), who emigrated from his native Italy; conducting first in São Paulo, Brazil, he led the OSSODRE from 1932 to 1941. Other Italian immigrants included Guido Santórsola (1904–94), who studied in London, played viola under Baldi, and sometimes conducted the OSSODRE. He composed nearly twenty orchestral works. Benone Calcavecchia (1886–1953), born in Sicily, did not begin composing until 1922 but turned out some orchestral works. The ensemble also played compositions by other members, such as the violist Luis Cluzeau Mortet (1889–1957), who wrote approximately two hundred (around one-tenth are published), and the trumpeter Vicente Ascone (1897–1979) (table 7.1).

Héctor Tosar (1923–2002) premiered several of his nineteen orchestral works with the ensemble (table 7.1). Tosar, whom Copland admired, was initially associated with Neoclassicism, which enjoyed wide currency in Latin America through the 1940s and, in the case of some composers, considerably later. His *Sinfonía para cuerdas* (Symphony for Strings), composed in 1950 and premiered by Kleiber in 1951, gives an idea of his versatility. Of the three movements, the second bears the critical weight, both in length (eleven minutes out of a total of twenty-six) and intensity, with searing dissonances and extended, chant-like melodies offsetting the terse motives of the outer movements. Among Tosar's orchestral works are two other symphonies and the serialist *Recitativo y variaciones*, performed at the 1968 Inter-American Music Festival.

The principal successor to these composer-conductors is José Serebrier (b. 1938). At age eighteen, he won a composition contest with his symphonic work *La leyenda de Faust* (The Faust Legend), which the OSSODRE performed. After enrolling at the Curtis Institute of Music in Philadelphia, Serebrier studied composition with Copland at the Berkshire Music Center as well as conducting with Pierre Monteux and Antal Dorati; he conducted the Cleveland Philharmonic Orchestra from 1968 to 1971. Sometimes Serebrier programmed his own works. In 1960, he led the National Symphony in his second symphony, titled *Partita para orquesta*, which the straight-talking Washington-based critic Paul Hume called "something of a musical junk shop."[25] Such barbs aside, Robert Whitney saw fit to record *Partita* with the Louisville Orchestra. In October 1963, Leopold Stokowski conducted Serebrier's *Poema elegíaco* (Elegiac Poem) in Carnegie Hall at a concert honoring the United Nations. His works have been recorded on the Naxos label (table 7.1).

Other Uruguayan composers of orchestral music include Antonio Mastrogiovanni (1936–2010), who studied with Tosar and later received two scholarships from the Organization of American States (the successor organization to the Washington, DC–based Pan American Union). Mastrogiovanni composed several symphonic works, including *Sol de América* for orchestra, chorus, and narrator, one of many "speaker pieces" composed in South America during the politically fraught 1960s and 70s.[26] The career of León Biriotti (1929–2020) reflects some political upheavals of the twentieth century. Among his teachers was Enrique Casal Chapí, one of several expatriate composers who contributed to musical life in the Americas in the aftermath of the Spanish Civil War. Biriotti's first symphony, *Sinfonía Ana Frank* (1964), commemorates the Holocaust (table 7.1). He also used twelve-tone techniques and electronics. The Grammy-nominated Miguel del Águila composes in a variety of styles and has received several prestigious prizes. Born in Montevideo in 1957, he has spent long periods in Europe and the United States. One symphonic work recognizes his connections to the latter: in 2004 he composed *Chautauquan Summer*, a "short concert opener (or closer)" as he describes it, to mark the seventy-fifth anniversary of the Chautauquan Symphony Orchestra; it pays homage to the three summers Águila spent at the Chautauqua Institution Summer Festival [New York] as a resident composer.[27] Other Uruguayan composers of symphonic music include Diego Legrand (1929–2014) and Sergio Cervetti (b. 1940). Several Uruguayan women composers deserve greater study.[28] Carmen Barradas (1888–1963), who lived for many years in Spain, left approximately 170 manuscripts at her death. Hiltrud Kelner (1913–2002), a student of Tosar's, wrote some orchestral music, as did Beatriz Lockhart (1944–2015).

Paraguay

In 1607, the Jesuit Province of Paraguay was established, embracing part of present-day Paraguay, Uruguay, Argentina, and Brazil. Its main purpose was to evangelize the Guaraní Indians. Even sharp critics of the church such as Jean-Jacques Rousseau praised the self-sustainability of the reductions (missions). Initially, Jesuits accepted religious and secular Guaraní music, although it was eventually phased out, erasing its influence on future generations, as the Indians learned European methods of singing, instrument making, and performing.[29] A Guaraní sensibility has nonetheless endured. Today a full 95 percent of Paraguay's population is mestizo and the country has two official languages, Spanish and Guaraní, which is also spoken in parts of Argentina, Bolivia, and Brazil.

Expert musicians from Europe were recruited for the evangelization project. Among them was Domenico Zipoli (1688–1726), the Italian organist and composer who became a Jesuit in 1716 and promptly set sail for Paraguay. He soon became the "most famous composer to have chosen the Jesuit order."[30] His religious music, dramatic works, and keyboard music were solicited in Lima, Sucre, and other locales.[31] In 1811, Paraguay won independence from Spain, and two years later, José Gaspar Rodríguez de Francia was proclaimed dictator. He ruled until his death in 1840, effectively isolating Paraguay from its neighbors, which allowed for little cultural exchange. Band music, dances, and theater music were paramount. In the War of the Triple Alliance (1865–70), Paraguay faced off against Argentina, Brazil, and Uruguay in a bloody conflict over borders and tariffs, which devasted the young nation.

A campaign for national reconstruction was undertaken in which music would play a role. To reinforce the idea that Paraguay was a nation of racial harmony, musicians drew on the Guaraní heritage, often through invented traditions such as the so-called Paraguayan harp, which many citizens began to play. (The harp, brought by Europeans, nonetheless became associated with several regions of South America.[32]) Classical composers also sought to fortify Paraguayan-Guaraní identity, often through the titles of their works. The violinist and composer Fernando Centurión (1886–1938), founder of the Cuarteto Haydn and recognized as Paraguay's first composer for symphony orchestra, composed *Serenata Guaraní* and *Capricho sobre un tema Paraguayo*. (The latter work, from 1929, was performed at the Pan American Union.) He also wrote *Marcha heroica*. Classical musical organizations also formed, such as the Sociedad Filarmónica La Lira, founded in 1881.

During the twentieth century, several Paraguayan artists and intellectuals were exiled, some during the dictatorship of General Alfredo Stroessner, who seized power in 1954. They included José Asunción Flores (1904–72), who popularized a genre known as the *guarania*.[33] Another, Carlos Lara Bareiro (1914–88), who studied in Brazil with Francisco Mignone and helped found the Orquesta Sinfónica de Asunción, composed two orchestral suites under the title *Aquarelas paraguayas*. Francisco Alvarenga (1910–57) composed several works on social themes and a symphonic *guarania* in homage to his compatriots who died in the Chaco War, a border dispute with Bolivia that lasted from 1932 to 1935. Other composers made their careers in Paraguay. Remberto Giménez (1899–1977), who studied at the Schola Cantorum, was also a conductor and teacher. Among his symphonic works is a *Rapsodía paraguaya*, which he once conducted with a German orchestra. Juan Carlos Moreno González (1911–82) studied in São Paulo; upon returning home, he directed the Conservatorio del Ateneo. His orchestral music includes *Kuarahy mimby* (Guaraní for "the flute of the sun") of 1944.[34] Luis Cañete (1905–85) wrote five symphonic poems.

The central figure in Paraguayan orchestral music was Florentín Giménez (1925–2021), whose long career spanned critical years in the history of his country. Born in Ybycuí, outside the capital, he and his family moved to Asunción, where he studied music. After a sojourn in Buenos Aires, Giménez conducted Paraguay's major ensembles: the Orquesta Sinfónica de la Ciudad de Asunción, the Orquesta de Cámara Municipal, and the Orquesta Sinfónica Nacional.[35] His opera *Juana la Lara*, which premiered in 1987, is based on a female independence fighter. Among his thirteen orchestral works are several numbered symphonies (table 7.1).

Argentina

As noted, Jesuit reductions extended through part of what is now Argentina. In Córdoba, Blacks (often kept as slaves by some of the Jesuits) participated in music making.[36] In Buenos Aires, religious music held relatively little sway. The city was designated an episcopal see in 1622, but, as one scholar puts it, ecclesiastical music was never compelling enough to "subalternize other musics."[37] One staple of those "other musics" was an orchestra consisting mainly of Afro-descended performers, mostly string players but also hornists, flutists, and oboists. Several festivals and celebrations involving music took place annually, and theaters maintained orchestras for performing *tonadillas* and *zarzuelas*.[38] During the viceroyalty (est. 1776) the orchestra of the Coliseo Provisional was conducted by Blas Parera, a Spanish musician who later composed the Argentine national anthem.[39] In 1810, after invasions by the British, Buenos Aires province declared independence from Spain, with other regions following suit after an 1816 congress at Tucumán.

In 1819, a Sociedad Filarmónica was founded in Buenos Aires, followed by approximately fifteen such societies established between 1840 and 1875. More theaters were built, including what is now called the "Old Colón," to distinguish it from the current Colón. In general, opera held sway. Yet Juan Pedro Esnaola (1808–78), who studied in Paris and Madrid, composed some orchestral works, including three symphonies.[40] After the fall of the strongman Juan Manuel de Rosas in 1852, German, Swiss, English, and Welsh immigrants took advantage of newly liberalized immigration policies to seek their fortunes in Argentina; Spaniards, Italians, and Russian Jews would arrive later. This influx of foreigners could be musically stimulating, but it also prompted xenophobia in some circles and outright racism in others. Forging the nation's image became an urgent matter for artists and intellectuals, including the composers of the so-called Generation of '80, most of whom were born in the 1860s. The most compelling national symbol was the gaucho, the free-spirited horseman of the pampas, whose resourcefulness and independence were widely celebrated, most notably by José Hernández in his two-part epic poem *Martín Fierro*, published in 1872 and 1879.[41]

The world of the gaucho attracted the composer Alberto Williams (1862–1952) who wrote the symphonic poem *Aires de la pampa*, along with nine symphonies. Julián Aguirre (1868–1924) invoked folk genres such as the *triste*, a free-flowing, plaintive, and often ornamented song of the pampas, and the *gato*, an Argentine social dance that juxtaposes patterns in duple and triple meters. Another symphonic composer was Eduardo García Mansilla (1871–1930).

Table 7.2 Symphonies and Other Orchestral Music from Argentina

Symphonies and Works of Symphonic Scope

Alberto Williams (1862–1952). Symphony No. 1 in B Minor (1907); Symphony No. 2 in C Minor, "La bruja de las montañas" (1910); Symphony No. 3 in F Major, "La selva sagrada" (1911); Symphony No. 4 in E-flat, "El ataja-caminos" (1935); Symphony No. 5 in B-flat Major (n.d.); Symphony No. 6 in B Major, "La muerte del cometa" (1937); Symphony No. 7 in D, "Eterno reposo" (1937); Symphony No. 8 in F, "La esfinge" (1938); Symphony No. 9 in B-flat, "Los batracios, La humorística" (1939).

Eduardo García Mansilla (1871–1930). Symphony (ca. 1890).

José María Castro (1892–1964). Sinfonía de Buenos Aires (1963).

Juan José Castro (1895–1968). Symphony No. 1 (1931); *Sinfonía bíblica* (1932); *Sinfonía argentina* (1934); *Sinfonía de los campos* (1939).

Jacobo Ficher (1896–1978). Symphony No. 1 (1932); Symphony No. 2 (1933); Symphony No. 3 (1938–40); Symphony No. 4 (1946); Symphony No. 5: *Así habló Isaís* (1947); Symphony No. 6 (1956); Symphony No. 7: *Epopeya de mayo* (1958–59); Symphony No. 8 (1965); *Hamlet* Symphony (1967); Symphony No. 9 (1973); Symphony No. 10 (1976–77).

Washington Castro (1909–2004). *Sinfonía breve para orquesta de cuerdas* (1961).

Alberto Ginastera (1916–1983). Symphony No. 1, "Porteña" (1942, withdrawn); Symphony No. 2, "Elegíaca" (1944, withdrawn); *Pampeana* No. 3 (1954); *Sinfonía de Don Rodrigo* (based on opera, with soprano solo, 1964).

Other Orchestral Works

Alberto Williams (1862–1952). *Primera obertura de concierto* (1889); *Segunda obertura de concierto* (1892); *Diez miniaturas*, first series (1890); *Diez miniaturas*, second series (1890); *Marcha del centenario, 1810–1910* (ca. 1910); *Poema de los mares australes* (1929); *El corazón de la muñeca* (1936); *Las milongas de la orquesta* (1938); *Poema del Iguazú* (1943); *Aires de la pampa: Diez nuevas milongas* (1944).

Julián Aguirre (1868–1924). *Preámbulo, triste y gato* (ca. 1910); *De mi país* (1916); *Belkiss* (ca. 1919); *Paisaje, canción y danza* (ca. 1920); *Poema sinfónico* (n.d.).

Eduardo García Mansilla (1871–1930). *La bandera nacional* (ca. 1890); *La course à la mort* (ca. 1890); *Leyenda sinfónica* (ca. 1890).

Pascual de Rogatis (1880–1980). *Zupay* (1910); *Atipac* (perf. 1929).

Felipe Boero (1884–1958). *Danzas argentinas* (1920–30); *El matrero*, suite (1930); *Magrugada en la pampa* (1930); *Suite argentina* (1930); *Camino solitario* (1930s); *Carnaval en la sierra* (1930s); *Crepúsculo pampero* (1930s); *Lluvia en el campo* (1930s); *Vidala riojana* (1939–40).

Juan Bautista Massa (1885–1938). *Canción gitana* (n.d.); *En la pampa* (n.d.); *Interludio* (string orch., n.d.); *Primera suite argentina* (1929); *Segunda suite argentina* (n.d.); *La muerte del Inca* (1932); *Las campanas* (n.d.); *Preludio para arcos* (string orch., n.d.); *Scherzo* (string orch., n.d.).

Athos Palma (1891–1951). *Cantares de mi tierra* (strings, 1914); *Jardines* (1926); *Los hijos del sol* (1929).

José María Castro (1892–1964). Concerto grosso (1932); *Obertura para una ópera cómica* (1934); *Georgia* (two ballet suites, 1937); *Concierto para orquesta* (1944); *Tres pastorales* (1945); *Arietta con variazione* (1948); *Suite de cinco piezas* (1948); *El sueño de la botella* (ballet suite, 1948); *Falarka* (ballet suite, 1951); *Tema coral con variaciones* (1952); *Diez improvisaciones breves* (1957); *Preludio, tema con variaciones y final* (1959).

Juan José Castro (1895–1968). *El jardín de los muertos* (1924); *A una madre* (1925); *La Chellah* (1927); *Suite infantile* (1928, lost); *Suite breve* (1929); *Allegro, lento e vivace* (1930); *Corales criollos* No. 3 (1953); *Fanfare for the Queen* (1953); *Adios a Villa-Lobos* (1960).

Table 7.2 *continued*

Jacobo Ficher (1896–1978). Suite (1924, rev. 1966); *Poema heróico* (1934); *Obertura patética* (1928, rev. as *Exodus*, 1960); *Sulamita* (1927, ver. 1960); *Tres bocetos sinfónicos inspirados en el Talmud* (1930); *Don Segundo Sombra* (1954); Variations and Fugue on a Theme of Mozart (1961); *Festival Overture* (1962).

Juan Carlos Paz (1897–1972). *Canto de Navidad* (1927; orch. 1930); *Movimiento sinfónico* (1930); *Suite para Juliano Emperador* (1931); *Tres piezas para orquesta* (1931); *Passacaglia* (1936, second version 1952–53); *Música para orquesta: Preludio y fuga* (1940); *Rítmica ostinato* (1942, rev. 1952); *Seis superposiciones para orquesta* (1954); *Continuidad 1960* (1960).

Washington Castro (1909–2004). *Concierto campestre: Suite según el cuadro de Giorgione* (1946); *Música para orquesta de cámara* (1951); *Obertura para niños* (1951); *Obertura jubilosa* (1957); *Tres piezas para orquesta* (1962); *Concierto para orquesta* (1963); *Música sinfónica para Juana de Arco* (1968); *Coral y toccata para orquesta de cuerdas* (1970); *Tres piezas para cuerdas* (1972); *Variaciones sobre un tema de Handel* (1970, rev. 1985); *Rapsodia en ritmo de tango* (1978); *Divertimento* (1982); *Cuadros de Picasso: Suite Sinfónica* (1983, rev. 1986); *Valses románticos* (1985); *Dos pastorales: Nocturno y danza rústica* (1988); *Música de circo y danza rústica, para pequeña orquesta* (1988); *Concierto de ángeles* (1989); *Variaciones sobre un tema de Mozart* (1990); *Paseo por la orquesta* (1991); *Momentos musicales* (1993); *Otoño y primavera en Mogotes* (1994); *Adagio y Scherzo fantástico* (n.d.).

Isabel Aretz-Theile (1909–2005). *Puñenas* (1937); *Dos aquarelas* (string orch., 1939); *Serie criolla* (1949).

Guillermo Graetzer (1914–93). Concerto for Orchestra (1939); *Danzas antiguas de la corte española* (1940); *Variations and ending on a theme by Salomone Rossi* (1941); *La parábola* (1946–47); *Sinfonietta* No. 1 (1947); *Sinfonietta* No. 2 (1951); Sonata for string orchestra (1953); *Triludium* (string orch. 1978); *Liberación* (1978–79).

Alberto Ginastera (1916–83). *Panambí* (ballet suite, 1935–37); *Estancia* (ballet suite, 1941); *Malambo* (suite based on film score, 1942); *Obertura para el "Fausto Criollo"* (1943); *Ollantay: Three Symphonic Movements* (1947); *Variaciones concertantes* (1953); *Concerto per corde* (1965, rev. 1967); *Music from Bomarzo* (suite based on opera, 1967–70); *Estudios sinfónicos* (1967); *Popul Vuh* (1975, sections 1–6 only finished); *Gloses sobre temes de Pau Casals* (1977).

Astor Piazzolla (1921–92). *Obertura dramatica para gran orquesta* (1944); *Rapsodía porteña para orquesta sinfónica* (1947); *Danza salvaje* (1950); *Buenos Aires: Tres movimientos sinfónicos* (1951); *Serie de tangos sinfónicos: Allegro, moderato, vivace* (1963); *Tangazo* (1975).

Hilda Dianda (b. 1925). *Nucleos* (1963); *Resonancias 3* (1966); *Ludus 1* (1969); *Ludus 2* (chamber orch., 1969); *Impromptu* (string orch., 1970); *Canto* (chamber orch., 1972); *Mitos* (string orch., perc., 1993).

Mario Davidovsky (1934–2019). *Suite sinfónica para el payaso* (1955, also a ballet suite); *Serie sinfónica* (1958); *Planos* (1960); *Transientes* (1972).

Oscar E. Bazán (1936–2002). *Exégesis II* (1968); *X 73* for string orchestra (1973); *Invocación* (1985).

Gerardo Gandini (1936–2013). *Variaciones para orquesta* (1962); *Cadencias II* (1967); *Laberynthus Johannes* (1973); *Soria Moria* for string orchestra (1974); *E sará* (1975); *Eusebius* (1984–85); *Música ficción III* (ca. 1990); *Mozartvariationen* (ca. 1991).

Pablo Ortíz (b. 1956). *Adagietto* (string orch., 1983); *Angel's Relics* (string orch., 1984); *Horse Latitudes* (1986); *Suomalainen Tango* (2008).

The son of a diplomat, García Mansilla studied in Vienna and then Saint Petersburg, where he worked with Rimsky-Korsakov. He called his earliest symphonic work *La bandera nacional* (The National Flag), composed circa 1890; he also wrote a symphony around the same time. In 1915, the Sociedad Nacional de la Música was established. One of its founding members, Felipe Boero (1884–1958), was known for his gaucho-themed works, some of which are for orchestra. Another composer, Juan Bautista Massa (1885–1938), was inspired by pre-Columbian traditions: in 1940, Stokowski conducted his mournful symphonic poem *La muerte del Inca*

(The Death of the Inca) in Buenos Aires, where critics praised the "Inca flavor" of the work.[42] As shown in table 7.2, Athos Palma (1891–1951) and Pascual de Rogatis (1880–1980) wrote Indigenous-themed works as well.

Later generations tended to look beyond national borders. The Teatro Colón attracted an impressive roster of international conductors including Ernest Ansermet, Fritz Busch, and Kleiber, all of whose roles in Latin American symphonic music deserve further study. Besides the orchestra of the Teatro Colón, the Orquesta Filarmónica de la Asociación del Profesorado Orquestal, founded in 1919, was active, as were radio orchestras such as the Sinfónica de Radio El Mundo. Two others, the Orquesta Sinfónica del Estado and the Orquesta Sinfónica Nacional, eventually joined forces, presenting an inaugural concert under Roberto Kinsky (1910–77), one of many Jews who immigrated to Argentina during the Nazi period and enriched musical life there.[43] (For example, Kinsky gave the Argentine premieres of Schoenberg's *Erwartung*, Hindemith's *Hin und zurück*, and Stravinsky's *Jeu de cartes*.) Another Jewish immigrant was Wilhelm Grätzer (1914–93), a former student of Paul Hindemith who arrived in Buenos Aires in early 1939.[44] Under the name Guillermo Graetzer, he composed in his new home a Concerto for Orchestra and other symphonic works, including *Danzas antiguas de la corte española* (Ancient Dances of the Spanish Court, 1940) and *La parábola* (The Parable, 1946–47).[45] Another prominent Jewish musician in Buenos Aires was Jacobo Ficher (1896–1978) of Russia, who composed ten numbered symphonies and other instrumental music. Sometimes he wove Jewish topics into his works, as in *Tres bocetos sinfónicos inspirados en el Talmud* (Three Symphonic Sketches Inspired by the Talmud) of 1930. His Second Symphony is a response to Hitler's anti-Semitism (table 7.2).

One Argentine symphonic composer who achieved worldwide acclaim was Juan José Castro (1895–1968). He came from a prominent musical family: his father was a cellist and two of his brothers, José María (1892–1964) and Washington (1909–2004), were composers. (Their orchestral works are found in table 7.2.) After lessons with d'Indy in Paris, Juan José traveled frequently to the United States, often to conduct. At home, he directed several orchestras, including that of the Colón, until speaking out against Juan Domingo Perón cost him his job in the 1940s.[46] Stravinsky, who seldom had a good word for any conductor, called Castro an "impeccable master of the baton."[47] Among Castro's eighty-odd compositions, a dozen are for orchestra, including four symphonies from the 1930s. Conductors such as Stokowski, Ansermet, and Alfredo Casella interpreted his works at venues such as the International Society for Contemporary Music (ISCM). (Castro's *Allegro, lento e vivace* for orchestra received an ISCM award in 1931.[48]) His compositions range from the mildly folkloric to a more identity-neutral Neoclassical style. In a 1953 review titled "A Convincing Neoclassicism," the Argentine critic Jorge d'Urbano called Castro "the great Argentine exponent of that current orientation in music known as 'neoclassicism,'" adding "it could almost be said that his 'neoclassicism' isn't so much of a school but . . . a question of temperament."[49] More than once, Castro decried what he called the "abuses" of folklore (i.e., unsubtle nationalism). He also held that "the authentic accent will appear in every note, every word, or every brushstroke if the interior [creative] process is a mature one," contending "all the rest is a disguise."[50]

One work of subtle national representation is Castro's variation set *Corales criollos* (Creole Chorales) of 1953. As noted, a *criollo/a* denotes a person born in Latin America of Spanish heritage (the term can also apply to a physical object or a concept). Residents of Buenos Aires, however, often use the term to refer to the provinces, particularly those of the north and northwest, which is the sense in which it should be understood here.[51] The work took first prize in 1954 at the First Festival of Latin American Music, held in Caracas. Copland, one of the judges and who was generally underwhelmed by Castro's music, wrote in his travel diary that the *Corales criollos* No. 3 was Castro's best work, noting its "brilliance and delicacy."[52] It opens with a sober theme in C minor of Castro's own creation. Among the highlights of the six variations that follow, No. 2, marked "rústico," contains many open fourths and fifths (some enhanced with seconds), long associated with rural environments. Variation 3 evokes Indigenous music, with the performance indication *quenas* referring to a type of Andean flute often heard in northern Argentina. Here, it is played by the piccolo and enhanced with subtle daubs of color in the celesta, which gives out the theme along with muted violas. Variation 5, on the other hand, whisks the listener away from this pastoral setting to urban life with a tango, a dance associated with the slums of turn-of-the century Buenos Aires but which combines European harmonic language with rhythms some claim to be African.[53] Variation 5 has little to do with the initial theme. When *Corales criollos* premiered in Buenos Aires in 1956, a critic for *La Nación* observed that Castro had achieved a "nationalist accent" without directly quoting folk music, effectively summarizing Castro's own priorities.[54]

Juan Carlos Paz (1897–1972) was Latin America's first serialist.[55] Born in Buenos Aires, he initially composed in a late-romantic vein and then flirted briefly with nationalism, which he came to disparage as his often-acerbic concert reviews abundantly confirm. After brief forays into Neoclassicism and jazz (the latter to "desensitize" music, as he put it), in the mid-1930s, Paz became intrigued with twelve-tone music, programming works of Schoenberg and Webern on his Buenos Aires piano recitals. As the only Argentine composer interested in Schoenberg's method, he began corresponding with Józef Koffler, a Polish student of Schoenberg, for advice on compositional specifics (during World War II, Koffler died in a concentration camp).[56] As a composer, Paz took Schoenberg's straightforward and formally conscious Woodwind Quintet (op. 26) as a model. He wrote ten orchestral works. One that attracted international notice was his *Passacaglia*, which Charles Munch performed at the 1937 ISCM in Paris. In several ways, the *Passacaglia* exemplifies Paz's approach. Permutations of the row tend to be confined to the prime and retrograde forms, with their transpositions.[57] Also, rows can yield third-based sonorities: even if Paz goes well beyond these tonal implications, the occasional flight into "momentary tonality" (to borrow David Sargent's label) may occur.[58] In the *Passacaglia*, the row (E—B♭—F♯—C—D♭—G—A♭—E♭—B—F—D—A) serves as the theme, appearing in the bass clarinet, with the lower strings enhancing each note. In every variation, it surfaces in its prime form. The row contains the consecutive triads (G♯)A♭—(D♯)/E♭—B and F—D—A in its second hexachord.

ALBERTO GINASTERA

Alberto Ginastera (1916–1983) is likely the Argentine composer with the greatest international reputation, in part due to his experience in the United States at midcentury. After becoming acquainted with Copland and taking advantage of a Guggenheim Fellowship in the 1940s, Ginastera shone at the Inter-American Festivals, where his twelve-tone works were hailed as "giant advances" in composition.[59] His operas were also performed in the United States, such as *Don Rodrigo*, which inaugurated the New York State Theater (now the David H. Koch Theater) in 1966, with Plácido Domingo in the title role. Ginastera also fashioned a "dramatic symphony" from this work (table 7.2). During the 1960s, he directed the Rockefeller-funded Centro Latinoamericano de Altos Estudios Musicales (Latin American Center for Advanced Musical Studies, or CLAEM), a center for avant-garde composition in Buenos Aires.[60]

Ginastera did not begin his career as a modernist, however. In the 1960s, he offered his principal biographer, Pola Suárez Urtubey, the tripartite scheme that has since informed criticism of his *oeuvre*: (1) objective nationalism, (2) subjective nationalism, and (3) neo-Expressionism.[61] "Objective" nationalism (1934–47) centered on Argentine folkloric song and dance genres whereas "subjective" nationalism (1947–57) treated Argentine folklore less explicitly. Neo-Expressionist works (1958–76) incorporated serialism, microtones, clusters, aleatory, or other avant-garde procedures.[62] In 2001, Deborah Schwartz-Kates pointed out that this model neglects a good many years of the composer's activity, and she proposed a scheme that includes the composer's final years, which he spent in Switzerland. This fourth period, or "final synthesis," effectively balances some forward-looking strategies with Latin American traditions, including indigenous music.[63] Of course, none of these four categories is watertight.

Although Ginastera's high-modernist works won him acclaim in the rarefied world of art music, his objective nationalist compositions remain popular favorites. His first "hit" was the ballet *Panambí* premiered under Juan José Castro at the Colón in 1937, when Ginastera was still a student. Mainly performed as an orchestral suite, the multimovement *Panambí* juxtaposes the parallel harmonies and shimmering accompaniments of French Impressionism with primitivist ostinati to depict an Indigenous tribe on the banks of the Paraná River. Four years later, Ginastera composed *Estancia*, an orchestral suite based on the eponymous ballet and inspired by gaucho culture (*estancia* means "ranch"). The spirited Finale is based on the *malambo*, an energetic gaucho dance that survives today.[64] During this early period, Ginastera also wrote two symphonies. He withdrew the first, titled *Sinfonía Porteña* (Buenos Aires Symphony, 1942) after Paz excoriated it in a review.[65] The second symphony, "Elegíaca" (Elegiac Symphony, 1944), was a war composition dedicated "To Those Who Died for Liberty"; several movements incorporate music from a film score of 1942, *Malambo*. Although the symphony won an award after its Buenos Aires premiere in 1946, he withdrew it as well.[66]

Ginastera's second-period orchestral works, their nationalist elements now more subdued, include the *Variaciones concertantes* of 1953. This tour de force in orchestral writing features Ginastera's signature "guitar chord," so called because it derives from the open strings of the guitar (E-A-d-g-b-e).[67] The guitar chord also appears in the early *Obertura para el Fausto Criollo* (Overture for the Creole Faust), a work that depicts a gaucho who attends a performance of Gounod's *Faust* and later relates his experience to a rustic companion. The *Variaciones concertantes* won the Cinzano Prize in 1957, awarded to the best Argentine composition, and John Taras of the New York City Ballet choreographed it under the title *Tender Night*.[68]

Pampeana No. 3, commissioned by the Louisville Orchestra and composed in 1954, is Ginastera's valedictory to nationalism. He described the three-movement work as a "symphonic pastorale" evocative of the pampas, intended to capture his own reactions to the pampas, with their "unlimited immensity."[69] He also aimed to write "a purely symphonic work, governed by the strict laws of musical construction, but whose essence would be taken from my subjective feelings."[70] Unlike most traditional orchestral works, *Pampeana* No. 3 begins and ends with a slow movement. Movement I, Adagio contemplativo, suggests the changing moods of the pampas. A melodic fragment grows gradually out of the lower strings, an additive melody that emphasizes fourths, undoubtedly to convey vastness, much the way the "open" sonorities of Copland and Roy Harris conjure up the middle and western United States. The fourths also hint at the guitar chord, which will close the work. Equally anticipatory are the insistent, syncopated thirds in the woodwinds and celestas, which will prove structurally important in each movement (see, for example, Movement III, Reh. 4).

At Reh. 2, Ginastera introduces a twelve-note theme (example 1). Repeated at several transpositions, the theme does not *generate* the piece, however, and cannot be properly described as a row. At Reh. 6, major thirds take over, resulting in an octatonic sonority, which he treats polyphonically (example 2). A subtle hint of folklore is found in the oboe line at Reh. 6 and later taken up by the trumpet in the mellifluous form of a *triste*, the gaucho genre Ginastera used in other works, such as his Second String Quartet. The climax of the movement (Reh. 9) involves a surging, third-based melody, also harmonized in thirds, and with a prominent ascending line in the horns (see also Movement III, Reh. 4).

Example 7.1 Ginastera. *Pampeana* 3, mvt. 1, reh. 2

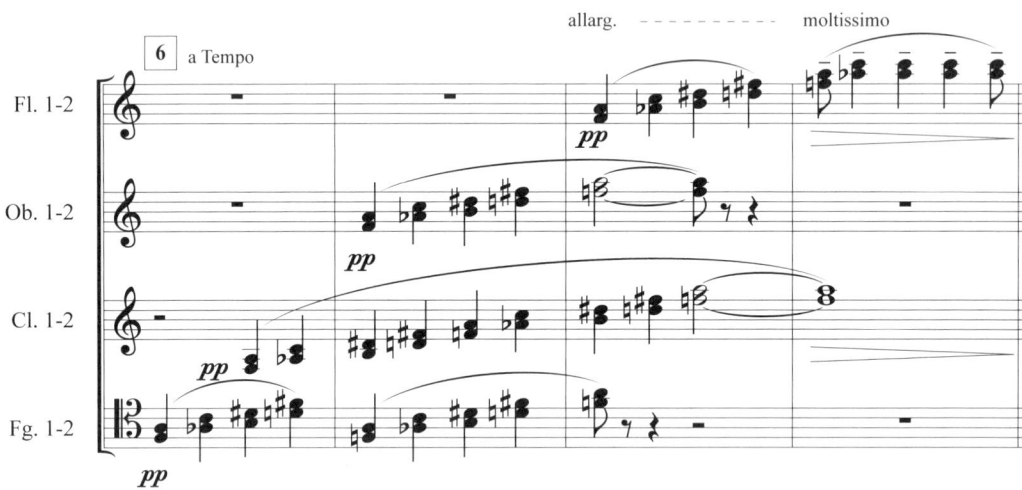

Example 7.2 Ginastera. *Pampeana* 3, mvt. 1, reh. 6

Movement II, with its duple- and triple-meter juxtapositions, recalls the "Malambo" from *Estancia*; this emblematic metric structure is intensified through many repeated notes, which reappear to humorous effect in the Trio (Reh. 19).[71] When Copland heard this movement, he remarked in his diary that it "sounded North American" (by which he means "US") although he does not explain further.[72] In fact, the section beginning at Reh. 21, with its alternating fourths and octaves, gawky melodic line, and duple and triple groupings—all articulated with a dry string timbre—could have been written by Copland himself. Movement III, marked Largo con poetica esaltazione, begins in the oboe with a typical Ginastera melody in that it expands from a repeated main note (E) and is metrically free. At Reh. 13, the entire composition comes full circle when the melody of the opening measures blossoms into a full-blown

Facing, **Example 7.3** Ginastera. *Pampeana* 3, mvt. 3, reh. 13 ("guitar chord")

statement of the guitar chord and the piece then vanishes into nothingness—*niente!*, as the composer cautions—and the memory of the pampas fades (example 3).

Those hints of US music that Copland heard in *Pampeana* No. 3 suggest one aspect of Ginastera's music ripe for further study, namely allusion. Might the trills and repeated notes in the oboe and English horn (Movement II, Reh. 9) suggest the "night music" of Béla Bartók, whose influence Ginastera freely acknowledged? Does the horn part, with its parallel minor thirds, triple division of selected beats, and dark timbres (Movement I, Reh. 5) echo the Ring motive that first appears at the end of Act I of *Das Rheingold*, the first in Wagner's famous operatic tetralogy? If the latter possibility seems remote, it pays to remember that Ginastera quoted the slow movement of Beethoven's Fourth Piano Concerto in Movement III of his own First Piano Concerto (1961) and that additional motives from the venerable German tradition surface in several other works, such as Schubert's *Winterreise* (in the cantata *Milena* of 1971) and Brahms's Second Piano Concerto (in the Second Cello Concerto of 1980–81).[73]

Among the next generation of Argentine composers, Pulitzer prize–winner Mario Davidovsky (1934–2019) composed *Suite sinfónica para el payaso* (Symphonic Suite for a Clown, 1955), although he is known mainly for electroacoustic works. Oscar E. Bazán (1936–2002) composed a few orchestral works but eventually dedicated himself to what he called *música austera* (austere music) for smaller forces—reducing music to its most essential elements and eschewing the *omnium-gatherum* of timbres that he believed represented the acquisitiveness of a consumer society, all to reflect his own status as a "third-world" composer. Another influential figure was Gerardo Gandini (1936–2013), whose international honors included a Guggenheim Fellowship and various European prizes.

For many listeners, the tango—especially when performed on the *bandoneón*, a button accordion with a plangent timbre—is the quintessential Argentine music. Astor Piazzolla (1921–92), who studied with Ginastera, is world-renowned for introducing unexpected elements into the tango such as dense counterpoint, chromaticism, jazz, or nontraditional instrumentation. Piazzolla also wrote several orchestral works, among them the early *Buenos Aires: Tres movimientos sinfónicos* (Three Symphonic Movements, 1951), which won the Fabien Sevitzky Prize and enabled him to study in France with Boulanger. Another work, *Tangazo*, dates from 1975. (The suffix "–azo" translates roughly as "to the nth degree" or "super.") Other composers who wrote symphonic tangos include Juan José Castro and Ginastera.

For a novel approach to the tango, we can look to Pablo Ortíz (b. 1956). A native of Buenos Aires, he studied with Davidovsky at Columbia University and now teaches at the University of California, Davis. His *Suomalainen Tango* dates from 2008. Since "Suomi" is the Finnish name for Finland, listeners might reasonably wonder about the title. In fact, from the 1930s many Finns who visited Argentina became enamored of the tango and took it back to their native land, with the result that a "Finnish tango" is no oxymoron. Superficial differences, such as Finnish lyrics, a keyboard accordion rather than the *bandoneón*, and the occasional drumbeat, fail to conceal the essentials of the genre, which Finns celebrate in tango festivals throughout the country and in the soundtracks of Finnish films, such as those directed by Aki Kaurismaki. Thanks to musicians such as Anssi Karttunen, whose repertory includes Ortíz's cello piece *Last Argentinian Tango* (the work was originally scored for viola), tangos have also made their way into Finnish art music.

When the National Orchestra of Catalonia (Spain) commissioned this work from Ortíz, it sought a tango that would complement Piazzolla's *Tangazo* and Sibelius's Seventh Symphony, both of which would be performed on the same program. Accordingly, Ortíz inserted several quotations (not always literal) from Sibelius's one-movement symphony, including the brief thud of the timpani that opens the work and the initial natural minor scale, which Sibelius caps off with a half-step ascent that yields an unexpected harmonic shift. We also hear the prominent trombone theme, marked "Aino" in the manuscript, a reference to Sibelius's wife. Around eight minutes into *Suomalainen Tango*, Ortíz highlights this theme by sustaining an unaccompanied note in the strings and allowing it to melt into the trombone sonority. (He also quotes "La Cumparsita," for many the most celebrated tango of all time—and by a Uruguayan.) Through this highly original composition, Ortíz shows how protean and versatile the Argentine genre can be.

Other Argentine composers of orchestral music include Salvador Ranieri (1930–2012), Mauricio Kagel (1931–2008), Marta Lambertini (b. 1937), Mariano Etkin (1943–2016), and Osvaldo Golijov (b. 1960). Women composers throughout history include the violinist and composer Celia Tomasa Torrá (1884–1962), who studied in France, where she gave benefit concerts for the Red Cross during World War I. In 1931, she composed the orchestral work *Rapsodía enterriana*, which received a national prize; another orchestral composition was *Suite incaica* (1937), which she conducted at the Colón in 1949.[74] Isabel Aretz-Theile (1909–2005), known mainly as a scholar and folk music specialist, studied composition with Athos Palma and wrote several orchestral works (table 7.2). Pía Sebastiani (1925–2015), another student of Ginastera's, composed *Coral, Fuga y Final* (perf. 1945) and *Estampas* (1946) for orchestra; Erich Kleiber conducted the latter. Also born in 1925 is Hilda Dianda, who studied electroacoustic music in France, working with Pierre Schaeffer's Groupe de Recherches Musicales of the Radiodiffusion-Télévision Française but also wrote several orchestral works (table 7.2).

Brazil

When Pedro Álvares Cabral sailed into Porto Seguro in 1500 (now the state of Bahia), he encountered the Tupi-Guaraní, who inhabited much of the coastline. As early as 1550, the year before the first Brazilian diocese was established at Salvador (in Bahia), Jesuits had begun teaching music. Other Indigenous groups, such as the Jiquabu, had lived for centuries in what is now the state of Minas Geraís, which would become an important musical center and boast the highest concentration of baroque churches in Brazil. When gold and diamond deposits were discovered, enslaved Africans were brought to work the mines along with Indigenous populations, and by the middle of the eighteenth century, more Africans and mixed-race individuals lived in Minas Geraís than any other group.[75] Their musical skills were known far and wide. One traveler, a Mr. Fletcher from the United States, reported that while in Minas Geraís, the lady of the house he was visiting announced that a concert would begin for her guests. Expecting "a wheezy plantation fiddle, a fife, a drum," Fletcher instead listened with pleasure to an all-Black and mixed-race orchestra that included strings, flutes, and trombones.[76] Although few descriptions of Africans or their descendants playing African instruments survive in Brazil, scholars have concluded that many were bimusical.[77]

The churches of Minas Geraís are an abundant resource, whose archives contain music by Haydn, Boccherini, and Beethoven. Music by freedmen (Africans freed before abolition in 1888) was performed in these same churches. These freedmen formed *irmandades*, musical guilds or unions that composed for the municipality or for religious institutions, turning out works for mixed chorus with orchestra of strings, horns, oboes, flutes, and continuo. One, Manoel Dias de Oliveira (1735–1813), was of mixed race; it is not clear that he had been enslaved, as his father was. A later composer, José Maria Xavier (1819–87), wrote with limited resources in mind: because there was no oboist in the Minas Geraís town where he lived, he relied on flute, clarinet, and trumpet for melodic lines in the higher ranges. Other noteworthy composers of the region were Marcos Coelho Netto (1746–1806) and Ignacio Parreiras Neves (*ca.* 1730–*ca.* 1793).

Other centers for music were São Paulo, where André da Silva Gomes (1752–1844) served as chapelmaster of the cathedral. Musical life also thrived in Rio de Janeiro: in 1766, when a convent was dedicated with a Metastasian oratorio, one chronicler described "an excellent sonata played by the orchestra composed of the best teachers and amateurs of the country."[78] Other events requiring music were bullfights, tournaments, parades, and dances, including Africans performing a *baile do Congo*. Visitors also described the *batuque*, or *dança de negros*, an umbrella term for gatherings of Blacks involving dance.[79] In 1808, when the Portuguese court moved to Rio, the mixed-race José Maurício Nunes Garcia (1767–1830) became chapelmaster at the cathedral.

After independence from Portugal in 1822, Italian and French styles predominated, especially in opera and salon music. The opera *Il Guarany* by Carlos Gomes (1836–96), whose overture has taken on a life of its own, was seen as a national statement despite its obvious Italianisms. Upper-class Cariocas (residents of Rio de Janeiro) read French-language music magazines and bought pianos from Paris, such as those by pianist and manufacturer Henri Herz, marketed as uniquely suited to the Brazilian climate. By the 1880s, an especially popular concert venue was the Eldorado, modeled on the Alcazar d'Été on the Champs-Élysées; Cariocas also flocked to mass concerts similar to Jules Pasdeloup's Concerts Populaires.[80] Brazilian composers responded: João Gomes de Araujo (1846–1943), for example, wrote four Italianate operas along with six symphonies.[81] The Sociedade de Concertos Populares, initiated in 1887, tended to celebrate Brazilian musical nationalism, programming works by Arthur Napoleão (1843–1925), Francisco Braga (1868–1945), and Alberto Nepomuceno (1863–1920). Braga composed several symphonic poems, including *Marabá*, based on Brazilian themes, whereas Nepomuceno, known mainly for winsome piano morceaux, wrote a handful of orchestral pieces, including a *Suite brasileira* with a "Batuque" for the final movement (table 7.3).[82] At least some of these orchestral compositions show the influence of Massenet, Chabrier, and Saint-Saëns.

HEITOR VILLA-LOBOS

This was the environment into which Brazil's best-known composer was born. Heitor Villa-Lobos (1887–1959), with his larger-than-life personality and catalog of more than one thousand works, began as a cellist. Early on, he professed an interest in Indigenous Brazilian music, which he pursued on various trips to the Amazon—excursions that furnished plenty of colorful stories, however debatable their musical significance (or indeed, their veracity).[83] The first significant concert of his works took place in Rio de Janeiro in 1915, which the more conservative critics failed to appreciate. Villa-Lobos immediately became known as an enfant terrible, a role he relished. It was in this capacity that he represented music at the Week of Modern Art in São Paulo in February 1922, even though his compositions were far more conservative than contemporaneous works by Stravinsky or Schoenberg. Shortly thereafter, Villa-Lobos left for Paris, where he composed some of his most extravagant pieces. The massively scored *Choros* No. 8 for orchestra, for example, enhanced his reputation among the French as a wild-eyed primitive. It also took the choro, an urban serenade in which players frequently improvised contrapuntal lines, to new heights.[84] Yet when he returned to Brazil in 1930, he adopted a more

Table 7.3 Symphonies and Other Orchestral Music from Brazil

Symphonies and Works of Symphonic Scope

Alberto Nepomuceno (1864–1920) Symphony in G Minor (1894).
Heitor Villa-Lobos (1887–1959). See table 7.4.
Oscar Lorenzo Fernândez (1897–1948). Symphony No. 1 (1945); Symphony No. 2 (1947).
Mozart Camargo Guarnieri (1907–93). Symphony No. 1 (1943–44); Symphony No. 2 (1945); Symphony No. 3 (1954); Symphony No. 4 (Brasilia, 1963); Symphony No. 5 (1977); Symphony No. 6 (1981); Symphony No. 7 (1985).
César Guerra-Peixe (1914–93). Symphony No.1 (1946); Symphony No. 2, "Brasília" (1960).
Cláudio Santoro (1919–1989). Symphony No.1 (two string orchs., 1939–40); Chamber Symphony (1941); Symphony No. 2 (1945); Symphony No. 3 (1947–48); Symphony No. 4, "da Paz" (1953); Symphony No. 5 (1955); Symphony No. 6 (1957–58); Symphony No. 7, "Brasília" (1959–60); Symphony No. 8 (1963); Symphony No. 9 (1982); Symphony No. 10 (1982); Symphony No. 11 (1984); Symphony No. 12 (1987); Symphony No. 13 (1988); Symphony No. 14 (1989).

Other Orchestral Works

Alberto Nepomuceno (1864–1920). *Série brasileira* (1892); *Scherzo vivace* (1893); *O Garantuja* (1904); *Suite brasileira* (ca. 1904).
Heitor Villa-Lobos (1887–1959). Several of the works listed below, such as *Rudepoema* and *Bachianas brasileiras* No. 4, are orchestrations of piano pieces. The dates given are for the orchestrated versions. *Tédio de Alvorada* (1916); *Naufrágio de Kleônicos* (1916); *Danças africanas* (1916); *Iara* (1917); *Amazonas* (1917); *Uirapurú* (1917, reorchestrated 1930); *Dança frenética* (1919); *Dança dos mosquitos* (1922); *Choros* Nos. 8 (1925); *Choros* Nos. 9 (1925); *Choros* Nos. 10, "Rasga o Coração" (chorus and orch., 1926); *Choros* Nos. 12 (1929); *Bachianas brasileiras* Nos. 2 (1930); *Rudepoema* (1932); *O Papagaio do moleque* (1932); *Caixinha de Boas Festas* (1932); *Evolução dos Aeroplanos* (1932); *Descobrimento do Brasil* (suites, 1937); *Bachianas brasileiras* Nos. 4 (1941); *Bachianas brasileiras* Nos. 7 (1942); *Bachianas brasileiras* Nos. 8 (1944); *Bachianas brasileiras* Nos. 9 (1945); *Madona* (1945); *Erosão* (1950); *Odisseia de uma raça* (1953); two suites, chamber orchestra (1959).
Oscar Lorenzo Fernândez (1897–1948). *Suite sinfônica* (ca. 1925); *Visões infantiles* (perf. 1927); *Imbapára* (1928); *Amaya* (1930, ballet); *Reisado do pastoreio* (1930); *Variações sinfônicas* (ca. 1947).
Francisco Mignone (1897–1986). *Congada* (1921); *Maracatu de Chico Rei* (1933); *Babaloxá* (1936); *Festa das igrejas* (1940); *Leilão* (ballet, 1941); *O espantalho* (ballet, 1941); *Sugestões sinfônicas* (1969); *Variações em busca de um tema* (1972); *O Caçador de esmeraldas* (ballet, 1980).
Mozart Camargo Guarnieri (1907–93). Some of the works listed below are orchestrated piano pieces or chamber works. *Suite infantil* (1929); *Toada* (1929); *Dança brasileira* (1931); *Dança selvage* (1931); *Em Memória dos Que Morreram por São Paulo* (1932); *Toada à Moda Paulista* (1935); *Toada triste* (1936); *A Flor de Tremembé* (1937); *Encantamento* (1941); *Abertura concertante* (1942); *Prologo e fuga* (1947); *Dança negra* (1947); *Improviso* No. 1 (1948); *Suite brasiliana* (1950); *Suite IV Centenário* (1954); *Suite Vila Rica* (1958); *Homenagem a Villa-Lobos* (1966); *Sequência, Coral e Ricercare* (1966); *Abertura festiva* (1971); *Improviso* No. 3 (1971); *Concerto for Strings and Percussion* (1972); *Improviso* No. 6 (1974).
Luiz Cosme (1908–65). *Salamanca do Jaráu* (1935); *Prelúdio* (1936); *Oração a Teiniaguá* (1939); *Falação de Anhangá-Pitã* (1939); *Idéia Fixa* nº 1 (1937, lost); *O Lambe-lambe* (1946, ballet).
César Guerra-Peixe (1914–93). *Divertimentos* Nos. 1 and 2 (1947); *Instantâneos sinfônicos* Nos. 1 and 2 (1947); *Variações* (1947); *Abertura solene* (1950); *Symphonic Suites* Nos. 1 and 2 (1955); *Ponteado* (1955); *A Inúbia do Cabocolinho* (1956); *6 peças de Microcosmos* (1966); *Assimilações* (1971); *A retirada da laguna* (1971); *Museu da inconfidência* (1972); *Tributo a Portinari* (1992).

Table 7.3 *continued*

Cláudio Santoro (1919–89). Adagio for Strings (1942); Three Small Divertimenti (1942); *Impressões de uma fundição de aço* (1942); Divertimento (1943); Variations on a Dodecaphonic Theme (1945); Music for Strings (1946); Overture (1947); *Canto de amor e paz* (string orch., 1950); Brazilian Dances Nos. 1 and 2 (1952); Funeral Ode (1953); *Ponteio* (string orch., 1953); *Entoando tristemente* (1953); *Brasiliana* (1954); *O alegre de vai nascer* (1954); Tragic Overture (1958); *Toada triste* (string orch., 1959); Introduction and Allegro, string orchestra (1962–63); Three Sketches for Orchestra (1964–65); *Tele Tonos Visionen* (1967); *3 Abstrações* (string orch., 1966); *Interações assintóticas* (1969); Divertimento for a Young Public and Orchestra (1972); *Pequena abertura universitária* (Short Academic Overture, 1979); *Mutationen XII* (string orch., with or without magnetic tape, 1976); Concerto grosso for string quartet and string orchestra (1980); Mini-Concerto grosso (string orch. playing in first position, 1981); *Frevo* (1982); Prelude (string orch., 1983); *Three Fragments on B-A-C-H* (string orch., 1985); Brasilia Suite (1986); Concerto for Chamber Orchestra (string orch., 1988).

Marlos Nobre (b. 1939). *Convergencias* (1968); *Ludus instrumentalis* (chamber orch., 1969); *Biosfera* (string orch., 1970); *Mosaico* (1970); *In memoriam* (1973); *Xingu* (1989); Passacaglia (1997); *Amazônia* (1998); *Kabbalah for Orchestra* (2004).

Paulo Chagas (b. 1953). *Eshu: la porte des enfers* (for Afro-Brazilian traditional perc. ensemble, orch., and electronic sounds, 1983); *Radiance* (2004); *Sinfonia de Câmara Brasileira* (wind orch., 2009); *Luzes* (chamber orch., 1992, rev. 2015); *Dança Marajoara* (2017).

Miguel Kertsman (b. 1965). *Amazônia* (1986); *Rosenfeld Variations for String Orchestra* (1990); Chamber Symphony No. 1 (1987); Chamber Symphony No. 2: *New York of 50 Doors* (2015).

---

restrained style, through which he purported, rather fancifully, to blend Brazilian folklore and indigenous musics with the style of Bach. The result was the nine *Bachianas brasileiras* for various instrumental combinations, including several for orchestra. Throughout his career, Villa-Lobos traveled several times to the United States, fearlessly assaying new genres and styles, including film scoring and a Broadway musical.[85]

Villa-Lobos is one of the most widely performed and recorded Latin American composers, with *Bachianas* No. 2, a four-movement work for orchestra, no less popular than its counterpart for soprano and eight cellos, *Bachianas* No. 5 (see table 7.3). Less familiar is the symphonic poem *Uirapurú*. It began as a ballet score and dates from World War I, when many artists unable to secure bookings in Europe tried their luck in Latin America, including Sergei Diaghilev's Ballets Russes.[86] When the company descended on Rio de Janeiro in 1917, Villa-Lobos met the dancer and choreographer Sergei Lifar, to whom he dedicated *Uirapurú*. Like Stravinsky's *Firebird*, Respighi's *Pines of Rome*, or Babbitt's *Philomel*, *Uirapurú* is inspired by birdsong: a paean to flight and freedom, the ballet is set in the jungle and recounts the legend of an enchanted bird (the uirapurú).[87] Natives worship and try to capture the uirapurú, and at one point it turns into a handsome young man. The piece reveals Villa-Lobos's sensitivity—some might say vulnerability—to existing styles. At Reh. 3 and parallel passages, for example, the motivic fragments, repeated-note accompaniments, vigorous down-bows, and off-beat punctuation in the brass and percussion recall the Infernal Dance of Kastchei from Stravinsky's *Firebird*. In orchestration, Villa-Lobos seems to have taken Rimsky-Korsakov's opulent scores as models: he adds chimes, celesta, piano, and harp in addition to the normal complement of strings, winds, and brass, and regales the listener with glissandi and *sul ponticello* passages, as well as prominent solos for flute, saxophone, and violin. In the opening flute gesture, which represents the uirapurú, the listener may well hear an echo of Petrushka's famous theme and even Debussy's *Syrinx* (example 4).

Example 7.4 Villa-Lobos. *Uiraparú*, mm. 19–23

One non-Russian element is the Latin American percussion, which includes the reco-reco, a metal scraper often used in Brazilian popular music. Villa-Lobos also calls for saxophone, which he adored. (When conducting Beethoven symphonies he would use saxophones if he lacked bassoons.[88]) Initially, the soprano saxophone represents the spirit of the young man but in other instances it doubles the piccolo (Reh. 12) or blends seamlessly into the clarinet line (after Reh. 20). Formally, the piece is simple, with several sections repeated, presumably for narrative reasons. Villa-Lobos's harmonic language comprises altered triads, altered quartal harmonies, additive rhythms, and the occasional octatonic harmony (2 mm. before Reh. 25).

Villa-Lobos composed twelve symphonies, which span most of his career (see table 7.4). The first five date from 1916 to 1920, each showing in various ways the influence of Vincent d'Indy, as in cyclic connections between movements in Symphonies No. 1 and 2. A gap of twenty-four years follows, after which he composed the Sixth Symphony; six others followed between 1945 and 1957, in which he takes a freer formal approach to the genre. Dedicatees of Villa-Lobos's symphonies include Olin Downes, senior music critic of the *New York Times* and one of the composer's great champions in the United States (the Eighth), and Serge Koussevitzky and his wife, Natalia (the Eleventh). The symphonies reveal the depths of Villa-Lobos's inspiration while also providing a window into some of the quirks and inconsistencies that riddle his vast *oeuvre*. Villa-Lobos seldom bothered to revise his music, claiming that in the time it took him to do so he could produce several new works—an idiosyncratic view of the creative process that caused Copland to call Villa-Lobos "the pride and despair" of Latin American composers.[89]

Several of the symphonies are programmatic. For the First, "The Unexpected" (1916), Villa-Lobos wrote out a program, a murky meditation on "the ancient Conscience" and "the mysterious vision of the Cosmos," which he distributed at the performance, just as Gustav Mahler did with several of his symphonies.[90] Other backward-looking features of the First Symphony are its expansive, long-breathed melodies (especially in Movement II),

Table 7.4 The Symphonies of Heitor Villa-Lobos (1887–1959)[a]

Title	Movements	Instrumentation	Comments
Sinfonietta No. 1, "À memória de Mozart" (1916)	1. Allegro giusto 2. Andante non troppo 3. Andantino	2 Flt., 2 Ob., 2 Clar., 2 Bssn., 2 Hr., 2 Tpt., 2 Trom., Timp., Strgs.	First performance (first and second movements only): Sociedade de Concertos Sinfônicos [São Paulo], conducted by the composer. First complete performance: January 12, 1954, by the Los Angeles Chamber Symphony Orchestra, conducted by the composer. Score published by Southern Music Publishing Co., 1955.
Symphony No. 1, "O Imprevisto" (The Unexpected) (1916)	1. Allegro assai—Moderato 2. Adagio 3. Scherzo: Allegro vivace 4. Allegro con brio	Grand plus 2 Picc., EH, Bclar., Cbssn., 2 Tpts., Tuba, Perc. (Tam-tam, BD, Sistrum, Cym., SD, Glsp.), 2 Harps, Cel.	According to the composer's program, the subtitle refers to the "soul and destiny of an artist." First performance (Movements 2 and 3): September 20, 1919, by the Grande Companhia Italiana, conducted by Gino Marinuzzi. First complete performance: August 30, 1920, by the Orquestra da Sociedade de Concertos Sinfônicos do Rio de Janeiro, conducted by the composer. Published by Editora da OSESP (Orquestra Sinfônica do Estado de São Paulo); rental score available at Academia Brasileira de Música (www.abmusica.org.br). Supersedes the 1916 Max Eschig edition.
Symphony No. 2, "Ascenção" (Ascension) (1917–44)	1. Allegro non troppo 2. Allegretto scherzando 3. Andante moderato 4. Allegro	Grand plus 2 Picc., EH, Bclar., Cbssn., 2 Tpts., Trom., Tuba, Perc. (Tam-tam, Bombo, Cym., SD, Tamb.), 2 Harps, Cel.	Begun in 1917 but not completed until 1943–44. Meaning of subtitle is unclear but may reflect the rising contour of all the principal themes. First performance: May 6, 1944, in a radio broadcast by the Orquestra Sinfônica da Rádio Nacional, conducted by the composer. Published by Editora da OSESP; rental score available at Academia Brasileira de Música (www.abmusica.org.br). Supersedes the 1978 Ricordi Americana Belwin edition.

Symphony No. 3, "A Guerra" (To War) (1919, rev. ca. 1955)	1. Allegro quasi giusto: "A vida e o labor" (Life and Labor) 2. Como um scherzo: "Intrigas e cochichos" (Rumors and Intrigues) 3. Lento e marcial: "Sofrimento" (Suffering) 4. Allegro impetuoso: "A batalha" (Battle)	Grand plus Picc., 2 Flt. (optional), EH, Bclar., 2 Bssn. (Bssn. 4 doubling Cbssn.), 4 Hr. (optional), 2 Tpts. (or 2 Cor.), Trom., Tuba, 3 Timp., Perc. (Tam-tam, Wood Block, Cym., Ratchet, BD, SD, Tri, Xylo.), 2 Harps, Pno., Cel. Marching band consisting of Picc. Bugle in E♭, 2 B♭ Bugles, 4 Cor., 2 Saxhorns, 4 Trom., 2 Bombardinos, 3 Tubas.	Created in response to a commission to write a symphony celebrating the Treaty of Versailles. First of a trilogy of war-inspired symphonies. Manuscript bears the subtitle "First Symbolic Symphony" ("1a Sinfônia Simbólica"). First performance (first and second movements only): July 31, 1919, by the Orquestra do Theatro Municipal, conducted by the composer, as part of a concert dedicated to Brazilian president Epitácio Pessoa. First complete performance in September 1920, by the Orquestra do Theatro Municipal, conducted by the composer, as part of a concert given for the king and queen of Belgium. The original version of the symphony had only three movements (Mvts. 1-2, 4). Around 1955, Villa-Lobos added the present-day third movement and lightened the instrumentation. Final version published by Editora da OSESP; rental score available at Academia Brasileira de Música (www.abmusica.org.br). Supersedes the 1978 Ricordi edition.
Symphony No. 4, "A Vitória" (To Victory) (1919)	1. Allegro impetuoso 2. Andantino 3. Andante 4. Lento—Allegro	Grand plus 2 Flt. (doubling Picc.), EH, E♭Clar., Bclar., Cbssn., Sopsax., Asax., Tsax., Barsax., 2 Tpts., Trom., Tuba, Perc. (Cym., BD, Tenor Drums of Provence, SD, Tam-tam, Bells, Sistrum, Small Frame Drum, Shaker, Sleigh Bells, Tri, Xylo.), 2 Harps, Pno., Cel. Marching band consisting of 3 Cor., 3 Bugles, 2 Hr., 2 Saxhorns, 2 Trom., Bombardino, 3 Tubas.	Second in the trilogy of war-inspired symphonies. Incorporates themes from the Third Symphony. First performance in September 1920, by the Orquestra do Theatro Municipal, conducted by the composer, as part of a concert given for the king and queen of Belgium. The composer recorded this symphony in Paris in 1955. Published by Editora da OSESP; rental score available at Academia Brasileira de Música (www.abmusica.org.br). Supersedes the 1978 Ricordi edition.

Table 7.4 *continued*

Title	Movements	Instrumentation	Comments
Symphony No. 5, "A Paz" (To Peace) (1920 [?])	1. Allegro 2. Scherzo 3. Moderato 4. Allegro grandioso	Not known; according to Villa-Lobos, this symphony, like its two predecessors, included a wind band; it also included a mixed chorus vocalizing on phonemes from various languages.	Last of the trilogy of war-inspired symphonies. Unclear if Villa-Lobos completed the work in 1920 or at a much later date (the 1940s or 1950s). The work was never performed, and the score is lost.
Symphony No. 6, *Sobre as Linhas das Montanhas do Brasil* (On the Outline of the Mountains of Brazil) (1944)	1. Allegro non troppo 2. Lento 3. Allegretto quasi animato 4. Allegro	Grand plus 2 Picc., EH, Bclar., Cbssn., 2 Tpt., Trom., Tuba, Perc. (Tam-tam, BD, SD, Cym., Surdo [large Brazilian Bass Drum], Indian Drum, Vbp.), 2 Harps, Cel.	Dedicated to the composer's companion, Mindinha (Arminda Neves d'Almeida Villa-Lobos). First performance: April 29, 1950, by the Orquestra do Theatro Municipal, conducted by the composer. Published by Editora da OSESP; rental score available at Academia Brasileira de Música (www.abmusica.org.br). Supersedes the 1978 Ricordi edition. Villa-Lobos carved out the principal theme by projecting the outline of the Serra dos Órgãos (Órgãos Mountains), visible from Rio de Janeiro) onto graph paper and deriving the melody from the resulting contour. He called this technique *milimetrazação* (milimeterization) or "graphing."
Symphony No. 7 (1945)	1. Allegro vivace 2. Lento 3. Scherzo: Allegro non troppo 4. Allegro preciso	Grand plus 2 Picc., Flt., Ob., 2 EH, Clar., 2 Bclar., Bssn., 2 Cbssn., 2 Hr., 2 Tpt., Trom., Tuba, Perc. (Tam-tam, Cym., Tri., Pandeiro [Frame Drum], Metal Rattle, Glsp., Reco reco [Güiro], Guizo, SD, Tenor Drum, BD, Sistrum, Xylo., Vbp.), 2 Harps, Pno., Cel., Novachord [a synthesizer]	Composed shortly after Victory in Europe Day for a competition in Detroit; as per its rules, Villa-Lobos submitted the symphony anonymously, under the pseudonym A. Caramurú. It did not win. The program note for the premiere entitled the symphony "Odisseéia da paz" (Peace Odyssey) and the four movements "Prologue," "Contrasts," "Tragedy," and "Epilogue," but none of these titles appear in the manuscript. First performance: March 27, 1949, by the London Symphony Orchestra, conducted by the composer. Published by Editora da OSESP; rental score available at Academia Brasileira de Música (www.abmusica.org.br). Supersedes the 1978 Ricordi edition.

Work	Movements	Instrumentation	Notes
Sinfonietta No. 2 (1947)	1. Animato 2. Moderato assai 3. Scherzando e Allegro (Final)	Flt./Picc., Ob./EH, Clar./Bclar., Eb Asax., Bssn., 3 Hr., 2 Tpt., 2 Trom., Timp., Perc. (Tam-tam, Cym., BD, Xylo.), Harp, Cel., Strgs.	Written for the Orchestra Accademia Filarmonica Romana. First performance: March 15, 1948, by the Orchestra Accademia Filarmonica Romana, conducted by the composer. Score published by Southern Music Publishing Co., 1960.
Symphony No. 8 (1950)	1. Andante 2. Lento (assai) 3. Allegretto scherzando 4. Allegro (giusto)	Grand plus 2 Picc., EH, Bclar., Cbssn., 2 Tpt., Trom., Tuba, Perc. (BD, Tam-tam, Cym., Xylo.), Harp, Pno., Cel.	Dedicated to Olin Downes (music critic of the *New York Times*). First performance: Carnegie Hall, January 18, 1955, by the Philadelphia Orchestra, conducted by the composer. Published by Editora da OSESP; rental score available at Academia Brasileira de Música (www.abmusica.org.br). Supersedes the 1978 Ricordi edition.
Symphony No. 9 (1950)	1. Allegro 2. Adagio 3. Scherzo (Vivace) 4. Allegro (giusto)	Grand plus Flt. (doubling Picc.), EH, Bclar, Cbssn., 2 Tpt., Trom., Tuba, Perc. (Tam-tam, Cym., Coco [Coconut Hulls], BD, Xylo., Vbp.), Harp, Cel.	Dedicated to Mindinha. First performance: May 16, 1966, in Caracas, Venezuela, by the Philadelphia Orchestra, conducted by Eugene Ormandy. Published by Editora da OSESP; rental score available at Academia Brasileira de Música (www.abmusica.org.br). Supersedes the 1952 Max Eschig edition.
Symphony No. 10, *Sumé, pater, patrium; Sinfonia amerindia com coros (Oratório)* (Sumé, Father of Fathers: Amerindian Symphony with Chorus) (1952–53)	1. Allegro: "A terra e os seres" (The Earth and Its Creatures) 2. Lento: "Grito de guerra" (War Cry) 3. Scherzo (Allegretto scherzando): "Iurupichuna" (Black-Mouthed Monkeys) 4. Lento: "A voz da terra e a aparição de Anchieta" (The Voice of the Earth and the Appearance of Anchieta) 5. Poco allegro: "Glória no céu e paz na terra!" (Glory in Heaven, and Peace on Earth!)	Grand plus 2 Flt. (doubling Picc.), EH, Clar., Bclar., Cbssn., 2 Tpt., Trom., Tuba, Perc. (Tam-tam, BD, Rattle, Coconut Hulls, Gongo, Guizos, Mrb., Tenor Drum of Provence, Pio [stick used to create bird-like chirp], Cym., Bells, Xylo.), 2 Harps, Pno., Cel., Org. Bass, Baritone, and Tenor Soloists, SATB Choir.	Written to celebrate the 400th anniversary of the founding of São Paulo. Texts drawn from several sources, including writings in the indigenous Tupi language as well as excerpts from poems by José de Anchieta, one of São Paulo's founders. Dedicated to Mindinha. First performance: April 4, 1957, by the Orchestre National et Choeur de la Radiodiffusion Française (Jean Giraudeau, tenor; Camille Maurane, bar.; Jacques Chalude, bass), conducted by the composer. Published by Editora da OSESP; rental score available at Academia Brasileira de Música (www.abmusica.org.br). Supersedes the 1953 Max Eschig edition.

Table 7.4 continued

Title	Movements	Instrumentation	Comments
Symphony No. 11 (1955)	1. Allegro moderato 2. Largo 3. Scherzo: Molto vivace 4. Molto allegro	Grand plus 2 Flt. (doubling Picc.), EH, Bclar., Cbssn., 2 Tpt., Trom., Tuba, Perc. (Tam-tam, Cym., Tri., Matraca [Wooden Rattle], BD, Xylo., Vbp.), 2 Harps, Pno., Cel.	Commissioned by the Koussevitzky Music Foundation in the Library of Congress and the Boston Symphony Orchestra to commemorate its 75th anniversary. Dedicated to the memory of Serge and Natalie Koussevitzky. First performance: March 2, 1956, by the Boston Symphony Orchestra, conducted by the composer. Published by Editora da OSESP; rental score available at Academia Brasileira de Música (www.abmusica.org.br). Supersedes the 1955 Max Eschig edition.
Symphony No. 12 (1957)	1. Allegro non troppo 2. Adagio 3. Scherzo: Vivace 4. Molto allegro	Grand plus Flt. (doubling Picc.), Bclar., Cbssn., 2 Tpt., Trom., Tuba, Perc. (Tam-tam, Cym., Coconut Hulls [low, medium, and high], Xyl.), Harp, Cel.	Completed on the composer's 70th birthday. Dedicated to Mindinha. First performance: April 20, 1958, by the National Symphony Orchestra, conducted by Howard Mitchell. Published by Editora da OSESP; rental score available at Academia Brasileira de Música (www.abmusica.org.br). Supersedes the 1957 Max Eschig edition.

a. Table by Brian Hart. Most of Villa-Lobos's symphonies were originally published by Max Eschig or Ricordi, but these scores are rife with errors and confusing annotations. In collaboration with various Brazilian musicologists, OSESP (the publishing house for the São Paulo Symphony), has created more reliable scores for the eleven existing symphonies. Most of the information for this table is derived from three online sources: Museu Villa-Lobos/OBRA, Gearhart/VILLA-LOBOS, and the site for Editoria de OSESP: https://editora.OSESP.art.br/en/compositores/heitor-villa-lobos-2/. Meters and measure lengths are not included in this table.

late-Romantic chromaticism, and thematic links across movements, although whole-tone fragments lend variety. Three other programmatic symphonies, all inspired by World War I, are the Third ("War"), Fourth ("Victory"), and Fifth ("Peace," lost). The first two are from 1919, when celebrations were held worldwide in the wake of the armistice. The Third Symphony commemorates the role of the Brazilian navy in the war, which, although limited and largely under British leadership, resulted in casualties. It combines formal freedom, motivic recall, and compelling themes, along with the unevenness critics often observe in Villa-Lobos's music. For example, whereas the cello melody in Movement III ("Suffering") is discreetly expressive, elsewhere Villa-Lobos indulges in pictorial writing that verges on the overly explicit (mickey-mousing, to borrow a term from film music). But the symphony can also be subtle, as in Movement II, a scherzo titled "Rumors and Intrigues," with its confused, twittering strings. Bombast is ever present: Villa-Lobos marshals a gigantic orchestra of 164 players (comprising both a full orchestra and a brass band) that includes four flutes, contrabassoon, eight horns, four harps, piano, and celesta. These vast forces, possibly a retort to the immense German war machine, are on display in Movement I ("Life and Labor"), with its glissandi in the piano, dissonant splashes, and whole-tone fragments.

They figure even more prominently in Movement IV. Like Biber's *Battalia* and Beethoven's *Wellington's Victory*, the finale of the Third Symphony is an example of instrumental combat music. Listeners naturally expect fanfares, explosions, march rhythms punctuated by snare drums, or quotations of national anthems. Villa-Lobos offers all in this concluding movement, subtitled "Battle," which he introduces with snare drums and a two-note fragment that recalls a principal motive of Movement I. (He also recalls the theme of Movement III.) At the climax, Villa-Lobos quotes the Brazilian national anthem, which, like many Latin American national anthems, could pass for a Donizetti melody. Some listeners may be surprised to hear it in tandem not with "God Save the King," the British national anthem, but "La Marseillaise." As noted, Brazilians had long revered French culture, a psychological bond that was stronger than any with Great Britain, whatever the partnerships of war. Representing the Allies, the French anthem enters subtly, with an internal phrase that barely surfaces beneath the bouncy, dotted rhythms of the Brazilian anthem. As "La Marseillaise" gains in profile, however, it gradually finds itself on an equal footing with its Brazilian counterpart, reminding the listener of Ives's collage technique. The piece ends abruptly on a blazing C-major chord.

During the mid-twentieth century, when high modernism peaked, Villa-Lobos was often attacked for hewing too closely to Brazilian popular music. By the 1950s, he had declared himself an anti-nationalist and tried his hand at less flamboyant or exotic styles, as in the symphonic work *Erosão* (Erosion). Yet as Simon Wright points out, his niche seemed to be to create "gigantic, colorful orchestral works."[91] When his final symphony, the Twelfth, premiered in Washington, DC, in 1958, Paul Hume noted a "wide-screen, multilux color effect." This feature was not necessarily a liability: Hume praised Movement I for its "big buildup not unlike that of a fine Broadway musical," adding, "this is the kind of work from which Broadway learns its lessons."[92] To date, such lessons have not been that widely available. Although all the symphonies are published and recorded (except for the lost Fifth), editions are marred by errors and sometimes-confusing annotations by the composer, all of which have discouraged performers.[93] Thanks, however, to a collaboration begun in 2010 among the São Paulo Symphony, various Brazilian musicologists, and Naxos records, listeners can sample all the symphonies in new editions sponsored by the orchestra and recorded in the Sala São Paulo, known for its splendid acoustics.[94]

Among Villa-Lobos's Brazilian contemporaries, Francisco Mignone (1897–1986) wrote orchestral music. He was inspired by the Afro-Brazilian tradition, especially the *maracatu*, a ritual that involves the symbolic crowning of an African king and queen. Mignone's *Maracatu de Chico Rei* is frequently performed in Brazil. Oscar Lorenzo Fernândez (1897–1948) wrote a few orchestral works, including two symphonies and the symphonic poem *Imbapára*, which quotes folk music. Fernândez is best known for his "Batuque," the final movement of *Reisado do pastoreio* (Epiphany of the Shepherds, 1930), which invokes Afro-Brazilian rhythms; Leonard Bernstein liked to program it. In the generation after Villa-Lobos, Luiz Cosme (1908–65) composed *Salamanca do Jaráu* (Salamander of Jaráu, 1935), a ballet and ballet suite that use popular materials from the state of Rio Grande do Sul.[95]

MOZART CAMARGO GUARNIERI AND CLÁUDIO SANTORO

One Brazilian composer often overlooked internationally is Mozart Camargo Guarnieri (1907–93), a native of São Paulo. (Mozart is not all that unusual a name in Brazil, where children are often given surnames of famous people, such as Edison or Milton. Guarnieri usually signed his name "M. Camargo Guarnieri" so as "not to offend a master," as he explained.[96]) Copland considered Guarnieri one of the best musicians in Latin America.[97] Equally impressed was Slonimsky, who commended Guarnieri's "Gallic neoclassicism."[98] This quality emerges in the *Abertura Concertante* (Concert Overture) of 1942, a work Slonimsky described as "of a strongly contrapuntal nature, in the neoclassical manner."[99] Several transparent, woodwind-dominated passages (m. 15, for example) support Slonimsky's claim, although other sections are scarcely Neoclassical at all. The overture begins with a vigorous motive based on the major second that, once extended, juxtaposes duple and triple meter. Assertive punctuation in the timpani previews that instrument's role in transitional passages, such as the two returns to the material of the A section (mms. 120, 259). The piece unfolds in tripartite form, with a lyrical B section, highlighting muted strings, sometimes with portamento.[100] The main motive is never far: in the B section, Guarnieri assigns it to the viola, albeit in an accompanimental role (mm. 183–84). The motive also accompanies the flute and clarinet (mm. 191), now in a more richly orchestrated passage; it weaves its basic shape into a long bassoon solo that ultimately yields to the timpani and the return of the A section, truncated to quickly surge into the exuberant coda (m. 370).

Guarnieri, who dedicated the overture to Copland, conducted its premiere in São Paulo. He then performed it with the Boston Symphony Orchestra in March 1943, at the height of the Good Neighbor period. Critic Warren Storey Smith noted that the *Overture* was "one more example of the prevalent neoclassicism," adding, "the music has both vigor and charm and is plainly the work of an expert hand."[101] Other critics observed the enthusiasm of the public, with one also describing the overture as "an amiable, ingratiating piece, well designed to cultivate good will between good neighbors."[102]

By the end of his long career, Guarnieri had composed numerous orchestral works, among them seven symphonies.[103] They encompass most of his career, with the First Symphony dating from 1943, when he was thirty-six, and the Seventh from 1985. (The First through the Fourth all received awards.) The symphonies also reflect a certain consistency in Guarnieri's style, several features of which are present in the *Overture*. As in that work, Guarnieri remains attached to traditional forms: the sonata form of Movement I of the Second Symphony is straightforward, as is that of Movement I of the Fourth Symphony, the themes of which are third related. Modestly departing from these norms are the Fifth Symphony, which uses arch form in the first movement, and the Sixth Symphony, which is in cyclic form; internal movements often follow ABA patterns. A similar conservatism informs Guarnieri's strongly tonal harmonic language, as in Movement I of the Fourth Symphony, solidly in C major despite numerous nonharmonic tones. Guarnieri's orchestration is also conventional, although he sometimes uses enhanced percussion: the Sixth Symphony, for example, calls for an *agogô* bell, common in Afro-Brazilian rituals. The Fifth Symphony employs a chorus, singing a text (by the composer's brother) about the Tietê River, which flows through São Paulo state. Counterpoint is frequent—for example, in Movement I of the Second Symphony. As in the *Overture*, a Neoclassical influence makes itself felt in Movement III of the Fourth Symphony and in the unison woodwind writing of Movement I of the Second Symphony, which recalls passages from Movement I of Stravinsky's *Symphony of Psalms*.

Some of Guarnieri's themes have a bluesy, Gershwinesque quality, thanks to the Brazilian composer's penchant for lowered sevenths. Among his more prominent modal melodies is the Mixolydian second theme of the Second Symphony, Movement I; Movement III of the Third Symphony is in Lydian mode. Other themes are angular, as in Movement I of the Second Symphony, which recalls 1920s machine music, as does its counterpart in the Fourth Symphony, dedicated to the establishment in 1960 of the new capital Brasília in the country's highlands. The Seventh Symphony uses a Hebrew melody, in homage to Leon and Antonietta Feffer, who commissioned the work. Some movements are monothematic, such as Movement II of the Second Symphony.[104] In the Third Symphony, Guarnieri uses an indigenous theme, a rare practice for him; he found it not through fieldwork but in a collection, *Rondonia*, published in 1916 by the author, anthropologist, and leader in Brazilian radio, Edgard Roquette-Pinto.

Guarnieri's symphonies have been performed in several Brazilian cities and internationally, including several performances in the United States during the composer's lifetime.[105] They deserve a wider hearing today, for the music is ingratiating and not without expressive breakthroughs in an often placid surface. One such moment occurs in Movement II of the Fourth Symphony. A unison violin line, more disjunct than Guarnieri's other melodies, wanders for nearly two minutes before the lower strings join in, also in unison, like a wordless recitative. After a full seven minutes, a dissonant chord punctuates the unison line, intensified with trills and chords from the piano before dying away several minutes later. Was this lonely and uncharacteristic theme intended to convey the "expansiveness of the flat horizon" out of which Brasília arose, as Marion Verhaalen suggests?[106] Whatever its raison d'être, the movement shows that Guarnieri could be profound when he wanted to be.[107]

From the late 1930s, several Brazilian composers became interested in serialism. Guarnieri denounced this trend as a threat to national identity (his own "Gallic neoclassicism" notwithstanding) and railed on this point in an "Open Letter to the Musicians and Critics of Brazil" that appeared in November 1950 in *O Estado de São Paulo*, one of Brazil's most respected newspapers.[108] His fears were not entirely groundless, for many Brazilian serialists were adamantly opposed to identity-conscious music. Their leader was the German-born composer Hans-Joachim Koellreutter (1915–2005), who trained at the Berlin Academy of Music before arriving in Rio de Janeiro in 1937. He gathered around him a group of likeminded young modernists, among them César Guerra-Peixe (1914–93), Eunice do Monte Lima Katunda (1915–91), and Cláudio Santoro (1919–89). Ultimately, most gave up serialism. (Surprisingly, Guarnieri himself used serialist procedures in his Fifth and Sixth Piano Concertos, which date from the 1960s.) Guerra-Peixe composed several orchestral works: one, *Tributo a Portinari* (Tribute to Portinari, 1992), is an homage to the Brazilian artist Cândido Portinari (1903–62), often compared to Diego Rivera for both his style and social vision. Guerra-Peixe also wrote two symphonies; like Guarnieri's Fourth, his Second, subtitled "Brasília," paid homage to the new capital and is scored for orchestra, chorus, and speaker. Katunda, an active and much-admired pianist, wrote little orchestral music and no symphonies although her *Homenagem a Schoenberg* (Homage to Schoenberg) was performed at the 1950 ISCM Festival in Brussels.

As for Santoro, he began his career by looking back to 1920s machine music with *Impressões de uma fundição de aço* (Impressions of a Steel Factory), which won a prize in the 1944 contest sponsored by the recently founded Orquestra Sinfônica de Brasil (OSB; now the Orquestra Sinfônica Brasileira), based in Rio de Janeiro.[109] While studying with Koellreuter, he wrote serial music. But as he became increasingly sympathetic to communism, which condemned such "formalism," he immersed himself in Brazilian folk and popular music, the influence of which surfaces in some of his orchestral works. He remained open to other styles, however. His *3 Abstrações* (Three Abstractions, 1966) for string orchestra, for example, is aleatoric.

Santoro's fourteen symphonies span his entire career.[110] He finished the First Symphony, for two string orchestras, in 1940, when he was twenty-one, and composed the Fourteenth in 1989, the year he died. Santoro's symphonies have been called "his major contribution to modern music," and nearly all have been published.[111] A few highlights give an idea of their import. The Fourth Symphony, composed in 1954, is subtitled "Sinfonia da Paz" (Symphony of Peace) and showcases broad themes subtly enhanced by Brazilian percussion. It remains one of Santoro's most frequently performed works, thanks in part to a recording by the USSR State Orchestra, also in 1954.[112] The Fifth Symphony, of the following year, affirms the composer's interest in Prokofiev and Shostakovich, and it was perhaps with the former in mind—at least the Prokofiev of four decades earlier—that Santoro conceived his Sixth Symphony for "classical" orchestra, in which he sought to "leave behind the direct idiom of popular and folkloric [music]," as he explained.[113] The Seventh Symphony continues in this vein, for it contains a French overture and a rondo in Movements I and IV, respectively. In the two-movement Eighth Symphony for orchestra and mezzo-soprano, Santoro returns to serialism. The Brazilian conductor Eleazar de Carvahlo, who led the St. Louis Symphony during the 1960s, premiered it in 1964.

Santoro's Ninth Symphony, from 1982, is noteworthy for its dark colors and dramatic contrasts, including the prolonged spotlighting of the woodwind choir in Movement I and the wandering unison writing in the low strings at the beginning of the Andante—a reference, perhaps, to the instrumental recitative in the lower strings in Beethoven's Ninth Symphony. The last movement is more explicitly Beethovenian: Santoro quotes the German composer's harmonically uncertain opening measures, twice interrupting with outbursts from the brass. Less obvious is the allusion shortly thereafter to Beethoven's Scherzo, a dissonant and jerky rendering of that movement's theme. Naturally, the listener wonders if Santoro will represent and then reject the other movements of Beethoven's Ninth ("not these tones!"). Instead, one minute before the end of the movement Santoro refers once more to the ambiguous opening before concluding this fascinating work with a brash chord. Santoro wrote five more symphonies between 1982 and 1989.

Marlos Nobre (b. 1939), a native of Pernambuco, studied in Recife and then with Gunther Schuller and Leonard Bernstein at the Berkshire Music Center. In his works, he embraces Brazilian popular music, serialism, aleatory, and tonality, and his orchestral compositions include *Kabbalah for Orchestra* (2004), an imaginative work filled with evocative colors and relentless energy (see table 7.3). Other Brazilian composers who have written for orchestra include Ricardo Tacuchian (b. 1939), Jamary de Oliveira (1944–2020), Ilza Nogueira (b. 1948), Rodolfo

Coelho de Souza (b. 1952), Paulo Costa Lima (b. 1954), Roberto Victorio (b. 1959), and Felipe Lara (b. 1979). Paulo Chagas (b. 1953) was born in Salvador, studied in São Paulo, and then worked with Henri Pousseur in Liège, Belgium. A victim of torture during Brazil's dictatorship, Chagas feels that this experience has marked his compositions. Of his 160-plus works, several are for orchestra. His *Eshu: la porte des enfers* (Eshu: The Gates of Hell, 1983) combines orchestra, electronics, and Afro-Brazilian percussion (table 7.3). Others are Miguel Kertsman (b. 1965), born in Recife and a student at the Berklee College of Music and the Juilliard School. The Vienna Symphony Orchestra, the London Philharmonic, the Bruckner Orchestra Linz, and the Saint Paul Chamber Orchestra have all commissioned his music. Like earlier Brazilian composers, he has written a symphonic poem titled *Amazônia* (1986). His works are recorded on the Naxos label. Alexandre Travassos (b. 1970), born in Rio de Janeiro, composed *Aurora australis* for orchestra.

Chile

At the time of the conquest, native populations in what is now Chile played flutes, trumpets made of bulls' horns, and drums, according to European chroniclers.[114] Enslaved Africans were first brought to Chile in 1536. As elsewhere in South America, the colonial system adhered to strict hierarchies: *español*, *indio*, and *negro* (Spaniard, Indian, Black) were the main categories, with Blacks occupying the lowest rung of society.[115] The traditional scholarly argument that the history of Chilean instrumental music coincided with independence, a multiyear campaign begun in 1810, has been recently challenged, as has the notion that Blacks played only a marginal role in music making.[116]

During the colonial period, most composers of orchestral music were employed by the church. Over the eighteenth century, concerted music took on greater significance, as confirmed in personnel records of the Santiago Cathedral and in Benedict XIV's encyclical of 1749.[117] We see this tendency away from strictly plainsong and unaccompanied polyphony in composers such as José de Campderrós (1742–1811), born in Spain and chapelmaster of the Santiago Cathedral between circa 1793 and 1811. The scoring for several of his works approximates that of the classical orchestra. A Mass in G Major, for example, contains differentiated oboe and flute parts; other masses of his called for trumpets and drums. Another practice was transcribing keyboard works for orchestra.[118]

Manuel Robles (1780–1837) is generally recognized as Chile's first native-born composer, writing an early version of the Chilean national anthem. In 1826, a philharmonic society was founded in Santiago; similar organizations in other cities followed (Concepción, 1829; Valparaiso, 1845; Valdivia, 1853). The Spanish émigré composer Isadora Zegers (1803–69), educated in Paris, organized concerts of instrumental music in her home. She also spearheaded projects such as establishing the National Conservatory in 1849 and launching *Seminario Musical*, Chile's first musical magazine.[119] As elsewhere in South America, opera was also a powerful force. Zegers, a Rossini enthusiast, persuaded the newly formed government to invite European singers to Chile, one of whom, the bass Henry Lanza, was employed as chapelmaster at the Santiago cathedral. During his tenure, many members of the cathedral orchestra played in the opera pit at night.[120] The German-born Aquinas Ried was the first composer to write an opera on a national subject, *Telésfora*, performed in Valparaiso in 1846.

Throughout the latter part of the nineteenth century, composers became interested in instrumental music. José Zapiola (1802–85) and Federico Guzmán (1836–85) wrote mainly for smaller instrumental ensembles; another German immigrant, Guillermo Frick Eltze

Table 7.5 Selected Symphonic Music from Chile, Peru, Bolivia, Ecuador, Colombia, and Venezuela

Chile

Carmela Mackenna (1879–1962). Orchesterstücke (1935).

Próspero Bisquertt (1881–1959). *Primavera Helénica* (1919); *Taberna al Amanecer* (1922); *Procesión del Cristo de Mayo* (1930); *Destino* (1934); *Nochebuena* (1936); *Metrópolis* (1940); *1945* (1945).

Enrique Soro (1884–1954). Andante appassionato (1902); Symphonic Suite No. 2 (1920); *Sinfonía romántica* (1921); *Tres Preludios Sinfónicos* (1929); *Tres aires chilenos* (1942).

Pedro Humberto Allende (1885–1959). Suite for String Orchestra (ca. 1903); Symphony in B-flat (ca. 1910); *Escenas campesinas* (1913); *La voz de las Calles* (1920).

Carlos Isamitt Alarcón (1887–1974). *Friso Araucano Americano* (1931); Symphonic Suite (1932); *Mito Araucano* (1935); Four Symphonic Movements (1960); *Lautaro* (1970).

Acario Cotapos (1889–1969). Three Preludes for Orchestra (1923); *Voces de gesta*, symphonic fragments (ca. 1927); Four Preludes for Orchestra (1930).

Juan Casanova Vicuña (1894–1976). *Cuatro bosquejos* (ca. 1931); *El Huaso y el Indio* (1940).

Domingo Santa Cruz (1899–1987). *Five Pieces* (1937); Sinfonia concertante for Flute and Orchestra, Op. 21 (1945); Symphony No. 1, Op. 22 (1945–46, rev. 1971); *Preludios dramáticos* (1946); Symphony No. 2 for Strings, Op. 25 (1948); Symphony No. 3 for Alto Solo and Orchestra, "In memoriam," Op. 34 (1964–65); Symphony No. 4, Op. 35 (1968).

Pablo Garrido (1905–1982). *Fantasía militar* (1932); *Fantasía submarina* (1934); *Rapsodia chilena* (1937).

Alonso Letelier Llona (1912–1994). *La vida del campo* (1937); *Suite grotesca* (1946); *Preludios vegetales* (1968); Symphony: *El hombre ante la ciencia* (1983–85).

Juan Orrego-Salas (1919–2019). *Escenas de cortes y pastores* (1946); *Obertura Festiva* (1948); Symphony No. 1, Op. 46 (1949); Symphony No. 2, "To the Memory of a Wanderer," Op. 39 (1954); Symphony No. 3, Op. 50 (1961); Symphony No. 4, "Of the Distant Answer," Op. 59 (1966); *Variaciones serenas* (1971); Symphony No. 5, Op. 109 (1995); Symphony No. 6 in One Movement, "Semper reditus," Op. 112 (1997).

Eduardo Maturana (1920–2003). *Gamma I* (1962); *Tres piezas* (1963); *Responso para el guerrillero* (1968); *Elegías* (1970).

Leni Alexander (1924–2005). *Música* (1951); *Fünf Epigramme* (1952); *Sinfonia Tríptico* (1954); *Divertimento Rítmico* (1955); *Aulicio* (1965); *. . . ils se sont perdus dans l'espace étoilé . . .* (1975).

Gustavo Becerra (1925–2010). Symphony No. 1 (1955); Symphony No. 2 (1957); Symphony No. 3 (1965).

Roberto Falabella (1926–58). Symphony No. 1 (1956); *Estudios emocionales* (1957).

Fernando García (b. 1930). *Estáticas* (1964); *Firmamento submergido* (1969); *Dos paisajes urbanos* (1997).

León Schidlowsky (1931–2022). *Nueva York* (1965); *Emanación* (1979); *Elegy* (1989); *Absalom* (1996); *I Will Lay Mine Hand Upon My Mouth* (1994); Three Pieces for Orchestra (2016); *Nebulae* (2019).

José Vicente Asuar (1933–2017). *Heterofonías* (1964).

Gabriel Brnčić (b. 1942). *Oda a la energía* (1963); *¡Volveremos a las montañas!* (1968); *Sinfonía* (1969); *Sinfonía concertante* (1988); *Polifonía de la lluvia* (1995).

Guillermo Rifo (1945–2022). *Suite al sur del mundo* (1981); *El ritual de al tierra* (1988); *Danza* (2001, rev. 2003).

Eduardo Cáceres (b. 1955). *Variaciones siete velos de un prisma* (1982); *Alunizaje en el Marga-Marga* (1982); *El quinto elemento* (2019).

Chañaral Ortega-Miranda (b. 1973). *A la sombra del Longino* (2001); *Un nocturno por Chacabuco* (2000); *Q'inti* (2004).

Miguel Farías (b. 1983). *Tessiture* (2008); *Fusion Point* (2009); *Ecos de un Color* (2009–10).

René Silva (b. 1984). *Y todavía tiene una pena . . .* (2012); *Cerro Chena, estación de la memoria* (2014); *Memorial de los Andes* (2017); *Wenu-Mapu* (2018).

Peru

Vicente Stea (1884–1943). *Sinfonía Autóctona* (1934); Symphony in F Minor (1943); *Burlesca*; *Danza per la orchestra*; *Danza* No. 2; *Meditazione*; *Notturno per orchestra*.

Luis Pacheco de Céspedes (1895–1982). *Danzas sobre un tema indio* (1940); *El paseo de aguas* (1941); *La reja* (1942); *La procesión del Señor de los Milagros* (1942); *Himno al Sol* (1943); *Gloria y ocaso del Inca* (1946); two symphonies.

Andrés Sas (1900–67). *Canción India* (1927); *Tres estampas del Perú* (1936); *Poema Indio* (1941); *La Parihuana* (1945).

Teodoro Valcárcel (1900–42). *Estampas del ballet Suray surita* (1928, orch. by Rodolfo Holzmann); *Suite incaica* (1929); *En las ruinas del Templo del Sol* (1940, orch. by Holzmann); *Ayaracha* (orch. by Holzmann).

Enrique Iturriaga (1918–2019). *Canción y muerte de Rolando* (1947); *Vivencias* (1965); *Homenaje a Stravinski* (1971); *Sinfonía Junín y Ayacucho* (1974).

Celso Garrido-Lecca (b. 1926). *Sinfonía en tres movimientos* (1960); *Sinfonía en un movimiento* (1961); *Laudes* (1963); *Retablos sinfónicos* (1973); *Pequeña suite peruana* (1986); *Elegía a Machu Picchu* (1965).

Gabriela Lena Frank (b. 1978). *Elegía andina* (2000); *Leyendas: An Andean Walkabout* (2001); *Peregrinos* (2009); *Escaramuza* (2010); *Concertino Cusqueño* (2012); *Raíces* (2012); *Karnavalingo* (2013); *Apu: Tone Poem for Orchestra* (2017); *Contested Eden* (2021).

Bolivia

José María Velasco-Maidana (1899–1989). *Ameríndia* (1934–35); *Cuento brujo* (1935); *Los Khuzillos* (1936); *Cory Wara* (perf. 1941); *Los hijos del sol* (perf. 1942); *Vida de Cóndores* (perf. 1942); *Los huacos* (perf. 1942); *Los Khusillos* (perf. 1943); *Cuento brujo* (perf. 1943).

Alberto Villalpando Buitrago (b. 1940). *Liturgías fantásticas* (1963); *Música para orquesta*, Nos. 1–5 (1974–2003); *Mística núm. 7* (1976); *Las transformaciones del agua y del fuego en las montañas* (1991).

Willy Pozadas (b. 1946). *Amtasiñani* (1986); *Paisajes para orquesta sinfónica* (1976); *Variamento para orquesta sinfónica* (1992); *Ancestrofonías para orquesta sinfónica* (2002).

Cergio Prudencio (b. 1955). *La ciudad* (indigenous instruments, 1980); *Cantos de tierra* (indigenous instruments, 1990); *Cantos Meridian* (indigenous instruments, 1996); *Cantos Crepuscular* (indigenous instruments, 1999); *Otra ciudad* (siku orch., 2005); *El alto nombre* (orch. and electronics, 2009).

Ecuador

Domenico Brescia (1866–1939). *Sinfonia ecuatoriana* (ca. 1910); *Life: Preamble and Three Episodes for Orchestra* (1919); *Truth* (1926).

Pedro Pablo Traversari (1874–1956). *Glorias andinas* (perf. 1930); *Tríptico Indoandino* (n.d.); *Huyanu (himno pentatónico)* (n.d.).

Segundo Luis Moreno (1882–1972). *Preludio para orquesta* (perf. 1910); Overture: *10 de agosto* (perf. 1911); *Suite Ecuatoriana* (1922); Overture: *9 de julio* (perf. 1925); *La coronación* (n.d.).

Luis Humberto Salgado (1903–77). *Atahualpa* (1933); *Suite coreográfica* (1946); *Pasillo-Intermezzo* (n.d.); *Homenaje a la danza criolla* (1959); *Sismo* (n.d.); eight symphonies.

Gerardo Guevara (b. 1930). *Yaguar shungo* (1958); *Ecuador* (1972); *Galería siglo XX de pintores ecuatorianos* (1976); *Historia* (1990); *De mestizo a mestizo* (1994).

Milton Estévez (b. 1947). *Campanas de bronce* (1982); *Cinco desencuentros con episodio cualquiera* (orch. and electroacoustics, 1986); *Apuntes con refrán* (orch. and electroacoustics, 1987); *Evbreves* (orch. and electroacoustics, 1988); *Bajo el peso de los guandos* (2003–04); *Sin título* (2010).

Arturo Rodas (b. 1954). *Entropía* (1981); *Clímax* (1985); *Güilli Gu* (for orch. and visual arts, 1985); *Fibris* (1986); *Melodías de Cámara* (chamber orch., 1987); *Full Moon Business* (chamber orch., 1997).

Table 7.5 *continued*

Diego Luzuriaga (b. 1955). *Felipillo* (1986); *Incensio* (chamber orch., perf. 1988); *Liturgia* (for shinobue, Japanese flute, and orch., perf. 2000); *Central Waltz* (for youth orch., perf. 2010); *El Capariche* (orchestral variations on an Ecuadoran theme, perf. 2012).

Juan Campoverde Quezada (b. 1964). *Tientos* (1990); *Crónicas* (1993), *Cánticos estudios en negative* (2013).

Colombia

José María Ponce de Léon (1845–82). *Sinfonía sobre temas colombianos* (1881); *Apoteósis a Bolívar: Himno de los Andes y Saludo de Colombia a Chile* (n.d.).

Pedro Morales Pino (1863–1926). *Suite Patria* (n.d.); *Brisas de los Andes* (n.d.).

Andrés Martínez Montoya (1869–1933). *Sinfonía "Isabel"* (prem. 1892); *Fuga, Preludio* (n.d.).

Santos Cifuentes (1870–1932). *Sinfonía "Albores musicales"* (1893); *Obertura* (ca. 1890); *Obertura ocho de marzo* (ca. 1890); *Scherzo* (ca. 1890); *La soledad* (ca. 1912).

Guillermo Uribe Holguín (1880–1971). Symphony No. 1, Op. 11 (1914, rev. 1947); Symphony No. 2, "Sinfonía del Terruño," Op. 15a (1924); *Suite típica* (1932); *Bochica*, Op. 73 (1939); *Sinfonieta campesina*, Op. 83 (1949); *Ceremonia indígena*, Op. 88 (1955); Symphony No. 3, Op. 91 (1955); Symphony No. 4, Op. 98 (n.d.); Symphony No. 5, Op. 100 (1956); Symphony No. 6, Op. 101 (1956); Symphony No. 7, Op. 102 (1957); Symphony No. 8, Op. 103 (1957, rev. 1958); Symphony No. 9, Op. 110 (1959); Symphony No. 10, Op. 112 (1960); Symphony No. 11, Op. 117 (1961).

Jesús Bermúdez Silva (1884–1969). Symphony in C (n.d.); *Torbellino* (n.d.); dances for orchestra.

José Rozo Contreras (1894–1976). *Alicia*, Tango-Serenata (1929); *Tierra Colombiana* (suite, 1930); *Burlesca* (1940).

Carlos Posada Amador (1908–93). *Obertura de recepción* (1934); *Rubaiatas: Suite lírica persa* (n.d., rev. 1990s); *La Coronación del Zipa en Guatavita* (ca. 1938, rev. 1991).

Adolfo Mejía (1909–73). *Pequeña Suite* (1938); *Preludio para la tercera salida de Don Quijote* (1938); *Acuarela* (1938); *Improvisación* (1941); *América* (1946); *Íntima* (1947); *Homenaje a Antonio Gómez Restrepo* (1941); *Homenaje a Luis López de Mesa* (1957).

Blas Emilio Atehortúa (1943–2020). *Tríptico* (1960); *Obertura simétrica* (1962); *Estudio sinfónico* (1968); *Cántico y cántico funebre* (1971); *Soggetto da Vivaldi* (1977); *Suite para orquesta de cuerdas* (1982); *Brachot* (1982); *Elegía sinfónica para Ginastera* (1983); *Música de orchestra para Béla Bartók* (1985); *Concertante antiphonal* (1996).

Francisco Zumaqué (b. 1945). *Porro novo* (1976); *1492: Génesis* (1992).

Andrés Posada (b. 1954). *Poema para una Catedral Invisible* (1984); *Obertura para un Concierto* (1986); *Danza para orquesta* (1992, rev. 1995); *Salmo 55* (1999–2000); *Variaciones sobre 12 segundos tristes* (2005, strg. orch.).

Gustavo Parra (b. 1963). *Cavatina para orquesta* (2014); *Pavec* (1998); *Bambaros* (2000).

Carlos Ágreda (b. 1991). *Abrazos de latina proveniencia* (2010); *Prólogo y danza fugitive* (2011); *¡Dejémonos de Vainas!* (2012).

Venezuela

Teresa Carreño (1853–1917). *Serenade* (strgs., 1896).

Juan Bautista Plaza (1898–1965). *Elegía* (1923); *El picacho abrupto* (1926); *Vigilia* (1928); *Campanas de pascua* (1930): *Fuga criolla* (1931); *Fuga romántica venezolana* (1950); *Marcha nupcial* (1959).

Juan Vicente Lecuna (1899–1954). *Rumbera* (1926–35); *Danza* (1954); *Movimiento* (1951–54).

Carlos Figueredo (1909–86). Symphony No. 1 (1947); Symphony No. 2 (1949); Symphony No. 3 (1952); Symphony No. 4 (1952); Symphony No. 5 (1953).

Evencio Castellanos (1915–84). *El río de las siete estrellas* (1946); *Avileña* (1947); *Santa Cruz de Parcairigua* (1954).

Inocente Carreño (1919–2016). *El pozo* (1946); *Margariteña* (1954); *Suite sinfónica* No. 1 (1955); Overture No. 1 (1956); Overture No. 2 (1961); Suite in Three Movements (strgs., 1963); *Obertura popular* (1973); *Obertura galleguiana* (1979); *Elegía sobre temas de Vicente Emilio Sojo* (strgs., 1980); *Estudio sinfónico* (1983).

Gonzalo Castellanos (1926–2020). *Suite caraqueña* (1947); *Antelación e imitación fugaz* (1954).

Alfredo del Mónaco (1938–2015). *Dos fugas académicas* (strgs., 1964); *Cromofonías II* (1968); *Tupac-Amaru* (1977); *Memorial* (2000).

Alfredo Rugeles (b. 1949). *Mutaciones* (strgs., 1974); *Camino entre lo sutil e inerrante* (1979); *Jugulares del video* (1991).

Josefina Benedetti (b. 1953). *Citas inocentes* (1996); *Misere mei* (1996); *Macuro* (1998); *Cantos del camino* (2001); *Rugeles '82* (2007).

Adina Izarra (b. 1959). *Oshunmare* (1982); *Mujer con telar* (1985); *Luna de aves* (chamber orch., 1988); *Cinco piezas para orquesta* (2014); *No me pidan atender a tantas voces* (prem. 2018).

Paul Desenne (b. 1959). *Táchira y frontera* (chamber orch. 1991); *Three Tropical Moves* (1999); *Three Orchestral Studies* (2001); *Sinfonía Burocrática ed Amazónica* (2004); Symphony for Brass and Percussion (2007); Sinfonía (2010–12); *Symphonía Clásica (La Teresa)* (2013); *Hipnosis Mariposa* (2014); Symphony No. 5 (2016); *El Caimán* (2016); *Guasamacabra* (2018).

Ricardo Lorenz (b. 1961). Concerto for Orchestra (1989); *Konex-Konex* (folk ensemble and orch., 2000); *El tren vá, Changó* (2001); *Rumba sinfónica* (Latin band and orch., 2007); *Habanera Science* (strgs., 2014); *Passacaglia Unrest* (strgs., 2014); *Olokun's Awakening* (2014).

Luis Ernesto Gómez (b. 1977). Concerto for Orchestra (2010); *El terremoto del Jueves Santo* (2012); *Rhythmic Toccata* (strgs., 2015).

(1813–1905), wrote incidental music. Carmela Mackenna (1879–1962), granddaughter of the independence fighter General Juan Mackenna, studied piano and composition in Berlin and worked as a cultural attaché. Her two *Orchesterstücke* date from 1935. Piano virtuoso Enrique Soro (1884–1954), who studied in Milan, wrote large- and small-scale symphonic works. The best known is the four-movement *Sinfonía romántica* (Romantic Symphony); his Symphonic Suite No. 2 was published by Ricordi (table 7.5).

Composer and teacher Pedro Humberto Allende (1885–1959) wrote several orchestral compositions, including a Suite for String Orchestra (premiered in 1903), an Overture in G Major, and a prize-winning Symphony in B-flat Major.[121] His *Escenas campesinas* (Rustic Scenes) of 1913 were performed in Santiago in 1941 alongside Copland's jazz-inflected Piano Concerto. His symphonic poem *La voz de las calles* (The Voice of the Streets) of 1920, which contains melodic cells based on *pregones* (the cries of street vendors), was performed at the Pan American Union. One of Allende's students, Carlos Isamitt Alarcón (1887–1974), was much taken with the culture of the Araucanians, the Indigenous population whose bravery and idealism in the face of the Spanish conquest have attracted many Chilean artists. (The current term for this community is *Mapuche*, albeit with some debate over the geographical region encompassed.) Some of Isamitt's orchestral works are *Suite Sinfónica*, the third movement of which is based on a native dance (table 7.5).[122] Two other similarly oriented symphonic works are *Friso Araucano Americano* (American Arucanian Frieze) and *Mito araucano* (Araucanian Myth). Similarly inspired was the Chilean-US composer Nino Marcelli (1890–1967), founder of the San Diego (California) Symphony; his *Suite Araucana* (Araucanian Suite) premiered in 1923 in New York.[123]

Several Chilean composers were independent spirits in that they had little formal training, instead trusting their own instincts. Among them was Próspero Bisquertt (1881–1959), some of whose symphonic poems, such as *Taberna al amanecer* (Tavern at Dawn) and *Metropolis*, have been published, along with other orchestral pieces (table 7.5). Another autodidact, Alfonso Leng (1894–1974), worked mainly as a dentist but composed *La muerte de Alsino* (The Death of Alsino) of 1921, a symphonic poem based on a novel by the Chilean author Pedro Prado about a conflicted hero. It reveals Leng's finesse with form and orchestration and is rooted in the tradition of Richard Strauss (the violin solos in *La muerte de Alsino* hint at *Ein Heldenleben*). *Canto de invierno* of 1933 is similarly romantic. (In 1941, the BBC Orchestra performed some of Leng's music.)[124] The well-traveled Acario Cotapos (1889–1969) was also largely self-taught. He became a member of the International Composers Guild, established under Edgard Varèse in New York City in 1921, as well as the Pan-American Association of Composers, founded there in 1928. Cotapos, who also lived in France, Spain, and Argentina, composed a vast stage work, *Voces de gesta* (Epic Voices), which he began in 1927 and completed only partly. Several symphonic fragments of *Voces de gesta* were performed in Paris (Salle Gaveau, 1932) and Madrid (Teatro Calderón, 1935). Another work was his *Cuatro preludios para orquesta* (Four Preludes for Orchestra, 1930), which Copland admired when the two met in 1941. Pablo Garrido (1905–82), on the other hand, formed the first Chilean jazz band and wrote copiously about jazz.[125] He composed a handful of symphonic works (table 7.5).

DOMINGO SANTA CRUZ, JUAN ORREGO-SALAS, AND GUSTAVO BECERRA

Chilean symphonists of the twentieth century include Domingo Santa Cruz (1899–1987), Juan Orrego-Salas (1919–2019), and Gustavo Becerra (1925–2010).[126] Santa Cruz taught a large class of students, and as an administrator he succeeded in incorporating music into the Chilean university system (it was previously confined to the conservatory). During the 1920s, he worked for the Chilean diplomatic service in Madrid, where he studied composition with Conrado del Campo (1878–1953). Among Santa Cruz's orchestral works are *Cinco piezas* (known in English as Five Short Pieces for String Orchestra) of 1937. When Lincoln Kirstein, founder of the American Ballet Caravan, heard the work during the company's 1941 goodwill tour of Latin America, he wanted to choreograph it but the company dissolved. Other orchestral compositions by Santa Cruz include *Preludios dramáticos* (Dramatic Preludes) and four symphonies, the third of which figured on the Third Inter-American Music Festival in Washington, DC (1965). Subtitled "In Memoriam," it was inspired by the poem "Tribulación" (Tribulation) by the Chilean poet-diplomat and Nobel laureate Gabriela Mistral (1889–1957). He is often categorized as a Neoclassicist: Slonimsky dubbed Santa Cruz "the Chilean Hindemith."[127]

Among Santa Cruz's students was Juan Orrego-Salas, who eventually made his career in the United States. Orrego-Salas earned a degree in architecture, which he practiced professionally before devoting himself full time to music. (His former students comment on their teacher's attention to music's architectural properties.) After teaching at the University of Chile and the Catholic University in Santiago, Orrego-Salas spent two years in the United States on a Rockefeller Foundation grant and the first of two Guggenheim Fellowships, beginning in 1945. He also studied at the Berkshire Music Center and worked with Randall Thompson, Paul Henry Lang, and Georg Herzog. Back in Chile, he resumed teaching and took up music criticism. In 1961, he returned to the United States to teach composition at Indiana University, where he established and directed the Latin American Music Center, combining his administrative responsibilities with teaching before his retirement in 1987. Among the many organizations that commissioned his works are the Koussevitzky and Coolidge Foundations, the Louisville Orchestra, the National Symphony of Washington, DC, and the National Endowment for the Arts.

Orrego-Salas composed nearly twenty orchestral works (table 7.5). Of his six symphonies, several bear subtitles. His Third Symphony, written in El Arrayán (Chile) in 1960, premiered with the National Symphony under Howard Mitchell in April 1961 at the second Inter-American Music Festival. Apropos that event, the often outspoken Cuban composer Aurelio de la Vega remarked to the Washington press that Latin American composers were no longer interested in "tourist music"—or, as one journalist put it, "jungle jingles."[128] On this point, Orrego-Salas's symphony proved persuasive.[129] The four-movement work opens with a dark-hued Allegro maestoso. Frequent snare drum rolls, fanfares in trumpets and trombones (before Reh. D), and a steady quarter-note accompaniment, repeated throughout the first several pages, suggest perhaps a "war symphony" or the *Weltschmerz* of Movement I of Mahler's Sixth Symphony, as does the angular, often screeching theme in the violins.[130] This dark mood eventually dissipates into a coloristic haze, characterized by a dearth of metrical tension and enhanced by the glockenspiel. Movement II, a buffa version of the symphonic Scherzo, is replete with jerky, square motives, although terse duple-meter fanfares recall Movement I. In the Trio, however, a sentimental violin solo in waltz time with an "oom-pah-pah" accompaniment takes over, as if fin de siècle café music was responding to the *Angst* of Movement I. A brief interlude with free counterpoint leads to a return of the Scherzo, now considerably truncated.

In Movement III, Recitativo-Lento, Orrego-Salas sustains a cello-dominated recitative against some arresting harmonies, which finally yield to a *più mosso* section, nearly at the movement's halfway mark. In the Interludio (two measures before Reh. M), the brass introduce the barest fragment of a new theme, one that begs for completion. Ostensibly in a major key, it also hints at optimism and thus at the narrative of *per aspera ad astra* familiar from many nineteenth-century symphonies. After a few brief fanfares, the gong cuts through the dying pizzicato in the strings and Movement IV begins, *attacca*. Over its course, the fragment blossoms into full realization as a Mixolydian theme, amid bustling accompaniment figures. The return of the screeching violin theme of the Allegro maestoso, along with the relentless march, suggests that light may not come, although the blazing E-flat major chord that concludes the thirty-two-minute work ultimately settles the question. Not for nothing did Ross Parmenter of the *New York Times* comment that Orrego-Salas's symphony was a "major work . . . deeply serious in its expressiveness."[131]

Like Orrego-Salas, Gustavo Becerra studied with Santa Cruz; and like his teacher, he was also a diplomat, serving as cultural attaché to West Germany. The few orchestral works he composed span his career: a *Divertimento for Orchestra* (1955), *Variationen oder?* (1992), and three symphonies, the first of which was performed in 1958 at the inaugural Inter-American Festival in Washington, DC. By this time, Fré Focke (1910–89), the Dutch pianist and serialist composer (he was former pupil of Anton Webern) had emigrated to Santiago, where he had a large class of composition students. Increasingly attracted to the avant-garde, Becerra helped establish Taller 44 (Studio 44), an institute for experimental composers such as Luis Advis (1935–2004), Gabriel Brnčić (b. 1942), Roberto Falabella (1926–58), and Fernando García (b. 1930). Other Chilean composers of orchestral music include Eduardo Maturana (1920–2003), Abelardo Quinteros (b. 1923), and José Vicente Asuar (1933–2017), a pioneer in Latin American electroacoustic music. Leni Alexander (1924–2005) was born in Breslau (today Wrocław, Poland). A Jew, she moved to Chile with her parents when Hitler came to power. When Augusto

Pinochet seized power in 1973 (with the aid of the Central Intelligence Agency), she underwent a second exile, now moving to France. She marked this event with two orchestral works, *Partitureintrag: 11/9/1974* and *. . . ils se sont perdus dans l'espace étoilé . . .* in memory of the protest singer Víctor Jara, murdered by Pinochet in the early days of the coup.[132]

Several composers were involved in politics: García's massive *América insurrecta* for orchestra and chorus (on a text by Pablo Neruda) is dedicated to the Chilean Communist Party, while Maturana's *Responso para el guerrillero* pays homage to Ernesto (Che) Guevara.[133] Some left South America, such as Falabella, who studied at the CLAEM but moved to Barcelona in 1974. Particularly prolific in the orchestral realm is León Schidlowsky (1931–2022), who emigrated to Israel in 1969 but maintained ties in Chile over his long career. Some of his seventy-plus orchestral works, such as *Absalom* and *I Will Lay My Hand Upon My Mouth*, were inspired by the Hebrew Bible.[134] Other stemmed from his commitment to social justice: Schidlowsky told Copland that his *Nueva York*, composed in 1965, was dedicated to "my black brothers of Harlem."[135]

A later generation includes Guillermo Rifo (1945–2022), who combines popular and classical elements in his compositions, including arrangements of Violeta Parra's song "Gracias a la vida." Eduardo Cáceres (b. 1955), similarly prolific, has written several orchestral works, including *Danza* for orchestra, composed upon receiving the Charles Ives Prizes given by the Instituto Chileno Norteamericano Cultural of Santiago (table 7.5). Some younger composers, such as Aliosha Solovera (b. 1963), have focused more on smaller ensembles. Chañaral Ortega-Miranda (b. 1973), who studied in Paris and Buenos Aires and worked with Jonathan Harvey and Brian Ferneyhough, also has composed some symphonic music. Miguel Farías (b. 1983), born in Venezuela, is the recipient of several international prizes (table 7.5). René Silva (b. 1984) has written several pieces for chamber orchestra. Valeria Valle (b. 1979), Katherine Bachmann (b. 1983), and Tamara Miller (b. 1992) have all composed symphonic music as well, and the organization Resonancia Femenina promotes music by women composers.

Peru

During the colonial period, Peru enjoyed a splendid tradition of religious music. One center was Cuzco, the capital of the Incan empire and whose cathedral was built over the remains of an Incan temple that was razed to the ground when Pizarro and his men entered the region. The cathedral was a center of musical life, employing from 1591 the Spanish-born Gutierre Fernández Hidalgo (ca. 1547–1623), one of the most respected sixteenth-century composers of the Americas and who wrote villancicos, hymns, motets, and other religious music. Beyond the cathedral, instrumental music figured in worship at monasteries, convents, and the nearby Seminario de San Antonio Abad. Civic ceremonies and processions marked special occasions with trumpets, drums, shawms, bells, sackbuts, and cornetts.[136] Andean songs and dances often coexisted with European music, and native musicians sometimes worked in religious institutions.[137] Yet Spanish singers (mostly clergy), ranked higher than Andean instrumentalists, especially the *ministriles* or woodwind players who, along with harpists, *bajoneros* (bassoonists), and violinists, give credence to the notion that instrumental music was the "manual labor" of colonial-era music.[138] Africans were fewer in number but no less audible, since as in Renaissance Europe, many became trumpeters.[139]

Even more impressive was Lima, the capital of the Viceroyalty of Peru and next to Mexico City the most powerful administrative center of Spanish America. Chroniclers described processions attended by extravagantly attired clergy, military, and officials, on which the viceroy looked down from his palace, noting the "excellent music" of trumpets, drums, and shawms.[140] Sometimes elaborate floats were involved: one, constructed to resemble Noah's Ark, housed two groups of instrumental musicians. Villancicos were performed for *autos-da-fé*, at which six thousand to twelve thousand people eager to see heretics meet their fates would flock, all to the accompaniment of instrumental music. So exuberant were these sounds that one poet, writing of the music that marked the birth of Philip IV's son Baltasar Carlos in 1639, rhapsodized that "the fifes cried out . . . the bugles whinnied; the trumpets roared; the cornetts shrieked." At one parade, about five hundred dancers of African descent participated. More intimate musical-religious performances took place in convents: one visitor to the convent of Nuestra Señora de la Encarnación recalled that thirty or so nuns would "sing and play a variety of instruments."[141]

The main site for instrumental music was the cathedral, however, consecrated in 1572. One of several celebrated chapelmasters employed at Lima was the Spanish-born Tomás Torrejón y Velasco (1644–1728), who we know today mainly through *La púrpura de la rosa* (The Blood of the Rose), the first opera of the Americas. For its 1701 performance, Torrejón y Velasco provided some newly composed music and arranged passages from an existing score of the same title by the Spanish composer Juan Hidalgo.[142] His villancicos, for voices and string ensemble, were widely performed in Spanish America. Another eminent chapelmaster was Roque Ceruti (1683–1760), who took the post in 1728. A native of Milan, he admired Corelli and wrote sacred music that showcased brilliant string writing and Italian taste in general. The first native-born composer of church music was José de Orejón y Aparicio (1706–65). Among his works is a *Passion for Good Friday*, scored for double chorus and orchestra. Another chapelmaster, José Bernardo Alzedo (1798–1878), wrote masses and villancicos and the Peruvian national anthem.

After independence, initially declared in 1821, another Italian immigrant, Carlo Enrico Pasta (1817–98), composed *Atahualpa* (1873–75), an opera on the plight of the last Incan king. Opera and salon music were the favored genres, although some composers ventured into orchestral music. José María Valle Riestra (1859–1925), who studied in London, Paris, and Berlin, wrote two operas, *Ollanta* and, like Pasta, an *Atahualpa*. A *Coronation March* from the latter is sometimes performed independently; another orchestral work is his *En Oriente: boceto para orquesta*. Daniel Alomía Robles (1871–1942) transcribed many Andean melodies and composed 238 original compositions, including a celebrated stage work, *El cóndor pasa*. Federico Gerdes (1873–1953) studied in Leipzig and was mainly a conductor but composed a *Marcha festiva* for orchestra. Vicente Stea (1884–1943), born in Italy, wrote a prize-winning *Sinfonía Autóctona* (1934) that incorporates Incan themes; he also composed a Symphony in F Minor as well as several smaller works. Renzo Bracesco (1888–1982) was born in Lima and studied in Milan. His Divertimento for chamber orchestra is published. Luis Pacheco de Céspedes (1895–1982), born in Lima, studied in Paris until the outbreak of World War II. Upon returning to Peru, he became very interested in local culture, as the titles of several of his orchestral works from the 1940s confirm, such as *Danzas sobre un tema indio* or *Gloria y ocaso del Inca* (see table 7.5). He also composed two symphonies. Also in Paris until the outbreak of the war was Raoul de Verneuil (1901–75), of French descent; he composed an orchestral work, *Las llamas* (Danza peruana).

Two other Europeans arrived in Lima: the Belgian violinist, composer, and musicologist Andrés Sas (1900–1967) and the German composer, ethnomusicologist, and author Rodolfo (Rudolph) Holzmann (1910–92). Sas, who opened his own conservatory, plunged into the indigenous heritage, composing several orchestral works such as *La Parihuana* (a *parihuana* is a South American flamingo). Holzmann introduced techniques of the Second Viennese School to Peruvian musicians. He also helped several Peruvian composers not entirely comfortable with orchestration, orchestrating a Prelude by Roberto Carpio Valdes (1900–1986), for example, and two movements of *Suite Cuzquena* by Franciso González-Gamarra (1890–1972). Teodoro Valcárcel (1900–1942), whose originality Slonimsky praised, was of indigenous parentage and studied with Felipe Pedrell in Spain. One of his several orchestral works (three of which Holzmann orchestrated) is the symphonic poem *En las ruinas del Templo del Sol* (In the Ruins of the Temple of the Sun, 1940), inspired by the Incan site Machu Picchu (table 7.5).

The next generations of Peruvian symphonic composers include José Malsio (1924–2007) and Francisco Bernardo Pulgar Vidal (1929–2012). Perhaps best known is Enrique Iturriaga (1918–2019), who studied at Lima's National Conservatory with Holzmann and then in Paris with Arthur Honegger. Of his half-dozen orchestral works, his *Sinfonía Junín y Ayacucho* of 1974 won a government-sponsored contest for the symphonic work that best depicted the battles against the Spanish at Junín and Ayacucho in 1824 during the wars of independence. Especially interesting is Iturriaga's *Homenaje a Stravinski* (Homage to Stravinsky) of 1971, scored for orchestra (without upper strings) and cajón, an Afro-Peruvian box drum made of wood and played with the hands. In his nineties, Iturriaga became something of a YouTube personality, and his engaging remarks on his music can be heard around the world.[143] Among Iturriaga's students is Sadiel Cuentas (b. 1973), who has written some electroacoustic music and the orchestral work *Cuentas: obertura sencilla* (Tales: Simple Overture).

Celso Garrido-Lecca (b. 1926) studied with Sas and Holzmann. Unusually receptive to different aesthetics (his musical approach has been described as "polystylistic"), he went to Santiago, where he worked with Santa Cruz, "the Chilean Hindemith," and also Fré Focke, the Dutch serialist mentioned above.[144] His ties to the United States were strong, in part because of Copland. Garrido-Lecca studied at the Berkshire Music Center and his *Sinfonía en un movimiento*, commissioned by the Fleisher Music Collection of Philadelphia, opened the 1961 Inter-American Music Festival in Washington, DC; another orchestral work, *Laudes*, was performed at the 1965 festival. Also in 1965, he commemorated the Incan heritage in his *Elegía a Machu Picchu*, commissioned by the German conductor Hermann Scherchen. An entire album of Garrido-Lecca's music is available on the Naxos label. César Bolaños (1931–2012), known mainly for electroacoustic and mixed-media compositions, wrote only a few orchestral works, including *Ensayo* (Essay) of 1956. In *Ñacahuasu* of 1970, scored for chamber orchestra and speaker, excerpts of Ernesto ("Che") Guevara's diaries are declaimed against an orchestral backdrop. (The Ñacahuasu was a group of guerillas led by Guevara.)

Edgar Valcárcel (1932–2010), nephew of Teodoro, took full advantage of international study. After working with Sas in Lima, he received a scholarship to attend Hunter College in New York City, where he studied with Donald Lybbert, a student of Elliott Carter and Otto Luening. During 1963–64, he was a scholarship student at the CLAEM, where he worked mainly with Ginastera. Thanks to a Guggenheim Foundation grant, Valcárcel pursued electroacoustic music at the Columbia-Princeton Center with Vladimir Ussachevsky during the years 1966–68. In his compositions, Valcárcel explored aleatory, polytonality, and integral serialism but also drew extensively on native Peruvian elements, as in his orchestral work *Checán II*, premiered in 1970 by the Mexican conductor Luis Herrera de la Fuente. The title refers to the word for "love" in Moche, an indigenous language of Northwest Peru spoken by a civilization known for making ceramic figures engaged in erotic acts. In *Checán II*, Valcárcel uses string harmonics, extreme ranges, rapidly shifting chromatic clusters, and flutter tonguing, all complemented by a strong presence in the brass.

Pozzi Escot, born in Lima in 1933, spent much of her youth in France and eventually became a US citizen, teaching theory at the New England Conservatory of Music. Her orchestral works have been performed in the United States, among them *Sands*, which Sarah Caldwell premiered in New York City in 1975.[145] Teófilo Álvarez (b. 1944), Douglas Tarnawiecki (b. 1948), José Carlos Campos (b. 1957), and Jorge Villavicencio Grossman (b. 1973) have composed orchestral music as well. Gabriela Lena Frank, born in California in 1978 to a Peruvian Chinese mother and a father of Lithuanian Jewish heritage, is a US citizen inspired by her Peruvian ancestry. She recalls that "while studying Bach's counterpoint, similar melodic treatments in Andean duo-panpipe songs from [her] mother's old LP records would come to mind," just as "Paganini's *Caprices* conjured up a hidden remembrance of the frenetic energy of Peruvian *kashwa* dances" (courtship circle dances).[146] Frank has studied Andean music in depth, as demonstrated in her orchestral works *Elegía andina* (Andean Elegy) of 2000 and *Leyendas: An Andean Walkabout* for string orchestra (2003, originally written in 2001 for string quartet). To date, she has composed seventeen orchestral works, and major US orchestras have played her music (table 7.5). Of roughly the same generation is Antonio Gervasoni Flórez-Estrada (b. 1973), who has received several prizes. Between 2009 and 2013 he directed the School of Music of the Universidad Peruana de Ciencias Aplicadas, where he teaches composition. Among his several orchestral works is *Fantastic episodes*, published by the American Society of Composers, Authors, and Publishers–affiliated press Cayambis, which specializes in Latin American music.

Bolivia

Over the first half of the sixteenth century, the Spanish conquered the Indigenous peoples of what is now Bolivia. The economy depended on mining, with Potosí affording a rich vein of silver. Due mainly to the Jesuits, the main musical centers were La Plata (Sucre after 1839), La Paz, Cochabamba, and Concepción.[147] Also, in missions at Moxos and Chiquitos, the Jesuits taught the Indians singing, instrument making, and instrumental techniques. Some religious processions incorporated native dances, and archives preserve some large-scale liturgical works in the Chiquitano language.[148]

Because Bolivia was part of the Viceroyalty of Peru until 1776, the history of its music is intertwined with that of Peru. Gutierre Fernández Hidalgo moved to Sucre having served as chapelmaster at Cuzco. Another highly regarded composer was Juan de Araujo (1646–1712), a pupil of Torrejón y Velasco, who worked in Sucre between 1680 and 1712. Over two hundred of his works are in the Sucre archives. They include liturgical music but also *negritos* and *jácaras*, lively vocal genres with alternating meters that were as common in the theater as in church. The cathedral at La Plata boasted a music school and a library that acquired works from Europe and Mexico City.[149] By the beginning of the eighteenth century, the cathedral chapter's musical forces, singers, and instrumentalists totaled around fifty.

In 1809, the struggle for independence began and in 1825, the republic of Bolivia was proclaimed, with La Paz as the legislative and judicial capital and Sucre the constitutional capital. In both locales, musical life was largely dominated by salon music and opera although the cathedral remained an important venue.[150] In Sucre, the chapelmaster Pedro Jiménez de Abril Tirado (1780–1856) sought to maintain the level of music making of the Araujo years, writing religious music but also minuets, symphonies, and a national anthem.[151] In 1833, the Spanish-born Mariano Pablo Rosquellas (1790–1856) arrived in Sucre, founding a Sociedad Filarmónica y Drámatica there two years later. Among his orchestral works is an overture called *El Pampero*. (Rosquellas had resided in Argentina before moving to Bolivia.) Two other composers wrote marches for orchestra: Eloy Salón (1842–89) composed a funeral march; and Alfredo Ballivián (1831–74), son of President José Ballivián, composed a "Great Military March for Orchestra." Additional societies were formed between 1880 and 1900, such as a Sociedad Haydn and a Sociedad Filarmónica in La Paz. In 1908, a conservatory was established there, and in 1910, a Círculo de Música.

Some composers active at the turn of the twentieth century wrote music that highlighted Bolivia's history. Teófilo Vargas Candia (1868–1961), a folklorist and choirmaster at the Cathedral at Cochabamba, published harmonizations of folk songs but also a symphonic poem, *La coronilla*. First performed in 1942, it marked a battle of May 27, 1812, when women armed with sticks and frying pans charged into the Spanish enemy lines.[152] Antonio González Bravo (1885–1961), who introduced the Dalcroze method into the Bolivian school system, orchestrated Aymara melodies in his *Trova a la Vírgen de Copacabana*, his homage to the basilica on the shore of Lake Titicaca.[153] Eduardo Caba (1890–1953), born in La Paz, studied in Madrid with Joaquín Turina and in Buenos Aires with Felipe Boero. The modal and pentatonic structures of his symphonic poem *Potosí* are intended to suggest indigenous life of the Andes.

José María Velasco-Maidana (1899–1989), also a film director, was one of the more renowned Bolivian composers of this period. He was also a beneficiary of cultural diplomacy: Velasco-Maidana spent nine months in Germany at the invitation of the Third Reich, where he prepared programs for shortwave radio broadcasts to South America and oversaw rehearsals of his ballet *Amerindia* (1934–35)—with three full months of rehearsal time—for its premiere in 1938 by the Berlin Opera and the Ballet corps of the *Deutsche Tanzbühne* to the enthusiastic response of audiences at the Theatersaal der staatlichen Hochschule and later at the Volkstheater.[154] In other words, just as the United States was beginning to foment solidarity in the hemisphere through cultural diplomacy, the Nazis had undertaken similar strategies. Other orchestral compositions by Velasco-Maidana, such as the symphonic poems *Cuento brujo* (1935) and *Los Khuzillos* (1936), are based on Aymara-Quechua legends. Back in La Paz, he conducted the Orquesta Sinfónica Nacional and started a concert series.

Also affected by Nazism was Erich Eisner (1897–1956), a Jewish musician born in Prague and once an assistant to Bruno Walter. Eisner was sentenced to indefinite detention in the Dachau concentration camp but managed through various connections to flee to Bolivia. His new home had its share of Nazi sympathizers, as elsewhere in the Americas, and Eisner did not always feel completely free, although his *Cantata boliviana*, for orchestra and voices, was a gesture of gratitude.[155] In 1945, when the Orquesta Sinfónica Nacional was established by government decree, Eisner served as its first music director. He gave it his all, copying by hand scores of Mahler and Bruckner and arranging them for the meager forces available to him. Like Holzmann in Peru, Eisner also orchestrated works by Bolivian composers, including Humberto Viscarra Monje (1898–1969), José Lavadenz (1883–1967), Armando Palmero (1899–1968), Teófilo Vargas (1866–1961), Simeón Roncal (1870–1953), and Eduardo Caba Valsalia (1890–1953).[156] One of Eisner's students, Atiliano Auza (b. 1928), studied at the CLAEM with Ginastera and Davidovsky, and in 1970 he composed *Estructuras* for chamber orchestra. Another, Gustavo Navarre (1931–2006), composed a symphony in two movements. Jaime Mendoza-Nava (1925–2005) studied at the Juilliard School and then worked with Boulanger. In addition to several film scores, Mendoza-Nava wrote three symphonic poems: *Don Alvaro*, *Antawara*, *Pachamama*.

Alberto Villalpando Buitrago (b. 1940) also studied at CLAEM. After returning to Bolivia, Villalpando established himself as a film composer and also wrote electroacoustic music, earning himself the moniker "the father of contemporary Bolivian music."[157] Villalpando is inspired by the geography of La Paz and feels rooted to his native country. He has written around ten works for orchestra, including *Música para orquesta* Nos. 1–5, composed between 1974 and 2003. *Música para orquesta* No. 1 describes La Paz acoustically.[158] An earlier work, *Liturgías fantásticas*, was completed in 1963 (that is, his period at the CLAEM) although it premiered only in 2000. Enhanced with quotations of the *Dies Irae*, the work represents Holy Week (*Semana Santa*); *Mística* núm. 7, for chamber orchestra, is also inspired by worship. Some of Villalpando's orchestral music includes electronics, such as *Yamar y Armor*, a ballet score for voice, tape and orchestra, or enhanced instruments, such as *Los diálogos de Tunupa* for string orchestra and viola profunda (a tenor viola).

Other living Bolivian composers are committed to their indigenous heritage. Cergio Prudencio (b. 1955), born in La Paz, founded an orchestra consisting of indigenous instruments, the Orquesta Experimental de Instrumentos Nativos. Among his works for that ensemble is *La ciudad* of 1980, to which he wrote an "answer" piece in 2005, *Otra ciudad*, scored for an orchestra of *sikus* (*siku* is the Aymara word for "panpipe"). The recipient of a Guggenheim Fellowship in 2008, Prudencio has also written electroacoustic music. From 2020, Prudencio has held a high position in the Ministry of Cultures, Decolonization, and Depatriarchalization, established the same year. Willy Pozadas (b. 1946) has used native instruments in works such as *Amtasiñani* (1986), performed by the Orquesta Experimental de Instrumentos Nativos. Among his works for traditional orchestra is the symphonic poem *Ancestrofonías para orquesta sinfónica* of 2002.

Ecuador

Several Indigenous peoples lived in Ecuador before the ascent of the Inca. In 1535, an order of Flemish Franciscans founded a convent in Quito, where they taught the natives to play shawms, sackbuts, flutes, trumpets, and stringed instruments. As one Franciscan observed, the Indians "easily learn to read and write and to play any instrument."[159] The Colegio de San Andrés, founded in 1555, focused on music education for natives. Several prodigies distinguished themselves, including two who took the European names Cristóbal of Caranqui and Juan Bermejo. The latter was a fine flutist and keyboardist.

The Quito cathedral had an excellent reputation for music. One chapelmaster was Diego Lobato (*ca*. 1538–*ca*. 1610), who assumed the position in 1574. A mestizo who claimed royal Incan blood, Lobato also became a priest, which members of the white Spanish clergy opposed, even though his fluency in Quechua could prove advantageous in evangelization. Church documents refer to his compositions although these have not been found. Lobato's successor was the peripatetic Gutierre Fernández Hidalgo (*ca*. 1547–1623), whom we have met in Peru and Bolivia, although he worked in Quito only a short time. Between 1682 and 1695, Manuel Blasco (*ca*. 1628–*ca*. 1696) served as chapelmaster and became the most eminent composer after Fernández Hidalgo. Outside the church, musicians were engaged for civic occasions, including players of harps, violins, "and other sonorous instruments," as one chronicler puts it.[160] Other centers for music were Cuenca and Guayaquil.

Known as the Audiencia de Quito, Ecuador was incorporated in the Viceroyalty of Peru. In 1822, when independence was declared, the nation became part of La Gran Colombia, a short-lived republic roughly encompassing modern-day Colombia, Panama, and Venezuela, as well as Ecuador. In 1830, one year before La Gran Colombia dissolved, Ecuador exited to become the Republic of Ecuador. Players in the orchestra at the Quito cathedral now addressed one another as "Citizen."¹⁶¹ A music school was established in Quito under the direction of the composer Agustín Baldeón (1815–47), who composed six *sinfonías*.¹⁶² He also founded a Sociedad Musical de Santa Cecilia de Quito. By the 1830s, there were so many fine instrumentalists in Quito that a theater impresario regretted having paid the travel expenses of musicians brought in from Lima. Clergy continued to affect Ecuadorian musical life. Fray Tomas Mideros, an Augustinian, started an orchestra, and others wrote both religious and secular music. The Quito Conservatory was established in 1870, and the following year, a German Jesuit then teaching in Ecuador wrote of the *quiteños* and their "natural bent" for music—adding, however, that the results were not always "calculated to soothe European ears."¹⁶³

In 1903, Domenico Brescia (1866–1939), Italian-born but resident in Chile, came from Santiago to direct the conservatory in Quito, a post he held until 1911. Despite his status as an outsider, he was one of the first composers in Ecuador to advocate for musical nationalism in the country, especially in his *Sinfonia ecuatoriana*. He eventually settled in San Francisco and taught music theory at Mills College. It was during this period that he wrote *Life: Preamble and Three Episodes for Orchestra*, which figured in a play at the exclusive Bohemian Grove; in 1926 he tackled *Truth*, also a Bohemian Grove project. Another director of the Quito Conservatory was Pedro Pablo Traversari (1874–1956), whose several orchestral works include the symphonic suite *Glorias andinas*. Segundo Luis Moreno (1882–1972) studied with Brescia. More a scholar and author than composer, he nonetheless wrote a *Preludio* for orchestra, two overtures, a *Suite Ecuatoriana*, and a "symphonic march," *La coronación* (table 7.5).¹⁶⁴

The music of Luis Humberto Salgado (1903–77) is still played today. He was once a pianist in silent films, and his orchestral music includes a symphonic suite on the familiar theme of *Atahualpa*.¹⁶⁵ Little is known about his eight symphonies, although the Sixth Symphony was recorded at the Festival de la Cultura Iberoamericana in Moscow in 2003; he also wrote two ballet scores. A multifaceted composer (one scholar calls him "the Quixote of music") Salgado departed from more academic styles to pay homage to the *pasillo*, a popular Ecuadoran genre (table 7.5).¹⁶⁶

Among the next generation of Ecuadoran composers, Gerardo Guevara (b. 1930) studied with Boulanger on a United Nations Educational, Scientific and Cultural Organization grant. Although he wrote mainly for voice and piano (sometimes with Quechua texts), he composed the ballet score *Yaguar shungo* in 1958; he also wrote two orchestral works. Mesías Maiguashca (b. 1938), born in Quito, began studies in his native country but received a Fulbright grant to enroll at the Eastman School of Music (1959–63). He also studied at the CLAEM and then in Europe, where he has remained. Greatly influenced by Stockhausen, Maiguashca worked in the electronic music studio of the Westdeutscher Rundfunk and in 1990 was appointed professor of electroacoustic music at the University of Freiburg. He mainly writes electroacoustic music but his *Iridiscente* of 2009 is scored for traditional orchestra, sound objects, and electronics. Milton Estévez (b. 1947) studied classical guitar at the conservatory in Quito and also earned a degree in architecture. He then went to the École Normale de Musique de Paris and the Sorbonne, where he studied electroacoustic and computer music. Most of his orchestral works call for electroacoustics although his *Sin título* (2010), commissioned by the Louisville Orchestra, is for string orchestra. Arturo Rodas (b. 1951) studied with Luciano Berio in Provence and with his compatriot Maiguashca in Metz, writing some works for orchestra.

Diego Luzuriaga (b. 1955) studied first in Ecuador and then at the Manhattan School of Music. In 1993 he received a Guggenheim Fellowship and earned a doctorate from Columbia University. He is credited with writing the first Ecuadorean opera, *Manuela y Bolívar*, about the storied relationship between Simón Bolívar and his mistress, which premiered in Sucre in 2006.[167] His *Responsorio* (a movement of his orchestral work *Liturgia*) has been performed as part of the program *Caminos del Inka*, a project of the conductor Miguel Harth-Bedoya, based in Texas. Luzuriaga has received commissions from major ensembles, such as the Tokyo Philharmonic Orchestra. Juan Campoverde Quezada (b. 1964) studied in Ecuador. He received a Fulbright grant to study at the Cincinnati Conservatory of Music; he took his PhD at the University of California, San Diego. His music for orchestra includes incidental music and other works (table 7.5). Jorge Oviedo (b. 1974), who studied at the conservatory in Quito, is an experienced conductor, directing national bands and orchestras as well as Quito Ensamble 6, created to disseminate both traditional and contemporary Ecuadoran music. Among his orchestral compositions are *Recreaciones*, *Huayra* (for youth orchestra), *Volcanic Suite*, and *Leyenda*, for Andean instruments.

Colombia

Early on in Colombia's history, a clash of identities between the Muisca natives and Spanish colonizers manifested itself musically. Representing the former were conch-shell trumpets and a variety of idiophones that enhanced a complex of song, dance, and ceremony while fifes, trumpets, and drums affirmed the military aims of the colonizers.[168] Some instruments conferred power: Governor Miguel Díaz de Armendariz made it a point to be seen in public with his mistress against a backdrop of trumpet fanfares.[169] The Muisca were eventually silenced in what Colombian musicologist Egberto Bermúdez describes as a "demographic catastrophe": by 1600, 80 percent of the Indigenous population had died. (An initially small number of enslaved Africans grew when gold mining increased.) Gonzalo García Zorro (*ca.* 1548–1617) was the first chapelmaster at the cathedral in Santafé (now Bogotá). A mestizo, he was prevented from advancing because of his race and was replaced in 1584, when the celebrated Gutierre Fernández Hidalgo took over.[170]

On the other hand, domestic music making in the colonial period relied on the vihuela, harp, guitars, and harpsichord, instruments often imported from Spain. Sometimes colonizers and colonists performed jointly, as at a pageant in 1747 at Popayán celebrating the ascension of Ferdinand VI.[171] In 1810, the multiyear process of gaining independence began, and from 1819, Colombia was part of La Gran Colombia, albeit briefly. During the first half of the nineteenth century, pianos were increasingly common in the homes of the elite. Opera and symphonic music began to be cultivated, thanks to figures such as Juan Antonio de Velasco (1802–59), who founded a concert series.[172] In 1847 a philharmonic society was established, presenting its first program in November 1848.[173] Composers of orchestral works included José María Ponce de Léon (1846–82), who studied with Charles Gounod and Ambroise Thomas at the Paris Conservatory. Besides his *Sinfonía sobre temas colombianos* and *Apoteósis a Bolívar: Himno de los Andes y Saludo de Colombia a Chile*, a tribute to the "Liberator," Ponce de León wrote religious music and two operas.[174] Various other composers tried their hand at symphonic music. Andrés Martínez Montoya (1869–1933) worked mainly with bands but composed a symphony, subtitled *Isabel*, that premiered in 1892. Santos Cifuentes (1870–1932), active in establishing music as a profession, wrote several orchestral works in the early 1890s as well as *La soledad*, a descriptive work for orchestra, probably from around 1912.[175] Orchestral works by Pedro Morales Pino (1863–1926) include *Suite Patria* and *Brisas de los Andes* (table 7.5).

The founding of the National Academy of Music in 1882 was a turning point. As of 1910, it became known as the National Conservatory, and many of Colombia's twentieth-century composers were associated with it. Chief among these was Guillermo Uribe Holguín (1880–1971), who, after studying with d'Indy at the Schola Cantorum, directed the Conservatory for twenty-five years. During his tenure, he founded the Sociedad de Conciertos Sinfónicos del Conservatorio, which lasted from 1920 until 1935.[176] The following year saw another important event in Colombian art music: the establishment of the Orquesta Sinfónica Nacional, whose first director, Guillermo Espinosa (1905–90), was active in musical Pan Americanism.

Uribe Holguín was a complicated individual who professed to reject the folkloric gestures of musical nationalism, insisting that "music knows no country."[177] Yet his thirty-odd orchestral works include a *Suite típica* of 1932 and a *Ceremonia indígena* (Indigenous Ceremony) of 1959. In May 1940, the *Suite típica* was featured on a "Salute to the Americas" broadcast on the New York radio stations WABC, WOR, and WEAH (later WNBC), conducted by Espinosa and with an address by Colombian president Eduardo Santos.[178] Of Uribe Holguín's eleven symphonies—the last seven of which he wrote in quick succession between 1956 and 1961—the second is probably the best known (table 7.5). Nicknamed "del Terruño" (From the Homeland), it contains several folkloric rhythms from the Andean region, while its overall form corresponds to European norms. After receiving a prize, the symphony premiered during the Colombian national holidays of 1924. Uribe Holguín's orchestral music has not been widely performed or recorded.[179]

Among his students was Jesús Bermúdez Silva (1884–1969), who also taught at the conservatory and wrote a few orchestral works, including a Symphony in C (table 7.5).[180] One of Silva's students was Adolfo Mejía (1909–73). While enrolled at the conservatory, he won the Ezequiel Bernal prize for his orchestral composition *Pequeña Suite*, thanks to which he was able to study in France with Boulanger and Charles Koechlin, where he remained until the outbreak of World War II. The *Pequeña Suite*, a nationalistic work that contains a cumbia, is still frequently played. Mejía's orchestral works have recently been edited and include two tributes (*homenajes*) to his compatriots: writer Antonio Gómez Restrepo (1869–1947) and scientist Luis López de Mesa (1884–1967) (as shown in table 7.5).[181]

Blas Emilio Atehortúa (1943–2020), a timpanist, violinist, and composer, studied at the Instituto Di Tella where he met Copland during the latter's visit of 1963. (Copland was impressed with the young man's intelligence and musicality, despite what he called "an overdose of conservatory ideas.") Between 1992 and 1994, Atehortúa taught at Duquesne University in Pennsylvania. Among his several works for orchestra is an elegy from 1983 on the death of Ginastera (see table 7.5). The versatile Francisco Zumaqué (b. 1945) studied at National University in Bogotá and then in France to work with Boulanger and Pierre Schaeffer. Zumaqué then served as cultural attaché of the Colombian Embassy in Bonn. As a composer he is at home with electroacoustic music and popular genres such as cumbia and protest songs. Andrés Posada (b. 1954) was born in Medellín, where he began his musical studies before enrolling at the Mannes School of Music in New York. He has written in numerous genres, including several orchestral compositions (table 7.5). Gustavo Parra (b. 1963), a native of Ipiales (western Colombia), has directed several orchestras, among them the Orquesta Sinfónica Nacional. His orchestral works are listed in table 7.5. More recent Colombian composers and sound artists include Carolina Noguera Palau (b. 1978), a native of Cali who studied in the United Kingdom, composing *Autumn Whisperings* for orchestra in 2010. Francisco Lequerica (b. 1978) has also written orchestral music A rising star in the conducting world is Carlos Ágreda (b. 1991) of Bogotá, who has written several orchestral works.

Venezuela

For many, classical music in Venezuela conjures up images of energetic young people delivering flawless performances of Beethoven, Bernstein, or Mahler, whose Second Symphony ("Resurrection") may well be the Venezuelan Youth Orchestra's signature work. These youngsters, many of whom are economically disadvantaged, are but one arm of El Sistema, the network of symphony orchestras that combines music making and social change.[182] Thanks to the late José Antonio Abreu, the visionary music-lover who launched the program in 1975, El Sistema now extends well beyond the touring orchestra of the top players, encompassing 125 musical centers and 350 orchestras, and impacting more than four hundred thousand young Venezuelans. The El Sistema model has also spread to Brazil, where the Bahia Orchestra Project was founded in 2007; branches also exist in the United States and Canada.

Yet European-style classical music established itself only slowly in what is now Venezuela. At the time of the conquest, the region was inhabited by the Mariches (who in turn descended from the Caribes) among other Indigenous peoples, whom Diego de Losada, founder of Caracas, ultimately exterminated. The population as a whole was scarce, with only around two thousand Europeans living in Venezuela by the mid-sixteenth century. Enslaved Africans were eventually brought to work the cocoa plantations. Franciscans and Dominicans were initially the principal missionary orders. In urban centers such as Caracas, celebrations such as the Fiesta de la Naval commemorated the Christian victory over the Turks at Lepanto in 1571. Its observance in the Americas involved at least three groups of musicians: white choir singers from the cathedral gallery; an ensemble of freedmen, many African descendants (musical details unknown); and a band of white and mixed-race buglers, trumpeters, drummers, fifers, and shawn players.[183]

Venezuela may have been one of the poorer areas of the Spanish empire, but by the eighteenth century, Caracas was a principal center for religious music. Composers included the mixed-race Juan Manuel Olivares (1760–97), who wrote a Good Friday Lamentation for violins, flutes, French horns, viola, and bass. José Ángel Lamas (1775–1814) composed numerous concerted works, including a *Popule meus* for violins, oboes, trumpets, viola, and bass, and a Mass in D for violins, oboes, horns, viola, cello, and bass.[184] In 1783 a music academy opened in Caracas and secular music became a greater presence. Venezuelan composers commemorated stirrings toward independence, which began in 1810. José María Isaza (1786–1840) composed *Canción a los Libertadores del sur* for soprano solo, chorus, and orchestra. His younger compatriot Juan José Landaeta (1780–1814), the son of free mulattos, wrote the music that was eventually adopted as the national anthem, "Gloria al bravo pueblo," in addition to religious works. Composers often assumed various roles: Lino Gallardo (*ca.* 1775–1837) was a church music composer, the director of an academy, and occasional conductor of a Sociedad Filarmónica. In 1854 the Teatro Caracas was inaugurated.

As for instrumental music without voices, the Caracas-based Juan Meserón (1779–1842) wrote two symphonies. A "musical dynasty," the Montero family contributed powerfully to instrumental music. José Lorenzo Montero (*ca.* 1800–1857) composed approximately 120 works, which were recently located in the National Library in Caracas; they establish him as a principal composer of the early postindependence period—that is, from circa 1830–60. Montero's Symphony No. 4 is the subject of a recent musicological study.[185] Other orchestral works, such as *Overture for Large Orchestra* and *Sinfonía concertada*, are now published.

Another member of the Montero family was José Angel (1839–81), who was chapelmaster at Caracas Cathedral and wrote religious music, zarzuelas, and the occasional orchestral piece, such as *Two Masonic Marches*. Federico Villena (1835–1900) wrote mainly church and salon music along with *zarzuelas*, but he also composed some orchestral music as well.

Two fundamental figures in Venezuelan twentieth-century music were the composer-teachers Emilio Vicente Sojo (1887–1974) and Juan Bautista Plaza (1898–1965). Armed with innovative pedagogical strategies and eager to reform musical infrastructure, they galvanized musical circles. Both witnessed the founding of the Orquesta Sinfónica de Venezuela, officially established in 1930, where artists of the stature of Stravinsky and Wilhelm Furtwängler guest conducted.[186] Plaza especially cast a wide net, embracing the music of the colonial past, musical nationalism, and twentieth-century trends with equal enthusiasm. Active in sacred music, he studied on a scholarship in Rome before becoming chapelmaster of the Caracas Cathedral, a post he held for twenty-five years. Deeply committed to enhancing Venezuelan musical life beyond the academy, conservatory, and church, he reached the general public through newspaper articles, radio broadcasts, and lectures. In 1942, Plaza visited the United States as a guest of the Pan American Union and introduced his US colleagues to Venezuelan colonial-period music, performing *Popule meus* and the Gloria of a Mass in D, both by José Ángel Lamas, along with other works.[187]

As a composer, Plaza was influenced by Romanticism, Impressionism, Neoclassicism, atonality, and nationalism to varying degrees, like others of his generation.[188] He is probably best known for his nationalist works, although in several of these Venezuelan referents are obscure. One of the more striking of Plaza's orchestral works (table 7.5) is *Vigilia* (Vigil, 1928). He vacillated between calling it a "small-scale symphonic poem" (*pequeño poema sinfónico*) and a "lyric poem" (*poema lírico*).[189] In fact, *Vigilia* is his longest orchestral work, lasting some fifteen minutes. The lyric element is conspicuous, however, as he based the work on the eponymous sonnet from the set *Sonetos espirituales* (Spiritual Sonnets) by the Spanish poet Juan Ramón Jiménez (1881–1958). It tells of a lover haunted by images of his beloved and unable to sleep. Not coincidentally, Plaza himself was "haunted" by Nolita Pietersz, whom he met early in 1928 and eventually married. The work floats along on several melodic fragments, some of which are derived from the pentatonic motive announced at the outset by the English horn. (A second pentatonic theme, 6 mm. after Reh. B, recalls Puccini.) Another motive consists of an elaborated descending major scale, first heard in the violins at Reh. C and perhaps expressing resignation to insomnia. Plaza uses added-note chords (harp, before Reh. A) and subtleties such as the unresolved V/I in m. 7, which subsequently juxtaposes an A-natural against the A-flat pedal in the low strings. Tonality is never far off, however, as many affirmations of tonal center attest, especially the A-flat major chord of the final cadence. Emphasizing English horn, viola, harp, and intermittent horns, Plaza's timbral palette is often dusky. One contrast, however, is the brass-dominated passage at Reh. G with its strongly profiled rhythms; perhaps this is the point at which the lover cries out "El dormir ¡ay de mí! se me ha olvidado" (Sleep, ah! it has forgotten me). The tender violin solo just after Reh. C is surely a secret utterance. Plaza wrote *Vigilia* with no small degree of optimism given that in 1928 Caracas had no ensemble that could perform it. When the work finally premiered in October 1938, critics reacted enthusiastically.[190]

Caracas gained prominence when the Cuban-born critic, novelist, and musicologist Alejo Carpentier (1904–80), then living in the Venezuelan capital, decided to replicate the international festivals at Bayreuth and Salzburg in Caracas but with a focus on Latin American symphonic music through a series of public concerts and a contest for orchestral composition. Thanks to him and the Orquesta Sinfónica de Venezuela and Ignacio Palacios (a generous donor who financed expenses for international jurors, salaries for orchestra personnel and staff, and substantial prize money for competition winners), the first Caracas Festival took place in 1954. Several works discussed in this essay were performed then and at a second festival in 1957.

Another Venezuelan composer was Antonio Estévez Aponte (1916–1988). He is probably best known for his *Cantata criolla* of 1954, which Gustavo Dudamel, music director of the Los Angeles Philharmonic and a product of El Sistema, has promoted in the United States. A composition student of Sojo's, Estévez played oboe in the Orquesta Sinfónica de Venezuela. During 1945–49, he lived in the United States, where he worked with Otto Luening at Columbia University and with Bernstein, Koussevitzky, and Copland at the Berkshire Music Center. It was there that Estévez began his Concerto for Orchestra—completed in 1949, four years after Bartók's definitive essay—which received the Premio Nacional de Música.[191] When it was performed at the first Inter-American Music Festival in Washington, DC (April 1958), one US critic remarked that it was "more international in character than [Estévez's] usual output."[192] The titles of its three movements recall the Western European tradition: Toccata, Passacaglia, and Ricercare, all played *attacca*. Estévez manipulates a three-note motivic cell, which combines a minor third with a minor second and appears in several transpositions and reorderings over the course of the sixteen-minute work. A vigorous introduction blends into the toccata proper, propelled by a repeated-note accompaniment. Eight bars into the movement we hear the basic cell, C♯—D—F, which Estévez promptly varies (clarinet, m. 12). A complementary lyrical motive arises in the strings and the cell jostles against other motives, sometimes hidden in the orchestral texture and sometimes exposed, as in the flute after Reh. 70. Just before Reh. 140, it is given out in the horns (in the form C♯—E—D♯) in augmentation, to be followed by the violins at Reh. 160, again in augmentation. As the texture thins, a passage marked Largo e maestoso evaporates into a unison line for the woodwinds, which leads to the passacaglia theme. It, too, derives from the three-note cell (example 5).

Example 7.5 Estévez. Concerto for Orchestra, mvt. 2. Passacaglia theme

Having introduced the eight-bar theme, Estévez maintains a fairly strict form over the movement, with only a few "parentheses" (i.e., passages without the theme). Mainly, the theme appears in the low strings, with new countermelodies emerging as the variations progress. Coloristic effects, such as the muted horns with dotted rhythms in the fifth statement of the theme, enliven the somber character. At times, Estévez transposes his materials (one measure before Reh. 50, one measure before Reh. 100): elsewhere, he employs thematic fragments, as in the flute line at the *pochissimo più animato*. Three repetitions of the theme, returned to the low strings, precede the transition to Movement III, a ricercare that lives up to its name: a "searching out" or exploration of a motive or theme (flute, mm. 6–9). Here, it undergoes extension, truncation, diminution, and augmentation, with an occasional hint at inversion (Reh. 60 + 5). A section marked Grave e maestoso—"Apotheosis"—reiterates the three-note motive yet again, now as part of a dramatic conclusion.

Plaza and Estévez may be the most prominent Venezuelan composers of orchestral music, but several others have distinguished themselves in this field as well. Plaza's contemporary Juan Vicente Lecuna (1899–1954), a pianist and diplomat (he worked in the Venezuelan Embassy in Washington) composed some orchestral works (table 7.5). Another composer-diplomat was Carlos Figueredo (1909–86), who posted in Paris, Copenhagen, and Madrid and wrote five symphonies, which date from the mid-twentieth century. Critic and composer José Antonio Calcaño (1900–1978) wrote at least one symphony. Evencio Castellanos (1915–84) and his brother Gonzalo (1926–2020) were also important figures. Evencio was a composer, pianist, and organist, employed at the Caracas Cathedral; an entire album dedicated to his works is available on the Naxos label. Gonzalo Castellanos was primarily a conductor until the late 1970s when he stopped to concentrate on composition. Besides orchestral works (table 7.5) he wrote for symphonic band. Inocente Carreño (1919–2016) studied with Sojo and distinguished himself primarily as a nationalist composer. One of his several orchestral works is a tribute to his teacher, *Elegía sobre temas de Vicente Emilio Sojo* (strings, 1980). Carreño also wrote film scores.

Alfredo del Mónaco (1938–2015) studied in Venezuela and at Columbia University. (He also earned a degree in law.) He was a pioneer in Venezuelan electroacoustic music, cofounding the Estudio de Fonología Musical in Caracas in 1966. In 1968 he helped established the Venezuelan branch of the International Society for Contemporary Music. He spent 1969 to 1975 at the Columbia-Princeton Electronic Music Center but, upon returning to Venezuela, he concentrated more on traditional instruments, producing several orchestral works.

Alfredo Rugeles (b. 1949), composer, conductor, and administrator, studied with Estévez and Gonzalo Castellanos. He writes aleatoric music and electroacoustic music but also some orchestral works (table 7.5).

Several Venezuelan women have composed orchestral music. Likely the most celebrated is Teresa Carreño (1853–1917). Known primarily for her virtuosic piano playing, she was also a singer, entrepreneur, and composer; she wrote a Chamber Symphony for Strings (1896), a "free transcription" of one of her string quartets.[193] The scholar, singer, and musical theater composer María Luisa Escobar (1898–1985) wrote a symphony-ballet called *Orquideas Azules* (1941).[194] Blanca Estrella Veroes de Méscoli (1910–86) was the first woman in Venezuela to receive a degree in composition, studying with Sojo among other teachers. She composed chamber works, piano pieces, and songs; her best-known work, however, is the symphonic poem *María Lionza* (1950), influenced by the histories, legends, and myths of the Venezuelan state of Yaracuy. Her *Ballet miniatura* for chamber orchestra is published.[195] Of another generation is Josefina Benedetti (b. 1953): besides composing for a variety of media, including electroacoustics, she served as president of the Juventudes Musicales in Venezuela and the National Philharmonic Orchestra Foundation and as cultural director of the Central University of Venezuela. Among her orchestral compositions is *Citas inocentes* (1996). Adina Izarra (b. 1959) studied with Alfredo del Mónaco and incorporated traditional Venezuelan music into her works, as in *Mujer con telar* (Woman with Loom), scored for an orchestra of Latin American instruments (see table 7.5).

Other Venezuelan orchestral composers born around 1960 include Ricardo Teruel (b. 1959), also a pianist. Besides writing electronic music, in 1985, he composed two orchestral works: *Orquestada num. 6: El fresco aroma de viejos placeres*, and *Orquestada num. 7: La Gran Aldea* (for orchestra or electronic instruments). Paul Desenne (b. 1959) studied in France and performs as a cellist. His compositions also draw on traditional elements and instruments, such as the four-string cuatro. He has written several orchestral compositions, including five symphonies, some with colorful titles, such as *Sinfonía Burocrática ed Amazónica* (2004) (table 7.5). Ricardo Lorenz (b. 1961) has recorded on the Naxos label and won several awards for his works. Like Estévez, he has composed a Concerto for Orchestra. His sense of humor manifests itself in the 2002 work for piano and chamber orchestra, *Fantasía del Equivocado Fritz*, loosely translated as "The Wrong Brahms"—that is, Johannes's brother Fritz, who spent several years in Caracas. Other orchestral scores combine traditional or popular elements with symphonic style, such as *Konex-Konex*, for folk ensemble and orchestra, and *Rumba sinfónica*, for Latin band and orchestra. Luis Ernesto Gómez (b. 1977) began his career with El Sistema and then studied in Venezuela and Peru. His Concerto for Orchestra received first prize in the Antonio Estévez National Composition Competition of the Symphonic Orchestra of Venezuela; the tone poem *El Terremoto del Jueves Santo*, which dates from 2012, marks an earthquake that caused incalculable material and human damage two hundred years earlier (see table 7.5).

Bibliographic Overview

No comprehensive survey of South American orchestral music exists. I have culled the information presented here from general-background sources related to orchestral music, reference works such as the *Diccionario de la música española e hispanoamericana*, genre studies, writings by individual composers, musical analyses, biographical studies (still rare in this repertory), and, in the case of living composers, websites. A useful source for works lists, especially for mid-twentieth-century composers, is COMPOSITORES/COMPOSERS, published by the Pan American Union. A "classic" general source on Latin American music and still worth consulting is the two-volume Mayer-Serra/MÚSICA. A more recent source is Miranda and Tello/LA MÚSICA, volume 4 of a series with the evocative title "The Ongoing Quest: The Particular and the Universal in Latin American Culture" (*La búsqueda perpetua: lo propio y lo universal de la cultura latinoamericana*).

For English-language accounts, Stevenson's work remains fundamental, as in Stevenson/AZTEC INCA, which has been rereleased as part of the University of California Press's Revived Voices series. Many of the composers covered here are discussed in Grove Music Online, albeit quite briefly in the case of lesser-known figures and with works often lacking dates of composition. Fortunately, other Grove entries (Schwartz-Kates/GINASTERA) introduce their respective composers far more substantively. Genre studies include Buch/TANGOS, which treats classical composers who wrote orchestral tangos; another genre study is Livingston-Isenhour and Caracas García/CHORO, which details the historical background of the urban popular genre that inspired more than one Brazilian orchestral composer. A still-useful source is Slonimsky/MUSIC, the result of his journey undertaken at the height of the Good Neighbor period to find orchestral scores by Latin American composers, analyzed in Ros-Fábregas/NICOLAS SLONIMSKY. These scores, many by composers discussed here, are part of the Edwin A. Fleisher Collection of Orchestral Music at the Free Library of Philadelphia (https://libwww.freelibrary.org/assets/pdf/fleisher/Latin-American-works.pdf). Many remain unperformed.

Uruguay and Paraguay. Few regions show the artificiality of present-day borders as markedly as those separating Uruguay, Paraguay, Bolivia, and northern Argentina. On colonial-period music in these territories, Celenza Hartwell and Del Donna/MUSIC AS CULTURAL MISSION offers a solid introduction, which can be complemented by Ayestarán/BARROCO, Waisman/MÚSICA COLONIAL, Illari/CARTA, Illari/ZIPOLI, and other authors cited in the text. Nineteenth-century musical life in Uruguay, principally centered in Montevideo, is discussed in Lange/LA MÚSICA URUGUAY; on the status of European music in Montevideo, see Hess/SAINT-SAËNS. The emblematic Teatro Solís receives detailed treatment in Salgado/TEATRO SOLÍS, to which Salgado/BREVE can serve as a companion.

For Paraguay, studies such as Nawrot/VESPERS and O'Malley/JESUITS amplify those on colonial music listed above. On changing musical attitudes in the nineteenth century, especially in the wake of the War of the Triple Alliance, see Colman/PARAGUAYAN. Slonimsky/MUSIC provides some detail on individual composers. Paraguay's principal composer, Florentín Giménez, is covered in the Paraguayan press, including obituaries since his death in March 2021.

Argentina. Many of the sources on colonial music apply to what is now Argentina. Especially compelling in terms of racial identity are Illari/SLAVE'S PROGRESS and Pedrotti/POBRES. On musical life in the nineteenth century, see Lange/LA MÚSICA ARGENTINA; another general study, albeit focused on Buenos Aires, is d'Urbano/BUENOS AIRES. Jewish musicians fleeing Nazi Germany for Argentina are detailed in Glocer/MELODÍAS; the same author focuses on Guillermo Graetzer (Wilhelm Grätzer) in Glocer/JUDAÍSMO. Women composers of orchestral music are discussed in Dezillio/LAS PRIMERAS. On avant-garde music (some of which involved orchestra) in Argentina and more generally in Latin America, see Herrera/ELITE.

As with several of the major figures in South American classical music, Ginastera has still not been the subject of a serious single-volume life-and-works biography, much less a study that addresses his orchestral works in detail. Suárez Urtubey/GINASTERA, which appeared in 1967, can be read alongside that Argentine scholar's other studies on the composer (1972, 2003); none have been translated into English. Suárez Urtubey, who knew Ginastera, offers a great deal of information, although with little musical analysis. In the absence of a comprehensive biography in English, the Grove article by Schwartz-Kates, cited above, should be read alongside her other studies, including Schwartz-Kates/RESEARCH, with its admirable catalog of works (more detailed than in Grove) and frequent references to orchestral works. The reception of several of Ginastera's orchestral works in the United States is discussed in Hess/REPRESENTING.

Musical analyses of Ginastera's works include Wallace/GINASTERA, which dates from 1964 and thus does not cover his later compositions. Wallace does, however, address Ginastera's Second Symphony ("Elegíaca"), soon to be available for performance. Although Fobes/INVESTIGATION does not discuss the orchestral music, his study offers insights into Ginastera's manipulation of pitch-class relations; the same can be said of Tabor/LATE. Scarabino/GINASTERA invites the reader to track a variety of style traits in the composer's orchestral works from 1930 to 1950, including instances of the "guitar chord," identifiable dance rhythms, and general harmonic and melodic tendencies. Abundant musical examples and charts make it easy enough for the reader unfamiliar with Spanish to follow Scarabino's observations.

Other valuable sources include Corrado/VANGUARDIAS, which explores the music of Paz. This Argentine scholar analyzes several of Paz's works in detail, with numerous musical examples that enable the reader to consider the influence of the Schola Cantorum and Paz's eventual path to serialism. (An earlier study is Sargent/PAZ.) Manso/CASTRO abounds in biographical detail, press clippings, and correspondence, but lacks musical discussion; we can nonetheless learn much about Castro's career as an orchestral conductor, as is also the case with Slim/HOLOGRAPH. Both studies can be complemented by García Muñoz/CASTRO, which emphasizes Castro the conductor, again without musical analysis. Arias/*CORALES CRIOLLOS* analyzes one of Castro's best-known orchestral works.

Brazil. Since the era of the German-born musicologist Francisco Curt Lange (Lange/MINAS GERAIS) various scholars of Brazil's colonial-period music have examined the African presence, including bimusicality (Budasz/RIO DE JANEIRO). Another study of eighteenth-century musical life is Castagna and Trindade/CHAPELMASTERS. In the past two decades, several recordings of eighteenth-century composers active in the churches of Minas Geraís have been released. The most valuable recent study of musical life in Rio de Janeiro is Magaldi/IMPERIAL RIO, in part for the author's contextualization of European influence.

The first biographies of Villa-Lobos appeared in Brazil during the composer's lifetime. He intervened in them so relentlessly, however, that at least one study has been said to approach *auto*biography.[196] Further, in these early studies the reader looks in vain for musical analysis. More recent essays include Appleby/VILLA-LOBOS, which refers in passing to some of the symphonies. Also on a modest scale is Wright/VILLA-LOBOS, which contains next to no commentary on the symphonies but a fair amount on orchestral works such as the choros and the orchestral *Bachianas brasileiras*. Enyart/SYMPHONIES is the only study dedicated solely to the symphonies. The catalog of works, published by the Villa-Lobos Museum in Rio de Janeiro (Museu Villa-Lobos/OBRA), suffers from some errors but is still a valuable source for information on first performances and publication; the explanatory notes, some of which are by the composer, offer food for thought. The German Brazilian critic Lisa Peppercorn wrote extensively on Villa-Lobos but devotes little space to the orchestral music in Peppercorn/VILLA-LOBOS. The principal Villa-Lobos scholar in the United States, the late Gerard Béhague, made no pretense of publishing a full-scale, critical biography, although Béhague/VILLA-LOBOS contains many valuable observations albeit with little discussion of orchestral music.

Studies of Camargo Guarnieri include Silva/GUARNIERI, which contains much correspondence and primary-source information, along with a detailed works list and an essay on Guarnieri's orchestral works by the Brazilian composer Ricardo Tacuchian. Verhaalen/GUARNIERI, the only full-scale English-language study of Guarnieri, devotes an entire chapter to the orchestral music. The Brazilian musicologist Vasco Mariz offers a detailed catalog of Santoro's works and a sympathetic portrait of the composer in Mariz/SANTORO. Mariz/FIGURAS catalogues orchestral music by lesser-known Brazilian composers.

Chile. Aracena/ARAUCANIAN contains much valuable information on indigenous music, building on ethnomusicological studies of earlier generations. Vera/SWEET PENANCE, a study of music at the Santiago cathedral, challenges the idea that Chilean music flourished only after independence. A valuable study on the long-neglected presence of Afro-Chileans and their musical influence (albeit with less relevance to instrumental classical music) is discussed in Wolf/STYLING. In Claro Valdés/SANTIAGO, a well-regarded musicologist discusses the beginnings of symphonic societies in Santiago during the nineteenth century, which, as noted above, flowed naturally from concerted religious music. A principal Chilean historian was Eugenio Pereira Salas, who was involved with Good Neighbor–era cultural exchange and wrote on music. His prolific writings include Pereira Salas/NOTES, on US-Latin American musical exchange, and Pereira Salas/LA VIDA, on nineteenth-century musical life; Merino/VALPARAISO focuses on the same period but with respect to Valparaiso. Several Chilean composers of the twentieth century deserve a full-scale biography. Two autobiographies, Santa Cruz/MI VIDA and Orrego-Salas/ENCUENTROS, make for thoughtful reading but contain little musical analysis. Studies of more recent composers, such as Paraskevaídis/MATURANA, Fugielle Videla/SCHIDLOWSKY, and Fugielle Videla/LENI ALEXANDER, are a welcome trend, as is Gonzalez/PENSAR, a refreshing survey of major trends and attitudes in Chilean music.

Peru. In recent years, many scholars have tackled music in Peru during the colonial period, including instrumental music. Building on prior work such as Claro Valdés and Chase/MÚSICA DRAMÁTICA, most emphasize Cuzco (Baker/IMPOSING) or Lima (Knighton/MUSIC AND RITUAL). In Lima, the first opera in the Americas was an important step for instrumental music (Stein/*PÚRPURA*). Whereas any number of scholars have researched folk and indigenous music from Peru, classical music is far less studied, although Carrizo/MUSICAL POLYSTLISM on Garrido-Lecca is an exception. More recent composers, such as Valcárcel, Escot, and Frank, are well worthy of study.

Bolivia and Ecuador. With respect to Bolivia, Kennedy/COLONIAL SOURCES surveys musical institutions at Cochabamba, Concepción, and La Plata; on La Plata, see also Illari/POLYCHORAL. Seoane Urioste and Eichmann/LÍRICA explores overlaps between indigenous and European cultures in Bolivia. Some of its nineteenth-century composers are briefly covered in standard sources. Twentieth-century composers are ripe for further study: just as Ramírez/DACHAU tells the moving story of the émigré Jewish musician Erich Eisner in Bolivia, a study of José María Velasco-Maidana would make fascinating reading, including his months in Hitler's Germany under the auspices of cultural diplomacy. Also worthy of further research are those Bolivian composers who embraced their native land despite its less-than-exalted status in the world of classical music. These include Villalpando (Zuleta/VILLALPANDO) and living composers who are especially committed to Bolivia's indigenous heritage, such as Pozadas and Prudencio. A similar situation presents itself with respect to the classical music of Ecuador. Stevenson's studies on the Quito cathedral during the colonial period are still among the most valuable (Stevenson/QUITO); Cuenca and Guayaquil merit similar attention. One champion of Ecuadoran classical music in the United States is John L. Walker, also founder of Cayambis Music Press (Walker/INCANS; Walker/YOUNGER GENERATION). Ketty Wong sheds light on the fascinating composer Luis Salgado (Wong/SALGADO) in addition to her work on Ecuadoran popular genres, which sometimes figure in classical music (Wong/SONG). The multifaceted career of Mesías Maiguashca, who worked on three continents with twentieth-century figures ranging from Copland to Stockhausen, would make a fascinating study.

Colombia and Venezuela. Egberto Bermúdez enhances our understanding of classical music in Colombia in nearly every period. He covers the colonial period (Bermúdez/GOLD) and the turn of the twentieth century (Bermúdez/SANTOS CIFUENTES) in addition to examining broader trends and historiography (Bermúdez/TOWARD), among other studies.

A respected general history is Perdomo Escobar/HISTORIA, which went through several editions. The entertaining autobiography by Colombia's foremost twentieth-century composer, Uribe Holguín/VIDA, can be read profitably alongside Castro Pantoja/ANTAGONISM, the latter shedding light on debate over national identity and "universalism" in Colombia's classical music circles, a topic also addressed in Bermúdez/SIGLO. In Venezuela, studies of colonial-period music revolve around the Caracas Cathedral (Stevenson/MUSICAL LIFE); secular music is discussed in Coifman/SPIRIT. José Lorenzo Montero, a distinguished member of the musical Montero family, wrote several symphonies, as recently explored in Arismendi Noguera/MONTERO. The history of the Orquesta Sinfónica de Venezuela is covered in Calzavara/ORQUESTA. Juan Bautista Plaza's numerous contributions to Venezuelan musical life, including his instrumental compositions, are covered in Labonnville/PLAZA. As elsewhere, women composers in Venezuela remain under researched, although Lunar Romero/MESCOLI is a welcome exception.

Notes

1. Ginastera/ORQUESTAS, p. 105.
2. Bermúdez/FORTRESSES.
3. Laird/DISSEMINATION.
4. Davies/MAKING MUSIC, p. 64.
5. Baker/IMPOSING, p. 45; see also Bermúdez/URBAN.
6. Vera/SWEET PENANCE, p. 250.
7. A good historical summary of this problem is Waisman/MÚSICA COLONIAL.
8. Pernet/"GENUINE CULTURE," pp. 136–42.
9. Blanco Aguinagua/MODERNISM, pp. 3–16.
10. Pasten/METROPOLIS; García Canclini/MODERNITY.
11. Hess/REPRESENTING, pp. 81–141.
12. Hess/COPLAND, p. xx; Ros-Fábregas/NICOLAS SLONIMSKY.
13. Slonimsky/MUSIC.
14. Hudde/NEGOTIATING.
15. De la Vega/COMPOSERS, p. 164.
16. Composers from Mexico (José Rolón and the Spanish-born Rosa García Ascot) and the Spanish-speaking Caribbean (Alejandro García Caturla and Argeliers León of Cuba, Héctor Campos-Parsi of Puerto Rico) who studied with Boulanger are discussed in the next chapter.
17. Glocer/MELODÍAS; Ramírez/DACHAU.
18. Lange/LA MÚSICA URUGUAY, p. 340.
19. Slonimsky/MUSIC, p. 282.
20. Salgado/TEATRO SOLÍS, p. 20; see also Salgado/BREVE.
21. Hess/SAINT-SAËNS, pp. 205–6.
22. Salgado/TEATRO SOLÍS, pp. 25–26.
23. Slonimsky/MUSIC, p. 287.
24. Salgado/TEATRO SOLÍS, p. 184.
25. Paul Hume, "Young Performers Fall Short of Being Fully Captivating," *Washington Post*, November 10, 1960, p. D9.
26. Hess/COPLAND, p. xx.
27. https://migueldelaguila.com/program-notes/.

28. At this writing I have been unable to uncover any information on Elisabetta M. S. de Pate, a composer and conductor who gave a concert at the Pan American Union in 1933. Pereira Salas/NOTES, p. 32.

29. Nawrot/VESPERS; Illari/CARTA.

30. Stevenson/ZIPOLI.

31. Illari/ZIPOLI.

32. Colman/PARAGUAYAN.

33. Slonimsky/MUSIC, p. 264.

34. Ibid., p. 265.

35. https://www.abc.com.py/espectaculos/musica/2021/03/11/fallecio-florentin-gimenez/.

36. Lange/LA MÚSICA ARGENTINA, p. 86; Pedrotti/POBRES, pp. 85–111.

37. Illari/SLAVE'S PROGRESS, p. 190.

38. Ibid., p. 199.

39. Lange/LA MÚSICA ARGENTINA, p. 87.

40. Ibid., p. 87.

41. Schwartz-Kates/*GAUCHESCO*; Schwartz-Kates/CONSTRUCTION, pp. 248–81.

42. "Leopoldo Stokowski Dió su Tercer Concierto Anoche en el Gran Rex," *La Prensa*, August 21, 1940.

43. Glocer/MELODÍAS.

44. Ibid., p. 177.

45. *Forbidden Music*, by Michael Haas [https://forbiddenmusic.org/2015/01/23/a-south-american-story-of-music-exile-guillermo-graetzer-wilhelm-gratzer/].

46. Manso/CASTRO, pp. 179–205.

47. Slim/HOLOGRAPH, pp. 447–58.

48. Arias/*CORALES CRIOLLOS*, pp. 26–50.

49. d'Urbano/EN BUENOS AIRES, pp. 38–39.

50. Cited in García Muñoz/CASTRO, p. 21.

51. Arias/*CORALES CRIOLLOS*, p. 28.

52. *Venezuela Visit—November 26–December 9, 1954/February 2–March 31, 1957*, BOX/FOLDER 244/15 and 16, Aaron Copland Collection, Library of Congress (hereafter CCLC). In 1947, Castro composed a *Corales criollos* for piano.

53. Arias/*CORALES CRIOLLOS*, p. 32.

54. Cited in García Muñoz/CASTRO (III), p. 395.

55. The birth date given for Paz in Grove Music Online is incorrect. See Corrado/VANGUARDIAS, p. 26.

56. Corrado/VANGUARDIAS, p. 139.

57. Sargent/PAZ, p. 101.

58. Ibid., p. 84; see also Corrado/VANGUARDIAS, p. 140.

59. Hess/REPRESENTING, pp. 147–54. See also Schwartz-Kates/GINASTERA.

60. Herrera/ELITE.

61. Suárez Urtubey/GINASTERA, pp. 68–69.

62. Wallace/GINASTERA, 219–309. See also Tabor/LATE, pp. 1–31, and Fobes/INVESTIGATION.

63. Schwartz-Kates/GINASTERA, accessed June 26, 2021.

64. The "Malambo" has become famous in arrangements for marching band. Also from *Estancia*, the "Danza del Trigo" (Dance of the Wheat) appeared in the 2011 movie *The Artist*. In the 1970s, the English progressive rock group Emerson, Lake, and Palmer recorded portions of Ginastera's first piano concerto under the title "Toccata" with the composer's enthusiastic endorsement on their album *Brain Salad Surgery*.

65. Buch/TANGOS.
66. See Schwartz-Kates RESEARCH, pp. 51 and 55, for details on these symphonies; the Latin American Music Center at Indiana University holds a manuscript copy of the Second Symphony. Melanie Plesch, who tracked down the one other surviving manuscript, is planning a performance by the University of Melbourne Symphony Orchestra.
67. Scarabino/ALBERTO GINASTERA, p. 75.
68. Wallace/GINASTERA, p. 177.
69. Program note for Louisville premiere, cited in ibid., p. 206. Ginastera wrote three *Pampeanas*, with No. 1 for violin and piano and No. 2 for cello and piano.
70. Ibid.
71. Scarabino/GINASTERA, pp. 109–10, 115–16.
72. Travel diary, *Venezuela Visit—November 26–December 9, 1954/February 21–March 31, 1957*, BOX/FOLDER 244/15 and 16, CCLC.
73. See Schwarz-Kates/GINASTERA, p. 38.
74. Dezillio/LAS PRIMERAS, pp. 23–27.
75. Castagna and Trindade/CHAPELMASTERS.
76. Lange/MINAS GERAIS, p. 426.
77. Budasz/RIO DE JANEIRO, p. 154.
78. Quoted in ibid., p. 151.
79. Ibid., p. 161.
80. Magaldi/IMPERIAL RIO, p. 8.
81. Slonimsky/MUSIC, p. 123.
82. Ibid., p. 137.
83. Principal studies on Villa-Lobos include Béhague/VILLA-LOBOS; Wright/VILLA-LOBOS. See also Peppercorn/WORLD.
84. Livingston-Isenhour and Caracas García/CHORO, pp. 18–38.
85. Hess/REPRESENTING, pp. 81–110, 120–26.
86. Villa-Lobos's other ballet scores include *Amazonas* and *Emperor Jones*, the latter based on Eugene O'Neill's play. Martha Graham choreographed several of his nonballet scores, giving them titles such as *Primitive Canticles* and *Primitive Mysteries*.
87. An uirapurú appears in Messiaen's 1964 work for winds and percussion, *Et exspecto resurrectionem mortuorum*.
88. Marx/PORTRAIT, p. 15.
89. Copland/FESTIVAL, p. 5.
90. Peppercorn/VILLA-LOBOS, p. 81.
91. Wright/VILLA-LOBOS, p. 121.
92. Cited in Hess/REPRESENTING, p. 140.
93. A catalog of Villa-Lobos's works is Museu Villa-Lobos/OBRA; on the symphonies, see pp. 169–72. Hess/REPRESENTING, p. 131. Nor were Villa-Lobos's symphonies played regularly in his lifetime: the Second, "Ascenção" (Ascension), composed in 1917, waited almost thirty years for its premiere, when the Werner Janssen Symphony in Los Angeles performed it in 1944 during the first of Villa-Lobos's several visits to the United States.
94. The complete Naxos set is now available. Between 1997 and 2000, Carl St. Clair also recorded the symphonies with the South West German Radio Symphony Orchestra of Stuttgart on the cpo label.
95. A catalog of works by Brazilian orchestral composers Brasilio Itibere (1846–1913), Frutuoso Viana (1896–1976), Radames Gnattali (1906–88), José Siqueira (1907–85), and Mário Tavares (b. 1928)—in addition to Cosme—can be found in Mariz/FIGURAS, pp. 125–205.
96. Verhaalen/GUARNIERI, p. 2.

97. Copland/COMPOSERS, pp. 79–80.
98. Slonimsky/MUSIC, p. 32.
99. Ibid., p. 131.
100. It is too much, however, to propose that each of the three sections has "its own exposition-development-recapitulation," as none contains a bona fide development. Verhaalen/GUARNIERI, p. 224.
101. Cited in ibid., p. 223.
102. Cited in ibid., pp. 223–24.
103. See Tacuchian, "O sinfonismo guarnieriano," in Silva/GUARNIERI, pp. 447–63.
104. Verhaalen/GUARNIERI, pp. 48–49.
105. Hess/COPLAND, p. xx.
106. Verhaalen/GUARNIERI, p. 238.
107. John Neschling, born in Rio de Janeiro in 1947 and grand-nephew of Arnold Schoenberg (his grandmother was a cousin of the Austrian composer), has recorded the first six symphonies with the São Paulo Symphony Orchestra on the BIS label.
108. Quoted in Silva/GUARNIERI, p. 144.
109. Other Brazilian orchestras included the Orquestra Filarmônica, founded in 1931 by conductor, composer, and pianist Burle Marx (it survived only three years); the Radio Nacional Orchestra; and orchestras for popular music, such as that directed by Radames Gnattali (1906–88) and sponsored by Coca Cola. The São Paulo Symphony was founded in 1954.
110. For Santoro's catalog, see Mariz/SANTORO, pp. 83 ff.
111. Ibid., p. 53.
112. Neschling has recorded the Fourth and Ninth Symphonies with the São Paulo Symphony Orchestra on BIS. Several others have recently appeared on Naxos (see Table 1.3).
113. Mariz/SANTORO, p. 53.
114. Aracena/ARAUCANIAN, pp. 4–6.
115. Wolf/STYLING, p. 18.
116. Vera/SWEET PENANCE, pp. 9–11; Wolf/STYLING.
117. Vera/SWEET PENANCE, p. 356.
118. Ibid., pp. 55–60, 80.
119. Claro Valdés/SANTIAGO, p. 50. On other aspects of nineteenth-century music in Chile, see Merino/VALPARAISO and Pereira Salas/LA VIDA.
120. Claro Valdés/SANTIAGO, p. 53.
121. Slonimsky/MUSIC, p. 154.
122. Ibid., p. 160.
123. Marcelli was born in Italy but moved to Chile at age five and then settled in the United States. Stevenson/MARCELLI, p. 116.
124. Slonimsky/MUSIC, p. 161.
125. Menanteau/JAZZ EN CHILE, pp. 29–39.
126. For an overview of twentieth-century classical music in Chile, see González/PENSAR, pp. 279–300.
127. See Santa Cruz's weighty autobiography. Santa Cruz/MI VIDA.
128. "Jungle Jingles Called Passé in Latin Music," *Washington Post*, April 25, 1961, p. B11.
129. Orrego-Salas addresses Symphony No. 3 and other issues in Oteri/ORREGO-SALAS.
130. Adorno/PHYSIOGNOMY, pp. 96–97.
131. Ross Parmenter, "Music: New Latin Furor." *New York Times*, April 24, 1961, p. 36.
132. Fugellie Videla/LENI ALEXANDER.
133. Paraskevaídis/MATURANA, pp. 63–66.
134. Fugielle Videla/SCHIDLOWSKY.

135. HESS/Copland, p. xx.
136. Claro Valdés and Chase/MÚSICA DRAMÁTICA.
137. Baker/IMPOSING, p. 2.
138. Illari/POLYCHORAL, p. 129.
139. Baker/IMPOSING, p. 86.
140. Knighton/MUSIC AND RITUAL, p. 32.
141. Quoted in Knighton/MUSIC AND RITUAL, p. 27.
142. Stein/*PÚRPURA*, pp. x–xii.
143. See https://www.youtube.com/watch?v=_DPoBmPUZSE.
144. Carrizo/POLYSTLISM.
145. Donal Henahan, "Music: Two 'Firsts' for Sarah Caldwell," *New York Times*, November 12, 1975, p. 48. Other orchestral compositions by Escot include *Cristos*, *Lamentos*, and *Visione*. See also Shirley Fleming, "Women Composers," *New York Times*, November 2, 1975, p. 155.
146. Frank/NOTE.
147. Kennedy/COLONIAL SOURCES.
148. Seoane Urioste and Eichmann/LÍRICA.
149. Illari/POLYCHORAL.
150. De Mesa and Seoane/LA MÚSICA.
151. Ibid., pp. 95, 118.
152. Slonimsky/MUSIC, p. 108.
153. Ibid., p. 107.
154. Smith/MUSICAL TOUR, p. 210.
155. Ramírez /DACHAU, p. 162.
156. Ibid., p. 165n27.
157. Zuleta/VILLALPANDO, p. 188.
158. Ibid., p. 193.
159. Stevenson/QUITO, p. 19.
160. Quoted in ibid., p. 32.
161. Ibid., p. 35.
162. Walker/YOUNGER GENERATION, p. 203.
163. Slonimsky/MUSIC, p. 199; cited in Stevenson/QUITO, p. 36.
164. Sigmund/MORENO.
165. Walker/YOUNGER GENERATION, p. 201.
166. Wong/SALGADO/Wong/SONG.
167. Walker/INCANS, pp. 1–5.
168. Bermúdez/GOLD, pp. 88–90.
169. Ibid., p. 90.
170. Bermúdez/TOWARD, p. 77.
171. Ibid., p. 79.
172. Triana y Altorveza/VELASCO.
173. Perdomo Escobar/HISTORIA, p. 53.
174. Ibid., pp. 57–59.
175. Bermúdez/SANTOS CIFUENTES, pp. 212–13.
176. Perdomo Escobar/HISTORIA, p. 76.
177. Reprint of a 1927 speech in Uribe Holguín/VIDA, pp. 127–41; see also Castro Pantoja/ANTAGONISM.
178. "The Microphone Presents," *New York Times*, May 19, 1940, p. 138.
179. As of this writing, a few performances, including of the Second and Fourth Symphonies, can be found on YouTube.

180. Slonimsky/MUSIC, p. 169.
181. Slonimsky records that Mejía's *Danza Ritual Africana* for orchestra was performed in Bogotá in December 1940. No work of that title appears in Mejía's catalog, although it may be the *Danza mora* of 1942. Slonimsky/MUSIC, p. 170.
182. The full name is Fundación del Estado para el Sistema Nacional de las Orquestas Juveniles e Infantiles de Venezuela.
183. Coifman/SPIRIT, pp. 106–15.
184. Stevenson/MUSICAL LIFE. Other composers included José Antonio Caro de Boesi, José Cayetano Carreño, Juan José Landaeta, José Luis Landaeta, and Juan Francisco Meserón. Many scores from the cathedral have been lost, but the archive of the Escuela de Música José Ángel Lamas does contain some eighteenth-century music.
185. Arismendi Noguera/MONTERO.
186. Calzavara/ORQUESTA.
187. Plaza/CARACAS, pp. 198–213.
188. Labonville/PLAZA, pp. 28–35.
189. Sans/VIGILIA, p. ii.
190. Labonville/PLAZA, p. 83.
191. Other Latin American composers who composed concertos for orchestra include José María Castro and Washington Castro (Argentina), Ricardo Lorenz and Luis Ernesto Gómez (Venezuela), and Roberto Sierra (Puerto Rico).
192. *The First Inter-American Music Festival*, program booklet, April 18–20, 1958 (Washington, DC: Pan American Union); cited in Payne/AMERICAS, p. 38.
193. Galván/FLEISHER, p. 7; see also Galván/ABCs.
194. Slonimsky/MUSIC, p. 292.
195. Lunar Romero/MESCOLI.
196. This is Béhague's apt description of Paula Barros's heavily supervised *O Romance de Villa Lobos* of 1951. Béhague/VILLA-LOBOS, p. 1.

Bibliography

Adorno/PHYSIOGNOMY	Adorno, Theodor W. *Mahler: A Musical Physiognomy*, translated by Edmund Jephcott. Chicago and London: University of Chicago Press, 1992.
Appleby/VILLA-LOBOS	Appleby, David P. *Heitor Villa-Lobos: A Life (1887–1959)*. Lanham, MD, and London: Scarecrow, 2002.
Aracena/ARAUCANIAN	Aracena, Beth K. "Viewing the Ethnomusicological Past: Jesuit Influences on Araucanian Music in Colonial Chile." *Latin American Music Review* 18, no. 1 (1997): pp. 1–29.
Arias/*CORALES CRIOLLOS*	Arias, Enrique Alberto. "Juan José Castro's *Corales Criollos*." *Latin American Music Review* 7, no. 1 (1986): pp. 26–50.
Arismendi Noguera/MONTERO	Arismendi Noguera, Coralys Margarita. "Sinfonía núm. 4 en sol mayor de José Lorenzo Montero." MM thesis, Caracas: Universidad Nacional Experimental de las Artes, 2009.
Ayestarán/BARROCO	Ayestarán, Lauro. "El Barroco musical hispano-americano: los manuscritos de la iglesia de San Felipe Neri

(Sucre, Bolivia) existentes en el Museo Histórico Nacional del Uruguay." *Yearbook, Inter-American Musical Research* 1 (1965): pp. 55–93.

Baker/IMPOSING — Baker, Geoffrey. *Imposing Harmony: Music and Society in Colonial Cuzco.* Durham, NC, and London: Duke University Press, 2008.

Béhague/VILLA-LOBOS — Béhague, Gerard. *Heitor Villa-Lobos: The Search for Brazil's Musical Soul.* Austin: Institute of Latin American Studies, University of Texas at Austin, 1994.

Bermúdez/FORTRESSES — Bermúdez, Egberto. "Sounds from Fortresses of Faith and Ideal Cities: Society, Politics, and Music in Missionary Activities in the Americas, 1525–1575." In *Listening to Early Modern Catholicism: Perspectives from Musicology*, edited by Daniele V. Filippi and Michael Noone, pp. 301–25. Vol. 49 of *Intersections: Interdisciplinary Studies in Early Modern Culture*. Leiden: Brill, 2017.

Bermúdez/GOLD — Bermúdez, Egberto. "'Gold was Music to their Ears': Conflicting Sounds in Santafé (Nuevo Reino de Granada), 1540–1570." In *Music and Urban Society in Colonial Latin America*, edited by Geoffrey Baker and Tess Knighton, pp. 83–101. Cambridge: Cambridge University Press, 2011.

Bermúdez/SANTOS CIFUENTES — Bermúdez, Egberto. "Santos Cifuentes (1870–1932): la profesión musical el Colombia." In *La hegemonía conservadora*, edited by Rubén Sierra Mejía, pp. 203–55. Bogotá: Universidad Nacional de Colombia, 2018.

Bermúdea/SIGLO — Bermúdez, Egberto. "Un siglo de música en Colombia: ¿Entre nacionalismo y universalismo?" *Revista Credencial* (2016) https://www.revistacredencial.com/historia/temas/un-siglo-de-musica-en-colombia-entre-nacionalismo-y-universalismo, accessed May 18, 2021.

Bermúdez/TOWARD — Bermúdez, Egberto. "Toward a History of Colombian Musics." In *The Colombia Reader: History, Culture, Politics*, edited by Ann Farnsworth-Alvear, Ana María Gómez López, Marco Palacios; translated by Ann Farnsworth-Alvear, pp. 75–87. Durham, NC: Duke University Press, 2017.

Bermúdez/URBAN — Bermúdez, Egberto. "Urban Musical Life in the European Colonies, 1530–1650." In *Music and Musicians in Renaissance Cities and Towns*, edited by Fiona Kisby, pp. 167–80. Cambridge: Cambridge University Press, 2001.

Blanco Aguinagua/MODERNISM — Blanco Aguinagua, Carlos. "On Modernism from the Periphery." In *Modernism and Its Margins: Reinscribing Cultural Modernity from Spain and Latin America,*

	edited by Anthony L. Geist and José B. Monleón, pp. 3–16. New York and London: Garland, 1999.
Buch/TANGOS	Buch, Esteban, ed. *Tangos Cultos: Kagel, J. J. Castro, Mastropiero y Otros Cruces Musicales*. Buenos Aires: Gourmet Musical, 2012.
Budasz/RIO DE JANEIRO	Budasz, Rogério. "Music, Authority, and Civilization in Rio de Janeiro, 1763–1790." In *Music and Urban Society in Colonial America*, edited by Geoffrey Baker and Tess Knighton, pp. 151–70. Cambridge: Cambridge University Press, 2011.
Calzavara/ORQUESTA	Calzavara, Alberto. *Trayectoria cincuentenaria de la Orquesta Sinfónica Venezuela, 1930–1980*. Mérida (Venezuela): Universidad de los Andes, 1980.
Carpentier/ESE MÚSICO	Carpentier, Alejo. *Ese músico que llevo dentro*, ed. Zoila Gómez (Havana: Editorial Letras Cubanas, 1980) 1: pp. 434–35.
Carrizo/POLYSTYLISM	Carrizo, Andrés. "'Don't knock the hybrids': Musical Polystylism in Celso Garrido-Lecca's Duo Concertante." *Perspectives of New Music* 56, no. 1 (2018): pp. 101–35.
Castagna and Trindade/CHAPELMASTERS	Castagna, Paulo, and Jaelson Trindade. "Chapelmasters and musical practice in Brazilian Cities in the Eighteenth Century." In *Music and Urban Society in Colonial America*, edited by Geoffrey Baker and Tess Knighton, pp. 132–50. Cambridge: Cambridge University Press, 2011.
Castro Pantoja/ANTAGONISM	Castro Pantoja, Daniel Fernando. "Antagonism, Europhilia, and Identity: Guillermo Uribe Holguín and the Politics of National Music in Early Twentieth-Century Colombia." PhD diss., University of California, Riverside, 2018.
Celenza Hartwell and Del Donna/MUSIC AS CULTURAL MISSION	Celenza Hartwell, Anna, and Anthony R. Del Donna, eds. *Music as Cultural Mission: Exploration of Jesuit Musical Practices in Italy and North America*. Philadelphia: St. Joseph University Press, 2014.
Chase/CARACAS	Chase, Gilbert. "Caracas Host to Second Latin American Festival." *Musical America* 77, no. 6 (May 1957): pp. 11–12.
Claro Valdés/SANTIAGO	Claro Valdés, Samuel. "Santiago de Chile Cathedral Music in the Nineteenth Century." *Inter-American Music Review* 4, no. 2 (1982): pp. 47–58.
Claro Valdés and Chase/MÚSICA DRAMÁTICA	Claro Valdés, Samuel, and Gilbert Chase. "Música dramática en el Cuzco durante el siglo XVIII y el

	catálogo de manuscritos de música de Seminario del San Antonio Abad." *Anuario* 5 (1969): pp. 1–48.
Coifman/SPIRIT	Coifman, David. "The 'Spirit of Independence' in the *Fiesta de la Naval* of Caracas." In *Music and Urban Society in Colonial Latin America*, edited by Geoffrey Baker and Tess Knighton, pp. 102–16. Cambridge: Cambridge University Press, 2011.
Colman/PARAGUAYAN	Colman, Alfredo C. *The Paraguayan Harp: From Colonial Transplant to National Emblem*. Lanham, MD: Lexington, 2015.
Copland/COMPOSERS	Copland, Aaron. "The Composers of South America." *Modern Music* 19, no. 2 (January–February 1942): pp. 75–82.
Copland/FESTIVAL	Copland, Aaron. "Festival of Contemporary Latin American Music." *Tempo* 35 (1955): pp. 4–5, 10.
Corrado/VANGUARDIAS	Corrado, Omar. *Vanguardias al Sur: La música de Juan Carlos Paz*. Havana: Fondo Editorial Casa de las Américas, 2010.
Davies/MAKING MUSIC	Davies, Drew Edward. "Making Music, Writing Myth: Urban Guadalupan Ritual in Eighteenth-Century New Spain." In *Music and Urban Society in Colonial America*, edited by Geoffrey Baker and Tess Knighton, pp. 64–82. Cambridge: Cambridge University Press, 2011.
de la Vega/COMPOSERS	de la Vega, Aurelio. "Latin American Composers in the United States." *Latin American Music Review* 1, no. 2 (1980): pp. 162–75.
de Mesa and Seoane/LA MÚSICA	de Mesa, J., and C. Seoane. "La música en Bolivia durante el siglo XIX." *Die Musikkulturen Lateinamerikas im 19. Jahrhundert*, edited by Robert Günther, pp. 93–120. Regensburg: Gustav Bosse Verlag, 1982.
Dezillio/LAS PRIMERAS	Romina Dezillio. "Las primeras compositoras profesionales de música académica en Argentina: logros, conquistas y desafíos de una profesión masculina." In *Música y mujer en Iberoamérica: haciendo música desde la condición de género*. Actas III Coloquio de Investigación Musical Ibermúsicas, edited by Juan Pablo González, pp. 22–45. Santiago, 2017.
d'Urbano/BUENOS AIRES	d'Urbano, Jorge. *Música en Buenos Aires*. Buenos Aires: Editorial Sudamericana, 1966.
Enyart/SYMPHONIES	Enyart, John William. "The Symphonies of Heitor Villa-Lobos (Brazil)." PhD diss., University of Cincinnati, 1984.
Fobes/INVESTIGATION	Fobes, Christopher A. "A Theoretical Investigation of Twelve-Tone Rows, Harmonic Aggregates, and Non-Twelve-Tone Materials in the Late Music of Alberto

	Ginastera." PhD diss., State University of New York at Buffalo, 2006.
Frank/NOTE	Frank, Gabriela Lena. "Composer's Note for *Elegía Andina*." DMA diss., University of Michigan, 2000.
Fugielle Videla/LENI ALEXANDER	Fugellie Videla, Daniela. "Leni Alexander (1924–2005) o la migración perpetua." In *Música y mujer en Iberoamérica: haciendo música desde la condición de género*. Actas III Coloquio de Investigación Musical Ibermúsicas, edited by Juan Pablo González, pp. 76–91. Santiago: Secretaría General Iberoamericana, 2017.
Fugielle Videla/SCHIDLOWSKY	Fugielle Videla, Daniela. "León Schidlowsky, Premio Nacional de Artes Musicales. Perspectivas de su trayectoria artística en Chile, Israel y Alemania." *Revista Musical Chilena* 59, no. 224 (2015): pp. 11–36.
Galván/ABCs	Galván, Gary. "The ABCs of the WPA Music Copying Project and the Fleisher Collection." *American Music* 26, no. 4 (2008): pp. 514–38.
Galván/FLEISHER	Galván, Gary, comp. *Latin American Orchestral Works in the Fleisher Collection*. Philadelphia: Free Library of Philadelphia, 2017.
García Canclini/MODERNITY	García Canclini, Néstor. *Hybrid Cultures: Strategies for Entering and Leaving Modernity*, translated by Christopher L. Chiappari and Silvia L. López. Minneapolis: University of Minnesota Press, 1995; originally published in Mexico City, 1989.
García Muñoz/CASTRO	García Muñoz, Carmen. "Juan José Castro (1895–1968)." *Cuadernos de música iberoamericana* 1 (1996): pp. 3–24.
García Muñoz/CASTRO (III)	García Muñoz, Carmen. "Castro (III)." *Diccionario de la música española e hispanoamericana*. Vol. 3, edited by Emilio Casares, pp. 357–98. Madrid: INAEM, 1999.
Gearhart/VILLA-LOBOS	Gearhart, Steven, ed. *Niewig Chart 2017: Villa-Lobos 12 Symphonies, Publication and Recording Details*. http://www.orchestralibrary.com/Nieweg%20Charts/Villa%20Lobos%20Chart%20Master%202017.pdf.
Ginastera/ORQUESTAS	Ginastera, Alberto. "Las orquestas sinfónicas en los Estados Unidos." *Sur* 145 (1946): p. 105.
Glocer/JUDAÍSMO	Glocer, Silvia. "Guillermo Graetzer. Judaísmo y exilio: las palabras ausentes." *Latin American Music Review* 33, no. 1 (2012): pp. 65–101.
Glocer/MELODÍAS	Glocer, Silvia. *Melodías del destierro: Músico judíos exiliados en la Argentina durante el nazismo (1933–1945)*. Buenos Aires: Gourmet Musical Ediciones, 2016.
González/PENSAR	González, Juan Pablo. *Pensar la música desde América Latina: problemas e interrogantes*. 2nd ed. Santiago: Ediciones Universidad Alberto Hurtado, 2018.

Herrera/ELITE	Herrera, Eduardo. *Elite Art Worlds: Philanthropy, Latin Americanism, and Avant-Garde Music.* New York: Oxford University Press, 2020.
Hess/COPLAND	Hess, Carol A. *Aaron Copland in Latin America: Music, Politics, and Cultural Diplomacy.* Champaign: University of Illinois Press, 2022.
Hess/EXPERIENCING	Hess, Carol A. *Experiencing Latin American Music.* Oakland: University of California Press, 2018.
Hess/REPRESENTING	Hess, Carol A. *Representing the Good Neighbor: Music, Difference, and the Pan American Dream.* New York: Oxford University Press, 2013.
Hess/SAINT-SAËNS	Hess, Carol A. "Saint-Saëns and Latin America." In *Saint-Saëns and His World*, edited by Jann Pasler, pp. 201–8. Princeton, NJ: Princeton University Press, 2012.
Hudde/NEGOTIATING	Hudde, Hermann. "Negotiating Politics and Aesthetics: The Untold History of Modern Latin American Art Music in the Berkshire Music Center at Tanglewood, 1940–1951." PhD diss., University of California, Riverside, 2021.
Illari/CARTA	Illari, Bernardo. "Carta de misiones: sobre la música jesuítico-guaraní en 1651 y su investigación actual." *Revista del Instituto de Investigación Musicológica "Carlos Vega"* 20, no. 20 (2006): pp. 97–113.
Illari/POLYCHORAL	Illari, Bernardo. "Polychoral Culture: Cathedral Music in La Plata (Bolivia), 1680–1730." PhD diss., University of Chicago, 2002.
Illari/SLAVE'S PROGRESS	Illari, Bernardo. "The Slave's Progress: Music as Profession in *Criollo* Buenos Aires." In *Music in Urban Society in Colonial Latin America*, edited by Geoffrey Baker and Tess Knighton, pp. 186–207. Cambridge: Cambridge University Press, 2011.
Illari/ZIPOLI	Illari, Bernardo. *Domenico Zipoli: para una genealogía de la música clásica latinoamericana.* Havana: Fondo Editorial Casa de las Americas, 2011.
Kennedy/COLONIAL SOURCES	Kennedy, T. Frank. "Colonial Sources from the Episcopal Archive of Concepción, Bolivia." *Latin American Music Review* 9, no. 1 (1988): pp. 1–17.
Knighton/MUSIC AND RITUAL	Knighton, Tess. "Music and Ritual in Urban Spaces: The Case of Lima, c. 1600." In *Music and Urban Society in Colonial America*, edited by Geoffrey Baker and Tess Knighton, pp. 21–42. Cambridge: Cambridge University Press, 2011.
Labonville/PLAZA	Labonville, Marie Elizabeth. *Juan Bautista Plaza and Musical Nationalism in Venezuela.* Bloomington and Indianapolis: Indiana University Press, 2007.

Laird/DISSEMINATION	Laird, Paul R. "The Dissemination of the Spanish Baroque Villancico." *Revista de Musicología* 16, no. 5 (1993): pp. 2857–64.
Lange/LA MÚSICA ARGENTINA	Lange, Francisco Curt. "La música en la Argentina del siglo XIX." In *Die Musikkulturen Lateinamerikas im 19. Jahrhundert*, edited by Robert Günther, pp. 93–120. Regensburg: Gustav Bosse Verlag, 1982.
Lange/LA MÚSICA URUGUAY	Lange, Francisco Curt. "La música en el Uruguay durante el siglo XIX." In *Die Musikkulturen Lateinamerikas im 19. Jahrhundert*, edited by Robert Günther, pp. 333–44. Regensburg: Gustave Bosse Verlag, 1982.
Lange/MINAS GERAIS	Lange, Francisco Curt. "La música en Minas Gerais: un informe preliminar." *Boletín Latino-Americano de Música* 6 (1946): pp. 409–94.
Livingston-Isenhour and Caracas García/CHORO	Livingston-Isenhour, Tamara Elena, and Thomas George Caracas García. *Choro: A Social History of a Brazilian Popular Music*. Bloomington: Indiana University Press, 2005.
Lunar Romero/MESCOLI	Lunar Romero, María Fernanda. "Nacionalismo musical presente en el poema sinfónico *María Lionza* de Blanca Estrella de Méscoli." MM thesis, Universidad Arturo Michelena (San Diego, Venezuela), 2018.
Magaldi/IMPERIAL RIO	Magaldi, Cristina. *Music in Imperial Rio de Janeiro: European Culture in a Tropical Milieu*. Lanham, MD: Scarecrow, 2004.
Manso/CASTRO	Manso, Carlos. *Juan José Castro*. Buenos Aires: De los Cuatro Vientos, 2006.
Mariz/FIGURAS	Mariz, Vasco. *Figuras de música brasileira contemporânea*. Brasília: Universidade de Brasília, 1970.
Mariz/SANTORO	Mariz, Vasco. *Cláudio Santoro*. Rio de Janeiro: Civilização Brasileira, 1994.
Marx/PORTRAIT	Marx, Burle. "Brazilian Portrait—Villa-Lobos." *Modern Music* 17, no. 1 (October–November 1939): pp. 10–17.
Mayer-Serra/MÚSICA	Mayer-Serra, Otto. *Música y músicos de Latinoamérica*. 2 vols. Mexico City: Editorial Atlante, 1947.
Menanteau/JAZZ EN CHILE	Menanteau, Álvaro. *Historia del jazz en Chile*, 2nd ed. Santiago: Ocho Libros Editores, 2006.
Merino/VALPARAISO	Merino, Luis. "Música y sociedad en el Valparaiso decimonónico." In *Die Musikkulturen Lateinamerikas im 19. Jahrhundert*, edited by Robert Günther, pp. 199–235. Regensburg: Gustav Bosse Verlag, 1982.
Miranda and Tello/LA MÚSICA	Miranda, Ricardo, and Aurelio Tello. *La música en Latinoamérica*. Vol. 4. *La búsqueda perpetua: lo propio y lo universal de la cultura latinoamericana*, edited by

	Mercedes de la Vega Armijo. Mexico City, Secretaría de Relaciones Exteriores, 2011.
Museu Villa-Lobos/OBRA	*Villa-Lobos, Sua Obra*. 2nd ed. Rio de Janeiro: Museu Villa-Lobos, 1972.
Nawrot/VESPERS	Nawrot, Piotr. *Vespers Music in the Paraguay Reductions*. PhD diss., Catholic University of America, 1993.
O'Malley/JESUITS	O'Malley, John W. *The Jesuits: Culture, Sciences, and the Arts (1540–1773)*. Toronto: University of Toronto Press, 1999.
Orrego-Salas/ENCUENTROS	Orrego-Salas, Juan. *Encuentros, Visiones y Repasos*. Santiago: Ediciones Universidad Católica de Chile, 2005.
Oteri/ORREGO-SALAS	Oteri, Frank J. "Juan Orrego-Salas: 'I've Written All That I Have to Write.'" http://www.newmusicbox.org/articles/juan-orrego-salas, accessed April 28, 2014.
Paraskevaídis/MATURANA	Paraskevaídis, Graciela. "Eduardo Maturana: un músico olvidado." *Revista Musical Chilena* 68, no. 222 (2015): pp. 58–69.
Pasten/METROPOLIS	Pasten, José Agustín. "Neither Grobalized or Glocalized: Fuguet's or Lemembel's Metropolis?" *Spanish Language and Literature* (2005). http://digitalcommons.unl.edu/modlangspanish (Modern Languages Commons).
Payne/AMERICAS	Payne, Alyson Marie. "Music of the Americas in the Cold War: Alberto Ginastera and the Festivals for Inter-American Music." MM thesis, Bowling Green State University, 2006.
Pedrotti/POBRES	Pedrotti, Clarisa Eugenia. *Pobres, negros y esclavos: música religiosa en Córdoba del Tucumán (1699–1840)*. Córdoba: Editorial Brujas, 2017.
Peppercorn/VILLA-LOBOS	Peppercorn, Lisa. *Villa-Lobos: The Music. An Analysis of His Style*, translated by Stefan de Haan. London: Kahn & Averill, 1991.
Peppercorn/WORLD	Peppercorn, Lisa. *The World of Villa-Lobos in Pictures and Documents*. Aldershot: Scolar Press, 1996.
Perdomo Escobar/HISTORIA	Perdomo Escobar, José Ignacio. *Historia de la Música en Colombia*. Bogotá: Editorial ABC, 1963.
Pereira Salas/LA VIDA	Pereira Salas, Eugenio. "La vida musical en Chile en el siglo XIX." In *Die Musikkulturen Lateinamerikas im 19. Jahrhundert*, edited by Robert Günther, pp. 237–59. Regensburg: Gustav Bosse Verlag, 1982.
Pereira Salas/NOTES	Pereira Salas, Eugenio. *Notes on the History of Music Exchange between the Americas before 1940*. Washington, DC: Music Division, Pan American Union, 1943; trans. of *Notas para la historia del intercambio musical entre las Américas*. Santiago de Chile: Universidad de Chile.

Pernet/"GENUINE CULTURE"	Pernet, Corinne A. "'For the Genuine Culture of the Americas.'" In *Decentering America*, edited by Jessica C. E. Gienow-Hecht, pp. 132–68. New York and Oxford: Berghahn, 2007.
Plaza/CARACAS	Plaza, Juan Bautista. "Music in Caracas During the Colonial Period." *Musical Quarterly* 29 (1943): pp. 198–213.
Ramírez/DACHAU	Ramírez, Miguel. "From Dachau to La Paz: Erich Eisner and the Confluence of Jewish, Austro-German, and Bolivian Musical Traditions." *Journal of Musicological Research* 38, no. 2 (2019): pp. 159–74.
Ros-Fábregas/NICOLAS SLONIMSKY	Ros-Fábregas, Emilio. "Nicolas Slonimsky (1894–1995) y sus escritos sobre música en Latinoamérica: reivindicación de un 'fishing trip.'" In *La Música y el Atlántico: relaciones musicales entre España y Latinoamérica*, edited by María Gembero Ustárroz and Emilio Ros-Fábregas, pp. 153–80. Granada: University of Granada, 2007.
Salgado/BREVE	Salgado, Susana. *Breve historia de la música culta en el Uruguay*. Montevideo, 1971.
Salgado/TEATRO SOLÍS	Salgado, Susana. *The Teatro Solís: 150 Years of Opera, Concert, and Ballet in Montevideo*. Middletown, CT: Wesleyan University Press, 2003.
Sans/VIGILIA	Sans, Juan Francisco, ed. *Vigilia (Poema sinfónico) de Juan Bautista Plaza (1898–1965)*. Caracas: Fundación Bautista Plaza, 2005.
Santa Cruz/MI VIDA	Santa Cruz, Domingo. *Mi vida en la música*, edited by Raquel Bustos Valderama. Santiago: Ediciones Universidad Católica de Chile, 2007.
Sargent/PAZ	Sargent, David H. "The Twelve-Tone Row Technique of Juan Carlos Paz." *Anuario Interamericano de Investigación Musical* 11 (1975): pp. 82–105.
Scarabino/GINASTERA	Scarabino, Guillermo. *Alberto Ginastera: Técnicas y Estilo (1935–1950)*. Buenos Aires: Instituto de Investigación Musicológica Carlos Vega, 1996.
Schwartz-Kates/CONSTRUCTION	Schwartz-Kates, Deborah. "Alberto Ginastera, Argentine Cultural Construction, and the Gauchesco Tradition." *Musical Quarterly* 86, no. 2 (2002): pp. 248–81.
Schwartz-Kates/*GAUCHESCO*	Schwartz-Kates, Deborah. "The *Gauchesco* Tradition as a Source of National Identity in Argentine Art Music (ca. 1890–1955)." PhD diss., University of Texas at Austin, 1997.
Schwartz-Kates/GINASTERA	Schwartz-Kates, Deborah. "Ginastera, Alberto (Evaristo)." In Grove Music Online. *Oxford Music Online*, http://www.oxfordmusiconline.com/subscriber/article/grove/music/11159, accessed June 26, 2010.

Schwartz-Kates/RESEARCH	Schwartz-Kates, Deborah. *Alberto Ginastera: A Research and Information Guide.* New York and London: Routledge, 2010.
Seoane Urioste and Eichmann/LÍRICA	Seoane Urioste, C., and A. Eichmann. *Lírica colonial boliviana.* La Paz: Editorial Quipus, 1993.
Sigmund/MORENO	Sigmund, Charles. "Segundo Luis Moreno (1882–1972): Ecuador's Pioneer Musicologist." *Yearbook for Inter-American Musical Research* 8 (1972): pp. 71–104.
Silva/GUARNIERI	Silva, Flávio. *Camargo Guarnieri: O Tempo e a Música.* Rio de Janeiro: Funarte, 2001.
Slim/HOLOGRAPH	Slim, H. Colin. "A Stravinsky Holograph in 1936 for Juan José Castro in Buenos Aires: 'maître impeccable de la baguette.'" In *Music Observed: Studies in Memory of William C. Holmes*, edited by Colleen Reardon and Susan Helen Parisi, pp. 447–58. Warren, MI: Harmonie Park, 2004.
Slonimsky/MUSIC	Slonimsky, Nicolas. *The Music of Latin America.* New York: Thomas Y. Crowell, 1945.
Smith/MUSICAL TOUR	Smith, Carleton Sprague. *Musical Tour through South America, June–October 1940.* New York: Typescript, 1940.
Stallings/COLLECTIVE	Stallings, Stephanie. "Collective Difference: The Pan-American Association of Composers and Pan-American Ideology in Music, 1925–45." PhD diss., Florida State University, 2009.
Stein/*PÚRPURA*	Stein, Louise K. ed. "Introducción." *La Púrpura de la rosa: fiesta cantada, ópera en un acto.* Madrid: Instituto Complutense de Ciencias Musicales, 1999.
Stevenson/AZTEC INCA	Stevenson, Robert M. *Music in Aztec and Inca Territory.* Oakland: University of California Press, 2022 [reprint 1976].
Stevenson/MARCELLI	Stevenson, Robert M. "Nino Marcelli, Founder of the San Diego Symphony Orchestra." *Inter-American Music Review* 10, no. 1 (1988): pp. 113–23.
Stevenson/MUSICAL LIFE	Stevenson, Robert M. "Musical Life in Caracas Cathedral to 1836." *Inter-American Music Review* 1, no. 1 (1978): pp. 29–71.
Stevenson/QUITO	Stevenson, Robert M. "Quito Cathedral: Four Centuries." *Inter-American Music Review* 3, no. 1 (1980): pp. 19–38.
Stevenson/ZIPOLI	Stevenson, Robert M. "Zipoli, Domenico." In Grove Music Online. *Oxford Music Online.* https://doi-org.auth.lib.niu.edu/10.1093/gmo/9781561592630.article.30997.
Suárez Urtubey/GINASTERA	Suárez Urtubey, Pola. *Alberto Ginastera.* Buenos Aires: Ediciones Culturales Argentinas, 1967.

Tabor/LATE	Tabor, Michelle. "Alberto Ginastera's Late Instrumental Style." *Latin American Music Review* 15, no. 1 (1994): pp. 1–31.
Triana y Antorveza/VELASCO	Triana y Antorveza, Humberto. "Las actividades de Juan Antonio Velasco, a favor de la educación musical en nuestra ciudad." *Boletín Cultural y Bibliográfico* 7, no. 5 (1964): pp. 783–84. Biblioteca Virtual Miguel de Cervantes. http://www.cervantesvirtual.com/portales/al_tall/obra/las-actividades-de-juan-antonio-velasco-en-favor-de-la-educacion-musical-en-nuestra-ciudad-907600/0.
Uribe Holguín/VIDA	Uribe Holguín, Guillermo. *Vida de un músico colombiano*. Bogotá: Librería Voluntad, 1941.
Vera/SWEET PENANCE	Vera, Alejandro. *The Sweet Penance of Music: Musical Life in Colonial Santiago de Chile*. New York: Oxford University Press, 2020.
Verhaalen/GUARNIERI	Verhaalen, Marion. *Camargo Guarnieri, Brazilian Composer*. Bloomington: Indiana University Press, 2005.
Waisman/MÚSICA COLONIAL	Waisman, Leonardo. "La música colonial en la Iberoamérica neo-colonial." *Acta musicologica* 76, no. 1 (2004): pp. 117–27.
Walker/INCANS	Walker, John L. "Incans, Liberators, and Jungle Princesses." *Latin American Music Review* 37, no. 1 (2016): pp. 1–33.
Walker/YOUNGER GENERATION	Walker, John L. "The Younger Generation of Ecuadorian Composers." *Latin American Music Review* 22, no. 2 (2001): pp. 199–213.
Wallace/GINASTERA	Wallace, David Edward. "Alberto Ginastera: An Analysis of His Style and Techniques of Composition." PhD diss., Northwestern University, 1964.
Wolf/STYLING	Wolf, Juan Eduardo. *Styling Blackness in Chile: Music and Dance in the African Diaspora*. Bloomington: Indiana University Press, 2019.
Wong/SALGADO	Wong, Ketty. *Luis H. Salgado, un Quijote de la música*. Quito: Banco Central del Ecuador y Casa de la Cultura Ecuatoriana Benjamín Carrión, 2004.
Wong/SONG	Wong, Ketty. "The Song of the National Soul: Ecuadorian Pasillo in the Twentieth Century." *Latin American Music Review* 32, no. 1 (2011): pp. 59–87.
Wright/VILLA-LOBOS	Wright, Simon. *Villa-Lobos*. Oxford and New York: Oxford University Press, 1992.
Zuleta/VILLALPANDO	Zuleta, Sebastián. "En torno a cincuenta años de la obra de Alberto Villalpando." *Ciencia y cultura* 32 (2014): pp. 185–203.

CHAPTER EIGHT

The Symphony in Mexico, Central America, and the Spanish-Speaking Caribbean

Carol A. Hess

Introduction

This chapter surveys orchestral music in Mexico, Central America (Guatemala, El Salvador, Honduras, Nicaragua, Costa Rica, Panama), and the Spanish-speaking Caribbean (Cuba, the Dominican Republic, Puerto Rico). Many of the factors relevant to South America apply to this region: a strong indigenous heritage, concerted Catholic church music after the conquest, the growth of instrumental music through philharmonic societies and orchestras during the nineteenth century, a flowering of symphonic music in the twentieth century, and new directions in orchestral music in the present century. As in South America, composers from this region have grappled with musical nationalism. Those bent on asserting identity could draw on the articles, recordings, and transcriptions that folklore studies yielded: as early as 1926 the Cuban government endorsed folk music study and even a poor country such as El Salvador established a National Committee for Folklore Research.[1] As in South America, musical nationalists clashed with modernists, just as composers from Mexico, Central America, and the Spanish-speaking Caribbean also assessed their relationship with Europe. But the United States loomed large. The Mexican composer Carlos Chávez, fluent in English, spent long periods in the United States, which he found more stimulating than Europe: as Carol J. Oja points out, for Chávez, "New York became Paris."[2] His compatriot Silvestre Revueltas lived in the United States, as did several other composers on an even more permanent basis, whether to study or work.[3]

To be sure, political strife with the United States left its mark. The Mexican-American War of 1846–48 was a prime example of US aggression. Other tensions are linked to slavery: Nicaragua, once part of the short-lived, postindependence Central American Federation (Guatemala, Honduras, Costa Rica, El Salvador, Nicaragua), caught the eye of one William Walker of Tennessee, who in 1856 usurped the Nicaraguan government to establish additional slave states in Central America. The Spanish-American War of 1898 was also divisive, especially for Cuba and Puerto Rico. Panama, part of the Republic of Colombia until 1903, came under what President Theodore Roosevelt famously called "the Big Stick" when the United States destabilized the Colombian government to build the Panama Canal. Another tool was dollar diplomacy, which often involved fiscal reorganization of other countries. All was undertaken in the spirit of Manifest Destiny, which rested on notions of Anglo-Saxon supremacy.

Music could be affected. One episode shows how the United States failed to take Puerto Rican classical music seriously, imagining that only folkloric styles were possible. In 1931, Theodore Roosevelt Jr. (son of President Theodore Roosevelt) was serving as governor of Puerto Rico. One day, he received a visit from some local musicians who wanted to establish a conservatory so that Puerto Ricans could study classical music "according to the standards established in [other] countries," as they put it.[4] Governor Roosevelt was delighted to talk music with his visitors: he told them how much he enjoyed *música jíbara* (a rural musical genre) and instruments such as the the güiro and the cuatro (a small guitar with steel strings arranged in courses). Politely, the musicians repeated their request. But the governor seemed not to hear them and instead continued to enthuse over traditional Puerto Rican music. Frustrated, the musicians left, and ultimately Roosevelt vetoed the measure to build the conservatory even though both the Puerto Rican House of Representatives and the Senate had approved it.

As in the chapter on South America, my main point here is that a considerable body of orchestral music hails from this region. We start with Mexico, the country most widely recognized for its orchestral culture, and proceed through Central America and the Spanish-speaking Caribbean.

Mexico

In 1519, when Hernán Cortés began the conquest of what is now Mexico, the Mexica people had at their disposal many musical instruments. (Although the term *Aztec* is common, *Mexica* refers to all the Nahutal-speaking communities in the region, including the Aztec, who lived around Tenochtitlán, present-day Mexico City.) Besides a staggering variety of aerophones were the *huehuetl*, a tall drum with an animal-skin head, and the *teponaztli*, a slit-drum made from the trunk of a tree with an H-shaped cut that allowed for variety of pitch. Europeans offered their impressions of native music, some describing it as "noise" but others showing greater insight, noting both the mournful quality of the teponatzli and its carrying power. Missionaries were impressed with the natives' aptitude for music. In 1523, three Franciscans arrived in Mexico, including Pedro de Gante (1480–1572), who learned Nahuatl and opened a music school for the Indians. From the mid-sixteenth century on, a printing press in Mexico City provided plainchant while polyphonic music was readily imported from Europe.[5]

Like the cathedral at Cuzco, its counterpart in Mexico City was built on a sacred indigenous site. The first chapelmaster was appointed in 1539 and followed by luminaries such as the Spanish-born Hernando Franco (1532–85) and later Manuel de Sumaya (*ca.* 1678–1755). Born in Mexico City and trained in Latin America, Sumaya was the first composer in New Spain to write "systematically" for violins and consider them an integral part of cathedral ensembles.[6] In his numerous villancicos, figuration in the instrumental parts is complemented by harmonic activity and ingenious motivic treatment.[7] Also at Mexico City was the Italian-born Ignacio de Jerusalem (1707–69), who wrote music in the *style galant* for choir and orchestra, in which ritornelli, unison singing, and counterpoint alternate for textural variety.[8] Equally spectacular was the cathedral music at Puebla.[9] Among its many fine chapelmasters was Juan Gutiérrez de Padilla (1590–1664).[10] In his masses for double choir, each choir had its own continuo of organ, harp, and bass viol. In Padilla's more than forty-five villancicos, recorders, chirimias (shawms), cornets, sackbuts, and treble, tenor and bass *bajons* (bassoons) might complement the foundational instruments. (From around 1800, more violins, as well as clarinets and timpani, were added to such ensembles.) The enterprising Padilla also operated an instrument-building workshop in Puebla, which employed several Black instrument makers and sold to other regions of Mexico and to Guatemala.[11]

Other cathedrals attracted fine musicians as well. Santiago Billoni (*ca.* 1700–*ca.* 1763) was born in Italy and arrived in New Spain in the 1730s. He played the violin in the cathedrals at Guadalajara and Valladolid (now Morelia), and in late 1749, he became chapelmaster at the Durango cathedral in northern New Spain.[12] Drawing on his experience as a violinist, he wrote idiomatically for strings, writing a set of *Fabordones* for orchestra and, according to some evidence, divertimenti for strings in addition to some vocal works that call for instruments. Another center for music was the Oaxaca cathedral.[13] Outside of formal worship, the faithful publicly celebrated their devotion to the Virgin of Guadalupe with "drums, bugles, and well-tuned instruments" or "drums, shawms, and 'flutes played harmoniously,'" according to one chronicler.[14] Music also enlivened the Inquisition. Its first trial in the Americas took place in Mexico City in 1536, accompanied by spectacle that included trumpets and drums. Sometimes musicians were among the condemned for singing "profane songs."[15]

As in South America, music thrived in the missions, with many in Mexico alone. The first of seven in the Sierra Gorda region (south central Mexico) was established in the late seventeenth century; others took hold on the northern frontier (Durango, Chihuahua, Sinaloa, Sonora).[16] Throughout New Spain, the friars encountered many Indigenous groups, including the P'urépecha, who lack a direct translation of the word *music* in their language.[17] In Alta California (now the state of California), the Franciscan Junípero Serra, fluent in Otomí, founded a total of nine of 21 missions, starting in 1769. Several boasted orchestras. At Mission Santa Barbara, inventories list four flutes, three trumpets and two valveless horns, one Turkish crescent (a percussion stick with jingles), one bass drum, two drums, three triangles, two cellos, twenty-four violins, organ with six registers, and a four-octave keyboard; the missions at San Antonio de Padua and Santa Clara also had full orchestras.[18] Often, experienced chapelmasters from Spain, such as Florencio Ibañez (1740–1818) and the Mallorcan Juan Bautista Sancho (1771–1830), were in charge of music.[19] As in South America, these ensembles laid a foundation for the symphonic music of Chávez, Revueltas, and many others.

Establishing the missions in Alta California concluded in 1823. All the while, important developments in music distribution were taking place in Mexico City. By around 1800, hundreds of orchestral scores could be purchased there, either imported from Europe or copied in the Americas. Works by Haydn, Pleyel, Mozart, and others were now available to the musical community, a market that could only have existed with a well-established orchestral infrastructure. An important resource was the Fernández de Jáuregui bookshop in Mexico City, a distribution center for these scores. By 1801, hundreds were listed in the inventory.[20] In 1821, Mexico won independence from Spain, after which Agustín de Iturbide reigned briefly as emperor. Amid fervor for Italian opera and salon music, philharmonic societies were established. One, the Sociedad Filarmónica, began as a salon in the home of the pianist Tomás León (1826–93) and attracted composers such as Melesio Morales (1838–1908) and Aniceto Ortega (1825–75); it laid the groundwork for a national conservatory, founded in 1866.[21]

Orchestral composition developed during the *porfiriato*, the long administration of Porfirio Díaz (1876–1911) that ultimately fell in the Mexican Revolution. Gustavo Emilio Campa (1863–1934) and Ricardo Castro (1864–1907) were best known for opera (Castro also wrote numerous character pieces for piano). In the early 1880s, however, Campa composed a *Himno sinfónico* and Castro a Symphony in C Minor (table 8.1) and Leonora Saavedra notes "the

Table 8.1 Symphonies and Other Orchestral Music from Mexico

Symphonies

Ricardo Castro (1864–1907). Symphony in C Minor (1883).

Julián Carrillo (1875–1965). Symphony in D Major (1901); Symphony in C Major (1905); *Sinfonía heroica atonal* (1945). Microtonal symphonies: *Primera sinfonía Colombia* (1926); *Segunda sinfonía Colombia* (1926); *Tercera sinfonía Colombia* (1931).

José Rolón (1876–1945). Symphony in E Minor (1918–19).

Arnulfo Miramontes (1882–1960). Symphony No. 1 (1917); Symphony No. 2 (1939); Symphony No. 3 (1947).

Candelario Huízar (1883–1970). Symphony No. 1 (1933); Symphony No. 2, "Oxpaniztli" (1936); Symphony No. 3 (1938); Symphony No. 4, "Cora" (1942); Symphony No. 5 (1960).

María Teresa Prieto (1896–1982). *Sinfonía asturiana* (1942); *Sinfonía breve* (1945); *Sinfonía cantabile* (1956); *Suite sinfónica* (1967).

Carlos Chávez (1899–1978). See table 8.2.

Eduardo Hernández Moncada (1899–1995). First Symphony (1942); Second Symphony (1943).

Silvestre Revueltas (1899–1940). *La noche de los Mayas* (film score, 1939; arranged by José Yves Limantour as symphonic suite, 1960).

Lan Adomián (1905–79). Symphony No. 1, "Lírica" (1950–51); Symphony No. 2, "La española" (1960); Symphony No. 4 (1958–63); Symphony No. 6, "Le cadeau de la vie" (1963); Symphony No. 7 (1963); Symphony No. 3 (1965); Symphony No. 8 (1966); Symphony No. 5, "Yaar Hak'doshim" (1974).

Luis Sandí (1905–96). *Sinfonía mínima* (string orchestra, 1978); Symphony No. 2 (1979).

Rafael Adame (1906–63). *Sinfonía folclórica* (1924–25).

Daniel Ayala (1908–75). *Sinfonía* (1936).

Salvador Contreras (1910–82). Symphony No. 1 (1944); Symphony No. 2 (1945); Symphony No. 3 (string orchestra, 1963); Symphony No. 4 (unfinished).

Miguel Bernal Jiménez (1910–56). *México: Sinfonía-poema* (1946).

Blas Galindo (1910–93). *Sinfonía breve* (Symphony No. 1, string orchestra, 1952); Symphony No. 2 (1957); Symphony No. 3 (1961).

José Pablo Moncayo (1912–58). *Sinfonía* (1942); *Sinfonietta* (1945); Symphony No. 2 (unfinished).

Carlos Jiménez Mabarak (1916–94). Symphony No. 1 (1945); *Sinfonía en un movimiento* (1962).

Manuel Enríquez (1926–94). First Symphony (1957); Second Symphony (1962).

Joaquín Gutiérrez Heras (1927–2012). *Sinfonía breve* (1992); *Suite sinfónica* (1992).

Federico Ibarra (b. 1946). Symphony No. 1 (1990); Symphony No. 2: *Las antesalas del sueño* (1993).

Other Orchestral Works

Gustavo Emilio Campa (1863–1934). *Himno sinfónico* (1884); *Lamento para gran orquesta* (1890); *Mélodie* (1890).

Rafael Tello (1872–1946). Suite (string orchestra, 1872); Overture to *Nicolás Bravo* (1910); *Madrigal* (string orchestra, 1916); *Patria heróica* (1929); *Elegidium* (chamber orchestra, 1931); *Tríptico mexicano* (orch. of piano piece, 1939).

Julián Carrillo (1875–1965). *Marcha México* (1895); *Suite de bagatelas* (1896); *Suite sinfónica "Los naranjos"* (1903); *Marcha nupcial* (1922); *Impresiones de la Habana* (1929); *Nocturnos* (1935); *Trozo sinfónia atonal* (1961). Microtonal works: *Nocturno al río Hudson* (1926); Concertino (1926); *Gran fantasía sonido 13* (1930).

José Rolón (1876–1945). *Andante malinconico* (1915); *Obertura de concierto* (1920); *Zapotlán. 1895* (1924); *El festín de los enanos* (1925); *Gavotte et musette* (string orchestra, 1928); *Escenas mexicanas* (ca. 1930).

Arnulfo Miramontes (1882–1960). *Primavera* (1910); *Allegro scherzando* (string orchestra, 1917); *Suite sinfónica Mexicana* (1917); *Canción nupcial* (n.d.); *Poema sinfónico de la revolución* (n.d.).

Manuel Ponce (1882–1948). *Interludio elegíaco* (1919); *Estampas nocturnas* (1923); *Merlín* (suite after opera by Isaac Albéniz, 1929); *Danse des anciens mexicains* (1930); *Suite en estilo antiguo* (1933); *Poema elegíaco* (1934); *Chapultepec* (1934); *Ferial* (1940); *Instantáneas mexicanas* (1947).

Candelario Huízar (1883–1970). *Minuetto* (1925); *Suite en estilo antiguo* (1926); *Imágenes* (1927); *Pueblerinas* (1931); *Surco* (1958).

Adolfo Salazar (1890–1958). *Estampas* (1914); *Arabia* (1923); *Pasajes* (1929); *Homenaje a Arbós* (1934).

Antonio Gomezanda (1894–1961). *Fantasía Mexicana* (1922); *Lagos* (1923); *Xiuhzitqüilo o La fiesta del fuego* (1925).

Vicente Mendoza (1894–1964). *Ballet de la revolución* (1931); *Danza tarahumara* (1931); *Tierras solares* (1936); *Azulejos* (1944); *Quetzal* (n.d.); *Suite extremeña* (1941).

María Teresa Prieto (1896–1982). *Chichen Itzá* (1942); *Variaciones y fuga* (1946); *Oración de quietud* (1949); *Sinfonía cantabile* (1956); *Suite sinfónica* (1967); *Cuadro de la naturaleza* (1967); *Tema variado y fuga dodecafónicos* (1968).

Carlos Chávez (1899–1978). *Los cuatro soles* (ballet, 1926, performed in concert version); *Caballos de vapor [H.P.]* (ballet, 1926–32, performed in concert version); *Cantos de México* (1933); *Chapultepec*, formerly *Obertura republican* (1935); *Toccata para orquesta* (1947); *Baile: cuadro sinfónico* (1953; original Finale of Fourth Symphony); *Resonancias* (1964); *Elatio* (1967); *Clío* (symphonic ode, 1969); *Discovery* (1969); *Initium* (1971); *Paisajes mexicanas* (1973).

Eduardo Hernández Moncada (1899–1995). *Marcha fúnebre* (1938); *Guelatao* (1957).

Silvestre Revueltas (1899–1940). *Obra para orquesta* (1929); *Cuauhnahuac* (1930); *Esquinas* (1930); *Ventanas* (1931); *Alcancías* (1932); *Colorines* (1932); *Janitzio* (1933); *Caminos* (1934); *Planos* (1934); *Homenaje a Federico García Lorca* (1935); *Redes* (suite from film score, 1938); *Sensemayá* (1938).

Rodolfo Halffter (1900–1987). *Suite para orquesta* (1924–28); *Dos impromptus y divertimento* (string orchestra, ca. 1931); *Preludio atonal. Homenaje a Arbós* (1933); *Don Lindo de Almería* (ballet suite, 1935); *La madrugada del panadero* (ballet suite, 1940); *Tres sonatas de Fray Antonio Soler* (1951); *Obertura festiva* (1952); *Tres piezas* (string orchestra, 1954); *Tripartita* (1959); *Diferencias para orquesta* (1970); *Dos ambientes sonoros* (1975–79); *Elegía. En memoriam Carlos Chávez* (string orchestra, 1978).

Lan Adomián (1905–79). *Pantomime* (1930); *Preludio* (1930); *Tempo di marcia* No. 1 (1945); *Israel* (1949); *Notturno patetico* (1953); *Tempo di marcia* No. 2 (1955); *Tamayana-mural* (1956–57); *Le matin de magiciens* (1966–67); *Interplay 1* (1971); *Interplay 2* (1975).

Jesús Bal y Gay (1905–93). *Suite para orquesta* (1931); *Serenata para orquesta de concerto grosso* (1941–42); *Tres piezas para gran orquesta* (1945); *Concerto grosso* (1951).

Luis Sandí (1905–96). *Sonora* (1933); *Suite banal* (1936); *La angostura* (1939); *La oja de plata* (string orchestra, ca. 1939); *Norte* (1940); *Tema y variaciones* (1944); *Esbozos sinfónicos* (1951); *Cuatro miniaturas* (1952); *América* (1967); *Cinco gacelas* (string orchestra, 1968); *Trenos* (string orchestra, 1978); *Díptico* (1987–88).

Rosa María Ascot (1908–2002). *Suite* (n.d.).

Daniel Ayala (1908–75). *Tribu* (1934); *Paisaje* (1935); *Panoramas de México* (1936); *El hombre maya* (1939); *Mi viaje a Norteamérica* (1947); *Yaux U ha* (1952).

Salvador Contreras (1910–82). *Tríada en modos griegos* (1935); *Suite indígena primitive* (string orchestra, 1937); *Suite para orquesta de cámara* (1938); *Música para orquesta sinfónica* (1940); *Tres movimientos sinfónicos* (1941); *Obertura en tiempo de danza* (1942); *Suite en tres movimientos* (1944, rev. 1956); *Obertura* (1960); *Danza negra* (1966); *Dos piezas dodecafónicas* (string orchestra, 1966); *Poema elegíaco* (1974); *Homenaje a Stravinski* (string orchestra, 1976); *Homenaje a Carlos Chávez* (string orchestra, 1978); *Símbolos* (1979).

Table 8.1 *continued*

Blas Galindo (1910–93). *Obra para orquesta Mexicana* (1938); *Impresión campestre* (1940); *Sones de mariachi* (1940–41); *Arroyos* (1942); *Arrullo a la niña del retrato* (string orchestra, 1945); *Notturno* (1945); *Homenaje a Cervantes* (1947); *Me gustas cuando callas* (string orchestra, 1948); *Pequeñas variaciones de "El sueño y la presencia": Chacona* (1951); *Scherzo mexicano* (string orchestra, 1952); *Obertura mexicano* No. 1, "Suite de la revolución" (1953); *Homenaje a Juárez* (1957); *Cuatro piezas* (1961); *Tríptico* (string orchestra, 1947); *Homenaje a Juan Rulfo* (1980); *Obertura mexicano* No. 2 (1981); *Suite* (string orchestra, 1985); *Homenaje a Rodolfo Halffter* (1989); *Popocatépetl* (1980).

José Pablo Moncayo (1912–58). *Hueyapan* (1938); *Huapango* (1941); *Tres piezas para orquesta* (1947); *Tierra de temporal* (1949); *Cumbres* (1953); *Bosques* (1954); *La potranca* (1954); *Canción india. Ofrenda* (n.d.).

Carlos Jiménez Mabarak (1916–94). *El nahual herido: preludio sinfónico* (1952); *Obertura* (string orchestra, 1963); *Sala de retratos* (1992); *Cantos de vida y esperanza* (1994).

Manuel Enríquez (1926–94). *Música incidental* (1952); *Suite* (1957); *Trayectorias* (1967); *Ixamatl* (1969); *Encuentros* (1972); *Ritual* (1973); *Raíces* (1977); *Fases* (1978); *Obertura sobre temas de Juventino Rosas* (1989); *Piedras del viento* (1991); *Visión de los Vencidos* (1993).

Joaquín Gutiérrez Heras (1927–2012). *Los cazadores* (1961); *Postludio* (string orchestra, 1986); *Ludus automni* (1991).

Mario Lavista (1943–2021). *Seis piezas* (string orchestra, 1965); *Continuo* (1971); *Lyhannh* (1976); *Ficciones* (1980); *Reflejos de una noche* (string orchestra, 1986); *Aura* (1989); *Clepsidra* (1990–91); *Lacrymosa a la memoria de Gerhart Muench* (1992); *Tropo para Sor Juana, sobre el Sanctus de la Misa a Nuestra Señora del Consuelo* (1995).

Federico Ibarra (b. 1946). *Cinco misterios eléusicos* (1979); *Obertura para un nuevo milenio* (1993); *Obertura para un encuentro fantástico* (1993); *Balada* (string orchestra, 1995).

Daniel Catán (1949–2011). *Hetaera esmeralda* (1975); *El árbol de la vida* (1980); *En un doblez del tiempo* (1982); *Tu son tu risa tu sonrisa* (1991); *El vuelo del águila* (1994); *Florencia en el Amazonas* (orch. suite, 2003).

Ana Lara (b. 1959). *La Víspera* (1989); *Ángeles de llama y hielo* (1993–94); *Canticum Sacrum* (string orchestra, 2000); *Atanor* (2010); *Of Bronze and Blaze* (winds and percussion, 2018); *Cuando caiga el silencio* (2018).

Gabriela Ortíz (b. 1964). *Patios* (1988); *Elegía* (1993); *Zócalo-Bastille* (1996).

development of a symphonic style" in Castro's opera *Atzimba* of 1900.[22] Another composer, Rafael Tello (1872–1946), was a sought-after teacher; Revueltas was among his students. Committed to developing a national opera, Tello composed *Nicolás Bravo* about a Mexican military hero. After its premiere in 1910, the overture was performed separately (table 8.1). José Rolón (1876–1945) founded the Orquesta Sinfónica de Guadalajara in his native city (now the Sinfonía Filarmónica de Jalisco). A student of Nadia Boulanger, he composed a Symphony in E Minor and other orchestral works.[23] Arnulfo Miramontes (1882–1960) composed three symphonies, and Candelario Huízar (1883–1970) wrote five; both also composed other orchestral music. The musicologist and folklorist Vicente Mendoza (1894–1964) is mainly known for his work on the corrido, a strophic narrative song that often recounts historical events. But he also composed music for orchestra, including a *Ballet de la revolución* and indigenous-themed works. Antonio Gomezanda (1894–1961), who studied in Berlin, composed the indigenous-themed orchestral work *Xiuhtzitzqüilo o La fiesta del fuego* (1925), and Eduardo Hernández Moncada (1899–1995), assistant conductor of the Orquesta Sinfónica de México in 1936, wrote two symphonies (see table 8.1 for all).

An important but difficult-to-classify composer of orchestral music is Julián Carrillo (1875–1965). He studied in Leipzig and Ghent, and eventually became convinced that music should embrace more than the 12 half steps of the chromatic scale. Accordingly, he began composing with microtones, writing three microtonal symphonies, among other works; he also composed three nonmicrotonal symphonies.[24] Drawn to New York, he moved there with his family, and in 1915 he conducted the first of the nonmicrotonal symphonies there, having already premiered the work in Leipzig.[25] In the 1920s, his microtonal music was performed under the auspices of organizations such as the New York–based League of Composers. An important work in this style was Concertino (1926), commissioned by Leopold Stokowski. Carrillo calls for six instruments using microtones (piccolo, horn, guitar, violin, harp, cello) and a nonmicrotonal orchestra, much in the format of the concertino and ripieno of the Baroque concerto grosso.

Since Mexico was the only country other than the Soviet Union to support the Republican side in the Spanish Civil War (1936–39), many Spanish expatriates unwelcome in Franco's Spain flocked to Mexico. They included the composer-critic Adolfo Salazar (1890–1958), Rodolfo Halffter (1900–1987), and Jesús Bal y Gay (1905–93), all of whom wrote orchestral music (table 8.1).[26] Two others were Rosa García Ascot (1908–2002), who studied with Boulanger from 1938 to 1939, and María Teresa Prieto (1896–1982), who came from Asturias (northwest Spain). In Mexico, Prieto composed the symphonic poem *Chichen Itzá*, along with *Sinfonía asturiana* (both 1942); as the composer herself acknowledged, the symphony expresses homesickness and nostalgia for her native region. In Mexico, she studied with Manuel Ponce (1882–1948) and later with Darius Milhaud at Mills College in Oakland, California. Her other orchestral works includes *Tema variado y fuga dodecafónicos* from 1968 (table 8.1).

Ponce is known as a standard-bearer for Mexican musical nationalism. As a young man, he studied composition in Bologna; a fine pianist, he then went to Berlin to have lessons with Martin Krause, who also taught Edwin Fischer and Claudio Arrau. Upon returning home, Ponce established himself in Mexican musical circles although he intermittently traveled to Havana, New York, and Paris. Over the course of his career, he mastered several styles and techniques. During the early years of the revolution, Ponce championed the Mexican cancion, seen as emblematic of Mexican identity and which he called "the soul of the people."[27] He harmonized canciones, appealing to composers far and wide to construct a national musical identity,[28] among them Luis Delgadillo of Nicaragua, discussed below. He also railed against the "Yankee invention" of the foxtrot and its undue influence.[29] Ponce's orchestral works, three of which are concertos (including *Concierto del sur* of 1941, a highly influential guitar concerto), reveal the breadth of his style.[30] Musical nationalism manifests itself in symphonic works such as *Ferial* (Feast Day, 1940), which contains indigenous and Mexican melodies. Another work is the "symphonic triptych" *Chapultepec*, which Stokowski performed in 1934 with the Philadelphia Orchestra.[31] Back in Mexico City, near the end of his restless life, he completed *Instantáneas mexicanas*, a seven-part series of miniatures (table 8.1).

CARLOS CHÁVEZ

In July 1947, Ponce's best-known student, Carlos Chávez (1899–1978), premiered the *Instantáneas mexicanas* with the Orquesta Sinfónica de México, which he conducted for years.[32] Chávez had studied piano with Ponce but not composition; indeed, lacking formal training in the latter, Chávez preferred to study treatises and scores on his own. Like other Latin American composers of his generation, Chávez was heir to a tradition of musical nationalism (e.g., the cancion); as a teenager, he published an article in which he argued that Mexican folklore could serve as a basis for modern music. The precocious Chávez tried his hand at a symphony at age sixteen. In 1921, he presented a debut concert in Mexico City, which critics found excessively modern. In the ensuing years, he was often at odds with the artistic program of José Vasconcelos, which privileged folk music above the modernist and so-called primitive (i.e., indigenous) musics that Chávez came to favor.[33] Increasingly at home in New York, Chávez met Varèse, Henry Cowell, and especially Aaron Copland, with whom he had much in common; his modernist-indigenist music was seen to represent an authentic voice of the Western Hemisphere, with more effusive critics hearing "Toltec divinities" and "high deserts" in his music.[34] Like many of his peers, Chávez ultimately downplayed musical nationalism and advocated for "universal" music.[35] Much admired as a conductor at home and abroad, Chávez taught at the conservatory and wrote lively and engaging music criticism in addition to composing.[36]

Chávez's six numbered symphonies reflect the immense variety of his *oeuvre* (table 8.2).[37] Initially, he conceived the first, *Sinfonía de Antígona* (Antigone Symphony), as incidental music for a performance of Jean Cocteau's adaptation of Sophocles's tragedy. Some of its quartal and quintal harmonies are based on Dorian and Hypodorian modes; Chávez, who often used oboe and English horn in his orchestral writing, enhances his instrumental palette here with the seldom-heard heckelphone, along with alto flute and eight horns. More than once, he was inspired by antiquity, either in terms of subject matter (as with *Sinfonía de Antígona*) or by classic principles such as restraint, clarity, and equipoise. What makes the label "neoclassical" less than satisfactory for much of Chávez's classically oriented scores is his tendency to weave in gestures associated with musical primitivism, such as repetition (rather than development) of motivic fragments of narrow melodic range, ostinati, and pentatonicism, such that the adjective *austere* frequently appears in criticism of his music.[38]

Chávez's second and best-known symphony, the *Sinfonía India*, is anything but austere, however.[39] Its Indianist elements include native melodies and indigenous percussion instruments such as the teponatzli and the huehuetl, described above. He also used strings of deer hooves, the water gourd, and *tenebari* (butterfly cocoon rattles), the latter used in the traditional Yaqui deer dance.[40] (If an orchestra might lack deer hooves or butterfly cocoons, Chávez recommends substitutes, as shown in table 8.2.) In accordance with twentieth-century primitivist signifiers, several themes have a narrow melodic range, as with the three-note melody beginning at Reh. 14; the piece also involves mixed meters (Rehs. 1–9, for example) and subtle use of cross-rhythms in the central slow section (from Reh. 27). The classicizing element of the one-movement work is its structure, which the experienced listener instinctively relates to sonata form. A formal diagram of the work, endorsed by the composer, appears in a biography by the Argentine scholar and composer Roberto García Morillo.[41] The fact that other readings of *Sinfonía India* are equally plausible confirms both the vitality of this work and the plasticity of the time-honored form. Do we really hear Rehs. 1–9 as an introduction, as Chávez proposes, or as *P*? To be sure, the material heard at Reh. 9, which Chávez considers the *P*, returns before the recapitulation of the opening material (at Rehs. 59 and 81, respectively), but Chávez would hardly be the first composer to reverse the order of the *P* and *S* material. Accordingly, the section beginning at Reh. 52 can be reasonably heard as a retransition, the music that anticipates the inevitable return. Given the exuberant percussion, dramatic accelerando, and peremptory unison writing (from Reh. 56), the passage in question could hardly fulfill this formal requirement more aptly.

Chávez's third symphony was commissioned by Clare Boothe Luce (1903–87), the first woman in the United States appointed to major ambassadorial positions (Italy, Brazil) and

Table 8.2 The Symphonies of Carlos Chávez (1899–1978)[a]

Title	Movements	Instrumentation	Comments
Sinfonía para orquesta (1915–18)	1. Preludio 2. Allegro maestoso 3. Adagio	2 Flt., 2 Ob., 2 Clar., 3 Bssn., 4 Hr., 4 Tpt., 3 Trom., Tuba, Timp., Strgs.	Begun at age 15. Completed but never performed or published, and not acknowledged by Chávez in his list of works.
Sinfonía de la Patria (1923)			Written for concert by the Orquesta Sinfónica Nacional on December 16, 1923, but taken off the program the day before the concert; see Saavedra/ SELVES, pp. 122–25. Work appears to follow an Aztec theme, but unclear if it was a program symphony or symphonic suite; manuscript lost until recently. Not listed in Halffter/CHÁVEZ.
Sinfonía de Antígona [Symphony No. 1] (1933)	One movement 2/4 (197 mm.)	Picc., Flt., Aflt., Ob., EH, Heckelphone, 2 Clar., E♭ Clar., Bclar., 3 Bssn., 8 Hr., 3 B Tpt., Tuba, 3 Perc. (Glsp., SD, Tenor Drum, Indian Drum, Small Cyms., Large Cyms.), Timp., 2 Harps, Strgs.	Originally written as incidental music for a 1932 production in Mexico City of Sophocles's play in a version by Jean Cocteau. Reorchestrated and lengthened from 7 to 12 minutes. Premiere: December 15, 1933, by the Orquesta Sinfónica de México, conducted by the composer. Published by G. Schirmer, 1948.

Table 8.2 continued

Title	Movements	Instrumentation	Comments
Sinfonía India [Symphony No. 2] (1935–36)	One movement 5/8 (491 mm.)	2 Picc. (Picc. 2 doubling 3rd Flt.), 2 Flt., 3 Ob., 2 Clar., E Clar., Bclar., 3 Bssn., 4 Hr., 2 B Tpt., 2 Trom., 4 Perc. (Player 1: Yaqui Drum, Clay Rattle, Yaqui Metal Rattle, Suspended Cym.; Player 2: Water Gourd, *Tenebari* [string of butterfly cocoons], Large Claves, 2 *Teponaztles* [two-keyed Xylos.]; Player 3: SD with snares off, *Grijutian* [string of deer hooves], Güiro; Player 4: *Tlapanhuéhuetl* [large cylindrical drum], Raspador Yaqui], Timp., Harp, Strgs. In the absence of Indigenous instruments, Chávez authorizes the following alternative scoring for percussion: Player 1: Indian Drum, 1 Maraca, Metal Rattle, Suspended Cym.; Player 2: Tenor Drum without snares, Soft Rattle made from pasteboard, Large Claves, Xylo.; Player 3: SD with snares off, Rattling String made of hard wooden beads, Güiro; Player 4: BD, Rasping Stick.	Quotes indigenous melodies of the Cora, Yaqui, Sonora, and Seri peoples; employs native percussion instruments (for which Chávez indicates alternatives if needed). Commissioned by William S. Paley for a CBS radio broadcast. Premiere: January 23, 1936, by the Columbia Broadcasting Symphony Orchestra, conducted by the composer. Published by G. Schirmer, 1950.
Symphony No. 3 (1951–54)	1. Introduzione—Andante moderato 3/4 (120 mm.) 2. Allegro 12/8 (198 mm.) 3. Scherzo 2/4 (183 mm.) 4. Finale: Molto lento 4/4 (91 mm.)	Picc., 2 Flt, 2 Ob., EH, 2 Clar., E Clar., 3 Bssn (3rd doubling Cbssn.), 4 Hr., 3 B Tpt., 3 Trom., Tuba, Timp., 3 Perc. (Player 1: Cyms., SD; Player 2: Tam-tam, Tenor Drum; Player 3: BD, Large Tam-tam, SD), Harp, Strgs.	Commissioned by Clare Booth Luce in memory of her daughter Ann Clare Brokaw, to whom the work is dedicated. Completed in 1954, after Chávez had written the Fourth and Fifth Symphonies. Premiere: December 11, 1954, at the First Festival of Latin American Music in Caracas by the Orquesta Sinfónica de Venezuela, conducted by the composer. Awarded the Caro de Boesi prize by the Institución José Angel Lamas, Caracas. Published by Boosey & Hawkes, 1955.

Symphony	Movements	Instrumentation	Notes
Symphony No. 4: *Sinfonía romántica* (1953)	1. Allegro 4/4 (172 mm.) 2. Molto lento 4/4 (62 mm.) 3. Vivo non troppo mosso 4/4 (240 mm.)	3 Flt. (3rd doubling Picc.), 2 Ob., EH, 2 Clar., 3 Bssn. (3rd doubling Cbssn.), 4 Hr., 2 B Tpt., 3 Trom., Tuba, Perc. (Player 1: Suspended Cyms., SD, Claves; Player 2: Tenor Drum, BD, Maraca, Suspended Cyms.; Player 3: Glsp., Xylo., BD), Timp., Strgs.	Commissioned by and dedicated to the Louisville Orchestra. Premiere: February 11, 1953, by the Louisville Orchestra, conducted by the composer. After the premiere, Chávez replaced the Finale with a new movement. He released the original Finale as *Baile: Cuadro sinfónico*. He added the subtitle *Sinfonía romántica* for the published score. Published by Boosey & Hawkes, 1959.
Symphony No. 5 (1953)	1. Allegro molto moderato 12/8 (122 mm.) 2. Molto lento 4/4 (112 mm.) 3. Allegro con brio 4/4 (145 mm.)	Strgs. (five parts: Vlc. and Cb. separate)	Commissioned by the Serge Koussevitzky Music Foundation in the Library of Congress. Premiere: December 1, 1953, by the Los Angeles Chamber Orchestra, conducted by the composer. Published by Affiliated Musicians, 1954.
VI Symphony (1961)	1. Allegro energico 4/4 (346 mm.) 2. Adagio molto cantabile 4/4 (53 mm.) 3. Con anima 9/8 (451 mm.)	Picc., 2 Flt., 2 Ob., EH, 2 Clar., 2 Bssn., Cbssn., 4 Hr., 2 B Tpt., 2 Trom., Btrom., Tuba, 2 Perc. (2 Suspended Cyms., SD, BD), Timp., Strgs.	Modeled on Brahms's Fourth Symphony, with a Passacaglia as the Finale. Commissioned by the New York Philharmonic in celebration of its opening season in the Lincoln Center for the Performing Arts. Dedicated to Leonard Bernstein and the New York Philharmonic. Premiere: May 7, 1964, by the New York Philharmonic, conducted by Bernstein. Published by Mills Music, 1965.
Symphony No. 7 (ca. 1960)	1. Allegro 2. Andante 3. Finale	3 Flt., 3 Ob., 3 Clar., 3 Bssn., 4 Hr., 3 Tpt., 3 Trom., Tuba, 3 Perc., Timp., 2 Harps, Strgs.	Listed in Halffter/CHÁVEZ, 61. Catalog does not indicate how much, if any, of the work was written.

a. Table by Brian Hart.

likely the first—if not the only—US diplomat to write a hit Broadway play, *The Women*. After losing her nineteen-year-old daughter in an automobile accident, Luce commissioned a musical tribute from Chávez, whom she had met in Italy. Initially, she wanted a piano concerto, stipulating that it be "the most beautiful and sad and gay thing [Chávez] ever wrote" and that it convey her daughter's "lovely face and my broken heart."[42] Between 1951 and 1954, Chávez labored over the commission, but for various reasons he completed the Fourth and Fifth Symphonies before getting to Luce's commission. He now conceived of the work as a symphony and by 1954 it was ready: the work premiered at the First Festival of Latin American Music in Caracas, taking second prize. Luce was unable to attend but she heard the symphony in New York City in early 1956, whereupon she gave it her full approval.

The four-movement symphony opens soberly, with several passages featuring the three percussionists in full and dire force. Counteracting this tragic mood, however, is a pentatonic chant sung by children worldwide: first heard in the flute at Reh. 16 and again at Reh. 24, it also returns in the last moments of the Finale, starting at 1 m. before Reh. 153 and recurring intermittently until the strife-ridden coda (Reh. 161). Robert L. Parker argues persuasively that, in inserting this tune, Chávez may have had in mind the extremes Luce specified—although, on the face of it, such a concession contradicts his stated desire to write an abstract work "whose expression lies in its purely musical values."[43] But for the pentatonic chant, Movement I conveys grief staggering under its own weight; the bizarrely elongated final cadence, spotlighting the piccolo, suggests only the most ephemeral of conclusions. Movements II and III, on the other hand, revel in wit. Both contain passages reminiscent of the cool woodwind timbres of Stravinsky's Octet, such as the Meno mosso of Movement II (example 1) or the playful fugato that opens Movement III (which, unlike the Octet, calls for contrabassoon). Chávez begins Movement II by transposing down the relentlessly repeated octave in the piccolo that closes Movement I—not unlike the transition between Movements I and II of Beethoven's String Quartet in C-sharp Minor, Op. 131—with closely spaced strings sighing on a nonfunctional F♯-minor ninth chord. For all its perkiness, though, Movement II concludes wistfully. The final bars of Movement III, with the prominent piccolo, recalls the quirky ending of Movement I; it, however, ends firmly in F major. Movement IV begins with a recitative-like solo for English horn and harp, which expands to wind trios (Rehs. 145, 147). Chávez delays the entrance of

Example 8.1 Chávez. Symphony No. 3, mvt. 2, reh. 50–51

the strings for five minutes into the movement. Despite the brief references to the pentatonic chant, the symphony ends in anguish, with only a fragment of the tune repeated three times in the horns (2 mm. before Reh. 164).

Copland wrote admiringly in his diary of the symphony after hearing it in Caracas. To be sure, he found it "uncompromising" and doubted that it would "make friends easily if at all."[44] He also noted "a kind of unevenness of interest peculiar to [Chávez], the tunes are unimportant; it is the brutal force and almost sadistic power that holds the attention . . . one cannot help but be impressed."[45] For some critics, however, Chávez would never be anything but the Mexican Indian. When the New York Philharmonic performed the Third Symphony in January 1956, Howard Taubman, who had supported the composer since the 1930s, noted the symphony's "primitive cast"; he asserted that, as in the past when Chávez "sought consciously to evoke Mexico's ancient Indian music," the Third Symphony too communicated "the spirit of an antique heritage in a mature form that has become Señor Chávez' personal style."[46]

Chávez wrote his Fourth Symphony, subtitled *Sinfonía romántica*, at white heat so as to meet a performance deadline by the Louisville Orchestra, which commissioned the work and premiered it in February 1953. Listeners differ on the suitability of the subtitle: although Parker attributes it to the symphony's "lyricism and buoyancy," Copland told Chávez that "the Romántica doesn't seem so romántica to me."[47] After a few performances, Chávez decided to replace the Finale; he wrote a new movement and released the rejected one separately as *Baile: Cuadro sinfónico* (Dance: Symphonic Picture). In a letter to the program annotator, Chávez referred to the symphony's classic features, noting the presence in Movement I of a *P, S* (Reh. 3) and *K* (Reh. 10); *I/P* returns in Movements II and III, slightly altered and sometimes enhanced with countermelodies.[48] The development section of the otherwise harmonically placid movement opens with a stinging dissonance (2 mm. before Reh. 14), anticipating the concluding sonority of the entire work (example 2). Movement II, a Molto Lento, scored for strings and brass, begins by citing *I/P* in counterpoint and with striking timbral contrasts. Movement III begins in the style of a *moto perpetuo*, with fragments of dance-like motives, occasionally prominent percussion, and restatements of *I/P*.

Chávez's Fifth Symphony, for strings alone, also dates from 1953 and was commissioned by the Koussevitzky Music Foundation in the Library of Congress. In April 1954 the composer premiered it with the Los Angeles Chamber Orchestra. The brief and compact work consists of three movements. Its principal theme dominates the first while the multisectional second movement features an array of contrasts: tempo changes; abrupt shifts of texture; and close, grating harmonies alternating with more consonant passages, such as that at Reh. 50. The final section is scored exclusively in natural harmonics, a "magical moment" according to one Los Angeles critic.[49] Movement III, filled with nonimitative counterpoint, proceeds along the lines of a vigorous invention. The Sixth Symphony (or VI Symphony, as the composer titled it) dates from 1961. As indicated in the score, Chávez composed it to mark the opening of the 1962 season of the New York Philharmonic at Lincoln Center. (Bernstein did not premiere the symphony until 1964.) Throughout this discreet work, Chávez spotlights the low brass, using the tuba to announce the theme of the passacaglia in Movement III, sometimes combining brass with contrabassoon. These dark colors contrast with the glassier, bell-like timbres in Movement I or the prominent low strings of Movement II.

For many listeners, Chávez's six numbered symphonies are the most eloquent written by any Latin American composer. Having such extensive experience as a conductor, he knew firsthand the potential of the orchestra. His writing for strings is often dry (even percussive)

Carol A. Hess

Example 8.2 Chávez. Symphony No. 4 ("Romántica), mvt. 1

rather than lyrical, and his preference for woodwinds over strings is evident in the trios in the Third Symphony, for example. He also features unusual instruments, such as the heckelphone and native percussion, as well as surprising combinations of more conventional instruments, such as English horn and E-flat clarinet in the opening of the Third Symphony. These timbral choices go beyond mere splashes of "color." Rather, in combination with formal discipline and clearly delineated structures, they reveal the logic and clarity of Chávez's musical thinking. In fact, Chávez often reduces symphonic form to its barest essentials even while departing from established procedures. Convinced that artists should always reinvent traditional forms, he was known for his concept of "non-repetition," as manifested in his chamber works *Soli I* and *Soli IV* (1933, 1966), which feature a continuous unfolding of new material in a kind of "eternal development."[50] In symphonies, of course, some repetition is necessary, but Chávez usually alters the instrumentation in such passages, drawing on the approaches just described. An "austere" outlook also prevails in Chávez's thematic material. As Copland pointed out, his themes are anything but tuneful, often relying on extreme ranges. Or they may be quite angular, with wide leaps. All told, Chávez brings to the symphony a wealth of techniques and a perspective all his own.

SILVESTRE REVUELTAS

Just as Haydn and Mozart, Debussy and Ravel, or Albéniz and Granados are often paired, Chávez is often mentioned in the same breath with his compatriot and direct contemporary Silvestre Revueltas (1899–1940).[51] Like Chávez, Revueltas tested his fortunes in the United States, living there for extended periods: in Austin and Chicago as a student and then in Mobile, Alabama, and San Antonio, Texas, as a professional musician.[52] Upon returning to Mexico, he served as an assistant conductor under Chávez starting in 1929, although the two eventually fell out. One of Revueltas's most celebrated works expresses his solidarity with the beleaguered Loyalist government during the Spanish Civil War: *Homenaje a Federico García Lorca* (Homage to Federico García Lorca). Dating from 1936, it honors the Spanish poet murdered by General Francisco Franco's forces early in the conflict.[53] Apart from the middle movement, "Duelo" (Sorrow), the work is anything but dirgelike, however, and listeners often express surprise at the exuberant outer movements, which convey the slain poet's childlike nature. As he does in other works, Revueltas draws on popular street idioms rather than the sound world of indigenous cultures.

Another well-known symphonic work by Revueltas is *Sensemayá*, inspired by a poem of the same title by the Afro-Cuban poet Nicolás Guillén (1902–89).[54] It concerns the Afro-Cuban rite of killing a snake (for Guillén, a symbol of imperialism): a skilled dancer carries a large figure representing the snake while participants chant a series of incantations and beat the snake with clubs. Revueltas's creative process for this piece was unusual. He first set the incantations to music, then deleted the words and used these passages as refrains. Several themes, including one derived from the octatonic scale, jostle against three main ostinati; the music mimics the slithering of the snake, the incantations, and the beating of the reptile. Thanks to bass clarinet, basses, bassoon, and a prominent tuba solo, dark timbres prevail, along with a generous percussion section of traditional and folk instruments, including xylophone, claves, maracas, rasp, gourd, small Indian drum, bass drum, high and low tom-toms, cymbals, large and small gongs, glockenspiel, celesta, and piano. The dissonant layering of textures, the jagged rhythms and shifting meters (within a prevailing 7/8), and ritualistic repetitions at the climax show

Revueltas's imaginative absorption of *Le Sacre du printemps*, conveyed within a captivating and often riotous sound world.

Revueltas was much taken with the then-new medium of cinema and composed a total of nine film scores. In 1935, by which time he had broken with Chávez, he began work on *Redes*, a tale of exploited fisherman that corresponded perfectly to the composer's social vision. Both the film and Revueltas's score made a powerful impression in leftist circles in New York during the 1930s (the literal translation of the title, "Nets," was modified as "The Wave" for English-language audiences).[55] Thanks to an arrangement by Erich Kleiber, it can be played as concert music.[56] Another film score, *La noche de los Mayas* (The Night of the Mayas), also treats the plight of a marginalized group. Director Chano Ureta shot the film on location in the Yucatán, depicting the clash between a traditional Mayan community and a tragic encounter with "civilization." After its 1939 premiere in Mexico City, the film attracted little notice. But in 1960, twenty years after Revueltas's death, the Mexican conductor and composer José Limantour arranged thirty-six cues into a four-movement suite, endowing it with "the shape of a symphony," as one commentator explains.[57] A weighty first movement ("Noche de los Mayas") is followed by a Scherzo ("Noche de Jaranas" or Night of Revelry). In the slow movement ("Noche de Yucatán"), some of Revueltas's most romantic passages alternate with a Yucatán evening song. The finale ("Noche de encantamiento" or Night of Enchantment) consists of a series of variations on a pentatonic theme. After the introduction of the theme, the thirteen-member percussion battery engages in a lively cadenza added in the late 1990s by the conductor Enrique Diemecke (with the approval of the Revueltas estate). In each of the variations that follow, increasingly frenzied layers of ostinatos in the percussion and shrieks from the woodwinds hurl the music, juggernaut style, toward its powerful climax, with *I/P* returning at the end to round off the composition. Thanks in part to riveting performances by the Venezuelan Youth Orchestra, *La noche de los Mayas* has become one of Revueltas's most frequently performed works.

That *chavistas* and *revueltistas* battle it out in Mexico today not only confirms the enduring significance of these two figures but highlights some significant differences between them. Certainly no one would accuse Revueltas of "austerity." His music is frequently more humorous than Chávez's, as in the outer movements of the *Homenaje*. Humor turns sardonic in the orchestral work *Janitzio*: with exaggerated high spirits that border on the grotesque, *Janitzio* masquerades as a paean to Lake Pátzcuaro but is really a dig at the tourist industry and commodification. If Chávez's unusual timbral combinations ultimately serve musical logic, Revueltas's orchestration was praised for "brilliancy and expert use of telling . . . colors," as the *New York Times* critic Olin Downes observed.[58] Copland, who believed that Chávez had greater command of form, nonetheless found that Revueltas left the listener "with a sense of the abundance and vitality of life."[59] Whereas Chávez employs spiky themes, Revueltas's melodies tend to be diatonic and folklike, frequently evoking popular idioms. An overarching organizational principle for Revueltas is rhythm, with ostinato one of his favorite devices. It confers on *Sensemayá*, with its three ostinati, a visceral drive, just as the final movement of *La noche de los Mayas* generates similarly raw excitement in contrast to the more orderly progression of ideas found in the climax of the *Sinfonía India* and other Chávez symphonies. If Chávez is often associated with Stravinskian Neoclassicism, Revueltas reaches back to the Russian composer's earlier folkloric period. Despite these differing approaches, the two composers have both been considered nationalists, showing the elasticity of that term.

The Symphony in Mexico, Central America, and the Spanish-Speaking Caribbean

AFTER CHÁVEZ AND REVUELTAS

Another twentieth-century Mexican composer who composed orchestral music was Luis Sandi (1905–96), mainly associated with the Coro de Madrigalists, which he founded in 1938; his orchestral works include several symphonic poems, an orchestral suite derived from his ballet *Bonampak* (after the Mayan archaeological site), and a *Suite banal*, as well as two symphonies from late in his career. The Ukrainian-born Lan Adomián (1905–79), who became involved in leftist causes such as the Composers Collective while living in the United States, wrote eight symphonies. Two composers who drew on Mexican idioms were Rafael Adame Gómez (1906–63), a native of Jalisco, who wrote *Sinfonía folclórica* (1924–25), and Miguel Bernal Jiménez (1910–56) of Morelia (Michoacán state). Known primarily for his religious music, Bernal Jiménez honored his birthplace in a symphonic poem *Noche en Morelia* (1941). His *México: Sinfonía-poema* dates from 1946 (table 8.1).

Daniel Ayala (1908–75), Blas Galindo (1910–93), Salvador Contreras (1910–82), and José Pablo Moncayo (1912–58) are known collectively as the *Grupo de los Cuatro*. They met as students at the National Conservatory of Music, where they enrolled in Chávez's class "Creación Musical." (According to Galindo, a class in "musical creation" was not quite the same thing as a composition seminar, since it required students to solve problems that went beyond conventional musical and aesthetic practices.[60]) When Chávez left the Conservatory in late 1934, the young men continued working together, and when they presented their works publicly in Mexico City in November 1935, a critic christened them as an entity. Like *Les Six* in France or the *Grupo de los ocho* in Spain, the *Grupo de los Cuatro* was united more by common purpose than by adherence to a particular compositional style, although the four identified most closely with Chávez and Revueltas. All wrote orchestral music. Ayala, who often drew on his Mayan heritage in his compositions, wrote the ballet score *El hombre maya* and a symphonic poem called *Tribu* (Tribe); he also wrote a symphonic work *Panoramas de México*, which was performed by the Orquesta Sinfónica de Yucatán and the Dallas Symphony.[61] In addition to several other orchestral works, Galindo composed three symphonies. Contreras's orchestral works include *Música para orquesta sinfónica*, *Tres movimientos sinfónicos*, and a Suite for Chamber Orchestra, all of which Copland examined when he visited Mexico City in 1941.[62]

Of all the works by any member of the *Grupo de los Cuatro*, surely Moncayo's *Huapango* (1941) is the most celebrated. He took as his point of departure the traditional Mexican dance from the Huasteca region, which is in a brisk tempo and based on alternating six- and three-beat patterns. The genre inspired more than one composer: the folklorist Gerónimo Baqueiro Fóster (1898–1967) orchestrated several huapangos. Thanks to Moncayo's deft balancing of instrumental groupings (especially spotlighting the harp), his gradual introduction of new themes, and an overall exuberant character, his *Huapango* remains popular worldwide. Moncayo also composed a symphony and a sinfonietta (a second symphony is unfinished) as well as other orchestral works with impressionistic titles, including *La potranca* (The filly) from his score for a portion of the 1955 film *Raíces* (table 8.1).[63]

Slightly younger than the members of the *Grupo de los Cuatro* were Carlos Jiménez Mabarak (1916–94), who studied in Brussels and Rome, and in Mexico City with Revueltas. Later, he worked with René Leibowitz in Paris. After receiving a prize for one of his film scores (*La deseada*, 1961), Jiménez Mabarak was much in demand in Mexican cinema. His orchestral works include a Symphony No. 1 in E-flat as well as a second symphony in one movement. He won a prize for his music for the 1968 Olympics in Mexico City. Committed to communicating with the broad public, Jiménez Mabarak was nonetheless among the first Mexican composers to use twelve-tone technique and electronic media. Another composer of orchestral music was Manuel Enríquez (1926–94) of Jalisco state. He studied with Bernal Jiménez and Stefan Wolpe, the latter in New York, and received several prizes and commissions. Enríquez also served as an arts administrator in Mexico and taught at two branches of the University of California (Los Angeles and San Diego). His compositions span Neoclassicism, minimalism, aleatory, indeterminacy with graphic notation, and other trends. Enríquez's orchestral works include two symphonies and other works (table 8.1). Joaquín Gutiérrez Heras (1927–2012) studied composition with Galindo and analysis with Rodolfo Halffter, with Olivier Messiaen in Paris and then, on a Rockefeller Foundation Scholarship, with William Bergsma and Vincent Persichetti at the Juilliard School in New York. Back in Mexico he directed a radio station and taught. He wrote several orchestral works (table 8.1).

Three major composers were born in Mexico City during the 1940s. Mario Lavista (1943–2021) studied composition with Chávez and analysis with Halffter. In 1967 he attended classes with Iannis Xenakis and Henri Pousseur in Paris and then went to Germany to study with Karlheinz Stockhausen (Cologne) and to attend the Darmstadt summer program in 1968. He has taken great advantage of avant-garde techniques, composing in 1969 a work for fifteen alarm clocks, appropriately called *Kronos*. Among his several orchestral works is *Ficciones*, which premiered in 1980. Influenced by the eponymous short story collection by the Argentine author Jorge Luis Borges, Lavista embedded into his score "mirrors, labyrinths, and harmonic circles" in addition to other allusive devices.[64] Another orchestral work, *Lacrymosa* (1994), was premiered by the American Composers Orchestra. Julio Estrada (b. 1943) studied initially with Julián Orbón (see below) and then, like Lavista, with Pousseur, Xenakis, and Stockhausen. Active in computer music, he has composed a few works for orchestra, among them *Naufragio* (Shipwreck) of 2003 for strings. Federico Ibarra (b. 1946) also studied with Stockhausen and Halffter, in addition to taking classes with Pierre Schaeffer. A fine pianist, he premiered works by Henry Cowell, John Cage, and George Crumb in Mexico. His orchestral works include two symphonies (table 8.1).

One of Ibarra's students was Arturo Márquez (b. 1950), who also studied with Gutiérrez Heras before spending 1980–82 in Paris, where he worked with Jacques Castérèrede. Back in Mexico City, he taught and for a time directed the Municipal Band. Although he has sometimes explored new formats through electroacoustic music and mixed media, he also cares deeply about writing music accessible to the ordinary listener—a tendency probably best exemplified in some of his orchestral works, especially a series of three *Danzones*, each a realization of the *danzón*, a popular genre. Daniel Catán (1949–2011), known mainly for his operas, also composed several orchestral works, one of which is a suite based on his 1996 opera *Florencia en el Amazonas* (table 8.1). Ana Lara (b. 1959) was educated in her native Mexico City, where she studied with Lavista, Ibarra, and Catán; she also studied at the Warsaw Academy and at the University of Maryland. Her orchestral work *Cuando caiga el silencio* invites the listener on an inner journey stimulated by shifting timbres (table 8.1). Ricardo Zohn-Muldoon, a native of Guadalajara (b. 1962), currently teaches at the Eastman School of Music and has written several works for large ensembles. Also teaching at the Eastman School is Carlos Sánchez-Gutiérrez (b. 1963), whose orchestral works include *Girando, danzando* (2015), performed at the Tanglewood Music Festival, and *Gota de Noche*, commissioned for performance in Mexico City. Gabriela Ortíz (b. 1964), also a former student of Lavista and Ibarra, has composed some symphonic works, such as *Patios* (1989) and *Altar de neón* for percussion quartet and chamber orchestra (1995). While Ortíz often pursues an avant-garde style, her almost exact contemporary Hebert Vázquez (b. 1963) draws on the folkloric genre of the *son* in orchestral works such as *El Árbol de la vida*. Gabriel Pareyón (b. 1974), who worked with Mario Lavista, composed *Preludio orquestal* in 1995. Sergio Luque (b. 1976), based in Madrid, writes mainly for smaller ensembles but in 2017 composed *Closing In* for large orchestra.

Central America: Guatemala

In 1524, the Spanish arrived in what is now Guatemala, where the impressive culture of the Maya had prevailed for more than two thousand years. During colonial times, musical life centered around the Guatemala City Cathedral, which employed eminent composers such as Hernando Franco (1532–85), who worked there before he went to Mexico City. Archival evidence confirms the presence of instruments: for example, a "caxa [box] de flautas grandes" was purchased in 1549.[65] Other composers included Manuel José de Quirós, chapelmaster from 1738 until his death in 1765. Among his villancicos is "Una escuela de muchachos," scored for SATB, four horns, violins, and continuo.[66] Quirós was succeeded by his nephew Rafael Antonio Castellanos, who also wrote villancicos, often accompanied by a chamber orchestra. Outside of Guatemala City, chapelmasters directed morning and evening music "with organs and other musical instruments."[67]

Early composers of symphonic music in Guatemala included José Eulalio Samayoa (*ca.* 1781–1866). His first six symphonies are lost but three are extant. No. 7, dedicated to a military victory, employs in its fourth movement a *son chapín*, a Guatemalan popular genre in 6/8 meter.[68] Other symphonies by Samayoa are nicknamed *Sinfonía Cívica* and *Sinfonía Histórica*; he also composed the series *Piezas para tocarse en la Iglesia* (Pieces to be Played in Church) for middle-sized to large orchestras.[69] Luis Felipe Arias (1862–1908), who studied in Naples, was a pianist and a distinguished conductor and composed a *Morisca* for orchestra. In 1873, a national conservatory was founded in Guatemala City, and in 1936, the Orquesta Sinfónica Nacional de Guatemala, known as the Orquesta Liberal Progresista until 1944.[70] One of its conductors, the Paris-trained Jorge Castañeda (1898–1983), wrote three symphonies and a ballet score, *La serpiente emplumada*, which takes as its subject matter the Mayan legend *Popol Vuh* and which premiered in 1958. Castañeda also participated in Good Neighbor–era cultural diplomacy.[71]

Other composers included Raúl Paniagua (1879–1953), largely self-taught. He based his symphonic poem *Mayan Legend* on elements of indigenous music; it was performed by the National Orchestral Association of New York on February 17, 1931. Downes found it "highly experimental and somewhat barbaric" with themes "of an exotic and primitive sort."[72] Downes also noted that Paniagua got some of his material for *Mayan Legend* from the composer and ethnomusicologist Jesús Castillo (1877–1946). Castillo, who began his studies in his native city of Quezaltenango, was regarded as a leading figure in Guatemalan musical nationalism and drew on indigenous music in his five *Oberturas indígenas*, among other works.[73] His symphonic poem *Tecún Umán* is based on a work by the Guatemalan poet Miguel Ángel Aturias (1899–1974), who also inspired Edgard Varèse's *Ecuatorial* (table 8.3). Castillo's younger half-brother Ricardo Castillo (1891–1966) also began music instruction in Quetzaltenango. He then studied violin and composition in Paris, the latter with Paul Vidal. (According to Slonimsky, Castillo was such a Francophile that he fought with the French army during World War I.) In 1922, he returned home and began teaching at the National Conservatory, a post he held for many years. He arranged his piano piece *Guatemala* as a symphonic work, a version that premiered in Guatemala City in November 1934.[74] Some of his orchestral works are based on indigenous narratives, such as the "symphonic evocation" *Xibalbá* (1944) whereas in others, such as *Abstracción* (1965), Castillo distances himself from the pre-Hispanic world (table 8.3).[75] An entire CD of his music, performed by the Moscow Symphony, is available on the Naxos label.

Another composer was Salvador Ley (1907–85), born in Guatemala of German-Jewish parents. After studying in Berlin, he returned to direct the National Conservatory. His orchestral works include *Dos trozos para danza*, a serenade for string orchestra, and an *Obertura jocosa*, which premiered in Guatemala in 1952. He then emigrated to the United States, where one of his two operas, *Afternoon of a Spawn* (*La tarde de un engendro*), was presented at the Westchester Conservatory in 1963.[76] Franz Ippisch (1883–1958), on the other hand, was born in Austria but came to Guatemala in 1938 because of his wife's Jewish origins and because he composed music considered "degenerate."[77] In his new home, he directed a military band and taught conducting and composition at the conservatory. Slonimsky refers to his "solid mastery of the [symphonic] medium."[78] Among his several symphonic works are *Eine Lustige Ouverture für Grosses Orcheskter* and four symphonies; the third, *Sinfonía Guatemalteca* (1941), pays tribute to Ippisch's adopted country.

Ippisch was an influential teacher. One of his students, Humberto Ayestas (1920–2007), composed the densely textured and highly chromatic orchestral work *Homenaje a un amigo* (1957). Another Ippisch student, Manuel Herrarte (1924–74), attended the Eastman School of Music, where he worked with Howard Hanson. As a send-off, the Orquesta Filarmónica de Guatemala performed his Divertimento in 1944, which one critic praised for its humor.[79] Herrarte's subsequent orchestral works include *Obertura pastoral* and a *Sinfonieta campestre*. Perhaps Ippisch's best-known student is Joaquín Orellana (b. 1930).[80] Orellana composed several symphonic works, such as the prize-winning *El Jardín encantado* (table 8.3). In 1967–68, he began studying at the CLAEM, where he worked with Ginastera and visiting professors such as Luigi Nono and Vladimir Ussachevsky. He also became interested in electroacoustic music, which he often juxtaposes with more traditional performing forces, as in *Humanofonía I* for orchestra and tape; he intended this work as a testimonial to the violence, hunger, and misery of daily life endured by oppressed peoples. At one point, Orellana began building electronic instruments, sometimes taking traditional Guatemalan instruments as models.[81]

Rodrigo Asturias (b. 1940), born in Guatemala City, studied with Ricardo Castillo before going to Lausanne, Switzerland, and eventually settling in Paris. His four symphonies (1981, 1984, 1986, 1990) are grouped under the title *Livre pour orchestre.*[82] Asturias has made it his mission to promote music by Guatemalan composers. He edited seventy-two works by Ricardo Castillo and Herrarte for the Parisian music publisher Max Eschig and located several symphonic works believed to be lost by his grandfather Manuel Martínez-Sobral (1879–1946): these include his *Cinco piezas características y una romanza*, *Vals brilliante de concierto*, and *Acuarelas chapinas*.[83] These efforts paid off: Naxos released not only the works by Ricardo Castillo, mentioned above, but also Martínez-Sobral's *Aquarelas chapinas*.

Jorge Sarmientos (1931–2012) was born in San Antonio Suchitepéquez and grew up in a rural environment. Thanks to his musical talent, he enrolled in the National Conservatory as a saxophone and clarinet student, studying composition with Ricardo Castillo. In the mid-1950s, he attended at the École Normale de Musique in Paris on a fellowship. He composed several orchestral works, including *Tres cuadros corales sinfónicos* (1964) for chorus and

Table 8.3 Symphonies and Other Orchestral Music from Central America

Guatemala

Jesús Castillo (1877–1946). *Oberturas indígena* Nos. 1–5 (1897–1910); *Tecún Umán* (1936); *Vartizanic* (1941); *Suite indígena* (n.d.); *Himno al sol* (n.d.); *Oda a la liberación de Guatemala* (overture, n.d.); *Preludio melodramático* (n.d.); *Procesión hierática* (n.d.); *El Quetzal* (overture, n.d.); *Las telas mágicas* (n.d.).

Ricardo Castillo (1891–1966). *Homenaje a Ravel* (1920); *Guatemala* (symphony, 1934); *La procesión* (1935); *La doncella ixquic* (1937); *Xibalbá* (1944); *Sinfonieta* (1945); *Trópico* (1948); *Instantáneas plásticas* (1963); *Abstracción* (1965).

Joaquín Orellana (b. 1930). *El Jardín encantado* (1958); Adagio and Scherzo (1962); *Contrastes* (1963, with tape); *Un extraño personaje* (1964); *Humanofonía I* (1971, with tape).

Jorge Sarmientos (1931–2012). *Estampas de Popol Vuh* (1958); *David y Betsabé* (1958); *El Destello de Hiroshima* (1994).

Dieter Lenhoff (b. 1955). Symphony No. 1 (1975); Symphony No. 2 (1990); *Tardes de feria* (2008); *Caribe Suite* No. 1 (2009).

El Salvador

María de Baratta (1894–1978). *Nahualismo* (orch. by Riacrdo Hüttenrauch, perf. 1936); *Danza del incienso* (orch. by Alejandro Muñoz, perf. 1937); *Ofrenda de la elegida: danza ritual* (orch. by Alejandro Muñoz, perf. 1937).

Nicaragua

Luis Abraham Delgadillo (1887–1961). *Escenas pastoriles* (1919); *Suite indígena o centroamericana* (1921); *Sinfonía mexicana* (1923); *Teotihuacán* (1925); *Sinfónia incaica* (1926); *Suite colonial nicaragüense* (1929); *Obertura indiana* (1929); *Invocación a la luna* (1930); *En el templo de Agat (danza indígena nicaragüense)* (1937); *12 Sinfonías breves* (1953–1955); *Schoenbergniana en los 12 tonos, capricho sinfónico* (1955).

Costa Rica

Alejandro Monestel (1865–1950). *El amante y la coqueta* (n.d.); *A orillas de un arroyo* (n.d.); *Seis canciones* (n.d.).

Julio Fonseca (1885–1950). *Maxixe* (n.d.); *Obertura húngara* (n.d.); *Suite Tropical* No. 1 (n.d.); *Suite Tropical* No. 2 (n.d.); *Gran Fantasía Sinfónica* (n.d.); *Tango Clemencia* (1927); *Marcha Heredia* (1927).

Panama

Roque Cordero (1917–2008). *Capricho interiorano* (1939); Symphony No. 1 (1945); *Movimiento sinfónico* (1946); *Introducción y alegro burlesco* (1950); *Rapsodia campesina* (1953); Symphony No. 2 in One Movement (1957); *Mensaje fúnebre: in memoriam Dimitri Mitropoulous* (1961); Symphony No. 3 (1965); *Sinfonía con un tema y cinco variaciones* (1965); *Circunvoluciones y móviles* (1967); *Elegía para orquesta de cuerdas* (1973); Symphony No. 4 (1986); *Tributo sinfónico a un centenario* (1997).

orchestra and based on "Tecún Umán," the poem that inspired Ricardo Castillo and Varèse. In 1965, Sarmientos became the first of the two Guatemalans who studied at the CLAEM (as noted above, Orellana arrived there in 1967) and later worked with Pierre Boulez. One of his later orchestral works is *El Destello de Hiroshima* (1994) for soprano, narrator, and orchestra, in which Sarmientos employs tonal, bitonal, polytonal, and microtonal referents.[84] In 2015, the Orquesta Sinfónica Heredia of Costa Rica performed his *Micro–Preludio Orquestal* (the orchestration of his 2003 piano Prelude No. 4) posthumously. Igor de Gandarias (b. 1953), who received a PhD from Catholic University, has devoted himself primarily to electroacoustic music, although he wrote the orchestral work *Desde la infancia*, which alludes to marches played during Holy Week. Dieter Lenhoff (b. 1955) also completed his PhD at Catholic University, where he studied composition with Conrad Bernier. He has composed several orchestral works, including two symphonies (table 8.3).

Central America: El Salvador

An important figure in Salvadoran classical music was the Guatemalan-born José Escolástico Andrino (1817–62). Leaving his birthplace, he traveled throughout the region, for a time playing violin in a Havana orchestra and settling in El Salvador in 1845.[85] He founded a music school in San Salvador, the capital, and in the 1860s, established an orchestra. Also a composer, Andrino wrote two symphonies.[86] In 1864, another school of music was founded under the auspices of the government-supported Academy of Fine Arts. Complementing the school was the Sociedad Orquestal Salvadoreña, under the direction of an Italian immigrant, Antonio Gianoli.[87] It was supplanted by band culture, however, and the Salvadoran composer Jesús Alas (1866–1952), who conducted the Banda de los Supremos Poderes, composed music mainly for that ensemble although he did write an *Obertura Patriótica* for orchestra.

The National School of Music (now known as the National Center for the Arts) was founded in 1930. Still, some Salvadoran composers went abroad to study, such as Domingo Santos (1892–1951), who went to Rome. Upon returning to El Salvador, Santos wrote various orchestral works, including two overtures, *Martita* and *Dorita*, and an intermezzo titled *La tarde*. María de Baratta (1894–1978) studied in Bologna. Primarily a folklore specialist, she composed a few orchestral works, some based on indigenous materials and others orchestrations of her piano pieces. Another Salvadoran composer who studied in Italy was Esteban Servellón (1921–2003), who spent 1973–76 in the United States. Among his orchestral works is the suite *Retrospectivas* (1959). Gilberto Orellana (b. 1920) studied with the US composer Charles H. Robb of the University of New Mexico as part of an exchange program. Orellana, who wrote several symphonic suites, is credited as the first Salvadoran twelve-tone composer, as in his orchestral piece *Psicosis*. His son, Gilberto Orellana Castro Jr. (b. 1938), studied with Servellón and composed electroacoustic music as well as the symphony *Sinfonía Pípil* (1980), inspired by pre-Columbian music.

Central America: Honduras

Europeans first arrived in Honduras in 1524. In the north, they met with such resistance that Spanish influence never fully took hold, although for the next 300 years, Honduras formed part of the Captaincy of Guatemala, an administrative division of the Spanish Empire. We know little about music during this period. One composer, José Trinidad Reyes (1797–1855), ordained as a priest in 1822, the year after Honduras became independent from Spain, spent part of his career in Guatemala. When he returned to Tegucigalpa, he established a music school in 1834. His compositions include masses and villancicos.

From the nineteenth century on, several top-notch bands were active, some established with the help of Europeans invited by the government. As in El Salvador, one was called the Banda de los Poderes Supremos. Its director from 1915, Manuel Adalid y Gamero (1872–1947), composed. He also made arrangements of European classics for band: as with Sousa's band in the United States, concert bands in Latin America routinely played such repertoire. Rafael Coello Ramos (1877–1967) established the short-lived Verdi Orchestra, and Ignacio Villanueva Galeano (1885–1954) composed a "Pan American Union March" (scored for strings as well as traditional band instruments) and a *Sinfonía patética* for string orchestra, among other works. Francisco Ramón Díaz Zelaya (1896–1977) wrote four symphonies and founded both a Wagner Orchestra and a national symphony. Composer and pianist Norma Erazo (b. 1947), who studied at the University of Montreal, has also composed for orchestra.

Central America: Nicaragua

After the first Spanish expedition to what is now Nicaragua, in the early sixteenth century, the Indigenous population decreased from around one million to merely tens of thousands. From 1609, Nicaragua was part of the Captaincy of Guatemala. Support from the Spanish crown for music was scant, likely because the region lacked strategic importance. Payments for religious observances that almost certainly involved music are documented, however, and inventories of European instruments exist. A series of earthquakes surely destroyed many materials that would shed light on colonial-era music making.

Nicaragua became independent from Spain in 1821 and subsequently part of the Central American Federation. Pablo Vega Raudes (1850–1919), the scion of a Nicaraguan musical dynasty, promoted symphonic music and conducted a chamber orchestra; he also founded Nicaragua's first music school. His son, Alejandro Vega Matus (1875–1937), composed masses in the style of Haydn and works for chamber orchestra; his son, Ramiro Vega Jiménez, was more involved with band music. Fernando Luna Jiménez (1853–1936) wrote an overture, *La cabaña de Lepha*. He also composed the first symphonic work based on Nicaraguan folk material, *El Toro Huaco*, named after a dance event that commemorates the patron saint of Diriamba (a city south of the capital, Managua) in which players wear ragged clothing and wooden masks.

Nicaragua was much affected by the "Big Stick." In 1909, the United States began to occupy the country in accordance with the overly broad premises of the Roosevelt Corollary of the Monroe Doctrine. The Nicaraguan poet Rubén Darío registered his displeasure in the scathing anti-ode "A Roosevelt" (To Roosevelt), the "invader of our native America." Yet the relationship between Nicaragua and the "Colossus of the North" was complicated: more than once, the Nicaraguan government requested US military protection. Roosevelt's successor, William Howard Taft, initiated so-called dollar diplomacy, presumably to ensure financial instability in the region although businesses friendly to the United States ultimately prospered and Nicaragua essentially became a protectorate. In 1933, when the Good Neighbor policy replaced the Big Stick, US troops withdrew from Nicaragua.

One manifestation of this fraught political relationship was "cultural ambivalence," to borrow Bernard Gordillo's term for this phenomenon.[88] Composers such as Luis Abraham Delgadillo (1887–1961) balanced the influence of US culture, a conservative turn in Nicaragua (supported by the Catholic Church), and their own desires for a musical identity. Delgadillo digested influences from the many countries in which he lived or visited, including Italy (where he studied), Mexico, Bolivia, Peru, Cuba, the United States, and Honduras. He involved himself in each of these nations' musical life. In Mexico, for example, where he moved in 1921, he publicly opposed Carrillo's microtonal system but admired Ponce and considered Mexico the "big sister of the Americas," paying tribute with his *Sinfonía mexicana* and *Teotihuacán*, a suite for orchestra.[89] Upon visiting Peru and Bolivia, Delgadillo composed a *Sinfonía incáica*. It was in Cuba, not Nicaragua, that Delgadillo premiered his *Suite colonial nicaragüense* (*diciembre*), his first orchestral composition to rely on Nicaraguan folklore and which contains traditional songs of the Christmas season (table 8.3). In the United States, where he lived from 1929 to 1932, he performed several of his symphonic works in piano arrangements, such as the *Teotihuacán* suite. On other occasions he conducted his own orchestral music, once at the Pan American Union in Washington, DC, in 1930.[90]

Like other Latin American composers, Delgadillo was influenced by Felipe Pedrell. Delgadillo wrote copiously on musical nationalism, arguing in his 1913 book, *Consideraciones generales sobre arte musical en Nicaragua*, for greater musical infrastructure and urged composers to cultivate a national voice, much as Pedrell did in *Por nuestra música* of 1891. Besides the *Suite colonial*, Delgadillo's nationalist compositions for orchestra include *Suite indígena o centroamericana* of 1921, which marked the centennial of independence. It evokes the indigenous legacy through modal melodies, drones, and ostinato; Delgadillo suggests the *chirimía* through English horn and oboe and the *quijongo* (a monochord associated with Central America) through various textural changes in the lower strings. All coexist with popular Nicaraguan mestizo melodies and Delgadillo's own approach to sonata form.[91] Nonnationalist works by Delgadillo include *12 Sinfonías breves* (1953–55) and a dodecaphonic work, *Schoenbergniana en los 12 tonos, capricho sinfónico* (1954).[92] In sum, he created two kinds of nationalist music: one he defined as music made of gestures "of the people" (and understood as such) and the other as music that lacks the specifics of nationalism but is nonetheless endowed with "a social and political function."[93]

One of Delgadillo's contemporaries, Carlos Ramírez Velásquez (1882–1976), founded several orchestras, including the Orquesta La Aspiración in Masaya. Nicaraguan tradition continues to influence musical creation into the present. The colonial-era street play *El güegüense*, celebrated on September 13 (St. Jerome's Day), uses texts in both Spanish and Nahuatl and mixes Baroque music and indigenous melodies.[94] One composer who has taken on this fascinating reflection of identity formation is Raúl Martínez Salas (b. 1958), the codirector and founder of the Nicaraguan chamber ensemble Camerata Bach, which has recorded his four-movement *Suite el güegüense* (2001) based on these traditional materials.[95] Another is Pablo Buitrago (b. 1954), one of a family of Nicaraguan composers. After studying in Rio de Janeiro, he began directing the conservatory at the Universidad Politécnica de Nicaragua. In addition to several noteworthy film scores and half a dozen works for chamber orchestra, Buitrago has been inspired by the traditional melodies of *El güegüense*, including the *son* "Los Borrachos" (The Drunkards) with its humorous accents.

The award-winning Nicaraguan-US composer Gabriel Bolaños Chamorro (b. 1984) worked with Buitrago at the Universidad Politécnica de Nicaragua while on a Fulbright Fellowship. Educated at Columbia University and the University of California, Davis, Bolaños writes multifaceted music informed by linguistics, the physical properties of sound, technology, and psychoacoustics—broad concepts he often realizes with Latin American instruments played in novel ways, such as the scratching of bongos or blending the Cuban *chekere* with twenty-first-century sonorities. One of Bolaños's orchestral works is *Cinco viñetas*, a five-movement programmatic composition for chamber orchestra that reveals the passage of time. The first movement, *Singularidad*, is scored for strings, B-flat clarinet, and flute, and represents the universe prior to the big bang, its point of origin. It is the most avant-garde of the five movements, featuring microtonality, graphic notation, multiphonics, and aleatory. String techniques include playing behind the bridge, crank bowing (pressing the bow hard on the strings and cranking it so that a creaking sound is produced by the hair of the bow), and creaking the hair of the bow on the body of the string instruments (example 8.3).

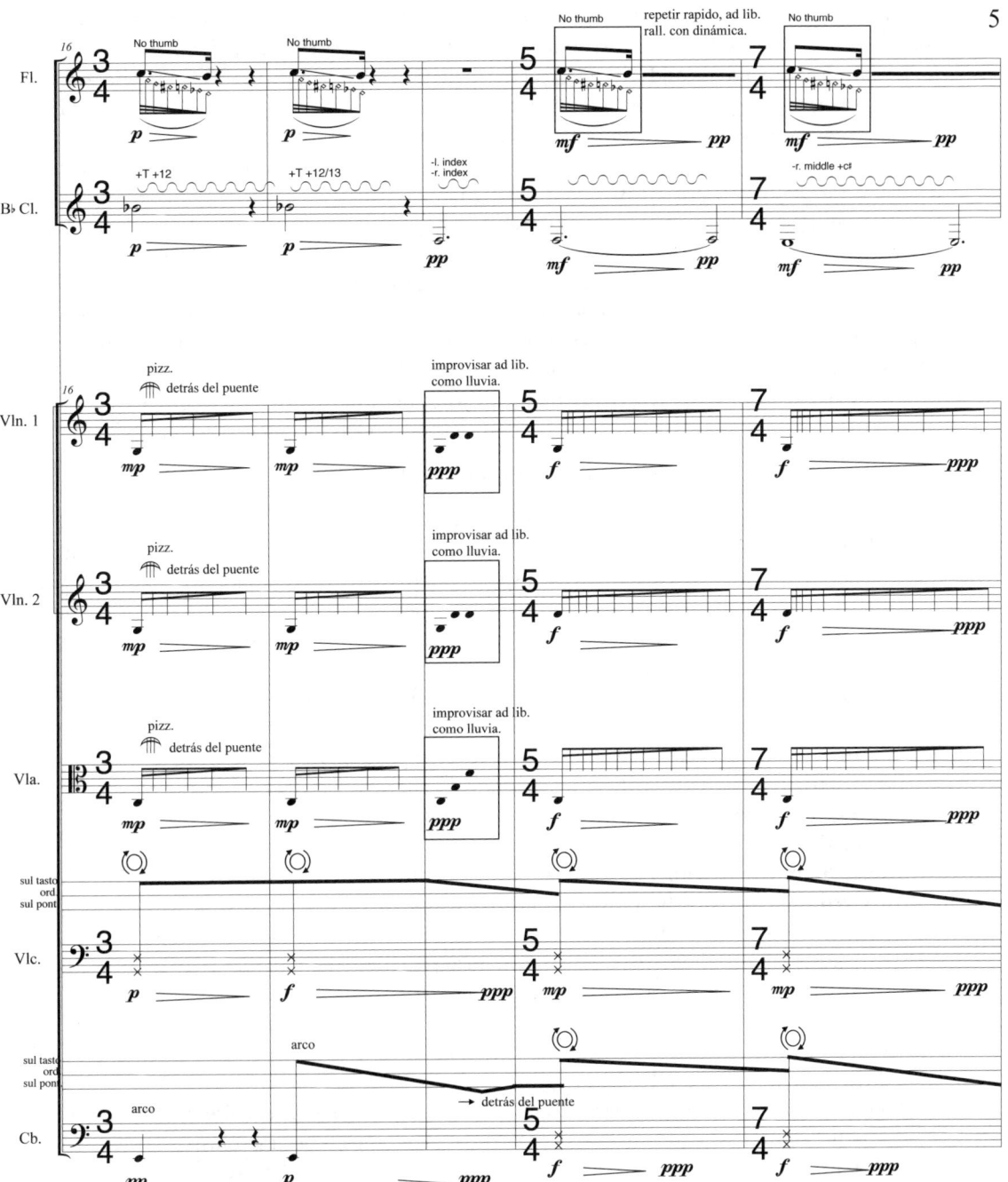

Example 8.3 Bolaños. *Singularidad*, mm. 16–20. Reproduced with kind permission of the composer.

The second movement, *Ex Machina*, is based on looping; the third, *Monodia*, on simple monodic melodies. By contrast, the fourth movement, *Irridentus Degeneratus*, is somewhat more complex in terms of meter and phrase structure. In the fifth movement, *Farruca*, Bolaños combines the flamenco genre of the farruca with J. S. Bach's Fugue in D-sharp Minor (Book I, *Well-Tempered Clavier*). All serve an overall strategy: each vignette is progressively less avant-garde such that *Farruca* is "quite easy-listening," to quote the composer. In sum, *Cinco viñetas* traces the trajectory of "time's arrow" from the big bang to the time and place of composition (2016, Nicaragua) by capturing key moments and feelings that can be described as universal.

Cinco viñetas premiered in July 2017 in Granada, Nicaragua, conducted by the composer.[96] It was part of *Proyecto Eco*, a new music series that featured music, audio-reactive visuals, multimedia, lighting, and other technologies. Also featured were works by Guillermo Norory and Juan Rosales. The project has stalled since the Nicaraguan political crisis of 2018, which has involved violent demonstrations against an increasingly authoritarian government. Of the five movements, *Singularidad*, the composer's favorite, became a stand-alone piece and was premiered as such in 2018 by the Orquesta Sinfónica de Santiago de Cuba.

Central America: Costa Rica

Columbus first glimpsed Costa Rica in 1502, on his fourth voyage to the Americas. Among the different Indigenous groups found there were the Diquis, skilled metal and stone workers. Due to the absence of gold and silver, along with a sparse population and geographic isolation from the administrative centers of New Spain (of which it was a part), Costa Rica was one of the poorer colonies and thus not conducive to support for classical music. Independent from Spain as of 1821, Costa Rica belonged to the Mexican Empire of Iturbide until 1823, when it joined the Central American Federation. In 1838, it became the Republic of Costa Rica. By that time, pianos began to be imported to Costa Rica, and in 1845, a network of bands was established. Serving as director of bands was one of the most coveted positions during the nineteenth century and various composers wrote for that medium.[97] Theaters were also constructed, among them the Teatro Nacional in San Juan, inaugurated in 1897 and still considered one of the best in Latin America.[98]

A Belgian immigrant, Jean Loots (1872–1929), established a symphony orchestra in 1926 but it survived only a year. The Orquesta Sinfónica Nacional was founded in San José, the capital, with state support in 1940, with the Italian violinist and conductor Hugo Mariani (1899–1965) at the helm. In 1962 the Costa Rican horn player and conductor Germán Alvarado launched the Orquesta Sinfónica de Heredia (in Heredia province), an ensemble that presents a broad range of musical styles with emphasis on Latin American music of the twentieth and twenty-first centuries. Two music schools were founded in the late nineteenth century, and the National Conservatory was established in 1942.

Although band music and operetta dominated Costa Rican musical life at the turn of the twentieth century, several individuals left their mark on orchestral music.[99] Alejandro Monestel (1865–1950) trained in Brussels and lived for a time in the New York area, where he composed and worked as an organist.[100] Back home in San José, he taught at the conservatory and composed several works (table 8.3). Like Monestel, Julio Fonseca (1885–1950) was an organist who spent several years in the United States (1914–18). He studied composition in Costa Rica, however, with Alvise Castegnaro, a graduate of the conservatory in Milan and one of several Italian musicians who immigrated to Costa Rica. Alongside *Suite Tropical*, which employs Costa Rican folklore, Fonseca's *Gran Fantasía Sinfónica* concludes with a fugue based on motives from the national anthem and from the folkloric "Punta Guanacasteco" (table 8.3).[101] (He is best known for the waltz *Leda*.) Julio Mata (1899–1969) studied in San José and then attended the Brooklyn Academy of Music. In addition to operettas, Mata composed the orchestral *Suite abstracta*, which features "disoriented tonality," as the composer described it.[102] The Spanish-born César Nieto (1892–1969) emigrated to Costa Rica in 1899, becoming a citizen in 1936. His ballet *La Piedra del Toxil* contains pentatonic melodies, presumably Incan, with nineteenth-century harmonizations.

The next generation includes Rocío Sanz (1933–93), who was born in Costa Rica but studied in Mexico with Halffter and Galindo as well as in Moscow. Sanz spent most of her life in Mexico City, where she taught and worked in radio. Many of her sixty-odd works are for voices, although she wrote the suite *Hilos* for orchestra, along with a *Suite de ballet* (1959).[103] Bernal Flores (b. 1937) earned three degrees at the Eastman School of Music, where his teachers included Howard Hanson. (He declined a scholarship to the CLAEM.[104]) Among his orchestral pieces are two symphonies. Benjamín Gutiérrez (b. 1937) studied at the conservatory in San José before a stint at the New England Conservatory of Music and the University of Michigan; in 1964, he worked with Ginastera at the CLAEM.[105] Gutiérrez used twelve-tone techniques and other contemporary resources but also paid homage to the musical past in some of his orchestral works, such as *Sinfonía no. 1: En Recuerdo de Johannes Brahms* (1980). Jorge Luis Acevedo (b. 1943), who composed two orchestral works, studied voice and ethnomusicology in Paris. Mario Alfagüell (b. 1948) studied at the National Conservatory in San José and then went to Freiburg, where he studied with the British composer Brian Ferneyhough, who taught at the Hochschüle für Musik between 1973 and 1986. Among Alfagüell's orchestral works are a *Symphony in Two Movements* and *Episodios sinfónicos* (1982). Luis Diego Herra Rodríguez (b. 1952) studied in Costa Rica, where Flores and Gutiérrez were his teachers. He then studied with Betsy Jolas in Paris. His orchestral works include ballet scores, a symphony (1990), and a suite. Alejandro Cardona (b. 1959) studied at Harvard University with Leon Kirchner. Upon returning to Costa Rica, he settled in Heredia province, where he has also researched indigenous music and composed *Sones mestizos* for orchestra. He maintained international ties, participating in ALEA III, the Boston-based experimental music group.

The Orquesta Sinfónica Heredia has promoted Costa Rican symphonic composers such as Eddie Mora (b. 1965), Guido Sánchez-Portuguez (b. 1974), José Mora Jiménez (b. 1977), Byron Latouche (b. 1980), Pablo Santiago Chin (b. 1982), and Andrés Soto (b. 1986). It has also commissioned new works, such as the prize-winning *Nocturnos a Debravo* (2019), by the clarinetist and composer Sergio Delgado (b. 1993) in honor of the Costa Rican poet Jorge Debravo.[106]

Central America: Panama

Little documentation on musical life in Panama prior to or during the colonial period is available. Even the much-admired Juan de Araujo, who worked there between 1676 and 1680, left scarcely a trace of his activities there. During the nineteenth century, bands played in various towns and villages throughout the country. Scholars have generally taken the early twentieth century as the starting point for orchestral music in the nation. After a state music school was founded in 1904, several of its wealthier students established the Círculo Filarmónico to promote orchestral music, and an orchestra was founded shortly thereafter. The school suffered financial difficulties but eventually reopened as the National Conservatory in 1941. Herbert de Castro founded the Orquesta de la Unión Musical and the Orquesta Sinfónica Nacional in 1939 and 1941, respectively. One Panamanian composer of symphonic music was Alberto

Galimany (1889–1974), who was born in Spain but emigrated to Panama and who conducted the Banda Republicana until 1937. In September 1928, he presented a concert at the Pan American Union.[107] One of Galimany's symphonic works is the suite *Vasco Nuñez de Balboa*; another, *Panama*, pays tribute to his new home and was published in Barcelona.[108]

The best-known Panamanian composer of symphonic music (and numerous other genres) was Roque Cordero (1917–2008). Born in Panama City, Cordero studied composition there. In 1943, he received a grant to study at Hamline University in Minnesota, where he had the good fortune to meet Dimitri Mitropoulos, then director of the Minnesota Symphony Orchestra (now the Minnesota Orchestra). Cordero studied conducting with Mitropoulos, who took a strong interest in developing the young man's talents. Also at Hamline was Ernst Krenek, the Viennese composer branded "degenerate" by the Nazis; he taught there from 1942 to 1947, when the young Panamanian numbered among his composition students. Cordero spent the next 16 years in Panama. In 1966 he returned to the United States, now as associate director of Indiana University's Latin American Music Center, which the Chilean composer Orrego-Salas had directed since 1961. In 1972 Cordero joined the faculty of Illinois State University. Thanks to numerous prizes, commissions, and honorary degrees, he received the title distinguished emeritus professor upon retiring in 1987.

Among Cordero's works for orchestra are four symphonies and several single-movement works (table 8.3). Some are folkloric and others stridently modernist. His Symphony No. 2 proved controversial at the 1957 Caracas Festival. According to Gilbert Chase, it "received the greatest public ovation."[109] Yet the first prize was divided between Blas Galindo for his Symphony No. 2 and Mozart Camargo Guarnieri of Brazil for his *Choros* for Piano and Orchestra, both less forward-looking than Cordero's symphony. (Cordero tied with the Peruvian composer Enrique Iturriaga for second place. In 1957 the symphony received the Caro de Boesi prize.) Like many other one-movement symphonies, this work, based on multiple tone rows, unfolds in discrete sections: Lento-Presto e furioso, Allegro, Vivace, and Andante quasi Adagio. It opens with a "cry of anguish," as Cordero put it, as a strident, fifth-based motive in the brass is answered by a flurry of dissonant thirty-second notes in the upper woodwinds.[110]

The symphony was also performed at the 1958 Inter-American Music Festival in Washington, DC, where the critic Paul Hume praised "the powerful phrases that [Cordero] so well commands" along with the composer's "delight in handling the large orchestra."[111] In a vehement essay titled "¿Nacionalismo versus dodecafonismo?" (Nationalism or Dodecaphony?), Cordero urged his fellow Latin Americans to leave the past behind and embrace "the technical advances of recent decades"—namely, twelve-tone music.[112] Yet he frequently honored the musical traditions of his native land: as Orrego-Salas put it, "Cordero manipulates serialism with great originality, without allowing [the system] to interfere with the free expression of his ideas or their elements—especially rhythm—to impede vernacular traditions that spontaneously manifest themselves."[113]

Despite his decades in the United States, Cordero's legacy is felt in Panama. A composition contest is held in his name, and the accomplishments of his students are noteworthy. José Luis Cajar Escala (1914–82), who studied both composition and conducting with Cordero, wrote a few orchestral works, as did Marina Saíz Salazar (1930–90), who composed an *Ensayo para*

Facing, Example 8.4 Carrizo. *Poliptico*, mm. 176–83. Reproduced with kind permission of the composer.

orquesta (Essay for Orchestra) published by the Pan American Union. Representing another generation is the composer and conductor Samuel Robles (b. 1974), whose orchestral works include *amanecer en tiempos de guerra*, commissioned by the Orquesta Sinfónica Nacional. It commemorates the months-long military operation by the United States dubbed "Just Cause," condemned by both the Organization of American States and the United Nations General Assembly; the composer dedicated it to "the Panamanian victims of the invasion of December 1989."[114] In another orchestral work, *Zafra* (2009), Robles incorporates Panamanian drumming patterns; in *Veraguas*, Robles evokes a city in Panama.

Andrés Carrizo was born in Panama City in 1982. He studied at Williams College (Williamstown, Massachusetts) and with Gerardo Gandini in Buenos Aires. His advanced degrees are from Bowling Green State University (Ohio) and the University of Chicago. Now a resident in the United States, Carrizo maintains strong ties with Panama, having founded the MusicArte Panama Contemporary Music Festival and served as Panama's cultural attaché to Israel. He has received many prizes and commissions and his music has been played in Taiwan, Italy, Israel, and in various cities in the Americas by ensembles such as the St. Paul Chamber Orchestra and the Orquesta Sinfónica Nacional of Panama. Carrizo's *Políptico* (2010) was commissioned by the Interlochen Symphony Orchestra. Its title, which translates as "polyptych" (multipaneled painting), invites the listener to recall this time-honored form, familiar from fifteenth-century altarpieces but realized here in contemporary musical guise. Does the viewer of a polyptych instinctively connect the various panels? Carrizo observes that with *Políptico* he was initially concerned with pulse rather than timbre, arranging "small shards of recurring material, rather than working with a single, unifying thematic idea, the piece's specific moments"—thus suggesting an ambiguous relationship between the different elements of the work, as might well happen in a visual polyptych. Timbre is an important factor: in addition to the standard instruments, Carrizo calls for four percussionists (tubular bells, sizzle cymbal, wind chimes, crotales, three timpani, among several other instruments), harp, piano, and celesta. Harmonics, a variety of mutes, and other arresting effects pervade the work. Another unifying factor is the tangible rhythmic structure: Carrizo sought to counter the often amorphous rhythms of contemporary music, which, in his view, often fail to communicate and fall short in comparison to the musical and social reality of Latin America itself—not to mention the highly rhythmic works of Ginastera, Piazzolla, and Stravinsky that initially prodded the young Carrizo toward a musical career. The following passage gives an idea of the timbral and rhythmic variety in *Políptico* (example 8.4).

The Spanish-Speaking Caribbean: Cuba

Principal Indigenous groups in the territory known today as Cuba were the Taíno, an Arawak people. As elsewhere, their population declined after the conquest due to forced labor and diseases introduced by Europeans. Enslaved Africans, mostly Yoruban, were imported as early as the 1550s. They sustained the plantation economy and remained a significant cultural presence, as detailed below. In classical music, activity initially centered around the cathedral in Santiago de Cuba, where the position of chapelmaster was established in 1682. One important composer was Esteban Salas y Castro (1725–1803), born in Havana but appointed to the cathedral in Santiago in 1764. He wrote mainly sacred music, much of which calls for string orchestra.[115]

Whereas other regions of Latin America declared independence in the 1820s, the colonial period in Cuba was protracted, with a series of smaller wars preceding the final break from Spain in 1898. During the nineteenth century, the Havana cathedral served as a center of musical life in that by the 1830s, both operatic and symphonic music were performed there; thus the cathedral was "transformed into a true conservatory," in the words of critic and novelist Alejo Carpentier, the lively chronicler of Cuban musical life.[116] Composers responded, among them the peripatetic violinist and priest Antonio Raffelín (1796–1882), who composed three symphonies. He also established an orchestra in Havana, lived in Paris, and published some of his music in the United States, founding a music magazine, *La lira católica*, in Philadelphia. Another violinist, Toribio Segura (d. 1860), who wrote a *Marcha triunfal* for orchestra, promoted concerts with Raffelín. Another violinist-composer was Laureano Fuentes Matons (1825–98): born in Santiago de Cuba, he wrote several orchestral works, including the symphonic poem *América* from 1892.[117]

One of Cuba's most celebrated composers (his music is still played today) was the pianist Ignacio Cervantes (1847–1905). Beginning his studies with Louis Moreau Gottschalk (1859–61), he went to the Paris Conservatory where he won various awards and then sojourned in Madrid. Upon returning to Havana, he gave piano recitals, taught, and directed an opera orchestra. When it became known that some of his concerts were fundraisers for the rebel side in the War of Independence (1868–78), Cervantes sensed danger and went to the United States, where he continued his musical fundraising. He also took his campaign to Mexico. In 1900, when the break with Spain was complete, Cervantes returned to Cuba and worked as an orchestral conductor. Known mainly for his graceful piano compositions, Cervantes also wrote a few works for orchestra, including a Symphony in C Minor (1879) and a *Scherzo caprichioso* (1886), along with some shorter pieces, all in a tonal idiom (table 8.4). He was among the first Cuban composers to suggest that music could reflect the character of a people.[118]

Gonzálo Roig (1890–1970) is best known for his hit song "Quiéreme mucho" (Yours) and the zarzuela *Cecilia Váldes*, a story of interracial love that was performed in Carnegie Hall and Lewisohn Stadium in the 1960s.[119] Yet some consider him a "pioneer of symphonic music" in Cuba in that he helped to establish the country's principal orchestra.[120] Throughout his career he promoted Cuban music and worked on behalf of Cuban union musicians.[121] Also fundamental to orchestral music in Cuba was Ernesto Lecuona (1895–1963). Known principally for his songs (especially *Malagueña* of 1933, most familiar as an instrumental standard), Lecuona wrote an orchestral suite (1945) and a *Rapsodía negra* for piano and orchestra (1943). His sister Ernestina (1882–1951) published several songs; also from the same distinguished family is Margarita Lecuona (1910–81), who mainly composed songs but whose orchestral composition *Toku: Indo-Cuban rumba* is in the Fleisher Collection (in an arrangement by Al Boss). Pedro Sanjuán (1886–1976) was born in San Sebastián, Spain, and studied in Madrid with Joaquín Turina. He arrived in Cuba in 1924 where he taught, composed, and became fascinated by Afro-Cuban culture, writing a *Liturgia negra* for orchestra. Other orchestral works include *Rondo fantástico* and *Sones de Castilla*, in which Sanjuán pays homage to his native land.

Taking a similar tack were Alejandro García Caturla (1906–40) and Amadeo Roldán (1900–39). (Both were also fine violinists.) Caturla, born in Remedios, studied law at the university in Havana and took composition lessons with Sanjuán. In June 1928 he left for France, where he studied briefly with Boulanger. Caturla's Afro-Cuban orchestral works include *Bembé* for chamber orchestra. (A bembé is a religious ritual involving call-and-response singing and dancing, to the accompaniment of bells and drums; unlike those in its more famous cousin Santería, however, bembé drums are not consecrated.) Caturla's *Tres danzas cubanas* (Three Cuban Dances, 1928) for large orchestra date from his studies with Boulanger; the first and third were originally for piano and, as an assignment, Caturla orchestrated them. The set

Table 8.4 Symphonies and Other Orchestral Music from the Spanish-Speaking Caribbean

Cuba

Ignacio Cervantes (1847–1905). Symphony in C Minor (1879); *Scherzo caprichioso* (1886).
Amadeo Roldán (1900–1939). *Obertura sobre temas cubanos* (1925); *Tres poemas pequeños* (1926); *La Rebambaramba* (1928); *El milagro de Anaquillé* (1929, re-orch. 1931); *Tres toques* (chamber orchestra, 1931).
Alejandro García Caturla (1906–40). *Berceuse* (1925); *Tres preludios para orquesta* (1925); *Poema de ambiente cubano* (1925); *Pequeña suite de conciertos* (1925); *Guajireñas* (1926); *Poema de Verano* (1927); *Rumba* (1928); *Tres danzas cubanas para orquesta* (1928); *Dos poemas afrocubanos* (1929); *Yamba-O* (1928–31); *Bembé* (chamber orchestra, 1929); *Suite para orquesta* (1937); *Obertura cubana* (1937).
José Ardévol (1911–81). *Dos trozos de música* (1933); Symphony No. 1 (1943); Symphony No. 2, "Homenaje a Falla" (1945); Symphony No. 3 (1946); *Suite Cubana* No. 1 (1947); *Tríptico de Santiago* (1949); *Suite Cubana* No. 2 (1949); *Tríptico de Pinar del Río* (1954); *Movimiento sinfónico* No. 1 (1967); *Movimiento sinfónico* No. 2 (1969).
Edgardo Martín (1915–2004). Fugues (string orchestra, 1947); *Concertante* (chamber orchestra, 1949); *Soneras* Nos. 1, 2, 3 (orch. of piano works from 1951, 1973, 1977); *Cuadros de Ismaelillo* (1970); *Dazones* No. 2 (1979); *Para niños* (1983); *Compañeros* (1991).
Harold Gramatges (1918–2008). Symphony in E (1945); *Serenata* (string orchestra, 1947); *Dos danzas cubanas* (1950); *Sinfonietta* (1955); *In memoriam. Homenaje a Frank País* (1961).
Argeliers León Pérez (1918–91). Sinfonia for Strings (1946); Symphony No. 1 (1946); Symphony No. 2 (1962).
Julián Orbón (1925–91). Symphony in C (1945); *Homenaje a la tonadilla* (1947); *Tres versiones sinfónicas* (1953); *Danzas sinfónicas* (1955); *Partita* (1965).
Aurelio de la Vega (1925–2022). *Obertura a una farsa seria* (1950); *Introducción y episodio* (1952); *Elegía* (string orchestra, 1954); Divertimento (chamber orchestra, 1956); *Sinfonía en cuatro partes* (1960); *Intrata* (1972); *Adiós* (1977); *Variación del recuerdo* (string orchestra, 1999).
Roberto Valera (b. 1938). *Chachachuá* (1963); *Música para cuerdas* (1964); *Devenir* (1969); *Extraplán* (1990); *Tierra del sol, cielo y mar* (1992); *Non divisi* (1999, string orchestra)
Magaly Ruíz (b. 1941). *Tres piezas para pequeña orquesta* (1977); *Estructura tritemática para orquesta sinfónica* (1977); *Tres ambientes sonoros* (1981).
Tania León (b. 1943). *Latin Lights* (1980); *Concierto criollo* (piano and eight timpani, 1980); *Pet's Suite* (1980); *Batá* (1985, rev. 1988); *Carabalí* (1991); *Indígena* (chamber orchestra, 1991); *Horizons* (1999).

Dominican Republic

Juan Francisco García (1892–1974). Symphony No. 1: *Sinfonía Quisqueya* (perf. 1941); *Scherzo clásico* (1941); Symphony No. 2 (ca. 1944).
Luis Emilio Mena (1895–1964). *Ecos de libertad* (n.d.); *Fantasía española* (n.d.); *Obertura* (n.d.); *Preludietto* (n.d.); *Recuerdos de infancia* (n.d.); *Sinfonía giocosa* (n.d.); *Tres preguntas* (n.d.); *Sinfonía de Juguetes* (n.d.).
Enrique Mejía-Arredondo (1901–51). Symphony No. 1 in A Major (perf. 1941); *Renacimiento* (n.d.); Symphony No. 2: *Sinfonía de la luz* (n.d.); *Dos evocaciones* (perf. 1942); *12 de julio* (overture); *Cuentos nocturnos* (n.d.); *Pequeña suite* (n.d.); *Suite de estampas* (n.d.).
Ninón Lapeiretta (1907–89). *Obertura Jocosa* (1940); *Pastoral* (chamber orchestra, 1941); *Abominación de la espera* (voice and orch., 1943); *Suite de danzas* (1963).
Margarita Luna (1921–2016). *Tres preludios* (string orchestra, 1964); *Mosaico* (1980); *Dicotomía* (1989).
Manuel Marino Miniño (1930–96). *Suite clásica* (1957); *Concerto grosso* (1959); *Poema* (1959); *Sinfonía masónica* (1960); *Dominicana* (1962); *Sideral* (1962); *Concertante* (1963); *Suite de danzas españolas del siglo XVI* (1963); *Suite mística* (1963); *Suite patria* (1963); *Canto a las montañas de mi tierra* (1976); *Suite dominicana* (1978).

Darwin Aquino (b. 1979). *Insomnia Suite* (2003); *Espacio Ritual* (2007); *Congofonía* (2008); *YOAminicana* (2010).

Puerto Rico

Juan Morel Campos (1857–96). *Alegoría fúnebre* (n.d.); *La lira* (overture, 1882); *Puerto Rico* (1893).
Héctor Campos Parsi (1922–88). *Divertimento del sur* (string orchestra, 1953); *Tureyareito* (1984); *Variations on a Theme by Mozart* (1990).
Ignacio Morales Nieva (1928–2005). Symphony No. 1, *Hebraica* (1974); Symphony No. 2, *De la América Hispana* (1976); *El Grito de Lares* (1976); *Ode à Hector Berlioz* (1980); Symphony No. 3 (1985); Symphony No. 4, *Virrenial* (1986); Symphony No. 5 (1990).
Francis Schwartz (b. 1940). *Plegaria* (1937); *Yo protesto* (1974); *The Tropical Trek of Tristan Trimble* (1975); *Amistad III* (1979); *Un sourire festif* (1981); *Gestos* (for orchestra and audience, 1983); *Fantasía de la Libertad* (1986); *Papageno's Dream* (1991).
William Ortiz-Alvarado (b. 1947). *Kantuta* (1976); *Antillas* (chamber orchestra, 1981); *Resonancia esférica* (1982); *Llegó la banda* (1984); *Joceo* (string orchestra, 1987); *Suspensión de soledad en tres tiempos* (1990); *Música de Ciudad* (1996); *Montaje para un sueño en Mi* (2001); *Elogio a la Plena* (2002); *Trova* (also arr. for concert band, 2005); *Tránsito* (2010); *Trilogía jabao* (string orchestra, 2014).
Roberto Sierra (b. 1953). *Júbilo* (1985); *Preámbulo* (1989); *Sasima* (string orchestra, 1990); *Ritmo* (1995); *Alegría* (1996); *El jardín de las delicias* (1997); *Concerto for Orchestra* (1999); Symphony No. 1 (2004); *Serenata* (chamber orchestra, 2004); Symphony No. 2 (2005); Symphony No. 3: *La salsa* (2005); *The Bacchae* (2006); *Carnaval* (2007); Symphony No. 4 (2009); *Montuno* (2013); Symphony No. 5: *Río Grande de Loíza* (with chorus, 2015); *Dos piezas para orquesta* (2017); Symphony No. 6 (2021).
Raymond Torres-Santos (b. 1958). *Sinfonietta concertante* (1980); *Exploraciones* (1982); *Areytos: A Symphonic Picture* (1985); *El país de los cuatro pisos: A Symphonic Poem* (1988); *La Canción de las Antillas: A Program Symphony* (1990); *Danza: Variation on a Theme by Mozart* (1991); *Fantasía caribeña* (1992); *Descarga Sinfónica* (1997); *1898 Overture* (1998); *Millennium Symphony: A Program Symphony* (2002); *Recordar es vivir* (2010); *Symphonia: Resonantia Luminosa Infinita* for Brass and Orchestra (2014).

was published in 1929 and performed at the Ibero-American Symphonic Festival at the Barcelona International Exhibition that same year and then in Havana in 1933.[122] Caturla calls for a large percussion section, including tam-tam, piano, harp, and celesta. Movement I, "Danza del tambor" (Dance of the Drum), is something of a curtain raiser, as it takes under a minute and a half. In it, Caturla concentrates fixedly on two main themes (with some motivic variation); ostinati ensure a fixed tonal center throughout, while tension between duple and triple meters plays out. Movement II, "Motivos de danzas" (Dance Motives), contrasts coloristically with harp glissandi, muted strings and horns, and prominent woodwind solos, which swap motives (Reh. 13 + 8). Movement III, "Danza lucumí," is both the most substantive and the most evocative. (Lucumí is a Yoruban language although the term also refers to one of several Afro-Cuban religions observed through music and dance, such as Santería.[123]) Less identity-conscious pieces include *Suite para orquesta* (Suite for Orchestra) of 1937 (table 8.4). In 1932 Caturla founded the Caibarién Concert Society, whose orchestra he conducted and which performed music by Gershwin, Cowell, Falla, Debussy, and others.[124] As an attorney, Caturla took the practice of law seriously rather than as a mere "day job"; among the causes he championed was the plight of juvenile delinquents.

Amadeo Roldán was born in Paris but took Cuban citizenship (his mother's nationality). He studied at the conservatory in Madrid: there Conrado del Campo served as his composition teacher and he won the Sarasate Prize for his violin playing. In 1919 he arrived in Cuba, where he performed with the symphony and also played with chamber ensembles and movie orchestras.[125] In 1925 he composed the first of several orchestral works, *Obertura sobre temas cubanos*. His best-known work for orchestra may be the high-energy, four-movement ballet suite *La Rebambaramba* (1928), the title of which refers to a gathering involving songs, dances, and sometimes poetry. (It can also mean "publicize" or "give attention to.") Another work, *El milagro de anaquillé* (1929, rev. 1931), is a restaging of an Abakuá ritual.[126] Roldán is best known, however, for his *Rítmicas* (1930), a series of short pieces for various instrumental ensembles. This pioneering opus features Nos. 5 and 6, scored solely for percussion ensemble; thus they precede Varèse's better-known *Ionisation* (1931), often hailed as the first autonomous work with this scoring. (The all-percussion interlude from Shostakovich's opera *The Nose* is from 1928.)[127] In 1931 Roldán composed *Tres toques* (1931) for chamber orchestra, and in 1933 he paid homage to a beloved Cuban musician who was murdered during Carnival in *Fanfarria para despertar a Papá Montero* (Fanfare to Awaken Papá Montero), which some consider Roldán's call to bring down Gerardo Machado, the Cuban dictator-president from 1925 to 1933 (table 8.4).[128] Caturla's nonorchestral *Fanfarria para despertar espíritus apolillados* (Fanfare to Awaken Worn-Out Spirits), also from 1933, has been seen in a similar light.

In collaboration with Carpentier, Roldán established a concert series for new music, and from 1932 he devoted himself increasingly to conducting. He also taught at the Havana Municipal Conservatory. But in 1939, just shy of his fortieth birthday, Roldán died of an illness. The following year, Caturla, now a district judge, was killed in his hometown of Remedios by a gunman who thought he was about to sentence him. The premature deaths of both these two energetic and highly creative musicians was a great tragedy for Latin American music.

Another Spanish composer who emigrated to Cuba was José Ardévol (1911–81). Born in Barcelona, he arrived on the island in 1931, eventually replacing Roldán at the Municipal Conservatory. (The conservatory was later renamed in Roldán's honor.) Less taken with local color than many of his colleagues, Ardévol changed his musical style frequently, although today he is best known as a Neoclassicist. Ardévol set forth these values in a book on music in his adopted country, in which he compared "the poverty of aboriginal artistic manifestations" with the virtues of Neoclassicism, which he considered both a useful pedagogical tool and a means of resisting *localismo*, which cosmopolitan composers considered a stigma.[129] Among his numerous works for small ensembles are three *Ricercare* and two concerti grossi; music for full orchestra includes three symphonies (all from the mid-1940s), two sets titled *Suite cubana* (Cuban Suite), and other works (table 8.4). After the revolution of 1959, through which Fidel Castro came to power, Ardévol began writing topical avant-garde works. His *Movimiento sinfónico* No. 1 (Symphonic Movement) draws on materials from his cantata *La Victoria de Playa Girón* (the title refers to a beach near the Bay of Pigs), which contains aleatoric passages. *Movimiento sinfónico* No. 2, composed in 1969 and published in 1975 in the Soviet Union, borrows from another of his political cantatas, *Che comandante* (Commander Che), portions of which are serialist.

Ardévol was extremely influential in Cuban musical life. After founding a chamber orchestra in 1934, which he conducted for eighteen years, he advised the Grupo Renovación Musical, established in 1942 to reject musical "nationalism for its own sake" and to promote contemporary music by Cuban composers.[130] Several of its members studied with Ardévol, such as Edgardo Martín (1915–2004), who composed nine symphonic works (three are orchestrations of his piano pieces). Gisela Hernández Gonzalo (1912–71), who studied with Ardévol from 1940 to 1944, composed two symphonic works, *Tríptico cubano* (Cuban Triptych) of 1954 and *Diálogo de octubre* (October Dialogue) of 1965, a reference to what is known in the United States as the Cuban missile crisis of October 1962. Another Ardévol student was María Isabel Rubirosa, who wrote a *Suite* for orchestra that was performed in 1941 on a program of Cuban-US music in which Copland participated.[131] Argeliers León (1918–91) took lessons with Ardévol before traveling to France in 1957 to study with Boulanger. An early orchestral work, the twelve-tone *Cántico homenaje* (Homage Canticle, 1958), established him as one of Cuba's first serialists. His other works for orchestra include two symphonies (table 8.4). León was also active as an ethnomusicologist. Julio Gutiérrez (1918–90) took a different path, touring as a pianist with a jazz band and later working in television. His *Me voy asi: beguín* (in an arrangement by Antonio Parral) is in the Fleisher Collection.

One of the more energetic figures in Cuban musical life was Harold Gramatges (1918–2008). Initially a student of Roldán's, he began working with Ardévol in the 1940s. Both he and Ardévol considered orchestral music the ideal vehicle for "showcasing a nation's cultural advancement and modernity" yet felt that Cuba fell short here.[132] It was not for lack of effort on Gramatges's part. In 1945, he won the Reichold Chemical prize for the Caribbean region, a Good Neighbor project initiated by Reichold Chemical of Detroit to promote Latin American symphonic music. In 1946, Gramatges studied with Copland at the Berkshire Music Center and then took classes with Ulysses Kay and Elliott Carter at Columbia. Once back home, he founded a youth orchestra and taught at the conservatory. His orchestral works include a Symphony in E and handful of other compositions (table 8.4). With another former Ardévol student, Juan Blanco (1929–2008), Gramatges was among the founding members of Sociedad Cultural Nuestro Tiempo, established during the 1950s to combat the extreme conservatism and Eurocentrism in Cuban musical circles, often blamed on Castro's predecessor Fulgencio Batista.[133] Blanco, who composed a few orchestral works in the 1950s, is widely recognized as the first electroacoustic composer in Cuba.

After the 1959 revolution, state funding for the arts increased, in part to add luster to the regime. This period saw the advent of a Cuban national ballet company, for example, and an Orquesta Sinfónica Nacional, the latter established as early as October 1959. Both entities were to promote national pride, practice cultural diplomacy with other nations (especially socialist governments), and showcase music by Cuban composers.[134] Cuban symphonic music was programmed alongside works from the European canon, such that compositions by Roldán, Caturla, and the younger generation appeared on an equal footing with Beethoven and Brahms. In sum, the Orquesta Sinfónica Nacional democratized "bourgeois"—if not elite—symphonic music, sometimes with programming targeted to select groups or explicitly tied to historical events. The latter included an April 1963 homage to victory over the United States in the Bay of Pigs invasion, featuring *Elegía (En memoria de los heroes del pueblo cubano caídos en la lucha y la justicia)* by Juan Blanco. Program notes by Edgardo Martín, a fervent revolutionary, helped set the mood.

Not all composers felt at home in postrevolutionary Cuba. Julián Orbón (1925–91), born in Spain, settled in Havana in 1940, where he studied with Ardévol. Having attended the Berkshire Music Center in 1946, Orbón received Guggenheim funding and various honors in the

United States. After 1959 he moved to Mexico, where he served as an assistant to Chávez in the latter's *taller de composición* before settling in New York. Orbón's orchestral works include an early Symphony in C, composed in 1945 (table 8.4). Two years later he wrote *Homenaje a la tonadilla* (Homage to the Tonadilla). The piece reflects Orbón's Spanish roots: a tonadilla is a skit, usually with music, inserted between the acts of a Spanish drama or opera; it was popular in eighteenth-century Madrid.[135] Orbón quotes several tonadilla themes in his score, which he tracked down through a 1933 study by the Spanish musicologist José Subirá.[136] He fragments the themes and also generates new material through them, enhancing them with celesta, harp, castanets, tambourine, gong, bells, and cymbals.

Another orchestral work by Orbón is *Tres versiones sinfónicas* of 1953. Here, he interweaves the gestures and colors of his adopted country with a decidedly free reading of distant European traditions. Movement I, "Pavana (Luis de Milán)," pays homage to the sixteenth-century Spanish theorist and vihuelist. Although the pavan is normally a slow, stately dance, Orbón takes a mercurial approach, inserting mixed meters and a variety of rhythmic patterns into the multisectional movement. Some of the quicker passages, such as that beginning at Reh. 2, approximate a galliard, with which the pavan was often paired. Sections are often demarcated by abrupt changes in texture, such as the bare octaves in the cello, highlighted with daubs of color in the harp and piano at Reh. 7. A simple, stepwise melody given at the outset in the horns effectively announces how overwhelmingly tonal this composition will be, despite frequent added-note chords. None of it sounds especially Spanish, least of all the maracas in the B section (Reh. 2) or the rocking, repeated octaves, punctuated by rests, along with the rhythmic figure, suggestive of Copland's *El salón México* (example 5). (When Copland heard the work, he commented in his diary, "Sometimes it sounds like me."[137])

Example 8.5 Orbón. *Tres versiones sinfónicas*, mvt. 1, reh. 2

Movement II, "Organum-Conductus (Perotin)," with its freewheeling *fiorature*, is less reminiscent of organum than of flamenco singing (Reh. 1, also 3 mm. before Reh. 8). Throughout, Orbón balances a variety of textures and orchestral colors, deftly manipulating harp, celesta, piano, standard percussion, and Latin instruments such as claves, bongos, and maracas. Latin percussion dominates the moto perpetuo Movement III, "Xilofono (Congo)." The claves lead off, isolated but with a steady trochaic pattern instead of the signature clave rhythm. Bongo, cymbals, and piano swap themes and rhythmic motives throughout, often punctuated with glissandi in the xylophone and smears in the low brass. Does Orbón's fanciful blending of Old and New World traditions suggest that to him such boundaries are artificial? Are these "versions" of tradition, identities, and expectation? Having broached such questions, the work took third prize in the First Festival of Latin American Music in 1954 and remains his best-known composition.

Another Cuban expatriate was Aurelio de la Vega (1925–2022). In the 1940s, he studied composition with Ernst Toch while serving as cultural attaché in the Cuban Embassy in Los Angeles. In 1959, effectively blacklisted by the Castro government, de la Vega took a position at San Fernando Valley State College, now California State University, Northridge, where he established an electronic music studio. His orchestral works include *Sinfonía en cuatro partes*, composed in 1960 (table 8.4). The prolific Leo Brouwer (b. 1939), on the other hand, studied in the United States at the Hartt College (now School) of Music and the Juilliard School but returned to Cuba. His orchestral works include *Arioso (Homenaje a Charles Mingus)* for orchestra and jazz combo, composed in 1965. He has also written scores for over sixty films, including the international hit *Como agua para chocolate* (Like Water for Chocolate) of 1992. One of Brouwer's students was Héctor Angulo (1932–2018), who worked with him from 1964 after a stint at the Manhattan School of Music. Angulo's orchestral works include a set of variations for string orchestra. Roberto Valera (b. 1938) studied first with Ardévol, then with Brouwer, and then in Warsaw on a grant from the Cuban government. His works for orchestra include *Devenir* (1969), with both serial and aleatoric techniques (table 8.4). Of the same generation was Carlos Fariñas (1934–2002), who studied with Ardévol and Gramatges and wrote experimental music, some of which was performed by the Orquesta Sinfónica Nacional. Like Valera, the Afro-Cuban composer José Loyola Fernández (b. 1941) studied in Warsaw. His orchestral works include *Sinfonietta* for chamber orchestra (1965), *Música viva* No. 2 (1976), and *Tropicalia I* (1987) and *Tropicalia II* (1988), richly suggestive of Cuban percussion. Magaly Ruiz (b. 1941), born in Santa Clara, has reinterpreted traditional Cuban genres through bitonality and polytonality and has composed several orchestral works as well as an oboe concerto (table 8.4).

Tania León (b. 1943) is a truly international figure. She moved to the United States in 1967 and is active as a composer, pianist, and conductor and is an advocate for the arts in New York City.[138] Long associated with the Dance Theatre of Harlem, León served as new music adviser to the New York Philharmonic and as a distinguished professor of the City University of New York. She has also served as music director for Broadway shows such as *The Wiz* and *Godspell*. Her orchestral works include *Carabalí* (the name of a rain forest park, 1991) and the percussion-oriented *Horizons* (1999). Carlos Malcolm (b. 1945), also involved with dance, wrote *Marionetas* (1964) for orchestra in addition to two concertos. One member of the Cuban avant-garde is Sergio Fernández Barroso (b. 1946), who writes music for electroacoustic media as well as for more traditional ensembles.[139] Guido López-Gavilán (b. 1944), on the other hand, who studied at the Moscow Conservatory, composes in a more accessible neotonal style, a point of view he explains in a 2015 interview titled "I Care If You Listen," a reference to Milton Babbitt's infamous essay "Who Cares If You Listen?" published in *High Fidelity* in 1958 (the editor chose this inflammatory title over Babbitt's more neutral "The Composer as Specialist").[140]

A healthy tension between the popular and the avant-garde continues to enliven Cuban classical music. José Lezcano, who teaches at Keene State College in New Hampshire and specializes in guitar music, composed a *Tango Suite* for string orchestra. Ileana Pérez Velázquez (b. 1964) of Cienfuegos studied in Cuba, where she received several prizes, and currently teaches at Williams College.[141] She writes for electronic instruments but also for more traditional media, as in her *Influoresence* (2005), commissioned by the Berkshire Symphony Orchestra and which draws on a "Cuban jazzy rhythmic style," as she describes it; another of her orchestral works is *Fragmented Memories* (1999).[142] Keyla Orozco (b. 1969), who studied with Gramatges, composed a *Concierto barroco* in 1991 but has mostly dedicated herself to smaller ensembles. The versatile Yalil Guerra (b. 1973) is a classical guitarist, producer, arranger, and composer in various musical styles. His orchestral works, mainly for strings, include two symphonies. Louis Aguirre Rovira (b. 1968) conducted the Camagüey Symphony from 1995 to 2002 and writes in a style that has been described as "not for the faint of heart."[143] His *Oggún-Oniré* for orchestra (2008–12), which evokes Santería, carries on the practice of honoring Afro-Cuban religious rituals through classical music.[144]

Spanish-Speaking Caribbean: Dominican Republic

In 1494 mass was sung in what is today the Dominican Republic, on the island of Hispaniola. Trumpeters and other instrumentalists participated in musical life, including in religious institutions. In 1586, when Francis Drake and his men sacked the city of Santo Domingo by order of Elizabeth I of England, church records and musical scores were unfortunately destroyed. The Spanish returned to recolonize the territory, followed by a Haitian occupation (1822–44) and four more years of Spanish rule (1861–65). A war beginning in 1863 resulted in independence from Spain two years later, by which time music schools had been established, along with several bands. Musicians of that era include Juan Bautista Alfonseca (1810–75), who composed the national anthem, and José Reyes (1835–1905).[145] As the classical music community grew, musicians became preoccupied with questions of identity, or "*criollismo* in universality," as one Dominican author labels the matter.[146] In the twentieth century, orchestral music assumed greater importance, especially after 1941, when a symphony orchestra was established in the capital, Santo Domingo. (Between 1936 and 1961, the capital was known as Ciudad Trujillo after the reigning dictator Rafael Trujillo.) A national conservatory was also founded.[147] As for composers, Manuel de Jesús Lovelace (1871–1956), who studied at the Peabody Conservatory, wrote the orchestral work *Escenas dominicanas*, although he was primarily a critic.

Another Dominican composer of symphonic music was self-taught. Juan Francisco García (1892–1974) composed *Sinfónia Quisqueya*, the indigenous name of the region, and other orchestral works (table 8.4). Also drawing on national materials was Enrique Mejía-Arredondo (1901–51), whose programmatic Symphony in A Major, which relates to the war of 1863, was performed at the inaugural concert of the Orquesta Sinfónica Nacional in October 1941; Mejía-Arredondo's symphonic poem *Renacimiento* (Renaissance) conveys optimism after the ravages of a hurricane in 1930 (table 8.4).[148] Rafael Ignacio (1897–1984), who played in a military band and conducted a dance orchestra, wrote a Symphony in C Minor and a *Suite Folklórica* for orchestra.[149] Two Black symphonic composers were José Dolores Cerón (1897–1969) and Esteban Peña Morell (1894–1939). Cerón's symphonic poem *Enriquillo*, named after a sixteenth-century Indigenous leader, was performed in 1941. Peña Morell, a bassoonist in the Havana Philharmonic Orchestra, wrote the symphonic poem *Anacaona*.[150]

Clearly the Orquesta Sinfónica Nacional was fundamental to the growth of symphonic music. Its conductor was the Spanish expatriate Enrique Casal Chapí (1909–77), the grandson of the zarzuela composer Ruperto Chapí y Lorente. Active in Republican cultural circles, Casal Chapí arrived in the Dominican Republic in April 1940 and became a naturalized citizen. (After extended stays in Uruguay, Argentina, and Puerto Rico, he returned to Spain in 1960.) His symphonic works include an overture, which he conducted in November 1942, a *Final para una sinfonía imaginaria*, a *Fantasía sinfónica*, and other works. Slonimsky found "technical mastery" befitting its "advanced modern style" in Chapí's music.[151]

In his programs with the Orquesta Sinfónica Nacional, Casal Chapí promoted Dominican composers, some of whom were his students. Luis Emilio Mena (1895–1964), for example, wrote an overture subtitled *El camino del cielo*, which Casal Chapí premiered in October 1941.[152] Among Mena's works for orchestra are a *Sinfonía de Juguetes* (Toy Symphony) based on children's themes, and *Ecos de la libertad*, a "symphonic fantasy" that incorporates Dominican national anthems (table 8.4). Another student of Chapí's was Ninón Lapeiretta (1907–89), who incorporated traditional sources in a handful of orchestral works, including a *Suite de danzas* (table 8.4).[153] Also inspired by folklore was Enrique de Marchena (1908–88), whose *Suite de Imagenes* was premiered by Casal Chapí in 1942. He also wrote a symphonic poem, *Arco Iris*, and spent part of 1943 in the United States as a guest of the US State Department to lecture on Dominican music.[154] Less interested in folklore was Manuel Simó (1916–88), who composed a *Pastoral*, an Overture, a Prelude and Fugue (for strings), and a symphony. He would eventually write twelve-tone music.[155]

In the next generation, Margarita Luna (1921–2016), a student of Simó's, wrote twelve-tone and aleatoric music. From 1964 to 1967 she studied at the Juilliard School and then returned to the Dominican Republic to direct the National Conservatory. She wrote three orchestral works (table 8.4). Manuel Marino Miniño (1930–96), opposed to Trujillo, was persecuted at various intervals; he composed several symphonic works (table 8.4). Bienvenido Bustamente (1923–2001) wrote an orchestral *Fantasía* that premiered when he was 18. His *Serenata para Cuerdas* was performed under the auspices of the Association of Dominican Classical Artists, based in the Washington Heights area of New York City, an organization dedicated to "projecting a different image of the Dominican diaspora."[156]

Darwin Aquino (b. 1979), born in the Dominican Republic, studied there before enrolling at the conservatory in Strasbourg, France. In 2008 he became composer-in-residence of the Orquesta Sinfónica Nacional. Aquino has received national and international prizes for his compositions, and distinguished ensembles such as the Simón Bolívar Orchestra of Venezuela and the Philharmonisches Staatsorchester Mainz have performed his works, which are published by Cayambis (table 8.4). Aquino's *Espacio Ritual* (2007) was premiered by the Orchestre Philharmonique de Radio France. He currently serves as conductor-in-residence at Washington University in St. Louis.

The Spanish-Speaking Caribbean: Puerto Rico

Whatever the views of Governor Theodore Roosevelt Jr. in the 1930s, a classical music tradition had existed for centuries before his administration. For example, the first bishop of Puerto Rico, Alonso Manso, who arrived in 1513, was well versed in music.[157] Construction of the cathedral was beset by various delays, however, and instruments and instrumentalists were hard to come by: as one observer stated in 1688, "The poverty of Puerto Rico causes musicians from everywhere else in the Indies to shun the island."[158] Yet the number of church musicians gradually increased as did their secular counterparts, who played for balls and comedias (theater), forming the basis of symphony orchestras in various locales. In 1851 an orchestra was established in the inland town of Caguas, for example. By the end of the nineteenth century, three church orchestras were active: one at the San Juan cathedral and the others at the churches of San Francisco and San José. Indeed, there were orchestral musicians aplenty: when Louis Moreau Gottschalk played in San Juan in 1858, an ensemble of 250 musicians was swiftly assembled.[159]

One influential classical composer was Manuel Gregorio Tavárez (1843–83), who shaped musical life in Puerto Rico partly through his teaching, despite his short career.[160] Among his students was Juan Morel Campos (1857–96), born in Ponce. After playing in a military band, he founded an orchestra in his native city and composed prolifically. Among his symphonic works is *Puerto Rico* (1893), a symphony based on popular melodies (table 8.4).[161] Also from

Ponce was Arístides Chavier Arévalo (1865–1942), who lived in France for a time and composed *Obertura Puerto Rico* for orchestra. Braulio Dueño Colón (1854–1934) wrote an Italianate overture called *La Amistad*; another overture, *Noche de otoño*, premiered in Spain. He also composed a *Sinfonía dramática* and *Ecos de mi tierra* for orchestra, which contains regional themes. Rafael Balserio Dávila (1867–1929) composed a funeral march and wrote so many waltzes he became known as the "waltz king." Full of picturesque titles (*El Niágra*, *Puerto Rico*, *Las Mariposas*), they have been recorded by the Orquesta Sinfónica de Madrid. José Ignacio Quintón (1881–1925) wrote a *Marcha Triunfal* and *Gran obertura de concierto*, both from around 1910.[162]

One fascinating figure in Puerto Rican music was Rafael Hernández Marín (1892–1965). A native of Aguadilla, he studied music in San Juan. In 1917, when the United States entered World War I—and granted limited citizenship to Puerto Rico so that its people could be drafted—the young Afro–Puerto Rican, then working as a musician in North Carolina, caught the eye of the jazz bandleader James Reese Europe, then assembling his Orchestra Europe (nicknamed the Harlem Hellfighters) to buck up the spirits of the troops.[163] After returning from France, Hernández Marín wrote many popular songs and is especially well-known for his *Lamento borincano*, which can be found in numerous arrangements, including one in the Fleisher Collection (arranged by Antonio del Parral) for strings, saxophones, trumpets and trombones, percussion, piano, and guitar. Herández Marín also founded Little League baseball in Puerto Rico and knew the niceties of cigar making. President John F. Kennedy praised his many talents.

More recent composers also developed ties with the United States. Héctor Campos-Parsi (1922–88), born in Ponce, studied first in Puerto Rico and then attended the New England Conservatory of Music. He spent two summers at the Berkshire Music Center, working with Copland (1949) and Messiaen (1950) and then studying in Fontainebleau with Boulanger. Back home, Campos-Parsi promoted Puerto Rican identity, in part motivated by the desire to distinguish Puerto Rico from the United States. For example, he preferred not to incorporate jazz into his works.[164] He taught at the Puerto Rico Conservatory, founded in 1959, when many musical activities on the island were dominated by the Spanish cellist Pablo Casals.[165] Campos-Parsi's trajectory followed a typical path: Neoclassicism in the 1950s, atonality and serialism in the 1960s, followed by aleatory and electronic music. He composed some orchestral music, including *Variations on a Theme by Mozart* (1990) commissioned by the Casals Festival to mark the bicentennial of Mozart's death and in which several Puerto Rican composers collaborated, somewhat like Diabelli's project in nineteenth-century Vienna.[166] Ignacio Morales Nieva (1928–2005), born in Spain, worked with Joaquín Turina at the Madrid Conservatory, earned a degree in theology, and moved to Puerto Rico in 1954. Among his orchestral works are five symphonies and *Oda a Berlioz* (table 8.4).

Rafael Aponte-Ledée (b. 1938) studied in Madrid at the Royal Conservatory with Cristóbal Halffter. He spent 1965–66 at the CLAEM, where his teachers were Ginastera and Gandini.[167] Aponte-Ledée once denied that he practiced musical nationalism, declaring that it was "too obvious."[168] He has marshaled a range of twentieth-century techniques, including serialism, electroacoustic music, aleatory, and indeterminacy, enhanced with various extended instrumental techniques.[169] Sometimes, however, he quotes popular song. For example, in one orchestral work, *La muchacha de las bragas de oro* (The Girl with the Golden Panties), he mixed excerpts from a guaracha (a Cuban genre noted, appropriately, for its double entendres) with Ravel's *La valse* in a "Caribbean rhythm."[170] Another one of his orchestral works is *In*

Memoriam Salvador Allende for orchestra and tape, one of several musical homages to the Chilean leader.

Another pathfinder in Puerto Rican music is Francis Schwartz (b. 1940). Born in Pennsylvania, he grew up in Texas, studied at the Juilliard School, and moved to Puerto Rico in 1965. Put off by the conservative mindset in Puerto Rican musical circles—due in part to the repertory of the Casals Festival and the Casals mystique in general—he began organizing on behalf of new music, insisting that "it's a habit one creates."[171] To help create that habit, in 1968 Schwartz founded the group Fluxus with Aponte-Ledée. His orchestral works tend toward the experimental: *Gestos* (1983) is scored for orchestra and audience whereas *Papageno's Dream* (1991) calls for "stereophonic lip gestures." William Ortiz-Alvarado (b. 1947), born in Puerto Rico, studied with Campos-Parsi and then went to the United States, where he completed his PhD at the State University of New York at Buffalo, working with Lejaren Hiller and Morton Feldman. Ortiz-Alvarado has made it his mission to realize musically the sounds of Latin and Black urban neighborhoods, principally those in New York City. He pays homage to what he calls the "violent beauty of urban life: the expression of the shouts in the street—those that are felt, that are muffled," a goal he realizes principally in chamber music but also in orchestral works such as *Música de Ciudad* (1996). His catalog contains eleven additional orchestral works, including *Elogio a la Plena* (2002), an homage to the plena, a popular Puerto Rican genre (table 8.4).[172]

Roberto Sierra (b. 1953) studied in Puerto Rico and at the Hamburg Hochschule für Musik, where he worked with György Ligeti between 1979 and 1982. His first major work for orchestra, *Júbilo*, premiered by the Milwaukee Symphony Orchestra in March 1987 at Carnegie Hall; the critic Will Crutchfield deemed it "skillfully scored."[173] Sierra became the ensemble's composer-in-residence, the first of several such residencies. He then began teaching at Cornell University. Known for his brilliant orchestration, Sierra has composed six symphonies. Of his Symphony No. 4, commissioned by the Boston Symphony Orchestra, one critic applauded Sierra's "knack for creating both razzle-dazzle and subtle shimmering from essentially traditional instrumentation."[174] Among Sierra's over twenty orchestral works is a *Concerto for Orchestra* (table 8.4). He also reorchestrated the overture *La lira* composed in 1882 by his compatriot, Juan Morel Campos.[175]

Ernesto Cordero (b. 1946) was born in New York, studied in Madrid, and then taught at University of Puerto Rico. His works for orchestra include a *Concierto Criollo*, with cuatro, the instrument so emblematic of Puerto Rico. He was especially drawn to music for orchestra and instruments in the guitar family, as his album on the Naxos label shows. Other compositions include *Mariandá para orquesta sinfónica* (2010) and *Añoranza* for string orchestra (2017).[176] Raymond Torres-Santos (b. 1958) studied initially in Puerto Rico and then at the University of California, Los Angeles. For a time, he worked with David Raksin on film scoring and then taught in the California State University system. His music reflects influences ranging from Stan Kenton to Aaron Copland. Among his sixteen orchestral works is the *1898 Overture*, completed exactly a century after the Spanish-American War helped decide Puerto Rico's status in the hemisphere (table 8.4).

An important younger composer is Johanny Navarro Huertas (b. 1992) of Bayamón. Extremely versatile, she has received commissions from the Catholic University of America Symphony Orchestra, the New World Symphony, and several prominent artists. Her *Videntes Stellam* for choir and orchestra (2016) premiered at the Basilica of the National Shrine of the

Immaculate Conception in Washington, DC.[177] Her orchestral work *Daño colateral: memorias del útero puertorriqueño* (Collateral Damage: Memories of a Puerto Rican Uterus) was commissioned by the Multicultural Music Group, who requested that the work take as a point of departure the tribulations Puerto Rican women underwent during World War I, when they were exposed to military and domestic violence. In three parts, the work explores numerous textures and timbral possibilities. *Daño colateral* was premiered by the Orquesta Sinfónica de Puerto Rico in October 2019.[178]

Bibliographic Overview

Several sources listed in the previous chapter are useful here. Again, the *Diccionario de la música española e hispanoamericana* is valuable, although well-maintained websites are often the best source for living composers. Press commentary, judiciously interpreted, can lead to fruitful investigation. Grove Music Online can also be helpful, especially with substantive essays such as Parker/CHÁVEZ. Although published in 1945, Slonimsky/MUSIC proves unusually informative for Central American composers not covered in other sources; also, the Fleisher Collection contains music by composers from Mexico, Central America, and the Spanish-speaking Caribbean as does COMPOSITORES/COMPOSERS. Mayer-Serra/MÚSICA, a standard source for decades, still offers useful perspectives. Avant-garde composers of Mexico, Central America, and the Spanish-speaking Caribbean are discussed in Herrera/ELITE. Still, few serious treatments of orchestral music by composers of Mexico, Central America, or the Spanish-speaking Caribbean exist.

Mexico. Stevenson/MEXICO remains authoritative and readable although naturally some details can be updated. On instrumental music from the colonial period, the following should be consulted: Davies/SUMAYA; Davies/MAKING MUSIC; Russell/SUMAYA: REEXAMINING; and Brill/OAXACA, along with other studies by these scholars. A sensitive discussion on the experience of native populations vis-à-vis music is Cayward/MISSIONS. For fascinating detail on intersections between the Inquisition, music in colonial Mexico, and musical scholarship, see Marín López/CONFLICTED, p. 61. As for mission music, Russell/SERRA offers a lively account of this phenomenon, one in which the author treats instrumental music and engages with prior research by Koegel/SPANISH, Summers/RECENTLY, and Wagstaff/FRANCISCAN.

Instrumental music of the nineteenth century remains ripe for further study. On availability of printed scores, however, see Suárez de la Torre/PAPELES and Rodríguez-Erdmann/TESOROS. Another general study is Sordo Sodi/MÚSICA MEXICANA; see also Saavedra/NUEVO. Miranda Pérez/ECOS contains essays on several aspects of Mexican music, including instrumental music. Composers who straddled the nineteenth and twentieth centuries and who have received extended scholarly treatment include Manuel Ponce and José Rolón. Barrón/PONCE offers a reasonable orientation on Ponce; an insightful essay is found in Miranda Pérez/ECOS. Miranda's study of José Rolón is also recommended (Miranda Pérez/ROLÓN). A valuable full-scale study on Carrillo is Madrid/CARRILLO.

Carlos Chávez remains the most researched Mexican composer. The first major study, García Morillo/CHÁVEZ, is by the Argentine composer and critic Roberto García Morillo. Chávez endorsed the book, which discusses all his orchestral music to 1960. Halffter/CHÁVEZ is a catalog of the composer's works, originally created to mark the composer's seventieth birthday but updated after his death. Of the literature in English, Robert Parker's studies (Parker/ORPHEUS, Parker/LUCE, Parker/COPLAND, and Parker/RECURRING) are rich in detail (see also Parker/MÚSICA). The leading Chávez scholar today is Leonora Saavedra. In Saavedra/SELVES, her 2001 dissertation, she raised important issues on cultural priorities in postrevolutionary Mexico and their effect on music, while addressing also the cultural-historical significance of orchestral works such as *Sinfonía India* and the ballet *Caballos de Vapor* (Horse-Power, often simply rendered *H.P.*). Her extended essay of 2015, Saavedra/POLYSEMIC, is equally pathbreaking, especially in terms of cultural analysis. Saavedra also edited an essay collection resulting from the 2015 Bard Music Festival, devoted to Chávez, which covers a great variety of topics (Saavedra/WORLD). One feature of this volume, for example, is Saavedra's annotated translation of Orbón/SINFONÍAS, which considers all Chávez's symphonies along with Chávez's understanding and approach to the genre.

As noted, Chávez is often mentioned in the same breath with his compatriot and contemporary Silvestre Revueltas (1899–1940). Clearly Revueltas, with his short but intense life, deserves a full-length life-and-works biography. In the meantime, studies by the principal Revueltas scholar Roberto Kolb can be consulted with great profit (Kolb and Wolffer/REVUELTAS). Hoag/*SENSEMAYÁ*, an early analysis of Revueltas's best-known orchestral work, explores, among other things, the composer's use of the octatonic collection; Zohn-Muldoon/*SENSEMAYÁ* is a more recent analytical study. On Revueltas's experience in the United States, see Candelaria/REVUELTAS, Parker/CHICAGO, and Parker/SAN ANTONIO, MOBILE. (On the experiences of Revueltas's contemporaries in New York, see Taylor Gibson/PONCE, CARRILLO, CHÁVEZ.) Hess/REVUELTAS explores the reception of several of the composer's orchestral works during his tour of Republican Spain during the civil war. Given that Chávez and Revueltas are so often paired, Miranda Pérez and Bitrán/DIÁLOGO is a fine source of observations about both composers, including some of their symphonic works; see also the articles by Roberto Kolb-Neuhaus and Howard Pollack in Saavedra/WORLD. Another important scholar, Ana Alonso-Minutti, has written extensively about Mario Lavista (Alonso Minutti/LAVISTA).

Central America. Studies of music in Guatemala during the colonial period include those by Alfred E. Lemmon and Robert M. Stevenson. (See, for example, Lemmon/GUATEMALA and Stevenson/GUATEMALA.) One of Stevenson's many former students is the conductor, composer, and musicologist Dieter Lehnhoff, a principal figure in Guatemalan musical life who has especially promoted early music. His survey of music in the nation, Lehnhoff/GUATEMALA, is the most comprehensive to date and therefore indispensable. In Nicaragua, Luis Abraham Delgadillo was a central figure in orchestral music. The principal specialist in his music is Bernard Gordillo, who has examined his activities from a variety of perspectives, including the relationship between Nicaragua and the United States (Gordillo/DELGADILLO). The main music scholar in Costa Rica is Bernal Flores (Flores/VIDA; Flores/COSTA RICA); Flores also wrote the entry on the nation for Grove Music Online. María Clara Vargas-Cullel emphasizes band music in her 2004 study of music in Costa Rica from 1840 to 1940 (Vargas-Cullel/FANFARRÍAS) although she discusses some orchestral music. As for Panama, articles by its principal twentieth-century composer Roque Cordero are enlightening (e.g., Cordero/NACIONALISMO). A full-scale study of Cordero would be welcome.

The Spanish-Speaking Caribbean. A few scholars have attempted to survey the totality of Cuban music. One lively albeit dated study is Carpentier/CUBA. In Ardévol/INTRODUCCIÓN, the Spanish-born José Ardévol largely represents his own views. Orovio/CUBAN MUSIC is in dictionary format and useful for quick basic facts, including those related to orchestral music, but should always be cross-checked. Escudero and Quevedo/CLASSICAL

CUBA provides an excellent orientation. Twentieth-century composers of instrumental music such as Roldán and Caturla were among the most frequently performed composers in the Pan-American Association of Composers; the reader finds insightful analyses of works by both in Stallings/COLLECTIVE. On Roldán's appropriation of the African legacy, see also Tomé/RACIAL. The Cuban Revolution of 1959 affected musical creation and the organization of musical life—a point covered in Quevedo/ORQUESTA, which gives good coverage to Harold Gramatges. Recent composers of instrumental music now working outside of Cuba (Ileana Velásquez, Louis Aguirre Rovira, and others) are discussed in Morales Flores/IDENTIDADES. Many Cuban composers merit full-scale biographies but unfortunately few exist. Madrid/TANIA is a happy exception.

A dated and biased view of musical life in Santo Domingo, the capital of the Dominican Republic, is Nolasco/MÚSICA. Published in 1939, it may offer historiographical interest. A leading US authority on music in the Dominican Republic was the versatile Jacob Maurice Coopersmith, organist, conductor, and musicologist who eventually worked for a recording company. Coopersmith/MUSIC was published by the Pan American Union; his two-part series in *Musical Quarterly* (Coopersmith/MUSIC 1, MUSIC 2) duplicates some of the information it presents but remains a reasonable initiation for readers unacquainted with classical music of the Dominican Republic. A full-scale biography of Enrique Casal Chapí, a Spanish expatriate who openly defied Franco and then contributed to musical life in various parts of Latin America, would make fascinating reading. A hint of his experience in the Dominican Republic is found in Llorens/MEMORIAS, a study of Spaniards seeking refuge in Santo Domingo from a Europe in which Hitler, Mussolini, and Franco had come to prevail, only to encounter a land under the dictator Rafael Trujillo.

The literature on classical music in Puerto Rico is more extensive. Among older studies, Muñoz/MÚSICA orients readers completely unfamiliar with this subject; it especially provides biographical information on composers of instrumental music from various periods. Quevedo/PUERTO RICO is extremely helpful. On the function of instrumental music in earlier periods in Puerto Rican music, see Thompson/PUBLIC and Stevenson/SAN JUAN. Thompson covers instrumental music of the nineteenth century in Thompson/NINETEENTH and later music in Thompson/MÚSICA. More than one scholar has related music to the often-troubled relationship between Puerto Rico and the United States. In Lazo/PROGRESS, Silvia Lazo relates these tensions to the Casals Festival, which, she argues, was intimately tied to tourism and capital accumulation—in short, the sort of "development," as it was known, engineered by the United States.

Several scholars have addressed Campos-Parsi and Aponte-Ledée either individually or in tandem, relating these two leaders in Puerto Rican twentieth-century music either to musical nationalism, as in Díaz Díaz/AFFIRMATION; modernism, as in Alonso/INICIOS; or in historical context, as in Caso/CAMPOS PARSI. Analyses of musical works include Montalvo/CAMPOS PARSI. González focuses on a representative selection of orchestral works by Puerto Rican composers born at midcentury (González/SELECTED).

Notes

1. Pernet/GENUINE CULTURE, pp. 137, 139.
2. Oja/MAKING, p. 278; see also Saavedra/POLYSEMIC, pp. 95–100.
3. Hudde/NEGOTIATING.

4. Glasser/MY MUSIC, p. 13.
5. Bermúdez/FORTRESSES, pp. 301–12.
6. Davies/SUMAYA, p. xii.
7. Russell/SUMAYA: REEXAMINING.
8. Summers/RECENTLY; see also Summers/MISA.
9. Stevenson/COLONIAL.
10. Querol Gavaldá/NOTAS.
11. Another eminent chapelmaster was Antonio de Salazar, who served at Puebla from 1679 to 1688. Stevenson/PUEBLA.
12. Davies/ITALIANIZED.
13. Davies/SUMAYA, p. xii. See also Brill/OAXACA.
14. Quoted in Davies/MAKING MUSIC, pp. 72, 66.
15. Marín López/CONFLICTED, p. 61.
16. Jackson/FRONTIERS, pp. 32, 7, 44–45.
17. Cayward/MISSIONS.
18. Russell/SERRA, pp. 352, 49.
19. Koegel/SPANISH; Wagstaff/FRANCISCAN. See also Kennedy/COLONIAL.
20. Suárez de la Torre/PAPELES; see also Rodríguez-Erdmann/TESOROS.
21. Sordo Sodi/MÚSICA MEXICANA, p. 303; Miranda Pérez/ECOS.
22. Stevenson, writing in the *Diccionario de la música española e hispanoamericana* (3:410) refers to a Symphony in D by Castro, which is either unfinished or unpublished. Castro's unfinished symphonic poem *Oithona* is in the Fleisher Collection. Saavedra/NUEVO, p. 97.
23. Miranda Pérez/ROLÓN, pp. 60, 64.
24. Madrid/CARRILLO.
25. Taylor Gibson/PONCE, CARRILLO, CHÁVEZ, p. 27.
26. Salazar began a *Moderato assai e semplice* for orchestra, dated 1934, but it likely remains unfinished. Trujillo/SALAZAR.
27. Taylor Gibson/PONCE, CARRILLO, CHÁVEZ, p. 41.
28. Saavedra/POLYSEMIC, p. 105.
29. Hess/REPRESENTING, p. 53.
30. Barrón/PONCE, pp. 31–41.
31. Ibid., pp. 32, 38.
32. Miranda Pérez/HEARTBEAT, p. 50.
33. Saaevdra/POLYSEMIC, pp. 107–8.
34. Parker/COPLAND, pp. 433–44; Hess/REPRESENTING, pp. 25–80.
35. Hess/COPLAND, p. xx.
36. Saavedra/WORLD.
37. Orbón/SINFONÍAS, pp. 148–58; see also Orbón/SYMPHONIES, pp. 62–75.
38. Hess/REPRESENTING, pp. 25–49, 77–80. See also Parker/MÚSICA, pp. 4–12.
39. See Parker/ORPHEUS, p. 70; Stevenson/MEXICO, p. 243; Saavedra/SELVES, pp. 302–16.
40. As Saavedra points out, Chávez occasionally misidentified a theme. Although he believed the melody at Reh. 9 to be a Huichol melody, it is actually a Cora tune. The theme heard at Reh. 29, so reminiscent of Copland, is a Seri tune, as is the theme at Reh. 88. Saavedra/SELVES, pp. 303–5.
41. García Morillo/CHÁVEZ, p. 94.
42. Parker/LUCE, p. 49.
43. Cited in ibid., p. 52. For other instances of this motive, see Parker/RECURRING, pp. 160–72.
44. *Venezuela Visit—November 26 through December 9, 1954* (Aaron Copland Collection, Library of Congress, box 244, folders 15 and 16).
45. Copland suppressed his criticisms in his article FESTIVAL.

46. Howard Taubman, "Music: A New Work from Mexico," *New York Times*, January 27, 1956, p. 19.
47. Parker/CHÁVEZ; Letter, Aaron Copland to Chávez, July 26, 1967.
48. Cited in García Morillo/CHÁVEZ, p. 158.
49. Quoted in Stevenson/CHÁVEZ, p. 144n9.
50. Parker/CHÁVEZ. See also Bauer/NON-REPETITION.
51. Miranda Pérez and Bitrán/DIÁLOGO; Kolb and Wolffer/REVUELTAS; see also Kolb-Neuhaus/DIALOGUE.
52. Candelaria/REVUELTAS, pp. 502–32; Parker/SAN ANTONIO, MOBILE; Parker/CHICAGO.
53. Hess/REVUELTAS, pp. 278–96.
54. Hoag/*SENSEMAYÁ* and Zohn-Muldoon/*SENSEMAYA*. Revueltas first wrote the work for chamber ensemble and rescored it for full orchestra a year later.
55. Alexander/FILM, p. 143.
56. The film has been restored on a DVD from Naxos.
57. John Henken, https://www.laphil.com/musicdb/pieces/2185/la-noche-de-los-mayas, accessed February 14, 2021.
58. Olin Downes, "American Music Heard at Museum," *New York Times*, May 25, 1941, p. 18.
59. Aaron Copland, "Mexican Composer," *New York Times*, May 9, 1937, p. X5.
60. Navarro/HACER, p. 31.
61. Hess/COPLAND, p. xx.
62. Ibid., p. xx.
63. Also contributing music to this multisectional film were Blas Galindo, Rodolfo Halffter, and Guillermo Noriega.
64. https://redmayor.wordpress.com/2010/09/27/mario-lavista-n-1943/, accessed April 12, 2021. See also Alonso Minutti/LAVISTA.
65. Stevenson/GUATEMALA, pp. 343–44; see also Stevenson/GUATEMALA CATHEDRAL.
66. Lehnhoff/GUATEMALA, p. 102.
67. Stevenson/SIXTEENTH-CENTURY GUATEMALA, p. 347n27; Lemmon/GUATEMALA.
68. Lehnhoff/GUATEMALA, p. 145.
69. Ibid., p. 140.
70. https://aprende.guatemala.com/cultura-guatemalteca/historia-orquesta-sinfonica-nacional-guatemala/.
71. Lehnhoff/GUATEMALA, p. 252; Hess/COPLAND, p. xx.
72. Olin Downes, "Music: Premiere of *Mayan Legend*," *New York Times*, February 18, 1931, p. 14. Paniagua also performed at the Pan American Union on November 26, 1926. Pereira Salas/NOTES, p. 32.
73. Lehnhoff/GUATEMALA, p. 247.
74. Slonimsky/MUSIC, p. 205.
75. Lehnhoff/GUATEMALA, pp. 268–69.
76. Ibid., pp. 269, 290.
77. Ippisch's *Pierrots Liebeswerben* (Pierrot's Courtship) for wind ensemble can be found at the website of the Center for Banned Music. https://exilarte.org/, accessed March 10, 2021.
78. Slonimsky/MUSIC, p. 206.
79. Lehnhoff/GUATEMALA, p. 270.
80. Herrera points out that Orellana has "insisted" that he was born in 1937 but that his application to the CLAEM gives the date 1930. Herrera/ELITE, p. 27.
81. Herrera/ELITE, p. 150.
82. Lehnhoff/GUATEMALA, p. 276.

83. Ibid., pp. 202, 276.
84. Ibid., p. 274.
85. Slonimsky/MUSIC, p. 280.
86. Ibid., p. 203.
87. Ibid., p. 280.
88. Gordillo/DELGADILLO, p. 33.
89. Ibid., pp. 76, 64.
90. "Brilliant Concert in Nation's Capital," *New York Times*, April 22, 1930, p. 24.
91. Gordillo/DELGADILLO, pp. 227–63.
92. COMPOSITORES/COMPOSERS: pp. 47–48.
93. Gordillo/DELGADILLO, p. 6.
94. Slonimsky/MUSIC, p. 256.
95. https://www.goethe.de/ins/mx/es/kul/mus/bel/thh.html.
96. http://unicornios-intergalacticos.blogspot.com/2017/07/concierto-de-nueva-musica-contemporanea.html.
97. Flores/VIDA, p. 265.
98. Ibid., p. 267.
99. Vargas-Cullel/FANFARRIAS.
100. Slonimsky/MUSIC, p. 177.
101. Flores/VIDA, p. 267; see also Flores/COSTA RICA.
102. Quoted in Slonimsky/MUSIC, p. 177.
103. http://archivomusical.ucr.ac.cr/catalogo/obras/suite-de-ballet.
104. Herrera/ELITE, p. 25.
105. Ibid., p. 25.
106. https://mcj.go.cr/sala-de-prensa/noticias/profesor-de-musica-del-sinem-recibe-premio-nacional-de-musica-2019.
107. Pereira Salas/NOTES, p. 3.
108. Slonimsky/MUSIC, p. 261.
109. Chase/CARACAS, p. 11.
110. Orosz/CORDERO.
111. Paul Hume, "Symphony Plays Four Premieres," *Washington Post and Times Herald*, April 19, 1958, p. B11.
112. Cordero/NACIONALISMO, p. 28.
113. Translation mine. Orrego-Salas/TÉCNICA Y ESTÉTICA, p. 187.
114. Robles/AMANECER.
115. Stevenson/ESTEBAN SALAS.
116. Carpentier/CUBA, p. 60.
117. Orovio/CUBAN MUSIC, p. 88.
118. Carpentier/CUBA, p. 124.
119. "Gonzalo Roig, 80, Composer, Dead," *New York Times*, June 15, 1970, p. 39.
120. Orovio/CUBAN MUSIC, p. 183.
121. Ibid., p. 184.
122. Stallings/COLLECTIVE, p. 112.
123. A lucumí pattern, transcribed by Cuban ethnographer Fernando Ortíz (1881–1969), can be found in Grove Music Online (use the search term *lucumí*); Caturla employed some elements of this pattern, such as the dotted-eighth-sixteenth and occasional off-beat in his piece.
124. Orovio/CUBAN MUSIC, pp. 90–91.
125. Ibid., p. 185.
126. Tomé/RACIAL OTHER.

127. Stallings/COLLECTIVE, p. 26.
128. Gómez/ROLDÁN, pp. 122–24.
129. Ardévol/INTRODUCCIÓN, pp. 5, 91.
130. Orovio/CUBAN MUSIC, p. 18.
131. Hess/COPLAND, p. xx.
132. Quevedo/ORQUESTA, pp. 22–23.
133. Ibid., p. 22; see also Quevedo/EXPERIMENTAL.
134. Quevedo/ORQUESTA, p. 24.
135. Le Guin/TONADILLLA.
136. Subirá/TONADILLA.
137. *Venezuela Visit—November 26 through December 9, 1954* (Aaron Copland Collection, Library of Congress, box 244, folders 15 and 16.
138. Madrid/TANIA.
139. Orovio/CUBAN MUSIC, p. 81.
140. "I Care If You Listen: 5 Questions to Guido López Gavilán (composer)," https://www.icareifyoulisten.com/2015/11/5-questions-guido-lopez-gavilan-composer/.
141. Morales Flores/IDENTIDADES.
142. Ileana Pérez Velázquez, http://ileanaperezvelazquez.com/nflorescence-for-symphonic-orchestra-2005-18/.
143. "5 Cuban Composers to Watch" (Baltimore Symphony Orchestra newsletter) https://www.bsomusic.org/stories/5-cuban-composers-to-watch/.
144. Morales Flores/IDENTIDADES.
145. Slonimsky/MUSIC, p. 191.
146. Nolasco/MÚSICA, pp. 81–98.
147. Coopersmith/MUSIC 2, p. 224 n191.
148. Slonimsky/MUSIC, p. 194.
149. Ibid., p. 194.
150. Ibid., p. 196.
151. Ibid., p. 193.
152. Ibid., p. 195.
153. On the works from the 1940s, see Coopersmith/MUSIC 2, pp. 32–33.
154. Coopersmith/MUSIC 1, p. 71n2.
155. Coopersmith/MUSIC 2, p. 223; see also *Enciclopedia Dominicana* http://enciclopediadominicana.org/Manuel_Sim%C3%B3.
156. Association of Dominican Classical Artists, https://www.adca.nyc/.
157. Stevenson/SAN JUAN, p. 74.
158. Quoted in ibid., p. 77.
159. Thompson/NINETEENTH, p. 330.
160. Muñoz/MÚSICA, p. 129.
161. Ibid., pp. 123–24.
162. Ibid., pp. 117–27.
163. Puerto Rico is a commonwealth of the United States known as the Estado Libre Asociado de Puerto Rico (Free Associated State of Puerto Rico, or ELA).
164. Díaz Díaz/AFFIRMATION, p. 11.
165. Lazo/PROGRESS.
166. Mark Carrington, "Music," *Washington Post*, November 28, 1991. Rafael Aponte-Ledée, Ignacio Morales-Nieva, and Raymond Torres-Santos each wrote a variation as well.
167. Herrera/ELITE, p. 25.
168. Díaz Díaz/AFFIRMATION, p. 12.

169. Alonso/INICIOS.
170. Díaz Díaz/AFFIRMATION, p. 13.
171. Katrina del Mar, "Who Is Francis Schwartz?" https://kdelmarr.wixsite.com/karinadelmar/post/who-is-francis-schwartz.
172. William Ortiz-Alvarado (composer), http://williamortiz.com/.
173. Will Crutchfield, "Concert: Milwaukee Symphony," *New York Times*, March 3, 1987, p. C16.
174. Roberto Sierra, http://www.robertosierra.com/reviews.html.
175. Roberto Sierra, http://www.robertosierra.com/work-catalogue.html.
176. Ernesto Cordero, compositor, https://www.ernestocordero.com/.
177. Johanny Navarro, https://johannynavarro.com.
178. https://www.periodicolaperla.com/la-orquesta-sinfonica-de-puerto-rico-estrena-pieza-de-joven-compositora/ (this website has been removed).

Bibliography

Alexander/FILM	Alexander, William. *Film on the Left: American Documentary Film from 1931 to 1942*. Princeton, NJ: Princeton University Press, 1981.
Alonso/INICIOS	Alonso, Ernesto. "Inicios de La Vanguardia Musical Puertorriqueña: Rafael Aponte Ledée." *Musiké: Revista Del Conservatorio de Música de Puerto Rico* 5, no. 1 (2016): pp. 35–49.
Alonso-Minutti/LAVISTA	Alonso-Minutti, Ana. "Resonances of Sound, Text, and Image in the Music of Mario Lavista." PhD diss., University of California, Davis, 2008.
Ardévol/INTRODUCCIÓN	Ardévol, José. *Introducción a Cuba: la Música*. Havana: Instituto del Libro, 1969.
Barrón/PONCE	Barrón, Jorge. *Manuel M. Ponce: A Bio-Bibliography*. Westport, CT: Praeger, 2004.
Bauer/NON-REPETITION	Bauer, Amy. "Non-repetition and Personal Style in the *Inventions* and *Solis*." In *Carlos Chávez and His World*, edited by Leonora Saavedra, pp. 165–77. Princeton, NJ: Princeton University Press, 2015.
Bermúdez/FORTRESSES	Bermúdez, Egberto. "Sounds from Fortresses of Faith and Ideal Cities: Society, Politics, and Music in Missionary Activities in the Americas, 1525–1575." *Listening to Early Modern Catholicism*, vol. 49. Intersections: Interdisciplinary Studies in Early Modern Culture, edited by Daniele V. Filippi and Michael Noone, pp. 301–25. Leiden and Boston: Brill, 2017.
Brill/OAXACA	Brill, Mark. "The Oaxaca Cathedral *Exámen de oposición*: The Quest for a Modern Style." *Latin American Music Review* 26, no. 1 (2005): pp. 1–22.
Candelaria/REVUELTAS	Candelaria, Lorenzo. "Silvestre Revueltas at the Dawn of his 'American' Period: St. Edward's College, Austin Texas (1917–1918)." *American Music* 22, no. 4 (2004): pp. 502–32.

Carpentier/CUBA	Carpentier, Alejo. *La música en Cuba*. Havana: Editorial Letras Cubanas, 1979.
Carpentier/ESE MÚSICO	Carpentier, Alejo. *Ese músico que llevo dentro*, edited by Zoila Gómez, pp. 1: 434–35. Havana: Editorial Letras Cubanas, 1980.
Caso/CAMPOS PARSI	Caso, Fernando H. *Héctor Campos Parsi en la historia de la música puertorriqueña del siglo XX*. San Juan: Instituto de Cultura Puertorriqueña, 1980.
Cayward/MISSIONS	Cayward, Margaret. "Missions and Transmissions: Music and the Spanish Missions of Alta California from 1769." PhD diss., University of California, Davis, 2012.
Celenza Hartwell and Del Donna/ MUSIC AS CULTURAL MISSION.	Celenza Hartwell, Anna, and Anthony R. Del Donna, eds. *Music as Cultural Mission: Exploration of Jesuit Musical Practices in Italy and North America*. Philadelphia: St. Joseph University Press, 2014.
Chase/CARACAS	Chase, Gilbert. "Caracas Host to Second Latin American Festival." *Musical America* 77, no. 6 (May 1957): pp. 11–12.
COMPOSITORES/COMPOSERS	*Compositores de América/Composers of the Americas*. Washington, DC: Pan American Union, 1956, vols. 1–19.
Coopersmith/MUSIC	Coopersmith, Jacob Maurice. *Music and Musicians of the Dominican Republic*. Washington, DC: Department of Cultural Affairs, Pan American Union, 1949.
Coopersmith/MUSIC 1	Coopersmith, Jacob Maurice. "Music and Musicians of the Dominican Republic: A Survey." Part 1. *Musical Quarterly* 31, no. 1 (1945): pp. 71–88.
Coopersmith/MUSIC 2	Coopersmith, Jacob Maurice. "Music and Musicians of the Dominican Republic: A Survey." Part 2. *Musical Quarterly* 31, no. 2 (1945): pp. 212–26.
Copland/COMPOSERS	Copland, Aaron. "The Composers of South America." *Modern Music* 19, no. 2 (January–February 1942): pp. 75–82.
Copland/FESTIVAL	Copland, Aaron. "Festival of Contemporary Latin American Music." *Tempo* 35 (1955): pp. 4–5, 10.
Cordero/NACIONALISMO	Cordero, Roque. "¿Nacionalismo versus dodecafonismo?" *Revista Musical Chilena* 13 (1959): pp. 28–39.
Davies/ITALIANIZED	Davies, Drew Edward. "The Italianized Frontier: Music at Durango Cathedral, Español Culture, and the Aesthetics of Devotion in Eighteenth-Century New Spain." PhD diss., University of Chicago, 2006.
Davies/MAKING MUSIC	Davies, Drew Edward. "Making Music, Writing Myth: Urban Guadalupan Ritual in Eighteenth-century New Spain." In *Music and Urban Society in*

	Colonial America, edited by Geoffrey Baker and Tess Knighton, pp. 64–82. Cambridge: Cambridge University Press, 2011.
Davies/SUMAYA	Davies, Drew Edward. "Manuel de Sumaya and His Music." In *Manuel de Sumaya: Villancicos from Mexico City*, edited by Drew Edward Davies, pp. xii–xv. Middleton, WI: A-R Editions, 2019.
de la Vega/COMPOSERS	de la Vega, Aurelio. "Latin American Composers in the United States." *Latin American Music Review* 1, no. 2 (1980): pp. 162–75.
Díaz Díaz/AFFIRMATION	Díaz Díaz, Edgardo. "Puerto Rican Affirmation and Denial of Musical Nationalism: The Cases of Campos Parsi and Aponte Ledée." *Latin American Music Review* 17, no. 1 (1996): pp. 1–20.
Escudero and Quevedo/ CLASSICAL CUBA	Escudero, Miriam, and Marysol Quevedo. "Classical Music in Cuba." Oxford Bibliographies Online. *Oxford Music Online*. Oxford University Press. https://www-oxfordbibliographies-com.auth.lib.niu.edu/view/document/obo-9780199757824/obo-9780199757824-0165.xml, accessed September 4, 2021.
Flores/COSTA RICA	Flores Zeller, Bernal. *La música en Costa Rica*. San José: Editorial Costa Rica, 1978.
Flores/REPUBLIC	Flores, Bernal. "Republic of Costa Rica." Grove Music Online. *Oxford Music Online*. Oxford University Press. https://www-oxfordmusiconline-com.auth.lib.niu.edu/grovemusic/view/10.1093/gmo/9781561592630.001.0001/omo-9781561592630-e-0000041086?rskey=F3x7Zv, accessed September 4, 2021.
Flores/VIDA	Flores, Bernal. "La vida musical de Costa Rica en el siglo XX." In *Die Musikkulturen Lateinamerikas im 19. Jahrhundert*, edited by Robert Günther, pp. 261–75. Regensburg: Gustav Bosse Verlag, 1982.
Galván/ABCs	Galván, Gary. "The ABCs of the WPA Music Copying Project and the Fleisher Collection." *American Music* 26, no, 4 (2008): pp. 514–38.
Galván/FLEISHER	Galván, Gary, comp. *Latin American Orchestral Works in the Fleisher Collection*. Philadelphia: Free Library of Philadelphia, 2017.
García Canclini/MODERNITY	García Canclini, Néstor. *Hybrid Cultures: Strategies for Entering and Leaving Modernity*, translated by Christopher L. Chiappari and Silvia L. López. Minneapolis: University of Minnesota Press, 1995; originally published in Mexico City, 1989.
García Morillo/CHÁVEZ	García Morillo, Roberto. *Carlos Chávez: vida y obra*. Mexico City and Buenos Aires: Fondo de Cultura Económica, 1960.

Glasser/MY MUSIC	Glasser, Ruth. *My Music Is My Flag: Puerto Rican Musicians and Their New York Communities, 1917–1940*. Berkeley: University of California Press, 1995.
Gómez/ROLDÁN	Gómez, Zoila. *Amadeo Roldán*. Havana: Editorial de Arte y Literatura, 1977.
González/SELECTED	González, Roberto. "Selected Orchestral Works by Puerto Rican Composers Born between 1945 and 1956." DA diss., Ball State University, 1983.
Gordillo/DELGADILLO	Gordillo, Bernard. "Luis A. Delgadillo and the Cultural Occupation of Nicaragua under U.S.-American Intervention." PhD diss., University of California, Riverside, 2019.
Halffter/CHÁVEZ	Halffter, Rodolfo, ed. *Carlos Chávez: Catálogo completo de sus obras*. Mexico City: Sociedad de Autores y Compositores de Música, 1971.
Herrera/ELITE	Herrera, Eduardo. *Elite Art Worlds: Philanthropy, Latin Americanism, and Avant-Garde Music*. New York: Oxford University Press, 2020.
Hess/COPLAND	Hess, Carol A. *Aaron Copland in Latin America: Music, Politics, and Cultural Diplomacy*. Champaign: University of Illinois Press, 2022.
Hess/EXPERIENCING	Hess, Carol A. *Experiencing Latin American Music*. Oakland: University of California Press, 2018.
Hess/REPRESENTING	Hess, Carol A. *Representing the Good Neighbor: Music, Difference, and the Pan American Dream*. New York: Oxford University Press, 2013.
Hess/REVUELTAS	Hess, Carol A. "Silvestre Revueltas in Republican Spain: Music as Political Utterance." *Latin American Music Review* 18, no. 2 (1997): pp. 278–96.
Hoag/SENSEMAYÁ	Hoag, Charles K. "*Sensemayá*: A Chant for Killing a Snake." *Latin American Music Review* 8, no. 2 (1987): pp. 172–84.
Hudde/NEGOTIATING	Hudde, Hermann. "Negotiating Politics and Aesthetics: The Untold History of Modern Latin American Art Music in the Berkshire Music Center at Tanglewood, 1940–1951." PhD diss., University of California, Riverside, 2021.
Jackson/FRONTIERS	Jackson, Robert H. *Frontiers of Evangelization: Indians in the Sierra Gorda and Chiquitos Missions*. Norman: University of Oklahoma Press, 2017.
Kennedy/COLONIAL	Kennedy, T. Frank. "Latin American Colonial Music: The Case for Mission Music as a New Genre." *Sonus: A Journal of Investigations into Global Music Possibilities* 21, no. 2 (2001): pp. 27–38.
Koegel/SPANISH	Koegel, John. "Spanish and French Mission Music in Colonial North America." *Journal of the Royal Music Association* 126 (2001): pp. 1–53.

Kolb and Wolffer/REVUELTAS	Kolb, Roberto, and José K. Wolffer, eds. *Silvestre Revueltas: Sonidos en rebellion*. Mexico City: Universidad Nacional Autónoma de México, Escuela Nacional de Música, Dirección General de Apoyo al Personal Académico, 2007.
Kolb-Neuhaus/DIALOGUE	Kolb-Neuhaus, Roberto. "Carlos Chávez and Silvestre Revueltas: Retracing an Ignored Dialogue." In *Carlos Chávez and His World*, edited by Leonora Saavedra, pp. 76–98. Princeton, NJ: Princeton University Press, 2015.
Labonville/PLAZA	Labonville, Marie Elizabeth. *Juan Bautista Plaza and Musical Nationalism in Venezuela*. Bloomington and Indianapolis: Indiana University Press, 2007.
Laird/DISSEMINATION	Laird, Paul R. "The Dissemination of the Spanish Baroque Villancico." *Revista de Musicología* 16, no. 5 (1993): pp. 2857–64.
Lazo/PROGRESS	Lazo, Silvia. "'Music for Progress': A Study of Pau Casals's Music Institutions in Puerto Rico as an Extension of US Neocolonialism." *Revista de Música Latinoamericana* 38, no. 2 (2017): pp. 185–211.
LeGuin/TONADILLA	LeGuin, Elisabeth. *The Tonadilla in Performance: Lyric Comedy in Enlightenment Spain*. Berkeley, Los Angeles, and London: University of California Press, 2014.
Lehnhoff/GUATEMALA	Lehnhoff, Dieter. *Creación musical en Guatemala*. Guatemala: Universidad Rafael Landívar, 2005.
Lemmon/GUATEMALA	Lemmon, Alfred, ed. *La música de Guatemala en el siglo XVIII. Music from Eighteenth-Century Guatemala*. Antigua Guatemala, Centro de Investigaciones Regionales de Mesoamérica: South Woodstock, VT: Plumsock Mesoamerican Studies, 1986.
Llorens/MEMORIAS	Llorens, Vicente. *Memorias de una emigración: Santo Domingo, 1939–1945*. Edited with notes and introduction by Manuel Aznar Soler. Series Biblioteca del exilio. Seville: Editorial Renacimiento, 2006.
Madrid/CARRILLO	Madrid, Alejandro L. *In Search of Julián Carrillo and Sonido 13*. New York: Oxford University Press, 2015.
Madrid/TANIA	Madrid, Alejandro. *Tania León's Stride: A Polyrhythmic Life*. Champaign: University of Illinois Press, 2021.
Marín López/CONFLICTED	Marín López, Javier. "A Conflicted Relationship: Music, Power, and the Inquisition in Viceregal Mexico." In *Music and Urban Society in Colonial America*, edited by Geoffrey Baker and Tess Knighton, pp. 43–63. Cambridge: Cambridge University Press, 2011.
Mayer-Serra/MÚSICA	Mayer-Serra, Otto. *Música y músicos de Latinoamérica*. 2 vols. Mexico City: Editorial Atlante, 1947.
Miranda and Tello/LA MÚSICA	Miranda, Ricardo, and Aurelio Tello. *La música en Latinoamérica*. Vol. 4, *La búsqueda perpetua: lo propio*

	y lo universal de la cultura latinoamericana, edited by Mercedes de la Vega Armijo. Mexico City: Secretaría de Relaciones Exteriores, 2011.
Miranda Pérez/ECOS	Miranda Pérez, Ricardo. *Ecos, Alientos y Sonidos: Ensayos sobre Música Mexicana*. Veracruz and Mexico City: Universidad Veracruzana and Fondo de Cultura Económica, 2001.
Miranda Pérez/HEARTBEAT	Miranda, Ricardo Pérez. "'The Heartbeat of an Intense Life': Mexican Music and Carlos Chávez's *Orquesta Sinfónica de México*, 1928–1948." In *Carlos Chávez and His World*, edited by Leonora Saavedra, pp. 46–61. Princeton, NJ: Princeton University Press, 2015.
Miranda Pérez/ROLÓN	Miranda Pérez, Ricardo. *José Rolón: Músico*. Guadalajara: Secretaría de Cultura Jalisco, 2012.
Miranda Pérez and Bitrán/DIÁLOGO	Miranda Pérez, Ricardo, and Yael Bitrán, eds. *Diálogo de resplendores: Carlos Chávez y Silvestre Revueltas*. Mexico City: CONACULTA, 2002.
Montalvo/CAMPOS PARSI	Montalvo, José A. "Héctor Campos Parsi, His Life and Music: A Biographical Study with an Analysis of Four Selected Works." PhD diss., New York University, 1992.
Morales Flores/IDENTIDADES	Morales Flores, César. *Identidades en proceso. Cinco compositores cubanos de la diáspora (1990–2013)*. Havana: Fondo Editorial Casa de las Américas, 2018.
Muñoz/MÚSICA	Muñoz, María Luisa. *La música en Puerto Rico: panorama histórico-cultural*. Sharon, CT: Troutman, 1966.
Navarro/HACER	Navarro, Antonio, ed. *Hacer música: Blas Galindo, compositor*. Guadalajara: University of Guadalajara, 1994.
Nawrot/JESUIT REDUCTIONS	Nawrot, Piotr. "Jesuit Reductions: The Infusion of the Indian Element into Musical Practice." *Studia Missionalia* 62 (2013): pp. 141–62.
Nolasco/MÚSICA	Nolasco, Flerida de. *La música en Santo Domingo y otros ensayos*. Ciudad Trujillo: Editora Montalvo, 1939.
Oja/MAKING	Oja, Carol J. *Making Music Modern*. New York: Oxford University Press, 2000.
O'Malley/JESUITS	O'Malley, John W. *The Jesuits: Culture, Sciences, and the Arts (1540–1773)*. Toronto: University of Toronto Press, 1999.
Orbón/SINFONÍAS	Orbón, Julián. "Las sinfonías de Carlos Chávez." In *En la esencia de los estilos y otros ensayos*, edited by Julio Estrada, pp. 148–58. Madrid: Editorial Colibrí, 2000.
Orbón/SYMPHONIES	Orbón, Julián. "Carlos Chávez's Symphonies." Translated, introduced, and annotated by Leonora Saavedra. In *Carlos Chávez and His World*, edited by Leonora Saavedra, pp. 62–75. Princeton, NJ: Princeton University Press, 2015.

Orosz/CORDERO	Orosz, Jeremy. "The Twelve-Tone Music of Roque Cordero." *Latin American Music Review* 39, no. 2 (2018): pp. 137–59.
Orovio/CUBAN MUSIC	Orovio, Helio. *Cuban Music from A to Z*. Durham, NC, and London: Duke University Press, 2004.
Orrego-Salas/TÉCNICA	Orrego-Salas, Juan. "Técnica y estética." In *América Latina en su Música*, edited by Isabel Aretz, pp. 174–98. Paris: UNESCO, 1977.
Parker/CHÁVEZ	Parker, Robert L. "Chávez, Carlos." Grove Music Online. *Oxford Music Online*. Oxford University Press. http://www.oxfordmusiconline.com/subscriber/article/grove/music/05495, accessed September 8, 2015.
Parker/CHICAGO	Parker, Robert L. "Revueltas, the Chicago Years." *Latin American Music Review* 25, no. 2 (2004): pp. 180–94.
Parker/COPLAND	Parker, Robert L. "Copland and Chávez: Brothers-in-Arms." *American Music* 5, no. 4 (1987): pp. 433–44.
Parker/LUCE	Parker, Robert L. "Clare Boothe Luce, Chávez, and *Sinfonía* No. 3." *Latin American Music Review* 5, no. 1 (1984): pp. 48–65.
Parker/MÚSICA	Parker, Robert L. "De música incidental a sinfonía: la *Antígona* de Chávez." *Heterofonía* 113 (July–September 1995): pp. 4–12.
Parker/ORPHEUS	Parker, Robert L. *Carlos Chávez: Mexico's Modern-Day Orpheus*. Boston: Twayne, 1983.
Parker/RECURRING	Parker, Robert L. "A Recurring Melodic Cell in the Music of Carlos Chávez." *Latin American Music Review* 12, no. 2 (1991): pp. 160–72.
Parker/SAN ANTONIO, MOBILE	Parker, Robert. "Revueltas in San Antonio and Mobile." *Latin American Music Review* 23, no. 1 (2002): pp. 114–30.
Pereira Salas/NOTES	Pereira Salas, Eugenio. *Notes on the History of Music Exchange Between the Americas before 1940*. Washington, DC: Music Division, Pan American Union, 1943, trans. of *Notas para la historia del intercambio musical entre las Américas*. Santiago de Chile: Universidad de Chile.
Pernet/GENUINE CULTURE	Pernet, Corinne A. "'For the Genuine Culture of the Americas.'" In *Decentering America*, edited by Jessica C. E. Gienow-Hecht, pp. 132–68. New York and Oxford: Berghahn, 2007.
Querol Galvadá/NOTAS	Querol Gavaldá, Miguel. "Notas bibliográficas sobre compositores de los que existe música en la catedral de Puebla." *Inter-American Music Review* 10, no. 2 (1989): pp. 49–60.
Quevedo/EXPERIMENTAL	Quevedo, Marysol. "Experimental Music and the Avant-garde in Post-1959 Cuba." In *Experimentalisms in*

	Practice: Music Perspectives from Latin America, edited by Ana R. Alonso-Minutti, Eduardo Herrera, Alejandro Madrid, pp. 251–78. New York: Oxford University Press, 2018.
Quevedo/ORQUESTA	Quevedo, Marysol. "The Orquesta Sinfónica Nacional de Cuba and Its Role in the Cuban Revolution's Cultural Project." *Cuban Studies* 47 (2019): pp. 19–34.
Quevedo/PUERTO RICO	Quevedo, Marysol. "Music of Puerto Rico." Oxford Bibliographies Online. *Oxford Music Online*. Oxford University Press. https://www-oxfordbibliographies-com.auth.lib.niu.edu/view/document/obo-9780199757824/obo-9780199757824-0254.xml, accessed September 4, 2021.
Robles/AMANECER	Robles, Samuel. *amanecer en tiempos de guerra*. Cincinnati, OH: University of Cincinnati, 2000.
Rodríguez-Erdmann/TESOROS	Rodríguez-Erdmann, Francisco Javier. *Tesoros del AGN: Dos inventarios musicales novohispanos*. Mexico City: Archivo General de la Nación, 2013.
Ros-Fábregas/NICOLAS SLONIMSKY	Ros-Fábregas, Emilio. "Nicolas Slonimsky (1894–1995) y sus escritos sobre música en Latinoamérica: reivindicación de un 'fishing trip.'" In *La Música y el Atlántico: relaciones musicales entre España y Latinoamérica*, edited by María Gembero Ustárroz and Emilio Ros-Fábregas, pp. 153–80. Granada: University of Granada, 2007.
Russell/SERRA	Russell, Craig H. *From Serra to Sancho: Music and Pageantry in the California Missions*. Currents in Latin American & Iberian Music, edited by Walter A. Clark. New York: Oxford University Press, 2009.
Russell/SUMAYA: REEXAMINING	Russell, Craig. "Manuel de Sumaya: Reexamining the *a cappella* Choral Music of a Mexican Master." *Encomium musicae: A Festschrift in Honor of Robert J. Snow*, edited by David Crawford and Grayson G. Wagstaff, pp. 91–106. Hillsdale, NY: Pendragon, 2002.
Saavedra/NUEVO	Saavedra, Leonora. "El nuevo pasado mexicano: estratégias de representación den *Atzimba* de Ricardo Castro." *Resonancias* 19, no. 35 (2014): pp. 81–83.
Saavedra/POLYSEMIC	Saavedra, Leonora. "Carlos Chávez's Polysemic Style: Constructing the National, Seeking the Cosmopolitan." *Journal of the American Musicological Society* 68, no. 1 (2015): pp. 99–150.
Saavedra/SELVES	Saavedra, Leonora. "Of Selves and Others: Historiography, Ideology, and the Politics of Modern Mexican Music." PhD diss., University of Pittsburgh, 2001.
Saavedra/WORLD	Saavedra, Leonora, ed. *Carlos Chávez and His World*. Princeton, NJ: Princeton University Press, 2015.

Slonimsky/MUSIC	Slonimsky, Nicolas. *The Music of Latin America*. New York: Thomas Y. Crowell, 1945.
Sordo Sodi/MÚSICA MEXICANA	Sordo Sodi, Carmen. "La música mexicana en la época del Presidente Benito Juárez." In *Die Musikkulturen Lateinamerikas im 19. Jahrhundert*, edited by Robert Günther, pp. 299–325. Regensburg: Gustav Bosse Verlag, 1982.
Stallings/COLLECTIVE	Stallings, Stephanie. "Collective Difference: The Pan-American Association of Composers and Pan-American Ideology in Music, 1925–45." PhD diss., Florida State University, 2009.
Stevenson/AZTEC INCA	Stevenson, Robert M. *Music in Aztec and Inca Territory*. Oakland: University of California Press, 2022 [rprt. 1976].
Stevenson/*CHÁVEZ*.	Stevenson, Robert. M. "Carlos Chávez's Los Angeles Connection." *Inter-American Music Review* 3, no. 2 (1981): pp. 133–50.
Stevenson/COLONIAL	Stevenson, Robert M. "Colonial Treasure in the Puebla Cathedral Music Archive." *Inter-American Music Review* 15, no. 1 (1996): pp. 39–51.
Stevenson/ESTEBAN SALAS	Stevenson, Robert M. "Esteban Salas y Castro (1725–1803): Cuba's Consummate Cathedral Composer." *Inter-American Music Review* 15, no. 2 (1996): pp. 73–102.
Stevenson/GUATEMALA	Stevenson, Robert M. "Music in Sixteenth-Century Guatemala." *Musical Quarterly* 50 (1964): pp. 341–52.
Stevenson/GUATEMALA CATHEDRAL	Stevenson, Robert M. "Guatemala Cathedral to 1803." *Inter-American Music Review* 2, no. 2 (1979–80): pp. 27–72.
Stevenson/MEXICO	Stevenson, Robert M. *Music in Mexico: A Historical Survey*. New York: Thomas Y. Crowell, 1952.
Stevenson/PUEBLA	Stevenson, Robert M. "Puebla Chapelmasters and Organists: Sixteenth and Seventeenth Centuries," pt. 2. *Inter-American Music Review* 6, no. 1 (1984): pp. 29–139.
Stevenson/SAN JUAN	Stevenson, Robert M. "Music in the San Juan, Puerto Rico, Cathedral to 1900." *Inter-American Music Review* 1, no. 1 (1978): pp. 73–95.
Suárez de la Torre/PAPELES	Suárez de la Torre, Laura, ed. *Los Papeles para Eurterpe: La música en la Ciudad de México desde la historia cultural, siglo XIX*. Mexico City: Instituto de Investigaciones Dr. José Luis Mora, Consejo Nacional de Ciencia y Tecnología, 2014.
Subirá/TONADILLA	Subirá, José. *La tonadilla escénica: sus obras, sus autores*. Barcelona: Editorial Labor, 1933.

Summers/MISA	Summers, William J. "The *Misa Viscaina*: An Eighteenth-Century Musical Odyssey to Alta California." In *Encomium Musicae: Essays in Memory of Robert J. Snow*, edited by David Crawford and Grayson Wagstaff, pp. 127–41. Hillsdale, NY: Pendragon, 2002.
Summers/RECENTLY	Summers, William J. "Recently Recovered Manuscript Sources of Liturgical Polyphony from Hispanic California." *Ars musica Denver* 7, no. 1 (1994–95): pp. 13–30.
Taylor Gibson/PONCE, CARRILLO, CHÁVEZ	Taylor Gibson, Christina. "The Music of Manuel M. Ponce, Julián Carrillo, and Carlos Chávez in New York, 1925–1932." PhD diss., University of Maryland, College Park, 2008.
Thompson/MÚSICA	Thompson, Donald. "La música contemporánea en Puerto Rico." *Revista Musical Chilena* 38, no. 162 (1984): pp. 110–17.
Thompson/NINETEENTH	Thompson, Donald. "Nineteenth-Century Musical Life in Puerto Rico." In *Die Musikkulturen Lateinamerikas im 19. Jahrhundert*, edited by Robert Günther, pp. 327–31. Regensburg: Gustav Bosse Verlag, 1982.
Thompson/PUBLIC	Thompson, Donald. "Music in Puerto Rican Public Ceremony: *Fiestas Reales*, *Fiestas Patronales*, *Ferias*, and *Exposiciones*: A Chronological List of Official Reports and Similar Documents." *Inter-American Music Review* 10, no. 2 (1989): pp. 135–41.
Tomé/RACIAL	Tomé, Lester. "The Racial Other's Dancing Body in *El milagro de anaquillé* (1927): Avant-Garde Ballet and the Ethnography of Afro-Cuban Performance." *Cuban Studies* 46 (2018): pp. 185–227.
Trujillo/SALAZAR	Trujillo, Jeremiah C. "Adolfo Salazar as Composer: A Musical Cosmopolitan in Early-Twentieth Century Spain." PhD diss., University of California, Davis, 2019.
Vargas-Culell/FANFARRÍAS	Vargas-Cullel, María Clara. *De las fanfarrías a las salas de concierto: música en Costa Rica (1840–1940)*. San José, Costa Rica: Editorial de la Universidad de Costa Rica, 2004.
Wagstaff/FRANCISCAN	Wagstaff, Grayson. "Franciscan Mission Music in California, c. 1770–1830: Chant, Liturgical and Polyphonic Traditions." *Journal of the Royal Music Association* 126 (2001): pp. 54–82.
Waisman/MÚSICA COLONIAL	Waisman, Leonardo. "La música colonial en la Iberoamérica neo-colonial." *Acta musicologica* 76, no. 1 (2004): pp. 117–27.
Zohn-Muldoon/*SENSEMAYÁ*	Zohn-Muldoon, Ricardo. "The Song of the Snake: Silvestre Revueltas's *Sensemayá*." *Latin American Music Review* 19 (1998): pp. 133–59.

CHAPTER NINE

The Symphony in the United States since 1970

Matthew Mugmon

Introduction

The story of the American symphony since 1970 is governed by a tension between the unspoken rules of a genre with deep historical roots and the exponentially expanded sonic possibilities of a digital, global age.[1] As has been argued before, the story begins with the symphony emerging with new clout among composers as a historically charged genre, in a way that coincided with the decline of high modernism in the 1960s.[2] Since then, as commentators have also suggested, the symphony has continued to provide a fertile home for many American composers who are oriented toward tonality and who have found traditional forms, genres, and conventions to be useful starting points for structured responses to circumstances both personal and societal—thus satisfying both their own interests as composers and the desires of patrons.[3] Indeed, the appearance of a large number of symphonies by American composers since 1970, and even more pointedly since the 1980s—a sense of which can be gleaned from the list of selected symphonies in table 9.1—has been powered largely by networks of patronage and of musical colleagues, and by an engagement with diverse musical and cultural perspectives and sources. The names of many of the same teachers, conductors, orchestras, and commissioning initiatives turn up repeatedly throughout this chapter—suggesting that a compact nexus of influential individuals and organizations has helped sustain the genre and propel it forward. Despite all this, or perhaps as a prerequisite of the symphony's recent success as a place of encounter between old and new in a postmodern age, techniques and styles associated with music after World War II—such as twelve-tone writing, indeterminacy, quotation, collage, electronics, and minimalism—have found their way into, and helped defined, a genre with a Romantic heritage and tenacious bonds to tonality.[4] And as with earlier periods, vernacular musics from the United States and around the world have played a significant role in shaping the American symphonic soundscape—now boosted by accelerated global communications.[5]

Beginning especially in the 1980s, but with several precedents in the 1960s and 1970s, American composers of diverse cultural backgrounds, generations, and stylistic orientations have turned to the genre in force.[6] Through a detailed survey of a number of recent American symphonists in their broader contexts, this chapter offers a sweeping view of the American

Table 9.1 Selected American Symphonies since 1970

Composer	Title	Year of Premiere
Leonardo Balada	*Steel Symphony*	1973
Lou Harrison	*Elegiac Symphony*	1975
George Rochberg	Symphony No. 4	1976
David Del Tredici	*Final Alice*	1976
Elliott Carter	*A Symphony of Three Orchestras*	1977
Easley Blackwood Jr.	Symphony No. 4	1978
Charles Wuorinen	*Two-Part Symphony*	1978
Gloria Coates	Symphony No. 1 ("Music for Open Strings")	1978
Glenn Branca	Symphony No. 1 ("Tonal Plexus")	1981
Ellen Taaffe Zwilich	Symphony No. 1 ("Three Movements for Orchestra")	1982
Olly Wilson	*Sinfonia*	1984
Stephen Albert	*RiverRun* (Symphony No. 1)	1985
John Adams	*Harmonielehre*	1985
Libby Larsen	*Symphony: Water Music* (Symphony No. 1)	1985
George Rochberg	Symphony No. 5	1986
Tobias Picker	Symphony No. 2 ("Aussöhnung")	1986
Christopher Rouse	Symphony No. 1	1988
Aaron Jay Kernis	*Symphony in Waves*	1989
Daniel Asia	Symphony No. 1	1990
William Bolcom	Symphony No. 5	1990
Shulamit Ran	Symphony	1990
John Corigliano	Symphony No. 1	1990
John Harbison	Symphony No. 3	1991
Philip Glass	Symphony No. 1 ("Low")	1992
Daniel Asia	Symphony No. 3	1993
David Maslanka	Symphony No. 4, for wind ensemble	1994
Kamran Ince	Symphony No. 2 ("Fall of Constantinople")	1994
Michael Daugherty	*Metropolis Symphony*	1994
Joseph Schwantner	*Evening Land Symphony*	1995
Michael Torke	*Brick Symphony*	1998
Elliott Carter	*Symphonia: sum fluxae pretium spei*	1998
Libby Larsen	*Solo Symphony* (Symphony No. 5)	1999
Adolphus Hailstork	Symphony No. 2	1999
Lowell Liebermann	Symphony No. 2	2000

Composer	Title	Year of Premiere
Kevin Puts	Symphony No. 2 ("Island of Innocence")	2002
Stephen Hartke	Symphony No. 3	2003
John Corigliano	Symphony No. 3 ("Circus Maximus"), for wind ensemble	2005
Richard Danielpour	*Rocking the Cradle, Symphony in Two Movements for Orchestra*	2007
Lera Auerbach	Symphony No. 2 ("Requiem for a Poet")	2007
William Bolcom	Symphony No. 8	2008
Aaron Jay Kernis	Symphony No. 3 ("Symphony of Meditations")	2009
Wynton Marsalis	Symphony No. 3 ("Swing Symphony")	2010
Steven Stucky	*Symphony*	2012
George Walker	Sinfonia No. 4 ("Strands")	2012
Mason Bates	*Alternative Energy*	2012
Mohammed Fairouz	Symphony No. 3 ("Poems and Prayers")	2012
Andrew Norman	*Play*	2013
Wang Jie	Symphony No. 2 ("To and from Dakini")	2014
Christopher Rouse	Symphony No. 4	2014
John Adams	*Scheherazade.2, Dramatic Symphony for Violin and Orchestra*	2015
Wynton Marsalis	Symphony No. 4 ("The Jungle")	2016
Aaron Jay Kernis	Symphony No. 4 ("Chromelodeon")	2018
Philip Glass	Symphony No. 12 ("Lodger")	2019

symphony since 1970, beginning with Elliott Carter (1908–2012) and concluding with Mohammed Fairouz (b. 1985). There are numerous ways these many composers could be grouped, but in this chapter they are placed in chronological order of birth year primarily to allow them—and each of their symphonies—to stand on their own rather than to be reduced to specific stylistic trends, which could inadvertently diminish the importance of individual works that do not seem to fit within a larger given category. Indeed, far from being defined by a single aesthetic orientation across their careers, each composer drew on a variety of techniques and artistic movements in shaping a varied symphonic output. Between Carter and Fairouz are Lou Harrison (1917–2003), George Rochberg (1918–2005), George Walker (1922–2018), Philip Glass (b. 1937), John Corigliano (b. 1938), William Bolcom (b. 1938), John Harbison (b. 1938), Ellen Taaffe Zwilich (b. 1939), Adolphus Hailstork (b. 1941), Stephen Albert (1941–1992), John Adams (b. 1947), Christopher Rouse (1949–2019), Libby Larsen (b. 1950), Daniel Asia (b. 1953), Tobias Picker (b. 1954), Aaron Jay Kernis (b. 1960), Lowell Liebermann (b. 1961), Wynton Marsalis (b. 1961), Mason Bates (b. 1977), and Wang Jie (b. 1980). I asked several of these composers directly for their views about their works and their attitudes and beliefs about the symphony in general; these interviews took place primarily in 2015 by phone, email, and Skype.

The discussion of these composers captures a range of intersecting issues associated with the recent American symphony. None of the themes discussed in this chapter is exclusive to any individual composer, and for many composers, multiple questions come into play. These include the broadly varying definitions of both the adjective *American* and the noun *symphony*; a wide spectrum of attitudes and approaches to symphonic form—generally within a multi-movement layout, but with a striking number of one-movement symphonies that build on a tradition established by Jean Sibelius's Symphony No. 7 (1924) in being called symphonies despite lacking multiple movements; the role of the symphony in helping to construct individual and group identities; the so-called return of tonality and the advent of Neoromanticism; the blending of avant-garde techniques with the traditional expectations of symphonic forms; the sometimes bewildering growth of the orchestra's sonic possibilities; and explorations of contemporary political and social issues as well as of personal emotion. I selected the composers highlighted in this chapter because their works, when considered together, speak to these matters.

Given the vast output of recent American symphonies, this survey must regrettably omit several notable and prolific symphonists, including figures such as Richard Danielpour (b. 1956) and Kevin Puts (b. 1972). Many of these composers and selected symphonies, along with the year of premiere, are represented in table 9.1. Also, this survey does not explore figures who have to date composed only a single symphony, and some of these works are also listed in the table. These include Shulamit Ran's (b. 1949) Pulitzer Prize–winning *Symphony* (1989–90), Joseph Schwantner's (b. 1943) *Evening Land Symphony* for soprano and orchestra (1995), Michael Torke's (b. 1961) *Brick Symphony* (1997), and Steven Stucky's (1949–2016) *Symphony* (2012). The latter marked Stucky's return to the genre after having composed four in his youth and then withdrawn them from his catalog, and his reflections demonstrate the historical weight of the term *symphony*, even for composers who tended to keep some distance from the genre. In program notes for his *Symphony*, Stucky suggested a disconnect between "progressive" composition and the writing of symphonies. He then asked, "So what does it mean for a composer of my generation to haul the title *Symphony* out of the closet in 2012?" He added, "Perhaps the very word is meant to assert that it's time for me to face squarely my own relation to the symphonic tradition? Perhaps it's a call for gravitas, an ambition to treat the material more 'symphonically,' including the possibility that ideas might return, develop, evolve?"[7] And Kevin Puts, composer of four symphonies, also pointed to a sense of gravitas that he saw latent in the genre: "The symphony is not a trifle. It is not cute or hip or light. It says something important—about life and death and cosmic stuff—and it does so without embarrassment."[8]

Ultimately, as in other periods, musical details alone cannot be used to determine whether a work is best understood as a symphony or as a representative of another genre—nor is creating that distinction one of this chapter's goals. Part of the symphony's richness as a genre has always been that a variety of factors—including formal characteristics, audience reception, or even a composer's simple decision to use the word *symphony* in a work's title—contribute to whether a work for orchestra (and possibly other forces), typically a substantial one that includes contrasting sections or movements as well as a unified sense of overarching trajectory, is productively understood as a symphony. Indeed, there are no fixed distinctions between the symphony and genres such as symphonic poem (especially given the large number of one-movement symphonies), concerto, orchestral song cycle, orchestral suite, or oratorio—nor are the parameters used to define these other genres fixed. Several symphonies in recent years, as in other periods, could be seen as belonging to multiple genres simultaneously. Far from diluting the symphony as a musical genre, this flexibility invites us to view a multitude of works through a symphonic lens. For practical reasons, though, the focus of this chapter is limited to works that contain *symphony* (or a closely related word, such as George Walker's sinfonias) in the title or have otherwise been understood as symphonies, primarily by their composers.

Even more ambiguous than *symphony* is the term *American*. To speak of an American symphony in any period—but perhaps most clearly in the period discussed in this chapter—is to speak of a global phenomenon, regardless of a particular composer's place of birth or training. Wang Jie, whose symphonies are considered in detail in this chapter, hails from China and left in 2000 to study at the Manhattan School of Music.[9] Wang and many symphonists from abroad have defined the genre in terms of their positions as global citizens and have contributed to American musical life. The Spanish-born composer Leonardo Balada (b. 1933) arrived as a student at the New York College of Music in 1956 and later studied at Juilliard; he went on to teach at Carnegie Mellon University in Pittsburgh.[10] Among his works are the *Sinfonía en Negro: Homage to Martin Luther King* (1968); the *Steel Symphony* (1972), inspired by the "multitude and power of the factories in and around Pittsburgh"; and the Symphony No. 5, "American" (2002–03), which both addresses the events of September 11, 2001, and explores American folk music styles, including spirituals.[11] Shulamit Ran, whose *Symphony* was mentioned above, was born in Israel and relocated to the United States in 1963 to study at the Mannes College of Music. Lera Auerbach (b. 1973), a pianist and poet as well as a composer of several symphonies rich with connections to literature, defected to the United States from the Soviet Union in 1991.[12] And it was in 1959 that the Czech-born composer Karel Husa (1921–2016) became an American citizen. As Husa wrote of his colorful and complex Symphony No. 2, "Reflections" (1982–83), in a gesture that points to the genre's longevity, "Although not written in a classical or romantic style, it nevertheless reflects the symphonic form."[13]

A list of relevant composers omitted here also includes figures primarily based abroad but whose ties to this side of the Atlantic are strong nonetheless, in the tradition of European composers like Antonín Dvořák and Gustav Mahler. These include Gloria Coates (1933–2023), who was born in Wisconsin but relocated to Germany in 1969.[14] The first of Coates's 16 symphonies, the texturally dense Symphony No. 1, "Music on Open Strings" (1972–73), experiments with shifts in tuning and incorporates a pentatonic scale provided for her by her mentor Alexander Tcherepnin (1899–1977).[15] (Tcherepnin was himself a transatlantic symphonist; originally from Russia, he became an American citizen in 1958.[16]) The prolific Polish symphonist Krzysztof Penderecki (1933–2020) taught at Yale University in the 1970s and developed an international profile as a conductor. Polish composer Henryk Górecki's (1933–2010) Symphony No. 3, "Symphony of Sorrowful Songs" (1976), perhaps the most popular symphony by any recent composer, had enormous success in the United States and internationally starting in the early 1990s.[17] And the Estonian composer Arvo Pärt's (b. 1935) meditative Symphony No. 4, "Los Angeles" (2008), for strings, harp, timpani, and percussion, was commissioned by the Los Angeles Philharmonic and was linked in part to the composer's examination of a Christian text on a guardian angel.[18] Pärt had composed his Third Symphony in 1971, making "Los Angeles" his first in nearly 40 years—and his first since creating his signature *tintinnabuli* style in the 1970s, a bell-evoking style based on triads and stepwise motion that clearly informs the symphony's sound world.[19] Incidentally, the Third (1983) and Fourth (1992) Symphonies of another major European figure, the modernist Witold Lutosławski (1913–1994), were commissioned by the Chicago Symphony Orchestra and Los Angeles Philharmonic, respectively; the Fourth was, in fact, his last major work. Both symphonies took the form of a continuous two-movement structure consisting of what Stucky, who admired Lutosławski's work, called a "preparation" followed by a "main event."[20] (Stucky's own *Symphony* was also commissioned by the Los Angeles Philharmonic, jointly with the New York Philharmonic.[21])

Although this chapter focuses on the orchestral symphony, one genre ripe for further study is the symphony for wind ensemble, perhaps best represented today by the works of David Maslanka (1943–2017), who wrote eight symphonies for wind ensemble (and two for full orchestra). Indeed, the wind symphony may well prove one of the most fruitful avenues for symphonic composition in the twenty-first century. In program notes for his Symphony No. 3, "Circus Maximus" (2004), one of the most celebrated large works for wind ensemble, John Corigliano included among the advantages of writing in this medium the observation that such groups may allot several weeks to preparing to perform new compositions.[22] In addition to Corigliano's work, this chapter will consider wind symphonies by Bolcom and Fairouz.[23]

In the tables for individual composers throughout the chapter, the dates listed in the leftmost column reflect the best possible information about the span of years in which it was created or (if only one year is included) the year of completion; dates of revisions ("rev.") are also provided where available, but these are not necessarily comprehensive, nor are they certain to reflect all possible moments at which a work has been revised. I gathered this information—and sometimes estimated it—from reference materials, data from publishers, and other sources. I also gathered instrumentation lists from various sources, and these lists may not always reflect the most updated information, especially when works have undergone further revision. Regarding wind instruments, "Clar." (for clarinet) refers to either that B-flat or A clarinet, and "doubling" indicates only how many—not which—of a given player is asked to play another part. Individual percussion instruments, and sometimes the division of labor itself among percussionists, are indicated in the instrumentation where available; these lists do not, however, generally indicate whether individual percussion instruments are shared between players. Comments about the symphonies in the table include details about commissions, texts, premieres, and score publishers. (Throughout the tables, all score publication dates have been omitted because of frequently spotty and inconsistent publication information.) I have also listed many commercial recordings of these works, although as of this writing, recordings of several of these works are also found on YouTube. As this chapter discusses very recent material, many sources are online; inevitably, some links to websites in the bibliography no longer function, but readers may consult the Internet Archive (https://archive.org/web) to find versions of these websites consulted for this chapter.

Elliott Carter (1908–2012)

In his vast musical output, Elliott Carter blended rhythmic complexity with a sense of melodic breadth, textural transparency, and intellectual rigor. His efforts as a symphonist culminated in the *Symphonia: sum fluxae pretium spei* (1993–96), but his works in the genre spanned more than 50 years and are listed in table 9.2. Shortly after returning to New York from his studies with Nadia Boulanger in Paris, Carter composed a symphony in 1937 that he later withdrew from his catalog.[24] But a few years after that early composition, his Symphony No. 1 (1942) joined a number of other orchestral works by American composers with a populist flavor that may be linked to the era of the Great Depression and World War II.[25]

As Carter described it, the Symphony No. 1 emerged from "a natural desire to write something many people could presumably grasp and enjoy easily at a time of social emergency, but I did so without appreciating just how serious was the audience paralysis engendered by this lack of interest in or familiarity with the new in any of its artistic forms. Thus I wrote

Table 9.2 The Symphonies of Elliott Carter (1908–2012)

Title	Movements	Instrumentation	Comments
Symphony No. 1 (1942, rev. 1954)	I. Moderately, wistfully (554 mm.) II. Slowly, gravely (212 mm.) III. Vivaciously (486 mm.)	Picc. (doubling Flt.), Flt, 2 Ob. 2 Clar. (1 doubling E♭ Clar.), 2 Bssn., 2 Hr., 2 Tpt., Trom., Timp., Strgs.	Dedicated to Carter's wife, Helen. First performance: April 27, 1944, Eastman-Rochester Symphony Orchestra. Score published by Associated Music Publishers. Recorded by Louisville Orchestra, conducted by Robert Whitney (LOU-611); American Composers Orchestra, conducted by Paul Dunkel (CRI CD 552); Nashville Symphony Orchestra, conducted by Kenneth Schermerhorn (Naxos 8.559151).
A Symphony of Three Orchestras (1976)	One movement (394 mm.)	Orchestra I: 3 Hr., 3 Tpt., 3 Trom., Tuba, Timp., Vln. (14–16 players), Vla. (6–8 players), Vlc. (4–6 players), Cb. (2–4 players) Orchestra II: E♭ Clar., Clar., BClar. (doubling Clar.), Perc. (2 Players: Vbp., Chimes, Xylo., Mrb., Long Drum with snares, Tom-tom [low]), Pno., Vln. (4 players), Vlc. (4–6 players), Cb. (2 players) Orchestra III: Picc., 2 Flt. (both doubling Picc.), 2 Ob., EH (doubling Ob.), 2 Bssn., Cbssn. (doubling Bssn.), 2 Hr., Perc. (1 Player: Anvil, Bell Tree, 2 Suspended Cyms. [high, low], 2 SD: [high, low], Tamb., 2 Tam-tams [small, large], Vln. (14–16 players), Vla. (6–8 players), Cb. (2–4 players)	Commissioned by the New York Philharmonic for the US Bicentennial as part of a series of commissions by a consortium of major orchestras. First performance: February 17, 1977, New York Philharmonic, conducted by Pierre Boulez, and dedicated to the orchestra and conductor. Score published by Associated Music Publishers. Recorded by New York Philharmonic, conducted by Pierre Boulez (Sony Classical SMK 68 334).

Table 9.2 *continued*

Title	Movements	Instrumentation	Comments
Symphonia: sum fluxae pretium spei (1993–96)	I. Partita (580 mm.) II. Adagio tenebroso (342 mm.) III. Allegro scorrevole (240 mm.)	Picc., 2 Flt. (1 doubling Picc.), 2 Ob., EH, 2 Clar. (1 doubling E♭ Clar.), BClar., 2 Bssn., Cbssn., 4 Hr., 3 Tpt., 3 Trom., Tuba, Timp., Perc. (4 Players; Player 1: Xylo., Glsp., SD, Tom-tom, Wood Block, Suspended Cym.; Player 2: 2 Metal Blocks [very high, medium high], 4 Temple Blocks, 2 Suspended Cyms., 2 Wood Blocks, 2 Cowbells, Wood Drum [log Drum], BD, Bongos, Güiro, Tom-tom; Player 3: Vbp., BD, 4 Bongos, 2 Tom-toms, 2 Wood Blocks, SD; Player 4: Vbp., Glsp. [with pedal damper], Mrb., Wood Drum, Gavel, 2 Bongos, 2 Tom-toms), Pno., Harp, Strgs.	Commissioned as separate movements by the Chicago Symphony Orchestra (Partita), BBC Radio 3 (Adagio tenebroso), and the Cleveland Orchestra (Allegro scorrevole). First Performance of complete symphony: April 25, 1998, BBC Symphony Orchestra, conducted by Oliver Knussen. Partita dedicated to the Chicago Symphony Orchestra and Daniel Barenboim. Adagio tenebroso dedicated to the BBC Proms and to Amira and Alexander Goehr. Allegro scorrevole dedicated to the Cleveland Orchestra and Oliver Knussen. Score published by Boosey & Hawkes. Recorded by BBC Symphony Orchestra, conducted by Oliver Knussen (DG 459 660-2); Bavarian Radio Symphony Orchestra, conducted by Emilio Pomarico (Neos 11420); Chicago Symphony Orchestra, conducted by Daniel Barenboim (Teldec 4509-99596-2; Partita only).

music which escaped the average listener, despite what seemed to me its directness."[26] Carter finished the three-movement work in Santa Fe, New Mexico, but his comment that he hoped the music would recall Cape Cod, Massachusetts, where he sketched the composition, suggests its transcontinental origins.[27] In a later interview, he said that at one time, "only Doctor's office orchestras" would perform the symphony "because it was easy to play it and easy to understand. For years I never heard a good performance of it."[28] Despite the flippant suggestion about its supposed simplicity, Carter's comments hint at the rhythmic and harmonic complexity of much of the symphony; the first movement, in fact, contains early examples of his characteristically intricate layering of meters.[29] What David Schiff has called the work's "pastoral" sensibility is apparent from the first movement's gently rocking accompaniments, extended tonality, and textures driven by playful and broadly outlined solo wind lines—all reminiscent of the music of his teacher at Harvard University, Walter Piston.[30] After the gently lyrical second movement comes a boisterous, spritely Finale, drawn from music Carter initially composed for his ballet *Pocahontas* (1936).[31] That movement's animated fugue and closing clarinet solo may have been what led Duke Ellington to tell Carter, "I think you're beginning to understand something about jazz."[32] Carter's significant 1954 revisions to the score included the addition of shimmering sonorities in the strings at the beginning of the symphony and the deletion in the final movement of a chorale-like section.[33]

Carter's musical style underwent a significant shift in the period between his Symphony No. 1 and his next symphony, during which he developed a highly complex personal idiom that centered on dense chromaticism and intricately layered rhythms.[34] This sense of layering is especially prominent in *A Symphony of Three Orchestras* (1976), which, like Igor Stravinsky's *Symphonies of Wind Instruments* (1920), refers not only to the classical genre but to a "sounding together"—here, of three "orchestras" (in reality, a reshaping of a single orchestra into three groups). A US Bicentennial commission by the New York Philharmonic, *A Symphony of Three Orchestras* appeared more than 30 years after the premiere of the first version of Symphony No. 1 but connects indirectly with it. Lincoln Kirstein, who commissioned *Pocahontas* (early material for which, as mentioned above, found its way into Symphony No. 1), included a passage from Hart Crane's poem *The Bridge* in the ballet scenario.[35] The striking opening passage of *A Symphony of Three Orchestras*, with its glistening strings, oscillating piano and piccolo, and luminescent trumpet solo—for trumpet virtuoso Gerard Schwarz, who in his career as conductor has championed American symphonies—relates to the beginning of Crane's poem and its evocation of New York Harbor through the dual lens of a seagull's flight and the Statue of Liberty (Carter lived most of his mature creative life in Greenwich Village).[36] Each of the three orchestras then follows with four interweaving "movements," making for 12 altogether.[37] As Carter himself described it, "The four movements of each orchestra, while differing in expression and speed, are related, of course, by spatial location and instrumental color and also characteristic harmonies and rhythms. While no orchestra plays two of its movements at a time, each of the twelve is introduced while another movement of another orchestra is being played, briefly surfaces to be heard alone and then becomes the background for another entrance of another movement."[38] Toward the end (beginning at m. 318), all three orchestras join together, frighteningly, to quash the solo violins; Schiff aptly described this moment as "the thunder-chords which blot out the last traces of expressive music."[39] Then emerges an ungainly ostinato-laden coda that has been viewed as a satire of minimalism.[40] Carter's signature practice of metric modulation, in which reinterpreted note values cause shifts in tempo, appears throughout the work.

Carter again turned to the symphony in the 1990s, amid a period of astonishing productivity in his eighties and nineties that saw a number of significant orchestral works, including *Three Occasions for Orchestra* (1986–89), the Violin Concerto (1990), the Clarinet Concerto (1996), the Cello Concerto (2000), and *Three Illusions for Orchestra* (2002–04). His most ambitious symphonic effort was his *Symphonia: sum fluxae pretium spei* ("I am the prize of inconstant hope"). Commissioned and premiered as three separate movements, the composition is titled after a line from the poem *Bulla* ("Bubble") by the English Jacobean poet Richard Crashaw (*ca.* 1613–49)—a poem that, as Carter described it, "personifies a floating bubble." Carter linked the generally bustling, outgoing energy of the first movement, *Partita* (1993), to a decidedly modern sensibility. He wrote, "My musical intention was to present the many changes and oppositions of mood that make up our experience of life. In general, my music seeks the awareness of motion we have in flying or driving of a car and not the plodding of horses or the marching of soldiers that pervades the motion patterns of older music." Despite this apparent eschewing of "older music," Carter named the movement "Partita"—mainly because one of the word's meanings is "game," and "like all games this piece adheres rather strictly to certain laid down rules within which it presents a large expanse of action and expression."[41] After a dark, mysterious, and meditative *Adagio tenebroso* (1994), the concluding *Allegro scorrevole* (1996) is a whimsical fast movement that Carter described as "a continuous flow of soft, rapid passages that move over the entire range of the sound spectrum, and here and there form into thematic material. Against this is a lyrical idea also developed throughout, sometimes slowing down to hesitantly separated notes and at other times tightly joined to form intensely expressive lines."[42] The symphony famously concludes with a single piccolo straining in its highest registers before it disappears—painting a musical picture of the "personified" bubble's impermanence.[43]

By ending a colossal work with such a breezy gesture, and by providing the entire composition with a high-sounding Latin title that at the same time refers to a playful, ephemeral phenomenon, the *Symphonia* seems both to celebrate and question the symphony's seriousness as a genre—as Schiff has suggested, to "ironize the monumental aspects of the project."[44] Specifically, Carter's use of a Latin title reflects, as Felix Meyer and Anne Shreffler have discussed, his long-standing "distance from the Germanic tradition."[45] Connecting the work's conclusion to contemporary politics, Carter said in the days leading up to the 2004 US election that he "couldn't write a grand finale after the manner of Bruckner or Mahler," and he added, "that kind of grandiose thing seems to me a little hard to do—and it would be even harder now, especially right before this election."[46]

Carter's three symphonies—despite the fact that their composition spanned five decades of his career—capture quite consistently his theatricality, innovative deployment of instrumental forces, and attraction to philosophy and literature. Along with his other orchestral works, the symphonies show that Carter's power as an instrumental composer is, as James Wierzbicki has put it, "as much visceral as intellectual."[47] And although their aesthetic worlds may seem far apart, Carter's virtuosic, colorful, and endurance-testing orchestral writing in these symphonies finds a parallel in the symphonic works of John Adams, which are discussed later in this chapter.

Lou Harrison (1917–2003)

Lou Harrison came of age as a musician in California—a protégé of the mystically minded ultramodernist Henry Cowell, an admirer of the music of Charles Ives, a colleague of John

Cage, a student of Arnold Schoenberg, and a champion of dance music. On moving to New York in 1943, he became both a noted music journalist and a conductor, and he won an early success with his performance of Ives's Third Symphony on April 5, 1946.[48] The primacy of melody, dance rhythms, non-Western sounds and scales, and eclectic combinations are all central components of his style. All these elements feature in various ways throughout his four symphonies, which appear in table 9.3.

Harrison's range of experiences early in his career offers a useful context for his varied *Symphony on G*, which he began composing in the late 1940s during a time of personal crisis (he felt overwhelmed by his new life in New York).[49] As Harrison explained of the work's unusual name, "The title itself (on G, not in G) refers to the fact that the whole work, though serially composed with twelve tones, is nonetheless tonally centered on the note G. In the first three movements the technique is classical 12-tone procedure, but in the Finale I have ignored the forbiddance concerning octave-conjunction, & have written freely in the 'grand-manner.'"[50]

Much is "classical" about the *Symphony on G*, which Harrison completed in the 1960s. A sonata-form first movement combines angular themes with lush harp-driven textures; it is followed by a slow second movement that proceeds from airy chamber music textures to a fuller orchestral soundscape before fading out in an extended harmonic world. Signaling its heritage in earlier twelve-tone music, the score of this movement includes *Hauptstimme* markings, which the composers of the Second Viennese School employed to show which voice carries the principal melody. The heart of the composition, though, is the third movement, itself a four-section dance suite—for Harrison, a natural enlargement of the classical symphonic idea of a third movement as a Minuet or Scherzo and Trio.[51] A playful Schoenbergian waltz for string sextet, which also includes *Hauptstimme* markings, is followed by a jazzy, polytonal polka. This section centers on a raucous clarinet tune with a boisterous accompaniment for the tack piano—a piano modified by placing tacks in the hammers, which yields a jangly timbre that here evokes honky-tonk. (In the polka, as Leta Miller and Fredric Lieberman have pointed out, Harrison suggested tonal grounding by "repeating groups of notes within the row and treating the twelve notes in a rotational fashion: within any row form, he could start on any note as long as he completed the cycle by circling back to the beginning to encompass all twelve."[52]) The next part of the suite, "Song"—an orchestral version of the fourth movement from the Suite for Cello and Harp of 1949, but originally completed in short score for the symphony in 1947—features aching melodies, cinematic chord shifts, and the constant underpinning of ethereal harp arpeggios.[53] Harrison called the atonal Rondeau, which highlights the harp, piano, and prepared piano, the symphony's "cadenza."[54] The Rondeau rounds out the suite and gives way to Harrison's "grand" Finale, which replaced an original Finale for the work's 1966 premiere.[55]

Harrison completed his second symphony, *Elegiac Symphony*, in 1975 as a commission from the Koussevitzky Foundation; he revised it in 1988, but some of the material dates back to 1942.[56] In 1953, Harrison returned to California, and he became fascinated with Asian musical traditions, in particular the gamelan. The title of the *Elegiac Symphony*'s first movement, "Tears of the Angel Israfel," refers to the lachrymose angel of Islamic tradition who was celebrated in an 1831 poem by Edgar Allan Poe. In this movement, the descending, modal melodies and lush, string-driven textures suggest weeping while a contrasting section for piano, tack piano, harps, and string drones hint at the exotic; here, Harrison treats strings and winds as distinct groups in dialogue. A sense of perpetual motion pervades the fast second movement, with its shifting meters and angular thematic material. The chamber-like third movement, which

Table 9.3 The Symphonies of Lou Harrison (1917–2003)

Title	Movements	Instrumentation	Comments

Symphony on G (1947–64, rev. 1966)	I. Allegro deciso (203 mm.)
	II. Largo (110 mm.)
	III. Scherzo:
	  1. Waltz (98 mm.)
	  2. Polka (67 mm.)
	  3. Song (41 mm.)
	  4. Rondeau (72 mm.)
	IV. Largo—Molto Allegro, vigoroso, poco presto (372 mm.)
		2 Flt., 2 Ob., EH, 2 Clar., Bclar., 2 Hr., 2 Tpt., 2 Trom., Timp., Perc. (BD, Tam-tam, Glsp., Chimes, Metal Wind Chimes [2 or 3 sets, high or low]), Pno., Tack Pno., 2 Harps, Strgs.	First performance: August 23, 1964, at the Cabrillo Music Festival, conducted by Gerhard Samuel. New finale composed in 1966. First performance of revised version: February 8, 1966, Oakland Symphony, conducted by Gerhard Samuel.
			
			Score published by Peermusic Classical.
			
			Recorded by Royal Philharmonic Orchestra, conducted by Gerhard Samuel (CRI CD 715).

Elegiac Symphony (1975, rev. 1988)	I. Tears of the Angel Israfel (171 mm.) II. Allegro, poco presto (137 mm.) III. Tears of the Angel Israfel (2) (127 mm.) IV. Praises for Michael the Archangel (175 mm.) V. The Sweetness of Epicurus (87 mm.)	3 Flt. (1 doubling Picc.), 3 Ob. (1 doubling EH), 3 Clar., 3 Bssn. (1 doubling Cbssn.), 4 Hr., 3 Tpt., 3 Trom., Tuba, Timp., Perc. (BD, Tubular Chimes, Tam-tam, Glsp., Vbp.), 3 Drones (one player each of Vln. 1, Vln. 2, and Vlc.), Pno., Tack Pno., Cel., Org., 2 Harps, Strgs.	Commissioned by the Koussevitzky Music Foundation. First performance: December 7, 1975, Oakland Symphony Youth Orchestra, conducted by Denis de Coteau. Score published by Peermusic Classical. Recorded by Oakland Symphony Youth Orchestra, conducted by Denis de Coteau (1750 Arch Records S-1772); American Composers Orchestra, conducted by Dennis Russell Davies (MusicMasters MMD 60204).

Third Symphony (1982, rev. 1985)	I. Allegro moderato (171 mm.)
	II.
	  A. Reel in Honor of Henry Cowell (100 mm.)
	  B. A Waltz for Evelyn Hinrichsen (60 mm.)
	  C. An Estampie for Susan Summerfield (271 mm.)
	III. Largo Ostinato (65 mm.)
	IV. Allegro (407 mm.)
		3 Flt. (1 doubling Picc.), 3 Ob. (1 doubling EH), 3 Clar., 3 Bssn., 4 Hr., 3 Tpt., 3 Trom., Tuba, Cel., Tack Pno., Harp, Mrb., Vbp., Perc., Strgs.	Composed for the twentieth anniversary of the founding of the Cabrillo Music Festival. First performance: August 9, 1982, Cabrillo Music Festival, conducted by Dennis Russell Davies.
			
			Score published by C. F. Peters.
			
			Recorded by Cabrillo Music Festival Orchestra, conducted by Dennis Russell Davies (MusicMasters 7073–2-C).

Fourth Symphony (*Last Symphony*) (1990, rev. 1991–95)	I. Largo (144 mm.) II. Stampede—poco presto (Offered to William Colvig) (693 mm.) III. Largo (123 mm.) IV. Intro / Coyote's Path / Story I / Coyote's Path / Story II / Coyote's Path / Story III / Finale (161 mm.)	3 Flt. (1 doubling Picc.), 3 Ob. (1 doubling EH), 3 Clar. (1 doubling Bclar.), 3 Bssn. (1 doubling Cbssn.), 4 Hr., 3 Tpt., 3 Trom., Tuba, Perc. (4 Players; Player 1: Sleigh Bells, Chimes, Güiro, Gong [preferably the Gong Ageng of a Gamelan], Rasp, Keprak, Box; Player 2: Rattles, Gentorak, 3 Muted gongs, 3 Chinese Drums; Player 3: Vbp., Cym., Box, Field Drum; Player 4: BD), Cel., Tack Pno., Strgs., Baritone Soloist	Commissioned by the Brooklyn Philharmonic Orchestra. First performance of original version: November 2, 1990, Brooklyn Philharmonic Orchestra, conducted by Dennis Russell Davies, with tenor Damon Evans. Dedicated to Dennis Russell Davies. Score published by Peermusic Classical. Fourth movement (which exchanged places with the second movement in the final version) contains three "Coyote Stories." Stories 1 and 3 are Amerindian tales, from Bruce Walter Brown, *The Tree at the Center* (Santa Barbara, CA: Ross-Erikson, 1980), and Story 2 is by Daniel-Harry Steward. Final version recorded by California Symphony, conducted by Barry Jekowsky, with Al Jarreau, baritone (Argo 455-590-2).

shares the first movement's title "Tears of the Angel Israfel" and its modal melodic quality, honors Koussevitzky with a duet for solo contrabasses; the emphasis on perfect intervals, along with the percussive sonorities of the contrasting section, evokes an antique splendor. The fourth movement, "Praises for Michael the Archangel," recaptures the angularity of the second movement and verges on atonality; here, chimes and celesta add to Harrison's colorful palette of percussive effects. Smooth contours, wistful melodies, and shimmering textures return in the meditative fifth and final movement, "The Sweetness of Epicurus."

Composed for the Cabrillo Music Festival, the Third Symphony (1982) incorporates a number of pieces originally written in earlier decades, and it recalls the *Symphony on G* in treating a middle movement as the home for a dance suite. The first movement, whose material dates back to 1958, suggests folk music in its modal, pentatonic inflection and a lullaby in its central plaintive violin solo.[57] The second movement is divided into three dances. Harrison initially composed the first, "Reel in Honor of Henry Cowell," for piano in 1939, and the symphonic version recalls his mentor's interest in Celtic cultures through the use of spoons as accompaniment.[58] The second, "A Waltz for Evelyn Hinrichsen," derives from a piano piece Harrison wrote for the president of C. F. Peters in 1977. And "An Estampie for Susan Summerfield" pays homage to a celebrated organist. The slow movement that follows, *Largo Ostinato* (originating in 1937) treats the uncanny oscillation between F major and D-flat major as a backdrop for flowing, languid songlike themes. It leads to a celebratory movement, a diatonic Finale that blends flowing, polyphonic dance-like passages and gamelan-like colors with heroically leaping melodies cut from the same cloth as Copland's Symphony No. 3 (1946). Like the first movement, this material also dates to 1958.

In his Fourth Symphony (initially titled *Last Symphony*, 1990, rev. 1991–1995), Harrison added Amerindian culture to his eclectic symphonic mix. The symphony's opening movement grows from an atmospheric duet for oboe and celesta into a lush sound world that suggests conventional Western sonic conceptions of East Asia, especially through the combination of celesta and tack piano, along with the string melody's modal character. The second movement (originally the Finale) is an estampie that bears the title "Offered to William Colvig," Harrison's life partner. Here, spiraling melodies in winds and strings, an emphasis on two six-note modes centered on D, and an array of percussion (including boxes with rasps) furnishes the especially boisterous quality of an imagined medieval dance.[59] The slow third movement derives its impassioned character from the fact that the melodies are made up of minor seconds, minor thirds, and perfect fifths; the first movement's melodic material is similarly prescribed, employing only major seconds, minor thirds, and minor sixths.[60] (Harrison used similar procedures of interval control in works throughout his career.[61]) The most striking part of the symphony, however, is the fourth movement (originally the second). Here, a baritone presents three Amerindian stories that focus, respectively, on multiculturalism, love, and sustainability; the first and third stories, traditional tales, are performed in a free rhythm over an improvised accompaniment in celesta, vibraphone, and harp, while the second (with words by Daniel-Harry Steward, of Wintu descent) is recited over percussion. Between each story is a refrain, "Coyote's Path," that evokes the bell-like timbres of the gamelan, and all the melodic and harmonic material in this movement derives from a five-note scale drawn from Javanese music.[62]

The lesson of the final "story" in the Fourth Symphony involves a warning about incontinence; the coyote, having eaten forbidden berries—berries belonging to the "children of the future"—finds that "his behind had fallen off." Thus, Harrison's symphonic output concludes with a joke. For both Carter and Harrison, who came of age in the period before World War II and held Ives in high regard, symphonies were less about making grand rhetorical statements than exploring new possibilities in sound, meaning, and reference. For Harrison in particular, they provided an opportunity to blend seemingly disparate components in new ways. And in exploring those possibilities, Harrison's symphonic works provide a reference point for the postmodernist juxtaposition of seemingly incongruous musical materials and ideas in the music of other recent symphonists.

George Rochberg (1918–2005)

George Rochberg was one of the most important transitional composers in the music of the later twentieth century. Born in Paterson, New Jersey, Rochberg served in Europe during World War II; on his return, he studied with Rosario Scalero at the Curtis Institute of Music and became a noted teacher at the University of Pennsylvania. Although he made a name for himself composing atonal and twelve-tone works, Rochberg famously turned away from the dominant high-modernist aesthetic of postwar serialism and toward a tonal idiom infused with the melodic and harmonic hallmarks of eighteenth- and nineteenth-century music. In notes on his landmark String Quartet No. 3, finished in 1972, he wrote that "by the beginning of the sixties, I had become completely dissatisfied" with the "inherently narrow terms" of serialism.[63] An important event in the reshaping of Rochberg's musical language was the death of his son Paul in 1964. Rochberg called this event the "catalyst" for his aesthetic shift away from serialism, adding that it was a "shock of a kind that necessitated a new sense of how I had to live the rest of my life."[64]

Rochberg's symphonies, which are shown in table 9.4, capture the stages of this shift, providing a panorama of his own personal stylistic and aesthetic evolution. His work has been credited with helping "to free the next generation of composers from the serial straightjacket to write music that was once again comprehensible to audiences."[65] Although Rochberg was also noted for chamber music, assessments like these carry a special significance for the symphony because of that genre's status as a vehicle for assembling large audiences and groups of performers.

Rochberg's five-movement Symphony No. 1 grew out of the larger discourse of the "Great American Symphony" that captured composers in the 1930s and 40s.[66] This particular work blends a harsh austerity with an almost expressionistic lyricism and a sense of grand gesture often found in midcentury American symphonies, such as Aaron Copland's Symphony No. 3 (1946). Rochberg composed the work in 1948–49, but he reduced it to three movements on the advice of friends and colleagues because of its length, removing the second and third movements and deleting parts of the others.[67] He reconstituted it as a five-movement work in the 1970s, with new choices in orchestration that lent the revised version what he called "a richer, more varied physical voice."[68] Repeated and interrupted phrases, chromatic and angular thematic material, an emphasis on extroverted brass, and the presence of piano recall early modernist essays like Carl Ruggles's imposing but far briefer *Men and Mountains* (1924), while the playfully irregular rhythms and spare orchestration hint at Copland's orchestral works. Although this work generally avoids clear tonal centers, stark moments of tonal focus—such as the lush B-flat major passages that begin and conclude the fourth movement, "Variations"— prefigure Rochberg's allusions to Romantic idioms in his later music. The second movement's title, "Night Music," along with the third movement's tempo instruction "Fast and impetuous, like a curtain-raiser," hints at Rochberg's theatricality. Strikingly, these evocative designations involve the two movements excised from the symphony in its time as a three-movement work

Table 9.4 The Symphonies of George Rochberg (1918–2005)

Title	Movements	Instrumentation	Comments
Symphony No. 1 (1948–49; rev. 1957, 1971–72, 1977, 2003)	I. Allegro molto ma un poco pesante; exultant! (481 mm.) II. Night Music. Poco adagio; like a slow march (196 mm.) III. Capriccio. Fast and impetuous; like a curtain raiser (613 mm.) IV. Variations. Molto adagio; very slow and stately (304 mm.) V. Finale. Adagio; parlando e molto rubato (321 mm.)	Picc. (doubling Flt.), 2 Flt. 2 Ob., EH (doubling Ob.), 2 Clar. (1 doubling E♭ Clar.), Bclar. (doubling Clar.), 2 Bssn., Cbssn., 4 Hr., 3 Tpt., 3 Trom., Tuba, Timp., Perc. (SD, Side Drum, Tom-toms, Bongos, BD, Crash Cyms., Suspended Cym. [large], Gongs [medium, low], Tubular Bells, Tri., Tamb.), Harp, Pno., Strgs.	All five movements originally composed in 1948–49, with the second and third movements left out of a revised three-movement version. First performance of three-movement version: March 28, 1958, Philadelphia Orchestra, conducted by Eugene Ormandy. Other movements reinstated in revision in the 1970s. Score published by Presser. Three-movement version recorded by Louisville Orchestra, conducted by Robert Whitney (Soundmark 48118); five-movement version with 2003 revisions recorded by Saarbrücken Radio Symphony Orchestra, conducted by Christopher Lyndon-Gee (Naxos 8.559214).
Chamber Symphony for Nine Instruments (1953)	I. Allegro tempo giusto (193 mm.) II. Adagio (48 mm.) III. Marcia (51 mm.) IV. Allegro assai (165 mm.)	Ob., Clar., Bssn., Hr., Tpt., Trom., Vln., Vla., Vlc.	Dedicated to Rochberg's wife, Gene. First performance: 1955, Baltimore Chamber Society, conducted by Hugo Weisgall. Score published by Presser. Recorded by members of the Oberlin Chamber Orchestra (Desto - DC 6444).

Symphony No. 2 (1955–56)	One movement in four sections: I. Declamando (mm. 1–255) II. Allegro scherzando (mm. 256–572) III. Molto tranquillo (mm. 573–656) IV. Tempo primo, ma incalzando (mm. 657–795)	Picc., 2 Flt., 2 Ob., EH, 2 Clar., Bclar., 2 Bssn., Cbssn., 4 Hr., 3 Tpt., 3 Trom., Tuba, Timp., Xylo., Perc. (SD, Tenor Drum, BD, Cym., Gong, Tri., Tamb.), Strgs.	Dedicated to the Cleveland Orchestra and George Szell. First performance: February 26, 1959, Cleveland Orchestra, conducted by George Szell. Score published by Presser. Recorded by New York Philharmonic, conducted by Werner Torkanowsky (CRI CD 768; Saarbrücken Radio Symphony Orchestra, conducted by Christopher Lyndon Gee (Naxos 8.559182).
Symphony No. 3 (1966–69)	One movement (677 mm.)	6 Flt. (2 doubling Picc.), 6 Ob. (1 doubling EH), 2 Eb Clar. (both doubling Clar.), 3 Clar., BClar., Cbclar., 5 Bssn., Cbssn., 6 Hr., 8 Tpt., 6 Trom., Cbtrom., 3 Tubas (1 doubling Cbtuba), Timp., Perc. (BD [large], 3 Tam-tams or Gongs [high, middle, low], Tubular Bells, Steel Bell Plates [low pitched], Antique Cyms., Tri. [small], Glsp., Vbp.), Pno., Pipe Org., Electric Org. [large], Cel., Strgs., Vocal Soloists (Soprano, Alto, Tenor, Bass), Chamber Chorus (2 Soprano, 2 Alto, 2 Tenor, 2 Bass; 2–4 per part), Double SATB Chorus (minimum of 80 per chorus)	Commissioned by the Juilliard School. First performance: November 24, 1970, Juilliard Orchestra and Chorus, Collegiate Chorale, conducted by Abraham Kaplan, with Joyce Mathis, soprano; Joy Blackett, alto; John Russell, tenor; Robert Shiesley, bass. Score published by Presser.
Symphony No. 4 (1976, rev. 1977)	I. Adagio—Andante con moto (289 mm.) II. Serenade—Scherzo (365 mm.) III. Introduction and Finale (mm. 862)	3 Flt. (1 doubling Picc.), 3 Ob. (1 doubling EH), 2 Clar., Bclar., 2 Bssn., Cbssn., 4 Hr., 3 Tpt., 3 Trom., Tuba, Timp., Perc. (Glsp., Tamb., Tri., SD, BD, Suspended Cyms. [large, small], Crash Cyms.), Cel., Harp, Strgs.	Dedicated to Vilem Sokol. Commissioned by the Seattle Youth Orchestra for the US Bicentennial. First performance: November 15, 1976, Seattle Youth Orchestra, conducted by Vilem Sokol. Score published by Presser.

Table 9.4 continued

Title	Movements	Instrumentation	Comments
Symphony No. 5 (1984, rev. 1985, 1986)	One movement in seven sections: I. Opening Statement (mm. 1–42) II. Episode 1 (mm. 43–62) III. Development 1 (mm. 63–140) IV. Episode 2 (mm. 141–76) V. Development 2 (mm. 177–275) VI. Episode 3 (mm. 276–322) VII. Finale (mm. 323–486)	3 Flt. (1 doubling Picc.), 2 Ob., 1 EH, 2 Clar., 1 Bclar., 2 Bssn., 1 Cbssn., 4 Hr., 4 Tpt., 3 Trom., Tuba, Timp., Perc. (Xylo., Tubular Bells, Roto-toms, SD, Tenor Drum, BD, Suspended Cym. [large], Crash Cyms., Vbp.), Cel., Pno., Harp, Strgs.	Dedicated to Sir Georg Solti and the Chicago Symphony Orchestra. Commissioned by the City of Chicago and the Chicago Office of Fine Arts for the Chicago Symphony Orchestra in celebration of the city's sesquicentennial, in memory of John S. Edwards. Winner of the 1986 Pulitzer Prize in Music. First performance: March 13, 1986, Chicago Symphony Orchestra, conducted by Georg Solti. Score published by Presser. Recorded by Saarbrücken Radio Symphony Orchestra, conducted by Christopher Lyndon-Gee (Naxos 8.559115).
Symphony No. 6 (1986–87)	I. Fantasia: Allegro (202 mm.) II. Marcia (501 mm.)	Picc., 3 Flt., 3 Ob., EH, E♭ Clar., 3 Clar., Bclar., 3 Bssn., Cbssn., 4 Hr., 4 Tpt., 3 Trom., Tuba, 2 Timp., Perc. (Xylo., Vbp., Tubular Bells, Tri., Suspended Cyms. [small, large], Crash Cyms., Tam-tam, Whip (slap-stick), Güiro, SD, Tenor Drum, BD), 2 Harps, Cel., Strgs.	Commissioned by the Pittsburgh Symphony Society. First performance: October 16, 1987, Pittsburgh Symphony Orchestra, conducted by Lorin Maazel. Score published by Presser.

(Rochberg gave them lives of their own in the 1950s). Perhaps it was in part Rochberg's engagement with musical tradition in the 1960s and 1970s (discussed below) that encouraged him to return the more programmatic movements of the Symphony No. 1 to their original positions.

Rochberg turned to twelve-tone compositions in the 1950s with his Twelve Bagatelles for piano (1952), dedicated to the Italian composer Luigi Dallapiccola.[69] And dodecaphonic writing characterizes his next two symphonies, the Chamber Symphony (1953) and Symphony No. 2 (1955–56); in a letter to William Schuman of May 24, 1957, Rochberg wrote, "12-tone as a way of thinking & feeling is right for me."[70] Looking back on his four-movement Chamber Symphony, Rochberg called it "the first large-scale instrumental work I attempted using a twelve-tone row to organize the melodic/harmonic levels and interrelationships."[71] (This contrasts with his use of "the most primitive kind of twelve-tone row" in the second theme of his Symphony No. 1, where "it functions only melodically and motivically rather than harmonically and contrapuntally and in no way actually affects the general tonal orientation of the music."[72])

As a symphonic composer, Rochberg's twelve-tone writing culminated in his Symphony No. 2, which proceeds in four continuous movements plus a coda and plays on the contrast between sections of thick and transparent orchestration. Recalling George Szell's work in shepherding the composition to its premiere with the Cleveland Orchestra in 1958, Rochberg wrote admiringly that "the Second had miraculously taken on, in Szell's hands, the quality of a work in the grand Romantic tradition that Szell and his orchestra had played many times before, knew intimately, and believed in thoroughly."[73] Rochberg's telling program notes demonstrate how a modernist technique—in his case, complex manipulations of the hexachords making up a symmetrical tone row—could connect readily to a Romantic heritage: "The problem was to find a way to employ a total chromatic palette, melodic and harmonic, on a large scale true to what the term 'symphony' has come to mean after Beethoven, without losing a sense of proportion, continuity, and growth. The language is contemporary but the adherence to concepts of logic of musical discourse is traditional."[74]

More than a decade passed between the premieres of Rochberg's Symphony No. 2 and Symphony No. 3 (1966–69), and the aesthetic gap between the two works is significant.[75] "Some who heard the premiere of George Rochberg's Symphony No. 3 at the Juilliard Theatre on Tuesday night," Allen Hughes wrote in the *New York Times* after the latter piece's first hearing in 1970, "may feel that the composer was trying to get away with wholesale larceny by filling up so much of the half hour of the piece with other people's music."[76] This work, for vocal soloists, chamber chorus, double chorus, and an immense orchestra, departs from Rochberg's earlier symphonies not just in its use of a significant force of vocalists and enlarged instrumental ensemble but in its frequent tonal writing, which typically takes the form of glosses on canonical works from the seventeenth to nineteenth centuries. In doing so, it joins the ranks of a number of other postmodernist compositions from the late 1960s, including Lukas Foss's *Baroque Variations* (1967), Luciano Berio's *Sinfonia* (1969), and Rochberg's own *Nach Bach* (1966) and *Music for the Magic Theater* (1965; orchestral version 1969). (Drawing on another characteristic of much music from that period, it even includes elements of performer choice, such as the final message to the conductor to "continue choral pattern as long as you wish, each repetition fainter and fainter as more and more voices drop out."[77]) Rochberg considered this composition to be more a "passion" than a "symphony"; he called it *A Passion According to the Twentieth Century*.[78] As he explained, "The texts—each of which has its associated 'music' drawn from a specific work of another composer—bear their load of awesome religious-theological meaning and unify themselves around my idea of twentieth century man's 'passion'—the terrible drama of his struggle with his own nature."[79] The symphony's center of gravity is seventeenth-century German composer Heinrich Schütz's sacred concerto *Saul, was verfolgst du mich* (SWV 415) from *Symphoniae sacrae III* (1650), which, as Rochberg noted, "is incorporated in its entirety—although its appearance is considerably altered from its first form."[80] Rochberg blends and juxtaposes the Schütz work with material from other musical warhorses, including Ludwig van Beethoven's *Missa Solemnis*, as well as echoes of Gustav Mahler's first two symphonies; Charles Ives's *The Unanswered Question*; and passages from Beethoven's Third, Fifth, and Ninth Symphonies.[81]

This symphony in particular clarifies the role of quotation, collage, and arrangement in constructing Rochberg's broader relationship with musical modernism at a transitional moment in his career. Rochberg said of his "collage/assemblage works" that they contain "an almost 'natural' sense of a strangely familiar musical speech even when the elements being worked come from other times and other composers."[82] Speaking of his use of Mozart's Divertimento K287 (1777) in *Music for the Magic Theater*, Rochberg claimed that by challenging audiences' perceptions of what counts as contemporary music, the Mozart excerpt "will make its presence felt even more if it is projected in a detached manner—floating out ever so gently, almost whispered at times."[83] Rochberg's framing of his musical quotations casts this practice as a modernist exercise rather than a wholehearted embrace of a specific style that carried weight in the past; as he explained, his use of Mozart in that work challenged "the whole concept of what is 'contemporary'" and "abrogates the nineteenth to early twentieth century notion of 'originality.'"[84] In the Symphony No. 3, about which Rochberg claimed not to care whether one called it a "contemporary" work, he hoped to enact "the impulse to speak to my fellow-man in the language I know best of the things closest to my heart."[85]

Rochberg's Symphony No. 4 (1976) has as its predecessor the String Quartet No. 3 (1972), the landmark work in which the composer employed tonality by adopting past styles without the protective screen of direct quotation. Of the three-movement symphony, he wrote, "The essential style of the language is tonal—a tonality which is broad-ranging enough to include not only the diatonic and the chromatic but the atonal as well."[86] The long opening movement presents and recapitulates several sets of material, including an oscillating motif in the low strings reminiscent of the opening of Hector Berlioz's *Harold in Italy* (1834), a lush songlike section, and a chromatic whirl. A section marked "Transcendent" (m. 246) restores the grounded tonal focus of the opening, and its string-driven textures contain shades of the *Adagietto* from Mahler's Fifth Symphony (1901–02). This first movement includes a clear long-term tonal trajectory, with its extended opening pedal on A eventually giving way to an embellished D major at the close. The second movement, "Serenade-Scherzo," is a recomposition of an orchestral piece Rochberg wrote in the late 1950s called *Waltz Serenade*.[87] Lurking behind it is the Scherzo of Mahler's Seventh Symphony (1904–05), with its cascades of eighth notes and convulsive energy (Rochberg admired Mahler's Seventh, and in particular the Scherzo).[88] The movement contains a tone row, but, as Rochberg wrote, "the atonality inherent (usually) in such a row (or series) I turned inside-out so it becomes essentially tonal, that is, key-centered and directional, with the inevitable resurrection of the cadence as marking points of arrival and defining articulation of musical speech"—an example, for Rochberg, "of reconciling opposites that seem to contradict each other but are, in reality, simply different faces of the same primary features."[89] Rochberg's discussion suggests a parallel to Lou Harrison's "tonal" use of twelve-tone writing in his *Symphony on G*, although in the "Serenade-Scherzo," any clear sense of a single key center scarcely penetrates the densely chromatic fabric.

Wagner and Haydn mingle in the final movement, "Introduction and Finale," where a sense of tonality is far more apparent. A songlike but fragmentary introductory section draws on and expands the Romantic lushness of the first movement. The music of this part of the Finale dates back to Rochberg's time as pianist for the Montclair State Teacher's College Dance Club in 1938, when he composed and improvised music for a program on the story of Tristan and Isolde.[90] Cleverly, this Wagner-inflected section serves as an amplified version of the slow introduction of a Haydn symphony; it jarringly precedes Rochberg's own take on a fast classical-era Finale. Although slower material does return toward the end of this movement, Haydn ultimately dominates with a suitably fast and rambunctious conclusion. Given this symphony's status as a Bicentennial commission, it is fitting that Rochberg's multistylistic salute to the birth of the United States—at a time of much discussion about founding fathers—ended with an overt reference to a Revolutionary-era, albeit European, composer often remembered as the "Father of the Symphony" (and who coincidentally was born only one month before George Washington).

Rochberg's Symphony No. 5 is perhaps his crowning achievement in the genre. In this work, he tied together many of the strands seen in his previous symphonies; he fused tonality with extreme chromaticism, stylistic allusions with direct quotations, and stunning displays of orchestral virtuosity with the dramatic demands of a continuous one-movement form. Composed in 1984 for the Chicago Symphony Orchestra in honor of the city's one hundred fiftieth anniversary, Rochberg's harmonic language moved away from the "soft romanticism" of the previous symphony's outer movements and toward what he called the "hard romanticism" that he also identified in the "Serenade-Scherzo" of the Symphony No. 4.[91] An anonymous "patron"—soon revealed to be the conductor Georg Solti himself—had made a special request of Rochberg for a concerto to highlight the orchestra's noted brass section, but the composer hoped to write a symphony because of "the freedom to make use of a wider palette."[92] Rochberg called the resulting composition, which earned the 1986 Pulitzer Prize, "an intense, passionate work of an emotional scale which I hope wholly befits the city, the occasion, the conductor, and the orchestra for which it was written."[93] Harmonically, the work evokes tonality as though stretched to a breaking point; Rochberg called its one movement in seven continuous sections "mainly chromatic with virtually no overt references to the tonal palette which most people have come to associate with my music."[94] In the ominous first section ("Opening Statement"), an intense string figure, which vacillates between semitones, battles with a Mahlerian turn figure that is first stated in the brass; this figure will pervade the entire composition. As seen in example 9.1, a brief English horn solo provides the transition from the turbulent "Episode 1" to the impassioned "Development 1." (As is the published score, this example is in C.) This first development section then expands the turn figure into a fully-fledged melody that recalls the heartrending anguish of the last movement of Mahler's Ninth Symphony (1908–09).

With the slow "Episode 2" comes a stark change in texture. Scored for four French horns with scant accompaniment, this passage evokes the obbligato horn solo in the Scherzo of Mahler's Fifth Symphony; as the center of gravity in Rochberg's work, the episode also contains several clear references to older works, a special showcase of the Chicago horns' prowess in the orchestral repertory. At m. 149, a suggestion of a prominent motive in Jean Sibelius's

Matthew Mugmon

Example 9.1 George Rochberg, Symphony No. 5, mm. 61–65. Copyright © 1986 by Theodore Presser Company. All rights reserved. Used with permission.

Lemminkäinen in Tuonela (from the *Lemminkäinen Suite*, 1893) leads to the climactic turn figure in the third movement of Shostakovich's Fifth Symphony (1937) at mm. 154–55; at mm. 161–62, an allusion to the opening of Tchaikovsky's Symphony No. 4 (1878) is heard. The whole orchestra enters with "Development 2," characterized by aggressive rising and falling motifs. This gives way to the dreamy, distant "Episode 3," where wind solos hover over shimmering strings; hazy vibraphone, celesta, and harp tone clusters evoke a Messiaen-like temporal stasis. In the "Finale," frantic energy gives way to a serene elaboration of the turn figure. But in the symphony's thunderous concluding moments, which especially highlight the brass, the Shostakovich and Tchaikovsky references mingle (mm. 447–54), and the work closes with an unforgiving final thud.

The specter of war haunts Rochberg's next and final symphonic effort, the Symphony No. 6 (1986–87). (A Symphony No. 7 was planned as the third and final installment of a symphonic trilogy begun by his Symphony No. 5, but it never materialized.[95]) With its similarly assertive brass writing and chromatic harmonic canvas, this two-movement symphony picks up where the Symphony No. 5 left off. The opening movement, "Fantasia," is filled with fanfares that for Rochberg suggested "not only the ancient association with what we now know to be the false glories of war but also the hidden, underlying tragic implications of mankind's perennial passion for making war and its inability to rid itself of a sophisticated barbarism rationalized as the military side of national defense."[96] The fanfares, he wrote, "come in unexpected ways and in unexpected places . . ., emerging out of or interrupting or taking over other kinds of musical ideas."[97] These fanfares always loom, contrasting with moments of tense calm and searing passion. But the first movement ends with a surprising lull, as though better forces have temporarily subdued the threatening fanfares. The second movement, "Marcia," consists of several marches, more modal than densely chromatic in flavor. All derive from material Rochberg composed previously. The main march originates in a 1947 orchestral suite, while the second is an orchestration of *Carnival Music*, a 1971 work for piano. But the third march has the most intriguing history: Rochberg wrote its primary theme for a parade march while serving in Mississippi during World War II.[98] With its pounding percussion and fierce brass, the symphony evokes large-scale war and struggle, and suggests Mahler's Symphony No. 6 (1903–04) as a precedent.

The tension between Rochberg's embrace of the past and his profile as a modernist is perhaps best reflected in a pair of statements by two quite different composers of the following generation, William Bolcom and Joseph Schwantner, written in 1988 to mark Rochberg's seventieth birthday. For Bolcom, Rochberg "became one of my heroes around 1965, when his use of past styles, quotations, etc. was a healthy reaction to a doctrinaire modernism that had most composers in a strangle-hold. He still is extremely high in my estimation, especially for the music that contains an emotional intensity and an openness of approach."[99] For Schwantner, however, the appeal went beyond the choice of musical language; he referred to Rochberg's "unswerving artistic vision" and said that his "seminal work during the sixties was of special significance to me and to many composers of my generation. His strong and direct music provided new and reinvigorated musical pathways for many of us to consider."[100] What may be the most lasting aspect of Rochberg's legacy as a symphonist, though, is that in making tonality a normal part of contemporary language across multiple genres, he boosted the aesthetic standing of such "traditional" genres as the symphony—and, in turn, the orchestra as an institution.

George Walker (1922–2018)

George Walker was already well established as a pianist and composer by the time he began writing symphonic works in the 1980s. His composition teachers included Rosario Scalero at the Curtis Institute of Music and Nadia Boulanger in Paris, and he went on to spend the bulk of his career teaching at Rutgers University.[101] Walker's most celebrated works include his *Lyric for Strings* (1946) and *Lilacs* for voice and orchestra (1995); for the latter he became the first Black composer to win the Pulitzer Prize in music. Regarding his symphonic compositions, listed in table 9.5, Walker calls them sinfonias rather than symphonies; as he explained, "I chose the title 'sinfonia' because its origin suggests an instrumental work that is less expansive" (though not, by implication, less significant) "than the concept of the 19th century 'symphony.' My sinfonias are tightly knit statements."[102] Before the sinfonias, however, Walker did compose a three-movement symphony, which was performed by the University of Colorado's orchestra when he was a visiting professor there in 1968; as he recalled, it "was read with considerable difficulty."[103] The second movement survives in revised form in the *Serenata for Chamber Orchestra* (1983), but Walker withdrew the symphony's first and third movements.[104] Walker's orchestral works prior to the sinfonias also include, among other compositions, his Concerto for Trombone and Orchestra and the *Address for Orchestra*, both composed in the 1950s, as well as *An Eastman Overture* (1983).

Walker's Sinfonia No. 1 (1984) was commissioned by the Fromm Foundation; as the composer recalled, he appreciated the opportunity to have his music performed at Tanglewood, but the relatively small fee motivated him to write a work of limited, rather than extended, length.[105] The first of its two movements contrasts several elements, including fanfare-like passages; angular thematic material; lyrical moments; and mysterious, sustained sonorities. In the second movement, meandering motives in the winds and strings interact with lively flourishes for a varied array of percussion; here, a "theme" consisting of several repeated notes, initially encountered in the first movement, emerges as the leading musical element, passed from instrument to instrument and leading to a conclusion on flurries of repeated clusters. Despite the impressively large forces involved in this work, Walker creates a clean sound reminiscent of chamber music—one in which individual sonorities are highlighted and blended, and in which motives are exchanged from voice to voice and subtly altered. After its premiere, John Rockwell of the *New York Times* baldly derided this work as "empty and blustery in the worst faceless contemporary orchestral manner."[106] Rockwell's hasty criticism ignores Walker's sensitive and subtle attention to the details of timbral combinations and an attention to melodic manipulation that reveals itself on repeated listening.

With the three-movement Sinfonia No. 2 (1990), Walker again exhibited his careful blending of orchestral sonorities. In the first movement, an angular, strident opening gesture gives way to the seductively placid transition and second section, and a version of the opening gesture returns to suggest a recapitulation. The slow second movement consists of an extended flute solo with spare accompaniment from cellos and guitar, providing a respite from the almost frenetic activity of the first movement before the sense of buoyant energy returns in the Finale. Rhythm drives this concluding movement, which centers on, in Walker's words, "the rhythmic impulse of five notes played initially by the English horn and bass clarinet. . . . The subtle emergence of an eighth note pattern with a steady pulse provides the basis for the imposition of rhythmic fragments above it. Interposed between these sections are brief sustained moments that interrupt the foot tapping insistence of the bass line of eighth notes.

Table 9.5 The Sinfonias of George Walker (1922–2018)

Title	Movements	Instrumentation	Comments
Sinfonia No. 1 (1984, rev. 1996)	I. (107 mm.) II. (95 mm.)	Picc. (doubling Fl. and Alto Fl.), 2 Flt., 2 Ob., EH, 2 Clar (1 doubling E♭ Clar.), Bclar., 2 Bssn., Cbssn., 4 Hr., 4 Tpt., 3 Trom., Tuba, Timp., Perc. (Glsp., Xylo., Chimes, Vbp., SD, BD, Tenor Drum, Roto-toms, Chocolo, Bongos, Timbales, Suspended Cym., Tam-tam, Gong, Anvil, Cowbells, Tri., Tamb., Ratchet, Castanets, Maracas, Whip, Güiro, Claves, Temple Blocks, Wood Blocks, Glass Wind Chimes), Pno., Harpsichord, Harp, Strgs.	Commissioned by the Fromm Foundation. Dedicated to Paul Kapp. First performance: August 1, 1984, Berkshire Music Center Orchestra, conducted by Gunther Schuller. Score published by Lauren Keiser Music Publishing. Recorded by Sinfonia Varsovia, conducted by Ian Hobson (Albany TROY1061).
Sinfonia No. 2 (1990)	I. Qtr=76 (151 mm.) II. Lamentoso e quasi senza misura (11 mm.) III. (99 mm.)	Picc., 2 Flt., 2 Ob., EH, 2 Clar., Bclar., 2 Bssn., Cbssn., 4 Hr., 4 Tpt., 3 Trom., Tuba, Timp., Perc. (Suspended Cym., SD, Glsp., Xylo., Vbp., Chimes), Pno., Harp, Gui., Strgs.	Commissioned by the Koussevitzky Music Foundation. First performance: April 15, 1993, Detroit Symphony Orchestra, conducted by Neeme Järvi. Score published by Lauren Keiser Music Publishing. Recorded by Sinfonia Varsovia, conducted by Ian Hobson (Albany TROY1178).
Sinfonia No. 3 (2002, rev. 2007)	I. (98 mm.) II. (69 mm.) III. (83 mm.)	Picc., 2 Flt., 2 Ob., EH, E♭ Clar, 2 Clar., Bclar., 2 Bssn., Cbssn., 4 Hr., 4 Tpt., 3 Trom., Tuba, Timp., Perc. (Glsp., Xylo., Vbp., Mrb., Chimes, Claves, Wood Block, Temple Blocks, Tamb., Güiro, Tri., Maracas [high], Roto-toms, SD, Tam-tam, BD, Tom-toms, Whip, Suspended Cyms., Crash Cyms.), Harp, Cel., Strgs.	First performance: January 16, 2004, Detroit Symphony Orchestra, conducted by Andrey Boreyko. Score published by Lauren Keiser Music Publishing. Recorded by Sinfonia Varsovia, conducted by Ian Hobson (Albany TROY1061).

Table 9.5 continued

Title	Movements	Instrumentation	Comments
Sinfonia No. 4, "Strands" (2011)	One movement (165 mm.)	Picc., 2 Flt., 2 Ob. (1 doubling EH), 2 Clar. (1 doubling Bclar.), 2 Bssn., Cbssn., 4 Hr., 3 Tpt., 3 Trom., Tuba, Timp., Perc. (Xylo., Glsp., Vbp., Mrb., Chimes, Tri., SD, Tom-toms, BD, Claves, Timbales, Wood Block, Glass Chimes, Suspended Cym., Sizzle Cym., Tamb., Temple Blocks, Tam-tam), Pno., Harp, Strgs.	Commissioned through Meet the Composer by the New Jersey Symphony Orchestra, the Cincinnati Symphony Orchestra, the National Symphony Orchestra, and the Pittsburgh Symphony Orchestra. First performance: March 30, 2012, New Jersey Symphony Orchestra, conducted by Jacques Lacombe. Score published by Bellegrove. Recorded by Sinfonia Varsovia, conducted by Ian Hobson (Albany TROY1430).
Sinfonia No. 5, "Visions" (2015–16)	One movement (326 mm.)	Picc., 2 Flt., 2 Ob., EH, 2 Clar., Bclar., 2 Bssn., Cbssn., 4 Hr., 4 Tpt., 3 Trom., Tuba, Timp., Perc. (4 Players: Glsp., Xylo., Mrb., Vbp., Tri., Small Cym., Suspended Cym., Sizzle Cym., SD, BD, Wood Blocks, Güiro, Temple Blocks, Chimes, Glass Chimes, Tam-tam, Anvil, Castanets, Jawbone), Harp, Pno, Amplified Harpsichord, Amplified Voices (Soprano, Tenor, 2 Baritones, Bass), Strgs.	Inscribed "In memoriam . . .", and relates to the 2015 attack at Emanuel African Methodist Episcopal Church in Charleston, SC. Text by George Walker. Video with image of Charleston shoreline to be projected during the work. Score published by Bellegrove. Recorded by Sinfonia Varsovia, conducted by Ian Hobson (Albany TROY1707).

The brilliant conclusion of the work incorporates the five notes heard at the beginning of the movement."[107]

Regarding his next sinfonia, Walker recalled in his autobiography that he called Detroit Symphony Orchestra executive director Emil Kang to inform him about his newest orchestral work, and Kang opted to program it.[108] Written at age 80, Sinfonia No. 3 (2002) is akin to its predecessor in its three-movement structure, but specific formal differences abound. The first movement sustains a dark, ominous mood through the repeated use of the interval of a semitone, both melodically and harmonically.[109] The tragic atmosphere continues in the second movement, which shares in none of the playfulness of the previous sinfonia's middle movement but does similarly exhibit Walker's mastery of timbral blending. In the Finale, the glimmering opening gesture in the flutes (also beginning with a semitone) yields to the vigorously driving motives in the brass and strings that dominate the movement, which closes with a series of unforgiving orchestral thuds.

Composed in 2011 at the age of 88 and commissioned for several orchestras through Meet the Composer, Walker's one-movement Sinfonia No. 4, "Strands," is named for what he called "the interplay of several melodic and motivic elements that are fused into a mosaic-like texture."[110] (Meet the Composer, founded in 1974, was an arts organization instrumental in creating the funding opportunities that led to the creation of a number of symphonies in this survey; in 2011 it joined the American Music Center to become New Music USA.) After a tense opening section, quotations from two spirituals—"There Is a Balm in Gilead" and "Roll, Jordan, Roll"—appear, but both are somewhat disguised through Walker's characteristically resourceful use of the orchestra. The first phrases of "There Is a Balm in Gilead" (beginning at m. 106)—exquisitely distributed among various registers and instruments in a *Klangfarbenmelodie*-like manner—are especially striking with their shimmering accompaniment and slow tempo. Example 9.2 shows this passage in Walker's score, with the melody of the spiritual beginning in the solo cello and migrating throughout the orchestra; the notes of the spiritual itself are boxed.

The sense of relief suggested by the source spiritual's title makes this delicate treatment seem especially appropriate. But the respite is brief. The conclusion of the "Gilead" quotation coincides with the forceful opening of "Roll, Jordan, Roll," heard as a flourish for brass and then in piano chords overlaid by increasing orchestral activity, and the unsettled energy of the work's opening rounds out this brief but weighty composition.[111] As Walker recalled, he decided to call this work a sinfonia after learning that it would share the program, on its premiere, with Beethoven's Third and Fifth Symphonies. For Walker, the title made clear that the composition was to be viewed as a serious one—not the expected light "concert opener" but, rather, a work that could stand aside the Beethoven symphonies.[112]

Walker's intricate treatment of spirituals in the Sinfonia No. 4—along with his investment in formal challenges and the details of orchestral technique and motivic manipulation—sheds light on his broader significance as both an American composer and a Black composer. In a video documentary about Walker on the premiere of his Sinfonia No. 4, he called it "important that my music should have a certain seriousness about it, and there's a certain scope I simply did not feel that what existed as important music on a purely musical level had been created by Black composers." He added, "I've always thought in . . . more universal terms, not just what is Black, or what is American, but simply what has quality."[113] Walker also noted that in his music he has quoted not just spirituals but Broadway tunes and folk songs as well.[114]

***Facing and below*, Example 9.2** George Walker, Sinfonia No. 4, mm. 103–16. Copyright © George Walker. Used with permission.

Walker's final work in this genre, the Sinfonia No. 5, "Visions" (2015–16), relates to the devastating attack on June 17, 2015, at Emanuel African Methodist Episcopal Church in Charleston, South Carolina, in which a white supremacist killed nine African Americans. The work contains a text by Walker as well as musical quotations, including from the spiritual "Swing Low, Sweet Chariot" and the Stephen Foster song "Jeanie with the Light Brown Hair."[115] In terms of its presentation, this one-movement sinfonia, whose score bears the inscription "In memoriam . . .," is Walker's most unconventional effort in the genre. Recalling the tradition of melodrama, five narrators (a soprano, a tenor, two baritones, and a bass), positioned stage right behind the orchestra, recite a text. And consistent with the work's subtitle "Visions," the score calls for an image of Charleston's shoreline to be projected partway through the work and to fade out near the very end.

Philip Glass (b. 1937)

That Philip Glass has composed multiple symphonies since the late 1980s is one of the more surprising details in the recent history of American music. How could one of the pioneers of minimalism, with its gradual processes, static harmonies, and mechanical sonorities for small ensembles thrive in a genre that often demands concretely perceptible events, harmonic and melodic contrast, and a lavish sound palette? Glass even seemed to shut the door on a career as an orchestra composer on the very eve of his shift toward symphony writing. In April 1987, he said there were few practical incentives for producing symphonies, arguing that they tended to be shelved after their premieres and were less economically and artistically rewarding than stage works. What is more, the self-proclaimed "theater composer" said, "No one ever asked me to do it. I get asked to write operas, but I don't get asked to write symphonies."[116]

In hindsight, Glass's emergence as a leading composer of symphonies is not so astonishing. On April 5, 1987—just a week before making the above comments—his Violin Concerto No. 1 had its premiere with the American Composers Orchestra under the baton of Dennis Russell Davies, who would go on to champion the symphonies of Glass and others. And Glass already had significant experience writing for orchestra through his operas *Satyagraha* (1980) and *Akhnaten* (1983).[117] Stylistically, Glass's symphonies mold the postminimalist Neoromantic language of works such as "Façades" and "Islands" from *Glassworks* (1981) and the score for the film *Koyaanisqatsi* (1982) into large symphonic structures. Arpeggios, repeated progressions, and asymmetric rhythms blend with lush orchestration and striking harmonic twists and turns—all within a framework that centers on triads, a wistful and sometimes intense lyricism often based on scalar material, and, in several symphonies, the power of the human voice. Glass's symphonies are shown in table 9.6.

Symphony No. 1, "Low" (1992), was Glass's first work to be labeled a symphony, even though it was preceded by the symphony-like *Itaipú* (1989), a four-movement work for chorus and orchestra, as well as two symphonic poems, *The Light* (1987) and *The Canyon* (1988). The first official "symphony" by Glass draws on songs on or associated with the 1977 album *Low* by David Bowie and Brian Eno and suggests with its name a collapsing of perceived cultural hierarchies and aesthetic distinctions between "popular" and "art" music.[118] In its first movement, "Subterraneans," two sections of contrasting mood—the opening one in a moody, atmospheric B minor and most clearly resembling the song's sound world minus the surreal electronic sonorities, the second incongruously festive with an A-major flavor—hold together through a pandiatonic focus on pitches native to B minor. The second movement, "Some Are," turns the subdued meditation of the original song into an energetic journey. In the opening

Table 9.6 The Symphonies of Philip Glass (b. 1937)

Title	Movements	Instrumentation	Comments
Symphony No. 1, "Low" (1992)	I. Subterraneans (374 mm.) II. Some Are (486 mm.) III. Warszawa (293 mm.)	Picc., 2 Flt., 2 Ob., E♭ Clar., 2 Clar., Bclar., 2 Bssn., 4 Hr., 3 Tpt., 3 Trom., Tuba, Perc. (SD, Tenor Drum, BD, Glsp., Tri., Chimes, Tamb., Cyms., Castanets, Tam-tam, Wood Block, 4 Tom-toms), Harp, Pno., Strgs.	Commissioned by the Brooklyn Philharmonic Orchestra. Based on songs from album *Low* (1977) by David Bowie and Brian Eno. First performance: August 30, 1992, Junge Deutsche Kammerphilharmonie, conducted by Dennis Russell Davies. Score published by Dunvagen. Recorded by Brooklyn Philharmonic Orchestra, conducted by Dennis Russell Davies (Point Music 438-150–2).
Symphony No. 2 (1994)	I. (561 mm.) II. (347 mm.) III. (434 mm.)	Picc., 2 Flt., 2 Ob. (1 doubling EH), E♭ Clar., 2 Clar., Bclar. (doubling Cbclar.), 2 Bssn., 4 Hr., 3 Tpt., 3 Trom., Tuba, Perc. (SD, Tenor Drum, BD, Glsp., Tri., Chimes, Hi-hat, Tamb., Cym., Tam-tam), 2 Harps, Electric Pno., Cel., Strgs.	Commissioned by the Brooklyn Philharmonic Orchestra. First performance: October 15, 1994, Brooklyn Philharmonic Orchestra, conducted by Dennis Russell Davies. (Score dedicated to this orchestra and conductor.) Score published by Dunvagen. Abridged version recorded by Vienna Radio Symphony Orchestra, conducted by Dennis Russell Davies (Nonesuch 79496–2); full version recorded by Bournemouth Symphony Orchestra, conducted by Marin Alsop (Naxos 8.559202).
Symphony No. 3 (1995)	I. Qtr=112 (104 mm.) II. Qtr=144 (201 mm.) III. Qtr=112 (242 mm.) IV. Qtr=144 (142 mm.)	Strgs. (6-4-3-2)	Commissioned by the Würth Foundation. First performance: February 15, 1995, Stuttgart Chamber Orchestra, conducted by Dennis Russell Davies. Score published by Dunvagen. Recorded by Stuttgart Chamber Orchestra, conducted by Dennis Russell Davies (Nonesuch 79581–2); Manitoba Chamber Orchestra, conducted by Anne Manson (Orange Mountain Music OMM0086); Bournemouth Symphony Orchestra, conducted by Marin Alsop (Naxos 8.559202).

Table 9.6 continued

Title	Movements	Instrumentation	Comments
Symphony No. 4, "Heroes" (1996)	I. Heroes II. Abdul Majid III. Sense of Doubt IV. Sons of the Silent Age V. Neu Köln VI. V2 Schneider	Picc., 2 Flt., 2 Ob., 2 Clar., Bclar., 2 Bssn., 3 Hr., 3 Tpt., 3 Trom., Tuba, Perc. (SD, Tenor Drum, BD, Tamb, Cyms., Tri, Vbp., Tam-tam, Castanets, Glsp.), Harp, Pno., Cel., Strgs.	Developed as ballet with choreography by Twyla Tharp. Based on songs from album "*Heroes*" (1977) by David Bowie and Brian Eno. Ballet Premiere: Tharp!, September 20, 1996. First performance: May 15, 1997, Academy of St. Martin in the Fields, conducted by Martyn Brabbins. Score published by Dunvagen. Recorded by American Composers Orchestra, conducted by Dennis Russell Davies (Point Music 454-388-2); Bournemouth Symphony Orchestra, conducted by Marin Alsop (Naxos 8.55925); Sinfonieorchester Basel, conducted by Dennis Russell Davies (Orange Mountain Music OMM0096).
Symphony No. 5, "Requiem, Bardo and Nirmanakaya" (1999)	Prologue (16 mm.) I. Before the Creation (198 mm.) II. Creation of the Cosmos (312 mm.) III. Creation of Sentient Beings (179 mm.) IV. Creation of Human Beings (199 mm.) V. Joy and Love (190 mm.) VI. Evil and Ignorance (166 mm.) VII. Suffering (303 mm.) VIII. Compassion (204 mm.) IX. Death, (187 mm.) X. Judgment and Apocalypse (288 mm.) XI. Paradise (234 mm.) XII. Dedication (198 mm.)	Picc., 2 Flt., 2 Ob., E♭ Clar., 2 Clar., Bclar., 2 Bssn., 4 Hr., 3 Tpt., 3 Trom., Tuba, Timp., Perc. (Glsp., SD, Tenor Drum, BD, Suspended Cym., Tri., Anvil, Chimes, Wood Blocks, Tamb., Cym., Xylo., Mrb., Castanets, Tam-tam [large, small]), Harp, Pno., Cel., Strgs., Vocal soloists (Soprano, Mezzo-soprano, Tenor, Baritone, Bass Baritone), SATB Chorus, Children's Chorus	Commissioned by Salzburg Festival with support of ASCII corporation. Texts from various religious traditions compiled and edited by Philip Glass, James Parks Morton, and Kusumita P. Pederson. First performance: August 28, 1999, Vienna Radio Symphony Orchestra, conducted by Dennis Russell Davies. Score published by Dunvagen. Recorded by Vienna Radio Symphony Orchestra, Morgan State University Choir, Hungarian Radio Children's Choir, and various soloists, conducted by Dennis Russell Davies (Nonesuch 79618-2).

Symphony No. 6, "Plutonian Ode" (2001)	Picc., 2 Flt., 2 Ob., E♭ Clar., 2 Clar., B clar. (doubling C♭clar.), 2 Bssn. (1 doubling C♭ssn.), 4 Hr., 3 Tpt., 3 Trom., Tuba, Timp., Perc. (Glsp., SD, Tenor Drum, BD, Suspended Cym., Tri., Anvil, Chimes, Hi-hat, Wood Blocks, Tamb., Cym., Xylo., Maracas, Castanets, Tam-tam [large, small], Tom-toms, Vbp.), Harp, Pno., Cel., Strgs., Soprano Soloist	Commissioned by Carnegie Hall Corporation and Brucknerhaus Linz for Glass's 65th birthday. Text by Allen Ginsberg. First performance: February 2, 2002, American Composers Orchestra, conducted by Dennis Russell Davies, with soprano Lauren Flanigan. Score published by Dunvagen. Recorded by Bruckner Orchester Linz, conducted by Dennis Russell Davies, with soprano Lauren Flanigan (Orange Mountain Music OMM0020).
	I. (What new element . . .) (542 mm.) II. (The Bard surveys Plutonian History) (285 mm.) III. (This ode to you O Poets) (243 mm.)	
Symphony No. 7, "A Toltec Symphony" (2004)	Picc., 2 Flt., 2 Ob., EH, 2 Clar. (1 doubling E♭ Clar.), Bclar., 2 Bssn., 4 Hr., 3 Tpt., 3 Trom., Tuba, Timp., Perc. (5 Players: Rattle, Wood Block, BD, Tam-tam [small], Glsp., Suspended Cym., Tamb., Tenor Drum, SD, Anvil, Castanets, Tri., Xylo., Tom-tom, Shaker, Mrb., Finger Cym.), Cel., Pno., Org., Harp, Strgs., SATB Chorus	Commissioned by National Symphony Orchestra for Leonard Slatkin's 60th birthday. First performance: January 20, 2005, National Symphony Orchestra and Master Chorale of Washington, conducted by Leonard Slatkin. Score published by Dunvagen. Recorded by Bruckner Orchester Linz and Linz Opera Chorus, conducted by Dennis Russell Davies (Orange Mountain Music OMM0061). Revisions reflected in recording include removal of coda (mm. 287–355) and brief extension of the previous section into the conclusion.
	I. The Corn (206 mm.) II. The Hikuri (The Sacred Root) (325 mm.) III. The Blue Deer (355 mm.)	

Table 9.6 continued

Title	Movements	Instrumentation	Comments
Symphony No. 8 (2005)	I. (604 mm.) II. (174 mm.) III. (101 mm.)	Picc. (doubling Flt.), 2 Flt., 2 Ob. (1 doubling EH), 2 Clar. (1 doubling E♭ Clar.), Bclar., 2 Bssn., 4 Hr., 3 Tpt. (1 doubling E♭ Tpt.), 3 Trom., Tuba, Timp., Perc. (4 Players: Xylo., Vbp., Glsp., Chimes, SD, Tenor Drum, BD, Suspended Cym., Hi-hat, Cowbell, Tri., Maracas, Castanets, Wood Block, Tamb., Slapstick), Pno. (doubling Cel.), Harp, Strgs.	Commissioned by the Bruckner Orchester Linz. First performance: November 2, 2005, Bruckner Orchester Linz, conducted by Dennis Russell Davies. Score published by Dunvagen. Recorded by Bruckner Orchester Linz, conducted by Dennis Russell Davies (Orange Mountain Music OMM0028).
Symphony No. 9 (2011)	I. (313 mm.) II. (516 mm.) III. (360 mm.)	2 Picc., 2 Flt., 2 Ob., EH, E♭ Clar, 2 Clar., Bclar., CBclar., 2 Bssn., 5 Hr., 4 Tpt., 4 Trom., Tuba, Timp. (6), Perc. (7 Players: Chimes, Glsp., Xylo., Mrb., Shaker, Castanets, Tamb., Wood Block, Tri., Crash Cyms., Tam-tam, Anvil, Temple Blocks, SD, Tom-toms, Tenor Drum, BD), Harp, Pno., Cel., Strgs.	Commissioned by the Bruckner Orchester Linz, Carnegie Hall, and Los Angeles Philharmonic. First performance: January 1, 2012, Bruckner Orchester Linz, conducted by Dennis Russell Davies. Score published by Dunvagen. Recorded by Bruckner Orchester Linz, conducted by Dennis Russell Davies (Orange Mountain Music OMM0081).
Symphony No. 10 (2011–12)	I. Qtr=138 (213 mm.) II. Qtr=104 (224 mm.) III. Qtr=152 (264 mm.) IV. Qtr=120 (149 mm.) V. Qtr=132 (217 mm.)	Picc., 2 Flt., 2 Ob., 3 Clar. (1 doubling E♭ Clar., 1 doubling Bclar.), 2 Bssn., 4 Hr., 3 Tpt., 3 Trom., Tuba, Timp., Perc. (6 Players: Chimes, Glsp., Xylo., Mrb., Tri., Anvil, Tamb., Crash Cyms., Castanets, Wood Block, SD, Tom-toms, Tenor Drum, BD), Cel., Pno., Harp, Strgs.	Commissioned by the Orchestre Français des Jeunes. First performance: August 9, 2012, Orchestre Français des Jeunes, conducted by Dennis Russell Davies. Score published by Dunvagen. Recorded by Bruckner Orchester Linz, conducted by David Russell Davies (Orange Mountain Music OMM0101).

Symphony No. 11 (2016)	I. Qtr=104 (136 mm.) II. Qtr=86 (181 mm.) III. Qtr=120 (216 mm.)	Picc., 2 Flt. (1 doubling Picc.), 2 Ob., EH, 2 Clar. (1 doubling E♭ Clar.), Bclar. (doubling Cbclar.), 2 Bssn., 4 Hr., 3 Tpt., 3 Trom., Tuba, Timp., Perc. (5–9 players; SD, Tenor Drum, BD, Tri., Hi-hat, Suspended Cym., Tam-tam, Anvil, Temple Blocks, 3 Tom-toms, Shaker, Tamb., Wood Block, Glsp., Xylo., Vbp.), 2 Harps, Pno., Cel., Strgs.	Commissioned by the Bruckner Orchester Linz, Istanbul Music Festival, and Queensland Symphony Orchestra. First performance: January 31, 2017, Bruckner Orchester Linz, conducted by Dennis Russell Davies. Score published by Dunvagen. Recorded by Bruckner Orchester Linz, conducted by Dennis Russell Davies (Orange Mountain Music OMM033). Chicago Symphony Orchestra conducted by Riccardo Muti (CSO Resound).
Symphony No. 12, "Lodger" (2018)	I. Fantastic Voyage II. Move On III. African Night Flight IV. Boys Keep Swinging V. Yassassin VI. Repetition VII. Red Sails	Picc., 2 Flt. (1 doubling Picc.), 3 Ob. (1 doubling EH), 3 Clar. (2 Clars. doubling E♭ Clar, 1 doubling BClar.), 2 Bssn., 4 Hr., 3 Tpt., 3 Trom., Tuba, Perc. (Glsp., Mrb. Xylo), Timp., Strgs., Solo Org., Solo vocalist	Commissioned by Los Angeles Philharmonic. Texts from album *Lodger* (1979) by David Bowie and Brian Eno. First performance: January 10, 2019, Los Angeles Philharmonic, conducted by John Adams, with Angélique Kidjo (vocalist) and James McVinnie (organ). Recorded by Filharmonie Brno, conducted by Dennis Russell Davies, with Angélique Kidjo (vocalist) and Christian Schmitt (organ) (Orange Mountain Music OMM0159).
Symphony No. 13 (2022)	Three movements	2 Flt. (1 doubling Picc.), 2 Ob., 2 Clar. (1 doubling Bclar.), 2 Bssn., 4 Hr., 3 Tpt., 2 Trom., Btrom., Tuba, Timp., Perc. (Tri., Tamb., Suspended Cym., Tam-tam, Wood Block, 3 Bongos, SD, Tenor Drum, BD), Harp, Strgs.	Commissioned by the National Arts Centre Orchestra (Canada). Symphony is a tribute to Canadian journalist Peter Jennings (1938–2005). First performance: March 30, 2022, National Arts Centre Orchestra, conducted by Alexander Shelley.
Symphony No. 14, "Liechtenstein Suite" (2021)	Three movements	Strgs.	Commissioned by LGT Young Soloists for the centennial of the Liechtenstein Global Trust. First performance: September 17, 2021, LGT Young Soloists, conducted by Alexander Gilman. Recorded by LGT Young Soloists, conducted by Mark Messenger (Orange Mountain Music OMM061).

and closing sections of this movement, descending scales contrast with the ascending ones that dominated the first movement, while a pensive, luminous middle section offers cinematic scoring and harmonic turns. The third movement, "Warszawa," features recitative-like passages for low strings, energy-building arpeggios, and a solemn resolution in B-flat major—a key with which the end of the first movement flirted. In 1996 Glass turned to the 1977 album *"Heroes,"* again by Bowie and Eno, for his Fourth Symphony ("Heroes"), which he composed as a ballet for the choreographer Twyla Tharp. In that score, Glass relied less on dense string-based textures and cultivated a lighter, more varied orchestral touch than that of the earlier rock-inspired symphony.

Sandwiched between "Low" and "Heroes" are two symphonies that offer a study in contrasts. In the three weighty movements of his Symphony No. 2, composed in 1994, Glass expanded on the possibilities of the postminimalist symphony by melding the sound world of his earlier works—particularly the propulsive irregular rhythms and generous repetition of short motives—with a stirring harmonic palette and expansive melodies. The first movement presents unusual juxtapositions of harmonies. This is heard clearly at the outset (see example 9.3), where broken E-minor triads set up a scalar E-minor melody in the English horn, which overlays soft A-flat major and F-sharp major triads.

Such moments connect closely to Glass's interest in polytonality in this symphony, which the composer linked to the work of a prior generation of modernist composers, including Darius Milhaud.[119] Turning to the second movement, broken triads in the celesta toward the end prefigure the beginning of the third movement, where the pulsing rhythms seem to take Glass's earlier music as a reference point.[120] Meanwhile, Symphony No. 3 (1995), in four relatively brief movements for a string orchestra of 19 players, shows Glass scaling his grander symphonic aspirations back to classical proportions. The lithe first movement contrasts with the feverish, almost militaristic second movement, a scherzo of sorts. The third movement, the work's longest, builds on the warmer sonorities of the lower strings and a recurring short-long-short motive, along with soaring solo violin passages and a gradual, dizzying division of the ensemble into its 19 constituent parts. With the brief fourth movement comes a return of the second movement's assertive temperament and frequent, unsettling meter changes.

For his next three symphonies, Glass turned to the human voice. Lasting more than an hour and a half, the 12 movements of Symphony No. 5, "Requiem, Bardo, and Nirmanakaya" (1999), comprise a syncretistic blend of texts from various religions translated into English, with most movements containing several excerpts from different texts in succession. This extensive work combines clear declamation and homophonic choral textures with Glass's characteristically panoramic harmonic language. In the Symphony No. 6, "Plutonian Ode" (2001), Glass sets Allen Ginsberg's poem of the same name for soprano and orchestra. The three movements correspond to the three sections of the poem; as Glass described it, "The first movement [is] a passionate outcry against nuclear contamination and pollution, the second a turn towards healing, and the final movement an epiphany arrived at through personal transformation."[121]

The Symphony No. 7, "A Toltec Symphony" (2004), revives the choral forces of the Symphony No. 5. Its title alludes to Mesoamerican culture, and its movement names refer to religious symbols of the Wixárika people of central Mexico, also known as the Huichol.[122] Glass entitled each movement after a Huichol deity: corn, peyote (the hallucinogenic cactus, also known as Hikuri), and the blue deer. The repetitious but unsteady rhythmic propulsion of the instrumental first movement, "The Corn," relies on linked strands of two, three, and

The Symphony in the United States since 1970

Example 9.3 Philip Glass, Symphony No. 2/I, mm. 1–8. Copyright © 1994 by Dunvagen Music Publishers, Inc., and Chester Music. All rights reserved. International copyright secured. Reprinted with permission.

four eighth notes, as well as on scalar melodies and stepwise oscillations; also noticeable is an austere lyricism driven by woodwinds and brass, which contrasts with the lush string-centered sonorities of his earlier symphonies. This coolness continues in the second movement, "The Hikuri (The Sacred Root)"; a chorus chants a set of syllables over a brief rising and falling, hypnosis-inducing ostinato figure that dominates the whole movement in various rhythmic and instrumental configurations—evoking, in its kaleidoscopic energy, a peyote-induced ritual. A more meditative and hymnlike third movement ("The Blue Deer") builds gradually on a series of phrases consisting of repeated chords, conspicuous grand pauses, and a more prominent and warmer role for the strings; toward the end, a striking entrance of choral chanting amplifies the alternating pattern of phrases and long rests.

In his later symphonies, Glass revisited the instrumental sound worlds of his first four efforts in the genre. He called the Symphony No. 8 (2005) "a return . . . to orchestral music where the subject of the work is the language of music itself, as in the tradition of the 18th and 19th century symphonies."[123] The whimsical, swirling, and motoric first movement, which builds to a dizzying climax of combined themes, gives way to a shorter second movement (a passacaglia), which is followed by the brief, atmospheric, rhythmically amorphous finale.[124] Especially notable among the three movements of the Symphony No. 9 (2011)—the West Coast premiere of which John Adams conducted in 2012—is the middle movement. Its sumptuous opening gives way to the composer's more familiar, insistent factorylike turbulence that dominates the movement, with blustery brass that recalls moments in Adams's own symphonic works (discussed below). The lusher, warmer opening material returns at the movement's end, this time haunted by rumbling percussion. Glass soon produced another symphonic work, having spoken jokingly about the "silly jinx" of the ninth symphony.[125] Despite that dismissal of symphonic superstition, Glass still evoked the age-old sense of a ninth symphony as a summative gesture by calling his Tenth (2012) a "Not-Nine Symphony."[126] This composition, a reworking of *Los Paisajes del Rio* (composed for the Philip Glass Ensemble to accompany the concluding fireworks display of the 2008 Expo in Zaragoza, Spain), features five movements instead of his usual three and ends with a thunderous climax that contrasts with the previous symphony's more serene conclusion.

With a significant output of large-scale symphonies that has continued into the third decade of the twenty-first century, many prestigious commissions, a steadfast advocate in conductor Dennis Russell Davies, and several performances and recordings of the works, Glass has far surpassed any expectations he or his audiences may have had for his potential role as a symphonic composer back in the late 1980s. His cosmopolitan outlook, along with the signature fusion of irregular rhythms, hypnotic repetition, large-scale instrumental effects, and political and literary themes, continues to resonate in the work of younger generations of symphonic composers. Glass's blending of texts in his Symphony No. 5, which finds its own ancestors in George Rochberg's immense Symphony No. 3 (1969) and Libby Larsen's Symphony No. 2, "Coming Forth into Day" (1986), provides a precedent for Mohammed Fairouz's more focused efforts in his own Symphony No. 3 (2010).

And Glass's own work as a symphonist has continued to move forward quickly. On January 31, 2017 (Glass's eightieth birthday), Dennis Russell Davies and the Bruckner Orchester Linz gave the world premiere of his Symphony No. 11 at Carnegie Hall.[127] And in the Symphony No. 12, "Lodger" (2019), Glass once again turned to David Bowie and Brian Eno, this time the album *Lodger* (1979)—completing his cycle of symphonies based on their Berlin Trilogy of albums. Contrary to the instrumental first and fourth symphonies, Glass employed the lyrics rather than the music from the source album; "Lodger" contains a vocal part, performed at the premiere by the Beninese singer Angélique Kidjo, whom Glass called "the first choice as singer and interpreter of the new work."[128] The premieres of two more symphonies by Glass have also taken place—the thirteenth in 2022 and the fourteenth slightly earlier, in 2021.[129]

John Corigliano (b. 1938)

John Corigliano, one of the most celebrated living American composers, has deep-seated connections to American orchestral culture. His father, John Paul Corigliano, was concertmaster of the New York Philharmonic from 1943 to 1966. In 1977, Leonard Bernstein, who worked with the elder Corigliano in that orchestra, led the premiere of John's Clarinet Concerto, with Stanley Drucker as soloist. Through Meet the Composer, Corigliano became the Chicago Symphony Orchestra's first composer-in-residence, from 1987 to 1990, and he wrote his First Symphony while in that role. A Metropolitan Opera commission generated his first opera, *The Ghosts of Versailles* (1991). In 1999, his score for the film *The Red Violin* won an Academy Award. And in 2001, his Symphony No. 2 won the Pulitzer Prize for Music. Just a few years later, his Third Symphony emerged as one of the leading works in the wind ensemble repertoire. Corigliano's three symphonies—for orchestra, string orchestra, and wind ensemble, respectively—are listed in table 9.7.

Like Glass and Walker, Corigliano did not turn to the symphony as a genre until well after achieving success as a composer. And though for Rochberg the symphony provided a fruitful venue for a return to nineteenth-century inspirations in serious music, Corigliano tended away from the avant-garde in the first place, despite his coming-of-age as a composer in the late 1950s and early 1960s.[130] He named as his early influences Walter Piston, Leonard Bernstein, Aaron Copland, and Samuel Barber, with their "combo of sounds that is clean and American, and not angst-filled, and has the kind of rhythmic profile American music has."[131] His mention of Bernstein in particular points to his eclecticism, which is a crucial component of his Symphony No. 1 (1988); Corigliano said that he "loved [Bernstein's] music, but more than that I learned so much from it. His eclecticism made it possible for me to produce works like my opera, *The Ghosts of Versailles*, and my first symphony."[132] Moreover, all those composers wrote symphonies, but Corigliano initially had no intention of doing so: "My thought [as a young composer] was that there were so many great symphonies in the repertoire that I could satisfy only my ego by writing yet another."[133]

By the late 1980s, however, Corigliano's perspective had changed. He continued, "Only the death of countless friends from AIDS prompted me to write in our largest orchestral form. Mahler once described writing a symphony as creating a world. My Symphony No. 1 was about world-scale tragedy and, I felt, needed a comparably epic form."[134] The symphony, which is one of the most performed and best-known American symphonies since 1970, capped off his tenure as the Chicago Symphony Orchestra's composer-in-residence and suggests the genre's continued resonance in the late twentieth century as a vehicle for serious and profound expression, commemoration, and nostalgia—in this case through an eclectic blend of indeterminate and gradually shifting textures and timbres.

As Corigliano described it, the first movement, "Apologue: Of Rage and Remembrance," is "highly charged and alternates between the tension of anger and the bittersweet nostalgia of remembering."[135] (An apologue, as Corigliano defined it in his program notes, is "an allegorical narrative usually intended to convey a moral."[136]) The agitated opening section features the contrast of rhythmic amorphousness with persistent pulse, as well as striking

Table 9.7 The Symphonies of John Corigliano (b. 1938)

Title	Movements	Instrumentation	Comments
Symphony No. 1 (1988)	I. Apologue: Of Rage and Remembrance (298 mm.) II. Tarantella (295 mm.) III. Chaconne: Giulio's Song (176 mm.) IV. Epilogue (64 mm.; measure numbers in score continue third movement, mm. 177–240)	Picc. (doubling Flt.), 3 Flt. (2 doubling Picc.), 3 Ob., EH, 4 Clar. (includes A, B♭, E♭, Bclar., and optional Cbclar.), 3 Bssn., Cbssn., 6 Hr., 5 Tpt., 4 Trom., 2 Tubas, Timp, Perc. (5–6 Players: Glsp, Crotales, Vbp., Xylo., Mrb., Chimes [2 sets], SD, 3 Tom-toms, 3 Roto-toms, Field Drum, Tenor Drum, 2 BD, Suspended Cym., Tam-tam, Finger Cyms., 3 Temple Blocks, Tamb., Anvil, Metal Plate [with Hammer], Brake Drum, Tri., Flexatone, Police Whistle, Whip, Ratchet), Harp, Pno. (also plays offstage Pno. part), Strgs. (1–2 stands of Vln. 2 doubling Mandolin)	Dedicated to the memory of Sheldon Shkolnik. Commissioned by the Chicago Symphony Orchestra through Meet the Composer. Winner of the 1991 University of Louisville Grawemeyer Award for Music Composition. Winner of 1991 Grammy Award for Best Contemporary Composition. First performance: March 15, 1990, Chicago Symphony Orchestra, conducted by Daniel Barenboim. Score published by G. Schirmer. Recorded by Chicago Symphony Orchestra, conducted by Daniel Barenboim (Erato 2292-45601-2), winner of 1991 Grammy for Best Orchestral Performance; National Symphony Orchestra, conducted by Leonard Slatkin (RCA Victor Red Seal 09026-68450-2), winner of 1996 Grammy for Best Classical Album; National Orchestral Institute Philharmonic, conducted by David Alan Miller (Naxos 8.559782).
Symphony No. 2 (2000)	I. Prelude (36 mm.) II. Scherzo (236 mm.) III. Nocturne (112 mm.) IV. Fugue (143 mm.) V. Postlude (119 mm.)	Strgs. (6-5-4-2 minimum)	Dedicated to Susan Feder. Commissioned by the Boston Symphony Orchestra. Based on Corigliano's String Quartet (1996). Winner of the 2001 Pulitzer Prize in Music. First performance: November 30, 2000, Boston Symphony Orchestra, conducted by Seiji Ozawa. Score published by G. Schirmer. Recorded by Helsinki Philharmonic, conducted by John Storgårds (Ondine ODE 1039-2); I Musici de Montréal, conducted by Yuli Turkovsky (Chandos CHSA5035).

| Symphony No. 3, "Circus Maximus" (2004) | I. Introitus (62 mm.)
II. Screen/Siren (measure count varies by instrument)
III. Channel Surfing (118 mm.)
IV. Night Music (31 mm.)
V. Night Music II (102 mm.)
VI. Circus Maximus (32 mm.)
VII. Prayer (62 mm.)
VIII. Coda: Veritas (18 mm.) | Large wind ensemble, divided into three groups:

Stage Band:
4 Flt. (2 doubling Picc.), 4 Ob. (1 doubling EH), 3 Clar. (9 players minimum), 2 Bclar., Cbclar., 3 Bssn., Cbssn., 4 B♭ Tpt. (2 doubling D Tpt.), 4 Hr., 4 Trom., 2 Euph., 2 Tubas, Pno., Harp, Timp., Perc. (4–5 players; includes a 12-gauge shotgun)

Surround Band (stationed individually and in specific groups around audience):
Clar., 4 Sax. (2 Asax., 1 Tsax., 1 Barsax.), 11 Tpt., 2 Hr., 3 Perc., Cb.

Marching Band:
Picc. (doubling Flt.), E♭ Clar., 2 Tpt. (Tpt. 5 and 7 from Surround Band), 2 Trom., Perc. (Perc. 2 from Surround Band) | Commissioned by the School of Music at the University of Texas at Austin for the University of Texas Wind Ensemble.

First performance: February 16, 2005, University of Texas Wind Ensemble, conducted by Jerry Junkin, to whom the score is dedicated.

Score published by G. Schirmer.

Recorded by University of Texas Wind Ensemble, conducted by Jerry Junkin (Naxos 8.559601). |

timbres that suggest painful screams and howls. This is achieved through aleatoric means: at the outset, for instance, strings begin by playing A but switch strings gradually, building from controlled vibrato to a fiery pitch fluctuation and an abrupt descent to G-sharp—a passage of shifting string clusters reminiscent of Gloria Coates' Symphony No. 1, "Music on Open Strings" (1972–73), and Krzysztof Penderecki's *Threnody to the Victims of Hiroshima* (1960). Later, selected instruments play notated passages *ad libitum* and unsynchronized, in a manner redolent of Witold Lutosławski's "aleatoric counterpoint." In the movement's nostalgic middle section, aching strings faintly suggestive of Shostakovich accompany a tango by Isaac Albéniz (in Leopold Godowsky's arrangement of 1921), played on offstage piano (m. 79)—an Ivesian flourish that recalls the trumpet playing "Taps" in *Decoration Day*. As Elizabeth Bergman aptly described this section of Corigliano's symphony, "Already nostalgic and wistful in its original character, the disembodied tango sounds as if it emanates from a recording that had been playing all the while, but is audible now only that the orchestral fury of the first section has subsided."[137] This tango had been frequently performed by Sheldon Shkolnik, Corigliano's friend and a noted concert pianist.[138] It thus memorializes Shkolnik in advance of his passing, as this movement was specifically dedicated to his memory.[139] (In fact, Shkolnik attended the first performances on March 15–17, 1990, but died the following week.[140]) The orchestra then engulfs the slow, lyrical material of the middle section, but the piano returns briefly at the end of the movement (m. 284). The striking first movement, then, provides an eclectic mix of styles and techniques drawn from various twentieth-century composers.

The symphony's Scherzo, an expansion of the "Tarantella" from Corigliano's *Gazebo Dances* (1973), thrives on abrupt disjunctions in melody, timbre, and rhythm as well as on extremes of tempo and dynamics. The movement is dedicated to the Baldwin Piano Company executive Jack Romann. "The association of madness and my piano piece"—by which Corigliano meant the tarantella's traditional role in southern Italian culture as a dance to cure insanity caused by a spider bite—"proved both prophetic and bitterly ironic," Corigliano wrote, "when my friend, whose wit and intelligence were legendary in the music field, became insane as a result of AIDS dementia." This frightening movement—designed, according to the composer, to "picture some of the schizophrenic and hallucinatory images that would have accompanied that madness, as well as the moments of lucidity"—juxtaposes deceptively gentle passages, including wistful clarinet solos, with pounding percussion and thunderous fanfares, often with no transition.[141] In a final section that evokes the third movement of Mahler's Symphony No. 9, the main tarantella melody travels from the low, dark registers of the contrabass clarinet, stated there at a glacial pace, to the frantic heights of the piccolos, seemingly at warp speed; what follows is an explosive, visceral orchestral spasm. On the whole, this striking movement draws its special emotional force from the way it transforms the tarantella, an innocuous dance, into a devastating depiction of both the suddenness and the turmoil of mental illness—a truly nightmarish application of Mahler's distortion of the familiar. In this way, one of the movement's ancestors is the third movement of Mahler's First Symphony (1888), which distorts the familiar tune of "Frère Jacques" into a funeral march.

The weighty third movement of the Symphony No. 1 is an Adagio in memory of the cellist Giulio Sorrentino and others. What Corigliano describes as a "chaconne, based on 12 pitches (and the chords they produce)" sets the stage for a series of richly chromatic melodies, each referring to a deceased friend who is named in the published score. The movement thus offers a musical parallel to the AIDS Memorial Quilt, which Corigliano identified as the inspiration for the entire symphony, especially because the individual panels were created by the victims' loved ones, and he similarly hoped "to memorialize in music those I have lost, and reflect on those I am losing." The idea of a musical quilt itself plays a special role in the third movement, in which, as Corigliano described it, "friends are recalled in a quilt-like interweaving of motivic melodies." The first melody, presented after the "hazily dissolving" string sonorities of the chaconne, begins at m. 9 and was inspired by a recording of Corigliano and Sorrentino improvising in 1962, with Corigliano on piano. To create the other melodies, Corigliano asked William M. Hoffman, librettist of *The Ghosts of Versailles*, to write sentences in their memory; Corigliano set the texts for solo instruments and then deleted those texts, leaving only the instrumental melodies. But just as the orchestra had earlier interrupted a nostalgic section in the first movement, large forces again take over, drowning out the sense of calm remembrance. Here, the chaos from the first movement morphs into a Mahlerian funeral march—the climactic point of the symphony. The brief final movement features what Corigliano called "waves" of cascading sonorities in the brass to suggest timelessness.[142] This epilogue (whose measure numbers in the published score continue from the previous movement), revives material from the other movements before disappearing into the distance—or the past. As seen in example 9.4, these "waves" intersect poignantly with the return of the offstage piano tango from the first movement. (As in the published score, this example is in C.)

Partly because of its powerful message, Corigliano' Symphony No. 1 resonated well beyond its premiere weekend. Fittingly, Mark Adamo called it "an occasion piece, for an occasion— AIDS—that, grimly, goes on and on."[143] After Daniel Barenboim led its premiere with the Chicago Symphony Orchestra, their recording garnered two Grammy Awards in 1991, one for Best Orchestral Performance and one for Best Contemporary Composition. The recording with Leonard Slatkin and the National Symphony Orchestra earned a Grammy for Best Classical Album for 1996. (The same year, incidentally, Corigliano's String Quartet, composed for the Cleveland Quartet's final tour and eventually to be developed into his Symphony No. 2, won for Best Classical Contemporary Composition.) The Slatkin record was named for the first track, *Of Rage and Remembrance* (1991), in which Corigliano refashioned the symphony's third movement into a haunting piece for mezzo-soprano, boy soprano, men's chorus, low strings, and chimes. Commissioned by the Seattle, New York, and San Francisco gay men's choruses, it restores Hoffman's memorial texts, which Corigliano had assigned to instruments in the symphony. The newer work suggests a more specific message than does the symphonic movement on which it is based: as Bergman observed, with its texts "the chaconne is no longer a generalized, tragic work about loss but a memorial piece that reckons openly with AIDS and its human toll."[144]

Even after the success of his first symphony, Corigliano remained a hesitant symphonist, initially declining the Boston Symphony Orchestra's commission for a symphony to recognize the hundredth anniversary of Symphony Hall's opening in 1900. Changing his mind, he turned to his String Quartet and decided to rework it for string orchestra as his Symphony No. 2 (2000). As he wrote, "This also satisfied my reservations about writing another symphony in a repertoire of masterpieces: the string symphony is another animal entirely, and there aren't many of them."[145] Indeed, this powerful composition shows Corigliano exploiting the string orchestra's sonic potential, including effects such as muting, harmonics, microtones, vibratoless playing, and the setting of the string quartet apart from the rest of the string body.

The slowly unfolding first movement of his Symphony No. 2, "Prelude," begins with staggered entrances of chromatically and microtonally sliding string passages, yielding a shifting mass of sound that recalls texture-centered works such as György Ligeti's *Atmosphères* (1961).

Example 9.4 John Corigliano Symphony No. 1/3–4, mm. 184–91. Copyright © 1990 by G. Schirmer, Inc. (ASCAP). International copyright secured. All rights reserved. Reprinted with permission.

The exhilarating arrival of a stable C-major sonority in m. 23 offers a moment of respite before the violently repeating clusters at the beginning of the second movement, "Scherzo." These repeating collections alternate with frantic, scurrying motives. A lyrical middle section, slightly more metrical than the opening, expands on the brief hint of C major from the opening movement before leading to a reprise of the clamorous opening.

In the third movement, "Nocturne," hazy textures from the Prelude return in a reminiscence of the composer's time in Fez, Morocco; in light of this recollection, the chromaticism here carries an exoticist tinge. As Corigliano wrote, "My room overlooked the Old City and during the night (about 4 a.m.) I was awakened by the calls of the muezzins from the many mosques in the city. First one, then another, and finally dozens of independent calls created a glorious counterpoint, and at one moment all of the calls held on to a single note (pure accident) and the result was a major chord." (Corigliano was referring to the gradual emergence of G-sharp major in mm. 79–81.) He continued, "The calls died away, a cock crowed and a dog barked to announce the sun. This Nocturne recalls that memory—the serenity of the Moroccan night, the calls (here composed of motivic fragments of repeated notes and minor thirds) and the descent to silence and the dawn."[146]

The fourth movement is a rhythmically inventive (and disorienting) fugue in which each voice seems to proceed at its own tempo. Occasional repeated passages centered on C-major chords offer respite. In the final movement, "Postlude," oscillating minor thirds (sometimes altered by quarter tones) recall the "Abschied" from Mahler's *Das Lied von der Erde* (1908–09). This connection to Mahler's own farewell-centered work is likely not a coincidence; as Corigliano wrote about his own movement, the "registral distance between the solo violin and the other strings" in the movement's opening "is meant to impart a feeling of farewell to the entire movement." The symphony closes with a brief return of the wavelike opening material of the first movement—fading out with what Corigliano called the composition's initial "asynchronous ambient-sounding threads."[147]

Corigliano again steered clear of the standard symphony orchestra with his most recent symphonic composition, the Symphony No. 3, "Circus Maximus," for large wind ensemble (2004). Composed for Jerry F. Junkin and the University of Texas Wind Ensemble, this theatrical work makes full and adventurous use of a concert hall space through its scoring for a stage band, a marching band, and a "surround band" positioned in the tiers; the score contains a detailed visual map of the placement of these forces throughout the hall. Named for the enormous ancient Roman stadium, the work evokes a pessimism about twenty-first-century life. As Corigliano wrote, "The parallels between the high decadence of Rome and our present time are obvious. Entertainment dominates our reality, and ever-more extreme 'reality' shows dominate our entertainment. Many of us have become as bemused by the violence and humiliation that flood the 500-plus channels of our television screens as the mobs of imperial Rome, who considered the devouring of human beings by starving lions just another Sunday show." He added that the symphony, with its eight continuous movements, "was built both to embody and to comment on this massive and glamorous barbarity." It begins with the "Introitus," in which aggressive fanfares emanate from the surround band before the stage group joins in for a cacophonous conclusion; here, the repeated and sustained D in the trumpets at the very start draw a startling link to the strings' screaming A at the outset of Symphony No. 1. "Screen/Siren" centers on a saxophone quartet and string bass with their "seductive inflections" from the hall's second tier; this leads to the riotous "Channel Surfing," in which percussion simulates the clicking of a remote control as rhythms, textures, and timbres shift.

Two complementary movements, "Night Music I" and "Night Music II," follow. The first is a nostalgic one that Corigliano described as "Tranquility in nature" but whose blanket of sound the quietly howling brass unsettles. In the contrasting second, "the hyper night-music of the cities pulse with hidden energy and sudden flashes."

In the sixth movement, "Circus Maximus," material from the other movements returns in a sort of hyperactive recapitulation that evokes the raucous *Circenses* movement of Ottorino Respighi's symphonic poem *Feste Romane* (1928): "A band marching down the aisles counterpoints the onstage performers and the surrounding fanfares. Exuberant voices merge into chaos and a frenzy of overstatement." The cacophony culminates in a deafening climax that yields to the serene "Prayer" movement, where "a long-lined serene melody is set against a set of plagal (IV-I) cadences that circle through all the keys. The rising line grows in intensity against the constantly changing harmonies as the chords overlap from stage to surround trumpets and back." That movement's vision of solace is, however, only an illusion. In the brief "Coda: Veritas," the alarming energy of the first movement returns, and the movement concludes with a gunshot—specifically, as the score hauntingly stipulates, a twelve-gauge shotgun firing a "full load/black powder 'popper' made by Winchester" that may require "a licensed pyro-technician" instead of a percussionist.[148] That gunshot occurs on a descent from a sustained A to a sudden G-sharp—the same gesture with which the Symphony No. 1 begins. According to Corigliano, though, this parallel between the two works was unintentional, a reflection of his personal musical style rather than a conscious choice to connect the two compositions.[149] In both cases, the jarring melodic turn aptly captures the sense of distress that permeates these compositions' programmatic conceptions.

Taken as a group, Corigliano's symphonies encompass a range of approaches typically associated with the later twentieth century—inventive timbral effects, asynchronous rhythms, twelve-tone writing, fragmented forms, a creative use of physical space and offstage effects, aleatory, and graphic notation. In creating these symphonic canvases, Corigliano has been called "eclectic" and an "American syncretist."[150] Indeed, his symphonies—especially the first movement of the Symphony No. 1—certainly offer evidence for such labels. But much as with other composers noted for innovative techniques—such as Mason Bates, one of Corigliano's successors as a Chicago Symphony Orchestra composer-in-residence—Corigliano did not incorporate innovative techniques into his symphonies for their own sake. Rather, with their vivid extramusical associations, these works have helped extend the Romantic program symphony—and the very idea of the symphony as a vehicle to convey profound, sometimes explicitly identified, personal and philosophical statements—into the twenty-first century.[151]

William Bolcom (b. 1938)

William Bolcom is one of the most prolific of recent symphonists. A pianist who has specialized in American vernacular music, Bolcom studied composition with Darius Milhaud, Olivier Messiaen, and Leland Smith, and he went on to teach at the University of Michigan from 1973 to 2008.[152] A highly acclaimed composer, Bolcom won the Pulitzer Prize for his *12 New Etudes for Piano* (completed in 1986), and he has written nine orchestral symphonies and one for band (with the third symphony technically a symphony for chamber orchestra). Notably, his first two symphonies, which employ tonal elements, predate Rochberg's much-touted conversion from serialism. Like Rochberg—whom, as we have seen, Bolcom admired for his "emotional intensity and an openness of approach"—Bolcom drew on a late nineteenth-century heritage. But in his symphonies, Bolcom went further than Rochberg in embracing

Table 9.8 The Symphonies of William Bolcom (b. 1938)

Title	Movements	Instrumentation	Comments
Symphony No. 1 (1957)	I. Allegro molto (256 mm.) II. Adagio (95 mm.) III. Tempo di menuetto (44 mm.) IV. Allegro (159 mm.)	2 Flt. (1 doubling Picc.), Ob., Clar., Bssn. 4 Hr., 2 Tpt, Btrom., Timp., Pno, Perc. (SD, BD, Cyms.), Strgs.	First performance: August 16, 1957, Aspen Music Festival student orchestra, conducted by Carl Eberl. Score slightly revised in 1989. Recorded by Louisville Orchestra, conducted by Lawrence Leighton Smith (First Edition LCD007/FECD-0033).
Symphony No. 2 ("Oracles") (1962–64)	One movement (346 mm.)	2 Flt. (1 doubling Picc.), 2 Ob. (1 doubling EH), E♭ Clar. (doubling E♭ Asax.), Clar. (doubling Bclar.), 2 Bssn., Cbssn., 2 Hr. (2 more Hr. optional), 2 Tpt., 3 Trom., Tuba, Perc. (Glsp., Chimes, Tri., Tamb, Tam-tam, SD, 2 graduated suspended Cyms., 4 graduated tom-toms, BD), Harp, Cel., Strgs.	First performance: Seattle Symphony Orchestra, May 2, 1965, conducted by Milton Katims. Score published by E. B. Marks.
Symphony No. 3 for chamber orchestra (1979)	I. Alpha (176 mm.) II. Scherzo Vitale (302 mm.) III. Chiaroscuro (87 mm.) IV. Omega (100 mm.)	Flt. (doubling Alto Flt. and Picc.), 2 Ob. (1 doubling EH), Clar. (doubling E♭ Clar. and Bclar.), 2 Bssn., 2 Hr., Pno. (doubling Cel. and Electric Pno.), Strgs.	Commissioned by Saint Paul Chamber Orchestra. First performance: September 15, 1979, Saint Paul Chamber Orchestra, conducted by Dennis Russell Davies. Score published by E. B. Marks. Recorded by Louisville Orchestra, conducted by Lawrence Leighton Smith (First Edition LCD007/FECD-0033).
Symphony No. 4 (1986)	I. Soundscape (Allegro; with great energy) (504 mm.) II. The Rose (Largo, misterioso) (367 mm.)	Picc., 2 Flt., 2 Ob., EH, 2 Clar. (1 doubling E♭ Clar.), Bclar., 2 Bssn. (1 doubling Cbssn.), 4 Hr., 4 Tpt., 4 Trom., Tuba, Timp., Perc. (3 SDs [small, large, tenor], Mrb., Glsp., Crotales, 3 Suspended Cyms. [small, medium, large], 4 Tom-toms, Tam-tam, Tri., Chimes, BD), Harp (amplified slightly), Pno., (doubling Cel.), Strgs., Mezzo-Soprano soloist	Commissioned by the St. Louis Symphony. Second movement sets the poem "The Rose" by Theodore Roethke. First performance: March 13, 1987, St. Louis Symphony Orchestra, conducted by Leonard Slatkin; Joan Morris, mezzo-soprano. Score published by E. B. Marks. Recorded by St. Louis Symphony Orchestra, conducted by Leonard Slatkin, with Joan Morris (mezzo-soprano) (New World 80356).

Table 9.8 continued

Title	Movements	Instrumentation	Comments
Symphony No. 5 (1989, rev. 1991)	I. Pensive/Active (233 mm.) II. Scherzo Mortale (245 mm.) III. Hymne à l'Amour (79 mm.) IV. Machine (87 mm.)	3 Flt. (1 doubling Picc.), 2 Ob., EH, 2 Clar. (1 doubling E♭ Clar.), Bclar., 2 Bssn., Cbssn., 4 Hr., 3 Tpt., 3 Trom., Tuba, Timp., Perc. (Button Gongs [Thai Gongs], Crotales, Bass Mrb., Small Cyms., Sizzle Cyms. [medium], Large Cyms. [suspended], SD, Tenor Drum, Piccolo Drums [all with snare], BD [small], Tam-tam [large], Glsp.), Harp, Strgs.	Commissioned by the Philadelphia Orchestra and composed in memory of Stephen Sell. First performance: January 11, 1990, Philadelphia Orchestra, conducted by Dennis Russell Davies. Score published by E. B. Marks. Recorded by American Composers Orchestra, conducted by Dennis Russell Davies (Phoenix PHCD164/Argo 433 077-2); fourth movement appears on *Earquake* (Ondine 894-2), recorded by the Helsinki Philharmonic Orchestra, conducted by Leif Segerstam.
Symphony No. 6 (1996–97)	I. Not too slow (158 mm.) II. Burlesk (241 mm.) III. Adagio lirico (74 mm.) IV. March II contre les Philistins (152 mm.)	3 Flt. (1 doubling Picc.), 3 Ob. (1 doubling EH), 3 Clar. (1 doubling E♭ Clar., 1 doubling Asax., 1 doubling Bclar.), 3 Bssn. (1 doubling Cbssn.), 4 Hr., 3 Tpt. (1 doubling Flugelhorn), 3 Trom., Tuba, Timp., Perc. (Glsp., Crotales, Tri., 2 Wood Blocks, Ratchet, Bongos, Tamb., Tenor Drum, Large Suspended Cym. [large], BD [large], Trap set), Harp, Pno., Strgs.	Commissioned by the National Symphony Orchestra as part of Meet the Composer/Arts Endowment Commissioning Music/USA. Score published by E. B. Marks. First performance: February 26, 1998, National Symphony Orchestra, conducted by Leonard Slatkin. *Adagio Lirico* is a newly orchestrated version of the *Molto Adagio*, which was commissioned by the Lancaster Symphony Orchestra for its 50th anniversary. *Burlesk* contains a quotation of "Soft Eyes" by Vincent Youmans.
Symphony No. 7 ("Symphonic Concerto") (2002)	Act I. Dramatis Personae: Exposition (235 mm.) Act II. Conspiracy: Confrontation (174 mm.) Interlude (60 mm.) Act III. Climax: Dénouement (224 mm.)	Solo instruments (Ob., Clar., Bssn., 3 Tpt., Trom., Vln., Vla., Vlc. Cb.), 3 Flt. (1 doubling Picc.), Ob., EH, Clar., Bclar., Bssn., Cbssn., 4 Hr., 3 Trom., Tuba, Timp., Perc. (Glsp., Crotales, Xylo., Thai Gongs, 4 Graduated Tom-toms, Tri., 3 Graduated Suspended Cyms., Chinese Cym., Pair of Crash Cyms., Tamb., SD, Tenor Drum, BD), Strgs.	Commissioned by the MET Orchestra. First performance: May 19, 2002, MET Orchestra, conducted by James Levine. Score published by E. B. Marks.

Work	Movements	Instrumentation	Notes
Symphony No. 8 (2005–7)	I. Rintrah Roars (79 mm.) II. The Shadowy Daughter of Urthona (170 mm.) III. This Theme Calls Me (109 mm.) IV. A Song of Liberty (249 mm.)	4 Flt. (2 doubling Picc.), 2 Ob., EH, 2 Clar. (1 doubling Eb Clar.), Bclar., 2 Bssn., Cbssn., 6 Hr., 4 Tpt., 4 Trom., Tuba, Timp., Perc. (Bass Mrb., Glsp., Vbp., Chimes, Crotales, Thai Gongs, SD, BD, 3 Suspended Cyms., Gong [large], Anvil, 4 Tom-toms, Suspended Cym. [large], 2 Tam-tams, Tri.), Harp, Pno. (doubling Cel.), Strgs., SATBB Chorus	Commissioned for the Boston Symphony Orchestra's 125th anniversary. Texts by William Blake, drawn from *Prophetic Books*. First performance: February 28, 2008, Boston Symphony Orchestra and Tanglewood Festival Chorus, conducted by James Levine. Score published by E. B. Marks. Recorded by Boston Symphony Orchestra and Tanglewood Festival Chorus, conducted by James Levine (BSO Classics 0903-D).
First Symphony for Band (2008)	I. Ô tempora ô mores (95 mm.) II. Scherzo tenebroso (195 mm.) III. Andantino pastorale (91 mm.) IV. Marches funéraires et dansantes (146 mm.)	6 Flt. (2 doubling Picc.), 3 Ob., EH, 9 Clar. (1 doubling Eb Clar.), 3 Bssn., Cbssn. (doubling Eb Cbclar. and/or Sax. *ad lib*.), Sopsax., Asax., Tsax., Barsax., Cornet, 6 Tpt. (1 doubling Picc. Tpt. *ad lib*.), 6 Hr., 3 Trom., 2 Euph., 3 Tubas, Harp, Pno. (doubling Cel.), Timp., Perc. (Concert BD, Trap Set, Bongos [4 graduated] Chinese Cym., Crotales, 2 Flexatones [4 optional, if 7 players], Glsp., Slapstick, Maracas, Mrb., Tam-tam [large], Temple Blocks [set of 5], Tenor Drum with snares, Thai Gongs, 4 Concert Tom-toms, Tri.), Cb.	Commissioned by the Big 10 Band Directors Foundation. Originally planned as Symphony No. 9. First performance: February 6, 2009, University of Michigan Symphony Band, conducted by Michael Haithcock. Score published by E. B. Marks. Recorded by Middle Tennessee State University Wind Ensemble, conducted by Reed Thomas (Naxos 8.572732).
Symphony No. 9 (2011–12)	One movement (348 mm.)	3 Flt. (1 doubling Picc.), 3 Ob. (1 doubling EH), 2 Clar., Bclar. (doubling Eb Clar.), 2 Bssn., Cbssn., 4 Hr., 3 Tpt. (1 doubling Flugelhorn), 3 Trom., Tuba, 4 Timp., Perc. (Crotales, Xylo., Slapstick, Tamb., SD, Gongs [Thai or pitched], Cyms. [small, medium, large], Pno. (doubling Cel.), Strgs.	Commissioned for the Centennial of Rice University. First performance: October 12, 2012, Shepherd School Symphony Orchestra, conducted by Larry Rachleff. Score published by E. B. Marks.

a wide spectrum of styles and effects, folding them into an impressively varied symphonic *oeuvre*. His symphonies are listed in table 9.8.

In both his boisterous four-movement Symphony No. 1 and his Sibelius-inspired one-movement Symphony No. 2, "Oracles," Bolcom foreshadowed the broader acceptance of tonality in compositional communities in the later twentieth century. The first symphony, composed while studying with Milhaud at the Aspen Music School in 1957, is, as Bolcom described it, "a short and sardonic symphony in the classical mold," with a fourth movement that sounds "vaguely like *The Yellow Rose of Texas* until the general melee at the end."[153] In his Symphony No. 2, "Oracles" (1962–64), Bolcom made use of a large orchestra that included a sizable percussion component—a change from the more chamber-like intimacy of the First Symphony, with its small wind section. Bolcom wrote in 2003 that in "Oracles," composed for his doctor of musical arts degree at Stanford, he saw "the emergence of my present style in my tonal underpinning of an essentially total-chromatic style, quite unusual for a time when the received wisdom was that tonality was dead."[154] Using Sibelius's Seventh Symphony as a reference point for its one-movement structure, Bolcom wrote that its "'oracular,' mystical atmosphere . . . was drawn from my personal experience. Despite the mood of that time, so dismissive of key centers or traditional harmonic practice, I could not find a clearer, better way to express the epiphany I'd felt than the resolution in C major that occurs at the end of this symphony."[155] (Of course, C major is also the key of Sibelius's work.)

With its eclectic embrace of techniques and styles, evocative movement titles and inscription from the Book of Common Prayer ("Man, that is borne of woman, hath but a short time to live, and is full of misery. He cometh up and is cut down, like a flower; he fleeth as it were a shadow, and never continueth in one stay"), Bolcom's Symphony No. 3 for chamber orchestra (1979) charts territory well beyond his first two symphonies. The first movement, "Alpha," layers a rhythmically free section of quiet string glissandi in high registers with animated solos for alto flute, bassoon, and English horn. Bolcom considered this a "half-humorous visualization of three spirits . . . who watch over the process of our birth and death." In m. 9, celesta and flute outline slowly unfolding D-major triads, but an orchestral climax transitions into a contrasting section with hints of an exposition (it even contains a repeat) and development; as Bolcom described the movement, it is "referentially" linked to classical models, not "any sort of attempt to write within the form." In the second movement, "Scherzo Vitale," a short, jazzy electric piano riff coexists with suggestions of chorales in the winds as well as a sweeping tune in the strings that evokes 1930s American popular song. But by the end of the movement, the material dissolves into what Bolcom called "no more than a handful of musical chromosomes."

A sense of disorientation continues with the brief third movement, "Chiaroscuro," a "delicate balance between atonal elements and D-flat Major," operating "as an extended 'leading tone' to the opening D Major triad of the last movement." The D-major arpeggio that starts "Omega" (and also concludes its opening section) recalls not just the similar arpeggio from the first movement but also, in its long-breathed string-driven texture, the conclusion of Mahler's Ninth Symphony. In m. 77, the rising chords of the electric piano suggest a heavenly ascent; they lead to the same descending D-major triads from the first movement in the celesta and flute, with a defamiliarizing modal countermelody in the oboe. The woodwind "spirits" return over the mysterious string glissandi from the first movement, but here they dissolve upward, as if into the ether. For Bolcom, the similarity between the beginning and end of the symphony relates to his "own feeling that we were born from the collective unconscious and eventually return to it."[156]

With his Symphony No. 4 (1986), Bolcom turned to the human voice. The relatively concise first movement, "Soundscape," juxtaposes contrasting sounds at a breakneck pace. It includes scurrying motives for high winds and strings that suggest a scherzo, arresting percussion flourishes, majestic brass fanfares—and, occasionally, a stunning, gleaming major triad. Time slows in the protracted second movement, a setting of "The Rose" by the American poet Theodore Roethke (1908–1963) sung by a mezzo-soprano. Here, Bolcom's subtle changes in orchestration evoke the poem's seascapes, birdsong, and machine-related imagery, and the vocal line ranges from speech through *Sprechstimme* to the resplendent triadic melody of the movement's coda. There, a diatonic C-major section realizes the full potential of the major sonorities heard sporadically throughout the symphony; this coda, beginning with "And I rejoiced in being what I was," at m. 347, provides a structural counterpoint to the earlier arrival on C-sharp major at the central word *roses* in m. 194. At m. 226, the work engages loosely with the perennial question of what defines the "American sound": Bolcom blends free rhythms and spare accompaniment with spoken recitation and *Sprechstimme* on the lines, "What do they tell us, sound and silence? / I think of American sounds in this silence."

Bolcom returned to purely instrumental forces for his next symphonic work. The road to the Symphony No. 5 (1989) was not a direct one, and Bolcom's comments about it reveal the weight the genre still carries. "When the time came to give the Philadelphia Orchestra its expected commission," he wrote, "I took the onus off by deciding not to write a symphony after all, only to find that the piece was becoming a symphony anyway!" Bolcom described the first movement as a "terse sonata-allegro." It suggests Mahler in its expressive melodic leaps, as well as Shostakovich in its quasi-tonality, humorous orchestration shifts, and martial use of percussion. As seen in example 9.5, the start of the second movement ("Scherzo Mortale"), a quotation of the wedding march from Wagner's *Lohengrin* in contrabassoon is layered with the hymn "Abide with Me" in the double bass, launching an incongruous journey in which motifs from *Tristan und Isolde* are transformed into a seductively swaggering dance. This hair-raising movement serves as a modern take on the ironically woeful third movement of Mahler's First Symphony, plugs into a tradition of humorous adaptations of material from *Tristan und Isolde*, and captures Bolcom's animated musical personality.

The "Hymne à l'Amour," a colorful orchestration of the final piece in Bolcom's *12 New Etudes for Piano*, provides what the composer called an "ironic contrast" to the following movement, "Machine." Bolcom wrote of this final movement that "the impersonal non-human regularity of current dance music is the metaphor" for the journey from G minor to "tonal entropy by the end"—a "mirror of the first movement." The work's "noisy conclusion," Bolcom added, "was part of the commission, Dennis Russell Davies having requested something with which to end a concert."[157] Throughout the symphony, Bolcom's exuberant orchestration, along with the playful use of serious materials in the second movement, places a lens of tragicomic ambiguity on the symphony's almost absurdly insistent ending, itself perhaps a riff on Beethoven's Fifth Symphony.

Like Symphony No. 5, composed in memory of Stephen Sell (the executive director of the Philadelphia Orchestra and a friend of Bolcom's), Symphonies Nos. 6 and 7 contend directly with death. The third movement of Symphony No. 6 (1996–97) serves as a memorial to Bolcom's mother, and the second movement includes a tune by the Broadway composer Vincent Youmans—highlighting Bolcom's fervent connection to American popular traditions.[158] The Symphony No. 7, "Symphonic Concerto" (2002), started as a request by James Levine for a concerto for orchestra—specifically the Metropolitan Opera Orchestra—but developed into

Example 9.5 William Bolcom, Symphony No. 5/2, mm. 1–6. Copyright © 1992 by Edward B. Marks Music Company and Bolcom Music. Used with permission.

"a work with deeper formal overtones than the usual concerto."[159] Calling it "an opera for opera orchestra," Bolcom likened the work to "a Shakespearean play, with prominent 'characters' and smaller supporting parts."[160] The tragic events of September 11, 2001, inspired the composition of the interlude—the symphony's third movement—between the second and third "acts." Anthony Tommasini, writing in the *New York Times*, called this interlude "the symphony's most immediately affecting music" in a larger fabric that melded hints of "soulful jazz, raucous rock, wistful folk song and Coplandesque Americana"—all "without a trace of condescension."[161]

With his immense Symphony No. 8 (2005–07), Bolcom returned to the human voice and produced his largest symphony—both in terms of forces and length. The origins of the work date back to his time at Stanford, where he wrote his Symphony No. 2. While there, "a musical phrase for chorus on 'Rintrah roars & shakes his fires in the burden'd air,' the opening line from Blake's *The Marriage of Heaven and Hell*, came to me. It has taken 40-odd years for that phrase to find its home, near the beginning of the first movement of my Eighth Symphony."[162] (Blake was far from new for Bolcom; his *Songs of Innocence and of Experience*, first performed in 1984, is a three-hour long oratorio that sets 46 Blake poems and occupied Bolcom for much of his career.) In the Eighth Symphony, Bolcom's choice of what he called "thorny Blake prophecy" to set in four consecutive choral movements was meant to comment on "our nation's survival and, by extension—since we are so powerful and so clumsy—the survival of the rest of the earth."[163] Angular melodies, choral roars, and forceful instrumental interjections—especially in brass and percussion—highlight this symphony's hefty ambitions.

Bolcom's First Symphony for Band (2008), commissioned by Big 10 band directors, was initially intended as his ninth symphony. At that time, in 2008 (anticipating Philip Glass's own dismissal of the storied curse of the ninth symphony), Bolcom wrote amusingly that it "has been suggested that making my Ninth for band instead of for orchestra might be a hedge against the old ninth-symphony-and-you-croak bugaboo. We'll see."[164] Of the work for band, which was inspired by Corigliano's Symphony No. 3, "Circus Maximus," Bolcom wrote that he was "counting on all that youthful fire and abandon" in its performances "to counteract any leaden premonitions associated with that number."[165] Ultimately, he decided to call the four-movement work his first band symphony rather than his official ninth symphony because "I wanted a one-movement, tight, and dramatic symphony as the last of the group, and the more I thought about it the less the Band Symphony felt like that sort of piece."[166]

Given the playfully unexpected nature of much of the music in his symphonies, it is appropriate that his one-movement Symphony No. 9 (2011–12), which disappears into the high registers much like Elliott Carter's *Symphonia*, is Bolcom's last official word in the genre—for, as the above quotation implies, he said that he does not intend to write any further orchestral symphonies.[167] This decision is unrelated to the aforementioned curse; rather, he "just got tired of writing them. I feel I've exhausted that direction for myself."[168] Moreover, mentioning Beethoven, Schubert, and Bruckner, he noted that he has "had a yen for keeping the number of works in a genre I'll write in conformity with a set by some composer I admire."[169] And stopping at nine official symphonies certainly invites Bolcom's audiences to view his symphonic output for orchestra as a unified body of work. "All have a seriousness and size befitting the genre," he reflected, calling them part of what he identifies as the "grand line of the form."[170] Bolcom's symphonies coincide with Rochberg's and Corigliano's in asserting a strong sense of Romantic heritage, but Bolcom has employed a far more heterogeneous palette to extend the nineteenth-century tradition and carry it into the twenty-first century, fusing poetry, striking effects, vernacular styles, and a polystylistic playfulness.

John Harbison (b. 1938)

John Harbison, who has taught at the Massachusetts Institute of Technology since 1969, studied with two eminent symphonists, Walter Piston at Harvard and Roger Sessions at Princeton. He has played a vibrant role in the cultural life of Boston throughout his career as a conductor, composer, and pianist; his own symphonies have emerged through commissions from major orchestras, including three from the Boston Symphony Orchestra, which has recorded all six. In considering the history of the symphony as a genre in this country and his place in it, Harbison sees the American symphony as following more solidly in the line of Sibelius than Mahler, with Mahler's expansive structures precluding a clear sense of what he calls "location in the form." Harbison avoids the sense of a grandiose "Great American Symphony"; speaking of predecessors such as Copland, for instance, he identifies more with the *Short Symphony* (1933) than the much larger Third Symphony (1946). His six symphonies, listed in table 9.9, thus incorporate a range of materials into coherent but expressive structures. And his close attention to melody derives in part from his studies with Sessions, whose melodic writing Harbison admires; for Harbison as a composer, melodic writing is "the hardest thing and the most necessary."[171]

Table 9.9 The Symphonies of John Harbison (b. 1938)

Title	Movements	Instrumentation	Comments
Symphony No. 1 (1981)	I. Drammatico II. Allegro sfumato III. Paesaggio: Andante IV. Tempo giusto	3 Flt. (doubling Picc. and Alto Flt.), 3 Ob. (1 doubling EH), 3 Clar. (1 doubling Bclar.), 3 Bssn. (1 doubling Cbssn.), 4 Hr., 2 Tpt., 3 Trom., Tuba, Timp., Perc. (Tubular Bells, Mrb., Vbp., 2 Gongs [low], Metal Blocks, Temple Blocks, Wood Blocks, Maracas, Claves, Tri., Wood Drum, Tamb., SD, 2 Tuned Drums, 3 Tom-toms, BDs), Harp, Strgs.	Commissioned by the Boston Symphony Orchestra for its 100th anniversary. First performance: March 22, 1984, Boston Symphony Orchestra, conducted by Seiji Ozawa. Score published by Associated Music Publishers. Recorded by Boston Symphony Orchestra, conducted by Seiji Ozawa (New World 80331); Boston Symphony Orchestra, conducted by James Levine (BSO Classics 1302).
Symphony No. 2 (1987)	I. Dawn (68 mm.) II. Daylight (117 mm.) III. Dusk (90 mm.) IV. Dark (163 mm.)	3 Flt. (1 doubling Picc.), 2 Ob., EH, 2 Clar., E♭ Clar., Bclar., 3 Bssn. (1 doubling Cbssn.), 4 Hr., 4 Tpt. (2 doubling Picc. Tpt.), 3 Trom., Tuba, Timp., Perc. (Glsp., Vbp., Crotales, Tri., SD, Suspended Cyms., Sizzle Cym., Tam-tam, Gong [low], 3 Tom-toms, SD [lower than Tom-toms], BD, Temple Blocks, Castanets, Thunder Sheet, Lion's Roar), Harp, Pno. (doubling Cel.), Strgs.	Dedicated to Michael Steinberg. Commissioned for the 75th anniversary of the San Francisco Symphony. First performance: May 13, 1987, San Francisco Symphony, conducted by Herbert Blomstedt. Score published by Associated Music Publishers. Recorded by San Francisco Symphony, conducted by Herbert Blomstedt (Decca 443 376-2); Boston Symphony Orchestra, conducted by James Levine (BSO Classics 1302).
Symphony No. 3 (1990)	I. Sconsolato (99 mm.) II. Nostalgico (90 mm.) III. Militante (122 mm.) IV. Appassionata (118 mm.) V. Esuberante (181 mm.)	3 Flt. (1 doubling Picc.), 3 Ob. (1 doubling EH), 3 Clar. (1 doubling Bclar.), 3 Bssn. (1 doubling Cbssn.), 4 Hr., 3 Tpt., 3 Trom., Tuba, Timp., Perc. (4 Players; Player 1: 4 Suspended Cyms., Tri., 4 Tom-toms, Bell [high], Chimes, Crotales, Xylo.; Player 2: Tamb., Timbales, Lujon, Temple Blocks, Mrb.; Player 3: Tenor Drum, SD, Brake Drums, Vbp.; Player 4: Cowbell, BD, Wood Block, Log Drum, Tam-tam, Glsp.), Pno., Strgs.	Dedicated to Christopher Rouse. Commissioned by the Baltimore Symphony Orchestra. First performance: February 26, 1991, conducted by David Zinman. Score published by Associated Music Publishers. Recorded by Albany Symphony Orchestra, conducted by David Alan Miller (Albany TROY390); Munich Philharmonic Orchestra, conducted by James Levine (Oehms 507); Boston Symphony Orchestra, conducted by James Levine (BSO Classics 1303).

Symphony No. 4 (2003, rev. 2006)	I. Fanfare (129 mm.) II. Intermezzo (101 mm.) III. Scherzo (301 mm.) IV. Threnody (65 mm.) V. Finale (175 mm.)	3 Flt. (1 doubling Picc.), 3 Ob. (1 doubling EH), 3 Clar. (1 doubling Bclar.), 3 Bssn. (1 doubling Cbssn.), 4 Hr., 2 Tpt., 2 Trom., Tuba, Timp., Perc. (3 Players: SD, Tenor Drum, BD, 2 Tom-toms, Tamb., Temple Blocks, Tri., Mrb, Vbp., Glsp., Tubular Bells, Suspended Cym., 2 Tam-tams), Pno., Harp, Strgs.	Commissioned by Constance Albrecht in celebration of the Centennial of the Seattle Symphony. First performance: June 17, 2004, Seattle Symphony, conducted by Gerard Schwarz. Score published by Associated Music Publishers. Recorded by Boston Symphony Orchestra, conducted by Ludovic Morlot (BSO Classics 1303); National Orchestral Institute Philharmonic, conducted by David Alan Miller (Naxos 8.559836).
Symphony No. 5 (2007)	I. Con forza (307 mm.) II. Andante cantabile (312 mm.) III. Grave (109 mm.) IV. Lento (118 mm.)	3 Flt. (1 doubling Picc.), 3 Ob. (1 doubling EH), 2 Clar. (1 doubling E♭ Clar., 1 doubling Bclar.), 2 Bssn., Cbssn., 4 Hr., 2 Tpt., 2 Trom., Tuba, Perc. (3 Players; Player 1: Glsp., Vbp., Metal Blocks, Güiro, Slapstick; Player 2: Concert Mrb., Bell [high], Tenor Drum, Maracas, Claves [high], Claves [highest], Sandpaper Blocks; Player 3: Bell [large], Tuned Gongs, Cowbells, SD, BD, Sandpaper Blocks), Pno., Harp, Electric Gui., Strgs., Vocal soloists (Mezzo-Soprano, Baritone)	Commissioned by the Boston Symphony Orchestra. First Performance: April 17, 2008, Boston Symphony Orchestra, conducted by James Levine, with Kate Lindsey, (mezzo-soprano) and Nathan Gunn (baritone). Text includes poems on Orpheus by Czesław Miłosz, Louise Glück, and Rainer Maria Rilke. Score published by Associated Music Publishers. Recorded by Boston Symphony Orchestra, conducted by Jiří Bělohlávek, with Gerald Finley (baritone) and Sasha Cooke (mezzo-soprano) (BSO Classics 1303).
Symphony No. 6 (2011)	I. Con moto (91 mm.) II. Con anima (153 mm.) III. Vivo, ruvido (167 mm.) IV. Moderato cantabile e semplice (223 mm.)	3 Flt. (1 doubling Picc.), 3 Ob. (1 doubling EH), 3 Clar. (1 doubling Bclar.), 3 Bssn. (1 doubling Cbssn.), 4 Hr., 3 Tpt., 3 Trom., Tuba, Timp., Perc. (Vbp., Glsp., Congas, Bongo, Tam-tams [large, small], Gongs [small, large], Mrb., SD, BD, Flexatone, Tubular Bells, Cyms., Metal Chain), Cimbalom (or Prepared Pno.), Strgs, Mezzo-Soprano Soloist	Commissioned by the Boston Symphony Orchestra and dedicated to James Levine. First movement is set to the text "Entering the Temple in Nîmes," by James Wright. First performance January 12, 2012, Boston Symphony Orchestra, conducted by David Zinman, with Paula Murrihy (mezzo-soprano). Score published by Associated Music Publishers. Recorded by Boston Symphony Orchestra, conducted by David Zinman, with Paula Murrihy (mezzo-soprano) (BSO Classics 1303).

Harbison's attention to well-shaped and contrasting melodies is clear in the first movement ("Drammatico") of the concise Symphony No. 1 (1981). A series of dissonant clashes at the beginning reflect the "metallic harmonies" that occurred to Harbison in a dream.[172] Those sonorities yield to four thematic areas: a hazy series of indistinct blocked harmonies, a poignant melody for French horns and violins that is replete with expressive leaps, a more energetic theme for winds, and a set of arpeggios in the lower strings. The latter material overtakes the orchestra in a persistent push to the return of the opening "metallic harmonies" and the eventual reprise of the resplendent horn/violin melody. After a brief, scherzoish second movement comes a slow movement that at one point highlights the earthy quartet of alto flute, English horn, bass clarinet, and contrabassoon; the quartet moves with winding counterpoint, and the movement unfolds with a Debussy-like shimmer toward a thunderous climax. This movement also quotes the chamber work *In Eius Memoriam* (1968) by the American composer Seymour Shifrin (1926–1979).[173] The bustling fourth movement evokes both jazz and early Copland with its syncopated rhythms, effectively transforming the first movement's "metallic harmonies" into a livelier soundscape.

Symphony No. 2 (1987) is cast in four continuous movements that explore the time cycle of a single day. After "Dawn," a slow and sensuous first movement, comes "Daylight," a raucous Scherzo whose sense of perpetual motion and large sound evoke the development section of the first movement of Mahler's Third Symphony (1896) in gesture, though not scope. It transitions without break to the mysterious slow movement, "Dusk," which centers on the unfolding of a string melody. The longest movement, "Darkness," opens with distorted, call-and-response fanfare-like figures in the brass that eventually envelop the entire palette of orchestral sounds—especially the lower registers—before a brief but intense climax; the descending trombone glissandi at m. 320, along with the calmer, more transparent section that follows, suggests recovery from the previous intensity. A later, more vigorous climax features the lion's roar before the music disappears on a series of repeated harmonies.

Harbison called his Symphony No. 3 (1990) "a continuous progression of temperamental movements each of which necessitates the next" and identified a "fluid psychological progression, with its momentary victories and defeats, and its release at the end."[174] His emphasis on percussion in this work, which contributes to its emotional landscape, prompted Harbison to dedicate the symphony to his fellow symphonist Christopher Rouse, who is especially known for his percussion writing.[175] The tumultuous first section ("Sconsolato") gives way to the second section ("Nostalgico"), where "a nostalgic phrase played by the clarinets" leads to a more foreboding "subterranean horn call."[176] "Eventually, the carillon of San Ilario, near Genoa, is heard. I once walked that hill often, wondering if the bells implied transcendence or impermanence." Of the following "Militante," he continued, "Massed horns take up the bell song, transforming it into something less comfortable. . . . The percussion section erupts twice in this scherzo, like a sinister jack-in-the-box, or worse, a Pandora's box." In the next section, "Appassionata," "a violin melody appears three times, first as a solo, then with marimba and vibraphone shadow, finally with full orchestra." This leads to the aptly named finale, "Esuberante," which concludes with a flourish that puts a special spotlight on percussion.

The emotional core of the Symphony No. 4 (2003) is the fourth movement, evocatively titled "Threnody." This passionate lament follows a first movement that, as Harbison describes it, features "a brash fanfare answered by solo instruments in a more informal friendly conversation"; a second movement that "questions these uncertainties—mysterious bell-sounds, pauses, long spun-out circling string solos"; and a third movement "reasserting the healthy energies of the first section." As Harbison explained of the highly personal genesis of the

"Threnody," "One morning at eight, in Bogliasco, Italy, where I was working, I receive a phone call—two o'clock the caller's time. I cannot describe the knowledge that struck during that call except to say that the breath of mortality, bearing at this moment on someone much in my care, came suddenly and radically close." Of the Finale that follows, Harbison wrote, its "ritual formality embraces, and perhaps chokes off, the frantic dance and march which attempt to modify its character."[177]

"Every piece with singers and instruments should be coherent as a lucid sequence of sounds," Harbison wrote in program notes on his Symphony No. 5 (2007). "These sounds, without reference to their verbal origins, aspired to a significant musical shape, something *symphonic*."[178] Although his first four symphonies were purely instrumental, Harbison ventured into the realm of vocal writing for the next two, but his skill as a writer for voice had long been established; *The Flight into Egypt* (1986), for soprano, baritone, chorus, and small orchestra, earned him the Pulitzer Prize in 1987. Symphony No. 5 presents a modern retelling of the Orpheus myth in which the stunning sonority of electric guitar stands in for Orpheus's lyre. A setting of Czesław Miłosz's "Orpheus and Euridice" (translated by Robert Haas) in the first two movements, sung by baritone, leads to a third movement that presents the story from Euridice's perspective, set to Louise Glück's poem "Relic." The Finale, a setting of Rainer Maria Rilke's "Sonnet to Orpheus II, 13" (translated by Stephen Mitchell), offers a baritone and mezzo-soprano duet in which the voices sing similar material but mostly with staggered entrances, suggesting the fateful moments in which Euridice followed Orpheus. Harbison begins the Symphony No. 6 (2011) where he left off in the previous symphony, this time with a setting for mezzo-soprano of James Wright's poem "Entering the Temple in Nîmes," another text that evokes ancient imagery. The final three movements are purely instrumental.

Like many others, including Walker, Corigliano, Glass, Zwilich, and Kernis, Harbison turned to the symphonic genre in the 1980s. As he wrote of that shift, "Eventually I felt convinced by the title 'Symphony.' I couldn't see why our big orchestral pieces needed to be called things like *Consternations or Entropies I* (the 1960s) or *Rimmed by a Veiled Vision* (the '70s) if they were symphonic in ambition and scale."[179] And just as William Bolcom concluded his symphonic output with his Symphony No. 9, Harbison said in 2015 that he does not plan to write any more symphonies. Conceiving of the genre as an opportunity to work out structural challenges, he said that "in terms of the formal issues of symphony writing, and the kind of instinctive set of interlocks that were not very planned . . . I think that the sixth symphony was further down the road than I expected it to be"; thus, he quipped, it serves as a sixth and seventh symphony combined.[180] (Harbison's reference to a seventh symphony might be seen as another gesture toward Sibelius.) In fact, much of what drove Harbison's symphonic output was a desire, closely linked to modernism, to explore new ground with each work. He wrote of approaching a composition in terms of "the conviction of not having done it this way before," continuing, "and once there is one piece, another comes from the determination to do something different. And another, to work away from the first two."[181] As with George Walker and his sinfonias, an important aspect of Harbison's legacy as a symphonist is his polished and, for the most part, succinct exploration of the genre's formal possibilities, which have yet to exhaust themselves in the early twenty-first century.

Ellen Taaffe Zwilich (b. 1939)

A distinguished composer and once a professional violinist who performed with the American Symphony Orchestra, Ellen Taaffe Zwilich made a promising start in the symphonic genre, winning the 1983 Pulitzer Prize in Music with her Symphony No. 1, "Three Movements for

Orchestra"—the first Pulitzer Prize in music awarded to a woman. Recalling the genesis of the work, composed in 1982, Zwilich said that she initially named the piece *Three Movements for Orchestra*, but that Gunther Schuller, who conducted the premiere, suggested to her—and she agreed—that the work was actually a symphony. So she decided to call it one, despite external pressure not to write in a genre some saw as obsolete (the addition of *symphony* to the title did not reach the Pulitzer committee, so it won the award as *Three Movements for Orchestra*).[182] Well before her first orchestral symphony appeared, though, Zwilich had become a notable figure in American composition. In 1975, she became the first woman to earn a doctor of musical arts in composition from Juilliard, where she had studied with Elliott Carter and Roger Sessions. In the same year, Pierre Boulez conducted her orchestral work *Symposium* (1973).[183]

A tragic personal event had significant aesthetic implications for Zwilich during the same decade: the death of her husband, the violinist Joseph Zwilich, in 1979. She was in the process of composing her Chamber Symphony at the time; reflecting on his death several years later in a way that recalls Rochberg's own reaction to his son's death, she said, "Suddenly all talk of method and style seemed trivial; I became interested in meaning. I wanted to *say* something, musically, about life and living."[184] In the highly chromatic Chamber Symphony, Zwilich contrasts sharply angular melodic material with gently sweeping and soaring lines. The short, one-movement composition is characterized by frequent motivic exchange and varied timbral combinations. Both these features are heard clearly throughout her symphonic *oeuvre*, which is shown in table 9.10.

The opening measures of Zwilich's Symphony No. 1, "Three Movements of Orchestra," define the entire composition, the first of five symphonies for full orchestra. "I have long been interested in the elaboration of large-scale works from the initial material," Zwilich explained of her "'organic' approach to musical form."[185] In this case, "Throughout the entire Symphony, the melodic and harmonic implications of the first 15 bars of the first movement are explored. My aim was to create a rich harmonic palette and a wide variety of melodic gestures, all emanating from a simple source."[186] The first movement contains what Zwilich calls a "'motto': three statements of a rising minor third, marked accelerando. Each time the 'motto' appears in the first movement, an accelerando occurs, prompting slight evolutions of character until an *Allegro* section is established. After the *Allegro*, the movement subsides in tempo and ends as quietly as it began."[187] In the first movement's haunting ending, shown in example 9.6, the sense of constant motivic development comes to a standstill on a repeated minor-ninth in the piccolo, flute, and second violins, which underpins a return of the opening thirds to create a hazy, chromatic wash of color.

The second movement, which like the first movement expands toward a climax and then contracts, builds on a chromatic figure that itself ascends through a minor third. In the final movement, which Zwilich characterized as a rondo, a feverish opening section, with its relentless rhythms and cascading thirds, yields to contrasting sections that unfold more gradually. A final cadence for the whole orchestra takes place on the pitch A, the note on which the symphony started.

In the aggressive Symphony No. 2, "Cello Symphony" (1985), a rhythmic motive—a fast, almost threatening short-short-short-short-long—pervades all three movements. In the opening movement, the motive competes with a sumptuous theme for the cellos, which eventually leads to a stunning cadenza for the whole section. In the slow second movement, the motive's appearance in the violins and solo trumpet offers an alarming reminder of the first movement's foreboding atmosphere. That sense of urgency returns in the fast third movement, which ends

Table 9.10 The Symphonic Works of Ellen Taaffe Zwilich (b. 1939)

Title	Movements	Instrumentation	Comments
Chamber Symphony (1979)	One movement (303 mm.)	Flt. (doubling Picc.), Clar. (doubling Bclar.), Vln., Vla., Vlc., Pno.	First performance November 30, 1979, by Boston Musica Viva, conducted by Richard Pittman. Score published by Presser. Recorded by Louisville Orchestra, conducted by Albert-George Schram (First Edition FECD-0004); Boston Musica Viva, conducted by Richard Pittman (CRI CD 621).
Symphony No. 1 ("Three Movements for Orchestra") (1982)	I. (243 mm.) II. (67 mm.) III. (223 mm.)	Picc., Flt. (doubling Picc.), Ob., EH, Clar., Bclar. (doubling Clar.), Bssn., Cbssn (doubling Bssn.), 4 Hr., 2 Tpt., 3 Trom., Tuba, Timp., Perc. (Orchestra Bells, Vbp. [also with bow], Crotales, Suspended Cyms. [small, medium], Suspended Sizzle Cym., 2 Cyms. [large], SD [picc.], BD [small], BD [large], Tamb., Güiro, Tubular Bells), Pno., Harp, Strgs.	Commissioned by American Composers Orchestra and the National Endowment for the Arts. Winner of 1983 Pulitzer Prize in Music. First performance: May 5, 1982, American Composers Orchestra, conducted by Gunther Schuller. Score published by Margun Music. Recorded by Indianapolis Symphony Orchestra, conducted by John Nelson (New World NW336-2).
Symphony No. 2 ("Cello Symphony") (1985)	I. Allegro (296 mm.) II. Lento (115 mm.) III. Presto (383 mm.)	Picc., 2 Flt., 2 Ob., EH, 2 Clar. (1 doubling E♭ Clar.), Bclar., 2 Bssn., Cbssn., 4 Hr., 3 Tpt., 3 Trom., Tuba, Timp., Perc. (SD [small], BD [large], Suspended Cyms. [small, medium], Suspended Sizzle Cym., Gong [medium-large], Slapstick, Crotales), Pno., Strgs.	Commissioned by Dr. and Mrs. Ralph I. Doorman for the San Francisco Symphony. First performance: November 13, 1985, San Francisco Symphony, conducted by Edo de Waart. Score published by Presser. Recorded by Louisville Orchestra, conducted by Lawrence Leighton Smith (First Edition FECD-0004).

Table 9.10 The Symphonic Works of Ellen Taaffe Zwilich

Title	Movements	Instrumentation	Comments
Symphony No. 3 (1992)	I. Maestoso e cantabile (167 mm.) II. Molto vivace (144 mm.) III. Largo (75 m.)	Picc., 2 Flt., 2 Ob., EH, 2 Clar., Bclar, 2 Bssn., Cbssn., 4 Hr., 3 Tpt., 3 Trom., Tuba, Timp., Perc. (Xylo., Vbp., Tamb., Suspended Cyms. [small; small, muted; hi-hat, closed], 2 Pedal BDs [high, low], Orchestral Cyms. [high (med.), low (large)], Sizzle Cyms. [high, low], BDs [small, large]), Strgs.	Commissioned by the New York Philharmonic for its 150th anniversary. First performance: February 25, 1993, New York Philharmonic, conducted by Jahja Ling. Score published by Presser. Recorded by Louisville Orchestra, conducted by James Sedares (Koch International Classics 3-7278); New York Philharmonic, conducted by Jahja Ling (New York Philharmonic Special Editions NYP 9914).
Symphony No. 4, "The Gardens" (1999)	I. Introduction: Litany of Endangered Plants (98 mm.) II. Meditation on Living Fossils (103 mm.) III. A Pastoral Journey (242 mm.) IV. The Children's Promise (164 mm.)	Picc., 2 Flt., 2 Ob., EH, 2 Clar., Cbssn., 4 Hr., 3 Tpt., 3 Trom., Tuba, Timp., Perc. (3 Players: Vbp., Glsp. [Orchestral Bells], Tubular Bells, Hi-hat Cyms., Suspended Cyms. [sizzle, small (splash), medium, and large], Tam-tams [medium, large], BD [large]), Strgs., SATB Chorus, Children's Chorus (also playing Handbells)	Commissioned by Michigan State University. Composition featured in the PBS documentary The Gardens: Birth of a Symphony. First performance: February 5, 2000, Michigan State University Symphony Orchestra, Choral Ensembles, and Children's Choir, conducted by Leon Gregorian. Score published by Presser. Recorded by Michigan State University Symphony Orchestra, Choral Ensembles, and Children's Choir, conducted by Leon Gregorian (Koch International Classics 3-7487-2).
Symphony No. 5 ("Concerto for Orchestra") (2008)	I. Prologue (105 mm.) II. Celebration (154 mm.) III. Memorial (101 mm.) IV. Epilogue (190 mm.)	Picc., 2 Flt., 2 Ob., EH, 2 Clar., BClar, 2 Bssn., Cbssn., 4 Hr., 3 Tpt., 3 Trom., Tuba, Timp., Perc. (4 Players: Vbp., Mrb., Suspended Cyms. [small, large], Zildjian Spiral Cym., Sizzle Cym., SD [picc.], BD [large], Djembes, Dumbek [or other hand drum], Drum Set [Ride Cym., Hi-hat, 4 Small Tom-toms, Pedal Bass Drum], Tuned Button Gongs), Strgs.	Commissioned by the Juilliard School for the composer's 70th birthday. First performance: October 27, 2008, Juilliard Orchestra, conducted by James Conlon. Score published by Presser.

Example 9.6 Ellen Taaffe Zwilich, Symphony No. 1, "Three Movements For Orchestra"/1, mm. 234–43. Copyright © 1983 by Associated Music Publishers (BMI). International copyright secured. All rights reserved. Reprinted with permission.

Example 9.6 *continued*

on the pitch A, just as the symphony itself begins. (Remarkably, the Symphony No. 1 also starts and concludes on A.)

Zwilich composed the Symphony No. 3 (1992) for an illustrious commission—the New York Philharmonic's one hundred fiftieth anniversary season. In this composition, following her usual three-movement pattern for a symphony, Zwilich again combines lyricism and timbral brightness with angularity and motivic incisiveness. Here, though, tonal centers are more present, and their off-kilter quality and the symphony's whirling motives recall Shostakovich. Once again in Zwilich's symphonic output, explicit extramusical references—common in several symphonies since 1970—are absent. In his review after the premiere, Bernard Holland of the *New York Times* praised Zwilich's skill but wrote that she "chooses to say little or nothing about the world around her," adding that this suggests "a certain avoidance."[188] That criticism, though, says less about Zwilich's music than it does about typical expectations for the symphony as a genre in the late twentieth century—that such works ought to deal directly and openly with pressing matters. It ignores the possible political associations of the symphony's initial pounding chords—Holland himself described them as "jolts of violence"—as well as the almost-thwarted F-sharp-major closing of the whole symphony, the poignant solo lines that weave throughout the work, and the spine-chilling interpolation of a jaunty subject for brass in the first movement that reappears piercingly in the winds in the fast second movement and is transformed into a cantabile theme in the contemplative third movement. Perhaps the then-recent success of John Corigliano's Symphony No. 1, with its clear references to the AIDS crisis, helped imbue (or reimbue) the symphony with the aura of communicating apparent or explicitly identified topical agendas in the minds of audiences and critics, at least in the United States.

Zwilich's Symphony No. 4, "The Gardens," composed in 1999, is immune to such criticisms of aloofness. As Denise Von Glahn has pointed out, this is one of Zwilich's rare works with a programmatic title.[189] Commissioned by Michigan State University and composed in recognition of its gardens, the work contains four movements that demonstrate Zwilich's engagement with environmental concerns. In the first movement, "Introduction: Litany of Endangered Plants," the chorus chants the Latin names of threatened plant life in the W. J. Beal Botanical Garden, starting with *castanea dentata*—the American chestnut—a tree that, as Von Glahn has pointed out, is an iconic tree in this country.[190] Zwilich plays with these terms for special effect by having the chorus repeat "folia" and "fragilis" apart from the names to which they belong—clearly meant as comments on human "folly" and nature's "fragility."[191] The instrumental second movement, "Meditation on Living Fossils," makes use of material from the first movement but is "personal and introspective" compared to the "public and outspoken" introductory movement, as Von Glahn observed.[192] In the third movement, "A Pastoral Journey," the chorus celebrates nature's beautiful simplicity by repeating "Behold the lilies of the field / They toil not, they spin not, but [even] Solomon in all his glory, was not adorned like one of these"—an adaptation of Matthew 6:28–29. Harmonic glissandi and handbells offer a mysterious, ethereal quality that complements the spiritual origins of the text.

Zwilich broke from her usual three-movement symphonic form by including a fourth movement, "The Children's Promise." Here, signaling a collective pledge of action, the children's chorus sings and repeats several lines penned by Erik LaMont especially for this symphony: "We will protect our heritage," "We will nourish our plants and trees," "We will nourish, from root to bough," "We will leave a verdant earth," "We will gather our corn and herbs," and "We will gather from forest to plow." The adult chorus joins in at times; they again intone

Latin names of plants, this time drawn from the Michigan 4-H Children's Garden, and here including *artemisia dracunculus* (tarragon) and *zea* (the genus that includes corn). The plants' presence in this movement helps bolster a sense of the human species' ancient, cyclical, and eternal reliance on nature's bounty for survival.

With Zwilich's recent Symphony No. 5 (2008), fittingly commissioned by her alma mater Juilliard for her seventieth birthday and premiered by its orchestra, the composer returned to her roots in more overtly absolute musical composition and seems to have drawn on a longstanding interest in highlighting the capabilities of a skilled orchestra. (Regarding Symphony No. 1, she had said, "I knew that I wanted to create something that would exploit the rich sonorities of the American Composer's Orchestra, and felt free, for example, to write a virtuosic tuba solo, because a modern symphony orchestra is really a stage full of virtuosos."[193]) Subtitled "Concerto for Orchestra" and thereby invoking a genre that came into its own in the twentieth century, this composition contains many of Zwilich's symphonic hallmarks, including fast ascending passages (scalar and arpeggiated), motivic density, varied orchestration, percussive forcefulness, pleading lyricism, and a sense of organic unity.

Zwilich's symphonic output challenges categories such as Neoromantic and Neoclassical—the latter a term not often used to describe twenty-first-century music. In a 1985 feature in the *New York Times Magazine* on Zwilich's music, Tim Page highlighted the tension between expressivity and technique in her music, arguing that "it would be simplistic to label Mrs. Zwilich a 'neo-Romantic,' for her work has a notable degree of classical poise in its careful structure and temperate demeanor. Yet it is more impulsive than most neo-Classicism."[194] Zwilich's symphonies suggest that, as for Beethoven and other nineteenth-century composers, divisions between "Romantic" and "classical" are in the ear of the beholder; a given work can be tightly or "classically" constructed and economical, building on a small amount of basic material, yet contain "Romantic" soaring themes, dramatic climaxes, lush textures, and profound messages, whether implicit or explicit.

Adolphus Hailstork (b. 1941)

As a young composer, Adolphus Hailstork had an experience shared by many symphonists of his generation. "When I was coming along in the '60s, anything that had melody, tonal harmony, a rhythmic pattern" was considered "so passé that it was practically forbidden as representative of what you should be doing."[195] Hailstork, who turned to symphonic writing in the late 1980s during a successful career as a composer, remarked that in his "later years" he has become "strongly fixed on a blending" in his music of his heritage as an African American and his training as a composer in the classical tradition.[196] His comments on generating a canon of music by Black composers shed light on this approach: "We need to create our own repertoire, and after we've created our sonatas, tone poems, symphonies, and whatever else we may invent, then perhaps we'll be called old fogies, but we would have created a black canon. I want to help establish a black canon, so that after I have gone away, I would have left a few symphonies, piano sonatas that black and white conductors will want to do. And they will say, 'Hey, this is great music.' But there will be a hint of African American experience in it."[197] Hailstork, who taught at Old Dominion University in Norfolk, Virginia, counts Nadia Boulanger and H. Owen Reed among his teachers. He is noted for his band, choral, chamber, and orchestral works—the latter of which include four symphonies, listed in table 9.11.

Hailstork explained the genesis of his Symphony No. 1 (1988), composed for the Ocean Grove Shore Festival of Classics (New Jersey), as follows: "Since the piece was to be twenty

Table 9.11 The Symphonies of Adolphus Hailstork (b. 1941)

Titles	Movements	Instrumentation	Comments
Symphony No. 1 (1988)	I. Allegro (164 mm.) II. Adagio: Lento ma non troppo (86 mm.) III. Scherzo: Allegretto (128 mm.) IV. Rondo: Vivace (209 mm.)	2 Flt., 2 Ob., 2 Clar., 2 Bssn., 2 Hr., 2 Tpt., Timp, Strgs.	Composed for the Ocean Grove Shore Festival of Classics in Ocean Grove, New Jersey. Score published by Lauren Keiser Music Publishing. Recorded by Virginia Symphony Orchestra, conducted by JoAnn Falletta (Naxos 8.559722).
Symphony No. 2 (1995–96)	I. Allegro (309 mm.) II. Grave (152 mm.) III. Allegro con brio (198 mm.) IV. Adagio—Allegro (438 mm.)	3 Flt. (1 doubling Picc.), 2 Ob., EH, 2 Clar., 3 Bssn. (1 doubling Cbssn.), 4 Hr., 3 Tpt., 3 Trom., Tuba, Timp., Perc. (3 Players; Player 1: SD [small], Large African Slit Drum, Xylo, Mrb; Player 2: Suspended Cym., 4 Tom-toms, Large Crash Cyms., Tam-tam, Mrb, SD, 2 Bongos; Player 3: BD, Crash Cyms, Suspended Cym., Tam-tam), Strgs.	Commissioned by the Detroit Symphony, in connection with the 1998 Unisys African American Composers Forum. First performance: Detroit Symphony Orchestra, February 12, 1999, conducted by Leslie Dunner. Recorded by Grand Rapids Symphony, conducted by David Lockington (Naxos 8.559295).
Symphony No. 3 (2002)	I. Vivace (384 mm.) II. Moderato (148 mm.) III. Scherzo: Vivace giocoso (199 mm.) IV. Finale: Moderato (325 mm.)	3 Flt. (1 doubling Picc.), 2 Ob. (1 doubling EH), 2 Clar., 2 Bssn., 4 Hr., 3 Tpt., 3 Trom., Tuba, Timp., Perc. (Timbales, Maracas [small], Double Cowbells, Xylo., Glsp., Suspended Cym., Crash Cyms., Mrb., Indian Tabla, Vbp., Tri. [small]), Strgs.	Commissioned by and dedicated to the Grand Rapids Symphony. Score published by Theodore Presser Company. Recorded by the Grand Rapids Symphony, conducted by David Lockington (Naxos 8.559295).
Symphony No. 4, "Survive" (2021)	I. Still Holding On II. Sometimes with a Lighter Touch III. While Still Remembering the Emanuel Nine and Many Others IV. Still Crossing That Bridge—Coda: A Time for Healing	3 Flt. (1 doubling Picc.), 2 Ob., 2 Clar., 3 Bssn. (1 doubling Cbssn.), E♭ Asax., 4 Hr., etc., 4 Hr., 3 Tpt, 3 Trom., Tuba, Timp., Perc., Strgs.	"Still Holding On" commissioned by Los Angeles Philharmonic. First performance ("Still Holding On"): Los Angeles Philharmonic, February 17, 2019, conducted by Thomas Wilkins.

minutes long and for a Haydn-sized orchestra, I decided that a simple first symphony would fit the bill."[198] The symphony begins with a sonata-form movement, complete with a playful first theme and a songlike woodwind-driven second theme. The slow second movement suggests Romanticism with its intense lyricism and diatonic simplicity. A giddy and at times prickly Scherzo features sparkling orchestration that highlights solo woodwinds; despite some surprising harmonic and textural shifts, it retains an overall air of sportive accessibility. The fast Finale begins and culminates with a reference to the music from the opening of the first movement, and trumpet flourishes offer appropriately energetic concluding gestures.

Hailstork's own words about his Symphony No. 2 (1988) demonstrate a direct connection to his African American heritage: "In the summer of 1996, I took a trip to Africa. There I visited the forts along the coast of Ghana, and saw the dungeons where the slaves were held before being shipped overseas. I put my reaction to that sad scene in movement two of this symphony. In movement four I sought to reflect the determination of a people who had arrived in America as slaves, but struggled, with courage and faith, against numerous odds."[199] Like the previous symphony, this work is shaped in four movements, but fittingly, it embodies a more solemn symphonic vision. The first movement starts with the same kind of ambiguous sonority that begins Beethoven's Symphony No. 9—here, open fifths beginning on A-flat that suggest a slow introduction is underway. But the texture quickly erupts with a dissonant A in the brass, fierce timpani rolls that develop into a persistent throbbing, and a spiky woodwind melody. The remainder of the movement features surprising moments of free dissonance in a tonal framework along with imposing textures of fierce percussive effects. The second movement, which Hailstork related directly to his visit to Ghana, begins with an English horn melody that suggests D minor; Hailstork's programmatic description of the symphony invites us to hear this melody as a trace of a spiritual, and the use of this instrument recalls the corresponding movement of Dvořák's "New World" Symphony. This passage gives way to a mysterious rumbling, and the movement builds to a tense climax in which low brass undergirds a straining string melody, suggesting an arduous struggle. The relaxed return of the English horn theme in D minor is interrupted violently by two unexpected sonorities in the brass—an A-flat-minor chord followed by an A-minor chord—and the movement concludes with the same rumbling heard earlier. After a relatively brief, feverish Scherzo, the fourth movement opens with a wandering clarinet solo followed by faintly glowing string sonorities. But this movement—which for Hailstork reflected the perseverance of newly arrived slaves—quickly blossoms into a swirling statement of exultation.[200]

With his Symphony No. 3 (2002), Hailstork aimed to write a piece that was "lighter" than the previous symphony, and it begins with a "snappy little trumpet tune." This melody—the first theme of this sonata-form movement—is marked by an intriguing rhythmic structure; although in 9/8, its 27 beats are divided into groups of six, eight, and thirteen. The second theme is also of rhythmic interest, as it features fast passages for flute, trumpet, marimba, and xylophone. In the second movement, an "extended string chorale" grows toward "an intense unison moment in the middle" and then recedes. As with his other symphonic slow movements, this one showcases Hailstork's facility with breathtaking diatonic writing. The symphony continues without pause into the third movement, described by Hailstork as "a jaunty Scherzo with many cross-rhythms and a lot of colorful percussion. The bluesy middle section with its 2 + 2 + 2 + 3 rhythm is begun by the unlikely combination of Marimba, Indian Tabla, and Glockenspiel." The trumpet solo at the beginning of the fourth movement recalls the "snappy" trumpet motive from the start of the symphony. A rhythmically buoyant movement builds to what Hailstork called a "flashy conclusion"—one that swirls and surges.[201]

Hailstork's Symphony No. 4, "Survive," responds directly to violence against Blacks in recent American history. In an interview with Frank J. Oteri from the summer of 2021, Hailstork spoke about the work: "I was reacting to all the black men who are getting shot in the back—16 bullets here, 7 bullets there . . . and so I just named the whole thing 'Survive.'" The first movement, "Still Holding On," commissioned by the Los Angeles Philharmonic, was first heard in February 2019 and quotes the spiritual "Keep Your Hand on the Plow." After the second movement, "Sometimes with a Lighter Touch," comes the third movement, "While Still Remembering the Emanuel Nine and Many Others," a reference—as with George Walker's Sinfonia No. 5, "Visions"—to the attack at Emanuel African Methodist Episcopal Church in Charleston, South Carolina, in 2015. Hailstork noted the contemporary resonance of the title of the fourth movement, "Still Crossing That Bridge": on March 7, 1965, John Lewis, in a protest march for voting rights, was beaten by state troopers in Selma, Alabama, after crossing the Edmund Pettis Bridge. A coda, titled "A Time for Healing," concludes the work, which Hailstork considers a "symphony of essays."[202] In a program note for the premiere of "Still Holding On," Hailstork pointed out connections with the music of William Grant Still—appropriate because "this premiere is at a concert saluting William Grant Still"—and, indeed, the concert also featured Still's own Symphony No. 4, "Autochthonous."[203]

The National Philharmonic (Maryland) premiered Hailstork's Fifth Symphony, a three-movement work for soloists, chorus, and orchestra, on June 4, 2023 (too late to include in table 9.11). As with the Fourth Symphony, selections of the work have already been performed separately.

Overall, Hailstork's symphonies blend classical symphonic structures with references to their composer's African American heritage and an individual flair for rhythmic animation, opulent orchestration, and vivid melodic and harmonic writing. His vibrant rhythms and conventional approach to symphonic form connect him with Walter Piston, Roger Sessions, and John Harbison, although Hailstork's musical surface is often more immediately inviting. And as a Black composer of symphonies, Hailstork—with his appealing melodic sensibility, luminous orchestration, and embrace of dissonance—occupies a middle ground between the jazz- and folk-inflected symphonies of Wynton Marsalis (discussed below) and the hard-edged modernist sensibility of George Walker.

Stephen Albert (1941–1992)

Like Hailstork, Stephen Albert opted out of the dominant trends of high modernism—specifically the use of tone rows—and achieved success by reevaluating his place in the classical tradition. But while Hailstork turned to Haydn for his first symphony, Albert looked to the models of the late nineteenth and early twentieth centuries. In 1990 Albert, who studied with Darius Milhaud and George Rochberg, summed up his compositional aesthetic, which has been described as "neo-Romanticism":

> The only real masterpieces after World War II had been by Shostakovich. The only place most new music was going was over a cliff into an abyss, and the so-called conservative alternative seemed to be mired in stasis. The only way out of it, it seemed to me, was to go back to where music had been shortly after the turn of the century. Eschewing the music of Schoenberg, Webern and Berg, I became interested in composers like de Falla, Sibelius and early Stravinsky. I

wanted a complexity of texture that bears repeated hearings and I wanted at the same time to have a surface accessibility.[204]

Albert's symphonies blend a clearly etched tonal focus with a symphonic grandeur that recalls Copland's Third Symphony, a work Albert admired.[205] His tendency toward the large scale in his two symphonies, shown in table 9.12, is reflected in both gesture (heroic themes, sweeping melodies, luminescent orchestration, and frequent pedal points) and length (both works contain multiple extended movements).

Albert's first symphony, *RiverRun* (1983–84), earned him the 1985 Pulitzer Prize in Music and emerged as part of a series of works inspired by the writings of James Joyce; Albert was composing another one, *TreeStone*, at the same time as *RiverRun*. As Albert explained, "riverrun" is the first word of Joyce's *Finnegans Wake* (1939); the movements' names, which he added after the symphony's composition, evince its relationship with *TreeStone*, which sets text from Joyce's novel (including "Leafy Speafing," the title of the second movement of *RiverRun* and a reference to Dublin's River Liffey).[206] Much of *RiverRun* centers on the ongoing transformation of a brief, five-note arching motive introduced in the horns in the first movement at m. 27. "Rain Music," the first movement, "is meant to convey the origins of a river," Albert reflected. "After the sharply accented chords of this movement's introduction"—a section that clearly conjures the opening melodic figure in Beethoven's *Pathétique* sonata, "the music shimmers with a tremulous atmosphere of expectancy."[207] In this "tremulous" passage, piano and winds combine to suggest the fluttering of birds over water, recalling the start of Elliott Carter's *Symphony of Three Orchestras*; indeed, the piano is prominent in *RiverRun* and the instrument has become a mainstay of the instrumentation of recent American symphonies.

In the next movement, "Leafy Speafing," soft passages for solo instruments are swallowed by scurrying rivers of sound. "At the end," Albert wrote of a section that bears a close relationship to the conclusion of "I am Leafy Speafing" from *TreeStone*, "is a coda in which the Voice of the River, held back until now, is heard for the first time from the horns in sharp relief over a rolling arpeggiated figure in the harps, woodwinds, and strings."[208] (Albert's program note as well as a review of the premiere indicate that this movement originally began with a winding solo for alto flute, but the published score and existing recordings begin with a clarinet.[209]) Albert called the third movement, which features the striking sonorities of piccolo clarinet and alto saxophone, a "fragmented march and scherzo": "It opens with a children's song. The march, for the pit band, follows, and we are engulfed in a boozy wake, a lively funeral in which the participants want to escape their own fears of death and disconnection."[210] The movement thus anticipates the "Scherzo Mortale" from Bolcom's Symphony No. 5. Toward the end of the movement, the children's song from the opening turns into "a raucous pub song for the piano, saxophone, and trumpet."[211] The fourth movement, "Rivers End," does suggest the completion of a grand journey. Here, as Albert described it, "Night is falling, and the river is moving quietly into darkness. As it approaches the open sea its momentum builds and it soon becomes a torrent spilling into the ocean. The movement ends quietly, bringing the entire symphony to a close in an atmosphere of suspension and stillness."[212] As seen in example 9.7, harps and bassoons outline the arching motive—reminiscent of one of the principal motives in Claude Debussy's *La Mer* (1905)—that plays such an important role throughout the symphony. (As is the published score, this example is in C.) The texture dissolves into calm oceanic vastness; the wavelike quality before the sonic dissolution here anticipates the "waves" that conclude Corigliano's Symphony No. 1.

Table 9.12 The Symphonies of Stephen Albert (1941–92)

Title	Movements	Instrumentation	Comments
RiverRun (Symphony No. 1) (1983–84)	I. Rain Music (203 mm.) II. Leafy Speafing (156 mm.) III. Beside the Rivering Waters (262 mm.) IV. Rivers End (150 mm.)	3 Flt. (1 doubling Alto Flt., 1 doubling Picc.), 2 Ob., EH, E♭ Clar., 2 Clar., Bclar., Asax., 2 Bssn., Cbssn., 4 Hr., 3 Tpt., 3 Trom., Tuba, Timp., Perc. (2 Vbp., Xylo., Cyms., Tri., Glsp., Gong, Chimes, BD), 2 Harps, Pno., Strgs.	Commissioned by the Sidney L. Hechinger Foundation. Winner of Pulitzer Prize for Music, 1985. First performance: National Symphony Orchestra, January 17, 1985, conducted by Mstislav Rostropovich. Score published by G. Schirmer. Recorded by National Symphony Orchestra, conducted by Mstislav Rostropovich (Delos D/CD 1016); Russian Philharmonic Orchestra, conducted by Paul Polivnick (Naxos 8.559257).
Symphony No. 2 (1992)	I. (229 mm.) II. (166 mm.) III. (204 mm.)	3 Flt. (1 doubling Picc.), 3 Ob. (1 doubling EH), 3 Clar. (1 doubling Bclar.), 3 Bssn., Cbssn., 4 Hr., 3 Tpt., 3 Trom., Tuba, Timp., Perc. (BD, Chimes, Glsp., SD, Suspended Cym., Tri., Vbp., Wood Block, Xylo.), Pno., Harp, Strgs.	Commissioned by the New York Philharmonic. Orchestration completed by Sebastian Currier in 1994. First performance: New York Philharmonic, November 10, 1994, conducted by Hugh Wolff. Score published by G. Schirmer. Recorded by Russian Philharmonic Orchestra, conducted by Paul Polivnick (Naxos 8.559257).

Above and facing, **Example 9.7** Stephen Albert, *RiverRun* (Symphony No. 1)/4, mm. 145–50. Copyright © 1989 by G. Schirmer. International copyright secured. All rights reserved.

The symphony was received quite well, thanks in part to its extramusical vividness and accessibility, and in part to the special moment of its premiere—the return of Mstislav Rostropovich, then conductor of the National Symphony Orchestra, from a sabbatical. Rostropovich, wrote Joseph McLellan, was greeted "with a bouquet so large that two ushers were needed to carry it; a standing ovation; and the National Symphony Orchestra, which played its heart out."[213] As for Albert's symphony, it was called "a brilliant, evocative symphony" that was "spectacularly orchestrated"—one that managed to "evoke the magic spell of Dublin's River Liffey in its many moods from the tentative, misty beginning of its course to its majestic merging with the sea."[214] Throughout, warm orchestral colors and an expansive sense of melody combine with layered textures to create one of the more vivid river journeys in music.

Tragedy struck on December 27, 1992, when Albert was killed in a car accident on Cape Cod, Massachusetts. He had nearly finished his Symphony No. 2, a commission from the New York Philharmonic for its one hundred fiftieth anniversary. The work is stylistically quite similar to *RiverRun* with its references to tonality and its suggestions of the pastoral. The task of completing it—which consisted of orchestrating about half of the three-movement work—fell to Albert's friend, the composer Sebastian Currier. Currier's comments on the work shed special light on the work's conclusion.

> Luckily, although Stephen in general mentioned very little about his work while it was in progress, he happened to have made a comment to his wife, Marilyn, which proved very helpful in the completion of this final section. He said to her once that she would like the ending of this piece because, unlike most of his other works, this piece would not end softly and serenely—a characteristic she had questioned from time to time—but with a forceful and climactic conclusion. Once I was aware of the overall effect Stephen intended, I was able to understand fully the significance of what was written in the score. On first glance, it looks like it might trail off to nothing as in his other pieces, but with this additional information I could see that many figures were meant to be repeated that Stephen had not bothered to write in the score, and rather than ending with a single line it built to a large orchestral tutti.[215]

Indeed, the work ends in dazzling fashion with an unambiguous C-sharp major chord for the whole orchestra, and similarly, the expansive first movement settles firmly on D major. Sandwiched between the large outer movements is a prickly Scherzo.

Albert's death was a shattering moment for the classical musical world. His legacy certainly lives on in works dedicated to his memory, including Aaron Jay Kernis's *Still Movement with Hymn* (1993), the third movement of Daniel Asia's Symphony No. 4 (1993), the second movement of Christopher Rouse's Symphony No. 2 (1994), and the second movement of Joseph Schwantner's Concerto for Percussion and Orchestra (1994). But Albert's own two symphonies occupy an important space all their own in the emerging symphonic canon of later twentieth-century works. As Holly Watkins has discussed, Albert's accessible style generated controversy, with some critics skeptical of its listener friendliness in particular and of late twentieth-century musical Romanticism in general.[216] But in these symphonies, Albert continued forging a path followed by Rochberg, Bolcom, and Corigliano, who embraced tonality and dissonance and—although Albert was less stylistically eclectic than those composers—drew quite openly on a late nineteenth and early twentieth-century symphonic heritage.

John Adams (b. 1947)

Like Philip Glass, John Adams is best known as a theater composer, having achieved canonical success with *Nixon in China* (1985–87), *Doctor Atomic* (2004–05), and the controversial *The*

Death of Klinghoffer (1989–91). And like Glass and several others discussed thus far, patrons and advocates in the orchestra world have played an important role in making possible Adams's output of symphonic works, which are listed in table 9.13. For Glass, support has come through conductor Dennis Russell Davies and groups such as the American Composers Orchestra and the Bruckner Orchester Linz, while for Adams, his association with the San Francisco Symphony early in his career proved pivotal. Adams became an adviser for the group in 1978, the same year in which he composed and premiered his immensely popular *Shaker Loops*. He was the orchestra's composer-in-residence from 1982 to 1985.[217]

Although in a younger generation of composers who drew on minimalism, Adams paved the way for Glass as a minimalist-turned-symphonist with a pair of symphonic works in the early 1980s that merged relentless repetition with melodies and harmonies that evoke Romanticism. Unlike Glass, Adams composed his first symphonies, *Harmonium* (1980–81) and *Harmonielehre* (1984–85), relatively early in his career, well before his operatic successes. And in contrast to Glass's more traditional orchestral sonorities, emphasis on repeated short harmonic patterns, triadic harmonies, and fairly constant musical surface, Adams's more frenetic symphonies showcase a varied timbral palette, extended harmonies, slow-moving and nebulous harmonic landscapes, and thunderous climaxes. The opening of *Harmonielehre*, shown in example 9.8, is typical of much of Adams's orchestral writing in its pounding repetition.

These traits are evident in his first symphonic work proper, *Harmonium*, for chorus and orchestra. (Adams called it "a curious piece, one of those odd birds in the classical music literature, a choral symphony."[218]) Sharing a name with the keyboard instrument but implying something of a much larger scale, the work carries cosmic resonances; as the composer wrote, "*Harmonium* began with a simple, totally formed mental image: that of a single tone emerging out of a vast, empty space and, by means of a gentle unfolding, evolving into a rich, pulsating fabric of sound."[219] (The title came from twentieth-century poet Wallace Stevens [1879–1955]; as Adams wrote, "So I began to search for a text . . . I first went to Wallace Stevens, thinking that I might share both his New England sensibilities and a common philosophical outlook. He'd published some of his first poems under the title *Harmonium*, and given that tonal harmony was very much at the forefront of my concerns, such a title seemed, well, harmonious. In the end the word 'harmonium' was all that I drew from Stevens."[220]) For Adams, "a balance between harmonic stability and the invention and variety of the sound 'surface'" was an important component of his composing at the time, as was a slowing of harmonic rhythm that allowed modulations to sound as "a kind of celestial gear shifting" (a contrast to Glass's more regular, patterned key shifts). A clear example of this approach appears in the first movement, "Negative Love," set to a text by John Donne. There, a sonic trickle builds to a pandiatonic wash of orchestral sound before a stunning switch (m. 239) to E-flat major at the words *My love*. The energetic first movement gives way to a more meditative second movement, a setting of Emily Dickinson's "Because I Could Not Stop for Death" that contains moments in which Adams's celestial gears seem almost startlingly frozen in place. It transitions stormily to the third movement's rhythmically unrelenting opening, which lives up to the title "Wild Nights" (another Dickinson poem). The excitement dissipates suddenly with the work's more contemplative conclusion, beginning at m. 236.

After this initial symphonic effort, and following such landmark works as *Grand Pianola Music* (1982), Adams composed the symphonic work for which he is still perhaps most celebrated: *Harmonielehre*, which Adams himself considers a symphony and whose title, as he explained, translates to "theory of harmony" or "harmony lesson"—meant to be "part

Table 9.13 The Symphonic Works of John Adams (b. 1947)

Title	Movements	Instrumentation	Comments
Harmonium (1980–81)	I. Negative Love (561 mm.) II. Because I Could Not Stop For Death (365 mm.) II. Wild Nights (435 mm.)	4 Flt. (3 doubling Picc.), 3 Ob., 3 Clar. (1 doubling Bclar.), 3 Bssn. (1 doubling Cbssn.), 4 Hr., 4 Tpt., 3 Trom., Tuba, Perc. (Glsp., Crotales, 2 Mrb., Metallophone, BD, Tubular Bells, Suspended Cym., Sizzle Cym., Crash Cyms., Xylo., Tri., Tom-toms [medium, large], Anvil, Cowbells, Tamb.), Harp, Cel., Pno., Synthesizer, Strgs., SATB Chorus (Divisi)	Commissioned by the San Francisco Symphony for the inaugural season of Davies Symphony Hall. Dedicated to Edo de Waart. First performance: April 15, 1981, San Francisco Symphony, conducted by Edo de Waart. Texts by John Donne (Movement 1) and Emily Dickinson (Movements 2 and 3). Score published by Associated Music Publishers. Recorded by San Francisco Symphony and San Francisco Symphony Chorus, conducted by Edo de Waart (ECM New Series 1277); Atlanta Symphony Orchestra & Chorus, conducted by Robert Shaw (Telarc CD-80365); San Francisco Symphony and San Francisco Symphony Chorus, conducted by John Adams (Nonesuch 79549).
Harmonielehre (1984–8)	Part I [no title] (595 mm.) Part II: The Anfortas Wound (205 mm.) Part III: Meister Eckhardt and Quackie (393 mm.)	4 Flt. (3 doubling Picc.), 3 Ob. (1 doubling EH), 4 Clar. (2 doubling Bclar.), 3 Bssn., Cbssn., 4 Hr., 4 Tpt., 3 Trom., 2 Tubas, Timp., Perc. (2 Mrb., Vbp., Xylo., Tubular Bells, Crotales, Glsp., 2 Suspended Cyms., Sizzle Cym., Small Crash Cyms., Bell Tree, 2 Tam-tams, 2 Tri., BD), 2 Harps, Pno, Cel., Strgs.	Commissioned as part of Meet the Composer. First performance: March 21, 1985, San Francisco Symphony, conducted by Edo de Waart. Score published by Associated Music Publishers. Recorded by San Francisco Symphony, conducted by Edo de Waart (Nonesuch 79115); City of Birmingham Symphony Orchestra, conducted by Simon Rattle (EMI 55051); San Francisco Symphony, conducted by Michael Tilson Thomas (SFS 0053); Royal Scottish National Orchestra, conducted by Peter Oundjian (Chandos CHSA 5129).

Chamber Symphony (1992)	I. Mongrel Airs (248 mm.) II. Aria with Walking Bass (175 mm.) III. Roadrunner (215 mm.)	Flt. (doubling Picc.), Eb Clar. (doubling Clar.) Bclar. (doubling Clar.), Bssn., Cbssn. (doubling Bssn.), Hr., Tpt., Trom., Perc. (Trap set: Cowbell, Hi-hat Cym., SD, Pedal BD, Wood Block, 2 Bongos, 3 Tom-toms, Roto-toms, Tamb, Timbale, Claves, Conga), Strgs.	Commissioned by the San Francisco Contemporary Music Players. First performance: January 17, 1993, Schönberg Ensemble (in The Hague, Netherlands), conducted by John Adams. Score published by Boosey & Hawkes. Recorded by London Sinfonietta, conducted by John Adams (Nonesuch 79219-2); Ensemble Modern, conducted by Sian Edwards (BMG/RCA 09026-68674-2); Absolute Ensemble, conducted by Kristjan Järvi (CCn'C 00492); Orchestre Philharmonique de Montpellier, conducted by René Bosc (Actes Sud OMA34102).
Naïve and Sentimental Music (1997–98)	I. Naïve and Sentimental Music (499 mm.) II. Mother of the Man (255 mm.) III. Chain to the Rhythm (401 mm.)	4 Flt. (2 doubling Picc.), 3 Ob. (1 doubling EH), 3 Clar. (1 doubling Bclar.), Bclar., 3 Bssn. (1 doubling Cbssn.), 4 Hr., 4 Tpt., 3 Trom., 2 Tuba, Timp., Perc. (5 Players; Player 1: Vbp., Almglocken, Xylo., 2 Tri., Suspended Cym., 2 Small Chinese Gongs, Small High-pitched Bell [higher], Glsp.; Player 2: Mrb., Shaker, Xylo., Crotales, Almglocken, Vbp., Suspended Cym.; Player 3: Xylo., Glsp., BD [large], Small High-pitched Bell [lower], Bowed Vbp., Suspended Cym.; Player 4: Chimes, Anvil [high], Tam-tam, "Ranch" Tri., 5 Japanese Temple Bowls; Player 5: 5 Gongs [low], Chimes, Sleighbells [large], 3 "Ranch" Tri., Tri. [high], Tam-tam, Suspended Cym., Suspended Sizzle Cym.), Pno., Cel., Keyboard Sampler, Gui. (Steel-string round-hole model with electric pickup), 2 Harps, Strgs.	Commissioned by Los Angeles Philharmonic Orchestra, Ensemble Modern, Vancouver Symphony, and Sydney Symphony Orchestra. First performance: February 19, 1999, Los Angeles Philharmonic Orchestra, conducted by Esa-Pekka Salonen. Score published by Boosey & Hawkes. Recorded by Los Angeles Philharmonic, conducted by Esa-Pekka Salonen (Nonesuch 79636-2).

Table 9.13 *continued*

Title	Movements	Instrumentation	Comments
Doctor Atomic Symphony (2007)	One movement: The Laboratory—Panic—Trinity (706 mm.)	Picc., 2 Flt., 3 Ob. (1 doubling EH), 3 Clar. (1 doubling E♭ Clar., 1 doubling B♭clar.), 3 Bssn. (1 doubling Cbssn.), 4 Hr., 4 Tpt. (1 doubling Picc. Tpt.), 3 Trom., Tuba, Timp., Perc. (4 Players: Chimes, Crotales, Glsp., BD, SD, Thunder Sheet, Tam-tams [medium, large], Suspended Cyms. [high, low], Tuned Gongs), Harp, Cel., Strgs.	Commissioned by Carnegie Hall Corporation, St. Louis Symphony Orchestra, and BBC Radio 3. Dedicated to David Robertson. Draws on music from opera *Doctor Atomic*. After its premiere, Adams shortened the work significantly. First performance: August 21, 2007, BBC Symphony Orchestra, conducted by John Adams. Score published by Boosey & Hawkes. Recorded by St. Louis Symphony Orchestra, conducted by David Robertson (Nonesuch 468220); Royal Scottish National Orchestra, conducted by Peter Oundjian (Chandos CHSA 5129).
Son of Chamber Symphony (2007)	I. (366 mm.) II. (198 mm.) III. (325 mm.)	Flt. (doubling Picc.), Ob., Clar., B♭clar., Bssn., Hr., Tpt., Trom., Perc. (2 Players; Player 1: Chimes, Keyboard Sampler [or Trash Can Lid or Chinese Cym.], 3 Bongos, Conga, Clave, Cowbell; Player 2: Keyboard Sampler, Glsp., Temple Blocks, Castanets, 3 Bongos, Conga, Clave, Wood Block, Closed Hi-hat, Suspended Cym., Cowbell, 3 Tom-toms [low], Pedal BD [very dry]), Pno. (doubling Cel. or sampled Cel.), Strgs.	Commissioned for Stanford Lively Arts in honor of the Bonnie J. Addario Lung Cancer Foundation and by the Carnegie Hall Corporation. Choreographed by Mark Morris as *Joyride* for San Francisco Ballet. First performance: November 30, 2007, by Alarm Will Sound, conducted by Alan Pierson. Score published by Boosey & Hawkes. Recorded by International Contemporary Ensemble, conducted by John Adams (Nonesuch 523014).

City Noir (2009)	I. The City and Its Double (462 mm.) II. The Song Is for You (173 mm.) III. Boulevard Night (340 mm.)	Picc., 3 Flt. (1 doubling Picc.), 3 Ob., EH, 3 Clar. (1 doubling BClar.), Asax, 2 Bssn., Cbssn., 6 Hr., 4 Tpt, 3 Trom., Tuba, Timp., Perc. (5 players; Player 1: Vbp., Bongos; Player 2: Tuned Gongs, Suspended Cym., Glsp., Mrb., Tam-tam [large], Vbp., Chimes, BD, SD, Mixed percussion [Castanets, Cowbell, Clave, Temple Block]; Player 3: Chimes, Glsp., Tamb., Tam-tam [medium], 2 Timbales, Suspended Cym., Crotales [opt. Glsp.], Xylo.; Player 4: BD, Tuned Gongs, SD, 2 Suspended Cyms., Crotales, Castanet, Tri., Glsp.; Player 5: 2 Tam-tams, BD, Suspended Cym., Tri., Temple Block, SD, Tamb., Bongo, Conga), Jazz Drummer (Hi-hat and Ride Cym.), SD, 3 Tom-toms [low], Cowbell, Timbales, Suspended Cym.), Cel., Pno., 2 Harps, Strgs.	Commissioned by Los Angeles Philharmonic Association, London Symphony Orchestra in association with Cité de la Musique-Salle Pleyel, Eduard Van Beinum Foundation, Dutch Radio Concert Series in the Concertgebouw Amsterdam, and Toronto Symphony Orchestra. First performance: October 8, 2009, Los Angeles Philharmonic, conducted by Gustavo Dudamel. Score published by Boosey & Hawkes (Hendon Music). Recorded by Los Angeles Philharmonic Orchestra, conducted by Gustavo Dudamel (world premiere; DG 28947906322); St. Louis Symphony Orchestra, conducted by David Robertson (Nonesuch 7559795644).
Scheherazade.2, Dramatic Symphony for Violin and Orchestra (2014–15)	I. Tale of the Wise Young Woman — Pursuit by the True Believers (452 mm.) II. A Long Desire (Love Scene) (318 mm.) III. Scheherazade and the Men with Beards (Doctrinal disputes—they argue among themselves—the judgment—Scheherazade's appeal—the condemnation) (312 mm.) IV. Escape, Flight, Sanctuary (263 mm.)	Picc., 2 Flt., 2 Ob., EH, 2 Clar., Bclar., 2 Bssn., Cbssn., 4 Hr., 2 Tpt., 3 Trom., Perc. (3 Players: Suspended Cym., Tam-tam, 2 BD [medium, large], Vbp., Tuned Gongs, Whip, Xylo.), Cimbalom, Cel., 2 Harps, Strgs., Solo Vln.	Commissioned by New York Philharmonic, Royal Concertgebouw Orchestra Amsterdam, Royal Concertgebouw, and Sydney Symphony Orchestra. First performance: March 26, 2015, New York Philharmonic, conducted by Alan Gilbert, with Leila Josefowicz, violin. Score published by Boosey & Hawkes. Recorded by St. Louis Symphony, conducted by David Robertson, with Leila Josefowicz, violin (Nonesuch 557150).

Example 9.8 John Adams, *Harmonielehre*/1, mm. 1–5. Copyright © 1985 Associated Music Publishers, Inc. All rights reserved. International copyright secured. Reprinted with permission.

whimsical, part an acknowledgment of my puzzling father-son relationship to the master" (meaning Arnold Schoenberg, whose theory treatise of 1911 carried the same name).[221] Adams called *Harmonielehre* a "wedding of fin-de-siècle chromatic harmony with the rhythmic and formal procedures of Minimalism," suggesting the kind of postmodernist blend of styles also observed in Harrison's and Rochberg's works.[222] In the symphony's untitled first part, the unforgivingly emphatic opening, with its resolute repeated chords and persistent rhythms, derives from the composer's fantastical dream of "a huge oil tanker" in the San Francisco Bay that "slowly rose up like a Saturn rocket and blasted out of the bay and into the sky."[223] Also, that passage begins to suggest the difficulty of performing Adams's orchestral music, particularly the sheer endurance required of wind and brass players. This austere material eventually gives way to a rapturous, sweeping cello solo (m. 258), which is soon joined by other strings and develops into a wide-ranging sensuous melody that pierces through and eventually supplants the pandiatonic, minimalist texture. Late-Romantic chromaticism then leads back to the more relentless rhythmic contours of the opening section, lending the movement an overall ternary arc.

The symphony's second part, "The Anfortas Wound," is a reference to the king of medieval legend who, as Adams described him, "symbolized a condition of sickness of the soul that curses it with a feeling of impotence and depression."[224] Its hazy, calm, harmonically and rhythmically indistinct undercurrent erupts into moments of anguish, as at the climax at mm. 149–65. Echoing the recent symphonic practice of quoting from late-Romantic music (seen above especially in the music of George Rochberg), the passage of screaming trumpet and violins—which Adams called an "obvious homage to Mahler's last, unfinished symphony"—is indeed quite clearly a gloss on the famous outcry in the Adagio of the Austrian composer's unfinished Symphony No. 10 (1910; mm. 203–12).[225] Adams's third movement, "Meister Eckhardt and Quackie," is named for a dream Adams had of his daughter (then nicknamed "Quackie") traveling on a medieval mystic's shoulder.[226] It opens dreamily with wind, piano, harp, and celesta arpeggios that underpin a soaring, sweeping theme in the violins, which gives way to a languid, chromatically descending line in the brass. Kinetic energy returns as the movement culminates in an austere, brass-forward E-flat-major climax. Adams described this conclusion—which he revised after the first recording with the San Francisco Symphony—as "a reworking for orchestra of the end of *Light Over Water*" (a work of 1983 for synthesizer and brass), "an illustration of the extent to which my musical thinking easily crossbred electronic and orchestrated music."[227]

Adams continued with the three-movement form in the even larger *Naive and Sentimental Music* (1997–98), which draws on Friedrich Schiller's essay "On the Naive and Sentimental in Poetry" (1795). Adams himself called it "a symphony informed by the symphonies of Bruckner, themselves informed by the operas of Wagner and the symphonies of Beethoven."[228] For Adams, *naive* and *sentimental* in the composition's title reflects the tension between purely natural, spontaneous expression (the "naïve"—"speaking through the medium of the orchestra has always been a natural and spontaneous gesture for me") and one's self-conscious efforts to achieve such a creative state (the "sentimental"—"writing for orchestra at a time when the epoch of great orchestral music has already flowered and passed is itself a deeply sentimental act").[229] Suggesting the boundaries between these states to be fluid, Adams centers the harmonically indistinct first movement (itself called "Naive and Sentimental") on what he calls a "'naïve/sentimental' tune"—a long-breathed melodic refrain that "leaves the nest and ventures out into the wide world like a Dickens child."[230] The quick pace at which wistful sections alternate with orchestral eruptions contrasts sharply with the "celestial gear shifting" of *Harmonium*.

Adams revealed that the second movement, "Mother of the Man," reinterprets Ferruccio Busoni's *Berceuse élégiaque*, Op. 42 (1909), subtitled "Der Mannes Wiegenlied am Sarge seiner Mutter" ("The man's lullaby at his mother's coffin"), which he had already arranged for chamber orchestra in 1989.[231] The first section of Adams's movement places a languid, circling solo for amplified steel-stringed guitar over a blanket of slowly shifting string-based sonorities that recalls *The Unanswered Question* of Charles Ives, a composer with whom Adams has consciously associated himself; a more agitated middle section culminates in a series of ascending scales that lead to a brief reprise of the movement's opening. The final movement, "Chain to the Rhythm," is replete with what Adams wryly labeled "familiar Adamsian flora and fauna"—a sign of the composer's awareness of his secure place in the classical canon.[232] In the movement's slow burn toward a final climax, the gradual shifting and layering of timbres and motives recalls the phasing effects of classic minimalism. The work's use of amplified sounds and two keyboard samplers also refers to an earlier minimalist idiom and places the instrumental forces of *Naïve and Sentimental Music* beyond the more standard symphonic ones of *Harmonium* and *Harmonielehre*. But the impact of such technological additions to the sound of *Naïve and Sentimental Music* remains subtle in the context of Adams's variegated orchestral palette, especially when compared to the sparkling sampler-driven conclusion of *Fearful Symmetries* (1988) or the haunting prerecorded sounds in the Pulitzer Prize–winning *On the Transmigration of Souls* (2002), which commemorates the victims of the terrorist attacks of September 11, 2001.

The period between *Harmonielehre* and *Naïve and Sentimental Music* was significant beyond the realm of symphonic writing. It saw the operas *Nixon in China* (1987) and *The Death of Klinghoffer* (1991); several orchestral works, including *The Chairman Dances* (1985), *Short Ride in a Fast Machine* (1986), the Grawemeyer Award–winning Violin Concerto (1993), and *Slonimsky's Earbox* (1996); and the *Chamber Symphony* (1992), a feverish, contrapuntally and rhythmically dizzying three-movement composition that combines Adams's love of cartoons with his interest in Arnold Schoenberg's *Chamber Symphony*, Op. 9.[233] (The title of the third movement, "Roadrunner," points to the former connection.) Its three-movement musical descendant, *Son of Chamber Symphony*, appeared in 2007—the same year as the *Doctor Atomic Symphony*, which draws directly on music from Adams's 2005 opera on the development and testing of the atomic bomb in New Mexico in 1945. Initially in four movements, as heard in its premiere, this symphony in its shorter, revised form has been understood as a one-movement composition (as described in a review by Anthony Tommasini) in three sections, convincing because these sections are continuous and because "The Laboratory"—the first section, or "movement"—is extremely short, functioning more as a prelude to the second section, "Panic," than as an independent structure. (At the same time, these are three separate movements in the published score.) The final section, "Trinity," is an instrumental version of J. Robert Oppenheimer's Act I aria "Batter My Heart"; here, the baritone part is reassigned to trumpet, and the piece retains the aria's insistent focus on D minor and its ritornello-like format.[234]

Adams thus brought to the recent symphony an eclectic mixture of minimalist rhythms, late-Romantic harmony and melody, stylistic allusions, a robust relationship with popular culture and technology, and an often quirky musical sensibility. Although his central works in the genre—*Harmonium*, *Harmonielehre*, and *Naïve and Sentimental Music*—were not officially given the title "symphony," their three-movement structures suggest large-scale contrast, tension, and release. Yet another work along these lines is *City Noir* (2009), a three-movement jazz-infused work that Adams called "a symphony inspired by the peculiar ambiance and mood of Los Angeles 'noir' films, especially those produced in the late forties and early fifties"; Adams grouped it with two earlier orchestral works "that have as their theme the California experience" (and that could very well be understood as symphonies): *El Dorado* (1991) and *The Dharma at Big Sur* (2003).[235] And his even more recent *Scheherazade.2* (2014–15) pushes boundaries as a rare work that is both a symphony and solo concerto. He composed the work for violinist Leila Josefowicz and employed a smaller ensemble than in his other symphonies. News stories about the treatment of women around the world led Adams to conceive of a

> "dramatic symphony" in which the principal character role is taken by the solo violin—and she would be Scheherazade. While not having an actual story line or plot, the symphony follows a set of provocative images: a beautiful young woman with grit and personal power; a pursuit by "true believers"; a love scene (who knows . . . perhaps her lover is also a woman?); a scene in which she is tried by a court of religious zealots ("Scheherazade and the Men with Beards"), during which the men argue doctrine among themselves and rage and shout at her, only to have her calmly respond to their accusations; and a final "Escape, Flight, Sanctuary," which must be the archetypal dream of any woman importuned by a man or men.[236]

Adams subtitled the work "Dramatic Symphony for Violin and Orchestra," a name that connects the work to nineteenth-century symphonic tradition through specific nods to Hector Berlioz (*Roméo et Juliette, symphonie dramatique*, from 1839) and Nikolai Rimsky-Korsakov (*Sheherazade*, the symphonic suite from 1888). And with its hints of a narrative, *Scheherazade.2* plugs into a network of recent symphonies linked to striking extramusical content, such as John Corigliano's Symphony No. 1 and Mason Bates's electronically bolstered multimovement orchestral works (discussed below).

Christopher Rouse (1949–2019)

Many of the works of Christopher Rouse (1949–2019) have been associated with an intense sense of despair and tragedy—so much so that a 1993 *New York Times* headline for an article on Rouse read, "A Composer Spreads a Little Sunshine (Very Little)."[237] Indeed, the harsh experience of another's death often informed Rouse's work. The Pulitzer Prize–winning Trombone Concerto (1991), which Rouse called "a dark, despairing piece," was dedicated to the memory of Leonard Bernstein.[238] The passing of his mother led to the orchestral work *Envoi* (1995).[239] Not pleased, however, with "being typecast in people's minds as a kind of prince of darkness," he decided he "would turn in the other direction, because I am interested in extremes."[240] Thus, his orchestral composition *Rapture* (2000) paints a more jubilant picture. But whether uplifting or somber, a sense of profound expression is central to Rouse's music, including his symphonies, which are listed in table 9.14. As he said in a 2008 interview, "It doesn't matter to me if a piece is tonal or atonal or what the organizing system is or even if there is one. All that matters to me is if there is a sense of urgency in the expression and that the listener needs to bring a certain urgency to the experience of hearing it, too."[241]

Rouse was composer-in-residence of his hometown Baltimore Symphony Orchestra from 1986 to 1989, and his Symphony No. 1 (1986) emerged from a Meet the Composer commission. Speaking to Glenn Watkins of this work, Rouse said, "I find writing a work called 'symphony' to be a rather daunting task and one which I don't take lightly—hence the long time before I actually composed one which I hoped would be deserving of the name."[242] This

Table 9.14 The Symphonies of Christopher Rouse (1949–2019)

Title	Movements	Instrumentation	Comments
Symphony No. 1 (1986)	One movement: Grave, Lamentoso (375 mm.)	2 Flt. (1 doubling Picc.), 2 Ob. (1 doubling EH and Oboe d'amore), 2 Clar. (1 doubling Bclar.), 2 Bssn. (1 doubling Cbssn.), 4 Hr. (2 doubling Tenor Wagner Tubas, 2 doubling Bass Wagner Tubas), 3 Tpt., 3 Trom., 1 Tuba, Timp., Perc. (3 Players: Player 1: Chinese Cym., SD, Bongo [high], Tam-tam [large], Glsp., Suspended Cym.; Player 2: Tenor Drum, BD, Xylo.; Player 3: Tamb., Metal Plate, Hammer [as in Mahler's Sixth Symphony], Tam-tam [large], Glsp., Suspended Cym.), Strgs.	Commissioned by Meet the Composer and dedicated to John Harbison. Awarded first prize in the 1988 Kennedy Center Friedhelm Awards for new orchestral works by American composers. First performance: January 21, 1988, Baltimore Symphony Orchestra, conducted by David Zinman. Score published by Helicon Music Corporation. Recorded by Baltimore Symphony Orchestra, conducted by David Zinman (Elektra/Nonesuch 9 79230-2); Royal Stockholm Philharmonic Orchestra, conducted by Alan Gilbert (BIS-CD-1386).
Symphony No. 2 (1994)	I. Allegro (516 mm.) II. Adagio (In memoriam Stephen Albert) (132 mm.) III. Allegro (499 mm.)	Picc., 2 Flt., 3 Ob., EH, 2 Clar., Bclar., 3 Bssn., 4 Hr., 3 Tpt., 3 Trom., Tuba, Timp., Perc. (Cyms., Xylo., Glsp., SD, Tam-tam, BD, Suspended Cym., Field Drum, Chinese Cym., Tenor Drum, Tamb., Bongo), Harp, Strgs.	Commissioned by Houston Symphony. First performance: March 4, 1995, Houston Symphony, conducted by Christoph Eschenbach, to whom the score is dedicated. Score published by Boosey & Hawkes. Recorded by Houston Symphony, conducted by Christoph Eschenbach (Telarc CD-80452); Royal Stockholm Philharmonic Orchestra, conducted by Alan Gilbert (BIS-CD-1586).

Symphony No. 3 (2011)	I. (536 mm.) II. (585 mm.)	Picc., 2 Flt., 2 Ob., EH, 2 Clar., Bclar., 2 Bssn., Cbssn., 4 Hr., 4 Tpt., 4 Trom., Tuba, Timp., Perc. (Xylo., Orchestra Bells, Chimes, Chinese Cym., Crash Cym., Suspended Cym., 2 Chinese Opera Gongs, Tam-tam, Tri., Wood Blocks, Tamb., SD, 2 Tenor Drums, Tom-toms, Timbales, BD), 2 Harps, Strgs.	Dedicated to John Merrill, the composer's high school teacher. Commissioned by St. Louis Symphony Orchestra, Singapore Symphony Orchestra, Baltimore Symphony Orchestra, and Royal Stockholm Philharmonic Orchestra. First performance: May 5, 2011, St. Louis Symphony Orchestra, conducted by David Robertson. Score published by Boosey & Hawkes. Recorded by New York Philharmonic, conducted by Alan Gilbert (Dacapo 8.226110).
Symphony No. 4 (2013)	I. Felice (499 mm.) II. Doloroso (169 mm.)	Picc., 2 Flt., 2 Ob., EH, 2 Clar., Cbclar., 2 Bssn., Cbssn., 4 Hr., 3 Tpt., 4 Trom., Tuba, Perc. (Vbp., Glsp., Tam-tam, Tri., Mrb., Cyms., BD, Chimes), Harp, Cel., Strgs.	Commissioned by New York Philharmonic. First performance: June 5, 2014, New York Philharmonic, conducted by Alan Gilbert. Score published by Boosey & Hawkes. Recorded by New York Philharmonic, conducted by Alan Gilbert (Dacapo 8.226110).
Symphony No. 5 (2015)	One movement (1134 mm.)	3 Flt. (1 doubling Bass Flt.), 3 Ob., 3 Clar., 3 Bssn., 4 Hr., 3 Tpt., 3 Trom., Tuba, Timp., Perc. (3 Players; Player 1: Chinese Cym., Suspended Cym., Crash Cym., 2 Wood Blocks; Vbp.; Player 2: SD, Tamb, Tam-tam; Player 3: BD, Glsp., Tamb.), 2 Harps, Strgs.	Commissioned by Dallas Symphony Orchestra, Nashville Symphony, and Aspen Music Festival and School. First performance: February 9, 2017, Dallas Symphony Orchestra, conducted by Jaap van Zweden. Score published by Boosey & Hawkes. Recorded by Nashville Symphony, conducted by Giancarlo Guerrero (Naxos 8.559852).
Symphony No. 6 (2019)	I. Desolato (141 mm.) II. Piacevole (230 mm.) III. Furioso (267 mm.) IV. Passacaglia (102 mm.)	2 Flt., 2 Ob., 2 Clar. (1 doubling Bclar.), 2 Bssn., 4 Hr., 2 Tpt. (1 doubling Flugelhorn), 3 Trom., Tuba, Timp., Perc. (2 players; Player 1: Suspended Cym., Cyms., Tam-tam, Glsp., Xylo., Gong; Player 2: Suspended Cym., SD, BD, Xylo.), Harp, Strgs.	Commissioned by Cincinnati Symphony Orchestra for its 125th anniversary season. First performance: October 18, 2019, Cincinnati Symphony Orchestra, conducted by Louis Langrée. The premiere took place posthumously, as the composer had died the previous month. Score published by Boosey & Hawkes.

symphony employs stylistic allusions and quotations to suggest grief, and it is cast in a single slow movement in which ethereal hymnlike passages morph into throbbing climaxes. The contrast between these two sensibilities reaches a sudden and shocking limit when, as Rouse described it, "as if an enormous earlier struggle is going to lift away, with a sense of reconciliation . . . instead what pops up is this orchestral scream."[243] This event, which takes place at Reh. 24, comes at the end of a lengthy, quiet passage for strings that transforms, with the help of French horns and bass drum, into a colossal orchestral explosion, derived in part from the "Montagues and Capulets" movement of Sergei Prokofiev's *Romeo and Juliet*.[244] The score at this moment also calls for a hammer, as in the final movement of Mahler's Sixth Symphony. Rouse called this moment in his own work a "totem," and he acknowledged reusing it in both the Trombone Concerto and the orchestral work *Jagannath* (1987) to capture a sense of "annihilation."[245] The work also includes a fugue, starting at Reh. 6, with its subject beginning with the first violins on D, E-flat, C, and B—Shostakovich's emblematic DSCH motive. It also features a striking recollection of the opening of the Adagio from Bruckner's Symphony No. 7, in a resolute statement by the Wagner tubas at two measures before Reh. 29. This reference leads to a slow, repeated short-short-long pattern in the timpani, a rhythmic pattern that figured earlier in the work, underneath violins softly straining in the high registers, all before a quiet conclusion in the low strings. Other references abound in the symphony. The short-short-long rhythm at Reh. 14 recalls the second movement of Ralph Vaughan Williams's Symphony No. 6, and the extended wind solos over pedal points, as at Reh. 26, suggest Shostakovich. The inscription "De profundis clamavi . . ." ("From the depths I have cried") connects these references to the highly personal nature of the despair in this symphony—as opposed to the collective anguish of Corigliano's First Symphony. And as a one-movement symphony, this work points back to Sibelius's Symphony No. 7 as well as the Symphony No. 6 of William Schuman, a work Rouse especially admired. He called that work "perhaps the most impressive score in Schuman's entire oeuvre" and "a true one-movement symphony, subtly constructed and highly rewarding for analysis."[246]

The unrelenting opening movement of Symphony No. 2 (1994), commissioned by the Houston Symphony Orchestra, is fast and full of colorful percussion (Rouse was a percussionist), prickly counterpoint, angular leaps, and a sense of rhythmic propulsion. This innocent, almost lighthearted material collides abruptly with the pounding brass and percussion that introduce the slow second movement, whose opening measures are seen in example 9.9. (As is the published score, this example is in C.)

This movement was written in memory of Stephen Albert who, as mentioned above, died in a car accident in Massachusetts in 1992. The violent musical interruption follows without warning and without break after the playful bassoon noodling at the end of the previous movement—as if to communicate the unanticipated trauma of such a tragic event, and the suddenness of a car accident in particular; as such, this moment captures the sense of uncensored intensity often found in Rouse's symphonies. Expressive leaps and more sudden orchestral "screams" throughout the movement paint a picture of all-consuming anguish. A bass clarinet solo leads directly into the fast Finale, in which a long crescendo ushers in a grim recapitulation of the playful first movement. As Rouse put it, the second movement "might be said to act as a tunnel through which the somewhat mercurially-mooded first Allegro passes; on the other end of the tunnel, this allegro music emerges recognizably both the same and different, with the lighter temperament of the originally heard music now darker and more

Example 9.9 Christopher Rouse, Symphony No. 2/2, mm. 1–4. Copyright © 1994 Hendon Music, Inc., a Boosey & Hawkes Company. Copyright for all countries. All rights reserved. Reprinted with permission.

threatening in tone. As a result, the arch-like form of the symphony brings the work to a close at virtually the same structural point at which it began, but the conclusion's emotional world is light years away from that at the beginning."[247]

Rouse's third effort in this genre did not arrive until 2011, but he returned to symphony writing with force in the 2010s. His two-movement Symphony No. 3, a large theme-and-variation structure, picked up where the Symphony No. 2 left off with a raucous opening. In the consistently loud introductory movement, a clarion call from the trumpets ushers in a whirlwind of strings, brass, and winds exchanging angular motives over a percussion-powered orchestral engine. Rouse drew the striking opening trumpet effect, as well as the symphony's two-movement structure and its second-movement theme-and-variations format, from Prokofiev's Symphony No. 2 (Beethoven's Piano Sonata No. 32 in C minor, Op. 111, served as another reference point).[248] Certainly, too, the raucous, unrelenting style found throughout Prokofiev's Symphony No. 2 points toward Rouse's third symphonic effort. The theme-and-variations proper takes place in the second movement, and as Rouse wrote, "the musical language ranges from the dissonant and barbaric to the overtly tonal."[249] The theme (m. 2, first heard in the English horn) is a concealed version of one of the introduction's motives, declaimed slowly and gently by various wind soloists over an oscillating, shimmering string accompaniment. In the celebratory first variation (m. 21), the speed and energy of the symphony's introduction returns. The slow second variation (m. 171) for strings and harp offers some of the movement's rare glimpses of triadic respite. It contrasts with the faster and louder third variation (m. 202), which again pits winds against strings and builds to the speedy fourth and fifth variations (m. 273, m. 393). The symphony ends where it began, as a restatement of the theme (at m. 568, again in the English horn) yields to a deafening trumpet call that conjures the symphony's opening. As with other moments in his symphonies, the calmer return of the theme only offers the illusion of a letup in musical ferocity.

Rouse wrote his Symphony No. 4 (2013) in his capacity as Marie-Josée Kravis Composer-in-Residence for the New York Philharmonic. In a review, Anthony Tommasini referred to Rouse's symphony in a way that recalls the extreme emotional variance familiar from Rouse's other works: "an intriguing 20-minute work structured in two connected movements of vastly contrasting character: the first bustling and seemingly cheerful, the second grim and despairing."[250] Unlike the Symphony No. 2, Rouse offered no hints about specific programmatic or autobiographical references. Rouse did write, however, that "while I did have a particular meaning in mind when composing my Symphony No. 4, I prefer to keep it to myself. Some listeners may find the piece baffling but will nonetheless have to guess."[251] Two more symphonies followed his fourth. The Symphony No. 5 (2015) alludes to and is in some ways modeled on Beethoven's Fifth Symphony.[252] Rouse's final symphony, the Symphony No. 6, which premiered in 2019 one month after the composer's death from cancer, features the flugelhorn and is his only symphony in four movements.[253]

One fascinating aspect of Rouse's musical persona—and one that provides context for his symphonies—was his relationship with popular music. He famously taught a rock music course at the Eastman School of Music, where he served on the faculty from 1981 to 2002. His music evokes rock; at times it does so explicitly, as in the percussion work *Bonham* (1988), named for the drummer of Led Zeppelin, but Rouse's embrace of overwhelming volume in his symphonies, which certainly finds an analog in some rock music, served—along with his direct references to past works—as an avenue for generating his signature Neoromantic aesthetic.

Libby Larsen (b. 1950)

Libby Larsen's symphonies, shown in table 9.15, paint a more visually vivid and less psychologically turbulent picture than those of Rouse. They do so through soundscapes that vibrantly combine an expanded diatonic palette with novel investigations of rhythm and texture—in Larsen's case, often from a specifically "American" angle. One of the few composers in recent years to compose symphonies that deal explicitly with questions of American identity, Larsen applies her interest in the sound qualities of American English to her symphonies and other works:

> The rhythmic complexity of American English, combined with its fluid and inventive nature, suggests (I would even say inspires) a kind of musical syntax which is distinctive and all its own. Many people characterize American music (non-texted as well as texted) as having a certain kind of drive and harmonic conditioning that is not involved in European modernism. Some suggest that the sheer size of the landmass of the Americas may affect both the texture and the architecture of music that is heard as "American." Whatever the influences may be, to me to be an American symphonic composer means to be cognizant of my musical wellsprings and invite them into the center of my process.[254]

Rhythm and texture are at the forefront of her first symphony (*Symphony: Water Music*). Larsen completed this "poetic symphony" in 1985 on a commission from the Minnesota Orchestra. It premiered less than two months before John Adams's *Harmonielehre*, and the first movement, "Fresh Breeze," calls to mind the lively rhythms and swelling effects of Adams's work, as well as the textural vibrancy of Aaron Jay Kernis's *Symphony in Waves* (1989); in its explorations of water in its different physical states, it also anticipates Mason Bates's *Liquid Interface* (2007). As Larsen described "Fresh Breeze," "The first quiet chord, emerging from the strings, is a stack of thirds pulsing in 6/8 time. It attempts to capture the fresh, oscillating, crystalline vibrancy of water moved by constant wind. The gestures move about the orchestra almost kaleidoscopically, pin-pointing here a quartet of horns and harp glissando, there trilling high in the winds or sandwiched in the violas; often vibrations of percussion are suspended weightlessly in the air. The motion is constant as the colorful images dart across the immensity of the full orchestra."[255] The first movement also contains a musical translation of the "Alla Hornpipe" from Handel's *Water Music* Suite in D Major (HWV 349)—a rhythmically altered recomposition of Handel's famous opening motive, which permeates the movement.[256] In the second movement ("Hot, Still!"), hazy harmonies and floating winds over a background of shimmering, sustained strings paint a picture of stillness, and its harmonic language departs from the more straightforward diatonicism of the first movement. Larsen also evokes specific natural sounds, such as that of a katydid at m. 66 through a suspended cymbal with sizzle, and crickets at m. 71 with flutes. The next movement, "Wafting," is a scherzo whose onrush of rising motives suggests the movement's title, and whose temple blocks add an unusual timbral flavor. The symphony culminates in the last movement, "Gale," where swirling, rising motives stir up a musical maelstrom. The final, turbulent sonority blends C major and B-flat major.

Larsen followed her first symphony with a towering, politically charged composition for multiple soloists and choruses, a narrator, and orchestra—in this case a fascinating cultural document of the Cold War. For this work, *Coming Forth into Day: A Choral Symphony* (1986), Larsen worked with the Egyptian activist and scholar Jehan Sadat to choose writings from a variety of sources to set to music—a gesture that prefigured Philip Glass's textually wide-ranging Symphony No. 5. Each movement begins with an optional reading by the narrator

Table 9.15 The Symphonies of Libby Larsen (b. 1950)

Title	Movements	Instrumentation	Comments
Symphony: Water Music (Symphony No. 1) (1985)	I. Fresh Breeze (165 mm.) II. Hot, Still (77 mm.) III. Wafting (130 mm.) IV. Gale (154 mm.)	Picc., 2 Flt., 2 Ob., 2 Clar., Bclar., 3 Bssn., 4 Hr., 3 Tpt., 3 Trom., Tuba, Timp., Perc. (3 Players: Vbp., Mrb., Orchestra Bells, Crotales, Bell Tree, Tri., Wind Chimes, Tam-tam [large], BD, Tenor Drum, Bongos, Tom-toms, SD, Temple Blocks, Tubular Bells, Sleigh Bells, Suspended Cym., Sizzle Cym., Wind Machine [optional synthesized white or pink noise], Harp, Pno. (doubling Cel.), Strgs.	Commissioned by the Minnesota Orchestra. Dedicated to Neville Marriner. First performance: January 30, 1985, Minnesota Orchestra, conducted by Neville Marriner. Score published by ECS Publishing. Recorded by Minnesota Orchestra, conducted by Neville Marriner (Elektra Nonesuch 9 79147-2); London Symphony Orchestra, conducted by Joel Revzen (Koch International Classics 3-7370-2).
Coming Forth into Day: A Choral Symphony (Symphony No. 2) (1986)	I. War (155 mm.) II. Heroes, Heroines (322 mm.) III. Innocents (264 mm.) IV. One World (162 mm.)	2 Flt. (1 doubling Picc.), 2 Ob., 2 Clar., 2 Bssn. (1 doubling Cbssn.), 4 Hr., 3 Tpt., 3 Trom., Tuba, Perc. (2 Players; Player 1: Chimes, Orchestra Bells, Tam-tam [large], SD, Suspended Cym., BD, Mrb., Xylo., Tri. [medium]; Player 2: Chimes, Orchestra Bells, Cel., SD, Bell Tree, Wind Chimes [brass], Timp.), Harp, Strgs., Vocal Soloists (Soprano, Baritone, Narrator), SATB Chorus, Children's Chorus (optional)	Commissioned by the Plymouth Music Series. Sets texts of Jehan Sadat, Mohammed Dib, Walt Whitman, the Stele of Antef, Bedros Tourian, Beulah Steele Jenness, Stephen Crane, Mother Goose, and John White Chadwick. First performance: April 14, 1986, Plymouth Festival Chorus and Orchestra, and Bel Canto Voices, conducted by Philip Brunelle, with Jehan Sadat, narrator; Lynda Russell, soprano; and Jubilant Sykes, baritone. Score published by ECS Publishing. Recorded at premiere, Plymouth Music Series 003 (LP).

Symphony No. 3 ("Lyric") (1991)	I. Deep Purple (180 mm.) II. Quiet (59 mm.) III. Since Armstrong (239 mm.)	3 Flt. (1 doubling Picc.), 3 Ob. (1 doubling EH), 3 Clar. (includes doubling of E♭ Clar, Aclar., and Bclar.), 2 Bssn., Cbssn., 4 Hr., 3 Tpt., 3 Trom., Tuba, Timp., Perc. (3 Players; Player 1: Vbp., Chimes, Tom-toms, Suspended Cym., Bell Tree, Hi-hat; Player 2: Suspended Cym., SD, Hi-hat, Mrb, Orchestra Bells, Tom-tom [low], Tri., Vbp., Sand Blocks; Player 3: BDs, Tam-tam [large], Chimes, Suspended Cym., Wood Block, Sleigh Bells, Vbp., Tom-toms), Keyboards (Pno., Cel., Synthesizer), Harp, Strgs.	Commissioned by the Albany Symphony Orchestra. Dedicated to Betty Hulings. First performance: March 6, 1992, Albany Symphony Orchestra, conducted by Joel Revzen. Recorded by London Symphony Orchestra, conducted by Joel Revzen (Koch International Classics 3-7370-2).
Short Symphony (for wind ensemble) (1995)	I. Allegro (75 mm.) II. Adagio in One Phrase (62 mm.) III. Scherzo-Rag (108 mm.) IV. Vivace (70 mm.)	Picc., 2 Flt., 2 Ob., EH, 3 Clar., Bclar., 2 Asax., Tsax., Barsax., 2 Bssn., 4 Hr., 3 Tpt., 3 Trom., Euph., 2 Tuba, Pno., Timp., Perc. (3 Players; Player 1: Vbp., Wood Block [high, low], Temple Blocks, Sarna Bell, Suspended Cym., Flat Ride Cym., Tri. [medium], BD, SD, Tubular Bells; Player 2: Mrb., Xylo., Glsp., Chinese Bells, Sleigh Bells, Tubular Bells; Tom-toms [high, medium, low]; Player 3: Suspended Cym., Hi-hat Cym., Crash Cym., Large Tam-tam, Maracas, Sleigh Bells, Tamb., Tri. [small], SD)	Commissioned by Lt. Col. Alan Bonner, commander of the US Air Force Band. First performance: December 22, 1996, US Air Force Band, conducted by Commander Lowell Graham. Published by Oxford University Press.
String Symphony (Symphony No. 4) (1998)	I. Elegance (166 mm.) II. Beauty Alone (156 mm.) III. Ferocious Rhythm (250 mm.)	Strgs.	Commissioned by the Minnesota Orchestra for the orchestra's centennial. First performance: December 5, 1998, Minnesota Orchestra, conducted by Eiji Oue. Score published by Oxford University Press. Recorded by Scottish Chamber Orchestra, conducted by Joel Revzen (Koch International Classics 3-7481-2).

Table 9.15 *continued*

Title	Movements	Instrumentation	Comments
Solo Symphony (Symphony No. 5) (1999)	I. Solo-Solos (177 mm.) II. One Dancer, Many Dances (225 mm.) III. Once Around (79 mm.) IV. The Cocktail Party Effect (143 mm.)	Picc., 2 Flt., 2 Ob., 2 Clar., Bclar., 2 Bssn., 4 Hr., 3 Tpt., 3 Trom., Tuba, Perc. (3 Players; Player 1: Mrb. [soft mallets], Tubular Bells, Large Log Drum, 2 Bongos [sticks], SD [sticks], Wire Brushes, Suspended Cym., Tri. [small, medium], Chimes, Wood Block [medium], Sweet Potato, Bee Bee Shaker; Player 2: Orchestra Bells, Vbp., Xylo., Suspended Cym. [sticks], Tenor Drum [mallets], Wire Brushes, 2 Congas [sticks], Hi-hat, Wood Block [medium]; Player 3: Pan Drum, Crotales, Steel Drum, Tam-tam [large], 5 Tom-toms [sticks], BD [soft mallets], SD [sticks], Wire Brushes, Drum Set, BD, 2 Congas, Tri., 2 Cowbells, Güiro, Temple Blocks), Timp., Pno., Strgs. (1 stand doubling Electric Bass with subwoofer)	Commissioned by the Colorado Symphony Orchestra. First performance: September 16, 1999, Colorado Symphony Orchestra, conducted by Marin Alsop. Score published by Oxford University Press. Recorded by Colorado Symphony Orchestra, conducted by Marin Alsop (Koch International Classics 3-7520-2).
Symphony: Forward (2011)	I. Boundless II. Here III. Forward	2 Flt. (1 doubling Picc.), 2 Ob., 2 Clar., 2 Bssn., 2 Hr., 2 Tpt., 2 Trom., Tuba, Timp., Perc. (3 Players; Player 1: Tubular Bells, Tamb., Orchestra Bells, Maracas, Brass Wind Chimes, Harmonica, Xylo., Suspended Cym., Mrb.; Player 2: Vbp., Tri. [medium], Suspended Cym., SD, Temple Blocks, 5 Tom-toms [high to low], Ratchet, Wood Blocks [medium, low], Ride Cym.; Player 3: Suspended Cym., Mrb., Tam-tam [large], BD, Wood Block [medium], Whip, Brake Drums [3 different pitches], Crash Cyms., Bongos, SD), Harp, Strgs.	Composed for the inaugural concert of the Norman Philharmonic. First performance: January 15, 2012, Norman Philharmonic, conducted by Richard Zielinski.

from Sadat's speeches (Sadat herself served as narrator at the premiere), but in the first movement, "War," the reading comes after an introductory fanfare. This first reading draws on a speech Sadat delivered after the assassination of her husband, the peacemaker Egyptian president Anwar Sadat; it includes the striking line "The Cold War is frozen stiff." The author also references the "failures of individual and collective endeavor in the cause of peace," but she proposes a "new meeting of hearts" and "an ideal forum, from which an appeal might go out to the world, for one more call for a common approach to try and find ways of rekindling the hope of peace in peoples' hearts." In Larsen's hands, the symphony itself—both this particular one and the genre as a whole—becomes such a forum. The rest of the opening movement consists of a rhythmically relentless choral setting of twentieth-century Algerian author Mohammed Dib's "The Mad Hour" and a brief duet for soprano and baritone soloists to a text from Walt Whitman's "Song of Myself." In the second movement, "Heroes, Heroines," Sadat refers directly to the work of Anwar Sadat, whose assassination in 1981 was still a fresh memory at the time Larsen composed the symphony. She sets passages from the *Maxims of the Stele of Antef* (a translation of an ancient Egyptian text), "Posthumous Decoration of Valor" by the twentieth-century writer Beulah Steele Jenness, and the nineteenth-century Armenian poet Bedros Tourian's "Complaint." These writings, Larsen explained, involve "the strong individual in the tangle of aggression and peace."[257] The extended, almost rhapsodic passage for the soprano soloist in the setting of Jenness's text suggests a eulogy by Jehan Sadat to her husband; the baritone's response ("Complaint"), after an orchestral interlude, is readily heard as Anwar Sadat's plea that his mission survive after his death.

The mood shifts, at least on the surface, for the third movement, "Innocents." Here, attention turns to youth and what Larsen called "the values of weakness, strength, and aggression we adults pass on to our children."[258] In this section, Stephen Crane's "The Trees in the Garden" joins with extracts from Mother Goose nursery rhymes. Playful rhythms and spare orchestration make this movement a scherzo of sorts, but it also represents the symphony's darkest moment. The melodic material for soprano, baritone, and children's chorus is deceptively straightforward; although it features triads and scalar runs, richly colored harmonies and pointed chromaticism interfere with a sense of clear simplicity and, in the work's broader context, cast an ominous shadow on the troubling rhymes "Rockabye Baby" and "There was a little man and he had a little gun." The symphony's final movement, "One World," offers a redemptive vision. A reading that emphasizes the possibility of peace is followed by a setting of nineteenth-century American poet John White Chadwick's "Eternal Rules of the Ceaseless Round," which, as Larsen described it, "sums up human understanding and striving to be one in our efforts to understand and exist."[259] This movement radiates joy through its triadic melodies and lush orchestration, and it concludes with a climax for the whole orchestra.

With her next two symphonies, Larsen addressed the questions of American cultural and musical identity mentioned above, specifically with respect to melody and its relationship with language—a subject she had begun dealing with in earlier works, such as *Cowboy Songs* (1979).[260] In her program notes for the Symphony No. 3, "Lyric" (1991), Larsen asked, "What is lyric in our times? Where is the great American melody?"[261] She identified American musical artists from across the spectrum of popular and classical music—Chuck Berry, Walter Piston, Dolly Parton, and James Brown, to name a few—and placed them among "composers who create melodies which are defined more by their rhythm than their pitch."[262] Contending with the age-old problem of defining "American" music in the face of the European tradition, she noted, "Here we speak American English, an inflected, complex, rhythmic language. It contains very little traditional European melodic (pitch) content."[263] The first movement, "Deep Purple," is anything but "melodic" in a traditional sense, with its murky harmonies, sudden textural effects, and vibrant rhythms. Following without break is a second movement, "Quiet," which is largely defined by scattered motives that seem to coalesce atop nebulous sonorities and a hypnotic harp ostinato. The Finale, "Since Armstrong," includes constant shifts of texture and timbre, unusual rhythms, snatches of melody, and strands of popular music. This movement shares its title with Larsen's Piano Concerto, composed just before this symphony; Larsen wrote that the concerto was "a bit like a dinner party. The guests at the table include the contemporaries Louis Armstrong, Igor Stravinsky, Maurice Ravel, Arnold Schoenberg, Jelly Roll Morton and Robert Johnson. . . . After dinner, we pose this question to our guests: Look ahead to the last decade of the 1900's. Who is the soloist and what is the piano concerto at the end of the 20th century?"[264] The first movement of the piano concerto contains a section called "Deep Purple," the name of the first movement of the symphony. And in fact, the symphony and the concerto contain some of the same material.[265]

In her Symphony No. 4, "String Symphony" (1999), Larsen continued to investigate linguistic questions—this time through the medium of the string orchestra, calling the composition "both an homage to strings and an essay about them."[266] In her program notes for this work, Larsen reflected on the decline of string-driven textures in the twentieth century—and of the lyricism such textures suggest. She asks, "What is the melody of American English? And can it be best expressed through orchestral strings?"[267] The first movement, "Elegance," is built on a gentle rising motive, and the second, long slow movement, "Beauty Alone," centers on a melodic fragment that recalls the *Dies irae*—lending an unsettling sensibility to some of the murkier moments. The third movement, "Ferocious Rhythm," features surprising rhythmic events, the return and mingling of melodic material from the previous movements, and a rapidly evolving musical surface that includes guitar-like strumming in the climactic final moments. Regarding her efforts to explore the relationship between melody and American English through this work, Larsen suggested that "plucked strings speak American English more effectively than bowed strings. So I am of a mind that writing abstract string music from the perspective of American English can be most effective when the composer uses plucked strings as a core rather than as an effect."[268]

The title of Larsen's Fifth Symphony, *Solo Symphony*, might imply a concerto for orchestra. Of course, a "symphony" and "concerto for orchestra" have not proved mutually exclusive, as we have seen with Ellen Taaffe Zwilich's Symphony No. 5, "Concerto for Orchestra," and William Bolcom's Symphony No. 7, "Symphonic Concerto." But Larsen's composition is perhaps more a symphony than a concerto because it explores ideas about the work of soloists more than it showcases individual orchestral skill, and ultimately, she considers the listener to be the "true soloist" of this work. In Larsen's words, "What is a solo? Is it the effort of one and only one, such as a solo violin, a solo flight? Is there such a thing as a solo effort? . . . Amelia Earhart's solo flights were only solos in that she was in the plane alone. But her ground crew was as responsible for each flight as she was." Following this line of argument, she suggested, "The effort of many becomes the effort of one to produce a unified sound, a unified music. This symphony is about the one and the many." The timbral polyphony of "Solo-solos," the first movement, leads to "One Dancer, Many Dances," an eclectic second movement made up of "a single melody seen through the lens of different dances, including funk, waltz, swing, square dance, tango, and jig." One of the many treasures found in this wide-ranging movement is seen in example 9.10, a passage that begins with electric bass, cello, tom-toms, and

The Symphony in the United States since 1970

Example 9.10 Libby Larsen, Solo Symphony (Symphony No. 5)/2, mm. 142–49. Copyright © 1999 Oxford University Press, Inc. Assigned to Oxford University Press 2010. Excerpt reproduced with permission. All rights reserved.

suspended cymbal underpinning trombone and tuba solos, and that is marked "Yma Sumac, poco animato"—an evocative performance direction that refers to the late Peruvian singer known for her vocal color and range. The brief third movement, "Once Around," is a "brash dash through the choirs of the orchestra," while the Finale, "The Cocktail-Party Effect," is a challenging "listening game" that explores "the ability to pick out and hear a single voice amidst chaos."[269]

Larsen's inclusion of electric bass in the *Solo Symphony*, although modest in the context of the multifarious second movement, coincides with one of her larger goals as a composer—to use "the symphony orchestra's instrumental choirs as vehicles for the sound and spirit of the time in which they evolved."[270] As she added, "I've thought for a long time now that if the symphonic ensemble is to remain true to its evolution as a cultural vehicle, it should be evolving a digital choir as part of its complement."[271] Although the *Solo Symphony* does not contain a "digital choir" *per se*, its inclusion of an electronic instrument can be related to her earlier use of synthesizer in the Symphony No. 3 and in the choral work *Canticle of the Sun* (1987), as well as recorded sound in *All Around Sound* (1999). In the latter case, Larsen collaborated with the children's book author John Coy to design an orchestral work that incorporates selected sounds captured on tape by students in Twin Cities schools. Furthermore, *Encircling Skies* (2009) is a seven-movement work for chorus and orchestra that features a sampler. By expanding the sonic profile of the orchestra through electronic means to create works with programmatic and local resonances, Larsen's compositions join works by John Adams (including *Naïve and Sentimental Music*) in anticipating the symphonic music of Mason Bates.

Other symphonies by Larsen include the *Short Symphony* for concert band (1996), commissioned by the US Air Force and first performed by its band in Chicago, and the *Symphony: Forward* (2011) for orchestra, composed for the first concert of the Norman Philharmonic in Oklahoma.

Daniel Asia (b. 1953)

In his six symphonies, shown in table 9.16, Daniel Asia incorporates colorful orchestral writing and nebulously tonal soundscapes into dynamic multimovement structures, at times contending explicitly with questions of Jewish identity along the way. The latter is an especially important part of Asia's musical persona, and is one that only a few other composers, including Leonard Bernstein and Aaron Jay Kernis, have also explored in the American symphonic tradition. Asia, born in Seattle, Washington, counts Jacob Druckman and Stephen Albert among his teachers. He has been teaching composition at the University of Arizona since 1988 and served as composer-in-residence of the Phoenix Symphony Orchestra from 1991 to 1994. Also an accomplished conductor, Asia founded the New York–based contemporary music group Musical Elements in 1977.

Asia's Symphony No. 1 (1987) takes as its starting point the seven-movement *Scherzo Sonata* (1987) for piano. A response to a commission from the Seattle Symphony Orchestra and the American Composers Orchestra, the work brings together five of its movements in orchestral versions, yielding an arch form with slow outer movements, two scherzos, and an inner Allegretto.[272] A fast ascending motive, introduced at the symphony's outset, permeates the entire work. In the first movement, a more tranquil melody, related to that hurried ascent and marked "delicately" in the score, hints at tonal stability. It is introduced in the trumpet and glockenspiel (m. 9), later restated in solo violin, celesta, and brass (m. 58), and finally reiterated in the solo violin alone (m. 106), leading to the movement's peaceful close. The brief, frantic

Table 9.16 The Symphonies of Daniel Asia (b. 1953)

Title	Movements	Instrumentation	Comments
Symphony No. 1 (1987)	I. Adagio (113 mm.) II. Scherzo (250 mm.) III. Allegretto (62 mm.) IV. Scherzo (280 mm.) V. Adagio (94 mm.)	3 Flt. (1 doubling Picc.) 3 Ob. (1 doubling EH), 3 Clar. (1 doubling Bclar.), 3 Bssn. (1 doubling Cbssn.), 4 Hr., 3 Tpt., 3 Trom., Tuba, Perc. (Mrb., 2 Xylo., Crotales, Vbp., 2 Glsp., 3 Cyms. [high, medium, low], Sizzle Cym. [large], 3 Tam-tams [high, medium, low], Gong [very large, unpitched, lower than lowest Tam-tam], 4 Tri. [2 sets, high and medium], 2 Timbales [or small Tom-toms], Medium Tom-tom, Large Tom-tom, SD [snares off], BD, Log Drum, 2 Wood Blocks, 5 Temple Blocks, Claves [high], Slapstick], Timp., Pno. (doubling Cel.), Harp, Strgs.	Commissioned by the Seattle Symphony Orchestra and the American Composers Orchestra. First performance: February 19, 1990, Seattle Symphony Orchestra, conducted by Christopher Kendall. Score published by Merion Music. Recorded by New Zealand Symphony Orchestra, conducted by James Sedares (Summit DCD 256).
Symphony No. 2, "Celebration Symphony" (1988–90)	I. Ma Tovu (174 mm.) II. Ashrenu (77 mm.) III. L'Kha Adonai (210 mm.) IV. Hine El Yeshuati (105 mm.) V. Halleluyah (464 mm.)	3 Flt. (1 doubling Picc.), 3 Ob. (1 doubling EH), 3 Clar. (1 doubling Bclar.), 3 Bssn. (1 doubling Cbssn.), 4 Hr., 3 Tpt., 3 Trom., Tuba, Timp., Perc. (4 Players; Player 1: Xylo., Vbp., Glsp., BD, Tam-tam [large]; Player 2: Glsp., Chimes, SD, Tom-toms [low, medium], 2 Timbales; Player 3: Mrb., BD; Player 4: 4 Cyms., 2 Tri.), Pno. (doubling Cel. and Synthesizer), Harp, Strgs.	Commissioned by the Syde family of Tucson, Arizona, in memory of Saul Syde. Score bears the inscription "In memoriam Leonard Bernstein." First performance: April 30, 1992, Tucson Symphony Orchestra, conducted by Robert Bernhardt. Score published by Merion Music. Recorded by Phoenix Symphony, conducted by James Sedares (New World 80447-2).

Table 9.16 *continued*

Title	Movements	Instrumentation	Comments
Symphony No. 3 (1992)	I. Largo—Lively (758 mm.) II. Adagio, mysterioso (399 mm.) III. Pensively—Lively (528 mm.)	4 Flt. (1 doubling Picc., 1 Flt. doubling Picc. and Aflt.), 4 Ob. (2 doubling EH), 4 Clar. (1 doubling E♭ Clar, 1 doubling Bclar.), 2 Bssn., 2 Cbssn., 6 Hr., 4 Tpt., 3 Trom., Tuba, Perc. (4 players; Player 1: Crotales [2 octaves], Tri., Suspended Cyms., Tam-tams, Glsp., Xylo., Wood Blocks, Temple Blocks, Anvil; Player 2: Tam-tams, Glsp., Mrb., Vbp., Wood Blocks, Temple Blocks, Cowbells, Suspended Cym.; Player 3: Tam-tams, Suspended Cyms., Suspended Sizzle Cym., Tri., Pitched Drums, Wood Blocks, Log Drum, SD, BD; Player 4: Tri., Wood Block, Suspended Cyms., Tam-tam, Anvil, BD, Timp. [4 drums]), Pno. (doubling Cel.), 2 Harps, Strgs.	Commissioned by the Phoenix Symphony and Meet the Composer. First performance: May 6, 1993, Phoenix Symphony, conducted by James Sedaris. Score published by Merion Music. Recorded by Phoenix Symphony, conducted by James Sedares (New World 80446-2).
Symphony No. 4 (1993)	I. Adagio (191 mm.) II. Allegro (Scherzo) (732 mm.) III. Adagio (in Memoriam Stephen Albert) (84 mm.) IV. Allegro (368 mm.)	2 Flt., 2 Ob., 2 Clar., 2 Bssn., 4 Hr., 2 Tpt., 2 Trom., Timp., Perc. (3 Players; Player 1: Tri. [large, small], BD, Wood Blocks, Suspended Cym. [large], Chimes, Timbales; Player 2: Crotales, Timbales, Suspended Cym. [large], Glsp., Claves, Tam-tam; Player 3: Vbp., Mrb., Glsp., Tri. [small], SD, Xylo, Wood Blocks), Pno. (doubling Cel.), Harp, Strgs.	Commissioned by the Phoenix Symphony. First performance: October 27, 1993, Phoenix Symphony, conducted by Daniel Asia. Score published by Merion Music. Recorded by New Zealand Symphony Orchestra, conducted by James Sedares (Summit DCD 256).

Symphony No. 5, "Of Songs and Psalms" (2008)	I. Psalm No. 115 Adonai Z'kharanu (103 mm.) II. The Ball Shem Tov (Pines) (25 mm.) III. God's Hand in the World (Amichai) (75 mm.) IV. Brooklyn (Pines) (40 mm.) V. Jerusalem (Amichai) (61 mm.) VI. Fluid Mechanics (Pines) (48 mm.) VII. Through Two Points Only One Straight Line Can Pass (Amichai) (74 mm.) VIII. Psalm No. 23 (174 mm.) IX. I Shall Cook Me Bacon, Lord (Pines) (44 mm.) X. Sonnet from the Voyage (Amichai) (56 mm.) XI. Where We Once Refused to Go (Pines) (60 mm.) XII. Almost a Love Poem (Amichai) (27 mm.) XIII. You See My Old Wandering Jew; Pont L'Archiveche (Pines) (49 mm.) XIV. A Young Soldier (Amichai) (128 mm.) XV. Barukh Adonai L'Olam (from Psalms 89, 135, and 72) (101 mm.)	Picc., 2 Flt., 2 Ob., EH, 3 Clar. (1 doubling Bclar.), 2 Bssn., Cbssn., 4 Hr., 3 Tpt., 3 Trom., Tuba, Timp., Perc. (Suspended Cyms. [high, medium, medium-low], Tam-tam [large], Crash Cyms., Bongos, Tom-toms, Tenor Drum, SD, BD, Vibraslap, Wood Blocks, Brake Drum, Tri. [small, medium], Tamb., Vbp., Xylo., Glsp., Crotales), Harp, Pno. (doubling Cel.), Strgs., Vocal soloists (Tenor, Bass-baritone), SATB Chorus	Commissioned by the America Israel Friendship League in honor of Israel's 60th birthday. The movements alternate settings of texts by Paul Pines (Movements 2, 4, 6, 9, 11, and 13) and Yehuda Amichai (Movements 3, 5, 7, 10, 12, and 14) with three psalm settings spread throughout (Movements 1, 8, and 15). First performance: November 7, 2008, Tucson Symphony Orchestra and Chorus, conducted by George Hanson, with Robert Swensen, tenor, and Kelly Anderson, bass-baritone. Score published by Presser. Recorded by Pilsen Philharmonic, conducted by Koji Kawamoto, with Robert Swensen, tenor; Chris Pedro Trakas, baritone; and New Czech Song Singers (Summit DCD 579).
Symphony No. 6, "Iris" (2018)	I. Jaunty (267 mm.) II. Slow (59 mm.) III. Impetuous (108 mm.)	Picc., 2 Flt., 2 Ob., EH, 2 Clar., Bclar., 2 Bssn., Cbssn., 4 Hr., 3 Tpt., 3 Trom., Tuba, Timp., Perc. (SD, BD, Suspended Cyms., Tamb., Tri., Bongos, Crotales, Tom-tom [high], Tam-tam [low], Wood Block [high], Glsp., Vbp., Xylo.), Strgs.	Orchestral version of *Iris* (2017, rev. 2018) for two pianos.

first Scherzo draws on and transforms the first movement's ascending motive, bubbling with constant energy, except for a brief songlike middle section. After the fragmented orchestration of the even shorter third movement, the next Scherzo begins with the ascending motive and retains the liveliness of the previous two movements, this time with an emphasis on bell-like percussive effects and colliding rhythms. In the final Adagio, the gentle melody from the first movement returns, in solo violin and trumpet (m. 41), in the flute (m. 76), and finally in the solo violin (m. 85); this last statement leads to the stunning but serene D-major sonority that closes the symphony.

Asia's instrumental Symphony No. 2 (1990), also in five movements, draws on music he had already composed for *Celebration* (1988) for baritone and mixed ensemble, a work for Temple Beth-El in Springfield, Massachusetts. The symphony, called "Celebration Symphony," bears the inscription "In memoriam Leonard Bernstein" (Bernstein died on October 14, 1990). The Hebrew movement titles are the names of prayers, and the English subtitles are passages in those prayers; Asia had previously set the texts to music in *Celebration*. The first movement, "Ma Tovu" ("Your love is great; answer me with true deliverance") centers on a circling motive, passed among different instrumental combinations, which suggests the rhythmic modes and modal harmony of Notre Dame discant; moments of textural swelling punctuate the gentle, almost dance-like musical flow. In "Ashrenu," subtitled "Therefore it is our duty to thank and praise you," a lush central section features broad string passages that frame a brief but expressive cello solo. The third movement, "L'Kha Adonai" ("Yours, O Lord, is the greatness and the power and the splendor"), appropriately features austere trumpet passages that alternate with imposing ones for an engine-like orchestra; here, the trumpet's role is like that of the flute in Edgard Varèse's *Amériques* (1921). The next movement, "Hine El Yeshuati" ("Behold, God is my deliverance; I am confident and unafraid"), highlights solo trombone over a shimmering orchestral texture with vibraphone, harp ostinati, and extended harmonies. The celebratory finale, "Halleluyah" ("Praise God in the Highest!"), draws on the nimble, scherzolike rhythms of the first movement. At times, the texture fractures, and layered birdsong interrupts the rhythmic vigor. What Asia called "a ghost of a Hasidic tune" faintly emerges out of that rhythmic pulse.[273] The appearance of the tune through a soundscape that evokes nature served, for Asia, as a way of amplifying a sense of "resonance . . . with a lost culture" in a post-Holocaust world.[274]

Like his first two symphonies and Larsen's Symphony No. 3, Asia's next two works in the genre also involve treatments of earlier material. He composed his third and fourth symphonies in short order for the Phoenix Symphony. Symphony No. 3 (1992) continues with the grandiosity of the second, but this time on a larger scale—and with a particularly large orchestra that includes two harps and piano. The symphony draws heavily on *At the Far Edge* (1991), a symphonic poem that Asia has said reflects Aaron Copland's "musical spirit, his striving for the simple statement, his distinctly American sense of rhythm, as well as a preference for high glistening sonorities."[275] The symphony begins with the same music as *At the Far Edge*—a broad, slow, sweeping melody that is rooted in tonality but embraces moments of pointed dissonance. The degree of dissonance increases throughout the first movement, which culminates in a raucous conclusion; a bustling Finale follows the slow second movement. With the four-movement Symphony No. 4 (1993), which draws on his guitar piece *Your Cry Will Be a Whisper* (1992), Asia scaled back his orchestral forces.[276] A first movement with a slow introduction gives way to a Scherzo with engaging rhythmic effects; the Finale is similarly lively. The slow movement—heart-wrenching at times—is dedicated to the memory of Stephen Albert.

After a fifteen-year break from writing symphonies, Asia returned to the genre in 2008 with the ambitious, wide-ranging Symphony No. 5, composed in honor of the sixtieth birthday of Israel. This work recalls Symphony No. 2 in its overt references to Jewish identity, but the more recent symphony charts new territory with its fifteen-movement form and employment of the voice; Asia calls it "an elaborate song cycle." It sets texts by the American poet Paul Pines and the late Israeli poet Yehuda Amichai and frames them with settings of psalms. Asia continued, "The texts, in their entirety, thus present an American Jewish experience, a modern Israeli experience, and the timelessness of the literature of the Jewish Bible, which provides the foundation that unites these different views of Jewish life in the 21st century."[277] Asia organizes these settings systematically; a tenor sings the Pines texts while the Amichai poems are performed (in English translation) by bass-baritone, and a choir takes the psalm settings. Psalm 23, the eighth and longest movement, is sung in English, and the opening and closing psalm movements are in Hebrew. Angular melodies, gauzy harmonies, and subtle instrumental effects and combinations that recall Asia's Symphony No. 1 abound, but moments such as the jaunty seventh movement suggest musical theater. The symphony ends with a luminescent but unsettling gesture: a quiet piano arpeggio and ghostly strings, emphasizing stacked fourths, cloak an extended C-major harmony on the word *Amen*.

This gesture encapsulates the difficulty of fully reconciling the various experiences and emotions suggested by Asia's combination of texts in this symphony and provides a striking summation of his work as a symphonist thus far—one who skillfully blends the familiar with the unconventional. As a fifteen-movement song cycle, the Symphony No. 5 also follows in the tradition of Mahler's *Das Lied von der Erde* and Shostakovich's Symphony No. 14 in demonstrating that the recent symphony as a genre continues to lack specific formal requirements and often is a "sounding together" of multiple elements within a clear, overarching structure. After that composition, Asia's work as a symphonist continued with the Symphony No. 6, "Iris" (2018), an orchestral version of his two-piano work *Iris* (2017).

Tobias Picker (b. 1954)

Tobias Picker is celebrated for his chamber, orchestral, and vocal works, but opera in particular has had a special place in output; he helped found Opera San Antonio, serving as its artistic director from 2010 to 2015, and he has composed five operas, dating back to the highly acclaimed *Emmeline* (1996). Like John Adams, Picker turned to opera after his success as a symphonic composer. He has written three symphonies (listed in table 9.17); two date from his time as composer-in-residence at the Houston Symphony Orchestra from 1985 to 1990, and all three evoke Romanticism in their dazzling melodies, warm orchestral textures, references to tonal harmony and, in the striking case of his Symphony No. 2, an open embrace of Romantic musical ancestry.

The most unusual of Picker's three symphonies, the Symphony No. 2, "Aussöhnung" (1986), points quite unequivocally to high Romanticism. The heart of the symphony is the radiant seventh movement, an orchestral setting of Johann Wolfgang von Goethe's poem "Aussöhnung" ("Reconciliation") for soprano and orchestra, sung in German. Strings accompany at first and lead the way, but the entire orchestra joins in a lush setting that recalls Richard Strauss or Gustav Mahler in its resplendent, expansive tonality and evocative text painting. The poem begins with the image (in David Luke's prose translation) of "an anguished heart that has lost too much" ("Beklommens Herz, dich, das zu viel verloren"), which Picker accompanies with a gently rocking extended C-major harmonic fabric—suggesting, perhaps, resignation rather

Table 9.17 The Symphonies of Tobias Picker (b. 1954)

Title	Movements	Instrumentation	Comments
Symphony No. 1 (1982)	I. Rhapsody (143 mm.) II. Variations (374 mm.)	3 Flt. (1 doubling Picc.), 2 Ob., EH, 2 Clar., Bclar, 3 Bssn., 4 Hr., 2 Tpt., 3 Trom., Tuba, Timp., Perc. (BD, Suspended Cym., Hi-hat, Chimes, Glsp.), 2 Harps, Pno., Strgs.	Commissioned by Dr. and Mrs. Ralph I. Dorfman for the San Francisco Symphony. Dedicated to Edo de Waart. First performance: April 20, 1983, San Francisco Symphony, conducted by Edo de Waart. Score published by Schott Helicon.
Symphony No. 2 ("Aussöhnung") (1986)	Prelude (30 mm.) Movement I (65 mm.) Movement II (75 mm.) Movement III (66 mm.) Movement IV (49 mm.) Movement V (78 mm.) Movement VI (68 mm.) Movement VII ("Aussöhnung") (130 mm.) Postlude (30 mm.)	3 Flt. (1 doubling Alto Flt., 1 doubling Picc.), 3 Ob. (1 doubling EH), 3 Clar. (1 doubling Bclar.), 3 Bssn. (1 doubling Cbssn.), 4 Hr., 3 Tpt., 3 Trom., Tuba, Timp., Perc. (2 Players: Glsp., Mrb., Cyms., Suspended Cym., Gong, 6 Tom-toms [low to high], SD, BD), Harp, Pno. (doubling Cel.), Strgs., Soprano Soloist	Commissioned by Meet the Composer for the Houston Symphony Orchestra. Dedicated to Sergiu Comissiona. Final movement is an orchestral song set to the poem "Aussöhnung" by Johann Wolfgang von Goethe. First performance: October 25, 1986, Houston Symphony, conducted by Sergiu Comissiona, with Judith Bettina (soprano). Score published by Schott Helicon. Recorded by Houston Symphony Orchestra, conducted by Sergiu Comissiona, with Leona Mitchell, soprano (First Edition FECD-0029).
Symphony No. 3 for string orchestra (1988)	I. Allegro (50 mm.) II. Largo (182 mm.) III. Allegro (65 mm.) IV. Adagio (218 mm.) V. Allegro (113 mm.)	Strgs.	Commissioned by Meet the Composer for the Houston Symphony. Adapted from Picker's String Quartet with Bass (1988). First performance: Houston Symphony, January 14, 1989, conducted by David Zinman. Score published by Schott Helicon.

than torment. The otherworldly sounds of harp and piano color a shift to A minor for the start of the second stanza, appropriate for the line "But now, on wings of angels, music comes forth and rises" ("Da schwebt hervor Musik mit Engelsschwingen"). After the ebullient image at the poem's end of the "double joy of music and love" ("Das Doppel-Glück der Töne wie der Liebe"), an ominous orchestral swell overtakes the musical texture (the start of the symphony's gloomy postlude), complicating the poem's overall trajectory of resolution.[278]

Suggesting the structure of Mahler's Fourth Symphony, the previous movements present variations on the song before it is heard. The Prelude and first movement both emphasize warm, dark colors and rich, varied orchestration—qualities that return in the even more intense third movement; between them is the second movement, a brief, energetic Scherzo. Again providing contrast, the fast fourth movement is almost diabolical in its insistent motor rhythms, quick meter shifts, abrasive brass, and percussive fabric. An equally brief fifth movement only slightly lightens the mood, leading to a melancholy-filled sixth movement for strings only; the song leads into a dark Postlude that is cut from the same cloth as the Prelude. Taken together, the range of emotions suggested by the various movements mirrors that of the poem, which concerns the pleasure of beauty and the pain of longing—and the power of music to elicit profound emotional responses. The symphony's bleak conclusion perhaps suggests that the pain of longing defeats, or at least outlasts, the pleasure of beauty. This symphony originally had 10 movements, plus the Prelude and Postlude. After its premiere, Picker removed three of the movements and reordered the rest; the Houston Symphony recorded the revised version.

Four years before the Symphony No. 2, Picker wrote his Symphony No. 1 (1982), which emerged from an invitation by John Adams to perform his chamber piece *Nova* (1979) as part of Adams's "New and Unusual Music" series in San Francisco. Edo de Waart, then music director of the San Francisco Symphony, asked Picker, through Adams, for a "major statement" for orchestra.[279] The forcefully repeated sonorities and the majestic scope of the opening measures of both movements of Picker's first symphony do suggest Adams's symphonic scores as a point of reference. Six years later (and two years after the Symphony No. 2), Picker adapted his String Quartet with Bass into the five-movement Symphony No. 3 for string orchestra (1988). A brief, fast first movement replete with scurrying fragments and only vague hints of a tonal center yields to a slow impassioned Largo that concludes on a shimmering, extended C-major chord. Next is a fast middle movement, followed by an extended Adagio that concludes on an embellished D major. The Finale revives the fluttering energy of the first and third movements.

Aaron Jay Kernis (b. 1960)

For the prolific composer Aaron Jay Kernis (b. 1960), the symphony "is a fundamentally open form that can contain a vast range of emotional and formal exploration."[280] Kernis studied with John Adams at the San Francisco Conservatory and Jacob Druckman at Yale, where he now teaches. An early success for Kernis came in an open reading of his work *"dream of the morning sky" (Cycle V)* in 1983 with Zubin Mehta and the New York Philharmonic as part of a festival showcasing the work of living composers.[281] A frequently recorded composer who won the Pulitzer Prize in 1998 for his String Quartet No. 2 ("Musica Instrumentalis"), Kernis composes symphonic works with evocative titles, striking and colorful orchestration, eclectic stylistic references, strong tonal grounding, and a sense of close engagement with matters of personal, emotional, and political import. His symphonies are shown in table 9.18.

Table 9.18 The Symphonies of Aaron Jay Kernis (b. 1960)

Title	Movements	Instrumentation	Comments
Symphony in Waves (1989)	I. Continuous Wave (474 mm.) II. Scherzo (154 mm.) III. Still Movement (194 mm.) IV. Intermezzo (80 mm.) V. Finale (218 mm.)	Flt. (doubling Picc.), 2 Ob. (1 doubling EH), Clar. (doubling Bclar. and Eb Clar.), 2 Bssn. (1 doubling Cbssn.), 3 Hr., 1 Tpt., Timp., Perc. (Chimes, Glsp., Vbp. [with motor], Mrb., Crotales, 6 Bell Plates, 4 Cowbells, 2 High-pitched Steel Pipes or Anvils, Tri., Crash Cyms. [medium], Suspended Cym. [medium], Ride Cym., Tam-tam [medium], Sleigh Bells on a leather strap, 4 Tom-toms, SD, Tamb., Wood Block [high]), Pno. (doubling Cel.), Strgs. (minimum 6-6-4-2)	Commissioned by Saint Paul Chamber Orchestra. Dedicated to John Adams. First performance (Movements 1 and 2): November 3, 1989, Saint Paul Chamber Orchestra, conducted by John Adams. First performance (all five movements): November 9, 1991, New York Chamber Symphony, conducted by Gerard Schwarz. Score published by Associated Music Publishers. Recorded by New York Chamber Symphony, conducted by Gerard Schwarz (Argo 436 287-2); Grant Park Orchestra, conducted by Carlos Kalmar (Cedille CDR 90000 105).
Second Symphony (1991)	I. Alarm (199 mm.) II. Air/Ground (132 mm.) III. Barricade (116 mm.)	3 Flt. (1 doubling Picc.), 2 Ob., EH, 2 Clar., Bclar., 3 Bssn. (1 doubling Cbssn.), 4 Hr., 4 Tpt., 4 Trom., Tuba, Timp., Perc. (SD [Picc. high], Tenor Drum, BD [small, large], Log Drum [medium], Brake Drum, Bongos, Congas, Wood Blocks, Reco-Reco, Lead Pipe, Mounted Handbells, Cowbells, Thunder Sheet, Crotales, Cabasa, Tri. [small, high], China Boy Cym., Cyms. [small, medium, large], Crash Cyms. [small, medium], Ride Cym., Vbp., Xylo., Glsp., Mrb., Chimes, Tam-tams [medium, large], Tom-toms), Harp, Pno., Strgs.	Commissioned by Carillon Importers Ltd., on behalf of Absolut Vodka. First performance: January 15, 1992, New Jersey Symphony Orchestra, conducted by Hugh Wolff. Score published by AJK Music and Associated Music Publishers. Recorded by City of Birmingham Symphony Orchestra, conducted by Hugh Wolff (Argo 448 900-2); Peabody Symphony Orchestra, conducted by Marin Alsop (Naxos 8.559830).

| Symphony No. 3 ("Symphony of Meditations") (2007–9) | I. Invocation (112 mm.)
II. Meditation on Oneness (286 mm.)
III. Supplication (716 mm.) | 3 Flt. (1 doubling Picc.), 3 Ob. (1 doubling EH), 3 Clar. (1 doubling Eb Clar., 1 doubling Bclar.), 3 Bssn. (1 doubling Cbssn.), 4 Hr., 3 Tpt. (1 doubling Picc. Tpt.), 3 Trom., Tuba, Timp., Perc. (4 Players; Player 1: Glsp., Xylo., Almglocken, Suspended Cym. [high; also with sizzles], Suspended Cym. [medium], Crash Cyms. [small, large], Tri., Bongos, SD, Roto-toms, Timp.; Player 2: Crotales, Pitched Gongs, 2 Tri. [high], Crash Cym. [medium], 2 Suspended Cyms. [medium; 1 also with sizzles], Suspended Cym. [low], 1 Wood Block [Picc.], 2 Wood Blocks [high], 2 Tom-toms [high], Thunder Sheet [large], Tamb.; Player 3: Vbp. [without motor], 2 Tri. [high], Suspended Cym. [medium], Suspended Cym. [large; also with sizzles], Crash Cym. [large], Tam-tam [low; also with chain], Bongos, 3 Tom-toms [2 low, 1 medium], Small BD, Tamb.; Player 4: Mrb., Suspended Cym. [high], Tam-tams [large, medium, small], Tri. [very high], Pitched Small Drums, BD [large], Bongos, 2 Wood Blocks [high], Tamb.), Pno., Harp, Electric Bass, Strgs, Vocal Soloists (Soprano, Baritone, Tenor), Large SATB Chorus | Commissioned by Seattle Symphony. Dedicated to Jeff and Lara Sanderson and Gerard and Jody Schwarz. In memory of the composer's parents. Third movement sets text by Solomon ibn Gabirol, translated by Peter Cole.

Score published by AJK Music/Associated Music Publishers.

First performance: June 25, 2009, Seattle Symphony and Chorale, conducted by Gerard Schwarz, with Hyunah Yu, soprano; Paul Karaitis, tenor; Robert Gardner, baritone. |

Table 9.18 *continued*

Title	Movements	Instrumentation	Comments
Symphony No. 4, "Chromelodeon" (2018)	I. Out of Silence (179 mm.) II. Thorn Rose	Weep, Freedom (After Handel) (237 mm.) III. Fanfare Chromelodia (171 mm.)	3 Flt. (1 doubling Picc.), 3 Ob. (1 doubling EH), 3 Clar. (1 doubling E♭ Clar., 1 doubling BClar.), 3 Bssn. (1 doubling Cbssn.), 4 Hr., 3 Tpt., 3 Trom., Tuba, Timp., Perc. (5 Players; Player 1: Glsp., Xylo, Mrb, Tom-toms [large and medium], Suspended Cym. [medium], Crash Cyms. [large], Bongos, Triangle, Wood Block [medium]; Player 2: Crotales, Nipple Gongs, 2 Suspended Cyms. [high], Suspended Cyms. [medium and low], Crash Cyms. [medium, large], Tam-tam [medium], 2 Tri. [high], 2 Wood Blocks [medium], 4 Tin Cans, Conga; Player 3: Vbp., Steel Plates [large], Nipple Gongs, Splash Cym., Suspended Cyms. [high, medium], Tam-tam [medium], 3 Tri. [high], Metal shaker, Tenor Drum; Player 4: Chimes, Steel Plates, Mrb., Tri., Splash Cym., Suspended Cyms. [high, medium, low], Tam-tam [medium], Wood Block [high], BD; Player 5 [auxiliary]: 2 Tri. [high], Suspended Cym. [medium], Crash Cyms. [medium], Tam-tam [large], SD, Tom-tom [low], Tamb.), Piano (doubling Cel.), Harp, Strgs.	Commissioned by the New England Conservatory of Music for its 150th anniversary; the Nashville Symphony; and the Bellingham Festival of Music. Score published by AJK Music/Associated Music Publishers. First performance: April 18, 2018, New England Conservatory Philharmonia, conducted by Hugh Wolff. Score published by AJK Music and Associated Music Publishers. Recorded by Nashville Symphony, conducted by Giancarlo Guerrero (Naxos 8.559838).

Already decorated by the late 1980s—among other achievements, he had earned a Guggenheim Fellowship and the Rome Prize—Kernis composed his first symphony, *Symphony in Waves*, on a commission from the St. Paul Chamber Orchestra (the same group that commissioned William Bolcom's Symphony No. 3) and dedicated it to John Adams. Like Glass and Corigliano, Kernis initially expressed hesitation about becoming a symphonist: as he wrote in his program notes, "Prior to writing this work in 1989, I never imagined I would write a symphony. It seemed such an outdated and irrelevant form." Having overcome his reluctance at age 29—suggesting the genre's cross-generational impact at that moment—he added, "I've become increasingly excited by the communicative potential, by the highly varied ideas and emotions, latent in traditional forms. I hope to find what 'symphony' means to me, to define the form for myself, by bringing my own experiences and passions to it." On the specific meanings of this work in particular, "I am not dealing with waves in a strictly programmatic sense. I think about waves of sound in addition to those of wind and water. Each movement uses some aspect of wave motion: swells and troughs of dynamics, densities, and instrumental color: the 'sounds' of light broken into flickering bits by the water's action."[282]

The first movement ("Continuous Wave") suggests minimalism—an aesthetic that interested Kernis—in the layering of fast ascending figures, whose beginnings are seen in example 9.11. (The example omits the quiet timpani gesture that inaugurates the section as well as the whole rests, which do not appear in the published score.[283]) Here, the ascending figures begin haltingly in the double basses and gradually widen in range and timbre, like a wave beginning to form in the open ocean.

In the brief Scherzo, pointillistic textures hint at the particle properties of waves, and the movement concludes with a piano part and the direction "Play it like Jerry Lee Lewis!"—a gesture that points to Kernis's use of popular idioms in such works as *100 Greatest Dance Hits* (1993). The longer third movement ("Still Movement") begins with a passage of harsh sonorities that gives way to a drawn-out section of aching melodies, sparse textures, and slow-moving, off-kilter harmonies; the unforgiving chords return before a brief but tranquil coda. A short intermezzo recalls the continuous wavelike strings of the first movement and leads to a Finale whose jubilant conclusion joins the pointillistic energy of the second movement to the first movement's smoother contours.[284]

Leta Miller has positioned Kernis's embrace of tonality in the *Symphony in Waves*, clearly evident in its opening measures, as part of a new concern with classic and romantic forms and idioms in his output.[285] Kernis's three-movement Second Symphony (1991), dealing with the Persian Gulf War, came soon after.[286] "The absurdity and cruelty of this war, in particular the 'surgical' nature of its reliance on gleaming new technological warfare used at a safe distance made an enormous and lasting impression on me," Kernis wrote in his notes on the work.[287] Motor rhythms, noisy percussion, and austere and angular thematic material—especially highlighting the brass section—dominate the opening movement, "Alarm." The title of the contrastingly meditative middle movement, "Air/Ground," plays on the names of war venues and cleverly reveals itself as an air with a ground bass, in the tradition of Baroque lament—a technique that parallels Corigliano's use of a chaconne in the slow movement of his then-recent Symphony No. 1.[288] "Air/Ground" offers passionate melodies and unexpected harmonic shifts that, despite clear hints of tonal focus, thwart any feeling of firm resolution.

For the final movement, "Barricade," Kernis drew on "news reports of a civilian apartment building (mistakenly thought to be a military installation) that was flattened by American bombs just before the end of the war—its 500 civilian inhabitants were killed instantly."[289]

Matthew Mugmon

Above and facing, **Example 9.11** Aaron Jay Kernis, *Symphony in Waves*/1, mm. 26–65. Copyright © 1991 by Associated Music Publishers, Inc. All rights reserved. International copyright secured. Reprinted with permission.

This movement begins with an aching violin passage that employs extreme registers. The colossal percussive swell at the symphony's conclusion, foreshadowed several times throughout the movement with smaller percussion rolls, suggests, in light of Kernis's inspiration, the senselessness of violence—and communicates a similar degree of raw, adrenaline-inducing physical and emotional force evoked in the symphonies of Christopher Rouse. Writing in the *New York Times* after the premiere, which came about through a commission from Carillon Importers Ltd. for a concert series called "Absolut Concerto" (after the brand of vodka imported by the company), Allan Kozinn likened the composition to Corigliano's Symphony No. 1. He called it "an angry, topical work" and added, "Mr. Kernis appears to agree with Mr. Corigliano that anger and anguish are best expressed in an unequivocal tonal language that is lyrical, colorfully orchestrated and punctuated by unrestrained percussion."[290] But as a symphony protesting a specific war, the American ancestry of the Symphony No. 2 dates back to Roger Sessions's Sixth (1966), Seventh (1967), and Eighth (1968) symphonies, inspired by the composer's opposition to the Vietnam War.[291]

For Kernis, the Second Symphony "began a series of works touched by world conflict and human suffering," including *Colored Field* (1994), a large-scale English horn concerto that Kernis adapted into a cello concerto in 2000, for which he won the 2002 Grawemeyer Award.[292] This work was prompted by Kernis's visits to the sites of Nazi concentration camps in 1989.[293] *Colored Field* is symphonic in scope, but his next symphony in name, the Symphony No. 3, "Symphony of Meditations," is even more immense. As with Daniel Asia, Kernis's Jewish identity has played an important role in his music, and in this symphony, he set texts by the eleventh-century Jewish poet Solomon ibn Gabirol, translated from Hebrew to English by Peter Cole. The work's origins date back to the 1990s, when Kernis received a copy of Gabirol's *Kingdom's Crown* from Cole on a visit to Jerusalem. After both of Kernis's parents died in 2004, he returned to Gabirol's poetry: "Memories of attending synagogue in my early years began to resurface for me. Though I am not religious in the sense of being consistently observant of holidays, ritual, and synagogue-going, I identify myself definitively as Jewish. I still have the sound of an unaccompanied cantor in my ear. I have repeatedly turned to spiritual issues and texts from many faiths as the basis for my vocal work, and at this point in my life the Gabirol text seemed utterly necessary for me to work with."[294] In the first two movements, which feature extended tonal harmonies and dazzling instrumental combinations, solo voices (baritone in the first, soprano in the second) frame thrilling choral surges. The symphony's center of gravity, though, is the third movement, itself lasting more than 40 minutes. According to Kernis, the movement "ranges in intensity from the baritone's recitatives and arias of reflection and desolation, to a searing, climactic orchestral interlude and very gradually calms toward the joyful and resolute concluding lines of prayer in Hebrew."[295] As a monumental composition that features chorus and orchestra, Kernis's Symphony No. 3 joins the growing tradition of recent American choral symphonies—works that often, but not always, point explicitly to matters of topical relevance; in addition to the works already discussed by Rochberg, Adams, Larsen, Glass, and Zwilich, the list includes symphonies by Lowell Liebermann and Mohammed Fairouz, discussed below.

For his Symphony No. 4, "Chromelodeon" (2018), Kernis did not employ the human voice, returning instead to the instrumental palette of his first two symphonies. The concept of color has played a significant role in Kernis's *oeuvre*, and for Kernis, the "particular meaning" of the title "Chromelodeon" (also the name of an organ invented by the composer Harry Partch) is "chromatic, colorful, melodic music performed by an orchestra." Perhaps more abstract than his previous three symphonies, this three-movement work "is created out of musical elements, not images or stories, though I would not be surprised if the influence of living in the chaos of the world today—at a 'molecular' emotive level—didn't play a part in its creation." Among the work's varied inspirations are the thought of John Cage—the first movement is titled "Out of Silence"—and George Frideric Handel, specifically in the second movement, "Thorn Rose | Weep, Freedom (After Handel)."[296]

Lowell Liebermann (b. 1961)

Lowell Liebermann (b.1961) is frequently connected to Neoromanticism, although he dislikes that label (and, indeed, all simplified labels) and would prefer the term *Neoclassicism* because of his emphasis on "formal balance and organic unity."[297] Tonality certainly figures in his music, but it is only one aspect among many—including atonality and serialism—that he uses when he finds them "necessary for the organic argument of a particular piece."[298] His experience as a young composer showed that the freedom to employ tonality was far from given in the early 1980s despite its role in the music of George Rochberg and David Del Tredici. As Liebermann wrote, "I remember in the early '80s, one teacher pointing to a passage of triads in my First Symphony saying 'You CAN'T write that—the critics will crucify you!'"[299] Today for Liebermann, who teaches at Mannes School of Music, tonality and atonality are "musical materials that can coexist in the same piece quite happily."[300] Like his other compositions, Liebermann's four symphonies, shown in table 9.19, demonstrate different ways of constructing large-scale orchestral forms through largely—but not exclusively—tonal materials.

Liebermann began writing his Symphony No. 1 in 1979 while a student of David Diamond at Juilliard. He called the composition a "coming to terms" with several elements, including tonality, atonality, and the whole symphonic tradition; as he described it, "the musical argument . . . is it keeps trying to resolve from complexity and dissonance to tonality" but without finally resolving to C major.[301] The brooding first movement centers on a slow, impassioned melody that develops from the basic interval of a tritone and contains only vague hints of a tonal center; a full orchestral climax dissolves into a ghostly coda that suggests a music box in highlighting flute and glockenspiel. After an animated second movement, the slow third movement climaxes with force in a chorale-like series of chromatically related triads that is cut off, violently, in a percussive swell. In the last movement, a duet for flute and harp toys with C major, and a passage of shimmering, distantly related triads, roughly centered on C major as well, seems to do battle with the more angular harmonies of the first movement. But the material is connected: Liebermann juxtaposes triads whose roots are a tritone apart, drawing a link between the seemingly tonal fabric of parts of the Finale and the melodic tritone that figures prominently at the symphony's beginning and conclusion.

For the Second Symphony, commissioned for the Dallas Symphony Orchestra's one hundredth anniversary in 2000, Liebermann—composer-in-residence from 1999 to 2002—was specifically asked for a celebratory piece that featured organ, chorus, and extra brass (Liebermann made the extra brass optional, in order to facilitate future performances).[302] As the composer said, one critic "interpreted the text as a kind of a naively optimistic drum-beating piece, and to me, it was exactly the opposite."[303] Liebermann continued that he drew on texts by Walt Whitman that dealt with "the search for a faith that doesn't necessarily exist. It's a longing for faith—it's about that longing rather than whether it exists or not."[304] In the opening section of this work, which is cast in one extended single movement, a sweeping melody unfolds slowly in the orchestra and then in the chorus. Here, chromatically related triads,

Table 9.19 The Symphonies of Lowell Liebermann (b. 1961)

Title	Movements	Instrumentation	Comments
Symphony No. 1, Op. 9 (1979–82)	I. Andante (148 mm.) II. Allegro con fuoco (239 mm.) III. Largo (255 mm.) IV. Largo e mesto (136 mm.)	3 Flt. (1 doubling Picc.), 2 Ob., EH, 2 Clar., E♭ Clar., Bclar., 2 Bssn., Cbssn., 4 Hr., 4 Tpt., 3 Trom., Tuba, Timp., Perc. (BD, Crash Cyms., Suspended Cym., BD with Cym. attached, SD, Tenor Drum, Xylo., Whip, Tamb., Tri. [large, small], Tubular Bells, Tam-tam [large]), Harp, Pno. (doubling Cel.), Strgs.	Dedicated to David Diamond. Awarded the Juilliard Orchestra Competition's first prize in 1987. First performance: February 19, 1988, Juilliard Orchestra, conducted by Paul Zukofsky. Score published by Presser.
Symphony No. 2, Op. 67 (1999)	One movement (1027 mm.)	Picc., 2 Flt., 2 Ob., EH, 2 Clar., Bclar., 2 Bssn., Cbssn., 4 Hr., 3 Tpt., 3 Trom., Tuba, Timp., Perc. (Tri. [small], Antique Cyms., Glsp., Vbp., Mrb., Tubular Bells, Crash Cyms., Tamb., Suspended Cym., Xylo., BD, SD, Large Tam-tam, Gong [small]), Harp, Pno., Cel., Org., SATB Chorus, Strgs., Optional Brass Band (3 Tpt., 3 Trom.)	Commissioned by Ford Lacy and Cece Smith for the Dallas Symphony Orchestra and Chorus for the orchestra's 100th anniversary. Texts drawn from poetry by Walt Whitman: section 5 of "Passage to India"; section 21 of "Song of Myself"; "Poets to Come!" from *Inscriptions*; section 5 of "Song of Myself"; section 4 of "Song of the Universal" from *Birds of Passage*; section 5 of "Proud Music of the Storm"; and section 8 of "The Mystic Trumpeter" from *Noon to Starry Night*. First performance: February 10, 2000, Dallas Symphony Orchestra, conducted by Andrew Litton. Score published by Presser. Recorded by Dallas Symphony Orchestra & Chorus, conducted by Andrew Litton (Delos DE 3256).

Symphony No. 3, Op. 113 (2010)	One movement (632 mm.)	3 Flt. (1 doubling Picc.), 3 Ob. (1 doubling EH), 3 Clar. (1 doubling Bclar.), 2 Bssn., Cbssn., 4 Hr., 3 Tpt., 3 Trom., Tuba, Timp., Perc. (BD, SD, Cyms., Suspended Cym., Medium Gong, Tam-tam, Sand Block, Wood Block, Temple Blocks, Tri., Anvil, Tubular Bells, Glsp., Xylo., Mrb., Vbp.), Harp, Pno. (doubling Cel.), Strgs. (Vlns. divided into 3 sections)	Commissioned through Magnum Opus Project. First performance: November 4, 2010, Virginia Symphony Orchestra, conducted by JoAnn Falletta. Score published by Presser.
Symphony No. 4, Op. 129 (2015)	One movement (388 mm.)	Picc., 2 Flt., 2 Ob., EH, 2 Clar., Bclar., 2 Bssn., Cbssn., 4 Hr., 3 Tpt., 3 Trom., Tuba, Timp., Perc. (Tri., Crotales, Glsp., Vbp., SD, Temple Blocks, Tamb., Mrb., Crash Cyms., Tubular Bells, BD, Suspended Cym., Wood Block, Gongs [large, small], Xylo., Slide Whistle, Flexatone, Siren), Harp, Pno., Cel., Strgs.	Commissioned for the Eastern Music Festival through the Bonnie McElveen-Hunter commissioning project. First performance: July 18, 2015, Eastern Music Festival, conducted by Gerard Schwarz.

along with lush orchestration, create an uncanny, cinematic effect. Just before the onset of a mysterious (and at times sinister) march, the ascending minor scales from the opening melody turn to become major. But in the march, the sense of tonal grounding is slightly less certain than in the first section; it casts a pall over the seemingly triumphant text of Whitman's "Poets to come!" that appears at the end of the section. The ensuing slow instrumental interlude, a respite from the march's intensity, begins with an opulent chorale that unfurls an aching melody rich with both chromaticism and triadic support. Leading to the symphony's conclusion, voices return singing passages from four different Whitman poems, beginning with a texted version of the chorale heard in the instrumental interlude and culminating in an energetic fugue followed by a reference to the chorale and finally an ethereal climax on the line "Joy! joy! all over joy!" from Whitman's "The Mystic Trumpeter." For Liebermann, the untempered exuberance of this ending was self-conscious and even ironic, with Dmitri Shostakovich's Fifth Symphony serving as a reference point.[305] The sardonic style of the march helps reinforce the Shostakovich link.

Because his Symphony No. 2 is "easily misinterpreted" as blindly cheerful (and unlikely to receive many performances because of the sizable forces required), Liebermann "very much wanted to write another symphony."[306] When the commission for a short orchestral work arose, he took the opportunity to produce his Symphony No. 3 (2010), a one-movement symphony whose "structural and thematic conciseness" Liebermann linked to Sibelius's Symphonies No. 4 (1911) and No. 7.[307] It recalls Liebermann's own Symphony No. 1 both in its opening, where a complex texture spins out from a slow melody, and in its conclusion, which strives for C major (the key of Sibelius's Seventh). In program notes for a performance by the Nashville Symphony Orchestra in 2012, Liebermann stated that he composed the work "during the unfolding of two devastating and catastrophic events: the Nashville flooding and the Deepwater Horizon oil spill," and that it is "dark and ironic, but not without its moments of humor and hope."[308] After an opening that expounds the basic thematic material—including a three-part chorale that prompted Liebermann to divide the violins into three groups instead of two—a middle section takes the form of "a jazz-inflected allegro which aspires to a kind of superficial jollity, but never loses its undercurrent of darkness and hysteria."[309] The conclusion "is the emotional core of the work. A reflection on the passage of time, it further develops the chorale theme, ending with an intrusive and unresolved recollection of the allegro."[310] Liebermann's Symphony No. 4 (2015), is a one-movement work composed for the Eastern Music Festival in Greensboro, North Carolina.

Wynton Marsalis (b. 1961)

The trumpeter, bandleader, impresario, and composer Wynton Marsalis (b. 1961) is one of the most prominent and multifaceted figures in recent music. In addition to his celebrated performances of jazz works—including original compositions—and of Baroque and Classical trumpet concertos, Marsalis has developed Jazz at Lincoln Center from a summer concert series in the 1980s into New York's most notable institutions for jazz performance and education in the twenty-first century. Marsalis has also earned acclaim as a composer of extended jazz compositions such as *In This House, On This Morning* (1992) and *Blood on the Fields* (1994), which in 1997 became the first such composition to win the Pulitzer Prize.

Less widely known than his work in these realms, but crucial to an understanding of Marsalis's mission "to put jazz on an equal social standing with Western art music," as Guthrie P. Ramsey has put it, are four immense, jazz-infused symphonies commissioned and performed

Table 9.20 The Symphonies of Wynton Marsalis (b. 1961)

Title	Movements	Instrumentation	Comments
All Rise (1999)	I. Jubal Step (475 mm.) II. A Hundred and a Hundred, a Hundred and Twelve (227 mm.) III. Go Slow (But Don't Stop) (226 mm.) IV. Wild Strumming of Fiddle (350 mm.) V. Save Us (214 mm.) VI. Cried, Shouted, Then Sung (131 mm.) VII. Look Beyond (124 mm.) VIII. The Halls of Erudition and Scholarship (Come Back Home) (217 mm.) IX. El "Gran" Baile de la Reina (311 mm.) X. Expressbrown Local (188 mm.) XI. Saturday Night Slow Drag (78 mm.) XII. I Am (Don't You Run from Me) (248 mm.)	3 Flt. (1 doubling Picc.), 3 Ob. (1 doubling EH), 3 Clar. (1 doubling B♭clar., 1 doubling Cbssn.), 3 Bssn. (1 doubling Cbssn.), 4 Hr., 3 Tpt., 3 Trom., 1 Tuba, Timp., Perc. (4 Players: Anvil, 2 BDs, Bongo Drums, Cabasa, Chimes, Flexatone, Glsp., Hand Drum, Low Bell, Mrb., Bass Mrb., Piatti, Sandpaper, Shaker, SD, Suspended Cym., Tamb., 4 Tom-Toms, Wood Block, Xylo.), Strgs., SATB Chorus, Jazz Ensemble (5 Reeds, 4 Tpt., 3 Trom., Pno., Bass, Drums)	Commissioned by the New York Philharmonic. First performance: December 29, 1999, New York Philharmonic, Lincoln Center Jazz Orchestra with Wynton Marsalis (trumpet), and Morgan State University Choir, conducted by Kurt Masur. Recorded by Los Angeles Symphony Orchestra, Lincoln Center Jazz Orchestra with Wynton Marsalis (trumpet), Morgan State University Choir, the Paul Smith Singers, and the Northridge Singers of California State University, Northridge, conducted by Esa-Pekka Salonen (Sony SK 89817).
Symphony No. 2, "Blues Symphony" (2009, rev. 2015 and after)	I. Born in Hope II. Swimming in Sorrow III. Reconstruction Rag IV. Southwestern Shakedown V. Big City Breaks VI. Danzón y Mambo, Choro y Samba VII. Dialog in Democracy	3 Flt. (2 doubling Picc.), 3 Ob. (1 doubling EH), 3 Clar. (1 doubling E♭ Clar., 1 doubling B♭clar.), 3 Bssn. (1 doubling Cbssn.), 4 Hr., 3 Tpt., 3 Trom., Tuba, Timp., Perc. (5 players; Agogo Bells, Anvil, BDs [small, concert, jazz], Bongo Bell, Brake Drum, Chimes, Chinese Cym., Congas, Cowbell, Field Drum, Glsp., Gong, Güiro, Hand Cyms., Hi-hat, Mrb., New Orleans BD Cym., Pandiero, Picc. SD, Police Whistle, Ride Cym., Sand Block, Sizzle Cym., Slapstick, SD, Splash Cym., Suspended Cyms. [small, medium, large], Tamb., Tam-tam, Temple Blocks, Timbales, Tom-toms, Tri., Washboard, Wood Blocks, Xylo.), Strgs.	Commissioned by the Atlanta Symphony Orchestra and the Boston Symphony Orchestra. First performance (selected movements): November 19, 2009, Atlanta Symphony Orchestra, conducted by Robert Spano. First performance of completed version: February 4, 2015, Shenandoah Conservatory Symphony Orchestra, conducted by Jan Wagner. Recorded by Philadelphia Orchestra, conducted by Cristian Măcelaru (Blue Engine Records, BE0039).

Table 9.20 *continued*

Title	Movements	Instrumentation	Comments
Symphony No. 3, "Swing Symphony" (2010, rev. 2013)	I. St. Louis to New Orleans II. All-American Pep III. Midwestern Moods IV. Manhattan to L.A. V. Modern Modes and the Midnight Moan VI. Think Space: Theory VII. The Low Down Up on High	3 Flt. (1 doubling Picc.), 2 Ob., EH., 3 Clar. (1 doubling Bclar.), 3 Bssn. (1 doubling Cbssn.), 4 Hr., 3 Tpt., 3 Trom., Tuba, Timp., Perc. (Tam-tams, Cyms., Tom-toms, BDs, SD, Xylo., Mrb, Vbp., Bongo Bell, Timbale Bell, Congas, Claves, Güiro, Tamb.), Strgs., Jazz Ensemble (5 Reeds, 4 Tpt., 3 Trom., Pno., Jazz Bass, Drum Set)	Commissioned by the Berlin Philharmonic Orchestra, London Symphony Orchestra, Los Angeles Philharmonic Orchestra, and New York Philharmonic. First performance: June 9, 2010, Berlin Philharmonic Orchestra, conducted by Simon Rattle. Score published by Skayne's Music. Recorded by Jazz at Lincoln Center Orchestra with Wynton Marsalis (trumpet) and St. Louis Symphony, conducted by David Robertson (Blue Engine Records BE0017).
Symphony No. 4, "The Jungle" (2014)	I. The Big Scream (Black Elk Speaks) (334 mm.) II. The Big Show (163 mm.) III. Lost in Sight (Post-Pastoral) (263 mm.) IV. La Esquina (281 mm.) V. Us (177 mm.) VI. Struggle in the Digital Market (355 mm.)	3 Flt. (1 doubling Picc.), 3 Ob. (1 doubling EH), 3 Clar. (1 doubling Bclar.), 3 Bssn. (1 doubling Cbssn.), 4 Hr., 3 Tpt., 3 Trom., Tuba, Timp., Strgs.	Commissioned by the New York Philharmonic for its 175th anniversary. First performance: December 29, 2016, New York Philharmonic, conducted by Alan Gilbert (first movement omitted). Recorded by Jazz at Lincoln Center Orchestra with Wynton Marsalis (trumpet) and Melbourne Symphony Orchestra, conducted by Nicholas Buc (Blue Engine Records BE 0040).

by leading orchestras and listed in table 9.20.[311] These works reflect their composer's identity as an American and an African American composer; in a video from 2010, he described his first three symphonies as works that "deal with the aspects of American music that . . . actually relate to American life, and our way of doing things in terms of improvisation and the blues, and swing—all those things that really bring us together as a country."[312] By incorporating vernacular music into large symphonic structures, Marsalis positioned his works not just within the legacy of the late-Romantic symphony but also in the context of long-standing efforts to combine jazz and classical music, including symphonic jazz and Third Stream music—Gunther Schuller's term for music that fuses jazz and classical norms.[313] Indeed, commenting on his first symphony, *All Rise* (1999), Marsalis said that he "intended to extend the continuum of jazz/symphonic orchestra collaboration foretold by Dvořák, initiated by Ellington and Gershwin, and furthered by Bernstein and Schuller."[314]

It was at the friendly prodding of his colleague at Lincoln Center, New York Philharmonic music director Kurt Masur, that Marsalis composed his blues-centered *All Rise* for orchestra, jazz orchestra, and choir. Suggesting the significance of embarking on a work that includes orchestra, and in a parallel to other symphonic late bloomers like Glass and Corigliano, Marsalis said, "I had no intention of ever writing for a classical orchestra." Masur would repeatedly ask Marsalis if he was "still scared to write for the New York Philharmonic . . . I got tired of hearing that. I said, OK, I'm not afraid to write for the New York Philharmonic."[315] Marsalis considers *All Rise* "the culmination of a ten-year odyssey during which I sought to realize more complex orchestrations for long form pieces based in American vernacular music and jazz."[316]

That *All Rise* contains 12 movements is no coincidence; it consists of three four-movement sections, meant to mirror the format of twelve-bar blues. Marsalis conceived of the composition both as a journey and as a means of fusing distinct musical elements under the umbrella of the blues: "Each section expresses different moments in the progression of experiences that punctuate our lives. It is a personal and communal progression. The first four movements are concerned with birth and self-discovery; they are joyous. The second four movements are concerned with mistakes, pain, sacrifice and redemption. They are somber and poignant. The last four are concerned with maturity and joy." Pointing to his wide-ranging use of vernacular materials and his cosmopolitan idea of American music, Marsalis added that the composition "contains elements of many things I consider related to the blues: the didgeridoo, ancient Greek harmonies and modes, New Orleans brass bands, the fiddler's reel, clave, samba, the down home church service, the Italian aria, and plain ol' down home ditties. Instead of combining many different styles on top of a vamp, I try to hear how they are the same."

The recording of *All Rise*, with Esa-Pekka Salonen leading the Los Angeles Philharmonic, was made just days after the terrorist attack of September 11, 2001. On learning of the assault on their hometown, Lincoln Center Jazz Orchestra members decided to remain in Los Angeles for a scheduled performance of the work and for the recording. As Marsalis related in his liner notes, a rehearsal of *All Rise* after the attack "was made forever memorable by the outpouring of concern and love from members of the Los Angeles Philharmonic." But the producer and engineer for the planned recording were stuck in the Midwest because flights were grounded after the attack. Miraculously, "several uncommon acts of dedication saved the sessions." Thanks to emergency car rides provided by friends, the engineer and producer made it to Los Angeles. "Even though time was limited and the recording schedule was tight," Marsalis wrote, "a deeper sense of community and inspiration guided us through these sessions."[317]

Marsalis's next two symphonic endeavors offer historical narratives through music. His seven-movement Symphony No. 2, "Blues Symphony," stands alone among his four symphonies in that it calls for orchestra without the addition of the jazz ensemble. Marsalis specifically called this work an Afro-American symphony, a label that suggests William Grant Still's Symphony No. 1, "Afro-American" (1930), as an antecedent.[318] As Marsalis explained in a 2009 video, "Every movement uses the blues form as its basis" and "has a specific sound and historic period, and it deals with things that exist in American folklore and Afro-American mythology."[319] In 2021, in liner notes for a recording of the symphony with the Philadelphia Orchestra, Marsalis wrote that the piece was "intended to further the legacy" of those "who were determined to add the innovations of jazz to the vocabulary of the symphonic orchestra. I believe there is an organic and real connection between all Western traditions regardless of instrumentation, and that the symphonic orchestra can and will swing, play the blues, feature melodic improvisation, and execute the more virtuosic aspects of jazz and American vernacular music with absolute authenticity."[320] The work's score has undergone several revisions since its partial world premiere in 2009 and again after its first complete performance in 2015.[321]

Like *All Rise*, Marsalis's Symphony No. 3, "Swing Symphony" combines jazz ensemble and orchestra, this time to present Marsalis's particular vision of jazz history—one that "traces the evolution of the swing rhythm from ragtime to this very moment in order to unite diverse instrumental techniques, musical personalities, song forms, dance grooves, and historic eras." As Marsalis himself described it, the first movement, "St. Louis to New Orleans," evokes ragtime and New Orleans, and the second, "All-American Pep," points to the "Charleston" and tango before "an optimistic, post-Depression" concluding section. The third movement, "Midwestern Moods," suggests Kansas City swing as well as Duke Ellington, Benny Goodman, Lionel Hampton, and Freddie Greene; this movement also highlights relationships between the saxes and cellos in recognition of tenor saxophonist Coleman Hawkins, who was also a skilled cellist. The fourth movement, "Manhattan to L.A.," explores bebop and mambo, and it includes an alto saxophone tribute to Benny Carter. In the fifth movement, "Modern Modes and the Midnight Moan," Marsalis considers the Third Stream as well as the sounds of Charles Mingus and Miles Davis. The sixth movement, "Think-Space: Theory," "focuses on the type of introspection that came into jazz through Bill Evans, Thelonius Monk, Wayne Shorter, and Herbie Hancock." And a varied finale, "The Low Down (Up on High)," ends with a highly unusual gesture: a communal sigh voiced by the entire orchestra.[322]

Marsalis's Symphony No. 4, "The Jungle" (2014), contains the same historical sweep as its predecessors in the genre while limiting its geographical scope to Marsalis's home of New York City. In the composer's words, the first movement, "The Big Scream (Black Elk Speaks)," "represents nervous energy, the primal soul of our city as maintained across time" and "reflects our Native American roots and the many forms of strife we have endured in an attempt to negotiate this small space with and without each other." With the next movement, "The Big Show," Marsalis leaps to modern times, providing a musical depiction of "the brash, brassy, razzle-dazzle of our city" with "the feeling of ragtime, of Broadway, and the European immigrant's transition to New Yorker through the syncopated spirit of the early 20th-century dance, animal movements like the turkey trot and fox trot." In the third movement, "Lost in Sight (Post-Pastoral)," Marsalis offers the other side of the coin, a reflection on "the homeless, the dispossessed, the out-of-luck, and the love-lost." "La Esquina," the fourth movement, celebrates the role of Afro-Latin music in New York's cultural landscape. On "Us," the fifth movement, Marsalis wrote of the sounds of "being with, against, and up against each other," and the concluding movement, "Struggle in the Digital Market" grapples with "the myth of unlimited growth for the purpose of ownership and seclusion."[323] Of that final movement, Anthony Tommasini observed that it combined "raw, wailing brass with spinning melodic twists, often hovering over obsessively repeated syncopated riffs." In a "surprising coda," as Tommasini put it, an extended trumpet-dominated passage "slowly splinters, as if the component parts are slipping away."[324]

Mason Bates (b. 1977)

Mason Bates (b. 1977) has emerged as one of the most popular living American symphonic composers. Using his experience as a DJ, he augments the timbral profile of the symphony orchestra with a wide spectrum of electronic sonorities ranging from straightforward techno beats to NASA spacewalk recordings. Bates uses arresting sounds not for their own sake but in the context of larger narrative considerations, especially as an extension of nineteenth-century program music. As Bates puts it, "I love infusing sprawling narrative ideas with the power of the orchestra and the drama of electronics."[325] Through the use of electronics—performed either manually by the composer as a member of the percussion section or automatically by means of a downloaded software patch running on a laptop—"those great nineteenth-century programmatic narrative forms can be looked at with fresh eyes," a result that Bates says places those forms "in technicolor."[326] And Bates's "technicolor" works have established lives well beyond their premieres. A survey of the 2014–2015 seasons in 21 major American orchestras showed that Bates's orchestral works (which also include brief "openers" and tone poems) were programmed more than those of any other living composer—American or not—except John Adams.[327] Michael Tilson Thomas and the San Francisco Symphony showcased Bates's symphonic music as part of its Beethoven and Bates festival in 2014; he served, along with Anna Clyne (b. 1980), as Mead Composer-in-Residence for the Chicago Symphony Orchestra from 2011 to 2015; and in 2015, he began his tenure as the first composer-in-residence in the history of the John F. Kennedy Center for the Performing Arts in Washington, DC (somewhat of a homecoming for the composer, as he grew up in nearby Richmond, Virginia). His symphonies—designated as such on the composer's website, http://masonbates.com, at the time of this writing—are shown in table 9.21.

Bates calls *Liquid Interface* (2007) a "water symphony" in that it examines the different physical states of water through musical development (recalling in this way Libby Larsen's *Symphony: Water Music* and Aaron Jay Kernis's *Symphony in Waves*).[328] The work, which Bates considers "a kind of Symphony No. 1" in its large-scale narrative form, is dedicated to his mentor at the Juilliard School, John Corigliano, whose own Symphony No. 1 Bates admires for a "weighty" narrative that is "often at the service of the music," functioning as "an imaginative way to unify a highly diverse musical endeavor."[329] Inspired by watching Berlin's Wannsee lake transition "from an ice sheet thick enough to support sausage vendors" to "a refreshing swimming destination heavy with humidity," *Liquid Interface* begins with the cold "Glaciers Calving" movement that combines an orchestral imitation of the fragmenting of glaciers— "huge blocks of sound drifting slowly upwards through the orchestra, finally cracking off in the upper register"—with authentic recordings of calving glaciers.[330] "As the thaw continues," Bates wrote, "these sonic blocks melt into aqueous, blurry figuration. The beats of the electronics evolve from slow trip-hop into energetic drum 'n bass, and at the movement's climax the orchestra blazes in turbulent figuration." "Scherzo Liquido," the second movement, "explores water on a micro-level: droplets splash from the speakers in the form of a variety of nimble

Table 9.21 The Symphonies of Mason Bates (b. 1977)

Title	Movements	Instrumentation	Comments
Liquid Interface (2007)	Glaciers Calving (116 mm.) Scherzo Liquido (113 mm.) Crescent City (140 mm.) On the Wannsee (73 mm.)	3 Flt. (all doubling Picc.), 3 Ob. (1 doubling EH), 3 Clar. (1 doubling Bclar. and Eb Clar.), 3 Bssn. (1 doubling Cbssn.), 4 Hr., 3 Tpt., 3 Trom., Tuba, Electronica (Laptop, Speakers, Monitors), Perc. (Timp., BD, Bongos, Trap Set, Vbp., Xylo., Mrb., Suspended Cym., Ride Cym., Splash Cym., Sizzle Cym., Chimes, High Tam-tam, Castanets, Tri., Glsp., Washboard [with spoon], Crotales, Harmonicas, Slide Gui., 6 Crystal Glasses, Wind Machine), Harp, Pno., Strgs.	Commissioned by the National Symphony Orchestra. Dedicated to John Corigliano. First performance: February 22, 2007, National Symphony Orchestra, conducted by Leonard Slatkin. Score published by Aphra Music. Recorded by San Francisco Symphony, conducted by Michael Tilson Thomas (SFS Media 0065).
The B-Sides (2009)	I. Broom of the System (118 mm.) II. Aerosol Melody (Hanalei) (86 mm.) III. Gemini in the Solar Wind (114 mm.) IV. Temescal Noir (99 mm.) V. Warehouse Medicine (141 mm.)	2 Flt. (1 doubling Picc.), 2 Ob. (1 doubling EH [optional]), 2 Clar. (1 doubling Bclar.), Eb Clar. (doubling Bclar.), 2 Bssn., Cbssn., 4 Hr., 3 Tpt., 3 Trom., Tuba, Electronica (Laptop, Speakers, Monitors), Perc. (Suspended Cym., Sizzle Cym., Ride Cym., Crash Cym., 2 Tri. [high], Sandpaper Blocks, Hi-hat, Tamb., Wood Block [high], Castanets, SD, BD, Glsp., Mrb., Vbp., Djembe, Large Broom, Typewriter, Oil Drum), Harp, Pno. (doubling Cel.), Strgs.	Commissioned by the San Francisco Symphony. First performance: May 20, 2009, San Francisco Symphony, conducted by Michael Tilson Thomas. Score published by Aphra Music. Recorded by San Francisco Symphony, conducted by Michael Tilson Thomas (SFS Media 0065).

Alternative Energy (2011)

Ford's Farm, 1896 (167 mm.)
Chicago, 2012 (99 mm.)
Xinjiang Province, 2112 (191 mm.)
Reykjavík, 2222 (92 mm.)

3 Flt. (all doubling Picc., 1 doubling Aflt.), 3 Ob. (1 doubling EH), 3 Clar. (1 doubling E♭ Clar.), 3 Bssn. (1 doubling Cbssn.), 4 Hr., 3 Tpt., 3 Trom., Tuba, Electronica (Laptop, Speakers, Monitor), Timp., Perc. (Car Parts, Scrap Metal, Glsp., Vbp., Hi-hat, Ratchet [huge], Rachet [small], Floor Tom, Mrb., Ride Cym., Picc., SD, Tam-tam, BD, Gong, Sizzle Cym., Splash Cym., Crotales, Suspended Cym., Wood Blocks [high, medium], Bundle of Wood Sticks, Bamboo Wind-chimes, Ceramic Wind-chimes, Tubular Bells, Tri. [high], Djembe, Shaker, Thai Gongs), Pno., Harp, Strgs.

Commissioned by the Chicago Symphony Orchestra.
First performance: February 2, 2012, Chicago Symphony Orchestra, conducted by Riccardo Muti.
Score published by Aphra Music.
Recorded by Chicago Symphony Orchestra, conducted by Riccardo Muti (CSO Resound); San Francisco Symphony, conducted by Michael Tilson Thomas (SFS Media 0065).

The Anthology of Fantastic Zoology (2014)

Forest: Twilight (15 mm.)
Sprite (94 mm.)
Dusk (26 mm.)
The A Bao A Qu (132 mm.)
Nymphs (123 mm.)
Night (5 mm.)
The Gryphon (219 mm.)
Midnight (15 mm.)
Sirens (78 mm.)
The Zaratan (20 mm.)
Madrugada (392 mm.)

3 Flt. (1 doubling Picc.), 3 Ob. (1 doubling EH), 3 Clar. (1 doubling E♭ Clar., 1 doubling Bclar.), Bssn. (1 doubling Cbssn.), 4 Hr., 3 Tpt. (1 doubling Picc. Tpt. [optional]), 3 Trom., Tuba, Perc. (Xylo., Glsp., Large Chinese Drum, Wood Blocks, Crash Cyms., Crotales, Tri., BD, SD, Castanets, Tam-tam, Ratchet, Asian Wood Block, 3 Suspended Cyms., Soprano Wind Machine, Conga, Tamb., Almglocken, Hi-hat, Whip, Vbp., Flexible Wood Switches, Asian Drum), Timp. (including additional Picc. Timp. or Rototoms), Harp, Pno. (doubling Cel.), Strgs.

Dedicated to Riccardo Muti. Commissioned by the Chicago Symphony Orchestra.
Score published by Aphra Music.
First performance: June 18, 2015, Chicago Symphony Orchestra, conducted by Riccardo Muti.
Recorded by Chicago Symphony Orchestra, conducted by Riccardo Muti (CSO Resound).

Table 9.21 continued

Title	Movements	Instrumentation	Comments
Children of Adam, songs of creation for chorus and orchestra (2017–18)	I. Walt Whitman, "From Pent-up Aching Rivers" (77 mm.) II. Psalms 144 & 128 (112 mm.) III. Walt Whitman, "I Sing the Body Electric" (63 mm.) IV. Mattaponi Indians of Virginia, "Tolepe Menenak" ("Turtle Island") (66 mm.) V. Carl Sandburg, "Prayers of Steel" & "Smoke and Steel" (85 mm.) VI. From the Book of Genesis (107 mm.) VII. Walt Whitman, "To the Garden, the World" (84 mm.)	2 Flt. (both doubling Picc.), 2 Ob. (1 doubling EH), 2 Clar., 2 Bssn. (1 doubling Cbssn.), 4 Hr., 3 Tpt., 3 Trom., 3 Perc. (Tri., Glsp., SD, Tamb., BD, Tam-tam, Rute, Crash Cyms., Mrb., Vbp., Castanets, Wood Block, Djembe, Finger Cym., Bowed Cym., Low Asian Drum, Anvil, Oil Drum, High Log Drum), Harp, Pno. (doubling Cel.), SATB div., Strgs.	Commissioned by Richmond Symphony Orchestra for its 60th anniversary. Dedicated to Sharon Sun Eagle. Texts from various sources (see second column); Whitman movements from "Children of Adam" in *Leaves of Grass*. Score published by Aphra Music. First performance: May 11, 2018, Richmond Symphony and Richmond Symphony Chorus, conducted by Steven Smith. Recorded by Richmond Symphony and Richmond Symphony Chorus, conducted by Steven Smith (Reference Recordings FR-732).
Art of War (2017–18)	I. Money as a Weapons System (227 mm.) II. Two Worlds (137 mm.) III. On the March (205 mm.)	3 Flt. (1 doubling Picc. and Alto Flt.), 3 Ob. (1 doubling EH), 3 Clar. (1 doubling E♭ Clar.), 3 Bssn. (1 doubling Cbssn.), 4 Hr., 4 Tpt., 3 Trom., Tuba, Timp., Electronica (Laptop, Speakers, Monitor), 4 Perc. (Field Drum, Crash Cyms., Vbp., BD, Cash Register Ding, Tri., Crotale, Xylo., Rute, Suspended Cym., SD, Hi-hat, "Cricket Percussion," Finger Cyms., Djembe, Marching SD, Floor Tom, 3 Tom-toms, Tam-tam, Siren, Some shouting), Pno. (doubling Cel.), Harp, Strgs.	Commissioned by Kennedy Center for the Performing Arts. Published by Aphra Music. First performance: December 6, 2018, National Symphony Orchestra, conducted by Gianandrea Noseda.

electronica beats, with the orchestra swirling around them." "Crescent City," by contrast, "examines the destructive force as water grows from the small-scale to the enormous"—a clear reference to Hurricane Katrina in 2005. Here, suggestions of New Orleans jazz transition into "an electronic hurricane of processed storm sounds," leading eventually to the redemptive vision of "On the Wannsee," which Bates describes as "a kind of balmy, greenhouse paradise." In this movement, "a simple, lazy tune bends in the strings above ambient sounds recorded at a dock on Lake Wannsee," and "the melody floats lazily upwards through the humidity and—at the work's end—finally evaporates."

The impetus for Bates's work *The B-Sides* (2009) came from Michael Tilson Thomas, who "suggested a collection of five pieces focusing on texture and sonority," with Arnold Schoenberg's *Five Pieces for Orchestra*, Op. 16, as a reference point. For his part, Bates "had often imagined a suite of concise, off-kilter symphonic pieces that would incorporate the grooves and theatrics of electronica in a highly focused manner. So, like the forgotten bands from the flipside of an old piece of vinyl, *The B-Sides* offers brief landings on a variety of peculiar planets, unified by a focus on fluorescent orchestral sonorities and the morphing rhythms of electronica." In the first piece, "Broom of the System" (titled after the David Foster Wallace novel), "To the ticking of a future clock, our broom—brought to life by sandpaper blocks and, at one point, an actual broom—quietly and anonymously keeps everything running, like a chimney sweep in a huge machine." The title of the second movement, "Aerosol Melody (Hanalei)," refers to the way in which "a gentle, bending melody evaporates at cadence points"; Bates associates this effect with a location on the Hawaiian island of Kauai, with "Aerosol" thus suggesting an ocean mist and recalling *Liquid Interface*. Bates's inventive percussive effects often do not rely on electronics; he notes that in this movement, "Djembe and springy pizzicati populate the strange fauna of this purely acoustic movement." The arresting third piece, "Gemini in the Solar Wind," launches into space, serving as "a re-imagination of the first American spacewalk, using actual communication samples from the 1965 Gemini IV voyage provided by NASA. In this re-telling, clips of words, phrases, and static from the original are rearranged to show Ed White, seduced by the vastness and mystery of space, deliriously unhooking from the spacecraft to drift away blissfully." White's mention of seeing California from space serves as a clever transition to the planetary surface:

> The initial grit of "Temescal Noir," like the Oakland neighborhood of the title, eventually shows its subtle charm in hazy, jazz-tinged hues. Unbothered by electronics, this movement receives some industrious help in the rhythm department by a typewriter and oil drum. At its end, the broom returns in a cameo, again altering the tempo, and this propels us into "Warehouse Medicine." An homage to techno's birthplace—the empty warehouses of Detroit—the final stop on *The B-Sides* gives no quarter. Huge brass swells and out-of-tune pizzicati emulate some of the visceral sonorities of techno, and on this pounding note *The B-Sides* bows out.[331]

Just as *Liquid Interface* is a "water symphony," *Alternative Energy* (2011), Bates's third symphony, is an "energy symphony" in that it "travels through ever greater and more powerful forces of energy," from nineteenth-century America to twenty-third-century Iceland.[332] Inspired thus by a futuristic scientific concept, Bates's approach in this work calls to mind the music of Edgard Varèse (1883–1965), but with a less esoteric tinge and often with the propulsive rhythmic profiles of minimalism.[333] Composed for the Chicago Symphony Orchestra, the work evokes the nineteenth-century symphonic tradition in that its movements are unified by what Bates considers an idée fixe. In the first movement ("Ford's Farm, 1896"), the melody, heard in the fiddle and "accompanied by junkyard percussion and a 'phantom orchestra' that trails the fiddler like ghosts," is meant to evoke Henry Ford.[334] The next movement, "Chicago, 2012," includes sound that was recorded from FermiLab equipment near the city of the work's commission and premiere, processed "to recreate the sound of a particle accelerator booting up."[335]

The remaining movements of *Alternative Energy* take a dim view of the future, tinted with nostalgia. In the third movement, "Xinjiang Province, 2112," the flute offers "a tragically distorted version of the fiddle tune, dreaming of a forgotten natural world. But a powerful industrial energy simmers to the surface, and over the ensuing hardcore techno, wild orchestral splashes drive us to a catastrophic meltdown." "Reykjavik, 2212" follows immediately and presents an "Icelandic rainforest on a hotter planet" where the fiddler from the first movement "returns over a woody percussion ensemble to make a quiet plea for simpler times." *Alternative Energy* also contains a second defining motif, the "accelerando cranking of a car motor," which serves as "a kind of rhythmic embodiment of ever more-powerful energy" and makes for an especially stunning transition between the first and second movements.[336]

Wynton Marsalis's epic symphonies offer one precedent for the vast time spans covered by Bates's *Alternative Energy*; another is a large symphony from nearly a hundred years earlier—*America: An Epic Rhapsody* (1926), by Ernest Bloch (1880–1959). The earlier composition's three extended movements journey from precolonial times through the cityscapes of the twentieth century, and its third movement is titled "1926: The Present—The Future."[337] Another precursor, also by Bloch, is the Suite for Viola and Orchestra (1919). The bustling quality of parts of the second movement of the Bloch suite, with its fiddle-like viola part and dance rhythms, anticipates "Ford's Farm, 1896." Moreover, Bloch's four movements initially carried the evocative titles "In the Jungle," "Grotesques," "Nocturne," and "Land of the Sun," and in a parallel to Bates's fanciful "Xinjiang Province, 2112," Bloch wrote in his program notes of "a vision of the Far East that inspired me: Java, Sumatra, Borneo—those wonderful countries I so often dreamed of, though I never was fortunate enough to visit them in any other way than through my imagination."[338] (Incidentally, Bates teaches at the San Francisco Conservatory of Music, which Bloch directed from 1925 to 1930; John Adams taught there from 1972 to 1982.)

Bates's entirely acoustic instrumental symphony, *The Anthology of Fantastic Zoology* (2014), is named for the 1954 book (better known in its later editions as the *Book of Imaginary Beings*) by the Argentine writer Jorge Luis Borges (1899–1986). Bates called this composition a "psychedelic *Carnival of the Animals*" in which different mythological and literary creatures are presented before their various themes are combined.[339] He has described the work as "a concerto for orchestra in the guise of a bestiary of mythological creatures," and one that "showcases different sections and soloists with the vividness of Russian ballet scores, a major inspiration for the piece."[340] This work has a recent ancestor in *A Scotch Bestiary* (2004) for organ and orchestra by Scottish composer James MacMillan (b. 1959); this work, incidentally, like *The B-Sides*, features a typewriter. *Anthology*, a Chicago Symphony Orchestra commission, uses acoustic means for narrative purposes. This is clearly demonstrated in the "Sprite" movement, in which a motif circulates, as Bates described it, "from music stand to music stand."[341] Another multimovement acoustic symphony is *Children of Adam* (2018), a seven-movement set of songs for chorus and orchestra that Bates composed for the sixtieth anniversary season of the Richmond Symphony Orchestra, his "hometown band." This work, as Bates put it, "explores seven exuberant perspectives of creation and rebirth, from American poets to sacred and Native American texts."[342]

Unlike in *Anthology of Fantastic Zoology* or *Children of Adam*, Bates employed electronic sounds in the three-movement *The Art of War* (2017–18), "a symphony exploring the perspective of soldiers, weapons, and the collision of civilizations." Bates, who composed the work as composer-in-residence of the Kennedy Center, wrote that he had "always been fascinated by the vividness of martial music" and that he "wanted to explore the musical possibilities of two civilizations becoming intertwined," which in this case meant a blend of the blues with Middle Eastern folk music in the symphony's second movement, "Two Worlds." Preceding this movement is "Money as a Weapons System," whose name is drawn from "the title of an actual US military handbook describing the use of money to achieve military goals, and I couldn't resist composing a musical analogue to the alarming idea of weaponized money." As he did in other symphonies, Bates created and used field recordings, this time from machines printing money at the Bureau of Engraving and Printing. "Lurching rhythms created from these sounds integrate with quicksilver, caffeinated musical textures that glitter like coins from a slot machine—only to spin wildly out of control over the course of the movement."[343] The finale, "On the March," incorporates recordings of the sounds of weapons at Marine Corps Base Camp Pendleton in California.[344]

With his symphonies, particularly *Liquid Interface, Alternative Energy, The B-Sides,* and *Art of War*, Bates has helped to realize Libby Larsen's hope, quoted above, that the orchestra of the future should develop "a digital choir as part of its complement."[345] Similarly, Bates calls the orchestra "an evolving creature throughout history. I do think electronic sounds are the current innovation in it."[346] Time will tell whether electronics will endure as a permanent part of the standard symphony orchestra and of the symphony as a genre, or if Bates's experiments in this realm will prove the exception. But if the growth of orchestral percussion (including the more frequent use of piano) over the last hundred years is any indication, the digital expansion may indeed be the next phase in the orchestra's ongoing transformation. Signs of such expansion, in fact, appear in film scores that fuse digital and acoustic sound, such as Thomas Newman's (b. 1955) score for the Disney/Pixar film *WALL-E* (2008), directed by Andrew Stanton. Set in the year 2805, *WALL-E*—like *Alternative Energy*—depicts an earth laid waste by the behavior of human beings, and both scores tell dystopian stories in part by testing the boundaries between noise and music. The similarities between the music of Newman and Bates—their emphasis on percussion, rhythmic energy, and vivid orchestral writing—point to the cinematic resonance of the symphonic works of Bates, who scored the 2015 film Gus Van Sant film *The Sea of Trees*.

The work of Newman and others has shown that Bates is hardly alone in exponentially enlarging the orchestra's timbral palette through electronics and, in turn, enlivening the symphonic genre's narrative possibilities. As documented by the composer Elliott Schwartz (1936–2016), experiments in combining electronic and orchestral sounds date back to the middle of the twentieth century.[347] One particularly prominent example is prolific Finnish symphonist Einojuhani Rautavaara's (1928–2016) dazzling *Cantus Arcticus*, subtitled "Concerto for Birds and Orchestra" (1972), which combines orchestral sounds with recorded samples of Nordic birdsong. (A much earlier example is found in Ottorino Respighi's 1924 symphonic poem *Pini di Roma*, whose third movement calls for a recording of a nightingale.) But Bates and others may well be ushering in the new "golden age of music for the orchestra involving circuits of some sort" that Schwartz predicted could emerge.[348] In 2014 the American Composers Orchestra released the album *Tech and Techno*, which includes compositions that blend orchestral and electronic sonorities by Bates (*Omnivorous Furniture*, 2004); his teacher at the University of California, Berkeley, Edmund Campion (*Practice*, 2005); and his fellow composer-in-residence at the Chicago Symphony Orchestra, Anna Clyne (*Tender Hooks*, 2008). A laptop also figures in the scoring for the opera *Ainadamar* (2003) by Argentinean American composer Osvaldo Golijov (b. 1960).

In recent years, as discussed in this chapter's introduction, a number of American composers of symphonies have shown their perspectives to be global ones, extending well beyond western Europe. To name a few others, Kamran Ince (b. 1960) was born in Montana and spent much of his childhood in Turkey, and he went on to teach at the University of Memphis; his symphonies have drawn directly on various aspects of Turkish culture. Tan Dun (b. 1957), the composer of the immense *Symphony 1997: Heaven Earth Mankind* (1997) and the concise Internet Symphony No. 1, "Eroica" (2008), was born in China and studied both there and in the United States. For Tan as for Ince, the term *American* is an incomplete designation. To be sure, these are far from the only composers with shares of American identity to have explored non-Western sounds and ideas in their symphonic works. As seen above, Lou Harrison's intense interest in Asian cultures permeated his symphonic works (as it did for Henry Cowell and Alan Hovhaness). But for recent composers, the symphony has become a home for blending Western and non-Western aspects of composers' personal identities. Because of their complex cultural identities, their stylistic amalgamations suggest not the sympathetic exoticism found in Harrison's gamelan-infused works or in the "Nocturne" of John Corigliano's Symphony No. 2, with its evocations of Morocco. Rather, their works demonstrate an organic intermingling of techniques and approaches drawn from the history of symphonic writing, from deeply ingrained personal experiences and senses of heritage, and from an Internet-powered world in which limitless literary and cultural inspirations rest at every creative artist's fingertips. This chapter concludes with two composers—Wang Jie and Mohammed Fairouz—who bring to the symphony their unique perspectives as global citizens.

Wang Jie (b. 1980)

The New York–based composer Wang Jie (b. 1980) was born and raised in Shanghai and traveled to the United States to study composition at the Manhattan School of Music. While Mason Bates looked directly to the nineteenth-century program symphony for inspiration, Wang places the symphony firmly in the camp of absolute music. Distinguishing between musical and verbal thought, Wang views the lack of verbal language in the symphony (as she defines it) as allowing her the "complete freedom" to generate a wholly musical discourse. As a large-scale genre that permits an especially wide range of possible sounds, the symphony "avails the total force" for Wang "to join everything from the slightest musical murmur" to the "monstrous sonic burst"—making possible "a truer reflection of my inner emotional world."[349] Wang's symphonies (shown in table 9.22) are not "absolute" in the strictest sense because, as will be seen below, she associates specific texts and images with the works. These works do not, however, project the kind of precise narrative account found in Bates's symphonies.

Wang composed her Symphony No. 1, a twelve-minute work in three continuous movements, as a student assignment at the Curtis Institute; with it she won the American Composers Orchestra's Underwood Emerging Composers Commission in 2009. With its tragic sensibility, as expressed in the accompanying poem "Awakening," which Wang also wrote, this symphony is a tribute to Gustav Mahler.[350] The poem speaks of people with "fragmented hearts" who are drawn together through pain—"By what brings us to ache / Not by what we celebrate."[351] The slow first movement shimmers, at times playfully, with melodic fragments

Table 9.22 The Symphonies of Wang Jie (b. 1980)

Title	Movements	Instrumentation	Comments
Symphony No. 1, "Awakening" (2008; rev. to 2018)	I. Andante comodo, con amore (58 mm.) II. Agitato, con moto (148 mm.) III. Adagio con rubato (53 mm.)	Picc., 2 Flt., 2 Ob., EH, 2 Clar., Bclar, 2 Bssn., Cbssn., 4 Hr., 3 Tpt., 3 Trom., Tuba, Timp., Perc. (3 Players; Player 1: Suspended Cym., Crash Cym., SD, Chimes, Xylo.; Player 2: Glsp., Suspended Cym. [14-inch high pitch], Kick Drum, 4 Tom-toms; Player 3: Tri. [high], Crotales, BD, 5 Wood Blocks), Pno, Cel., Harp, Strgs.	Winner of the 2009 American Composers Orchestra's Underwood Emerging Composers Commission. First performance April 14, 2008, Curtis Symphony Orchestra, conducted by Lio Kuokman. Score published by Wang Jie Music.
Symphony No. 2, "To and from Dakini" (2013)	One movement (357 mm.)	Picc., 2 Flt., 2 Ob., EH (doubling Ob.), 2 Clar., Bclar. (doubling Clar.), 2 Bssn., 1 Cbssn., 4 Hr., 3 Tpt., 3 Trom., Tuba, Timp., Perc. (3 Players; Player 1: Vbp., 5 Wood Blocks, BD, Tamb.; Player 2: Xylo., Slapstick, 2 Bongos, 2 Tom-toms, Kick Drum, 1 Suspended Cym. [medium]; Player 3: Glsp., Mrb., Tri. [high], SD, Crash Cyms.), Harp., Strgs.	Commissioned by the Detroit Symphony Orchestra in honor of Elaine Lebenbom. First performance: March 26, 2014, Detroit Symphony Orchestra, conducted by Leonard Slatkin. Score published by Wang Jie Music.
The Winter that United Us (2020–22)	One movement (628 mm.)	Picc., 2 Flt., 3 Ob., 2 Clar., Bclar. (doubling Eb Clar.), 2 Bssn., Cbssn., 4 Hr., 3 Tpt., 3 Trom., Tuba, Timp., Perc. (Tri., Tamb., SD, Xylo, Vbp., Slap Stick, Crash Cyms., Suspended Cyms., BD, Sleigh Bells, Chimes), Strgs.	First performance: June 11, 2022, Buffalo Philharmonic Orchestra, conducted by JoAnn Falletta.
Flying on the Scaly Backs of Our Mountains (2020–22)	One movement (514 mm.)	Picc., 2 Flt., 2 Ob., EH, 2 Clar. (1 doubling Eb Clar., Bclar, 2 Bssn., Cbssn., 4 Hr., 3 Tpt., 3 Trom., Tuba, Timp., Perc. (2 Players; Player 1: SD, Tam-tam; Player 2: Tri., Suspended Cym., Xylo., Sleigh Bells, Vbp., Tamb., Tam-tam [shared with Player 1]), Strgs.	Commissioned by the Colorado Music Festival. First performance: August 4, 2022, Colorado Music Festival Orchestra, conducted by Peter Oundjian.

that evoke birdsong as well as a generally light touch with orchestration. But menacing orchestral rumbles and swells prefigure the work's tragic trajectory. The second movement, with its pulsating, unpredictable rhythms and swirling textures, suggests the more explosive side of the poem's scenario. The final movement returns to the serene character of the first movement, and the tranquility is tinged with tragedy through a blend of anguished leaps and bell-like sonorities; although present in the first movement, here they take on a tragic, funereal tone. Wang's revisions to the work since 2008 include the addition of material for cello at the beginning of the first movement and for brass in the second movement.[352]

Wang related her one-movement Symphony No. 2, "To and From Dakini," to her own mother as well as to Elaine Lebenbom (1933–2002), in whose honor the work was commissioned by the Detroit Symphony Orchestra through an annual award for women composers. In doing so, Wang referred specifically to what she calls "feminine forces": "I blinked my eye and the first draft of the symphony was finished. When I read it over, the broad range of character transformation bewildered me. At times, the feminine force sings with utmost tenderness. But other times, she can't stop dancing, as if gravity ceased to exist and all terrestrial boundaries disappeared. This dreamy female becomes a nurturer of calming introspection. But in an instant, she reveals herself to be a tempestuous dancing goddess!"[353] Research on dancing goddesses—specifically through one of the early twenty-first-century world's ubiquitous research tools, the Internet ("I immediately googled 'dancing goddess,'" she noted)—led Wang to the third female force, Dakini, a deity in Tibetan Buddhism who Wang described as "elusive, playful, the female embodiment of enlightenment and an accomplished teacher of realities that cannot be grasped intellectually."[354]

The music of Symphony No. 2 continues literally where Symphony No. 1 left off, with the same hushed string sonority found in the earlier work's final measures and shown in example 9.12. Remarkably, this gesture plays three simultaneous roles: as the endpoint for one work, the start of another, and a transitional hinge between them. And because the gesture gently swells from ***ppp*** to *piano* and back, it serves as a microcosm of the sense of departure and return that is central to musical form.

From this opening sonority, the texture grows and pace accelerates as instruments exchange motives. The first section centers on an impassioned, concerto-like dialogue between solo violin and orchestra. In the ensuing climactic section (*Subito vivace*, beginning at m. 162) slow-moving wind melodies overlay fast, spiraling scales in the strings, creating a sense of temporal dissonance; this leads to an energetic passage strongly reminiscent of the "Jeu du Rapt" from Igor Stravinsky's *Le sacre du printemps* (beginning at m. 223 of Wang's work)—an especially fitting association given the symphony's explicit connections to dance. At various points in

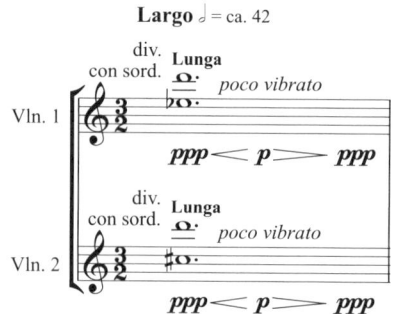

Example 9.12 Wang Jie, Symphony No. 2, "To and From Dakini," m. 1. Copyright © 2014 Wang Jie Music. All rights reserved. Used with permission.

the composition, harmonics, slides, microtones, and col legno string effects generate an otherworldly atmosphere. The symphony ends with an airy passage in which the final measure—like the symphony's opening one—moves from ***ppp*** to ***p*** and back to ***ppp***.

The Winter That United Us (2020–22), Wang's third symphony, begins with the same gesture that ends Symphony No. 2, following the pattern established at the opening of that work. (This pattern does not extend, however, to *Flying On the Scaly Backs of Our Mountains* [2020–22], a work that connects to Wang's experiences as a rock climber and that she has also identified as a symphony.[355]) Such uniquely intentional linkages among works may bear an intriguing relationship to Wang's attitude toward national identity. With her transnational background, she does not consider her music to have a particular Chinese or American quality; she is more interested in exploring what she considers a humanistic sense of connectedness through musical beauty—a task for which she believes the symphony is especially fertile ground.[356]

Mohammed Fairouz (b. 1985)

Mohammed Fairouz (b. 1985), an American composer of Arab descent, takes the word *symphony*, and its classic meaning of "sounding together," as a starting point for exploring the genre's social implications in a multicultural world. Fairouz's symphonies, shown in table 9.23, vary in scope and performing forces, but they embrace a cosmopolitan perspective and engage explicitly with issues of contemporary political importance. Fairouz's four-movement Symphony No. 1, "Symphonic Aphorisms" (2005) shows his early interest in musical structures; as Fairouz noted, it is "based on the idea of the aphorism as a flexible and serviceable form for the concise expression of ideas."[357] An eclectic mixture of styles and references, the symphony includes a third movement, "Remembrance of Things Played," which reflects the music of twentieth-century modernists such as Milton Babbitt and Pierre Boulez, and a fourth movement, "Homage to a Belly-Dancer," which employs the sonorities of an Arabic orchestra.[358]

After his three-movement Symphony No. 2 for chamber orchestra in 2009 (itself preceded by Chamber Symphony No. 1, "Sabra," in 2005, for musicians and actors—a work that evokes the Sabra and Shatila massacre in Beirut in 1982 and includes texts from the testimonies of survivors), Fairouz composed the ambitious Symphony No. 3, "Poems and Prayers" (2010). Fairouz labeled it a "poetic Middle Eastern journey," and it incorporates a range of texts from Middle Eastern traditions, boldly juxtaposing the Aramaic, Hebrew, and Arabic languages.[359] At the outset, in an assertive statement of the *Kaddish* (in Aramaic), the Jewish prayer of mourning, textures swell and recede as a plaintive English horn solo leads to the first movement's hushed conclusion. In this movement, the *Oseh Shalom* (the Hebrew addendum to the Kaddish), which serves as a refrain throughout the symphony, first appears. "Lullaby," the first part of the second movement, is a duet for mezzo-soprano and solo clarinet with atmospheric accompaniment from the orchestra. It sets an Arabic text by Mahmoud Darwish in which a mother sings to her son at his funeral; here, the clarinet's extended techniques suggest a mother's memory of her child's sobbing and wailing. This leads to "Minyan" (the term for a group of male Jewish worshippers), the conclusion of the movement, in which the *Oseh Shalom* returns with the men's chorus. Like "Lullaby," "Night Fantasy," the third movement, is also a duet, this time between mezzo-soprano and violin. The text, by noted Palestinian poet Fadwa Tuqan, expresses the suffering of her people, and is again followed by *Oseh Shalom*.[360]

In its combined use of orchestra and voice, as well as its sheer length, the Finale places Fairouz's work in the tradition of symphonies that close with extended vocal/choral movements,

Table 9.23 The Symphonies of Mohammed Fairouz (b. 1985)

Title	Movements	Instrumentation	Comments
Symphony No. 1, "Symphonic Aphorisms" (2007)	I. Funeral March: The Order of the Burial of the Dead (119 mm.) II. Scherzo (54 mm.) III. Intermezzo: Remembrances of Things Played (63 mm.) IV. Homage to a Belly-Dancer (153 mm.)	2 Flt., 2 Ob., 2 Clar., 2 Bssn., 2 Hr., 2 Tpt., 2 Trom., Timp., Perc. (Tam-tam [large], Tubular Chimes, Suspended Cym., Xylo., BD, SD, Tenor Drum, Darabuka, Claves), Strgs.	Commissioned by the New England Conservatory Composers' Series Orchestra. Score published by Peermusic Classical.
Symphony No. 2 (2009)	I. Memorial for the War Dead (123 mm.) II. Dubkeh (82 mm.) III. Apotheosis (56 mm.)	Flt. (doubling Picc.), Ob., Clar., Bssn., Hr., Tpt., Trom., Timp., Perc. (Tam-tam [large], Tubular Chimes, Suspended Cym., Tamb., Xylo., Large BD, SD), Pno., Harp, Strgs.	Commissioned by ALEA III contemporary music ensemble at Boston University. First performance: January 27, 2010, ALEA III, conducted by Theodore Antoniou. Score published by Peermusic Classical.
Symphony No. 3, "Poems and Prayers" (2010)	I. Kaddish (113 mm.) II. Lullaby—Minyan (170 mm.) III. Night Fantasy—Oseh Shalom (156 mm.) IV. Memorial Day for the War Dead (463 mm.)	Picc., 2 Flt, 2 Ob., 2 Clar., 2 Bssn., 4 Hr., 2 Tpt., 3 Trom., Timp., Perc. (1 Player: Chimes, Cyms., BD [large], Suspended Cym., SD, Tamb, Xylo., Tam-tam), Harp, Strgs., Vocal Soloists (Mezzo-Soprano, Baritone), Mixed Chorus, Children's Chorus (or women of the mixed chorus)	Commissioned by the Middle East Center for Peace, Culture and Development at Northeastern University for the Zamir Chorale of Boston. Sets the Mourner's Kaddish from the Jewish tradition, in Aramaic and Hebrew; poetry by Mahmoud Darwish and Fadwa Tuqan, in Arabic; and poetry by Yehuda Amichai, in Hebrew. First performance: February 16, 2012, Ensemble 212 and the Young New Yorkers Chorus, conducted by Yoon Jae Lee, with Rachel Calloway (mezzo-soprano) and David Kravitz (baritone). Score published by Peermusic Classical. Recorded by UCLA Philharmonia, Chorale, and Chorus, conducted by Neal Stulberg, with Sasha Cooke (mezzo-soprano) and David Kravitz (baritone) (Sono Luminus DSL92177).

Symphony No. 4, "In the Shadow of No Towers" (2012)	I. The New Normal (198 mm.) II. Notes of a Heartbroken Narcissist (76 mm.) III. One Nation Under Two Flags (199 mm.) IV. Anniversaries (138 mm.)	Wind Ensemble: 4 Flt. (doubling Picc.), 3 Ob., EH, 6 Clar, 2 Bclar, Cbclar, 2 Asax., Tsax., Barsax., 4 Bssn., 2 Cbssn., 8 Hr., 6 Tpt., 6 Trom., 3 Tuba, Timp., Perc. (6 Players; Player 1: Chimes, BD, Xylo., Suspended Cym., SD, Tam-tam, Wood Block; Player 2: Tri, Xylo., Suspended Cym., Cyms., Chimes, Claves; Player 3: Suspended Cym., BD, Xylo.; Player 4: Tenor Drum, Chimes, Xylo.; Player 5: Tenor Drum, Suspended Cym., BD, Chimes, Tri, Xylo.; Player 6: BD, Suspended Cym., Cyms.), Harp [amplified], Pno. [amplified], Cb. [amplified]	Commissioned by Reach Out Kansas Inc., and inspired by the graphic novel *In the Shadow of No Towers* by Art Spiegelman. First performance: March 26, 2013, in Carnegie Hall, Kansas University Wind Ensemble, conducted by Paul W. Popiel. Score published by Peermusic Classical. Recorded by University of Kansas Wind Ensemble, conducted by Paul W. Popiel (Naxos 8.573205).
Symphony No. 5 (2021)	I. David's Symphonic Feat (279 mm.) II. Solomon: The Kingdom of Time (161 mm.) III. The Infinite Variations 218 mm.) IV. Light in Ascent: the Illumination (454 mm.)	2 Flt. (1 doubling Picc.), 2 Ob., 2 Clar., 2 Bssn., 2 Tpt., 3 Trom., Timp., Perc., Pno. (doubling Cel.), Harp, Strgs.	Commissioned by the Abu Dhabi Music & Arts Foundation. Score published by Presser. Recorded (January 2022) by London Symphony Orchestra, conducted by Lee Reynolds, for its digital world premiere broadcast, May 19, 2022, for the Abu Dhabi Festival.

such as Beethoven's Symphony No. 9; Mahler's Symphony No. 2, "Resurrection"; Bernstein's Symphony No. 3, "Kaddish"; and Kernis's Symphony No. 3, "Symphony of Meditations." This movement sets Israeli poet Yehuda Amichai's poignant "Memorial Day for the War Dead" and concludes with another statement of the *Oseh Shalom* by all vocal forces—this time in a version, recited by Jews in Reform traditions, that refers to peace not just in Israel but within the global community of nations.[361] For Fairouz, this change reflects "a transformation of an ancient prayer of peace not only for the tribe but for all the Earth."[362] When this work was performed in Los Angeles in 2003, Mark Swed wrote in the *Los Angeles Times* that it was "a young man's extraordinary effort to say what needs to be said, feel what needs to be felt and demonstrate what needs to be demonstrated about the Israeli and Palestinian morass in the Middle East."[363]

Fairouz's Symphony No. 4 (2012) contends with the collective experience of the terrorist attacks of September 11, 2001—a subject explored in different ways in other recent symphonies by American composers, including Kevin Puts's Symphony No. 2, "Island of Innocence" (2002), and Leonardo Balada's Symphony No. 5, "American" (2003). Fairouz's work, from 2012, is scored for wind ensemble and named after Art Spiegelman's graphic novel *In the Shadow of No Towers*; the individual movement titles are drawn from text in panels in the Spiegelman work. The first of four movements, "The New Normal," draws on three panels by Spiegelman that depict a family watching television before, during, and after the attacks.[364] The opening recalls minimalism in its hypnotic layering of D-major and E-flat-major sonorities, and Fairouz related this section to the "electronic monotony" of life before the attacks. The fiery middle section suggests the family's reaction at the moment of the attacks, and a Mahlerian funeral march leads to a reprise of the opening oscillation, this time overlaid with an ominous trumpet solo (in the panel that corresponds to this final section, Spiegelman depicts the family as in the first panel, but with frazzled hair and an American flag hanging on the wall.) Here, in Fairouz's words, "It seems that nothing has *really* changed. Everything is the same, but not quite." The repeated pitch A, which serves as connective tissue throughout the movement, emphasizes this paradoxical sense of dynamic motionlessness.

Percussive effects define "Notes of a Heartbroken Narcissist," the contemplative, sonically enigmatic second movement that evokes the sounds of digging through rubble.[365] The scherzolike third movement, "One Nation Under Two Flags," offers a literal representation of the country's divided political landscape in 2012—what Fairouz calls his "most explicit critique of loud nationalism." Just as Elliott Carter split the orchestra into three groups in his 1976 symphonic study of New York, *Symphony of Three Orchestras*, Fairouz bisects the wind ensemble, with the two resulting groups called the "United Red Zone of America" and the "United Blue Zone of America." Highlighting the fracture between the "zones" is a stylistic divergence; the "Red Zone" plays distorted Sousa-esque music with "a jingoistic, fanfare-y thrust," while the "Blue Zone" often evokes Philip Glass with its rapid arpeggios. The juxtaposition of these "zones" recalls the works of Charles Ives, as "the music of each band is pitted relentlessly against the other with the two sides not listening to one another." A quiet middle section makes rapprochement seem possible, but tempers between the "zones" flare anew in the movement's thunderous conclusion. In the extended, slow Finale, "Anniversaries," ticking percussion evokes a clock's second hand. The movement, meant as a comment on the complex interplay of time and memory, is a drawn-out crescendo that lasts, significantly, 9 minutes, 11 seconds. After the University of Kansas Wind Ensemble's first performance of this work in

2013, Steve Smith in the *New York Times* called the symphony "technically impressive, consistently imaginative and in its finest stretches deeply moving."[366]

Both Fairouz's Symphony No. 5 (2021) and its predecessor are shaped in the standard four movements of the classical symphony, but Fairouz considers the Symphony No. 5 to be his most clearly "classical"; in fact, Fairouz specifically refers to it as a "classical symphony" as those words "describe this symphony's design to bear a certain self-aware sensibility about itself." But he also views this symphony and the Symphony No. 4 as "polar magnetic opposites" with a certain "kinship"; the Symphony No. 5, for orchestra (rather than wind ensemble), "reflects the preceding work through the projection of its brilliant electric light just as the earlier symphony carries within it a certain formal mirror of the later work cast entirely in the dark matter of its shadows." Both works might be considered as, simultaneously, both classical and epic in scope. Fairouz noted that the construction of the first movement of Symphony No. 5, "David's Symphonic Feat"—and the symphony's unfolding as a whole—explores aspects of King David's musical imagination. The other movement titles, "Solomon: The Kingdom of Time," "The Infinite Variations," and "Light in Ascent: The Illumination," suggest a certain monumentality, and the work's Romantic heritage is echoed in the composition's dazzling scoring and expansive lines.[367] This symphony, commissioned by the Abu Dhabi Music & Arts Foundation, was recorded in January 2022 by the London Symphony Orchestra, conducted by Lee Reynolds, and its world premiere took place as a digital broadcast of this recording on May 19, 2022, as part of the Abu Dhabi Festival.

Conclusion: The American Symphony into the Future

When discussing in 2015 his desire to compose more symphonies, Fairouz responded that his impulse to do so derives from "the infinite combinations of the colors of the orchestra and all of the new opportunities that are open to us as composers living in the cosmopolitan age."[368] Remarking on the "poetry of wordless symphonic expression," Fairouz added, "I don't think that the poetry of the form has even begun to be exploited to its full potential."[369]

Such symphonic optimism reflects a stark turn from the ambivalence of Leonard Bernstein just 50 years earlier, and even the reluctance of composers like Corigliano and Glass to tackle the genre even 25 years prior. On the eve of the period considered in this chapter, Leonard Bernstein asked if symphonies were "a thing of the past." His conflicted response only raised more questions:

> No, obviously, since they are still being written in substantial quantity. But Yes, equally obviously, in the sense that the classical concept of a symphony, depending as it does on a bifocal tonal axis, which itself depends on the existence of tonality—that classical concept *is* a thing of the past.
>
> Does that mean that symphonies can no longer be created? No; in a loose sense the word "symphony" can be applied to all kinds of structures. On the other hand, Yes; in a strict sense the decline of the symphony can perceivably be dated back to the beginning of our century.[370]

By the beginning of *our* century, as the above survey shows, the symphony—far from completing its so-called decline—had absorbed a range of meanings, purposes, and sonic possibilities and still managed to remain recognizable. On a musical level, this is partly because since 1970 tonality ceased to be simply "a thing of the past"—and thus composers could continue to use the symphony as a place to explore the large-scale formal questions that occupied earlier symphonists, and to draw on examples ranging from Mahler's multimovement choral-orchestral leviathans to Sibelius's one-movement statement. In addition, a range of musical components from all ends of the stylistic spectrum—indeterminacy, electronics, extended techniques, and contemporary vernacular idioms, to name a few—have enabled composers to continue to tell musical stories in new ways. Composers still reflect on the weight and durability of the genre, as well as the place of their own symphonies in what they tend to view as a grand tradition; this, too, testifies to the symphony's endurance. William Bolcom's comments in 2008, centering on his substantial Symphony No. 8, illustrate that a tension between the genre's continued expressive potential and its sometimes overbearing historical tradition in fact help sustain it:

> I suppose we expect symphonies to deal more with larger spiritual and philosophical subjects than other musical forms of their length and heft. In our culture we have sanctified the form by calling the ensemble that plays such pieces a "symphony orchestra." All this is well and good, but the symphonic form is so historically and financially freighted that its own weight may doom it relatively soon, like so many other dinosaurs of our history. I hope not. I suppose I still write them in this late day because some things can only be expressed in a symphony, at least by me. I cannot imagine having written my Eighth in a lesser form than that of a symphony.[371]

Significantly, for recent American symphonists, the long-standing and occasionally overwhelming pressure to create *the* "Great American Symphony"—a work that somehow encapsulates a monolithic idea of American culture—has become a distant memory. In place of that burden is a new freedom to employ an even greater diversity of materials and performing forces than before, and to create works with a wide range of formal plans, extramusical connections, political resonances, and philosophical underpinnings. Far from diluting the integrity of the symphony as a genre, though, this diversity seems to have enriched it. If there is anything particularly "American" about this heterogeneity, it is perhaps best reflected in Libby Larsen's comment that to be an "American" symphonic composer for her means "to be cognizant of my musical wellsprings and invite them into the center of my process."[372] One need only take into account the blossoming of the symphony in the different approaches, or "wellsprings," of the three youngest composers above—Wang Jie's poetic organicism, Mason Bates's far-reaching expansion of the orchestral palette, and Mohammed Fairouz's cosmopolitan and message-oriented musical perspective—to predict that the genre's future seems bright.

Bibliographic Overview

At this stage, the scholarly literature on recent American symphonies is scant, with no full-length studies focusing specifically on the symphony in the period after 1970. Two broader surveys of American symphonies, Butterworth/SYMPHONY and Tawa/GREAT, contain brief sections on the more recent symphony, but these books are geared toward earlier periods. Butterworth surveys the symphonies of Lou Harrison, Easley Blackwood, Jr., William Bolcom, John Harbison, John Corigliano, Gloria Coates, Ellen Taaffe Zwilich, and Daniel Asia; he also offers a list of symphonies and a discography. Tawa/GREAT discusses Rochberg's symphonies in some detail and mentions Harrison, Rouse, Harbison, Zwilich, Corigliano, Kernis, and others. Although Bernard/TONAL does not focus specifically on the symphony, it considers works of Rochberg, Zwilich, and Corigliano, as well as Michael Daugherty, Richard Danielpour, Stephen Albert, Aaron Jay Kernis, Libby Larsen, David Del Tredici, William Bolcom, Philip Glass, John Adams, and Christopher Rouse. Taruskin/OXFORD mentions

Corigliano's Symphony No. 1 and Glass's Symphony No. 5 in the context of the "New Topicality" and "New Spirituality" that spoke to the expectations of patrons. Wilson/SURVIVAL provides a brief but insightful overview of the recent symphony and its aesthetic contexts with respect to modernism and tradition; it focuses mainly outside the United States but does mention Rochberg, Bolcom, and Corigliano. And although it does not concentrate specifically on the symphonies, Ritchey/BATES links Mason Bates's embrace of technology in his music to neoliberal ideology.

Some symphonic composers have whole studies devoted to their works. There exist several useful ones on Elliott Carter, including Meyer & Shreffler/CARTER, Schiff/CARTER, and Wierzbicki/CARTER. Lou Harrison's output, including his symphonies, has been discussed in great detail in Miller & Lieberman/COMPOSING (which includes an information-filled catalog of works as well as a compact disc), Miller & Lieberman/HARRISON, Miller/AESTHETICS, and Alves & Campbell/HARRISON. Many details of George Rochberg's life and works, including a helpful collection of program notes, are found in Dixon/ROCHBERG. John Corigliano's life and works are summarized concisely in Adamo/CORIGLIANO. May/ADAMS READER serves as a valuable source for commentators' writings on Adams's works, including his symphonies. Miller/KERNIS brings to light many details of the life and compositions of Aaron Jay Kernis and contains extended discussions of his symphonies and the circumstances surrounding those works. And a quite recent study, Von Glahn/LARSEN, contends with Libby Larsen's life and work.

Discussions of certain symphonies may be found in several broader scholarly efforts. One study of women composers, Von Glahn/SKILLFUL, considers Larsen's *Symphony: Water Music* and Zwilich's Symphony No. 4, "The Gardens" (the latter is also explored in Von Glahn/SOUNDS). A few individual scholarly articles contend with one more of a particular composer's symphonies in detail: Bergman/RAGE (Corigliano's Symphony No. 1); Grimshaw/HIGH (Glass's Symphony No. 1), Watkins/PASTORAL (Albert's Symphony No. 1), Grimley/SYMPHONY (Carter's *Symphony of Three Orchestras*), Wlodarski/CAVERNOUS and Wlodarski/ROCHBERG (Rochberg's Symphony No. 3), and Miller & Lieberman/GAMELAN (Harrison's Fourth Symphony). Some commentary on individual works from this period is also found in Steinberg/SYMPHONY (Harbison's Symphony No. 2) and Fanning/SYMPHONY.

A number of composers have produced memoirs that consider their symphonies in the broader contexts of their music and lives. These include Elliott Carter (Edwards/FLAWED), George Rochberg (Rochberg/LINES), George Walker (Walker/REMINISCENCES), John Adams (Adams/HALLELUJAH), and, most recently, Philip Glass (Glass/WORDS).

Finally, several books contain enlightening interviews with recent American symphonists. Banfield/CONVERSATIONS contains the reflections of George Walker and Adolphus Hailstork. McCutchan/MUSE includes conversations with Bolcom, Corigliano, Harbison, Adams, Rouse, Larsen, and Kernis, among others. More recently, Raines/DIGITAL WORLD features interviews with Zwilich, Rouse, Larsen, Kernis, and Fairouz. As far as specific composers are concerned, Maycock/GLASS includes some relevant interviews with Philip Glass and includes lively discussions of his first six symphonies; and Swafford/ASIA, although not strictly an interview, engages personally with Daniel Asia's symphonic output.

The bulk of published matter on recent American symphonies has yet to be mined by scholars, as it resides in program notes (often written by the composers), CD liner notes, composer websites, publishers' websites, and published scores (many of which have been scanned and placed online, accessible through publishers' websites). Journalistic sources, including reviews and profiles of composers appearing in newspapers, and publications geared toward those interested in orchestral music and institutions (such as *Symphony*, published by the League of American Orchestras) and contemporary music (such as *New Music Box*, published by New Music USA), also offer valuable material that will occupy scholars of American symphonic music for years to come.

Notes

1. I am grateful to the following individuals for assisting me in this project: Daniel Albertson, Ethan Allen, Daniel Asia, Nathan Ball, Mason Bates, Arian Baurley, Steve Biagini, William Bolcom, Mitch Brodsky, Holli Clements, John Corigliano, Elizabeth Craft, Richard Danielpour, Madeleine deBlois, Cindy Elliott, Louis Epstein, Mohammed Fairouz, James Forger, Richard Guérin, Adolphus Hailstork, John Harbison, Brian Hart, Evan Hause, Barbara Haws, Bill Holab, Phillip Huscher, Maria Iannacone, Kamran Ince, Nicole Jordan, Margo Kieser, Aaron Jay Kernis, Ellen Knight, Libby Larsen, Frank Lehman, Hannah Lewis, Lowell Liebermann, Noah Luna, David Maslanka, Leta Miller, Tammy Moore, John Muniz, David Murray, Jennifer Nichols, Andrew Norman, Sarah Peterson, Tobias Picker, Emily Richmond Pollock, Erin Rogers, Jim Schneeberg, Jason Senchina, Liz Silver, Gabryel Smith, Andrea Steele, Stephen Steele, Robert Sutherland, Frank Villella, George Walker, Wang Jie, Jan Wagner, Norman Weinberg, Allison Weissman, Scott Wollschleger, and Ellen Taaffe Zwilich.

2. See Wilson/SURVIVAL; Tawa/GREAT, pp. 17–18; and Bernard/TONAL, p. 538.
3. See Tawa/GREAT, pp. 17–18; Taruskin/OXFORD, pp. 514–28; and Wilson/SURVIVAL.
4. See Taruskin/OXFORD, p. 516; Bernard/TONAL, p. 555–59; and Wilson/SURVIVAL.
5. See Bernard/TONAL, pp. 538, 564–65; and Fanning/SYMPHONY, p. 126.
6. See Tawa/GREAT, pp. 210–13.
7. Information and quotations on Stucky's *Symphony* from this paragraph drawn from Stucky/SYMPHONY.
8. Puts/SYMPHONY.
9. Anonymous/UNDERWOOD.
10. Stone/BALADA, p. 86.
11. Balada/STEEL and Balada/SYMPHONY 5.
12. Schweitzer/LISTENING.
13. Husa/SYMPHONY 2.
14. Gojowy/COATES, p. 68.
15. Arias/TCHEREPNIN, p. 233.
16. Arias/TCHEREPNIN NG, p. 185.
17. Howard/MOTHERHOOD.
18. Anonymous/PÄRT SYMPHONY 4.
19. Ibid.
20. Stucky/LUTOSŁAWSKI.
21. Stucky/SYMPHONY.
22. Corigliano/SYMPHONY 3.
23. See chapter 6 for an analysis of Vincent Persichetti's Symphony No. 6 for Band and chapter 5 for a brief discussion of Hindemith's Symphony in B-flat.
24. Wierzbicki/CARTER, p. 27.
25. See Meyer & Shreffler/CARTER, p. 49.
26. Edwards/FLAWED, p. 58.
27. See Meyer & Shreffler/CARTER, p. 49.

28. Baker/INTERVIEW.
29. Meyer & Shreffler/CARTER, p. 49.
30. See Schiff/CARTER, p. 131, where the influence of Piston on Carter is discussed and the symphony is considered part of Carter's "brief bucolic phase." For Piston's symphonies, see chapter 5.
31. Ibid., p. 276.
32. Baker/INTERVIEW.
33. See Meyer & Shreffler/CARTER, p. 51, for greater detail on these changes.
34. Ibid., pp. 12–19.
35. See Schiff/CARTER, p. 15.
36. See Meyer & Shreffler/CARTER, p. 225, and Schiff/CARTER, pp. 300–307.
37. The complex scheme is discussed in detail in Schiff/CARTER, pp. 303–07.
38. Carter/THREE ORCHESTRAS.
39. Schiff/CARTER, p. 307.
40. Meyer & Shreffler/CARTER, p. 227, and Schiff/CARTER, pp. 306–07.
41. The above quotations in this paragraph are drawn from Carter/PARTITA.
42. Carter/ALLEGRO SCORREVOLE.
43. See Schiff/CARTER, pp. 316–23, for more detail on the *Symphonia*.
44. Ibid., p. 316.
45. Meyer & Shreffler/CARTER, p. 296.
46. Dyer/BOSTON, as quoted in ibid., p. 296.
47. Wierzbicki/CARTER, p. 4.
48. On Harrison's biography, see Miller & Lieberman/COMPOSING, pp. 25–76.
49. Ibid., pp. 37–38.
50. Harrison/SYMPHONY ON G.
51. Ibid.
52. Miller & Lieberman/HARRISON, p. 87.
53. See Miller & Lieberman/COMPOSING, p. 300, n. 187, and Miller/AESTHETICS, pp. 91–94, for information on the origins of the movements. For more detail on this symphony, also see Alves & Campbell/HARRISON, pp. 133–36.
54. Harrison/SYMPHONY ON G.
55. See von Gunden/MUSIC, pp. 77–86, as well as Alves & Campbell/HARRISON, pp. 320–22, for more detail on this symphony.
56. See Miller & Lieberman/COMPOSING, p. 303, n. 211, for information on the origins of the movements.
57. See ibid., p. 307, n. 243, and Miller/AESTHETICS, pp. 94–100, for information on the origins of the movements.
58. Miller & Lieberman/COMPOSING, p. 303, n. 211.
59. Harrison/FOURTH NOTE.
60. Ibid.
61. Miller & Lieberman/COMPOSING, pp. 206–07.
62. See Harrison/FOURTH NOTE and Harrison/FOURTH ABOUT. Also see Miller & Lieberman/COMPOSING, p. 312, n. 281, for information on the origins of the movements, and Alves & Campbell/HARRISON, 397–99, for greater detail on this symphony.
63. As quoted in Dixon/ROCHBERG, pp. 139–40.
64. Reilly/RECOVERY, p. 9.
65. Ibid., p. 8.
66. Rochberg/LINES, p. 80. See chapters 1 and 5 for more on the "Great American Symphony" during the interwar period.

67. Dixon/ROCHBERG, pp. 153–54. Also see Rochberg/LINES, p. 85.
68. As quoted in Dixon/ROCHBERG, p. 154.
69. Dixon/ROCHBERG, p. 182.
70. As quoted in Swayne/ORPHEUS, p. 317.
71. As quoted in Dixon/ROCHBERG, p. 64.
72. As quoted in ibid., p. 152.
73. Rochberg/LINES, p. 17.
74. As quoted in Dixon/ROCHBERG, p. 156. Also see Rochberg/LINES, p. 16.
75. For more detail on the Third Symphony, see Wlodarski/ROCHBERG, pp. 83–99.
76. Hughes/JUILLIARD.
77. Rochberg/SYMPHONY 3, p. 163.
78. Rochberg/LINES, p. 168. See Wlodarski/CAVERNOUS, pp. 248–51.
79. As quoted in Dixon/ROCHBERG, p. 159.
80. As quoted in ibid., p. 160.
81. Ibid.
82. Rochberg/LINES, p. 172.
83. As quoted in Dixon/ROCHBERG, p. 97.
84. As quoted in ibid.
85. As quoted in ibid., p. 161.
86. As quoted in ibid., p. 162.
87. Rochberg/LINES, p. 200.
88. See ibid., pp. 211, 242.
89. Ibid., p. 202.
90. Ibid., pp. 201–02.
91. Ibid., pp. 203–04, 207.
92. Ibid., pp. 208, 204–05.
93. As quoted in Dixon/ROCHBERG, p. 163. A 2003 recording by Christopher Lyndon-Gee with the Saarbrücken Radio Symphony Orchestra (Naxos 8.559115)—the work's first performance since its premiere—also earned the symphony a Grammy nomination as Best Classical Composition.
94. As quoted in ibid., p. 163.
95. Ibid., p. 165.
96. As quoted in ibid., pp. 165–66.
97. As quoted in ibid., p. 166.
98. Rochberg/LINES, p. 209.
99. As quoted in Dixon/ROCHBERG, p. xiv.
100. As quoted in ibid., p. xviii.
101. See Walker/REMINSCENCES, pp. 46–49, 94–101, 116–17, 144–45.
102. Walker/FEB 3 EMAIL.
103. Walker/REMINISCENCES, p. 115.
104. Ibid.
105. Walker/INTERVIEW.
106. Rockwell/MUSIC.
107. Walker/SINFONIA 2.
108. Walker/REMINISCENCES, p. 167.
109. Anonymous/WALKER SINFONIA 3.
110. Walker/SINFONIA 4.
111. This and other details of the work's structure are described in ibid.
112. Walker/INTERVIEW.

113. As quoted in Schultz/WALKER.
114. Walker/INTERVIEW.
115. Anonymous/WALKER SINFONIA 5.
116. Clark/DISCUSSION, p. 195. Also see Grimshaw/HIGH, pp. 472–73.
117. See Clark/DISCUSSION, p. 195, for Glass's comments on the premiere of his concerto and his experience as an orchestra composer in his theater works.
118. See Grimshaw/HIGH, pp. 480–81, and Rothstein/GLASS.
119. Keller/SYMPHONY 2.
120. See Grimshaw/HIGH, p. 474, and Maycock/GLASS, p. 86.
121. Glass/SYMPHONY 6.
122. Glass/SYMPHONY 7.
123. Glass/SYMPHONY 8.
124. See ibid. for further detail on the structure of this composition.
125. Taylor/GLASS.
126. Guérin/GLASS.
127. Robin/GLASS.
128. Glass/SYMPHONY 12.
129. Guérin/EMAIL. See table 9.6 for details.
130. Broyles/MAVERICKS, p. 163.
131. As quoted in McCutchan/MUSE, p. 34.
132. LaFave/BERNSTEIN, p. 185.
133. Corigliano/SYMPHONY 2, p. 25.
134. Ibid.
135. Corigliano/SYMPHONY 1.
136. Ibid.
137. Bergman/RAGE, pp. 345–46.
138. von Rhein/SHKOLNIK.
139. Ibid. This issue is discussed in Bergman/RAGE, p. 344.
140. von Rhein/SHKOLNIK.
141. Corigliano/SYMPHONY 1.
142. Details and quotations above in this paragraph are drawn from ibid.
143. Adamo/CORIGLIANO, p. 23.
144. Bergman/RAGE, p. 343.
145. Corigliano/SYMPHONY 2, p. 27.
146. Ibid., p. 31.
147. Ibid., p. 33.
148. Details and quotations above in these paragraphs are drawn from Corigliano/SYMPHONY 3.
149. Corigliano/INTERVIEW.
150. Adamo/CORIGLIANO, p. 49.
151. See Bates/MECHANICS.
152. See Johnson/BOLCOM.
153. As quoted in Bolcom/SYMPHONY 1.
154. Bolcom/SYMPHONY 2.
155. Ibid.
156. Details and quotations in these paragraphs are drawn from Bolcom/SYMPHONY 3.
157. Details and quotations in this paragraph are drawn from Bolcom/SYMPHONY 5.
158. See Doyle/BOLCOM.
159. As quoted in Clague/SYMPHONY 7.

160. As quoted in ibid.
161. Tommasini/OPERA.
162. Bolcom/PROPHETIC, pp. 15–16.
163. Ibid., p. 18.
164. Ibid., p. 19.
165. Ibid.
166. Bolcom/EMAIL JUNE 2.
167. Bolcom/EMAIL FEB 3.
168. Bolcom/EMAIL FEB 18.
169. Bolcom/EMAIL JUNE 2.
170. Bolcom/EMAIL FEB 18.
171. Details and quotations in this paragraph are drawn from Harbison/INTERVIEW.
172. Harbison/SYMPHONY 1.
173. Ibid.
174. Harbison/SYMPHONY 3.
175. Ibid.
176. Details and quotations here and below in this paragraph are drawn from Harbison/SYMPHONY 3 ALBANY.
177. Details and quotations above in this paragraph are drawn from Harbison/SYMPHONY 4.
178. Harbison/SYMPHONY 5.
179. Harbison/SYMPHONIES.
180. Harbison/INTERVIEW.
181. Harbison/SYMPHONIES.
182. Zwilich/INTERVIEW.
183. Page/ZWILICH, p. 29.
184. Ibid, p. 30.
185. Zwilich/SYMPHONY 1.
186. Ibid.
187. Ibid.
188. Holland/COMPOSERS.
189. Von Glahn/SOUNDS, p. 235.
190. Ibid., pp. 236–37.
191. Ibid., p. 239.
192. Ibid., p. 244.
193. Page/ZWILICH, p. 32.
194. Ibid, p. 28.
195. Hailstork/SYMPHONY OF HOPES.
196. Ibid.
197. Banfield/CONVERSATIONS, p. 100.
198. Hailstork/SYMPHONY 1.
199. As quoted in Anonymous/HAILSTORK SYMPHONIES.
200. See ibid.
201. Details and quotations above in this paragraph are drawn from ibid.
202. Oteri/HAILSTORK. The full symphony premiered in June 2023.
203. Hailstork/STILL HOLDING ON. See chapter 5 for Still's symphonies.
204. As quoted in Wigler/ALBERT.
205. Duffie/ALBERT.
206. Albert/RIVERRUN.

207. Ibid.
208. Ibid.
209. See ibid. and McLellan/ROSTROPOVICH.
210. Albert/RIVERRUN.
211. Ibid.
212. Ibid.
213. McLellan/ROSTROPOVICH.
214. Ibid.
215. Currier/SYMPHONY 2.
216. Watkins/PASTORAL, p. 11.
217. See Cahill/ADAMS.
218. Adams/HALLELUJAH, p. 114.
219. Adams/HARMONIUM.
220. Adams/HALLELUJAH, p. 111.
221. Ibid., p. 129.
222. Ibid., p. 130.
223. Ibid.
224. Adams/HARMONIELEHRE.
225. Ibid.
226. Adams/HALLELUJAH, p. 130.
227. Ibid., pp. 132, 130.
228. Ibid., p. 257.
229. Adams/NAIVE.
230. Ibid.
231. Ibid.
232. Ibid.
233. See Adams/HALLELUJAH, pp. 172–73.
234. Maddocks/EXPLOSIVE and Tommasini/DEMYSTIFYING.
235. Adams/CITY.
236. Adams/SCHEHERAZADE.2.
237. Jepson/COMPOSER.
238. Ibid.
239. See McCutchan/MUSE, p. 131.
240. As quoted in Druckenbrod/GLOOMY.
241. Oteri/ROUSE.
242. As quoted in Watkins/INTERVIEW.
243. McCutchan/MUSE, p. 128.
244. Ibid.
245. Ibid.
246. Rouse/DOCUMENTARY, p. 16.
247. Rouse/SYMPHONY 2.
248. Rouse/SYMPHONY 3.
249. Ibid.
250. Tommasini/ROUSE.
251. Rouse/SYMPHONY 4.
252. Rouse/SYMPHONY 5.
253. Rouse/SYMPHONY 6.
254. Larsen/EMAIL APRIL 21.

255. Larsen/WATER MUSIC.
256. See Von Glahn/SKILLFUL, p. 244.
257. Larsen/SYMPHONY 2.
258. Ibid.
259. Ibid.
260. Larsen/COWBOY SONGS.
261. Larsen/SYMPHONY 3.
262. Ibid.
263. Ibid.
264. Larsen/PIANO CONCERTO.
265. Larsen/EMAIL APRIL 30.
266. Larsen/SYMPHONY 4.
267. Ibid.
268. Larsen/EMAIL APRIL 24.
269. Details and quotations above in this paragraph are drawn from Larsen/SOLO SYMPHONY.
270. Larsen/EMAIL APRIL 21.
271. Ibid.
272. See Reel/ASIA 1 AND 4.
273. Asia/SYMPHONY 2.
274. Asia/INTERVIEW.
275. Asia/FAR EDGE. See Reel/ASIA 2 AND 3, p. 7, on the relationship between Symphony No. 3 and *At the Far Edge*.
276. See Reel/ASIA 1 AND 4.
277. Asia/SYMPHONY 5.
278. Poem texts are drawn from Luke/VERSE, pp. 316–17.
279. Picker/INTERVIEW.
280. Kernis/EMAIL.
281. See Miller/KERNIS, pp. 26–38.
282. Details and quotations in this paragraph are drawn from Kernis/SYMPHONY IN WAVES.
283. See Miller/KERNIS, p. 17.
284. See Miller/KERNIS, pp. 55–58, for more detail on the *Symphony in Waves*.
285. Ibid., p. 55.
286. See ibid., pp. 81–85, for more detail on the Second Symphony.
287. Kernis/SECOND SYMPHONY.
288. Miller/KERNIS, p. 84.
289. Kernis/SECOND SYMPHONY.
290. Kozinn/PREMIERES.
291. Olmstead/SESSIONS, p. 357. See chapter 6 for details on these works.
292. Kernis/SECOND SYMPHONY.
293. Miller/KERNIS, p. 71.
294. Kernis/SYMPHONY OF MEDITATIONS.
295. See ibid., pp. 136–48, for more detail on the "Symphony of Meditations."
296. Kernis/CHROMELODEON.
297. Liebermann/NEO-ROMANTIC.
298. Ibid.
299. Ibid.
300. Liebermann/INTERVIEW.
301. Ibid.

302. Liebermann/INTERVIEW.
303. Ibid.
304. Ibid.
305. Ibid.
306. Ibid.
307. As quoted in Marx/SYMPHONY 3, p. 47.
308. As quoted in ibid., p. 47. Despite the Nashville connection, the symphony premiered with the Virginia Symphony Orchestra under JoAnn Falletta in 2010.
309. As quoted in ibid., p. 48.
310. As quoted in ibid.
311. Ramsey/RACE, p. 163.
312. Marsalis/SWING SYMPHONY.
313. See chapter 5 for a discussion of James P. Johnson's *Harlem Symphony*, an example of symphonic jazz from 1932.
314. As quoted in Anonymous/MARSALIS SYMPHONY 4, p. 35.
315. Ibid.
316. Marsalis/ALL RISE.
317. Details and quotations in this and the previous paragraph are from ibid.
318. See chapter 5 for a study of Still's symphonies.
319. Marsalis/BLUES SYMPHONY VIDEO.
320. Marsalis/BLUES SYMPHONY NOTE.
321. Kelly/BLUES SYMPHONY.
322. The quotations and details in this paragraph are drawn from Marsalis/SWING SYMPHONY NOTE.
323. Details and quotations above are drawn from Marsalis/GLANCE.
324. Tommasini/SYMPHONY 4.
325. Bates/MECHANICS.
326. Bates/INTERVIEW.
327. O'Bannon/2014–15 SEASON.
328. Bates/INTERVIEW.
329. Bates/MECHANICS.
330. Details and quotations here and below in this paragraph are drawn from Bates/LIQUID INTERFACE.
331. Details and quotations above in this paragraph are drawn from Bates/B-SIDES.
332. Bates/ALTERNATIVE NOTE.
333. See Anderson/VARESE.
334. Bates/ALTERNATIVE NOTE.
335. Bates/ALTERNATIVE BLOG.
336. Bates/ALTERNATIVE NOTE. "Reykjavik" (without the í) is Bates's spelling.
337. See chapter 5 for a discussion of *America* and Bloch's other symphonies.
338. Bloch/PROGRAMS, p. 54. See chapter 5 for more on Bloch's *America*.
339. Bates/INTERVIEW.
340. Bates/ZOOLOGY.
341. Bates/INTERVIEW.
342. Bates/MAY DAYS.
343. The above details and quotations in this paragraph are drawn from Bates/ART OF WAR BLOG.
344. Bates/ART OF WAR NOTE.

345. Larsen/EMAIL APRIL 21.
346. Bates/INTERVIEW.
347. Schwartz/ELECTRONICS.
348. Ibid.
349. Wang/EMAIL NOV 4.
350. Wang/INTERVIEW.
351. Wang/SYMPHONY 1.
352. Wang/INTERVIEW 2.
353. Wang/SYMPHONY 2.
354. Ibid.
355. Wang/EMAIL NOV 30.
356. Wang/INTERVIEW.
357. Fairouz/SYMPHONY 1.
358. Ibid.
359. Fairouz/SYMPHONY 3.
360. See ibid.
361. Ibid.
362. Ibid.
363. Swed/POEMS.
364. Details and quotations below in this paragraph and the following are drawn from Fairouz/SYMPHONY 4.
365. See Knight/ARTS.
366. Smith/HARSH.
367. Quotations and details above in this paragraph are drawn from Fairouz/EMAIL.
368. Fairouz/INTERVIEW.
369. Ibid.
370. Bernstein/WHAT I THOUGHT. See chapter 6 for more on Bernstein's attitudes toward and personal contributions to the symphony.
371. Bolcom/PROPHETIC, p. 19.
372. Larsen/EMAIL APRIL 21.

Bibliography

Anonymous/HAILSTORK SYMPHONIES	Program note on Adolphus Hailstork, Symphonies Nos. 2 and 3. From liner notes, *Hailstork: Symphonies Nos. 2 and 3.* Naxos, 8.559295. https://www.naxos.com, accessed August 20, 2021.
Anonymous/MARSALIS SYMPHONY 4	Program note on Wynton Marsalis, Symphony No. 4, "The Jungle." In New York Philharmonic Program book, December 28, 2016–January 3, 2017: pp. 35–36.
Anonymous/PÄRT SYMPHONY 4	Program note on Arvo Pärt, Symphony No. 4, "Los Angeles." Universal Edition. Description of Study Score. https://www.universaledition.com/sheet-music-and-more/symphony-no.-4-los-angeles-fuer-streichorchester-harfe-pauken-und-schlagzeug-paert-arvo-ue34562, accessed July 10, 2017.
Anonymous/UNDERWOOD	"Wang Jie Wins ACO's Underwood Commission." *NewMusicBox.* https://nmbx.newmusicusa.org/wang

	-jie-wins-acos-2009-underwood-commission/, accessed August 20, 2021.
Anonymous/WALKER SINFONIA 3	Program note on George Walker, Sinfonia No. 3. From liner notes, *George Walker: Great American Orchestral Works, vol. 1*. Albany Records, TROY1061.
Anonymous/WALKER SINFONIA 5	Program note on George Walker, Sinfonia No. 5 ("Visions"). From liner notes, *George Walker: Great American Orchestral Music, vol. 5*. Albany Records, TROY1707.
Adamo/CORIGLIANO	Adamo, Mark. *John Corigliano: A Monograph*. Todmorden, Lancs, UK: Royal Northern College of Music in association with Arc Music, 2000.
Adams/CITY	Adams, John. Program note. *City Noir*. https://www.boosey.com/cr/music/John-Adams-City-Noir/53958, accessed August 7, 2021.
Adams/HALLELUJAH	Adams, John. *Hallelujah Junction: Composing an American Life*. New York: Farrar, Straus and Giroux, 2008.
Adams/HARMONIELEHRE	Adams, John. Program note. *Harmonielehre*. Earbox. http://www.earbox.com/harmonielehre/, accessed June 4, 2015.
Adams/HARMONIUM	Adams, John. Program note. *Harmonium*. New York: Associated Music Publishers, n.d.
Adams/NAIVE	Adams, John. Program note. *Naive and Sentimental Music*. http://www.earbox.com/naive-and-sentimental-music/, accessed June 4, 2015.
Adams/SCHEHERAZADE.2	Adams, John. Program note. *Scheherazade.2*. In New York Philharmonic program book, March 26–28, 2015: p. 33.
Albert/RIVERRUN	Albert, Stephen. Program note. From liner notes, *Albert, S.: RiverRun / Symphony No. 2*. Naxos 8.559257. https://www.naxos.com, accessed August 20, 2021.
Alves & Campbell/HARRISON	Alves, Bill, and Brett Campbell. *Lou Harrison: American Musical Maverick*. Bloomington: Indiana University Press, 2017.
Anderson/VARESE	Anderson, John D. "Varèse and the Lyricism of the New Physics." *Musical Quarterly* 75, no. 1 (1999): pp. 31–49.
Arias/TCHEREPNIN	Arias, Enrique Alberto. *Alexander Tcherepnin: A Bio-Bibliography*. New York: Greenwood, 1989.
Arias/TCHEREPNIN NG	Arias, Enrique Alberto. "Tcherepnin, Alexander." *New Grove Dictionary* 2 (25): pp. 185–86.
Asia/FAR EDGE	Asia, Daniel. Program note. *At the Far Edge*. http://www.danielasia.net., accessed May 5, 2015.
Asia/INTERVIEW	Asia, Daniel. Telephone interview with the author. February 16, 2015.

Asia/SYMPHONY 2	Asia, Daniel. Program note. Symphony No. 2 ("Celebration Symphony"). http://www.danielasia.net, accessed May 5, 2015.
Asia/SYMPHONY 5	Asia, Daniel. Program note. Symphony No. 5 ("Of Songs and Psalms"), p. iii. n.p.: Theodore Presser, n.d.
Baker/INTERVIEW	Baker, Alan. "An Interview with Elliott Carter" (transcript). American Public Media. July 2002. http://musicmavericks.publicradio.org/features/interview_carter.html, accessed May 27, 2015.
Balada/STEEL SYMPHONY	Balada, Leonardo. Note on *Steel Symphony*. From liner notes, *Balada, L.: Symphony No. 6 / Concerto for 3 Cellos and Orchestra / Steel Symphony*. Naxos 8.573298. https://www.naxos.com, accessed July 10, 2017.
Balada/SYMPHONY 5	Balada, Leonardo. Note on Symphony No. 5. From liner notes, *Balada, L.: Symphony No. 5 / Prague Sinfonietta / Divertimentos*. Naxos 8.557749. http://www.naxos.com, accessed July 10, 2017.
Banfield/CONVERSATIONS	Banfield, William C. *Musical Landscapes in Color: Conversations with Black American Composers*. Lanham, MD: Scarecrow Press, 2003.
Bates/ALTERNATIVE BLOG	Bates, Mason. "Alternative Energy." Blog post. http://www.masonbates.com/blog/alternative-energy/, accessed June 8, 2015.
Bates/ALTERNATIVE NOTE	Bates, Mason. Program note. *Alternative Energy*. http://www.masonbates.com/work/work-alternative energy.html, accessed June 8, 2015.
Bates/ART OF WAR BLOG	Bates, Mason. "Art of War." Blog post. December 3, 2018. https://www.masonbates.com/artofwar-blog/, accessed August 13, 2021.
Bates/ART OF WAR NOTE	Bates, Mason. "Art of War." Program note. https://aphramusic.com/products/art-of-war, accessed August 13, 2021.
Bates/B-SIDES	Bates, Mason. Program note. *The B-Sides*. http://www.masonbates.com/work/work-bsides.html, accessed June 8, 2015.
Bates/INTERVIEW	Bates, Mason. Telephone interview with the author. April 3, 2015.
Bates/LIQUID INTERFACE	Bates, Mason. Program note. *Liquid Interface*. http://www.masonbates.com/work/work-liquidinterface.html, accessed June 8, 2015.
Bates/MAY DAYS	Bates, Mason. "May Days." Blog post. https://www.masonbates.com/may-days/, accessed August 12, 2021.
Bates/MECHANICS	Bates, Mason. "The Mechanics of Musical Narrative." Blog post. http://www.masonbates.com/blog/the-mechanics-of-musical-narrative/, accessed May 30, 2015.

Bates/ZOOLOGY	Bates, Mason. "A Mythological Zoo." Blog post. https://www.masonbates.com/a-mythological-zoo/, accessed August 12, 2021.
Bergman/RAGE	Bergman, Elizabeth. "*Of Rage and Remembrance*, Music and Memory: The Work of Mourning in John Corigliano's Symphony No. 1 and Choral Chaconne." *American Music* 31, no. 3 (2013): pp. 340–61.
Bernard/TONAL	Bernard, Jonathan W. "Tonal Traditions in Art Music Since 1960." In *The Cambridge History of American Music*, edited by David Nichols, pp. 535–66. Cambridge: Cambridge University Press, 1998.
Bernstein/WHAT I THOUGHT	Bernstein, Leonard. "Bernstein: What I Thought . . ." *New York Times*, October 24, 1965, p. X19.
Bloch/PROGRAMS	Bloch, Suzanne, and Irene Heskes. *Ernest Bloch: Creative Spirit: A Program Source Book*. New York: Jewish Music Council of the National Jewish Welfare Board, 1976.
Bolcom/EMAIL FEB 3	Bolcom, William. Email message to the author. February 3, 2015.
Bolcom/EMAIL FEB 18	Bolcom, William. Email message to the author. February 18, 2015.
Bolcom/EMAIL JUNE 2	Bolcom, William. Email message to the author. June 2, 2015.
Bolcom/PROPHETIC	Bolcom, William. "A Prophetic Symphony." *Symphony: The Magazine of the League of American Orchestras* 59, no. 1 (January–February 2008): pp. 15–19.
Bolcom/SYMPHONY 1	Bolcom, William. Program note. Symphony No. 1. From liner notes, *William Bolcom: The Louisville Orchestra*. First Edition Music, FECD-0033.
Bolcom/SYMPHONY 2	Bolcom, William. Program note. Symphony No. 2 in One Movement, "Oracles." New York: Edward B. Marks, 2007.
Bolcom/SYMPHONY 3	Bolcom, William. Program note. Symphony No. 3. From liner notes, *William Bolcom: The Louisville Orchestra*. First Edition Music, FECD-0033.
Bolcom/SYMPHONY 5	Bolcom, William. Program note. Symphony No. 5. From liner notes, *Violin Concerto; Fantasia Concertante for Viola and Cello; Fifth Symphony*. Argo 433-077-2.
Broyles/MAVERICKS	Broyles, Michael. *Mavericks and Other Traditions in American Music*. New Haven, CT: Yale University Press, 2004.
Butterworth/SYMPHONY	Butterworth, Neil. *The American Symphony*. Aldershot, UK: Ashgate, 1998.
Cahill/ADAMS	Cahill, Sarah. "John Adams." *New Grove Dictionary 2* (1): pp. 143–46.

Carter/ALLEGRO SCORREVOLE	Carter, Elliott. Program note. *Allegro Scorrevole.* Boosey & Hawkes. http://www.boosey.com/cr/music/Elliott-Carter-Allegro-scorrevole/6115, accessed May 27, 2015.
Carter/PARTITA	Carter, Elliott. Program note. *Partita.* Boosey & Hawkes. http://www.boosey.com/cr/music/Elliott-Carter-Partita/7364, accessed May 27, 2015.
Carter/THREE ORCHESTRAS	Carter, Elliott. Program note. *A Symphony of Three Orchestras.* New York: Associated Music Publishers, n.d.
Clague/SYMPHONY 7	Clague, Mark. Program note. William Bolcom, Symphony No. 7. Detroit Symphony Orchestra. October 26–28, 2007. http://dso.org/upload_files/content_pdfs/res/backstage/history/0708_programnotes/BolcomSymphonyNo7.pdf, accessed June 2, 2015.
Clark/DISCUSSION	Clark, J. Bunker, ed. "The Composer and Performer and Other Matters: A Panel Discussion with Virgil Thomson and Philip Glass, Moderated by Gregory Sandow." *American Music* 7, no. 2 (1989): pp. 181–204.
Corigliano/INTERVIEW	Corigliano, John. Telephone interview with the author. April 3, 2015.
Corigliano/SYMPHONY 1	Corigliano, John. Program note. Symphony No. 1. New York: Schirmer, 1990.
Corigliano/SYMPHONY 2	Corigliano, John. Program note. Symphony No. 2. In program book for Week 8 of Boston Symphony Orchestra 2000–2001 Season: 25–33.
Corigliano/SYMPHONY 3	Corigliano, John. Program note. Symphony No. 3, "Circus Maximus." New York: Schirmer, 2005.
Currier/SYMPHONY 2	Currier, Sebastian. Program note. Stephen Albert, Symphony No. 2. From liner notes, *Albert, S.: RiverRun / Symphony No. 2.* Naxos 8.559257. http://www.naxos.com, accessed June 4, 2015.
Dixon/ROCHBERG	Dixon, Joan DeVee. *George Rochberg: A Bio-Bibliographic Guide to His Life and Works.* Stuyvesant, NY: Pendragon, 1992.
Doyle/BOLCOM	Doyle, Rebecca A. "Bolcom's Symphony No. 6 Premieres in Washington." *University Record* (University of Michigan). February 25, 1998. http://ur.umich.edu/9798/Feb25_98/bol.htm, accessed June 2, 2015.
Druckenbrod/GLOOMY	Druckenbrod, Andrew. "Classical Music Preview: Gloomy Composer Christopher Rouse Turns Toward the Light with 'Rapture.'" *Pittsburgh Post-Gazette,* May 5, 2000. http://old.post-gazette.com/magazine/20000505rouse5.asp, accessed June 5, 2015.

Duffie/ALBERT	Duffie, Bruce. Transcript of telephone interview with Stephen Albert. December 9, 1990. http://www.bruceduffie.com/albert.html, accessed June 5, 2015.
Dyer/BOSTON	Dyer, Richard. "Inside His Compositions, Life's Complexities Take Shape." *Boston Globe*, November 7, 2004.
Edgers/WALKER	Edgers, Geoff. "In Life's Coda, Master Composer George Walker Has a Symphony in Mind." *Washington Post*, August 22, 2015. http://www.washingtonpost.com/entertainment/music/2015/08/20/d6e9e6c2-3beb-11e5-9c2d-ed991d848c48_story.html, accessed September 8, 2015.
Edwards/FLAWED	Edwards, Allen. *Flawed Words and Stubborn Sounds: A Conversation with Elliott Carter*. New York: W. W. Norton, 1971.
Fairouz/EMAIL	Fairouz, Mohammed. Email message to the author. March 23, 2023.
Fairouz/INTERVIEW	Fairouz, Mohammed. Telephone interview with the author. February 27, 2015.
Fairouz/SYMPHONY 1	Fairouz, Mohammed. Program note. Symphony No. 1 ("Symphonic Aphorisms"). http://mohammedfairouz.com/symphony-no-1-symphonic-aphorisms-2007/, accessed June 8, 2015.
Fairouz/SYMPHONY 3	Fairouz, Mohammed. Program note. Symphony No. 3 ("Of Poems and Prayers"). http://mohammedfairouz.com/symphony-no-3-poems-and-prayers-2010/, accessed June 8, 2015.
Fairouz/SYMPHONY 4	Fairouz, Mohammed. Program note. Symphony No. 4 ("In the Shadow of No Towers"). http://mohammedfairouz.com/in-the-shadow-of-no-towers/, accessed June 8, 2015.
Fanning/SYMPHONY	Fanning, David. "The Symphony since Mahler: National and International Trends." In Horton/SYMPHONY, pp. 96–130.
Glass/SYMPHONY 6	Glass, Philip. Program note. Symphony No. 6. http://www.philipglass.com/music/compositions/symphony_6.php, accessed May 30, 2015.
Glass/SYMPHONY 7	Glass, Philip. Program note. Symphony No. 7. http://www.philipglass.com/music/compositions/symphony_7.php, accessed May 30, 2015.
Glass/SYMPHONY 8	Glass, Philip. Program note. Symphony No. 8. http://www.philipglass.com/music/recordings/symphony_8.php, accessed May 30, 2015.
Glass/SYMPHONY 12	Glass, Philip. Program note. Symphony No. 12, "Lodger." https://www.laphil.com/musicdb/pieces/4784/symphony-no-12-lodger-lyrics-by-david-bowie

	-and-brian-eno-world-premiere-la-phil-commission-with-generous-support-from-lenore-s-and-bernard-a-greenberg, accessed August 13, 2021.
Glass/WORDS	Glass, Philip. *Words Without Music: A Memoir*. New York: W. W. Norton, 2015.
Gojowy/COATES	Gojowy, Detlef. "Coates, Gloria." *New Grove Dictionary 2* (6): pp. 68–69.
Grimley/SYMPHONY	Grimley, Daniel M. "Symphony/Antiphony: Formal Strategies in the Twentieth-Century Symphony." In Horton/SYMPHONY, pp. 285–310.
Grimshaw/HIGH	Grimshaw, Jeremy. "High, 'Low,' and Plastic Arts: Philip Glass and the Symphony in the Age of Postproduction." *Musical Quarterly* 86, no. 3 (2002): pp. 472–507.
Guérin/EMAIL	Guérin, Richard. Email message to the author. August 12, 2021.
Guérin/GLASS	Guérin, Richard, ed. "Philip Glass—NEW ALBUM—Symphony No. 10/Concert Overture (2012)." *Glass Notes*. July 9, 2015. http://philipglass.typepad.com/glass_notes/2015/07/philip-glass-new-album-symphony-no10-concert-overture-2012.html, accessed September 9, 2015.
Hailstork/EMAIL	Hailstork, Adolphus. Email message to the author. June 4, 2015.
Hailstork/STILL HOLDING ON	Hailstork, Adolphus. Program Note. "Still Holding On." Los Angeles Philharmonic. https://www.laphil.com/musicdb/pieces/4820/still-holding-on-world-premiere-la-phil-commission, accessed August 10, 2021.
Hailstork/SYMPHONY 1	Hailstork, Adolphus. Program note. Symphony No. 1. From liner notes, *An American Port of Call*. Naxos 8.559722. http://www.naxos.com, accessed June 4, 2015.
Hailstork/SYMPHONY OF HOPES	Hailstork, Adolphus. "A Symphony of Hopes and Dreams." Interview with Sarah McConnell. *With Good Reason* (radio broadcast). February 19, 2011. http://withgoodreasonradio.org/2011/02/a-symphony-of-hopes-and-dreams/, accessed June 4, 2015.
Harbison/INTERVIEW	Harbison, John. Telephone interview with the author. January 27, 2015.
Harbison/SYMPHONIES	Harbison, John. "John Harbison on His Symphonies: Introduction to a Cycle." In Boston Symphony Orchestra Concert program book, October 14–16, 2010: p. 45.
Harbison/SYMPHONY 1	Harbison, John. Program note. Symphony No. 1. In Boston Symphony Orchestra program book, March 23–25, 1984: p. 29.

Harbison/SYMPHONY 3	Harbison, John. Program note. Symphony No. 3. http://www.musicsalesclassical.com/composer/work/627/24249, accessed March 23, 2023.
Harbison/SYMPHONY 3 ALBANY	Harbison, John. Program note. Symphony No. 3. From liner notes, *John Harbison: The Most Often Used Chords, Symphony No. 3, Flute Concerto*. Albany Records, TROY390.
Harbison/SYMPHONY 4	Harbison, John. Program note. Symphony No. 4. New York: Associated Music Publishers, n.d.
Harbison/SYMPHONY 5	Harbison, John. Program note. Symphony No. 5. New York: Associated Music Publishers, n.d.
Harrison/FOURTH ABOUT	Harrison, Lou. "About My Fourth Symphony." *Current Musicology* 67 (Fall 1999): pp. 129–32.
Harrison/FOURTH NOTE	Harrison, Lou. Program note. *Fourth Symphony*. Peer International Corporation, 1993.
Harrison/SYMPHONY ON G	Harrison, Lou. Program note. *Symphony on G*. From Jacket for LP recording by Gerhard Samuel and the Royal Philharmonic Orchestra. CRI 236 USD-B.
Holland/COMPOSERS	Holland, Bernard. "From Two American Composers." *New York Times*, March 4, 1993, p. C20.
Horton/SYMPHONY	Horton, Julian, ed. *The Cambridge Companion to the Symphony*. New York: Cambridge University Press, 2013.
Howard/MOTHERHOOD	Howard, Luke B. "Motherhood, Billboard, and the Holocaust: Perceptions and Receptions of Górecki's Symphony No. 3." *Musical Quarterly* 82, no. 1 (1998): pp. 131–59.
Hughes/JUILLIARD	Hughes, Allen. "Juilliard Offers Rochberg's No. 3: Abraham Kaplan Conducts Premiere of Symphony." *New York Times*, November 26, 1970, p. 58.
Husa/SYMPHONY 2	Husa, Karel. Program note. *Reflections (Symphony No. 2)*. New York: Associated Music Publishers, 1992.
Jepson/COMPOSER	Jepson, Barbara. "A Composer Spreads a Little Sunshine (Very Little)." *New York Times*, January 3, 1993, pp. H25, H33.
Johnson/BOLCOM	Johnson, Steven. "William Bolcom." *New Grove Dictionary 2* (3): p. 818.
Keller/SYMPHONY 2	Keller, James. Program note. Philip Glass, Symphony No. 2. http://www.musicsalesclassical.com/composer/work/6353, accessed May 30, 2015.
Kelly/BLUES SYMPHONY	Kelly, Jonathan. "The Making of Blues Symphony." *Wynton's Blog*. May 21, 2021. https://wyntonmarsalis.org/blog/entry/the-making-of-blues-symphony, accessed August 12, 2021.
Kernis/CHROMELODEON	Kernis, Aaron Jay. Program note. Symphony No. 4, "Chromelodeon." From liner notes, *Kernis, A.J.:*

	Color Wheel / Symphony No. 4, "Chromelodeon." Naxos 8.559838. https://www.naxos.com, accessed August 20, 2021.
Kernis/EMAIL	Kernis, Aaron Jay. Email message to the author. January 28, 2015.
Kernis/SECOND SYMPHONY	Kernis, Aaron Jay. Program note. Second Symphony. http://www.musicsalesclassical.com/composer/work/29558, accessed June 7, 2015.
Kernis/SYMPHONY IN WAVES	Kernis, Aaron Jay. Program note. *Symphony in Waves.* http://www.musicsalesclassical.com/composer/work/29566, accessed June 7, 2015.
Kernis/SYMPHONY OF MEDITATIONS	Kernis, Aaron Jay. Program note. Symphony No. 3, "Symphony of Meditations." In program book for East Coast Premiere. Yale School of Music, 2009. http://issuu.com/yalemusic/docs/symphony_of_meditations, accessed June 7, 2015.
Knight/ARTS	Knight, Christina. "10 Years after Iraq, a Symphony on the 9/11 Aftermath." *NYC-ARTS.* http://www.nyc-arts.org/collections/56268/10-years-after-iraq-a-symphony-on-the-911-aftermath, accessed June 8, 2015.
Kozinn/PREMIERES	Kozinn, Allan. "3 Premieres, and Debut of a 29-Year-Old Work." *New York Times,* January 19, 1992, p. 48.
LaFave/BERNSTEIN	LaFave, Kenneth. *Experiencing Leonard Bernstein: A Listener's Companion.* Lanham, MD: Rowman & Littlefield, 2015.
Larsen/COWBOY SONGS	Larsen, Libby. Program note. *Cowboy Songs.* https://libbylarsen.com/index.php?contentID=241&profileID=1345, accessed July 19, 2017.
Larsen/EMAIL APRIL 21	Larsen, Libby. Email message to the author. April 21, 2015.
Larsen/EMAIL APRIL 24	Larsen, Libby. Email message to the author. April 24, 2015.
Larsen/EMAIL APRIL 30	Larsen, Libby. Email message to the author. April 30, 2015.
Larsen/PIANO CONCERTO	Larsen, Libby. Program note. *Piano Concerto: Since Armstrong.* http://libbylarsen.com/index.php?contentID=242&profileID=1389, accessed June 6, 2015.
Larsen/SOLO SYMPHONY	Larsen, Libby. Program note. *Solo Symphony.* New York: Oxford University Press, n.d.
Larsen/SYMPHONY 2	Larsen, Libby. Program note. *Coming Forth into Day: A Choral Symphony* (Symphony No. 2). Boston: ECS, n.d.
Larsen/SYMPHONY 3	Larsen, Libby. Program note. Symphony No. 3 ("Lyric"). Boston: ECS, n.d.

Larsen/SYMPHONY 4	Larsen, Libby. Program note. *String Symphony* https://libbylarsen.com/index.php?contentID=236&profileID=1194, accessed July 11, 2017.
Larsen/WATER MUSIC	Larsen, Libby. Program note. *Symphony: Water Music* (Symphony No. 1). http://libbylarsen.com/index.php?contentID=236&profileID=1196, accessed June 5, 2015.
Liebermann/INTERVIEW	Liebermann, Lowell. Telephone interview with the author. February 19, 2015.
Liebermann/NEO-ROMANTIC	Liebermann, Lowell. "Would You Describe Yourself as a Neo-Romantic? Why (Not)?" *New Music Box*, September 1, 2003. http://www.newmusicbox.org/articles/Would-you-describe-yourself-as-a-neoromantic-Why-not-Lowell-Liebermann/, accessed June 7, 2015.
Luke/VERSE	Luke, David (ed.). *Goethe: Selected Verse*. New York: Penguin Classics, 1986.
Maddocks/EXPLOSIVE	Maddocks, Fiona. "Explosive Account of the First A-Bomb." *London Evening Standard*, August 22, 2007.
Marsalis/ALL RISE	Marsalis, Wynton. Program Note, *All Rise*. From liner notes, *Wynton Marsalis: All Rise*. Sony Classical, SK 89817. http://wyntonmarsalis.org/discography/title/all-rise/P8, accessed July 10, 2017.
Marsalis/BLUES SYMPHONY NOTE	Marsalis, Wynton. Program note, Symphony No. 2, "Blues Symphony." From liner notes, Symphony No. 2, "Blues Symphony." Blue Engine Records, BE0039. https://wyntonmarsalis.org/discography/title/blues-symphony, accessed August 12, 2021.
Marsalis/BLUES SYMPHONY VIDEO	Marsalis, Wynton. "Talking About the Blues Symphony—Movement I-II." YouTube Video. 2009. https://www.youtube.com/watch?v=YoviRVjC9cQ, accessed July 10, 2017.
Marsalis/GLANCE	Marsalis, Wynton. "The Work at a Glance." In New York Philharmonic program book, December 28, 2016–January 3, 2017, p. 36.
Marsalis/SWING SYMPHONY NOTE	Marsalis, Wynton. Program note, *Swing Symphony*. From liner notes *Swing Symphony*. Blue Engine Records, BE0017. https://wyntonmarsalis.org/discography/title/swing-symphony, accessed August 20, 2021.
Marsalis/SWING SYMPHONY VIDEO	Marsalis, Wynton. "Wynton Marsalis on Composing his 'Swing Symphony.'" YouTube Video. New York Philharmonic, 2010. https://www.youtube.com/watch?v=2eDKrSmThjg, accessed July 10, 2017.
Marx/SYMPHONY 3	Marx, Jonathan (ed.). Program note. Lowell Liebermann, Symphony No. 3. *InConcert* (May 2012): pp. 46–48.

May/ADAMS READER	May, Thomas, ed. *The John Adams Reader: Essential Writings on an American Composer.* Pompton Plains, NJ: Amadeus, 2006.
Maycock/GLASS	Maycock, Robert. *Glass: A Portrait.* London: Sanctuary, 2002.
McCutchan/MUSE	McCutchan, Ann. *The Muse That Sings: Composers Speak about the Creative Process.* New York: Oxford University Press, 1999.
McLellan/ROSTROPOVICH	McLellan, Joseph. "Rostropovich's Triumphant Return." *Washington Post*, January 18, 1985, p. C3.
Meyer & Shreffler/CARTER	Meyer, Felix, and Anne Shreffler. *Elliott Carter: A Centennial Portrait in Letters and Documents.* Woodbridge, Suffolk: Boydell, 2008.
Miller/AESTHETICS	Miller, Leta E. "Lou Harrison and the Aesthetics of Revision." *Twentieth Century Music* 2, no. 1 (2005): pp. 79–107.
Miller/KERNIS	Miller, Leta E. *Aaron Jay Kernis.* Urbana: University of Illinois Press, 2014.
Miller & Lieberman/COMPOSING	Miller, Leta E., and Fredric Lieberman. *Composing a World: Lou Harrison, Musical Wayfarer.* Rev. ed. Urbana: University of Illinois Press, 2004.
Miller & Lieberman/GAMELAN	Miller, Leta E., and Fredric Lieberman. "Lou Harrison and the American Gamelan." *American Music* 17, no. 2 (1999): pp. 146–78.
Miller & Lieberman/HARRISON	Miller, Leta E., and Fredric Lieberman. *Lou Harrison.* Urbana: University of Illinois Press, 2006.
O'Bannon/2014–15 SEASON	O'Bannon, Ricky. "The 2014–15 Orchestra Season by the Numbers." Baltimore Symphony Orchestra. http://bsomusic.org/stories/the-2014-15-orchestra-season-by-the-numbers.aspx, accessed June 7, 2015.
Olmstead/SESSIONS	Olmstead, Andrea. *Roger Sessions: A Biography.* New York: Routledge, 2008.
Oteri/HAILSTORK	Oteri, Frank J. "Adolphus Hailstork: Music Is a Service." Interview with Adolphus Hailstork, July 23, 2021. *New Music Box,* August 4, 2021. https://newmusicusa.org/nmbx/adolphus-hailstork-music-is-a-service/, accessed August 10, 2021.
Oteri/ROUSE	Oteri, Frank J. "Christopher Rouse: Going to Eleven." Interview with Christopher Rouse, February 8, 2008. *New Music Box,* July 1, 2008. https://nmbx.newmusicusa.org/christopher-rouse-going-to-eleven/, accessed August 10, 2021.
Page/ZWILICH	Page, Tim. "The Music of Ellen Zwilich." *New York Times Magazine.* July 14, 1985, pp. 26, 28–30, 32.
Picker/INTERVIEW	Picker, Tobias. Telephone interview with the author. March 30, 2015.

Porter/JAZZ	Porter, Eric. *What Is This Thing Called Jazz? African American Musicians as Artists, Critics, and Activists.* Berkeley and Los Angeles: University of California Press, 2002.
Puts/SYMPHONY	Puts, Kevin. "A Pulitzer Winner Asks: Why Write Symphonies?" *Deceptive Cadence.* National Public Radio Classical, August 13, 2013. http://www.npr.org/sections/deceptivecadence/2013/08/05/208280751/a-pulitzer-winner-asks-why-write-symphonies, accessed October 27, 2017.
Raines/DIGITAL WORLD	Raines, Robert. *Composition in the Digital World: Conversations with 21st-Century American Composers.* New York: Oxford University Press, 2015.
Ramsey/RACE	Ramsey, Guthrie P., Jr. *Race Music: Black Cultures from Bebop to Hip-Hop.* Berkeley and Los Angeles: University of California Press, 2003.
Reel/ASIA 1 AND 4	Reel, James. "Daniel Asia: Symphonies." From liner notes, *Symphonic Works of Daniel Asia,* Summit DCD-256: 2000.
Reel/ASIA 2 AND 3	Reel, James. "Symphonies Nos. 2 and 3." From liner notes, *Daniel Asia: Symphony No. 2/Symphony No. 3,* pp. 3–8. New World Records, 80447–2: 1993.
Reilly/RECOVERY	Reilly, Robert R. "The Recovery of Modern Music: George Rochberg in Conversation." *Tempo* 219 (January 2002): pp. 8–12.
Ritchey/BATES	Ritchey, Marianna. "'Amazing Together': Mason Bates, Classical Music, and Neoliberal Values." *Music & Politics* 11, no. 2 (2017). https://quod.lib.umich.edu/m/mp/9460447.0011.202/--amazing-together-mason-bates-classical-music-and-neoliberal?rgn=main;view=fulltext.
Robin/GLASS	Robin, William. "Philip Glass Celebrates His 80th Birthday with an 11th Symphony." *New York Times,* January 27, 2017. https://www.nytimes.com/2017/01/27/arts/interview-philip-glass-celebrates-his-80th-birthday-with-an-11th-symphony.html, accessed July 10, 2017.
Rochberg/LINES	Rochberg, George. *Five Lines, Four Spaces: The World of My Music,* edited by Gene Rochberg and Richard Griscom. Urbana: University of Illinois Press, 2009.
Rochberg/SYMPHONY 3	Rochberg, George. *Symphony No. III (1969) for Solo Voices, Chamber Chorus, Double Chorus, and Large Orchestra.* n.p.: Theodore Presser Co., n.d. http://issuu.com/theodorepresser/docs/symph-3-re, accessed May 29, 2015.
Rockwell/MUSIC	Rockwell, John. "Music: 2 Scores on Homeric Theme." *New York Times,* August 3, 1984, p. C10.

Rothstein/GLASS	Rothstein, Edward. "Philip Glass Shows Another Side." *New York Times*, November 16, 1992, p. C11.
Rouse/DOCUMENTARY	Rouse, Christopher. *William Schuman: Documentary*. New York: Schirmer, 1980.
Rouse/SYMPHONY 2	Rouse, Christopher. Program note. Symphony No. 2. New York: Boosey & Hawkes, n.d.
Rouse/SYMPHONY 3	Rouse, Christopher. Program note. Symphony No. 3. http://www.christopherrouse.com/sym3press.html, accessed June 5, 2015.
Rouse/SYMPHONY 4	Rouse, Christopher. Program note. Symphony No. 4. http://www.christopherrouse.com/sym4press.html, accessed June 5, 2015.
Rouse/SYMPHONY 5	Rouse, Christopher. Program note. Symphony No. 5. Boosey & Hawkes. https://www.boosey.com/cr/music/Symphony-No-5/101536, accessed July 10, 2017.
Rouse/SYMPHONY 6	Rouse, Christopher. Program Note. Symphony No. 6. http://www.christopherrouse.com/sym6press.html, accessed August 12, 2021.
Schiff/CARTER	Schiff, David. *The Music of Elliott Carter*. 2nd ed. Ithaca, NY: Cornell University Press, 1998.
Schultz/WALKER	Schultz, Eric (producer). *George Walker: Composer*. Video. State of the Arts series, NJTV. 2012. https://www.youtube.com/watch?v=tYnEXI3WyRQ, accessed May 29, 2015.
Schwartz/ELECTRONICS	Schwartz, Elliott. "Stars, Stripes, Batons and Circuits: American Music for Orchestra and Electronics." *New Music Box*, October 1, 2001. http://www.newmusicbox.org/articles/Stars-Stripes-Batons-and-Circuits-American-Music-For-Orchestra-and-Electronics/, accessed June 8, 2015.
Schweitzer/LISTENING	Schweitzer, Vivien. "Listening to a Disconnected Society." *New York Times*, July 5, 2013. http://www.nytimes.com/2013/07/07/arts/music/the-blind-lera-auerbachs-opera-confronts-isolation.html, accessed July 10, 2017.
Smith/HARSH	Smith, Steve. "The Harsh and Haunting Winds of Sept. 11.: University of Kansas Wind Ensemble, at Carnegie Hall." *New York Times*, March 29, 2013. http://www.nytimes.com/2013/03/30/arts/music/university-of-kansas-wind-ensemble-at-carnegie-hall.html, accessed June 8, 2015.
Steinberg/SYMPHONY	Steinberg, Michael. *The Symphony: A Listener's Guide*. New York: Oxford University Press, 1995.
Stone/BALADA	Stone, Peter Eliot. "Leonardo Balada's First Half Century." *Symphony Magazine* 34, no. 3 (1983): pp. 85–90.

Stucky/LUTOSŁAWSKI	Stucky, Steven. Program note. Witold Lutosławski, Symphony No. 4. http://www.musicsalesclassical.com/composer/work/7712, accessed July 10, 2017.
Stucky/SYMPHONY	Stucky, Steven. Program Note. *Symphony*. http://www.stevenstucky.com/docs/Symphony-note.html, accessed July 10, 2017.
Swafford/ASIA	Swafford, Jan. "On Daniel Asia's Symphonies." In *The Jewish Experience in Classical Music: Shostakovich and Asia*, edited by Alexander Tentser, pp. 89–94. Newcastle upon Tyne, UK: Cambridge Scholars, 2014.
Swayne/ORPHEUS	Swayne, Steve. *William Schuman and the Shaping of America's Musical Life*. New York: Oxford University Press, 2011.
Swed/POEMS	Swed, Mark. "Review: 'Poems and Prayers' Lands with Compelling Force at Royce Hall." *Los Angeles Times*, December 10, 2013. http://articles.latimes.com/2013/dec/10/entertainment/la-et-cm-mohammed-fairouz-review-20131210, accessed June 8, 2015.
Taruskin/OXFORD	Taruskin, Richard. *The Oxford History of Western Music*. Vol. 5, *The Late Twentieth Century*. New York: Oxford University Press, 2005.
Tawa/GREAT	Tawa, Nicholas. *The Great American Symphony: Music, The Depression, and War*. Bloomington: Indiana University Press, 2009.
Taylor/GLASS	Taylor, James C. "Philip Glass, 75, Has an iTunes Hit with His Ninth Symphony." *Los Angeles Times, Culture Monster* (blog). February 2, 2012. http://latimesblogs.latimes.com/culturemonster/2012/02/philip-glass-75-has-an-itunes-hit-with-his-ninth-symphony.html, accessed May 30, 2015.
Tommasini/DEMYSTIFYING	Tommasini, Anthony. "Demystifying Messiaen, with a Little Help from the Birds." *New York Times*, February 18, 2008.
Tommasini/OPERA	Tommasini, Anthony. "An Opera in Which Instruments Are Singers." *New York Times*, May 23, 2002, p. E5.
Tommasini/ROUSE	Tommasini, Anthony. "A Work Is Rushed to Debut, By Design." *New York Times*, June 6, 2014.
Tommasini/SYMPHONY 4	Tommasini, Anthony. "Review: Wynton Marsalis's Urban Symphony for the Philharmonic." *New York Times*, December 30, 2016.
Von Glahn/LARSEN	Von Glahn, Denise. *Libby Larsen: Composing an American Life*. Urbana: University of Illinois Press, 2017.

Von Glahn/SKILLFUL	Von Glahn, Denise. *Music and the Skillful Listener: American Women Compose the Natural World.* Bloomington: Indiana University Press, 2013.
Von Glahn/SOUNDS	Von Glahn, Denise. *The Sounds of Place: Music and the American Cultural Landscape.* Boston: Northeastern University Press, 2003.
Von Gunden/MUSIC	Von Gunden, Heidi. *The Music of Lou Harrison.* Metuchen, NJ: Scarecrow Press, 1995.
von Rhein/SHKOLNIK	von Rhein, John. "Sheldon Shkolnik, 52, Leading Concert Pianist." *Chicago Tribune,* March 25, 1990.
Walker/FEB 3 EMAIL	Walker, George. Email message to author. February 3, 2015.
Walker/INTERVIEW	Walker, George. Telephone interview with author. February 5, 2015.
Walker/REMINSCENCES	Walker, George. *Reminiscences of an American Composer and Pianist.* Lanham, MD: Scarecrow, 2009.
Walker/SINFONIA 2	Walker, George. Program note. Sinfonia No. 2. From liner notes, *George Walker: Great American Orchestra Works, vol. 2.* Albany Records, TROY1178.
Walker/SINFONIA 4	Walker, George. Program note. Sinfonia No. 4 ("Strands"). From liner notes, *George Walker: Great American Orchestral Works, vol. 4.* Albany Records, TROY1430.
Wang/EMAIL NOV 4	Wang Jie. Email message to the author. November 4, 2015.
Wang/EMAIL NOV 30	Wang Jie. Email message to mailing list. November 30, 2022.
Wang/INTERVIEW	Wang Jie. Skype interview with the author. February 18, 2015.
Wang/INTERVIEW 2	Wang Jie. Zoom interview with the author. August 12, 2021.
Wang/SYMPHONY 1	Wang Jie. Program note. Symphony No. 1. Fourth Edition. New York: Wang Jie Music, 2017.
Wang/SYMPHONY 2	Wang Jie. Program note. Symphony No. 2. New York: Wang Jie Music, 2013.
Watkins/INTERVIEW	Watkins. Glenn. "An Interview with the Composer." From liner notes, *Rouse: Symphony No. 1 / Phantasmata.* First Edition CD-0026. http://www.naxos.com, accessed June 5, 2015.
Watkins/PASTORAL	Watkins, Holly. "The Pastoral after Environmentalism: Nature and Culture in Stephen Albert's *Symphony: Riverrun.*" *Current Musicology* 84 (Fall 2007): pp. 7–24.
Wierzbicki/CARTER	Wierzbicki, James. *Elliott Carter.* Urbana: University of Illinois Press, 2011.

Wigler/ALBERT	Wigler, Stephen. "Stephen Albert, His Melodious Music Helped Define the 'New Romanticism.'" *Baltimore Sun*, December 29, 1992.
Wilson/SURVIVAL	Wilson, Charles. "The Survival of the Symphony." *New Grove Dictionary 2* (24): pp. 847–49, in Jan LaRue et al. "Symphony." *New Grove Dictionary 2* (24): pp. 812–49.
Wlodarski/CAVERNOUS	Wlodarski, Amy Lynn. "Cavernous Impossibilities: Jewish Art Music after 1945." In *The Cambridge Companion to Jewish Music*, edited by Joshua Walden, pp. 244–57. Cambridge: Cambridge University Press, 2015.
Wlodarski/ROCHBERG	Wlodarski, Amy Lynn. *George Rochberg, American Composer: Personal Trauma and Artistic Creativity*. Rochester, NY: University of Rochester Press, 2019.
Zwilich/INTERVIEW	Zwilich, Ellen Taaffe. Telephone interview with the author. January 28, 2015.
Zwilich/SYMPHONY 1	Zwilich, Ellen Taaffe. Program note. Symphony No. 1 ("Three Movements for Orchestra"). Newton Centre, MA: Margin Music, n.d.

CONTRIBUTORS

Katherine Baber is Professor of Music History at the University of Redlands and Associate Dean of the College of Arts and Sciences. She is author of *Leonard Bernstein and the Language of Jazz* (University of Illinois Press, 2019), and her work on Leonard Bernstein as an international musical and political figure can be found in German- and English-language publications. She resides in Salzburg, Austria, where she serves as the Alice Mozley Director of the University of Redlands international campus.

E. Douglas Bomberger is Professor of Music at Elizabethtown College, where he teaches music history and piano. His PhD dissertation for the University of Maryland, College Park, examined nineteenth-century American musicians who studied in Germany. He spent a year as a DAAD fellow in Mainz gathering materials for the study. His subsequent publications have built on the topic of German American musical interactions, including *A Tidal Wave of Encouragement: American Composers' Concerts in the Gilded Age* (Praeger, 2002), *MacDowell* (Oxford, 2013), and *Making Music American: 1917 and the Transformation of Culture* (Oxford, 2018).

J. Peter Burkholder is Distinguished Professor Emeritus of Musicology at the Indiana University Jacobs School of Music. He has written or edited five books on Ives, most recently the award-winning *Listening to Charles Ives: Variations on His America* (Amadeus Press, 2021), and has published dozens of articles and book chapters on topics ranging from borrowing to modernism, from musical meaning to music history pedagogy, and from fifteenth-century masses to Berg and Schoenberg. His research has won awards from the American Musicological Society; the Society for American Music; the American Society of Composers, Authors, and Publishers; and the Association for Recorded Sound Collections. He is most widely known as the primary author of *A History of Western Music* and the *Norton Anthology of Western Music* (W. W. Norton), the leading music history texts in the English language. His writings have appeared in Japanese, Korean, Chinese, Arabic, Italian, German, Spanish, and Braille. He is a former president of the Charles Ives Society and an honorary member and former president of the American Musicological Society.

Brian Hart is Professor of Music History at Northern Illinois University. He is author of "The French Symphony after Berlioz: From the Second Empire to the First World War" in *The Symphonic Repertoire, Volume III, Part B*. He has written and presented on various topics relating to French symphonic music and culture, including Vincent d'Indy's influence on French symphonic development, Debussy and the symphony, the French organ symphony, the symphonies of Arthur Honegger, and competing cultural and political interpretations of the symphony in fin de siècle France. He is author of the entries on César Franck, Arthur Honegger, Vincent d'Indy, Albert Roussel, and Ernest Chausson for *Oxford Bibliographies Online*.

List of Contributors

Carol A. Hess is a professor at the University of California, Davis. Her research explores the intersections between musical style and political currents, with emphasis on links between music criticism and political rhetoric in the Spanish-speaking world. Her grants and awards include Fulbright Fellowships, NEH Summer Stipends, two Robert M. Stevenson Awards for Outstanding Scholarship in Iberian Music, the Society for American Music's Irving Lowens Article Award, the ASCAP-Deems Taylor Award, and several teaching and mentoring awards. Her textbook, *Experiencing Latin American Music* (University of California Press, 2018), received the American Musicological Society's Teaching Award. Her most recent scholarly book is *Aaron Copland in Latin America: Music, Diplomacy, and Cultural Politics* (University of Illinois Press, 2022).

Susan Key is a public musicologist, combining roles in academe and performing arts. Most recently she was based at Chapman University, where she taught in the honors program and coordinated a partnership with the Pacific Symphony. She was Special Projects Director at the San Francisco Symphony, where she worked on a variety of projects in media and education. Dr. Key earned a doctorate in historical musicology and has taught at the University of Maryland, the College of William and Mary, Stanford University, and Chapman University. She has published on a variety of topics in American music and on arts education. She has developed public programs for the San Francisco Symphony, the J. Paul Getty Museum in Los Angeles, and the Los Angeles Philharmonic, and has served on the boards of the Society for American Music, the Los Angeles Public Library, and the chamber music organization Pacific Serenades. She also works on projects for the Star Spangled Music Foundation and baritone Thomas Hampson's Song of America initiative.

Drew Massey holds a PhD in Historical Musicology from Harvard University. He is a noted scholar of American and British music working at Schubertiade Music.

Matthew Mugmon is Associate Professor of Musicology at the University of Arizona. He has served as the New York Philharmonic's Leonard Bernstein Scholar-in-Residence, and his research appears in the *Journal of Musicology*, *Music & Letters*, the *Journal of Musicological Research*, and the essay collection *Rethinking Mahler*. His monograph *Aaron Copland and the American Legacy of Gustav Mahler* was published in 2019 by the University of Rochester Press.

Douglas W. Shadle is Associate Professor of Musicology and Chair of the Department of Musicology and Ethnomusicology at Vanderbilt University's Blair School of Music. He is author of the award-winning *Orchestrating the Nation: The Nineteenth-Century American Symphonic Enterprise* and *Antonín Dvořák's New World Symphony*. With Samantha Ege, he is preparing a volume on the life and music of Florence Price.

INDEX

Note: Page numbers in **bold** indicate primary discussion of a topic.
Page numbers in *italics* indicate tables and charts.

Abakuá people, 768
Abel, Carl Friedrich, 61, 62
Abendzeitung, 72
Abertura Concertante (Guarnieri), 692
abolitionism, 215
Abraham Lincoln: A Likeness in Symphony Form (Bennett), 452, 454
Abreu, José Antonio, 711
Absalom (Schidlowsky), 702
"Absolut Concerto" (concert series), 900
absolute music, 916
Abstracción (Vidal), 754
abstract nationalism, 3, 337
Abu Dhabi Festival, 923
Abu Dhabi Music & Arts Foundation, 923
academic serialism, 635
Academy Awards (Oscars), 449–450, 455, 459
Academy of Fine Arts, 756
Academy of Music (Boston), 63
Academy of Music (Philadelphia), 528, 530, 668
Academy of Music (Rome), 32
Acevedo, Jorge Luis, 761
Acuarelas chapinas (Martínez-Sobral), 754
Adagio for Strings (Barber), 354
Adagio tenebroso (Carter), 802. See also *Symphonia: sum fluxae pretium spei* (Carter)
Adalid y Gamero, Manuel, 756
Adame Gómez, Rafael, *738,* 751
Adamo, Mark, 835
Adams, John, **864–873**; and Bates, 909, 914; and Carter, 802; and distinctive qualities of American symphony, 23, 24; and evolution of American symphonic style, 795; and Glass, 830; and Ives's orchestral sets, 286; and Kernis, 893, 897; and key influences on American repertoire, 21–22; and Larsen, 878, 886; and Picker, 891; and Sibelius, 22; symphonies' movements and instrumentation, *866–869*; symphony premiere dates, *794, 795*. See also *specific composition titles*
Adams, John Luther, 559
Adaskin, Murray, 37
Addison, Adele, 625
Address for Orchestra (Walker), 816
Adeste fideles (Wade), 253–254, 295n115
Adler, F. Charles, 392
Adomián, Lan, *738, 739,* 751
Adventures of Huckleberry Finn, The (Twain), 50n17, 451
Adventures of Robin Hood, The (film; score by Korngold), 455
Advis, Luis, 701
Aeolian Hall, 425
Africa (Still), 431
African American culture and heritage: African American Renaissance, 382; Afro-Brazilian tradition, 692, 695; Afro-Caribbean culture, 30, *111,* 112–114, 418–419, 749, 765, 767, 771–772; Afro-Cuban culture, 765, 771; Afro-Latin music, 908; Afro-Uruguayan identity, 668; and Argentinian composers, 672; and Blitzstein, 317; and Brazilian composers, 681; and Dvořák's support of American idioms, 312; and Hailstork, 856–859; and influential works of the 1930s, 32; and Perry, 630, 634; and Second New England School composers, 126. See also Black composers and musical influences; *specific composers*
Afro-American Symphony. See Symphony No. 1, *Afro-American Symphony* (Still)
Afternoon, An (Ives), 285
Afternoon of a Spawn (Ley), 754
Agate Beach, Oregon, 436
Age of Anxiety, The. See Symphony No. 2, *The Age of Anxiety* (Bernstein)

953

Index

Age of Anxiety, The (Auden), 589, 592
Age of Innocence, The (Wharton), 484
Ágreda, Carlos, *698,* 710
Águila, Miguel del, 668, 670–671
Aguirre, Julián, 672, *673*
AIDS epidemic, 23, 831, 834–835, 855
Ainadamar (Golijov), 916
"Ain't Got No Tears" (Bernstein), 589, 593
Airborne Symphony (Blitzstein), 22, 32, *316,* **316–319**, 358–359, 451, 463n48, 595–596
Aires de la pampa (Williams), 672
Akhnaten (Glass), 822
Alarcón, Carlos Isamitt, *696*
Alas, Jesús, 756
Albéniz, Isaac, 22, 24, 834
Albert, Stephen, *794, 795,* **859–864**, *861,* 876, 886, 890. See also specific composition titles
Albion, The, 106
Aldrich, Richard, 137
Alessandro, Victor, 431
Alexander (von Tilzer), 285
Alexander, Leni, *696,* 701
Alfagüell, Mario, 761
Alfonseca, Juan Bautista, 772
Algonquin culture, 83
Alice M. Ditson Fund, 493
Alien (film), 374
All Around Sound (Larsen), 886
Allegro scorrevole (Carter), 802. See also *Symphonia: sum fluxae pretium spei*
Allegro symphonique (Martinů, unfinished), 441
Alleluia (Thompson), 381
Allende, Pedro Humberto, *696,* 699
All on a Summer's Day (Sowerby), 377
All Rise. See *Symphony No. 1, All Rise* (Marsalis)
Alsop, Marin, *13,* 418
Alta California, 737
Altar de neón (Ortíz), 753
Alternative Energy (Bates), *795, 911,* 913–914, *915*
Altizer, J. J., 608
Alvarado, Germán, 760
Alvarenga, Francisco, 671
Álvarez, Teófilo, 705
Amador, Carlos Posada, *698*
Amazônia (Kertsman), 695
América (Matons), 765
America: An Epic Rhapsody (Bloch), *9,* 313, 436–439, 441, 452, 914. See also individual movements

American Academy in Rome, 314, 354, 365, 376, 456–457, 560
American Academy of Arts and Letters, 488
American Academy of Arts and Sciences, 488
American Art Journal, 67, 160
American Ballet Caravan, 700
American Composers' Concerts, 166
American Composers' Contest, 457
American Composers on American Music (Cowell), 404
American Composers Orchestra, 362, 574, 752, 822, 856, 865, 886, 915–916
American Composition Award, 493
American Conservatory, Chicago, Illinois, 410
American Conservatory, Fontainebleau, France, 32, 314, 624
American Conservatory, Hammond, Indiana, 374
American Eagle's Musical Flight to the World's Fair, The (Heinrich), 80
American Festival of Microtonal Music, 268
American Festival Overture (Schuman), 519
American Guild of Organists, 511
American identity and idioms: "American" rhythm, 29; and Antheil, 395; and Blitzstein, 318; and the *Boulangerie,* 315; and Chadwick, 138; and Copland, 322; and Cowell, 405; and Creston, 505, 511, 512; and Diamond, 565, 568; and evolution of American symphonic style, 796, 797; and future of American symphony, 924; and Ives, 212, 215, 217; and Larsen, 883; and linguistics issues, 883–884; and MacDowell, 165–166; and Marsalis, 906; maverick tradition, 29; and Paine, 138; and social environment of 1920 to 1950, 309–314; and Stravinsky, 448; and Tan, 916; and Thompson, 379, 382; and Thomson, 350. See also "Great American Symphony" trope
American in Paris, An (Gershwin), 313, 462n22
American Jewish World, 607
American Music Center, 362, 819
American Music Research Center, 655n397
American National Theater and Academy, 485
American Negro Ballet, 415, 418
American Opera Center, 610
American Record Guide, 632
American Revolution, 60, 71, 274–276
American School of the Air: Folk Music of America, 456

American Society of Composers, Authors, and Publishers, 505, 610
American sounds, 199, 201
American Symphony, 1938 (Harris), *328*
American Symphony Orchestra, 228, 411
American Symphony Orchestra League, 484
American-trained composers, **381–433**
American Woods, The (Ives), 199
America's Music: From the Pilgrims to the Present (Chase), 48–49
"America the Beautiful" (Bates), 212
Ameríndia (Velasco-Maidana), 706
Amerindian culture, 806. *See also* Indigenous music, instruments, and idioms; Native American culture
Amériques (Varèse), 890
Amichai, Yehuda, 891, 922
Amidah ("standing" prayers), 591
À Montevideo (Gottschalk). *See* Symphony No. 2, *À Montevideo* (Gottschalk)
Amtasiñani (Pozadas), 707
Ancestrofonías para orquesta sinfónica (Pozadas), 707
Andante from Symphony No. 3 in B Minor (Hadley), *9*
Anderson, Martin, 447
André, Franz, 447
Andrew W. Mellon Foundation, 7
Andrino, José Escolástico, 756
And They Lynched Him on a Tree (Still), 432
Angelus Domini descendit de caelo (Willaert), 509
Anglican Church, 184, 282
Angulo, Héctor, 771
Anhalt, István, *38*
Añoranza (Cordero), 775
Ansermet, Ernest, 675
Ansky, S., 596
Antheil, George, **383–396**; and American musical pedagogy, 381, 382–383; and Bloch, 438; and contributions of American-educated composers, 314; and distinctive qualities of American symphony, 23; and film music, 468n233, 468n244; Guggenheim Fellowship, 471n337; and key influences on American repertoire, 21; on political and economic crises, 309; and social context of symphonic repertoire, 311; symphonies' movements and instrumentation, 384–386. *See also specific composition titles*

Antheil, Henry, 392
Anthology of Fantastic Zoology, The (Bates), *911*, 914
Anthony Adverse (film; score by Korngold), 455
anti-Semitism, 675, 701–702
Antonio Estévez National Composition Competition, 715
apocalyptic themes, 597
Aponte-Ledée, Rafael, 774, 775
Apoteósis a Bolívar: Himno de los Andes y Saludo de Colombia a Chile (Ponce de León), 709
Appalachian Spring (Copland), 323
Appalachian Spring (Gottlieb), 599
"April in Harlem" (arr. of Mvt. II of *Harlem Symphony*), 471n333
Apthorp, William F., 125, 142, 144
Aquarelas chapinas (Martínez-Sobral), 754
Aquarelas paraguayas (Bareiro), 671
Aquino, Darwin, *767*, 773
Arabic music, 919
Aramaic language, 599
Araucanians, 699
Araujo, João Gomes de, 682
Araujo, Juan de, 705, 761
Arawak Indians, 764
Archer, Violet, *38*
Ardeatine Caves, 531–532
Ardévol, José, *766*, 768, 769, 771
Arens, Franz Xavier, 137, 166
Aretz-Theile, Isabel, *674*, 681
Arévalo, Arístides Chavier, 774
Argentina, 665, 667, **672–681**, *673–674*
Arias, Luis Felipe, 753
Arioso (Homenaje a Charles Mingus) (Brouwer), 771
Arizaga, Rodolfo, 667
Arkansas Traveler, 275
Armenian Cathedral and Cultural Center Project, 554
Armenian music, 553–555, 556
Armstrong, Louis, 884
Arteaga, Edward, *44*
Artist, The (film), 720n64
Art of War, The (Bates), *912*, 915
Arvey, Verna, 431, 432
Ascone, Vicente, *669*
Ascot, Rosa María, *739*
Asia, Daniel, 21, 29, 35, *794*, 795, 864, **886–891**, *887–889*, 900. *See also specific composition titles*

Index

Asian idioms and influences, 553, 916
Aspen Music School, 842
Assembly (bugle call), 262
Association of American Colleges, 377
Association of Dominican Classical Artists, 773
Asturias, Rodrigo, 754
Asuar, José Vicente, *696*, 701
asymmetrical phrases, 137
Atahualpa (Pasta), 703
Atahualpa (Riestra), 703
Atahualpa (Salgado), 708
Atehortúa, Blas Emilio, *698*, 710
Atlantic, The, 112, 131
Atmosphères (Ligeti), 835
atomic (nuclear) weapons, 484, 493–495, 596–597, 600, 601
atonality, 362, 513, 534, 604, 626, 667, 901
At the Far Edge (Asia), 890
Aturias, Miguel Ángel, 753
Atzimba (Castro), *740*
Auden, W. H., 317, 586, 594
Audiencia de Quito, 707
Audubon, John James, 79
Audubon, Lucy, 79
Auerbach, Lera, *795*, 797
Augenmusik (example in Paine Symphony No. 1), *132–134*
Augusteo Orchestra, 354
Aurelia the Vestal (Fry), 100
Aurora australis (Travassos), 695
"Aussöhnung" (Goethe), 891
Austin, Larry, 268–269, 297n139
Austin, William, 326, 346
autogenesis, 29, 335–336, 337, 520, 524
Auza, Atiliano, 706
Avance et Retraite (Heinrich), 72
avant-garde music: and Ardévol, 768; and Barroso, 771; and Beccera, 701; and Bernstein, 606; and Bolaños, 758, 760; and Corigliano, 831; and evolution of American symphonic style, 796; and Ginastera, 676–677; and Hanson, 374; and Ives's orchestral sets, 286; and Lavista, 752; and Lourié, 456; and maturation of American symphonic activity, 309; and Mennin, 624; and Ortíz, 753; and Piston, 341; and scope of American symphonic repertoire, 3; and Sessions, 501; and Sowerby, 376; and tensions within midcentury American symphony, 635; and Toch, 459
Avshalomov, Aaron, 636

Ayala, Daniel, *738, 739*, 751
Ayestas, Humberto, 754
Aymara people, 706
Azmon (Gläser), 219, *220–221*, 223, *224*, 266, 292n70
Aztec culture, 736

Babbitt, Milton, 565, 630, 683, 771, 919
Baber, Katherine, 33
Bach, J. C., 61
Bach, Johann Sebastian: and Bolaños, 760; and Chadwick, 150; and Creston, 502, 509; and Hovhaness, 556; and Ives, 182, 199, 201, 206, 212–213, 215, 244; and Johnson, 415; and Paine, 137; and Persichetti, 583
Bacharach, Burt, 445
Bachianas brasileiras No. 2 (Villa-Lobos), 683
Bachianas brasileiras No. 5 (Villa-Lobos), 683
Bachmann, Katherine, 702
Bacon, Elmore, 453
Bacon, Ernst, 311, 438, 452, 471n337
Bacon, Leonard, 265, 296n126
Bad Boy of Music, The (Antheil), 383
Badea, Christian, 623
Badian, Maya, *43*
Bahia Orchestra Project, 711
Bahr, Ehrhard, 434
Baile: Cuadro sinfónico (Chávez), 746–747
Bailey, Lillian, 124
Baker, Michael Conway, *41*
Baker, Theodore, 166–167
Balaban, Emanuel, 625
Balada, Leonardo, *794*, 797, 922
Baldeón, Agustín, 708
Baldi, Lamberto, 670
Baldwin Wallace Conservatory, 584
Bales, Richard, 185
Ballade for Piano and Orchestra in F-sharp Major (Fauré), 570
Ballad of Baby Doe, The (Moore), 456
ballad symphony form, 317
ballet: and Antheil, 383; and Bates, 914; and Bernstein, 593, 596; and Carter, 801; and Castañeda, 753; and Copland, 322, 323, 463n55; and Cuban nationalism, 769; and Escobar, 714; and Ginastera, 677; and Glass, 828; and Hovhaness, 553; and Johnson, 415, 418; and Korngold, 455; and Mennin, 636; and Milhaud, 446; and Nieto, 761; and Piston, 345; and Rodríguez, 761; and Roldán, 768; and Salgado, 708; and Sandi,

751; and Schuman, 513; and SODRE, 669; and Stravinsky, 449; and Velasco-Maidana, 706; and Villa-Lobos, 683–684, 692, 721n86; and Villalpando Buitrago, 707
Ballet mécanique (Antheil), 383
Ballet miniatura (Estrella), 714
Ballets Russes, 683
Ballivián, Alfredo, 706
Ballivián, José, 706
Baltasar Carlos, Prince of Asturias, 703
Baltimore Symphony Orchestra, 873
Bal y Gay, Jesús, *739*, 741
Banda de los Supremos Poderes, 756
Banda Republicana (Panama), 762
bandoneón, 680
banjos, 428, 430
Banshee, The (Cowell), 404
"Baptist Mission" (Johnson; Mvt. IV of *Harlem Symphony*), 418
Baqueiro Fóster, Gerónimo, 751
Baratta, María de, *755*, 756
Barber, Samuel, **354–362**; and commercial recordings of symphonic works, 11; and Copland, 323; and Corigliano, 831; and Creston, 511; and European influences, 314; and "Great American Symphony" trope, 5; Guggenheim Fellowship, 471n337; and Hanson, 373; and Hovhaness, 534; and key influences on American repertoire, 21; and Piston, 341; symphonies' movements and instrumentation, 355. *See also specific composition titles*
barbershop quartets, 318
Barcelona International Exhibition, 767
Bareiro, Carlos Lara, 671
Barenboim, Daniel, 617, 835
Barlow, Howard, 453, 455, 518
Barnes, Milton, *40*
Baron, Carol K., 289n10
Baroque era and music, 206, 374–376, 500, 502, 534, 555, 556, 614, 904
Baroque Variations (Foss), 811
Barradas, Carmen, 671
Barros, Antonio Cayetano, 668
Barroso, Sergio Fernández, 771
Bartók, Béla, 433, 458, 492, 555, 572, 578, 680
Bates, Katherine Lee, 212
Bates, Mason, **909–916**; and Adams, 873; and Corigliano, 838; and evolution of American symphonic style, 795; and future of American symphony, 924; and Larsen, 886; and Rouse, 878; symphonies' movements and instrumentation, *910–912*; symphony premiere dates, *795*. *See also specific composition titles*
Batista, Fulgencio, 769
Battalia (Biber), 691
Battle Cry of Freedom, The (Root), 255, 272–273, 275
Battle Hymn of the Republic, The (Howe), 256, *259–261*, 262
Battle of Bunker Hill, 66
Battle of Stalingrad, 391
batuque dance, 682
Bautista Massa, Juan, *673*
Bayly, Thomas Haynes, 213
Bay of Pigs invasion, 768, 769
Bazán, Oscar E., *674*, 680
Bazelon, Irwin, 636
BBC Orchestra, 438, 624
Beach, Amy, **156–159**; background and education, 156–157; and Boston's influence, 116; and Dvořák's "New World" Symphony, 53n52, 127; and "Great American Symphony" trope, 6; and key influences on American repertoire, 21; and scope of American symphonic repertoire, 3; and Second New England School, 125; symphonies' movements and instrumentation, *157*; Symphony in E Minor, "Gaelic," **157–159**
Beach, Henry Harris Aubrey, 156
Beautiful River, The (Lowry), 242
Beaux Arts, 665
bebop, 908. *See also* jazz
"Because I Could Not Stop for Death" (Dickinson), 865
Becerra, Gustavo, *696*, 700, 701
Becker, John J., 218
Becket, Thomas a', 201
Beckwith, John, 36
Beecham, Thomas, 457
Beethoven, Ludwig van: and Adams, 871; and Antheil, 387; the "Beethoven problem," 4; and Bernstein, 586, 590, 605; and Blitzstein, 318–319; and Bristow, 92; and Chávez, 746; death of, 60; and Diamond, 567, 569; and first American symphonists, 63, 66; and founding of permanent orchestras in US, 124; and "Great American Symphony" trope, 4; influence on concert music in US, 1; and Ives, 184, 185, 188, 270; and key influences on American repertoire, 21; and Martinů, 441, 444; and Mennin, 613, 614; and Paine, 127–135, 136, 167; and Rochberg, 811, 812;

and Rouse, 878; and Schuman, 531; and South American composers, 681; and Stravinsky, 448; and Strong, 161; and tensions within midcentury American symphony, 635; and Uruguayan composers, 668; and Venezuela's El Sistema, 711; and Villa-Lobos, 685, 691
Behrend, Jeanne, 115
Bekker, Paul, 31
Belgian Radio, 447
Belkin, Alan, *44*
Bellamann, Henry, 230–231, 243
Bellugi, Piero, 625
Bembé (Caturla), 765
Benedetti, Josefina, *699*, 714
Benedict XIV, Pope, 695
Ben-Hur (film), 555
Bennett, Robert Russell, 310, 452–453, 454, 471n337. *See also specific composition titles*
Benson, Warren, 636
Berceuse élégiaque (Busoni), 872
Berezowski, Nikolai, *9*, 453
Berg, Alban, 570, 599, 619
Berger, Arthur, 322–323, 325–326, 344, 582, 616
Bergman, Elizabeth, 834
Bergmann, Carl, 90, 92, 95, 98
Bergsma, William, 752
Berio, Luciano, 708, 811
Berklee College of Music, 695
Berkshire Music Center (Tanglewood): and Campos-Parsi, 774; and Gramatges, 769; and Hindemith, 439; and Hovhaness, 533; and Perry, 624, 625; and Read, 457; and South American composers, 667, 700, 704, 713; and Uruguayan composers, 670; and Walker's works, 816
Berkshire Music Festival, 624
Berkshire Symphony Orchestra, 771
Berlin Academy of Music, 439, 639, 693
Berlin Philharmonic Orchestra, 455
Berlin Phonogramm-Archiv, 396
Berlin Symphony Orchestra, 115
Berlioz, Hector, 21, 99, 104, 163, 201, 445, 594, 812, 873
Bermejo, Juan, 707
Bermúdez, Egberto, 709
Bermúdez Silva, Jesús, *698*, 710
Bernadette Soubirous, Saint, 449
Bernal Jiménez, Miguel, *738*, 751, 752
Bernier, Conrad, 756

Bernstein, Leonard, **585–609**; and Antheil, 387; and Asia, 886; and Blitzstein, 318; and Cold War cultural politics, 485; and commercial recordings of symphonic works, 11; and Copland, 325; and Corigliano, 831; and Creston, 506, 507; critiques of nineteenth-century composers, 116; and Diamond, 559, 566, 569–570, 574–575; and distinctive qualities of American symphony, 24; and elements of American modernism, 486–487; and emergence of postmodern style, 634; and future of American symphony, 923; on German influence on American symphonic traditions, 656n432; and Gottschalk, 115; and "Great American Symphony" trope, 4–6, 484; and Hanson, 373; and Hill, 455; and Hovhaness, 533; and Ives, 200, 214, 215–216, 286; and Mahler, 22; and Mennin, 613, 616, 617, 619; "musical kindergarten" comment, 36, 54n99; New York Philharmonic recordings, *19*; and Perry, 626; and Persichetti, 580, 583; and Piston, 340–341; premiere of key works during Koussevitsky's tenure, *9*; and Rouse, 873; and Schuman, 513, 517, 519, 527–528, 530–531, 533; and scope of American symphonic repertoire, 6; and Sessions, 500; and Shapero, 458; and South American composers, 713; and support for American symphony, 7, 485; symphonies' movements and instrumentation, *587–588*; and tensions within midcentury American symphony, 486–488, 635; and Venezuela's El Sistema, 711; and Villa-Lobos, 692. *See also specific composition titles*
Bernstein, Samuel J., 591, 609
Berry, Chuck, 883
Bethany (Mason), 232–234, 245–246, *246, 247–248, 255–256*, 267, 293n83
Bethlehem, Pennsylvania, 61–62
Bethlehem Philharmonic, 66
Betts, Lorne, *38*
Beulah Land (Sweney), 188, 211–212, 230, 235, 241–242, 244
Beyoncé, 286
Big Band, 431
Big Stick diplomacy, 735, 757
Billings, William, 405
Billoni, Santiago, 737
Billy the Kid (Copland), 323
Birchard, C. C., 271

Bird, Robert Montgomery, 86
Biriotti, León, *669*, 670
"Birth of the Ocean Waters" (Ives *Universe Symphony*), 269
Bischoff, Ludwig, 70
Bishop, Henry R., 242, 251
Bisquertt, Próspero, *696*, 700
bitonality, 353, 381, 449, 553–556, 755, 771
Black, Brown and Beige (Ellington), 454
Black composers and musical influences: and Argentinian composers, 672; Black church, 626; and Brazilian composers, 681–682; and Chilean composers, 695, 702; and commercial recordings of symphonic works, 11; and Dvořák's support of American idioms, 312; and education/training of American composers, 32–33; and key influences on American repertoire, 21; and Perry's works, 625–630, 632, 633–634; and popular music, 633; and Uruguayan composers, 668; and Walker's works, 819. *See also* African American culture and heritage; *specific musicians and composers*
Blackwood, Easley, Jr., 55n105, 636, *794*
Blake, William, 501–502, 608, 844
Blanco, Juan, 769
Blasco, Manuel, 707
Blitzstein, Marc: *Airborne* Symphony, *316*, **316–319**; and Bernstein, 595–596; death, 596; on democratization of American symphony, 312; and "Great American Symphony" trope, 450–451; Guggenheim Fellowship, 471n337; and key influences on American repertoire, 22; and radio broadcasting, 310; and Schuman, 517
Bloch, Ernest, **436–439**; and American musical pedagogy, 381; and Antheil, 383; and Bacon, 452; and Bates, 914; and Bernstein, 598; and commercial recordings of symphonic works, 11; and conflicts over modernism, 313; and "Great American Symphony" trope, 450; and Gruenberg, 454; and Hindemith, 441; and Moore, 456; and Porter, 457; premiere of key works during Koussevitsky's tenure, 9; and Sessions, 488; and social context of symphonic repertoire, 311; symphonies written in America, *434*; and Thompson, 379. *See also specific composition titles*
Block, Adrienne Fried, 30, 158–159
Blondel, Jorge Urrutia, 667

Blood on the Fields (Marsalis), 904
blues: and Bates, 915; and Bernstein, 589–590, 593; and Black American composers, 32; and Blitzstein, 318; and Copland, 323; and Creston, 507; and emergence of Black composers, 382; and Hailstork, 858; and Johnson, 415, 417; and Liebermann, 907–908; and Perry, 33, 626, 630, 632–634; and Price, 422–424; and Sowerby, 374; and Still, 428–430; and tensions within midcentury American symphony, 487; and Thompson, 379; and Villa-Lobos, 693
Blutopia (Ellington), 454
Boccherini, Luigi, 681
Boepple, Paul, 559
Boero, Felipe, *673*, 674, 706
Boethius, 440
Bohemia, sinfonia romantica (Heinrich), *76*, 81, *81*
Bohemian Grove, 708
Bohemian influences, 126, 442
Bok, Mary Louise Curtis, 383, 387
Bolaños, César, 704
Bolaños Chamorro, Gabriel, 758–760
Bolcom, William, **838–845**; and Albert, 864; and distinctive qualities of American symphony, 23; and evolution of American symphonic style, 795; and future of American symphony, 924; and Harbison, 849; and key influences on American repertoire, 21; and Larsen, 884; and Rochberg, 815; and scope of American symphonic repertoire, 1; and Sibelius, 22; symphonies' movements and instrumentation, *839–841*; symphony premiere dates, *794, 795*. *See also specific composition titles*
Bolívar, Simón, 709
Bolivia, 665, 667, *697*, **705–707**
Bomberger, E. Douglas, 4, 30, 53n52, 309, 310, 312–313
Bonampak (Sandi), 751
Bonds, Estelle, 420
Bonds, Margaret, 420, 626
Bonham (Rouse), 878
Book of Imaginary Beings (Borges), 914
Borges, Jorge Luis, 752, 914
Borowski, Felix, 381, 453
Borroff, Edith, 373, 623
Boston, Massachusetts: and Bernstein's background, 609; Boston Common, 272; and Bristow's career, 98; and Chadwick's background,

141, 151–152; and critiques of listening public, 51n22; cultural influences, 6; and émigré composers, 310; and first generation of American symphonists, 63; influence on character of American symphony, 116; reception of Paine's works, 136, 137; rivalry with New York City, 51n22, 147, 608. *See also* Boston Symphony Orchestra (BSO)
Boston Conservatory, 533
Boston Globe, 135, 147
Boston Handel and Haydn Society, 141
Boston Herald, 126, 157, 278, 518
Boston Post, 51n22, 144, 145, 518
Boston Symphony Orchestra (BSO): and Barber's works, 358; and Beach's works, 158; and Berezowski's works, 453; and Bernstein's works, 590, 594, 595, 596, 609; and Boulanger's students, 315; and Chadwick's works, 141, 142, 146, 153, 154, 156; and Copland's works, 323; and Corigliano's works, 835; and Cowell's works, 404–405; and Diamond's works, 566, 567; founding and early repertoire of, 124–125; and Hadley's works, 454; and Hanson's works, 365; and Harbison's works, 845; and Harris's works, 334, 339; and Hindemith's works, 439; influence on character of American symphony, 116; and Ives's works, 200, 218, 271–272, 297n154; and Josten's works, 455; Latin American symphonies premiered, 8; and Lourié's works, 456; and Martinů's works, 442, 445; and Mennin's works, 616; and Milhaud's works, 446; and Paine's works, 138; and Piston's works, 341–344, 345, 348, 349; and Schuman's works, 518, 519–520, 523, 527, 530; and Second New England School composers, 126; and Sessions's works, 492, 496; and Shapero's works, 458; Shepherd's tenure with, 458; and Sierra's works, 775; and social context of symphonic repertoire, 311; and South American composers, 667, 692; and Sowerby's works, 377; and support for American symphony, 6–7, 485
Boston Transcript, 137, 144, 152
Botstein, Leon, 100, 315
Bottesini, Giovanni, 107
Boulanger, Lili, 315
Boulanger, Nadia: and Bennett, 452; and Blitzstein, 316; and Carter, 798; contrasted with Rome Academy training, 354; and Copland, 319–322; and Cuban composers, 769; and Diamond, 559; and Hailstork, 856; and Harris, 326; and Lockwood, 456; and Mexican composers, 741; and Perry, 624; and Persichetti, 583; and Piston, 340, 349–350; and Puerto Rican composers, 774; and Rolón, 740; and Sessions, 492–493; and Shapero, 458; and South American composers, 667, 706, 708, 710; students of the *Boulangerie,* **315**; and Walker, 816
Boulez, Pierre, 115, 586, 755, 850, 919
Bowie, David, 822, 828, 830–831
Bowling Green State University, 764
Bowring, John, 233
Bracesco, Renzo, 703
Bradbury, William B., 221, 244, 279
Brady, Timothy, *45–46*
Braga, Francisco, 682
Brahms, Fritz, 715
Brahms, Johannes: and Beach, 159; and Bernstein, 585; and Chadwick, 146, 147; and founding of civic orchestras in US, 123; and Ginastera, 680; and Ives, 184, 188, 194, 195, 199, 208, 210–214, 291n36; and key influences on American repertoire, 21; and Martinů, 441–442; and Mennin, 623; and Paine, 131; and Schuman, 520; and Sowerby, 376; and tensions within midcentury American symphony, 635
Brain Salad Surgery (Emerson, Lake, and Palmer), 720n64
Branca, Glenn, viii, *794*
Brandeis Creative Arts Award, 488
Brant, Henry, 36
Braslovsky, Solomon, 596–597
Brazil, 665, **681–695**, 711
Breaking Heart, The (Fry), *102,* **104–105,** *105,* 109
Brescia, Domenico, *697,* 708
Brewster, Lyman, 298n161
Brick Symphony (Torke), *794,* 796
Bridge, The (Crane), 801
Briggs, John, 584
Bringing in the Sheaves (Minor), 210, 280–281
Brinkmann, Reinhold, 433
Bristow, George Frederick, **85–100**; background and education, 85–86; and early years of New York Philharmonic, 67; and ethnic conflict in early American symphony, 68, 69–70; and Fry, 101, 109, 110; and Heinrich, 71; and key influences on American repertoire, 21; and support for American symphony, 6; symphonies' movements and instrumentation, *87–88*;

Symphony No. 2, *Jullien,* **90–92**; Symphony No. 3 in F-Sharp Minor, **92–95,** *93*; Symphony No. 4, *Arcadian,* **95–98**; Symphony No. 5, *Niagara,* **98–100**; views on American subject matter, 51n27
British Grenadiers, The (traditional), 274–276
Britten, Benjamin, 607
Brnčić, Gabriel, *696,* 701
Broadway, 313, 746, 771
Broder, Nathan, 358, 362
Brodhead, Thomas M., 234
Bronzeville neighborhood (Chicago), 382
Brooklyn Academy of Music, 761
Brooklyn Civic Orchestra, 382
Brooklyn Daily Eagle, 95
Brooklyn Daily Union, 95
Brooklyn Philharmonic, 86, 95
Brooklyn Seidl Society, 162
Broqua, Alfonso, 668, *669*
Brott, Alexander, *38*
Brouwer, Leo, 578, 770
Brown (Bradbury), 244
Brown, A. Peter, vii, 290n20
Brown, Carol Vanderbilt, vii
Brown, Gwynne Kuhner, 410, 412, 470n300
Brown, James, 883
Brown, Rae Linda, 382, 420, 422, 423, 472n350
Brown, Stephen, *43*
Brubeck, Dave, 445
Bruce, Neely, 85
Bruckner, Anton, 125, 613, 871, 876
Bruckner Orchester Linz, 695, 830, 865
Brunelle, Philip, 511
Brunswick, Mark, 439
B-Sides, The (Bates), *910,* 913, 915
Büchlein vom Leben nach dem Tode (Fechner), 569
Buck, Dudley, 182, 184
Buczynski, Walter, *41*
Buenos Aires, Argentina, 665, 672, 675, 676
Buenos Aires: Tres movimientos sinfónicos (Piazzolla), 680
Buhr, Glenn, *45*
Buitrago, Pablo, 758
Bulla (Crashaw), 802
Bunyan, John, 234
Burg, William van den, 411
Burge, John, *46*
Burgin, Richard, 272, 298n154, 334
Burk, John N., 523, 530
Burkhardt, Charles, 106, 108
Burkholder, J. Peter, 30–31
burlesque, 150
Burritt, Lloyd, *42*
Burton, Humphrey, 519
Busch, Fritz, 675
Busoni, Ferruccio, 872
Bustamente, Bienvenido, 773
Butterworth, Neil, 534, 613, 617
Byron, George Gordon, Lord, *93,* 108

Caba, Eduardo, 706
Cabot, John, 668
Cabral, Pedro Álvares, 681
Cabrillo Music Festival, 806
Cáceres, Eduardo, *696,* 702
Cadman, Charles Wakefield, 453
Cage, John, 286, 289n7, 353, 534, 752, 802–803, 901
Cahn, Judah, 598
Caibarién Concert Society, 767
Calcaño, José Antonio, 714
Calcavecchia, Benone, *669,* 670
Caldwell, Sarah, 705
call-and-response: and bembé ritual, 765; and Creston, 511; and Dawson, 412, 414; and Diamond, 575; and Harbison, 848; and Hindemith, 439–440; and Hovhaness, 554; and Johnson, 418; and Perry, 633; and Price, 421, 423; and Schuman, 529; and Still, 429, 431
Camagüey Symphony, 771
Cambridge History of American Music (Nicholls, ed.), 641
Cambridge History of Twentieth-Century Music (Cook and Pople, eds.), 641
Caminos del Inka (Luzuriaga), 709
Campa, Gustavo Emilio, 737, *738*
Campbells Are Coming, The (traditional), 251
Campderrós, José de, 695
Campion, Edmund, 916
camp-meetings, 293n71
Campo (Fabini), 669
Campo, Conrado del, 768
Campos, José Carlos, 705
Campos, Juan Morel, 767, 773, 775
Campos-Parsi, Héctor, 774
Campoverde Quezada, Juan, *698,* 709
Camptown Races (Foster), 213–214, 215, 251, 291n42
Canadian composers and symphonies, 36–48, *37–47*

Canadian Music Centre, 48
Candide (Bernstein), 559, 595, 600
candombe genre, 668
Cañete, Luis, 672
Canonic Choruses (Schuman), 517
Cantata Boliviana (Eisner), 706
Cantata criolla (Estévez), 713
Canticle of the Sun (Larsen), 886
Canticle of the Sun (Sowerby), 374
Cántico homenaje (León), 769
Canticum sacrum (Stravinsky), 572
Cantus Arcticus (Rautavaara), 915
Canyon, The (Glass), 822
Capricho sobre un tema Paraguayo (Centurión), 671
Captaincy of Guatemala, 756, 757
Carabalí (León), 771
Caracas Cathedral, 712, 714
Caracas Festival, 712–713, 762
Cardona, Alejandro, 761
Caribbean, **764–776**
Carillon Importers Ltd., 900
Carlyle, Thomas, 84
Carmel Bach Festival, 452
Carnegie Foundation, 377
Carnegie Hall: and Antheil's works, 383; and Bristow's works, 99–100; and Dawson's works, 411; and Ellington's works, 454; and Glass's works, 830; and Hovhaness's works, 554; and Ives's works, 216, 228; and Johnson's works, 415; and Serebrier's works, 670; and Sierra's works, 775
Carnegie Mellon University, 797
Carnival Music (Rochberg), 815
Carolina Shout (Johnson), 415
Carolinian Symphony (Vardell), 459
Carpenter, John Alden, 453
Carpentier, Alejo, 712, 765
Carr, Benjamin, 62
Carrabré, T. Patrick, *46*
Carreño, Inocente, *699,* 714
Carreño, Teresa, *698,* 714
Carrillo, Julián, 34, *738,* 741
Carrizo, Andrés, 35, 764
Carter, Benny, 908
Carter, Elliott, **798–802**; and Albert, 860; and Bolcom, 845; and Boulanger's influence, 315; and distinctive qualities of American symphony, 29; and evolution of American symphonic style, 795; and Fairouz, 922; and Gramatges, 769; and Hill, 455; and Lybbert, 704; and Piston, 341; and Sessions, 492, 499; symphonies' movements and instrumentation, *799–800*; symphony premiere dates, *794*; and Zwilich, 850. *See also specific composition titles*
Carvahlo, Eleazar de, 667, 694
Casa de Comedias, 668
Casal Chapí, Enrique, 670, 772
Casals, Pablo, 774, 775
Casals Festival, 774, 775
Casella, Alfredo, 488, 675
Casey at the Bat (Schuman), 513, 524
Cassaro, James, 458
Castañeda, Jorge, 753
Castegnaro, Alvise, 760
Castellanos, Evencio, *698,* 714
Castellanos, Gonzalo, *699,* 714
Castellanos, Rafael Antonio, 753
Castelnuovo-Tedesco, Mario, 434, 451
Castérèrede, Jacques, 752
Castillo, Jesús, 753, *755*
Castillo, Ricardo, 753–755, *755*
Castro, Fidel, 768, 770
Castro, Herbert de, 761
Castro, José María, *673,* 675
Castro, Juan José, 34, *673,* 675–676, 677, 680
Castro, Ricardo, 737, *738*
Castro, Washington, *673,* 674
Catalan Overture (Preti-Bonati), 668
Catán, Daniel, *740,* 752
Catherine of Siena, Saint, 633
Catholic Church, 34, 352, 508, 735
Catholic University of America Symphony Orchestra, 775
Caturla, Alejandro García, 35, 765–768, *766,* 769. *See also specific composition titles*
CBS. *See* Columbia Broadcasting System
CBS Symphony Orchestra. *See* Columbia Symphony Orchestra
Cecilia Váldes (Roig), 765
Celebration (Ellington), 454
Celebration Concertante (Schuman), 528, 530
Celestial City, 234–242
Celestial Railroad, The (Hawthorne), 230–232, 234–243, 294n86, 298n162
Cello Concerto (Carter), 802
Celtic idioms and influences, 3, 29, 150, 156, 159, 335, 583
Centennial Symphony for Band (Gould), 454
Center Church, 199, 264

Center for Black Music Research, 655n397
Central America, **756–764**; Costa Rica, 760–761; El Salvador, 756; Guatemala, 753–756; Honduras, 756–757; Nicaragua, 757–760; Panama, 761–764; symphonies and orchestral works, *755*
Central American Federation, 735, 760
Central Europe, 625. *See also* European idioms and influences; *specific countries*
Central Park in the Dark (Ives), 289n1
Central Presbyterian Church, 217, 296n128
Central Washington State College, 505
Centrediscs label, 48
Centro Latinoamericano de Altos Estudios Musicales (CLAEM), 676, 702, 704, 706–708, 754–755, 761, 774
Centurión, Fernando, 671
Ceremonia indígena (Holguín), 710
Cerón, José Dolores, 772
Ceruti, Roque, 703
Cervantes, Ignacio, 34, 765, *766*
Cervetti, Sergio, 671
Chabrier, Alexis-Emmanuel, 682
Chaco War, 671
Chadwick, George Whitefield, **138–156**; and American musical pedagogy, 381; background and education, 138–141; and Beach, 159; and Boston's influence, 116; and Bristow, 98; and distinctive qualities of American symphony, 24; and diversity of American symphonic styles, 167; and Dvořák's enthusiasm for folk influences, 127; and European influence on American repertoire, 54n99; and "Great American Symphony" trope, 4; and Hadley, 455; and key influences on American repertoire, 21; and Mason, 456; and premiere of key works during Koussevitsky's tenure, 9; and Price, 420; and scope of American symphonic repertoire, viii, 1, 3; and Second New England School, 125–126; and Shepherd, 458; *Sinfonietta*, **151–153**; and Still, 425; *Suite Symphonique*, **153–156**; *Symphonic Sketches*, **147–151**; symphonies' movements and instrumentation, *139–140*; Symphony No. 1, **141–142**; Symphony No. 2, **142–145**; Symphony No. 3, **146–147**
Chadwick, John White, 883
Chagas, Paulo, *684, 695*
chamber music, 433
Chamber Orchestra of Boston, 271
Chamber Symphony (Adams), *867,* 872

Chamber Symphony (Eisler), 454
Chamber Symphony (Rochberg), 811
Chamber Symphony (Zwilich), 850, *851*
Chamber Symphony for Nine Instruments (Rochberg), *808*
Chamber Symphony for Strings (Carreño), 714
Chamber Symphony No. 1, "Sabra" (Fairouz), 919
Chamber Symphony No. 1 (Schoenberg), 458, 872
Chamber Symphony No. 2 (Schoenberg), 458
Champagne, Claude, 36, *37*
Chance, John Barnes, 636
Chandos label, *20*
Chanler, Theodore, 438
chant, 591, 747. *See also* hymns
Chapí y Lorente, Ruperto, 772
Chapultepec (Ponce), 741
Charke, Derek, *47*
Charles Eliot Norton Lectures, 591
Charles Ives Prize, 702
Charles Ives Society, 268
Charleston, South Carolina, 61, 62
Charrúa Indians, 668
Chase, Gilbert, 48, 762
Chausson, Ernest, 52n41
Chautauqua Institution Summer Festival, 671
Chautauquan Summer (Águila), 670–671
Chautauquan Symphony Orchestra, 670
Chávez, Carlos, **741–749**; and commercial recordings of symphonic works, 11; and Copland, 322; and Cowell, 396; and distinctive qualities of American symphony, 24; and expanding role of music in South America, 666; and key compositions from Mexico, *738, 739*; and Lavista, 752; and Orbón, 770; premiere of key works during Koussevitsky's tenure, 9; and radio broadcasting, 310; recording labels featuring, 52n50; and scope of American symphonic repertoire, 2; symphonies' movements and instrumentation, *743–745*; time in US, 735. *See also specific composition titles*
Checán II (Valcárcel), 704
Cheney, Amy Marcy. *See* Beach, Amy
Chicago Black Renaissance, 382
Chicago Club of Women Organists, 420
Chicago Daily News, 500
Chicago Defender, 420
Chicago Music Association, 420
Chicago Symphony Orchestra: and Bates's works, 909, 913–914, 916; and Bernstein's works,

596; and Corigliano's works, 831, 835, 838; and Elgar's works, 453; and evolution of American symphonic style, 797; and Ives's works, 188, 279; and Milhaud's works, 446; and Price's works, 420, 422; and Rochberg's works, 813; and Schuman's works, 532; and Sessions's works, 497; and Sowerby's works, 374, 376, 377; and Stravinsky's works, 448; and Thomas's influence, 123; and works by Black composers, 382, 410

Chicago Tribune, 163–164, 374
Chichen Itzá (Prieto), 741
Chihara, Paul, 438
Childe Harold (Byron), 108
Childe Harold (Fry), *102,* **108–109**
Children of Adam (Bates), *912,* 914
Children's Day, 227
Chile, 665, **695–702,** *696*
Chilean Communist Party, 702
Chin, Pablo Santiago, 761
Chinese music, 396
Chopin, Frédéric, 156, 193, 502
Chorale, 294n89
Choreographic Poem (Schuman), 517–518
Choros for Piano and Orchestra (Guarnieri), 762
Choros No. 8 (Villa-Lobos), 682
Christian evangelism, 665
Christian Science Monitor, 607
Christmas (Handel), 244
Christus resurgens ex mortuis, 509
Christy, Edwin P., 252
chromaticism: and Adams, 871; and Ayestas, 754; and Barber, 357, 359; and Bernstein, 593, 605; and Bolcom, 842; and Bristow, 89, 96, 99; and Carrillo, 741; and Carter, 801; and Corigliano, 834, 835, 837; and Cowell, 404–405, 408; and Creston, 506–507, 509; and Diamond, 560, 566, 570, 571, 574; and *Five Folksongs in Counterpoint,* 471n343; and Ginastera, 680; and Hanson, 362; and Harris, 336; and Heinrich, 84–85; and Hovhaness, 534; and Ives's *Holidays Symphony,* 252, 258, *260–261,* 262, 264, 266; and Ives's orchestral sets, 275–278, 279–281, 282; and Ives's Symphony No. 1, 193–194; and Ives's Symphony No. 2, 211, 214; and Ives's Symphony No. 3, 218, 223, 226–227; and Ives's Symphony No. 4, 228, 233, 235, *237–239,* 242, *247–248*; and Ives's *Universe Symphony,* 269; and Johnson, 417; and Kernis, 900; and Larsen, 883; and Liebermann, 901–902, 904; and MacDowell, 165; and Mennin, 610, 613–614, 618, 621–622; and Perry, 631, 633; and Persichetti, 578–580; and Piston, 345, 346, 349; and Price, 420, 423–424; and Rochberg, 807, 811–813, 815; and Schuman, 513, 529–530, 531, 532; and Sessions, 495; and Sowerby, 377; and Still, 429, 432; and Strong, 163; and Thompson, 380; and Valcárcel, 704; and Villa-Lobos, 691; and Zwilich, 850

Chromatic Ramble, A (Heinrich), 72
chronological order of compositions, 184, 289n10
Church Triumphant (Elliott), 244
Cifuentes, Santos, *698,* 709
Cincinnati Philharmonic Orchestra, 268
Cinco piezas (Santa Cruz), 700
Cinco piezas características y una romanza (Martínez-Sobral), 754
Cinco viñetas (Bolaños), 758–760
cinema, 750. *See also* film music; *specific film titles*
Cinque canti (Schuman), 528
cinquillo (dance), 112
Cinzano Prize, 677
Círculo Filarmónico, 761
Citas inocentes (Benedetti), 714
Citizen Kane (film; score by Hermann), 455
City Noir (Adams), *869,* 873
City University of New York, 771
civil rights movement, 626, 859
Civil War (Spain), 666, 670, 741, 749
Civil War (US): and Bloch, 437; and first generation of US symphonists, 60; and Fry, 110; and "Great American Symphony" trope, 4; and Harris, 340; influence on character of American symphony, 116, 123; and Ives's background, 175; and Ives's works, 242, 253, 255, 272; and National Peace Jubilee, 148; and Still, 431
Clarinet Concerto (Carter), 802
Clarinet Concerto (Corigliano), 831
Clarke, Frederick, R. C., *40*
class conflict and divisions, 123, 167
Cleveland Institute of Music, 436, 453, 488, 559
Cleveland News, 453
Cleveland Orchestra, 358, 442, 453, 460, 526, 610, 617, 811
Cleveland Philharmonic Orchestra, 670
Cleveland Quartet, 835
Cleveland Symphony, 309
Cloeter, Tim, 100
Clurman, Harold, 319
Cluzeau Mortet, Luis, 670
Clyne, Anna, 909, 916

CMC label, 48
Coates, Gloria, *794, 797,* 834
Cochrane, Donald, *40*
Cocteau, Jean, 742
Coello Ramos, Rafael, 757
Cohen, Abe, 600
Cold War, 33, 338, 485, 559–560, 600, 667, 878–883
Cole, Peter, 900
Coleridge-Taylor, Samuel, 420
Coliseo Provisional, 672
College-Conservatory's Percussion Ensemble, 268
College of Church Musicians, 374
College of the Pacific, 362
Collegiate Chorale, 614
collegium musicum, 61–62, *62–63*
Collins, William, *93*
Colombia, *698,* **709–710**
Colón, Braulio Dueño, 774
Colored Field (Kernis), 900
Columbia, the Gem of the Ocean (A'Becket), 201, 213, 214, 216, 230, 242, 258, *259–261,* 262, 285
Columbia Broadcasting System (CBS), 310, 311, 369, 370, 414, 453, 456
Columbia Composer's Commissions, 310
Columbiad, The (Heinrich), 71–72, *73, 77,* 78–79, *79,* 81–82, 84–85
Columbia-Princeton Electronic Music Center, 714
Columbia Symphony Orchestra, 200, 458, 518
Columbia Teachers' College, 354
Columbia University, 164, 218, 344, 493, 613, 714
Columbia University Opera Workshop, 625
Columbia University Orchestra, 115
Columbus (Bristow), 86
Columbus Symphony Orchestra, 623
Colvig, William, 806
Coming Forth into Day: A Choral Symphony (Larsen), 878, *880*
Commemoration Symphony, A (Bennett), 452–453
Como agua para chocolate (film), 771
Comoedia, 278
"Complaint" (Tourian), 883
Composers Collective, 751
Composers' Committee to Aid Spanish Democracy, 517
Composers' Conference, 447
Composers Recording, Inc. (CRI), 11, *17–19,* 21, 631
Concertino for Jazz Quartet and Orchestra (Schuller), 487

concert jazz, 33, 313, 454
Concerto for Orchestra (Estévez), 713, *713*
Concerto for Orchestra (Gómez), 715
Concerto for Orchestra (Sessions), 501
Concerto for Orchestra (Sierra), 775
Concerto for Percussion and Orchestra (Schwantner), 864
Concerto for Trombone and Orchestra (Walker), 816
Concert Spirituel concert series, 78
Concerts Populaires, 682
"Conchobhar ua Raghallaigh Cluann" (Irish tune), 158
Concierto barroco (Orozco), 771
Concierto criollo (Cordero), 775
Concord Sonata (Ives), 183, 212, 230, 242, 284–285, 298n162. *See also* Piano Sonata No. 2: *Concord, Mass., 1840-60*
Cone, Edward T., 448–449
Connotations (Copland), 530–531
Consecration of the House Overture (Beethoven), 531
Conservatorio del Ateneo, 672
Conservatory of Fine Arts, 362
Consideraciones generales sobre arte musical en Nicaragua (Pedrell), 758
Contradanza de los militares y empelados (Furriol), 668
Contreras, Salvador, *738, 739,* 751
Converse, Charles, 219
Converse, Frederick S., 453, 533
"Convincing Neoclassicism, A" (d'Urbano), 675
Cook, Will Marion, 415
Coolidge Foundation, 610, 701
Coolidge String Quartet, 453
Cooney, Myron, 98
Cooper Union, 632
Copland, Aaron, **319–326**; and Antheil, 387; and Asia, 890; and Barber, 356; and Bernstein, 589, 591, 593, 594, 595, 599, 609; and Boulanger's influence, 315; and Chávez, 742, 747; and Cold War cultural politics, 485, 486; and commercial recordings of symphonic works, 11; and Corigliano, 831; and Creston, 506–507, 511–513; critiques of nineteenth-century composers, 116; *Dance Symphony,* 463n55; and Diamond, 559, 565–566, 570; and distinctive qualities of American symphony, 24, 29; and emergence of postmodern style, 634; and "Great American Symphony" trope, 6, 451; and Gruenberg,

965

454; Guggenheim Fellowship, 471n337; and Harbison, 845; and Harris, 335, 336, 468n238; and Hovhaness, 533–534; and Ives's influence on later generations, 286; and key influences on American repertoire, 22; and Martinů, 442–443; and maturation of American symphonic activity, 309; and Mennin, 614, 623; and Mexican composers, 751; and Orbón, 770; and OSSODRE, 670; and Persichetti, 578, 579; premiere of key works during Koussevitsky's tenure, 9; and Puerto Rican composers, 774; and radio broadcasting, 310; and Read, 457; and Revueltas, 750; and Rochberg, 807; and Schuman, 513, 517, 524, 531; and scope of American symphonic repertoire, 1, 2; and Sessions, 492; and social context of symphonic repertoire, 311–312; and South American composers, 667, 676–677, 680, 692, 699–700, 713; and Still, 430; and support for American symphony, 7; symphonies' movements and instrumentation, *320–321*; and tensions within midcentury American symphony, 487; and Torres-Santos, 775. *See also specific composition titles*

Copland-Sessions concerts, 445
Coral, Fuga y Final (Sebastiani), 681
Corales criollos, 675–676
Cordero, Ernesto, 775
Cordero, Roque, 34, *755,* 762
Corigliano, John, **831–838**; and Adams, 873; and Albert, 864; and Bates, 909, 916; and Bolcom, 845; and commercial recordings of symphonic works, 11; and distinctive qualities of American symphony, 23, 24; and evolution of American symphonic style, 795, 798; and future of American symphony, 923; and Ives's influence on recent music, 286; and Kernis, 897; and key influences on American repertoire, 22; and Rouse, 876; and support for American symphony, 9; symphonies' movements and instrumentation, *832–833*; symphony premiere dates, *794, 795*. *See also specific composition titles*
Corigliano, John Paul (father), 831
Cornell College, 439
Coro de Madrigalists, 751
Coronation (Holden), 244
Coronation March (Pasta), 703
corporate funding for symphonic works, 485, 580
Cortège Macabre (Copland), 322
Cortés, Hernán, 736

Corwin, Norman, 608
Cosme, Luiz, *684,* 692
cosmopolitanism, 3, 34, 36, 67, 138, 488, 492, 513
Costa Rica, *755,* **760–761**
Cotapos, Acario, *696,* 700
Coulthard, Jean, 37
Country Band March (Ives), 242, 275
Cours de composition musicale (d'Indy), 666
COVID-19 pandemic, 11
Cowell, Henry, **396–409**; and American musical pedagogy, 382, 383; and Antheil, 383; and Bloch, 438, 439; and Chávez, 742; and contributions of American-educated composers, 314; and Creston, 502, 509; and Cuban composers, 767; and distinctive qualities of American symphony, 23; Guggenheim Fellowship, 396, 471n337; and Harrison, 802, 806; imprisonment, 404, 405, 469n271; and Ives, 200, 215, 216, 267–268; and Mennin, 613–614, 616; and scope of American symphonic repertoire, 6; and Still, 430; symphonies' movements and instrumentation, *397–403*; and Thomson, 350. *See also specific composition titles*
Cowell, Sidney, 267–268
Cox, Sidney Thurber, 335
Cradle Will Rock, The (Blitzstein), 316
Crane, Hart, 801
Crane, Stephen, 883
Crashaw, Richard, 802
Crawford, Richard, 484
Crawford, Ruth. *See* Seeger, Ruth Crawford
Creation, The (Haydn), 270
Creole Rhapsody (Ellington), 454
Creston, Paul, 5, 11, 33, 376, 486–487, **502–513,** *503–504,* 575, 613. *See also specific composition titles*
criollos, 666
Cristóbal of Caranqui, 707
Cross, Benjamin, 62
Crouch, Frederick Nicholls, 89
Crucible, The (Ward), 459
Crucifixus, 509
Crump, Michael, 441, 445
Crusader's Hymn (Mason), 233
Crutchfield, Will, 775
Crystal Palace, 109
Cuando caiga el silencio (Lara), 752
Cuarteto Haydn, 671
Cuba, 601, 735, **764–772,** *766, 769*

Cuban missile crisis, 601, 769
Cuentas, Sadiel, 704
Cuento brujo (Velasco-Maidana), 706
Cullen, Countee, 420
cultural diplomacy, 706
Cultural Presentations Program, 513
cumulative form movements: and Ives's *Holidays Symphony*, 249, 258, *259–261*, 265; and Ives's orchestral sets, 273, 280, 282, *283*, 284; and Ives's Symphony No. 3, 198, 217, 219, *222*, 223, 227–228; and Ives's Symphony No. 4, 230, 231, 234, 246, *247*; and Ives's *Universe Symphony*, 269
Curious Flights, 463n53
Currie, Neil, *45*
Currier, Sebastian, 864
Curtis Institute of Music, 316, 575, 670, 807, 816, 916
cyclic construction of symphonies, 365, 372
Czech Philharmonic, 442

Dahl, Ingolf, 315
Dahlhaus, Carl, 125
Daily Eagle, 97
Daily News, 388
Daily Union, 97
Daily Worker, 316
Dallapiccola, Luigi, 487, 488, 502, 528, 624–625, 630, 811
Dallas Public Library, 447
Dallas Symphony Orchestra, 439, 447, 452, 486, 527, 615, 751, 901
Damrosch, Walter, 154, 185, 199, 200, 218, 290n13, 322
Danbury, Connecticut, 253
dança de negros, 682
dance, 341, 405, 508, 553, 682, 749, 751, 757, 803, 908. *See also* ballet
Dance Symphony (Copland), *320*, 454, 463n55
Dance Theatre of Harlem, 771
Daniel (Bristow), 86
Daniel, Oliver, 11
Danielpour, Richard, *795*, 796
Daño colateral: memorias del útero puertoriqueño (Huertas), 776
Danuser, Hermann, 450
Danza (Cáceres), 702
Danzas sobre un tema indio or *Gloria y ocaso del Inca* (Pacheco de Céspedes), 703

Danzones (Márquez), 752
Darío, Rubén, 757
"Dark Is the Night!" (Beach), 158
Darwish, Mahmoud, 919
Das Lied von der Erde (Mahler), 270, 592, 597, 598, 837, 891
Das Rheingold (Wagner), 270, 680
Daugherty, Michael, *794*
Daughters of the American Revolution, 251
Davidovsky, Mario, 667, *674*, 680, 706
Davidson, Mary Wallace, 560
Davidson, Matthew de Lacey, *46*
Davies, Dennis Russell, 534, 822, 830, 843, 865
Dávila, Rafael Balserio, 774
Davis, Miles, 908
Dawning of Music in Kentucky, The (Heinrich), 71, 78, 84
Dawson, Ted, *44*, 383, 470n300
Dawson, William Levi, **410–415**; and American musical pedagogy, 381; and commercial recordings of symphonic works, 11; and contributions of American-educated composers, 314; and emergence of Black composers, 382; and key influences on American repertoire, 21; and radio broadcasting, 310; and scope of American symphonic repertoire, 6; symphonies' movements and instrumentation, *410*. *See also specific composition titles*
Day in the Country, A (Fry), *102*, 104, **105–106**, *106*, 107, 110
Deane, James, 188
Death and Transfiguration (Strauss), 594
"Death of God" theology, 608
Death of Klinghoffer, The (Adams), 864–865, 872
Debravo, Jorge, 761
Debussy, Claude, 153, 154, 322, 447–448, 502, 505, 589, 607, 684, 767, 848
Decoration Day (Ives), *177*, 249, **252–256**, *257*, 267, 295n110, 295n113, 295n115, 834. *See also Symphony: New England Holidays, A* (Ives)
"Dedication" (Longfellow), 574
Deep South Suite (Ellington), 454
Deepwater Horizon oil spill, 904
DeForest, John William, 50n17
Delacroix, Eugène, 395
DeLamarter, Eric, 453
Delgadillo, Luis Abraham, 34, *755*, 757
Delgado, Sergio, 761
Delos record label, 11

Index

Del Tredici, David, 22, 488, *794,* 901
DeMille, Cecile B., 388
democracy and democratic themes, 311–312, 362, 396, 666
De Organizer (Johnson), 418
Desclos, Anne, 497
Desde la infancia (Gandarias), 756
Desenne, Paul, *699,* 715
Des Knaben Wunderhorn, 604
Dethier, Gaston, 502
Detroit Civic Orchestra, 422
Detroit Symphony Orchestra, 11, *20,* 819, 918
Deutsche Tanzbühne (Velasco-Maidana), 706
Dewey, John, 517
Dharma at Big Sur, The (Adams), 873
Diaghilev, Sergei, 683
Diálogo de octubre (Gonzalo), 769
Diamond, David, **559–575**; and Blitzstein, 317; and Boulanger, 315; and commercial recordings of symphonic works, 11; and Copland, 323; and Creston, 505; and elements of American modernism, 486–487; and the Federal Music Project, 311; and Hovhaness, 534; and Liebermann, 901; and Mennin, 617, 619; and Perry, 626; and Persichetti, 580, 583; and Schuman, 513; and Sessions, 488, 492, 496; and shifting center of American symphonic activity, 486; symphonies' movements and instrumentation, *561–564;* and tensions within midcentury American symphony, 635. *See also specific composition titles*
Dianda, Hilda, *674,* 681
Dias de Oliveira, Manoel, 681
Díaz, Porfirio, 737
Díaz de Armendariz, Miguel, 709
Dib, Mohammed, 883
Dick, Marcel, 453
Dickinson, Emily, 865
Die Harmonie der Welt Symphony (Hindemith), 440
Die Jakobsleiter (Schoenberg), 271
Diemecke, Enrique, 750
Die Sarazenen (MacDowell), 126, 164
Die schöne Aldâ (MacDowell), 126, 164
Dies irae (Gregorian chant), 884
"Dies irae" movement from Verdi's Requiem Mass (1873), 620
d'Indy, Vincent, 456, 457, 666, 685
Din-Torah, 600, 601, 605

Diquis culture, 760
"Dirge, The" (from Symphony No. 2, *The Age of Anxiety;* Bernstein), 589
Distant Choir, 232–234, 245, 282–283, *283*
distinctive qualities of symphonies from U.S., **23–36,** 51n25
Divertimento (Herrarte), 754
Divertimento for Orchestra (Becerra), 701
Divertimento No. 15 in B-flat Major (Mozart), 812
Dixie (Emmett), 262
Dixon, Dean, 377, 631
DJs, 909
Doctor Atomic (Adams), 864, *868,* 872
dodecaphony, 758, 762, 811
Dodworth, Harvey B., 67, 68
Dolin, Samuel, *38*
dollar diplomacy, 735–736, 757
Domingo, Plácido, 676
Dominican order, 711
Dominican Republic, *766–767,* **772–773**
Donizetti, Gaetano, 182
Donne, John, 865
Don Rodrigo (Ginastera), 676
Dorati, Antal, 7, 264, 346, 439, 485, 527, 532, 670
Dorian, Frederick, 440
Dorian mode, 742
"Dorian" Toccata and Fugue in D Minor (Bach), 182, 244
Dorita (Santos), 756
Dorrnance (Woodbury), 246, 277
Dorsey, Tommy, 337–338
Dos trozos para danza (Ley), 754
double consciousness, 382, 634
Douglas, Paul, *41*
Dover Air Force Base, 500
Down East Overture (Ives), 199, 291n27
Downes, Edward, 558, 570–571, 584
Downes, Olin: on Chadwick's *Sinfonietta,* 151; on *chavistas/revueltistas* conflict, 750; on Creston's Symphony No. 2, 508; on influence of traditionalism, 648n140; on Ives's Symphony No. 2, 215; on Ives's Symphony No. 4, 249; on Naumburg awards, 496; on Paniagua's *Mayan Legend,* 753; on Persichetti's Symphony No. 4, 579; on Schuman's Symphony No. 3, 525; on Still's *From the Land of Dreams,* 425; support for Villa-Lobos, 685
Drake, Francis, 772

"Dream of a Witches' Sabbath" (Berlioz *Symphonie fantastique*), 579
"dream of the morning sky" (Cycle V) (Kernis), 893
Drucker, Stanley, 831
Druckman, Jacob, 886, 893
Drury Lane Theatre, 71
Du Bois, W. E. B., 382, 625, 634
Dudamel, Gustavo, 713
Duffalo, Richard, *12*
Dukas, Paul, 163, 340, 459
Dukelsky, Vladimir (Vernon Duke), *9*, 453
Duke Street (Hatton), 265, 266, 296n128
Dun, Tan, 916
Dunbar, Paul Laurence, 428–429, 430
d'Urbano, Jorge, 675
Dürer, Albrecht, 162
During Camp Meetin' Week-One Secular Afternoon (Ives), 285. *See also Orchestral Set No. 3* (Ives)
Dvořák, Antonín: advocacy of African American music, 410; and Beach, 53n52, 157, 159, 167; and Bristow, 98–99; and Chadwick, 146–147; and Dawson, 412; and emergence of Black composers, 382; enthusiasm for folk influences, 126–127; and evolution of American symphonic style, 312, 797; and "Great American Symphony" trope, 4, 6; and Hailstork, 858; and Hanson, 372; and Ives, 185, 188, 193, 194–195, 201, 291n24, 291n43; and Johnson, 415; and key influences on American repertoire, 21; and Marsalis, 907; and Price, 420, 423, 424; and tensions within midcentury American symphony, 635; and Thompson, 381
Dwight, John Sullivan: and ethnic conflict in early American symphony, 69–70; on Fry, 101, 108; on idealization of classical orchestral music, 123; on Paine's compositions, 137; and scope of American symphonic repertoire, 1, 3; and social context of symphonic repertoire, 311
Dwight's Journal of Music, 92, 95
Dybbuk, The (Bernstein), 596
Dying Soldier, The (Fry), *103*, 109–110

Earth Is Born, The (film; score by Schuman), 513, 528
East Asian idioms and influences, 553
Eastern Europe, 391
Eastern Music Festival, 904
East Germany, 454
Eastman Overture, An (Walker), 816
Eastman School of Music: and Diamond, 559; and Flores, 761; and Guevara, 708; and Hanson, 362, 365; and Herrarte, 754; and Hovhaness, 533; and Mennin, 610, 613; and Read, 457; and Rouse, 878; and Vardell, 459; and Zohn-Muldoon, 752
Eberl, Anton, 62
Eckhardt-Gramatté, Sophie-Carmen, *37*
eclecticism: and Adams, 872; and Albert, 864; as analytical tool, 314; and Antheil, 396; and Bernstein, 607, 609; and Blitzstein, 318, 463n53; and Bolcom, 842; and briefly mentioned midcentury composers, 641; and Chadwick, 151, 153; and Corigliano, 831, 834, 838; and Cowell, 404, 406, 409; and education of American composers, 32; and Fairouz, 919; and "forgotten modernisms," 34; and Harrison, 803, 806; and Hindemith, 440; and Ives, 286; and Kernis, 893; and key influences on American repertoire, 22–23; and Larsen, 884; and Perry, 626, 634; and Persichetti, 580; and scope of American symphonic repertoire, 6; and Sessions, 501; and South American composers, 667; and Thompson, 380
École Normale de Musique de Paris, 459, 708, 754
economic conditions, 123, 309, 450. *See also* Great Depression
Ecos de la libertad (Mena), 773
Ecos de mi tierra (Colón), 774
Ecuador, *697–698,* **707–709**
Ecuatorial (Varèse), 753
Edition Adler, 256
Edward, Michel, *47*
Edwards, Jonathan, 249
Edwards, Michelle, 631
Edwin A. Fleisher Collection, 185
Ehrenberg, Carl, 164
Eichmann, Adolf, 601
1898 Overture (Torres Santos), 775
1861-1865-Hours of Joy-Hours of Sorrow (Bloch), 437. *See also America: An Epic Rhapsody* (Bloch)
eight-movement works, *28*
Eine Lustige Ouverture für Grosses Orchester (Ippisch), 754
Einstein, Albert, 598
Eisenhower, Dwight D., 513

Index

Eisfeld, Theodore, 68, 90
Eisler, Hanns, 454
Eisler, Paul, 252
Eisner, Erich, 667, 706
El Árbol de la vida (Ortíz), 753
El Destello de Hiroshima (Orellana), 755
El Dorado (Adams), 873
Eldorado (concert venue), 682
electronic and electroacoustic music: and Bates, 913, 915–916; and Cuban composers, 769, 771; and El Salvadoran composers, 756; and evolution of American symphonic style, 793; and future of American symphony, 924; and Guatemalan composers, 756; Márquez, 752; and Mónaco, 714; and South American composers, 667; and Villalpando, 708
Elegía (En memoria de los heroes del pueblo cubano caídos en la lucha y la justicia) (Blanco), 769
Elegía a Machu Picchu (Garrido-Lecca), 704
Elegía andina (Frank), 705
Elegiac Symphony (Harrison), *794*, 803, *804*
Elegía sobre temas de Vicente Emilio Sojo (Carreño), 714
Elegy to Our Forefathers, An (Ives), **279–280**, 284. See also *Orchestral Set No. 2* (Ives)
Elfrida Whiteman Scholarship, 559
Elgar, Edward, 147, 453
El güegüense (street play), 758
El hombre maya (Ayala), 751
Elizabeth I, Queen of England, 772
Elizabeth Sprague Coolidge Medal, 457
El Jardín encantado (Orellana), 754
Elkus, Jonathan, 200–201, 264
Ellington, Edward Kennedy ("Duke"), viii, 11, 33, 313, 382, 454, 487, 801, 908
Elliott, Charlotte, 221
Elliott, J. W., 244
El milagro de anaquillé (Roldán), 768
Elogio a la Plena (Ortiz-Alvarado), 775
El salón México (Copland), 323, 770
El Salvador, 735, *755*, **756**
El Sistema (Venezuela), 711, 715
Elson, Louis C., 4, 125, 141, 147
El Terremoto del Jueves Santo (Gómez), 715
El Toro Huaco (Jiménez), 757
Eltze, Guillermo Frick, 695–699
Elwell, Herbert, 438
Emancipation Proclamation, 340
Emanuel African Methodist Episcopal Church, 822, 859
Emerson, Lake, and Palmer, 720n64
émigré composers, 310–311, 314, **433–450**, *434–435*, 486
Emmeline (Picker), 891
Emmett, Daniel, 262
Emperor Jones, The (Gruenberg), 454
Empress Queen of the Magyars, The (Heinrich), 76, 81, *82*, 84
Encircling Skies (Larsen), 886
Endo, Akira, *12*
Enescu, George, 340
En las ruinas del Templo del Sol (Pedrell), 704
Eno, Brian, 822, 828, 830–831
En Oriente: boceto para orquesta (Riestra), 703
Enríquez, Manuel, *738, 740,* 752
En Saga (Sibelius), 365
Ensayo (Bolaños), 704
Ensayo para orquesta (Salazar), 762–764
Entartete Musik Exhibition, 439
Envoi (Rouse), 873
Episcopal Cathedral of Saint James, 374
Episodios sinfónicos (Alfagüell), 761
Erazo, Norma, 757
Erickson, Frank, 636
Ericson, Raymond, 559
Erie (Converse), 219, *220–221*
Erosão (Villa-Lobos), 691
Escala, José Luis Cajar, 762
Escenas campesinas (Allende), 699
Escenas dominicanas (Lovelace), 772
Eschig, Max, 754
Escobar, María Luisa, 714
Escot, Pozzi, 705
Eshu: la porte des enfers (Chagas), 695
Esnaola, Juan Pedro, 672
Espacio Ritual (Aquino), 773
Espinosa, Guillermo, 710
Estacio, John, *47*
Estampas (Sebastiani), 681
Estancia (Ginastera), 667, 677–678, *678–679*, 720n64
Esterhazy, Hildy, 593
Estévez, Milton, *697*
Estévez Aponte, Antonio, 34, 667, 713–715
Estrada, Julio, 752
Estrella Veroes de Méscoli, Blanca, 714

Estudio de Fonología Musical, 714
E.T. (film), 374
"Eternal Rules of the Ceaseless Round" (John White Chadwick), 883
ethnic identity and conflict, 50n2, 67–70, 451, 553–555, 666
Etkin, Mariano, 681
Etude, 309
Europe, James Reese, 774
European idioms and influences: and Bernstein, 54n99, 585; and Bloch, 438; and distinctive qualities of American symphony, 29; and education of American-based composers, 314; of émigré composers, 433; European-trained composers, **315–381**; and first generation of American symphonists, 60–62, 62–66; and founding of permanent orchestras in US, 124–125; and Hindemith, 440–441; and Hovhaness, 554; and Ives, 199, 201, 215, 217, 286; key influences on American repertoire, 21–23; and Larsen, 883–884; and maturation of American symphonic activity, 310; and Perry, 634; and Schuman, 517; and Sessions, 492; in South America, 665; and South American composers, 666; and Still, 433; and Stravinsky, 448; and Strong, 160; and tensions within midcentury American symphony, 487, 635; and Thomson, 354; and Venezuela's El Sistema, 711
Euterpiad, The (periodical), 71
evangelism, 665. *See also* missionaries
Evans, Bill, 908
Evening Land Symphony (Schwantner), 794, 796
"Evenings on the Roof" concerts, 447
Ewen, David, 358
Ewing, Alexander, 284
Ex Machina (Bolaños), 760
experimental music, 289n1, 349, 409, 633. *See also* avant-garde music; electronic and electroacoustic music
Ezequiel Bernal prize, 710

Fabien Sevitzky Prize, 680
Fabini, Eduardo, 668–669, *669*
Fabordones (Billoni), 737
Fairouz, Mohammed, **919–923**; and evolution of American symphonic style, 795; and future of American symphony, 923, 924; and Ives, 286; and key influences on American repertoire, 23; and Mahler, 22; and scope of American symphonic repertoire, 2; symphonies' movements and instrumentation, *920–921*; symphony premiere dates, *795*. *See also specific composition titles*
Falabella, Roberto, *696*, 701
Fall 1961 (Lowell), 597
Falletta, JoAnn, *13*
Fancy Free (Bernstein), 593
Fanfare for the Common Man (Copland), 323, 324
Fanfarria para despertar a Papá Montero (Roldán), 768
Fanfarria para despertar espíritus apolillados (Caturla), 768
Fantasia and Fugue in G Minor (Bach), 150
Fantasía del Equivocado Fritz (Lorenz), 715
Fantasía sinfónica (Casal Chapí), 772
Fantasy in Space (Luening), 408
Farías, Miguel, *696*, 702
Fariñas, Carlos, 771
Farnsley, Charles, 486
Farruca (Bolaños), 760
Farský, Pavel, 85
Farwell, Arthur, 126, 326
Faucett, Bill F., 150
Fauser, Annegret, 2, 313
Faust (Goethe), 162, 598
Faust (Gounod), 677
Faust Symphony, A (Liszt), 99
Fearful Symmetries (Adams), 872
Fechner, Gustav, 569
Federal Music Project (FMP), 31, 311, 422, 517
Federal Street (Oliver), 265, 296n128
Federation of Musical Clubs, 154
Feffer, Antonietta, 693
Feffer, Leon, 693
Feldman, Morton, 775
Fennell, Frederick, 583
Ferdinand I, Emperor of Austria, 81
Ferdinand VI, King of Spain, 709
Ferguson, Donald, 346
Ferial (Ponce), 741
Fernández, José Loyola, 771
Fernández, Oscar Lorenzo, *683*, 692
Fernández de Jáuregui bookshop, 737
Fernández Hidalgo, Gutierre, 702, 705, 707
Ferneyhough, Brian, 761
Feste Romane (Respighi), 838

Index

Festival de la Cultura Iberoamericana, 708
Festival of American Music, 188, 310, 362, 459
Fiala, George, *39*
Ficciones (Lavista), 752
Ficher, Jacobo, *673, 674,* 675
Fiedler, Max, 124
Fiesta de la Naval, 711
fiestas, 666
54th Regiment, Massachusetts Volunteer Infantry, 272, 273
Figueredo, Carlos, *698,* 714
film music: and American musical pedagogy, 383; and Antheil, 396; and Bates, 915; and Brouwer, 771; contributions to symphonic repertoire, 468n231; and Eisler, 454; and evolving audiences for symphonic music, 451–452; and Glass, 822; and Herrmann, 455; and Hovhaness, 555; and hybrid orchestral styles, 313; and Johnson, 415, 417; and Korngold, 455; and Mónaco, 714; and Moncayo, 751; and Revueltas, 750; and Schuman, 513; and Still, 432, 433–434; and Stravinsky, 447, 449–450; and Toch, 459; and Torres-Santos, 775
Filtz, Anton, 61, 62
Final Alice (Del Tredici), *794*
Final para una sinfonía imaginaria (Casal Chapí), 772
Fine, Irving, 405–406, 531, 637
Finnegans Wake (Joyce), 860
Finney, Ross Lee, 637
"Finnish tango," 680
Firebird (Stravinsky), 683–684
First Choral Symphony (Holst), 614
First Congregationalist Church (Danbury), 182
First Edition Music label, 11, *12,* 21, 580
First Festival of Latin American Music, 676, 746, 770
first generation of American symphonists, **60–117**; Bristow, **85–100**; early New York Philharmonic, **66–67**; and ethnic conflict, **67–70**; first American symphonists, **62–66**; first US orchestras, **61–62**; Fry, **100–110**; Gottschalk, **110–116**; Heinrich, **71–85**
First Symphony for Band (Bolcom), *841,* 845
Fisher, Marjory M., 496
Fisher's Hornpipe (fiddle tune), 251
Five Folksongs in Counterpoint (Price), 471n343
five-movement works, *27–28*
Five Pieces for Orchestra (Schoenberg), 913

Flagello, Nicolas, viii, 637
Fleisher Collection, 774
Flight into Egypt, The (Harbison), 849
Florencia en el Amazonas (Catán), 752
Flores, Bernal, 761
Flores, José Asunción, 671
Flórez-Estrada, Antonio Gervasoni, 705
Fluxus, 775
Flying on the Scaly Backs of Our Mountains (Wang), *917,* 919
Focke, Fré, 701
folk idioms and influences: and Antheil, 395; and Barber, 358; and Bates, 915; and Beach, 158, 159; and Blitzstein, 317; and Bloch, 438; and Bolcom, 844; and Chávez, 741–742; and Copland, 324; and Cordero, 762; and Cowell, 406; and Dawson, 410–411, 412; and Diamond, 565; and distinctive qualities of American symphony, 29; and Dvořák, 126; and evolution of American symphonic style, 797; folk-based nationalism, 30; and folk jazz, 54n93; and Fonseca, 760–761; and "Great American Symphony" trope, 4, 451; and Hailstork, 859; and Hanson, 365; and Harrison, 806; and Heinrich, 80; and Holguín, 710; and Honduran composers, 756–757; and huapangos, 749–750; and key influences on American repertoire, 21; and Liebermann, 908; and Lorenz, 715; and Marchena, 773; and Martinů, 443–444; and Mexican composers, 740; and Nicaraguan composers, 757–758; and Ortíz, 753; and Perry, 626, 632; and Persichetti, 583; and Piston, 348; and Powell, 457; and Price, 422–423; and radio broadcasting, 313; and Revueltas, 749–750; and scope of American symphonic repertoire, 3; and South American composers, 666–667, 672, 675–678, 681, 683, 692, 694; and Sowerby, 374, 377; and Stravinsky, 450; and Thompson, 379; and Thomson, 353; and Vargas Candia, 706; and Walker, 819. *See also* vernacular idioms and influences
Fonseca, Julio, *755,* 760
Foote, Arthur, 125, 126
Forbes, Elliot, 379–380
Ford, Clifford, *43*
Ford, Henry, 914
Ford Foundation, 7, 485
For He's a Jolly Good Fellow (traditional), 251, 353
Forsyth, Malcolm, *41*
Forte, Allen, 507

Fort Smith (Arkansas) Symphony, 424
Fortspinnung, 502, 510, 511–512, 572
Forty-Eighters, 68
Foss, Lukas, 439, 513, 594, 637, 811
Foster, Stephen: and Gottschalk, 112–114; and Ives, 175, 206, *207*, 212, 213, 215, 230, 242, 251, 272, 275, 279; and Price, 472n350; and Walker, 822. *See also specific composition titles*
Fountain (Mason), 227
Fountain, Robin, 110
Four Freedoms—A Symphony after Four Paintings by Norman Rockwell (Bennett), 452
Four Saints in Three Acts (Thomson), 350
Fourth of July, The (Ives), *178, 240,* 241, 249, **256–264,** *263,* 265, 267, 280, 285. See also *Symphony: New England Holidays, A* (Ives)
Fragmented Memories (Velázquez), 771
France, 52n41, 153, 350, 446, 560, 677
Franciscan order, 665, 668, 707, 711, 736, 737
Francis of Assisi, Saint, 339
Franck, César, 188, 193, 194, 635
Franco, Francisco, 667, 741, 749, 778
Franco, Hernando, 736, 753
Frank, Gabriela Lena, *697,* 705
Frankenstein, Alfred, 409, 437
Frank Leslie's Illustrated Newspaper, 92
Freed, Isadore, 439
Freed, Richard D., 573
Freedman, Harry, *39*
Free Library, 667
Freeman, Paul, 377
French Ministry of Education, 446
French Neoclassicism, 560
Friso Araucano Americano (Isamitt), 699
From Hanover Square North (Ives), **281–284**. See also *Orchestral Set No. 2* (Ives)
Fromm Foundation, 816
From the Land of Dreams (Still), 425
From the Northland (Sowerby), 376, 377
Frost, Robert, 500
Fry, Joseph, 100
Fry, William Henry, **100–110**; background and education, 100–104; and *The Breaking Heart,* 104–105; and Bristow, 90, 91; and *Childe Harold,* 108–109; and *A Day in the Country,* 105–106; and distinctive qualities of American symphony, 24; and *The Dying Soldier,* 109–110; and ethnic conflict in early American symphony, 68, 69; and Gottschalk, 110, 112, 115; and *Hagar in the Wilderness,* 109–110; and key influences on American repertoire, 21; and *Niagara,* 109; and *Santa Claus: Christmas Symphony,* 107–108; and scope of American symphonic repertoire, 5–6; and support for American symphony, 6; symphonies' movements and instrumentation, *102–103*. See also *specific composition titles*
fugal techniques, 573
Fugue in D-sharp Minor (Bach), 760
Fujihara Music Company, 559
Fulbright Scholarships, 553, 560, 758
Fuleihan, Anis, 454
funereal symphonies, 392
Furriol, Jacinta, 668
Furtwängler, Wilhelm, 439, 712
"Future: Heaven, the Rise of All to the Spiritual" (Ives *Universe Symphony*), 269
futurism, 456. *See also* avant-garde music; experimental music

Gabirol, Solomon ibn, 900
Gade, Niels, 67
Gaelic idioms and influences, 158
gagaku music, 553
Galimany, Alberto, 761–762
Galindo, Blas, *738, 740,* 751–752, 761–762
Gallardo, Lino, 711
Gallic idioms and influences, 150
Gandarias, Igor de, 756
Gandini, Gerardo, *674,* 680, 764
Gann, Kyle, 23, 100, 417
Gante, Pedro de, 736
García, Fernando, *696,* 701
Garcia, José Maurício Nunes, 682
García, Juan Francisco, 766, 772
García Ascot, Rosa, 741
García Mansilla, Eduardo, 672, *673*
García Morillo, Roberto, 742
García Zorro, Gonzalo, 709
Garrido, Pablo, *696,* 700
Garrido-Lecca, Celso, *697,* 704
Garryowen (traditional), 242, 251
Gate 5 Records, 635
Gayfer, James, *38*
Gazebo Dances (Corigliano), 834
Gebhard, Heinrich, 533
Gebrauchsmusik, 379
Geechee culture, 415
Gellman, Steven, *43*

Index

Gemini IV mission, 913
Genesis, Book of, 620
Gentry, Philip, 595
Gericke, Wilhelm, 124, 125
Gerk, Sarah, 159
German cultural influences: and Bernstein, 592, 656n432; and Chadwick, 153, 156; and ethnic conflict in early American symphony, 68; German Romanticism, 21; and Ginastera, 680; and Hindemith, 440–441; influence on American repertoire, 310; and Second New England School, 125; and Strong, 160; and Velasco-Maidana, 706
Germania Musical Society, 68
Gershwin, George, 313, 415, 429–430, 462n22, 487, 589–590, 594, 767
Gershwin Memorial Award, 613
Gestos (Schwartz), 775
"Gettysburg Address" (Lincoln), 339, 340
Ghana, 858
Ghosts of Versailles, The (Corigliano), 286, 831, 835
Giannini, Bruto, 382, 415
Giannini, Vittorio, viii, 637–638
Gianoli, Antonio, 756
Gilbert, Henry, 126
Gilded Age, 123, 167
Gillis, Don, 638
Gilman, Laurence, 249
Gilmore, Patrick, 148
Giménez, Florentín, 54n97, *669,* 672
Giménez, Remberto, 672
Ginastera, Alberto, **676–681**; and "American" identity issues, 48; and Bolivian composers, 706; and expanding role of music in South America, 666; and Gutiérrez, 761; and influence of Berkshire Music Center, 667; orchestral works, *674*; return to Argentina, 665; symphonic works, *673. See also specific composition titles*
Ginsburg, Allen, 828
Girando, danzando (Sánchez-Gutiérrez), 752
Girl I Left behind Me, The (traditional), 281
Gläser, Carl Gotthelf, 219
Glass, Philip, **822–831**; and Adams, 864–865; and Boulanger's influence, 315; and commercial recordings of symphonic works, 11; and evolution of American symphonic style, 795; and Fairouz's works, 922; and future of American symphony, 923; and "Great American Symphony" trope, 6; and Persichetti, 578; and Rouse, 878; and support for American symphony, 9; symphonies' movements and instrumentation, *823–827*; symphony premiere dates, *794, 795. See also specific composition titles*
Glassworks (Glass), 822
Glick, Srul Irving, *41*
Globe Theater, 250
Gloria of a Mass in D (Lamas), 712
Glorias andinas (Traversari), 708
Glück, Louise, 849
Gnattali, Radames, 722n109
God Be with You (Tomer), 242
God Save the Emperor variations (Heinrich), 72
Goethe, Johann Wolfgang von, 891
Goetschius, Percy, 415, 458
Goldberg, Albert, 434, 446
Goldman, Richard Franko, 409, 440, 531
Goldman Band, 583–584
Golijov, Osvaldo, 681, 916
Gomes, André da Silva, 682
Gomes, Carlos, 682
Gómez, Luis Ernesto, *699,* 715
Gomezanda, Antonio, *739,* 740
Gómez Restrepo, Antonio, 710
González Bravo, Antonio, 706
González-Gamarra, Franciso, 704
Gonzalo, Gisela Hernández, 769
Goodman, Benny, 908
Good Neighbor policy, 666–667, 692, 757, 769
Goodnight, Ladies (Christy), 252
Goossens, Eugene, 228, 454
Gordillo, Bernard, 757
Górecki, Henryk, 797
gospel music, 182, 211, 282, 630. *See also* hymns
Goss, Robert, 409
Gota de Noche (Sánchez-Gutiérrez), 752
Gotham, Nic, *46*
Gottlieb, Jack, 590–591, 593, 595, 597–600, 604
Gottschalk, Louis Moreau, **110–116**; and *À Montevideo,* **114–115**; background and education, 110–112; and Cervantes, 765; and key influences on American repertoire, 21; performances in Puerto Rico, 773; and *Symphonie romantique,* **112–114**; symphonies' movements and instrumentation, *111*
Gould, Glenn, 586
Gould, Morton, 188, 279, 313, 454, 506
Gounod, Charles, 709

Index

"Gracias a la vida" (Parra), 702
Graetzer, Guillermo, *674*, 675
Graham, Martha, 404, 449, 513, 553
Gramatges, Harold, *766*, 769, 771
Grammy Awards, 835
Grand Army of the Republic, 295n110
Grand Pianola Music (Adams), 865
Grand Slam Jam (Ellington), 454
Grand Symphonie (Barros), 668
Grand Testimonial Concert (for Bristow), 92
Grand Valedictory Concert (Heinrich), 72, 80
Gran Fantasía Sinfónica (Fonseca), 760–761
Gran obertura de concierto (Quintón), 774
Gran sinfonia eroica (Heinrich), *73*, 78
Grant, Stewart, *43*
Grätzer, Wilhelm, 675
Grawemeyer Award, 872, 900
"Great American Symphony" trope: and Bernstein, 585, 595; and Blitzstein's *Airborne Symphony*, 319; and Chadwick, 147; and Copland, 326; and Cowell, 409; establishment of "Great American Symphony Orchestra," 309; evolving meaning of, 484; and future of American symphony, 924; and Great American novel model, 50n17; and Harbison, 845; and Harris, 334, 520; impact on American symphonic development, 3–5, 450–451; and interwar optimism, 312; and maturation of American symphonic activity, 309; and postwar era, 314; and Rochberg, 807; and tensions within midcentury American symphony, 487; and Thompson, 379
Great Depression, 3, 31, 309, 311, 313, 323, 798
Great Dictator, The (film; score by Willson), 460
Great Migration, 420
Great Military March for Orchestra (Ballivián), 706
Great Republic, The (Bristow), 86
Great River Symphony (Bacon), 452
Greene, Freddie, 908
Greenwich Orchestra, 517–518
Greenwich Village, 425
Gregorian chant, 362, 506, 508, 509
Gregory, Eugenia Giannini, 625
Grohg (Copland), 463n55
Grossman, Jorge Villavicencio, 705
Groupe de Recherches Musicales, 681
Grove Music Online, 636
Gruenberg, Louis, 454
Grupo de los Cuatro, 751

Grupo Renovación Musical, 768–769
Gruppen (Stockhausen), 286
guaranía genre, 671
Guaraní Indians, 668, 681
Guarnieri, Mozart Camargo, 34, 52n50, *683*, *684*, **692–694**, 762
Guatemala, **753–756**, *755*
Guatemala (Castillo), 753–754
Guatemala (Vidal), 754
Guatemala City Cathedral, 753
Guerra, Yalil, 771
Guerra-Peixe, César, *683*, *684*, 693–694
Guerrero, Giancarlo, *14*
Guevara, Ernesto ("Che"), 702, 704
Guevara, Gerardo, 667, *697*, 708
Guggenheim Foundation and Fellowships: and Cowell, 396, 471n337; and Creston, 505; and Diamond, 559; and Ginastera, 665, 676, 680; and Harris, 471n337; and Hovhaness, 553; and Johnson, 418; and Kernis, 897; and Luzuriaga, 708; and Mennin, 610; and Orbón, 769–770; and Orrego-Salas, 700; and Perry, 624; and Persichetti, 584; and Piston, 471n337; and Prudencio, 707; recipients listed, 471n337; and Schuman, 519, 527; and Sessions, 488; and Still, 425, 471n337; and Thompson, 380, 471n337; and Thomson, 471n337; and Valcárcel, 704
Guidelines for Style Analysis (LaRue), xiii
Guillén, Nicolás, 749
Gullah culture, 415
Gutiérrez, Benjamín, 761
Gutiérrez, Julio, 769
Gutiérrez Heras, Joaquín, *738, 740*, 752
Guzmán, Federico, 695
Gyrowetz, Adalbert, 61

Ha'aretz, 606
Haas, Robert, 849
habanera (dance), 112, 424
Hadley, Henry Kimball, viii, *9*, 454
"Haffner" Symphony (Symphony No. 35, Mozart), 520
Hagen, Theodore, 91, 92, 95, 108–109
Hahn, Christopher, 655n397
Hail! Columbia (Phile), 115, 242, 262, 276
Hailstork, Adolphus, 35, *794*, *795*, **856–859**, *857*. *See also specific composition titles*
Halcyon community, 396
Hale, Philip, 125, 146, 151, 159

Index

Halffter, Cristóbal, 774
Halffter, Rodolfo, *739*, 741, 752, 761
Hall, Lillian, 625
Hamburg (Mason), 211
Hamburg Hochschule für Musik, 775
Hamilton, Charles, 608
Hamlet and Ophelia (MacDowell), 126
Hamm, Charles, 484
Hampton, Lionel, 908
Hampton Institute, 625
Hancock, Herbie, 908
Handel, George Frideric, 99, 244, 878, 901
Handy, W. C., 387, 415, 424–425
Hangmen Also Die! (film; score by Eisler), 454
Hannah, Ronald, *43*
Hanslick, Eduard, 101
Hanson, Howard, **362–374**; and Cold War cultural politics, 485; and commercial recordings of symphonic works, 11; and conflicts over modernism, 313; and Cowell, 405; and emergence of Black composers, 382; and European aesthetic and training, 354; and the Federal Music Project, 311; and Gutiérrez, 761; and Herrarte, 754; and key influences on American repertoire, 21; and Mennin, 610; Mercury recordings, *20*; and Oldberg, 457; and Piston, 341, 344; premiere of key works during Koussevitsky's tenure, *9*; and radio broadcasting, 310; and scope of American symphonic repertoire, 2, 6; and shifting center of American symphonic activity, 486; and Still, 425, 430, 433; and support for American symphony, 7; symphonies' movements and instrumentation, *363–364*; and Thompson, 379, 380; and Ward, 459. *See also specific composition titles*
Happy Day (traditional), 280–281
Harbison, John, 9, 22, 24, 35, 488, *794, 795*, **845–849**, *846–847*, 859. *See also specific composition titles*
Harlem, 313, 382, 425, 430
"Harlem Love Song" (Johnson; from Mvt. II of *Harlem Symphony*), 417
Harlem Mendelssohn Union, 86
Harlem Renaissance, 33, 54n93, 382, 422, 626
Harlem stride, 415
Harlem Symphony (Johnson), 33, 313, 382, 410, **415–418**, *416*
Harmonic Materials of Modern Music (Hanson), 373

Harmonielehre (Adams), viii, 24, *794*, 865, *866*, *870*, 871–872, 878
Harmonium (Adams), 865, *866*, 872
Harold in Italy (Berlioz), 812
Harris, Roy, **326–340**; and Antheil, 387; and Barber, 356; and commercial recordings of symphonic works, 11; and Creston, 513; and Diamond, 565; and distinctive qualities of American symphony, 24, 29; and emergence of postmodern style, 634; Fourth and Fifth Symphonies, **337–340**; and "Great American Symphony" trope, 6, 451; Guggenheim Fellowship, 471n337; and Hovhaness, 534, 555; and influence of émigré composers, 433; and Ives, 200, 286; and Johnson, 415; and key influences on American repertoire, 21, 22; and Mennin, 623; and Persichetti, 578, 579, 582; premiere of key works during Koussevitsky's tenure, *9*; and radio broadcasting, 310; and Schuman, 513, 517, 519, 524, 527, 531; and scope of American symphonic repertoire, 2, 5–6; and Sibelius, 468n238; and social context of symphonic repertoire, 311; and South American composers, 677; symphonies' movements and instrumentation, *327–333*; and tensions within American art music, 486; Third Symphony, **334–337**; and Thompson, 379. *See also specific composition titles*
Harrison, Jay S., 616, *804–805*, 812
Harrison, Lou, **802–807**; and Bates, 916; and Cowell, 409; and distinctive qualities of American symphony, 23; and evolution of American symphonic style, 795; and "Great American Symphony" trope, 6; and Hovhaness, 534; and Ives, 200, 215, 218; symphonies' movements and instrumentation, *804–805*; symphony premiere dates, *794*. *See also specific composition titles*
Hart, Weldon, 406
Harth-Bedoya, Miguel, 709
Hartke, Stephen, *795*
Hartsough, Lewis, 244, 280
Hartt College of Music, 771
Harvard Musical Association Orchestra, 141
Harvard University, 340, 453, 488, 519, 590–591, 801
"Harvest Work Theme" (Ives), 264–265
Harvey, Jonathan, 702
Hasidism, 890
Hatton, John, 265
Haubiel, Charles, 519

Haupt, Carl August, 127
Hauptstimme markings, 803
Havana Municipal Conservatory, 768
Hawkins, Coleman, 908
Hawthorne, Nathaniel, 50n17
Haydn, Joseph: and Bernstein, 585; and Bristow, 91, 92; and Diamond, 571; and European influence on American repertoire, 60; and first American symphonists, 63; and Ives, 184, 270; and Mexican symphonic music, 737; and origins of American orchestras, 61–62; and Persichetti, 579, 583; and Rochberg, 813; and South American composers, 681; and Stravinsky, 448
Heard, Alan, *42*
Hebrew Children, The (Walker), 210
Hebrew language, 591, 654n356, 693, 702
Heiden, Bernard, 55n105
Heifetz, Jascha, 451
Heinrich, Anthony Philip, **71–85**; American national symphonies, 78–80; background and education, 71–72; and ethnic conflict in early American symphony, 68; and Gottschalk, 110, 114; and key influences on American repertoire, 21; and memorial symphonies, 84–85; and national symphonies, 80–82; symphonies' movements and instrumentation, *73–77*; symphonies on Native American subjects, 82–84
Heiress, The (film; score by Copland), 451
He Is There! (Ives), 298n162
Hell's Kitchen neighborhood, 415
Helvetia (Bloch), 437, 454
hemiolas, 148, 150, 256, 337, 362, 372, 376, 623, 631
Hemsley, David, *42*
Henahan, Donal, 319
Henderson, W. J., 21
Hendl, Walter, 486, 613, 615
Henschel, Georg, 124
Herbert, Victor, 454
Hernández, José, 672
Hernández Marín, Rafael, 774
Hernández Moncada, Eduardo, *738, 739,* 740
"Heroes" Symphony (Glass), 35. *See also* Symphony No. 4, "Heroes" (Glass)
Hérold, Ferdinand, 201
Herrarte, Manuel, 754
Herrera de la Fuente, Luis, 704
Herrmann, Bernard, 5, 200, 218, 228, 455
Herz, Henri, 682
Herzog, Georg, 700

Hess, Carol A., 34–35
Hétu, Jacques, 36, *42*
Hewitt, James, 62
Hexachord and Its Relation to the Twelve-Tone Row, The (Rochberg), 528
Hidalgo, Fernández, 707
Higginson, Henry Lee, 124–125, 141, 311
High Fidelity, 632, 771
Hill, Edward Burlingame, 455
Hill, Ureli Corelli, 70
Hiller, Lejaren, 775
Hilsberg, Alexander, 584
Himno sinfónico (Campa), 737
Hindemith, Paul, **439–441**; and Argentinian composers, 675; and "Great American Symphony" trope, 451; and influence of émigré composers, 433, 434; and Mennin, 613, 614; and OSSODRE, 670; and Persichetti, 578, 582, 585; and Shapero, 458; symphonies written in America, 435. *See also specific composition titles*
Hiroshima bombing, 484
Hirschorn Museum and Sculpture Garden, 532
Histoire du soldat (Stravinsky), 318
History of the Sonata Idea (Newman), viii
Hitler, Adolf, 601, 675, 701–702, 778
Ho, Vincent, 47
Hoffman, William M., 835
Holden, Oliver, 244
Holguín, Guillermo Uribe, 34, *698,* 710
Holidays Symphony (Ives). *See Symphony: New England Holidays, A* (Ives)
Holland, Bernard, 319, 855
Holland, Charles, 318
Hollywood, California, 382, 417, 425, 451, 459, 506, 594. *See also* film music
Hollywood Bowl, 453, 486
Holocaust, 596, 600, 670
Holy Wars of Vartan, 554
Holzmann, Rodolfo (Rudolph), 667, 703–704
Homage to Vivaldi (Perry), 630, 632. See also *Requiem for Orchestra* (Perry)
Homenagem a Schoenberg (Katunda), 694
Homenaje a Federico García Lorca (Revueltas), 749, 750
Homenaje a la tonadilla (Orbón), 770
Homenaje a Stravinski (Iturriaga), 704
Homenaje a un amigo (Ayestas), 754
Homer, Sidney, 358
Home! Sweet Home! (Bishop), 242, 251, 252

Hommann, Charles, 62–63, *63*, 66
Honduras, **756–757**
Honegger, Arthur, 365, 704
Hopkins, Charles Jerome, 110
Hopkinson, Joseph, 276
Horace, 379
Horn, Charles E., 99
Horner Institute of Fine Arts, 410
Horowitz, Joseph, 7, 484–485, 585
Horwood, Michael S., 43
Housatonic at Stockbridge, The (Ives), **276–278**. See also *Orchestral Set No. 1*, *Three Places in New England* (Ives)
Housatonic River, 277
House Committee on Un-American Activities (HUAC), 559–560
Houston Symphony Orchestra, 486, 555, 876, 891, 893
Hovhaness, Alan, **533–559**; and commercial recordings of symphonic works, 11; and Converse, 453; and Cowell, 408; and Creston, 505–506, 512; and distinctive qualities of American symphony, 29; and emergence of postmodern style, 634; and scope of American symphonic repertoire, 6; and shifting center of American symphonic activity, 486; symphonies' movements and instrumentation, 535–552; Symphony No. 2, *Mysterious Mountain*, *536*, **555–558**, *557*; Symphony No. 9, "Saint Vartan," *538*, **554–555**; Symphony No. 19, "Vishnu," *541*, **558–559**; and tensions within midcentury American symphony, 487–488. See also *specific composition titles*
Howard, John Tasker, 326
Howard, Sidney, 294n89
"How Firm a Foundation" (hymn), 350, 353
Howland, John, 313
Huapango (Moncayo), 751
Huckleberry Finn (Twain), 295n119
huehuetls, 736
Huertas, Johanny Navarro, 775
Hughes, Allen, 811
Hughes, Langston, 418, 420
Hughes, Rupert, 127, 137
Huichol people, 828–830
Huízar, Candelario, *738*, *739*, 740
Humanities Commons, 655n397
Hume, Paul, 340, 670, 691, 762
Hunter College, 704

Hupfeld, Charles, 62
Hurricane Katrina, 913
Husa, Karel, 797
hybrid musical forms, 357
"Hymn and Fuguing Tunes" (Cowell), 405
hymns: and Albert, 864; and Bernstein, 591, 597; and Bloch, 437–438; and Bolcom, *840*, 843; and Copland, 322–324; and Cowell, *397–399, 402–403*, 405, 408; and Creston, 508–509; and distinctive qualities of American symphony, 29; and Glass, 830; and Harris, 335, 338; and Hidalgo, 702; and Hovhaness, *536, 548, 551, 552, 556, 557*; and Ives, 175, 182, 188, 210–212, 215, 217–219, 221, 223, 225, 227–228, 230–231, 233, 235, *239*, 241, 243–246, 249, 250, 253, 255–256, 265, 271, 276–285, 290n18, 291n35, 293n71, 296n126, 296n128, 299n168; and Johnson, 418; and Martinů, 442; and Perry, 633; and Persichetti, 487, 583, 584, 651n248; and Price, 421, 424; and Rouse, 876; and Schuman, 533; and Thompson, 380–381; and Thomson, 350–353, *351, 352*. See also *specific titles*
Hymns and Responses for the Church Year (Persichetti), 583, 584
Hyperion Theater Orchestra, 185, 199
Hypodorian mode, 742

Ibañez, Florencio, 737
Ibarra, Federico, *738, 740*, 752
Ibero-American Symphonic Festival, 767
"I Care If You Listen" (López-Gavilán), 771
Iceland, 6
Ichmouratov, Airat, *47*
Ignacio, Rafael, 772
"I Got Rhythm" (Gershwin), 429–430
Il Guarany (Gomes), 682
Illinois Symphony Orchestra, 452
. . . ils se sont perdus dans l'espace étoilé (Alexander), 702
Imbapára (Fernândez), 692
Imbrie, Andrew, 488
immigration: and Argentinian composers, 672; and ethnic conflict in early American symphony, 67–68; and origins of American orchestras, 62; and South American composers, 666–668, 670, 672, 675, 695–696, 701–703; Spanish expatriates in Mexico, 741
imperialism, US, 666–667
Imperial Philharmonic Orchestra of Tokyo, 631

Impressionism, 156, 381, 502, 677
Impressões de uma fundição de aço (Santoro), 694
improvisation: and Bernstein, 593; and Corigliano, 835; and Creston, 507, 512; and Hanson, 373; and Harrison, 806; and Hovhaness, 555; and Ives, 182, 217–218, 262, 269, 275, 280; and Liebermann, 907–908; and Price, 424; and Rochberg, 813; and Siegmeister, 458; and Still, 429, 431; and Villa-Lobos, 682
Inca people, 674–675, 707
Ince, Kamran, viii, **794**, 916
Incredible Flutist, The (Piston), 345
Independence Day, 256
independence movements, 705
indeterminacy, 793
Indian Carnival, The (Heinrich), 74, 82, 84
Indian idioms and influences, 553, 682–683, 693
Indianist movement, 453
Indian music, 396, 533
Indigenous music, instruments, and idioms: and Alarcón, 699; Argentina, 676; Bolivia, 705; Brazil, 681; and Chávez, 742; Chile, 695; Costa Rica, 760; Cuba, 764; Ecuador, 707; Guatemala, 753–754; and Holguín, 710; Mexico, 736–737; and Prudencio, 707; Venezuela, 711. *See also* Native American culture
Indonesian music, 396
In Eius Memoriam (Shifrin), 848
Influoresence (Velázquez), 771
In Memoriam Salvador Allende (Aponte-Ledée), 774–775
Inquisition, 737
Instantáneas mexicanas (Chávez), 741
Institute of Musical Art, 362, 396
Instituto Chileno Norteamericano Cultural of Santiago, 702
Inter-American Music Festival, 667, 670, 676, 700–701, 704, 713, 762
Interlochen Center for the Arts, 369, 373
Interlochen Symphony Orchestra, 764
"Interlochen" theme (from Hanson Symphony No. 2, "Romantic"), 369
International Anthony Philip Heinrich Society, 85
International Composers Guild, 425, 445, 700
International Society for Contemporary Music (ISCM), 675, 676, 714
Internet Symphony No. 1, "Eroica" (Dun), 916
intervallic composition, 600
In These United States (Ives), 199

In the Shadow of No Towers (Spiegelman), 922
In the Sweet By-and-By (Webster), 233, 241–242, 266, 282–284, *283*
In This House, On This Morning (Marsalis), 904
Ionisation (Varèse), 430, 768
Ippisch, Franz, 754
Iridiscente (Maiguashca), 708
Irish idioms and influences, 144, 158, 159, 251, 262, 279, 396, 405. *See also* Gaelic idioms and influences
Irish Washerwoman (traditional), 242, 251
Iroquois culture, 83
Irridentus Degeneratus (Bolaños), 760
Isamitt Alarcón, Carlos, 699
Isaza, José María, 711
Israel Philharmonic Orchestra, 596, 600, 606
Israel Symphony (Bloch), 436
Itaipú (Glass), 822
Italy, 358
Iturbi, José, 453
Iturbide, Agustín de, 737, 760
Iturriaga, Enrique, *697*, 704
Ives, Charles, **175–289**; and Adams, 872; birth and death, 55n105; Burkholder on Ives's borrowing, 290n11; and commercial recordings of symphonic works, 11; context of compositions, 175–184; and Cowell, 396, 469n271; and Fairouz's works, 922; and "Great American Symphony" trope, 6; and Harrison, 802, 807; health issues, 284–285; *Holidays Symphony*, **249–267**, *254–255*, *257*, *259–261*, *263*; and key influences on American repertoire, 21–23; orchestral sets, *180–181*, **271–286**, *283*; overtures, 289n1; and Rochberg, 812; and Schuman, 533; and scope of American symphonic repertoire, 2, 3, 5; symphonies' movements and instrumentation, *176–181*; Symphony No. 1, **185–199**, *186–187*, *189–190*; Symphony No. 2, **199–217**, *202–205*; Symphony No. 3 *The Camp Meeting*, 31, 54n83, 175, *176*, 200, **217–228**; Symphony No. 4, **228–249**, *229*, *236–240*, *246*, *247–248*; *Universe Symphony*, **267–271**
Ives, Harmony, 201, 215, 285, 292n70
I Will Lay My Hand Upon My Mouth (Schidlowsky), 702
Izarra, Adina, *699*, 714

Jackson, E. A., 415
Jacobi, Frederick, 311, 439, 459

Jadassohn, Salomon, 138
Jagannath (Rouse), 876
James, William, 569
Janabar (Hovhaness), 554
Janiculum Hill, 584
Janitzio (Revueltas), 750
Janus, 584
Japan idioms and influences, 553
Järvi, Neeme, 11, *20*
jazz: and Adams, 873; and Antheil, 387; and authenticity criticisms, 462n23; bebop, 908; and Bernstein, 589–590, 591, 593–595, 601–603; and Bloch, 438; and the *Boulangerie,* 315; and Copland, 319, 322, 324; and Creston, 505, 507; and Ellington, 454; and emergence of Black composers, 382; and evolution of American symphonic style, 312; and folk idioms, 54n93; and Hovhaness, 533; and Johnson, 417; and Marsalis's works, 904, 907–908; and Mennin, 613; and Orbón, 771; and Perry, 630, 632, 633; piano jazz, 593–594; and Price, 423, 424; and Puerto Rican composers, 774; and Schuman, 513; and Sessions compositions, 492; and South American composers, 676, 700; and Sowerby, 376; and Still, 425, 430, 431; symphonic jazz, 313, 376, 487, 906; and tensions within midcentury American symphony, 487; and Thompson, 380–381
Jazz at Lincoln Center, 904
Jazz Symphony (Antheil), 383, *384*
"Jeanie with the Light Brown Hair" (Foster), 822
Jenness, Beulah Steele, 883
Jeremiah. See Symphony No. 1, *Jeremiah* (Bernstein)
Jerusalem, Ignacio de, 736
Jesuits, 340, 665, 668, 671–672, 681, 705, 708
Jesus Loves Me (Bradbury), 279, 350, 353
Jeter, John, 424
Jewish Advocate, The, 594
Jewish Chronicle, 607
Jewish Cycle (Bloch), 437
Jewish themes and idioms, 586–592, 594–595, 596–609, 886, 890–891, 900
Jew's harp, 24
Jibbenainosay (Bristow), 86
Jim Crow, 420
Jiménez, Fernando Luna, 757
Jiménez, José Mora, 761
Jiménez, Juan Ramón, 712

Jiménez Mabarak, Carlos, *738, 740,* 751–752
jingoism, 559–560. *See also* nationalism, musical
Jiquabu Indians, 681
John C. Borden Auditorium, 574
John D. and Catherine T. MacArthur Foundation, 7
John F. Kennedy Center for the Performing Arts, 7, 484, 623, 909
Johnson, Harriet, 623
Johnson, James Price, 33, 311, 313–314, 381–383, 410, **415–418,** 487. *See also specific composition titles*
Johnson, James Weldon, 33
Johnson, John Andrew, 414
Johnson, Robert, 884
Johnson, Robert Underwood, 276, 299n168
Johnston, Richard, *38*
Joliet, Louis, 340
Jones, Raymond Durward, 376
Joplin, Scott, 382, 415, 429
Jordá, Enrique, 447
Josefowicz, Leila, 873
Joseph H. Bearns Prize, 613
Joseph II, Holy Roman Emperor, 82
Josephson, Nors, 285
Jost, Franz, 162
Josten, Werner, 455
Journey into Jazz (Schuller), 487
Joyce, James, 860
Joy of Music, The (Bernstein), 484, 590
Juana la Lara (Giménez), 672
Juba ("Pattin' Juba") dance, 421–422, 424
Juilliard Orchestra, 497, 528
Juilliard Publication Award, 455
Juilliard School of Music: and Bates, 909; and Bolivian composers, 706; and Diamond, 560; and evolution of American symphonic style, 797; and Gutiérrez Heras, 752; and Hanson, 362; and Ives, 218; and Liebermann, 901; and Luna, 773; and Mennin, 610, 614, 617, 624; and Orbón, 771; and Perry, 625; and Persichetti, 575, 585; and Piston, 348; and Puerto Rican composers, 775; and Schuman, 513, 533; and Sessions, 488; and South American composers, 695; and Wagenaar, 459; and Ward, 459; and Whithorne, 460; and Zwilich, 850, 856
Juilliard Theatre, 811
Julia Perry Working Group, 655n397
Julius Hartt School of Music, 436

Jullien, Louis Antoine, 69–70, 90–92, 101, 106–108
Jung, Carl, 592
Jungle (Josten), 455
Junkin, Jerry F., 837
Juventudes Musicales, 714

Kabbalah, 595, 609
Kabbalah for Orchestra (Nobre), 694
Kaddish. See Symphony No. 3, *Kaddish* (Bernstein)
Kaddish prayer, 599, 919
Kagel, Mauricio, 681
Kalliwoda, Johann Wenzel, 67
Kalnins, Janis, *37*
Kang, Emil, 819
Kapellmeister, 68
Kaplan, Abraham, 596, 609
Karnatic music, 553
Karttunen, Anssi, 680
Katunda, Eunice do Monte Lima, 693
Katy Darling (traditional), 262
Katz, David, 228
Kaurismaki, Aki, 680
Kay, Ulysses, 769
Keats, John, 614–615
Keene, Christopher, 85
Keene State College, 771
Kelner, Hiltrud, 671
Ķeniņš, Tālivaldis, *38*
Kennedy, Jacqueline, 484
Kennedy, John F., 595, 606, 608–609, 774
Kenton, Stan, 775
Kepler, Johannes, 440
Kerner, Leighton, 500
Kernis, Aaron Jay, **893–901**; and Albert, 864; and Asia, 886; and Bates, 909; and evolution of American symphonic style, 795; and "Great American Symphony" trope, 6; and key influences on American repertoire, 22; and Mahler, 22; and Rouse, 878; symphonies' movements and instrumentation, *894–896*; symphony premiere dates, *794, 795. See also specific composition titles*
Kernodle, Tammy, 626
Kertsman, Miguel, *684,* 695
Key, Susan, 31–32, 461n1
Kimberling, Victoria, 560, 570
Kindler, Hans, 334, 344, 388, 391

Kingdom Coming (Work), 262
Kingdom's Crown (Gabirol), 900
Kinsky, Roberto, 675
Kirchner, Leon, 439, 447, 761
Kirkpatrick, John, 184, 285, 295n119, 338
Kirstein, Lincoln, 700, 801
Kittredge, Walter, 255
Klangfarbenmelodie, 498, 572–573, 604, 619–620, 819
Kleiber, Erich, 670, 675, 681, 750
Klein, Lothar, *41*
Kletzki, Paul, 447
Knaebel, Simon, 66
Knight, Death and the Devil, The (Dürer), 162
Kodály, Zoltán, 458
Koechlin, Charles, 710
Koellreutter, Hans-Joachim, 693
Koffler, Józef, 676
Kolodin, Irving, 463n53
Konex-Konex (Lorenz), 715
Koprowski, Peter, *43*
Korea, 6
Korn, Peter, 337
Korndorf, Nikolai, *43*
Korngold, Erich Wolfgang, 374, 433–435, 451, 455. *See also specific composition titles*
Kosok, Paul, 382
Kostal, Irwin, 595
Kostelanetz, André, 115, 558–559
Kotzschmar, Hermann, 127
Koussevitzky, Natalie, 345, 348, 446, 527–528, 567
Koussevitzky, Serge: advocacy of American symphonists, 486; and Barber, 358; and Berezowski, 453; and Bernstein, 585, 589–590, 593–594, 597, 609; and briefly mentioned midcentury composers, 636; and Cold War cultural politics, 485; and Copland, 319–325; and Diamond, 566–567, 569; and distinctive qualities of American symphony, 24; and Gruenberg, 454; and Hanson, 365; and Harris, 334, 339; and Harrison, 806; and Hindemith, 439; and Hovhaness, 533, 555; and Ives, 200, 215, 218, 297n154; and Josten, 455; Latin American symphonies premiered, *8*; and Lourié, 456; and Martinů, 441; and maturation of American symphonic activity, 309; and Mennin, 616; and Milhaud, 446; and Piston, 348; premiere of key works under, *9*; and Price, 418, 423, 424; and Schuman, 518, 519, 525, 527, 530; and Sessions,

488, 492, 496; and South American composers, 667, 713; and Sowerby, 374, 377; and support for American symphony, 6–7, 485; support for Villa-Lobos, 685; and Thomson, 353

Koussevitzky Music Foundation: and Berezowski, 453; and Bernstein, 588, 595; and Chávez, *745, 747*; and Copland, *321*; and Cowell, *401*; creation and goals of, 7; and Diamond, *561, 567*; and Finney, 637; grants by year, *10*; and Harris, *330*; and Harrison, 803, *804*; and Mennin, 610; and Orrego-Salas, 701; and Overton, 638; and Piston, *342, 345, 348*; postwar challenges, 485; and Riegger, 639; and Russo, 639; and Schuman, 513, *515*, 527; and Shapero, 458; and Smit, 640; and Tcherepnin, 640; and Trimble, 640; and Villa-Lobos, *690*; and Walker, *817*. *See also* Serge Koussevitzky Foundation in the Library of Congress

Kowalke, Kim, 441
Koyaanisqatsi (Glass), 822
Kozinn, Allan, 900
Krásná Pocestná (Heinrich), 72
Krehbiel, Henry E., 4, 126, 147, 160–161, 164
Krenek, Ernst, 433–434, 455, 458, 762
Krommer, Franz, 61
Kronos (Lavista), 752
Krueger, Karl, 100
Kuarahy mimby (Giménez), 672
Kuchar, Theodore, *14*
Küffner, Joseph, 91
Kunz, Alfred, *40*
Kurka, Robert, 638
Kurtz, Efrem, 438
Kushner, David, 437

La Amistad (Colón), 774
La bandera nacional (Mansilla), 674
La cabaña de Lepha (Jiménez), 757
Lachner, Franz, 67
La ciudad (Prudencio), 707
La coronación (Moreno), 708
La coronilla (Vargas Candia), 706
Lacrymosa (Borges), 752
La deseada (Jiménez Mabarak), 751
La Gran Colombia, 707, 709
La leyenda de Faust (Serebrier), 670
La lira (Sierra), 775
La lira católica (magazine), 765

"La Marseillaise," 691
Lamas, José Ángel, 711–712
Lambertini, Marta, 681
Lamentations, Book of, 589
Lamento borincano (Hernández Marín), 774
Lamia (MacDowell), 126
Lamond, Felix, 354, 379
LaMont, Erik, 855
La Motte-Fouqué, Friedrich Heinrich Karl, 162
La muchacha de las bragas de oro (Aponte-Ledée), 774
La muerte de Alsino (Leng), 700
La muerte del Inca (Massa), 674–675
La Nación, 676
Lancelot and Elaine (MacDowell), 126
Landaeta, Juan José, 711
Lang, B. J., 141
Lang, Paul Henry, 700
La noche de los Mayas (Revueltas, arr. Limantour), 24, 34, 750
Lanza, Henry, 695
La Parihuana (Holzmann), 703–704
Lapeiretta, Ninón, *766*, 773
La Piedra del Toxil (Nieto), 761
La potranca (Baqueiro Fóster), 751
La púrpura de la rosa (Torrejón y Velasco), 703
Lara, Ana, *740*, 752
Lara, Felipe, 695
La Rebambaramba (Roldán), 768
La Rhapsodie (Martinů, unfinished), 441
Larsen, Libby, 35, *794*, 795, 830, **879–886**, *880–882*, 909, 915, 924. *See also specific composition titles*
LaRue, Jan, xiii
La serpiente emplumada (Castañeda), 753
Last Argentinian Tango (Ortíz), 680
La Symphonie (Martinů, unfinished), 441
La tarde (Santos), 756
Latin American composers, 3, 34. *See also* Caribbean; Central America; South America; *specific countries*
Latin American Music Center, 700, 762
Latin Holiday (¡Fiesta!), 667
Latouche, Byron, 761
Laudate Dominum, 622
Lausanne Orchestra, 164
La valse (Ravel), 774
La Victoria de Playa Girón (Ardévol), 768

La Vie joyeuse (Chadwick), 153
Lavista, Mario, *740*, 752
La voz de las calles (Allende), 699
Lawrence of Arabia (film), 555
League of American Orchestras, 450
League of Composers, 341–344, 445, 741
Leaves of Grass (Whitman), 373
Le banjo (Gottschalk), 115
Lebenbom, Elaine, 918
Lecuna, Juan Vicente, *698,* 714
Lecuona, Ernestina, 765
Lecuona, Ernesto, 765
Led Zeppelin, 878
Lees, Benjamin, 638
Le Flem, Paul, 278
Leginska, Ethel, 439
Legrand, Diego, 671
Lehman, Frank, 373
Leibowitz, René, 751
Leighton, Lawrence, *12*
Leinsdorf, Erich, 349, 392, 442
Leipzig Conservatory, 141, 160, 459
Lemminkäinen in Tuonela (Sibelius), 21, 815
Leng, Alfonso, 700
length of American symphonies, 25–28
Lenhoff, Dieter, *755,* 756
León, Argeliers, 769
León, Tania, *766,* 771
León, Tomás, 737
Leonard, Kendra Preston, 655n397
Leonard, Peter, *12*
Leonora (Fry), 100
Lequerica, Francisco, 710
Leschetizky, Theodor, 457
Les Huguenots (Meyerbeer), 150
Les Six composers, 383
Levee Land (Still), 425
Levine, James, 124, 843
Levi Yitzhok of Berditchev, Rabbi, 600
Levy, Beth, 326
Lewis, John, 859
Ley, Salvador, 754
Leyendas: An Andean Walkabout (Frank), 705
Lezcano, José, 771
Liberian Suite (Ellington), 454
Liberty Bell March (Sousa), 275
Liberty Leading the People (painting by Delacroix), 395

Library of Congress, 7, 72, 528, 747
Lieberman, Fredric, 803
Liebermann, Lowell, 21, 578, *794,* 795, **901–904,** *902–903*. See also specific composition titles
Lieberson, Goddard, 370
Liebling, Leonard, 312, 525
Lifar, Sergei, 683
Life: Preamble and Three Episodes for Orchestra (Brescia), 708
"Life Pulse Prelude" (Ives *Universe Symphony*), 268–269
Ligeti, György, 619, 775, 835
Light, The (Glass), 822
Light Over Water (Adams), 871
Like Water for Chocolate (film; score by Brouwer), 771
Lilacs (Walker), 816
Lima, Paulo Costa, 695
Lima, Peru, 702–703
Limantour, José, 750
Lincoln, Abraham, 101–104, 311, 436
Lincoln Center Festival, 531
Lincoln Center for the Performing Arts, 7, 484, 513, 531, 533, 610, 747
Lincolnova symfonie (Weinberger), 459
Lincoln Portrait (Copland), 317, 323, 506
Lind, Jenny, 86, 90
linguistics, 883–884
Liquid Interface (Bates), 878, 909, *910*, 913, 915
Lischer (Mason), 244
Liszt, Franz: and Bernstein, 594; and Bristow, 99; and Fry, 101; and Heinrich, 80; and Ives's Symphony No. 1, 194; and MacDowell, 164; and Strong, 162; and symphonic poem genre, 126; and Thomas's concerts, 123
Little Orchestra Society, 631
Little Rock, Arkansas, 418, 420
Little Symphony (Gould), 454
Little Symphony (Krenek), 455
Little Symphony No. 1 (Sanders), 457
Little Symphony No. 2 (Sanders), 457
Little Symphony No. 3 (Sanders), 457
Liturgia negra (Sanjuán), 765
Liturgías fantásticas (Villalpando), 707
Lobato, Diego, 707
Locke, Alain, 33, 54n93, 382, 414, 422, 630
Lockhart, Beatriz, 671
Lockwood, Normand, 456, 610

Index

Loder, George, 67, 69, 85–86
"Lodger" Symphony (Glass), 35, *795, 827,* 830–831
Loeffler, Charles Martin, 153
Lohengrin (Wagner), 843
Lomax, John, 456–457
London Musical Standard, 98
London Philharmonic, 695
London's Great Exhibition (1851), 80
London Symphony Orchestra, 923
Long, Long Ago (Bayly), 213
Longfellow, Henry Wadsworth, 126, 459, 574
"Long Time Ago" (minstrel song), 99
Loots, Jean, 760
Lopatnikoff, Nikolai, *9,* 456
López de Mesa, Luis, 710
López-Gavilán, Guido, 771
L'Orchestre de l'Institut National Radiodiffusion-Belge, 447
Lord, Charles Walker, 99
Lorenz, Ricardo, *699,* 715
Losada, Diego de, 711
Los Angeles Chamber Orchestra, 747
Los Angeles Philharmonic, 456, 797–798, 859
Los Angeles Symphony Orchestra, 309, 486
Los Angeles Times, 434, 922
Los Khuzillos (Velasco-Maidana), 706
Los Paisajes del Rio (Glass), 830
Louisville Orchestra: and Chávez's works, 747; and commercial recordings of symphonic works, 11; and Cowell's works, 406; and Estévez's works, 708; First Edition recordings, *12;* and Ginastera's works, 677; and Hovhaness's works, 559; Latin American works commissioned, 667, 677; and Mennin, 616; and Orrego-Salas's works, 701; and Persichetti's works, 580; and Santoro's works, 694; and Serebrier's works, 670; and shifting center of American symphonic activity, 486; and Sowerby's works, 377; and support for American symphony, 485, 635; and tensions within American art music, 484
Lourié, Arthur Vincent, 456
Lovelace, Manuel de Jesús, 772
Lowell, Robert, 597
Lowry, Robert, 242
Luce, Clare Boothe, 742
Lucia di Lammermoor (Donizetti), 182
Luening, Otto, 11, 408, 704, 713
Luke, David, 891

Luna, Margarita, *766,* 773
Luque, Sergio, 753
Lusitania sinking, 281–282
Luther College, 362
Lutosławski, Witold, 24, 797, 834
Luzuriaga, Diego, *698,* 708
Lybbert, Donald, 704
Lyric for Strings (Walker), 816
lyricism, 293n83, 317, 358, 430

Macbeth (film), 415
MacDonald, Andrew Paul, *46,* 126, 164
MacDowell, Edward A., **164–167**; background and education, 164; and scope of American symphonic repertoire, 5; and Second New England School, 125; and Strong, 160, 162; *Suite für Grosses Orchester, 165,* **165–167**; and symphonic poem genre, 126
MacDowell, Marian, 166
MacDowell Colony, 513, 595, 624
MacDowell Medal, 488
Machado, Gerardo, 768
machine music, 694, 915
Machu Picchu, 704
MacIntyre, David, *45*
Mackenna, Carmela, *696,* 699
Mackenna, Juan, 699
Mackkatananamakee, 84
MacMillan, Ernest, 36
MacMillan, James, 914
"Mad Hour, The" (Dib), 883
Madrid Conservatory, 774
"Magdalena stod i grönan lund" (folk tune), 365
Magee, Gayle Sherwood, 184, 200, 218, 232, 256, 280, 289n10, 299n173
Magellan, Ferdinand, 668
Mahler, Fritz, 506
Mahler, Gustav: and Adams, 871; and Antheil, 387, 391, 392; and Asia, 891; and Bernstein, 585–586, 590, 592, 594, 597–599, 601, 604–609; and Bolcom, 842, 843; and Corigliano, 831, 837; and Diamond, 575; and distinctive qualities of American symphony, 24; and evolution of American symphonic style, 797; and future of American symphony, 924; and Harbison, 845, 848; and Ives's *Holidays Symphony,* 267; and Ives's Symphony No. 3, 218; and Ives's *Universe Symphony,* 270; and Picker, 891; and Rochberg, 812; and Rouse, 876; and Sessions, 500; and

Sibelius, 22; and Strong, 162; and Venezuela's El Sistema, 711; and Villa-Lobos, 685; and Wang, 916
Maiguashca, Mesías, 708
Mainz Stadttheater, 454
Major John Andre (Brewster), 298n161
Malagueña (Lecuona), 765
Malambo (Ginastera), 674, 677, 678, 720n64
Malcolm, Carlos, 771
Malsio, José, 704
mambo, 908
Mandel, August, 78–79, 80
Manhattan School of Music, 560, 574, 708, 771, 797, 916
Manhattan Symphony Orchestra, 454
Manifest Destiny, 736
Manitou Mysteries (Heinrich), 74, 83
Mannes School of Music, 436, 710, 797, 901
Mansilla, García, 674
Manso, Alonso, 773
Manuscript Society of New York, 98
Marabá (Braga), 682
"maracas and drums" style, 667
Maracatu de Chico Rei (Mignone), 692
maracatu ritual, 692
Marcelli, Nino, 699
Marcha festiva (Riestra), 703
Marcha heroica (Centurión), 671
Marcha triunfal (Quintón), 774
Marcha triunfal (Segura), 765
Marchena, Enrique de, 773
Marching Band Symphony (Perry), 629
Marching Through Georgia (Work), 242, 253, 259–261, 272–276, 295n115
María Lionza (Estrella), 714
Mariandá para orquesta sinfónica (Cordero), 775
Mariani, Hugo, 760
Maria Theresa, Empress of Austria, 82
Marie-Josée Kravis Composer-in-Residence, 878
Marionetas (Malcolm), 771
Marquette, Jacques, 340
Márquez, Arturo, 752
Marriage of Heaven and Hell, The (Blake), 844
Marsalis, Wynton, 35–36, 632, 795, *795,* 859, **904–909,** *905–906,* 914. *See also specific composition titles*
Marsh, Simeon B., 241
Martín, Edgardo, *766,* 769
Martínez Montoya, Andrés, 709

Martínez-Sobral, Manuel, 754
Martín Fierro (Hernández), 672
Martinon, Jean, 497
Martinů, Bohuslav, 433–435, **441–445,** 471n337, 533. *See also specific composition titles*
Martita (Santos), 756
Martyn (Marsh), 241–242, 244–246, *247–248*
Marx, Burle, 722n109
Masefield, 574
Maslanka, David, viii, *794,* 798
Mason, Daniel Gregory, viii, *9,* 456
Mason, Lowell, 211, 219, 227, 233, 242–244, 291n37. *See also specific composition titles*
Mason, William, 92
Mass (Bernstein), 591, 596, 609
Massa, Juan Bautista, 674–675
Massachusetts Institute of Technology, 845
Massa's in de Cold Ground (Foster), 206, *207,* 213, 215, 242, 251, 272–273, 275, 279–280, *283,* 284
Massenet, Jules, 682
Massey, Drew, 461n1
Mass in G Major, A (Campderrós), 695
mass media, 312, 323
Mastodon, The (Heinrich), 74, *83,* 84
Mastrogiovanni, Antonio, *669, 670*
Masur, Kurt, 575
Mata, Julio, 761
Materna (Ward), 211–212
Mathis der Maler Symphony (Hindemith), 439, 440
Matons, Laureano Fuentes, 765
Matthews, Michael, 36, *44*
Maturana, Eduardo, *696,* 701–702
Má vlast (Smetana), 271
Maxims of the Stele of Antef (Larsen), 883
Mayan Legend (Paniagua), 753
Mayan people and culture, 751, 753
Mayflower (ship), 265
Mazzeo, Rosario, 524, 529
McCarthyism, 559–560, 595
McDonald, Harl, 456
McIntosh, John, 82, 83
McIntyre, Paul, *41*
McLellan, Joseph, 608, 864
Mead Composer-in-Residence, 909
Meckna, Michael, 350–352
Meet the Composer, 7, 819, 831, 873
Mehdizadeh, Daniel, *47*
Mehta, Zubin, 893

Meignen, Leopold, 63–66, *64,* 100–101, 107. See also *Symphonie militaire* (Meignen)
Mejía, Adolfo, 667, *698,* 710
Mejía-Arredondo, Enrique, *766,* 772
melodic concatenation, 593
Melpomene (Chadwick), 144
Melville, Herman, 50n17
Memorial Day, 295n110
"Memorial Day for the War Dead" (Amichai), 922
Memorial Slow March (Ives), 230
memorial symphonies (Heinrich), **84–85**
Memos (Ives), 185, 193, 200, 218, 243, 250, 264, 268, 294n101, 295n104
Mena, Luis Emilio, *766,* 772–773
Men and Mountains (Ruggles), 807
Mendelssohn, Felix, 21, 71, 85, 95, 137, 148, 150, 156, 349
Mendelssohn Union, 86
Mendoza, Vicente, *739,* 740
Mendoza-Nava, Jaime, 667, 706
Mengelberg, Willem, 459
Mennin, Peter, **610–624**; and commercial recordings of symphonic works, 11; and Creston, 505; and emergence of postmodern style, 634; and Hovhaness, 534; and Persichetti, 582, 585; and shifting center of American symphonic activity, 486; and sources from Hebrew Scriptures, 654n356; and support for American symphony, 9; symphonies' movements and instrumentation, *611–612;* and tensions within midcentury American symphony, 487, 635. *See also specific composition titles*
Mercury Living Presence, *20*
Meserón, Juan, 711
Mesoamerican culture, 828–830
Message Bird, 67, 89, 101
Messiaen, Olivier, 752, 774, 838
Messiah (Handel), 99
Mester, Jorge, 11, *12*
metaphysics, 592
Metropolis (Bisquertt), 700
Metropolis Symphony (Daugherty), *794*
Metropolitan Hall, 101
Metropolitan Opera, 98, 831, 843
Me voy así: beguín (Gutiérrez), 769
Mexican-American War, 735
Mexico, **736–753**
México: Sinfonía-poema (Bernal Jiménez), 751
Meyer, Felix, 802

Meyerbeer, Giacomo, 150
Michelangelo, 574–575
Michigan 4-H Children's Garden, 856
Michigan State University, 855
Micro–Preludio Orquestal (Sarmientos), 756
microtonal music, 268, 558, 636, 677, 741, 757, 835, 919
Middle Eastern traditions, 919
Mideros, Tomas, 708
Midsummer Night's Dream, A (Mendelssohn), 95
Midsummer Night's Dream, A (Shakespeare), 150
Mignone, Francisco, 671, *683,* 692
Milhaud, Darius, **445–447**; and Albert, 859; and Bolcom, 838, 842; and Copland, 324; and Diamond, 559; and Glass, 828; and influence of émigré composers, 433–434; and Prieto, 741; symphonies written in America, 435. *See also specific composition titles*
Miller, David Alan, *14*
Miller, Leta, 803, 897
Miller, Rebecca, 100
Miller, Tamara, 702
Mills College, 445, 708, 741
Miłosz, Czesław, 849
Milwaukee Symphony Orchestra, 775
Minas Geraís, Brazil, 665, 681–682
Mingus, Charles, 908
minimalism: and Adams, 865, 871, 872; and Bates, 913; and Carter, 801; and Diamond, 575; and Enríquez, 752; and evolution of American symphonic style, 793; and Fairouz, 922; and Glass, 822; and Kernis, 897; and Perry, 633; and scope of American symphonic repertoire, 3
Miniño, Manuel Marino, *766,* 773
Minneapolis Symphony Orchestra, 218, 264, 439, 486
Minnesota Centennial, 496
Minnesota Orchestra, 346, 762, 878
Minor, George A., 210, 280
minstrelsy, 213
Miramontes, Arnulfo, *738, 739,* 740
Miron, Dan, 596
Missa Deus sempiterne, 508
Missa Solemnis (Beethoven), 812
missionaries, 736
Missionary Chant (Zeuner), 212, 246, *246, 247–248,* 299n168
Missionary Hymn (Mason), 243–244
Mission Santa Barbara, 737

Mistral, Gabriela, 700
Mitchell, Howard, 510, 701
Mito araucano (Isamitt), 699
Mitropoulos, Dimitri: and Cordero, 762; and Diamond, 565, 566, 574; and Dick, 453; and Hindemith, 439; and Ives, 218; and Mennin, 613; and Sessions, 493, 496; and Swanson, 458
Mitze, Clark, 582
mixed-race persons, 668, 681
Moby Dick (Mennin), 613
modernism and modernity: and Adams, 871; and American musical pedagogy, 382–383; and Antheil, 387, 392, 396; and Barber, 356; and Bernstein, 585–586, 589–590, 597, 604, 606–608; and Bloch, 437; and Bolcom, 843; and briefly mentioned midcentury composers, 636–637, 639–640; and Carter, 802; and Casal Chapí, 772; and Chadwick, 153; and Chávez, 742; and Copland, 319, 322; and Cordero, 762; and Cowell, 404–406, 409; and Creston, 502, 511–513; and Dawson, 414; Depression-era conflict over, 313–314; and Diamond, 565, 571, 574–575; and distinctive qualities of American symphony, 23; and European influences in South America, 666; and evolution of American symphonic style, 793, 797; and Fairouz, 919; and Ginastera, 677; and Glass, 828; and Gramatges, 769; and Guarnieri, 693–694; and Hailstork, 859; and Harbison, 849; and Hindemith, 439; and Hovhaness, 533–534, 555; and influence of émigré composers, 433; and Ives, 184, 216, 218, 228, 230, 278; and key influences on American repertoire, 21; and Larsen, 879; and MacDowell, 166; and Marsalis, 908; and Martinů, 442; and maturation of American symphonic activity, 309; and Mennin, 610, 614, 618–619; modern traditionalism, 610; and Paine, 127, 136; and Perry, 626, 630, 632; and Persichetti, 651n248; and Piston, 340–341; and programming of symphonic performances, 451; and Rochberg, 807, 811–812, 815; and Schuman, 527, 533; and scope of American symphonic repertoire, 2; and Sessions, 495, 501; and social tensions in Mexico, Central America, and the Spanish-speaking Caribbean, 735; and South American composers, 666; and Sowerby, 374, 376; and Still, 425, 428, 430; and Strong, 163; and tensions within midcentury American symphony, 486–488, 634–635; and Thompson, 379; and Thomson, 350, 354; and Villa-Lobos, 691; and Zwilich, 856

Modern Music, 309, 493, 495, 534
Module for Orchestra (Perry), 626, 632
Moeser, James, 511
Moller, John Christopher, 62
Mónaco, Alfredo del, *699*, 714
Moncayo, José Pablo, *738, 740,* 751
Monestel, Alejandro, *755*
Money Musk (traditional), 251
Monje, Viscarra, 706
Monk, Thelonius, 908
Monodia (Bolaños), 760
Monotony (Sowerby), 376
Monroe Doctrine, 666, 757
Montclair State Teacher's College Dance Club, 813
Montealegre, Felicia, 596
Montero, José Angel, 712
Montero, José Lorenzo, 711
Monteux, Pierre, 395, 493, 615, 670
Montevideo, Uruguay, 668
Montezuma (Sessions), 497, 498
Montoya, Andrés Martínez, *698*
Moore, Douglas, 11, 313, 438, 456
Moore, Undine Smith, 626
Mora, Eddie, 761
Morales, Melesio, 737
Morales Nieva, Ignacio, 774
Morales Pino, Pedro, *698*
Moran, Jason, 286
Morawetz, Oskar, *38*
Moreno, Segundo Luis, *697,* 708
Moreno González, Juan Carlos, 672
Moross, Jerome, 310, 456–457
Mortet, Luis Cluzeau, *669*
Morton, "Jelly Roll," 424, 884
Morton, Lawrence, 457
Mosaic Quartet (Cowell), 408–409
Moscheles, Ignaz, 156
Moscow Symphony, 754
Moss, Julia, 110
Mosses from an Old Manse (Hawthorne), 234
Mother of Us All, The (Thomson), 350
Mount Scopus, 606
Moussa, Samy, *47*
Movement for String Quartet (Cowell), 408, 409
movement structure of American symphonies, 25–28
Movimiento sinfónico No. 1 (Ardévol), 768

Movimiento sinfónico No. 2 (Ardévol), 768
Mozart, Wolfgang Amadeus: and Bernstein, 585; and Bristow, 91, 92; and Diamond, 571; and European influence on American repertoire, 60; and first American symphonists, 63; and Ives, 175, 184; and Mexican symphonic music, 737; and origins of American orchestras, 61, 62; and Persichetti, 579; and Rochberg, 812; and Sessions, 492
Mozetich, Marjan, *44*
Muck, Karl, 124
Mugmon, Matthew, 35
Muisca people, 709
Mujer con telar (Izarra), 715
Multicultural Music Group, 776
multimedia, 667. *See also* electronic and electro-acoustic music
Munch, Charles, 349, 445–446, 485, 496, 615–616, 676
Municipal Conservatory (Cuba), 768
Musgrave, Thea, 315
música austera, 680
Música de Ciudad (Ortiz-Alvarado), 775
Music Advisory Panel, 485, 513, 517
música jíbara, 736
Musical America, 309, 436, 452, 496, 500, 569, 573–574
Musical Congress, 109
Musical Courier, 160, 188, 249, 309, 569
Musical Elements, 886
Musical Fund Society, 62, 63, 66, 100
Musical Quarterly, 216, 531
musical theater, 425, 460, 746. *See also* Broadway
Música para orquesta No. 1 (Villalpando), 707
Música para orquesta sinfónica (Contreras), 751
MusicArte Panama Contemporary Music Festival, 764
Música viva No. 2 (Fernández), 771
Music Copying Project, 185
Music Educators National Conference (MENC), 582, 583
Music for Strings, Percussion and Celesta (Bartók), 555
Music for the Magic Theater (Rochberg), 811–812
Music in the Making Concerts, 632
Music Man, The (Willson), 460
Music Teachers National Association, 162
Musik-Verein of Graz, 78
Mussolini, Benito, 778

Muti, Riccardo, 532
Mutual Broadcasting System, 310, 475n467
My Father Knew Charles Ives (Adams), 286
My Old Kentucky Home (Foster), 284
Myrick, Julian S., 183
Mysterious Mountain. *See* Symphony No. 2, *Mysterious Mountain* (Hovhaness)
Mysterium (Scriabin), 270
mysticism, 362, 505, 609
"Mystic Trumpeter, The" (Whitman), 904

Ñacahuasu (Bolaños), 704
Nach Bach (Rochberg), 811
Naïve and Sentimental Music (Adams), 22, *867*, 871, 872
Nancarrow, Conlon, 408, 488
Naomi (Mason), 211, 227–228
Napoleão, Arthur, 682
Nashville Symphony Orchestra, *14*, 904
National Academy of Music (Colombia), 709
national anthems, *111*, 115, 454, 672, 691, 695, 703, 705, 711, 761, 772–773
National Association for American Composers and Conductors, 505
National Association for Music Education, 582
National Association of Negro Musicians, 420
National Committee for Folklore Research, 735
National Conservatory (Chile), 695
National Conservatory (Colombia), 709
National Conservatory (Dominican Republic), 773
National Conservatory (Mexico), 751
National Conservatory (New York), 98, 126, 146
National Conservatory (Panama), 761
National Endowment for the Arts, 701
National Federation of Music Clubs, 153
National Foundation on the Arts and the Humanities, 584
National Gallery of Art, 188
National Gallery Orchestra, 185
National Institute of Arts and Letters, 374, 457, 584, 610
nationalism, musical: and Argentinian composers, 676; and Castillo, 753; and Creston, 513; in Cuba, 769; and Delgadillo, 758; and Ginastera, 677; and Piston, 341, 348; and Plaza, 712; and Ponce, 741; and Schuman's Symphony No. 3, 525–526; and scope of American symphonic repertoire, 3, 6; and social tensions in Mexico,

Central America, and the Spanish-speaking Caribbean, 735; and South American composers, 666; and Uruguayan composers, 668–669; and Wang, 919
National Memories: Grand British Symphony (Heinrich), 80
National Music Camp, 373
National Orchestral Association (Guatemala), 753
National Orchestral Institute Philharmonic, *14*
National Orchestra of Catalonia, 680
National Peace Jubilee, 148
National Philharmonic (Maryland), 859
National School of Music (El Salvador), 756
National Symphony (Chile), 701
National Symphony (Uruguay), 670
National Symphony Orchestra (US): and Albert's works, 864; and Antheil's works, 388, 391; and Corigliano's works, 835; and Creston's works, 510, 511; and Harris's works, 334; and Ives's works, 252; and Mennin's works, 610, 623; and Piston's works, 344; and Schuman's works, 532; and shifting center of American symphonic activity, 486; and tensions within American art music, 484; and works of Chilean composers, 701
Native American culture, **82–84**, 96–97, 166, 312, 437, 908. *See also* Indigenous music, instruments, and idioms
Naufragio (Estrada), 752
Naumburg Award, 349, 610
Naumburg Foundation, 485, 493, 496, 513, 533, 610, 613
Navarre, Gustavo, 706
Navrátil, Karel, 457
Naxos Records, 11, *13–17,* 21, 52n50, 110, 695, 714, 754, 775
Nazism, 433, 706, 762
NBC: *Carolinian Symphony* broadcast, 475n467; and growth of radio broadcasting, 310; NBC Orchestral Awards, 310; NBC Radio, 391; NBC Symphony Orchestra, 32, 323, 370, 388, 456
Neale, Alasdair, 463n53
Nearer, My God, to Thee (Mason), 233
"Near the Lake Where Drooped the Willow" (Horn), 99
Ned McCobb's Daughter (Howard), 294n89
Negev Desert, 589
negritos, 666
Negro and His Music, The (Locke), 422

Negro Folk Symphony (Dawson), 6, 21, 32, 310, *410,* **410–415,** *412, 413*
Neoclassicism: and Antheil, 383, 387, 396; and Ardévol, 768; and Argentinian composers, 675–676; and briefly mentioned midcentury composers, 636–637, 640; and Campos-Parsi, 774; and Chávez, 742; and content of South American compositions, 667; and Creston, 502, 509; and Diamond, 560, 565–567, 570; and Enríquez, 752; and grouping composers, 314; and Guarnieri, 692–693; and Hanson, 362; and Harris, 338; and Liebermann, 901; and Mennin, 610, 614; and Perry, 626, 632; and Persichetti, 578, 579, 583, 584; and Piston, 344, 346; and Plaza, 712; and Revueltas, 750; and Santa Cruz, 700; and Sessions, 488–492, 493; and Stravinsky, 448, 450; and Swanson, 459; and tensions within midcentury American symphony, 635; and Thomson, 350, 354; and Uruguayan composers, 670; and Zwilich, 856
Neo-Expressionism, 677
Neoromanticism: and Albert, 859; and Barber, 356; and briefly mentioned midcentury composers, 636, 637; and Creston, 505–506, 508, 510; and Diamond, 560, 565–567, 569, 571, 574; and distinctive qualities of American symphony, 23; and evolution of American symphonic style, 796; and Glass, 822; and key influences on American repertoire, 22; and Liebermann, 901; and Mennin, 610; and Rouse, 878; and scope of American symphonic repertoire, 5; and Still, 431; and Zwilich, 856
Nepomuceno, Alberto, 682, *683*
Nettl, Bruno, 656n432
Nettl, Paul, 656n432
Nettleton (hymn), 241–242, 245–246, 279, 291n35
Netto, Marcos Coelho, 682
Neuendorff, Adolf, 156
Neue Zeitschrift für Musik (Schumann), 91
Neves, Ignacio Parreiras, 682
"New and Unusual Music" (concert series), 891
New Chamber Orchestra, 228
New Deal, 326, 485, 517
New England Conservatory of Music, 138, 141, 420, 453, 457–458, 533, 589, 705, 761, 774
New England Triptych (Schuman), 523
New German School, 30, 96, 162, 167
New Jersey Symphony Orchestra, 497
Newman, Alfred, 449, 451

Newman, Thomas, 915
Newman, William S., viii
New Music, 250, 404
New Musical Resources (Cowell), 404, 409
New Music Quarterly, 231
New Music Quarterly Recordings, 404
New Music Society, 250, 404
New Music USA, 819
New Negro movement, 33, 382, 626
"New Orleans Blues" (Morton), 424
New Orleans jazz, 913
New Orleans Symphony, 486
New School Auditorium, 228
New School of Music, 559
New World a-Comin' (Ellington), 454
New World Records, 11–21, *17–19*
New World Symphony, 775
New World Symphony (Symphony No. 9; Dvořák): and Beach's Symphony in E Minor, 157–158; and Chadwick's *Symphonic Sketches,* 150; and Chadwick's Symphony No. 2, 146–147; and Dawson's *Negro Folk Symphony,* 412; and Hailstork's Symphony No. 2, 858; and Hanson's Symphony No. 3, 372; and Ives's Symphony No. 1, 188, 193, 194, 198, 291n24; and Ives's Symphony No. 2, 291n43; and key influences on American repertoire, 21; and Price's Symphony No. 1, 420
New York City: and critiques of listening public, 51n22; cultural influences, 6; and émigré composers, 310; and first generation of American symphonists, 60; and German immigrants, 68; and Heinrich's background, 71; and Mennin's works, 616; rivalry with Boston, 51n22, 147, 608; and Schuman's works, 513. *See also* New York Philharmonic Orchestra
New York City Ballet, 677
New York City Composers' Forum-Laboratory, 311, 517, 610
New York City Symphony, 318
New York College of Music, 797
New Yorker, 500–501, 570
New York Harmonic Society, 86
New York Herald, 98, 157
New York Herald Tribune, 216, 249, 358, 534, 584
New York Little Symphony, 218
New York Magazine, 856
New York Music Critics' Circle Award, 218, 345, 349, 458–459, 505, 506, 526, 565, 590, 648n140

New York Negro Symphony Orchestra, 410, 418
New York Philharmonic Orchestra: and Albert's works, 864; and Barber's works, 358; and Berezowski's works, 453; and Bernstein's works, 585, 586, 590, 594, 595; and Boulanger as conductor, 315; and Bristow's works, 86, 89, 90–93, 98, 100; and Carter's works, 801; and Chávez's works, 747; and commercial recordings of symphonic works, 11; and Copland's works, 322; and Corigliano's works, 831; and Creston's works, 508; and Diamond's works, 560, 565, 569, 570, 575; early years, **66–69**; and first generation of American symphonists, 63; and Fry's works, 101, 108, 110; and German musicians, 68; and Gottschalk's works, 115; and Hadley's works, 454; and Harris's works, 340; and Heinrich's works, 71; and Herrmann's works, 455; and Hovhaness's works, 554, 558–559; and Ives's works, 200, 218, 228; and Kernis's works, 893; and León's works, 771; and Mennin's works, 610, 613, 614, 615, 617; and Moore's works, 456; origins of, 61; and Perry's works, 631; and radio broadcasting, 311; and recordings of symphonic works, *19*; and Rouse's works, 878; and Sanders's works, 457; and Schuman's works, 530, 531; and Sessions's works, 493, 500; and shifting center of American symphonic activity, 486; and Stravinsky's works, 449; and Strong's works, 162; and support for American symphony, 6, 485; and Swanson's works, 458; and Thomson's works, 353; and Zwilich's works, 855
New York Philharmonic Symphony Orchestra, 459
New York Philharmonic-Symphony Society, 457
New York Public Library for the Performing Arts, 100
New York State Theater, 676
New York Sun, 160
New York Symphony Orchestra, 154, 185, 200, 595
New York Times: on Bernstein's *Kaddish* Symphony No. 3, 607; on Bolcom's Symphony No. 7, 844; on Dawson's *Negro Folk Symphony,* 414; on Diamond's Symphony No. 8, 574; on Fairouz's Symphony No. 4, 923; on Hovhaness's Symphony No. 2, 559; on Hovhaness Symphony No. 9, 555; on Ives's Symphony No. 2, 215; on Ives's Symphony No. 3, 228; on Ives's Symphony No. 4, 183, 249; on Kernis's *Symphony in Waves,* 900; on MacDowell's *Suite für*

Grosses Orchester, 166; on Mennin's Symphony No. 8, 623; on Orrego-Salas's Symphony No. 3, 701; on Perry's *Short Piece for Orchestra,* 631; on Revueltas's *Janitzio,* 750; on Rochberg's Symphony No. 3, 811; on Rouse, 873; skepticism of neoromantic style, 356; on Strong's Symphony No. 2, 163, 164; support for Villa-Lobos, 685; on Walker's *Sinfonia No. 1,* 816; on Zwilich's Symphony No. 3, 855
New York Tribune, 101
Niagara (Fry), *103,* **108–109,** *109*
Nicaragua, 735, *755,* **757–760**
Nickel, Christopher, 47
Nick of the Woods (Bird), 86
Niederrheinische Musik-Zeitung, 70
Nielsen, Carl, 585
Nieto, César, 761
Nieva, Ignacio Morales, 767
"Night Club, The" (Johnson; Mvt. III of *Harlem Symphony*), 417–418
Night Creature (Ellington), 454
Night Flight (Barber), 359
Night in the Tropics. See Symphony No. 1, *Symphonie romantique: La nuit des tropiques* (Gottschalk)
Nikisch, Arthur, 124, 125
1926 . . . the Present—the Future (Anthem) (Bloch), 437. *See also America: An Epic Rhapsody* (Bloch)
Nixon in China (Adams), 864, 872
Nobody Knows the Trouble I've Seen (spiritual), 279
Nobre, Marlos, *684,* 694
Noche de otoño (Colón), 774
Noche en Morelia (Bernal Jiménez), 751
Nocturnos a Debravo (Delgado), 761
Nogueira, Ilza, 694
Noguera Palau, Carolina, 710
Nono, Luigi, 754
non-repetition concept, 749
non-touring orchestras, 123
Non-violent Integration (Ellington), 454
Nordic epics, 365
Nordoff, Paul, 575
Norlin Foundation, 513, 635
Norman, Andrew, *795*
Norory, Guillermo, 760
North by Northwest (film; score by Herrmann), 455
North-South relations, 666
North Star, The (film; score by Copland), 451

Northwestern University, 362, 457, 459
Noss, Luther, 440, 441
Notre Dame of Paris (Fry), 101, 104
Notturno for Strings and Harp (Fine), 531
Nova (Picker), 891
nuclear (atomic) weapons, 484, 493–495, 596–597, 600, 601
Nuestra Señora de la Encarnación, 703
Nuit des tropiques. See Symphony No. 1, *Symphonie romantique: La nuit des tropiques* (Gottschalk)
NYA Symphony Orchestra, 506

Oberlin Conservatory, 610
Obertura jocosa (Ley), 754
Obertura para el Fausto Criollo (Ginastera), 677
Obertura pastoral (Herrarte), 754
Obertura Patriótica (Alas), 756
Obertura Puerto Rico (Arévalo), 774
Oberturas indígenas (Castillo), 753
Obertura sobre temas cubanos (Roldán), 768
Ocean Grove Shore Festival of Classics, 856
"Ode to Freedom" (Beethoven, arr. Bernstein), 586
Ode to Joy (Beethoven), 135, 509, 586
Oedipus Rex (Stravinsky), 574
O Estado de São Paulo, 693
Offenbach, Jacques, 115
Of Mice and Men (film; score by Copland), 451
Of Rage and Remembrance (Corigliano), 835
Oggún-Oniré (Rovira), 771
Oja, Carol J., 354, 374, 430, 735
Oklahoma Symphony Orchestra, 431
Oldberg, Arne, 457
Old Black Joe (Foster), 213, 215, 242, 272–273, 279–280
Old Colón, 672
Old Dominion University, 856
Old Folks at Home (Foster), 251
Old Home Day (Ives), 256, *259–261,* 262, 264
Olivares, Juan Manuel, 711
Oliveira, Jamary de, 694
Oliver, Henry K., 265
Ollanta (Riestra), 703
Olmstead, Andrea, 492, 494, 496, 501–502
Olympic Theatre, 85
Omnibus television programs, 485
Omnivorous Furniture (Bates), 915–916
"O Mother Dear, Jerusalem" (hymn), 212
100 Greatest Dance Hits (Kernis), 897

114 Songs (Ives), 276, 285
one-movement symphonies: and Barber, 356; and Chávez, 742; and distinctive qualities of American symphony, 29; and film music, 468n231; and key influences on American repertoire, 21–22; key works, *25–26*; and Persichetti, 584; and Stravinsky, 447–448; Symphony No. 7 (Harris), 339
"On the Naive and Sentimental in Poetry" (Schiller), 871
On the Town (Bernstein), 593–595
On the Transmigration of Souls (Adams), 286, 872
"Open Letter to the Musicians and Critics of Brazil" (Guarnieri), 693
opera: and Bristow, 86; and Corigliano, 831; and early New York Philharmonic, 67; and first generation of US symphonists, 60; and Fry, 100; and Glass, 822; and Ley, 754; and Picker, 891; and Sessions, 502; and South American composers, 703; and tensions within American art music, 484
Operation Just Cause, 764
Orbón, Julián, 35, 752, *766*, 769–770
Orchesterstücke (Mackenna), 699
Orchestra Europe, 774
Orchestral Set No. 1, *Three Places in New England* (Ives), viii, 6, 184, 200, 215, **271–278**, 285, 297n154. See also *Housatonic at Stockbridge, The* (Ives); *Putnam's Camp, Redding, Connecticut* (Ives); *"St. Gaudens" in Boston Common, The* (Ives)
Orchestral Set No. 2 (Ives), viii, 24, 215, **278–284**, 285. See also *Elegy to Our Forefathers, An* (Ives); *From Hanover Square North* (Ives); *Rockstrewn Hills Join in the People's Outdoor Meeting, The* (Ives)
Orchestral Set No. 3 (Ives), **284–286**
Orchestra Now, 100
Orchestre Philharmonique de Radio France, 773
Orchestre Symphonique de Paris, 256
Orejón y Aparicio, José de, 703
Orellana, Gilberto, 756
Orellana, Joaquín, 754, 755, *755*
Orellana Castro, Gilberto, Jr., 756
Organization of American States, 670, 764
Origin of the North American Indians, The (McIntosh), 82
Ormandy, Eugene: and Antheil, 392–393; and Hanson, 372; and Harris, 339; and Martinů, 442; and Mennin, 616; and Persichetti, 578, 579, 584; and Piston, 349; and Schuman's works, 526; and Sowerby, 377; and support for American symphony, 7, 485
Ornithological Combat of Kings, The (Heinrich), 71–72, *73*, 78–80, 85
Ornstein, Leo, 350
Orozco, Keyla, 771
Orphée aux enfers (Offenbach), 115
"Orpheus and Euridice" (Miłosz), 849
Orquestada num. 6: El fresco aroma de viejos placeres (Teruel), 715
Orquestada num. 7: La Gran Aldea (Teruel), 715
Orquesta de Cámara Municipal, 672
Orquesta de la Unión Musical (Panama), 761
Orquesta Experimental de Instrumentos Nativos, 707
Orquesta Filarmónica de Guatemala, 754
Orquesta Filarmónica de la Asociación del Profesorado Orquestal, 675
Orquesta Filarmónica de la Habana, 252
Orquesta La Aspiración, 758
Orquesta Sinfónica de Asunción, 671–672
Orquesta Sinfónica de Guadalajara, 740
Orquesta Sinfónica de Heredia, 756, 760
Orquesta Sinfónica del Estado, 675
Orquesta Sinfónica del Servicio Oficial de Difusión Radio Eléctrica (OSSODRE), 669–670
Orquesta Sinfónica de Madrid, 774
Orquesta Sinfónica de México, 740, 741
Orquesta Sinfónica de Puerto Rico, 776
Orquesta Sinfónica de Venezuela, 712, 713
Orquesta Sinfónica de Yucatán, 751
Orquesta Sinfónica Heredia, 756, 760, 761
Orquesta Sinfónica Nacional (Argentina), 675
Orquesta Sinfónica Nacional (Bolivia), 706
Orquesta Sinfónica Nacional (Colombia), 710
Orquesta Sinfónica Nacional (Costa Rica), 760
Orquesta Sinfónica Nacional (Cuba), 769, 771–773
Orquesta Sinfónica Nacional (Dominican Republic), 772
Orquesta Sinfónica Nacional (Panama), 761, 764
Orquesta Sinfónica Nacional (Paraguay), 672
Orquesta Sinfónica Nacional de Guatemala, 753
Orquestra Filarmônica (Brazil), 722n109
Orquestra Sinfônica de Brasil (OSB), 694
Orquideas Azules (Escobar), 714
Orrego-Salas, Juan, 34, 667, *696*, 700–701, 762
Ortega, Aniceto, 737

Ortega-Miranda, Chañaral, *696*, 702
Ortíz, Gabriela, *740*, 752–753
Ortíz, Pablo, *674*, 680–681
Ortiz-Alvarado, William, *767*, 775
Oseh Shalom (prayer), 919, 922
Oskanondonha, 84
Osmond-Smith, David, 641
Oteri, Frank J., 859
Otra ciudad (Prudencio), 707
Our Town (film; score by Copland), 323, 451
Overton, Hall, 638
Overture and March "1776" (Ives), 275, 285
Overture for Large Orchestra (Montero), 711
Overture in G Minor (Ives), 289n1
Overture to "As You Like It" (Paine), 135
Overture: Town, Gown and State (Ives), 199, 291n27
Oviedo, Jorge, 709

Pacheco de Céspedes, Luis, *697*, 703
Paderewski Fund Competition, 457
Paderewski Prize, 454–455
Padilla, Juan Gutiérrez de, 736–737
Page, Tim, 856
Paine, John Knowles, **127–138**; and Beach, 157; and Boston's influence, 116; and Bristow, 98, 100; and Chadwick, 141; and diversity of American symphonic styles, 167; and Hill, 455; and key influences on American repertoire, 21; and Mason, 456; and scope of American symphonic repertoire, 1, 5; and Second New England School, 125; symphonies' movements and instrumentation, *128*; Symphony No. 1 in C Minor, **127–135**; Symphony No. 2 in A Major, "Spring," **135–138**
Palacios, Ignacio, 713
Palestine, 589
Palma, Athos, *673*, *675*, 681
Palmero, Armando, 706
Pampeana No. 3 (Ginastera), viii, 34, *678–679*, 680
Panama, *755*, **761–764**
Panama Canal, 735
Panambí (Ginastera), 677
Pan American Association of Composers, 404, 700
Pan Americanism, 115, 710
Pan American Union, 671, 699, 712, 757–758, 762, 764
Paniagua, Raúl, 753
Panoramas de México (Ayala), 751

Papageno's Dream (Schwartz), 775
Papineau-Couture, Jean, *38*
Parade (Satie), 570
Paraguay, 665, *669*, **671–672**
Paraná River, 677
Parera, Blas, 672
Pareyón, Gabriel, 753
Paris Conservatoire, 315, 459, 709, 765
Parker, Henry T., 151, 154
Parker, Horatio: and Beach, 159; and Ives, 182–185, 188, 193, 198, 230, 290n18; and Porter, 457; and Second New England School, 125; and Sessions, 488; and Smith, 458
Parker, John Rowe, 71
Parker, Robert L., 746–747
Parkman, Francis, 127
Parmenter, Ross, 531, 608, 631, 701
Parra, Gustavo, *698*, 710
Parra Violeta, 702
Parsi, Héctor Campos, *767*
Pärt, Arvo, 633, 797
Partch, Harry, 635, 900
Partita (Carter), 802, *Symphonia: sum fluxae pretium spei* (Carter)
Partita para orquesta (Serebrier), 670
Partitureintrag: 11/9/1974 (Alexander), 702
Parton, Dolly, 883
Pasdeloup, Jules, 52n41, 682
Passacaglia (Paz), 676
passenger pigeons, 79, 81–82
Passion According to the Twentieth Century, A (Rochberg), 811
Passion for Good Friday (Orejón y Aparicio), 703
Passions, The (Collins), 93
Pasta, Carlo Enrico, 703
"Past: Formation of the Waters and Mountains" (Ives *Universe Symphony*), 269
Pater, si non potest hic calix (Creston), 509
Pathétique Sonata (Piano Sonata No. 13; Beethoven), 860
Pathétique Symphony (Symphony No. 6; Tchaikovsky), 188, 197, 201, 520
Patios (Ortíz), 753
patriotic themes, 200–201, 262, 338–339. *See also* nationalism, musical
patronage of American symphonic music, 6–21
Paumgartner, Bernhard, 517
Paumgartner, Hans, 166
Paur, Emil, 124, 158
Paz, Juan Carlos, 34, *674*, 676

Index

Peabody Conservatory, 610, 772
Peaceable Kingdom, The (Thompson), 381
Pearl Harbor attack, 313, 526
Pedrell, Carlos, 668
Pedrell, Felipe, 668, 704, 758
Peermusic Classical, 560
Peña Morell, Esteban, 772
Penderecki, Krzysztof, 23, 619, 797, 834
pentatonic scale: and Beach, 158; and Caba, 706; and Chadwick, 142, 144, 148; and Chávez, 742, 746–747; and Cowell, 408; and Dawson, 411; and evolution of American symphonic style, 797; and Hanson, 372; and Harrison, 806; and Ives, 194, 208, 213, 231, 233–234, 242, 272, 277, 279; and key influences on American repertoire, 21; and Nieto, 761; and Plaza, 712; and Price, 420, 423; and Revueltas, 750; and Sowerby, 377; and Still, 430, 431
Pentland, Barbara, 36, *38*
Pépin, Clermont, *40*
Pequeña Suite (Mejía), 710
Pérez, Argeliers Léon, *766*
Pergolesi, Giovanni Battista, 598
period music, 437
Perkins, Francis, 358
Perkins, Theodore, 233
Perón, Juan Domingo, 675
Perry, Julia, 33–34, 487, **624–634**, *627–629*, 635. *See also specific composition titles*
Persephone (Graham ballet), 449
Persian Gulf War, 897
Persichetti, Dorothea, 578, 580, 651n242
Persichetti, Vincent, **575–585**; and Creston, 505; and elements of American modernism, 486–487; and emergence of postmodern style, 634; and Gutiérrez Heras, 752; and Hovhaness, 534; marriage, 651n240; and Mennin, 610, 617, 618; and support for American symphony, 9; symphonies' movements and instrumentation, *576–577*. *See also specific composition titles*
Peru, *697*, **702–705**
Peter, Johann Friedrich, 62
Peter and the Wolf (Prokofiev), 318
Peters, C. F., 806
Petrushka (Stravinsky), 383, 684
Pettis, Ashley, 356
Peyser, Joan, 600
Philadelphia, Pennsylvania, 62
Philadelphia Conservatory, 575, 651n240

Philadelphia Orchestra: and Antheil's works, 393; and Bolcom's works, 843; and Boulanger, 315; and Dawson's works, 410, 414; and emergence of Black composers, 382; and Hanson's works, 372; and Josten's works, 455; and Martinů's works, 442; and Persichetti's works, 578, 579, 584; and Piston's works, 349; and Ponce's works, 741; and radio broadcasting, 311; and Schuman's works, 526, 528, 529; and Still's works, 431; and Vardell's works, 459
Philadelphia Orchestra Association, 339
Philadelphia Public Ledger, 101
philanthropy, 580. *See also* patronage of American symphonic music
Phile, Philip, 242, 276
Philharmonic Hall (Lincoln Center), 531
Philharmonic Society (Bethlehem), 62–63
Philharmonic Society (New York), 61. *See also* New York Philharmonic Orchestra
Philharmonic Society (Philadelphia), 100
Philharmonisches Staatsorchester Mainz, 773
Philip Glass Ensemble, 830
Philip IV, King of Spain, 703
Philomel (Babbitt), 683
Phoenix Symphony, 886, 890
Piano Concerto (Copland), 699
Piano Concerto (Larsen), 884
Piano Concerto No. 1 in E-flat Major (Liszt), 194
Piano Concerto No. 2 in B-flat Major (Brahms), 194, 680
Piano Concerto No. 2 in F Minor (Chopin), 156
Piano Concerto No. 2 in D Minor (Mendelssohn), 156
Piano Concerto No. 2 in E-flat Major (Moscheles), 156
Piano Concerto No. 3 (Bartók), 458
Piano Concerto No. 3 in C Minor (Beethoven), 518
Piano Concerto No. 4 (Saint-Saëns), 570
piano jazz, 593–594
Piano Quintet in F Minor (Franck), 194
Piano Sonata No. 2: *Concord, Mass., 1840-60* (Ives), 183. *See also Concord Sonata* (Ives)
Piano Sonata No. 32 in C minor (Beethoven), 878
Piano Variations (Copland), 430, 599
Piazzolla, Astor, 34, 315, 667, *674,* 680
Picker, Tobias, *794, 795,* **891–893,** *892*
Pierrot lunaire (Schoenberg), 498
Pietersz, Nolita, 712

Piezas para tocarse en la Iglesia (Samayoa), 753
Pig Town Fling (traditional), 206, *207,* 213–214, 242, 252
Pilgrims, 264–265
Pilgrim's Progress, The (Bunyan), 234
Pilot, The (McLellan), 608
Pines, Paul, 891
Pini di Roma (Respighi), 683, 915
Pinkham, Daniel, 638–639
Pinochet, Augusto, 701–702
Pisar, Samuel, 596
Piston, Walter, **340–350**; and Boulanger's influence, 315; and Carter, 801; and commercial recordings of symphonic works, 11; and Corigliano, 831; Guggenheim Fellowship, 471n337; and Hailstork, 859; and Harbison, 845; and Harris, 334–335; and influence of émigré composers, 433; and Larsen, 883; premiere of key works during Koussevitsky's tenure, 9; and radio broadcasting, 310; and Shapero, 458; and shifting center of American symphonic activity, 486; and support for American symphony, 7; symphonies' movements and instrumentation, 342–343. *See also specific composition titles*
Pittsburgh Symphony (Hindemith), 439, 440, 451
Pittsburgh Symphony Orchestra, 440, 454, 459, 590, 631
Pizzetti, Ildebrando, 457
plainchant, 508–509
Play (Norman), 795
Plaza, Juan Bautista, 34, *698,* 712, 714
Pleyel, Ignaz, 61, 737
Plow That Broke the Plains, The (film; score by Thomson), 451
Pocahontas (Carter), 801
Pocahontas (Heinrich), 82
Poe, Edgar Allan, 803
Poema elegíaco (Serebrier), 670
poetry, 428–429, 430, 501–502, 511, 574, 669, 674–675
Políptico (Carrizo), *763,* 764
Polisi, Joseph, 513, 524, 527, 528
political advances, 309, 310
political ideologies, 626. *See also* nationalism, musical
polka, 91–92
Pollack, Howard, 317, 319, 324, 349, 356, 359–360
polyphony: and Bristow, 91; and Chilean music, 695; and Cowell, 404, 405; and Creston, 508; and ethnic diversity, 50n2; and Ginastera, 678; and Harris, 336, 338; and Harrison, 806; and Hovhaness, 534; and Ives, 198, 216; and Larsen, 884; and Martinů, 442; and Mennin, 610, 619, 624; and Mexican culture, 736; and Paine, 134; and Schuman, 527; and Sessions, 492; and Stravinsky, 449–450
polyrhythms, 29, 235, *237–240,* 630
polytonality: and briefly mentioned midcentury composers, 639, 641; and conflicts over modernism, 313; and Garrido-Lecca, 704; and Glass, 828; and Harris, 335, 336; and Harrison, 803; and Hovhaness, 554; and Ives, 182–183, 218, 230, 252, 265, 278, 280; and Milhaud, 446–447; and Persichetti, 578; and Price, 423–424; and Ruiz, 771; and Sarmientos, 755; and Schuman, 518
Ponce, Manuel, *739,* 741
Ponce de Léon, José María, *698,* 709
Popol Vuh legend, 753
popular culture and music: and Bernstein, 589–590, 597–598; and Chadwick, 156; and Cowell, 408; and Creston, 505; and distinctive qualities of American symphony, 29; and Dukelsky, 453; and emergence of Black composers, 382; and Gershwin, 313; and Ives, 175, 215; and Johnson, 415, 417; and Kernis, 897; and Price, 472n350; rock music, 878; and Rouse, 878; and Sessions, 492; and Sowerby, 374; and Still, 430; and Thompson, 381; Tin Pan Alley, 313, 318, 505, 513–514; vaudeville, 150, 381; and Villa-Lobos, 691
Popule meus (Lamas), 712
populism, 3, 91, 317, 319, 356. *See also* nationalism, musical
Porter, David, 268–269, 285, 297n139
Porter, Quincy, 315, 380, 438, 457
Portinari, Cândido, 693–694
Portugal, 666, 668
Posada, Andrés, *698,* 710
Poscimur (Horace), 379
Poseidon Records, 559, 635
postmodernism: and Adams, 871; and Bernstein, 589; and Cowell, 409; and criticisms of American compositions, 33–34; and Diamond, 575; and distinctive qualities of American symphony, 23–24; and evolution of American symphonic style, 793; and Harrison, 807; and Ives, 293n76; key figures of, 634; and key influences

on American repertoire, 22; and Perry, 626; and Rochberg, 811; and scope of American symphonic repertoire, 3
Pousseur, Henri, 695, 752
Powell, John, 457
Pozadas, Willy, *697*, 707
Prague Conservatory, 459
Prairie (Sowerby), 376, 377
prairie sound, 32, 96, 396
prayers, 589, 591, 594, 599, 919. *See also* hymns
Prelude for a Great Occasion (Schuman), 532
Prelude to the Afternoon of a Faun (Debussy), 154
Preludio (Moreno), 708
Preludios dramáticos (Santa Cruz), 700
Premio Nacional de Música, 713
Presbyterian Church, 296n128
"Present: Earth, Evolution in Nature and Humanity" (Ives *Universe Symphony*), 269
President's March, The (Phile), 276
Presser, Theodore, 528
Preston, Katherine K., 100
Preti-Bonati, Luigi, 668
Price, Florence, **418–424**; and American musical pedagogy, 381; and Converse, 453; and Dawson, 410; and education of American-based composers, 314; and emergence of Black composers, 382–383; and key influences on American repertoire, 21; and Perry, 630; and social context of symphonic repertoire, 311; and Still, 425; symphonies' movements and instrumentation, 419. *See also specific composition titles*
Price, Thomas Jewell, 420
Prieto, María Teresa, *738, 739,* 741
primitivism: and Antheil, 387; and Beach, 159; and Blitzstein, 317; and Chávez, 34, 742, 747; and Cowell, 405; and Ginastera, 677; and Hanson, 369; and Heinrich, 80; and Johnson, 415; and Ortíz, 753; and Rochberg, 811; and Stravinsky, 450; and Villa-Lobos, 682
Princeton, 488, 501, 845
Principles of Rhythm (Creston), 505
print culture, 666
Private Lives of Elizabeth and Essex, The (film; score by Kongold), 455
Prix de Rome, 315, 379, 565
Prix Fontainebleau, 624
Prokofiev, Sergei: and Antheil, 387, 393, 395; and Bernstein, 589–590, 594; and Blitzstein, 318; and Copland, 324; and Hanson, 365; and Rouse, 876, 878; and Sessions, 496
Pro Musica, 228
Proprior Deo (Sullivan), 233, 234, 245
Protestantism, 29, 163, 182, 199, 215, 280, 335
Proyecto Eco, 760
Prudencio, Cergio, *697,* 707
Pruett, Laura Moore, 115
Psalm 150, 622
Psalm Symphony (Sowerby), *375*
Psicosis (Orellana), 756
Psycho (film; score by Herrmann), 455
public education, 86, 112, 669
Puerto Rico, 735, 736, *767,* **773–775**
Puerto Rico (Campos), 773
Puerto Rico Conservatory, 774
Pulitzer Fellowships, 452
Pulitzer Prizes: Adams, 872; Albert, 860; Bacon, 452; Bolcom, 838; Corigliano, 831; Davidovsky, 680; Hanson, 372; Harbison, 849; Ives, 218, 272; Kernis, 893; Marsalis, 904; Piston, 345, 349; Ran, 796; Rochberg, 813; Rouse, 873; Sessions, 488, 501; Sowerby, 374; Toch, *435,* 459; Walker, 816; Zwilich, 849, 850
Punta Guanacasteco, 761
P'urépecha people, 737
Puritans, 231
Pushmataha (Heinrich), 82
Putnam, Israel, 274
Putnam's Camp, Redding, Connecticut (Ives), **274–276,** 278, 280, 284, 298n161, 298n162. *See also* Orchestral Set No. 1, *Three Places in New England* (Ives)
Puts, Kevin, viii, 1–2, 11, *795,* 796, 922
Pye, Richard, 520

Queens College, 528
"Quiéreme mucho" (Roig), 765
Quiet City (Shaw; score by Copland), 524
Quinteros, Abelardo, 701
Quintón, José Ignacio, 774
Quirós, Manuel José de, 753
Quito Conservatory, 708
Quodlibet (Schickele), 212

Rachmaninoff, Sergei, 594
racial identity, 53n52, 215, 414, 625–626, 709. *See also* ethnic identity and conflict

Index

radio broadcasting, 11, 52n48, 310, 312, 447, 456, 460, 608, 710
Radiohead, 286
Radio Nacional Orchestra, 722n109
Radio's Best Plays, 318
Rae, Allan, 42
Raff, Joachim, 96, 125, *136,* 160, 164, 167
Raffelín, Antonio, 765
ragtime, 276, 280–281, 415, 421, 423, 431, 908
Ragtime Dances (Ives), 280
Raíces (Baqueiro Fóster), 751
Raid, Kaljo, *39*
Raksin, David, 775
Ramin, Sid, 595
Ramsey, Guthrie P., 904–907
Ran, Shulamit, *794, 796,* 797
Ranieri, Salvador, 681
Rao, Nancy, 408
Rapsodía enterriana (Torrá), 681
Rapsodía negra (Lecuona), 765
Rapsodía paraguaya (Giménez), 672
Rapsodie d'Auvergne (Furriol), 668
Rapture (Rouse), 873
Rasmussen, Karen, 599
Rational Metric Notation (Creston), 505
Rautavaara, Einojuhani, 915
Ravel, Maurice, 153, 502, 505, 559, 560, 607, 774, 884
Read, Gardner, 457
Réage, Pauline, 497
Recitativo y variaciones (Tosar), 670
recording industry, 11–21
Red, White and Blue. See *Columbia, the Gem of the Ocean* (A'Becket)
Redes (Revueltas), 750
Red Pony, The (film; score by Copland), 451
Red Scare, 559–560
Reed, Herbert Owen, 639, 856
Reeves, David Wallis, 253, 256
Reich, Steve, 445, 578
Reichold Chemical Prize, 769
Reinagle, Alexander, 62
Reinecke, Carl, 138
Reiner, Fritz, 575, 590
Reinhard, Johnny, 268, 270, 271, 297n139
Reisado do pastoreio (Fernândez), 692
"Relic" (Glück), 849
Reminiscing in Tempo (Ellington), 454

Renacimiento (Mejía-Arredondo), 772
Renaissance era, 336, 534, 555, 610, 614, 624
Representing the Good Neighbor: Music, Difference, and the Pan American Dream (Hess), 54n97
Requiem for Orchestra (Perry), 632. See also *Homage to Vivaldi* (Perry)
Respighi, Ottorino, 354, 362, 369, 456, 683, 838, 915
Responso para el guerrillero (Maturana), 702
Responsorio (Luzuriaga), 709
Retrospectivas (Servellón), 756
Reveille (bugle call), 214, 242
Revueltas, Silvestre, 24, 34, 453, 666, 735, *738,* **749–750**. See also specific composition titles
Reyes, José Trinidad, 756, 772
Reynolds, Christopher, 135, 162
Reynolds, Lee, 923
Rhapsody in Blue (Gershwin), 313, 383, 415
Rheinberger, Josef, 138, 141, 457
Ribaupierre, André de, 559
Ribeiro, León, 34, 668, *669*
Rich, Alan, 458
Richmond Symphony Orchestra, 914
Ried, Aquinas, 695
Riegger, Wallingford, viii, 319, 487, 639
Riestra, José María Valle, 703
Rifo, Guillermo, *696,* 702
Rilke, Rainer Maria, 849
Rimsky-Korsakov, Nikolai, 362, 447, 457, 674, 684, 873
Ringwall, Rudolph, 358
Rio de Janeiro, Brazil, 682
Rip Van Winkle (Bristow), 86
Rip Van Winkle (Chadwick), 138
Rite of Spring (Stravinsky), 450, 591, 750
Rítmicas (Roldán), 768
Rival, Robert, 47
Rivera, Diego, 694
RiverRun. See *Symphony No. 1, RiverRun* (Albert)
Robb, Charles H., 756
Robbins, Jerome, 596
Robert Browning Overture (Ives), 285
Roberts, George, 267–268
Roberts, Luckey, 415
Robertson, E. John, *42*
Robles, Manuel, 695
Rochberg, George, **807–815**; and Adams, 871; and Albert, 859, 864; and Bolcom, 845; and distinctive qualities of American symphony,

997

23, 24; and evolution of American symphonic style, 795; and Glass, 830; and key influences on American repertoire, 21, 22; and Liebermann, 901; and Schuman, 513, 528; symphonies' movements and instrumentation, *808–810*; symphony premiere dates, *794*; and Zwilich, 850

Rochester Philharmonic Orchestra, 11, *20*, 382, 406, 410, 425, 430, 453

Rock-a-bye Baby, 281

Rockefeller Foundation, 7, 11, 485, 486, 580, 752

Rocking the Cradle, Symphony in Two Movements for Orchestra (Danielpour), 795

rock music, 878

Rockstrewn Hills Join in the People's Outdoor Meeting, The (Ives), **280–281**, 284. *See also* Orchestral Set No. 2 (Ives)

Rockwell, John, 532, 816

Rodas, Arturo, *697,* 708

Rodeo (Copland), 323

Rodgers, Richard, 506

Rodríguez, Luis Diego Herra, 761

Rodríguez de Francia, José Gaspar, 671

Rodríguez Socas, Ramón, 669

Rodzinski, Artur, 200, 215, 358, 508

Roethke, Theodore, 843

Rogatis, Pascual de, *673,* 675

Rogers, Bernard, 438, 457, 459, 610

Rogers, Delmer, 100

Rogers, Harold, 607

Roig, Gonzálo, 765

Roldán, Amadeo, 252, 765, *766,* 768–769. *See also specific composition titles*

"Roll, Jordan, Roll" (spiritual), 819

Rolón, José, *738,* 740

Romann, Jack, 834

Romanticism: and Adams, 865, 871–872; and Albert, 864; and Antheil, 393, 396; and Argentinian composers, 676; and Barber, 356; and Beach, 159; and Bernstein, 593; and Bolcom, 845; and Chávez, 747; and Chilean composers, 700; and content of South American compositions, 667; and Corigliano, 838; and Cowell, 404, 406; and Creston, 502; and Diamond, 560, 567, 569; and distinctive qualities of American symphony, 23; and evolution of American symphonic style, 793, 797; and Fairouz, 923; and folk idioms, 54n93, 313; and Glass, 822; and grouping composers, 314; and Hailstork, 858; and Hanson, 362, *363,* 365–369, 373; and Hovhaness, 534, 553; and Ives, 175, 184, 185, 194, 214, 227, 230, 271, 286; and Johnson, 417; and Kernis, 897; and key influences on American repertoire, 21; and Marsalis, 907; and Mennin, 613, 617–618, 624; and Paine, 133, 136; and Perry, 630; and Picker, 891; and Piston, 340–341, 344, 346; and Plaza, 712; and Revueltas, 750; and Rochberg, 807, 811, 813; and scope of American symphonic repertoire, 2–3; and Sowerby, 376–377; and Strong, 162; and tensions within midcentury American symphony, 635; and Thomson, 350; and Toch, 459; and Villa-Lobos, 691; and Zwilich, 856. *See also* Neoromanticism

Romberg, Andreas, 62, 63

Romeo and Juliet (Prokofiev), 876

Rome Prize, 362, 374, 488, 897

Roncal, Simeón, 706

Rondano, Miguel Ángel, 667

Rondo fantástico (Sanjuán), 765

Rondonia (Roquette-Pinto), 693

Roosevelt, Franklin Delano, 455, 493, 517, 593, 666–667

Roosevelt, Theodore, 735

Roosevelt, Theodore, Jr., 736, 773

Roosevelt Corollary, 757

Root, George F., 188, 227, 242, 255, 265, 272. *See also specific composition titles*

Roquette-Pinto, Edgard, 693

Rorem, Ned, 374, 639

Rosales, Juan, 760

Rosas, Juan Manuel de, 672

Rosenberg, Richard, 115

Rosenfeld, Paul, 4, 425, 437, 493

Rosenwald Fellowship, 458

Rosquellas, Mariano Pablo, 705

Ross, Alex, 575

Ross, Hugh, 624

Ross, James, *14*

Rossini, Gioachino, 182

Rostropovich, Mstislav, 623, 864

"Round Me Falls the Night" (hymn), 583

Rounds for String Orchestra (Diamond), 566, 651n239

Rouse, Christopher, **873–878**; and Albert, 864; and evolution of American symphonic style, 795; and Harbison, 848; and Kernis, 900; and key influences on American repertoire, 21; and

support for American symphony, 9; symphonies' movements and instrumentation, *874–875*; symphony premiere dates, *794, 795*. *See also specific composition titles*
Rousseau, Jean-Jacques, 671
Roussel, Albert, 344, 365, 559
Rovina, Hannah, 596
Rovira, Louis Aguirre, 771
Rowe, Tony, 110
Royal Northern Sinfonia, 100
Royal Philharmonic Orchestra, 100, 438
Royal Philharmonic Society, 66
Royal School of Church Music, 374
Royal Scottish National Orchestra, 110
Rozo Contreras, José, *698*
Rózsa, Miklós, 434
Rubirosa, María Isabel, 769
Rugeles, Alfredo, *699*, 714
Ruggles, Carl, 350, 807
Ruíz, Magaly, *766*, 771
Rumba sinfónica (Lorenz), 715
rural cultural influences, 6
Rural Symphony (Schoenefeld), 126
Russian Revolution, 309, 433
Russo, William, 639
Rutgers University, 816
Ryder, Luemily, 215

Saavedra, Leonora, 737–740, 779n40
Sabin, Robert, 395, 573–574
Sachs, Joel, 396
Sacred Service (Bloch), 598
Sacred Symphony No. 3, *Hagar in the Wilderness* (Fry), *103*, 108, 109–110
Sadat, Anwar, 883
Sadat, Jehan, 878–883
Sailor's Hornpipe (traditional), 251
Saint-Domingue, 61
Saint-Gaudens, Augustus, 272
Saint Patrick's Day (traditional), 251
Saint Paul Chamber Orchestra, 695
Saint-Saëns, Camille, 52n41, 159, 511–512, 570, 668, 682
Salamanca do Jaráu (Cosme), 692
Salas, Raúl Martínez, 758
Salas y Castro, Esteban, 764
Salazar, Adolfo, *739*, 741
Salazar, Marina Saíz, 762–764
Sale, J. B., *93*

Salgado, Luis Humberto, *697*, 708
Salón, Eloy, 706
"Salute to the Americas" (broadcast), 710
Salzburg Festival, 358, 517
Samaroff, Olga, 575
Samayoa, José Eulalio, 753
Sambucetti, Luis, 668
Saminsky, Lazare, 457
Sammartini, Giovanni Battista, 582
Samuel, Gerhard, 268
San Antonio de Padua mission, 737
Sánchez-Gutiérrez, Carlos, 752
Sánchez-Portuguez, Guido, 761
Sancho, Juan Bautista, 737
Sandburg, Carl, 608
Sanders, Robert L., 457
Sandí, Luis, *738, 739*, 751
Sands (Escot), 705
San Fernando Valley State College, 771
San Francisco Conservatory of Music, 436, 452, 893, 914
San Francisco Symphony: and Adams's works, 865, 871; and Antheil's works, 395; and Bacon's works, 452; and Bates's works, 909; and Hadley's works, 454; and Ives's orchestral sets, 299n168; and maturation of American symphonic activity, 309; and Milhaud's works, 446, 447; and Picker's works, 891; and Sessions's works, 493; and shifting center of American symphonic activity, 486
Sanjuán, Pedro, 765
San Quentin prison, 404, 405
Santa Clara mission, 737
Santa Claus: Christmas Symphony (Fry), 21, 24, 101, *102, 107*, **107–108**, 110, 115
Santa Cruz, Domingo, 34, *696*, 700
Santiago Cathedral, 695
Santo Domingo, Dominican Republic, 772
Santoro, Cláudio, 34, 52n50, 667, *683, 684*, **693–694**
Santórsola, Guido, 670
Santos, Domingo, 756
Sanz, Rocío, 761
São Paulo Symphony, 691, 722n109
Sarah Lawrence College, 519
Sarasate Prize, 768
Sargeant, Winthrop, 500–501, 570
Sargent, Malcolm, 438
Sarmientos, Jorge, 754, *755*

Index

Saroni, Hermann, 67, 89–90
Saroni's Musical Times, 67
Sas, Andrés, *697,* 703
Sasaki, Miho, 424
Satie, Erik, 560, 570
Saturday Review, 582
Satyagraha (Glass), 822
Saul, was verfolgst du mich (Schütz), 812
Sauvé, Martial, *47*
Scalero, Rosario, 807, 816
Scarlatti, Domenico, 502
Schaeffer, Pierre, 681, 710, 752
Schafer, R. Murray, 36, *41*
Scheff, Walter, 318
Scheherazade.2, Dramatic Symphony for Violin and Orchestra (Adams), *795, 869,* 873
Schenkerian analysis, 290n17, 293n76
Schenkman, Edgar, 218, 517
Scherchen, Hermann, 704
Scherman, Thomas, 631
Schermerhorn, Kenneth, *14,* 497
Scherzo: All the Way Around and Back (Ives), 268–269
Scherzo capricioso (Cervantes), 765
Scherzo Sonata (Asia), 886
Schickele, Peter, 212, 340
Schidlowsky, León, 667, *696,* 702
Schiff, David, 801
Schiller, David, 594–595, 599–602, 604–605
Schiller, Friedrich, 84, 586, 871
Schiller: Grand sinfonia dramatica (Heinrich), *73,* 84
Schipizky, Frederick, *45*
Schippers, Thomas, 486
Schmidt, Arthur P., 137, 165
Schmidt, Franz, 459
Schmidt, Heather, *47*
Schmidt, John C., 137
Schnepel, Julie, 4, 5, 6, 51n25, 127, 315, 382, 452
Schoenberg, Arnold: and Adams, 872; and Argentinian composers, 676; and Bates, 913; and Bernstein, 594; and Blitzstein, 316; career summary, 457–458; and factionalism in American music, 484; and Harrison, 803; and influence of émigré composers, 433, 434; and Ives's *Universe Symphony,* 271; and key influences on American repertoire, 21; and Larsen, 884; and Sessions, 492, 495, 498, 501; and Stravinsky, 447. *See also specific composition titles*

Schoenbergniana en los 12 tonos, capricho sinfónico (Delgadillo), 758
Schoenefeld, Henry, 126
Schola Cantorum, 672
Schonberg, Harold C., 110, 501, 574, 623, 631
Schubert, Franz, 31, 185, 188, 193, 194, 680
Schudel, Thomas, 42
Schuller, Gunther, 487, 639–640, 906
Schuman, William, **513–533**; and Antheil, 387; and Cold War cultural politics, 485; and commercial recordings of symphonic works, 11; and Creston, 505, 506; and Diamond, 559, 565; and distinctive qualities of American symphony, 24; and elements of American modernism, 486–487; and the Federal Music Project, 311; and "Great American Symphony" trope, 6; and Harris, 337, 340; and Hovhaness, 534; and key influences on American repertoire, 21; and Mennin, 610, 617, 618, 619, 620, 623; and Perry, 626; and Persichetti, 579, 580, 582, 583, 585; premiere of key works by Koussevitzky, 9; and Rochberg, 811; and Rouse, 876; and scope of American symphonic repertoire, 1; and shifting center of American symphonic activity, 486; and support for American symphony, 9; symphonies' movements and instrumentation, *514–516*; and tensions within midcentury American symphony, 635; and "traditional modernism," 634; and Wagenaar, 459. *See also specific composition titles*
Schumann, Robert, 91, 95, 125, 136, *136,* 167, 525
Schütz, Heinrich, 812
Schwantner, Joseph, *794,* 796, 815, 864
Schwartz, Elliott, 915
Schwartz, Francis, *767,* 775
Schwartz-Kates, Deborah, 677
Schwarz, Gerard, 11, *13, 20,* 575, 801
Schwass, Frederick, 422
Schwindl, Friedrich, 61
Scotch Bestiary, A (MacMillan), 914
Scotch idioms and influences, 251, 279
Scotch snaps, 381, 412, 414
Scriabin, Alexander, 270
Scriven, Joseph, 219
Sea of Trees, The (film; score by Bates), 915
Seasons (Thomson), *93*
Sea Symphony, A (Vaughan Williams), 614
Seattle Symphony, 11, *20,* 454, 457, 486, 533–534, 559, 560, 575, 886

Sebastiani, Pía, 681
"Second Age of the Symphony, The" (Dalhaus), 125
Second New England School, **123–168**; and Beach, **156–159**; and Chadwick, **138–156**; and MacDowell, **164–167**; and Paine, **127–138**; and scope of American symphonic repertoire, 2, 3; and Strong, **160–164**
Second Regiment Connecticut National Guard March (Reeves), 253
Second (Indian) Suite (MacDowell), 126, 166
Second Viennese School, 565, 704, 803
Seeger, Ruth Crawford, 350, 396, 430
Segura, Toribio, 765
Seidel, Frederick, 597
Seidl, Anton, 98, 162
Sell, Stephen, 843
Seminario Musical, 695
Semper fideles (Sousa), 275
Sensemayá (Revueltas), 749, 750
senza misura passages (Hovhaness), 553–554, 558–559
September 11, 2001, terrorist attacks, 844
Serebrier, José, 228, 497, *669*, 670
Serenata for Chamber Orchestra (Walker), 816
Serenata Guaraní (Centurión), 671
Serenata para cuerdas (Bustamente), 773
Serge Koussevitzky Foundation in the Library of Congress, 7, *10*, 485, 528. *See also* Koussevitzky Music Foundation
serialism: academic serialism, 635; and Ardévol, 768–769; and Beccera, 701; and Bernstein, 590, 593; and Blitzstein, 319; and Bolcom, 838; and Brazilian composers, 693–694; and briefly mentioned midcentury composers, 636, 637, 639; and Campos-Parsi, 774; and Cordero, 762; and Creston, 502; and Diamond, 565, 570–572; Garrido-Lecca, 704; and Ginastera, 676–677; and Harrison, 803; and Hovhaness, 534; and Liebermann, 901; and Mennin, 614, 616, 624; and Perry, 626, 631, 632; and Persichetti, 578; and Piston, 349; and Rochberg, 807; and Schuman, 513, 529–530, 531, 532; and Sessions, 492, 493, 495–496, 500–501; and South American composers, 667; and Stravinsky, 450; and tensions within midcentury American symphony, 486–488; and Uruguayan composers, 670; and Valera, 771
Serly, Tibor, 458

Serra, Junípero, 737
Servellón, Esteban, 756
service music, 182, 184. *See also* hymns
Servicio Oficial de Difusión Radio Eléctrica (SODRE), 669
Sessions, John, 496
Sessions, Roger, **488–502**; and Antheil, 383; and Bloch, 438; and Creston, 512; and Diamond, 559, 560, 565; and distinctive qualities of American symphony, 29; and elements of American modernism, 486; and Hailstork, 859; and Harbison, 845; and Kernis, 900; and Mennin, 613; and Perry, 626, 630; and Persichetti, 582, 583; and Schuman, 517; and scope of American symphonic repertoire, 5; and support for American symphony, 9; symphonies' movements and instrumentation, *489–491*; and tensions within midcentury American symphony, 487, 635; and Zwilich, 850. *See also specific composition titles*
seven-movement works, *28*
Shadle, Douglas W., 4, 29, 30, 110
Shaker Loops (Adams), 865
Shakespeare, William, 135, 150
Shakespeare's Tempest (Paine), 135
Shanet, Howard, 110, 115, 632
Shankar, Uday, 533
Shapero, Harold, 458, 471n337
Sharman, Rodney, *46*
Shavitch, Vladimir, 669
Shaw, David T., 201
Shaw, Irwin, 524
Shaw, Robert (conductor), 614
Shaw, Robert Gould (Colonel), 272, 278
Shelley, Harry Rowe, 182
Shepherd, Arthur, *9*, 458
Sherman, William Tecumseh, 253
Sherwood, Gayle. *See* Magee, Gayle Sherwood
Shifrin, Seymour, 848
Shining Shore, The (Root), 188, 265–266, 285, 296n128
Shkolnik, Sheldon, 834
"Sh'ma Yisrael" prayer, 589, 591, 594
Sholem Aleichem, 597
Shorter, Wayne, 908
Short Piece for Orchestra, A (Perry), 624, **630–632**
Short Ride in a Fast Machine (Adams), 872
Short Symphony. See Symphony No. 2, *Short Symphony* (Copland)

1001

Index

Short Symphony (for wind ensemble) (Larsen), *881*, 886
Short Symphony (Swanson), 458
Shostakovich, Dmitri: and Antheil, 387, 388–392, 468n233; and Asia, 891; and Bernstein, 589–590, 594; and Blitzstein, 318; and Bolcom, 843; and Corigliano, 834; and Diamond, 565; and key influences on American repertoire, 22; and Liebermann's works, 904; and Rouse, 876; and wartime nativism, 313. *See also specific composition titles*
Shreffler, Anne, 802
Shuman, Davis, 438
Sibelius, Jean: and Antheil, 387, 388, 391; and Barber, 356–357, 358; and Bolcom, 842; and distinctive qualities of American symphony, 29; and evolution of American symphonic style, 796; and Hanson, 362, 365, 370–371; and Harbison, 845; influence on Harris, 468n238; and Ives, 217; as key influence on American repertoire, 21–22, 53n54; and Liebermann, 904; and Read, 457; and Rochberg, 813–815; and Rouse, 876; and Schuman, 519. *See also specific composition titles*
Sides, Patricia, 626
Siegmeister, Elie, 458, 459
Sierra, Roberto, 54n97, *767*, 775
Sierra Gorda, 737
Silva, René, *696*, 702
Simmons, Walter: on Barber's Symphony No. 2, 359; on Creston's Symphony No. 1, 506; on Creston's Symphony No. 2, 507; on Creston's Symphony No. 3, 509–510; on Creston's Symphony No. 5, 511; on Creston's Symphony No. 6, 512; on Mennin's Symphony No. 4, 615; on Mennin's Symphony No. 8, 613, 621, 622; on Persichetti's ecumenism, 578; on Persichetti's Symphony No. 7, 579, 584; on Schuman's Symphony No. 6, 527; on Schuman's Symphony No. 7, 528–530; on Schuman's works, 526
Simó, Manuel, 773
Simón Bolívar Orchestra, 773
Sinclair, James B., 252, 272, 298n164
Sinfonia (Berio), 811
Sinfonia (Mennin), 618, 620
Sinfonia (Wilson), *794*
Sinfonía Ana Frank (Biriotti), 670
Sinfonía asturiana (Prieto), 741
Sinfonía Autóctona (Stea), 703
Sinfonia breve (Bloch), 438
Sinfonia breve (Van Vactor), 459
Sinfonía Burocrática ed Amazónica (Teruel), 715
Sinfonía Cívica (Samayoa), 753
Sinfonía concertada (Montero), 711
Sinfonía de Juguetes (Mena), 772–773
Sinfonía de la Patria (Chávez), *743*
Sinfonía dramática (Colón), 774
Sinfonía en cuatro partes (Vega), 770
Sinfonía en Negro: Homage to Martin Luther King (Balada), 797
Sinfonía en un movimiento (Garrido-Lecca), 704
Sinfonía folclórica (Adame), 751
Sinfonía Histórica (Samayoa), 753
Sinfonía incáica (Delgadillo), 757
Sinfonía India. See Symphony No. 2, *Sinfonía India* (Chávez)
Sinfonía Junín y Ayacucho (Iturriaga), 704
Sinfonía mexicana (Delgadillo), 757
Sinfonia No. 1 (Walker), 816, *817*
Sinfonía no. 1: En Recuerdo de Johannes Brahms (Gutiérrez), 761
Sinfonia No. 2 (Walker), 816, *817*
Sinfonia No. 3 (Walker), *817*, 819
Sinfonia No. 4, "Strands" (Walker), *795*, *818*, *819*, *821*
Sinfonia No. 5, "Visions" (Walker), *818*, 822, 859
Sinfonía para cuerdas (Tosar), 670
Sinfonía para orquesta (Chávez), *743*
Sinfonía patética (Coello Ramos), 757
Sinfonía Pípil (Orellana Castro), 756
Sinfonía Porteña (Ginastera), 677
Sinfónia Quisqueya (García), 772
Sinfonía romántica (Soro), 699
Sinfonía sobre temas colombianos (Ponce de Léon), 709
Sinfónica de Radio El Mundo, 675
Sinfonieta campestre (Herrarte), 754
Sinfonietta (Berezowski), 453
Sinfonietta (Chadwick), *9*, *140*, **151–153**, *152*
Sinfonietta (Fernández), 771
Sinfonietta (Korngold), 455
Sinfonietta (Lopatnikoff), *9*
Sinfonietta (Piston), *9*
Sinfonietta for Chamber Orchestra (Cowell), 404
Sinfonietta for Chamber Orchestra (Piston), *342*
Sinfonietta No. 1, "À memória de Mozart" (Villa-Lobos), *686*
Sinfonietta No. 2 (Villa-Lobos), *689*

single-movement works, 334–337
Singleton, Kenneth, 268
Singspiel, 484
Singularidad (Bolaños), 758, *759*, 760
Sintram and His Companions (La Motte-Fouqué), 162
Six-Day War, 606
six-movement works, *28*
1620–the Soil–the Indians–(England)–the Mayflower–the Landing of the Pilgrims (Bloch), 437. See also *America: An Epic Rhapsody* (Bloch)
Slater, Nicholas, *39*
Slatkin, Leonard, 486, 835
Slattery, Paul, 430, 432
slavery, 61, 158, 208, 215, 273, 340, 668, 672, 695, 711, 735, 764
sliding tones, 408
Slonimsky, Nicolas: and Guarnieri, 692; and Ippisch, 754; and Ives's *Holidays Symphony*, 250, 256; and Ives's orchestral sets, 285, 297n154, 298n164; and Ives's Symphony No. 4, 232; and Santa Cruz, 700; and Shapero, 458; and South American composers, 667; and Uruguayan composers, 668
Slonimsky's Earbox (Adams), 872
Smetana, Bedřich, 271
Smit, Leo, 640
Smith, Catherine Parsons, 425–428
Smith, Cecil, 569, 614–615
Smith, David Stanley, 457, 458
Smith, Helen, 590, 600
Smith, Leland, 838
Smith, Melville, 315
Smith, Moses, 518
Smith, Steve, 923
Smith, Warren Storey, 518, 692
Smith, Willie "The Lion," 415
Smith College, 455
Smithsonian Institution, 532
Snow-Bound: A Winter Idyl (Whittier), 250
Sociedad Cultural Nuestro Tiempo (Cuba), 769
Sociedad de Conciertos Sinfónicos del Conservatorio (Colombia), 710
Sociedade de Concertos Populares (Brazil), 682
Sociedad Filarmónica (Argentina), 672
Sociedad Filarmónica (Bolivia), 706, 737
Sociedad Filarmónica (Mexico), 737
Sociedad Filarmónica (Uruguay), 668
Sociedad Filarmónica (Venezuela), 711
Sociedad Filarmónica La Lira (Paraguay), 671
Sociedad Filarmónica y Drámatica (Bolivia), 705
Sociedad Haydn (Bolivia), 706
Sociedad Musical de Santa Cecilia de Quito (Ecuador), 708
Sociedad Nacional de la Música (Argentina), 674
Sociedad Orquestal Salvadoreña (El Salvador), 756
Society for the Preservation of the American Musical Heritage, 100
Sojo, Emilio Vicente, 712
Sokoloff, Nikolai, 311
Sol de América (Mastrogiovanni), 670
Soli I (Chávez), 749
Soli IV (Chávez), 749
Solís, Juan de, 668
Solomon, Maynard, 184, 289n10
Solovera, Aliosha, 702
Solti, Georg, 813
Somers, Harry, 36, *40*
Somervel, Stephen, 278
Something for Thee (Perkins), 233, 234, 245
Something Wild (film; score by Copland), 451
Sones de Castilla (Sanjuán), 765
Sonetos espirituales (Jiménez), 712
Song of Bernadette, The (film), 449
"Song of Harlem" (Johnson; Mvt. II of *Harlem Symphony*), 417
Song of Hiawatha, The (Longfellow), 126
"Song of Myself" (Whitman), 883
Song of Orpheus, A (Schuman), 530
Song of Roland, The, 126, 164
Songs of Innocence and of Experience (Bolcom), 844
sonic exuviation, 232
Sonneck, Oscar, 72, 374, 376
"Sonnet to Orpheus II, 13" (Rilke), 849
Son of Chamber Symphony (Adams), *868*, 872
Sorbonne, 708
Sorcerer's Apprentice, The (Dukas), 163
Soro, Enrique, *696*, 699
Sorrentino, Giulio, 834
Soto, Andrés, 761
Sousa, John Philip, 242, 275, 460, 922. See also specific composition titles
South America, **665–715**; Argentina, 672–681, *673–674*; Bolivia, *697*, 705–707; Brazil, 681–695, *683–684*; Chile, 695–702, *696*; Colombia, *698*, 709–710; Ecuador, *697–698*, 707–709; Paraguay, *669*, 671–672; Peru, *697*, 702–705;

political and social background, 665–668; Uruguay, 668–671, *669*; Venezuela, *698–699*, 711–715
South Asian idioms and influences, 553
Southern Baptists, 350
Souvenir de Porto Rico (Gottschalk), 115
Souza, Rodolfo Coelho de, 694
Soviet Union, 317, 338, 694
Sowerby, Leo, 310, 354, **374–377**, *375*, 634. *See also specific composition titles*
Space Symphony (Perry), *629*
Spain, 517, 666–667, 671
Spalding, Esperanza, 286
Spanish-American War, 735, 775
Spiegelman, Art, 922
Spies, Claudio, 667
spirit sounds, 554
spiritual minimalism, 633
spirituals, 422–423, 438, 819–822. *See also* hymns
Spohr, Louis, 92
Sprechstimme, 843
Springfield Festival, 141
Stabat Mater, Pergolesi's setting of text, 598
Stabat Mater, Perry's setting of text, 624, 625
Stabat Mater sequence (Gregorian chant), 509
Star-Spangled Banner, 115, 264, 276
State University of New York, 775
St. Cecilia Society, 61, 62
Stea, Vicente, *697*, 703
Steel Symphony (Balada), *794,* 797
Stehman, Dan, 334, 336
Stein, Gertrude, 350
Steinberg, Michael, 445, 474n421, 500, 607–608
Steinberg, William, 440, 631
Steiner, Max, 434, 451
Sternberg, Constantine von, 383
Stevens, Halsey, 640
Stevens, Wallace, 865
Steward, Daniel-Harry, 806
"St. Gaudens" in Boston Common, The (Col. Shaw and His Colored Regiment) (Ives), 272–274, *275,* 279, 284. *See also Orchestral Set No. 1, Three Places in New England* (Ives)
Still, William Grant, **424–433**; and American musical pedagogy, 381; and commercial recordings of symphonic works, 11; and Dawson, 410; and education of American-based composers, 314; and emergence of Black composers, 382; and European influences, 314; Guggenheim Fellowship, 425, 471n337; and Hailstork, 859; and Johnson, 415, 417; and Marsalis's works, 908; and Perry, 630; and Price, 418–420; and radio broadcasting, 310; and scope of American symphonic repertoire, 2; and social context of symphonic repertoire, 311; symphonies' movements and instrumentation, *426–427. See also specific composition titles*
Stiller, Andrew, 85
Still Movement with Hymn (Kernis), 864
Stites, Edgar P., 241
"St. Louis Blues" (Handy), 424
St. Louis Symphony Orchestra, 486, 584
St. Malachy's Church, 502–505
Stock, Frederick, 374, 376–377, 382, 420
Stockhausen, Karlheinz, 286, 752
Stokowski, Leopold: and Antheil's works, 388, 391; and Argentinian composers, 675; and Carillo, 741; and Copland, 323; and Dawson, 411, 414; and emergence of Black composers, 382; and Hovhaness, 555; and Ives's Symphony No. 4, 228; and Josten, 455; and maturation of American symphonic activity, 309; and Ponce, 741; and Still, 431; and Uruguayan composers, 670
Story of O, The (Réage), 497, 500
Stothart, Herbert, 451
Stowell, Edgar, 200
St. Patrick's Day (fiddle tune), 242
St. Paul Chamber Orchestra, 897
St. Petersburg Conservatory, 456
Straus, Joseph, 495
Straus, Noel, 228, 565
Strauss, Johann, 123, 164, 594, 607
Strauss, Richard, 194, 588, 594, 607, 669, 700, 891
Stravinsky, Igor, **447–450**; and Antheil, 383, 387; and Argentinian composers, 675; and Bernstein, 591, 607, 609; and Carter, 801; and Copland, 319, 322; and Cowell, 408; and Creston, 505; and Diamond, 572; and factionalism in American music, 484; and Hanson, 365; and influence of émigré composers, 433, 434; and key influences on American repertoire, 21; and Larsen, 884; and Mennin, 614; and OSSODRE, 670; and Perry, 632; and Persichetti, 578; and Schuman, 524; and Sessions, 488, 492, 493, 496; and South American composers, 712; symphonies written in America, 435; and Villa-Lobos, 683. *See also specific composition titles*

Stravinsky, Vera, 447
Street Beat (drum pattern): and Ives's *Holidays Symphony,* 256, 262; and Ives's orchestral sets, 273–274, 275; and Ives's Symphony No. 2, 210, 213; and Ives's Symphony No. 4, 233, 234, 242, 245
Strickland, William, 631
stride piano style, 415
String Quartet (Creston), 506
String Quartet 1931 (Seeger), 430
String Quartet in C-sharp Minor (Beethoven), 318, 746
String Quartet No. 1 (Diamond), 565
String Quartet No. 1 (Schuman), 517
String Quartet No 2. (Ginastera), 677
String Quartet No 2. (Ives), 232
String Quartet No 2. (Thomson), 354
String Quartet No. 2, "Musica Instrumentalis" (Kernis), 893, *894*
String Quartet No. 3 (Rochberg), 807, 812
String Quartet No. 3 (Schuman), 527
String Quartet No. 4 (Schuman), 530–531
String Quartet with Bass (Picker), 893
String Symphony (Serly), 458
Stroessner, Alfredo, 671
Strong, George Templeton, 30, **160–164**, *161,* 167. *See also specific composition titles*
Stucky, Steven, *795,* 796, 797–798
Suárez Urtubey, Pola, 677
subscriptions and ticket sales, 66, 67, 124
"Subway Journey, A" (Johnson; Mvt. I of *Harlem Symphony*), 417
Suite (Sowerby), 376, 377
Suite abstracta (Mata), 761
Suite Araucana (Marcelli), 699
Suite banal (Sandi), 751
Suite brasileira (Nepomuceno), 682
Suite colonial nicaragüense (diciembre) (Delgadillo), 757–758
Suite cubana (Ardévol), 768
Suite Cuzquena (González-Gamarra), 704
Suite de danzas (Lapeiretta), 773
Suite de Imagenes (Marchena), 773
Suite d'orchestre (Preti-Bonati), 668
Suite Ecuatoriana (Moreno), 708
Suite el güegüense (Salas), 758
Suite for Cello and Harp (Harrison), 803
Suite for Chamber Orchestra (Contreras), 751
Suite for String Orchestra (Allende), 699
Suite for String Orchestra (Schoenberg), 458
Suite für Grosses Orchester (MacDowell), **165–167**
Suite incaica (Torrá), 681
Suite indígena o centroamericana (Delgadillo), 758
Suite para orquesta (Caturla), 767
Suite sinfónica para el payaso (Davidovsky), 680
Suite symphonique (Chadwick), *140,* **153–156**, *155*
Suite típica (Holguín), 710
Suite Tropical (Fonseca), 760
Sullivan, Arthur, 233
Sumaya, Manuel de, 736
Summerfield, Susan, 806
"Sunset" Symphony (Hovhaness), *535*
Suomalainen Tango (Ortíz), 680–681
Švanda dudák (Weinberger), 459
Swafford, Jan, 293n83
Swanson, Howard, 458
Swayne, Steve, 513, 517–519, 527–530, 532
Swed, Mark, 922
Sweney, John R., 188, 241
"Swing Low, Sweet Chariot" (spiritual), 822
swing music, 908
Switten, Henry, 625
Switzerland, 448
Sylviad, The (Heinrich), 71
Symphomaniac (Ellington), 454
Symphoniae sacrae III (Schütz), 812
Symphonia serena (Hindemith), 439
Symphonia: sum fluxae pretium spei (Carter), *794, 798, 799,* 802, 845
Symphonic Dances (Hindemith), 440
Symphonic Interlude (Lockwood), 456
symphonic jazz, 313, 376, 487, 906
Symphonic Metamorphosis on Themes by Carl Maria von Weber (Hindemith), 439
Symphonic Orchestra of Venezuela, 715
Symphonic Picture of Carousel, A (Bennett), 453
Symphonic Sequences (Lockwood), 456
Symphonic Serenade for Strings in B-flat (Korngold), 455
Symphonic Sketches (Chadwick), viii, *140,* **147–151**, *149,* 156
Symphonic Story of Jerome Kern, A (Bennett), 452–453
Symphonic Variations for Audience and Orchestra (Serly), 458
Symphonie en fa pour grand orchestra (Antheil), *385,* 387
Symphonie fantastique (Berlioz), 99, 104, 163, 579

Index

Symphonie gaspésienne (Champagne), 36
Symphonie militaire (Meignen), 64, *64–65*, 100, 107
Symphonies of Wind Instruments (Stravinsky), 383, *447–448*, 801
Symphony (Lockwood), 456
Symphony (Moross), 457
Symphony (Ran), *794*, 796, 797
Symphony (Stucky), *795*, 796, 798
Symphony 1933 (Harris), *327*
Symphony 1997: Heaven Earth Mankind (Dun), 916
Symphony-American Portrait (Harris), *327*, 334
Symphony for Band, "West Point" (Harris), *330*, 339
Symphony for Classical Orchestra (Shapero), 458
Symphony for Concert Band (Sanders), 457
Symphony for Five Instruments (Antheil), 383, *384*
Symphony for Organ and Orchestra (Copland), 511. See also Symphony No. 1, *Symphony for Organ and Orchestra* (Copland)
Symphony for Trombone and Orchestra (Bloch), 438
Symphony for Voices (Harris), 334
Symphony: Forward (Larsen), *882*, 886
Symphony for Winds and Percussion (Krenek), 455
Symphony Hall (Boston), 147, 272, 835
Symphony in A (Sanders), 457
Symphony in A, "Virginia Symphony" (Powell), 457
Symphony in A Major (Mejía-Arredondo), 772
Symphony in B-flat for Band (Hindemith), 440, 582
Symphony in Black (Ellington), 454
Symphony in Brown (Johnson), *416*, 418
Symphony in C (Orbón), 770
Symphony in C (Stravinsky), **448–449**, 632
Symphony in C Minor (Castro), 737
Symphony in C Minor (Cervantes), 765
Symphony in C Minor (Converse), 453
Symphony in C Minor (Oldberg), 457
Symphony in D for the Dodgers (Bennett), 452
Symphony in D Minor (Borowski), 453
Symphony in E-flat (Bloch), 438
Symphony in E-flat (Hindemith), 439, 440
Symphony in E-flat (Stravinsky), 447
Symphony in E Minor (Borowski), 453
Symphony in E Minor (Converse), 453
Symphony in E Minor (Rolón), 740
Symphony in E Minor, "Gaelic" (Beach), 6, 21, 30, *157*, **157–159**, 167
Symphony in E Minor, "Pennsylvania" (Cadman), 453
Symphony in F (Josten), 455
Symphony in F Major (Converse), 453
Symphony in F Minor (Converse), 453
Symphony in F Minor (Oldberg), 457
Symphony in Four Cycles (Serly), 458
Symphony in Four Movements and Coda (Lockwood), 456
Symphony in F-sharp Major (Korngold), 455
Symphony in G (Sowerby), 374
Symphony in G Major (Borowski), 453
Symphony in One Movement (Vauclain), 459
Symphony in Three Movements (Stravinsky), **449–450**
Symphony in Two Movements (Alfagüell), 761
Symphony in Waves. See Symphony No. 1, *Symphony in Waves* (Kernis)
Symphony: New England Holidays, A (Ives), **249–267**; cumulative form of, *259–261*; *Decoration Day*, *177*, 249, **252–256**, *254–255*, *257*, 258, 267, 295n110, 295n113, 295n115, 834; and diversity of American symphonic styles, 175; *The Fourth of July*, **256–264**, *259–261*, *262*, *263*; and Ives's diverse musical background, 183–184; and Ives's orchestral sets, 274, 285; and Ives's Symphony No. 2, 200, 215; and Ives's *Universe Symphony*, 270–271; movements and instrumentation, *177–178*; premiere of, 54n83; and scope of American symphonic repertoire, 6; suite and symphony, 266–267; and "symphony" designation, 294n101, 297n153; *Thanksgiving and Forefathers' Day*, *178*, 249, 256–264, *259–261*, *262*, **264–266**, 296n130; *Washington's Birthday*, 24, *177*, 249, **250–252**, 253, 256, 264, 267, 284, 295n104
Symphony No. 1, *RiverRun* (Albert), *794*, 860, *861*, *862–863*
Symphony No. 1 (Antheil), *384*, 387
Symphony No. 1 (Asia), *794*, 886, *887*, 891
Symphony No. 1 (Bacon), 452
Symphony No. 1 in One Movement (Barber), 5, 11, 21, *355*, **356–358**, *357*, *358*, 511
Symphony No. 1 (Berezowski), *9*
Symphony No. 1, *Jeremiah* (Bernstein), *9*, 586, *587*, 589, **590–592**, *591*, 601–602, 606, 609
Symphony No. 1 (Bolcom), *839*, 842

Symphony No. 1 in C Minor (Brahms), 134, 201, 206, 210, 213
Symphony No. 1, "Tonal Plexus" (Branca), *794*
Symphony No. 1 in E-flat Major (Bristow), 69, *87*, **89–90**
Symphony No. 1, "Sermons in Stones" (Carpenter), 453
Symphony No. 1 (Carter), 798, *799*
Symphony No. 1 in C Major (Chadwick), 138, *139*, **141–142**, 151, 156
Symphony No. 1, *Sinfonía de Antigona* (Chávez), 9, *742, 743*
Symphony No. 1, "Music on Open Strings" (Coates), *794*, 797, 834
Symphony No. 1, *Symphony for Organ and Orchestra* (Copland), 9, **319–322**, *320*, 326
Symphony No. 1 (Corigliano): and Adams's *Scheherazade.2,* 873; and Bates's *Liquid Interface,* 909; and commercial recordings of symphonic works, 11; and Corigliano's composer-in-residence tenure, 831; and distinctive qualities of American symphony, 23; epilogue, 835, *836*; and Ives, 286; on Kernis's *Symphony in Waves,* 900; and key influences on American repertoire, 22; links to Symphony No. 3, 837–838; movements and instrumentation, *832*; and Rouse's Symphony No. 1, 876; symphony premiere dates, *794*; third movement described, 834–835
Symphony No. 1 (Cowell), *397*
Symphony No. 1 (Creston), 503, *503, 505,* 506
Symphony No. 1 (Diamond), 560, *561,* 565
Symphony No. 1 (Dick), 453
Symphony No. 1 in F Major (Dukelsky), *9*
Symphony No. 1, "Symphonic Aphorisms" (Fairouz), 919, *920*
Symphony No. 1 in C Minor (Gade), 67
Symphony No. 1, "Low" (Glass), 35, *794*, 822, *823*
Symphony No. 1, *Symphonie romantique: La nuit des tropiques* (Gottschalk), 21, 112–115, *113, 114*
Symphony No. 1 (Gould), 454
Symphony No. 1 (Guarnieri), 692
Symphony No. 1 in D Minor, "Youth and Life" (Hadley), 454
Symphony No. 1 (Hailstork), 856, *857*
Symphony No. 1 in E Minor, "Nordic" Symphony (Hanson), 6, *9*, 344, *363*, **365**, *366–368*, 369
Symphony No. 1 (Harbison), *846,* 848
Symphony No. 1 (Honegger), 365

Symphony No. 1, *Exile Symphony* (Hovhaness), *535*
Symphony No. 1 in D Minor (Ives), **185–199**, 201; American theme, 290n18; cyclic theme, *192, 196*; and diversity of American symphonic styles, 175; first theme, *189–190*; formal plan, *186–187*; harmonies, *194*; and key influences on American repertoire, 21; main ideas, *195*; movements and instrumentation, *176*; premiere of, 54n83; publication and performance, 183–184; and Symphony No. 2, 200, 210–211; and Symphony No. 3, 226; theme sources, *207*
Symphony No. 1, *Symphony in Waves* (Kernis), *794*, 878, *894, 897, 898–899*, 909
Symphony No. 1, 455
Symphony No. 1, *Water Music* (Larsen), *794*, 878, *880*, 909
Symphony No. 1 (Liebermann), 901, *902*
Symphony No. 1 (Lopatnikoff), 456
Symphony No. 1, *Sinfonia dialectica* (Lourié), 456
Symphony No. 1 in D Major (Mahler), 162, 299n168, 843
Symphony No. 1, *All Rise* (Marsalis), *905, 907*
Symphony No. 1 (Martinů), 441
Symphony No. 1 in C Minor (Mason), 9, 456
Symphony No. 1, "The Santa Fe Trail" (McDonald), 456
Symphony No. 1 (Mennin), 611
Symphony No. 1 (Milhaud), 446
Symphony No. 1 in C Minor (Paine), **127–135**; and Bristow, 100; contrasted with Symphony No. 2, 137; first movement, *129–130, 131, 132–134*; and key influences on American repertoire, 21; movements and instrumentation, *128*; and scope of American symphonic repertoire, 1; and Strong's Symphony No. 1, 161
Symphony No. 1, *Symphony in One Movement for Violas and String Basses* (Perry), 627
Symphony No. 1 (Persichetti), *576,* 578–579
Symphony No. 1 (Picker), 891, *892*
Symphony No. 1 (Piston), **341–344**, *342,* 348
Symphony No. 1 in E Minor (Price), 32, 42, 410, **420–422**, *421,* 423
Symphony No. 1 (Read), 457
Symphony No. 1 (Rochberg), 807, *808,* 811
Symphony No. 1 (Rouse), *794,* 873, *874*
Symphony No. 1, "Of the Great Rivers" (Saminsky), 457
Symphony No. 1 (Santoro), 694
Symphony No. 1 (Schuman), *514,* 517–519

Index

Symphony No. 1 in B-flat Major, "Spring" (Schumann), 136
Symphony No. 1 (Serly), 458
Symphony No. 1 in E Minor (Sessions), *489*, **492–493**
Symphony No. 1, "Horizons" (Shepherd), 458
Symphony No. 1 (Siegmeister), 458
Symphony No. 1 (Somers), 36
Symphony No. 1 in E Minor (Sowerby), *375*, 376
Symphony No. 1, *Afro-American Symphony* (Still), **428–431**; and Dawson, 410; first performance, 425; and Johnson's *Harlem Symphony,* 417; and Marsalis's "Blues Symphony," 908; movements and instrumentation, *426*; and Price's Symphony No. 1, 421; and scope of American symphonic repertoire, 2
Symphony No. 1 in F Major, "In the Mountains" (Strong), 160, *161*
Symphony No. 1 (Thompson), *378*, **379–380**
Symphony No. 1, *Symphony on a Hymn Tune* (Thomson), **350–353**, *351*, *352*, 508
Symphony No. 1 (Toch), 459
Symphony No. 1 in D Minor (Van Vactor), 459
Symphony No. 1, "O Imprevisto" (Villa-Lobos), 685–691, *686*
Symphony No. 1, "Awakening" (Wang), 916, *917*
Symphony No. 1 (Whithorne), 460
Symphony No. 1 in F Minor, "A Symphony of San Francisco" (Willson), 460
Symphony No. 1, "Three Movements for Orchestra" (Zwilich), *794*, 849–850, *851*, *853*, 855
Symphony No. 2 (Albert), *861,* 864
Symphony No. 2 (Antheil), *385,* 387, 506–508
Symphony No. 2, "Celebration Symphony" (Asia), *887*, 890, 891
Symphony No. 2, "Requiem for a Poet" (Auerbach), 795
Symphony No. 2 (Bacon), 452
Symphony No. 2 (Barber), *355*, **358–362**, *360–361*
Symphony No. 2 (Berezowski), 453
Symphony No. 2, *The Age of Anxiety* (Bernstein), 24, 495, 527, 586, *587,* 589–590, **592–595**, 599, 605–606
Symphony No. 2, "Oracles" (Bolcom), 21, *839,* 842, 844
Symphony No. 2 in D Major (Brahms), 159
Symphony No. 2, in D Minor, "Jullien" (Bristow), *87,* **90–92**, *91*, 100
Symphony No. 2 (Carpenter), 453

Symphony No. 2 in B-flat Major (Chadwick), 3, 51n22, *139*, *142*, **142–145**, *143*, *145*, 152
Symphony No. 2, *Sinfonía India* (Chávez), 2, *9*, 11, 24, 34, 36, 742, *744,* 750
Symphony No. 2, *Short Symphony* (Copland), 319, *321*, **322–323**, 326, 845
Symphony No. 2 (Cordero), 762
Symphony No. 2 (Corigliano), *831*, *832,* 835, 916
Symphony No. 2, "Anthropos" (Cowell), *397*
Symphony No. 2 (Creston), *503*
Symphony No. 2, "After Walt Whitman" (DeLamarter), 453
Symphony No. 2 (Diamond), *561,* *565,* 566–567, 569
Symphony No. 2 (Fairouz), *919*, *920*
Symphony No. 2 (Ficher), 675
Symphony No. 2 (Galindo), 762
Symphony No. 2 (Glass), *823,* 828, *829*
Symphony No. 2, *À Montevideo* (Gottschalk), *111*, 114–115
Symphony No. 2, "On Marching Tunes" (Gould), 454
Symphony No. 2 (Gruenberg), 454
Symphony No. 2 (Guarnieri), 692, 693
Symphony No. 2 in F Minor, "The Four Seasons" (Hadley), 454
Symphony No. 2 (Hailstork), 35, *794,* 857, 858
Symphony No. 2 in D-flat Major, "Romantic" (Hanson), 2, 11, *363,* **365–369**, *369,* 373–374
Symphony No. 2 (Harbison), *846,* 848
Symphony No. 2 (Harris), *327,* 334
Symphony No. 2 (Hétu), 36
Symphony No. 2, *Mysterious Mountain* (Hovhaness), *536,* **555–558**, *557*
Symphony No. 2, "Fall of Constantinople" (Ince), *794*
Symphony No. 2 (Ives), **199–217**; and commercial recordings of symphonic works, 11; and distinctive qualities of American symphony, 23; and diversity of American symphonic styles, 175; formal plan, *202–205*; harmonic structure, 194; main ideas, *195*; movements and instrumentation, *176*; premiere of, 54n83; publication and performance, 183–184; and Symphony No. 1, 185, 198; and Symphony No. 3, 227; theme and theme sources, *207, 209*
Symphony No. 2 (Kernis), 35, 897, 900
Symphony No. 2 (Krenek), 455
Symphony No. 2 (Larsen), 830

Index

Symphony No. 2 (Liebermann), *794,* 901, *902,* 904
Symphony No. 2 (Lopatnikoff), 456
Symphony No. 2, *Kormtchaia* (Lourié), 456
Symphony No. 2 in C Minor, "Resurrection" (Mahler), 586, 601, 604, 606, 711, 922
Symphony No. 2, "Blues Symphony" (Marsalis), *905,* 908
Symphony No. 2 (Martinů), 442
Symphony No. 2 in A Major (Mason), 456
Symphony No. 2, "The Rhumba" (McDonald), 456
Symphony No. 2 in B-flat Major, "Lobgesang" (Mendelssohn), 98
Symphony No. 2 (Mennin), *611,* 613
Symphony No. 2 (Milhaud), 446
Symphony No. 2 in A (Moore), 456
Symphony No. 2 in A Major, "Spring" (Paine), 30, *128,* **135–138,** 166
Symphony No. 2 (Perry), *627*
Symphony No. 2 (Persichetti), *576,* 578–579
Symphony No. 2, "Aussöhnung" (Picker), *794, 891, 892*
Symphony No. 2 (Piston), *9, 342,* **344–345,** 349
Symphony No. 2 in D Minor (Prokofiev), 878
Symphony No. 2, "Island of Innocence" (Puts), 2, *795,* 922
Symphony No. 2 (Read), 457
Symphony No. 2 (Rochberg), *808,* 811
Symphony No. 2 (Rouse), 864, *874,* 876, *877*
Symphony No. 2, *Symphonie des sommets* (Saminsky), 457
Symphony No. 2 (Schuman), *9,* 21, *514,* 517, 517–519, 525–526
Symphony No. 2 (Serly), 458
Symphony No. 2 (Sessions), *489,* **493–496,** *494*
Symphony No. 2 in D Minor (Shepherd), *9,* 458
Symphony No. 2 in D Major (Sibelius), 520–522
Symphony No. 2 (Siegmeister), 458
Symphony No. 2 in B Minor (Sowerby), 376, 377
Symphony No. 2 in G Minor "Song of a New Race" (Still), 425, *426,* 431
Symphony No. 2 in G Minor, "Sintram: The Struggle of Man against Evil Powers" (Strong), *161,* **162–164**
Symphony No. 2 in E Minor (Thompson), 5, *9, 378,* 379, *380,* **380–381**
Symphony No. 2 in C Major (Thomson), 350, *351,* **353–354**
Symphony No. 2 (Toch), 459
Symphony No. 2, "Music for the Marines" (Van Vactor), 459
Symphony No. 2, "Ascenção" (Villa-Lobos), *686,* 691, 721n93
Symphony No. 2, "To and from Dakini" (Wang), *795, 917, 918,* 918–919
Symphony No. 2 (Whithorne), 460
Symphony No. 2 in E Minor, "Missions of California" (Willson), 460
Symphony No. 2, "Cello Symphony" (Zwilich), 11, 850, *851*
Symphony No. 3, "American" (Antheil), 21, *385,* **387–388**
Symphony No. 3 (Asia), *794,* 888
Symphony No. 3 in E-flat Major, "Eroica" (Beethoven), 620, 668, 812, 819
Symphony No. 3 (Berezowski), *9*
Symphony No. 3 (Bernard), 599
Symphony No. 3, *Kaddish* (Bernstein), **595–609;** and conceptions of symphonic form, 586; and emergence of early postmodernist styles, 626; and Fairouz's Symphony No. 3, 922; and key influences on American repertoire, 22; and Mennin's Symphony No. 8, 619; movements and instrumentation, *588,* 590; reception of, *585;* rhythmic profile, 591–592; twelve-tone rows, 599–605, *602, 603*
Symphony No. 3 for chamber orchestra (Bolcom), *839,* 842
Symphony No. 3 in F Major (Brahms), 146, 210
Symphony No. 3 in F-Sharp Minor (Bristow), 21, *87,* **92–95,** *93, 94,* 100
Symphony No. 3 in F Major (Chadwick), 4, 21, 51n22, *126, 139,* **146–147,** 151
Symphony No. 3 (Chávez), 34, 742–746, *744, 746,* 749
Symphony No. 3 (Copland), **323–326;** and commercial recordings of symphonic works, 11; and distinctive qualities of American symphony, 24; and "Great American Symphony" trope, 5, 451; and Harbison, 845; and Harrison's Symphony No. 3, 806; influence on Albert, 860; and key influences on American repertoire, 22; movements and instrumentation, *321;* opening theme, *324;* and scope of American symphonic repertoire, 2; "strumming" gesture, 527; and twelve-tone system, 599
Symphony No. 3, "Circus Maximus" (Corigliano), 9, *795,* 798, 831, *833,* 837–838, 845

Index

Symphony No. 3, *Gaelic Symphony* (Cowell), *397*

Symphony No. 3, "The Three Mysteries" (Creston), *503*, 506, 508–510

Symphony No. 3 in E (DeLamarter), 453

Symphony No. 3 (Diamond), *561,* 566, *566*

Symphony No. 3, "Poems and Prayers" (Fairouz), 22, *795*, 919, 920

Symphony No. 3 (Glass), *823,* 828

Symphony No. 3, "Symphony of Sorrowful Songs" (Górecki), 797

Symphony No. 3 (Gould), 454

Symphony No. 3 (Gruenberg), 454

Symphony No. 3 (Guarnieri), 693

Symphony No. 3 in B Minor (Hadley), *9,* 455

Symphony No. 3 (Hailstork), *857,* 858

Symphony No. 3 (Hanson), *363,* **369–372,** *370–371*

Symphony No. 3 (Harbison), 24, *794, 846,* 848

Symphony No. 3 (Harris), **334–337**; and Antheil, 387; and commercial recordings of symphonic works, 11; and distinctive qualities of American symphony, 24, 29; and "Great American Symphony" trope, 5; and key influences on American repertoire, 21; movements and instrumentation, *328*; opening, *336*; and Schuman's Symphony No. 2, 519; and scope of American symphonic repertoire, 2

Symphony No. 3 (Harrison), *804,* 806

Symphony No. 3 (Hartke), *795*

Symphony No. 3 (Hétu), 36

Symphony No. 3 (Hovhaness), *536*

Symphony No. 3, *Sinfonía Guatemalteca* (Ippisch), 754

Symphony No. 3, *The Camp Meeting* (Ives), **217–228**; culminating statement, *224, 225, 226*; and cumulative form, 198, 222, 282; and diversity of American symphonic styles, 175; harmonic structure, 194; and Harrison, 803; and *Holidays Symphony,* 265; and Ives's orchestral sets, 271, 272; movements and instrumentation, *176*; premiere of, 54n83; publication and performance, 183–184; and rejected movement from Third Symphony, 299n183; and Symphony No. 1, 185; and Symphony No. 2, 200; theme sources, *220–221*; and Thomson, 350

Symphony No. 3, "Symphony of Meditations" (Kernis), 6, 22, *795, 895,* 900, 922

Symphony No. 3 (Krenek), 455

Symphony No. 3, "Lyric" (Larsen), *881, 883,* 886, 890

Symphony No. 3 (Liebermann), 21, *902,* 904

Symphony No. 3 (Lopatnikoff), 456

Symphony No. 3 (Lutosławski), 797

Symphony No. 3 in D Minor (Mahler), 597, 598, 848

Symphony No. 3, "Swing Symphony" (Marsalis), *795,* 905

Symphony No. 3 (Martinů), 442

Symphony No. 3, "A Lincoln Symphony" (Mason), 456

Symphony No. 3, "Lamentations of Fu Hsuan" (McDonald), 456

Symphony No. 3 (Mennin), *611,* **613–614,** 624

Symphony No. 3, "Te Deum" (Milhaud), 446

Symphony No. 3 (Orrego-Salas), 701

Symphony No. 3 (Pärt), 797

Symphony No. 3, *Symphony for Ten Parts* (Pentland), 36

Symphony No. 3 (Perry), *627*

Symphony No. 3 (Persichetti), *576,* 578–579, 615

Symphony No. 3 for string orchestra (Picker), *892*

Symphony No. 3 (Piston), *342,* **345–346,** 349

Symphony No. 3 in C Minor (Price), **422–424,** *423*

Symphony No. 3 in F Major, "Im Walde" (Raff), 160

Symphony No. 3 (Rochberg), 807, *809,* 811, 812, 830

Symphony No. 3 (Rouse), 9, *875,* 878

Symphony No. 3 in G Minor (Roussel), 365

Symphony No. 3 in C Minor, "Organ" Symphony (Saint-Saëns), 511

Symphony No. 3, "Symphony of the Seas" (Saminsky), 457

Symphony No. 3 (Schuman), **519–526**; chorale theme, *523*; and Diamond's Symphony No. 1, 565; fugue subject, *522*; and "Great American Symphony" trope, 5; movements and instrumentation, *514*; passacaglia theme, *521–522*

Symphony No. 3 in E-flat Major, "Rhenish" (Schumann), 125

Symphony No. 3 (Sessions), *489,* 496

Symphony No. 3 in C Major (Sibelius), 518

Symphony No. 3 (In One Movement) (Siegmeister), 458

Symphony No. 3 in F-sharp Minor (Sowerby), *375,* 377

Symphony No. 3, "The Sunday Symphony" (Still), *425, 426,* 431

Symphony No. 3 (Thompson), *378,* **381**

1010

Symphony No. 3 (Thomson), 350, *351*, **354**
Symphony No. 3 (Toch), 459
Symphony No. 3 in C Major (Van Vactor), 459
Symphony No. 3, "A Guerra" (Villa-Lobos), *687*
Symphony No. 3 (Zwilich), *852*, 855
Symphony No. 4, "1942" (Antheil), 23, *385*, **388–392**, *389–390*, 468n233
Symphony No. 4 (Asia), 864, *888*, 890
Symphony No. 4 (Bacon), 452, 502
Symphony No. 4 (Blackwood), *794*
Symphony No. 4 (Bolcom), *839*, 843
Symphony No. 4 in E Minor (Brahms), 358, 573, 623
Symphony No. 4, in E Minor "Arcadian" (Bristow), 51n27, 88, **95–98**, *97*, 100
Symphony No. 4, *Sinfonía romántica* (Chávez), 34, *745*, 746, *748*
Symphony No. 4, "Short Symphony" (Cowell), 350, *397*, **404–406**
Symphony No. 4 (Creston), *503*, 510–511
Symphony No. 4 (Diamond), *561*, 566, **567–569**
Symphony No. 4, "In the Shadow of No Towers" (Fairouz), 23, 35, 286, *921*, 922–923
Symphony No. 4, "Heroes" (Glass), 35, *824*, 828
Symphony No. 4 for Band (Gould), 454
Symphony No. 4 (Gruenberg), 454
Symphony No. 4 (Guarnieri), 692–693
Symphony No. 4 in D Minor, "North, East, South, and West" (Hadley), *9*, 455
Symphony No. 4, "Survive" (Hailstork), *857*, 859
Symphony No. 4, "Requiem" (Hanson), 364, 372–374
Symphony No. 4 (Harbison), *846*, 848
Symphony No. 4, *Folk-Song Symphony* (Harris), 9, 329, **337–338**, 451
Symphony No. 4 (Harrison), 6, *805*, 806
Symphony No. 4 for Wind Orchestra, (Hovhaness), *536*
Symphony No. 4 (Ives), **228–249**; analytical approaches to, 293n76; and distinctive qualities of American symphony, 23; and diversity of American symphonic styles, 175; finale and borrowed tunes, 247–248; fourth movement theme, *246*; and "Great American Symphony" trope, 5; and Ives's background, 183; and Ives's orchestral sets, 271, 298n162, 299n168; movements and instrumentation, *177*; premiere of, 54n83; second movement programmatic structure, *236–240*; and Symphony No. 2, 215

Symphony No. 4, "Chromelodeon" (Kernis), *795*, *896*, 900
Symphony No. 4 (Krenek), 456
Symphony No. 4, "String Symphony" (Larsen), *881*, 884
Symphony No. 4 (Liebermann), *903*
Symphony No. 4 (Lopatnikoff), 456
Symphony No. 4 (Lutosławski), 797
Symphony No. 4 in G (Mahler), 586, 597, 604, 607
Symphony No. 4, "The Jungle" (Marsalis), *795*, *905*, 908
Symphony No. 4 (Martinů), 442
Symphony No. 4 for wind ensemble (Maslanka), *794*
Symphony No. 4, "Festival of the Workers" (McDonald), 456
Symphony No. 4, "The Cycle" (Mennin), *611*, 613, **614–615**, 618
Symphony No. 4, *Composée à l'occasion de Centenaire de la Révolution de 1848* (Milhaud), 446
Symphony No. 4 (Montero), 711
Symphony No. 4, "Los Angeles" (Pärt), 797
Symphony No. 4 (Perry), *627*, 630, 632
Symphony No. 4 (Persichetti), 576, 578–579
Symphony No. 4 (Piston), *342*, **346–348**, *347*, *348*, 349
Symphony No. 4 in C (Prokofiev), 365
Symphony No. 4 (Rochberg), *794*, 809, 812
Symphony No. 4 (Rouse), *795*, *875*, 878
Symphony No. 4, "Sinfonia da Paz" (Santoro), 694
Symphony No. 4 (Schuman), *515*, 519, **526–527**
Symphony No. 4 in D Minor (Schumann), 125
Symphony No. 4 (Sessions), *489*, 495, 496, 497
Symphony No. 4 in A Minor (Sibelius), 904
Symphony No. 4 (Siegmeister), 458
Symphony No. 4 in B♭ (Sowerby), *375*, 377
Symphony No. 4 in F Major, "Die Weihe der Töne" (Spohr), 92
Symphony No. 4, "Autochthonous" (Still), 424, 425, *427*, **431–432**, 859
Symphony No. 4 in F Minor (Tchaikovsky), 201, 412, 527, 815
Symphony No. 4 (Toch), 459
Symphony No. 4, "Walden" (Van Vactor), 459
Symphony No. 4, "A Vitória" (Villa-Lobos), *687*
Symphony No. 4, "The Gardens" (Zwilich), *852*, 855
Symphony No. 5, "Joyous" (Antheil), 21, *386*, **392–395**, *393–394*

Symphony No. 5, "Tragic" (Antheil, unpublished), *386*, 392
Symphony No. 5, "Of Songs and Psalms" (Asia), 22, *889*, 891
Symphony No. 5, "American" (Balada), 797, 922
Symphony No. 5 in C Minor (Beethoven), 66, 127, 132, 134–135, 212, 613, 812, 819, 843, *844*, 878
Symphony No. 5 (Bolcom), *794, 840,* 843
Symphony No. 5 in C Major, *Niagara* (Bristow), 88, **98–100**, *99*
Symphony No. 5 (Chávez), 34, 651n239, *745, 746*–747
Symphony No. 5 (Cowell), *398*
Symphony No. 5 (Creston), *504,* 510–511
Symphony No. 5 for Large Orchestra (Diamond), *562*, **570**, 573–574
Symphony No. 5 (Fairouz), *921,* 923
Symphony No. 5, "Requiem, Bardo, and Nirmanakaya" (Glass), 6, *824,* 828, 830, 878
Symphony No. 5 (Guarnieri), 692–693
Symphony No. 5 in C Minor, "Connecticut" (Hadley), 455
Symphony No. 5 (Hailstork), 859
Symphony No. 5, "Sinfonia sacra" (Hanson), *364, 372*–374
Symphony No. 5 (Harbison), *846,* 849
Symphony No. 5 (Harris), 22, *329*, **338–339**
Symphony No. 5, "Short Symphony" (Hovhaness), *536*
Symphony No. 5 (Krenek), 456
Symphony No. 5, *Solo Symphony* (Larsen), *794, 882, 884, 885,* 886
Symphony No. 5 in C-sharp Minor (Mahler), 812, 813, *814*
Symphony No. 5 (Martinů), **442–444**, *443, 444*
Symphony No. 5 (Mennin), 9, *611,* **615–616**
Symphony No. 5, "Integration" (Perry), 626, *627,* 632
Symphony No. 5, Symphony for Strings in One Movement (Persichetti), *576, 580*, **580–582**, *581*
Symphony No. 5 (Piston), *343*, **348–349**
Symphony No. 5 in B-flat Major (Prokofiev), 393
Symphony No. 5 (Rochberg), 21, 24, *794, 809,* **813**, 815
Symphony No. 5 (Rouse), *875,* 878
Symphony No. 5, *Jerusalem, City of Solomon and Christ* (Saminsky), 457
Symphony No. 5 (Santoro), 694

Symphony No. 5 Symphony for Strings (Schuman), *515,* 524, **527**, 651n239
Symphony No. 5 (Sessions), *490,* 497
Symphony No. 5 in D Minor (Shostakovich), 494, 815, 904
Symphony No. 5 in E-flat Major (Sibelius), 371, 388
Symphony No. 5, "Visions of Time" (Siegmeister), 458
Symphony No. 5 (Sowerby), *375,* 377
Symphony No. 5, "Western Hemisphere" (Still), *425, 427,* 431, **432–433**
Symphony No. 5 (Toch), 459
Symphony No. 5 (Van Vactor), 459
Symphony No. 5, "A Paz" (Villa-Lobos), *688*
Symphony No. 5, *Canticles of America* (Ward), 459
Symphony No. 5, "Concerto for Orchestra" (Zwilich), *852,* 856, 884
Symphony No. 6, "after Delacroix" (Antheil), *386*, **395–396**
Symphony No. 6, "Iris" (Asia), *889*
Symphony No. 6 in F Major, "Pastoral" (Beethoven), 66
Symphony No. 6 (Bolcom), *840,* 843
Symphony No. 6 (Chávez), *745,* 747
Symphony No. 6 (Cowell), *398*
Symphony No. 6 for Organ and Orchestra (Creston), *504*, **511–513**, 575
Symphony No. 6 (Diamond), *562*, **570**
Symphony No. 6, "Plutonian Ode" (Glass), *825,* 828
Symphony No. 6 (Guarnieri), 693
Symphony No. 6 (Hanson), *364,* 373
Symphony No. 6 (Harbison), *846*
Symphony No. 6, "Gettysburg" (Harris), *330,* 339
Symphony No. 6, "Celestial Gate" (Hovhaness), *537*
Symphony No. 6 in A Minor, "Tragic" (Mahler), 701, 815, 876
Symphony No. 6, *Fantaisies symphoniques* (Martinů), **445**, 474n421
Symphony No. 6 (Mennin), *612,* 615, **616–617**, 624
Symphony No. 6 (Milhaud), 446
Symphony No. 6 for Winds (Perry), *627*
Symphony No. 6, Symphony for Band (Persichetti), 9, *576,* 580, **582–584**, *585*
Symphony No. 6 (Piston), *343,* **348–349**

Symphony No. 6 (Rochberg), *810,* 815
Symphony No. 6 (Rouse), *875,* 878
Symphony No. 6 (Salgado), 708
Symphony No. 6 (Santoro), 694
Symphony No. 6 in One Movement (Schuman), 9, 21, 485, *515,* 520, **527–528**
Symphony No. 6 (Sessions), 488, *490,* 497, 500, 900
Symphony No. 6 (Siegmeister), 458
Symphony No. 6 (Toch), 459
Symphony No. 6 (Van Vactor), 459
Symphony No. 6, *Sobre as Linhas das Montanhas do Brasil* (Villa-Lobos), 685, 688
Symphony No. 6 (Williams), 876
Symphony No. 7 (Antheil), 21, *386,* 528–530
Symphony No. 7 (Bennett), 452–453
Symphony No. 7, "Symphonic Concerto" (Bolcom), *840, 843,* 884
Symphony No. 7 in E Major (Bruckner), 876
Symphony No. 7 (Chávez), *745*
Symphony No. 7 for Small Orchestra (Cowell), *398*
Symphony No. 7 (Diamond), *562,* **570**
Symphony No. 7, "A Toltec Symphony" (Glass), *825,* 828–830
Symphony No. 7 (Guarnieri), 692, 693
Symphony No. 7, "A Sea Symphony" (Hanson), *364,* 373
Symphony No. 7 (Harris), *330,* 339
Symphony No. 7 for Wind Orchestra, "Nanga Parvat" (Hovhaness), *537*
Symphony No. 7 in E Minor (Mahler), 812
Symphony No. 7, "Variation-Symphony" (Mennin), 9, *612,* **617**
Symphony No. 7 (Milhaud), 446–447
Symphony No. 7, "Symphony USA" (Perry), *628*
Symphony No. 7, "Liturgical" (Persichetti), 577, **584–585**
Symphony No. 7 (Piston), *343,* **349–350**
Symphony No. 7 (Santoro), 694
Symphony No. 7 (Schuman), 9, *515,* 518, 524, **528–530**
Symphony No. 7 (Sessions), 9, 488, *490,* **497–500**, 501, 900
Symphony No. 7 in C Major, "Leningrad" (Shostakovich), 22, 313, 391
Symphony No. 7 in C Major (Sibelius), 356, 519, 680–681, 796, 842, 876, 904

Symphony No. 7 (Siegmeister), 458
Symphony No. 7 in C Major (Spohr), 67
Symphony No. 7 (Toch), 459
Symphony No. 7 (Van Vactor), 459
Symphony No. 7 (Villa-Lobos), *688*
Symphony No. 8 (Bolcom), 1, 35, *795, 841, 844,* 924
Symphony No. 8 for Orchestra, Chorus, and Optional Contralto Solo (Cowell), *398*
Symphony No. 8 for Large Orchestra (Diamond), **560–565,** *562,* **570–574,** *571, 572, 573,* 599, 619
Symphony No. 8 (Glass), *825,* 830
Symphony No. 8, "San Francisco Symphony" (Harris), *331,* 339
Symphony No. 8, "Arjuna" (Hovhaness), *537*
Symphony No. 8 in E-flat Major, "Symphony of a Thousand" (Mahler), 598
Symphony No. 8 (Mennin), *612,* 613, *614,* **617–623,** *618, 621*
Symphony No. 8, "Rhodanienne" (Milhaud), 447
Symphony No. 8 (Perry), *628*
Symphony No. 8 (Persichetti), 9, 577, **584–585**
Symphony No. 8 (Piston), *343,* **349–350**
Symphony No. 8 in A Major, "Spring" (Raff), 136
Symphony No. 8 (Santoro), 694
Symphony No. 8 in B Minor, "Unfinished" (Schubert), 188, 193
Symphony No. 8 (Schuman), 9, *516,* **530–531**
Symphony No. 8 (Sessions), 488, *491,* 492, 500, 501, 900
Symphony No. 8 in C Minor (Shostakovich), 24
Symphony No. 8 (Siegmeister), 458
Symphony No. 8 (Villa-Lobos), *688*
Symphony No. 9 in D Minor (Beethoven): and Blitzstein, 319; and Bristow's *Niagara* symphony, 98; and conceptions of symphonic form, 586; and Creston, 509; and Fairouz's Symphony No. 3, 922; and Fry's *Santa Claus: Christmas Symphony,* 107–108; and Hailstork's Symphony No. 2, 858; and Ives's Symphony No. 1, 188, 197; and Ives's *Universe Symphony,* 270; and Paine's compositions, 132–133; and Paine's Symphony No. 1, 135; and Rochberg's Symphony No. 4, 812; and Santoro, 694
Symphony No. 9 (Bolcom), *841,* 845
Symphony No. 9 (Cowell), *399*
Symphony No. 9 (Diamond), *563,* **574–575**
Symphony No. 9 in E Minor (Dvořák). See *New World Symphony*

Symphony No. 9 (Glass), *826, 830*
Symphony No. 9 (Harris), *331,* 339
Symphony No. 9, "Saint Vartan" (Hovhaness), *538,* **554–555**, 556, 559
Symphony No. 9 in D Minor (Mahler), 592, 813, 834, 842
Symphony No. 9 (Mennin), 9, *612,* **623–624**
Symphony No. 9 (Milhaud), 447
Symphony No. 9, *A Suite Symphony* (Perry), 626, 628, 632
Symphony No. 9, *Sinfonia Janiculum* (Persichetti), *577,* **584–585**
Symphony No. 9 (Santoro), 694
Symphony No. 9, "Le fosse ardeatine" (Schuman), *516,* **531–532**
Symphony No. 9 (Sessions), *491,* 502
Symphony No. 9, "Figures in the Wind" (Siegmeister), 458
Symphony No. 9 (Villa-Lobos), 688
Symphony No. 10 (Cowell), *399*
Symphony No. 10 (Diamond), *563,* **574–575**
Symphony No. 10 (Glass), *826, 830*
Symphony No. 10, "Abraham Lincoln Symphony" (Harris), *331,* 340
Symphony No. 10, "Vahaken" (Hovhaness), *539*
Symphony No. 10 (Mahler), 871
Symphony No. 10 (Milhaud), 447
Symphony No. 10, "Soul Symphony" (Perry), *628,* **632–634**
Symphony No. 10, "American Muse" (Schuman), 9, *516,* **532–533**
Symphony No. 10, *Sumé, pater, patrium: Sinfonia ameríndia com coros* (Villa-Lobos), 24, 34, 689
Symphony No. 11, "Seven Rituals of Music" (Cowell), *400,* **406–408**, *407*
Symphony No. 11 (Diamond), *564,* **574–575**
Symphony No. 11 (Glass), *826, 830*
Symphony No. 11 (Harris), *332,* 340
Symphony No. 11, "All Men Are Brothers" (Hovhaness), *539*
Symphony No. 11 (Milhaud), 447
Symphony No. 11 (Perry), *629*
Symphony No. 11 (Villa-Lobos), *690*
Symphony No. 12 (Cowell), *400*
Symphony No. 12, "Lodger" (Glass), 35, *795, 827,* **830–831**
Symphony No. 12, "Père Marquette Symphony" (Harris), *332,* 340
Symphony No. 12 (Hovhaness), *539*
Symphony No. 12 (Perry), *629*
Symphony No. 12 (Villa-Lobos), *690*
Symphony No. 13, "Madras" (Cowell), *400*
Symphony No. 13 (Glass), *827*
Symphony No. 13 (in one movement), "Ardent Song" (Hovhaness), *539*
Symphony No. 13 for Wind Quintet (Perry), *629*
Symphony No. 13, *Bicentennial Symphony 1976* (Harris), *332,* 340
Symphony No. 14 (Cowell), *401*
Symphony No. 14, "Liechtenstein Suite" (Glass), *827*
Symphony No. 14, for Wind Orchestra, "Ararat" (Hovhaness), *540*
Symphony No. 14 (Santoro), 694
Symphony No. 14 (Shostakovich), 891
Symphony No. 15, "Thesis" (Cowell), *401,* **408–409**
Symphony No. 15, "Silver Pilgrimage" (Hovhaness), *540*
Symphony No. 16, "Icelandic" (Cowell), 6, *401,* 409
Symphony No. 16, "Kayagum" (Hovhaness), 6, *540,* 553
Symphony No. 17, "Lancaster" (Cowell), *402*
Symphony No. 17, "Symphony for Metal Orchestra" (Hovhaness), *541,* 553
Symphony No. 18 (Cowell), *402*
Symphony No. 18, *Circe* (Hovhaness), *541,* 553
Symphony No. 19 (Cowell), *403*
Symphony No. 19, "Vishnu" (Hovhaness), *541,* **558–559**
Symphony No. 20 (Cowell), *403*
Symphony No. 20, "Three Journeys to a Holy Mountain" (Hovhaness), *542*
Symphony No. 21 (Cowell), *403*
Symphony No. 21, "Etchmiadzin" (Hovhaness), *542*
Symphony No. 22, "City of Light" (Hovhaness), *542*
Symphony No. 23, "Ani" (Hovhaness), *543*
Symphony No. 24, "Majnun" (Hovhaness), *543*
Symphony No. 25, "Odysseus" (Hovhaness), *543*
Symphony No. 26 (Hovhaness), *544*
Symphony No. 27 (Hovhaness), *544*
Symphony No. 28 (Hovhaness), *544*
Symphony No. 29 (Hovhaness), *545*
Symphony No. 30 (Hovhaness), *545*
Symphony No. 31 (Hovhaness), *545*

Symphony No. 32, "The Broken Wings" (Hovhaness), 545
Symphony No. 33 (Hovhaness), 545
Symphony No. 34 (Hovhaness), 545
Symphony No. 35 (Hovhaness), 546
Symphony No. 36 (Hovhaness), 546
Symphony No. 37 (Hovhaness), 546
Symphony No. 38 (Hovhaness), 546
Symphony No. 39 (Hovhaness), 547
Symphony No. 39 in E-flat Major, K. 543 (Mozart), 89
Symphony No. 40 (Hovhaness), 547
Symphony No. 41 (Hovhaness), 547
Symphony No. 42 (Hovhaness), 547
Symphony No. 43 (Hovhaness), 547
Symphony No. 44 (Hovhaness), 547
Symphony No. 45 (Hovhaness), 548
Symphony No. 46, "To the Green Mountains" (Hovhaness), 548
Symphony No. 47, "Walla Walla, Land of Many Waters" (Hovhaness), 548
Symphony No. 48, "Vision of Andromeda" (Hovhaness), 548
Symphony No. 49, "Christmas Symphony" (Hovhaness), 549
Symphony No. 50, "Mount St. Helens" (Hovhaness), 549, 553
Symphony No. 51 (Hovhaness), 549
Symphony No. 52, "Journey to Vega" (Hovhaness), 549
Symphony No. 53, "Star Dawn" (Hovhaness), 549
Symphony No. 54 (Hovhaness), 549
Symphony No. 55 (Hovhaness), 549
Symphony No. 56 (Hovhaness), 550
Symphony No. 57, "Cold Mountain" (Hovhaness), 550
Symphony No. 58, "Symphony sacra" (Hovhaness), 550
Symphony No. 59 (Hovhaness), 550
Symphony No. 60, "To the Appalachian Mountains" (Hovhaness), 551
Symphony No. 61 (Hovhaness), 551
Symphony No. 62, "Oh, Let Not Man Forget These Words Divine" (Hovhaness), 551
Symphony No. 63, "Loon Lake" (Hovhaness), 551
Symphony No. 64, "Agiochook" (Hovhaness), 551
Symphony No. 65, "Artstakh" (Hovhaness), 551
Symphony No. 66, "Hymn to Glacier Peak" (Hovhaness), 552
Symphony No. 67, "Hymn to the Mountains" (Hovhaness), 552
Symphony of Autumn, A (Moore), 456
Symphony of Psalms (Stravinsky), 365, 449, 614, 632, 693
Symphony of Spirituals (Gould), 454
Symphony of the Spirit (Heinrich), 75
Symphony of Three Orchestras, A (Carter), 794, 799, 801, 860, 922
Symphony on a Hymn Tune. See *Symphony No. 1, Symphony on a Hymn Tune* (Thomson)
Symphony on College Themes (Bennett), 452
Symphony on G (Harrison), 803, *804*, 806, 813
Symphony-Our Heritage (Harris), 327, 334
Symphony "Pallas Athene" (Krenek), 456
Synchrony (Cowell), 404
Synconata (Sowerby), 376
syncopation: and Antheil, 388, 393, 395; and Blitzstein, 318; and Bloch, 438; and Chadwick, 144, 146–148, 151–152, 154; and Copland, 323, 325; and Cowell, 405, 408; and Creston, 505, 506, 507, 509, 510; and Diamond, 560, 565–566, 568, 571; and distinctive qualities of American symphony, 23, 29; and Ginastera, 677; and Hanson, 362; and Harbison, 848; and Harris, 338; and Heinrich, 81; and Ives, 233–234, 235, 237, 239, 251, 270, 276, 280–281; and Johnson, 417–418; and Marsalis, 908–909; and Martinů, 442–443; and Mennin, 613, 615–616, 620, 623; and Perry, 631, 633; and Persichetti, 578, 583; and Piston, 341, 345–346, 348–349; and Price, 421, 422–423; and Schuman, 523, 527, 529–530, 532; and Sessions, 502; and Sowerby, 376–377; and Thompson, 379, 380; and Thomson, 353
synthesizers, 886. See also electronic and electroacoustic music
Syracuse Symphony, 669
Syrinx (Debussy), 684
Szell, George, 7, 617, 811

Taberna al amanecer (Bisquertt), 700
Tacuchian, Ricardo, 694
Taft, William Howard, 757
Taggard, Genevieve, 317
Taíno Indians, 764
Taller 44 (Studio 44), 701
Talma, Louise, 315
Tam's Copying Bureau, 250
Tangazo (Piazzolla), 680

Tanglewood Music Festival, 752. *See also* Berkshire Music Center (Tanglewood)
Tango in D (Albéniz), 22, 24, 834, *836*
tangos, 22, 24, 680, 771, 834, 908
Tango Suite (Lezcano), 771
Tanner, David, 44
Tannhäuser (Wagner), 163
Taps (bugle call), 253, 255–256
Taras, John, 677
Tarnawiecki, Douglas, 705
Taruskin, Richard, 270, 271
Tattooed Bride, The (Ellington), 454
Taubman, Howard, 496, 616, 747
Tavárez, Manuel Gregorio, 773
Tavener, John, 633
Tawa, Nicholas E.: on Barber's Symphony No. 2, 359; on Creston's rhythmic profile, 505–506; on Creston's Symphony No. 3, 508, 509; on Harris's later symphonies, 339; on Moore's Symphony No. 2 in A, 456; on Piston's legacy, 349; on Piston's Symphony No. 2, 345; on Schuman's Symphony No. 3, 525; on Schuman's Symphony No. 4, 526; on tensions within American art music, 485
Taxi Driver (film; score by Herrmann), 455
Taylor, Clifford, 349
Taylor, Davidson, 311
Taylor, Raynor, 62
Taylor, Robert, 607
Tchaikovsky, Pyotr Ilyich, 31, 123, 125, 185, 188, 197, 201, 448, 635. *See also specific composition titles*
Tcherepnin, Alexander, 640, 797
Teatro Caracas, 711
Teatro Colón, 665, 675
Teatro Nacional (Cuba), 252
Teatro Nacional (Spain), 760
Teatro Solís, 668
Tech and Techno (American Composers Orchestra), 915
technological advances, 309. *See also* electronic and electroacoustic music
techno music, 909
Tecún Umán (Castillo), 753, 755
Te Deum, 282, *283*
Telésfora (Ried), 695
Tello, Rafael, *738*, 740
Tema variado y fuga dodecafónicos (Prieto), 741

Tender Night (ballet set to Ginastera's *Variationes concertantes*), 677
Tenting on the Old Camp Ground (Kittredge), 255
Teotihuacán (Delgadillo), 757, 758
Teruel, Ricardo, 715
Thanksgiving and Forefathers' Day (Ives), *178,* 249, 256–264, *259–261, 262,* **264–266,** 296n130. *See also Symphony: New England Holidays, A* (Ives)
Tharp, Twyla, 828
Theosophy, 396
"There Is a Balm in Gilead" (spiritual), 819
There Is a Happy Land (Mason), 227, 242, 245–246
theremins, 24
There's Music in the Air (Root), 227
They Are There! (Ives), 298n162
Third Stream, 906, 908
Third Street Music Settlement School, 200
Thomas, Ambroise, 709
Thomas, Michael Tilson, 299n168, 326, 909, 913
Thomas, Theodore, 30, 95, 123, 135, 141, 156
Thompson, Randall, **377–381**; and Antheil, 383; and Bloch, 437, 438; on challenges faced by American composers, 312; and European training, 354; and "Great American Symphony" trope, 5; Guggenheim Fellowship, 380, 471n337; and Hanson, 362; and Orrego-Salas, 700; premiere of key works, *9*; and Sowerby, 374. *See also specific composition titles*
Thomson, James, *93*
Thomson, Virgil, **350–354**; and Antheil, 393; and Bernstein, 590, 594; and Blitzstein, 317; and Boulanger's influence, 315; and briefly mentioned midcentury composers, 639; and Bristow's Symphony No. 3, 93; and Cold War cultural politics, 485; and Copland, 322; and Creston, 508; and Diamond, 559–560, 565–566, 565–567; and distinctive qualities of American symphony, 23; and the Federal Music Project, 311; and film music, 451; Guggenheim Fellowship, 471n337; on Harris, 338; and Hill, 455; and Hovhaness, 534; influence of midcentury composers, 486; and Ives, 216; and Johnson, 418; and key influences on American repertoire, 22; and Mennin, 613, 615; and Schuman, 513, 517, 526; and Still, 430; and support for American symphony, 485; symphonies' movements and instrumentation, *351*
Thoreau, Henry David, 250

Thorne Music Fund, 574
Three Illusions for Orchestra (Carter), 802
Three New England Sketches (Piston), 349
Three Occasions for Orchestra (Carter), 802
Three-Part Invention in F Minor (Bach), 206, 213
Three Places in New England. See *Orchestral Set No. 1, Three Places in New England* (Ives)
Three Poems for Kaddish (Lowell), 597
Three Quarter-tone Pieces (Ives), 294n89
Threnody to the Victims of Hiroshima (Penderecki), 834
Throw Out the Life-Line (Ufford), 242, 279
Thuille, Ludwig, 458
Thurber, Jeannette, 98
Thurman, Kira, 625, 634
Tibetan Buddhism, 918
Tides of Manaunaun (Cowell), 404
Tietê River, 694
Time (magazine), 325–326, 608
Timm, Henry Christian, 86
Tin Pan Alley, 313, 318, 505, 513–514
Tirado, Pedro, 705
Toccata and Fugue in D Minor, "Dorian" (Bach), 182, 244
Toch, Ernst, 434, 435, 459, 770
Todd, Mabel, 625
Toku: Indo-Cuban Rumba (Lecuona), 765
Tomb of Genius; To the Memory of Mendelssohn-Bartholdy, The (Heinrich), 76, 84, 85
Tomer, William G., 242
Tommasini, Anthony, 844, 872, 878, 909
"To Music" (Masefield), 574
To Music: Choral Symphony (Diamond), 563, 574
Tone Parallel to Harlem, A (Ellington), 454
tone poems, 289n1, 317, 338, 359, 437, 558, 715. See also specific titles
tone rows: and Albert, 859; and Bernstein, 593, 599, 601; and Cordero, 762; and Diamond, 570, 571, 572–574; and Perry, 631; and Rochberg, 811, 812; and Schuman, 528–529; and Sessions, 496, 501
Torke, Michael, 794, 796
Torrá, Celia Tomasa, 681
Torrejón y Velasco, Tomás, 703, 705
Torres-Santos, Raymond, 767, 775
Tosar, Héctor, 667, 669, 670, 671
Toscanini, Arturo, 356, 668
To the Spirit of Beethoven (Heinrich), 84

Tourel, Jennie, 596, 609
Tourian, Bedros, 883
Trajetta, Filippo, 62
Tramp, Tramp, Tramp (Root), 242
Transatlantic (Antheil), 468n233
Transcontinental Railroad, 468n244
Travassos, Alexandre, 695
Travels in the Interior of North America (Wied-Neuwied), 82
Traversari, Pedro Pablo, 697, 708
Treaty of William Penn with the Indians, The (Heinrich), 82
Treemonisha (Joplin), 415, 429
"Trees in the Garden, The" (Crane), 883
TreeStone (Albert), 860
Tres danzas cubanas (Caturla), 765
Tres movimientos sinfónicos (Contreras), 751
Tres toques (Roldán), 768
Tres versiones sinfónicas (Orbón), 770, 770
Tribu (Ayala), 751
"Tribulación" (Santa Cruz), 700
Tributo a Portinari (Santoro), 693
Trimble, Lester, 640
Tríptico cubano (Gonzalo), 769
Tristan und Isolde (Wagner), 211, 507, 600, 813, 843
Trombone Concerto (Rouse), 873, 876
Tropicalia I (Fernández), 771
Tropicalia II (Fernández), 771
Trova a la Vírgen de Copacabana (González Bravo), 706
Trujillo, Rafael, 773
Truth (Brescia), 708
Tudor, Antony, 513
tumba francesca tradition, 112
Tupi-Guaraní Indians, 681
Tuqan, Fadwa, 919
Turina, Joaquín, 706, 774
Turin Symphony Orchestra, 631
Turkey in the Straw (traditional), 213, 242, 251, 252, 291n43
Turkish culture, 916
Turner, Robert, 39
Tuskegee Institute, 410–411
Tuthill, Burnet C., 376
Twa, Andrew, 39
Twain, Mark, 50n17, 295n119, 451
12 New Etudes for Piano (Bolcom), 838, 843
12 Sinfonías breves (Delgadillo), 758

Index

Twelve Bagatelles for piano (Rochberg), 811
twelve-tone system: and Argentinian composers, 676; and Bernstein, 590, 593, 599, 601, 604; and Bloch, 438; and briefly mentioned midcentury composers, 637, 639–640; and Cordero, 762; and Corigliano, 838; and Creston, 513; and Diamond, 560–566, 570–574, *571*; and Dick, 453; and evolution of American symphonic style, 793; and Ginastera, 676, 678; and Gutiérrez, 761; and Harrison, 803; and Hovhaness, 534; and Ives, 214; and Jiménez Mabarak, 752; and Krenek, 456; and León, 769; and Mennin, 617, 619, 623; and Orellana, 756; and Perry, 630–631; and Persichetti, 578, 580; and Rochberg, 807, 811, 813; and Schuman, 513, 528–532; and scope of American symphonic repertoire, 3; and Sessions, 493, 495–497, 500–501; and Simó, 773; and tensions within midcentury American symphony, 487–488, 635; and Uruguayan composers, 670
Twentieth Century Harmony (Persichetti), 578, 585
"Twentieth-Century Problems in Music" (concert series), 598
Twichell, Harmony. *See* Ives, Harmony
Two Masonic Marches (Montero), 712
two-movement works, *26–27*
Two-Part Symphony (Wuorinen), *794*
"Tyger, The" (Blake), 501–502

Ufford, Edward S., 242
Uirapurú (Villa-Lobos), 683–685, *685*
Uke (Bennett), 452
Ukraine National Symphony Orchestra, *14*
ultramodernism: and American musical pedagogy, 382; and Antheil, 383, 387; and briefly mentioned midcentury composers, 639; and Cowell, 396, 404, 406; and Diamond, 565; and education/training of American composers, 32; and Harrison, 802–803; and Ives, 184; and maturation of American symphonic activity, 309; and Sessions, 495; and Still, 425, 428, 430; and Thomson, 350. *See also* modernism and modernity
Unanswered Question, The (Ives), 22, 289n1, 524, 590, 601, 812, 872
Underwood Emerging Composers Commission, 916
Unfinished Symphony. See Symphony No. 8 in B Minor, "Unfinished" (Schubert)

Union (Gottschalk), 115
Union Army, 175
Union of Soviet Socialist Republics, 317, 338
Union Pacific (film), 388
United Nations (UN), 589, 764
United Nations Educational, Scientific and Cultural Organization (UNESCO), 513, 708
United States. *See* first generation of American symphonists; Second New England School; *specific composers*
United States Army Band, 440
Universe Symphony (Ives), 31, 175, *179*, 183, 184, **267–271**
Universidad Peruana de Ciencias Aplicadas, 705
University of Arizona, 886
University of Buffalo, 439, 560
University of California-Berkeley, 436, 447, 488
University of California-Davis, 447
University of Chicago, 764
University of Cincinnati College-Conservatory of Music, 268
University of Colorado Boulder, 655n397, 816
University of Kansas Wind Ensemble, 922–923
University of Michigan, 497, 761, 838
University of Minnesota, 346
University of Northern Colorado Symphony Orchestra, 268
University of Pennsylvania, 807
University of Rome, 560
University of Texas Wind Ensemble, 837
Ureta, Chano, 750
Uribe Holguín, Guillermo, 710
Urmotiv, 293n83, 605
Uruguay, **668–671**, *669*
US Air Force, 886
US Constitution, 340
US Department of State, 485, 513, 517, 610, 631, 773
US Information Service, 624
US Military Academy, 339
"Usonian" term, 48
Ussachevsky, Vladimir, 704, 754
USSR State Orchestra, 694

"Vagrom Ballad, A" (Chadwick), 150–151. *See also Symphonic Sketches* (Chadwick)
Valcárcel, Edgar, 667, 704
Valcárcel, Teodoro, *697*, 704
Valdes, Roberto Carpio, 704
Valera, Roberto, *766*, 771

1018

Valle, Valeria, 702
Valsalia, Eduardo Caba, 706
Vals brilliante de concierto (Martínez-Sobral), 754
Van Buren, Paul, 608
Vanderbilt University Orchestra, 110
Van der Stucken, Frank, 160, 162
Vanity Fair (from Hawthorne's "The Celestial Rail-Road"), 234, 235, 242
Van Sant, Gus, 915
Van Vactor, David, 459
Vardapet, Komitas, 553
Vardell, Charles, 459
Varèse, Edgard, 381, 425, 428, 430, 700, 753, 755, 890, 913. *See also specific composition titles*
Vargas Candia, Teófilo, 706
Variaciones concertantes (Ginastera), 677
Varian, John, 396
Variations on a Theme by Mozart (Casals), 774
Variety, 607
Vasconcelos, José, 742
Vasco Nuñez de Balboa (Galimany), 762
Vassar College, 457
Vauclain, Constant, 459
vaudeville, 150, 381
Vaughan Williams, Ralph, 31, 613, 614, 876
Veale, John, 494
V-E Day, 318–319
Vega, Aurelio de la, 667, 701, *766*, 770–771
Vega Jiménez, Ramiro, 757
Vega Matus, Alejandro, 757
Vega Raudes, Pablo, 757
Velasco, Juan Antonio de, 709
Velasco-Maidana, José María, *697*, 706
Velásquez, Carlos Ramírez, 758
Velázquez, Ileana Pérez, 771
Venezuela, *698–699*, **711–715**
Venezuelan Youth Orchestra, 711, 750
Veraguas (Robles), 764
Verdi, Giuseppe, 620
Verdi Orchestra, 757
Verhaalen, Marion, 693
vernacular idioms and influences: and Antheil, 395; and Bernstein, 599; and Blitzstein, 318; and Bolcom, 838, 845; and Bristow, 99; and Cordero, 762; and Cowell, 396, 404; and Creston, 507; and European training, 354; and evolution of American symphonic style, 793; and *Five Folksongs in Counterpoint*, 471n343; and future of American symphony, 924; and Gottschalk, 112; and "Great American Symphony" trope, 451; and Harris, 53n72, 334, 337; and Ives, 200, 250, 286; and Marsalis, 906, 907–908; and Perry, 630, 632; and Price, 421; and Schuman, 520; and scope of American symphonic repertoire, 3, 6; and social context of symphonic repertoire, 311; and Sowerby, 376; and Still, 429, 430–431; and tensions within midcentury American symphony, 635; and Thompson, 379, 381; and Thomson, 354; Twain as model for, 451. *See also* folk idioms and influences
Verneuil, Raoul de, 703
Vertigo (film; score by Herrmann), 455
Viceroyalty of Peru, 702–703, 705, 707
Victimae paschali laudes, 509
Victoria, Queen of England, 80
Victoria's and Albion's Young Hope, the Prince of Wales; A Royal Symphony (Heinrich), 74, 80–81, *81*
Victorio, Roberto, 695
Vicuña, Juan Casanova, *696*
Vidal, Francisco Bernardo Pulgar, 704
Vidal, Paul, 753–754
Videntes Stellam (Huertas), 775–776
Vides ut alta (Horace), 379
Vienna Music Academy, 459
Vienna Philharmonic, 624, 669
Vienna State Opera Orchestra, 115
Vienna Symphony Orchestra. *See* Wiener Symphoniker
Vier ernste Gesänge (Brahms), 213
Vierne, Louis, 374
Vietnam War, 500, 900
Vigilia (Plaza), 712
Villa Aurelia, 584
Villa-Lobos, Heitor, 24, 52n50, 666, **682–692**, *683*, *686–690*, 721n93. *See also specific composition titles*
Villalpando Buitrago, Alberto, *697*, 706–707
villancicos, 666, 702–703, 736, 753, 756
Villanueva Galeano, Ignacio, 757
Villena, Federico, 712
Vincent, John, 641
Viola Concerto (Serly), 458
Viola Sonata (Perry), 624
Violin Concerto (Adams), 872
Violin Concerto (Barber), 354
Violin Concerto (Berg), 570, 619
Violin Concerto (Carter), 802

Index

Violin Concerto (Sessions), 496
Violin Concerto No. 1 (Glass), 822
Violin Concerto No. 3 in B Minor (Saint-Saëns), 159
Violin Sonata No. 1 (Ives), 230
Violin Sonata No. 3 (Ives), 183
Virgin of Guadalupe, 737
Viscarra Monje, Humberto, 706
Vivaldi, Antonio, 556, 632
Vivier, Claude, 36
V-J Day, 319
Voces de gesta (Cotapos), 700
Von Glahn, Denise, 855
Von Tilzer, Harry, 285
Vox label, 52n50

Waart, Edo de, 891
Wadsworth, Mary C., 569
Wagenaar, Bernard, 459, 517
Wager, Michael, 600
Wagner, Richard: and Adams, 871; and Beach, 158; and Beethoven's influence, 135; and Bernstein, 589; and Bolcom, 843; and Bristow, 95; and Ginastera, 680; and Gottschalk, 114; and "Great American Symphony" trope, 4; and Ives, 194, 199, 201, 211–212; and MacDowell, 166; and Rochberg, 813; and Rouse, 876; and Sessions, 502; and Strong, 160, 162–163; and Thomas's concerts, 123; and Thompson, 380
Wagner Orchestra, 757
Wake Nicodemus (Work), 208–210, *209*, 215
Walden (Thoreau), 250
Walker, David, 210
Walker, George, 35, 36, 795, *795*, 797, **816–822,** *817–818,* 859. *See also specific composition titles*
Walker, William, 735
Walker-Hill, Helen, 624–626, 630–633, 655n397
Wallace, David Foster, 913
WALL-E (film; score by Newman), 915
Walter, Arnold, *37,* 597
Walter, Bruno, 453, 592, 706
waltzes, 774
Waltz Serenade (Rochberg), 812
Wanamaker Prize, 420
Wang Jie, 35, 36, 795, *795,* 797, **916–919,** *917,* 924. *See also specific composition titles*
Ward, Robert E., 459
Ward, Samuel A., 211

Ware, Peter, 44
War of Independence (Cuba), 765
War of the Austrian Succession, 82
War of the Triple Alliance, 671
Washington Post, 340
Washington Post March (Sousa), 242
Washington's Birthday (Ives), 24, *177,* 249, **250–252,** 253, 256, 264, 267, 284, 295n104. *See also Symphony: New England Holidays, A* (Ives)
Washington University, 582
Watchman (Ives), 230, 231, 233, 244
Water Music Suite in D Major (Handel), 878
Watjen Organ, 575
Watkins, Glenn, 873
Watkins, Holly, 864
Watts, Isaac, 296n128
Waxman, Franz, 434, 451
Webern, Anton, 440, 572, 586, 676, 701
Webster, James P., 232
Week of Modern Art (São Paulo), 682
Weidig, Adolph, 381
Weil, Irving, 437
Weill, Kurt, 517
Weinberger, Jaromír, 459
Weisgall, Hugo, 404, 409, 531
Weisgall, Nathalie, 531
Welch, Roy D., 493
Welcome Voice (Hartsough), 244, 280–281
Welles, Orson, 318, 415
Wellington's Victory (Beethoven), 691
Wells College, 439
Well-Tempered Clavier (Bach), 206, 213, 760
Werfel, Franz, 449
Werner, Jules, 517
Werner Janssen Symphony, 721n93
Wesley, Charles, 241
West African dance, 421
Westchester Conservatory, 754
Westdeutscher Rundfunk, 708
Western films, 432
Western Minstrel, The (Heinrich), 71
Westminster Chimes (Ives), 233–234, 242, 245, *246, 247*–248
Westminster College, 624–625
West Redding, Connecticut, 274
West Side Story (Bernstein), 528, 595–596, 602–603, 608–609
Wevers, Harold, 44
Wharton, Edith, 484

"Whatever Occurred to the Great American Symphony?" (Bernstein), 484
When Johnny Comes Marching Home—an American Overture (Harris), 338
Where, O Where Are the Verdant Freshmen? (college song), *209*, 210
White, Ed, 913
White Cockade (traditional), 251
White Flood (film), 454
Whiteman, Paul, 376, 383
Whitesitt, Linda, 388
Whithorne, Emerson, 460
Whitman, Walt: and Bloch, 436; and Chadwick's symphonic sketches, 151; and the Federal Music Project, 311; and "Great American Symphony" trope, 4, 50n17; and Hanson, 373; and Harris, 334, 340; and Hindemith, 441; and Larsen, 883; and Liebermann, 901, 904; and Mennin, 614; and Ward, 459
Whitney, Robert, 7, 11, *12*, 311, 377, 486, 580, 616, 635, 670
Whittier, John Greenleaf, 250, 295n104
"Who Cares If You Listen?" (Babbitt), 771
Widor, Charles-Marie, 374, 455, 458
Wied-Neuwied, Maximilian von, 82
Wiener Symphoniker, 377, 695
Wieprecht, Friedrich Wilhelm, 127
Wierzbicki, James, 802
"Wild Nights" (Dickinson), 865
Wildwood Troubadour, The (Heinrich), 72
Wilkinson, E. Scott, *46*
Willan, Healy, 36, *37*
Williams, Alberto, 34, 672, *673*
Williams, Alexander, 518, 526
Williams, John, 374
Williams, John McLaughlin, *14*
Williams, Mary Lou, 487
Williams College, 764, 771
Williamson, John Finley, 625
William Tell Overture (Rossini), 182
Willis, Richard Storrs, 69–70, 72, 91, 95, 101, 108
Willis, Thomas, 188
Willson, Meredith, 460
Wilson, Charles, *41*
Wilson, Frederic, 381
Wilson, Olly, 634, *794*
Wind Band Classics series, *16–17*
Winterreise (Schubert), 680
Winter that United Us, The (Wang), *917*, 919
Wixárika people, 828–830
W. J. Beal Botanical Garden, 855
Wolff, Albert, 670
Wolffers, Jules, 569, 594
Wolpe, Stefan, 752
Women, The (musical), 746
Woodbury, Isaac, 246
Woodworth (Bradbury), 221–223, *222*, *224*, 227–228, 285
Worcester Festival, 141, 166
Work, Henry Clay, 208, 242, 253, 262, 272. *See also specific composition titles*
Works Progress Administration (WPA), 185, 317, 422, 517, 533
World's Columbian Exposition (Chicago, 1893), 3
World War I: and American musical pedagogy, 381; and Argentinian composers, 681; and European migration to South America, 683; and "Great American Symphony" trope, 4; and Hernández Marín, 774; impact on American symphonic activity, 309, 450; impact on German repertoire in US, 310; impact on Puerto Rican women, 776; and Ives's *Holidays Symphony*, 253; *Lusitania* sinking, 281–282; postwar optimism, 312; and Sowerby, 374; and support for American symphony, 6; and Villa-Lobos's works, *691*
World War II: and Antheil, 392; and Antheil's works, 391; and Argentinian composers, 676; and Barber's works, 358, 362; and Diamond, 565; and emergence of postmodern style, 634; and European influences in South America, 666; and evolution of American symphonic style, 793; and Hindemith, 441; and influence of émigré composers, 433–434; and Ives's Symphony No. 3, 218; and key influences on American repertoire, 22; and Krenek's composing career, 455–456; and maturation of American symphonic activity, 309; and Mennin, 610; and Milhaud, 445, 446; and Perry, 626; and populist influences in music, 798; and Rochberg, 807, 815; and Schuman's Symphony No. 3, 525; and scope of American symphonic repertoire, 3; and Sessions, 493, 494; and South American composers, 667, 703; and Stravinsky, 449; and tensions within American art music, 484; and Thompson, 379; and wartime nativism, 313
"Wounded Cities" movement (Blitzstein *Airborne Symphony*), 463n53

Index

Wright, David, 624
Wright, Frank Lloyd, 48
Wright, Orville, 317–318
Wright, Simon, 691
Wuensch, Gerhard, *40*
Wuorinen, Charles, *794*

Xavier, José Maria, 681–682
Xenakis, Iannis, 752
Xibalbá (Vidal), 754
Xiuhtzitzqüilo o La fiesta del fuego (Gomezanda), 740

Yaddo Colony, 565
Yale hymnal, 296n126
Yale-Princeton Football Game (Ives), 243, 285
Yale University, 439, 457, 458, 488, 797, 893
Yamekraw (Johnson), 415
"Yankee Doodle" (traditional), 115, 154, 242, 262, 275
Yankee Doodleiad, The (Heinrich), 72
Yardumian, Richard, 641
"Year's Chronicle, A" (Lockwood), 456
Yellin, Victor, 141–142, 144, 146, 150, 154
Yigdal hymn, 597
Yon, Pietro, 502
Yoruban people, 764
Young People's Concerts, 110, 115, 597
Your Cry Will Be a Whisper (Asia), 890
YouTube, 11, 48, 52n48, 798

Zador, Eugene, 434
Zafra (Robles), 764
Zampa (Hérold), 201
Zapiola, José, 695
Zappa, Frank, 286
Zegers, Isadora, 695
Zeisl, Eric, 434
Zelaya, Francisco Ramón Díaz, 757
Zephaniah, Book of, 620, 654n356
Zerrahn, Carl, 141
Zhang, David, *42*
Ziegler, Oskar, 297n154
Zionism, 594
Zipoli, Domenico, 671
Zobel, Mark, 218
Zohn-Muldoon, Ricardo, 752
Zorn, John, 286
Zuckert, León, *37*
Zumaqué, Francisco, 667, *698,* 710
Zwilich, Ellen Taaffe, **849–856**; and commercial recordings of symphonic works, 11; and evolution of American symphonic style, 795; and key influences on American repertoire, 21; and Larsen, 884; and Sessions, 488; symphonies' movements and instrumentation, *851–852*; symphony premiere dates, *794. See also specific composition titles*
Zwilich, Joseph, 850